PROVINCIAL STRATEGIES OF ECONOMIC REFORM IN POST-MAO CHINA

Studies on Contemporary China

Studies on Contemporary China

PROVINCIAL STRATEGIES OF ECONOMIC REFORM IN POST-MAO CHINA

Leadership, Politics, and Implementation

Peter T.Y. Cheung, Jae Ho Chung, and Zhimin Lin, editors

Feng Chongyi
Keith Forster
David S.G. Goodman

Lijian Hong
Kevin P. Lane
Shawn Shieh

 An East Gate Book

M.E. Sharpe
Armonk, New York
London, England

An East Gate Book

Copyright © 1998 by M. E. Sharpe, Inc.

Library of Congress Cataloging-in-Publication Data

Provincial strategies of economic reform in post-Mao China:
Leadership, politics, and implementation / edited by
Peter T.Y. Cheung, Jae Ho Chung, and Zhimin Lin.
p. cm. — (Studies on contemporary China)
"An East gate book."
Includes bibliographical references and index.
ISBN 0-7656-0146-X (alk. paper). —
ISBN 0-7656-0147-8 (pbk : alk. paper)
1. China—Economic policy—1976– 2. China—Economic
conditions—1976– 3. Investments, Foreign—China. I. Cheung,
Peter T. Y., 1958– . II. Chung, Jae Ho, 1960– .
III. Lin, Zhimin. IV. Series.
HC427.92.P765 1998
338.951′009′049—dc21 97-32756
CIP
Printed in the United States of America

BM (c)   10   9   8   7   6   5   4   3   2   1
BM (p)   10   9   8   7   6   5   4   3   2   1

Contents

PROVINCIAL STRATEGIES OF ECONOMIC REFORM IN POST-MAO CHINA

Introduction

Provincial Leadership and Economic Reform in Post-Mao China

Peter T.Y. Cheung

Few scholars can afford to ignore the vast differences in the extent of economic reform and the contrasting patterns of economic development among China's thirty-one provincial units.* Chinese and Western scholars alike have done considerable research on the uneven patterns of economic reform and development in post-Mao China.[1] In order to account for such provincial and regional variations, some highlight the disparate endowments and overseas connections of the provinces while others emphasize the preferential treatment by the central government.[2] However, most have neglected the critical role of provincial leadership in explaining provincial variations in reform and economic accomplishments.[3] This study, therefore, aims to examine the reform experience of China's provinces by focusing on the role of provincial leadership in the initiation and implementation of economic reform. We will examine eight provincial cases and their reform strategies in two policy areas. Our studies of resource allocation include Shanghai, Guangdong, Zhejiang and Shaanxi, and our studies of foreign capital and investment cover Shandong, Fujian, Hainan, and Sichuan. The fol-

---

*Exclusive of Taiwan, Hong Kong, and Macau, China has twenty-two provinces, four centrally administered cities, and five autonomous regions, all enjoying provincial level status. For the sake of simplicity, these thirty-one units will be referred to as "province" in this book. "Localities" refer to administrative units at the subprovincial level such as municipalities or counties. "Regions" refer to groupings of several provinces sharing similar geographical attributes. The "Center" (*zhongyang*) refers to the "State Council and its commissions, ministries, and leadership small groups in Beijing as well as the party Politburo, Secretariat, and the organs of the Central Committee." This will be used interchangeably with the "central government" for the sake of simplicity. See Kenneth Lieberthal and Michel Oksenberg, *Policy Making in China: Leaders, Structures, and Processes* (Princeton: Princeton University Press, 1988), p. 138. Similarly, the term "province" or "provincial government" will be used to refer to provincial party and state authorities.

lowing sections of this chapter will discuss the significance of this study, examine the key concepts of province and provincial leadership, outline our research design and analytical framework, and provide a summary of the chapters.

Objectives and Significance of this Study

This study aims to contribute to the research on the political economy of economic reform, provincial politics, as well as central-provincial relations in the post-Mao era. First, studying the reform experience of the provinces, a topic still not well researched, is an excellent way of examining the political economy of China's reforms in the post-Mao era. Economic reform and open policy (*kaifang zhengce*) have led to significant decentralization of economic authority and resources to provincial authorities, hence enabling them to blaze their own path of reform. For instance, the rapid economic growth of Jiangsu and Zhejiang is fueled by the rise of township and village enterprises while that of Guangdong and Fujian is mainly driven by the huge influx of Hong Kong and Taiwanese investment. The preferential treatment of some of the coastal provinces by the central government, together with increasing provincial competition for domestic and foreign investment, has significant repercussions for the outcome of economic reform and economic development. The ensuing diversities in provincial reform experience, an area which has become increasingly relevant to our understanding of post-Mao China and yet far from fully explored, urgently call for more scholarly analysis.[4]

Second, this study on provincial leadership and economic reform will contribute to our knowledge of the emerging issue of provincial politics. The differential impact of reform and open policy has affected the interests between as well as within the provinces. For instance, the case studies of resource allocation and acquisition of foreign capital and investment in this study are excellent examples reflecting the conflict of interest among different sectors (e.g. between heavy industry and light industry) and among different localities (e.g. between affluent localities and poor localities). The rise of new social forces, such as a managerial and entrepreneurial class and other social organizations, that are keen on pursuing their own agendas and protecting their vested interests also reflects the growing pluralization of Chinese society.[5] The role of provincial leadership in resolving conflicts precipitated by these competing interests will illuminate our understanding of the evolving pattern of provincial politics in the reform era. Although our study does not focus on provincial politics per se, it will still shed new light on this increasingly salient issue in Chinese politics.[6] Jae Ho Chung's appendix in this volume will systematically discuss the changing substance of provincial politics, set out a research agenda for the future and provide a select list of key reference and source materials for the study of provincial politics and development issues.

Third, the provinces and their leaders are fast becoming pivotal actors in the

Chinese political system in the reform era. As Susan Shirk has argued, Deng Xiaoping and his associates have successfully marshalled the support of the provinces for his reform program through decentralization of economic and fiscal power in his "playing to the provinces" strategy.[7] Having gained initial success in claiming more economic power from the central government in the early 1980s, provinces and cities have eagerly competed with one another and made ever more demands for power from the central government since then. The opening of the fourteen coastal cities in early 1984 and Zhao Ziyang's advocacy of a coastal development strategy in 1987–1988 further highlight the important economic roles that could be performed by the coastal provinces in China's modernization. While China's pursuit of reform remained uncertain after the disruption caused by the political crisis in 1989 and three years of economic austerity since 1988, provincial enthusiasm was again mobilized and encouraged by Deng Xiaoping's celebrated tour to southern China in early 1992 in order to promote faster growth and bolder reform. The heightened economic and political role of the provinces was reflected in the promotion of party leaders of Sichuan and the centrally administered cities, namely Beijing, Shanghai and Tianjin, into the Politburo elected after the 13th National Party Congress in late 1987, which contributed over one-fifth of its total membership. Such a slate of provincial officials was further expanded to five in the twenty-two–member Politburo elected after the 14th National Party Congress in November 1992, including those from the above three centrally administered cities as well as Guangdong and Shandong. With the growing media coverage and public relations activities both inside and outside China, provincial leaders have become widely watched politicians in the reform era.[8] Starting from 1996, a series of speeches and documents issued by provincial leaders are being published by the press of the Central Party School, something rarely observed in the prereform era.[9] The growing attention on provincial events and the activities of provincial leaders in the Chinese mass media not merely sharpened our attention on these officials, but also reflected the increasing use of the media as a channel for local interest articulation and aggregation in the public sphere. For instance, Shanghai's People's Broadcasting Station and the East China Branch of the *People's Daily* jointly organized a radio hotline program for provincial leaders from six provincial units in East China in 1995, during which these leaders tried to show their concern for the people and their ability to articulate local interests by exploring ways to boost local economic development.[10] The analysis of the profile of top provincial leaders provided in this study is among the first steps toward a better understanding of their role in Chinese politics.

Last but not least, difficulties in central-provincial relations revealed in the 1990s also capture our attention on the important political role played by the provincial leaders. The purge of Beijing's party secretary, Chen Xitong, in April 1995 underlines the challenge posed by a recalcitrant strongman against the Center under the leadership of Deng Xiaoping's successor, Jiang Zemin. In many speeches made by top leaders in the mid 1990s, tensions in central-local relations remained a constant theme. For instance, in a key speech made at the Fifth Plenum held in September 1995, General Secretary Jiang Zemin not only openly recognized the existence of contradictions between the Center and localities, but also called for more compliance from the localities toward the Center. As he put it,

> Some localities and departments have paid undue attention to their own partial interests, and have failed to do what they should in implementing the central principles and policies, and some even went so far as to disobey orders and defy prohibitions. The power belonging to the central authorities has not been completely centralized, and in some aspects, it is over-centralized . . . We will not allow the existence of either local interests or departmental interests that jeopardize the interests of the country as a whole.[11]

Parts of the difficulties in central-provincial relations are related to the growing inequalities between the provinces. One recent study pointed out that the growth rate of the real per capita gross domestic product (GDP) in the eastern region was 15.5 percent while those in the middle and western regions were respectively only 10.3 percent and 9.2 percent during the 1991–1994 period.[12] The ratio of real per capita GDP in the east to that in the middle and western parts of China has sharply changed from 100:63.8:55.8 in 1990 to 100:53.0:44.5 in 1994, indicating that the gap between the richer and the poorer regions has become further widened in the 1990s. Provincial leaders from the poor inland areas have also become increasingly assertive in voicing their concerns over such disparities.[13] The Ninth Five-Year Plan (1996–2000) approved in March 1996 has thus attempted to address inter-regional inequalities by putting more emphasis on investment in basic construction and energy exploration, encouraging the relocation of manufacturing industries, adjusting prices of raw materials, gradually increasing more fiscal assistance and organizing more anti-poverty projects in the inland areas as well as promoting better economic cooperation between the southeastern coastal regions and the central and western regions.[14] The critical role of provincial leaders in Chinese economic reform and politics, which will become even more significant in the post-Deng era, indeed demands serious scholarly attention. To sum up, this study promises to fill a gap in the literature on the post-Mao period by focusing on an important, but not yet fully explored area: the performance of provincial leadership and provincial experience in introducing and implementing economic reform.

Province as a Key Political Unit in China

Province (*sheng*) has been a key political and administrative unit in China since the Yuan dynasty in the thirteenth century. The provincial system has undergone radical changes over time in Chinese history, but it remains the most important level of government between the central authorities and the localities. A total of eleven provinces was first established in the Yuan dynasty, but their number increased to thirteen in the Ming dynasty.[15] By the end of the Qing dynasty, the number further rose to twenty-three. In the last days of the Nationalist regime, a total of forty-eight provincial units could be found in China. After the People's Republic of China (PRC) was established in 1949, the number of provincial units fluctuated over time, ranging from the height of fifty-two in 1950–1951 to twenty-eight during 1955–1956 and 1958–1966 (this figure and the following ones exclude Taiwan). During the 1949–1954 period, six supraprovincial units—the Great Administrative Areas—were established to facilitate the political consolidation during the early days of the regime, but they did not last very long. The total number of provincial units stood constant at thirty from 1967 to 1987. The recent trend is to further divide up these fairly large administrative units so that they can deal with their own problems in social and economic development in a more effective manner. Hainan Island was hived off from Guangdong to become a province and a Special Economic Zone (SEZ) in 1988. Chongqing, which covers the Three Gorges area, was upgraded from one of the centrally planned cities (*jihua danlieshi*) to be the fourth centrally administered city after Beijing, Shanghai and Tianjin, in March 1997. As of March 1997, China has a total of twenty-two provinces, four centrally administered cities, and five autonomous regions, excluding Taiwan. Hong Kong became a Special Administrative Region on July 1, 1997, as will Macau on December 20, 1999. Despite various administrative restructuring introduced in the reform era, such as empowering cities with provincial-level economic status (i.e., the designation of centrally planned cities), and giving subprovincial-level cities more economic authority, these changes have not fundamentally altered the crucial role of the provinces as the immediate subordinate level under the central government.

China's provinces are mammoth units, whether in terms of population, size, or even economic power, yet they are marked by extreme disparities (see Table I-1).[16] While the PRC is the third largest country after Russia and Canada, the number of its constituent provinces (31) is smaller than the number of states in the United States (50), which is about the same size as China. With over 1.6 million square kilometers, the size of China's largest province, Xinjiang, is that of a big country while the smallest provincial unit, Shanghai, occupies only 6,341 square kilometers. On average, each province measures 270,000 square kilometers. China's provinces, while smaller than the average size of provinces in Canada or Australia, are bigger than the states in the United States. Before the promotion of Chongqing into a centrally administered city, Sichuan province claimed a population of over 113 million people and would be ranked the eighth most populous "country" if counted alone as a single unit.[17] After Chongqing's separation, Sichuan still has a population of over 83 million! Each of the top five most populous provinces, namely Henan, Shandong, Sichuan, Jiangsu, and Guangdong, has a population between 68 and 91 million people, which are already much bigger than most nation-states in the world. For an average prov-

Table I.1

Basic Statistics of China's Provinces, 1995

Provinces	Size	Population	GDP	GDP per capita	Agri. output	Industrial output	Foreign investment
Beijing	16,807	1,251	1,394	11,150	164	1,733	1,106
Tianjin	11,305	942	920	9,767	133	1,725	1,586
Hebei	180,000	6,437	2,849	4,426	1,147	2,589	613
Shanxi	156,000	3,077	1,092	3,550	299	1,121	93
Inner Mongolia	1,280,000	2,284	832	3,646	373	648	88
Liaoning	145,700	4,092	2,793	6,826	761	3,544	1,568
Jilin	180,000	2,592	1,129	4,356	490	1,233	481
Heilongjiang	469,000	3,701	2,014	5,443	670	1,951	624
Shanghai	6,431	1,415	2,462	17,403	182	4,703	3,005
Jiangsu	100,000	7,066	5,155	7,295	1,686	8,987	5,325
Zhejiang	100,000	4,319	3,524	8,161	891	4,497	1,289
Anhui	130,000	6,013	2,003	3,332	980	2,063	516
Fujian	120,000	3,237	2,160	6,674	765	1,747	4,149
Jiangxi	166,600	4,063	1,205	2,966	631	990	345
Shandong	150,000	8,705	5,002	5,746	1,857	5,686	2,764
Henan	167,000	9,100	3,002	3,299	1,304	2,763	649
Hubei	180,000	5,772	2,391	4,143	988	2,785	886
Hunan	200,000	6,392	2,195	3,435	1,046	1,646	560
Guangdong	178,000	6,868	5,381	7,835	1,445	7,189	10,669

Guangxi	230,000	4,543	1,606	3,535	743	1,140	708
Hainan	34,000	724	364	4,988	202	154	1,184
Sichuan	570,000	11,325	3,534	3,120	1,520	3,229	619
Chongqing	82,000	3,002	473	1,575	n.a.	n.a.	n.a.
Guizhou	170,000	3,508	630	1,796	344	476	90
Yunnan	390,000	3,990	1,206	3,024	474	1,038	119
Tibet	1,200,000	240	56	2,332	35	8	n.a.
Shaanxi	200,000	3,514	1,000	2,845	381	948	392
Gansu	450,000	2,438	553	2,269	289	694	82
Qinghai	720,000	481	165	3,436	55	142	2
Ningxia	66,000	513	169	3,309	56	182	6
Xinjiang	1,600,000	1,661	834	5,024	415	764	188

Sources: Guojia tongjiju (ed.), *Zhongguo tongji nianjian 1996* (China Statistical Yearbook 1996) (Beijing: Zhongguo tongji chubanshe, 1996), pp. 43, 70, 365, 404 and 600; Zhou Shunwu (ed.), *China Provincial Geography* (Beijing: Foreign Languages Press, 1992).

Notes: size = square kilometers ; population = 10,000; agri. output = gross output value of farming, forestry, animal husbandry and fishery (100 million yuan); industrial output = gross output value of industry at township level and above (100 million yuan) ; gross domestic product (GDP) = 100 million yuan (current prices); GDP per capita = yuan; foreign investment = total foreign capital and investment actually acquired in US$ million; n.a. = not available.

ince like Jiangxi or Zhejiang, which has a population of over 40 million people, the population is as large as a medium-sized country. The differences of economic strength are even more striking. For instance, the GDP of Guangdong, the largest provincial economy in China, is 96 times that of Tibet, the smallest. On a per capita GDP basis, Shanghai ranks number one with an annual figure of 17,403 yuan, but it is about ten times that of Guizhou, the poorest province before the upgrading of Chongqing.

As the primary political unit under the central authorities, the provincial government and party apparatus constitute an indispensable link in China's political system. Constitutionally, not only do they carry out the decisions of the provincial people's congresses, but they also have to work under the unified leadership of the State Council, the highest executive organ of the Chinese government. The State Council regularly issues directives to the provincial governments for implementation, refinement, and transmission to subprovincial units such as cities, prefectures, counties, townships and towns. Policy implementation in China allows for flexibility and fine-tuning at the provincial level because the provincial government is often given the discretion to decide on the details and schedule of implementation. For instance, the scale of minimum wage, as required by the labor law passed in 1995, is determined by the provinces rather than the central government. The central government has prerogative over foreign policy and national defense, but this does not reduce the substantial role of the provinces in the Chinese policy process. With a bureaucratic rank similar to the ministries and commissions in the State Council, only provinces and provincial-level economic units, such as the centrally planned cities, are represented in national-level policy-making bodies, such as the annual national economic work conference and the annual national planning conference. The provincial people's congresses, plus special areas like Shenzhen, Xiamen and the Hong Kong Special Administrative Region, are granted the power to promulgate local legislations, but the National People's Congress (NPC) and its Standing Committee can annul local legislations if they are found to be in violation of the Constitution or national laws. The representation in the annual meetings of the NPC is organized along provincial jurisdiction and all subprovincial delegates operate as part of a provincial delegation, especially during small group deliberations. Given the vastness of China, provincial-level units are thus important in both administration and legislation. On the other hand, the provincial party committees and the party secretaries still continue to perform critical functions for the Communist party-state. The appointment of provincial party leaders and the formation of the provincial party committee, consists of a dozen or so important leaders from the Party, state and other functional areas, have to be screened and approved by the highest level of the Party. Provincial party officials and organs have to observe tight Party discipline in accordance with the principles of democratic centralism. In addition, provincial party committees and their members have to follow the policy line of the Central Committee and carry out united front, organizational and ideological work. However, while the Communist party committees have to implement the policies of the central party authorities, many of the members of the provincial party committees are also responsible for functional work directly linked to local interests, hence compelling them to serve two "masters" at the same time. Such competing demands on the provincial leaders make the study of provincial leadership and their reform performance even more fascinating as they are now given much more discretion in policy initiation and implementation in the reform era. The provinces, in short, remain a critical component of the Chinese political system and their leaders are a unique group of actors in Chinese politics.

The Study of Political Leadership

Studies of political leadership can be traced to Max Weber's typology of three ideal-types of authority, namely traditional, legal-rational, and charismatic authority, which correspond to different social formations in the modern world. Such a conception has been employed in studies of the deradicalization and demobilization of communist revolutions and the changing role of communist leadership.[18] Similarly, studies of western capitalist societies have also examined their changing political leadership and their management of the challenges facing industrialized societies.[19] These studies, while useful contributions in political science, are not particularly pertinent for our study of provincial leaders because they are concerned with the general trends of regime or societal transformation. Nonetheless, the relationship between the leaders and the socio-economic context within which they operate remains a key concern for scholars of political leadership. With the economic takeoff of East Asia, scholarly attention has focused on the role of technocrats in managing the developmental state and charting a development strategy for these newly industrializing countries.[20] In these works, political leadership is conceptualized as a highly autonomous state elite who formulates and implements an export-oriented development strategy through industrial policy and administrative guidance for business in an authoritarian political system.

In contrast to the above structural and comparative-historical approaches, recent contributions in political science theories tend to apply formal, mathematical models to the exercise of political leadership. Three major theoretical perspectives, namely the principal-agent approach, the agenda-setter approach and the political entrepreneur approach, can be identified in the recent literature.[21] The agency theory sees leadership as an institutional arrangement created by a principal (or principals) in order to achieve "some objective more efficiently, more effectively, or with higher probability than he, or they, could without the coordination and enhanced productivity provided by the leadership institution."[22] Empirical research following this approach then examines the incentive schemes of and interactions between the principals (e.g. the followers) and the agents (e.g.

the leaders). The agenda-setting approach emphasizes the agenda-setting aspect of leadership and examines how leaders manipulate their agenda-setting power to influence decision outcomes disproportionately to their individual voting power and in favor of their own preferences. Research in this tradition hence focuses on issues such as representation, voting, committee politics, and legislative leadership. The political entrepreneur approach analyzes the supply of political leadership in collective actions, especially in coordination and organization. Viewing the political arena as a political marketplace, this approach identifies a mutually beneficial relationship between the entrepreneur (or leader) and the followers in the supply of a collective good (such as collective action or organization). This perspective has been employed especially to explain various interest group activities. These three approaches, however, draw mainly upon the experience of democratic political systems, emphasize the interactions between the leaders and the followers, and require sophisticated analysis of the incentives, calculus and strategies of these players. The authoritarian nature of the Chinese political system renders the application of these approaches difficult. Huang Yasheng's study of central-provincial relations over investment, which adopts a rational, value-maximizing actor approach, offers insights on the politics between the Center and the provinces, but even this impressive study looks at provinces as an aggregate and has not fully addressed the actual political dynamics in central-provincial relations or the performance of provincial leaders in implementing reform.[23]

Our study examines political leadership at the subnational level from a behavioral perspective. Broad approaches to the study of political leadership can be classified into mainly two types in accordance with their scope of analysis: (a) studies that focus on the leading actors, whether in the form of elite analysis which examines leaders as collectivities or the study of individual leaders which focuses on their biographies or psychobiographies, and (b) studies which focus on the interactions between leaders and their context.[24] Instead of focusing on the incentive structures of actors and interactions between the leaders and the led, we will focus on the interactions between the leaders and their policy environments, namely how provincial leaders make use of the new opportunities created in the reform era and confront the new policy challenges facing their provinces. Rather than assuming that provincial leaders are only agents of the Center and that political institutions determine the policy process and policy outcomes, we examine how provincial leaders have shaped their policy agendas, coped with institutional constraints, and attempted to bring about change within a largely hierarchical, Leninist political system. Hence we see provincial leaders not only as participants in national government and politics, but also as active players in the provincial political system which involves coordinating, bargaining and mediating with subprovincial units as well as promoting local social and economic development.

The Critical Role of Provincial Leadership

Do leaders count in China's reform era? If they do, under what circumstances would provincial leaders play an active role in the Chinese policy process? The death of Deng Xiaoping in mid February 1997 reminds us of the critical difference that individual leaders make in contemporary Chinese politics. Deng himself indeed fully appreciated the significance of the leadership factor when he began to introduce reform. In 1984, when China's door was about to be opened further, Deng sharply pointed out that in order to implement the open policy, the key was whether leaders in the localities were open-minded and energetic.[25] The study of leadership was once the dominant paradigm in the study of Chinese politics, with an emphasis on a dozen or so national leaders. With the demise of charismatic leaders like Chairman Mao Zedong and the growing institutionalization of the Chinese political system, scholarly attention on individual leaders has been replaced by increasing interest on the role of bureaucracy, bureaucratic politics and organizational dynamics of the policy process in post-1978 China, and less on the exercise of political leadership, whether at the central or the provincial level.[26] With the exceptions of, for instance, Fujian, Guangdong, Guizhou, Shanghai, Sichuan, and Zhejiang, there are not even political histories of the provinces.[27] Indeed, the study of provincial leaders and their performance, whether in the prereform or reform era, has not received sufficient scholarly attention. There has been an increasing number of aggregate studies of the profile and careers of provincial elites, but few make a systematic analysis of the role of individual leaders in the policy process.[28] Maria Chan Morgan's study of the leadership style of a provincial leader, Tao Zhu, Guangdong's party secretary in the pre–Cultural Revolution era, is a rare exception.[29]

In contrast to the focus on the top national leaders as found in studies of Maoist China, the emphasis on provincial leaders and their performance offers an excellent opportunity for further scholarly research not only because the complexities and challenges of governing the administrative units under their jurisdiction are in many ways similar to that of an ordinary nation-state, but also because these leaders play a vital role in engendering social and economic change in the reform era.[30] First, the role of the provinces and their leaders is critical in China's reform endeavor since 1978. Even in the prereform era, provincial leaders allied with particular central leaders in their efforts to launch new policy initiatives.[31] The key role of the provinces in bringing about policy change has actually become even more salient with the launching of reform and open policy in the post-Mao period.[32] Reminiscent of Chairman Mao's rallying of provincial support for his radical economic policies in the late 1950s, Deng Xiaoping's political strategy of economic reform hinges upon the support and initiative of provincial governments to introduce reform despite the resistance of central bureaucracies.[33] The delegation of economic power to the provinces and localities, rather than economic agents such as enterprises, created vested interests and intensified their demands for more economic power from the central government since 1978. Further, as David S.G. Goodman has rightly pointed out, "national decision-making was frequently an incremental process involving provincial experimentation before a final decision was reached."[34] The Chinese policy process itself has thus institutionalized the involvement of provincial leaders. Their role in national policy making has become even more critical in the reform era because of their enhanced control over power and resources.

Second, as aptly pointed out by one former official from Guangdong, the reason why leaders mattered a great deal in the reform era was because China did not have a reform model to emulate and the Chinese political system was not sufficiently institutionalized.[35] In fact, the incrementalist approach of China's reform process enables provincial leaders to interpret central policies more liberally than if central policies are more clearly defined and their implementation more effectively monitored. In the early days of reform, when ideological and political resistance to change the Maoist system was still prevailing, provincial leaders did play a key role in emancipating people from the Maoist mindset, promoting reform-minded officials to replace the revolutionary old guards, as well as encouraging local development initiative and flexibility in implementing reforms. In other words, once more systematic rules and regulations are used to institutionalize the Chinese political and economic systems, then the role for leadership might be sharply reduced.

Third, provincial leaders perform the role of policy entrepreneurs in the Chinese policy process. In an authoritarian political system like China, the "policy window" (i.e. the opportunity to force an authoritative decision) was often opened by the top central leaders because of the hierarchical nature of the government. While the "policy window" might be opened by central leaders, as often found in the inspection visits of preeminent leaders, or by other regular events in the political system like the convening of major party and state meetings, provincial leaders could take advantage of such openings and influence the policy-making process by acting as "policy entrepreneurs."[36] In particular, the granting of preferential policies by the Center to the localities actually requires provincial leaders to be attentive toward the opening of such "policy windows." They have to find the most opportune time to lobby on behalf of their provinces, bring specific policy solutions to the issues that arise, and shape the output of policy making in their favor. The provincial party and state leaders are given many such opportunities to perform these tasks because they are also national politicians who can legitimately shape the policy-making process. Indeed, whether they have done so skillfully makes a good test of their political leadership.

Fourth, provincial leaders are agents for multiple principals, one in the capital and one in their own province. On the one hand, as the Center still commands power over personnel appointment, the tenure of provincial party and state leaders is ultimately decided by the highest level of authority in the Party, not by their home province. In fact, most provincial leaders do not serve a five-year term and are often transferred to other postings after three or four years (if not an even shorter period) in one province. China's unitary political system ensures that the legislative and executive power of provincial governments and people's congresses are be constrained by the higher, national levels such as the Central Committee, the State Council and the NPC and its Standing Committee. Despite the weakening of central control over economic management in the localities, the Center has never given up the power over personnel appointment and has further developed other mechanisms of administrative monitoring in the reform era, such as monitoring appointment decisions and conduct through auditing, collecting information and disciplinary inspection.[37] On the other hand, as provincial party secretaries are "elected" by the corresponding party congresses and governors by the provincial people's congresses, they are also responsible to the local community and people. Most importantly, just as provincial leaders have to take their demands to the central government in Beijing, subprovincial units also have to make their cases to the provincial authorities for arbitration and resolution. Provincial leaders, as agents of the Center and implementors of national policy, also have to act as advocates and representatives of the provinces. Indeed, as rightly pointed out by David S.G. Goodman, provincial leaders play the role of "political middlemen" in the Chinese political system. Provincial leaders, therefore, have to walk a fine line between blind imposition of central directives and excessive promotion of local interests. Such cross-cutting pressures and constraints actually require a delicate act of political leadership and offer both opportunities and challenges for provincial leaders. If circumstances permit, it would be best for provincial leaders to please both the Center and their own provinces. When such a nice scenario is impossible, however, they have to make tough decisions. In short, the competing demands on provincial leaders in the Chinese political system only make a study of provincial political leadership even more fascinating.

Fifth, as officials governing sizable territories, provincial leaders are not only prominent political figures in their own jurisdictions but also a ready source for elite recruitment to the Center. The ex–party secretary from Shanghai, Jiang Zemin, was promoted to be the general secretary of the Party after a fairly successful tenure in China's largest metropolis. Two of the four premiers in the entire history of the PRC, Hua Guofeng and Zhao Ziyang, were former provincial officials. Former vice premiers such as Ke Qingshi and Tao Zhu in the Mao era as well as Wan Li, Tian Jiyun, Zhu Rongji, Jiang Chunyun and Wu Bangguo in the post-Mao era all came from a provincial career background. Similarly, in other important organs of the Chinese political system, former provincial officials are holding key positions, including Tian Jiyun, a close aide of Zhao Ziyang from Sichuan who is the current vice chairmen of the NPC, as well as Li Ruihuan and Ye Xuanping, formerly leaders of Tianjin and Guangdong who are respectively chairman and vice chairman of the Chinese People's Political Consultative Conference. A rising political star, Hu Jintao, a member of the Standing Committee of the Politburo, has served as a party secretary in Guizhou (1985–1988) and Tibet (1988–1992). Provincial experience not only serves to bridge national and local politics. but also provides useful exposure to the challenges of territorial administration for budding politicians. In the Politburo, the highest policy-making organ of the Party, provincial party secretaries have been regularly represented since 1979. Although the official representation of provincial leaders only includes Xie Fei from Guangdong, Huang Ju from Shanghai and Wei Jianxing from Beijing in the 1995–1996 period, at least four other members of the Politburo have maintained close ties with the provinces, including most notably Jiang Zemin, Zhu Rongji, Li Ruihuan, Jiang Chunyun and Wu Bangguo. These ex-provincial leaders still exercise a great deal of influence in their former place of posting. For instance, Li Ruihuan frequently commented on Tianjin's affairs and installed his own associates in the municipal government since his promotion to the Center in 1989.[38] Postings in Shanghai, in particular, have served as a launching pad for careers at the highest level, as one study reveals that its leaders were far more likely than those from other areas to be further promoted, or demoted.[39] The above cursory review, in short, shows that provincial leaders are not only pivotal actors in the Chinese political process but also key agents in undertaking economic reform.

Research Design

The primary goal of this book is to study how different types of provincial leadership have emerged, formulated provincial reform strategies and shaped patterns of economic reform in post-Mao China. Our earlier discussion has already examined the critical role of provincial leadership in the Chinese policy process, hence the following sections will analyze the choice of provincial reform strategies and provincial patterns in implementing economic reform as case studies for this project.

Provincial Reform Strategies

The performance of provincial leaders in crafting an effective reform strategy as well as making adjustments along the way to overcome difficulties and coping with the changing environment presents a crucial test of their leadership visions and skills in the reform era. Even in the implementation of the household responsibility reform, which is commonly understood as having relied heavily upon local initiatives, provincial leadership played crucial roles of both actively supporting (in the case of Anhui) and vehemently opposing (in the case of Heilongjiang) the policy.[40] The reform strategies of provincial authorities remain a key determinant of the fate of reform. As Kenneth Lieberthal and Michel

Oksenberg have rightly observed, "the provincial level is a gatekeeper guarding and providing access to the local levels."[41] In other words, not only can the provincial authorities channel demands between the Center and localities, but they can also coordinate and facilitate the implementation of central policies, or initiate policies that largely benefit their own provinces. In the 1980s, provincial leaders who were able to capitalize on the proper timing and sequencing of reforms, such as in Guangdong and Jiangsu, have also achieved faster economic progress in these provinces than those that lack such pioneering spirit and competence. In short, the reform strategies formulated by provincial leaders not only constitute a critical factor shaping the success or failure of reform, but also furnish a meaningful indicator to evaluate the performance of provincial leadership.

Case Studies of Resource Allocation and Acquisition of Foreign Capital and Investment

In addition to provincial strategies of economic reform, our inquiry allows for detailed case studies of provincial implementation of economic reform. Our focus in the domestic arena is on provincial policies toward resource allocation and our focus in the external arena is on provincial foreign economic policies, namely policies toward acquisition of foreign capital and investment. While many other reforms also deserve serious scrutiny, our focus on the above two policies is based on sound intellectual grounds, especially in view of the theme of this book. First, these two policies have experienced substantial changes and are both critical issues in the reform era. Fiscal management and investment have gained growing attention among scholars not only because of their major role in shaping the fate of economic reform, but also because of the many policy reforms that have been launched since 1978. Most recently, for instance, the fiscal arrangements between the Center and the provinces have moved away from the fiscal contracting regime to the revenue-sharing system since 1994 so that more revenue would be accrued to the central government.[42] Central control over investment in the provinces has become weakened, but the central government has also regularly resorted to administrative recentralization in order to alleviate economic overheating, the latest being the macro-economic retrenchment introduced in the summer of 1993. Similarly, as the largest recipient of foreign investment in the developing world, China's foreign economic policy has attracted widespread attention because its foreign trade and acquisition of overseas capital have not merely become vital components in its economic transformation but have also figured prominently as an issue in bilateral relations with countries like the United States. Second, and more importantly, changes in these policies directly affect not only the interests of different economic sectors and localities inside the provinces, but also the relationship between the Center and the provinces as well as between the provinces. Both policy issues are also highly political because of their conspicuous role in the contest between the market-oriented and the conservative wings of the top leadership in China. For example, the market-oriented reformers tended to favor more decentralization of power and resources to the provinces and enterprises as well as a more liberal policy toward the absorption of foreign capital and investment.[43] On the contrary, their conservative colleagues favored more centralization of power and resources at the central level and were more cautious about opening up China for foreign investment and acquiring foreign loans and credits. In sum, the pivotal role of provincial leadership in dealing with competing interests inside the provinces, bargaining with central leaders and government organs, as well as capturing domestic and external economic opportunities is well reflected in these two policy cases.

Selection of Provincial Cases

Comparative studies of subnational units in large countries, such as the states in the United States and India, provide a useful research design for analyzing contrasting governing styles of political elites and policy implementation.[44] As Gary King, Robert O. Keohane and Sidney Verba advise, "students of social policies can often look at governmental units that are subunits of the national state in which they are interested to test their hypotheses about the origins of various kinds of policies."[45] Recent works in comparative politics also begin to employ a subnational research strategy. Robert D. Putnam's majestic work on the origins of effective governments in modern Italy, which compares the social and economic performance of different regional governments, is an excellent example.[46] Studying variations across space and variations across time helps to improve qualitative research by increasing the number of observations. Similarly, disaggregating China into provincial units not only boosts the number of observations but also allows for closer scrutiny of empirical evidence. In China studies, comparative analysis of politics and policy implementation in provincial units is still not popular because of the complexity involved in data collection and research, although some new works begin to adopt this approach.[47] This study follows a comparative design by examining eight provincial cases. Each of the eight provinces in this book are absorbing cases on their own because of their variations in the paths of reform and the degree of economic achievements, but a systematic comparison and contrast of their experiences along the two policy dimensions opens an excellent window for assessing the performance of provincial leadership and provincial implementation of economic reform. This research design will maximize our room for comparison within the constraints of this book.

Each of China's thirty-one provinces is arguably a unique case because of the vast geographical and socio-economic diversities across these units, which also makes a representative sample of them difficult if not impossible. Some have chosen one particular province as a microsome of China and examined its role in policy implementation. Jean-Luc Domenach's major work on the Great Leap

Forward in Henan is a prime example.[48] Others have selected one province as a detailed case study in order to chart its particular path of social and economic development, whether in the reform or the prereform era.[49] Still others have explored a single case, such as Guangdong or Shanghai, from a multi-disciplinary perspective in order to illuminate the many facets of their drastic social, economic and spatial transformation in the reform era.[50] As our objective is to investigate the role of provincial leadership in the reform process, our choice of provincial cases is based on their significance in revealing contrasting provincial reform strategies and provincial patterns in the implementation of economic reform. In other words, we do *not* claim to provide a representative sample of China's thirty-one provinces.

It may be best to incorporate all of China's provinces in any study of provincial experience, but the limitation of space and our expertise makes it imperative to focus only on what we consider to be some of the most interesting cases. In order to illustrate contrasting provincial leadership, strategies and implementation of economic reform, we have selected a total of eight cases which reflect different levels of economic development, namely Fujian, Guangdong, Hainan, Shaanxi, Shandong, Shanghai, Sichuan and Zhejiang. These eight cases also diverge in their scope and pace of reform, with Guangdong, Shandong, Fujian, Hainan, and more recently, Shanghai, taking the lead. This sample has, however, already encompassed a cohort of key economic and political actors among the provinces. With over 401 million people, about one-third of China's population, these eight units contribute over 40 percent of the nation's GDP, 45 percent of industrial output, and 44 percent of total investment in fixed assets.[51] Because of their important social and economic characteristics, their reform experiences already merit attention on their own. Until the recent resurgence of Shanghai, Guangdong has been the shining star in the reform era and is still the largest provincial economy in terms of GDP and the most influential actor in China's foreign economic relations. Its recent economic slowdown nonetheless confirms the spread of economic dynamism to and the growing importance of Shanghai and the Yangtze Delta as one of the major growth zones in China. These recent developments aside, both Guangdong and Fujian will remain critical links in China's efforts to unify Hong Kong, Macau, and Taiwan. Shanghai, on the other hand, is a special provincial unit not simply because it is the largest metropolis and the future commercial and financial center for China, but also because its leaders have been far more active and prominent than those from other provinces in national politics.[52] Studying Shanghai's provincial leaders and their reform strategies since the mid 1980s sheds light not only on how these officials tried to re-invigorate China's most dynamic city, but also on the governing styles of its ex-officials such as Jiang Zemin and Zhu Rongji, who are now in charge of national affairs. Sichuan is a weighty province not just because it is the most populous (before the separation of Chongqing) but also because it is considered the leading region in China's southwest. Six of these units, namely Fujian,

Guangdong, Hainan, Shandong, Shanghai, and Zhejiang, are located in the coastal region and hence they have played an indispensable role in China's open door policy. With about 58 percent of China's registered foreign enterprises clustered in these eight cases, these eight provincial units contribute over 50 percent of the foreign capital and investment actually acquired by China, not to mention over two-thirds of its exports. To be sure, there are only two inland provinces and none of the five autonomous minorities areas are included. In sharp contrast to the other economic heavyweights, Hainan, a recently created province, is very small in terms of size and output. Shaanxi is similarly much weaker in economic strength. However, as suggested in the above overview, this sample of eight provincial units has already covered some of the most prominent political and economic actors that will continue to play leading roles in post-Deng China.

In the study of resource allocation, Shanghai and Guangdong provide two intricate extremes because the former had to hand over the bulk of its revenue to the Center while the latter was granted a favorable lump-sum transfer regime in the 1980s. How these two provinces dealt with the central government as well as with their localities would thus be exceptionally captivating. Further, if compared with other provinces, Guangdong has clearly taken a giant step ahead in economic reform in the 1980s and served as a reform model for other provinces. Shaanxi and Zhejiang, on the other hand, are radically different stories in terms of economic reform and economic development. Shaanxi is plagued with the problems left over not only from decades of central planning and the revolutionary legacies of the Mao era, but also by the difficulties of transforming from a resource-based economy to a modern, competitive economy in the reform era. One of its pressing missions is how to survive in view of dwindling central investment and support. Zhejiang, on the contrary, has a thriving economy, yet its political leadership for most of the reform era has been occupied by people who were conservative in political and economic orientation because of historical political reasons. While Zhejiang is an economic powerhouse and its GDP ranks fifth among the provinces, its leadership is still trying to define an effective development strategy in an increasingly competitive environment. In the study of foreign capital and investment, we have also covered rather interesting yet different provincial cases. Fujian used to be a backward coastal province, but like Guangdong, it has been endowed with special policies since 1979 and has become a major site in absorbing the growing Taiwanese investment. In 1995, the foreign capital and investment acquired was a sizable US\$ 41 billion, hence making it the fourth largest recipient of such funds among the provinces.[53] Shandong, another coastal economic heavyweight, has emerged as a front runner in acquiring foreign capital and investment since the late 1980s. In 1995, the total of foreign capital and investment acquired amounted to US\$ 27 billion, which put it as the fifth largest recipient of overseas funds. In contrast, despite its status as one of China's SEZs, Hainan lags far behind these two provinces in attracting foreign investment. Worse still, Sichuan, a land-locked province, obtains only a little more than half of the foreign capital and investment absorbed by Hainan. Such divergent provincial experiences provide an excellent opportunity for comparing the performance of provincial leadership and its impact on reform. Our research design, to be sure, is not perfect, but it is a step in the right direction. For instance, since various specific policy measures are introduced in each of our two policy areas and they have also changed over time, even more meticulous studies of each of these measures can still be attempted. Our design allows us to compare not only the performance of different provincial leaders in the same policy area, but also the achievements of different kinds of provincial leaders in two policy areas across different time spans. This research design, therefore, enables us to attempt substantively meaningful as well as methodologically sophisticated observations.

Provincial Leadership and Economic Reform:
An Analytical Framework

The framework outlined below will articulate a broad analytical scheme in order to facilitate comparison of our eight provincial cases. Although refinements will be made in individual chapters in order to fit each case, they are kept to a minimum in order to maintain the maximum degree of analytical coherence throughout the book. A variety of information, including interviews with provincial officials and researchers, statistics, documentary sources, and journalistic accounts, will be utilized in this study. Further, contributors have gauged the views of informants, be they officials, scholars, journalists, businessmen, or citizens, on provincial leadership and economic reform through interviews whenever possible. The leadership factor is considered as the *independent variable* while the strategies and implementation of economic reform the *dependent variable* of this study. Individual contributors have their own distinctive writing and argumentative style, yet such diversities enrich rather than weaken this project since their analyses all center on the key questions set out in our analytical framework.

Provincial Leadership

Definition

In order to analyze the performance of provincial leadership, it is first necessary to define our scope of analysis. By provincial leaders we refer to provincial party secretaries (or provincial first party secretaries in the early 1980s) and deputy party secretaries as well as provincial governors and vice governors. While the party secretary and governor work closely with their half a dozen or so deputies, these two key officials have evidently played a much more decisive role in defining the policy orientation of the province. The exercise of leadership is still primarily on their shoulders. While taking into account the performance and background of the above eight to ten provincial leaders as a group, our attention will inevitably concentrate on the party secretary and governor in each province. In each provincial case study, we will focus on various characteristics of provincial leaders in order to account for different provincial approaches to the strategy and implementation of economic reform. These characteristics include:

(1) Personal Background
   (a) age: which age cohort did these provincial leaders fall into (forties, fifties, or sixties)? how old were they when they were recruited into key provincial posts such as deputy party secretary or vice governor before becoming top provincial leaders? (i.e. were they high-flyers?) were they still in office beyond official retirement age?
   (b) native issue: were they natives of the provinces that they served and how long had they served in the same province? had they married natives from the province they served?
   (c) family background: what kind of families (e.g. cadres, intellectuals, workers, or peasants) did they come from? were they the offsprings of the first generation revolutionary leaders or close relatives of prominent leaders at the central level?
   (d) career history: what were their previous postings before becoming party secretary or governor? were they elevated all the way up from the local units to the highest posts within the province? were they transferred from another province or a central organ? which functional system (*xitong*) did they belong to before their appointment as top provincial leaders? what were their areas of expertise (e.g. engineering, economic management, state administration, or party work such as ideological, organizational or united front work)?
   (e) party history: when did they join the Communist Party? what happened to them during the Cultural Revolution? when were they appointed alternate or full members of the Central Committee? how did their seniority compare with other senior members in the provincial party-state organs? had they ever studied at the Central Party School?
   (f) education: what were their educational credentials? did they have university degrees or professional qualifications? were they majors in humanities and social science, natural science, or engineering in college?
   (g) personal styles: what were their personal managerial styles? did they prefer a low or high profile? did they make an effort to make themselves popular inside the province? did they spend a lot of effort in inspecting and cultivating the support of localities? were they decisive or non-decisive in dealing with key decisions? did they prefer

traveling overseas and forging ties with foreign businessmen during their tenure?

(2) Central Patronage. Did these provincial leaders enjoy close relations with key leaders in the Center? were these provincial leaders former subordinates of central leaders? were they picked and groomed by particular central leaders during the 1980s?

(3) Political and Economic Orientations. What were the professed views of these provincial leaders on reform and opening? did they have a distinctive orientation toward political reform and ideological issues? did they fully and immediately approve of the Center's crackdown in the aftermath of the June 4 incident?

Each contributor to this book will address most, if not all, of the above questions in individual chapters. Recent aggregate studies of provincial elites have identified the emergence of a new group of leaders in the provinces. A study of provincial elites in 1988 suggests that about 44.9 percent and 38 percent of these leaders respectively can be classified as party officials or government administrators and technocrats who are former engineers, factory managers, or directors of economic bureaus.[54] In particular, in stark contrast to the pattern in the prereform era where non-natives were more often top provincial leaders, the reform era witnessed the rise of locals in taking up provincial positions. For instance, over 43 percent of the party secretaries and governors are natives and some 73 percent of provincial leaders have spent their entire careers in the provinces they served. Useful as these data are, these aggregate results do not tell us more about the implications of such characteristics and how such background factors affect these leaders in action. Hence while acknowledging the impact of the changing domestic political and economic contexts on the calculation of provincial leaders, we consider the characteristics of provincial leaders as a key factor accounting for the varying performance of provincial leadership.

Three Types of Provincial Leaders

Studies of political leadership have devised various typologies to differentiate between leadership types, their goals and their impacts on society.[55] For instance, James MacGregor Burns' grand study of leadership postulates two broad categories, the transforming leaders and the transactional leaders. As the transforming leaders help and motivate followers to achieve a hierarchy of human needs ranging from basic needs to more lofty goals like self-actualization, they can be found in intellectual, reform, revolutionary, and heroic settings. On the other hand, transactional leaders assist the operation of existing social relationships and processes and they may take various forms, such as in opinion groups, party, executive and legislative leadership. In another detailed study of political leadership, Jean Blondel has suggested a two-dimensional typology of leadership, defined in accordance with the scope and degree of potential change that they have on society. For those who seek a wide scope of change, we can identify "saviors," "paternalists/populists," and "ideologues." For those who aim at a moderate scope of change (e.g. scope of a system), there are "comforters," "redefiners," and "reformists." And for those who attempt change with a specialized scope (e.g. policy area), one can find "managers," "adjusters/tinkerers," and "innovators." Nonetheless, these conceptions are too broad to capture the critical roles played by provincial leaders in the reform era. Nor do they tackle the special circumstances of the Chinese case.

Analyzing Chinese politics and policy from the perspective of leadership is not novel. Most of the existing studies, however, focus on top central leaders and distinguish them in accordance with their policy tendencies. Studies of Chinese politics in the reform era have employed different typologies to characterize leaders at the central level, as exemplified by the famous distinction between "reformers" and "conservatives."[56] Other more elaborate typologies include, for instance, Harry Harding's differentiation of top leaders into "restorationists," "radical reformers," and "conservative reformers" in his study of reform politics; Carol Lee Hamrin's distinction between "conservatives," "orthodox reformers," and "pragmatic reformers" in her studies of domestic and foreign policies as well as Dorothy Solinger's classification of central leaders into "marketeers," "bureaucrats," and "radicals" in her study of commercial policy.[57] Nonetheless, we think that to classify leadership into three categories of leadership types, namely pioneers, bandwagoners, and laggards can best capture the most important aspects of leadership qualities regarding the introduction and implementation of economic reform.[58] Hence this typology may not necessarily reflect other leadership qualities which may be equally essential for the discharge of other official provincial responsibilities. Several qualifications should be stated at the outset. The use of different classifications of leadership types does not imply that such types should be applied indiscriminately to China's provincial leaders. First, while we recognize that there are disagreements about reform and open policy within the thirty-one provincial party committees and provincial governments, these differences are not as important as the overall orientation of these provincial leaders in this study. Second, we believe that a province may be governed by different types of leaders during the post-Mao era. For instance, some provinces may be continuously governed by a provincial leadership that is especially enterprising and aggressive in undertaking economic reform, as in the case of Guangdong, while others may have a succession of different types of leaders during the 1980s, as in the case of Shandong. In fact, it is even possible to distinguish the changing performance of the same group of leaders as some of them may have been ambitious and reform-minded in the early 1980s but have become less entrepreneurial and more conservative in the early 1990s. While this conception already takes into account policy orientation, these three types of leaders are mainly differentiated on the basis of their performance in initiating and implementing economic reform. Specifically, our primary concern is on (a) their efforts to depart from central policies; (b) their efforts to take provincial initiatives and innovate in economic reform; and (c) their efforts to defend provincial interests and bargain with central leaders. By generalizing provincial leadership into these three categories does not imply that there are no other analytical categories that may be used in examining provincial leadership. However, the following categories offer a useful first step in studying the role of provincial leadership in initiating and implementing economic reform.

Pioneers

This kind of leader first tends to maximize the room for provincial initiative within the constraints of central policy. Not only do they often push central policy to the limit, but they are also willing to try path breaking and effective reform measures that may not be condoned by the central authorities. Second, they are far more willing to take risks in order to take full advantage of the opportunities made available in the reform era as China mainly follows an open-ended approach to economic reform. Since the central government may not even have an official reform program in certain policy areas, this type of leader is keen and skillful in exploiting such opportunities. Because of their ability to take initiatives in the reform era, these leaders lead their provinces ahead of the rest of the nation in economic reform, whether in depth or pace. Hence they often establish their own distinctive paths of reform. Further, this type of leaders is most daring in defending provincial interests and bargaining with central leaders whenever conflicts between provincial and central objectives and policies erupt. All of the above actions will, of course, entail criticism and intervention by the central government from time to time. However, their willingness to innovate and determination to defend provincial interests earn them support and popularity inside their own provinces.

Bandwagoners

In the first systematic study of bandwagoning in Chinese politics, Avery Goldstein argues that bandwagoning can be found in political systems in which "functional differentiation is low and influential resources are tightly concentrated in the hands of superordinate actors."[59] While our view is similar to his conception, we do not plan to extend it to a systematic analysis of the Chinese political system. Instead of trying to push the parameters of central policy to the maximum latitude, bandwagoners tend to operate within the confines of central policies. Consequently, while experimenting with reform schemes under central directives, they seldom deviate from central policy in the initiation and implementation of economic reform. Still, they often become ardent implementors of economic reform *after* these schemes are officially promulgated. These leaders want to be in the winning coalition and hence they are cautious before undertaking reform. Some of them may even be able to make a mark in implementing reforms enshrined by the Center. Second, perhaps because of their fear of unexpected policy consequences or because of their concern about their own careers, these leaders are less likely than the pioneers to initiate reforms that are not yet officially sanctioned by the Center. In other words, they are rather apathetic toward opportunities for experimenting with reforms. Finally, if compared with the pioneers, this type of leader is less enthusiastic in protecting and promoting provincial interests, hence they often yield to central demands without putting up a tough fight. Nonetheless, if central demands severely affect the vital interests of their provinces, they do face up to the Center.

Laggards

This type of leader, contrary to the above two types, is the least innovative, enterprising, and unyielding. The most conservative group of this type of leader does not favor change at all and is unwilling to depart from existing institutions or policies. Because of their personality and career concerns or their own political orientation, these cadres are skeptical of market-oriented reform and they still cling to some of the Maoist policies such as collectivized agriculture or the planning system, especially in the early days of reform. Some behave in a conservative manner because of their ideological and political affinity with Mao's ideas. Others act conservatively because of their inability to adapt to the new political and economic environment. They paid lip service to reform but did little to bring about change in practice. Most of these provincial leaders were replaced by more reform-minded leaders by the mid 1980s because of their old age, political conservatism or inability to launch economic reform. These leaders generally share the following characteristics. First, these leaders very much follow central policies to the word and are reluctant to take risks in introducing reforms that may bring about unpredictable consequences. Hence the provinces under their governance may lag behind the thrust of central policy. Secondly, if compared with the bandwagoners, these leaders are extremely unenthusiastic about provincial initiative and experimentation, hence they are also often called "conservatives" in many accounts of Chinese reform. They even fall behind the demands of the central government in economic reform because of their overly cautious inclination. By the time they recognize the benefits of some reform schemes, they have to learn from the experience of other provinces. Thirdly, instead of defending provincial interests, these leaders subscribe to central demands almost all the time, even at the cost of resistance from their provinces. Hence they become rather unpopular inside their own provinces whenever such central-provincial conflicts occur.

Provincial Strategies of Economic Reform

The following section attempts to develop a preliminary framework for examining provincial strategies of economic reform. Some elements outlined below may be more applicable to some cases than others, while the relative significance of these elements may also vary in each case because of the specific economic and political conditions of the province concerned. While individual contributors may capitalize on different aspects of the strategies embraced by a particular provincial leadership, they address most, if not all, of the following issues because this framework helps to suggest a common analytical perspective for the entire project and forms a basis for comparison across different provincial cases. Recent studies of central-local relations have enlightened us about the complex dynamics involved in these intricate relations. However, with only some exceptions, most of these studies offer insights on the overall pattern of central-provincial relations rather than on the details of individual provincial cases.[60]

Formulating an Effective General Program of Reform

An effective reform program requires appropriate timing and sequencing in implementing market-oriented economic reforms. There is, of course, no single universal law about the proper timing and sequencing of reform because a great deal of controversy over such issues exists in the literature in economics and political science. Nonetheless, it is possible to probe whether provincial leaders have a systematic program of reform and whether these programs are feasible and effective in view of the special economic, social, and political attributes of that particular province. First, the timing of introducing reform is critical. The timing of reform demands an astute analysis of the rapidly changing economic and political circumstances in the reform era. In other words, the issue of proper timing reflects a shrewd identification by provincial leaders of the most advantageous moment to introduce reform in view of developments in central-provincial relations, social and political reactions to initial reform moves, as well as opportunities created by the external economic environment. A second and related issue concerns the sequencing of reform. The sequencing of reform is a multi-faceted issue because we can examine this problem in different dimensions (e.g. economic reform and political reform), in different sectors (e.g. industry, agriculture, and service), as well as in different priorities (e.g. price reform and ownership reform). For instance, the provincial leadership in Guangdong implemented price reform in the first half of the 1980s as a spearhead for reforms in other sectors. Such a bold move not only avoided the economic difficulties of implementing price reform in the late eighties when almost every province was deregulating prices, but also served to overcome the psychological barriers among the people toward market reform in general. Similarly, the successful implementation of rural reform also has a major demonstration effect on industrial and other reforms introduced in China and other countries.[61]

Management of Central-Provincial Relations

One of the primary challenges for provincial leaders in the reform era is the management of central-provincial relations, which includes such actions as securing favorable fiscal and investment regimes, getting test sites for reform, acquiring more policy discretion in different issue areas, lobbying for privileged treatment or exceptions, coping with central interventions and courting support from central leaders.

Creating Institutional Support for Reform

An adroit strategy of reform inevitably involves the creation of institutional support that would sustain the reforms. Examples of building institutional support include the recruitment and promotion of capable and reform-minded officials as allies at the subprovincial level and re-organization of governmental institutions and administrative procedures.

Winning Social Support and Mobilizing Political Allies

In addition to institutional support in party and state apparatus, provincial leaders also have to secure support from society. Efforts to win the trust and backing of local people are reflected in the implementation of popular reform measures (or conversely the alleviation of undesirable effects caused by reform) and measures that helped to prepare people psychologically for unpopular repercussions of reform such as inflation. Provincial encouragement and protection of local reform experiments and decentralization of provincial power to the localities also serve to mobilize political allies at the subprovincial level.

Alleviating Side-Effects of Economic Reform

Economic reform in socialist systems has been accompanied by various social and economic outcomes that are often deemed undesirable by the government and the people. Although the provincial leadership may have won support from society through various measures identified above, it is imperative for them to demonstrate that they can effectively deal with problematic consequences caused by reform.[62] Alleviation of extreme polarization of society and attacks on official corruption and criminal activities, for instance, are some prominent examples.

Acquiring External Assistance

Finally, provincial leaders enlist various kinds of external assistance in undertaking economic reform. A wide range of efforts in this respect can be noted, such as borrowing new ideas from overseas businessmen and international financial institutions like the World Bank, or absorption of foreign capital and investment through overseas Chinese ties.[63]

Provincial Implementation of Economic Reform

After analyzing the general provincial strategy of economic reform, we will focus on the provincial patterns of implementation in two areas, namely policy toward resource allocation and policy toward foreign capital and investment. We do not seek to provide a comprehensive and exhaustive analysis of the implementation process, nor do we attempt to cast a definitive assessment of the outcomes of these reform policies. Rather, our focus is on the impact of provincial leadership on the patterns of implementation.

Provincial Policy toward Resource Allocation

The key issues to be explored in our study of provincial policy toward resource allocation center around fiscal and investment policies. By fiscal policy we refer not only to the fiscal regimes between the central government and the province but also to provincial budgetary priorities and subprovincial fiscal arrangements. Important changes in China's fiscal system have been introduced since 1978 in order to clarify and enhance the economic responsibility of the provinces in allocating resources and their incentives in extracting revenue.[64] In fact, a recent study indicates that whether a provincial leader was to be promoted or demoted depended not simply upon economic performance of the province under his or her leadership. Rather, leaders who showed a better record in generating revenue were more likely to be promoted than demoted.[65] In this study, we will concentrate on how provincial leaders manage a host of critical fiscal issues. For instance, how were revenue and expenditure shared between the central government and the provinces as well as between the provinces and their localities? What were the major changes in the pattern of budgetary transfers between different sectors and localities inside the province? What were the impacts of burgeoning extra-budgetary funds on the provincial budgets and how did they influence central-provincial fiscal relations and subprovincial fiscal arrangements?

In addition, we will examine the province's priorities in capital investment, discretion in capital investment, and control over capital investment within the province. This dimension of resource allocation directly affected the relationship between the provincial governments and the central government because central control over capital investment was reasserted regularly in order to ensure macro-economic stability in the post-Mao era.[66] Further, some provinces have made strategic shifts in their sectoral emphasis in investment, such as augmenting the development of light industry or the service sector. Not only have such changes in investment altered the financial relationship between the province and its subordinate enterprises and localities, but they have also incited competition for resources and power among different industrial sectors and enterprises with different kinds of ownership systems. In sum, our study of resource allocation will illuminate how provincial leaders balance the conflict and cooperation in central-provincial relations as well as the contending social, sectoral and local interests within the provinces.

Provincial Policy toward Foreign Capital and Investment

Similar to the issue of resource allocation, provincial policy toward foreign capital and investment frames not only central-provincial relations but also the relationship among provinces as well as between the provincial and subprovincial authorities. Further, this policy deals with the multi-faceted linkages between China and the capitalist world economy. The acquisition of foreign capital and investment is undoubtedly one of the core elements of China's open policy. Not only does it affect local economic development, employment, and technology transfer, but it also shapes foreign trade and other ties with the outside world. Although some contributors analyze other related dimensions of open policy, such as foreign trade, in their chapters, our primary concern is on various issues about the acquisition of foreign capital and investment. Key areas in our inquiry of provincial policy toward foreign capital and investment involve the degree of provincial discretion in the acquisition of foreign capital and investment vis-a-vis the central government and provincial priorities in the attraction of foreign funds.

(a) Provincial discretion in the acquisition of foreign capital and investment: A host of questions will be explored in order to ascertain the degree of provincial discretion in attracting outside funds. Has the province been granted a great deal of freedom by the Center? Or has it circumvented central policies in order to realize its own objectives? Has the province decentralized its control over the acquisition of foreign capital and investment to subprovincial authorities?

(b) Provincial priorities in acquiring foreign capital and investment: Another related issue in the study of provincial policy over foreign capital and investment concerns a province's priorities in acquiring outside resources. The forms of foreign direct investment and foreign capital have clear economic and political implications. For instance, foreign borrowing may allow the province more freedom in using such funds while foreign direct investment may entail stronger economic and cultural influence of foreigners or Hong Kong and Taiwanese businessmen in their localities. The concentration of foreign investment in one industrial sector may also have both positive and negative consequences for local industries in the provinces. Provincial priorities in attracting foreign capital and investment will also fashion the overall pattern of industrial growth in China, which will inevitably arouse the attention of the central government.

In sum, while recognizing that policy areas that are not related to resource allocation or foreign investment may have a different dynamic from those suggested in this study, we will be able delineate a preliminary generalization of provincial leadership and its impacts on provincial strategies of economic reform and provincial policy implementation through comparing and contrasting the eight provincial cases. Some interesting observations, though not universal generalizations, about different provincial cases, e.g. industrial versus rural provinces, coastal versus inland provinces, rich versus poor provinces, can also be sketched.

Provincial Leadership and Reform Strategies: An Overview

The theme that emerges from our eight provincial studies is that provincial leadership really matters in initiating and implementing economic reform and open policy. With the exception of Zhejiang where a conservative and risk-averse leadership was regarded as peripheral to its economic transformation, the role of a pioneering leadership is a critical factor in the economic reform and development in Fujian, Guangdong, Hainan, Shandong and Shanghai. In Sichuan, Zhao Ziyang's leadership did help to spearhead rural and enterprise reform since the late 1970s, but his departure in 1980 and the absence of sufficient support from the Center were not conducive to its efforts to tackle the many challenges facing this land-locked province. In Shaanxi, a combination of leadership failures and long-standing conservatism among its leaders imposed serious constraints on economic reform.

Effective extraction and allocation of resources are essential tasks for economic reform and economic growth. Two of our cases, Shanghai and Guangdong, are successful examples while the other two, Shaanxi and Zhejiang, reveal a somewhat different story. Shanghai's experience is especially striking in this respect. The straitjacket of central planning, the heavy burden of fiscal remittance to the Center and the urban decay caused by socialist development prevented Shanghai from re-gaining its vitality in the early days of the reform era. However, the reshuffling of the municipal leadership since 1985 opened the door for major policy change in this former industrial base of China's planned economy. As Zhimin Lin's study shows, the appointment of relatively younger, technocratic leaders like Rui Xingwen, Jiang Zemin, Zhu Rongji, Wu Bangguo and Huang Ju as the city's leaders marked a turning point in the city's post-1978 history. Unlike most of their predecessors who were near retirement age when they were appointed, these leaders (who were mostly in their fifties) were young enough to devote their energy to bring about Shanghai's economic recovery so that their accomplishments could be recognized by the Center in the future. These leaders were able to articulate, and constantly revise, a new and coherent development strategy, operationalize measures to put grand ideas into practice, and conceive innovative strategies to mobilize resources in order to achieve the above goals. Key features of this new game plan are to develop Pudong as a new growth pole for Shanghai, embark upon a large-scale improvement of its aging infrastructure, establish Shanghai as China's foremost center for trade and finance, as well as to build up modern industries and render other support for development. Their innovative strategies to mobilize resources are multi-dimensional, which include the bargaining over a new fiscal arrangement with the Center, the mobilization of resources from non-budgetary sources such as domestic and overseas markets, the establishment of new companies to manage such funds more effectively for urban reconstruction and local industries, and adjustment of budgetary allocations such as reforming the delivery of subsidies. Investment in neglected areas such as housing, urban construction and transportation, not only improved the city's investment environment but also galvanized the support of the local people for this novel development strategy. While some of these accomplishments could not have been possible without approval by the central government, it is amply clear that these leaders are the key driving forces that translate these policies into splendid practice.

Similarly, according to Peter T.Y. Cheung, the main secret why Guangdong was able to develop rapidly since 1978 was its leaders' ingenious mobilization and allocation of resources for economic development. Most of Guangdong's leaders in the post-Mao era, beginning from Ren Zhongyi and Liang Lingguang to Xie Fei and most recently, Lu Ruihua, can be considered as pioneers in reform, although their specific tasks and challenges have changed over time. The role of Guangdong's leaders is critical in securing a favorable fiscal arrangement with the central government and in decentralizing resources and authority to subprovincial governments. The lump-sum transfer regime was adopted as the primary fiscal arrangement between the province and the central government as well as between the provincial government and subprovincial governments. Despite various deficiencies, this regime has helped to stimulate local enthusiasm in revenue collection, facilitate economic reform, and foster rapid economic growth. Guangdong's leaders were equally skillful and successful in mobilizing resources for investment from both domestic and international sources, acquiring favorable treatment from the central government in investment, setting priorities for capital investment and technical renovation, and reforming the investment system. Not only did these efforts help to multiply the sources available for investment, but they also encouraged flexibility, competition, as well as economic responsibility in the investment process. This chapter highlights the contribution of Guangdong's leaders in taking advantage of the changing economic and political environments and in setting out an effective reform strategy in accordance with the unique conditions of the province.

In contrast to the above two cases, Keith Forster maintains that the role of provincial leadership in robust Zhejiang was really marginal to its phenomenal economic growth since 1978. Most of Zhejiang's provincial officials from 1978 to the early 1990s were very cautious and reactive cadres, rather than a group of highly capable leaders who could lead reform. Hence they were mostly laggards and bandwagoners. The entrenchment of such a leadership was the product of political dynamics that can be traced to the prereform era, such as the influence of a former leader, Jiang Hua, but it was hardly conducive to the launching of economic reform. For instance, the province fell behind the nation in inaugurating agricultural reform and was undecided or apathetic toward urban reform and greater opening to the outside world. Unlike leaders in other coastal areas who championed reform, Zhejiang's leaders were not noted for orchestrating major reform initiatives, yet they did not, or were perhaps unable to, stop the radical changes unleashed in the reform era, such as the rise of township and village enterprises and the private sector. The province failed to invest adequately in agriculture and other basic infrastructure, or offer sufficient support to the rural enterprises, yet its favorable geographical location and the momentum of the reform program of the central government continued to facilitate its sustained economic growth. To be sure, the inability of the leaders to play a more positive role in reforming the economy or formulating a more dexterous development strategy might have inhibited Zhejiang from fully exerting its strengths. The province, in other words, could have been even more better off if not for its leadership.

Shaanxi's provincial leadership and middle-level cadres, as Kevin Lane's study argues, not only failed to find solutions to the economic difficulties of this inland province, but had actually become part of the obstacles to economic reform themselves. He shows that the revolutionary heritage of this former Communist stronghold, the legacy of the centrally planned economy, and the lack of adequate backing from the central government, created a highly unfavorable context for transforming a resource-based economy like that of Shaanxi. Shaanxi's leaders were apparently laggards. With a history of aggressively pursuing Maoist policies and the deep influence of egalitarian values among the cadre corps, provincial leaders opposed the implementation of the household responsibility system in agriculture until 1982, which was two to three years behind the other provinces, and failed to promote rural collective enterprises as the engine of growth in the countryside. Nor were they enthusiastic about implementing the enterprise responsibility system and supportive of private enterprises. In particular, Zhang Boxing's long tenure as Party boss from 1987 to 1994 was distinguished by his poor performance and an ongoing conflict with the governor, Bai Qingcai. The tradition of appointing natives, the domination of the Northern Shaanxi Gang in the provincial administration, the poor education level and parochial outlook of the cadres, and their ideological affinity with Maoist egalitarianism together served to perpetuate the conservatism among officials and forestall policy changes. The designing of a coherent development strategy and the implementation of economic reform hence became extremely difficult under these circumstances. With the dwindling of central investment and policy support and a growth record below that of the national average, the province experienced a deepening fiscal crisis after 1978. Various fiscal reforms introduced in the reform era further aggravated Shaanxi's predicament as it was so used to the fruits of the previous "iron rice bowl." In sharp contrast to coastal areas like Shanghai or Guangdong, the provincial leadership was not active in exploring and utilizing alternative sources of capital. Given the worsening economic crisis, new difficulties created in the reform era, such as the flow of capital and the brain drain to the coastal areas and the rising expenditure precipitated by fiscal decentralization and popular demands, were creating additional constraints on the province's economic development. Whether a more enterprising leadership could have made a major difference in Shaanxi can never be known, but comparison with the recent experience in neighboring Shanxi is instructive. Unlike his conservative colleagues in Shaanxi, Hu Fuguo, Shanxi's party secretary, developed and applied innovative strategies to deal with the central government and campaign for popular support for his policy initiatives.[67]

While Shanxi could not be transformed overnight, such a pioneering leadership displays a striking comparison with its conservative counterparts in neighboring Shaanxi.

Our four studies of foreign capital and investment also unveil interesting cases of contrasts. Jae Ho Chung's chapter maintains that as a leading coastal province, Shandong's recipe for reform and development can be captured in a set of key components. With a rich cultural heritage, a favorable coastal location and an endowment of natural resources including energy, Shandong possesses some of the important ingredients that are vital to development. But these conditions could not be turned into positive factors for growth until policy innovations were introduced by its leaders. In the prereform era, due to the looming political shadow of Beijing, the province had exhibited compliant and opportunistic behavior. Although its leaders in the early reform period were either bandwagoners or failed reformers, the situation began to change remarkably when Jiang Chunyun was made governor, and later party secretary, of the province in the late 1980s. In the reform era, Shandong's leaders managed to get considerable preferential treatment from the central government by using personal networks, and, equally importantly, to exploit such policies to the fullest extent. These included, in particular, central preferential policies in foreign economic relations such as the designation of coastal open cities, development zones and free trade zones for various cities in the province. Aside from devising an appropriate regional development strategy, consistently pursuing a balanced approach to industrial development, and skillfully mustering resources for infrastructural projects, these leaders were also adept at promoting foreign trade and taking advantage of a favorable international factor—the improvement and later normalization of bilateral relations between South Korea and China. By maximizing the province's own internal strengths and actively seeking Hong Kong, South Korean and other investments, Shandong's pioneering leadership succeeded in developing its economy into the second largest provincial powerhouse.

Our second case on foreign investment concerns another front runner in China's reform era, Fujian. As one of the two provinces given the "special policies" in 1979, Fujian's reform experience offers an immediate comparison with neighboring Guangdong. Shawn Shieh's study suggests that the province has experienced quite distinct types of leaders and different phases of reform and open policy. After a short stint by a laggard who was unenthusiastic toward reform, the province came under the leadership of Xiang Nan. If Guangdong's early foundation for economic reform was laid by Ren Zhongyi, Fujian's reform gained momentum under Xiang's pioneering leadership. Xiang introduced a number of key initiatives, such as decentralizing powers to lower levels and recruiting younger and more competent officials, but he was also burdened with a lot of problems which obstructed the successful execution of his ideas. Hence he acted more like a bandwagoner than a pioneer at times. His successor, Chen Guangyi, was more suitably called a bandwagoner as he was less enterprising and skillful in introducing reform. Nonetheless, the relaxation of economic ties between the mainland and Taiwan during his term brought a growing inflow of Taiwanese investment to the province. If compared with Guangdong, however, Fujian's leaders were less pioneering and assertive, yet they also had to cope with difficulties left over by their predecessors and to influence developments well beyond their control. Given the preferential policies ordained by the Center, a favorable geographical location, and the warming of relations across the Taiwan Strait, Fujian has been able to acquire Hong Kong and Taiwanese investment and emerge as a star in China's open door policy.

Hainan is, in many ways, a special case of our sample because it was formerly part of Guangdong and was established as a province as late as 1988. Feng Chongyi and David S.G. Goodman argue that Hainan's leadership should be traced back to that of Lei Yu, head of Hainan's administration before it was made a province. They choose to characterize him as a "pathbreaker" because he lobbied for preferential policies and zealously attracted domestic and foreign investment, but such traits are indeed very much those of a pioneer. However, the illegal trade of imported cars snowballed into a large-scale scandal which not only led to his downfall, but even more seriously, policy setbacks for Hainan. Despite such a debacle, Hainan was lucky to get support from central leaders to upgrade it into a province and grant it SEZ-styled preferential policies in 1988. Xu Shijie and Liang Xiang, Hainan province's first party secretary and governor, masterminded a bold development program and were deft in obtaining central preferential policies and other support for their projects. However, in the aftermath of the June 4 crackdown, Liang was disciplined and Xu was forced to resign, and the implementation of their strategies disrupted. Their successors, who were apparently bandwagoners, adopted a very cautious approach to reform and were even unable to work together harmoniously. Ruan Chongwu, who took over both party and state posts, cannot be considered a pioneer, but more appropriately, a cautious reformer, in other words a bandwagoner who brought small scale but important improvements in various areas of government administration. The short tenure of Hainan's leaders and the complicated problems facing Hainan's development further tarnished their performance. In short, Hainan offers a unique case of reform because of its ethnic composition, its long rivalry with its superior Guangdong, and its special legacies as an island with abundant natural resources which were heavily extracted by the central government after 1949.

Sichuan, often dubbed the "heavenly kingdom" in Chinese history, is a huge province endowed with a wealth of natural and labor resources. The combined consequences of the damage caused by radical Maoist policies, the onus of the "Third Front" project for military and industrial construction, as well as the long tenure of a Mao favorite, Li Jingquan, in the prereform era were devastating for the province. Before 1978, local interests were often sacrificed in order to pursue radical revolutionary ideals, or to support other areas as dictated by the central government. Lijian Hong's chapter argues that Zhao Ziyang did help to push the province ahead in rural and enterprise reform since the late 1970s. After Zhao's promotion to the post of premier in 1980, a number of natives took over the helm of Sichuan's leadership. His immediate successor, Yang Rudai, failed to build upon such reform momentum and instead took a very cautious approach to reform. His failure to solve the troubles haunting the ailing state-owned enterprises, his consent to the unpopular Three Gorges construction project, and his inability to plot an effective reform strategy, for instance, were some hallmarks of his incumbency. If Yang's bandwagoner leadership style did not propel the province toward further reform, his successor, Xiao Yang, also floundered in his bid for reform and probably is the most controversial figure in Sichuan's contemporary history. While Xiao attempted to be a pioneer in economic reform, he could not translate his bold ideas into a viable reform program. He also tried to curry favor with the Center and compromised Sichuan's interests in his ill-fated lobby for promotion to the central level. His unpopularity in the province, however, only complicated his efforts to successfully master reform. Their successors were equally lackluster in their reform performance. While a number of strategies, such as strengthening ties among southwestern provinces, grooming economic relations with the former Soviet Union and Eastern Europe, and even selling state-owned enterprises to foreign investors, were espoused by Sichuan's leaders, the province was conspicuous in its failure to attract foreign investment. The fact that the province only attracted less than 1.3 percent of the total foreign investment absorbed by China as a whole in 1995 showed how poor its leaders had responded to the daunting task of raising the much needed capital for its economic revival!

Jae Ho Chung's appendix offers a substantive contribution addressing the sources, issues, and methodological considerations on the study of provincial politics in China. Economic reform has evidently reshaped the nature, process, and rationale of provincial politics in the Chinese polity because it has compelled provinces to become more assertive, stimulated inter-provincial linkages and politics, infused an economic logic into provincial politics, and complicated politics at the subprovincial levels. As he has cogently observed, three dimensions of provincial politics call for further inquiry. First, the institutional and procedural dimensions of provincial politics—such as the organizational evolution of the provincial party and state apparatus, the provincial policy-making processes, and the interactions among Beijing, the provinces and their subprovincial units—remain to be fully investigated. Second, the identification and explanation of local variations in provincial politics and policy also deserve far more research. Third, understanding the intensity and rationale of local compliance and resistance toward central policies demands much more scholarly work. In order to facilitate future research, he has also reviewed the existing sources on the provinces and offered valuable bibliographic advice.

The conclusion by Zhimin Lin summarizes our research findings and compares and contrasts the different cases in a more coherent and systematic manner. Since the role of provincial leaders, their strategies of reform, and the provincial patterns in implementing reform have not been adequately examined in the existing literature on post-Mao China, this study is a major step in the right direction. To be sure, more provincial cases and policy issues remain to be explored, changes and continuities in provincial policy between the prereform and reform eras await further scrutiny, and our analytical framework needs refinement in view of fresh empirical evidence and theoretical development. As pioneers in this research direction, we hope that this works with scholarly contributions from three continents can stimulate more systematic and sophisticated research on provincial leadership and their reform strategies. If the growing prominence of the provinces has recast Chinese political economy since 1978, the performance of their leaders and their reform strategies will continue to be key factors shaping China's future. Studying provincial China, in short, will provide one of the best keys to understand the political and economic dynamics of post-Deng China.

Notes

The author has benefited greatly from the valuable comments on an earlier draft of this chapter made by the co-editors, Jae Ho Chung and Zhimin Lin. The author would like to express his sincere appreciation for their generous advice, assistance, and, most importantly, patience throughout the project. Most of the chapters of this book have been presented at the annual meeting of the Association for Asian Studies in Washington in April 1995 as well as a series of seminars held at the Centre of Asian Studies at the University of Hong Kong in the summer and early fall of 1995. As the main editor, organizer and administrator of this project, the author would like to acknowledge the generous logistical support offered by the Department of Politics and Public Administration, University of Hong Kong, under the enlightened leadership of Professor John P. Burns. Veronica Sze, Cecilia Lung and especially Peter Lovelock provided efficient and indispensable editorial assistance. Special thanks should also be extended to the anonymous reviewer of the manuscript for valuable comments as well as to Mr. Doug Merwin, Vice President, Ms. Mai Shaikhanuar-Cota, Assistant Editor, and Ms. Angela Piliouras, Project Editor, of M.E. Sharpe for their support of this project.

1. For useful Chinese studies of uneven patterns of economic reform and development in post-Mao China, see, e.g., Ma Hong and Fang Weizhong (eds.), *Zhongguo diqu fazhan yu chanye zhengce* (China's Regional Development and Industrial Policy) (Beijing: Zhongguo caizheng jingji chubanshe, 1991); Shu Wei et al. (eds.), *Zhongguo diqu bijiao youshi fenxi* (An Analysis of Regional Comparative Advantage in China) (Beijing: Zhongguo jihua chubanshe, 1992); Jiang E and Liu Gen (eds.), *Zhongguo diqu jingji zengzhang bijiao yanjiu* (A Comparative Analysis of Regional Economic Development in China) (Shenyang: Liaoning renmin chubanshe, 1992). For English works, see, e.g., Philippe Aguignier, "Regional Disparities since 1978," in Stephan Feuchtwang et al. (eds.), *Transforming China's Economy in the Eighties*, Vol. II. (Boulder: Westview Press, 1988), pp. 93–106; Roger C.K. Chan, Tien-tung Hsueh and Chiu-Ming Luk (eds.), *China's Regional Economic Development* (Hong Kong: Institute of Asia-Pacific Studies, The Chinese University of Hong Kong, 1996); Victor Falkenheim, "The Political Economy of Regional Reform: An Overview," in Bruce L. Reynolds (ed.), *Chinese Economic Policy* (N.Y.: Paragon House, 1988), pp. 285–310; Feng-cheng Fu and Chi-keung Li, "Disparities in Mainland China's Regional Economic Development and Their Im-

plications for Central-Local Economic Relations," *Issues & Studies*, Vol. 32, No. 11 (1996), pp. 1–30; David S.G. Goodman (ed.), *China's Regional Development* (N.Y.: Routledge, 1989); David S.G. Goodman and Gerald Segal (eds.), *China Deconstructs: Politics, Trade and Regionalism* (London: Routledge, 1994); G.J.R. Linge and D.K. Forbes (eds.), *China's Spatial Economy: Recent Developments and Reforms* (Hong Kong: Oxford University Press, 1990); Susan Paine, "Spatial Aspects of Chinese Development Issues, Outcomes and Policies, 1949–1979," *Journal of Development Studies*, Vol. 17, No. 2 (1981), pp. 133–195; Dorothy Solinger, "Uncertain Paternalism: Tensions in Recent Regional Restructuring in China," *International Regional Science Review*, Vol. 11, No. 1 (1987), pp. 23–42; Kai Yuen Tsui, "China's Regional Inequality, 1952–1985," *Journal of Comparative Economics*, Vol. 15 (1991), pp. 1–21; Dali Yang, "Patterns of China's Regional Development Strategy," *China Quarterly*, No. 122 (June 1990), pp. 230–257 and "China Adjusts to the World Economy: The Political Economy of China's Coastal Development Strategy," *Pacific Affairs*, Vol. 64 (Spring 1991), pp. 42–64.

2. In fact, there are very few detailed studies of economic reform at the provincial level. Most of the English-language publications concentrate only on coastal provinces such as Guangdong and Shanghai. See, e.g., James Cotton, "China and Tumen River Cooperation: Jilin's Coastal Development Strategy," *Asian Survey*, Vol. 36, No. 11 (1996), pp.1086–1101; Reginald Yin-Wang Kwok and Alvin So (eds.), *The Hong Kong-Guangdong Link: Partnership in Flux* (Armonk: M.E. Sharpe, 1995); Sen Lin, "A New Pattern of Decentralization in China: The Increase of Provincial Powers in Economic Legislation," *China Information*, Vol. 7, No. 3 (1992–1993), pp. 27–38 and *China's Decentralization and Provincial Economic Legislation, 1980–1989*, unpublished Ph.D. dissertation, University of Calgary, 1993; Toyojiro Maruya (ed.), *Guangdong: "Open Door" Economic Development Strategy* (Hong Kong: Centre of Asian Studies, University of Hong Kong and Tokyo: Institute of Developing Economics, 1992); Gang Tian, *Shanghai's Role in the Economic Development of China: Reform of Foreign Trade and Investment* (Westport: Praeger, 1996); Ezra Vogel, *One Step Ahead in China: Guangdong under Reform* (Cambridge: Harvard University Press, 1989); Y.M. Yeung and David K.Y. Chu (eds.), *Guangdong: Survey of a Province Undergoing Rapid Change* (Hong Kong: The Chinese University Press, 1994; 2nd ed. forthcoming); Y.M. Yeung and Sung Yun-wing (eds.), *Shanghai: Transformation and Modernization under China's Open Policy* (Hong Kong: The Chinese University Press, 1996); Yun-wing Sung et. al., *The Fifth Dragon: the Emergence of the Pearl River Delta* (Singapore: Addison-Wesley, 1995). Two useful studies of the politics of reform in the Special Economic Zones in Guangdong and Fujian are respectively George Crane, *The Political Economy of China's Special Economic Zones* (Armonk: M.E. Sharpe, 1990) and Jude Howell, *China Opens Its Doors: The Politics of Economic Transition* (Boulder: Lynne Rienner, 1993). Starting from the March issue of 1997, *Provincial China: a research newsletter* will carry bibliographies on the provinces. A bibliography of English works on Guangdong province under reform compiled by this author will be the first of this series.

3. In his survey of the field, Avery Goldstein has noted works on "the growing prominence of provincial and subprovincial leaders," but his review does not elaborate on this theme. See his "Trends in the Study of Political Elites and Institutions of the PRC," *China Quarterly*, No. 139 (Sept. 1994), pp. 714–730. Various studies that have touched upon the issue of provincial leadership and reform include, e.g., Peter T.Y. Cheung, *Local Government and Economic Reform in Post-Mao China: The Guangdong Experience*, unpublished Ph.D. dissertation, University of Washington, 1993; Jae Ho Chung, *The Politics of Policy Implementation in Post-Mao China: Central Control and Provincial Autonomy under Decentralization*, unpublished Ph.D. dissertation, University of Michigan, 1993; Zhimin Lin, *The Retreat of the Center: Changing Central-Provincial Fiscal*

Relations in China, 1979–1992, unpublished Ph.D. dissertation, University of Washington, 1993; Dorothy Solinger, *China's Transition from Socialism: Statist Legacies and Market Reform 1980–1990* (Armonk: M.E. Sharpe, 1993).

4. There are some useful works on the profile of provincial leaders and mayors in the post-Mao era, but they mainly provide aggregate analysis of the leadership transition in the 1980s and its implications for Chinese politics rather than detailed case studies of how such leaders have shaped the process of economic reform. See, e.g., Zhiyue Bo, "Native Political Leaders and Political Mobility in China: Home Province Advantage?" *Provincial China: a research newsletter*, No. 2 (Oct. 1996), pp. 2–15 and "Economic Performance and Political Mobility: Chinese Provincial Leaders," *Journal of Contemporary China*, Vol. 5, No. 12 (1996), pp. 135–154; Cheng Li and David Bachman, "Localism, Elitism, and Immobilism: Elite Formation and Social Change in Post-Mao China," *World Politics*, Vol. 42 (Oct. 1989), pp. 64–94; William deB. Mills, "Leadership Change in China's Provinces," *Problems of Communism*, Vol. 34 (May-June 1985), pp. 25–40; Hsin-yi Ou-yang, "The Impact of the Tiananmen Incident on Mainland China's Provincial Leadership Appointment—A Brief Explanation of Second-Generation Elite Studies," *Issues & Studies*, Vol. 31, No. 7 (1995), pp. 100–117; Xiaowei Zang, "Provincial Elite in Post-Mao China," *Asian Survey*, Vol. 31, No. 6 (June 1991), pp. 512–525. For works which include some interesting discussion of the role of provincial leaders in the policy process in the reform era, see, e.g., Jae Ho Chung, "The Politics of Agricultural Mechanization in the Post-Mao Era, 1977–87," *China Quarterly*, No. 134 (June 1993), pp. 264–290; Kenneth Lieberthal and Michel Oksenberg, *Policy Making in China: Leaders, Structures, Processes* (Princeton: Princeton University Press, 1988); James Tong, "Fiscal Reform, Elite Turnover and Central-Provincial Relations in Post-Mao China," *Australian Journal of Chinese Affairs*, No. 22 (July 1989), pp. 1–28; Lynn T. White III, *Shanghai Shanghaied? Uneven Taxes in Reform China* (Hong Kong: Centre of Asian Studies, University of Hong Kong, 1989). For works on provincial leaders in the prereform era see, e.g. Parris Chang, *Power and Policy in China* (University Park, PA: The Pennsylvania State University Press, 1978); Victor Falkenheim, "Provincial Leadership in Fukien: 1946–66," Parris Chang, "Provincial Party Leaders' Strategies for Survival During the Cultural Revolution," and Lynn T. White III, "Leadership in Shanghai, 1956–69," in Robert A. Scalapino (ed.), *Elites in the People's Republic of China* (Seattle: University of Washington Press, 1972), pp. 199–244, 302–377 and 501–539; Robert A. Scalapino, "The CCP's Provincial Secretaries," *Problems of Communism*, Vol. 25, No. 4 (1976), pp. 18–35; David S.G. Goodman, "The Provincial First Party Secretary in the People's Republic of China, 1949–1978: A Profile," *British Journal of Political Science*, Vol. 10, Part I (January 1980), pp. 39–74, "Li Jingquan and the South-West Region: 1958–66: The Life and 'Crimes' of a 'Local Emperor'," *China Quarterly*, No. 81 (March 1980), pp. 66–96, "The Provincial First Party Secretaries in National Politics: A Categoric or a Political Group," in David S.G. Goodman (ed.), *Groups and Politics in the People's Republic of China* (Cardiff: University College Cardiff Press, and Armonk: M.E. Sharpe, 1984), pp. 68–82; David M. Lampton, *Paths to Power: Elite Mobility in Contemporary China* (Ann Arbor: Center for Chinese Studies, University of Michigan, 1979); Peter R. Moody, Jr. "Policy and Power: The Career of T'ao Chu, 1955–1966," China Quarterly, No. 54 (April/June 1973), pp. 266–293; David Shambaugh, *The Making of a Premier: Zhao Ziyang's Provincial Career* (Boulder: Westview, 1984); Dorothy J. Solinger, "Politics in Yunnan Province in the Decade of Disorder: Elite Factional Strategies and Central-Local Relations," *China Quarterly*, No. 92 (December 1982), pp. 628–662; Frederick Teiwes, *Provincial Leadership in China: The Cultural Revolution and Its Aftermath* (Ithaca: Cornell University East Asian Papers, No. 4, 1974). Keith Forster has written extensively on the political careers of Zhejiang's leaders and provincial politics; see his *Rebellion and Factionalism in a Chi-*

nese Province: Zhejiang, 1966–1976 (Armonk: M.E. Sharpe, 1990), which contains a useful bibliography and a list of his own writings on Zhejiang.

5. See, e.g., Gordon White, Jude Howell and Shang Xiaoyuan, *In Search of Civil Society: Market Reform and Social Change in Contemporary China* (Oxford: Clarendon, 1996), which also includes an extensive bibliography on the subject.

6. The role of local government during the democratic transition from former authoritarian states has recently received more attention. See, e.g., Theodore H. Friedgut and Jeffrey W. Hahn (eds.), *Local Power and Post-Soviet Politics* (Armonk: M.E. Sharpe, 1994); Tamara J. Resler and Roger E. Kanet, "Democratization: The National-Subnational Linkage," *In-Depth* (special issue on Establishing Democratic Rule: The Reemergence of Local Governments in Post-Authoritarian Systems) (Winter 1993), pp. 5–22.

7. For an argument emphasizing the role of politics in the strategy of economic reform, especially the "playing to the provinces" strategy, see Susan Shirk, *The Political Logic of Economic Reform* (Berkeley: University of California Press, 1993), ch. 9.

8. A collection of interviews and biographical accounts of ministers and provincial leaders in the magazine *Zhonghua yingcai* (Chinese Talents), is published as Wang Xiaopeng (ed.), *Zhongguo jingguan he fengjiang daili* (China's "Ministers in Beijing" and "Officials Assigned to the Border Areas") (Beijing: Zhonggong dangshi chubanshe, 1994). Coverage of provincial leaders seems to have increased significantly in the rapidly growing Chinese mass media since 1978. Provincial leaders often appeared in press conferences during the annual meetings of the National People's Congress or during their provincial-level meetings. They are also regularly interviewed by both the printed and electronic media both at home and abroad. Some of these are printed in book form; see, e.g., Wang Maolin et al. (eds.), *Zouchu fengbi—Zhongguo neilu shengfeng gaige kaifang dasilu* (Breaking Out of Containment—Grand Ideas on the Reform and Opening of China's Inland Provinces) (Changsha: Hunan chubanshe, 1992) or incorporated into journalistic accounts of China's reform; see, e.g., Jiang Yaping, *Gaige kaifang de longtou—Guangdong* (The Dragon Head of Reform and Opening—Guangdong) (Hong Kong: Mirror Post Cultural Enterprise Co., 1994).

9. Among those provincial leaders that have published in this series include He Zhukang (Jilin), He Zhiqiang (Yunnan), Hu Fuguo (Shanxi), Huang Huang (Anhui), Jia Qinglin (Fujian), Wu Guanzheng (Jiangxi), Xie Fei (Guangdong), Xie Shijie (Fujian), Yang Rudai (Sichuan), and Yue Qifeng (Liaoning). Biographies and autobiographies of provincial leaders, especially in Chinese, also began to appear. Biographies, speech and document collections, and journalistic accounts of the careers of provincial leaders in the prereform era are too numerous to cite, and a considerable number of such works are devoted to those who later became prominent national leaders such as Chen Yi, Li Xiannian, Peng Zhen, Tan Zhenlin, Tao Zhu, Ye Jianying, as well as the Shanghai members of the "Gang of Four." See, e.g., Zheng Xiaofeng and Shu Ling, *Tao Zhu zhuan* (A Biography of Tao Zhu) (Beijing: Zhongguo qingnian chubanshe, 1992); 'Huainian Li Xiannian tongzhi' Bianjizu (ed.), *Weida de renmin gongpu: huainian Li Xiannian tongzhi* (A Great Servant of the People: Remembering Comrade Li Xiannian) (Beijing: Zhongyang wenxian chubanshe, 1993); Jin Ye (ed.), *Huiyi Tan Zhenlin* (Remembering Tan Zhenlin) (Hangzhou: Zhejiang renmin chubanshe, 1992); Huang Weichi (ed.), *Ye Jianying zai Guangdong* (Ye Jianying in Guangdong) (Beijing: Zhongyang wenxian chubanshe, 1996); Quan Yanchi, *Tianjin shizhang* (Tianjin's Mayor) (Beijing: Zhongyang dangxiao chubanshe, 1993). For biographical works on provincial leaders in the reform era, see, e.g., He Pin, *The New Lords of P.R. China* (Hong Kong: Mingjing chubanshe, 1996); Gao Xin and He Pin, *Zhu Rongji zhuan* (A Biography of Zhu Rongji) (Taibei: Xinxinwen wenhua shiye youxian gongsi, 1993); Liang Lingguang, *Liang Lingguang huiyilu* (Liang Lingguang's Memoir) (Beijing: Zhonggong dangshi chubanshe, 1996); Shi Dongbing,

Cong kuanggong dao shengwei shuji—Ji Wang Maolin (From Miner to Provincial Party Secretary: On Wang Maolin) (Hong Kong: Jingji daobao youxian gongsi, 1996); Yang Zhongmei, *Jiang Zemin zhuan* (A Biography of Jiang Zhemin) (Taibei: Shibao wenhua chuban qiye gufen youxian gongsi, 1996); Zheng Yi, *Li Ruihuan zhuanqi* (A Biography of Li Ruihuan) (Hong Kong: Mingchuang chubanshe, 1991), *Jiang Zemin zhuanqi* (A Biography of Jiang Zhemin) (Hong Kong: Mingchuang chubanshe, 1992), *Zhu Rongji zhuanqi* (A Biography of Zhu Rongji) (Hong Kong: Mingchuang chubanshe, 1994). However, most of the biographies are not systematic or scholarly studies but broad-gauged overviews of their careers.

10. Transcripts of these broadcast programs as well as a sample of newspaper interviews of these leaders are published in Chen Wenbing (ed.), *Zoujin sheng, shizhang—'95 huadong sheng shizhang rexian jishi* (Getting Close to Provincial Governors and Mayors: A Factual Account of the Hotlines of Provincial Governors and Mayors from Eastern China 1995) (Shanghai: Fudan daxue chubanshe, 1996).

11. *Xinhua* news release, Oct. 8, 1995.

12. The eastern region includes Shanghai, Beijing, Tianjin, Liaoning, Guangdong, Zhejiang, Jiangsu, Shandong, Fujian, Hainan, Hebei and Guangxi. The middle region refers to Heilongjiang, Jilin, Hubei, Shanxi, Inner Mongolia, Hunan, Anhui, Jiangxi and Henan. The western region refers to Xinjiang, Qinghai, Ningxia, Tibet, Shaanxi, Yunnan, Sichuan, Gansu and Guizhou. The data for this paragraph draw from Woo Tun-oy, "Regional Economic Development and Disparities," in Maurice Brosseau, Suzanne Pepper and Tsang Shu-ki (eds.), *China Review 1996* (Hong Kong: The Chinese University Press, 1996), pp. 286–290.

13. Dali L. Yang, "The Dynamics and Progress of Competitive Liberalization in China," *Issues & Studies*, Vol. 32, No. 8 (1996), p. 13.

14. *Zhongguo gongchandang dishisijie zhongyang weiyuanhui diwuci quanti huiyi wenjian* (Documents of the Fifth Plenum of the 14th Central Committee of the Chinese Communist Party) (Beijing: Renmin chubanshe, 1995), pp. 45–47.

15. The following discussion mainly draws from Zhang Wenfan (ed.), *Zhongguo shengzhi* (China's Provincial System) (Beijing: Zhongguo dabaike quanshu chubanshe, 1995), pp.71–84. The number of provinces in the Yuan Dynasty refers to the number at the beginning of the dynasty while those of Ming and Qing refer to the numbers at the end of these dynasties, see ibid., pp. 70–71.

16. Ibid.

17. This and the following social and economic data in this paragraph are from *Zhongguo tongji nianjian 1996* (China Statistical Yearbook 1996) (Beijing: Zhongguo tongji chubanshe, 1996), passim.

18. Studies on Communist leadership are too numerous to cite. Samples include, e.g. Carl Beck et al. (eds.), *Comparative Communist Political Leadership* (New York: David McKay, 1973); Seweryn Bialer, *Stalin's Successors* (Cambridge: Cambridge University Press, 1980); George Breslauer, *Khrushchev and Brezhnev as Leaders* (London: Allen & Unwin, 1982); Archie Brown (ed.), *Political Leadership in the Soviet Union* (London: Macmillan, 1989); R. Barry Farrell (ed.), *Political Leadership in Eastern Europe and the Soviet Union* (London: Butterworths, 1970); A.G. Meyer, "Authority in Communist Political Systems," in Lewis Edinger (ed.) *Political Leadership in Industrialized Societies* (New York: John Wiley & Sons, 1978), pp. 84–107; W.J. Tompson, "Khrushchev and Gorbachev as Reformers: A Comparison," *British Journal of Political Science*, Vol. 23, Part 1 (January 1993), pp. 77–105. For an early study of the Chinese Communist leadership, leadership techniques and leadership doctrines, see John Wilson Lewis, *Leadership in Communist China* (Ithaca: Cornell University Press, 1963).

19. Lewis Edinger (ed.), *Political Leadership in Industrialized Societies* (New York: John Wiley & Sons, 1978).

20. See, e.g., Joel D. Aberbach et al. (eds.), *The Role of the State in Taiwan's Development* (Armonk: M.E. Sharpe, 1994); Alice H. Amsden, *Asia's New Giant: South Korea and Late Industrialization* (Oxford: Oxford University Press, 1989); Richard P. Appelbaum and Jeffery Henderson (eds.), *States and Development in the Asia Pacific Rim* (New York: Sage, 1992); Frederic C. Deyo (ed.), *The Political Economy of the New Asian Industrialism* (Ithaca: Cornell University Press, 1987); Chalmers Johnson, *MITI and the Japanese Miracle* (Stanford: Stanford University Press, 1982) and *Japan: Who Governs? The Rise of the Developmental State* (New York: Norton, 1995); Hyung-Ki Kim (ed.), *The Japanese Civil Service and Economic Development* (Oxford: Clarendon Press, 1995); Dae-Sook Suh and Chae-Jin Lee (eds.), *Political Leadership in Korea* (Seattle: University of Washington Press, 1976); Robert Wade, *Governing the Market* (Princeton: Princeton University Press, 1990).

21. For a summary and analysis of these three approaches as well as useful bibliographic information, see Morris P. Fiorina and Kenneth A. Shepsle, "Formal Theories of Leadership: Agents, Agenda Setters, and Entrepreneurs," in Bryan D. Jones (ed.), *Leadership and Politics: New Perspectives in Political Science* (Lawrence: The University Press of Kansas, 1989), pp. 17–40.

22. Ibid., p. 20.

23. Huang Yasheng, *Inflation and Investment Controls in China* (Cambridge: Cambridge University Press, 1996).

24. See the editor's introduction in Lewis J. Edinger (ed.), *Political Leadership in Industrialized Societies*, p. 12. A very useful conceptual discussion of leadership is Jean Blondel, *Political Leadership* (London: Sage, 1987). Both works have an extensive bibliography. Also see Robert D. Putnam, *The Comparative Study of Political Elites* (Englewood Cliffs, N.J.: Prentice Hall, 1976); Robert Elgie, *Political Leadership in Liberal Democracies* (London: Macmillan, 1995).

25. This is reported in the Deng Xiaoping TV documentary. For a verbatim account of the script, see Zhonggong zhongyang wenxian yanjiushi and Zhongyang dianshitai (eds.), *Daxing dianshi wenxian jilupian: "Deng Xiaoping" jieshouci* (Explanatory Notes of a Large Scale TV Documentary Program: "Deng Xiaoping") (Hong Kong: Liwen chubanshe, 1997).

26. See, e.g., Carol Lee Hamrin and Zhao Suisheng (eds.), *Decision-Making in Deng's China* (Armonk: M.E. Sharpe, 1995); Kenneth Lieberthal and David M. Lampton (eds.), *Bureaucracy, Politics, and Decision-Making in Post-Mao China* (Berkeley: University of California Press, 1992); Kenneth Lieberthal, *Governing China* (New York: Norton, 1995); Lieberthal and Oksenberg, *Policy Making in China;* Shirk, *The Political Logic of Economic Reform in China*.

27. Studies which contain considerable political histories of provinces include, e.g., June Dreyer, *China's Forty Millions: Minority Nationalities and National Integration in the People's Republic of China* (Cambridge: Harvard University Press, 1976); Keith Forster, *Rebellion and Factionalism in a Chinese Province: Zhejiang, 1966–1976;* Donald H. McMillen, *Chinese Communist Power and Policy in Xinjiang, 1949–1977* (Boulder: Westview, 1979); Vogel, *Canton Under Communism* (Cambridge: Harvard University Press, 1969); Goodman, *Centre and Province: Sichuan and Guizhou, 1955–1965* (Cambridge: Cambridge University Press, 1986); Christopher Howe (ed.), *Shanghai: Revolution and Development in an Asian Metropolis* (Cambridge: Cambridge University Press, 1981); and Lynn T. White III, *Policies of Chaos* (Princeton: Princeton University Press, 1989), which includes a useful bibliography of his works and other studies on Shanghai.

28. Please refer to note 4.

29. Maria Chan Morgan, *Leadership Strategy at the Intermediate Level: Tao Zhu's Political Strategies in Guangdong Province: The People's Republic of China: 1959–1967*, unpublished Ph.D. dissertation, Stanford University, 1987.

30. Examples of works that pay attention to the role of the provincial leadership in the reform process, see, e.g., Vogel, *One Step Ahead*, chs. 3 and 10 and Peter T.Y. Cheung, "Relations between the Central Government and Guangdong," in Yeung and Chu (eds.), *Guangdong*, pp. 19–51 and "The Case of Guangdong in Central-Provincial Relations," in Jia Hao and Lin Zhimin (eds.), *Changing Central-Local Relations in China: Reform and State Capacity* (Boulder: Westview, 1994), pp. 207–237; Jae Ho Chung, *The Politics of Policy Implementation*.

31. Important studies of the interactions between central and provincial leaders in the prereform era include Vogel, *Canton under Communism*; Goodman, *Centre and Province*; Dorothy J. Solinger, *Regional Government and Political Integration in Southwest China, 1949–1954* (Berkeley: University of California Press, 1977).

32. Please refer to note 30. For a case study of the issue of agricultural mechanization in Heilongjiang, see Chung, "The Politics of Agricultural Mechanization."

33. Shirk, *The Political Logic of Economic Reform in China*, ch. 9.

34. Goodman, *Centre and Province*, p. 181.

35. Interview with a provincial official in charge of economic reform in Guangdong province, May 1994.

36. These concepts are from John W. Kingdom, *Agendas, Alternatives, and Public Policies*, 2nd ed. (Boston: HarperCollins, 1995).

37. See, e.g., Huang Yasheng, "Administrative Monitoring in China," *China Quarterly*, No. 143 (Sept. 1995), pp. 828–843.

38. Interview with a Tianjin researcher, March 1997.

39. Bo, "Economic Performance and Political Mobility," p. 151.

40. Chung, *The Politics of Policy Implementation*, chs. 3–5.

41. See Lieberthal and Oksenberg, *Policy Making in China*, p. 344.

42. For an analysis of this reform, see Jae Ho Chung, "Beijing Confronting the Provinces: The 1994 Tax-Sharing Reform and Its Implications for Central-Provincial Relations," *China Information*, Vol. 9, No. 2/3 (1994–95), pp. 1–23 and Tsang Shu-ki and Cheng Yuk-shing, "China's Tax Reforms of 1994," *Asian Survey*, Vol. 34, No. 9 (1994), pp. 769–788.

43. For some of the most important studies of policy differences among the post-Mao elites, see, e.g., David Bachman, "Differing Visions of China's Post-Mao Economy: The Ideas of Chen Yun, Deng Xiaoping, and Zhao Ziyang," *Asian Survey*, Vol. 26, No. 3 (1986), pp. 292–321; Joseph Fewsmith, *Dilemmas of Reform in China: Political Conflict and Economic Debate* (Armonk: M.E. Sharpe, 1994); Carol Lee Hamrin, "Competing 'Policy Packages' in Post-Mao China," *Asian Survey*, Vol. 29, No. 1 (1984), pp. 487–518 and *China and the Challenge of the Future* (Boulder: Westview, 1991); Harry Harding, *China's Second Revolution* (Washington, D.C.: Brookings Institution, 1987), ch. 4; Dorothy Solinger, "The Fifth National People's Congress and the Process of Policymaking: Reform, Readjustment, and the Opposition," *Asian Survey*, Vol. 22, No. 12 (1982), pp. 1238–1275.

44. See, e.g., Malcom L. Goggin et al., *Implementation Theory and Practice: Toward a Third Generation* (Glenview: Scott, Foresman, 1990), chs. 2 and 4; Malcolm E. Jewell and Marcia Lynn Whicker, *Legislative Leadership in the American States* (Ann Arbor: University of Michigan Press, 1994); Atul Kohli, *The State and Poverty in India* (Cambridge: Cambridge University Press, 1987).

45. Gary King, Robert O. Keohane and Sidney Verba, *Designing Social Inquiry: Scientific Inference in Qualitative Research* (Princeton: Princeton University Press, 1994), p. 220.

46. Robert D. Putnam, *Making Democracy Work: Civil Traditions in Modern Italy* (Princeton: Princeton University Press, 1994).

47. Early exceptions include David S.G. Goodman, *Centre and Province*; Frederick Teiwes, "Provincial Politics in China: Themes and Variations," in John Lindbeck (ed.), *China: Management of a Revolutionary Society* (Seattle: University of Washington Press, 1971). Recent works that take a multiple case design include, e.g., Jae Ho Chung, *The Politics of Policy Implementation*; Kevin Patrick Lane, *The Life of the Party: Implementing Agricultural Policy in China, 1956–1957 and 1961–1965*, unpublished Ph.D. dissertation, Harvard University, 1992; Linda Chelan Lee, *Shifting Central-Provincial Relations in China: The Politics of Investment in Shanghai and Guangdong, 1978–1993* (Oxford: Oxford University Press, forthcoming); Lin Zhimin, *The Retreat of the Center*; Dali Yang *Calamity and Reform in China* (Stanford: Stanford University Press, 1996); Yong-Nian Zheng, "Perforated Sovereignty: Provincial Dynamism and China's Foreign Trade," *Pacific Review*, Vol. 7, No. 3 (1994), pp. 309–321.

48. Jean-Luc Domenach, *The Origins of the Great Leap Forward: The Case of One Chinese Province* (Boulder: Westview, 1995).

49. See, e.g., Chris Bramall, *In Praise of Maoist Economic Planning: Living Standards and Economic Development in Sichuan since 1931* (Oxford: Clarendon Press, 1993); Eduard B. Vermeer, *Economic Development in Provincial China: The Central Shaanxi since 1930* (Cambridge: Cambridge University Press, 1989); Howe (ed.), *Shanghai*; Vogel, *Canton under Communism*.

50. See, e.g. Yeung and Chu (eds.) *Guangdong*; Yeung and Sung (eds.) *Shanghai*. Another project on Fujian led by Professor Yeung Yue-man is also underway. A major project organized by Professor David S.G. Goodman, *China's Provinces in Reform*, aims to cover the broad social and political change in every province in the reform era, but some of the chapters also deal with the impact of provincial leadership on reform. The first volume will cover Guangxi, Hainan, Liaoning, Shanghai, Shandong, Sichuan and Zhejiang, and the second volume will cover Shanxi, Shaanxi, Hubei, Jiangsu, Jiangxi, Guizhou, and Tianjin. The first volume is David S.G. Goodman (ed.), *China's Provinces in Reform: Class, Community and Identity* (London: Routledge, 1997).

51. These and the following figures are 1995 data calculated from *Zhongguo tongji nianjian 1996*, passim.

52. Please refer to my "The Political Context of Shanghai's Economic Development," in Yeung and Sung (eds.), *Shanghai*, pp. 48–82.

53. *Zhongguo tongji nianjian 1996*, p. 600.

54. The definition of provincial elite refer to party secretaries, deputy secretaries, as well as governors and vice governors. See Zang Xiaowei, "Provincial Elite in Post-Mao China," pp. 523–524.

55. The following discussion draws from James MacGregor Burns, *Leadership* (New York: Harper & Row, 1978); Blondel, *Political Leadership*, ch. 3. For a survey of literature on the study of leadership in general, see Bernard M. Bass, *Stogdill's Handbook of Leadership* (New York: Free Press, 1981).

56. See, e.g., Richard Baum, *Burying Mao: Chinese Politics in the Age of Deng Xiaoping* (Princeton: Princeton University Press, 1996); Willy Wo-Lap Lam, *China After Deng Xiaoping: The Power Struggle in Beijing Since Tiananmen* (Hong Kong: P.A. Professional Consultants Ltd., 1994); Ruan Ming, *Deng Xiaoping: Chronicle of an Empire* (Boulder: Westview, 1994).

57. Hamrin, "Competing 'Policy Packages' in Post-Mao China," and *China and the*

Challenge of the Future; Harry Harding, *China's Second Revolution*; Dorothy J. Solinger, *Chinese Business Under Socialism: The Politics of Domestic Commerce, 1949–1980* (Berkeley: University of California Press, 1984).

58. After finding out their common interest in provincial reform and politics, the three editors have exchanged ideas extensively in developing the following analytical framework. This author wrote the original book proposal and develops the ideas further in this introduction, but he would like to acknowledge the valuable contributions from his co-editors. The two concepts, bandwagoner and laggard, draw from Chung, *The Politics of Policy Implementation*, chs. 4–5.

59. Avery Goldstein, *From Bandwagon to Balance-of-Power Politics: Structural Constraints and Politics in China, 1949–1978* (Stanford: Stanford University Press, 1991), p. 49.

60. Exceptions include, e.g., Shaun Breslin, *China in the 1980s: Centre-Province Relations in a Reforming Socialist State* (London: Macmillan, 1996); chapters by Peter T.Y. Cheung and Lin Zhimin in Jia Hao and Lin Zhimin (eds.), *Changing Central-Local Relations in China*, pp. 207–237; Peter T.Y. Cheung, "Relations between the Central Government and Guangdong," in Y.M. Yeung and David K.Y. Chu (eds.), *Guangdong*, pp. 19–51; brief analysis of the relations between the central government and Shanghai can also be found in Peter T.Y. Cheung's chapter on the political context of Shanghai's development, Lam Tao-chiu's chapter on interest articulation, and Ho Lok-sang and Tsui Kai-yuen's chapter on fiscal relations in Y.M. Yeung and Sung Yun-wing (eds.), *Shanghai*, chs. 3, 5, and 6; Goodman (ed.), *China's Provinces in Reform: Class, Community and Identity*; Huang Yasheng, *Investment and Inflation Controls*; and Linda Chelan Li, *Shifting Central-Provincial Relations*. Both the studies by Huang Yasheng and by Shaun Breslin focus on relations between Beijing and all the provinces rather than individual provincial examples, but they include useful information of individual cases. Christine Wong's study, *Fiscal Management and Economic Reform*, (Hong Kong: Oxford University Press, 1995), also offers useful information on central-provincial fiscal relations. For an excellent literature review of central-local relations, see Jae Ho Chung, "Studies of Central-Provincial Relations in the People's Republic of China: A Mid-Term Appraisal," *China Quarterly*, No. 142 (June 1995), pp. 487–508. Also see Gabriella Montinola, Yingyi Qian, and Barry R. Weingast, "Federalism, Chinese Style: The Political Basis for Economic Success in China," *World Politics*, Vol. 48 (Oct. 1995), pp. 50–81.

61. Yu-shan Wu, *Comparative Economic Transformations: Mainland China, Hungary, the Soviet Union, and Taiwan* (Stanford: Stanford University Press, 1994).

62. See Jae Ho Chung, "The Political Economy of Development and Inequality in Shandong," in Goodman (ed.), *China's Provinces in Reform: Class, Community and Identity*, pp. 127–157.

63. For an insightful analysis of the influence of outside ideas and institutions on China's reform and open policy, see Hamrin, *China and the Challenge of the Future*.

64. See, e.g., Ma Jun, *Intergovernmental Relations and Economic Management in China* (London: Macmillan, 1997), which also contains a useful bibliography; Michel Oksenberg and James Tong, "The Evolution of Central-Provincial Fiscal Relations in China, 1971–1984: The Formal System," *China Quarterly*, No. 125 (March 1991), pp. 1–32; Christine P.W. Wong, "Central-Local Relations in an Era of Fiscal Decline," *China Quarterly*, No. 128 (Dec. 1991), pp. 691–715 and Christine P.W. Wong et al., *Fiscal Management and Economic Reform in the People's Republic of China*; Christine P.W. Wong (ed.), *Financing Local Government in the People's Republic of China* (Hong Kong: Oxford University Press, 1997); Susan Shirk, "Playing to the Provinces: Deng Xiaoping's Political Strategy of Economic Reform," *Studies in Comparative Communism*, Vol. 23 (Autumn/Winter 1990), pp. 227–258.

65. Bo, "Economic Performance and Political Mobility," pp. 151–152.

66. Huang, *Investment and Inflation Controls*.

67. David S.G. Goodman, "King Coal and Secretary Hu: Shanxi's Third Modernization," paper presented at the 2nd workshop for *China's Provinces in Reform*, Hangzhou, Oct. 20–24, 1996. For Hu Fuguo's ideas on reform, see his, *Jiang zhenhua, banshishi, zuo biaoshuai: Zai chuang sanjin hui huang* (Speak the Truth, Do Practical Work, Be an Example: Establish Another Glorious Period for the Three-Jin Area) (Beijing: Zhonggong zhongyang dangxiao chubanshe, 1996).

Part I

**Provincial Reform Strategy and Policy
Toward Resource Allocation**

1

Shanghai's Big Turnaround since 1985

Leadership, Reform Strategy, and Resource Mobilization

Zhimin Lin

Introduction

The Chinese economic reform movement, started by Deng Xiaoping in the late 1970s, has been a roller-coaster experience for Shanghai. At the outset of the reform, the city led the nation's provinces in virtually all important economic categories such as Gross National Product (GNP), industrial output, export and government revenue.[1] However, during the initial phase of the reform (1978–1984), Shanghai had great difficulties in keeping up with the changes and digesting adverse consequences. As a result, Shanghai's economy grew slower than the national average for consecutive years for the first time after 1949; local revenue,[2] once a cash cow for the national coffers, became stagnant; and the city's industrial products, almost always the envy of the nation, were severely challenged by the rising provinces such as Guangdong. In short, Shanghai in the mid-1980s appeared to be a laggard in the reform and a loser in a comparative sense.

Yet, signs began to emerge after 1985 indicating a shift of fortune was in the making. The arrival of a new leadership team led by Rui Xingwen and Jiang Zemin in 1985 brought with them some renewed hope for economic revival. The city's industrial output, after showing dismal performance between 1978 and 1984, picked up steam after 1985. Shanghai's exports, down four out of five years in the first half of the 1980s, showed a consistent increase after 1986. Investment in urban infrastructure increased by almost 150 percent in 1985 and never looked back. Finally, the growth of GNP, after trailing the national average for most of the 1980s, began to outperform the rest of the nation (see Table 1.1).

By the beginning of the 1990s, what was a stream of incremental im-

Table 1.1

Shanghai's GNP Growth Rates Compared with National Averages, 1979–1996

Year	National	Shanghai	Difference	Year	National	Shanghai	Difference
1979	7.6	7.4	−0.2	1988	11.3	10.1	−1.2
1980	7.8	8.4	+0.6	1989	4.2	3.0	−1.2
1981	4.4	5.6	+1.2	1990	4.2	3.5	−0.7
1982	8.8	7.2	−1.6	1991	9.1	7.1	−2.0
1983	10.4	7.8	−2.6	1992	14.1	14.9	+0.8
1984	14.7	11.6	−3.1	1993	13.1	14.9	+1.7
1985	13.2	13.4	+0.2	1994	12.5	14.3	+1.7
1986	8.5	4.4	−4.1	1995	10.2	14.1	+3.9
1987	11.5	7.5	−4.0	1996	9.6	13.0	+3.4

Sources: Yao Xitang, ed., *Shanghai jingji shiwu nian* (Fifteen Years of Shanghai's Economy) (Shanghai: Shanghai Academy of Social Sciences Press, 1994), p. 12; *Zhongguo tongji nianjian 1996* (China Statistical Yearbook) (Beijing: Zhongguo tongji chubanshe, 1966) p. 42; *Shanghai nianjian 1996* (Shanghai Almanac) (Shanghai: Renmin chubanshe, 1996); p. 33; *Jiefang Ribao* (Shanghai), February 14, 1997.

provements turned into a torrent of breathtaking changes. With the highly touted Pudong new district[3] open for business and the systematic effort to turn Shanghai into the nation's trade and financial center, the Shanghai fever was on. The city once again was seen as a shining example of the "roaring economic development" in China.[4] The *Economist* magazine even suggested in 1995 that "if China were like Shanghai, the rest of the world might as well concede defeat tomorrow."[5]

The case of Shanghai is thus interesting in two ways. A stronghold of central planning for decades, the transition to a market economy was more painful in Shanghai than in many other provinces. How Shanghai was able to revive its stumbling economy under a new environment serves as a good example of the successes and difficulties encountered by China's reform. Moreover, unlike most other provinces whose experience under the reform was more or less straightforward, Shanghai's tortuous path toward economic revival calls for more study of the complexity of the Chinese reform process and the driving forces behind it.

This chapter deals with a central question based on Shanghai's economic turnaround after 1985, namely, what was the role of local leadership in helping to engineer and guide such a change especially in the area of mobilization of financial resources? Section one reviews the background of reform in Shanghai and the evolution of municipal leaders before 1985. Section two examines the new municipal leaders and the evolving reform and development strategy for Shanghai after 1985. Finally, section three is a case study of the successes and limits of resource mobilization in Shanghai.

An Overview of Shanghai before 1985

Shanghai became one of the five open ports[6] after China was forced to open its door in the wake of the Opium War. Soon after, Shanghai emerged as China's most important commercial, financial and industrial center. By the late 1930s, for example, Shanghai accounted for over 40 percent of the nation's industrial assets, 43 percent of industrial workers, and more than half of the nation's industrial output.[7] The subsequent Japanese occupation and the Civil War between the Nationalist and Communist forces interrupted the so-called golden era of capitalism in Shanghai. Still, by the time the Communist forces "liberated" Shanghai in 1949, the city remained a economic heavyweight unrivaled by others—over 60 percent of China's imports and exports, over 80 percent of foreign capital, more than half of industrial production, and nearly all international financial transactions were handled through Shanghai.[8]

Shanghai's fortune was thus destined to shift after 1949 as the new regime embarked on a drastically different course of development. Yet, the actual transformation was more complicated than many had anticipated. On the one hand, Shanghai benefited from the policies of the new masters in Beijing. The area under Shanghai's jurisdiction, for example, expanded by almost tenfold from 636.2 to 6,185.5 square kilometers between 1949 and 1958 as part of the nationwide redistricting.[9] Together with an increase of population from 5.02 to 9.99 million during the same period, Shanghai became more than a metropolitan town; it now possessed a sizable area and population on which the city could base its ambitious plan to develop into a self-sustained powerhouse. In addition, by being designated as one of the three municipalities (the other two were Beijing and Tianjin) under the direct supervision of the central government, Shanghai enjoyed a higher status than most other provinces including the privilege of having a seat in the powerful Politburo in normal times.

Shanghai also retained its prominence in the national economy with a changed role and hence a price. After 1949, the central government opted to make Shanghai the nation's largest *zonghe gongye jidi* (comprehensive industrial base).

Accordingly, Shanghai was provided with the best a central planning system could offer: stable supply of low-priced raw materials and guaranteed market shares. In return, Shanghai was to produce and distribute over one-third of all the goods made in China.[10] However, the overwhelming emphasis on manufacturing industries, especially heavy industries such as metallurgical, chemical, and heavy-machinery industries and the politically motivated decision to cut the city from the world economic system deprived Shanghai of the opportunity to concentrate on what its traditional strength was: serving as a center for trade, finance and other service industries. In 1957, for example, the ratio of light vs. heavy industries in Shanghai's total industrial output was 71 to 29; by 1978, the same ratio changed to 49 to 51.[11]

The more damaging consequence, however, was the loss of local autonomy to the heavy-handed and constant intervention by the central government. From 1949 to 1980, Shanghai contributed to about one-sixth of overall government revenue in China. Yet, the city managed to retain less than 13 percent of what it collected locally.[12] While some of the remitted revenue to the central government was remitted back to the city in the form of investment projects funded and administered by various central ministries, the amount was relatively small.[13] To make things worse, of those projects invested in Shanghai, most of them had little to do with what the city really needed. Reflecting a Maoist, general bias against investment in non-industrial projects, these central-administered projects paid scarce attention to things such as roads, public housing, and transportation. As a result, the city became heavily *qianzai* (in debt) in maintaining adequate urban infrastructure, much less able to bring it up to the standard of compatible cities in other parts of the world. The impact of the chronic underfunding in local infrastructure was devastating. In 1975, for example, 36.4 percent of the families in Shanghai lived in houses with less than four square meters per person reflecting the fact that less than 400 million yuan or 5.1 percent of the total investment on capital construction was spent on housing units from 1966 to 1975.[14] Nor were Shanghai's industries in good shape. Shanghai's labor productivity was 1.3 times that of the national average in 1942; it rose to 2.4 times in 1978. However, scholars argued that the gain had more to do with the price distortion in favor of Shanghai than progress made from increase of input or technological advancement.[15]

On the political front, Shanghai's experience was even more controversial. For years, Mao used Shanghai as his political stronghold and a springboard to launch many political campaigns. During the 1957 "Anti-rightist" campaign, the former mayor of Shanghai, Ke Qingshi, became one of the staunchest supporters of Mao's policy.[16] His severe crackdown on intellectuals won him Mao's trust but left the city with some of its best intellectuals being purged and silenced. Shanghai's role in national politics reached a new height during the Cultural Revolution period. Not only was the city used to set the stage for the radical mass movement, some of the radical local officials later moved on to become members of the top elite. Three of the so-called "Gang of Four," the leftist faction, came from Shanghai—Yao Wenyuan whose criticism of a literary work became the first shot of the Cultural Revolution, Zhang Chunqiao who masterminded key leftist programs, and Wang Hongwen who rose to the position of vice chairman of the CCP.[17]

The rise of Shanghai leaders to prominence in national politics had complicated effects. On the one hand, the city was exempted from extreme chaos which plagued so many provinces in China during the heyday of the Cultural Revolution largely because Mao and the leftist faction wanted to keep Shanghai as a model of success. Because of the special treatment,[18] Shanghai was able to post decent economic growth during this period while most other provinces were on the verge of collapse. On the other hand, being so close to one political faction had its down side. Once the leftist group was purged shortly after Mao's death in

Table 1.2

Names and Tenures of Shanghai Top Leaders, 1976–96

Party Secretary	Mayor
Su Zhenhua (10/76–1/79)	Su Zhenhua (10/76–1/79)
Peng Chong (1/79–3/80)	Peng Chong (1/79–3/80)
Chen Guodong (3/80–6/85)	Wang Daohan (10/80–7/85)
Rui Xingwen (6/85–11/87)	Jiang Zemin (7/85–4/88)
Jiang Zemin (11/87–8/89)	Zhu Rongji (4/88–4/91)
Zhu Rongji (8/89–3/91)	Huang Ju (4/91–2/95)
Wu Bangguo (4/91–9/94)	Xu Kuangdi (2/95–present)
Huang Ju (10/94–present)	

Source: Dangdai Zhongguo de Shanghai (Shanghai in Contemporary China) (Beijing: Zhongguo dangdai chubanshe), pp. 657–660; *Jiefang Ribao*, September 29, 1994.

1976, Shanghai was left in a bind. The whole municipal leadership was purged soon afterward.[19] The new team of leaders sent to Shanghai by the post-Mao leadership was instructed to scrutinize the city lest the remnants of the leftist group would regroup. For more than a decade, no one from Shanghai's own Party and government hierarchy was allowed to serve as its top leaders.

The political fallout was devastating to Shanghai in other ways as well. For example, while many provinces took advantage of the policy changes of the late 1970s and early 1980s to promote local reform and open policy, Shanghai was in the midst of a leadership reshuffle, not once but twice. Table 1.2 lists the names and tenures of Shanghai's top leaders since 1976.

To make things worse, the first two groups of leaders sent to Shanghai were either too preoccupied with their own political agenda or lacked commitment to reform Shanghai. They failed to provide the leadership needed for Shanghai to make effective adjustments to the changed environment and to embark on a new course of development.

The first group of leaders included a trio, Su Zhenhua, a Politburo member and the political commissar of the PLA's navy, Ni Zhifu, also a Politburo member and the leader of China's official National Workers Trade Union, and Peng Chong, the Party chief of Jiangsu province. Their ability to lead Shanghai's reform was questionable from the very beginning. Most of them were known for their closer ties with Hua Guofeng—Mao's immediate successor—than with the rising reformist group led by Deng Xiaoping.[20] Nor were they popular leaders in the eyes of the Shanghai public. Peng, for example, had difficulties in establishing control in Shanghai in part because of his leadership style and in part because he was never well received by the people in Shanghai, many of whom considered him a lightweight politician from a rival province. After Deng re-emerged in the political center in late 1978, the last remaining leader of the first group—Peng—was quickly recalled.[21]

In early 1980, the second group of leaders was dispatched to Shanghai. Chen Guodong and Hu Lijiao became the first and second party secretary respectively. In theory, this second group of leaders was in a better position to lead Shanghai out of its current difficulties. Both Chen and Hu had a close working relationship with Chen Yun, which might explain why they were chosen in the first place.[22] They were also longtime administrators serving mostly at the ministerial level. Chen and Hu were also joined by Wang Daohan, who served as the mayor of Shanghai from April 1981 to July 1985 (he became the acting mayor after October 1980). The most capable and skillful administer of the three, Wang was chosen for his talent in managing complex places such as Shanghai. Unfortunately, this second group of leaders, while much more committed to and focused on Shanghai's own development than their predecessors, was ultimately unable to turn the city around economically.

There were several reasons why the second group of leaders did not fare as well as expected. First, no one in this group had the national political status to exert a strong influence on central policies and to speak effectively for Shanghai.[23] This was crucial as many of the important reform policies were adopted during the period. The lack of presentation on behalf of Shanghai at this important juncture was very detrimental to the interests of the city. For example, China's economic reform was spearheaded by several measures of economic decentralization including fiscal decentralization. However, when the package concerning fiscal decentralization was being worked out between the central government and key provinces in 1979 and 1980, Shanghai was literally left in the cold.[24] As the following section will show, the missing of the first train of reform cost the city hugely.

Second, there was a lack of clear direction from above as to where Shanghai's development should go. The central government was divided in the early 1980s over the issue of whether or not to apply policies given to the Special Economic Zones (SEZs) to other places such as Shanghai.[25] Deng himself later regretted that he did not include Shanghai as one of the first SEZs. He said, "In retrospect, one of my big mistakes was that I had not included Shanghai when we were working on the four SEZs. Or otherwise, the Yangtze Delta, the entire Yangtze River area, and indeed, the whole nation's situation of reform and opening would have been different."[26]

The second group of leaders was partially to blame for the lack of progress. With the exception of Wang who was more cosmopolitan and open-minded,[27] the other two leaders (who by virtue of serving as the Party boss had more influence than Wang did) had not shown much innovation nor strong commitment to tough reform programs. They were long-term central planners after all.

While there was little question that they shared the overall goal of reform, they were either poorly trained or simply unwilling to take on the risk necessary for Shanghai to break away from the past. Both were near retirement age and hence had little incentive to try radical, however useful, reform programs.[28]

There were a lot of discussions in Shanghai especially among the experts on the need to take drastic measures to deal with the deteriorating situation in the city's economy.[29] Three problems were mentioned most frequently during these discussion. One problem was the need to repair and upgrade the city's aging infrastructure. Without massive improvement, many scholars argued that the city would never be able to attract the much-needed investment nor to rally public support for the economic reform. Another problem was the need to upgrade Shanghai's traditional industries. Most of these industries were either outdated or poorly equipped by that time. For Shanghai to compete with other provinces, the city needed to develop new and viable industries which were competitive domestically and internationally. Finally, there was the challenge for Shanghai to regain its leadership in the national economy by shifting the priority of the local economy to where the city traditionally did best such as commerce and finance, and by tapping into the city's strengths, such as the rich human resources and managerial excellence.

Clearly, to tackle these problems Shanghai would have to do more than patching things up. Nor would the city solve these problems by treating them as if they were separate and isolated issues. For a number of scholars in Shanghai, the key to overcome Shanghai current economic woe was threefold: a reform and development strategy that set appropriate goals, a set of policy tools to implement the strategy, and sufficient resources to back up these policies. However, without a reform-minded and effective leadership, none of these could be put together easily. Since the first and second groups of leaders showed little leadership of this caliber, the task was left for their successors. The question was, could they pass the test?

Municipal Leadership and Reform Strategy after 1985

In 1985, Shanghai's leadership underwent yet another round of wholesale change, the third since 1976.[30] Rui Xingwen became the first party secretary in June 1985 and Jiang Zemin the mayor in July 1985. Zhu Rongji came to Shanghai in early 1988 to succeed Jiang as the mayor of Shanghai after Jiang replaced Rui who was promoted as a member of the Secretariat in Beijing a few months earlier.[31]

Compared with the last two groups of leaders, the new municipal leadership enjoyed a number of advantages. These advantages put them in a better position in trying to reverse the relative economic decline in Shanghai.

Under normal circumstances, personnel changes like this would not necessarily lead to drastic changes in either local policies or the relationship with the

Center. However, the transfer of Rui, Jiang, and later Zhu to Shanghai was different. In a sense, their arrivals changed the dynamism of the relationship between Shanghai and Beijing.

Most previous leaders were sent to Shanghai by the central government to ensure that its policy line was strictly followed. Rui and Jiang came to Shanghai with a different mandate: They were asked to find ways to revitalize Shanghai's troubled economy and, in the process, help the national economy. Rui and Jiang were thus in a far better bargaining position vis-à-vis the Center than their predecessors. Both Rui and Jiang requested that the central government give the city concrete assistance so that they would have a better chance of achieving the goal of moving Shanghai out of its current slump.[33] The central government, under Hu Yaobang and Zhao Ziyang, concurred. Before Rui and Jiang left for Shanghai, Beijing had already agreed to provide Shanghai with a new revenue-sharing package.[34] Soon after their arrival, at the request of Jiang Zemin, the Center further gave the city the authority to raise funds in the international market independent of the central ministries.[35] While there was a limit as to how much the Center could meet the demands of the new Shanghai leaders, there was no question that the concessions Rui and Jiang had won played a significant role in boosting Shanghai's economy and paved the way for the eventual turnaround. More important, the requests made by Shanghai's new team of leaders and the swift, positive responses to these requests from the central government set up a new pattern in the relationship between the two. Instead of suspicion and mutual complaints, the two sides seemed to have reached a *quid pro quo* of some sort. Under the new relationship, Shanghai would promise better economic performance (and logically some larger contribution to the national economy) while the central government would offer various forms of assistance to the city based on the anticipated returns.

This new relationship proved to be critical to both sides. From the point of view of the central government, the change meant that Shanghai could now not only become another growth pole for China but also serve as an alternative model of reform and development, substantially different from the one exemplified by the experience of Guangdong. Deng Xiaoping and Chen Yun, for example, were known for their differences over certain aspects of the reform including the merits of introducing and expanding SEZs in southern China. However, the two seemed to have almost complete agreement on the need to give Shanghai more leeway and assistance to revitalize the local economy in its own style.[36] Shanghai, on the other hand, was more than happy with such a change. While in public the new leaders tried to downplay the image of being the favorite son of the central government, they nevertheless worked diligently to maximize the advantages associated with the new relationship with the Center.

Secondly, when Rui, Jiang and Zhu assumed their respective positions in Shanghai, they were, on average, about five years younger than the second group of leaders was when they took over.[37] This age difference might not seem to be particularly significant to some. However, in the Shanghai case, it made a big difference. The second group of leaders was only a few years away from their expected retirement when they arrived.[38] Since none of them had high expectations to move onto higher positions in the political hierarchy, there was little incentive for them to introduce drastic measures that involved huge risks. It was natural for them to be on the conservative side when dealing with controversial and touchy issues. Nor were they likely to take long-term perspectives on issues that they knew they would have very little to do with after their retirement.

The three new leaders, Rui, Jiang and Zhu, had obviously different motivations. Even after serving one full term in Shanghai,[39] they would still be young enough to assume higher positions in the central government. Given the fact that after the Cultural Revolution the central government had relied increasingly on provincial leaders to staff key positions, the possibility of moving upward certainly was not something that would easily skip their attention. They also knew that they had to earn the opportunity particularly by proving themselves while working in Shanghai. This meant that, regardless of their personal preferences, they were more committed to achieving concrete and visible results, especially those that would bear their names.

Finally, the educational and professional backgrounds and the personalities of Rui, Jiang and Zhu also helped them to exercise a more effective leadership than their predecessors. Jiang and Zhu received full-time university education after 1949. Rui completed most of the college-level courses. Some of them, such as Jiang, had extensive working experience in Shanghai. Others such as Rui and Zhu had only a brief encounter with the city. However, because their previous work focused mainly on the management of the urban sectors of the Chinese economy, they had the necessary experience to handle the types of issues cities like Shanghai were most likely to face after their arrival. Moreover, the personalities of the three tended to be by and large complementary rather than mutually exclusive. Rui, for example, was known for his steadiness and low-key style. Jiang, on the other hand, was known for his flamboyance but was also quick to learn and had a tendency to seek out new ideas and suggestions among other leaders or people working for him. Zhu was known for his strict and demanding style of leadership. He made his inferiors fearful of him. But because of that, he proved to be extremely efficient in administration. This, in turn, made him very popular among Shanghai residents who regarded him as the kind of leader they could truly count on to remedy the numerous problems left by the leaders and policies of the past.[40] It was not as if the three were always in harmony; on the contrary, trails of disagreements among them did appear from time to time. However, what was important was the fact that they at least did not allow such personal differences to escalate into major power and policy struggles as often happened in the past decade. As a result, Shanghai now had a leadership team that was balanced and maintained a higher degree of internal unity,[41] something the residents of Shanghai had not seen for quite some time.

Despite these strengths, however, there were still a number of important steps the new leadership had to take before they could actually turn Shanghai around. Most importantly, they had to search for a reform strategy that would help define how the city would get back on its feet and move forward.

There had been no shortage of debate or discussions in Shanghai in terms of what reform and development strategy the city should adopt since 1978. Unlike many less developed provinces, Shanghai had a rich intellectual tradition and a sound institutional base for such discussions to take place and play a role in actual policy making.[42] As a result, for years, Shanghai was known for its slow pace of reform but not so in terms of the number of policy discussions it conducted.

In early 1981, for example, several leading economists from Shanghai's Academy of Social Sciences had openly called for redirecting Shanghai's development efforts.[43] According to them, the time had come for Shanghai to rethink its development strategy. In particular, they called for moving away from the city's traditional industries (even though some of them were still fairly competitive nationwide at that time) and to focus on high-tech and high value-added industries.[44] Others made more specific proposals. One of the proposals argued that Shanghai should practice a *"neilian waiji"* policy (linking up with neighbors and pushing itself outward). Under this proposed policy, Shanghai would overhaul its economy by moving its traditional industries out to the neighboring areas while making itself more open to the outside world and using that access to upgrade its industries, especially the export sectors.[45]

However, most of these discussions remained what they were—suggestions—for years. Until the mid-1980s, Shanghai had neither the committed leadership nor the resources necessary to translate these proposals into actions. In fact, had there not been a series of major economic problems in the mid-1980s that forced both the central and local leadership to take a drastically different look at Shanghai reform strategy, real changes might have come even later.

Fortunately for Shanghai, the mounting problems it had to face in the mid-1980s were so serious that they simply denied the local and the central leaders the luxury of doing business as usual. The slowdown of the economic growth of Shanghai from 1981 to 1983 (see Table 1.1) alarmed the Center. The sharp decline in Shanghai's exports[46] and in its local revenue led the city's leaders to make repeated pleas to the Center for help.

In August 1984, after several top central leaders such as Hu Yaobang and Zhao Ziyang toured Shanghai to see the problems firsthand, the central government sent a working group to the city to work out possible solutions.[47] With the help from this working group and based on the recommendations from a variety of experts from Beijing, Shanghai and several other provinces, the Shanghai municipal government finally decided on a new development strategy. The strategy, later incorporated into a report Shanghai submitted to the Center identified three key goals in transforming Shanghai's economy.[48] The three goals were:

(1) to underscore Shanghai's role as a multi-functional central city and to use that advantage to help the city regain its leadership in areas such as commerce, international trade, finance, and science and technology; (2) while continuing to update the existing industries, concentrate on developing new ones, especially the high-tech and service sectors;[49] and (3) to further open up the city's economy so that Shanghai could serve as a key link between China and the world economy.

The report on the new strategy was submitted to the Center in December 1984 and approved in February 1985. Since then the document has served as a standard description of what Shanghai should do to revitalize its economy.

Rui Xingwen and Jiang Zemin inherited the 1984 development strategy from their predecessors and found many of the aspects to their liking. For example, the new strategy stressed the role of Shanghai government in initiating and coordinating various reform programs and efforts. Given their background and experience, especially their long-time involvement in central planning and management, the stress on government-guided reform fit their philosophy rather well. However, both of them also realized that in order to successfully revive Shanghai's economy, they had to make additional adjustments beyond what was subscribed by the 1984 strategy. For example, the 1984 strategy focused almost exclusively on economic development. The two, Rui in particular, believed Shanghai's revival needed improvements in other areas as well. Soon after their arrival, they pushed to develop a so-called cultural development strategy. They also placed much more importance on the need to improve the city's infrastructure both as a precondition and a major part of its economic revival.[50]

The 1984 strategy did not have the foresight to include a full discussion of the need and impact of transition to a market system.[51] Jiang, on the other hand, had traveled several times to Hong Kong and Guangdong in the early 1980s, so he knew perfectly well what was the real key to the economic success of these places. More importantly, even though the 1984 strategy contained several high goals, it did not have a well-thought-out plan to help translate these goals into actions and realities. In particular, the 1984 strategy did not spell out exactly how the issue of financing the economic transformation would be solved. Rui, by contrast, knew the significance of this problem only too well. In his first major speech to the leaders of Shanghai, he warned specifically, "It costs a lot of money and takes a long time to build the infrastructure. The lack of sufficient funds will be a very salient problem for years to come."[52]

Rui and Jiang's worry about the money issue was based on another concern. As soon as they took over the leading positions in Shanghai in 1985, they began to emphasize the need to target government spending for projects that were popular and linked directly to the livelihood of local residents. For example, starting from 1984, the municipal government would include in its annual economic and social development plan a promise to complete a certain number (usually 10 to 25) of projects as *weimin shishi* (practical projects for the people).[53] These projects were part of an effort to insert a populist dimension to the city's reform and development strategy so that the public would be more understanding and supportive of the transformation. Most of such projects involved things like building more residential housing units, creating a fund for and a system to help stabilize the supply and the prices of produce and other staples, improving the environment, and upgrading public transportation. These projects were highly popular but were costly. Moreover, since the city would usually promise to complete these projects within the year they were announced, it often had to divert money from other projects to keep its promise. As a result, the city was under constant pressure to find more money to finance and complete these projects, in addition to all its other undertakings.

It was thus not surprising that both Rui and Jiang devoted a considerable amount of their energy and time during the first two years in office to help mobilize financial resources. They did so in a number of ways. They started, of course, by asking the central government for help. This was not only the easiest way, but also a logical one. In the 1984 report on the proposed development strategy, Shanghai made it clear that in order for the strategy to work, "It is necessary for various central ministries concerned to offer some help, including delegating authority, assigning special policies, and providing necessary funds [to Shanghai]."[54]

The new Shanghai leadership under Rui and Jiang was more successful than its predecessors in securing such help from the central government. Thanks to the 1985 revenue-sharing fiscal regime worked out before they arrived, Shanghai was able to retain 1.8 billion yuan more revenue from 1985 to 1986.[55] On September 4, 1986, Shanghai received the permission from the Center to raise up to US$ 3.2 billion in the international markets to help finance projects ranging from infrastructure to industrial renovation and adjustment.

However, the 1985 fiscal regime failed to boost Shanghai's overall revenue significantly. Indeed, the local revenue actually fell from 18.42 billion yuan in 1985 to 16.61 billion yuan in 1988.[56] Shanghai once again called upon the Center for help. In late 1987, after several key central leaders inspected the city, Shanghai wrote a new report to the Center.[57] In the report, Shanghai proposed, based on the 1984 development strategy, that it be given greater autonomy in finance and other economic management so that the city could accelerate economic growth and the transition toward an economy geared to compete internationally. The report, known as Document 123, was approved by the central government in February 1985 along with several preferential policies. These policies were known as "one contract and four supporting programs." The one contract referred to the new revenue-sharing regime, also known as the lump-sum contract system. Under this regime, which was to start in 1988 and was good for five years, Shanghai would only need to remit to the Center a fixed amount of 10.5 billion yuan a year. Compared with the old regime, the new one was supposedly able to provide Shanghai with 1.4 billion yuan extra money a year or even more if the city could collect more than 16.5 billion yuan in revenue. The four supporting programs referred to the policies that authorized Shanghai to manage trade, price, distribution system, and local finance on a more autonomous basis.[58]

However, even with these preferential policies and arrangements, the recovery of Shanghai's economy proved to be far more difficult than initially thought. From 1986 to 1988, Shanghai's economy continued to grow considerably slower than the national average (see Table 1.1). The city's revenue showed little growth. The same was true for Shanghai's efforts to internationalize its economy. For example, the city received a mere total of US$ 371 million in direct foreign investment from 1985 to 1987 despite an extensive campaign aimed at attracting more inflow of foreign capital.[59] By contrast, during the same period, Guangdong attracted a total of US$ 1.75 billion in foreign investment. Moreover, the programs to transform Shanghai's traditional industries into modern ones did not proceed as planned largely due to shortage of funds and a lack of true control of how and when such transformation should take place as the central policies in this regard wavered quite often themselves.

In 1988, after Rui was promoted to the Center, Zhu Rongji, one of China's most capable economic administrators, was sent to Shanghai. During his youth, Zhu applied to a Shanghai university but ended up enrolling in the more prestigious Qinghua University in Beijing. A victim of the Anti-rightist campaign in the 1950s and the Cultural Revolution in the 1960s, Zhu managed to go back to work in several government jobs in the early 1980s after showing his talent for economic analysis and management. Although he confessed that he did not ask for the job in Shanghai, he was nevertheless intrigued by the prospect of managing one of China's largest economies on his own terms and determined to make his impact felt.[60]

Zhu's arrival gave Shanghai's efforts to revitalize its economy a new boost. In particular, his heavy-handed leadership style was well received by a city yearning for quick and tangible results. His prior ties to China's top economic management officials also fanned the expectation that he could secure more help from the central government in a more effective way. Zhu went to work in a hurry. Soon after his arrival, Zhu made it known that he was not happy with the status quo. He started, first, by looking for a new approach toward economic development that would not only help overcome Shanghai's current economic woes but also pave way for long-term economic well-being.

During his relatively short (1988 to 1991) stint in Shanghai, Zhu was instrumental in bringing about a new interpretation of the development strategy adopted in 1984. In theory, Shanghai had never formally abandoned the 1984 strategy, but Zhu and others had added so many new dimensions to it that by the time he left for Beijing in 1991, Shanghai's development strategy had already moved beyond a set of abstract principles symbolized by the 1984 strategy to a full-blown and operational strategy that had four key pillars.

The first was the focus on developing Pudong as a new pole of economic growth for Shanghai. It was also hoped that by building up Pudong, a large area relatively underdeveloped and hence less constrained by the old system of central planning, it could generate the momentum to reshape the city including its image, industrial structure, management style or even government organizations.

To be sure, Shanghai had long discussed the possibility of developing Pudong. In both the 1984 development strategy and the 1985 revised overall plan for the city, the issue of Pudong was given particular attention. However, the real momentum came only as a result of a critical meeting held in May 1988. During the meeting which was attended by both Jiang and Zhu, a decision was made to speed up the preparation for developing Pudong, including the establishment of a small leading group to coordinate the efforts.[61] At that time, the main rationale for developing Pudong was that it would help transform the old city center. However, as more and more attention was paid to Pudong, the importance attached to the development of the area also grew. According to Huang Ju, the deputy mayor of Shanghai at that time, the development of Pudong served three purposes: (1) as a key to make Shanghai a more open and modern metropolitan area; (2) as a magnet for the development of the Yangtze Delta area;[62] and (3) as a driving force for upgrading Shanghai's industries and infrastructure.[63]

After more than a year of discussion and preparation, Shanghai submitted to the Center a proposal outlining its plan to develop the Pudong area in February 1990.[64] The next month, the deputy premier, Yao Yilin, went to Shanghai for further inspection. In April, the central government formally approved Shanghai's request to develop Pudong and gave the city a variety of preferential treatments designed to ensure a quick start to the development process.[65] In addition to enjoying many special policies previously reserved only for SEZs, Shanghai also received 6.5 billion yuan from the central government for the next five years as *qidong zijin* (seed money) and the authority to raise more funds on its own including issuing local bonds for the purpose of financing major construction projects in the Pudong area.[66]

The decision to focus on developing Pudong turned out to be a strategic move. Because of the huge inflow of capital, Pudong moved from the sideline to emerge as the most important growth pole for Shanghai. From 1991 to 1994, Pudong's GDP grew from 7.2 billion yuan to 29.1 billion yuan, twice as fast as the growth rate of Shanghai as a whole and its share in Shanghai's GDP rose from 8.1 percent to 14 percent.[67] In 1994, Pudong attracted one-fourth of the foreign direct investment the city received even though the current area of Pudong was only one-tenth of the size of the old city.[68] More importantly, Shanghai managed to use the Pudong project to receive positive attention from the central government. Not only did the Center repeatedly list the development of Pudong as one of the highest national priorities, it also became more receptive to other demands Shanghai put forward given the high profile the central government attached to the development of Pudong.[69]

The second pillar was an unprecedented, large-scale campaign to renovate Shanghai's aging infrastructure. In 1986, Rui Xingwen already argued that building up the infrastructure was one of the three keys to Shanghai's development (the other two keys were attracting foreign investment and promoting export and making progress in science, technology and human development).[70] Since then other Shanghai leaders had put similar emphasis on drastically improving the city's infrastructure as a must for economic revival.

There were several reasons behind Shanghai's commitment to infrastructure. One had to do with plain reality. Shanghai's infrastructure was notoriously outdated by the mid-1980s. The city, on the other hand, was in the midst of a major transformation of its economic structure. The gap between the two was so obvious that Shanghai leaders had little choice but to concentrate on bringing the infrastructure up to the standard however expensive that might be. Another reason was the political benefits one could reap from the renovation of the city. Unlike the effort to reinvigorate the declining state-owned enterprises, improvements in the city's infrastructure tended to bring more visibility to the local leaders and more tangible results. Indeed, many of the projects designed to improve the infrastructure were immensely popular among local residents. There was thus sufficient incentive for Shanghai's leaders to devote their attention to the task. Moreover, it did not take long for the leaders in Shanghai to realize that the investment boom associated with the renovation effort could serve Shanghai in more than one way. For example, the construction boom could provide more jobs and opportunities for the city which in turn could accelerate the growth of the local economy. Better infrastructure could also make Shanghai more attractive to potential investors and hence give the city a competitive edge vis-à-vis other provinces such as Guangdong. Finally, the emphasis on improving infrastructure also seemed to fit the fundamental policies of the central government. China's reform was known for its emphasis on high growth or, as Barry Naughton put it, "growing out of the plan."[71] After the mid-1980s, especially in the wake of the economic slowdown following the 1989 Tiananmen crackdown, the central government particularly encouraged investment in infrastructure over other types of investments as a way to boost long-term development. Shanghai's decision to put more emphasis on infrastructure was not only logical, it was politically astute as well.

The third pillar of the new development strategy was the emphasis on reestablishing Shanghai as China's foremost center for domestic and foreign trade and finance and other service industries. This was one of the original goals identified in the 1984 development strategy. However, serious implementation did not start until the late 1980s. For example. while there had been calls to create markets of various production factors such as materials, capital, labor and land, most of the markets established were either small in size or isolated.[72] However, after 1985, the efforts to create various exchange centers in Shanghai picked up speed. In 1987, Shanghai began this endeavor by creating the Iron and Steel Market and by the end of 1993, Shanghai had fifteen such markets which handled a large portion of nationwide trade of key industrial goods and materials. In 1986, Shanghai was the first in China to open internal borrowing among banks. The next year, Shanghai formed an unified capital market which handled a variety of financial transactions. Shanghai began to issue stocks in 1984 but in December 1990, Shanghai became the second city to open a formal stock market since 1987. The Shanghai Stock Market quickly surpassed the one in Shenzhen in volume and in the number of listed companies to become the most important financial center in China. These moves, especially the opening of the stock market, gave Shanghai a number of direct benefits: high publicity, huge inflow of capital from other provinces, and proceeds from taxation on financial transactions. More importantly, by reclaiming the leadership in what is known in China as the *disan chanye* (tertiary industry as opposed to traditional industry and agriculture) and putting its most valuable resources—the experience, entrepreneurship, and managerial skills of local business persons—to this sector, Shanghai was able to reassert itself as a leader in the national economy.

The final pillar of Shanghai's new development strategy was a two-prone attack on the old problem of upgrading the city's enormous but outdated industries. When Zhu Rongji and other leaders tackled the problem, they were fully aware of the difficulties involved. Instead of relying on traditional solutions such as giving more autonomy to managers, they decided to take on a dual-track approach. In regard to the existing state-owned enterprises of which many were losing money chronically, they chose to make changes that would help alleviate the problems these enterprises had long faced without causing major disturbance. On the other hand, they put much more emphasis on developing new, key industries, hoping that in time these new industries would help phase out the old, less efficient ones. In 1988, Shanghai selected fourteen industrial projects as key development projects. The initial hope was that in three to five years, these new enterprises could substitute for the traditional industries as the leading sectors in Shanghai's economy.[73] In 1990, Shanghai further narrowed down the list to ten hi-tech and leading-edge industries as the key sectors for the 1990s and promised to give preferential policies and financial support to these sectors.[74]

To sum up, four years after the third group of leaders was sent to Shanghai, the city had significantly modified the 1984 development strategy. The goal of the revised strategy was to make Shanghai *yige longtou, sange zhongxin* (become the head of the dragon of the entire Yangtze river area and serve as three centers, namely, the economic, international finance, and trade center of China). To achieve this goal, the city decided to focus on four key areas defined by the revised development strategy: developing Pudong as the engine for change and development, launching a large-scale campaign to renovate the city's infrastructure to serve long-term growth, emphasizing the service industries to help strengthen Shanghai's economic leadership, and gradually moving Shanghai to hi-tech industries to phase out the old ones without causing too much socioeconomic pain.

The initial results in implementing this development strategy were encouraging. Shanghai's economy showed significant improvement from 1985 to 1990.[75] Despite the fact that the growth of the overall economy remained slow relative to other provinces, a number of important changes took place with positive impact on the future development. Shanghai moved steadily but consistently away from a center of traditional industries to a center of rising industries and service industries. While the GNP grew only by an average of 7 percent a year during this period, the service industries such as banking grew by more than 10 percent a year. The second half of the 1980s also saw rapid increase in capital accumulation. There was less outflow of national income. In 1985, 25.7 percent of Shanghai's national income flowed to other areas, largely through the city's remittance, to the central coffers. In 1989, only 7.2 percent of the generated national income left Shanghai. Of the national income used in Shanghai, more than half was saved and used as investment. From 1978 to 1984, the average saving rate was 43 percent; from 1985 to 1990, it was 52 percent. As a result, the total investment in fixed assets from 1986 to 1990 was 50 percent more than the amount invested in the previous five years. The total investment on urban infrastructure was 233 percent more. Together with the increasing amount of inflow of overseas capital, Shanghai was poised to enter a period of faster economic growth in the coming years.

The event in 1989 and its aftermath had a major impact on the composition of Shanghai's top leadership. Jiang Zemin was promoted to become the general secretary of the CCP after June 1989. Less than two years after Jiang left, Zhu Rongji was brought back to the Center to supervise the country's economic operations. Succeeding them were the fourth group of leaders led by Wu Bangguo and Huang Ju. After 1991, Wu served as the party secretary, and Huang the mayor. When Wu was called to serve in the central government in 1994, Huang took over both the party secretary and the mayor's job. In February 1995, Xu Kuangdi was elected as mayor of Shanghai while Huang retained his title as the party secretary.

Unlike the third group of leaders, the current Shanghai leaders had much to thank for their immediate predecessors. They had the benefit of running an economy that had already bottomed out thanks to the efforts by Rui, Jiang and Zhu. They were provided a development strategy that had generally worked well for the city and helped lay the foundation for further development. At a personal level, both Wu and Huang, and later Xu, owed a great deal of their careers to Jiang and Zhu as they worked as the latter's lieutenants for quite some time before they took over.

However, the current leaders had to deal with a different kind of challenges. With Shanghai's economy showing more and more signs of recovery, expectations rose too. Deng Xiaoping, in particular, had become obsessed with the changes in the city. In early 1992, Deng made the famous southern tour during which he called upon local leaders to seek faster economic growth. In a similar fashion, Deng challenged the Shanghai leaders to show that they could achieve *niannian you bianhua, sannian da bianyang* (improvements in every year and major facelift every three years) in Shanghai's overall economy and development.[76] This goal alone kept the current leaders' hands full.

The current leaders also belong to a different category of rulers of Shanghai. Both Wu and Huang grew up and worked exclusively in the Shanghai area, although they both received higher educations in Beijing.[77] Before they became the top municipal leaders, both of them had served in various capacities in the municipal government since 1983. Born in Zhejiang, Xu also studied and worked briefly in Beijing before he was transferred to Shanghai in 1963 where he stayed since.[78] They were, in a true sense, the first group of home-grown leaders in Shanghai's post-1949 history. They were also the first group of leaders who shared the changes in Shanghai on a personal basis.

The high expectations and personal background and credentials created a complicated task for the current leaders in Shanghai. First, they had to do more. Unlike in the past where some improvements alone could be touted as a major success, they had to beat the past record to prove themselves. Indeed, anything short of a spectacular economic boom would have been seen as a failure on their part. Secondly, they had to so with more local considerations in mind. Their power base was narrower than their predecessors', derived almost exclusively from the Shanghai area. In addition to keeping on good terms with their superiors, they had all the more reason to be sensitive to local demands.

Since 1991, the current leaders had by and large succeeded in this task. The growth rate of GDP more than doubled that of the previous five years. The share of service industries in GDP rose from 30.8 percent in 1990 to 40.1 percent in 1995. The share of high-tech, high value-added industries in total industrial output rose from 34.5 percent to 45.1 percent during the same period. Export increased by more than 20 percent a year between 1991 and 1995. Direct foreign investment passed the US$ 15 billion mark. Mandatory government planning now affected only 3 percent of major economic transactions. To the liking of Shanghai's citizens, the city's infrastructure had been improved beyond even the most optimistic expectation.[79]

The current leaders had their share of problems too. The transformation of SOEs was far from complete. More SOEs were losing money than ever before. More than half a million workers lost their jobs due to restructuring. The city as a whole still had to struggle with an inadequate urban infrastructure and other problems, such as a deteriorating environment, that were exacerbated by the economic boom.

Still, the last five years showed the strength of the current leaders. The strength was particularly evident in several areas. First, while the current leaders did not have a brand new reform and development strategy of their own, they were committed to improve upon the development strategy they inherited from Jiang and Zhu in the way they saw fit. In 1990 and 1994, the municipal government organized two rounds of discussions aimed at producing a new blueprint that would place Shanghai's development on a more solid ground.[80] The blueprint contained several interesting aspects. For example, more emphasis was now on how to integrate the various pillars of Shanghai's development into a well-coordinated effort designed to build a complete market system. This meant that things such as improvement of infrastructure would not be seen as an ad hoc measure but rather as the first step toward building a mega-metropolitan center. Similarly, unlike in the past where economic development was often defined in narrow terms, the new blueprint called for balanced development across the sectors, paying more attention to the so-called software of such development— better utilization of human resources, technological advancement, community life, and rearranging social organizations, among others. While Shanghai had a long way to go to fully implement the blueprint, the effort to adjust its reform and development strategy on a regular basis demonstrated the level of maturity of its leadership.

Another strength of the current leadership was its ability to try and introduce more market mechanisms into the overall development effort. Shanghai had always stressed the role of government in guiding reform. The current leaders were no different. However, compared with the previous leaders. the current leaders seemed to be more open to combine government guidance and market mechanisms together. Xu Kuangdi explained this point rather convincingly in 1994 before he became Shanghai's mayor. According to him, because the municipal government wanted so much to make the city a center for international trade and finance, the best way to do so was to take a lead in the nation in fully relying upon the market. The government would still play an active role in such a system like establishing rules, norms and laws, he argued, but it was the fundamental reliance on market mechanisms that would keep Shanghai attractive and make it a true economic center.[81] The last few years saw Shanghai moving consistently in that direction.

Resource Mobilization, Shanghai Style

The three versions of reform and development strategy Shanghai adopted after the mid-1980s had one thing in common: they were all predicated on the city's ability to mobilize a huge amount of financial resources. Whether it was the development of Pudong, renovation of the city's infrastructure, or creation of new core industries, the demand for input, especially capital input, was overwhelming. In a sense, Shanghai's reform strategy after the mid-1980s was a strategy of high-input, high-risk and a high level of reliance on government guidance. The leaders in Shanghai were not only fully aware of this, they actually hoped that the strategy could do two things for them. They hoped the investment boom would give Shanghai's slumping economy a shot in the arm. They also hoped that once the local economy began to show signs of revival,

Shanghai would be able to attract even more investment which would in turn help generate more revenue to be used in areas where the city needed it the most.[82] There was a catch, however. For such a strategy to work, Shanghai would have to mobilize huge amounts of funds in a short period of time in order to "kick off" the benign circle the city had hoped for. There was no surprise that a major part of Shanghai's efforts of reform and development after the 1980s was concentrated on mobilizing exactly such resources. The efforts were multi-faceted but well coordinated.

Seeking Greater Control Over Local Revenue

Shanghai's resource mobilization campaign started with the efforts to bring more revenue under its own control. Until 1991, Shanghai generated more local revenue than any other provinces did.[83] Yet, Shanghai had been largely unsuccessful in trying to retain more local revenue for itself between 1978 and 1984. On average, 14.61 billion yuan or 86 percent of the city's revenue was remitted to the central government.[84] This was caused mainly by the fact that Shanghai had to continue to live under the most unfavorable revenue-sharing arrangement known as *dingshou, dingzhi* (fixed revenue and expenditures targets). This arrangement left Shanghai with virtually no fiscal autonomy since the central government set fixed quotas for both local revenue collection and expenditures and took in what was left.

Shanghai's woe was exacerbated by the impact of the economic reform. The reform hit hard on Shanghai's SOEs (state-owned enterprises) which had produced most of the revenue for the city in the past. Since Shanghai had little control over its revenue, it could not provide sufficient funds needed for the SOEs to remain competitive. As a result, at a time when Shanghai's overall revenue remained stagnant, the tax expenditures in the form of subsidizing money-losing SOEs were growing at a fast rate.[85]

After 1984, Shanghai sought aggressively to rearrange its fiscal relationship with the central government. The focus was to replace the existing arrangements with ones that would give the city more control over its revenue and greater flexibility in local spending. In 1984, 1988 and 1994, three such arrangements were made with Shanghai getting more favorable treatment each time. One of the best indicators of Shanghai's gain can be seen in the changes in the percentages of local revenue remitted to the central government, as Table 1.3 shows.

The gradual but steady reduction of remittances to the central government coincided nicely with the introduction of the three new revenue-sharing regimes. The first regime was adopted in 1984 known as *heding jishu, zhong fenchen* (ratifying the base amount and sharing the total).[86] The new regime gave the city several concrete benefits. The local share of revenue went up from the average of 11.8 percent between 1976 and 1984 to 23.54 percent starting from 1985.[87] Since the percentage of remittances was fixed for six years, Shanghai in theory could

Table 1.3

Shanghai's Remittance as Percent of Local Revenue, 1984–1996
(unit: billion yuan)

	Remittance to center[a]	Local revenue	Remittance as % of local revenues	Budgetary balance
1984	14.09	16.39	85.97	+0.03
1985	13.42	18.42	72.86	+0.29
1986	13.37	17.95	74.49	−1.53
1987	12.88	16.89	76.26	−0.09
1988	10.55	16.16	65.28	b/ms[b]
1989	10.50	16.69	62.91	b/ms
1990	10.95	17.00	64.41	−0.17
1991	11.07	17.55	63.08	−0.49
1992	11.21	18.66	60.40	−0.69
1993	11.40	24.23	47.05	+0.30
1994	12.10	17.53[c]	68.45	+0.51
1995	12.00	21.99	54.57	b/ms
1996	12.00	28.85	41.59	+0.60

Sources: The 1985–1990 figures are from *Shanghai caizheng shuiwuzhi* (History of Shanghai's Finance and Taxation) (Shanghai: Shehui kexue chubanshe, 1995), p. 90. The other figures are from annual budget reports which can be found in *Shanghai caishui*, No. 5, 1991, pp. 4–7, No. 5, 1992, pp. 3–7, No. 3, 1993, pp. 4–7, No. 3, 1994, pp. 3–9, No. 3, 1995, pp. 4–7; and *Jiefang Ribao*, May 3, 1991, May 14, 1992, and February 27, 1997.

[a]The figures did not include remittance to the Center from the Energy and Key Transportation Project Construction Funds (EKTPCF) and the Budgetary Adjustment Funds (BAF). Provinces were required to remit to the Center 50 percent of what they collected under these two tax categories.

[b]b/ms = balance with minor surplus. This is a common term in Chinese budgeting indicating an insignificant amount of budgetary surplus.

[c]Because of the new revenue-sharing system introduced in 1994, the amount of local revenue is incompatible with that of the past.

gain more if local revenue grew. Finally, under the new regime, the central government would no longer issue mandatory spending quotas. The city could decide how to distribute local funds on its own.

Unfortunately, Shanghai's gain from the 1984 regime was temporary. In the first year of implementation, the budgetary outlays for infrastructure and education rose by 74.5 percent and 41.5 percent respectively.[88] However, once the overall revenue fell again in 1986, Shanghai was back to the same fiscal predicament, unable to spend as much as it wanted on key items. More significantly, even with the 1984 regime, the burden of remittance was still exceedingly heavy on Shanghai.

In 1988, Shanghai bargained and received a new revenue-sharing regime known as *da baogan* (lump-sum transfer system), the same regime Guangdong received in 1980. Under the new regime, Shanghai's remittance to the central government was fixed at 10.5 billion yuan per year. Revenue collected above that amount went to Shanghai. The central government did, however, put in a catch. After three years, Shanghai would share with the Center half of what it collected above the 16.5 billion yuan mark.[89]

Similar to what happened after the 1984 regime was introduced, the 1988 regime provided Shanghai with only some short-term gains. From 1988 to 1990, the local share of revenue rose to 33.79 percent. In 1988 alone, the city figured that the new regime allowed it to retain 1.4 billion yuan more than it would have under the old regime.[90] Yet, the 1988 regime failed to do the same wonder to Shanghai as it did to Guangdong in 1980. In the latter case, revenue collection rose from 3.95 billion yuan in 1981 to 6.55 billion yuan in 1985 while the amount of remittance remained largely unchanged.[91]

By the end of the 1980s, Shanghai finally realized that incremental changes in revenue-sharing would provide the city with only limited help. In fact, one Shanghai official was so disappointed by the results of the 1988 regime that he bluntly called it a rotten deal the city had to swallow.[92]

He might have been expressing his own views on this point, but the thrust of Shanghai's effort clearly shifted after 1988. The city became more committed than ever to look beyond the regular budgetary system for possible sources of funds (the efforts in this regard will be discussed in the next section). On the other hand, the city, along with economically more advanced regions such as Guangdong, pressed the central government to adopt a new fiscal regime not based on arbitrary revenue-sharing but on a clear and binding delineation of local, central, and shared taxes.[93]

The revenue picture meanwhile became more complicated as far as Shanghai was concerned. Shanghai's direct gain from the 1988 regime was tempered by the lackluster growth in overall revenue especially if the inflation rate is taken into account. On the other hand, the *ke zhipei caili* (disposable fiscal resources) available to the city rose rather quickly after 1987. These resources included not only the amount of revenue retained by Shanghai based on the sharing contract, they also included *zichou shoulu* (self-raised income outside the regular budgetary process) and the amount of central transfers (subsidies) to the city. Table 1.4 shows the changes.

The increase in disposable fiscal resources was important to Shanghai at least up to the end of the 1980s. This was the period in which Shanghai faced severe budgetary shortages but was unable to boost its total revenue collection one way or another. The increase of funds available to the city, though relatively small, helped to take some pressure away. Meanwhile, the municipal government used other means as well such as deficit spending to meet urgent needs.

The macro-environment changed after 1991. As the local economy began to take off, overall revenue rose. Ironically, the 1988 regime was adopted to help Shanghai relieve some pressure caused by the severe *huapo* (slide) in revenue collection. It was not until 1993 when Shanghai's revenue collection had already

Table 1.4

Total Disposable Fiscal Resources, 1987–1996 (unit: billion yuan)

Year	Disposable fiscal resources	Retained revenue	Non-budgetary incomes	Shared funds[a]	SM-incomes[b]	Central subsidies, grant-in-kind,[c] and rebate[d]
1987	5.32	4.01	0.38		0.38	0.55
1988	7.83	5.61	0.81	0.39	0.42	0.61
1989	8.62	6.19	0.82	0.43	0.39	0.79
1990	8.98	6.05	0.73	0.30	0.46	1.44
1991	10.12	6.48	1.01	0.33	0.68	1.62
1992	11.74	7.35	1.00	0.26	0.74	2.39
1993	18.06	12.83	1.67	0.40	1.28	1.98
1994	20.20	5.43				14.67
1995	27.41	9.99				16.68
1996	34.87	16.85				17.42

Sources: Same as Table 1.3.

ᵃ Shared funds include the tax revenue from the EKTPCF and BAF, 50 percent of which is shared by the provinces.

ᵇThese incomes include various user fees the city charged on public services.

ᶜThis item includes central subsidies such as the food price stabilization funds and other grants-in-kind.

ᵈAfter 1994, the central government rebates to Shanghai the same amount it remits to the Center plus 75 percent of revenue collected from VAT and business taxes and above the amount of fixed remittance.

turned around when the true benefits of the regime began to show. In 1993, Shanghai was able to retain more than half of the local revenue for the first time.

After years of preparation, the central government introduced a brand new tax system known as *fenshuizhi* (tax-sharing system) in 1994. Based on the new system, the central government also revised the revenue-sharing regimes with various provinces including Shanghai. Under the new regime, Shanghai would retain all the revenue collected under the "local tax" categories.[94] It would share with the central government several "shared taxes" such as the value-added tax (VAT), consumption tax and stock transaction tax. Shanghai's share for the first two taxes are 25 percent and its share for the last one is 50 percent. Shanghai would continue to "remit" to the central government a fixed amount of 12.0 billion yuan a year. However, this amount would be fully rebated by the central government since it collected more from its share in Shanghai's VAT and consumption tax income. In addition, it was stipulated that if the amount of the revenue Shanghai collected from the VAT and consumption tax surpassed the 1993 base amount, the city would receive an additional "rebate" equivalent to 30 percent of the increment.[95]

Of all the revenue-sharing regimes, the 1994 regime proved to be the most favorable to Shanghai in a number of ways. The regime provided a basically level field for Shanghai to compete with other provinces such as Guangdong. The regime was particularly beneficial to provinces where there was a strong revenue base for local taxes. In 1995, roughly 33 percent of the local revenue Shanghai collected was from various local taxes.[96]

Shanghai also benefited greatly from some of the remaining shared taxes such as the stock transaction tax. After the nation's second stock market opened in Shanghai in 1991, the volume of transactions and number of listed companies increased by leaps and bounds. This market along with other future and commodity markets provided Shanghai with a revenue bonanza.[97] In 1992, Shanghai collected a little over 100 million yuan in stamp tax.[98] The next year, the amount jumped to over 1.4 billion yuan.[99] In 1995, it further rose to 1.77 billion yuan.[100]

Ultimately, however, it was Shanghai's own efforts that helped it make the best out of the 1994 regime. Shanghai's success in turning the economy around provided a solid base for revenue increase. The city's intensified revenue collection also made a difference. For example, the initial budget report of 1994 by the municipal government forecasted a total income of 11.38 billion yuan from various local taxes (the 1993 figure was 10.59 billion yuan). However, with the economy growing faster than anticipated and target efforts to collect revenue from such taxes as personal income and business tax from overseas-owned enterprises, the city eventually generated a total of 17.53 billion yuan in revenue, 54 percent more than what was planned.[101]

Shanghai also introduced policies of its own to either find more revenue sources or to provide more incentives for revenue collection. The city gradually delegated more fiscal power to the lower level of government units such as counties and urban districts. These units in turn generated more revenue for their own sake. In 1995, for example, the revenue from these units rose by 40.3 percent, far outpacing the growth of revenue generated by the municipal government itself.[102] By the same token, as Shanghai introduced more market transactions or opened its door wider, it created instant and potential revenue sources. Over the last few years, Shanghai has been aggressive in luring foreign banks to open their branches in Shanghai especially in the Pudong area. The result: the city collected 81 percent more income tax from these banks in 1996 than in 1995.[103]

Mobilizing Resources from Non-budgetary Sources

Shanghai had thus come a long way in mobilizing fiscal resources within the traditional budgetary system. However, as mentioned earlier, Shanghai's leaders had realized early on that a major upturn in tax revenue collection like the one that happened after 1992 would not be enough to finance what was required by their high-input based development strategy. Indeed, probably the most interesting aspect of Shanghai's financial mobilization was the consistent and concerted efforts to seek input from non-budgetary sources. Without the success in this regard, Shanghai's turnaround after the mid-1980s would have been far less spectacular.

There was little doubt that Shanghai's efforts were out of necessity. Jiang and Zhu's reform and development strategy called for rebuilding Shanghai's massive and outdated infrastructure. The cost of actually doing so, however, was so high that there was simply no way that the municipal government alone could afford it. Yet, at the same time, Shanghai enjoyed several advantages few places had. The city's real estate was highly sought after by many. Shanghai's location and ties with overseas markets made it an ideal conduit for business transactions. Shanghai's close ties to the political center made it all the more attractive to those who wanted to establish a stronghold in China.

Out of necessity and using its various advantages, Shanghai was able to change the way how projects related to the city's infrastructure were funded. In the past, budgetary appropriations bore the bulk of spending on public projects; now the funding became much more diversified. Table 1.5 shows the breakdown of sources of investment in infrastructure from 1982 to 1995.

The changes were striking. The total investment went up sharply while the amount of funding from the government budget remained largely unchanged. How was Shanghai able to do that? The answer lies in several parts. Shanghai received several preferential authorizations from the central government which specifically allowed the city to raise funds from overseas sources. In 1986, for example, the State Council authorized Shanghai to borrow up to US$ 3.2 billion from overseas markets (including loans from foreign governments and multinational financial institutions such as the World Bank and the Asia Development Bank) to help finance local projects related to infrastructure and industrial development.[104] Shanghai would be fully responsible for raising and repaying these funds.

The policy undoubtedly gave Shanghai a shot in the arm. But what was more significant was Shanghai's decision to not only raise the funds through a well-thought-out plan but also to use the funds in such a way that they could serve more purposes than the dollar amount would indicate. Shanghai's first step was to set up a separate management company known as *Jiusi* Company to handle the anticipated flow of funds.[105] Later, the company received further authorization to borrow an additional US$ 1 billion for projects related to industrial renovation. In addition, Shanghai managed to give the company permission to engage in the domestic "currency swap." Since foreign currency was still in short supply at that time and the company possessed hard currency yet to be distributed, the company could use the time differential to earn additional income.[106]

It turned out that *Jiusi* Company played a key role in helping mobilize and distribute resources for the renovation of infrastructure in Shanghai. From 1988 to 1992, the company raised a total of 15 billion yuan not only from the international market but also from domestic sources as well.[107] It then distributed the funds to a total of 285 projects. Among these projects were the so-called big-five

Table 1.5

Sources of Investment in Infrastructure, 1982–95 (unit: 100 million yuan)

Year	Total investment in city infra-structure[a]	Budgetary appropriations		Loans[c]	Social funds[d]	Others[e]
		Amount	As %[b]			
1982	7.22					
1983	7.62					
1984	9.77	9.03	92.43			
1985	23.17	17.50	75.53			
1986	24.78	14.85	59.93			
1987	32.64					
1988	37.08	11.70	31.55			
1989	36.09	12.55	34.77			
1990	47.22	15.88	33.63	4.33	7.46	19.55
1991	61.38	16.03	26.11	6.86	9.01	29.48
1992	84.35	12.20	14.46	5.67	10.09	56.39
1993	172.53	21.23	12.36	6.62	23.33	121.35
1994	223.39					
1995	258.08					

Sources: Shanghai tongji nianjian 1994 (Statistical Yearbook of Shanghai), p. 87. 1994 figure is from *Jiefang Ribao* (Shanghai), February 8, 1995. 1995 figure is from *Shanghai touzi* (Shanghai Investment), No. 6, 1996, p. 11.

[a]Investment in public housing, roads, utility, public transportation, communications, etc.

[b]Budgetary appropriations came from two sources, budgetary appropriations earmarked as urban maintenance funds and a portion of the investment in capital construction that was devoted to projects related to the city's infrastructure.

[c]Loans refer to the loans received from multinational financial institutions or from foreign governments.

[d]Social funds refer to proceeds from the issuance of local bonds and other forms of fund-raising.

[e]All other sources include funds to build housing units by state-owned enterprises and payments by individual house owners.

undertakings, namely, the building of the Nanpu Bridge, the expansion of Shanghai's Hongqiao Airport, the completion of the first stage of the city's subway system, a massive sewage processing project, and a key communication center.[108] Without funding from *Jiusi* company, few of these projects would have been completed so fast. And without completing those projects, Shanghai's plan to overhaul its infrastructure would have been significantly delayed.

Not only was Shanghai creative in raising funds, it was also good at using the funds effectively. For example, the 1988 revenue-sharing regime provided the city with 1.4 billion yuan in disposable revenue in 1985 alone. Instead of putting the money into a regular a budgetary account, the city used the revenue as seed money to open up a new company known as *Shisi* Company.[109] Unlike the *Jiusi* Company, *Shisi* Company would devote its funds exclusively to supporting local industries especially exporting industries. Though *Shisi* Company could not match *Jiusi* Company in capital endowment, its role was no less critical. The company charged a fee on loans it gave out so that it could provide funding on a continuous basis. More important, the large discretion the company enjoyed enabled the city to target certain industries for special help without going through the regular and more complicated budgetary process.

Encouraged by the success of these companies, Shanghai relied increasingly on these market-based or semi-market–oriented entities to carry out the task tradition-ally reserved for government agencies in charge of urban maintenance and renova-tion. More companies were created using government funding as initial capital but moving on to raising and distributing funds mainly through various markets. Unlike private companies, however, the business of these companies was generally "guided" by the policies of the municipal government. One such company was called *Shanghai Chengjian Touzi Kaifa Zhonggongsi* (General Company of Shang-hai Urban Construction). This company had a variety of means to raise funds rang-ing from receipts from user fees charged on various city utilities, development funds from pre-tax profits paid by enterprises, budgetary outlays earmarked for urban renovation, bank loans designed to build infrastructure in designated development zones to county and urban district funds devoted to infrastructure, among others. The broad mandate and wide range of sources available to the company made it possible to finance many costly projects the municipal government wanted to build but could not if it relied completely on its own funds.

As Shanghai moved further down the road toward a market system, the munic-ipal government became more versed in combining its power and the market force to raise more funds for public projects and use these funds in determined ways. Taking the wholesale land leasing for example. Shanghai started wholesale land leasing in 1986. By 1994, land leasing generated more than 77 billion yuan in income for the city. Moreover, by selective land leasing and through differentia-tion in leasing prices, the city was able to set the basic tone as to how the renovation of the old city should be done, in what form, by whom, and when.[110]

Mobilizing funds from the society was another means through which Shang-hai was able to raise huge amounts of funds for urgent projects such as residen-tial housing. In addition to encouraging SOEs to partially fund the purchase of such housing units by their members, the city also expanded incentive programs for the residents to either buy out the housing units they currently lived in or purchase newly built housing units. While Shanghai, a city of more than 13 million regular residents and 1.5 million temporary residents, was still struggling to find more living space for its people, the overall situation had improved so much that Shanghai recently announced that it would complete the process of renovating the whole old city center by year 2,010, or 40 years ahead of the original date of year 2,050, a goal set in 1990.

Shanghai's efforts to mobilize financial resources were not limited to the infrastructure sector. Indeed, in recent years, Shanghai had increasingly turned its attention to finance industrial projects which were costly but critical to the goal of strengthening the city's edge in high-tech and high value-added industries. For example, in 1987, Shanghai faced a dilemma in the development of its budding automobile industry. The city was eager to boost the output of passenger cars to over 100,000 units by 1994. To do so, it would have had to upgrade various production facilities. However, neither the company nor the city could afford it. As a solution, Shanghai began, under the recommendation of then-mayor Zhu Rongji, collecting a fee of about 20,000 yuan for each car sold under the name of *guochanhua jijin* (funds for promoting domestically made car parts). While the stated purpose of the fee was to help defray the costs involved in raising the proportion of domestically-made parts, the huge amount of fees collected from 1988 to 1992—a total of 3.5 billion yuan!—was sufficient to help consolidate Shanghai's position as one of the major players in China's automobile industry.[111]

To some extent, the mobilization of non-budgetary resources was one of the several keys to Shanghai's economic revival. Once breaking the narrow definition of government finance, the city was able to find rich and diverse sources of funding. The enhanced ability to raise funds, on the other hand, helped Shanghai to turn the economy around much faster and more effectively than otherwise would have been possible.

Adjusting Budgetary Allocations

After the mid-1980s, Shanghai's budgetary allocations also underwent several major changes. Unlike the mobilization of budgetary and non-budgetary resources, changes in budgetary allocations themselves did not bring additional revenue to the city. However, shifts in budgetary allocations reflected the priorities of the city and its ability to use the resources effectively. Table 1.6 on pages 78–79 shows the pattern of budgetary allocations between 1985 to 1995.

The overall budgetary expenditure had increased drastically reflecting the growing resources available to the city. However, did the increase or the speed of the increase in specific spending categories fit the goals of the municipal government?

The changes in budgetary expenditures can be grouped into five categories. Some of the spending items received noticeable increase as a result of popular demand and the commitment on the part of the Shanghai government. The spending on education, cultural affairs, science and public health, for example, received the largest increase in funding for good reasons. In each of the three reform and development strategies Shanghai adopted after 1984, the municipal government specifically committed itself to more funding in these areas. In 1988, the city made a further commitment to keep the growth in spending on education higher than the growth of revenue income of a particular year. As a result, the percentage of budgetary expenditures on education rose from 20.4 percent in

1985 to 24 percent in 1994. The gradual increase in urban maintenance fell in the same category.

Some of the budget items showed ups and downs in spending over different periods of time. The spending on capital construction and technical updates showed wider fluctuation. These changes reflected the changing priorities of the city as well as government policies. In the mid-1980s, the general trend was to change government appropriations on capital construction to bank loans while the funds saved would be used primarily for helping technical renovation. However, entering the 1990s, the budgetary outlays on capital construction shot up again for two reasons. On the one hand, the deteriorating financial situation of many SOEs forced the city to appropriate more funds for construction projects. On the other hand, the city deliberately increased input into capital construction as part of the investment boom it wanted to create.

Still there were several spending items whose increase in funding was not necessarily what the city actually had planned. For example, almost every year, the city called for reduction in the size of the bureaucracy and the total spending on government administration. However, with a few exceptions, an increase in this category was a norm. Indeed, if one counts the spending on public security apparatus, the increase in spending on the government itself was substantial.

In addition to these more traditional spending items, there were quite a few new spending categories not listed in Table 1.6 that had become increasingly important in recent years in determining how the city allocated budgetary expenditures. In 1995, for example, for the purpose of supporting various reform programs while maintaining social stability, the city allocated 500 million yuan for a fund designed to help ease the pain many enterprises faced in making structural adjustment; 480 million yuan for helping families with financial difficulties;[112] 840 million yuan to stabilize the prices of food; and 180 million yuan to pay those whose health benefits were not paid by the SOEs they worked for. These new spending categories put even more pressure on Shanghai's budget. While some of the spending appeared to be a one-time outlay, much was likely to stay and grow as China's economic reform entered the more difficult phase.

Finally, there is the category of government subsidies. Chinese budgeting lists only price subsidies as part of the government expenditures. Subsidies to money-losing SOEs were counted as offsetting government revenue. However, the impact of the two on budgetary allocations was essentially the same. More subsidies means less appropriations available for other projects. Table 1.7 on page 80 shows the size of budgetary subsidies to SOEs.

In theory and in public statements, the leaders in Shanghai always maintained that both price subsidies and subsidies to SOEs were transitional in nature. Spending on various subsidies would eventually be phased out. In reality, however, the issue was more complicated. Price subsidies, for example, reached the peak in 1989 and then showed a gradual decline until they rose again in 1995 (see Table 1.6). The changes before 1995 were the results of a three-pronged

Table 1.6

Allocations of Budgetary Expenditures, 1985–1995 (unit: 100 million yuan)

Item	1985	1986	1987	1988	1989	1990	1991	1992	1993	1994	1995
ACC	14.2	14.2	10.0	5.7	5.5	14.0	12.8	18.7	22.2[a]	34.4	—[b]
TUF	9.4	13.5	7.4	16.8	17.4	7.3	8.3	3.8	12.4	14.2	—
ESAPA	1.5	2.0	1.7	2.0	3.5	4.0	4.4	4.5	5.2	6.6	—
CESHC	9.1	10.9	12.0	14.3	16.5	18.5	20.6	24.5	32.8	45.8	—
PSWRF	0.5	0.6	0.6	0.5	0.6	0.7	0.8	1.0	1.3	1.9	—
UMF	2.8	3.9	4.6	4.6	5.8	6.7	7.3	9.4	4.8	6.0	—
GA	1.8	2.1	2.3	1.7	1.9	2.3	2.7	3.6	5.7	7.8	—
APSPC	—	—	—	1.6	2.0	2.5	2.7	3.5	5.3	10.6	—
PS	—	6.5	10.2	11.9	13.6	11.8	12.0	10.4	6.2	10.5	—
ESE/EPCF	—	—	—	—	—	—	5.2	4.3	3.5	—	—
Others	6.8	5.9	5.1	6.5	6.3	7.9	9.3	13.8	18.4	45.5	—
Total[c]	46.1	59.1	53.9	65.6	73.1	75.7	86.1	94.9	119.7	190.8	267.9

Sources: 1985–86 figures are from *Shanghai tongji nianjian, 1986*, p. 48 and *Shanghai tongji nianjian, 1988*, p. 67. 1987–1991 figures are based on *Zhongguo caizheng tongji, 1950–1991* (China Financial Statistics, 1950–1991) (Beijing: Kexue chubanshe, 1992), p. 147, but adjusted based on Shanghai's yearly budget reports. 1992–93 figures are from, *Shanghai caishui*, No. 7, 1993, pp. 4–5; *Shanghai caishui*, No. 9, 1994, pp. 3–4, and, *Shanghai tongji nianjian 1993*, p. 57. The 1994 figures are from *Zhongguo caizheng tongji nianjian 1995* (Financial Statistical Yearbook of China) (Beijing: Zhongguo caizheng chubanshe, 1995), p. 361.

[a]This figure includes both ACC and TUF.

[b]— indicates data not available.

[c]Not all the expenditure items are included in the table. Hence they do not add up to the total in this line.

(continued)

Notes:

ACC: Appropriations for capital construction

TUF: Technical updates and transformation of enterprises, and new product promotion funds

ESAPA: Expenditures supporting agricultural production and administration

CESHC: Culture, education, science, and health care

PSWRF: Pensions and social welfare relief funds

UMF: Urban maintenance funds

GA: Government administration

APSPC: Appropriations for public security, prosecutors, and courts

PS: Price subsidies

ESE/EPCF: Educational surcharge expenditure and electricity power station construction funds.

OTHERS: This item includes all other expenditures that were not accounted for in published statistics. The Chinese accounting system often leaves a huge amount of budgetary outlays in the "all other" category. Possible items of expenditure in this category include circulating funds for state-owned enterprises, disaster relief funds, etc.

Table 1.7

Budgetary Subsidies to SOEs, 1988–94 (unit: billion yuan)

1988	1.48
1989	2.82
1990	2.87
1991	2.53
1992	2.48
1993	3.36
1994	4.21

Sources: See Table 1.3.

program launched by the municipal government after 1989. First, the city used a number of administrative means including quotas to slow down the growth of or even cut the amount of subsidies allowed each year. Secondly, it tried to introduce more market mechanisms into the provision and operation of many government programs like privatizing government facilities or abolishing ration coupons. Finally, for the subsidies that were still essential to the daily lives of the residents, the city would try to manage them in a more effective way. For example, under a program known as *cailanzi gongchen* ("vegetable basket project"), the city pooled together all the subsidies for the supply of vegetables to the urban area and tried to coordinate them into a coherent program. Starting from 1988, Shanghai spent, on average, 800 to 900 million yuan a year on this project to secure the production and supply of vegetables. While still costly, the money spent on the project actually helped to keep the supply and prices of vegetables stable and hence prevent government subsidies from growing even bigger. However, there were still limits as to how far the city could cut price subsidies as the 1996 rebound of spending on price subsidies indicated.

A more difficult challenge was to contain the subsidies to SOEs. A large portion of the subsidies went to food processing factories whose losses reflected the government policy of trying to keep the prices of food and non-staple food from rising too fast. The rest of the subsidies went to SOEs which were losing money but were not allowed to go bankrupt for political reasons. Neither types of subsidies were likely to be cut soon. In fact, with more and more SOEs facing financial strains and difficulties, such subsidies would most likely rise to an even higher level.

Conclusion

Shanghai's economic revival after the mid-1980s can be linked directly to the active role played by the key leaders of the municipal government and the quality of leadership they exercised in a number of areas. Unlike the first two groups of leaders sent to Shanghai between 1976 and 1984, the third and fourth groups of leaders spent enormous efforts in developing and refining a reform and development strategy that would serve as a road map for Shanghai's search for economic revival. They made it, and that made a huge difference. Without such a strategy, it would be difficult to imagine how Shanghai would be able to launch a concerted assault on the city's fundamental problems and turn the local economy around in such a short order and grand fashion.

The leaders in Shanghai after 1985 were also more determined and aggressive in pursuing their goals. Unlike their predecessors who were more conservative, the third and fourth groups of leaders took risks. Even with a well-developed strategy, there was no guarantee that the changes would be successful nor would there be less uncertainty. For their part, the last two groups of Shanghai leaders showed the kind of characteristics critical to the success of economic reform and development at a scope as large as the one in Shanghai. They were more determined yet flexible enough to deal with complexity and uncertainty and to take advantage of opportunities whatever and whenever they showed up as long as they were beneficial to the city. They were more open-minded and willing to learn from others as well as from their own mistakes. They were equally more open to new ideas, often ready to find alternatives if the planned route did not work. They were more creative and because of that could turn even adverse situations into advantages. They paid great attention to building up a massive institutional network not only to feed them with new ideas or suggestions but also to serve as a link to the views outside the rigid official channels. They were, especially the last group of leaders, more tuned to the demands of local residents. They acted for both personal and political reasons. However, by favoring populist programs, they were able to build a support base for reform strong enough to endure the inevitable pains associated with the social and economic transformation.

Shanghai still faced enormous problems. But the dramatic turnaround after 1985 showed what a strong local leadership could accomplish even in a country where the formal political system remained highly rigid and centralized. In a way, this is what made the experience of the Chinese reform so interesting.

Notes

The author would like to thank Peter T. Y. Cheung and Jae Ho Chung for their valuable comments on the draft of this chapter. The author is responsible, of course, for all the remaining mistakes.

1. In 1978, Shanghai's shares of China's GDP, import and export, industrial output, and government revenues were 7.6 percent, 14.7 percent, 12.1, and 15.1 percent, respectively. If measured on a per capita basis, Shanghai's lead was even larger. In 1978, Shanghai's per capita national income, government revenue, and import and export were 7.13, 13.23, and 12.85 times that of the national average, respectively. Figures from *Quanguo gesheng zizhiqu zhixiashi lishi tongji ziliao huibian, 1949–1989* (A Compendium of Historical Statistical Data of Provinces, Autonomous Regions, and Centrally Administered Cities in China, 1949–1989) (Beijing: Zhongguo tongji chubanshe), 1990, various pages.

2. Including only taxes and profits from locally administered enterprises and local taxes. Revenues from enterprises located in Shanghai but administered by the central government were not included. The taxes and profits generated by the centrally administered enterprises showed a consistent and rather impressive increase during most of the years after 1978. The total local revenue was 17.47 billion yuan in 1980. In 1990, it was 17.0 billion yuan. *Shanghai tongji nianjian 1994* (Statistical Yearbook of Shanghai) (Beijing: Zhongguo tongji chubanshe, 1994), p. 21.

3. In 1990, the central government formally agreed to designate the Pudong area as an economic development zone entitled to most of the preferential policies previously given only to the special economic zones.

4. *The Economist*, December 24, 1994–January 6, 1995, p. 40.

5. *The Economist*, March 18, 1995, p. 19.

6. As part of the Treaty of Nanjing (1842) signed between China and Britain, Shanghai and four other Chinese cities were designated as treaty ports open to foreign merchants. For more on Shanghai's pre-1949 history, see Rhoads Murphey, *Shanghai, Key to Modern China* (Cambridge: Harvard University Press, 1953).

7. *Dangdai Zhongguo de Shanghai* (Shanghai in Contemporary China) (Beijing: Dangdai Zhongguo chubanshe, 1993), Vol. 1, p. 33.

8. For a review of this period in Shanghai's history, see Marie-Claire Bergere, "The Other China, Shanghai from 1919 to 1949," in Christopher Howe, ed., *Shanghai, Revolution and Development in an Asian Metropolis* (New York: Cambridge University Press, 1981), pp. 1–34.

9. *Shanghai shehui jingji jianshe fazhan jianshi, 1949–1985* (A Brief History of the Development of Socialist Economy in Shanghai, 1949–1985) (Shanghai: Renmin chubanshe, 1989), p. 859. While the size of Shanghai changed little after 1958, the number of urban districts and counties fluctuated significantly. In 1978, Shanghai had ten suburban counties and ten urban districts. In 1993, Shanghai had only six counties and fourteen districts, reflecting the impact of increasing urbanization.

10. *Dangdai Zhongguo de Shanghai*, Vol. 1, p. 67.

11. *Quanguo gesheng zizhiqu zhixiashi lishi tongji ziliao huibian, 1949–1989*, p. 323.

12. See Zhimin Lin, "Reform and Shanghai, Changing Central-Local Fiscal Relations," in Hao Jia and Zhimin Lin, eds., *Changing Central-Local Relations in China: Reform and State Capacity* (Boulder, CO: Westview Press, 1994), pp. 239–60.

13. In the 1950s and 1960s, for example, only 3.6 percent of nationwide investment on capital construction was devoted to Shanghai. Wang Zhang, "Zhongguo jingji chengzhang zhongde 'Shanghai xianxiang'"(The "Shanghai Phenomenon" in China's Economic Development), *Shanghai gaige* (Shanghai Reform), No. 5, 1991, p. 17. In the 1970s, the nation's total amount of investment on capital construction increased sharply. However, because most of the investment concentrated in inland China (especially on the so called *da sanxian* (the third front) projects for strategical purposes, Shanghai's share of national total investment was still a meager 2.3 percent. Figures are from *Quanguo gesheng zizhiqu zhixiashi lishi tongji ziliao huibian, 1949–1989*, pp. 23, 331.

14. *Shanghai shehui jingji jianshe fazhan jianshi, 1949–1985*, pp. 570–578. *Quanguo gesheng zizhiqu zhixiashi lishi tongji ziliao huibian, 1949–1989*, p. 330.

15. Wang Zhang, "Zhongguo jingji chengzhang."

16. Ke served as the first party secretary of Shanghai from July 1956 to May 1965 when he died suddenly.

17. After Mao's death in 1976, all three, along with Mao's wife, went through a public trial and received long jail sentences. Yao was released from the prison in 1996.

18. The practice is known as *"quanguo bao Shanghai"* (the whole country protects Shanghai). Wang Zhang, "Zhongguo jingji chengzhang," p. 17.

19. In addition to the three mentioned above, all seven top Party officials of Shanghai and sixteen of the twenty mayor and deputy mayors at the time were purged. *Dangdai Zhongguo de Shanghai*, volume two, pp. 655-58.

20. For example, they were accused of suppressing the discussions in Shanghai in the summer of 1978 over the issue of the criterion of truth. The discussions were initiated by Deng's supporters largely to discredit Hua. *Dangdai Zhongguo de Shanghai*, Vol. 1, pp. 293–94.

21. Su and Ni were recalled in January 1979. Peng was formally recalled in March 1980, but he lost most of his influence in late 1979 due to his harsh treatment of some of the activists opposed to the leftist group and his low popularity among other Shanghai leaders.

22. Chen Guodong worked briefly in the Finance Ministry. He then worked for a long time in the Ministry of Grain. Hu Lijiao worked mostly in the Finance Ministry and in China's People's Bank. In these capacities, they came to know Chen Yun well and were generally considered to be more receptive to his economic views than to Deng's more radical proposals.

23. Of the three, Chen Guodong and Hu Lijiao were only full members of the 12th Central Committee of the CCP. This was not only unusual given the fact that top leaders from Shanghai usually would have at least a seat in the Politburo but was also in sharp contrast with provinces such as Guangdong and Sichuan which had several of their former leaders serving as key national leaders (for example, Zhao Ziyang was from Sichuan and Xi Zhongxun and Yang Shangkun were from Guangdong).

24. See Zhimin Lin, "Reform and Shanghai."

25. The original four SEZs are Shenzhen, Xiamen, Zhuhai, and Shantou, all in southern China. Shanghai was designated in 1984 as one of the fourteen open coastal cities. However, unlike the SEZs, such a designation carried only limited benefits, including expanded authority in approving overseas-funded adventures and providing favorable treatment to them. For details of these benefits, see, *Shanghai jingji, 1983–1985* (Shanghai Economy, 1983–85) (Shanghai: Shanghai Renmin chubanshe, 1986), pp. 129–130.

26. Quoted from Zhou Kaida and Li Qi, "Shijixing de zhanlüe: Deng Xiaoping lun Shanghai de fazhan" (Strategy of the Century: Deng Xiaoping on Shanghai's Development), *Jiefang Ribao* (Shanghai: Liberation Daily), April 10, 1995, p. 11.

27. Wang had a major impact on Shanghai's development even after he retired. He had a close working relationship with his successors and his views were highly valued (he reportedly was responsible for promoting Jiang to become the deputy director of the State Import and Export Commission after he himself left the commission. See Li Guoqiang, *Jiang Zemin pouxi* (Analyze Jiang Zemin) (Hong Kong: Wide Angle Press Ltd., 1989), p. 34. However, Wang never became the dominant leader in Shanghai. He also suffered from some personal problems as well. For example, in 1983, Wang was criticized for getting housing arrangements beyond what was considered appropriate.

28. Deng, for example, criticized Shanghai's leadership for being not bold enough in implementing the open-door policy in 1984.

29. For example, from 1979 to 1982 Shanghai produced a blueprint for the overall design of the city. Yet, the lack of funds and uncertainty over which direction Shanghai's economy was moving stalled the implementation of the plan. Similarly, in the 1984 development strategy, the portion on implementation contained few specific programs.

30. For a more detailed and excellent discussion of the changes in Shanghai's political leadership, see Peter T. Y. Cheung, "The Political Context of Shanghai's Economic Development," in Y. M. Yeung and Sung Yun-wing, eds., *Shanghai, Transformation and*

Modernization under China's Open Policy (Hong Kong: The Chinese University Press, 1996), pp. 49–92.

31. Rui was called to serve as a member of the Secretariat of the Central Committee of the CCP. He was dismissed after June 1989 officially for "mistakes in his work" but unofficially for being too sympathetic to Zhao Ziyang's stance during the student movement.

32. Based on interviews conducted in Shanghai in the summers of 1993 and 1994.

33. Of the two, Hu was reportedly more supportive of Shanghai than Zhao. During his visit to Shanghai in April 1983, Hu mentioned that Shanghai should be a "vanguard" of reform and the open-door policy. Zhao, on the other hand, was more interested in Shanghai experimenting with reform methods, such as the *da baogan* (comprehensive contract system) first used by other places such as Guangdong. Another indicator of Hu's ties to Shanghai was that just a few weeks before his dismissal from his post in 1987, his visit to Shanghai was highly publicized in the city's media. Based on interviews conducted in Shanghai in June 1990.

34. The new revenue-sharing package allowed Shanghai to keep about 23 percent of its revenue as opposed to the 18.49 percent it retained in 1984. The new ratio was reached using 1984 actual expenditures as a base point plus 1 billion yuan of additional funds available to Shanghai. *Shanghai jingji, 1983–1985*, pp. 832–33.

35. During an executive meeting of the municipal government in early 1986, Jiang suggested that Shanghai should borrow up to US$ 3.2 billion to invest in the city's industries and infrastructure. The suggestion was later submitted to the central government and became the basis of a preferential policy accorded to Shanghai. *Jiefang Ribao*, April 10, 1995.

36. Chen, a native of Qingpu county, now part of Shanghai, was generally regarded as favoring giving more attention to places such as Shanghai where central planning impacted the most in the past. Deng was known for his low regard for the leftist faction of which many came from Shanghai. What made Deng change his attitude toward Shanghai is not known. However, from 1990 to 1994, Deng made it a habit to spend the spring festival in Shanghai every year. (Chen had spent most of his time in Shanghai since the mid-1980s.)

37. For example, the ages of the six leaders when they started their duties in Shanghai were, Chen, 63, Hu, 65, Wang, 65, Rui, 59, Jiang, 61, Zhu, 60.

38. The Chinese system determines how long one can hold his/her political position depending on the level of his/her position. For key provincial leaders, the retirement age normally is 65. For main central leaders, the retirement age is 70 or above.

39. Which usually means four years as normally this is how long one session of the provincial level of the Party congress and the People's Congress last. However, the Center can promote, demote, and transfer provincial leaders at any time.

40. Based on interviews, conducted in Shanghai in the summers of 1993 and 1994.

41. This may be seen from the fact that after Zhu and Jiang were promoted to the Center, they tapped deep into their former colleagues in Shanghai for a number of important positions in the central government.

42. In addition to several key government think tanks, Shanghai had also established various channels through which the views of experts could be quickly and directly transmitted to the decision makers. For example, under Jiang's recommendation, Shanghai organized bimonthly forums focusing on economic reform. These forums were attended by both top city officials and various experts. Similarly, the city would often ask academic communities to engage in policy-oriented research and surveys. The results of such studies were often reflected in actual decisions.

43. See, Chen Minzhi, *Shanghai jingji fazhan zhanlue yanjiu* (Study of Shanghai's Economic Development Strategy) (Shanghai: Renmin chubanshe, 1984).

44. They summarized their arguments in a report entitled, "New Technological Revolution and the Adjustment of Shanghai's Economic Structure." *Shanghai jingji shiwu nian*, pp. 4–5.

45. Ibid., pp. 5–6.

46. From 1981 to 1986, Shanghai's total exports declined from US$ 3.81 billion to US$ 3.58 billion. By contrast, during the same period, Guangdong's total exports increased from US$ 2.37 billion to US$ 4.25 billion. *Quanguo gesheng zizhiqu zhixiashi lishi tongji ziliao huibian, 1949–1989*, pp. 335 and 636.

47. The group was led by Song Ping and Ma Hong. They were joined in Shanghai by a group of senior officials and prominent economists from both Beijing and Shanghai.

48. The report, known as "Guanyu Shanghai jingji fazhan zhanlue de huibao tigang" (The Outline of the Report of Shanghai's Economic Development Strategy), can be found in, *Shanghai jingji, 1983–1985*, pp. 25–34.

49. For that purpose, the report specifically asked that Shanghai's economic performance be measured primarily by GNP and not by the more traditional category of total industrial output.

50. For the two documents, see, *Shanghai jingji, 1987* (Shanghai's Economy, 1987) (Shanghai: Renmin chubanshe, 1987), pp. 4–16 and 26–28.

51. China did not formally endorse the phrase, "socialist market economic order" until 1987 and the phrase "socialist market economy" until 1992.

52. "Speech to the Fifth Party Congress of Shanghai's Communist Party," *Jiefang Ribao*, March 3, 1986.

53. The practice was initiated by Wang Daohan and has continued since. By the end of 1994, a total of 123 projects were planned, most of which were completed on time.

54. *Shanghai jingji, 1983–1985*, p. 34.

55. *Shanghai tongji nianjian, 1993* (Statistical Yearbook of Shanghai, 1993) (Beijing: Zhongguo tongji chubanshe, 1993), p. 55.

56. Ibid.

57. *Shanghai jihua jingji tansuo* (Exploring Shanghai's Planned Economy), No. 2, 1989, pp. 2–8.

58. Ibid.

59. In 1986, Shanghai promulgated sixteen preferential policies designed to encourage foreign investors. At the same time, the Center agreed that Shanghai set up two economic and technological development zones (one in Minhang and another in Hongqiao) which were also designed to provide a better, more attractive environment for outside investors.

60. *Zhonghua yingcai* (China's Talent), No. 58, 1993, pp. 9–10.

61. *Shanghai jingji nianjian, 1990* (Shanghai Economy Yearbook, 1990) (Shanghai: Sanlian shudian, 1990), p. 23. The group was headed by two deputy mayors of Shanghai.

62. This area includes some of China's most prosperous provinces such as Jiangsu and Zhejiang.

63. *Shanghai jingji, 1983–1985*, pp. 34–35.

64. Deng was actually the one who pushed the Pudong plan. Without his strong support, Pudong development might still be limited to discussions. For more on Deng's involvement, see, *Liaowang* (Outlook), No. 17, 1996.

65. The decision and the preferential policies were formally announced by Prime Minister Li Peng in Shanghai on April 15, 1990.

66. The ten major construction projects planned for between 1991 and 1995 alone cost 25 billion yuan. Another ten construction projects were planned for 1996–2000. The estimated total cost was 40 billion yuan.

67. *Pudong kaifa* (Development of Pudong), No. 1, 1995, p. 10.

68. *Jiefang Ribao*, February 8, 1995. Pudong's population is also about one-tenth of Shanghai's total.

69. The latest example of this support was the announcement made in September 1996 in which the central government authorized Shanghai to accept trading companies of other provinces to open subsidiaries in Pudong. The decision enhanced Pudong's role as China's most important center of international trade. See, *Jiefang ribao*, September 13, 1996.

70. *Shanghai jingji, 1983–1985*, p. 7.

71. Barry Naughton, *Growing Out of the Plan: Chinese Economic Reform, 1978– 1993* (New York: Cambridge University Press, 1995).

72. For example, the first trading center for consumer goods did not open until October 1984. The same was true of such centers for producers' goods. Figures used in this paragraph are from, *Shanghai jingji tizhi gaige shinian* (Ten Years of Economic System Reform in Shanghai), (Shanghai: Renmin chubanshe, 1989), pp. 40–48.

73. *Shanghai jingji, 1989* (Shanghai Economy Yearbook, 1989) (Shanghai: Sanlian Shudian, 1989), p. 148.

74. These ten industries included automobiles, computers, and home electronics, among others.

75. The figures quoted in this paragraph are from, Cai Laixin, ed., *Manxiang xiandai hua de juece* (Alternatives on the Road toward Modernization) (Shanghai: Yuandong chubanshe, 1993), pp. 279–312.

76. *Shanghai jingji, 1993* (Shanghai Economy, 1993) (Shanghai: Shanghai shehui kexueyuan), p. 3. The three-year time frame has since been used by Shanghai to set economic targets. In 1994, for example, Shanghai launched a city-wide discussion over what the city should strive to accomplish in the new three- year period (1995–1997).

77. They were, in fact, classmates from 1960 to 1963 at Qinghua University of Beijing. Wu majored in electronics while Huang in electronic engineering.

78. See *Guangjiaojing* (Hong Kong: Wide Angle), No. 6, 1996, pp. 18–23.

79. All figures are from *Jiefang ribao*, February 11, 1996.

80. For a summary of the 1990 discussions, see, Cai Laixin, eds., *Manxiang xiandaihua de juece*. For more on the 1994 discussions, see, *Mianxiang ershiyi shiji de Shanghai*.

81. Xu Kuangdi, "Shanghai shuaixian jinglu shehui zhuyi shichang jingji yunxin jizhi de ruogan tantao" (Exploring How Shanghai Will Take the Lead to Enter the Operational Mechanism of the Socialist Market Economy), *Shanghai zonghe jingji*, No. 5, 1994, pp. 4–9.

82. Some analysts in Shanghai argue that if investment in fixed assets grows by 1 percent, GDP will grow correspondingly by 0.42 percent. Moreover, for every dollar spent on fixed assets, 40 cents will be transformed into consumption demand. The push led by investment demand and consumption demand are, according to them, two major driving forces for Shanghai's economic growth. *Shanghai jihua jingji tansuo*, No. 30, 1994, p. 9.

83. Guangdong's total revenue in that year was 17.74 billion yuan vs. Shanghai's 17.55 billion yuan.

84. *Shanghai jihua jingji tansuo*, No. 23, 1993, pp. 2–3.

85. Unlike standard international practice, the Chinese system deducts such subsidies from revenue rather than counting them as expenditures.

86. For details of the regime, see, *Shanghai jingji, 1983–85*, pp. 830–31.

87. The new regime figured that Shanghai's expenditures in 1985 would be 3.37 billion yuan (1983 actual spending plus 1.5 billion yuan additional allowance) and the local revenue to be 15.16 billion. The local share of revenue was thus fixed at 23.54 percent. *Shanghai caizheng shuiwuzhi* (History of Shanghai's Finance and Taxation) (Shanghai: Shehui kexue chubanshe, 1995), pp. 67–68.

88. *Shanghai shehui jingji jianshe fazhan jianshe, 1949–1985* (The Construction of the Development of Shanghai's Socialist Economy) (Shanghai: Shanghai kexue jishu wenxian chubanshe, 1989), p. 774.

89. For more details of this regime, see *Shanghai jingji nianjian, 1989*, pp. 73–74.

90. The figure of 1.4 billion yuan was based on the assumption that if Shanghai collected the anticipated 15.3 billion yuan of revenue in 1988, after the remittance the city would retain 1.4 billion yuan more than it would have under the old revenue-sharing regime. Ibid..

91. Some in Guangdong argued that the province actually contributed more to the central government than the revenue remittances would indicate. Still, if one takes other forms of contribution such as loans to the Finance Ministry into consideration, Guangdong's share of its rapidly growing revenue still rose from 64.77 percent in 1981 to 70.67 percent in 1985. Calculated from Toyojiro Maruya, "The Development of the Guangdong Economy and Its Ties with Beijing," *China Newsletter*, No. 96, 1992, p. 4; and *Quanguo gesheng zizhiqu zhixiashi lishi tongji ziliao huibian, 1949–1989*, p. 636.

92. *Sheke xingxi jiaoliu*, No. 44, 1989, p. 5.

93. There is no agreement on who benefits most from the latter system. However, since more prosperous provinces have the most potential to raise revenue through local taxes, it is, in the author's view, provinces such as Guangdong and Shanghai that are bound to benefit more from the system than many less developed regions.

94. Including business tax, land-use tax, local enterprise and personal income tax, urban maintenance and construction tax, etc.

95. For details of the 1994 regime, see, *Caizheng guizhang zhidu xuanbian* (Selected Documents on Regulation of the Fiscal System) (Beijing: Zhongguo caizheng chubanshe, 1994), pp. 96–105.

96. *Shanghai nianjian, 1996*, p. 225.

97. There is a 0.3 percent tax on all financial transactions. Shanghai and the central government each shares half of the revenue generated.

98. Starting from 1995, a new tax—the stock transactions tax—was introduced to replace part of the stamp tax.

99. *Shanghai jingji, 1994*, pp. 396–97.

100. *Shanghai nianjian, 1996*, p. 225.

101. *Shanghai caishui*, No. 3, 1995, p. 4. In 1995, revenue from the personal income tax alone reached 880 million yuan, a 103 percent increase from the previous year. *Jiefang Ribao*, February 12, 1996.

102. *Jiefang ribao*, February 12, 1996.

103. *Shanghai nianjian, 1996*, p. 226.

104. Of the US$ 3.2 billion, 1.4 billion was to be used for infrastructure, 1.3 billion for industrial renovation, and 0.5 billion for the development of the service sector. The policy was good for fifteen years. *Shanghai zonghe jingji* (Shanghai Macroeconomy), No. 1, 1993, p. 27.

105. Jiusi is the Chinese homonym for ninety-four which was the serial number of the document in which the State Council authorized Shanghai to borrow funds from overseas.

106. *Shanghai zonghe jingji*, No. 1, 1993, p. 27.

107. *Jiefang ribao*, December 31, 1992.

108. Jiusi Company raised US$ 1.1 billion for these five projects. *Shanghai zonghe jingji*, No. 2, 1993, p. 30.

109. Shisi is the Chinese homonym for fourteen (100 million, the Chinese equivalent of 1.4 billion yuan). From 1990 to 1991, the company was temporarily merged with the Jiusi Company. However, it became a separate entity again in 1992.

110. There were many problems in land leasing, of course. One of the most common

problems occurred when local levels of government units decided either to lease land without permission or at discounted prices or both.

111. *Shanghai touzi* (Shanghai Investment), No. 3, 1994, p. 7. Shanghai produced 200.000 passenger cars a year in 1996.

112. According to the official estimate, Shanghai had about 600,000 people currently unemployed or semi-unemployed due to restructuring of the local economy and increasing competition. The fund was established mainly to help this group of workers.

2

The Guangdong Advantage: Provincial Leadership and Strategy Toward Resource Allocation since 1979

Peter T.Y. Cheung

Introduction

Guangdong's provincial leadership has played a critical role in implementing the "special policies, flexible measures" granted by the central government since 1979.[1] These policies granted Guangdong greater autonomy over economic policies, including budgeting, planning, material allocation, pricing, investment, labor management, and foreign economic policy, including the establishment of three Special Economic Zones (SEZs). Of particular significance among these policy privileges concerned powers that gave the province greater latitude in resource allocation and mobilization.[2] This chapter aims to examine the efforts of Guangdong's provincial leadership in mobilizing and allocating resources for economic development in the 1979–1995 period, focusing on fiscal and investment reform.

Guangdong: An Overview

Guangdong is situated on the southern coast of China, bordering Fujian, Jiangxi, Hainan, and Guangxi. In 1995, Guangdong had 21 prefecture-level cities, 32 county-level cities, 46 counties, 42 urban districts and 1,531 towns. As the fifth most populous province after Henan, Sichuan, Shandong and Jiangsu, Guangdong has over 67 million people, or about 5.6 percent of China's total population, yet its size of around 180,000 square kilometers occupies slightly less than 2 percent of the total land area of the nation.[3] The province has a hilly topography, except in the delta areas in the south and the east, but its coastline, the longest among China's provinces, enables it to tap the advantages offered by aquatic resources, maritime transport and trade. Sharp regional disparities characterize the province's spatial economy. The Pearl River Delta, which measures 41,596 square kilometers, is the largest delta as well as the key agricultural, commercial, and industrial center in the province. In 1995, the delta, which claimed only about one-third of the province's population, produced over 70 percent of its gross domestic product (GDP), 76 percent of gross value of industrial output (GVIO), 38 percent of gross value of agricultural output (GVAO), and about 64 percent of total investment in fixed assets.[4] The delta's GDP of 389 billion yuan was already larger than some of China's major provinces, such as Liaoning, Hebei, Zhejiang, and even Sichuan.[5] Hainan Island, formerly under Guangdong's jurisdiction since 1949, is also richly endowed with natural resources, but it was hived off to become a separate province in 1988. The mountainous areas in the northern, northeastern, and northwestern parts of the province are more rural and backward if compared with the Pearl River Delta. In 1995, while these less developed areas claimed about 65 percent of the territory and about 41 percent of the population of Guangdong, they contributed only 13 percent of its GVIO and 20 percent of GDP![6] The tropical and subtropical climate and the highly favorable geographical location have made the province a prime agricultural base, commercial center, and transportation hub for centuries. There are also reputedly over 30 million overseas Cantonese scattered in Hong Kong, Macau, Southeast Asia as well as North America. Such a valuable social asset is not available to most other provinces.[7]

Guangdong's distinctive subculture and dialects, commercial acumen, external social and economic ties, as well as its geographical distance from the capital often made it a political and administrative headache for central governments in the history of the Middle Kingdom.[8] The political role of Guangdong and its people in modern Chinese history is indeed substantial. Since the mid-nineteenth century, the challenge from Western powers aggravated the socio-economic difficulties of a declining imperial regime and sparked off the Taiping Rebellion led by a Cantonese, Hong Xiuquan (1816–1864), from today's Guangzhou area that almost toppled the Qing dynasty. Aside from being the home province of prominent reformers such as Kang Youwei (1858–1927) and Liang Qichao (1873–1929) in late Qing, Guangdong produced many activists in the Republican revolution. The Canton uprising in April 1911, though suppressed, was a forerunner of the successful Republican revolution in October. Because of Yuan Shihk'ai's efforts in imperial restoration, Dr. Sun Yat-sen (1866–1925) established his Nationalist government in Guangzhou in 1917 while his successor, Chiang Kaishek, began the northern military expedition there in an attempt to unify China. After the devastating defeat during the Civil War, the Nationalist government moved to Guangzhou in April 1949 before it was driven out of the mainland to Taiwan. Many political figures active in the Nationalist era were Cantonese. Perhaps the better known personalities included, among others, Dr. Sun who was a native from Zhongshan in the Pearl River Delta, the Soong family members who were Cantonese natives born in Shanghai, Wang Jingwei (1883–1944) who was Chiang's rival but later collaborated with the Japanese, and Chen Jitang (1890–1954), the Nationalist military official who established a strong reputation for his effective governance of Guangdong from 1929 to 1936.[9] Quite a few prominent Communist revolutionaries were also Guangdong natives, but the province remained a key base for the Nationalists rather than the Communists after the anti-Communist crackdown in 1927.

Despite their active involvement in Republican politics and the early phase of the Communist revolution, the Cantonese were not as prominent as their counterparts from other provinces in national politics after the establishment of the People's Republic of China (hereafter PRC) in 1949. There were some most important exceptions though, such as Ye Jianying (1897–1986), a key statesman in post–Cultural Revolution politics, his son Ye Xuanping (1924–), a former Guangdong governor and a vice chairman of the Chinese People's Political Consultative Committee since 1991, and Liao Chengzhi (1908–1983), the son of the prominent Kuomintang politician Liao Zhongkai and a former vice chairman of the Standing Committee of the National People's Congress (NPC). Two former Party leaders from Guangdong, Tao Zhu (1908–1969) and his lieutenant Zhao Ziyang (1919–), respectively a Hunanese and a Henanese, later became key politicians at the national level. Other notable Cantonese officials included, for instance, Chen Yu (1901–1974), a former minister of coal industry and later Guangdong governor, Ye Jizhuang (1893–1967), a former minister of foreign trade, Zeng Sheng (1910–1995), a former vice governor of Guangdong, Guangzhou mayor, and minister of communications, as well as Zhang Yunyi (1892–1941), a former People's Liberation Army (hereafter PLA) general and leader of Guangxi.

In the Maoist era, Guangdong was at best a mediocre province in economic development. The centrally planned economic system and radical economic policies were imposed on the province just like other areas in China, but such detrimental impacts were probably even greater in Guangdong because its previous strengths in commercialized agriculture and trade were hardly tapped during Mao's revolutionary reign. Not only did the province start with a weak industrial and technological base, but it also failed to fulfill its aspiration of building more industries after 1949.[10] The hostile relations between the U.S. and China and the subsequent embargo against the PRC after the Korean War further impaired the development of Guangdong because the central government deliberately concentrated investment in the inland areas that were less vulnerable to outside military assault. Only after the promulgation of special policies in 1979 did Guangdong's economy begin to take off. In the 1953–1978 period, the province's national income grew at only 5.3 percent per annum, which was lower than the national average of 6 percent. Guangdong began to take one step ahead of the country in economic growth after 1979. In the 1979–1994 period, however, for instance, the province's GDP grew at an annual rate of 14 percent, 4 percent higher than the national average, while its GVIO, total retail sales (TRS), as well as exports all

Table 2.1

Annual Economic Growth Indicators of Guangdong and China, 1979–1994
(unit = percent)

	Guangdong Province	National average
Gross domestic product	14.2	9.8
GVIO	21.7	14.9
GVAO	6.6	6.2
Export	22.5	17.0
Total retail sales	22.0	9.3

Sources: Guojia tongjiju (ed.), *Zhongguo tongji nianjian 1995* (China Statistical Yearbook 1995) (Beijing: Zhongguo tongji chubanshe, 1995), pp. 20–25; Guangdongsheng tongjiju (ed.), *Guangdong tongji nianjian 1995* (Statistical Yearbook of Guangdong 1995) (Beijing: Zhongguo tongji chubanshe, 1995), pp. 82–92.

Notes: GVIO = gross value of industrial output; GVAO = gross value of agricultural output.

increased at about 22 percent per annum, respectively 7 percent, 12 percent, and 5.5 percent higher than the national norm (see Table 2.1). In 1995, Guangdong's GDP registered another year of rapid growth, with GDP growing at 15 percent, GVIO at 25 percent, GVAO at 8 percent, and total export at 18.5 percent.[11]

After seventeen years of reform, Guangdong has already consolidated its position as a prime manufacturer of industrial goods, especially light industrial and textile products. Among China's provinces, not only was Guangdong the number one producer of electrical and electronic consumer durables, but it was also a second or third ranking manufacturer of other light industrial goods such as paper products, bicycles and canned food.[12] Because of the lack of sufficient mineral deposits, energy sources and a strong technical base, the province was not noted for its heavy industries, especially iron and steel, heavy chemicals, and energy, and most of these raw materials and heavy industrial products would have to be bought from other provinces or imported from abroad. Since 1979, the province has always been the largest recipient of foreign investment. Its total export was bigger than the total export of Shanghai, Jiangsu, Fujian, and Shandong lumped together! Compared with China's other provinces, Guangdong ranked second in GVIO, but number one in GDP, total retail sales, export, and acquisition of foreign investment.[13] In terms of living standards, Guangdong has also become one of the richest among China's provinces. In 1995, per capita net income of an average urban household in the province already reached 7,445 yuan, about 71 percent higher than the national average and the highest in the nation.[14] The net income per capita in the province's rural households also amounted to 2,699 yuan, or 71 percent above the national norm, and ranked fourth after Shanghai, Beijing, and Zhejiang.[15] By 1995, Guangdong has already become an undisputed economic center in China, contributing 9.3 percent of GDP, 12 percent of total investment in fixed assets, 12 percent of household savings, 11 percent of total retail sales, 25 percent of foreign investment actually acquired and 37 percent of export in China.[16]

Guangdong's Provincial Leadership

The reason why Guangdong has achieved high-speed growth since 1979 is not simply because it enjoys favorable geographical conditions and extensive ties with Hong Kong, but also because the provincial leaders have dealt with the central government effectively, formulated an effective reform strategy and exploited the opportunities in the reform era to the fullest. In a centralized Leninist political system like China, central decision making still remains a critical factor shaping provincial policy initiatives. Trying to take advantage of Guangdong's proximity to Hong Kong was not novel in the province's contemporary history. Given its relative backwardness, its leaders had no choice but to consider economic links with the neighboring and rapidly developing Hong Kong. As early as 1956, Guangdong's party secretary, Tao Zhu, reported to the Center about using Hong Kong capital in developing industries in the coastal area, an idea that was path breaking at that time, but this failed to be acted on until later.[17] In the aftermath of the Great Leap Forward, Tao made another attempt by sending an official from Foshan, a major town adjacent to Guangzhou, to the central and provincial governments who reported on a detailed plan to sell high-value agricultural products to Hong Kong in order to earn foreign exchange to buy more grain for the province. While this deal did go through, it did not result in further opening of the province. Similarly, Governor Chen Yu favored the promotion of foreign trade not just to expand export but also to stimulate domestic trade and invigorate Guangdong's economy.[18] These episodes from the prereform era aptly demonstrated that, even if the provincial leadership had an innovative idea, it could not be fully turned into a workable policy should it be deemed to be unacceptable by the central government. Central policies, however, were transformed since Deng Xiaoping's return to political preeminence in December 1978.

In order to succeed in reform, as Guangdong's former leader Lin Ruo pointed out, leaders had to experiment, explore and develop a pioneering spirit.[19] Guangdong's leaders in the post-Mao era were mostly successful pioneers who fully exploited central policies and propelled the province onto the fast track of reform and development. The only exceptions were Xi Zhongxun and Yang Shangkun, whose short stint in the province was characterized by a bandwagonering leadership style. But their successors, Ren Zhongyi, Liu Tianfu, Liang Lingguang, Lin Ruo and Ye Xuanping are typical examples of successful pioneers (see Table 2.2).[20] Because of the differences in their background, personality and the changing policy context, their contributions to Guangdong's reform endeavor inevitably varied. Partly because of their weaker political background and the shifting political constellation at the Center, Xie Fei and Zhu

Table 2.2

Guangdong's Party Secretaries and Governors since 1949

Provincial party secretaries	Governors
Ye Jianying (1949.8–1955.5)	Ye Jianying (1949.11–1953.9)
Tao Zhu (1955.6–1965.2)	Tao Zhu (1953.9–1957.6)
Zhao Ziyang (1965.2–Cultural Rev.)	Chen Yu (1957.8–Cultural Rev.)
Liu Xingyuan (1970.12–1972.3)	Huang Yongsheng (1968.2–1969.6)
Ding Sheng (1972.3–1973.12)	Liu Xingyuan (1969.6–1972.3)
Zhao Ziyang (1974.4–1975.10)	Ding Sheng (1972.3–1973.12)
Wei Guoqing (1975.10–1978.12)	Zhao Ziyang (1974.4–1975.10)
Xi Zhongxun (1978.12–1980.11)	Wei Guoqing (1975.10–1978.12)
Ren Zhongyi (1980.11–1985.7)	Xi Zhongxun (1978.12–1981.2)
Lin Ruo (1985.7–1991.1)	Liu Tianfu (1981.3–1983.4)
Xie Fei (1991.1–)	Liang Lingguang (1983.5–1985.7)
	Ye Xuanping (1985.8–1991.5)
	Zhu Senlin (1991.5–1996.2)
	Lui Ruihua (1996.2–)

Sources: Guangdong nianjian bianzuan weiyuanhui (ed.), *Guangdong nianjian 1987* (Guangdong Yearbook 1987) (Guangzhou: Guangdong renmin chubanshe, 1987), pp. 83–85 and 89–90; Ma Qibin et al. (eds.), *Zhongguo gongchandang zhizheng sishinian* (The Chinese Communist Party in Power for Forty Years) (Beijing: Zhonggong dangshi chubanshe, 1991), p. 611; *China Directory* (Tokyo: Radiopress, various years).

Senlin were more careful than their predecessors in pursuing Guangdong's interests. Hence they would be best described as cautious reformers or pioneers. What was noteworthy in Guangdong's case was that the continuous tenure of reform-minded leaders in the 1980s had emboldened local officials and contributed to the entrenchment of a norm among Guangdong officials: taking one step ahead of the nation in reform has become the rule rather than the exception. In fact, recent leaders from Shenzhen, Zhuhai, and Guangzhou, not to mention their other counterparts in the Pearl River Delta, have all tried to establish their own reputations as pioneers of reform.[21] Before examining the contributions and reform strategies of Guangdong's top leaders, it would be first necessary to analyze central concerns over Guangdong localism, the backgrounds of these provincial leaders, their ties with the Center, as well as their policy orientations.

Central Concern over Guangdong Localism

From the perspective of the central government, not only was Guangdong far away from Beijing (more than 2,300 kilometers away from the capital), but its southern culture, dialects and lifestyles also aroused suspicion and concerns about compliance. After 1949, Ye Jianying, the ranking Cantonese in the Communist movement, took over as the top Party leader in Guangdong, but natives like him were soon edged out by outsiders. In order to ensure sufficient central control, central policy toward the province was to appoint non-Guangdong cadres to the highest positions and replace local officials by cadres sent south by the Center because local Guangdong cadres opposed the harsh land reform policies in the early 1950s (for a list of Guangdong's leaders, see Table 2.2).[22] With the departure of Ye Jianying and his subordinate Fang Fang and the rise of Tao Zhu in 1952–1953, the Center finally managed to establish firm political control over this once recalcitrant province. Ye Jianying actually asked Chairman Mao to let him continue to work in Guangdong in early 1953, but was instead transferred to the central military system.[23] A localist rebellion eventually broke out in Hainan in December 1956, only to be suppressed by a campaign against localism by the provincial authorities with strong central support. Soon after the crackdown, Tao Zhu himself initiated the transfer of Chen Yu, a Guangdong native and then minister of coal industry, to become governor in August 1957, partly to alleviate the pent-up sentiments against outside cadres like himself.[24] During the 1950s and 1960s, Tao Zhu was noted for his efforts to use the province as an example of implementing Maoist policies, and he was elevated to be a vice premier and also a member of the Standing Committee of the Politburo in 1965–1966. Tao was succeeded by Zhao Ziyang, a close Tao associate who spent most of his career in Guangdong, but both fell from grace during the Cultural Revolution. Huang Yongsheng, who headed Guangdong's Provincial Revolutionary Committee from 1968 to 1969, was Lin Biao's right-hand man. Lin Biao and his followers in Guangdong were later accused of plotting to use the province as a base for a separate Party Center if their schemes fell apart. On the other hand, although Chen Yu served as governor until the Cultural Revolution, he lost power to the Maoists.[25] After the fall of Zhao Ziyang, two military officials, Ding Sheng and Liu Xingyuan, governed Guangdong from 1970 to 1973, yet Zhao soon re-emerged as Guangdong's leader in 1974–1975 before his replacement by another PLA official, Wei Guoqing, from Guangxi in October 1975.

The issue of "locals" versus "outsiders" remained a sensitive issue in Guangdong politics ever since the bitter experience of the 1950s. By the early 1970s, non-Guangdong cadres in the province had, however, become veteran local cadres since their arrival in the early fifties. The key leaders that had shaped Guangdong's early reform drive, such as Ren Zhongyi and Liang Lingguang, were not natives of the province, but outsiders. In fact, while they might have to deal with Guangdong's divisive political legacies, they brought new perspectives and dynamism. Localist officials who were victimized in the 1950s were also rehabilitated in the reform era, seemingly as a gesture to mollify the discontent of Guangdong cadres.[26] At the outset of reform, with the exception of top provincial leaders like Xi Zhongxun and Ren Zhongyi, the remaining party secretaries, deputy party secretaries, governors and vice governors were either natives or veteran cadres who probably saw themselves more as locals rather than outsiders. In 1983, only-one third of the secretaries and deputy secretaries of the Guangdong Provincial Party Committee were natives, but by 1993, all of them were Cantonese.[27] Similarly, over 14 percent of the governors and vice governors in 1983 were natives, but the share further rose to 57 percent by 1993. The trend toward localization in Guangdong's leadership has become amply evident since 1979.

Guangdong's Leaders since 1979: Their Backgrounds, Policy Orientations and Ties with the Center

In Deng Xiaoping's era, the first and second batches of Guangdong's leaders were the most senior in political background.[28] Xi Zhongxun, a Shaanxi native born in 1913, was a former political commissar of the First Field Army who had held many important positions before his purge by Chairman Mao in 1962. These posts included second secretary of the Northwest Bureau of the Party (1950–1954) and head of the Party Center's Propaganda Department (1952–1954). Similarly, Yang Shangkun, a Sichuan native born in 1907, was a veteran Party leader, a former director of the General Office of the Party's Central Committee (hereafter CC) as well as a key victim of the Cultural Revolution. Yang was also one of Deng Xiaoping's closet political allies in the reform era. Their appointment to the province helped Deng in accomplishing critical tasks in 1978–1979—cleaning the ideological and political influence of the "Gang of Four," rectifying injustices and rehabilitating veteran cadres victimized during the Cultural Revolution, as well as drumming up support for Deng's pragmatic line. Most importantly, they managed to secure the first batch of "special policies, flexible measures" for Guangdong. Nonetheless, they were soon transferred out of the province in 1980 not simply because they were able to play a more important role in national politics, but also because they were too cautious in introducing reform in Guangdong.[29] Such cautious behavior could be explained by their inadequate leadership skills as well as their concern for their own careers. Given their very senior status in the Party before 1978, both were planning for their political comeback. Hence they probably did not want to risk their own future by clashing with the conservative wing of the Center because Chen Yun, the conservative Party elder, took charge of economic policy in the late 1970s and early 1980s.

On the contrary, the second batch of provincial leaders was appointed by Deng Xiaoping with a mission to translate reform policies into successful practices in Guangdong. Hence not only were they even more open-minded than their predecessors, but they were also noted for determination and action. Ren Zhongyi, a Hebei native born in 1914, spent his entire career in Party and state positions in the northeast. Although he was tortured and purged during the Cultural Revolution, he was rehabilitated in 1973 and assumed leading positions in the Party and state organs in Heilongjiang (1973–1977) and Liaoning (1977–1980), one of the strongholds of Maoist radicals. While in Liaoning, Ren was already well known for his reform orientation and strong leadership. Despite his relatively old age of 67 in 1981, his reformist credentials were the key considerations for his appointment.[30] Already a full member of the CC elected in 1977, he continued to enjoy this status in the CC elected in 1982. Liu Tianfu, a Sichuan native born in 1908 who served as Guangdong's governor from 1981 to 1983, was also a strong advocate of economic reform and local interests. He was a former vice governor of Guangdong from 1963 to 1965 and a secretary of the provincial party committee from 1960 to 1965. He was already 72 when he was made governor in 1981, hence he was succeeded by Liang Lingguang in 1983. Liang, a Fujian native born in 1916, was a former veteran cadre and vice governor of Fujian province. Right before his appointment to Guangdong, he was a minister of light industry who enjoyed full CC membership since 1982. His reform orientation, experience in local administration and knowledge of light industry were vital assets for his transfer to Guangdong.

The third batch of leaders, Lin Ruo and Ye Xuanping, was also known to be staunch defenders of local interests and market-oriented reform. Their appointment was the first time for Guangdong to have natives in both Party and state leadership positions. A graduate of Guangdong's prestigious Zhongshan University, Lin Ruo had served in the East River communist guerrillas in the late 1940s. Lin was a Guangdong native born in 1924 who spent his entire career in the province's localities. Because of his extensive grass-root and administrative experience in Guangdong, he was keenly aware of the ill consequences of Maoist policies and had become a staunch supporter of reform and opening to the outside world.[31] Partly because of his career history as a Party official, he was politically more conservative than his counterpart Ye Xuanping, as reflected, for instance, in his opposition to the weakening of the Party's role over economic affairs and his emphasis on building spiritual civilization.[32] Noted for his strict discipline and clean record, he was a determined economic reformer.[33] Lin was also elected a full member of the CC in 1982 and 1987. After his departure from the post of party secretary, he became the chairman of Guangdong's Provincial People's Congress from 1985 to 1996 and had earned a reputation for speeding up legislative work, especially economic legislation, during his incumbency. Ye Xuanping, on the other hand, had a far more elitist background because he was first of all the eldest son of Marshal Ye Jianying, the top military official who helped orchestrate the coup against the "Gang of Four" in 1976. A Guangdong native born in 1924, he was an engineer by training and had studied in the Soviet Union in 1952–1953. Unlike Lin Ruo, he spent most of his career outside of Guangdong, mostly in Beijing, before returning to his home province in 1980. Having first served as vice governor and later mayor of Guangzhou, he was promoted to the post of governor in 1985. He was made an alternate member of the CC in 1982 and later promoted to a full member at the National Party Conference held in 1985. During his entire tenure as governor, he had earned a reputation as a highly popular, pragmatic, and skillful provincial leader. In fact, both Lin and Ye were well known for their defense of the province's interests against recentralization of economic power by the Center in the aftermath of the June 4th incident in 1989. Compared with their predecessors, Lin Ruo and Ye Xuanping had a somewhat different kind of central patronage. These leaders were not the founding fathers of the Communist revolution like Xi Zhongxun or Yang Shangkun, but they joined the movement as followers in the late 1940s. They were also not as close to the preeminent leader Deng as their predecessors were, but they did have their own strengths in dealing with the Center. In addition to his eminent family background, Ye possessed extensive connections inside the central Party and military systems while Lin was known to enjoy close personal ties with Zhao Ziyang since he worked in the localities when the former premier and general secretary was a leader in Guangdong in the prereform era.[34]

Xie Fei and Zhu Senlin, the fourth batch of leaders, were both veteran Guangdong cadres. Xie Fei, a Guangdong native born in 1932, joined the Communist Party in 1949 and worked for a decade in his hometown in eastern Guangdong before being promoted to various positions at the provincial level. After the Cultural Revolution, he further moved up and later became party secretary of Guangzhou in 1986, executive deputy provincial party secretary in 1988, and later provincial party secretary in 1991. An alternate member of the CC since 1982, he was elevated to a full CC member in 1987. At the fourteenth Party Congress held in 1992, he was inducted into the Politburo and became the first ever incumbent Guangdong leader in this highest policy-making body. Zhu Senlin was actually a Shanghainese born in 1930, but after his college education in the prestigious Qinghua University, he was sent as part of the southbound cadres to Guangdong in the early 1950s. Nonetheless, he never moved out of the province and spent his entire career in Guangzhou, the provincial capital, and its suburban counties. An alternate member of the CC since 1987, he was later promoted to be a full CC member in 1992 and was considered to be Ye Xuanping's preferred choice of a successor.

While Xie Fei was made a member of the Politburo in 1992, thanks largely to Guangdong's economic might rather than his political influence, both he and Zhu Senlin were even less well-connected with prominent central leaders than their predecessors. Since they spent most of their careers in Guangdong, they lacked the opportunity to forge close ties with other top central leaders. When they were promoted to provincial leadership posts in 1991, the Center was already dominated by conservative leaders like Li Peng and Yao Yilin. The tasks confronting Guangdong's leaders have also changed substantially with the deepening of economic reform. In the early and mid 1980s, its leaders had to lobby for special treatment when such policies were rare and encourage inept localities and enterprises to embark upon reform. By the early 1990s, however, they had to adjust to Guangdong's growing economic prowess, the ascent of a new central leadership under Jiang Zemin, the growing competition with other coastal provinces, as well as the need to formulate a novel development strategy under these new circumstances. Hence their primary task would be to develop new areas of strength for the province and to defend its record in the face of rising criticism and competition. Further, despite repeated lobbying by Guangdong's leaders, it was the central government that steadfastly tried to groom Shanghai, now the power base of central leaders like Jiang Zemin and Zhu Rongji, as China's future commercial and financial center and refused to accommodate Guangdong's request for more of a role in financial reform, such as the establishment of another stock exchange in Guangzhou and the expansion of foreign banking operations in the province. Unlike the early days of reform, it would be extremely difficult for Guangdong's leaders to ignore the central government if it wanted to introduce financial reforms or attract foreign investors into sectors hitherto closed to overseas business. Although Xie and Zhu did not have a record as shining as their predecessors, it would be wrong, however, to characterize them as bandwagoners because both supported bolder reform.

Key leadership changes were further introduced in February 1996. Zhu Senlin stepped down as governor and replaced Lin Ruo as the chairman of Guangdong's Provincial People's Congress while a native and veteran Guangdong cadre, Lu Ruihua, took over as governor.[35] Lu was the first governor with post-graduate education (in physics) from Zhongshan University. A former executive vice governor in charge of economic management and leader of one of Guangdong's most prosperous cities, Foshan, he was made a governor at the age of 57. Although he joined the Party only in 1972 and his political status was not as senior as his predecessor, he was made an alternate member of the fourteenth CC in 1992 and considered a popular provincial official. The above changes revealed the emergence of a new generation of provincial leaders in the 1990s. Lu's promotion reflected a broader trend that was taking place not only in Guangdong but also in other parts of China. If our scope is expanded from these top Party and state officials to the Standing Committee of the Guangdong Provincial Party Committee (GPPCSC), which encompassed all the party secretaries, governors, most vice governors, and other important political figures, the same pattern is still clear. Being younger, better educated, and professionally more qualified, the rising provincial leaders were mostly local in native background and much more junior in Party seniority.[36] In the 5th GPPCSC constituted in March 1983, none of the 14 members were in their forties, but in the 15-member 7th GPPC elected in March 1993, 6 (40 percent) were in their mid and late forties and another 7 (47 percent) were in their fifties. By 1993, only the two most senior members, Xie Fei and Zhu Senlin, were in their early sixties. In addition, most of the members of the GPPCSC in 1983 (54 percent) only had high school or below education, but by 1993, over 93 percent of the members had college or an equivalent level of education. All of the GPPCSC members in 1983 had 33 years or above of Party membership. In 1993, merely 9 of the 15 members (60 percent) had 20 to 30 years of seniority; only 4 joined the CCP in the late 1940s and 1950s, 6 joined in the 1960s, and 5 joined after 1971. One even joined the Party as late as 1978! Such changes in leadership background suggested that Guangdong's leaders would remain pragmatic and sensitive to the province's interests.

The policy orientation of Guangdong's leaders was strongly in favor of market economic reform and open policy. On the one hand, the political inclination of these leaders was part of the reason why they were appointed in the first place because Deng Xiaoping wanted to use Guangdong and Fujian as spearheads in his reform drive. On the other hand, reformist central leaders like former General Secretary Hu Yaobang and Vice Premiers Gu Mu and Wan Li also encouraged Guangdong's leaders to take a step ahead in reform because it could offer valuable lessons for China and promised to stand by the province if other central ministries obstructed the implementation of special policies.[37]

Three other factors were also at work in explaining the policy orientations of Guangdong's leaders, however. First, Guangdong's geographical distance from Beijing made it more difficult for the Center to exercise tight supervision as in other places like Beijing, Tianjin, Hebei, or Shandong. Guangdong leaders generally took a more flexible approach to policy interpretation in order to twist central policies in their favor. Numerous schemes to evade central monitoring have been devised by Guangdong's cadres. Given the political sensitivity toward the special policies granted to the province, especially in the early days of reform, Guangdong's leaders would never oppose the Center overtly, yet they were ready to stretch the limits of central policies and exploit whatever loopholes to the fullest in order to serve local interests.[38] For instance, Guangdong officials would rather spend energy on practical work and avoided ideological or policy debates by simply keeping quiet on reform initiatives, as in the early phase of rural reform, or they would relax central policies and make exceptions when they were implemented, as in the tax-for-profit reform for state-owned enterprises (SOEs).[39]

Second, the history of central neglect of Guangdong in economic development compelled provincial leaders to fend for themselves, who could not but be amazed by the rapid development of neighboring Hong Kong. Guangdong people were clearly aware that while most Hong Kong people were Cantonese, including many who fled the PRC since 1949, they were able to create an economic miracle under a different political and economic setting.[40] Since 1949, Hong Kong people had continuously provided all kinds of material support to their families and relatives in the mainland. These contacts and contributions back home amply showed the Guangdong people that they were doing much worse than their friends and relatives in capitalist Hong Kong. Many from Guangdong had also taken the risk to flee to Hong Kong by crossing the border illegally. Together with the growing contacts between the province and the out-side world, the demand for change among Guangdong's cadres would only get stronger since 1979. Third, the pro-reform orientation among Guangdong's leaders also had to do with the tenure of the liberal and reform-minded Ren Zhongyi, who was among one of the first provincial secretaries who strongly supported Deng Xiaoping in the debate about the criterion of truth in 1978. Aside from a pioneering spirit, Guangdong's leaders also made other concrete, indispensable contributions to its success in the reform endeavor.

Contributions of Provincial Leaders

Guangdong's success in reform, to be fair, could be attributed to both central support as well as provincial innovations, yet the contributions of its leaders might well be decisive. Central support for Guangdong was reflected not simply in granting special policies, but also in providing political support for its leaders to implement them. For instance, before Ren Zhongyi and Liang Lingguang were sent to the province in late 1980, they met with a host of top central leaders.[41] In particular, Deng Xiaoping made it clear that special policies should apply to the two provinces, not just the SEZs. Wan Li even suggested that these provincial leaders should invigorate Guangdong's economy with an open-mind and even if they committed mistakes, the State Council would shoulder the responsibility! The support of these central patrons was especially important in helping the province weather difficult periods in the reform era, such as the crack down against economic crimes in 1982 and the criticisms against the SEZs in 1985.[42] If central policies opened the "policy window" for provincial initiatives, they still could not fully account for Guangdong's remarkable economic success because the Center seldom dictated the specific policies to be adopted. Rather, it was the provincial government that ultimately implemented these policies in a rapidly changing policy environment.

First, the getting of special treatment from the central government by itself was a critical act of leadership.[43] The "special policies, flexible measures" granted to Guangdong were indeed path breaking because they enabled the prov-ince to enjoy a great deal of autonomy over a wide range of economic policies. Despite their lack of knowledge of Guangdong, Xi Zhongxun and Yang Shangkun, together with other members of the Provincial Party Committee, car-ried out research on its economic strengths and weaknesses and tried to act on the basis of a consensus among provincial officials.[44] These provincial leaders took advantage of the "policy window" that was opened at that particular historic juncture as Deng Xiaoping was groping for a path of reform for China. The skills of the provincial leadership in articulating local demands and arguing for more favorable treatment were essential in successfully lobbying the central leaders. Together with another vice governor, Wang Quanguo, Xi Zhongxun made a strong case for Guangdong in 1979 by reiterating the province's problems, such as slow agricultural growth, insufficient supply of energy and inadequate transportation facilities, as well as its potential strengths, such as earning foreign exchange, in the Central Work Conference in April 1979.[45] Even more significantly, by taking advantage of their close relationship with Deng Xiaoping, Xi Zhongxun and Yang Shangkun were able to lobby Deng directly and secure his approval of Guangdong's special policies during the conference, after briefing him about how the province could exert its strength and jump-start economic growth. When Deng was beginning to feel nostalgic about the ability of the Communist Party to fight its way for national power from its remote revolutionary bases, he agreed with Guangdong's suggestion to build the special zones with policy support, not resources, from the central government.[46] Highlighting that he spoke on the basis of a thorough discussion with the Provincial Party Committee, Xi even made a powerful analogy by suggesting that if Guangdong were an independent country, its economy could have taken off in just a few years.[47] Deeply impressed by Xi's comments, Deng immediately approved his request. This package of special policies, including the fiscal contract, was later promulgated as Central Document No. 50 in 1979.[48] After successful lobbying by Guangdong's leaders, these special policies were expanded and consolidated with the promulgation of Central Document No. 41 in 1980 and Central Document No. 27 in 1981. These three documents formed the first package of Guangdong's "special policies, flexible measures." Such a policy package was further renewed and expanded for another five years in State Council Document No. 46 in 1985. During Lin Ruo's tenure, he managed to make a bold request to the central government on the eve of the thirteenth National Party Congress in late 1987. Such an effort was strategically timed because Zhao Ziyang was exploring ways to implement his coastal development strategy. In late October 1987, Zhao Ziyang personally met Lin and Ye and talked about Guangdong's request and proposed turning the province into a "comprehensive reform experimental area."[49] A third policy package was issued as State Council Correspondence No. 25 in 1988, which vastly expanded Guangdong's economic powers. While this document was never fully implemented, its contents showed the extent to which provincial leaders were able to seize a favorable opportunity and secure the maximum preferential treatment from central leaders. Other less strategic but also equally important handling of central patronage was to ask sympathetic central leaders to solve particular problems for the province. For instance, in 1984, Governor Liang Lingguang lobbied Yang Shangkun, who was then the executive vice chairman of the Central Military Commission (CMC), to persuade the PLA to turn the military airport in Shantou into a dual-purpose airport (i.e. for both military as well as civilian use). Such a concession was critical because building a new airport required enormous amounts of resources and time.[50] While the PLA initially opposed the idea, they conceded only after several rounds of CMC meetings with Yang's support for the proposal. Such a success later paved way for opening three other military airports in the province into dual-use airports as well.

Second, provincial leaders also played a key role in encouraging experimentation by sub-provincial units and defending reform against criticisms from conservative critics. Among Guangdong's leaders in the reform era, Ren Zhongyi was particularly important in encouraging local reform initiatives. In one of his first speeches to Guangdong's cadres, he revealed the detailed statements made by central leaders to reassure them of central support for the province.[51] In 1983, he promoted the cause of reform with his famous slogan, "to the outside, more open; to the inside, looser; to those below, more leeway" (*duiwai, gengjia kaifang; duinei, gengjia fangkuan; duixia, gengjia fangquan*).[52] His reform strategy, which emphasized decentralization of provincial economic authority to sub-provincial units, encouraged local officials in launching reform. According to Ren, flexibility in implementing central policies would be allowed under three kinds of circumstances. First, cadres should first look for whatever policies that could be applied to a particular situation rather than do nothing; second, if there was certain latitude within central policy, cadres should implement the policy flexibly in order to stimulate economic production; third, should there be some reforms that were conducive to the interests of the people and the nation, test sites for such reforms should be allowed even if no provisions could be found in existing policy documents and such test sites might go beyond the limits of existing policies.[53] Such a bold interpretation of local discretion in policy implementation earned him popularity inside the province and among the circle of reformers but the dislike of conservatives in Beijing. In fact, even before the special policies were implemented, Xi Zhongxun and Liu Tianfu were shocked to learn that one of the vice premiers even threatened to mount a 7,000–kilometer iron fence to separate Guangdong from the neighboring provinces.[54] But Guangdong's provincial leadership did not retreat, even during such precarious periods as 1979–1981 and 1984–1985, when the special policies were often questioned by conservative critics. Rather, they had made every effort to get more concessions and maximize their demands within the broad policy parameter set by the central government or secure top level support in dealing with the resistance from central units. For instance, in cooperation with Gu Mu, then vice premier in charge of open policy, Guangdong's provincial leadership demanded a host of unprecedented economic powers ranging from planning, fiscal management, and pricing to material allocation and labor management during the drafting of the first document on special policies.[55] When these policies were initially implemented in 1979–1980, Guangdong officials also complained to the Center about the lack of cooperation among central ministries. After successful lobbying by Guangdong's leaders, the document issued after a Party Secretariat meeting in December 1980 even stated that:

> The central government has delegated power to Guangdong province to adopt a flexible method in dealing with the directives and various departments at the central level by implementing measures that are appropriate and not implementing those that are inappropriate or handling them in a flexible manner.[56]

By getting such a broad central endorsement, Guangdong could use it as a shield in dealing with intervention from central government units.

When the Center was about to reduce Guangdong's special policies because of the eruption of economic irregularities in 1982, Governor Liu Tianfu strongly defended the conduct of his subordinates and instead argued that the entire Provincial Party Committee and provincial government should take the blame.[57] In 1985, Ren himself made self-criticisms for letting smuggling and other problems get out of control in Hainan rather than blaming his subordinates and washing his hands of the matter. According to one retired provincial official, such leadership behavior was extremely rare in the PRC and was most conducive in encouraging their subordinates to undertake economic reform.[58] After the province began to develop at a fast pace in the first half of the 1980s, provincial leaders like Lin Ruo and Ye Xuanping had fiercely defended Guangdong's record by stressing the success of its own reform initiatives and its contribution to the national economy when other provinces began to envy its accomplishments and the special policies. Such personal examples by provincial leaders were exceptionally important in encouraging local subordinates to follow suit. The close ties that developed between these leaders and Guangdong were reflected in the fact that they all stayed in the province after they retired and were frequently invited as honorable guests in many social and business occasions. Guangdong's provincial leadership and its reform strategies, in short, constitute some of the province's most important advantages since 1979.

Resource Mobilization Through Fiscal Reform

Changes in Central-Provincial Fiscal Relations

One of the most significant elements of Guangdong's economic take off was its success in mobilizing and allocating resources through fiscal and investment policies.[59] The reform of the fiscal system was the foundation from which Guangdong's special policies flourished.[60] In the prereform era, while the central government hardly invested in the province, Guangdong, though still backward, often had to contribute as many resources to the central government as it could spend on local social spending, economic development, and administration (see Table 2.3). Since 1952, the province had contributed around 600 to 800 million yuan to the Center every year until it was hit by the Great Leap Forward. Guangdong's contribution fell drastically to a low point of 388 million yuan in 1961, but later its remittance rose again to about 1 billion yuan between 1964 and 1969 (with the exception of 1968). As the provincial economy began to recover from the Cultural Revolution, its contribution further rose to the range of 1.3 to 1.7 billion yuan in the first half of the 1970s. The persistent trend of substantial extraction of revenue from the province was, however, a major burden on the provincial economy. The absolute amount of Guangdong's net remittance amounted to 40 to 50 percent of its local revenue and about 10 to 14 percent of its national income between 1952 and 1975 (see Table 2.3). Even more significantly, this level of remittance was more or less the same as, if not higher than, the actual amount of local expenditure during the same period.[61] By 1978, the province still contributed 1.11 billion yuan, which equaled 25 percent of its revenue, 39 percent of its expenditure, and 6.4 percent of its national income.[62] Only after the implementation of fiscal reform and the rapid growth of its economy since 1979 did the share of fixed remittance to the Center in Guangdong's national income fall, dropping from 10 to 14 percent in the prereform era to about 4 to 5 percent in the reform era (see Table 2.4).

Guangdong's strategy of fiscal reform carried the following characteristics. First, the provincial leadership would lobby and bargain for the most favorable fiscal contract with the Center as a means of protecting the autonomy granted to the province and minimizing fiscal remittance to the central government. Second, paralleling the special fiscal arrangement with the Center, the provincial leadership had struck a number of fiscal deals with sub-provincial units in order to stimulate their incentive to generate revenue, encourage the initiation of economic reform as well as promote local economic development. Third, accompanying its remarkable economic growth, Guangdong was able to tap the increasing amount of resources available for social and economic development. After 1982, Guangdong's budgetary expenditure began to surpass other provincial units.[63] Provincial expenditure rose from 2.7 billion yuan in 1978 to 15 billion yuan in 1990 and 52.5 billion yuan in 1995.[64] The province's revenue increased at 15.6 percent per annum, or about 5 percent higher than the national average, during the 1979–1993 period.[65] Since 1991, Guangdong has replaced Shanghai as China's largest revenue-generating province, and in 1993, its revenue of 34.65 billion yuan amounted to one-tenth of total local revenue in China.[66] The province's revenue has jumped from a meager 3.95 billion yuan in 1978 to 13 billion yuan in 1990 and 38 billion yuan in 1995 (excluding the 16 billion yuan rebate from the central government).[67] By 1993, the revenue of 30 counties and county-level cities in Guangdong already reached 1 billion yuan or more.[68] In 1995, Guangdong's share in national revenue and expenditure were 5.7 percent and 7.2 percent respectively, both the highest among the provinces in the nation.[69]

Further, the amount of social spending (education, public health and research) jumped sharply from 679 million yuan in 1979 to 4.35 billion yuan in 1990 and 15.7 billion yuan in 1995.[70] The share of such spending in total budgetary expenditure rose from about 24 percent in 1979 to 30 percent in 1995. While the share of social spending was usually around 30 percent of the total budget in the reform era, the absolute increase of such expenditure should not be overlooked. In 1979, social spending was only about 43 percent of the budgetary expenditure for economic construction, but by 1995, it had already surpassed this item of expenditure. In particular, a huge amount of budgetary resources was used as

Table 2.3

Guangdong's Net Remittances to the Central Government in the Prereform Era, 1952–1978 (selected years)

		Net remittance as a percentage of		
	(a) Net remittance (mill. yuan)	(b) Local revenue (%)	(c) Local expenditure (%)	(d) National income (%)
1952	301	40.0	86.0	11.1
1957	544	50.0	108.0	10.0
1962	613	42.7	89.8	10.1
1965	1,077	49.0	110.6	13.3
1970	1,342	47.8	99.4	14.0
1975	1,749	46.3	94.1	13.1
1978	1,118	25.2	39.0	6.4

Sources: Guangdongsheng tongjiu (ed.), *Guangdongsheng guoming jingji tongji tiyao, 1949–1981* (Summary of Guangdong Province's National Economic Statistics, 1949– 1981) (internal publication, November 1981), pp. 184–187.

Notes: All figures were rounded. (a) Net remittances referred to Guangdong's fiscal remittance to the central government after deducting various kinds of central subsidies. (b) Local revenue included surplus from previous years and other income granted to the province. (c) Local expenditure did not include the net remittance and the surplus to be allocated into the next fiscal year.

Table 2.4

Guangdong's Net Remittances as a Share of Revenue, Expenditure, and National Income (unit = percent)

	Net Remittance as a Percentage of		
	Provincial revenue	Provincial expenditure	National income
1980	27.7	40.0	4.80
1985	29.3	32.0	3.96
1987	25.0	25.8	3.50
1990	40.0	35.0	5.12
1991	39.4	38.0	5.72
1992	33.5	33.9	4.25
1993	25.3	26.4	3.46

Sources: For figures on revenue, expenditure, and remittance, see the sources in Table 2.6; for figures of national income, see, Guangdongsheng tongjiju (ed.), *Guangdong tongji nianjian 1994*, p. 72.

price subsidies in order to cushion the people from price fluctuations caused by Guangdong's economic reform. Price subsidies during the 1987–1991 period were in the range of 1.2 to 1.7 billion yuan per year.[71] Together with the substantial improvements in living standards, such increases in social spending served to consolidate popular support for reform.

The Lump-Sum Transfer Regime, 1980–1984

The fiscal contract or lump-sum transfer regime (often referred to as *caizheng dabaogan*) between the Center and Guangdong during 1980–1984 was undoubtedly the most favorable revenue sharing deal for the province since 1979.[72] (For annual figures on Guangdong's remittances, please refer to Table 2.5). In Central Document No. 50 in 1979, the lump sum to be remitted to the central government was set at 1.2 billion yuan, but after lobbying by provincial leaders, it was scaled down to only 1 billion yuan for a five-year period from 1980 to 1984.[73] The above-quota surpluses would be accrued to the province. Except for customs duties and the income from enterprises (such as railway, ports, post and telecommunications, civil aviation, and banks) and non-profit units owned by the central government, all revenue would be designated as provincial income. Nonetheless, most expenses, except those for centrally owned enterprises and non-profit units as well as specialized funds for major natural calamities, would come solely from the coffers of Guangdong. Further, funding for capital construction (except that for centrally owned units) would also be entirely shouldered by the province. After deducting central transfers, the actual amount of remittance in 1979 was set at 960 million yuan.[74] As long as Guangdong's economy grew and more revenues were collected, the province could count on the increasing revenue accruing to fund its rising expenditures.

Fiscal reform since 1979 greatly facilitated Guangdong's economic growth and reform.[75] First, the contracting system enhanced the incentives of the provincial and sub-provincial governments in generating and collecting revenue because the above-quota revenue would be allocated to the province rather than to the central government. The contracting system also made it easier for the province to implement fiscal decentralization to sub-provincial units. Since provincial remittances to the Center would be fixed, the province could assign sub-provincial remittance targets and, more importantly, introduce a similar contracting system to its localities. While scholars, both inside and outside China, have criticized fiscal contracting as the cause of local protectionism and investment explosion, there was little doubt that the system served Guangdong's interests well.[76]

Second, and even more importantly, the contracting system expedited Guangdong's economic reform. The stability and security of fiscal arrangements within the contracting period not only facilitated better budgetary planning, but also protected the implementation of economic reform from drastic policy reversals, which were often the norm in the prereform era. The increased flexibility in fiscal policy was also critical because the Center would have less incentive to monitor how reforms were actually carried out in the localities. For instance, in order to allow more profit retention by enterprises, the provincial government not only redefined the classification of small enterprises, but also raised the level of retained profits for enterprises and allowed a higher level of per capita retained profits for enterprises.[77] While national policies clearly spelled out standardized tax rates in the tax-for-profit reform, Guangdong still handed out more tax privileges to stimulate the growth of local and foreign-funded enterprises. On the other hand, the reduction of fiscal remittances to the Center allowed the province to have more resources available for subsidizing reform. Guangdong researchers called this practice *zifei gaige* (or self-paid reform) because the province could carry out such reforms as wage reform, price reform, or enterprise reform ahead of other provinces by paying subsidies and allowing enterprises more tax exemptions without risking major social upheavals.

Third, the contracting system also encouraged responsibility and innovation in fiscal management. For instance, the clear-cut delineation of provincial responsibility in expenditure had compelled the provincial government to draw upon a variety of sources for funding capital investment and other services. The provincial government also introduced contracting with non-profit units (*shiye danwei*) and government units so that they could also be more entrepreneurial with their budgetary allocations.[78] Further, the contracting system facilitated the increased use of fiscal credit (*caizheng xinyong*) so that provincial revenue would be issued as credits for technical renovation of enterprises and poorer mountainous areas inside the province.[79]

A Modified Lump-Sum Transfer Regime, 1985–1987

The renewal of Guangdong's fiscal contract in 1984 was no longer as controversial as during the first time when China just began to introduce reform and open policy. On the one hand, Guangdong's economic growth was evident after implementing the special policies. For instance, if compared with the prereform era, the major economic indicators showed rapid growth during the 1979–1984 period: national income 10.2 percent, agricultural output 8.5 percent, industrial output 11.1 percent, and exports 9.6 percent.[80] On the other hand, Deng Xiaoping's southern tour in early 1984 led to the opening up of fourteen coastal cities in March and ushered in a second wave of reform, which cumulated in the adoption of a key decision on economic reform by the CC in October. Zhao Ziyang's visit to the Pearl River Delta and Yangtze River and his efforts to articulate a policy on the further opening of the coastal area also served to sustain the momentum for reform.[81] The renewal of the province's special policies, including the fiscal contract, was approved after a meeting on open cities and SEZs between Guangdong and Fujian and relevant departments under the State Council was held in early January 1985. As Guangdong's special policies were becoming politically less sensitive, the document was only issued as State Council Document No. 46, rather than the more prominent Central Committee Document, in March 1985.[82] The provincial leaders did not have to bargain fiercely with the Center over the renewal of the fiscal contract as before, although they had to overcome thorny problems in implementing the special policies, especially over the SEZs and Hainan.[83] More importantly, Guangdong's leadership had to agree to adjustments to the original fiscal contract in view of the province's economic progress and the changes in national fiscal policy and to raise its contributions as the province's economy had begun to take off. This contract, albeit modified, remained effective from 1985 to 1987.[84]

Owing to the adoption of the tax-for-profit reform nationwide, several modifications in Guangdong's contract with the Center were introduced. First, a number of profitable enterprises were classified as central-level enterprises. Second, the business tax from banks and insurance companies was incorporated as part of the local fixed income. Third, 70 percent of the three important newly created taxes, namely product tax, value added tax, and business tax from enterprises in the petroleum, petro-chemical, and metallurgical sectors, would be designated as central fixed income and only 30 percent would be designated as local fixed income. Fourth, the Center began to claim 50 percent of the increment above the 1984 baseline of the industrial and commercial taxes (hereafter ICT) collected by the customs administration and other specialized adjustment taxes. While the province was responsible for paying the construction and administrative costs of the customs system, the province could only get the remaining 50 percent of the ICT. The Center also raised the contracted lump sum upwards by adding the actual amount lent to the central government as part of the new 1984 remittance. Such borrowing amounted to 380 million yuan in 1981, 300 million yuan in 1982, and 460 million yuan in 1983–1984.[85] Owing to the changes in the transfer of ownership of enterprises, the actual amount of remittance was scaled down from 1 billion yuan in 1980 to 778 million yuan in 1987.[86] This "reduction" in contribution did not mean the actual contribution of the province to central coffer had declined because part of the central income came directly from the newly recentralized enterprises and the rest came from the sharing of various new taxes discussed above.

Incremental Contracting, 1988–1993

Guangdong's leadership was reshuffled in 1985 when, for the first time since 1955, two Guangdong natives, Lin Ruo and Ye Xuanping succeeded Ren Zhongyi and Liang Lingguang as Guangdong's party secretary and governor. Despite their different career backgrounds and political styles, they were eager to secure the continuation of special treatment for the province. The latest fiscal contract was part of the policy request made by Guangdong asking for more special treatment in late 1987. This request received a positive response from

Zhao Ziyang, who even promised that Guangdong did not have to implement the tax-sharing regime, as favored by some researchers, but could carry out a total sharing system.[87] The State Council issued an approval of Guangdong's request as State Council Correspondence No. 25 in February 1988. The year 1988 witnessed the universalization of fiscal contracting between most of the provinces and the central government. Hunan and Guangdong were the only two provinces that adopted an incremental contract with the Center. Instead of moving to the total sharing formula as promised by Zhao, Guangdong succeeded in securing the continuation of the more favorable fiscal contract, albeit with some modifications. This incremental fiscal contract was implemented from 1988 to 1991, and later extended to 1993. This departure from the original lump-sum regime was meant to increase the province's contribution to the Center. Guangdong's fixed remittances would be raised from 778 million yuan in 1987 to 1.41 billion yuan as the baseline for remittance in 1988. Again, the lending of 635 million yuan from Guangdong to the Center would be added to the 1988 figure. Adding such figures to the provincial contract baseline had by then become a common practice by the Center to raise contributions from the provinces. Guangdong was no exception. Further, Guangdong had to remit an additional increment of 9 percent of its revenue each year for three years until 1990. In 1990, the incremental contract was allowed to continue, using the actual amount of provincial remittance of 1.623 billion yuan (minus the reduction of Shenzhen's remittance of 207 million yuan, which would be remitted to the Center directly as the SEZ would be listed separately in the fiscal plan) as the baseline and adding an annual increment of 9 percent.[88] Agreeing to the increment and other changes, however, was a shrewd compromise which allowed the province to keep the contracting system for a few more years. Economic retrenchment introduced in late 1988 and the subsequent political and economic crisis in summer 1989 which led to Zhao's downfall, however, made it impossible for the province to fully carry out reform as promised in the above document.

When the central government, now dominated by conservative leaders like Premier Li Peng and Vice Premier Yao Yilin, tried to extract more resources from the provinces in view of the economic slowdown since 1989, provincial leaders were not reluctant to openly challenge criticisms which they deemed unfair. In an article published in *Qiushi*, September 1989, Lin Ruo defended the province by arguing that its economic success should not be simply attributed to the Center's special policies because it had mainly relied upon its own efforts in promoting economic growth.[89] He suggested that "Guangdong's construction funds have changed from depending upon central appropriation to mainly depending upon the province's own acquisition." During 1979–1988, "the proportion of central investment was very small" in Guangdong's fixed asset investment: 6 percent in the building of bridges, 13.6 percent in electricity supply, and 0.7 percent in education.[90] More importantly, he pointed out that Guangdong's success had to do with its ties with the world economy because by

1989, one-quarter of Guangdong's GDP and national income was realized in the international market while one-third of its construction funds came from abroad.[91] In another article published simultaneously in *Nanfang Ribao* and *Renmin Ribao*, on March 11, 1991, Lin also cited a host of statistics to argue that the province had contributed far more to the Center than the basic contracted remittances.[92] In view of the increasingly restrictive economic policy environment, these responses from provincial leaders were major efforts to defend the province.

Did Guangdong Contribute a "Fair" Share to the Central Government?

Whether Guangdong province had paid a fair share to the central government was a controversy not only between the Center and the province, but also between scholars inside and outside China. This section hence tries to clarify how much Guangdong had contributed to the central coffer.[93] The amount of Guangdong's fiscal remittance to the central government actually comprised two sources: the "narrow" category and the "broad" category. The "narrow" category consisted of (a) the basic remittance as specified in the fiscal contract between the Center and the province, and (b) a host of different kinds of remittances. What most observers had paid attention to concerned only the basic remittance from Guangdong. Under the fiscal contract with the Center from 1980 to 1984, the province would pay a fixed remittance of 1 billion yuan to the central government, but this did not include specialized funds that would be transferred back to the province by the Center.[94] The amount of the basic remittance was nonetheless raised to 1.41 billion yuan in 1988, and a further 9 percent increment would be imposed on the province during the 1988–1993 period.

The second source of the "narrow" category of remittance involved six kinds of remittances: (a) extra contribution (*duozuo gongxian*) since 1988, (b) specific remittance (*zhuanxiang shangjiao*), (c) remittance of two funds (State Energy, Transportation, and Key Construction Fund and State Budget Adjustment Fund), (d) customs-collected industrial and commercial taxes (which were incorporated as central revenue since 1990), (e) revenue from enterprises re-classified as centrally owned, and (f) borrowing through squeezing provincial expenditure (*yazhi jiekuan shangjiao*) since 1988.[95] The Center had increasingly relied upon such irregular means to raise income from Guangdong and other provinces in order to cover its growing deficit. In short, aside from imposing "involuntary" borrowing in the early 1980s, the Center had also "borrowed" extra money through the reduction of provincial expenditure in 1988 and 1989, demanded extra contributions since 1988, and even re-classified a local source of revenue (i.e. the industrial and commercial tax collected by the customs), as a central revenue since 1990. In 1987, the central government imposed an involuntary "loan" of 677 million yuan for Guangdong and starting from 1990, Guangdong was simply asked to contribute 1 billion yuan more each year as extra remittance to the central government.[96] Further, while central investment in Guangdong had dwindled, various kinds of expenditure that were part of central expenditure had been delegated to the province. In fact, the growth rate of net provincial remittance to the Center (even if based on the narrow category) had increased from 817 million yuan in 1979 to 6.9 billion yuan in 1991, which meant an annual growth rate of 19.6 percent between 1979 and 1991, or 4.3 percent higher than the growth of provincial revenue.[97]

The "broad" definition of remittance from Guangdong included mainly various sources of income which the central government earned directly and indirectly from the province. These remittances referred to: (a) custom-collected tariff, (b) revenue from enterprises in the banking and insurance systems, (c) remittance from other centrally owned enterprises in Guangdong, (d) remittance of foreign exchange earnings, as well as (e) state bonds and treasury bills sold in Guangdong. Owing to Guangdong's fast economic growth, the increase in the first three sources, namely tariffs, income from the banking system, and enterprise remittance jumped sharply, reaching respectively 53.2 percent, 28 percent, and 58.3 percent per annum during the 1979–1990 period.[98] The amount of the first three categories of remittance from Guangdong had shot up from 499 million yuan in 1980 to over 10.45 billion yuan in 1990. At the same time, the amount of foreign exchange remitted to the central government during the 1979–1989 period was a substantial US$ 15 billion. Quotas for provinces to sell state bonds and treasury bills were also issued to Guangdong, which amounted to a sum of 2.45 billion yuan for Guangdong in the 1981–1989 period.[99] Tax and profit remittances from enterprises, customs and banks under the central government also increased from less than 500 million yuan to more than 10 billion yuan during the 1979–90 period. Tables 2.4 and 2.5 provide a list of available figures on Guangdong's remittances to the Center.[100]

Several features in Guangdong's remittances to the central government should be mentioned. First, the net remittances (based on the narrow category) had increased significantly from around 1 billion yuan in 1980 to almost 8.7 billion yuan in 1993 (see Table 2.5). Second, the share of this remittance in Guangdong's economy was nonetheless lower than the prereform era and remained so in the 1980s. Whereas Guangdong contributed 10 percent to 14 percent of its national income to the central government, the share fell to 3 percent to 6 percent in the reform era (see Table 2.4). In 1992 and 1993, Guangdong had remitted a total of over 7.45 and 8.7 billion yuan, within this narrow category, respectively 34 percent and 25 percent of its revenue![101] Therefore, to argue whether Guangdong paid a fair share to the central government depends on the specific criteria used, but it is nonetheless clear that Guangdong paid quite a substantial amount since the late 1980s. An exact comparison with official remittances from other provinces should also take into account other kinds of factors, such as the availability of central investment and subsidies.

Table 2.5

Guangdong's Net Remittance to the Center since 1980
(unit = $100 million yuan)

	Provincial revenue	Provincial expenditure	Net remittances*
1980	36.10	24.93	9.99
1981	39.45	27.18	13.97
1982	40.53	30.75	12.86
1983	42.28	34.27	13.58
1984	45.17	42.65	12.43
1985	65.46	60.84	19.20
1986	79.82	82.91	16.73
1987	92.92	89.87	23.19
1988	107.57	115.20	33.35
1989	136.87	141.16	37.40
1990	131.02	150.69	52.41
1991	177.35	182.48	69.85
1992	222.64	219.61	74.53
1993	345.56	331.27	87.37
1994*	298.70	416.83	N.A.

Sources: Guangdong tongjiju (ed.), *Guangdong tongji nianjian 1990*, p. 412; *Guangdong tongji nianjian 1994*, p. 338; *Guangdong tongji nianjian 1995*, p. 102; Guangdongsheng tongjiju (ed.), *Guangdongsheng qiwu shiqi jingji he shehui fazhan chengxiu (1986–1990)* (Economic and Social Achievements of Guangdong Province during the 7th Five-Year Plan) (Guangzhou: Guangdongsheng tongjiju, 1991), p. 9 (appendix of statistical tables); Wang Zou et al., *Guangdong gaige kaifang pingshuo* (Comments on Guangdong's Reform and Opening to the Outside World) (Guangzhou: Guangdong renmin chubanshe, 1992), pp. 7–8 & 47–86; Lin Dengyun, "Gaige de tupokou ziyi: Guangdong caizheng gaige de youyichangshi," *Guangdong caizheng*, No. 4, 1992, pp. 8–10; Liu Peiqiong, ed., *Guangdong jingji touzi zonglan* (A Comprehensive Overview of Guangdong Investment and Economy) (Hong Kong: Shangwu yinshuguan, 1996), p. 222; Shi Ri, "Guangdong shinian caizheng zhichu de shizheng Fengxi" (An Analysis of Implementation of Ten Years Financial Foundation in Guangdong), *Guangdong caizheng*, No. 2, 1991, pp. 17–21; Zhou Kai, "Dui Guangdong caizheng shangjiao zhuangkuang de bianzheng renshi," *Guangdong caizheng*, No. 2,1992, pp. 47–50.

Note: Net remittances referred to Guangdong's "narrow" category of remittance minus Central subsidies.

Central-Provincial Fiscal Relations Under the Tax-Sharing System

The tax-sharing system (*fenshuizhi*; hereafter TSS) was introduced universally to all provinces on January 1, 1994. The fiscal contract and its incremental version that Guangdong and other provinces once enjoyed finally ended. This landmark in fiscal and tax reform was the result of extensive negotiation and bargaining between the Center and the provinces. Guangdong also agreed to the existing compromise, i.e., the 1994 reform, after several visits by Vice Premier Zhu

Rongji to the province and his acceptance of a suggestion made by Guangdong. The TSS was introduced in order to reduce the incessant bargaining between the Center and the provinces, raise the central share of overall revenue, and bring the Chinese tax system in line with international standards.[102] Several major changes in central-provincial fiscal relations under the new system were especially noteworthy.[103] First, there would be a clearer division of central and local revenue, with shared revenue coming from the important value added tax (VAT), securities tax, and resources tax.[104] In particular, while the securities tax would be shared equally between the Center and the provinces, 75 percent of the VAT would accrue to the Center and only 25 percent would be shared by the provinces. Second, instead of relying upon the localities to collect taxes, national tax bureaus would be set up to collect central and shared revenue while a local tax bureau would be established to collect only local revenue. Third, local governments no longer enjoyed the power to grant tax exemptions to enterprises as a uniform tax reform for the enterprise income tax was introduced. Nonetheless, the increment in the VAT and consumption tax would be shared between the Center and the provinces in accordance with the ratio of 1:0.3 for nationwide increases of these two taxes. The implementation of the TSS would not be introduced entirely in 1994 as the provinces would not get less than what they would get from their previous arrangements in 1993 as the Center promised to offer a rebate as a transitional measure.

Arduous bargaining between the Center and the provinces took place, especially in the summer and early fall of 1993 when Vice Premier Zhu Rongji made a dozen trips to convince provincial leaders about the merits and urgency of the reform.[105] Guangdong was his number one target because it was the largest revenue-generating province and its cooperation would be crucial for the Center to convince others to follow suit. Having been tried in a number of test sites, the TSS was considered unpopular by the provinces because it would not only restrict their fiscal autonomy but also raised the sum of central revenue at their own expense. One report even suggested that a meeting between Vice Premier Zhu Rongji and Guangdong's Party Secretary Xie Fei and Governor Zhu Senlin ended in a shouting match, although the actual confrontation between the Center and the province over this issue was never publicly reported.[106] Even prior to its introduction, Guangdong researchers with official backgrounds had criticized that the proposal on TSS suggested by the ministry of finance (hereafter MOF) failed to introduce a clear division of powers and responsibilities of the two levels of government and took away the most important sources of revenue for the localities as central revenue.[107] Such a view was of course not shared by researchers and officials in the central government who believed that China's fiscal system had to be thoroughly revamped.[108] Despite the repeated resistance by Guangdong's leaders, the province's economic prowess, the continual provision of special treatment as well as the growing envy of inland provinces toward the coastal areas made it increasingly difficult for Guangdong to resist central initiatives, especially given the strong determination of central leaders in imposing the reform on the provinces.

The original proposal suggested by the MOF for the 1994 reform was even more stringent than the actual reform introduced in 1994 because the Center would claim most of the important taxes.[109] Understandably, this proposal was not well received by the provinces, but at this juncture, a prominent economist and former director of Guangdong's Provincial Economic System Reform Office, Wang Zuo, suggested a compromise formula to Zhu Rongji directly, who soon referred the letter to the MOF and General Secretary Jiang Zemin. Zhu himself personally led a group of MOF officials to Guangdong and discussed the tax reform proposal with provincial officials.[110] In particular, he agreed with Wang's suggestion of sharing the increment in revenue between provinces and the central government within the framework of tax-sharing.[111] While there were undoubtedly disputes over the imposition of the TSS nationwide, the central government relied upon arduous bargaining and persuasion to cajole the provinces into accepting the TSS. The Center's success in urging Guangdong to accept the reform proposal, albeit with some changes, surely helped it to negotiate with other provinces. The compromise as reflected in the 1994 reform incorporated the principle of revenue sharing according to different kinds of taxes as well as a concern for provincial interests by promising that provincial revenue would not be worse off in 1993 and there would be inter-governmental rebates from the Center to the provinces in accordance with the 1:0.3 ratio for increments in VAT and consumption tax.

It is too early for detailed analysis of the implementation of the TSS in Guangdong. However, Guangdong has already tried to voice concerns over perceived problems and bargain for better treatment in the process of implementation. Four impacts of the new system on provincial revenue deserved special attention. First, the province would have to pay a larger amount of tax, although the Center promised to remit some of the revenue as an ad hoc measure during 1994–1996. The exact conditions that would allow Guangdong to get a rebate were the result of bargaining with the Center at the National Taxation Conference held in the fall of 1994, which decided that Guangdong's baseline for the central rebate be set at 11.93 billion yuan for 1993.[112] The TSS actually underwent subtle change in the process of implementation.[113] The ratio of the 1:.03 rebate was not to be implemented as suggested whereby the growth of the two taxes was based on the average national figures. On the one hand, the MOF agreed not to use the national growth rate of the two taxes for rebate. Rather, the rebate would be calculated on the basis of the growth rates of the actual amount of the VAT and consumption tax that were transferred from Guangdong (or other provinces) to the central treasury. On the other hand, the MOF issued a growth target of 20.4 percent for the VAT and consumption tax for Guangdong in 1993 (as compared with the national target of 16 percent). This rate of 20.4 percent constituted one-third of the estimated growth of the two kinds of taxes and this would apply universally to all areas, not just Guangdong. In other words, only if Guangdong had achieved this growth target for the above two taxes could the sharing rate of 1:0.3 be applied to the province. Should the above two types of revenue in the province fail to increase 20.4 percent and the actual amount of tax fall below the baseline of 11.93 billion yuan, the tax rebate for the province would be scaled down accordingly. Should the growth of the above two types of revenue fail to reach 20.4 percent, the province could still get a rebate if the actual revenue surpassed the baseline of 11.93 billion yuan.

Second, the power of local governments in exempting taxes for enterprises would be nullified because only the central government would have the authority to do so. This recentralization of the tax exemption authority has severely reduced the autonomy of Guangdong's subprovincial governments in promoting local industrialization through the manipulation of taxation. Third, the new tax system did not simply complicate the tasks of intergovernmental fiscal transfer (from the Center to the provinces and from the provinces to cities and counties), but also put the prerogative of transfer in the hands of the central government. Many local governments in Guangdong and elsewhere had complained about the delay in tax rebates, which created enormous cash-flow problems in 1994–1995 because there was a time lag before such remittances could reach the localities. Finally, the year 1994 turned out to be a poor time to implement fiscal reform in Guangdong because there was large-scale flooding in central and southern China in the summer of 1994. Moreover, the central government had not loosened the tight supply of credit for enterprises since the summer of 1993. The experience in the introduction of the TSS suggested that there would still be bargaining and negotiation between Guangdong and the Center, but given the new political and economic circumstances Guangdong's provincial leaders could no longer easily extract concessions from a determined central leadership that felt its fiscal resources were depleted by the local governments.

Guangdong's Subprovincial Fiscal Reform

Changes in Subprovincial Fiscal Management, 1979–1993

In line with the changing fiscal regimes with the Center, Guangdong's provincial leadership mobilized support from subprovincial levels for economic reform by fiscal decentralization. The province had established a number of contracts with subprovincial units in the reform era so that they, too, could benefit from the fiscal contract between the Center and Guangdong. There was a great deal of continuity in terms of provincial strategy, which was established when Ren Zhongyi and Liang Lingguang were the top provincial leaders, although the exact contracting methods evolved over time. Four characteristics of the provincial strategy merit analysis. The first aspect of the provincial leaders' strategy was its continual adoption of a differential approach whereby the rich areas would pay more and the poor areas would pay less, although the details of each deal would differ from case to case. The SEZs were dealt with most favorably at the beginning as they enjoyed special treatment and constituted a key part of Guangdong's open policy. Guangzhou, the provincial capital as well as a major generator of revenue, was also singled out for separate but less favorable treatment. Then the province would differentiate between the average cities or counties and those which were the poorest and which depended upon provincial subsidies. As a former director of finance in Guangdong suggested, the rich counties and cities in the Pearl River Delta would be given a stable, fixed remittance for a certain period of time so that they could embark upon rapid economic growth, except for sharing the extra remittances imposed by the central government. Similarly, the poor areas would be given less burden for sharing such responsibilities and would be granted subsidies to upset price increases as a result of economic reform.[114] A second feature of the provincial strategy was its commitment to support local economic growth. In fact, when the Center abolished fiscal contracting in 1994, the province still tried to retain some elements of the earlier contracting system with some of the cities so that they could enjoy more flexibility in promoting local economic development. Nonetheless, Guangdong's provincial leaders still had to seek progressive concessions from the localities in order to pay for its increasing remittances to the Center. A third characteristic of the provincial strategy was its continual emphasis on contracting in subprovincial fiscal management. In the early phase (1980–1984), the province contracted directly with both the cities/prefectures and counties, yet the result of this first contracting period was not favorable and the provincial leadership began to shift to another formula. Since 1985, the provincial government began to contract only with the cities/prefectures so that these cities would enjoy a greater degree of autonomy in establishing fiscal deals with counties under their jurisdiction. Paralleling the four fiscal regimes with the Center, the province's fiscal arrangement with subprovincial units could be roughly divided into four periods: (a) phase one, 1980–1984; (b) phase two, 1985–1987; (c) phase three, 1988–1993, and (d) phase four, since 1994.

In the first phase (1980–1984), a number of contracts between the province and cities and counties had been tried out as the province began to adapt to the contracting system with the central government. Four major systems were introduced in this scheme.[115]

(a) The three SEZs, which were established in 1979, enjoyed the most preferential treatment because they could keep all their revenue and the provincial government would pay for their expenditures in order to foster their construction and development.[116] This preferential policy had, however, been watered down over time as the zones had developed rapidly.[117] Since Shantou SEZ was rather backward, it was able to get construction funds from the province.

(b) Guangzhou, the provincial capital, adopted the system of "one linkage" (yibiangua) in 1981 and "sharing of total revenue" from 1982 to 1984.[118] In

1981, Guangzhou had a "one linkage" deal with the province whereby its revenue would be differentiated into (a) fixed income and (b) adjustment income. Of its fixed income, 82 percent would be reserved for Guangzhou while the remaining 18 percent would be remitted to the province, but all of its adjustment income would be accrued to the province. This treatment was immediately changed one year later. During 1982–1984, a total sharing regime was adopted whereby 68 percent of Guangzhou's total revenue would be remitted to the province and only 32 percent would be left for Guangzhou. This undesirable treatment was imposed on the provincial capital because it remained a "cash-cow" of the province.

(c) Another favorable method was "contracting over revenue and expenditure, providing fixed subsidies for five years," which applied to the poorer Hainan and minorities counties.

(d) The remaining nine cities or prefectures adopted one of the following four systems: (i) "one linkage" (*yibiangua*) meant that the revenue would be divided into two kinds: fixed income and adjustment income, and their total expenditure would be fixed. If their fixed income was smaller than the specified amount of expenditure, the adjustment income would be used to pay for the shortfall in accordance with a fixed ratio. (ii) "two linkages" (*liangbiangua*) were also introduced whereby two ratios for local sharing of revenue would be calculated on the basis of expenditure and the share over fixed income and adjustment income. The two remaining forms were (iii) sharing of total revenue and (iv) providing fixed subsidies for deficit areas.

In the second phase (1985–1987), the province had adopted another four types of contracts with sub-provincial units.[118] What was most significant for this period was that the overall method of contracting had been modified because since 1984, the province would only contract with prefectural-level cities or prefectures rather than the counties to ensure that these county-level units would not simply plead for more fiscal support from the province and provide an incentive for them to generate more revenue through contracting between them and their immediate superiors—the prefectural level. The provincial leadership was keenly aware of the relative slower growth of revenue as compared to the rapid economic growth rates. Comparing 1984 with 1980, Guangdong's revenue increased only 25 percent while its GDP and national income grew in the range of 70–80 percent.[119] As counties had to deal directly with their immediate administrative superior, there would be better division of fiscal responsibilities and more effective supervision over the achievement of contracts between these two levels. The roughly comparable increase in economic growth rates and revenue since the mid-1980s partly testified to the positive impact of this change in the contracting method.

(a) The SEZs could still keep their own revenue without paying a fixed amount of remittance to the province, but they had to shoulder more of their expenditure and remit a number of other remittances to the province as well as to the Center.[120] Starting from 1984, the SEZs had to be responsible for all of their own expenses, but they still did not have to remit to the province until the 1990s. Both the province, as well as the Center, had encroached upon both the autonomy and the resources of the SEZs since the early 1980s, however. First, Shenzhen was pressured into providing ad hoc and newly established remittances ever since its establishment in 1979.[121] Hence given the growing economic might of the SEZs, the "special" zones were no longer immune to the increasing demands for fiscal remittance from both the province and the Center. Second, the province, and especially the Center, would not exempt the SEZs from extractions that were applied universally to other areas in the nation.[122] In 1990, because of the growing economic strength of the SEZs, Shenzhen was listed separately in the state budget so that it would have to remit directly to the central government.

(b) During phase two (1985–1987), Guangzhou had a "fixed baseline, fixed remittance, and sharing of increment" regime with the province whereby the increment over a fixed amount of the remittance to the province would be shared with 60 percent for Guangzhou and 40 percent for the province. The reason for persistent unfavorable treatment of the provincial capital was quite simple. On the one hand, the provincial government had traditionally relied upon the city to provide the bulk of its revenue. On the other hand, conflict between provincial and municipal authorities was well known, so the province had adopted a more restrictive arrangement with Guangzhou in order to ensure that it would be under control. In 1992, for instance, Guangzhou's remittance to the Center and province amounted to 90 percent of its own expenditure in that year.[123]

(c) For five cities that had budgetary surpluses, they would follow an incremental contract whereby four of them, namely Foshan, Jiangmen, Shaoguan, and Maoming, would pay an additional remittance above a fixed remittance at an annual increment rate of 7 percent and the remaining one, Zhanjiang, at 6 percent.

(d) Hainan, Shantou and three prefectures (Zhaoqing, Huiyang, and Meixian) that suffered from budget deficits would get a fixed amount of subsidies from the province. For minorities areas, they would have a fixed amount of subsidies with an annual increment of 10 percent.

During the third phase (1988–1993), no drastic changes were introduced in subprovincial fiscal management because contracting had become widely implemented. Modifications of the various contracts, however, were carried out because the central government had extracted more funds from the province as it suffered from serious deficits during the retrenchment period of 1989–1991. For instance, starting from 1988, the fiscal arrangement between the province and Guangzhou was changed to a fixed remittance contract of 1.83 billion yuan, with annual incremental remittance of 60 million yuan fixed for three years. In the 1988–1991 period, Guangzhou had to share a total of 305 million yuan as part of Guangdong's remittance to the Center.[124] Further, in order to discourage over-spending, deficit counties and cities would no longer get subsidies or loans easily from the provincial government; instead, those units which could achieve a balanced budget would get a reward.[125]

Subprovincial Fiscal Changes since 1994

Subprovincial fiscal management, however, also underwent important changes with the introduction of the tax-sharing system in 1994. Similar to the revenue sharing between the Center and the province, the provincial government defined a set of fixed income, such as the business taxes from the financial sector and the income tax of provincial enterprises as provincial fixed revenue, whereas cities and counties would also have its fixed revenue such as income from enterprises under their ownership, the business tax, as well as a host of other taxes like the resources tax. Of the shared revenue, the most important concerned the VAT because the province could only claim 25 percent after sharing with the Center.[126] While the province seized the VAT from some of the biggest provincial enterprises such as the Guangzhou Petro-chemical Plant, it allowed cities and counties to share the remaining VAT. Further, the province would still share some of the taxes from a number of other areas with subprovincial units, such as 50 percent of stamp duties, 25 percent of land-use tax in urban areas, and 50 percent of above-1993 base figure since 1994, as well as 19 percent of land-use tax for arable land and 20 percent of above-1993 increment since 1994.

Contrary to the central government's centralizing efforts, the process of adjusting subprovincial fiscal relations was carried out incrementally. Instead of applying the tax-sharing regime immediately to the cities and counties, the strategy of Guangdong's leadership was to maintain the basic features of the contracting system with the cities in the interim period. In other words, the provincial leadership had attempted to take into account the vested interests of these lower levels and preserve the flexibility allowed in the previous contracting systems but raised the actual amount of remittance in view of its obligations to the Center.[127] Xie Fei and Zhu Senlin had prepared meticulously for implementing the new system in the province. Six major meetings were convened by the provincial party Committee and provincial government from late September until the end of December 1994.[128]

The provincial government allowed a more moderate approach in subprovincial fiscal management since 1994. This deliberate, conciliatory approach was based on the provincial leadership's pragmatic and strategic considerations. The continuation of contracting with cities was pragmatic because officials from cities and counties had voiced their concern over the TSS. But the provincial leaders' approach was also strategic because the fiscal contracting with subprovincial units was the key to rapid local economic development. The contracting system not only allowed a greater degree of fiscal, and hence policy autonomy, but also generated more incentives for collecting more revenue as above-contract remittances would be kept by these units. Since the TSS might hurt local revenue, the province did not simply extract resources from subprovincial units. First, using the 1992 revenue as a baseline, the provincial government would only use about 15 percent of the above-1992 figure of subprovincial revenue while allowing cities and counties to keep the remaining 85 percent. The 15 percent would be extracted in accordance with the economic circumstances of the cities. Four rates, namely 20 percent, 15 percent, 10 percent, and 0 percent would be differentially applied to different localities. Second, the 1993 increment over the 1992 baseline would then be included into the 1993 baseline as a new baseline for remittance for two years. Third, regarding the transfer of the VAT and consumption tax from the Center to the province, the provincial government would share with cities and counties in accordance with a 0.1:0.20 ratio. Provincial revenue obtained through these various channels was estimated to be around 1.4 billion yuan, which would be used in agriculture, education, science, public health, law and order, and anti-poverty programs. The subsidies to the poorer areas would remain the same despite the introduction of TSS. To sum up, while seeking additional remittances from the localities so that the province could adapt to the new TSS, the provincial leadership under Xie Fei and Zhu Senlin had tried to limit the impact of the new fiscal reform to a minimum through a number of compromises with the cities and counties. Nonetheless, fiscal reform in Guangdong, important as it is, still cannot account for the huge amount of resources that were made available for economic development since 1979. Two other major sources of resources concern domestic and foreign investment. Since Guangdong's attraction of foreign capital and investment has received extensive analysis, the following discussion focuses more on the domestic mobilization and allocation of investment resources.

Resource Mobilization Through Investment Reform

The massive investment in Guangdong's infrastructure and technical capacity was critical to its phenomenal economic growth since 1979.[129] Guangdong's investment in fixed asset, which consisted mainly of investment in capital construction and technical renovation, increased at a staggering rate of 30 percent during the 1979–1995 period. Such investment jumped sharply from 2.8 billion yuan in 1978 to 38.11 billion yuan in 1990 and a record 232.7 billion yuan in 1995 (for details, see Table 2.6).[130] Consequently, the share of Guangdong in China's total investment in fixed assets rose sharply from 4.2 percent in 1981 to 7.3 percent in 1985 and 12 percent in 1995.[131] In the 1979–1995 period, the province also managed to secure a record US$ 52.9 billion of foreign capital and investment, about one-quarter of the total amount acquired by the whole country, of which 74 percent was in foreign direct investment, 22 percent in loans, and 4 percent in other forms.[132] Aside from enhancing production capacity, the massive amount of investment brought about impressive upgrading of Guangdong's infrastructure, especially in electricity generation, telecommunications and transportation since the mid 1980s (see Table 2.7). For instance, the number of bridges increased more than 60 percent, the length of roads increased 65 percent, the amount of electricity generated jumped almost seven times, and the number

Table 2.6

Growth of Guangdong's Investment in Fixed Assets, 1979–1995

	Total invest- ment	(a) Capital construct.	(b) Tech. renovat.	(c) Real estate	(d) Others	(e) Coll.	(f) Individ.
1981–1985	54.88	24.69	9.83	—	0.89	7.22	12.25
1986–1990	154.99	68.03	28.22	12.91	2.21	21.84	21.79
1991–1995	749.82	285.74	87.48	145.98	45.28	104.37	80.97
1991	47.82	21.48	7.49	4.96	0.36	7.12	6.40
1992	92.18	33.87	12.86	12.56	1.05	20.93	10.91
1993	162.98	54.66	18.39	31.65	17.53	23.97	16.78
1994	214.12	85.13	23.18	40.41	14.91	28.39	22.08
1995	232.72	90.60	25.56	56.39	11.44	23.95	24.79

Sources: Guangdongsheng tongjiju (ed.), *Guangdong tongji nianjian 1996* (Statistical Yearbook of Guangdong 1996) (Beijing: Zhongguo tongji chubanshe, 1996), p. 260.

Note: Unit = billion yuan; total investment = total societal investment; coll. = collective investment in both rural and urban areas; individ. = individual investments in both rural and urban areas.

of telephones owned rose twenty times between 1985 and 1995. The following section examines Guangdong's investment record, strategies and mechanisms in mobilizing and allocating investment, and various problems in its investment process.

The Record

Similar to other coastal provinces, Guangdong received little central investment in the prereform era because its coastal location was vulnerable to foreign military attack. Consequently, Guangdong suffered from the lack of a strong industrial base as well as insufficient infrastructural facilities, both of which greatly constrained its economic growth. For instance, during the 1953–1975 period, the share of Guangdong in China's total investment in fixed assets was small (about 3 to 4 percent of the national total), which was lower than that of such provinces as Hebei, Liaoning, Heilongjiang and Sichuan.[133] The central government did not invest in any major, technologically advanced projects in the province.[134] None of the 156 projects sponsored by the Soviet Union in the 1950s was located in the province. Of the 26 major industrial facilities introduced from overseas in 1972, only one, Guangzhou's Petro-chemical Plant, was in Guangdong, but none of the 22 whole plant facilities brought from abroad in 1978 benefited the province. The absence of central investment prompted Guangdong's leaders to look for alternative ways to obtain investment when the reform era promised new hopes and opportunities.

In the reform era, Guangdong's pattern of investment exhibited a number of

Table 2.7

Select Indicators of Guangdong's Infrastructural Development

	1985	1990	1995	1995/1985	1995/1990
Local Railways (kilometers)	323	323	1,177	364%	364%
Roads (kilometers)	51,288	54,671	84,563	165%	155%
No. of Berths	1,219	1,938	2,709	222%	140%
No. of 10,000–ton Berths	36	61	93	258%	152%
Bridges (permanent)	9,797	10,996	15,806	161%	144%
Electricity (10,000 kilowatt)	25	74	178	691%	242%
Petroleum pipelines (kilometers)	182	182	324	178%	178%
Telephones	356,792	1,554,259	7,299,340	2,046%	470%

Sources: Guangdongsheng tongjiju (ed.), *Guangdong tongji nianjian 1996* (Statistical Yearbook of Guangdong 1996) (Beijing: Zhongguo tongji chubanshe, 1996), pp. 243, 245, and 259; *Guangdong tongji nianjian 1992*, pp. 213, 215, and 229.

Table 2.8

Composition of Investment in Fixed Assets in Guangdong (total = 100 percent)

	Capital construction	Technical renovation	Real estate investment	Collective investment	Individual investment	Others
1981–1985	44.9	17.0	—	13.2	22.3	1.6
1986–1990	43.9	18.2	8.3	14.1	14.1	1.4
1991–1995	38.2	11.7	19.5	13.9	10.8	6.0

Source: Guangdongsheng tongjiju (ed.), *Guangdong tongji nianjian 1996* (Statistical Yearbook of Guangdong 1996) (Beijing: Zhongguo tongji chubanshe, 1996), p. 260.

distinctive features. First, during the 1979–1995 period, Guangdong's investment in fixed assets increased at an annual rate of 30 percent, which was substantially higher than the annual GDP growth rate of 14 percent or the industrial growth rate of 22 percent.[135] Such a huge inflow of investment was thus a key source of Guangdong's rapid economic growth. The growth rates of investment in capital construction and technical innovation in the state sector, still the most important areas of fixed investment, were respectively 26.0 percent and 32.3 percent per annum during this period, which were higher than that of the other provinces. Second, the composition of investment in fixed assets also shifted since 1979 as capital construction and technical innovation, especially by the state sector, were no longer as dominant as in the prereform era. For instance, investment in these two areas fell from 62 percent of total investment in the 1981–1985 period to only 50 percent in the 1990s (see Table 2.8). Further, the share of investment in technical renovation in the total, which was around 17 percent in the 1980s, fell to only 12 percent in the 1990s while real estate development rose sharply to almost one-fifth of total investment.

Third, the source of investment also experienced radical changes since 1979 (see Table 2.9). Especially for investment in capital construction and technical renovation, the share of budgetary allocations, the most important source of investment in the prereform era, dropped sharply since 1979, falling rapidly from 45 percent in 1980 to 10 percent in 1985 and only 2 percent in 1995! Instead, the proportion of self-raised funds in such investment had risen significantly from 37 percent in 1980 to over 50 percent in 1995. As the investment system underwent reform, domestic lending had emerged as an important source of capital, accounting for about 20 percent of such investment in the 1980s. However, foreign investment had surpassed domestic lending as the second important source of funding since the late 1980s. The share of foreign capital in Guangdong's total investment in capital construction and technical renovation rose from about 6

Table 2.9

Sources of Guangdong's Investment in Capital Construction and Technical Renovation, selected years (unit = percent)

	Budgetary funding	Domestic lending	Foreign investment	Self-raised funds	Others
1980	44.6	12.9	5.8	36.7	—
1985	10.6	28.2	13.1	39.6	8.6
1990	6.0	19.6	18.9	38.2	17.3
1995	2.0	15.0	22.2	50.6	10.2

Sources: Guangdongsheng tongjiju (ed.), *Guangdong tongji nianjian 1996* (Statistical Yearbook of Guangdong 1996) (Beijing: Zhongguo tongji chubanshe, 1996), p. 259; *Guangdong tongji nianjian 1992*, p. 229.

Note: These two kinds of investment contributed respectively 68.5%, 61.5%, and 50% of Guangdong's total investment in fixed assets in 1985, 1990 and 1995. The remaining investments referred to those in real estate, individual investments, collective investments and others.

percent in 1980 to 13 percent in 1985 and 22 percent in 1995.[136] By 1995, foreign capital and investment already accounted for 24 percent of investment in capital construction and 16 percent of investment in technical renovation.[137]

Finally, similar to the experience in other areas, extra-budgetary funds (EBFs) constituted another important source of investment in fixed assets. Extra-budgetary revenue rose from 2.9 billion yuan in 1982 to 9.8 billion yuan in 1990 while extra-budgetary expenditure increased respectively from about 3.4 billion yuan to 9.2 billion yuan.[138] For instance, during the 1986–1990 period, of the accumulated 35.7 billion yuan of EBFs spent, about 30 percent (10.7 billion yuan) was used for investment in fixed assets.[139] This amount accounted for roughly 11 percent of total investment during this period. By seeking as many preferential policies from the central government as possible and encouraging local initiatives and expanding local discretion, the provincial leadership managed to mobilize a huge amount of domestic and foreign investment outside of the restrictive planning system while building up support from local levels for economic reform within a short period of time. Guangdong crafted a wide variety of strategies and mechanisms to mobilize investment, only four of which will be examined below because of the limitation of space.

Lobbying the Central Government for More Investment Power

Guangdong's leaders have consistently, and often successfully, lobbied the central government for more power over the acquisition of foreign as well as domestic investment since 1979.[140] In the first policy package issued in the 1979–1981 period, the province was not only granted the fiscal contract discussed earlier, but it was also given autonomy to decide on its own budgetary priorities and development plan. In return, the province would be responsible for its own capital investment without much support from the central government. Aside from establishing the SEZs and gaining other economic powers, the province was given power to approve foreign investment projects in export-processing, compensation trade and joint ventures that did not affect national balances (in funding and material supply) and utilize foreign investment in infrastructure. Further, additional financial powers, such as the power to issue bonds and stocks and to establish an investment firm in Hong Kong as a vehicle to absorb foreign capital, were granted. More privileges in the issuance of bank loans were also offered to Guangdong. In order to promote its energy and transport sectors, the province was authorized to exempt tax and withhold profit remittance for enterprises in the infrastructural sectors. Such powers were indeed unprecedented in the history of the PRC.

The second batch of central preferential policies for Guangdong, issued as State Council document No. 46 in 1985, further confirmed and expanded its privileges.[141] The province could approve on its own investment projects that were built with self-raised funds, although the scale of their investment would still be incorporated into the national plan. In particular, the province could approve projects of capital construction up to 200 million yuan, an amount equivalent to the approval ceiling to be decided by the State Planning Commission (SPC) in association with the State Council, as long as they did not affect the national plan. Nonetheless, this provision could not be put into full practice because of economic retrenchment in 1985.[142] The province's approval ceiling for technical renovation projects was set at 30 million yuan, which was again the same as that of the SPC. By mid-1985, therefore, Guangdong's leaders were already able to secure more favorable treatment from the Center over investment than other provinces.

Another boost in Guangdong's investment authority was achieved in 1988. The province's investment authority was further raised in the third package of special policies approved by the Center. Although this policy package, i.e. State Council Correspondence No. 25 issued in February 1988, was not fully implemented because of deflationary policies introduced since late 1988, the province's investment authority was already raised in this document. In fact, since the earlier approval power of 200 million yuan could not be exercised as a result of central control since 1985, Guangdong asked for raising the investment approval ceiling to 100 million yuan in the first request. After getting a favorable reception from Zhao Ziyang and the Central Economic and Finance Small Leading Group, however, the province submitted a final request which asked for raising the ceiling to 200 million yuan and getting the power to decide on total investment scale for projects that did not affect national planning. This request was approved because Guangdong's leaders were able to lobby Zhao Ziyang and other central leaders at an opportune time when Zhao wanted to allow the province a greater role in his emerging coastal development strategy.[143] Nonetheless, as economic overheating led to another retrenchment since the last quarter of 1988, these privileges could not be fully exercised. Still, this episode illustrates the extent to which an effective provincial leadership was able to seize preferential treatment from the central government.

Similarly, Guangdong's leaders also aggressively argued for expanding investment authority over overseas capital, which constituted a new but increasingly important source of funding. For instance, while the privilege of establishing the SEZs was already quite substantial, these zones were too small to make a big difference. In 1984, Guangdong was able to get two of its cities, Guangzhou and Zhanjiang, included in the list of fourteen coastal open cities. Guangzhou was also granted the status of a city separately in the plan (*jihua danlieshi*) from 1985 to 1993. More importantly, Guangzhou's foreign investment power was raised from US$ 5 million in the early 1980s to US$ 10 million in October 1984.[144] In the special policy (i.e. State Council Document No. 46) approved in 1985, Guangdong was allowed to approve productive projects with foreign investment up to US$ 10 million while there would be no ceiling for non-productive projects. But by 1988, Guangdong's approval ceiling for productive projects was raised three times to US$ 30 million.

The persistent lobbying by Guangdong's leaders for enlarging provincial power over both domestic and foreign investment has significant implications. On the one hand, more power over investment enabled the province to fully decide on projects without the bureaucratic delay caused by going through central government agencies. Many central government agencies were not receptive to economic reform because their own prerogative over economic management would be severely weakened. In particular, the investment ceiling could hardly offer an effective control because these projects could be broken into several components, hence effectively bypassing the central government, and as a result of further decentralization of investment power from the province to the localities, effective central monitoring became exceptionally difficult, if not impossible. On the other hand, by shielding investment projects from the central government, Guangdong attempted to avoid, or at least alleviate, the regular and disruptive central retrenchment policies that curbed provincial investment. Such retrenchment, often imposed through administrative control, not only caused uncertainties over central policy toward investment but also seriously affected construction and planning.[145] Last but not least, empowering subprovincial authorities through fiscal and investment policies proved to be a very effective instrument in rallying local support for reform and development initiatives. For a province bigger than South Korea or most European nations in size and population, reliance on local initiatives seemed to be a far more appropriate strategy than a master provincial development plan. In view of the regular policy reversals and deprivation of central investments in the prereform era and the emerging contention between the reformist and conservative leaders at the central level in the reform era, Guangdong leaders' strategy was proven to be rather effective under such a precarious policy environment.

Decentralization of Investment Authority

Aside from seeking central preferential treatment, Guangdong's leaders adopted a "decentralization" strategy to investment, namely by delegation of administrative and economic powers to sub-provincial governments so that they would be encouraged to explore the best strategy in view of their own circumstances. This strategy began with Ren Zhongyi, but was basically followed by his successors. Four former consultants to Guangdong's provincial government summed up this strategy well: all powers belonging to the provincial level would be decentralized to the city (prefecture) level and all power available to the city level would be decentralized to the county level.[146] Since Guangdong could not change China's centrally planned economy overnight, one remedy was to loosen the straitjacket of the old system by decentralizing as much power, especially the prerogative to approve investments, as possible within the constraints of the existing policy framework in order to stimulate local development initiative. This strategy also encouraged all kinds of economic and administrative reform because the local authorities would have to shoulder the responsibility to promote economic growth, mobilize resources for development and attract foreign investment. By further decentralizing investment approval and other related powers to subprovincial governments, central monitoring of Guangdong's investment activities would also become even more tenuous. On the other hand, the provincial government relaxed its control over subprovincial governments in other ways, such as stopping the mandatory targets over labor planning and wage level, so that cities and counties could make their own economic decisions within a much broader policy framework. Coupled with the fiscal contract whereby subprovincial governments would be responsible for their own expenditure after fulfilling the remittance of a contracted sum, this strategy helped sub-provincial units to support enterprises with a more flexible financial arrangement.

Guangdong's leaders also used other decentralizing strategies to circumvent central policies and facilitate local initiatives. Although widely criticized by some researchers, "loan payment before tax payment" for enterprises was a practice that was widely undertaken in Guangdong and some other provinces since 1979. This basically meant that enterprises would pay less tax because tax regulations would be "softened" and greater discretionary power would be given to local authorities. Party Secretary Lin Ruo even openly endorsed this practice and maintained that whether to continue this practice would be at the discretion of the cities as long as it was approved under proper procedures and the localities could fulfill their quota in fiscal remittance to the province.[147] Localities might also resort to other tax evasion or tax leniency measures in order to attract foreign investment or boost local industrial production. Allowing enterprises to retain more profits at their disposal provided enterprises with much-needed funds for technical renovation or further investment when the demand for capital became increasingly strong in the province in the 1980s.

Expansion of Preferential Policies over Acquisition
of Foreign Capital

Another important strategy adopted by Guangdong's leaders in mobilizing resources was to attract all sorts of foreign capital and investment.[148] In contrast to the periodic crackdown on excessive domestic investment, the acquisition of foreign investment would not be subject to investment quotas issued by the central government, which consistently favored the attraction of overseas funding as a key component of its open policy.[149] In particular, during periods of retrenchment, such as 1989–1991, Guangdong's provincial leaders also encouraged domestic investment projects to link up with foreign investment so that they could be exempted from central restrictions.[150]

To the envy of other provinces, Guangdong has consistently and often successfully lobbied for the expansion of central preferential policies over foreign investment in the reform era as this constituted one of the essential elements of the special policies.[151] Guangdong's provincial leaders were able to secure central support and applied such special policies to an increasing number of localities throughout the province since 1979. Such efforts were reflected, for instance, in the establishment of three SEZs (Shenzhen, Zhuhai, and Shantou) in 1979, the designation of Guangzhou and Zhanjiang as coastal open cities in 1984, the establishment of Economic Development and Technological Zones in Guangzhou and Zhanjiang in 1984 and in Dayawan (or Daya Bay, under Huizhou city) and Nansha (under Panyu city, one of Guangzhou's subordinate units) in 1993, the designation of about 59 smaller development zones (such as hi-tech, tourist, and bonded zones), as well as the incorporation of the Pearl River Delta into the Pearl River Delta Open Economic Area.[152] These areas were all able to enjoy varying degrees of preferential treatment over foreign trade and the acquisition of foreign investment.

As early as 1983, Governor Liang Lingguang sought to open up the entire Pearl River Delta, but it was only after getting support from Zhao Ziyang and Gu Mu were more concrete measures formulated. Zhao's visit to the Pearl River Delta in December 1994 prompted him to open up not just the Pearl River Delta, but also the Yangtze Delta and other peninsulas.[153] Backed by Gu Mu, Guangdong's leaders asked for applying the same preferential policies of the fourteen coastal open cities to the Pearl River Delta, which received central support as part of the opening up of the Yangtze, Pearl River and Minnan deltas in February 1985. The Pearl River Delta Open Economic Area was later expanded from a total of 4 cities and 12 counties in 1985 to 28 cities and counties in 1987.[154] The area's total investment in fixed assets amounted to 149 billion yuan, which was higher than that invested in the entire Shandong province, while foreign capital and investment actually acquired was US$ 8.5 billion, which was higher than the combined sum utilized by Shanghai and Jiangsu![155] Riding the tide of the open policy since Deng's southern tour in 1992, Guangdong was again able to utilize this golden opportunity to attract foreign investment. Three cities in the mountainous region—Shaoguan, Heyuan and Meizhou—were allowed to adopt preferential policies of the coastal open areas.[156] By the early 1990s, the most economically vibrant areas of Guangdong were all receiving some sort of preferential policies, including investment approval power, the power to issue bonds and shares, greater authority over foreign trade, and preferential tax treatment for foreign investment, especially in energy, ports, and other technology-intensive projects. In short, by securing support from pro-reform leaders in the Center and expanding preferential policies from the SEZs to the entire Pearl River Delta and beyond, the provincial leadership was able to fully exploit the opportunities of China's open policy.

In addition to attracting foreign direct investment, negotiating foreign loans or getting investment in export processing, Guangdong was empowered by the special policies to set up investment corporations in Hong Kong and elsewhere in order to facilitate its acquisition of foreign capital. Developing business ties with Hong Kong brought many advantages. On the one hand, Hong Kong companies that invested in Guangdong had access to the financial market in Hong Kong and elsewhere for funding investments in the province. On the other hand, Guangdong's provincial and subprovincial governments were able to establish offices in Hong Kong in order to absorb foreign investment and explore other business opportunities.[157] Guangdong Enterprise (Holdings) Ltd., wholly owned by the Guangdong provincial government, has already emerged as a leading company with a diverse portfolio in Hong Kong since the 1980s. It is also the parent company of several other companies in Hong Kong, including Guangdong Investment (GDI), a company listed in the Hong Kong stock market with assets valued at HK$ 11.17 billion in 1995. Similarly, other local governments from Guangdong have also set foot in the territory. For instance, Yue Xiu Enterprises, owned by the Guangzhou municipal government, was established in Hong Kong in 1985 as a trading and investment house. One of its subsidiaries, Guangzhou Investment, was listed in Hong Kong with assets valued at HK$ 9.1 billion in 1995. In sum, central preferential policies enabled Guangdong to forge extensive links with Hong Kong far ahead of other areas and to utilize fully the opportunities in overseas financing in the reform era.

Experimenting with New Mechanisms for Infrastructural Investment

In order to finance infrastructural projects when budgetary allocations could hardly meet the needs created by high-speed economic growth, Guangdong's leaders formulated a host of new fund-raising strategies.[158] First, owing to the shortage of electricity exacerbated by rapid economic growth, Guangdong's provincial government set up various funds to finance electricity generation since the mid 1980s. While maintaining overall management of the electricity networks, the provincial government introduced a number of reform measures, including the delegation of power to the provincial Electricity Bureau over management and approval of electricity projects, adoption of the contracting system for the electricity sector, exemption of various taxes related to electricity generation, and provision of subsidies for sub-provincial governments affected by such shortfalls in revenue.[159] Various partnerships between the provincial government and lower-level governments (or parties) were also formed to facilitate the mobilization of investment. While encouraging cities and counties to build up their own smaller-scale electricity plants, the provincial government also enticed cities and counties to contribute funds to the construction of provincial-level electric networks by guaranteeing them user rights in return. The provincial government set up an electricity share-holding company in August 1984 to attract subprovincial governments or enterprises to invest in this sector. These units could enjoy membership in the board of directors of this company in accordance with the amount of their contributions.[160] Surcharges were also imposed on electricity consumers in order to build up a specialized fund, the Electricity Development Fund, to finance such infrastructural projects. In 1986–1990, investment in power generation amounted to 8.28 billion yuan, about eight times higher than that in the 1981–1985 period.[161]

Second, beginning from the early 1980s when Ren Zhongyi was in power, he encouraged the borrowing of money from banks as the initial construction funds for building roads and bridges and then repaid these loans with toll fees and surcharges.[162] After the successful completion of the first bridge using Hong Kong funds in 1983–1984, the provincial government quickly learned the benefits of borrowing for infrastructural projects. This strategy was so successful that it was emulated all over Guangdong. During 1985–1990, for instance, over 5,000 bridges were built in the province by using mostly domestic loans. Starting from 1985, the provincial government further introduced other measures to augment funding for these projects, including the imposition of a surcharge on passengers to build up a road construction fund and a road maintenance fee as well as a special toll fee for using newly constructed bridges. Surcharges on passengers were used to raise funds for highway construction while surcharges on the use of gasoline and diesel as well as the use of urban land were used to fund transportation projects such as highways, railroads, ports, and airports. Similar to the case of power generation, local governments were also encouraged to participate in such infrastructural development.

Third, special policies granted by the central government allowed Guangdong to aggressively absorb foreign investment in infrastructural development, especially in electricity generation, highway construction, telecommunications, ports and other projects. For instance, aside from building several major power plants, Hong Kong tycoon Gordon Wu's Hopewell Holdings adopted the build-operate-transfer (BOT) method to build the 123–km superhighway linking Guangzhou and Shenzhen.[163] The Daya Bay Nuclear Plant, Guangdong's first nuclear power plant, was constructed with the participation of Hong Kong's China Light and

Power Company, which enjoyed a 25 percent share.[164] Fourth, the provincial government also adopted various new financial arrangements to expand funding for capital construction, including the issuance of stocks and bonds, because the province had an increasing amount of household savings accumulated from years of rapid growth. As Lin Ruo has aptly pointed out, these fund-raising schemes were particularly useful when the central government imposed restrictions on bank lending.[165] Following the relaxation of control over real estate in the late 1980s, another more recent method to raise funds for construction has been the development of real estate near the sites of ports, airports and terminals, a practice that was widely popular in Hong Kong.

Achievements and Problems

Guangdong's decentralization strategy had served the province well in the 1980s. However, such an approach also made it very difficult for the provincial government to coordinate investment efforts. Four inter-related problems were particularly obvious by the mid 1990s. First, the efficiency of investment in Guangdong was unsatisfactory because local governments, rather than enterprises or entrepreneurs, remained the driving force of investment. Various indicators showed that the efficiency of Guangdong's investment in fixed assets was declining. For instance, the amount of newly created national income generated per 100 yuan of investment in 1994 was only 32 percent, about 20 percent lower than the figure in 1991.[166] As sharply pointed out by two Guangdong researchers from the Provincial Planning Commission,

> under the current system, various levels of governments and their leaders are eager to compete for projects and funding. If they successfully compete for projects and funding, that means they have performance. If the projects are successfully implemented, their performance is even better . . . If the projects are not successfully implemented, no one is responsible . . . the government and collectives have to shoulder the losses and the burden.[167]

Second, the investment in Guangdong, though massive, failed to strengthen a few targeted industrial sectors. Despite rapid industrial growth in the reform era, the province's industrial structure remained quite fragmented. Of the key industries, only the following branches contributed more than 5 percent of total industrial output: chemicals (5.3 percent), clothing and textile (6.2 percent), food and beverages (7.5 percent), electronics and communication equipment (18.5 percent), electrical machinery and equipment (11.6 percent).[168] Guangdong's automobile industry, despite support from the provincial government, failed to establish a reputation in China's domestic market. Guangdong's R & D capacity remained to be improved. Only one-third of Guangdong's large and medium-sized enterprises had R & D units, while the national average was 51 percent.

The number of technicians and scientists per 10,000 population was 12.7 in Guangdong, about ten times lower than that of Shanghai and even lower than the national average and other coastal provinces.[169] Guangdong's researchers believed that the slow development of its technical base and fragmentation of its industrial structure were very unfavorable in the increasingly keen competition with other technologically advanced provinces.[170]

Third, investment in real estate since 1992 used an enormous amount of funds that should have been used more effectively and created a long-term problem that defied easy solution. During 1991–1995, investment in industry grew at 27.3 percent per annum while that in real estate increased at a staggering 76.7 percent.[171] Real estate investment shot up from 3 billion yuan in 1990 to a staggering 12.5 billion yuan in 1992 and 56.4 billion yuan in 1995 (see Table 2.8). Starting from 1992, such investment surpassed the amount spent on technical renovation and had become twice the size of the latter by 1995 (see Table 2.6). Many of these development projects in the Pearl River Delta were stopped, if not completely abandoned, because of the lack of sufficient demand and the imposition of macro-economic control by the central government since mid-1993. The decentralized investment system formed in the reform era made it possible for sub-provincial authorities to make very risky investments on a grand scale.

Finally, another conspicuous consequence of Guangdong's experience was the duplication in infrastructural development, especially in the Pearl River Delta. In view of the imminent improvement in road transport, especially the completion of the Guangzhou-Shenzhen-Zhuhai expressway, experts questioned the wisdom for each city in the delta building one or more ports.[172] For instance, aside from half a dozen smaller ports for freight in the delta, three major deep water ports—Yantian port in Shenzhen, Huizhou port in Daya Bay, and Gaolan port in Zhuhai—were being built in the 1990s. All these facilities were located in the vicinity of Hong Kong, which already accommodated the busiest container terminal in the world and handled about 80 percent of the mainland's exports. Similarly, at least eight airports were built within a parameter of 200 square kilometers in the Pearl River Delta. Although Hong Kong's modern Chek Lap Kok airport would be opened in spring 1998, three international airports located in Macau, Shenzhen, and Zhuhai were already completed in the 1994–1995 period. With the growing improvement of sea and land transport, whether these international airports in the delta can achieve efficiency is rather questionable. The lack of effective coordination among localities in infrastructural investment made it very difficult to achieve the economies of scale.

Conclusion: Whither Guangdong?

In stark contrast to the early 1990s when the overseas media portrayed Guangdong as the future model for China, perceptive analysts are writing about its deteriorating economic and investment environments, as reflected in poor administration, lack of respect for rules and regulations, rising labor and land costs, environmental degradation, inefficient use of capital as well as inadequate supply of qualified professional and technical staff.[173] Many challenges ahead will offer an astute test for Guangdong's present and future leaders.

First, as the relationship between Guangdong's leaders and the central government in the 1990s was not as intimate as in the 1980s, the influence of the provincial leaders vis-a-vis the Center has declined. Shanghai and the Yangtze Delta have now replaced Guangdong as the key area for policy support by the central government. Shanghai is also the power base of many central leaders such as Jiang Zemin, Zhu Rongji and Wu Bangguo. On the other hand, Guangdong's growing economic strength also makes it difficult to claim more special treatment from the Center. Inland provinces critical of the preferential policies granted to the coastal areas are also becoming increasingly vocal about their backwardness and pleading for more central support. In 1995, such anger was vented against Shenzhen by various critics.[174] As a result of the rise of a new central leadership, the universalization of open door policies all over China and the growing inter-regional disparities, Guangdong will find it hard to seek special treatment from the central government in the future.

Second, Guangdong will have to explore a new development strategy because the ill consequences of excessive economic decentralization have become amply evident. In a study of the social and political consequences of economic growth in Guangdong, I have highlighted the tensions and difficulties caused by uneven development inside Guangdong and between it and other nearby regions, the rise of collective conflicts, the deterioration of public order, and the slow development of a reliable administrative and legal framework as some of the most critical challenges facing this former star of China's reform era.[175] To be sure, the provincial leaders tried to consolidate investment and coordinate development strategies of the localities in the Pearl River Delta by setting up the Pearl River Delta Economic Region under direct provincial supervision in 1994, but whether effective coordination can be achieved remains to be seen. Unless the provincial leaders are able to take a step ahead in administrative and legal reform, which is essential to the proper functioning of the increasingly marketized economy and its competition for foreign investment with other coastal regions, it is unclear whether Guangdong's rapid growth can be sustained in the longer run.

Finally, although the return of Hong Kong to China after July 1, 1997 and the growing interdependence between the territory and Guangdong have fueled hopes of greater prosperity in the South China region, overseas investment has actually been diverted to other growth poles along China's "gold coast." For instance, total foreign investment acquired by Shanghai already jumped 1.6 times from US$ 3.2 billion in 1992 to US$ 5.3 billion in 1995.[176] If the figures of the three provinces of the Yangtze Delta—Jiangsu, Zhejiang, and Shanghai— were put together, the total foreign investment utilized by this "Greater Shanghai area" had already shot up from US$ 7 billion in 1993 to US$ 9.3 billion in 1995 and will likely surpass Guangdong in the near future. By the 1990s, Guangdong's pioneering efforts in reform and opening were widely copied by other areas in China. Coupled with the erosion of Guangdong's edge in preferential policies and labor-intensive manufacturing and the deterioration of its investment environment, even Hong Kong's labor-intensive processing operations may move out of Guangdong.

Guangdong's decentralizing reform strategy has jump-started rapid economic growth in the past seventeen years, but by the mid-1990s, the problems of inefficiency in investment, the duplication of infrastructural projects, the excessive investment in real estate and the lack of policy coordination among local authorities have become painfully evident. The light industrial products from Guangdong which once dominated the China market are now manufactured by other provinces ranging from Sichuan to Shandong, all of which are equally eager to get a share of this lucrative market. Further, these consumer goods are not likely to spearhead the next phase of China's economic growth. Guangdong does not seem to have an advantage in producing chemicals, pharmaceuticals, automobiles and other machinery equipment which are more competitively produced in other areas endowed with a more qualified workforce and a more solid technical base.

To be sure, Guangdong's recent leaders, such as Xie Fe, Zhu Senlin, and Lu Ruihua, were eagerly trying to find viable solutions. For instance, in early 1993, Party Secretary Xie Fei already postulated a three-pronged strategy (the so-called *"san ge san gongcheng"*)—(a) to establish three mechanisms, namely a socialist market economy, democracy and the rule of law, and clean government, (b) to strengthen three foundations, namely agriculture, transportation, energy and communication, as well as education, science and technology, and finally, (c) to improve Guangdong's industrial structure, ecology and environment, and quality of the people.[177] Similarly, provincial researchers pleaded for a "second industrial revolution" to foster pillar industries such as consumer appliances, automobiles, electronics, heavy chemicals and construction.[178] However, as Xie Fei aptly pointed out, "some of our cadres are only interested in special policies, but not enthusiastic about science and technology." He rightly concluded that with the exception of the SEZs, special policies could no longer provide the foundation for Guangdong's future development.[179] The results of such recent provincial efforts cannot be easily assessed, however. For instance, the benefits of an improved infrastructure cannot be immediately demonstrated right after the completion of such projects while recent investments in R & D and education can only yield concrete results in the longer run. On the other hand, inefficiency in management and investment cannot be easily rectified overnight while feasible solutions to newly emerging problems such as the gutted real estate market and the declining public order were yet to be identified. The success of Guangdong's industrial upgrading and restructuring depends not solely upon its own efforts, but also upon the catching up of other provincial competitors, developments in national politics, and international market changes, all of which are well beyond Guangdong's grasp. Recent shifts in central policy, as exemplified by restrictions over export processing and prohibition of such practices as "tax payment before loan payment" have further affected the business environment for Guangdong. Having experienced a period of exceptional economic growth and prosperity based on local autonomy and initiatives, to ask Guangdong's local officials and managers to chart a completely new developmental path would be a Herculean task.

Guangdong, though still an economic powerhouse in the post-Deng era, will no longer be the lone shining star of China's modernization drive in the future. Will the miracle of Guangdong come to an abrupt end? Will the provincial leadership deal effectively with the social and economic dilemmas that have emerged after years of rapid growth? Will they also manage to build up an administrative and legal structure which would make the province more competitive vis-a-vis other areas? The formulation of an innovative development strategy appropriate for Guangdong under the new circumstances is indeed indispensable. If a pioneering reform leadership was critical to the province's economic take-off in the past, maybe a different type of leadership would be needed to respond to the daunting economic and political challenges ahead.

Notes

An earlier draft of this paper was presented at the 47th Annual Meeting of the Association for Asian Studies in Washington, D.C. on April 6–9, 1995. I would like to thank the co-editors, Kevin Lane and other participants in the panel for valuable comments. Research for this chapter was sponsored by a CRCG grant from the University of Hong Kong.

1. Studies of Guangdong during the reform era in Chinese are too numerous to list; some of the most important works will be cited in this chapter. For analysis of Guangdong's reform and open policy in English, see Peter T.Y. Cheung, "The Case of Guangdong in Central-Provincial Relations," in Jia Hao and Lin Zhimin (eds.), *Changing Central-Local Relations in China: Reform and State Capacity* (Boulder: Westview Press, 1994), pp. 207–237 and "Pearl River Development," in Joseph Y.S. Cheng and Maurice Brosseau (eds.), *China Review 1993* (Hong Kong: Chinese University Press, 1993), pp. 18.1–18.29; Toyojiro Maruya (ed.), *Guangdong: "Open Door" Economic Development Strategy* (Hong Kong: Centre of Asian Studies, University of Hong Kong, and Tokyo: Institute of Developing Economies, 1992); Pak-Wai Liu, et al., *China's Economic Reform and Development Strategy of the Pearl River Delta* (Hong Kong: Nanyang Commercial Bank Ltd., 1992); Yeung Yueman and David Chu (eds.), *Guangdong: Survey of a Province under Rapid Change* (Hong Kong: Chinese University Press, 1994); Ezra Vogel, *One Step Ahead in China: Guangdong Under Reform* (Cambridge: Harvard University Press, 1989). For a bibliography of Guangdong under reform, see my bibliography in *Provincial China*, No. 1, March 1997, pp. 50–63. Also see Graham E. Johnson and Glen D. Peterson, *Historical Dictionary of Guangzhou and Guangdong* (London: Scarecrow Press, forthcoming).

2. For a detailed analysis of the evolution of these policies, see my chapter, "Relations between the Central Government and Guangdong," in Yeung and Chu (eds.), *Guangdong*, ch. 2.

3. Guangdongsheng tongjiju (ed.), *Guangdong tongji nianjian 1995 (Guangdong Sta-*

tistical Yearbook 1995) (Beijing: Zhongguo tongji chubanshe, 1995), p. 53. 1995 data will be included whenever available and appropriate.

4. Ibid, p. 93. The definition of the delta used here follows that of the Pearl River Delta Economic Zone (Zhujiang Sanjiaozhou Jingjiqu), which comprises a total of fourteen counties and cities.

5. Guojia tongjiju (ed.), *Zhongguo tongji nianjian 1995 (China Statistical Yearbook 1995)* (Beijing: Zhongguo tongji chubanshe, 1995), p. 33.

6. *Guangdong tongji nianjian 1996*, p. 94. These areas contributed 42 percent of the GVAO in Guangdong.

7. Guojia tongjiju (ed.), *A Statistical Survey of China 1996* (Beijing: Zhongguo tongji chubanshe, 1996), p. 60.

8. The biographical and historical data in this chapter, if unspecified, draw from Guangdong baikequanshu bianzuanweiyuanhui (ed.) *Guangdong baikequanshu (An Encyclopaedia of Guangdong)* (Beijing: Zhongguo daibaikequanshu chubanshe, 1995).

9. While Chen's hometown was later incorporated into Guangxi, it would still be appropriate to consider him a Cantonese.

10. Ezra Vogel, *Canton Under Communism* (New York: Harper and Row, 1969), ch. 4.

11. *Guangdong tongji nianjian 1996*, pp. 58–60.

12. Guojia tongjiju (ed.), *Zhongguo tongji nianjian 1996 (China Statistical Yearbook 1996)*, pp. 433–437.

13. *Guangdong tongji nianjian 1996*, pp. 89–90.

14. *Zhongguo tongji nianjian 1996*, pp. 288 and 302.

15. Ibid.

16. *Guangdong tongji nianjian 1996*, pp. 88–90.

17. This little known episode was recounted in Yu Jian, *Zhonghua renmin gongheguo lishijishi: gaige yangfan (1976–1984) (A Real Historical Account of the People's Republic of China)* (Beijing: Hongqi chubanshe, 1994), pp. 180–182.

18. Writing group of Huiyi Chen Yu Tongzhi (ed.), *Huiyi Chen Yu tongzhi (Remembering Comrade Chen Yu)* (Beijing: Gongren chubanshe, 1984), p. 226.

19. Lin Ruo et al., *Gaige kaifang zai Guangdong (Reform and Opening in Guangdong)* (Guangzhou: Guangdong gaodeng jiaoyu chubanshe, 1992), p. 39.

20. While it might be too early to classify Lu Ruihua, most indications suggest that he, too, could be considered a pioneer.

21. For instance, Guangzhou's former mayor, Li Ziliu, could well be considered a pioneer who was successful in promoting rapid growth for the city during his tenure. For a preliminary analysis of his development strategy, see my "Guangzhou's Municipal Leadership and Development Strategy in the 1990s," in Stewart MacPherson and Joseph Y.S. Cheng (eds.), *Economic and Social Development in South China* (Cheltenham: Edward Elgar, 1996), pp. 122–139.

22. Vogel's classic, *Canton Under Communism*, remains the best study of Guangdong politics in the prereform era.

23. Fang Shuo (ed.), *Ye Jianyingzhuan (A Biography of Ye Jianying)* (Beijing: Dangdaizhongguo chubanshe, 1995), p. 757.

24. Writing group of Huiyi Chen Yu tongzhi (ed.), *Huiyi Chen Yu tongzhi*, p. 218; Vogel, *Canton Under Communism*, p. 218.

25. Although he lost power, Chen still served as a member of the Provincial Revolutionary Committee until his death in 1974.

26. These included most notably the rehabilitation of Gu Dachun (1897–1966) and Feng Baiju (1903–1973), who led the 1956 rebellion in Hainan, in 1983 and Fang Fang (1904–1971) in 1994.

27. The data come from my paper, "Prosperity and Politics: Guangdong," presented to

the 92nd meeting of the American Political Science Association, San Francisco, Aug. 31, 1996.

28. Unless otherwise specified, data on personnel changes in this chapter draw from Liu Jintian and Shen Xueming (eds.), *Lijie zhonggong zhongyang weiyuan renming cidian (A Biographical Dictionary of Members of Central Committees)* (Beijing: Zhonggong dangshi chubanshe, 1992); the appendix in Ma Qibin, et al. (eds.), *Zhongguo gongchandang zhizheng sishinian (The Chinese Communist Party in Power for Forty Years)* (Beijing: Zhonggong dangshi chubanshe, 1991), pp. 587–618. Editorial Board of Who's Who in China (ed.), *Who's Who in China: Current Leaders* (Beijing: Foreign Languages Press, 1989 and 1994).

29. Interview with a retired provincial official, May 1994.

30. Vogel, *One Step Ahead*, pp. 88–90 and 314–317.

31. For a collection of his policy views, see Lin Ruo, *Zougou de lu—Guangdong gaige kaifang jicheng (A Path Already Taken—A Chronicle of Guangdong's Reform and Opening)* (Guangzhou: Guangdong gaodeng jiaoyu chubanshe, 1994).

32. Ibid., pp. 141–153.

33. Interview with a retired provincial official, May 1994.

34. Information provided by an informed source.

35. *Far Eastern Economic Review*, Feb. 22, 1996, p. 20.

36. The following information comes from my paper, "Prosperity and Politics." With the exception of the PLA officials of the Guangdong Military District, who were usually non-Guangdong cadres, all the members of the GPPCSC elected in 1983 and 1993 were already Guangdong natives or veteran Guangdong cadres.

37. For Gu's talk with Guangdong's leaders during the drafting stage of the special polices for Guangdong and Fujian in May 1979, see Zhonggong Guangdongshengwei bangongting (ed.), *Zhongyang dui Guangdong gongzuo zhishi huibian (A Compilation of Central Directives on Guangdong's Work) (hereafter ZDGGZH) (1978–1982)* (internal publication, 1988), pp. 9–17 and for comments by Hu and Wan, pp. 107–108.

38. Interview with a provincial official, November 1994.

39. Please refer to the section on fiscal reform.

40. The author had maintained contacts with relatives in Guangdong in the mid 1970s and had visited the province regularly in the reform era.

41. The key contents of these conversations were revealed in Ren's first major speech delivered after his arrival to Guangdong, "Jiefang sixiang, jiaqang tuanjie, ba guangdong jingji gaoshanqu" (Emancipate Thinking, Strengthen Unity, Strive To Upgrade Guangdong's Economy), *Dangdai Guangdong*, inaugural issue, 1995, pp. 12–17.

42. Please see my chapter in Yeung and Chu (eds.), *Guangdong*, ch. 2.

43. The difficulties in getting these policies are well documented in *ZDGGZH* (four volumes, 1988).

44. See Xi Zhongxun's preface in Lin Ruo, et al., *Gaige kaifang zai Guangdong*, p. 2.

45. Ibid., p. 3.

46. Ibid.

47. Ibid., p. 2.

48. The text of this document is in *ZDGGZH (1979–1982)*, pp. 20–30.

49. See *ZDGGZH (1986–1987), Vol. II* , pp. 384–386.

50. Liang Lingguang, *Liang Lingguang huiyilu (Liang Lingguang's Memoir)* (Beijing: Zhonggong dangshi chubanshe, 1996), pp. 561–562.

51. See note 41.

52. Vogel, *One Step Ahead*, p. 88.

53. Kuang Ji (ed.), *Dongdai Zhongguo de Guangdong (Guangdong in Contemporary China), Vol. I* (Beijing: Dangdai Zhonggguo chubanshe, 1991), p. 149.

54. See Liu Tianfu, "Guangdong zhixing teshu zhengce, linghuo cuoshi de huigu" (A Review of Guangdong's Implementation of Special Policies, Flexible Measures), *Dangdai Guangdong*, inaugural issue 1995, p. 18.

55. See Gu Mu's speech, *ZDGGZH (1979–1982)*, pp. 9–13.

56. *ZDGGZH (1979–1982)*, p. 110.

57. See Liu's account of the implementation of special policies in *Dangdai Guangdong*, inaugural issue 1995, pp. 18–41.

58. Interview, May 1994.

59. Because of the complexity of the issues involved and the lack of space, this chapter will focus on central-provincial fiscal relations and subprovincial fiscal management.

60. For studies of Guangdong's fiscal reform in Chinese, see, for instance, Huang Haichao, et al., *Mengxiang chengzhen (The Realization of Dreams: Guangdong Advancing to Market Economy)* (Guangzhou: South China University of Technology Press, 1993), ch.2 ; Kuang Ji (ed.), *Dangdai Zhongguo de Guangdong, Vol. I*, ch. 10; Lin Dengyu, "Guangdong caizheng gaige de youyi changshi," (Useful Trials in Guangdong's Fiscal System Reform," in Lin Ruo, et al., *Gaige kaifang zai Guangdong*, pp. 137 149; Lin Hanshu and Li Xinsheng, "Guangdong caizheng tixi gaige de goushi" (Thoughts on Guangdong's Fiscal System Reform), in Guangdong Renmin Zhengfu Bangongshi (ed.), *Gaige kaifang yu Guangdong (Reform, Opening, and Guangdong)* (Guangzhou: Guangdong renmin chubanshe, 1988), pp. 240–254.

61. This pattern of provincial remittance nonetheless began to change after 1975, which registered the highest level of remittance (1.74 billion yuan) in the 1952–1978 period.

62. See the sources in Table 2.5.

63. Zhonghua renmin gongheguo caizhengbu zhonghejihuasi (eds.), *Zhongguo caizheng tongji (1950–1985) (China's Financial Statistics)* (Beijing: Zhongguo caizheng jingji chubanshe, 1986), pp. 92 and 138.

64. *Guangdong tongji nianjian 1996*, p. 384.

65. On the expenditure side, Guangdong's annual increase of 18.2 percent was also much higher than the national average of 11 percent during the 1979–1993 period. See *Guangdong tongji nianjian 1994*, p. 626; *Zhongguo tongji nianjian 1994*, pp. 20–21.

66. Guojia tongjiju (ed.), *Dangdai Zhongguo zhizui (The Number Ones in China)* (Beijing: Zhongguo tongji chubanshe, 1994), p. 334.

67. *Guangdong tongji nianjian 1996*, pp. 385–386.

68. Guangdong nianjian bianzuanweiyuanhui (ed.), *Guangdong nianjian 1995* (Guangzhou: Guangdong nianjianshe, 1995), p. 387.

69. *Guangdong tongji nianjian 1996*, pp. 385–386; *Zhongguo tongji nianjian 1996*, pp. 221–222.

70. *Guangdong tongji nianjian 1996*, p. 386.

71. General Planning Department, Ministry of Finance, *China Finance Statistics (1950–1991)* (Beijing: Science Press, 1992), p. 157.

72. For a useful analysis of the content and importance of Guangdong's fiscal reform, see Wang Zou, et al., *Guangdong gaige kaifang pingshuo (Comments on Guangdong's Reform and Opening to the Outside World)* (Guangzhou: Guangdong renmin chubanshe, 1992), ch. 2.

73. *ZDGGZH (1979–1982)*, p. 67.

74. Huang, *Mengxiang chengzhen*, p. 31.

75. See the chapter by a former director of Guangdong's Financial Bureau, Lin Dengyun in Lin Ruo, et al., *Gaige kaifang zai Guangdong*, pp. 137–149.

76. See studies by researchers from the Ministry of Finance, Wei Liqun (ed.), *Central-Local Relations in the Market Economy* (Beijing: Zhongguo jingji chubanshe, 1994), pp. 45–62.

77. These practices, which were evidently not in line with central policy at that time, are now openly recognized by Guangdong scholars and officials. See Lin Ruo, et al., *Gaige kaifang zai Guangdong*, p. 140.

78. Ibid., p. 142.

79. Ibid., p. 143.

80. *Guangdong tongji nianjian 1995*, pp. 33–35.

81. For Zhao's views, see *ZDGGZH (1983–1985)*, pp. 248–262.

82. The text can be found in *ZDGGZH (1983–1985)*, pp. 377–385.

83. Please refer to my chapter in Yeung and Chu (eds.), *Guangdong*, ch. 2.

84. Kuang (ed.), *Dangdai Zhongguo de Guangdong*, p. 687; Huang, *Mengxiang chengzhen*, pp. 30–31.

85. Huang, *Mengxiang chengzhen*, pp. 30–31.

86. Ibid., p. 31.

87. The text is in *ZDGGZH (1986–1987) Vol. II*, p. 385.

88. Huang, *Mengxiang chengzhen*, p. 30–31.

89. All quotations are my own translation, see Lin Ruo, "Gaige kaifang yu Guangdong jingji di fazhan (Reform and Opening and Guangdong's Economic Development), *Qiushi*, No. 18, Sept. 16, 1989, p. 27.

90. Ibid., p. 29.

91. Ibid., p. 30.

92. Lin Ruo, "Several Points of Understanding on Developing the Socialist Commodity Economy," *Nanfang Ribao*, March 11, 1991, p. 3 in FBIS-CHI-91–054, March 20, 1991, p. 35.

93. This section draws selectively from my chapter in Jia Hao and Lin Zhimin (eds.), *Reform and State Capacity*, pp. 226–228.

94. As mentioned earlier, this basic remittance was scaled down to $778 million yuan in 1985 because of the recentralization of a number of provincial enterprises to the central government and the changes in taxation brought about by the tax-for-profit reform in 1984–1987.

95. The industrial and commercial tax was shared equally between the Center and Guangdong after exceeding a centrally decided baseline in the pre-1990 period, but it was turned into a source of central revenue since 1990.

96. *Guangdong nianjian 1988*, p. 77 and *Guangdong nianjian 1991*, p. 308.

97. Lin Dengyun in Lin Ru et al., *Gaige kaifang zai Guangdong* p. 138.

98. Wang Zou et al., *Guangdong gaige kaifang pingshuo* (Comments on Guandong's Reform and Opening to the Outside World) (Guangzhou: Guangdong renmin chubanshe, 1992), p. 74.

99. *Guangdong nianjian 1989*, p. 205.

100. Since the province has never openly published a detailed account of its remittances, there may still be missing figures or incomplete reporting. But these figures offer the best available information on this key issue.

101. Wang, *Guangdong gaige kaifang*, p. 62.

102. Christine Wong (ed.), *Financing Local Governments in the People's Republic of China* (Hong Kong: Oxford University Press, 1997), ch. 1.

103. The reform of central-provincial fiscal relation can be found in State Council Document No. 85 issued on Dec. 15, 1993. The full text is in *Caizheng*, No. 2, (1994), pp. 18–20.

104. There will be a different sharing formula for different kinds of resources, but the central government already laid claim to taxes from maritime petroleum.

105. For an analysis of the recent power struggle between the Center and the regions in the context of succession politics, see Willy Wo-lap Lam, *China After Deng Xiaoping* (H.K.: P. A. Professional Consultants Ltd., 1995), pp. 106–133.

106. Ibid., p. 121. Another informed source, however, suggested that instead of confronting Zhu Rongji themselves, Xie Fei and Zhu Senlin asked the executive vice governor, Lu Ruihua, to defend Guangdong's case. Zhu Rongji, as expected, did not budge. Interview in Hong Kong, March 1996.

107. Wang, *Guangdong gaige kaifang*, p. 80.

108. The best non-technical introduction to the tax-sharing reform is Christine Wong (ed.) *Financing Local Governments*, ch. 1.

109. These included the VAT, resources tax and some others. Interview with a scholar from Beijing in Hong Kong. February, 1995.

110. The author would like to express his deep thanks to Prof. Wang for sharing his insights on the TSS reform and providing a copy of his second article, "Tax Sharing System with Chinese Characteristics," in *Shanxi Development Herald*, January 21, 1994.

111. Wang later wrote a second article to Zhu explaining the rationale of the compromise solution, and Zhu not only endorsed this second article but also recommended this be published in the newspaper.

112. Reports in *Guangdong caizheng*, Oct. 5, 1994, pp. 4–5.

113. Reports in *Guangdong caizheng*, Oct., 1994, pp. 6–10.

114. Lin Dengyuan in Lin Ruo, et al., *Gaige kaifang zai Guangdong*, p. 144.

115. Wang, *Guangdong gaige kaifang*, pp. 62–63.

116. This section relies heavily upon two useful studies by Chen Xitao et al., *Shichang jingji yu caizheng gaige (Market Economy and Fiscal Reform)* (Shenzhen: Haitian chubanshe, 1993) and Chen Xitao et al., *Tequ caizheng lilun yu shixing (Theory and Practice of Special Economic Zone's Public Finance)* (Shenzhen: Haitian chubanshe, 1992), pp. 41–42 and 70.

117. The following draws from Kuang (ed.), *Dangdai Zhongguo de Guangdong*, p. 687; Wang, *Guangdong gaige kaifang*, p. 63.

118. Ibid.

119. *Guangdong tongji nianjian 1991*, p. 339; *Guangdong tongji nianjian 1994*, p. 50 and pp. 337–338.

120. Huang, *Mengxiang chengzhen*, p. 33.

121. For instance, similar to the province, the SEZ had to provide further contributions and share more of its revenue with the central government from time to time. For details, see Chen Xitao, et al., *Shichang jingji yu caizheng gaige*, p. 31.

122. See, e.g. Chen Xitao et al, *Tequ Caizheng Lilun yu Shixing*.

123. *Guangzhou nianjian 1993*, p. 336.

124. *Guangdong nianjian 1989*, pp. 39, 205 and 354.

125. *Guangdong nianjian 1989*, p. 205.

126. The document is from *Guangdong zhengbao*, No. 3, 1994, pp. 146–152.

127. This policy, as contained in "Concrete Proposal on the Reform of Guangdong Province's Fiscal Management System," was promulgated as Guangdong Provincial Government Document No. 19, 1994. See *Guangdong caizheng*, March 1994, pp. 146–152. Also see *Nanfang ribao*, July 2, 1994, p. 2.

128. *Nanfang ribao*, July 2, 1994, p. 2.

129. Most English works on Guangdong under reform have not examined domestic investment systematically, with only some exceptions. For instance, for analysis of Guangdong's finance and banking system in English, see Tsang Shu Ki, "Banking, and Finance," in Yeung and Chu (eds.), *Guangdong*, ch. 8; for finance and infrastructural development, see Liu Pak-wai et al., *The Fifth Dragon*, ch. 9; for a detailed account of central-provincial interactions over investment, see Linda Li, *Shifting Central-Provincial Relations* (Oxford: Oxford University Press, forthcoming). Numerous Chinese studies on

this subject are, however, available. See articles published in local journals, especially *Guangdong caizheng (Guangdong Public Finance)*, *Guangdong fazhan daokan (Development Journal of Guangdong)* and *Guangdong jinrong (Guangdong Banking)*. Useful Chinese works include, e.g. Wang Zou, et al., *Guangdong gaige kaifang*, ch. 1. Owing to the very rapid development of Guangdong's investment and financial sector in the 1990s, the following discussion offers at best a preliminary overview of the momentous changes in investment policy. More technical analysis of Guangdong's changing investment policy demands another study that is beyond the scope of this chapter.

130. For sources, see Table 2.6.

131. *Zhongguo tongji nianjian*, various years.

132. *Zhongguo tongji nianjian 1996*, p. 597.

133. The only exception was the 1963–1965 period when Guangdong's share reached 4.7 percent of the national total. Guojia tongjiju guding zichan touzi tongjishi (ed.), *Zhongguo guding zichan touzi tongji, 1950–1985 (Statistics on Investment in Fixed Assets in China, 1950–1985)* (Beijing: Zhongguo tongji chubanshe, 1986), p. 51. The figure refers to investment in the state sector, the primary source of investment in the prereform era.

134. Ibid., pp. 196–212. For a summary of investment in capital construction in the prereform and early reform period, see Dangdai Zhongguo congshu bianji bu (ed.), *Dangdai Zhongguo de jibenjianshe (Capital Construction in Contemporary China) Vol. II* (Beijing: Zhongguo shehui kexue chubanshe, 1989), pp. 66–117.

135. *Guangdong tongji nianjian 1996*, p. 60.

136. *Guangdong tongji nianjian 1991*, p. 191; *Guangdong tongji nianjian 1996*, pp. 90 and 259.

137. *Guangdong tongji nianjian 1996*, p. 259.

138. *Zhongguo caizheng tongji (1950–1985)*, pp. 144–145.

139. *China Finance Statistics (1950–1991)*, pp. 204 and 232.

140. For a study of central-provincial interactions over the special policies and an analysis of the key contents of these policies, see my chapter in Yeung and Chu (eds.), *Guangdong*, ch. 2. For a detailed account of central-provincial interactions over investment, see Li, *Shifting Central-Provincial Relations*.

141. The text can be found in *ZDGGZH (1983–1985)*, pp. 378–385.

142. Wu Huanchao (ed.), *Dangdai Zhongguo touzi tixi gaige (Reform of Contemporary China's Investment System)* (Harbin: Heilongjiang renmin chubanshe, 1992), pp. 612–613.

143. For Zhao's comments on the request and the views of the Small Leading Group, see respectively, *ZDGGZH (1986–1987) Vol. II*, pp. 384–396, and 387–390.

144. *ZDGGZH (1983–1985)*, p. 168.

145. For a systematic analysis of inflation control and investment behavior, see Huang Yasheng, *Inflation and Investment Controls in China* (Cambridge: Cambridge University Press, 1996).

146. Peng Zukang and Luo Kangning (eds.), *Zouxiang shijie zhi kanke zhilu—Guangdong gaige kaifang fansilu (Running Through a Difficult Path Towards the World—A Collection of Reflections on Guangdong's Reform and Opening)* (Guangzhou: Guangdong jiaoyu chubanshe, 1995), pp. 84–85.

147. Lin, *Zouguo de lu—Guangdong gaige kaifang jicheng*, pp. 200–201. This practice was only authoritatively prohibited by the tax-sharing reform in 1994.

148. Studies of Guangdong's open policy are too numerous to cite. Please refer to my bibliography in *Provincial China*, No. 1, March 1997. A useful summary can be found in Liu Jianchang, *Deng Xiaoping duiwai kaifang lilun yu Guangdong shijian (Deng Xiaoping's Theory of Opening to the Outside and Guangdong's Practice)* (Guangzhou: Guangdong renmin chubanshe, 1995), ch. 2.

149. Linda Li described this as the playing of the "foreign card." See her, "Guangdong Playing the 'Foreign Card' in Central-Provincial Relations and Economic Development, 1978–96," paper presented to the international conference, "Sub-regionalism in East Asia: Comparative Approaches," City University of Hong Kong, December 6–7, 1996.

150. Ibid., pp. 17, 22 and 23.

151. This section will focus only on the expansion of preferential policies because, aside from the lack of space, other aspects of Guangdong's external economic relations, such as the SEZs and foreign trade, have already received a great deal of scholarly attention.

152. *Guangdong nianjian 1996*, p. 181.

153. For a detailed account on this issue, see Liang, *Liang Lingguang huiyilu*, pp. 573–585

154. *Guangdong tongji nianjian 1996*, p. 93.

155. *Guangdong tongji nianjian 1996*, p. 73; *Zhongguo tongji nianjian 1996*, p. 140.

156. *Guangdong nianjian 1993*, p. 118.

157. For a very informative analysis of these issues, see Liu et al., *The Fifth Dragon*, chs. 9–10. The following information draws from China Equity Research, Nikko Research Center (HK) Ltd., *Red Chips*, Feb. 18, 1997.

158. This complicated issue demands a study far beyond the limitation of this section or chapter, hence the following examples are used mostly as illustrations. The following discussion draws from: Yeung Yueman, "Infrastructure Development in the Southern China Growth Triangle," in Myo Thant, Min Tang and Hiroshi Kakazu (eds.), *Growth Triangles in Asia: A New Approach to Regional Economic Cooperation* (Hong Kong: Oxford University Press, 1994), pp. 73–93; Liu, et al., *The Fifth Dragon*, ch. 9; Liu Peiqiong (ed.), *Guangdong jingji touzi zonglan (A Comprehensive Overview of Guangdong Investment and Economy)* (Hong Kong: Shangwu yinshuguan, 1996), ch. 4.

159. Zhonggong Guangdongshengwei bangongting (ed.), *Guangdong gaige kaifang qishi lu (A Chronicle of Insights of Guangdong's Reform and Opening)* (Guangzhou: Guangdong renmin chubanshe, 1993), pp. 212–219.

160. Zhonggong Guangdongshengwei bangongting and Guangdongsheng jihua weiyuanhui (jingji jihuasi) bianjishi (eds.), *Guangdongsheng jingji jihua wenjian xuanbian (A Selective Compilation of Guangdong's Economic Planning Documents) (Vol. 3, 1981–1990)*, pp. 394–395.

161. Zhonggong Guangdongshengwei bangongting (ed.), *Guangdong gaige kaifang qishi lu*, pp. 215–216.

162. Ibid., pp. 203–211.

163. *Distribution*, Jan. 1995, p. 26.

164. Liu et al., *The Fifth Dragon*, p. 207.

165. Lin, *Zouguo de lu—Guangdong gaige kaifang jicheng*, p. 218.

166. Luo Liufa and Gu Zhiwei, "Guangdong 'bawu' touzixiaoyi fenxi ji 'jiuwu' duice sikao" (An Analysis of Guangdong's Investment Efficiency in the 8th Five-Year Plan and Coping Strategies for the 9th Five-Year Plan), *Guangdong fazhan daokan*, No. 1, 1996, p. 23.

167. Ibid., p. 25.

168. *Guangdong tongji nianjian 1996*, p. 204.

169. Ibid., p. 34.

170. Ibid., pp. 34–39.

171. *Guangdong tongji nianjian 1996*, p. 30.

172. This section draws mainly from Liu et al., *The Fifth Dragon*, chs. 9–10.

173. See, e.g., an article by a mainland researcher working in Hong Kong, *Hong Kong Economic Times*, Aug. 12, 1996, p. A18; *Sunday Morning Post*, May 11, 1997, p. 4.

174. See *Jiushi niandai (The Nineties)*, Oct. 1995, pp. 49–51; *South China Morning Post*, Sept. 20, 1995, p. 21.

175. See my paper "Prosperity and Politics: Guangdong."

176. Shanghaishi tongjiju (ed.), *Shanghai tongji nianjian 1996 (Shanghai Statistical Yearbook)* (Beijing: Zhongguo tongji chubanshe, 1996), p. 12.

177. Xie Fei, *Guangdong gaige kaifang tansuo (Exploration of Guangdong's Reform and Opening)* (Beijing: Zhonggong zhongyang dangxiao chubanshe, 1996), pp. 37–49.

178. For a recent discussion, see, e.g., the various reports in *Guangdong tongji nianjian 1996*, pp. 18–48.

179. Ibid., p. 79.

3

The Political Economy of Post-Mao Zhejiang

Rapid Growth and Hesitant Reform

Keith Forster

This chapter explains the reasons behind the phenomenal rise of the Zhejiang economy to the forefront of provincial units during the reform period. It examines the role of leadership, provincial developmental strategies and policy priorities in the fields of resource allocation (in particular fiscal and investment policy) as factors in this growth, and comes to the rather paradoxical conclusion that these variables seem to have had little direct relationship with the economic outcomes. The paper argues rather that the extraordinarily dynamic growth of the provincial economy since the late 1970s can be attributed more to the change in direction embarked upon in Beijing, and that the role of the provincial leadership seems to have largely been confined to cautious and sometimes divided responses to these initiatives. On the other hand, there seems to have been a semi-spontaneous, creative response to central initiatives on the part of the people of Zhejiang who, with the active assistance or passive acquiescence of grassroots leaders more in tune with local realities, have been quick to take advantage of the opportunities which the new dispensation has thrown up.

It appears that the peculiar structure of the Zhejiang economy meant that it would inevitably develop rapidly once the constraints of the past were released. The reform endeavor assisted Zhejiang greatly in that, for the first time since 1949, priority was granted to those areas of economic activity in which its strengths had traditionally lain: agricultural raw materials, light industrial manufacturing and rural industry: in short those sectors of the economy which were least affected by the operations of the central planning system. Reforms to the production and marketing of agricultural and industrial commodities, in particular the decontrols over prices and the downgrading of the role of the state in the allocation of agricultural and industrial materials, allowed Zhejiang's industrial sector to obtain, process and sell goods which found a ready market among

China's vast rural population. Finance, materials, labor and markets were found predominantly within the country. The second dimension in Deng Xiaoping's strategy—opening to the outside world—was only seriously taken up by the Zhejiang authorities in the 1990s, after the collapse of domestic demand in the late 1980s.

Taking three large elements of the national reform program—agriculture, industry and foreign trade and investment—we see different sets of responses in Zhejiang. First, it is clear that until 1982 the provincial authorities deliberately lagged behind on reforming the production and distribution systems in agriculture, and were eventually forced to comply by a combination of central pressure (involving changes in key personnel), and by the actions of the peasants (presumably supported by local cadres) who went ahead and broke up the old collective structures. In relation to urban and industrial reform, the provincial authorities proved to be indecisive, faltering as a result of hesitations within the central leadership as well as doubts within their own ranks and their fear of provoking discontent from among such groups as industrial workers and urban citizens who stood to lose long-standing benefits in the process. In the third area, that of relations with the outside world, the Zhejiang leadership seemed to go hot and cold on the issue, partly in response to the perception of shifting trends at the national level and partly due to a diffidence in throwing off the security blanket provided by the domestic market and venturing into the international arena.

Overall, Zhejiang has been a major beneficiary of the reform agenda at the national level and has supplemented its general thrust with policy initiatives of its own. In terms of the ownership structure of the economy, the state today plays less of a direct role in its operation than anywhere else in China. This was also the case when the reform project commenced in 1979, and the difference now is one of degree, albeit one of considerable dimensions. Such an outcome has occurred largely as a result of the implementation of national program objectives which in themselves proved most beneficial to the kind of economy which had evolved in the province by the end of the Maoist era. While the provincial authorities at various times pushed the reform agenda forward, just as at other times they held it up or resisted its general thrust, they seem to have acted in the belief that the dynamic, indeed volatile, economy over which they presided requires the kind of supervision and constraint which cannot be entrusted entirely to the operations of the market. Thus, the traditional Confucian view that the merchants run enterprises while the bureaucrats supervise them seems to be a feature of the contemporary political economy of Zhejiang, and a major inhibition on the road to the further loosening of government control over entrepreneurial activity.

Provincial Overview

A few statistics starkly illustrate the incredible rate of development of the Zhejiang economy during the reform period (see Table 3.1). Between 1978 and

Table 3.1

Annual Rates of Increase in Major Indices 1979–95, Zhejiang and China

	1979–95	1981–95	1986–95	1991–95
Population	0.9	0.9	0.8	0.6
National	1.4	1.4		
GDP	13.8	13.7	13.2	19.1
National(GNP)	9.3	9.1		
Per capita GDP	12.8	12.7	12.3	18.3
GVIO	23.8	23.8	25.0	34.4
National	14.2	16.9		
GVAO	5.5	5.6	5.0	6.9
National	6.1	5.2		
Grain output	–0.1	0.0	–1.2	–2.0
National	2.4	3.3		
Cotton output	–0.9	–1.9	–2.6	–0.5
National	3.7	–1.3		
Coal output	–1.4	–0.9	–1.8	–1.8
National	4.2	3.5		
Freight (railway)	8.0	6.4	3.9	7.7
National	5.5	4.9		
Road	16.3	15.5	12.9	16.6
National	19.7	11.6		
Waterways	2.0	0.9	–3.5	–1.9
National	9.1	7.6		
Self–managed exports	38.8	26.7	24.5	30.2
National	16.1	16.3		
Consumer retail price index (CPI)	8.6	9.1	11.6	12.1
National	6.4	9.0		
Social agricultural procurement prices	11.2	10.5	13.3	14.3
National	7.9	8.3		

Source: Zhejiang tongji nianjian [hereafter *ZJTJNJ*] *1996* (Zhejiang Statistical Yearbook 1996), pp. 9, 11 and 13; *Jingji yanjiu cankao*, No. 58, August 26, 1992, p. 32.
Note: Figures for China are for the period 1979–1993.

1995 Zhejiang's Gross Domestic Product (GDP) increased by over nine times, against a national average of just over four times (between the years 1980 and 1995), Gross Value of Industrial Output (GVIO) by nearly 38 times, compared to the national average of just under nine times (1980—95), while Gross Value of Agricultural Output (GVAO) rose by nearly 2.5 times (compared to the national average of 2.7 times). Taking one outstanding statistic, between 1979 and 1995 the average annual growth rate of GVIO in Zhejiang was 24 percent, compared to the national average of 14.2 percent (1978 to 1993).[1] Zhejiang's ranking as an industrial power leapt from fourteenth in 1978 to sixth in 1988, and on to fourth by 1995, contributing 6.2 percent of national GVIO in 1988 and 8.8 percent in

1995.[2] Between 1978 and 1989 Zhejiang stood first in growth rates among all Chinese provinces in terms of Gross National Product (GNP), national income, Gross Value of Industrial and Agricultural Output (GVIAO), GVIO and volume of social retail sales. It stood fifth in terms of growth rates for budgetary revenue. Only in its growth rate for GVAO did Zhejiang lag behind the national average.[3] Nevertheless, in 1995 the province's GVAO, at 4.4 percent of the national total and ranking ninth,[4] indicated that Zhejiang was still producing more than its share of agricultural products. Taken as a whole, these figures not only illustrate that Zhejiang shared fully in the rapid growth of the Chinese economy over the period, but that it outperformed most, if not all, of its provincial counterparts.

An assessment of Zhejiang's economy published at the beginning of the 1990s argued that this rapid growth had been brought about by a large increase of inputs, primarily capital, and, only to a minor extent, had resulted from the impact of technological advances. It found that there was a very high coefficient between seasonal industrial output and industrial borrowings. Growth was powered along by inflation in consumer demand, which showed up in the high correlation between social retail sales on the one hand and GVIAO and national income on the other. The backbone of economic growth lay in the industrial sector, manufacturing in particular, whilst basic infrastructure and raw materials industries struggled to support this rapid growth. The engine driving the enormous speed of industrial growth was the township and village enterprise (TVE) sector, creating a particular kind of rural industrialization which had established for itself a pivotal (*juzu qingzhong*) position in the provincial economy.[5] By the mid 1990s, the Zhejiang economy seemed to represent the epitome of crude, extensive, high-speed quantitative growth, and was facing the huge challenge of transforming itself into a more intensive, technology-driven, qualitative and efficient economic unit.

By international standards, in 1988, and the situation remained basically the same in 1995, the economy of Zhejiang was in a transition phase from middle to late stage industrialization. This could be measured in terms of per capita GNP, the proportion of secondary industry in GDP (48.7 percent),[6] the proportion of manufactured goods in commodity exports (26 percent), per capita exports (US$ 10.09) and the shift of labor from agriculture to non-agricultural pursuits. By 1988 the proportion of Zhejiang's labor force engaged in agriculture in the rural areas had fallen to 63.4 percent from 92 percent ten years earlier, and comprised 51 percent of the province's total labor force. This figure was 15 percent below the national average (the annual average rate of transition had been 10 percent higher than the national average).[7] We now examine briefly the factors of production with which the province is endowed or that it has created for itself.

Zhejiang occupies about 1 percent of China's territory and is the smallest mainland province. However, with a population which stood at 43.7 million at the end of 1995, it contains almost 4 percent of the national population.[8] Zhejiang has the third highest provincial population density after Jiangsu and

Table 3.2

Per Capita Index of Resources for Zhejiang (national average = 100)

Water	89.6
Energy	0.5
Minerals	4.5
Useable land	40.0
Cultivated land and climate	117.2
Zhejiang's comprehensive index	11.5
Shanghai	10.4
Tianjin	10.6
Guangdong	26.0
Jiangsu	26.0

Source: *Zhejiang jingji nianjian 1988* (Zhejiang Economic Yearbook 1988), p. 417.

Shandong, and over 3.5 times the national average.[9] One unremitting feature of Zhejiang which its leadership has to contend with (but on many occasions since 1949 has seemingly been unable to accept) is the paucity of many of the mineral resources for industrial development which are found in abundance elsewhere in China. Table 3.2 indicates that Zhejiang has the lowest index of natural resources of all the Chinese provinces (excluding the centrally led cities of Shanghai and Tianjin). As a location for growing a fairly complete range of food and industrial crops, Zhejiang is blessed with a favorable climate and location, although its ability to grow these on any great scale is severely constrained by the nature of the terrain, which is roughly seven parts mountains and hills, one part water and two parts arable land (*qi shan yi shui erfen tian*).

Of course, the economic development of a region or country does not depend entirely on its natural resource base (Japan being a good example to the contrary) because account must be taken of other important inputs such as human resources, the availability of capital, the state of scientific knowledge and technology and the general stock of information. In relation to human resources the situation for Zhejiang is somewhat ambiguous. In 1987 65 percent of the population of the province was considered to be sources of labor power, compared to the national average of 61 percent, with a participation rate of 91 percent, well above the national average of 80 percent.[10]

On the other hand, for a province which has traditionally been considered one of the most cultured in China (particularly from the Song dynasty onward when Hangzhou became capital of the Southern Song during the twelfth and thirteenth centuries) the quality of this labor force is below national standards. Figures taken from 1987 clearly reveal this shortcoming. Taking the national average as 100, Zhejiang then had 76 university graduates in employment, 27 enrolled, and

88 higher secondary students at school. Although the illiteracy rate at 20 percent is below the national average, it is still unacceptably high.[11] In addition, Zhejiang has failed to meet its targets in spreading the nine-year compulsory education system across the province.[12]

In state units of employment in 1987, the number of scientific and technical personnel in Zhejiang was well below the national average, and only a little over a third of the proportion in Liaoning Province. The number of university graduates employed in such units in Zhejiang was also below the national average, and less than half that of Liaoning. And even the number of secondary and vocational students similarly employed was below the national average and considerably less than the proportion in Liaoning.[13] Even in the 1950s, enrollment in primary and secondary schools in Zhejiang was below the national average, as was provincial per capita social expenditure.[14]

The availability of capital is one area, however, where Zhejiang rates favorably. According to one source, in 1991 Zhejiang was only one of two provinces in China (the other was Fujian) where bank deposits exceeded bank loans.[15] Official statistics for *total* savings (both in Renminbi and U.S. dollars) for the years 1991 to 1995 (the only years for which these figures have been included in provincial almanacs) reveal that the province has indeed had a surplus of deposits over loans during these years (excepting in 1995 when foreign currency loans exceeded deposits by about 3 percent).[16] The figures also reveal an enormous increase in bank deposits, particularly deposits held by enterprises as well as those held by urban residents, in the 1990s. For example, in 1994, a year of very high inflation, total Renminbi deposits rose by 45 percent over 1993, while loans increased by 30 percent.[17]

A complicated and comprehensive measurement of the overall economic strength of China's provinces, carried out in the 1980s, and which measured two indices of "comprehensive efficiency" and "overall scale," ranked Zhejiang seventh on the former index and ninth on the latter. Comprehensive efficiency refers to per capita and productivity data, while overall scale ranks gross values. Clearly, efficiency indices provide a fairer base for comparison. The report on the first ten years of economic reform in Zhejiang used such categories as gross social product, national income, depth in industrial structure, foreign trade, social infrastructure, savings deposits, advances in science and technology, and management standards to measure the efficiency and ranking of the provincial economy.[18]

Between 1978 and 1995 Zhejiang's population grew by 16.5 percent, considerably slower than the national increase of 23 percent (between 1980 and 1995). Its share of national population therefore fell slightly from 3.7 percent to 3.6 percent. In 1994 Zhejiang's share of national GDP stood at 5.9 percent, well above its population proportion. Its standing in terms of GDP was fifth in 1994 and, with continued rapid growth in 1995, had almost overtaken Sichuan Province (with a population of over twice its size) by the end of that year. Zhejiang's ranking in terms of national income rose from twelfth in 1978 to seventh in 1988 and to fifth in 1992. Per capita national income ranking increased from thirteenth to fifth between 1978 and 1988, falling back to sixth in 1992.[19] Zhejiang's share of national income rose from 3.6 percent in 1978 to 5.5 percent in 1987. In terms of per capita national income, in 1978 Zhejiang's number was 7 points below the national average, while in 1987 it was 43 points above, a graphic illustration of its vastly increased standing in the Chinese economy.[20]

In terms of technical depth in industrial structure, taking five industries considered to be technologically intensive (electricity, petroleum, chemicals, communications and transport equipment, and electronics) Zhejiang's share of national output in three industries increased from 1982 to 1988, while in one it remained steady (figures for the fifth are incomplete). The share of these five industries in provincial GVIO almost tripled over the same period, suggesting that the degree of technical concentration in Zhejiang's industrial structure had advanced. But six years later in 1994, the proportion of these industries in GVIO had stabilized at just over 15 percent.[21]

In 1981 Zhejiang supplied 2 percent of China's exports. In 1988 this percentage had risen to 3.4 percent, and to 5.4 percent by 1995. In terms of the construction of basic infrastructure (social capital) in transport and communications, however, the fundamental weakness of the Zhejiang economy becomes immediately apparent. Provincial investment in this sector comprised 0.9 percent of national investment in 1983, rising to 2.1 percent in 1988. This proportion was strikingly at odds with Zhejiang's relative economic strength.[22] Thus, not only was Zhejiang's performance in this vital area of economic construction poor by national standards, it was creating a steadily growing bottleneck for the further development of the provincial economy. Finally, in 1980, total urban and rural savings deposits in Zhejiang stood at 4 percent of the national total, increasing their share to 4.3 percent in 1988. The reform period has thus witnessed the remarkably swift return of Zhejiang to the ranks of leading economic provincial powers in the country. This has been a retarded but inevitable trend in China's modernization process.

In 1949 Zhejiang's economy was almost entirely agriculturally based with what industry there was almost entirely devoted to the production of consumer goods. For example, in 1952 after three years of economic recovery, heavy industry only comprised 3 percent of the gross value of GVIAO. Agriculture contributed over 70 percent, with light industry making up 25 percent (the national proportions in 1952 were 57 percent agriculture, 28 percent light industry and 15 percent heavy industry). In the balance between light and heavy industry in Zhejiang, the latter only contributed 11 percent. Gross Domestic Product (GDP) was distributed two-thirds to agriculture, 20 percent to the tertiary sector and 10 percent to the secondary sector.[23]

Zhejiang's economic structure was basically at odds with the Soviet-inspired planned model based on heavy industry which characterized the most part of the following Maoist years. Consumer cities were considered parasitic, and industry was very quickly developed, often inappropriately and at great cost to the environment and to the health of urban citizens who lived near such polluting plants.[24] The concept of self-sufficiency and economic independence at the provincial level encouraged local leaders to develop a heavy industrial base. However, in Zhejiang this approach was both unsuitable and counter-productive. A high level of accumulation meant that consumer demand took second place to the development of the industrial base, and the preponderance of investment was directed into building an industrial structure at odds with the existing economy, and one which would have to rely on outside supplies of materials and energy to be viable, in an autonomous, autarchic economic structure which inhibited domestic trade except via planned allocations.

Compounding the problem was a provincial leadership which until the Cultural Revolution was dominated by three officials: Tan Zhenlin (1949–52), his deputy and successor Tan Qilong (1952–54), who were known as the "two Tans of Zhejiang" (*Zhejiang liangtan*), and then by Jiang Hua (1954–67), Tan Qilong's deputy and, like Tan Zhenlin, a peasant cadre who had close personal relations with Chairman Mao Zedong dating back to the revolutionary base of Jinggangshan in the late 1920s. From 1949 until the Cultural Revolution Zhejiang was a bastion of Maoism in all its permutations, a model of compliance to the unpredictable and erratic policy preferences of the Chairman,[25] and largely a willing victim to various economic, political and social experiments which were carried out during this period.[26] Frederick Teiwes' conclusion, based on his study of pre–Cultural Revolution politics and policies, that it was a "steady and lasting performance" rather than political activism which ensured the political survival of provincial leaders,[27] seems to apply most aptly in Jiang Hua's case.

The economic costs of pandering to the Leader's whims were enormous. During the Great Leap Forward for example, the provincial leadership under Jiang Hua devoted vast amounts of resources in a vain and foolish attempt to prove that Zhejiang had sufficient supplies of coal and iron to support a viable metallurgy industry.[28] When the inevitable collapse came the consequences were dramatic for the economy and people of Zhejiang. Huge amounts of capital, labor, raw materials (for example timber) were invested in an endeavor whose folly was only matched by the pretensions of those who carried it out. The magnitude of the commitment and ambition of the leadership was breathtaking in its audacity. In 1958, for example, industrial output rose by a phenomenal 202 percent, and investment in capital construction by an even more staggering 539 percent! Those who doubted the wisdom or correctness of the undertaking, or the capacity of the province to follow such a developmental strategy, were ridiculed or condemned as pessimists and conservatives.

Although a number of backbone enterprises were built during this period, some of which today remain among the core of certain industries in Zhejiang, the developmental strategy contained in this approach condemned the province to limp along at a below average growth rate compared to the rest of the country.

For example, in 1949 per capita national income in Zhejiang was 85 percent of the national average, while by 1976 it had fallen to 81 percent.[29] In 1957 per capita industrial output was only three-quarters of the national average. In 1974 this had fallen to 58 percent, recovering to 85 percent in 1979 and then forging ahead to 123 percent in 1984.[30] The situation in the agricultural sector was different, however. Zhejiang had always kept ahead of the national average (taking 1957 and 1979 as two indicative points), and by 1984 the margin had increased to 42 percent.[31]

By 1965 the structure of GVIAO had changed considerably since 1952. Agriculture's share had fallen to 45 percent, light industry (in spite of the planning and investment bias against it) had risen to 41 percent and heavy industry comprised 14 percent. The light/heavy industry share stood at 75:25. These proportions were quite different from those at the national level. In 1965 light industry and heavy industry split 50:50 in their respective contributions to national GVIO, while in the breakdown of GVIAO agriculture contributed 30 percent, light industry 35 percent and heavy industry 35 percent.[32] In terms of GDP, Zhejiang's primary industry made up 47 percent, its tertiary sector remained largely unchanged at 23 percent, and the industrial sector had increased to 30 percent. In the period 1953–65 the rate of growth for heavy industry was twice that for light industry, which in turn was over twice that for agriculture.[33]

During the Cultural Revolution a renewed attempt was made in the early 1970s to find the elusive sources of coal in Zhejiang. A developmental strategy characterized by small and complete (or large and complete), which emphasized heavy industry, accumulation and agriculture (grain) was pursued, this time by a military provincial leadership completely unfamiliar with the conditions in the province and caught up in the midst of violent factionalism which continued virtually unabated until the death of Mao.[34] The strategy of industrializing Zhejiang continued, with the share of heavy industry in GVIO increasing to 40 percent in 1978 and doubling to 26 percent of GVIAO in the same year. Light industry's share of GVIAO actually declined over this period to 38 percent, while the share of tertiary industry in GDP fell back to 19 percent, below the level of 1952.

It has been pointed out that it was during the Cultural Revolution that a large amount of authority in relation to investments and industry was devolved by the center to the provinces.[35] Provinces were encouraged to build up their own industrial bases according to the philosophy of "independent and complete" industrial systems. One might have expected the small-scale, collectively owned and consumer-oriented industrial economy of Zhejiang would have benefited from this devolution of authority. However, industrial policy emphasized heavy industry and those sectors serving agriculture (the "five small industries" of coal, iron and steel, cement, agricultural machinery and hydro-power stations). Accordingly, the provincial military-dominated leadership directed the bulk of investment funds into heavy industry. Additionally, destabilizing political factors exerted a strong countervailing influence. In the mid 1970s Hangzhou experienced wild swings in industrial output as a result of chronic factionalism in its industrial enterprises.[36] In the southern city of Wenzhou, the average annual growth rate of GVIAO during the "ten years of disaster" was a mere 1.85 percent, and the growth rate for GVIO in the third five-year plan (1966–70) was only 90 percent of that for the second five-year plan (1958–62), a period which included the years of natural and man-made disasters.[37] Provincial GVIO fell in 1967, 1968 and 1974, while GVAO dropped in 1967, 1971, 1973 and 1975.[38]

The Zhejiang which emerged from the throes of these violent years was a province fractured politically and socially, and further weakened economically by the continued application of strategies inappropriate and counter-productive to its development. The intraprovincial cleavages between the richer northern and eastern parts of the province and their more backward south-eastern and central-western counterparts were, if anything, exacerbated by the pursuit of local self-reliance and independent development. The backward western region lagged behind, while the neglected and isolated south of Zhejiang, centered on the enigmatic city of Wenzhou, went its own way along the "capitalist road."[39] A great gap between north-east and south-west Zhejiang had appeared in terms of the distribution of GVIO, national income, efficiency in state enterprises and the level of industrialization and development.

By 1978, from the provincial leadership down to at least the county level Zhejiang had been run by outsiders for the center for almost thirty years. Many of these outsiders by then may well have considered themselves as honorary locals! This domination by outsiders was most apparent among county party and government administrations. An examination of the relevant pages in the fifty or so county gazetteers published to date reveals an almost total domination by Shandong cadres who came south with the victorious 3rd Field Army in 1949, a domination which was only partially broken during the Cultural Revolution. A central cadre (who was a native of Zhejiang) on a tour of inspection in Zhejiang in 1956 commented on the total lack of local cadres in the county establishments which he visited.[40]

At the provincial level there was no such replication of Shandong cadre domination. However, there was, during and after the Jiang Hua years of rule, a seeming obsession with gaining credentials from obedience to and compliance with central line and policy. The Great Leap Forward was only an extreme manifestation of this tendency. Several factors seem to have contributed to this proclivity. First, the Party Chairman was a regular visitor during the years 1953 to 1975, when he made over forty visits, convened several crucial informal meetings of senior central and regional leaders and drafted several key documents.[41] Mao elicited from his "loyal lieutenants" unquestioning obedience bordering on sycophancy. To this day Jiang Hua continues to write emotional reminiscences of his personal and political indebtedness to the late Helmsman.[42]

Second, Zhejiang was an important source of fiscal remissions to the center.[43]

Despite the best efforts of central dictates and local directives, which ignored or neglected the main source of such revenues—that is, light industrial enterprises which were small in size, owned by the collective sector and made large profits from the scissors gap between the price of agricultural inputs and the ex-factory price of its processed goods—this sector continued to provide the main thrust behind the slow and below average growth which occurred in Zhejiang. Relying largely on its own agricultural raw materials, and lacking the minerals and ferrous metals for heavy industrialization, in the discretely planned regional strategy in force Zhejiang had no option but to continue to produce consumer goods.

By the end of the Maoist period the economy of the province showed an interesting divergence from the mainstream of the national economy This was a result of the influence of both the traditional structure, central neglect and the weakness of the planned state sector. A Chinese analyst has pointed to four aspects in which the economy of Zhejiang differed from the country as a whole, and which factors assisted it to advance so rapidly in the reform period.[44]

First, the proportion of non-state sectors in the provincial economy was high. In 1978 village industrial output value comprised 16 percent of GVIO, compared to 9 percent nationally. Urban collective industrial output value at 23 percent of GVIO stood 9 percent above the national average. In the retail sector, the value of sales from state outlets at 43 percent of social consumer retail sales[45] was 12 percent less than the national average, while sales from collective and private outlets were 10 percent and 2 percent respectively above the national average. Budgetary revenues, at 22 percent of GDP, were only two-thirds the national average of 31 percent.

Second, there were few centrally run enterprises and large and medium enterprises in the industrial structure, notwithstanding the aspirations and investment efforts of the provincial authorities to the contrary. The great majority of industrial enterprises came under the aegis of the local plan, and their inputs were allocated and their activities coordinated by the province. A mere 1.5 percent of state investment during the years 1953 to 1978 had been directed into Zhejiang. By 1978 the output of centrally managed industrial enterprises came to only 2.5 percent of provincial GVIO at the village level and above. The output of large and medium enterprises contributed 16 percent to GVIO. These figures were 4 percent and 27 percent respectively below the national average.

Third, the scope of mandatory planning for the supply, production and distribution of enterprise goods was narrow. Because most enterprises produced consumer goods and small agricultural tools they were allowed some flexibility, and the influence of market forces was not insignificant in investment allocations. Some of these enterprises had the power to sell their products themselves and even to fix the prices of these products.

Fourth, there was a strong consciousness of the commodity economy among these economic entities. This is most probably an indirect reference to the Zhejiangese well-known proclivity and acumen for business. Thus, the Zhejiang economy was not only ripe for reform, it possessed the preconditions and advantages to take advantage immediately and without any great adjustment of any shift from the planned, heavy industry strategy which had prevailed for the previous thirty years.

Provincial Leadership in the Reform Era

This section will attempt to explicate and clarify the relationship between provincial leadership and economic reform in the post-Mao period. The general thrust of the argument is that the Zhejiang leaders rarely took the initiative in pushing the reform program forward. On the contrary they either stonewalled (as in the case of agricultural reform), prevaricated and were undecided (as in the case of urban reform), or expressed doubt and diffidence (as in the case of opening to the outside world). Fortunately for them, the provincial economy continued to grow at a rapid rate for most of the whole reform period, despite the inaction, hesitation and lack of political will on the policy front. Ironically, the response of the leadership to reform was in inverse relationship to the province's economic success during the Maoist period, when the agricultural sector had out-performed the national average and the industrial sector has lagged behind. Ironically then, Zhejiang's leaders were most pro-active in policy initiative when the issue concerned was of only marginal importance to the local economy (but was high on the agenda of the central leadership such as reform of state enterprises), while in areas of key concern such as the TVE sector they were inactive or passive. This fact in itself reveals much about the compliance and subservience of the provincial leaders to the central agenda.

Up until 1982 analysts had observed five completed economic cycles in Zhejiang since 1950, roughly paralleling in timing and movement a national economic cycle.[46] On the basis of the reasoning of the report, the sixth cycle could be considered to have ended in 1990. In 1996 Zhejiang was in the sixth year of a seventh economic cycle which was finally showing signs of entering a phase of slowdown in the rate of growth.[47] From Table 3.3 it is apparent that these economic cycles have a high degree of correspondence to political cycles of upsurges in radicalism followed by periods of consolidation or retrenchment. However, this is not the place to pursue an analysis of such phenomena.

The fifth cycle roughly coincided with Tie Ying's leadership of Zhejiang, during which time reform was focused on the agricultural sector. During this period GVIAO grew by an annual average rate of 12.7 percent, hitting a peak of 21.7 percent in 1978. 1982 was the year of lowest growth at 10.7 percent. Tie's successors, Wang Fang and Xue Ju, presided over most of the sixth cycle and the shift to urban reform. Between 1983 and 1988, before the economic downturn which started in 1989, GVIAO grew at an even higher rate of 20.9 percent. The present provincial party leader Li Zemin has been in power during the running of the present cycle, which has also displayed the highest rates of growth during reform, and when Zhejiang's economy has finally and somewhat belatedly

Table 3.3

Cyclical Movements in the Zhejiang Economy, 1950–1983

	Length of cycle	Annual growth rate	Trough	Peak	Gap
1950–55	6	13.0	5.6	21.8	16.2
1956–61	6	6.5	−28.5	38.1	66.6
1962–67	6	5.5	−4.2	13.6	17.8
1968–74	7	6.5	−6.6	18.2	24.8
1975–82	8	12.7	10.7	21.7	11.0
1983–	unfinished	20.9			

Source: Feng Renyi and Wang Jie, "Jingji zengzhangde zhouqi fenxi" (Analysis of economic growth cycles), in *Zhejiang 1979–1988 nian jingji fazhan baogao*, p. 109.

opened to the outside world. GVIAO increased at an average annual rate of 30.8 percent between 1991 and 1995, after an average rate of growth of only 7.1 percent between 1989 and 1990.[48] From this perspective alone it would appear that economic growth has accelerated over time. Whether this has been due to the quality of provincial leadership and its ability to implement economic strategies and policies appropriate to the conditions of Zhejiang is an issue to be explored further in this chapter. However, only Li Zemin, of the three provincial party leaders since Tie Ying, has had to contend with a sustained economic slump in what has at times seemed to be a never-ending upward spiral of economic growth.

During the post–Tie Ying leadership period of the last twelve years, Zhejiang's economy has experienced three sustained periods of high economic growth. Between June 1983 and January 1986 it went through 32 months of high speed growth. Then, after six months' respite, from August 1986 to December 1988 the economy experienced a further 28 months of sustained growth. After passing through almost two years of retrenchment, in October 1990 the economy moved back into top gear, and by the end of 1992 this cycle had lasted for another 26 months.[49] Rapid economic growth, which has at times threatened to get out of control, was sustained throughout 1993 and 1994. In June 1993, at the height of this growth, industrial production rose at the amazing and alarming rate of 58 percent over the same month of 1992, the highest monthly increase since 1949.[50] Growth continued into 1995 and 1996, although this frenetic pace slowed somewhat.

Against this background of a sustained period of remarkable economic growth, since 1978 the tradition and policy (if there has indeed been one) of appointing outside cadres to run Zhejiang has been maintained. Only one native has held the position of provincial governor in these seventeen years. Not one of the provincial party leaders appointed during the reform period has had any

Table 3.4

Zhejiang Provincial Leadership, 1978–95

CCP Zhejiang Party Committee leaders	Government leaders
	Chairman, Provincial Revolutionary Committee
Tie Ying[ab] (Henan) 2/77–3/83	Tie Ying[ab] (Henan) 2/77–12/79
	Governor
Wang Fang[b] (Shandong) 3/83–3/87	Li Fengping[b] (Sichuan) 12/79–4/83
Xue Ju[b] (Shanxi) 3/87–12/88	Xue Ju[b] (Shanxi) 4/83–2/88
Li Zemin (Sichuan) 12/88–	Shen Zulun[b] (Zhejiang) 2/88–11/90
	Ge Hongsheng[b] (Shandong) 1/91–1/93
	Wan Xueyuan (Hubei) 1/93–

Source: Zhonggong Zhejiang shengwei zuzhibu, Zhonggong Zhejiang shengwei dangshi yanjiushi, Zhejiangsheng dang'anguan (ed.), *Zhongguo Gongchandang Zhejiangsheng zuzhishi ziliao, 1922.4–1987.12) (Materials on the organizational history of the CCP Zhejiang province, 1922.4–1987.12)* (Liangzhu: Renmin ribao chubanshe, 1994).
   Note: [a] PLA leader; [b] previous work experience in the province.

formal training or background in economic affairs: one being a military cadre (Tie Ying), another a public security official (Wang Fang), the third a generalist civilian cadre (Xue Ju), and the fourth and present party secretary, Li Zemin, being a graduate in party history at Beijing's People's University. Table 3.4 lists provincial party and government leaders since 1978 with their place of birth and tenure of office.

The first and most striking feature of the above table is the fact that even in the reform period Zhejiang has never had a native in the post of party leader, replicating the state of affairs which pertained during the Maoist period. The only native who has held the post of governor resigned (under pressure) in 1990, again replicating the situation of the pre-reform period when the only other two natives to have held the post were purged, one (Sha Wenhan) in the anti-Rightist struggle of 1957 and the other (Zhou Jianren) in the Cultural Revolution, although Zhou re-emerged as a vice-chairman of the Provincial Revolutionary Committee when that body was formed in March 1968. Even more noteworthy is the fact that the present incumbents of Zhejiang are distinguished from their predecessors by the fact that they had never served in the province before their appointments to the top party and government posts in 1988 and 1993 respectively.

A military political officer with a background in the judicial arm of the army, Tie Ying was 60 when he took over the leadership of the province immediately after the downfall of the Gang of Four in late 1976. In 1972 Tie had been elevated to deputy leader of the province (behind Tan Qilong) following the purge of the Cultural Revolution military leadership, which was accused of being implicated with the Lin Biao central military group. Tie survived for the next seven years despite his reservations about and resistance to some of the key planks of the reform program.[51] Early in his stewardship over Zhejiang Tie made clear his devotion to the new central leader, Hua Guofeng. In September 1977, at a rally in Hangzhou to mark the opening of the Chairman Mao Memorial Hall in Beijing, Tie recited his "three-musts": "We must love Chairman Hua the way we did Chairman Mao; we must defend Chairman Hua the way we did Chairman Mao; and we must carry out Chairman Hua's instructions the way we did Chairman Mao's."[52]

Despite his printed efforts in semi-retirement to associate himself with the once revered figure of Zhou Enlai[53] it is difficult to understand how Tie survived so long as the leader of Zhejiang. One important factor was the reserves of credit and goodwill he had built up among veteran cadres during his resolute struggle against the local rebel cum radical leaders between 1974 and 1976. Tie was the provincial leader singled out by the rebels for interrogation, kidnap and various other forms of political humiliation.[54] Tie obtained great political capital from his exploits during these difficult years of the mid 1970s. After 1977, many of Jiang Hua's pre–Cultural Revolution senior subordinates such as Li Fengping, Wang Fang and Xue Ju returned to leading posts in the provincial leadership and, with their better knowledge of local conditions, previous experience in administration and superior credentials as victims of the Cultural Revolution, they appeared to take over the running of the provincial administration. But Tie was anything if not energetic, and it was only at the end of 1982 that he backed down over his opposition to agricultural decollectivization.[55]

Nevertheless, despite the Zhejiang leadership dragging its feet in permitting the widespread introduction of the household contract responsibility system, economic data reveal an interesting pattern in relation to the development of the agricultural sector in the province. In 1982 the value of agricultural production had increased 73 percent over that of 1977, an annual 11.5 percent average increase. This has far exceeded any growth rates recorded since, and far exceeded the 4.4 percent per annum increase recorded between 1949 and 1977. Output figures for important provincial crops such as grain, tea, silk cocoons, citrus, hemp and sugar cane were at their highest ever, and income from commune-run enterprises was up 200 percent on 1977. In 1982 grain output had increased 65 percent over 1977, a 13 percent average annual increase. Part of the explanation for this impressive growth was that it was taking place from a low base, but it may have been difficult to condemn Tie for policy deviation in the light of these impressive results. The decline in growth rates in Zhejiang's agricultural sector since 1985 makes the achievements in the early years of reform even more outstanding. Taking the whole period 1979 to 1995, the average annual growth in GVAO in Zhejiang of 5.5 percent has lagged behind the na-

Table 3.5

Per Annum Increase in Economic Indices by Plan Periods

	Gross social output	GVIAO	National income
1st (1953–57)	10.4	9.5	9.2
2nd (1958–62)	2.2	2.3	–0.2
3rd & 4th (1966–75)	4.5	13.2	3.4
5th (1976–80)	16.4	16.1	14.5
6th (1981–85)	18.8	17.8	15.8
7th (1986–90)	7.3[a]	14.3	7.8

Source: Zhejiang jingji nianjian 1986, p. 86; JPRS-CAR-91–032, p. 22.
Note: [a] GDP.

Table 3.6

Speed of Economic Development, 1953–1984

	1953–57	1958–65	1966–78	1979–84	1953–84	1981–84
GVIAO	9.5	5.6	7.3	15.8	8.7	14.8
GVAO	6.1	2.6	3.7	11.9	5.3	13.3
GVIO	15.1	8.7	9.7	17.8	11.7	15.5
Light industry	13.1	7.0	7.0	18.9	10.1	16.6
Heavy industry	28.0	15.9	14.9	16.2	17.3	13.8

Source: Zhejiang shengqing (The Affairs of Zhejiang), pp.1009–14.

tional average of 6.1 percent (to 1993), and by the mid 1990s the agricultural "base" of the economy in Zhejiang had become very shaky indeed.

It was during Tie's term in office that the provincial economy made its initial lift-off into the high-speed pattern of growth which has characterized its performance for the most part of the reform period. Figures released in April 1983 at the provincial people's congress in the immediate aftermath of Tie's replacement by Wang Fang illustrate this very clearly.[56] Between 1977 and 1982 industrial and agricultural output doubled, while national income increased by 96 percent. Table 3.6 indicates that except for the heavy industry sector, growth rates were considerably higher in the first five years of the post-Mao period than for any period before 1979.

It is clear from the figures in Tables 3.5 and 3.6 that Tie Ying presided over an impressive growth in the Zhejiang economy between 1977 and 1982. However, these achievements were not sufficient to allow him to retain his position when a major shake-up of provincial leaders occurred in 1983. In March of that year, under the personal direction of key central leaders such as Deng Xiaoping and Peng Zhen, the commander of the Nanjing Military Region, and the still highly influential Jiang Hua, Tie was replaced by a deputy-secretary Wang Fang, a public security official who had worked in Zhejiang since 1949 and who was a core member of the Jiang Hua pre–Cultural Revolution group.[57]

At the age of 63, Wang was only four years younger than Tie Ying and, except for his greater experience working in Zhejiang, he was hardly any more suited to lead a program of economic modernization and reform than his predecessor. Two examples illustrate the dilemma in which the cautious, conservative Wang was placed in 1984, as the strategy of reform and opening to the outside world forged further ahead. In that year the center declared fourteen coastal cities, including Ningbo and Wenzhou in Zhejiang, open to the outside world. Yet it was a national leader, Gu Mu, rather than a provincial leader, who promoted the developmental experience of Wenzhou. Gu, who was then a state councillor, made an extensive trip to the region in 1984.[58] Wang Fang did not publicly endorse the city's unique approach to development until he visited the area in August 1985.[59]

The second area of reform concerned devolving increased power to the managers of industrial enterprises.[60] In this instance, the CCP's practice of propagating the experience of models placed Wang in a quandary. In Zhejiang the most publicized and controversial case concerned Bu Xinsheng, the manager of the Haiyan shirt factory, a collective enterprise in Jiaxing municipality in the northeast of the province. In April 1983, shortly after Wang's promotion to provincial party secretary, the provincial daily carried a full-page article singing the praises of the factory and its manager.[61] Bu was one of a new breed of managers who wished to run his enterprise with the minimum of even formal consultation with the workforce through its trade union representatives. He appears to have learnt from Japanese management practices by providing his staff with smart new uniforms, a factory song and a badge. He banned spitting on the premises, and smoking and tea-drinking in the workshops. He attempted to rein in expenditure on various kinds of leave benefits which the workers had enjoyed. However, it appears that the local party committee expressed its reservations about some of Bu's more draconian edicts. In particular, workers complained about their treatment, and Bu's attempt to suppress the factory trade union aroused opposition within the enterprise itself as well as from the local authorities.

In late 1983 the national press also carried an article praising Bu's accomplishments. Output in that year was reported to have increased 4.3 times over that in 1978, while state taxes were up 2.6 times. Bu's approach, it seemed, was paying dividends, and Wang Fang was forced to act. In early 1984 the provincial party committee convened a meeting at which it announced its decision on how to assess the factory and its manager.[62] Wang Fang summed up the view of the provincial authorities by stating that overall Bu, for his creative spirit and enterprise, could be affirmed as a reformer. Although he had made mistakes, for example by the way in which he had disposed of the factory trade union, it would be unrealistic to expect that major reforms of the kind he was instituting could be accomplished without errors. The difficulty for the provincial party was that the case arose in the middle of a major party rectification campaign. Even the central group in charge of rectification was involved in the decision to endorse Bu and his management style.[63] In two tests of his reform credentials in 1984, then, Wang had displayed the kind of cautious approach very much in keeping with a cadre of his experience and bureaucratic background.

When Wang Fang was promoted to the post of provincial party secretary in 1983 he was joined at the top of the provincial leadership by his deputy and concurrent governor, Xue Ju, another of Jiang Hua's most loyal pre–Cultural Revolution subordinates.[64] And when Wang was transferred from Zhejiang in April 1987 to become national minister of public security Xue took his place as provincial party secretary. Xue had been sent to work in East Zhejiang in 1947 by the Shanghai Bureau and Central China party organization.[65] He had served as chairman of the provincial party office from 1953 to 1955 and then held the post of deputy secretary-general of the provincial party committee from 1955 until the Cultural Revolution. As deputy to Wang Fang, Xue presided over the drawing up of a fifteen-year strategic program for economic development (1986–2000) as well as the seventh five-year plan (1986–1990),[66] and presented these for approval to the provincial people's congress in May 1986.[67] As with many economic targets which have been set by the provincial authorities throughout the reform period, these predictions invariably erred on the conservative side, and most were eventually met and exceeded well in advance.

In February 1988 Xue relinquished his governorship to a local, Shen Zulun, who had only joined the provincial leadership as late as March 1983. Shen was the first native of Zhejiang to head the government administration since 1966. He had experienced a meteoric rise from county deputy-secretary in 1976 to provincial deputy-governor seven years later. It could be assumed that his pre–Cultural Revolution posts in the provincial bureaucracy working under such men as Xue Ju were key factors in his rise. Born in 1931 in the major port city of Ningbo, Shen joined the CCP in 1948 and worked in his local area until 1952, before transferring to provincial party headquarters. Before the Cultural Revolution Shen had served as Jiang Hua's secretary, before being purged in the Cultural Revolution. After his return to office in 1976, Shen served in leading posts in Shaoxing and Jiaxing before transferring to Hangzhou.

Shen was elected to the provincial party committee at its seventh congress in November 1983, its standing committee in January 1985, and was then promoted to deputy secretary in September 1987 in preparation for his promotion to provincial governor. When, in late 1987/early 1988, Zhao Ziyang launched his coastal development strategy, provinces such as Zhejiang were key targets of this initiative. Both Shen and Xue, the former in particular, revealed themselves as staunch and enthusiastic supporters of a cause which was shortly to be tainted somewhat as the political fortunes of its sponsor declined. At the end of 1988 Zhejiang convened its eighth party congress. While it was Xue Ju who presented the political report on behalf of the outgoing party committee, it was a man who was not even a delegate to the congress, Li Zemin, who emerged at the end of the congress as provincial party secretary.

Like his predecessor Wang Fang, Xue Ju was transferred to a post in Beijing (as director of the central party school), ending his eighteen-month reign as provincial party leader. Li Zemin's appointment and Xue Ju's departure were as sudden as they were unanticipated. While the stranglehold of the Jiang Hua group over the province was dealt a strong blow, the center again preferred an outsider to rule Zhejiang. Li's appointment seems to have been part of a pattern in 1988 of appointing cadres with experience in running large cities (he had previously been party secretary of Shenyang) to provincial posts.[68] It may also be viewed as an attempt to shake Zhejiang out of the policy drift of the previous five years, a period during which despite continued rapid economic growth and transformation of the economy the reform agenda had stalled on several important occasions. Wang Fang and Xue Ju were both men from the past. Their promotion to provincial leadership may be seen as a belated reward for services rendered and careers cut off in their prime by the Cultural Revolution. This was vividly illustrated by Wang Fang's quandary in dealing with the legacy of the Cultural Revolution during the campaign to negate it in 1984. As an active participant and factional leader himself he found it impossible to sum up objectively the experience of those years.

Within the space of 1988 Zhejiang found itself with a new Governor in Shen Zulun, an official with proven reform credentials. Li Zemin, on the other hand, was an unknown quantity in Zhejiang. He was to face an entirely different challenge to that which had confronted him in Liaoning, situated as it is in the heartland of Chinese heavy industry. A native of Sichuan, Li was, at 54, three years younger than Shen Zulun. He had served in the Korean War in the early 1950s before joining the CCP in 1954. In 1960 he graduated from the People's University in party history and remained at his alma mater as a teacher until the outbreak of the Cultural Revolution. In the mid 1970s he was assigned to Liaoning, where he worked at Shenyang Agricultural College. Li rose swiftly through the party apparatus in Liaoning, becoming head of the provincial propaganda department. Then in 1985 he was appointed provincial deputy-secretary, concurrent with his Shenyang post.

In retrospect, Li could hardly have come to Zhejiang at a worse time in the post-Mao period. Several months earlier, a retrenchment policy had been implemented to rein in an economy out of control with booming consumer spending and high inflation threatening to undermine the whole financial system. The repercussions of this austerity program and tight credit policy were to be felt very severely in Zhejiang in 1989 to 1990. However, it appears that compliance with the retrenchment measures occurred mainly as a result of the change in the political environment after June 1989.[69]

In 1989, the student movement erupted across the country. Hangzhou and other cities in Zhejiang immediately became involved.[70] As a newcomer to his post, Li was still in the process of taking stock of his new surroundings when he was confronted by this stern challenge to his leadership. In the aftermath of the tragedy in Beijing, when the streets and railway lines in Hangzhou were blockaded, Li did not resort to harsh measures but seems to have reached an agreement that so long as the students allowed the free movement of goods and rubbish in and out of the city at night, no force would be used to break their blockade during the day.

Also, Li moved quickly to demonstrate to the new central leadership that it could have confidence in his stewardship over the province. He brought in a fellow *Renda* graduate, Liu Feng, who at that time was chairman of the Qinghai provincial branch of the People's Consultative Conference, as deputy-secretary in charge of propaganda and organization systems. The head of the propaganda department, Luo Dong, who had been promoted with great fanfare as part of the 1983 leadership reshuffle, was removed from office because he had failed to "stand firm" in the 1989 test of party leadership. Two other *Renda* graduates were brought in to head the propaganda and organization departments, so that word soon got around that Zhejiang was being ruled by People's University graduates. The leadership of the party's media arms was also shaken up. The dichotomy between economic reform and political orthodoxy, which has been a feature of Chinese politics since 1989, thus very quickly became evident in Zhejiang.

In late 1990 Shen Zulun, who had allegedly sent a telegram to Li Peng at a most inopportune time requesting that the center use democratic, legal and rational means to deal with the protesting students,[71] was forced to resign as governor of Zhejiang (while retaining his deputy-secretary's position until December 1993). It is unlikely that this was the only factor behind Shen's resignation because, according to a contemporary report, it was Li Zemin who had contacted the center on May 18, 1989 and conveyed such a message[72] and, on this basis, he would have seemed to have been as vulnerable to disciplinary action as Shen.

Shen Zulun had already pinned his colors to the mast of Zhao Ziyang's coastal economic development strategy, an act of political commitment which may have contributed more to his falling into disfavor with the post-June central leadership. Also, in 1988 a silk cocoon war had broken out between Zhejiang and the provinces of Jiangsu, Sichuan and Anhui.[73] The State Council intervened and instructed that in 1989 no unauthorized price hikes were to be offered to silk farmers in order to procure cocoons. However, it seems that Zhejiang defied this edict, and was accordingly rebuked by the State Council in late 1989.[74] This incident may have provided the central leadership with the opportunity or excuse to remove Shen from office for organizational indiscipline.

Table 3.7

Value of Social Commodity Retail Sales and Percentage Increase over Previous Years, Zhejiang 1981–90

Year	Value (billion yuan)	% increase
1981	10.38	12.0
1982	11.20	8.8
1983	12.54	11.0
1984	14.92	19.0
1985	19.78	32.6
1986	23.32	17.9
1987	27.94	19.8
1988	37.70	35.0
1989	40.03	6.2
1990	40.89	2.2

Source: *Zhejiang jingji nianjian 1991*, p. 106.

Shen was replaced as governor by Ge Hongsheng, an official of the same age who had served in Zhejiang since 1949 but was not a native of the province. After working in Taizhou district in south-east Zhejiang from 1949–56, Ge had spent the following 26 years until 1982 in the electrical power generation industry. Between 1981 and 1983 he held the post of vice-chairman of the provincial economic commission, before being sent to Ningbo as party leader in 1983. He was promoted to the provincial party standing committee in 1986 before being transferred back to Hangzhou as party deputy-secretary in July 1988. It soon became apparent that Ge and Shen held different opinions regarding the future of the provincial economy.

In the meantime Zhejiang had to navigate two difficult years of economic slowdown and retrenchment between 1989 and 1990. Chinese analysts have claimed, with justification, that the austerity program hit Zhejiang particularly severely because of the structure of the province's industrial sector, based as it is on the production of consumer goods. When domestic consumer demand collapsed in 1989 the impact was immediately felt in Zhejiang which, up until that time, had failed to broaden its markets by expanding into the international arena. Even its penetration of the national market was limited. In 1988, the year before the recession, only 37.6 percent of the value of sales by industrial enterprises at the county level and above were either ex-province or exported.[75] Table 3.7 illustrates the force of the slump in local consumer demand in 1989 and 1990. In these same years increases in output of collective industry, rural industry in particular, slowed dramatically to single-digit numbers, the only time this has occurred during the reform period,[76] and the close link between industrial output and retail sales has been referred to above.[77]

Given his bureaucratic background, it was probably no surprise that Ge proved to be a spokesman for and strong advocate of the development of heavy and basic industries in the province. While this was a readjustment of priorities which was clearly required in order to provide Zhejiang's industry with a broader base, it may well have sent alarm bells through the thousands of the province's counties, villages and townships whose economic revival had stemmed from the rapid growth of their light, small-scale, collective, manufacturing sectors. In April 1991, in an interview with a *Renmin Ribao* reporter, Ge expressed great confidence in the project to revive the state industrial sector, stating that it was not ownership per se but leadership and management which were the key to its revival.[78] However, he was referring to the industrial sector whose proportion of GVIO in the province was falling rapidly.[79]

At the annual session of the provincial people's congress in January 1993, a session marked by an unusually defiant mood by normally placid provincial delegates, Ge was voted out of office. It appears that there was a high level of dissatisfaction with his conservative approach to economic growth combined with his ideological orthodoxy. Even Hangzhou's traffic problems, which were very bad that Chinese New Year, were sheeted home to the governor.[80] Ge failed to receive sufficient votes to continue in his post, despite the fact that the central Organization Department had not nominated any alternate. With the number of candidates nominated for the posts of deputy-governor exceeding the quota, delegates nominated an alternate candidate for governor, and in so doing cleverly mitigated the wrath of the center by choosing a man who was both a newcomer and a non-native as their candidate ahead of more experienced locals. Suddenly, and very unexpectedly, deputy-governor Wan Xueyuan found himself governor of Zhejiang.[81]

Zhejiang now found itself led by a party secretary and governor, both non-natives, whose work experience in the province totaled four years. Wan, who was 52 at the time of his elevation to the post, had spent his working life in the adjacent metropolis of Shanghai. There, he had graduated from Jiaotong University in marine mechanics and had stayed on at his alma mater working in the Youth League. Wan continued in this work in the city branch before moving over to the general office of the municipal government. From 1988 until 1992 he occupied the twin posts of secretary-general and director of the municipal government office. Wan's patrons in Shanghai were none other than the present deputy-premier and standing committee member of the CCP CC, Zhu Rongji, and a powerful city politician Wang Daohan.

Despite the extraordinary events surrounding his appointment, Wan fits a pattern of Zhejiang leaders dating back to 1949: party generalists who have spent most of their careers working in party and government general offices rather than in specialist systems within the bureaucracy.[82] There have been exceptions to this pattern, however, with cadres in the military-security complex ruling the province for considerable periods of time. The most striking feature of the leadership has been the total lack of Zhejiang natives occupying both the top party position and, with the exception of Shen Zulun's short stint as governor, the top government post. For a developed province such as Zhejiang this is a remarkable phenomenon.

Despite the continued presence of Ge Hongsheng within the provincial leadership, in early 1992 Zhejiang responded quickly and with great enthusiasm to Deng Xiaoping's call for a renewed rapid economic growth. For the first time since reform had commenced in 1979, the province embarked on a massive capital construction program to build up its infrastructure while simultaneously experiencing the fastest rate of growth in industrial output since 1949, a growth powered by the non-state, non-urban TVE sector. Zhejiang also took more decisive steps to orient its economy to the international market.

Since 1992 Li Zemin has played a clever hand by maintaining a close ideological and political conformity with the center whilst at the same time being an enthusiastic supporter of economic reform. He seems to have dropped some of his early reservations about high-speed growth while keeping an ear out for the slightest shift in central priorities. Thus he is playing the classic role of middleman in the political system analyzed so thoroughly by Frederick Teiwes twenty-five years ago.[83] The 1995 push for grain production is an excellent case of the Zhejiang leadership, despite the misgivings it may hold about the renewed push for self-sufficiency in provincial grain output, pulling out all stops in a highly visible propaganda campaign.[84]

There is very little evidence to suggest that the successive leaders of Zhejiang over the past twenty years have come into any prolonged or significant conflict with the center. Tie Ying's loyalty to Hua Guofeng and his resistance to agricultural reform may have disadvantaged the province, but in exactly what way is difficult to tell. It is most fitting that the central leader who had perhaps the highest profile in Zhejiang after Mao's death was Chen Yun, the epitome of caution and discipline. Chen made publicly reported visits to Hangzhou in 1980, 1983, 1985, 1986 and 1990.[85] His 1990 meeting with the provincial leaders was publicized in the national press in January 1991, with Li Zemin penning an article in *Renmin Ribao* to explain what he and other provincial leaders had learned from Chen's instructions on dialectical materialism.[86]

Another feature of post-Mao Zhejiang politics has been the influence of "retired" provincial leaders who either make regular trips to the province or who reside there and continue to show a fatherly concern for Zhejiang's affairs. Jiang Hua, who was 90 in 1996, is a regular visitor to Hangzhou.[87] Since his formal retirement from the Supreme Court in 1983 Jiang has visited Zhejiang virtually every year.[88] A selection of Jiang's writings and speeches from the pre–Cultural Revolution period, as well as his memoirs concerning events prior to 1949, have been published in handsome editions by the provincial press.[89] It is rumored that at the time of his retirement Jiang Hua requested that he be allowed to live in Hangzhou, but calculating that his presence would not be helpful to the new provincial leadership then only recently installed, the center refused. However, it appears that Jiang has now obtained such approval, for he resides in a villa beside the West Lake and makes occasional appearances at state functions.[90]

Tie Ying and Li Fengping (Jiang Hua's deputy prior to the Cultural Revolution and an official who culminated his lengthy service in the province by serving as governor from 1979 to 1983) have retired in Hangzhou, and both are accorded places of honor at important party and government meetings. Their activities are regularly reported in the provincial press.[91] Another former governor, Shen Zulun, joined the Zhejiang delegation at the National People's Congress session in March 1995 to put forward a four-point opinion on how to handle the grain question in Zhejiang. The present governor, Wan Xueyuan, who spoke immediately after Shen, seemed to rebut his pessimism regarding the prospects for grain production.[92] Shen later presented his views on the future of Zhejiang markets into the next century to a provincial symposium.[93]

The activities and influence of veteran cadres can, as Hu Yaobang and Zhao Ziyang found to their great cost, be highly negative and destabilizing. Indeed, the very concept of retirement is alien to the traditions of Chinese political culture. In Zhejiang, these high-ranking former officials put the present leadership to some trouble and inconvenience. Given the Chinese traditions of respect for senior leaders, they have to be formally received, briefed on recent developments, escorted on major trips and their personal comfort and reception attended to in accordance with their status.[94] Whether the general tenor of their advice to the current provincial leadership tends in the direction of caution (along the lines of Chen Yun's 1990 talk) or encouragement for more rapid advance and change is difficult to calculate, although the odds would favor the former.

Provincial Strategies of Economic Reform

It has been argued by one of the more acute and insightful observers into the Zhejiang economy that with a plentiful supply of labor common to all provinces, regional economic development in China is decided by a combination of natural resource endowment, the ability to accumulate funds and technology. During the pre-reform period under a highly centralized plan, natural resource endowment and state investment greatly influenced regional development and the division of labor, and the growth of resource-led industries was superior to those which were guided by the market. Thus, regional superiority did not lie in Zhejiang, which was responsible for its below-average growth rates during the Maoist years. For example, between 1953 and 1976 national GVIO grew at an annual average rate of 11.1 percent while in Zhejiang the rate was only 9.4 percent. In the reform period four major changes have occurred.

First, with the change in the mode of allocation and variation in investment entities the proportion of state investment in total fixed assets has fallen, and local investment and enterprise investment (extra-budgetary funds) in replacement and reconstruction has increased. The proportion of bank loans in investment has increased, so that bank deposits have become a major source of accumulation. There has also been a regional discrepancy in foreign investment. Second, the strengthening of the role of the market has meant that technological factors have played a broader role in the assertion of regional comparative advantage. Third, despite regional blockades and protectionist tendencies, the market has played an increased role in the circulation of production materials and finished products. Fourth, the open-door policy of increased trade and use of foreign capital has favored coastal provinces, and increased their comparative advantage in relation to technology and capital endowments.[95]

The operating mechanisms of the economy have undergone major reform with a series of consequences for economic growth in Zhejiang.[96] First the role of the plan in allocating materials has been eroded and replaced by that of the market. This national trend has been beneficial to Zhejiang for the reasons mentioned above. The approach of concurrently relaxing and adjusting (mainly increasing) prices has been applied first to agricultural and sideline products as well as to consumer goods, and then to production materials, the transport and communication sector, labor products and service fees. Second, various business responsibility systems have been established in agricultural households, industrial and commercial enterprises and with local governments (fiscal contracting). Third, and most relevant to this section of the paper, what have been termed "intermediate-level adjustment and control mechanisms" (zhongguan tiaokong jizhi) have been utilized by provincial governments to encourage the development of various industrial sectors and departments.

These mechanisms include fiscal, monetary, financial and administrative policies, and indicate the priorities and preferences of provincial authorities toward reform and economic growth. It is here where the Zhejiang authorities have attempted to give expression to a provincial economic strategy. However, this strategy has shifted several times since 1979, reflecting uncertainty within the provincial leadership about the general thrust of central policy, and indecision and division in relation to the direction of economic reform. The strategy has also been hostage to macro-economic controls, political events and the conflict of wider interests over which the provincial authorities can exercise little control.

This section will first briefly discuss the overall strategy of economic reform in Zhejiang, and then examine its implementation in relation to three major sectors of the economy: agriculture, industry, and foreign trade and investment. It will focus on the role of provincial leadership in relation to reform in these three sectors, and attempt to explain the contradictory differences in both outputs and outcomes in each example. While reform to the collective structure of the agricultural economy was initially resisted very strongly, agricultural growth was most impressive in the early to mid 1980s but this sector has since become the Achilles Heel of the provincial economy. While the provincial authorities moved quickly to make fundamental readjustments to industry policy, the larger sphere of urban and industrial reform proved a difficult and arduous undertaking. But throughout the whole period (except during the center-contrived recession of 1989–90) the rate of industrial growth went ahead at fantastic proportions. A series of measures were taken to open the economy to the outside world, and a large number of special zones were established throughout the province, both by the center and the local authorities, yet Zhejiang's foreign trade and investment performance has lagged behind that of other coastal provinces. A preliminary conclusion could be that the basis of the Zhejiang economy (rural, collective, small-scale processing), which is both its strength and its weakness, is highly resilient, self-sustaining and self-directed.

In the immediate aftermath of the Cultural Revolution the provincial leadership immediately set about to repair the economy from the ravages of the ten years of upheaval. In late 1977, at the provincial people's congress, a plan was put forward for the development of a relatively comprehensive economic system, meaning the all-round development of agriculture, light industry and heavy industry with an emphasis on heavy industry.[97] This strategy, which was a continuation of a decision made at the national planning conference in 1970 and endorsed by the then military provincial leadership,[98] was ratified at the provincial party congress in 1978,[99] and seems to have been part of a national developmental strategy focusing on regional development.[100]

The first steps away from this previously discredited and inappropriate strategy occurred in the wake of the 3rd plenum of 1978 when, in 1979, the development of light industry was given priority in terms of the allocation of raw materials, funds and energy.[101] In 1980 the Zhejiang provincial planning commission commented that,

> In the past Zhejiang failed to study seriously its economic advantages and characteristics while endeavoring for industrial development. An unrealistic proposal was even made to build a so-called independent comprehensive industrial system in Zhejiang. With very poor coal and iron resources, we made extraordinary efforts to produce coal and iron. As a result, not only have the coal and iron industries not been developed but other industries with good potential in Zhejiang have not been well developed either.[102]

Recognition of the mistakes of the past was the first step toward dropping this strategy and moving toward a new approach to Zhejiang's economic development. In 1981 the provincial authorities issued a "Report on the economic situation and problems in economic development" (*Guanyu jingji qingkuang he jingji fazhan wentide baogao*) which affirmed that Zhejiang's industry was based on light industry, and that the province possessed good port facilities which had been under-utilized.[103]

During the sixth five-year plan (1981–85) the provincial authorities decided upon a series of preferential policies for the light and textile industries in relation to the supply of inputs (capital, including foreign currency for imports, and raw materials including electricity, coal, oil, ferrous metals and timber). In 1985 the provincial authorities set out a series of preferential policies for the TVE sector in relation to taxation, loans and profit retention rate which played a major role in its subsequent galloping growth rate.[104] With the encouragement of lateral links among provinces, cities and enterprises, Zhejiang strove to compensate for its raw material deficiencies by signing all kinds of agreements with other provinces, central ministries and state companies. In the five years from 1980 to 1985 one-third of the province's coal and two-fifths of its steel were obtained by such agreements, which have expanded from materials to funds, technology and personnel. In return, 60 percent of the province's industrial output during this period was sold outside the province or overseas, a proportion higher than that in 1988.[105]

In 1984 and 1985 two meetings were held in Beijing and Hangzhou to draw up a fifteen-year medium-range strategic outline for Zhejiang's social and economic development. The finished document was made public in mid-1986.[106] Emphasis was placed on fostering the role of cities as economic centers and building up Beilun port in Ningbo. The province would rely primarily upon its own sources of accumulation to finance an expansion in capital construction, with state investment being provided on an unprecedented scale. Four provincial economic regions were identified, based on major cities, and a division of labor would see each region concentrate on utilizing its own resource base to best effect, supplemented by inter-provincial and international trade. However, this regional distribution was challenged by some, who argued that Zhejiang should be divided into two economic regions radiating from the ports of Ningbo in the north and Wenzhou in the south. This would have been a controversial division because it would have in effect downgraded the importance of the provincial capital Hangzhou in the province's economic development.[107] It was thus overruled in the final version of the strategic outline.

Lobbyists for the Hangzhou cause may well have been able to co-opt the poorer interior districts of the province to support the retention of four provincial regions where their interests were better protected than in the two-division schema. For, as Table 3.8 reveals, extremes of economic wealth prevailed in Zhejiang in the 1980s. While neighboring Anhui Province was clearly poorer than Zhejiang, its per capita gross output was concentrated in the lower brackets, while the spread in its richer eastern neighbor was far greater. There was a less than 1:4 ratio between the poorest and richest counties in Anhui, while in Zhejiang the ratio was almost 1:10. The author comments that:

> The *xian* with high output per person were nearly all concentrated in the coastal plain area in the north of the province, close to the cities of Ningbo, Shaoxing and Hangzhou, and adjacent to the rich area of southern Jiangsu (Jiangnan) and, of course, the great metropolis of Shanghai. Particularly striking is the very high level of output per person from rural industries in these areas, ranging from around 1300 *yuan* in Yin and Shaoxing *xian* to less than

Table 3.8

1984 Per Capita GVIAO in the Counties of Zhejiang and Anhui
(unit = yuan)

	Number of counties	
GVIAO per capita	Zhejiang	Anhui
>2,000	2 (highest: 2180)	0
1,500–999	10	0
1,000–499	10	0
500–999	32	22 (highest: 886)
<500	13 (lowest: 239)	53 (lowest: 241)

Source: Peter Nolan, *The Political Economy of Collective Farms: An Analysis of China's Post-Mao Rural Reforms* (Cambridge: Polity Press, 1988), p. 171.

50 *yuan* in Songyang, Jingning, Yunhe, Qingyuan, Wencheng and Taishun *xian* ... The *xian* with low levels of output per person were all concentrated in the mountainous areas in the south and west of the province.[108]

Other statistics reinforce this picture of the unequal distribution of economic wealth in Zhejiang in the mid 1980s. In 1984 the five sub-provincial cities of northeast Zhejiang (Hangzhou, Ningbo, Shaoxing, Jiaxing and Huzhou) and the island chain Zhoushan district comprised 43 percent of the area of the province, had a population equal to 51 percent of the provincial total, but produced 72 percent of Zhejiang's GVIAO and 77 percent of its GVIO. Per capita GVIAO at 1,833 yuan in the northeast districts was 2.5 times higher than the 735 yuan in the five southeast cities and districts (Wenzhou, Jinhua, Quzhou, Taizhou and Lishui). Per capita GVIO, at 1,262 yuan in the northeast districts, was 3.2 times higher than the 389 yuan in the southwest. Thus, the issue of intra-provincial regional economic inequality was a very real one in Zhejiang.

It appears, from a series of articles published in local journals such as *Zhejiang jingji* (Zhejiang Economy) and *Zhejiang jingji yanjiu* (Studies in the Zhejiang Economy) in 1985 and 1986 that the other controversial aspect of the strategy which was formulated in the mid 1980s related to opening to the outside world. Some participants in the debate over Zhejiang's economic strategy advocated that the province take advantage of its membership in the Shanghai Economic Zone[109] as a conduit to both the wider domestic market and the world market.[110] Another contributor argued that Zhejiang should rely primarily on its own resources and markets.[111] The issue remained unresolved until Zhao Ziyang's intervention in late 1987 to involve coastal provinces such as Zhejiang in his strategy of deepening economic relationships with the outside world.

In late 1987, after the CCP's 13th National Party Congress, the newly installed General Secretary Zhao Ziyang launched his coastal development strategy by making two visits to eastern provinces in November 1987 and early January 1988.[112] Zhejiang was one of the key targets of the visits, with Zhao inspecting the northern municipality of Jiaxing between November 23 and 25, and then the port city of Ningbo between January 4 and 6, 1988.[113] Whilst he was in Zhejiang he was accompanied by Xue Ju and his deputy Shen Zulun. In Ningbo, Party Secretary Ge Hongsheng acted as host together with the city's mayor.

Zhao's coastal strategy was summed up by the slogan "two heads pointing out with the middle directed inward" (*liangtou zaiwai, zhongjian zainei*). This referred to the strategy of the coastal provinces importing raw materials, processing them and then exporting the manufactured goods to the international market (*yuan ziliao zaiwai, shichang zaiwai, ziji jiagong*). It called for a strengthening and broadening of the strategy of integration into the world market for the coastal region as a whole, and in particular emphasized the export potential of the fast growing TVE sector in the Yangtze River Delta region.[114] After Zhao's first visit to Zhejiang the local authorities responded in early December 1987 with a commentary entitled "Strike out for the international market!" (*da xiang guoji shichang qu!*), which argued that in the past Zhejiang had relied on the domestic market for both supplies of raw materials and for the consumers of its manufactured goods. However, this approach, the commentary pointed out, could not be sustained because interior provinces were striving to process their materials and would compete with Zhejiang on the domestic market. This meant a re-orientation to the international market. However, hedging its bets in a manner for which Zhejiang was renowned, the commentary warned that just as food could only be consumed one mouthful at a time, then the road ahead could only be trodden one step at a time.[115]

At a meeting held by the provincial party committee in late December 1987 to discuss the documents from the 13th National CCP Congress, Shen Zulun delivered a substantive report in which he expressed whole-hearted support for the shift in the province's economic strategy.[116] Shen also tackled head on some of the most controversial issues concerning provincial developmental strategy. These included, first, the importance assigned to the outward-looking strategy of engaging the world market. Shen observed that previous attempts to extend lateral links had, in practice, been confined mainly to the domestic market, primarily the "three norths" (north, north-east and north-west China). At only 10 percent of GDP, Zhejiang's export industry was, in his view under-developed.[117] Shen also referred to the relative importance assigned to light industry and heavy industry. He pointed out that some people wished to increase the proportion and importance assigned to the heavy and chemical industries relative to the light and textile industries. Shen disagreed with this approach. He also dismissed the perennial desire of striving for internal balance (that is self-sufficiency) within the provincial economy, and pointed out that the approach of strengthening lateral links with other provinces was preferable. Finally, Shen referred to the long-standing problem of low efficiency in the province's industrial enterprises. He pointed out that the root of the problem lay not with the equipment or technology (he provided figures to refute the notion that these were outmoded) but in the management of the existing stock of capital and labor.

In February 1988, after the closure of the first session of the 7th provincial people's congress where Shen Zulun was elected governor, an official editorial described Zhao's initiative as involving a strategic shift in Zhejiang's economic strategy (*jingji zhanlüe zhuanbian*).[118] Xue Ju's government work report to the congress devoted one section to the outward-looking strategy, and outlined five specific measures to implement Zhao's strategy.[119] These included reform of the foreign trade system in which foreign trading corporations would be responsible for their own profits and losses in a contractual arrangement with Beijing;[120] the opening and promotion of new markets with preferential treatment to Taiwanese businessmen (who had just benefited from the liberalization of contacts with the mainland announced by the government on Taiwan in 1987); a relaxation of policies to encourage foreign investment; utilization of foreign funds to transform and upgrade enterprises; and the increase in foreign currency revenue from non-merchandise trade through tourism and the export of labor and technology.[121]

The ink was hardly dry on the series of policy documents drawn up to give effect to this strategic shift when economic retrenchment combined with political upheaval shifted the attention of the provincial leadership elsewhere. By the end of 1990 Zhejiang had emerged badly scathed from the short-lived but serious economic recession. Early in 1991 Governor Ge Hongsheng presented the eighth five-year plan and a ten-year medium-term program to the provincial people's congress.[122] An official editorial, entitled "Laying a foundation, improving standards and raising economic efficiency," and released on the eve of the congress session, described the proposals as reflecting a change in the province's economic strategy.[123] Laying a foundation referred to agriculture, basic industries, infrastructure, science and technology, education and economic management. Improving standards referred to the necessity to improve the utility rate of the existing stock of equipment by raising technological levels, employees' skills and product quality. Raising economic efficiency was defined as taking the road of high output with low input and low consumption, and paying attention to social and ecological benefits. It is clear that most of these sectors and issues had been neglected during the previous decade in the mad rush into manufacturing. A strategic shift of investment into heavy industries was foreshadowed, but this time, unlike in the Maoist period, the enterprises were to be located on the coast and primarily in Ge Hongsheng's former bailiwick of Ningbo.

Events again overtook the provincial leadership. The impact of Deng Xiaoping's southern tour of early 1992 was felt immediately in Zhejiang, where a powerful constituency in favor of economic growth per se, if not for reform in all its manifestations, had evidently been established. An official editorial in February sounded the clarion call for a renewal of the reform program.[124] Zhejiang's economy immediately slipped back into high gear in the same vehicle which had driven it through the 1980s—rural industry. So rapid was the rate of growth that targets set down in Ge Hongsheng's 1991 report were surpassed well in advance. For example, the target of 140 billion yuan for GDP and 3,000 yuan per capita GDP by the year 2000 were met in 1993 (the latter target was almost attained in 1992). Conservative but respectable annual rates of growth targets were soon made to look ridiculous. GVIO was estimated to grow at a rate of 8 percent, but between 1991 and 1994 it grew by nearly five times this figure at a rate of 38 percent. Budgetary revenue was predicted to grow by 5.5 percent per annum, when the actual figure between 1991 and 1994 was nearly 20 percent. The planned increase in investments in social fixed assets was fixed at 5 percent, while in reality the rate hit 50 percent. The export target for 2000 was surpassed in 1992, with the estimated growth rate of 7 percent being more than quadrupled at 29 percent. Output targets presented by Ge to the 1992 session of the provincial people's congress were adjusted upward within two months.[125]

The lessons of Zhejiang's experience in the 1989–90 recession were quickly learnt. The strategy of opening to the outside world has become a reality rather than a platitude repeated ad nauseum to satisfy the demands of political correctness. A series of open zones and technology zones have been approved by the center and the province.[126] In 1993 the Ningbo free-trade zone (baoshuiqu) went into operation. The provincial authorities have also approved the opening of vast tracts of territory as economic zones with preferential tax and other policies designed to attract foreign investment.

To sum up, Zhejiang's economic strategy in the reform period has been characterized less by an incremental process of building upon previous gains as by a series of advances, halts and retreats. The provincial leadership has endeavored to keep the province in step with the beat of the central drum, even if the pace of that beat has varied from time to time, or unpredictable pauses have occurred between beats. This approach applies particularly to the middle period of reform from 1983 to 1991. Prior to 1983 an almost inevitable economic recovery occurred as Zhejiang's political situation stabilized and the province was gradually freed from the constraints imposed by the central plan and was allowed to build on its inherent strengths. Since 1992 when the direction and speed of reform have been less plagued by controversy, the Zhejiang leadership has felt more secure in shifting, albeit ever so cautiously, from the ranks of laggards to bandwagoners.

In the earlier stages the provincial leadership was reluctant to implement agricultural decollectivization. The detailed and illuminating discussion of reform in the agricultural sector contained in an official account of the first six years of rural reform[127] sums up the provincial leadership's attitude in words which could be applied equally to the past forty-odd years as a whole. Rural reform, it is argued, came about not as the result of directives from above, but as a result of the action of the peasants creating reform in practice. The leadership lagged behind the masses, and its thinking lagged behind reality and was stuck in

Table 3.9

Foreign Trade and Investment in Zhejiang, 1979–95 (unit = US$ million)

Year	Exports	Imports	Contracted items	Contracted value	Utilized investment
1979–83			3	22.2[a]	
1984	736.9	55.5	19		11.6
1985	957.7	185.8	83	89.1	62.1
1986	1,156.1	133.6	57	52.7	49.4
1987	1,370.3	213.5	84	143.3	114.0
1988	1,620.2	399.5	202	268.1	188.0
1989	1,879.2	450.1	248	345.3	269.2
1990	2,259.6	290.8	296	247.9	162.3
1991	2,912.6	538.4	592	374.8	171.9
1992	3,702.7	953.2	2,343	33,240.9	409.7
1993	4,560.4	1,690.2	4,497	4,043.3	1,219.9
1994	6,319.4	2,138.8	2,537	3,177.4	1,370.7
1995	8,445.0	3,080.7	1,861	4,221.5	1,539.7

Source: Dangdai Zhongguode Zhejiang, Vol. I, p.148; *ZJTJNJ*, various years).
Note: There are three major categories of foreign investment: foreign loans (government, international financial institutions and private financial institutions), direct investment (joint ventures, cooperative ventures, completely foreign owned ventures) and other investments by foreign business. [a]Includes compensatory trade, processing imported materials, leasing and borrowings, etc.

old grooves. The Tie Ying leadership believed, rightly or wrongly, that the rural socialist collective economy then in existence was the only suitable form, and that breaking out of this pattern would shake the public ownership system and depart from the socialist orientation. The leadership allegedly absolutised the public system and believed that egalitarianism in distribution was a sign of the superiority of socialism. It equated household business with the small peasant economy, and argued that to revert to this institutional arrangement would be a retrograde step.[128]

The provincial leadership under Wang Fang and Xue Ju did not attempt to block urban reform but found the enterprise a most difficult undertaking. The official description of the issue uses such phrases as heated discussion, not proceeded with, further explored, tested and explored,[129] indicating the controversy and semi-paralysis which the urban reform agenda engendered within the provincial authorities. When the center decided to decentralize foreign trade policy in the mid 1980s, for example, there was a nervous reaction in Zhejiang, and doubt as to whether the province could rise to the challenge. In the latest phase since 1992, however, the province has given the appearance of having thrown off much of its previous caution.

Many local observers have noted the wide discrepancy between the speed

Table 3.10

Zhejiang Ownership Proportions, 1978–95

	1978	1980	1985	1990	1995
1. Employees by enterprise ownership					
State	10.2	11.2	10.4	11.0	11.1
Urban collective	7.2	8.2	7.9	7.4	6.5
Other economic types			0.1	0.2	1.4
Urban private and individual	0.1	0.2	0.5	1.2	3.1
Rural	82.5	80.4	81.1	80.2	76.7
Other employees					1.2
2. GVIO by ownership					
State	61.3	56.4	37.2	31.2	16.1
Collective	38.7	43.0	60.4	60.1	56.0
TVE[a]	16.0	19.7	37.3	46.3	63.5
Other		0.5	0.7	2.1	10.1
Individual		0.1	1.7	6.6	17.8
3. Social consumer retail sales					
State	41.3	39.1	26.4	27.6	24.0
Collective	53.5	56.0	47.1	31.1	17.7
Joint			0.1	0.6	0.5
Private	0.4	0.6	16.7	27.6	38.5
Rural to non-agricultural population	4.8	4.3	9.7	13.1	19.3

Source: ZJTJNJ 1996, p.16.
Note: [a]TVEs can be collectively or individually owned.

with which state influence in the economy of Zhejiang has fallen (see Table 3.10) compared to the tardiness with which contentious reform policies have been implemented, and have contrasted Zhejiang unfavorably with Guangdong on this score. The restructuring of the ownership composition of the provincial economy in favor of the non-state sectors has in many respects been an irreversible trend which only the most obdurate and counter-productive resistance could have prevented or even slowed. On the other hand, mapping out and following a strategy for reform involves a much more pro-active role on the part of the provincial leadership. In many respects the credit for Zhejiang's rapid growth rate can be attributed more to the overall reform program launched by Beijing together with the entrepreneurial skills and hard work of the Zhejiangese people combined with the location and resource base which had been transformed from a liability into an advantage, than to the leadership skills and drive of the provincial authorities.

A comparison of the economies of Zhejiang and Guangdong provinces as of 1986 noted that since 1978 Zhejiang had caught up and even overtaken its larger southern counterpart as a result of higher rates of growth, particularly in industrial output. This was attributed to the greater development of rural industry and urban collective industry as well as a slower rate of population increase. Yet in terms of underlying industrial strength (*houjin*), measured in terms of the more developed nature of tertiary industry, a more balanced relationship between light and heavy industry accompanied by less reliance on the agricultural sector for industrial inputs, a more balanced departmental structure of industry in terms of the relationship among extractive, raw materials and processing industries, a more even distribution of enterprises by size, a greater proportion of modern industries, and finally a far more active engagement with the international economy, the writers concluded that Guangdong's economy was superior to that of Zhejiang.[130]

Analysts in the 1990s were recounting a similar story. For example, a Zhejiang delegation which inspected enterprises in the TVE sector in the Pearl River Delta in 1991 was amazed at the superiority of technology and equipment which it discovered.[131] While it has been acknowledged that Zhejiang has led the way in the transition from a state-dominated economy to a more mixed ownership system (while maintaining the predominance, it is alleged, of the public economy over the private) continued government interference in the operation of markets and the functioning of the commodity economy were compared unfavorably to the situation in Guangdong.[132] In an attempt to quantify this, a researcher from the provincial bureau of statistics noted that between 1979 and 1986 Zhejiang's GDP increased at an annual average rate of 14.4 percent compared to Guangdong's 12 percent. However, between 1987 and 1991, a period which covered the recession which bit deeply in Zhejiang, its rate of increase in GDP slowed to 8.3 percent per annum while Guangdong's increased to 14.5 percent. Answering his own question as to why this had occurred, the writer attributed the increased growth rate in Guangdong to its greater consciousness of and performance in undertaking reform and opening than Zhejiang, where it was claimed enterprise policy and market adjustment still suffered from undue government interference.[133]

Provincial Policy over Resource Allocation

One of the major paradoxes in Zhejiang's economy during the Maoist period was the stark contrast between the comparative wealth of its budgetary revenues and the paucity of investment in social infrastructure and capital construction. While Zhejiang was a major budgetary revenue remitter to the central government, for security and strategic reasons the center located few investment projects in the province. It was the inability or the unwillingness of the provincial leadership to put the case to Beijing for a better fiscal arrangement and greater central commitment to the economic growth of Zhejiang which contributed to this state of affairs.[134] The legacy of this historical injustice has spilled over into the reform period. Several indicators illustrate the imbalance between Zhejiang's economic status, fiscal effort and investment outlays into the early years of reform.

In 1983 provincial GSP (gross social product) equaled 4.4 percent of the national total, while state investment in fixed assets comprised only 2.2 percent of the national sum, ranking Zhejiang twentieth in China. By 1988, GSP in Zhejiang had grown to comprise 5.7 percent of China's total, ranking the province seventh, while investment at 2.5 percent of the national total placed Zhejiang fourteenth. In 1981 50 percent of revenues collected in the province were remitted to the center, and in 1987 the figure was still 45 percent. In 1988 Zhejiang's net remittances of 1.7 billion yuan was the fifth highest of all provincial-level units. This remittance may have been commensurate with its economic strength—in terms of national income Zhejiang ranked seventh in the country—but its investment ranking lagged far behind.[135] Thus, Zhejiang's ability to control and direct resources was impeded by a combination of the redistributive policies of the Chinese state combined with its regional investment priorities. In short, the center took financial resources from Zhejiang but located few construction projects in the province.

1. Fiscal Policy

From 1949 until 1980, when a major reform to the fiscal relations between center and provinces took place, Zhejiang's basic fiscal priority was to fulfill central remittance targets and then, on the basis of the funds left under its control, fulfill expenditure line commitments laid down by the center. Table 3.11 shows the proportion of local revenues collected in Zhejiang which have been remitted to the center in different periods since 1949. Along with the three centrally administered cities, and Liaoning, Jiangsu and Shandong provinces, Zhejiang has been a major contributor to central coffers over the whole post-Liberation period.[136]

An official account of Zhejiang's public finances between 1949 and 1985 makes the observation that the state of government finances depends on the coordination and development of the national economy, which in turn is closely related to the political situation.[137] An example from Wenzhou illustrates this point. During the upheavals of the Cultural Revolution Wenzhou was badly affected by factionalism.[138] In the most tumultuous years of 1967 and 1968 GVIO fell successively by 13 percent and 7 percent. In the renewed instability of the anti-Confucius anti–Lin Biao campaign of 1974 industrial output fell 17 percent on 1973. With well over 90 percent of budgetary revenue coming from enterprise profits and taxes, it is not surprising that budgetary revenue suffered badly in those same years, 1967, 1968 and 1974. In 1967, budgetary revenue fell over 40 percent and then another 25 percent in 1968, so that budgetary revenue for 1968 was only 38 percent of the sum in 1964. In 1969 industrial output rose by 26 percent and budgetary revenue shot up, from its nadir, by almost 100 percent. Then in 1974 budgetary revenue fell by almost 50 percent, on top of a 12 percent fall in 1973. However, even with a small recovery in industrial output in

Table 3.11

% Total Budgetary Revenue Remitted to the Center since 1949

1949–84	43.9[a]
1951–85	43.6
1953–57	63.0[b]
1965	63.3
1976–78	27.0
1979–85	40.4
1987	45.0
1988	20.0
1993–94	26.3

Source: Zhejiang shengqing, pp. 627, 639; *Zhejiang 1979–1988 nian jingji fazhan baogao*, pp.2–3; *Dangdai Zhongguode Zhejiang*, Vol. I, pp. 532, 534, 541, 549; 1993 and 1994 budgest speeches.

Note: [a]45 percent of "loans" and the purchases of state bonds are included; [b]71 percent if central taxes collected in Zhejiang are included.

1975 government finances continued to hemmorage, with a further fall of almost 50 percent in that year. Despite a slight recovery in 1976 budget revenue in 1975 and 1976 was lower than that for 1952! Massive deficits were incurred for the three years 1974 to 1976.[139]

The percentage of GDP accruing to government has sometimes been seen as an indication of the state's extractive capacity, and there are differing views as to how great China's extractive capacity is and to what extent it has declined during the reform period.[140] Just as the state sector in Zhejiang has comprised a lower proportion of economic activity compared to other provinces, so its budgetary revenues as a percentage of GDP have been below the national average. Table 3.12 illustrates that the government's share of provincial income has declined dramatically since 1978, when it was already at a low point both by national and international standards. For China as a whole, in 1978 budgetary revenue at 31 percent of GNP was 50 percent higher than that in Zhejiang, while by 1993, at 17 percent, it was almost double the rate of Zhejiang. Looking further at the distribution of national income, in 1978 in addition to the 25 percent which accrued to government, the remaining 75 percent was divided between personal (60 percent) and collective income (15 percent). Ten years later, in 1988, state finances had halved to 13 percent of national income, individual incomes had fallen to 50 percent, while collective income had more than doubled to 37 percent,[141] an indication of the large increase in extra-budgetary funds held by enterprises.

Considering its rapid industrial growth over the reform period, the rate of increase in Zhejiang's budgetary revenues has not been impressive (see Table 3.13). The situation has improved markedly in the years 1991–95, with an annual growth rate of 20 percent, but this can largely be accounted for by an unprecedented 41 percent increase in budgetary revenues in fiscal year 1993 (the

Table 3.12

Zhejiang's Extractive Capacity, 1978–95

	1978	1980	1985	1990	1995
Budgetary revenue as % GDP	22.2	17.3	14.1	12.1	7.9
Budgetary revenue as % GVIAO	13.6	10.5	8.0	5.7	3.2
Budgetary revenue as % GVIO	22.0	16.7	10.6	7.1	3.7
Budgetary revenue as % national income	25.0	19.5	15.9	14.0	11.0[a]

Source: Zhejiang jingji tongji nianjian 1985 (Yearbook of Zhejiang Economic Statistics), p.III-24; calculated from *ZJTJNJ 1993*, p. 24; *ZJTJNJ 1994*, pp. 24 and 323; *ZJTJNJ 1995*, pp. 9 and 11.
Note: [a]1992.

Table 3.13

Annual Rate of Increase in Budgetary Revenue and Outlays: Zhejiang and China

	1979–95	1981–95	1986–95	1991–95
Budgetary revenue (Zhejiang)	13.8	14.9	15.6	19.6
All governments	10.6	13.4		
Central	16.8	11.5		
Local	8.8	14.4		
Budgetary expenditure (Zhejiang)	14.7	16.9	17.0	17.6
All governments	11.0	14.1		
Central	9.2	11.2		
Local	12.2	16.2		

Source: ZJTJNJ 1996, p. 9, 11 and 13; *Jingji yanjiu cankao*, No. 58, August 26, 1992, p. 32.

reasons for which will be discussed below), after very disappointing, single-digit increases over the previous three years.

Over the period 1978 to 1995 the annual average increase in budgetary revenue was about 50 percent less than the increase in GVIAO and national income (see Table 3.14). Thus, a decreasing portion of the increased growth in public wealth which has been generated in Zhejiang over the past fifteen years has gone into the hands of government, constraining its ability to provide public services and facilities, to assist poorer regions of the province by redistributing income, and to utilize its "intermediate-level" adjustment and control mechanisms. In the late 1980s the World Bank calculated the tax effort of China's provinces, that is, the ratio of tax collection to estimated taxable capacity, for the year 1986. Zhejiang was ranked seventeenth out of a total of twenty provinces surveyed.[142]

Table 3.14

Annual Rates of Increase in GVIAO, National Income, and Budgetary Revenue, 1978–95

Year	% Increase GVIAO	% Increase national income	% Increase budgetary revenue
1978	21.7	22.6	37.4
1979	16.3	17.0	4.9
1980	19.5	15.3	20.2
1981	11.5	12.4	10.3
1982	10.7	12.4	6.5
1983	11.2	6.8	2.2
1984	26.5	23.1	12.2
1985	36.7	32.2	24.8
1986	19.6	15.3	17.8
1987	24.7	20.4	11.3
1988	31.7	25.6	12.0
1989	15.3	9.3	14.8
1990	7.9	4.0	3.4
1991	22.5	17.8	7.2
1992	31.4	25.1	8.6
1993	56.8	—	40.8
1994	37.2	—	25.7
1984:1978	141.4	123.5	69.7
Per annual average	15.8	14.3	9.2
1984:1980	73.5	66.4	48.5
Per annual average	14.8	13.6	10.4
1994:1978	1,959.2		762.8
Per annual average 1979–94	20.4		13.5

Source: Zhejiang jingji tongji nianjian 1985, p. III-24; calculated from *ZJTJNJ 1993*, p. 24; *ZJTJNJ 1994*, pp. 24, 323; *ZJTJNJ 1995*, pp. 9, 11; *ZJTJNJ 1996*.

Budgetary Revenues

Budgetary revenue grew at an annual average rate of 13.8 percent between 1978 and 1995, and the rate of growth picked up speed during the seventeen years.[143] In 1985 Zhejiang budgetary collections per capita amounted to 145 yuan (the national mean was 169 yuan), and total collections comprised 4.95 percent of the national total. Zhejiang's share of national budgetary revenue ranked it eighth in

Table 3.15

Composition of Zhejiang Budgetary Revenue, 1978–95
(unit = billion yuan)

Year	Total	ERa	(Industry)	(Com-merce)	Industrial & com-mercial tax	Salt tax	Agr. tax
1978	2.74	0.99	0.62	0.34	1.51	0.04	0.15
1979	2.59	0.72	0.61	0.37	1.66	0.04	0.15
1980	3.13	1.01	0.78	0.42	1.88	0.04	0.14
1981	3.43	1.03	0.83	0.45	2.16	0.05	0.15
1982	3.66	0.89	0.80	0.40	2.51	0.06	0.16
1983	4.18	1.00	0.88	0.38	2.88	0.05	0.17
1984	4.68	0.91	0.80	0.35	3.46	0.05	0.18
1985	5.82	0.76	0.69	0.24	4.74	0.04	0.22
1986	6.86	0.94	0.71	0.24	5.52	0.06	0.24
1987	7.64	0.93	0.79	0.25	6.26	0.05	0.24
1988	8.55	0.44	0.80	0.21	7.47	0.04	0.25
1989	9.82	0.20	0.76	0.19	8.58	0.05	0.33
1990	10.16	0.00	0.61	0.11	8.86	0.03	0.33
1991	10.89	0.19	0.48	0.07	9.65	0.04	0.33
1992	11.84	−0.25	0.40	0.08	10.90	0.04	0.34
1993	16.66	−1.01	−0.06	−0.02	16.41	0.03	0.33
1994	20.94						
1995	23.63b						

Source: ZJTJNJ 1996; annual budget speeches.

Note: Columns 3 and 4 are components of column 2, but column 2 is greater than the total of columns 3 and 4. Total revenue is greater than the combined total of columns 2, 5, 6 and 7.

aER = enterprise revenue.

bCalculated by adding the "two central taxes" (sales tax plus 75 percent of value-added tax) to local budgetary revenues.

China, one below its national income ranking and one above its population ranking.[144] By 1987 Zhejiang's ranking in terms of per capita fiscal revenue had risen to fifth, a position it held in 1990. Only the three centrally administered cities and Liaoning Province outperformed Zhejiang.[145] It appears, then, that in the past ten years Zhejiang's revenue-raising performance has improved.

During the reform period, the sources of budgetary revenues have changed considerably (see Table 3.15). Industrial and commercial indirect taxes have become the mainstay of government finance. In 1978 these comprised 55 percent of budgetary revenues, 60 percent in 1980, rising rapidly to 81 percent in 1985, 87 percent in 1990, and hitting a remarkable 98 percent in 1993 before dropping back to 84 percent in 1994. Enterprise revenues have fallen from 36 percent of budgetary revenues in 1978 to become a deduction from revenues by 1992. This is a nation-wide phenomenon, and the reasons behind the decline in enterprise revenues collected by the state have been analyzed at length.[146]

Expenditures

The rate of growth in budgetary expenditures, at 14.7 percent per annum, has been almost one percentage point more rapid than that of revenues for the whole period 1979 to 1995. But the gap in growth rates between revenues and outlays has narrowed over the fifteen years, and in the period 1991 to 1995 revenues have out-grown expenditures by 2 percent per annum.[147] In 1985 per capita budgetary expenditure in Zhejiang was calculated to be 93 yuan (well below the national mean of 152 yuan) and total expenditures comprised 3.6 percent of national outlays, over one percentage point less than Zhejiang's national revenues. Zhejiang's ranking in terms of per capita fiscal outlays fell from twelfth in 1985 to eighteenth by 1990.[148] So that while in 1985 figures showed that Zhejiang had a relatively poor tax effort, and its per capita budgetary revenues were only 86 percent of the national average, its per capita outlays were even lower, at 61 percent of the national average. Zhejiang's ratio of expenditures to collections was 0.53 in 1983, increasing to 0.74 in 1986. These were the fifth and fourth lowest respectively across China.[149] The ratio in 1995 remained at 0.73. Public finance in Zhejiang thus seems to be characterized by a low and inefficient extraction and a conservative fiscal stance in which budgetary surpluses are a major policy objective.[150]

In terms of where the provincial government spends its money, Tables 3.16 and 3.17 reveal a major shift in priorities from economic to non-economic items. For example, in 1978 (Table 3.16) columns 2 and 3 comprised 44 percent of total outlays, whereas in 1995 their share had fallen to 12 percent. The administration's share of the budget had risen from 44 percent in 1978 to 70 percent in 1995. Of this item, in 1995 nearly half was committed to education, culture and health. Price subsidies have fallen dramatically from 15 percent of outlays in 1990 to less than 3 percent in 1995. Because state industrial enterprises occupy a much less significant place in the provincial economy than elsewhere, Zhejiang is not subject to the same budgetary pressures on this front, although losses from state enterprises continue unabated.[151] Overall, these trends reflect a major change in government priorities as well as in the nature of the economy over which the government presides but no longer directs.

Central-Provincial Fiscal Relations

Since 1980, when the center introduced a fiscal contracting system with the provinces, the arrangements setting out central-local relations in this critical area of public administration have undergone frequent adjustments. Initially, Zhejiang was included in an arrangement involving a division of revenues and outlays contracted to different levels (*diceng baogan*). In 1980 and 1981 the province

Table 3.16

Composition of Budgetary Outlays, 1978–95

Year	Total	CC[a]	RR[b]	Sci/tech.	Admin.	WC[c]	UU
1978	1.71	0.61	0.14	0.02	0.75	0.11	0.02
1979	1.77	0.53	0.13	0.03	0.88	0.07	0.04
1980	1.73	0.38	0.17	0.03	0.99	0.07	0.05
1981	1.71	0.28	0.20	0.02	1.06	0.05	0.06
1982	1.89	0.30	0.18	0.03	1.21	0.08	0.07
1983	2.19	0.36	0.20	0.04	1.42	0.04	0.12
1984	2.88	0.44	0.25	0.06	1.90	0.01	0.18
1985	3.74	0.48	0.31	0.05	2.21	0.02	0.29
1986	5.10	0.56	0.30	0.05	2.83	0.06	0.42
1987	5.12	0.43	0.36	0.04	3.00	0.07	0.34
1988	6.31	0.40	0.44	0.05	3.83	0.08	0.48
1989	7.45	0.39	0.40	0.06	4.69	0.09	0.52
1990	8.02	0.38	0.41	0.08	5.06	0.08	0.55
1991	8.49	0.42	0.51	0.09	5.73	0.07	0.56
1992	9.53	0.54	0.63	0.10	6.80	0.06	0.63
1993	12.50	0.68	1.06	0.11	8.94	0.06	0.85
1994	15.30	0.72	1.07	0.13	10.65	0.05	1.11
1995	16.50	0.78	1.50	0.34			1.31

Source: ZJTJNJ 1996; annual budget speeches.

Notes: [a]CC = capital construction. [b]RR = replacement and reconstruction. [c]WC = working capital. [d]UU = urban upkeep.

received 13 percent of the industrial and commercial tax, the most lucrative source of budgetary revenue.[152] In 1982 Zhejiang reverted to the Jiangsu model of division of total revenues (*zonge fencheng*) with the 1979 budget final accounts used as the contracted base figure (*baogan jishu*). The proportion of outlays to revenue became that percentage retained by the province, and was fixed at 56 percent in 1982 and 51.8 percent in 1983. The province could then spend these monies as it saw fit.[153]

From 1985 a new fiscal system involving a division of taxes, fixed revenues and outlays, and contracting to different levels (*huafen shuizhong, heding shouzhi, fenji baogan*) was instituted. In 1988, one year after the center elevated Ningbo to the status of a separately-listed city in the state plan (*jihua danlie shi*), the system was changed again to an incremental increase contracting system (*diceng baogan*), and this remained in place until 1992. Under the 1988 arrangements Zhejiang and Ningbo were placed on a marginal retention rate of 100 percent when revenues exceeded specified levels,[154] and Zhejiang's contracted baseline figure increased by a rate of between 3.6 percent and 6.5 percent per annum.[155]

In 1994 a new tax-sharing system was introduced across China, after experiments had been conducted since 1992 in nine provinces and cities including

Table 3.17

Composition of Zhejiang's Local Budgetary Revenues and Outlays, 1985–95
(unit = billion yuan)

	1985	1990	1995
Budgetary revenue	5.8	10.2	20.9
Industrial & commercial taxes	4.7	8.9	
Industrial & commercial tax	3.4	6.7	
Enterprise revenue	0.8	0.0	
Industrial enterprises	0.7	0.6	
Commercial enterprises	0.2	0.1.	
Agricultural taxes	0.2	0.3	
Budgetary outlays	3.7	8.0	15.3
Capital construction	0.5	0.4	0.7
Replacement and reconstruction	0.3	0.4	0.7
Simple construction	0.01	0.02	0.03
Science/tech.	0.05	0.08	0.1
Circulating funds	0.02	0.08	0.05
Administration	2.2	5.1	10.7
Culture/educ./health	1.1	2.2	4.9
Administration	0.4	0.7	2.0
Support for agriculture	0.3	0.8	0.8
Urban renewal	0.3	0.5	1.1
Price subsidies	0.3	1.2	0.4

Source: ZJTJNJ, various years.
Note: There is no breakdown of 1994 revenues.

Zhejiang. The experimental period was originally scheduled to last for four years from 1992 to 1995, but in late 1993 the CCP Central Committee decided to introduce a new central-local fiscal arrangement and tax system from the following year. There were some differences between the experimental arrangements, and the new system which emerged in 1994 that are worth mentioning. First, in the 1992 arrangement all shared taxes between the center and province were split 50:50. In the 1993 reform the center took 75 percent of the value-added tax and 100 percent of the resource tax on off-shore petroleum. In 1992 about 30 sources of taxation and revenue were assigned to the province, while by 1993 this number had been consolidated to around a score. Third, the 1992 experiment took the final budgetary accounts for 1989 as the base year, while the 1994 reform took the final accounts for 1993 as the base figure, a concession by the center which enabled, as will be shown below, the provinces to boost their revenues considerably before the year expired. In a peculiar twist to the reform, and one typical of the "mongrel" economy which the Chinese state presides over, and characterized by intense bargaining between center and localities, those provinces such as Zhejiang which had been under the fiscal contract system which entailed the remission of a proportion of all revenue increases to the center, were now faced with an increased fiscal burden by the addition of the "shared taxation" system alongside this remnant element of the old system. Provincial cadres estimate that, by the year 2000, apart from remitting 15.5 billion yuan more under the tax-sharing scheme Zhejiang will remit an extra 3.9 billion yuan as a legacy of the former contract fiscal system.[156]

The impact of the new arrangements is difficult to gauge based on figures from their first year of implementation. Nevertheless, it appears that both the province and the center would have been pleased at the outcome. Provincial revenues rose 19 percent, while remittance to the center of the value-added tax and the consumption tax (which is levied on luxury consumer items such as jewelry and alcohol) increased by 12.5 percent.[157] The collection of these two taxes (one of which is assigned totally to the center and the other shared) is important to the continuing growth of provincial revenues, because for every 1 percent increase in their collection over the 1993 base figure the provinces receive a rebate of 0.3 percent.[158] On the other hand if contracted incremental increases are not met, the sum will be deducted from that portion being returned to the province.[159]

However, with the center agreeing to use 1993 as the base figure to calculate rebates on shared taxes,[160] it is interesting to observe that, in that year, fiscal revenue in Zhejiang increased by an unprecedented 41 percent. Revenue from the industrial and commercial tax rose by 51 percent, while extra-budgetary revenues fell dramatically by one-third, reversing a five-year trend in the opposite direction.[161] Such a trend was not confined to Zhejiang, with sub-national governments everywhere striving to increase their budgetary revenue (particularly the collection of the VAT and consumption tax) so as to raise the base figure and thus qualify for larger rebates in the future.[162]

Fiscal Arrangements with Subordinate Administrations[163]

At the beginning of the reform period Zhejiang split total revenues 60–40 with municipalities, prefectures and counties. In 1980 contracting to lower-level administrations was implemented, and four sets of arrangements were established with 80 municipal (prefecture) and county-level administrations, according to their relative fiscal capacities. The first arrangement, which applied to 20 units, was a fixed remission quota with a fixed division of increased revenues. The second was division of total revenues, and was implemented for 13 administrations. The third arrangement allowed 31 lower-level units to retain all their fixed quotas, with topping up where necessary from the industrial and commercial tax. The final arrangement, which applied to 16 units, involved fixed quotas with an incremental increase in subsidies.[164]

In 1985, when Zhejiang changed its arrangements with the center, it instituted three sets of arrangements with its 79 counties. The principle behind these arrangements was that gains and losses were to be shouldered equally (*quanheng libi*). The first arrangement, which applied to 29 counties, involved fixed remittances to the province, whereby except for the three taxes which comprised the industrial and commercial tax, all other taxes were to accrue to the counties as fixed revenues based on calculations using the 1983 contracted figures for revenues and outlays as the base year. If this fixed revenue contracted figure exceeded that for outlays, then the surplus would be remitted to the province as a fixed amount. Seventy percent of the revenue which exceeded the contracted base figure could be retained by the county. If revenue did not meet the contracted base figure the county would compensate the province. That is to say the fixed remittance figure could not be lowered. Five to 15 percent of annual increases in the collection of the industrial and commercial tax could be kept by the county.

The second set of arrangements involved an adjusted share of revenue and was to apply to 34 counties. If the fixed revenue base was insufficient to meet the contracted outlay commitment, the gap was to be made up from the industrial and commercial tax collected by the county at a proportion fixed according to the size of the gap. All additions to fixed revenue could be retained by the county, together with 10–15 percent of increases in industrial and commercial taxes after the subsidy component had been deducted. The third system applied to the poorer 16 counties in the province. If the fixed revenue and locally collected industrial and commercial tax were insufficient to meet the contracted expenditure base figure, then the province would subsidize the gap at an annual incremental rate of 5–10 percent. If revenue collections exceeded contracted outlays then the county or district could retain them all.[165] The World Bank commented on the complexity of this tax-sharing arrangement between province and locality, which differed from that prevailing elsewhere in China.[166] It also pointed out that "There are negotiated variations from this general pattern" and that the provincial government held the power to alter the sharing formula as it pleased.

The 1992 trial-run of the tax assignment system in Zhejiang divided its cities, prefectures and counties (or county-level cities) into four categories. Depending on the level of economic development and fiscal wealth, their revenue retention rate increased from a low of 30 percent, through 50 percent, 70 percent and up to 100 percent for administrations which were considered to be poor or in special difficulty. The 1994 system, however, dropped this initiative and reverted to the former arrangements between province and cities and counties as outlined above. Of all revenues shared between the center and province the latter would share its proportion in entirety with cities and counties. In addition, on the basis of the former division of revenues the province would hand over its 10 percent share of the land-use tax on cultivated land and quotas for grain subsidies. All revenues obtained in excess of the quota would be divided 20:80 between the province and counties.[167]

Since the late 1980s fiscal contracting seems to have made even more unequal the distribution of wealth among the province's counties. In 1988 it was claimed

Table 3.18

Provincial-level Budgetary Situation, 1990–96 (billion yuan)

Year	Total Revenue	Prov. Revenue	%	Total Expend.	Prov. Expend.	%
1990	10.16	0.34	3.35	8.02	0.34	4.24
1991	10.89	0.62	5.69	8.49	2.15	25.32
1992	11.84	n.a.	—	9.53	n.a.	—
1993	16.66	0.90	5.4	12.50	0.26	2.08
1994	20.94	0.76	3.63	15.29	2.94	19.23
1995	78.01	0.96	17.71	18.01	3.19	17.71
1996[a]	22.70	3.46	16.79	21.38	3.59	16.79

Source: Annual budget speeches, *ZJRB*.
Note: n.a. = not available; [a] adjusted to include province's share of two central taxes and central subsidies.

that the number of counties with budgetary revenue below 10 million had declined to five, while the number whose revenue exceeded 100 million had reached fourteen.[168] However, in the late 1980s and early 1990s finance ministers have regularly referred to the widening gap between the rich and poor counties of Zhejiang. In 1990 eighteen counties raised over 100 million yuan in budgetary revenues, and their combined revenues equaled 33 percent of provincial revenue and 57 percent of all budgetary revenue raised at the county level.[169]

It was reported that in 1993 thirty-nine counties had surpassed the 100 million yuan budgetary revenue mark, of which fourteen had exceeded 200 million yuan, up 12 percent and 6 percent respectively on 1992. However, forty-six counties were reported to have been in the red, but this number was seventeen less than the sixty-three counties reported to be in deficit in 1992.[170] The coffers of Xiaoshan and Shaoxing counties, both in close proximity to Hangzhou, have benefited greatly from the rapid expansion of their TVE sectors, and they now rank among the richest counties in China.[171] Remote mountain counties in the west of the province, however, are still waiting for the much-vaunted "trickle-down effect" to reach them.

A debate has arisen in relation to the consequences of fiscal contracting, in particular the question of whether it has been the center or the localities that have gained most.[172] However, it seems that the provincial level of government has gained least from the system. Its proportion of total local budgetary revenue is slight, while its expenditure commitments are heavy. It has been observed that the province depends on both higher and lower levels of government for its revenue, leaving it little independent discretion.[173] Zhejiang has released figures for provincial revenue and expenditures since 1990 (see Table 3.18). The figures themselves, particularly on the outlay side, seem erratic and unreliable. However, what is striking about them is the large gap between revenue sources and

Table 3.19

Zhejiang: Budget Estimates and Outcomes 1984-1995 (billion yuan)

Year	Revenue		Discrepancy (%)	Expenditure		Discrepancy (%)
	Estimate	Outcome		Estimate	Outlay	
1984	n.a	4.58	10.40	n.a	2.88	40.8
1985	4.99	6.07	21.70	2.68	3.74	6.9
1986	6.71	6.86	2.20	3.65	5.09	39.5
1987	7.41	7.64	3.10	4.00	5.12	0.1
1988	8.25	8.50	3.10	5.50	6.30	14.6
1989	9.20	9.74	5.90	6.84	7.40	8.2
1990	10.40	9.95	0.50	7.70	7.81	1.4
1991	10.90	10.89	−0.10	7.81	8.49	2.3
1992	11.63	11.80	1.40	9.05	9.30	2.8
1993	13.00	16.65	28.20	10.10	12.49	23.7
1994	8.02	9.46	18.00	13.22	15.30	15.7
1995	10.46	11.68	11.70	16.50	18.00	9.1

Source: Annual budget speeches in *ZJRB.*
Note: Figures for 1994 and 1995 include local revenue only.

expenditure commitments. Nevertheless, the province, like the center, has the capacity to extract funds at will from its subordinate administrations to meet the large deficits it seems to incur each year.

A final feature of the operation of Zhejiang's fiscal system during the reform period has been the wide discrepancy between budget statements and final accounts on both the revenue and outlays sides (see Table 3.19). Mini-budgets, which have adjusted budgetary forecasts for revenues and outlays both upward and downward, have been approved by plenums of the standing committee of the provincial people's congress (meeting between the annual sessions of the provincial people's congress) in 1986, 1987, 1990 and 1991. In 1992 it appears that revised estimates did not even go through the rubber-stamping procedure of referral to the people's congress standing committee but were approved by a plenum of the provincial party committee. Some budget forecasts have been revised due to unanticipated fluctuations in economic growth. Other adjustments were due to sudden shifts in central-provincial fiscal arrangements as the result of policy changes in Beijing.

Extra-budgetary Finances

The provincial government has issued several documents since the early 1990s in an attempt to control and manage extra-budgetary funds.[174] In March 1995 a provincial meeting on the issue, which was addressed by Governor Wan

Table 3.20

Zhejiang Extra-budgetary Revenues and Expenditures, 1986–94
(billion yuan)

Year	EB revenue	EB outlays	EBE as % EBR	EBR as % BR	EBE as % BE
1986	4.22	3.64	86	61	71
1987	5.74	4.69	82	75	92
1988	6.78	5.60	83	79	89
1989	7.35	6.72	91	75	90
1990	7.70	7.59	99	76	95
1991	9.36	9.16	98	86	108
1992	12.66	10.89	86	107	114
1993	8.37	7.58	90	50	61
1994	11.84	11.16	94	57	73

Source: ZJTJNJ 1995, pp. 315–16; *Zhongguo caizheng tongji (1950–1991)* (Statistics on China's Public Finances), pp. 200, 224; *Zhongguo caizheng nianjian 1994*, pp. 430–31; *1995*, pp. 423–24.

Note: EBR = extra-budgetary revenue; EBE = extra-budgetary expenditure; BR = budgetary revenue; BE = budgetary expenditure.

Xueyuan and executive Deputy-governor Chai Songyue, stated that the task of clearing up these funds had to be completed by the end of July 1995. The meeting declared that this was not only an economic task but one that would assist in the campaign against corruption. The meeting decided that by the end of April 1995 a full account and inspection of extra-budgetary income and expenditures since 1991, and especially for the years 1993 and 1994, would be carried out. Following this, in May 1995 an inspection of extra-budgetary funds of government departments and their enterprises would be undertaken.[175]

Table 3.20 shows that Zhejiang has maintained a surplus in the disposition of extra-budgetary funds, and that there has been a steady growth in the proportion of both extra-budgetary revenues and outlays to budgetary funds. This ratio reached a peak in 1992, with extra-budgetary funds actually surpassing budgetary funds. During the seventh five-year plan (1986–90) the 73.2 percent ratio of extra-budgetary revenues to budgetary revenues in Zhejiang was significantly less than the national proportion of 89.3 percent. In a province whose state sector was well below the national average the reverse would have been expected.

Extra-budgetary revenues are controlled by three kinds of public entities; local finance departments which levy tax and other surcharges; public utilities and administrative units which collect fees and charges; and state enterprises and their administrative departments which control funds for replacement and reconstruction, funds for major maintenance, and their retention share of various profits. Over the period 1986–90 extra-budgetary revenues belonging to the first group increased their share from 3.5 percent to 8.6 percent, those accruing to the second group rose from 25.6 percent to 31.4 percent, while those controlled by the third group fell from 71 percent to 60 percent. About 25 percent of extra-budgetary outlays was directed to replacement and reconstruction.[176]

In 1993 a reversal of the consistent trend toward the increased proportion of extra-budgetary to budgetary funds suddenly took place. Both extra-budgetary revenues and expenditures dropped dramatically both in real terms and as proportions of budgetary funds.[177] What may well have occurred in the lead-up period to the introduction of the new fiscal and taxation arrangements in 1994 was that local governments requisitioned funds from enterprises and departments and included them in the budget (the rise in budgetary revenues and expenditures in 1993 was unprecedented in scope) so as to raise the base figures from which future taxation rebates would be received from the center.[178]

2. Investment

For several reasons there was little central investment in Zhejiang during the Maoist period. First, there was a deliberate bias toward redirecting investment to the inland provinces and away from the coastal areas, although the economic benefits of this policy have been questioned.[179] Second, Zhejiang suffered from its geographic location for another reason—its proximity to Taiwan as an enemy regime across the Taiwan straits. For the whole of the Maoist period the province received only 1.5 percent of central state investment. Within the province, prior to 1978 one-half of total investment in Zhejiang occurred in Hangzhou and at key points along the interior railway line south from the provincial capital through central Zhejiang into Jiangxi Province.[180] Examples include the Quzhou Chemical Works and eight major factories in the heavy industrial sector which were located in the suburbs of Hangzhou. Some of these plants produced equipment for the defense forces.

Strategic and defense considerations dictated these priorities, but their effect was to neglect the development of the two port cities of Ningbo and Wenzhou, and thus reduce their ability to take advantage of their coastal location and to radiate economic influence into their respective hinterlands. During the Cultural Revolution the military leadership, acting on central instructions, concentrated investment in the "five small industries."[181] Zhejiang also pursued a "mini third front" strategy. In 1970, 50 percent of investment in capital construction was made in the backward, interior mountain districts, at the expense of agriculture, light industry, transport and ports. This strategy led to an imbalance in the industrial structure and was greatly to the detriment of the more developed eastern and coastal areas. The non-material (or non-productive) branches of the economy, such as social infrastructure, particularly housing and social services, were badly neglected.[182]

During the sixth five-year plan (1981–85) investment priorities were shifted toward the replacement and reconstruction of existing facilities, and into non-productive branches. The housing sector had suffered from years of neglect, and the stock of urban housing was in a decrepit state, with rental income only bringing in a mere fraction of the cost of upkeep and replacement.[183] It was in the seventh five-year plan that Zhejiang started, with central support, to invest heavily in the construction of social infrastructure and basic industries. Central and provincial investment in capital construction was estimated to be equal to 85 percent of total investment over the previous thirty years. Ninety key-point projects were targeted: eleven in the energy sector, twenty-two in transport and six in post and telecommunications. Investment in energy, transport, telecommunication and raw materials was to comprise 60 percent of total state investment over the five years. As if to justify the commitment of such large sums from the center, Zhejiang's governor claimed that in the 1950s Zhejiang had provided financial and material assistance to 160 key projects across the country.[184]

The proportion of investment directed to basic industries and infrastructure development increased from 31.7 percent in the sixth five-year plan period to 46.6 percent. During this five-year period, investment by units of public ownership in enterprise replacement and reconstruction increased 1.6 times over the sixth five-year plan. A substantial addition to the stock of fixed assets occurred through the construction of major projects.[185] Production capacity rose considerably, thus strengthening the foundation for further economic development. In particular the capacity of power generation and transmission, water storage, port cargo handling and highway facilities were improved, and the building materials industry strengthened.[186]

Investment in social fixed assets for the eighth five-year plan (1991–95) were initially estimated to increase at an annual average rate of 5 percent.[187] In actual fact between 1991 and 1995 the average annual increase was a massive 49 percent, hitting an extraordinary 87 percent in 1993. In 1994 the rate of increase was 48 percent, double the planned figure.[188] Table 3.21 shows that for the entire reform period the rate of increase in productive investments in Zhejiang has outstripped the national average by a considerable margin.

Table 3.22 indicates the sectors of the provincial economy to which investment in capital construction has been directed. By 1994 investment in agriculture had fallen to unprecedentedly low levels, with possible disastrous consequences for the future of this sector. Light industry's share of investment in capital construction was consistently highest between the years 1980 to 1983, and consistently lowest between 1990 and 1992 at the time when Ge Hongsheng was provincial governor. Since Ge's replacement investment in this sector has returned to near its previous highest ratio, while the proportion of investment in heavy industry has fallen to about 50 percent of the peak level which it recorded in 1990. Investment in the energy industry fell significantly in 1993 and 1994 after following an upward trend from 1985 to 1990. The proportion of investment in the transport and communications industries lagged behind in the early and mid 1980s, increased its share markedly into the 1990s but failed, until 1994, to surpass the proportion attained in 1980.[189] Over the

Table 3.21

Annual Rates of Increase in Investment: Zhejiang and China

	1979–95	1981–95	1986–95	1991–95
1. Investments in fixed assets	24.6	25.5	25.9	49.4
National	14.8	17.8		
2. Same by state units	23.4	25.1	29.1	46.1
National	14.8	17.0		
3. Capital construction	18.4	19.7	23.1	46.2
National	12.4	15.2		
4. Replacement & reconstruction	25.3	25.4	24.2	39.1
National	18.7	17.1		

Source: ZJTJNJ 1996, pp. 9, 11 and 13.
Note: The period covered for China is 1979–1993.

Table 3.22

Proportion of Investment in Capital Construction by Industrial Sectors

Year	Agriculture	Light industry	Heavy industry	Energy	trans./ comm.
1980	11.3	10.1	29.4	12.3	17.3
1981	7.3	10.3	37.4	14.8	8.1
1982	5.6	13.8	37.8	16.7	8.3
1983	6.0	12.3	38.8	24.2	5.8
1984	6.3	9.5	33.1	21.5	12.6
1985	4.5	8.7	29.3	19.3	9.2
1986	3.1	5.6	30.7	20.6	11.4
1987	3.2	11.7	30.8	22.7	10.8
1988	3.2	8.9	38.7	33.4	10.7
1989	3.6	8.7	41.6	36.5	11.2
1990	3.9	6.0	43.2	36.5	16.7
1991	5.4	5.9	39.0	33.3	15.4
1992	6.1	6.3	36.6	27.4	11.9
1993	1.2	9.9	22.6	17.6	16.0
1994	0.9	10.8	20.5	15.7	21.7
1995	0.5	10.8	21.0	16.4	21.3

Source: Quanguo gesheng, zizhiqu, zhixiashi lishi tongji ziliao huibian (1949–1989) (A Compendium of Historical Statistical Data on China's Provinces, Autonomous Regions and Centrally Administered Cities), p. 395; *ZJTJNJ 1994*, pp. 238–39; *ZJTJNJ 1996*, p. 14.

Note: The table does not include investment in commerce, education, health and culture (that is, in the non-material production sectors).

whole period 1980 to 1995 the pattern has been for the proportion of investment in capital construction to have fallen in the agricultural and heavy industry sectors, to have remained stable in light industry, and to have increased marginally in the energy and transport and communications branches. However, the

Table 3.23

Percentage of Investment in Material and Non-material (productive and non-productive) Construction

	Material	Non-material	(of which housing)
1980	67.8	32.2	19.0
1981	59.8	40.2	25.5
1982	59.1	40.9	25.8
1983	60.0	40.0	23.3
1984	60.6	39.4	20.7
1985	52.3	47.7	22.8
1986	54.2	45.8	21.3
1987	58.8	41.2	16.0
1988	65.9	34.1	11.8
1989	65.7	34.3	11.5
1990	69.4	30.6	8.8
1991	68.7	31.3	9.0
1992	68.3	31.7	8.6
1993	59.0	41.0	9.3
1994	63.6	36.4	8.0
1995	60.7	39.3	6.7

Source: ZJTJNJ 1994, p. 238; *ZJTJNJ 1995*, p. 14; *ZJTJNJ 1996*, p. 14.

proportion of investment directed into these five branches has fallen from about 80 percent of total investment in 1980 to almost 70 percent in 1994.

Despite the large sums invested in social capital the funds applied still failed to keep pace with the rapid economic development in the province. Between 1978 and 1988 there was an annual average increase of 14.2 percent in electricity generation. However, this was 50 percent below the 22 percent increase in GVIO for the same period. The impact of these trends in investment upon the structure of industry which, as mentioned above is weak in basic industries and over-reliant upon processing, was therefore minimal. In 1982 the proportion of provincial national income which was derived from the transport and communications industries was a mere 1.9 percent. By 1988 it had risen to 3.5 percent. In 1988 the structure of GVIO by branches broke down into 2 percent (energy), 4.1 percent (raw materials), and over 90 percent (processing).

From a proportion of 32 percent in 1980, investment in non-material capital construction was held at 40 percent during the sixth five-year plan, reaching 48 percent in the final year. Since then the percentage has fallen back to a low of 31 percent in 1990, rising to 41 percent in 1993 and then returning to 36 percent in 1994.[190] In the early to mid 1980s massive investment occurred in peasant housing. In more recent years greater attention has been given to investment in education, science and technology, health and culture.

Since the decision in 1985 to cease the system of allocating budgetary funds

Table 3.24

Source of Investment Funds in Capital Construction

	1980	1985	1990	1995
Budget	38.8	21.7	10.1	2.1
Domestic loans (banks & other				
financial institutions)	11.6	14.7	18.4	14.6
Credit	0.6			
Foreign funds	11.0	0.8	7.6	11.8
Self-raised (extra-budgetary)	38.6	52.1	48.9	58.7
Central depts.	2.1	2.8		
Provincial	11.1	9.3		
District (city)	12.7	11.8		
County	7.2	9.9		
Enterprise/utility	18.1	26.9		
Share issues	0.6			
Other sources	10.7	15.0	12.8	
Investment in fixed assets by				
ownership				
State	48.1	38.7	42.7	48.3
Collective	26.3	30.6	21.3	36.0
Individual	25.6	30.7	36.0	15.7

Source: ZJTJNJ 1996, pp. 14, 72; *Jingji cankao yanjiu*, No. 58, August 26, 1992, p. 32; *Zhongguo caizheng nianjian 1994*, pp. 430–31.

free of charge to enterprises for investment purposes, Zhejiang has pursued a variety of avenues to raise funds for economic development. This has meant greater recourse to extra-budgetary funds, domestic loans and to world capital markets, both government and private. Table 3.24 illustrates the great transformation in the sources of investment during the reform period. The major development has been that the proportion of investment from the budget has fallen thirteenfold between 1980 and 1994, with funds from extra-budgetary and other sources together making up the difference. Foreign funds still play a relatively insignificant role in provincial investment, and only in 1994 did they surpass the proportion provided in 1980. The proportion coming from domestic loans has also remained relatively stable, except for the years 1990 to 1993, when they reached a peak of 20 percent in 1991. In terms of the contributions to investment in fixed assets by ownership, the relative proportions coming from the state, collectives and individuals have remained remarkably stable. The proportion provided by collective entities has increased 10 percent while that from individuals has fallen 10 percent. In 1988, of every extra 100 yuan in investment by these

Table 3.25

Accumulation Rates in Zhejiang and China, 1953–92

Period	Zhejiang rate	National rate
1st 5–year plan	11.4	24.2
2nd 5–year plan	24.8	29.4
1963–65	15.2	22.3
3rd 5–year plan	19.7	25.8
4th 5–year plan	22.9	33.0
5th 5–year plan	28.0	33.2
1978–87	37.1	32.5
6th 5–year plan	35.3	30.7
7th 5–year plan	39.6	34.4[a]
1991–92[b]	40.1	

Source: Guomin shouru tongji ziliao huibian (1949–1985) (A Compendium of Statistical Materials on National Income), p. 221; *Zhejiang 1979–1988 nian jingji fazhan baogao*, p. 55; and calculated from *Quanguo gesheng, zizhiqu, zhixiashi lishi tongji ziliao huibian (1949–1989)*, p. 7; *ZJTJNJ 1993*, p. 27.

Note: [a]1986–89 only; [b]*Jingji yanjiu cankao*, No. 427, February 16, 1994, p. 30 gives a figure of 46.9 percent for 1992.

three ownership categories, entities of the whole people invested 63 percent in productive investment, collectives 92 percent and individuals 17 percent.[191]

Zhejiang has maintained a very high accumulation rate during the reform period. In the first five years of reform, prior to 1983, the relation between accumulation and consumption was in the range of 30:70, slightly higher than levels recorded in the Cultural Revolution. In 1984 the rate increased from 21 percent to 36 percent in one year. It rose further to a peak of 43 percent in 1987. Zhejiang's accumulation rate increased four points in the seventh five-year plan over the previous plan, and then rose a further half point in the first two years of the eighth five-year plan (1991–95). Before the beginning of the reform period, Zhejiang's accumulation rate was significantly lower than the national average. Since 1978, however, it has been consistently higher, too high according to one observer. However, this same observer believes that the figure of 43 percent for 1987 is probably an over-estimation. Deducting the construction of peasant housing would lower the rate 10 percent. Productive accumulation, he claims, was only 13 percent of utilized national income, and productive investment comprised only 14.5 percent of GNP, figures which are not excessively high during a period of industrialization.[192] Over the decade 1978 to 1988, the faster growth in non-productive accumulation compared to productive accumulation meant that the latter's proportion of total accumulation fell from 71.5 percent in 1978 to 55.1 percent in 1988.

Table 3.26

Structure of Investment Entities in Agriculture during the 7th Five-Year Plan
(unit = billion yuan)

	Social	State	Urban collective	Rural collective	Household
Investment in agri.	6.15	0.94	0.05	1.53	3.63
% investment in agri.	100.00	15.30	0.80	24.90	59.00
% trend of investment[a]	6.90	2.90	0.70	8.40	6.60

Source: Jingji yanjiu cankao, No. 63, July 3, 1992, p. 48.

Note: [a]The trend of investment refers to the proportion of that entity's total investment which is directed toward agriculture.

Investment outcomes in Zhejiang between 1979 and 1994 only partly met the government's objective of reallocating resources into those areas of the economy most in need. While the total sum of funds available for investment increased rapidly along with the incredible growth of the provincial economy, the agricultural sector was starved for funds, and the shift of funds to the energy, and transport and communications departments was rather less than desired or required. The greatest proportion of productive investments continued to go to industry, although its share fell from about 40 percent in 1980 to 30 percent in 1994. The crude, extensive, rural-based TVE processing sector of the economy has an unquenchable thirst for investment funds, and local governments are loathe to ignore its plea for favored consideration.

The dramatic fall in investment in agriculture over this period has exacerbated an already grave situation. Table 3.26 reveals that even rural collectives and households invested less than 10 percent of their total investment in agriculture during the seventh five-year plan. In 1988 the provincial government took two measures to attempt to halt the slide in agriculture, grain production in particular. First it levied a grain surtax to be used as a price subsidy in linking grain procurement agreements and the supply of chemical fertilizer, and second it explored new mechanisms to increase accumulation in agriculture.[193] Clearly its efforts in this direction have not brought about significant results.

Conclusions

Zhejiang has clearly out-performed most other provinces in terms of its rate of economic development during the fifteen years of reform. David Denny has argued that provinces such as Zhejiang, which were disadvantaged by Maoist regional economic policies, progressed rapidly first because they benefited from the influence of nearby major metropolitan regions (Shanghai in this case), second because they were able to exploit their own resources free from previous constraints, and finally because post-Mao China witnessed a return to a "more normal economic pattern."[194] Certainly Shanghai is a major market for agricultural raw materials, surplus labor and some processed goods from Zhejiang, but Zhejiang has often struggled to establish its own identity free from the overwhelming presence of its giant neighbor.[195] The second point has been addressed in this paper, and I have discussed the historical, cultural and social aspects of Zhejiang's experience during reform in detail elsewhere.[196]

In retrospect, the legacy of the Maoist period, nevertheless, was not completely negative for Zhejiang, which benefited from a distortion in price policy which under-priced industrial raw materials and energy sources and rewarded industrial processors with substantial profits. However, with the increased marketization of the Chinese economy, fierce domestic and foreign competition has already impacted on industrial profitability,[197] and the effects of the rises in and decontrols over the prices of these raw materials have been felt in Zhejiang.[198] Local observers are aware of the potential impact on the province of a major shift in regional priorities in the national ninth five-year plan.

In drawing up the provincial ninth five-year plan (1996–2000) and a fifteen-year medium-term economic program it appears that the economic regions of Zhejiang have been rearranged. Regions have been delineated not merely on the basis of geographic location (although this plays a role) or previous patterns of development, but according to lines of communication based on existing and planned railway systems. The Zhejiang authorities have divided the province into three economic zones. The first includes those counties bordering on or in the vicinity of the Zhe-Gan railway south from Hangzhou to the Jiangxi border,[199] as well as those along the Jinhua-Wenzhou line now under construction. The second encompasses the Wenzhou-Taizhou coastal zone of the south-east, while the third covers the rest of the province, that is the north and north-east plains across which traverse the Hang-Lu and the Hang-Yong railway lines from Hangzhou to Shanghai and Ningbo respectively.[200] This division gives greater prominence to the development of the more backward districts of the province by grouping them into two separate zones.

A review of the Zhejiang economy published in 1992 characterized it as being in transition from a directly-administered to an indirectly-administered entity, and concluded that the basic transition to a market economy had still to take place.[201] Yet in the allocation of material goods, by 1991 only eight agricultural commodities came under planned allocation, while the rest had been deregulated. Only thirty-five industrial products came within the orbit of the national and provincial mandatory planning systems, and their output value amounted to less than 4 percent of GVIO. Another 15 percent were regulated by guidance planning and the remaining 80 percent by the market. Almost two-thirds of the products of industrial enterprises at the county level and above were sold directly by the enterprise, compared to less than one-third in 1983. Only 12 percent of steel products, 11 percent of cement, 16 percent of ferrous metals and 15 percent of coal sold in Zhejiang in 1991 came under the planning distribution system. The power to scrutinize prices, which had been recentralized by the province during the recession of 1989–90, had again been devolved.[202]

Outwardly, it appears that the present leadership holds unified views on the future of Zhejiang, although from time to time leading officials have made cryptic comments which suggest that disputes about the implementation of reform policies persist.[203] In January 1995, provincial Deputy-secretary and executive Deputy-Governor Chai Songyue, a native of Zhejiang, stated at the provincial conference on economic restructuring:

> Reform is a pioneering undertaking. If we regard something as correct, we should just try it and go ahead, developing in accordance with the criteria of the "three conducives" [conducive to developing the productive forces of socialist society; to increasing the overall strength of socialist society; and to improving the people's living standards]. Even if there are different views with regard to a reform measure, we should try and review it in the course of practice. When a deviation occurs, we should promptly rectify it. We should not stand still whenever differences of opinion arise. This is an important point in the reform experience over the past sixteen years.[204]

During the reform period the provincial leadership has often faltered when tough decisions were required. It stonewalled on agricultural decollectivization, floundered over urban reform and prevaricated over opening to the outside world. Obviously, this indecisive and sometimes divided leadership was reflected in the performance of the economy, but not to the extent it may have been in other Chinese provinces. Zhejiang's collective and private economies have flourished in such an uncertain political context. In the future however, strong and decisive leadership will certainly be required to shift Zhejiang's economy onto a growth path which is qualitative, intensive, technologically advanced and of greater depth and breadth. Zhejiang's economy, as it is now structured, can probably sustain rapid growth rates into the foreseeable future. But for the longer term a fundamental restructuring of its industrial base will be required. Otherwise, in its race to stay at the head of the provincial pack, Zhejiang will be overtaken and left struggling in the slipstream.

Notes

The research for this chapter was carried out while the author was Visiting Fellow in the Department of Management, Hong Kong Polytechnic University. Appreciation is expressed to the department staff, in particular its chairman, Peter Yuen, and Carlos Lo, K. C. Cheung and T. C. Lam for the many considerations and facilities provided during a most productive and pleasurable eight months in the department. The author also benefited greatly from the series of seminars on the provinces presented at the Centre of Asian Studies, University of Hong Kong, in the first half of 1995 under the chairmanship of John Burns, at which he first presented some of the findings of his research. Interactions at these seminars with other contributors to this volume were most instructive. Appreciation is expressed to Peter T. Y. Cheung, Jae Ho Chung, Jane Ru and the Institute of International Studies, University of Technology, Sydney, for guidance to or the provision of research material. The author also thanks Jae Ho Chung and John Fitzgerald for comments on an earlier draft of this paper (in different formats) and to the participants at the October 1995 Suzhou conference on China's provinces under reform for their stimulating contributions.

1. Zhejiangsheng tongjiju (ed.), *Zhejiang tongji nianjian (Zhejiang Statistical Yearbook), 1996* [hereafter *ZJTJNJ*] (Yichun: Zhongguo tongji chubanshe, 1996), pp. 6-9; *Zhongguo tongji nianjian (China Statistical Yearbook), 1996* (Beijing: Zhongguo tongji chubanshe, 1996), pp. 22-25.

2. Table 12-5, *Provincial China: a research newsletter*, No. 3 (April 1997), p. 53. The figure for Zhejiang's GVIO in *ZJTJNJ 1996*, p. 9 is slightly higher.

3. Guojia tongjiju zonghesi (ed.), *Quanguo ge sheng zizhiqu zhixia chengshi lishi ziliao huibian (1949-1989) (A Compendium of Historical Statistical Data of Provinces, Autonomous Regions and Centrally Administered Cities)*, pp. 46-53. One analyst of comparative regional growth in China has cautioned against the accuracy of gross indicators. See Suzanne Paine, "Spatial Aspects of Chinese Development: Issues, Outcomes and Policies 1949-79," *Journal of Development Studies*, Vol. 17, No. 2 (1981), pp. 178-82.

4. Guojia tongjiju (ed.), *Zhongguo tongji gaiyao 1996 (A Statistical Survey of China)* (Beijing: Zhongguo tongji chubanshe, 1996), p. 64.

5. Fang Minsheng, "Zhejiang shinian (1979-1988) jingji fazhande xitong fenxi" (A systematic analysis of ten years of economic development in Zhejiang, 1979-1988)," in Zhejiang shinian (1979-1988) jingji fazhande xitong fenxi ketizu (Group for the Systematic Analysis of Zhejiang's Economic Development 1979-1988), *Zhejiang 1979-1988 nian jingji fazhan baogao (Report on Zhejiang's Economic Development, 1979-1988)*, (Hangzhou: Hangzhou daxue chubanshe, 1990), pp. 10-16. Unlike the situation in Sunan (southern Jiangsu) where the TVE sector is essentially collective in nature, in Zhejiang it seems to be overwhelmingly private, thus giving rise to the term "Zhejiang model." Field trip to Yiwu city, October 1996.

6. By 1995 this proportion had risen to 53.4 percent. See *Zhejiang zhengbao* [hereafter *ZJZB*], No. 145, 1995, p. 9.

7. *Zhejiang 1979-1988 jingji fazhan baogao*, pp. 8-9; *ZJTJNJ 1994*, pp. 9-17.

8. "Dangdai Zhongguo congshu" bianjibu (ed.), *Dangdai Zhongguode Zhejiang (Contemporary China's Zhejiang)* (Beijing: Zhongguo shehui kexue chubanshe, 1989), Vol. 1, p. 2.

9. Dong Junshu, "Zhejiang jingji zonghe shilide bijiao yu fenxi" (A comparison and analysis of the comprehensive economic power of Zhejiang), *Zhejiang jingji nianjian 1990 (Almanac of Zhejiang's Economy)*, [hereafter ZJJJNJ], p. 432.

10. See *ZJJJNJ 1990*, p. 432. Zhejiang also has a higher percentage of its population above the age of 60, which has great implications for its labour force and the future provision of social security benefits.

11. Ibid., p. 432.

12. The seventh five-year plan set a goal of a 75 percent coverage by 1990. See *ZJJJNJ 1987*, p. 22. However, its implementation rate only covered 53.7 percent of the province's population. See *Zhejiang ribao* [hereafter *ZJRB*], April 4, 1991.

13. *ZJJJNJ 1990*, p. 434.

14. Paine, "Spatial Aspects of Chinese Development," pp. 164-65.

15. Zhejiangsheng shehui kexueyuan jingji xingshi fenxi ketizu, "Zhejiang jingji 1991 nian fazhan baogao—1991 nian jingji xingshi fenxi he 1992 nian fazhan gaige celue" (Report on Zhejiang's economic progress in 1991—an analysis of economic trends in

1991 and a strategy for pushing forward reform in 1992), *Jingji yanjiu cankao (Economic Studies)*, No. 63, July 3, 1992, p. 34. However, official statistics reveal that only in 1992 and 1993, and before that in 1983, was this the case. An added imponderable relates to the fact that the post 1984 figures appear incomplete. See Zhejiang jingji yanjiu zhongxin, *Zhejiang shengqing (1949-1984) (The Affairs of Zhejiang, 1949-1984)* (Hangzhou: Zhejiang renmin chubanshe, 1986), p. 1033; *Zhejiang nianjian 1994 (Zhejiang Yearbook)* [hereafter *ZJNJ*], p. 524; *1995*, p. 549; *1996*, p. 590.

16. See *ZJNJ 1996*, pp. 280-81. These figures would not include transactions through non-official financial institutions.

17. *ZJTJNJ 1996*, p. 338; *1995*, p. 318.

18. *Zhejiang 1979-1988 nian jingji fazhan baogao*, pp. 3-7. Where possible these figures have been updated. On the measurement of economic strength, see also the article in *ZJJJNJ 1990*, pp. 432-34.

19. *ZJJJNJ 1990*, p. 433; *Qianjiang wanbao*, July 15, 1995.

20. *Zhejiang 1979-1988 nian jingji fazhan baogao*, p. 6.

21. Calculated from *ZJTJNJ 1995*, pp. 228-29.

22. *Zhejiang 1979-1988 nian jingji fazhan baogao*, pp. 6-7; *Zhongguo tongji gaiyao 1996*, p. 109.

23. *Quanguo gesheng, zizhiqu, zhixiashi lishi tongji ziliao huibian*, pp. 56, 59; *ZJTJNJ 1995*, p. 18.

24. See Chun-Shing Chow and Hang Chen, "Wenzhou: Development in Regional and Historical Contexts," in Yue-man Yeung and Xu-wei Hu (eds.), *China's Coastal Cities: Catalysts for Modernization* (Honolulu: University of Hawaii Press, 1992), pp. 188-89.

25. The controversy over "resolute contraction" in the agricultural collectivization movement in 1955 is a case in point. I have discussed this issue, among others, in Keith Forster, "Localism, Central Policy and the Provincial Purges of 1957-58: The Case of Zhejiang," in Tim Cheek and Tony Saich (eds.), *New Perspectives on State Socialism in China* (Armonk: M. E. Sharpe Inc., 1997), pp. 191–233.

26. Lucian Pye's scathing comment in the early 1980s concerning the Shanghai municipal leadership applies equally to its Zhejiang counterparts: "Shanghai's political leaders have consistently failed to assert the special economic and cultural interests of their city. Indeed, quite to the contrary, they have over considerable periods advocated policies and programs diametrically opposed to the interests and the welfare of the people they presumably represented." Cited in Lam Tao-chiu, "Local Interest Articulation in the 1980s," in Y.M. Yeung and Y.W. Sung (eds.), *Shanghai: Transformation and Modernisation under China's Open Policy* (Hong Kong: Chinese University Press, 1996), pp. 144–145.

27. Frederick Teiwes, "Provincial Politics in China; Themes and Variations," in John M. H. Lindbeck (ed.), *China: Management of a Revolutionary Society* (Seattle: University of Washington Press, 1971), pp. 173-74.

28. See the detailed account of the campaign in *Dangdai Zhongguode Zhejiang*, Vol. 1, pp. 68-78.

29. See *Provincial China: a research newsletter*, No. 1 (March 1996), p. 71.

30. Peter Ferdinand, "The Economic and Financial Dimension," in David S. G. Goodman (ed.), *China's Regional Development* (London: Royal Institute of International Affairs, 1989), p. 53; Dali Yang, "Patterns of China's Regional Development Strategy," *China Quarterly*, No. 122 (June 1990), p. 239.

31. Ferdinand, "The Economic and Financial Dimension," p. 54.

32. *Zhongguo tongji nianjian 1980*, p. 18.

33. *Zhejiang shengqing*, pp. 1009-14.

34. I have written about the political dimensions of the Cultural Revolution in *Rebellion and Factionalism in a Chinese Province: Zhejiang, 1966-76* (Armonk, NY: M. E. Sharpe,

1990), and more recently in "Researching the Cultural Revolution in Zhejiang," *Provincial China: A research newsletter*, No. 1 (March 1996), pp. 9-28; and "The Cultural Revolution 30 years on," *Hong Kong Journal of Social Sciences*, (article commissioned to mark the 30th anniversary of the Cultural Revolution), No. 11, Spring 1998.

35. Barry Naughton, "Industrial Policy during the Cultural Revolution: Military Preparation, Decentralization, and Leaps Forward"; Christine P.W. Wong, "The Maoist 'Model' Reconsidered: Local Self-Reliance and the Financing of Rural Industrialization"; and Penelope B. Prime, "Central-Provincial Investment and Finance: The Cultural Revolution and Its Legacy in Jiangsu Province," all in William A. Joseph, Christine P.W. Wong and David Zweig (eds.), *New Perspectives on the Cultural Revolution* (Cambridge, MA: Council on East Asian Studies, Harvard University, 1991), pp. 153-81, 183-96, and 197-215.

36. Forster, *Rebellion and Factionalism in a Chinese Province*, chs. 8-9.

37. Wenzhou tongjiju (ed.), *Wenzhou tongji nianjian 1994*, p 18. Figures based on 1980 fixed prices.

38. *ZJTJNJ 1994*, pp. 160, 205. Of course natural factors play a major part in the swings in agricultural output, a fact often conveniently overlooked for political purposes. See Paine, "Spatial Aspects of Chinese Development," p. 182, fn. 47. In 1975 the dying Zhou Enlai lamented the fact that rough grains from North China were being shipped to Zhejiang. Some wag had painted the slogan, "a gift to the lazybones of Zhejiang" (*song gei Zhejiang lanhan chi*) on the side of the goods carriage containing the shipment. See Tie Ying, "Nanwangde 1975 nian" (The unforgettable year of 1975), "Mianhuai Mao Zedong" bianjizu (ed.), *Mianhuai Mao Zedong (Cherish the Memory of Mao Zedong)* (Beijing: Zhongyang wenxian chubanshe, 1993), Vol. 1, pp. 347-56.

39. See Keith Forster, "The Wenzhou Model for Economic Development: Impressions," *China Information*, Vol. 3 (Winter 1990-1991), pp. 53-64; Forster and Yao Xianguo, "A Comparative Analysis of Economic Reform and Development in Hangzhou and Wenzhou Cities," in Jae Ho Chung (ed.), *Agents of Development: Sub-Provincial Cities in Post-Mao China* (London: Routledge, forthcoming).

40. Zhonghua renmin gongheguo guojia nongye weiyuanhui bangongting (Office of the State Agricultural Committee of the PRC (ed.), *Nongye jitihua zhongyao wenjian huibian* (A Collection of Important Documents on Agricultural Collectivization) , Vol. 1, 1949-1957 (Beijing: Zhonggong zhongyang dangxiao chubanshe, 1981), pp. 600-603. At a rough guess, about 90 percent of county-level party secretaries, deputy-secretaries and county magistrates working in Zhejiang between 1949 and 1966 seem to have been born in Shandong. A major grievance of locals was the low educational levels of these outsiders. One retired low-ranking cadre recounted to me that when he went to have a document signed by a Shandong cadre the illiterate official held it upside down!

41. See *Mao Zedong yu Zhejiang (Mao Zedong and Zhejiang)* (Beijing: Zhongyang dangshi chubanshe, 1993). Mao was attracted by the beauty and serenity of the West Lake, and he stayed in guest-houses around its perimeter.

42. See *ZJRB*, December 26, 1983; December 26, 1994.

43. From 1949 to 1984 about 45 percent of all locally-collected revenues were remitted to Beijing. See *Zhejiang shengqing*, p. 627.

44. "Jingji gaigezhong jihua he shichang guanxide bianhua ji qi qishi" (Changes and enlightenment therein from the relations of plan and market in economic reform), *Jingji yanjiu cankao*, No. 58 (June 28, 1992), pp. 29-43.

45. *ZJTJNJ 1994*, p. 9 gives a figure of 41 percent.

46. *Zhejiang 1979-1988 nian jingji fazhan baogao*, pp. 107-29.

47. In the first nine months of 1996 GDP was up by 12.5 percent on the same period for 1995. *ZJRB*, November 3, 1996.

48. *ZJTJNJ 1996*, pp. 9, 24.

49. Wang Jie, "1992 nian Zhejiang jingji shikuang fenxi" (An analysis of the state of Zhejiang's economy in 1992), *Jingji yanjiu cankao*, No. 219, February 4, 1993, p. 51.

50. *Jingji yanjiu cankao*, No. 427, February 16, 1994, p. 26.

51. See Keith Forster, "The Reform of Provincial Party Committees in China—The Case of Zhejiang," *Asian Survey*, Vol. 24, No. 6 (1984), pp. 618-36; "Tie Ying—Chairman of the Zhejiang Provincial Advisory Commission," *Issues & Studies*, Vol. 20, No. 10 (1984), pp. 84-92; "Leaders of Chinese Provinces," correspondence in *Problems of Communism*, Vol. 34, No. 6 (1985), pp. 85-87.

52. Zhejiang Provincial Service, September 9, 1977 in BBC, *Summary of World Broadcasts/ The Far East* [hereafter *SWB/FE*], 5615/BII/8-9. Revealingly, *Zhejiang Ribao* did not carry Tie's speech.

53. See *ZJRB*, January 9, 1985; January 8, 1986 (Tie Ying wrote an inscription for the renovated Zhou Enlai family residence in Shaoxing). Tie has also gone into print with articles concerning his ties with Ye Jianying and Xu Shiyou. See *ZJRB*, October 17, 1996 and October 21, 1995 respectively.

54. See a recent account regarding Mao's last trip to Hangzhou between February and April 1975 in *ZJRB*, March 18, 1995.

55. See Keith Forster, "The Repudiation of the Cultural Revolution in China: The Case of Zhejiang," *Pacific Affairs*, Vol. 59, No. 1 (1986), pp. 5-27.

56. *ZJRB*, April 22, 1983.

57. See *ZJRB*, January 9, 1958 for Wang's attack on "bourgeois rightists" in the judicial system.

58. *ZJRB*, May 1, 5; June 6, 1984. He visited Ningbo again in 1986. See *ZJRB*, March 23, 26, 1986.

59. See Forster, "The Wenzhou Model for Economic Development."

60. In 1984 the provincial daily carried a series of articles on reformist entrepreneurs. See *ZJRB*, May 1, 15; July 23, 29, 30, 1984.

61. *ZJRB*, April 26, 1983.

62. *ZJRB*, February 27, 1984; *Dangdai Zhongguode Zhejiang*, Vol. 1, p. 141.

63. If Wang had reservations about Bu, he may have felt vindicated by the feisty entrepreneur's later disgrace and forced retirement. See *Beijing Review*, February 15-28, 1988, pp. 8-9.

64. See *ZJRB*, June 28, 1968, which alleged that Xuc Ju was behind the attempt in Zhejiang to reverse the verdict on Jiang Hua as a capitalist-roader.

65. Zhonggong Zhejiang shengwei dangshi ziliao zhengji yanjiu weiyuanhui (ed.), *Zhonggong Zhejiang dangshi dashiji 1919-1949 (A Chronology of the History of the CCP in Zhejiang)* (Hangzhou, Zhejiang renmin chubanshe, 1990), p. 246.

66. See *ZJJJNJ 1987*, pp. 44-60.

67. Ibid., pp. 16-31.

68. See Keith Forster, "Li Zemin—Secretary of the CCP Zhejiang Provincial Committee," *Issues & Studies*, Vol. 26, No. 3 (1990), pp. 119-34; Joint Publications Research Service [hereafter JPRS] JPRS-CAR-89-095, pp. 52-53.

69. An article in the central publication, *Jingji cankao*, dated April 1989, contained a mixed picture concerning the implementation of the austerity campaign. See Joint Publications Research Service [hereafter *JPRS*] JPRS-CAR-89-077, pp. 16-20.

70. See Keith Forster, "Popular Protest in Hangzhou, April/June 1989," *Australian Journal of Chinese Affairs*, No. 23 (1990), pp. 97-119, reprinted as "The Popular Protest in Hangzhou," in Jonathan Unger (ed.), *The Democracy Movement in China: Reports from the Provinces* (Armonk, NY: M. E. Sharpe Inc., 1991), pp. 166-86, and available on the World Wide Web at http://www.nmis.org/Gate/links/KEITH.html.

71. See *Jiushi niandai*, January 1991, p. 6.

72. See *ZJRB*, May 19, 1989.

73. See *ZJRB*, May 23, 1988, August 13, 1988.

74. Xinhua, September 29, 1989, in *SWB/FE*/0578/G1-2.

75. Zhang Xuwei, "Zhejiangsheng shichang jingji fazhande xiankuang, wenti he duice" (The present state of Zhejiang's market economy, its problems and counter-measures), *Jingji yanjiu cankao*, No. 246 (1993), p. 26. In 1991 the percentage had risen to 43 percent. For a detailed discussion of domestic trade during the reform period, see Anjali Kumar, "Economic Reform and the Internal Division of Labour in China: Production, Trade and Marketing," in David S. G. Goodman and Gerald Segal (eds.), *China Deconstructs: Politics, Trade and Regionalism* (London: Routledge, 1994), pp. 99-130.

76. *ZJTJNJ 1995*, p. 227.

77. In a worrying sign, in May 1996 state commercial enterprises experienced their first drop in retail sales since 1989. *ZJRB*, August 2, 1996. During my research in Zhejiang from October to December 1996 everyone whom I met doing business complained that the market was soft during the year.

78. See *FBIS-CHI-91* 089, pp. 62-64; *FBIS-CHI-91-077*, p. 48.

79. In 1990 the output of state industry made up 31.2 percent of provincial GVIO. By 1995 this figure had fallen to 13.9 percent. *ZJTJNJ 1996*, p. 16.

80. Oral source. I can personally vouch for the accuracy of this observation, having spent that Chinese New Year in Hangzhou.

81. See a rather confused and somewhat inaccurate interpretation of the replacement of Ge in the electronic journal *Dignity*, No. 9408, October 20, 1994. Xinhua has recently made the first official mention of Wan's unusual election. See *South China Morning Post* [hereafter *SCMP*], June 15, 1995. Other interpretations are that Wan's posting to Zhejiang in November 1992 as deputy-governor was precisely a move to prepare him for elevation to the governorship, or alternatively that the central Organization Department having been made aware of Ge's unpopularity, assigned Wan to the province in preparation for any such contingency.

82. This pattern has been noticed on a nationwide basis. See Xiaowei Zang, "Provincial Elite in Post-Mao China," *Asian Survey*, Vol. 31, No. 6 (1991), p. 519.

83. Teiwes, "Provincial Politics in China; Themes and Variations," pp. 116-89.

84. See, for example, *ZJRB*, January 8, 10, 11, 24; March 4, 21, 23, 25, 30; April 3, 5, 8, 10, 11, 1995.

85. See *ZJRB*, May 2, 1980, May 1, 1983, May 2, 1985, May 2, 1986. The other veteran leader who has made regular trips to Zhejiang is Peng Zhen, who published an article on Marxism in *Hongqi* after visiting Zhejiang University in 1986. He visited the province every year between 1983 and 1986, and again in 1991. See *ZJRB*, February 7, 1984, February 28, 1985, February 9, 1986, February 14, 1991, March 13, 16, 19, 1991.

86. *Renmin Ribao*, January 18, 1991, translated in *SWB/FE*/0979 B2/1-5.

87. His most recent trip took place during the 1995 Chinese New Year. *ZJRB*, January 30, 1995. Jiang Hua was joined by two previous party leaders (Wang Fang and Xue Ju), one former governor (Ge Hongsheng) and a former political commissar of the military district! Wang Fang also attended the opening of the first section of the Jinhua-Wenzhou railway line at Jinyun county. *ZJRB*, March 6, 1995.

88. See Zhejiang Provincial Service, February 13, 1983 in *SWB/FE*/7261/BII/1; *ZJRB*, May 2, 1985, February 9, 1986, May 2, 1986.

89. *Zhuiyi yu sikao; Jiang Hua huiyilu (Recollections and Reflections: The Reminiscences of Jiang Hua)* (1991) and *Jiang Hua zai Zhe wenji (Selection of Writings by Jiang Hua in Zhejiang)* (1992).

90. See *ZJRB*, February 18, 1996; October 16 1996 when the nonagenarian spoke for two hours on the occasion of the 60th anniversary of the Long March.

91. The most recent example has been the publication of a joint article by the two former leaders concerning the burning issue of agriculture, which allegedly has provoked widespread interest across the province. See *ZJRB*, June 22, 1995, and for the reaction *ZJRB*, July 3, 10, 1995. On August 8 the provincial agricultural technical extension foundation (*sheng nongye jishu tuiguang jijinhui*) was established with Tie, Li and Shen Zulun as honorary chairmen. *ZJRB*, August 9, 1995. See also the article by Tie Ying reminiscing on his experiences in the anti-Japanese War, in *ZJRB*, June 4, 1995.

92. *ZJRB*, March 7, 1995.

93. *Qianjiang wanbao*, July 15, 1995. It appears that Shen, who was shunted off to the Political Consultative Conference, may have had his reputation somewhat restored.

94. In late 1995 Tie Ying's status was further enhanced when he was chosen as one of the province's nine elders (*jiulao*). *ZJRB*, November 2, 1995.

95. Zhu Jialiang, "Gaosu zengzhangde jiyu, chengyin he bianhua qushi" (The circumstances, origins and changing trends in high-speed growth), in *Zhejiang 1979-1988 nian jingji fazhan baogao*, pp. 97-98.

96. *Zhejiang 1979-1988 nian jingji fazhan baogao*, pp. 23-30.

97. *ZJRB*, December 31, 1977.

98. *Dangdai Zhongguode Zhejiang*, Vol. 1, pp. 102-106; Suisheng Zhao, "From Coercion to Negotiation: The Changing Central-Local Economic Relationship in Mainland China," *Issues & Studies*, Vol. 28, No. 10 (1992), p. 11.

99. *ZJRB*, June 7, 1978.

100. Dorothy J. Solinger, "The Shadowy Second Stage of China's Ten-Year Plan: Building Up Regional Systems, 1976-1985," *Pacific Affairs*, Vol. 52, No. 2 (1979), pp. 241-64, esp, pp. 243-45, 257-61.

101. *Dangdai Zhongguode Zhejiang*, Vol. 1, pp. 126-27.

102. Xinhua, May 7, 1980, in FBIS-CHI-91-03.

103. *Zhejiang 1979-1988 nian jingji fazhan baogao*, p. 98.

104. *Dangdai Zhongguode Zhejiang*, Vol. 1, pp. 126-27; *Zhejiang 1979-1988 nian jingji fazhan baogao*, pp. 28-29.

105. *Dangdai Zhongguode Zhejiang*, Vol. 1, pp. 147-48.

106. The documents can be found in *ZJJJNJ 1987*, pp. 16-31, 44-55, 52-60. See the article on the meetings by then deputy-governor, Wu Minda, in *ZJJJNJ 1986*, pp. 399-401.

107. Zhu Jialiang, "Zhejiang diqu jingji buju zhanlüe tantao" (A discussion of the strategic disposition of Zhejiang's regional economy), *Zhejiang jingji yanjiu*, No. 3, 1986, pp. 9-14.

108. Peter Nolan, *The Political Economy of Collective Farms: An Analysis of China's Post-Mao Rural Reforms* (Cambridge: Polity Press, 1988), p. 170.

109. The short-lived and aborted Shanghai Economic Zone was established in 1982, covering the southern districts of Jiangsu, the northern districts of Zhejiang and the metropolis itself. It was in some ways a precursor to Zhao Ziyang's outward strategy, but confined to the most developed areas of East China. In 1985 the zone was expanded to include the remaining districts of Jiangsu and Zhejiang as well as Anhui and Jiangxi provinces. See Lynn T. White III, "Shanghai's 'Horizontal Liaisons' and Population Control" (manuscript, pp. 18-22); Larsen, *Regional Policy of China, 1949–85* (Manila and Wollongong: Journal of Contemporary Asia Publishers, 1992), p. 93.

110. Xu Miaoquan et al., "Jianli Lu-Hang-Yong jingji fazhan kaifangdaide zhanlüe yiyi jiqi gousi" (The strategic significance of establishing a Shanghai-Hangzhou-Ningbo economic development open belt and its conception), *Zhejiang jingji yanjiu*, No. 10, 1985, pp. 9-12: He Wei, "Ba Zhejiang jingji fazhan zhanlüe fangdao Shanghai jingjiqude fanweinei lai yanjiu" (Studying the incorporation of Zhejiang's economic development strategy into the context of the Shanghai Economic Zone), *Zhejiang jingji yanjiu*, No. 14, pp. 2-7.

111. Li Wenqing, "Fazhan Zhejiang jingji ying yi neilian wei zhu" (In developing its economy Zhejiang should rely firstly on internal links), *Zhejiang jingji yanjiu*, No. 1, 1986, pp. 25-26.

112. Deng Xiaoping also inspected Zhejiang in January 1988. See *ZJRB*, June 14, 1996.

113. *ZJRB*, November 26, 1987; January 7, 1988. *ZJRB*, January 23, 1988 carried the gist of Zhao's ideas, which were later reprinted in *ZJJJNJ 1989*, pp. 3-6.

114. See the article by provincial deputy-governor and agricultural specialist Xu Xingguan, "Jiefang sixiang zhuazhu shiji shixian xiangzhen qiye xiangwai xiangxing jingji fazhande zhanlüe zhuanbian" (Open our minds, grasp the moment and realize the strategic shift of village and township enterprises turning outward), *Zhejiang jingji*, No. 7, 1988, pp. 2-5.

115. *ZJRB*, December 4, 1987. See a number of articles citing examples of the successful application of the outward strategy in *ZJRB*, December 8, 9, 1987; January 2, 4, 1988.

116. *ZJRB*, December 30, 1987; Shen's speech of December 24, 1987 is to be found in *ZJJJNJ 1988*, pp. 49-52.

117. A similar point was made in Zhejiangsheng shehui kexueyuan jingji xingshi fenxi ketizu, "Zhejiang jingji 1991 nian fazhan baogao—1991 nian jingji xingshi fenxi he 1992 nian fazhan gaige celue" (Development report on Zhejiang's economy in 1991—An analysis of the economic situation in 1991 and a strategy for pushing forward reform in 1992), *Jingji yanjiu cankao*, No. 63, 3 July 1992, p. 37.

118. *ZJRB*, February 5, 1988.

119. *ZJJJNJ 1989*, pp. 22-23.

120. In his December 1987 report Shen Zulun had viewed this further decentralization as a challenge which had to be accepted, so that Zhejiang could make use of its foreign trade powers to import technology and raw materials for its booming industrial sector. *ZJJJNJ 1988*, p. 50.

121. See also *Zhejiang 1979-1988 nian jingji fazhan baogao*, p. 29. Factory managers of state enterprises, interviewed at a symposium convened on the strategy in the same month, warned, however, that they would require the assistance of, and removal of impediments by, government departments to ensure the success of the strategy. See *ZJRB*, February 11, 1988.

122. *ZJNJ 1992*, pp. 8-20.

123. *ZJRB*, February 21, 1991, in FBIS-CHI-91-044, pp. 60-61.

124. *ZJRB*, February 20, 1992.

125. *ZJRB*, March 15, May 13, 1992.

126. See the list of economic zones in *ZJNJ 1995*, p. 273; *Hangzhou nianjian 1993*, p. 171; *Zhongguo jingji tequ kaifang diqu nianjian 1994*, pp. 46, 50, 115-20, 484-87.

127. *Dangdai Zhongguode Zhejiang*, Vol. 1, pp. 130-37.

128. Ibid., p. 133.

129. Ibid., pp. 137-51.

130. Feng Renyi and Shen Guoliang, "Zhejiang: Guangdong jingji bijiao fenxi" (A comparative analysis of the economies of Zhejiang and Guangdong), *Zhejiang jingji*, No. 1, 1988, pp. 40-44.

131. *Jingji yanjiu cankao*, No. 63, July 3, 1992, pp. 29-30, 37.

132. See *Jingji yanjiu cankao*, No. 58, June 28, 1992, p. 39; No. 63, July 3, 1992, pp. 27, 29, 37; No. 219, February 4, 1993, p. 50.

133. *Jingji yanjiu cankao*, No. 219, February 4, 1993, p. 52.

134. An exception to this pattern occurred in 1957 when Jiang Hua took advantage of his frequent access to Mao Zedong to plead for central investment in a plant to produce chemical fertilizers and pesticides so as to help meet the ambitious targets of the national

program for agricultural development. Mao agreed, the center approved funds, and the Quzhou Chemical Works in central Zhejiang was constructed. See Quzhou shizhi bianzuan weiyuanhui bian, *Quzhou shizhi (Quzhou City Gazetteer)* (Hangzhou: Zhejiang renmin chubanshe, 1994), pp. 415-16.

135. *Zhejiang 1979-1988 nian jingji fazhan baogao*, pp. 2-3.

136. Larsen, *Regional Policy of China, 1949-85* (Manila and Wollongong: Journal of Contemporary Asia Publishers. 1992), p. 196.

137. *Dangdai Zhongguode Zhejiang*, Vol. 1, p. 550.

138. See Forster, *Rebellion and Factionalism*, chs. 2-3.

139. *Chongman shengjide Wenzhou*, pp. 80, 90-91.

140. See Dali Yang, "Reform and the Restructuring of Central-Local Relations," in David S. G. Goodman and Gerald Segal (eds.), *China Deconstructs: politics, trade and regionalism* (London: Routledge, 1994), pp. 60-62; Wang Shaoguang, "Central-Local Fiscal Politics in China," in Jia Hao and Lin Zhimin (eds.), *Changing Central-Local Relations in China: Reform and State Capacity* (Boulder, CO: Westview Press, 1994), pp. 98-100.

141. *Zhejiang 1979-1988 nian jingji fazhan baogao*, p. 20.

142. *China: Revenue Mobilization and Tax Policy: A World Bank Country Study* (Washington, DC: The World Bank, 1990), p. 97.

143. *ZJTJNJ 1996*, p. 11.

144. *China: Revenue Mobilization and Tax Policy*, p. 147.

145. *Zhongguo caizheng tongji (1950-1991)*, p. 336; Huang Xiaoguang, "Caizheng tizhi gaige yu difang baohuzhuyi" (The relationship between fiscal reform and local protectionism), *Jingji yanjiu* (Economic Studies), No. 2, 1996, p. 40.

146. See Christine P. Wong, "Fiscal Reform and Local Industrialization: The Problematic Sequencing of Reform in Post-Mao China," *Modern China*, Vol. 18, No. 2 (1992), pp. 197-227.

147. *ZJTJNJ 1986*, p. 11.

148. *China: Revenue Mobilization and Tax Policy*, p. 147; *Zhongguo caizheng tongji (1950-1991)*, p. 337.

149. *China: Revenue Mobilization and Tax Policy*, p. 149.

150. However, in 1991 Zhejiang ran a budgetary deficit. The center has decreed that provincial-level administrations cannot run deficit budgets, nor can they resort to overseas borrowings to fund budgetary expenditures.

151. For example, in 1994 losses from state industrial enterprises at the county level and above increased by 34 percent over the previous year, and between January and September 1996 nearly one-half of state enterprises incurred losses, a figure up 11 percent over the same period for 1995. *ZJNJ 1995*, p. 169; *ZJRB*, November 3, 1996.

152. Michel Oksenberg and James Tong, "Evolution of Central-Provincial Fiscal Relations, 1971-1984," *China Quarterly*, No. 125 (March 1991), p. 20, fn 63.

153. *Zhejiang shengqing*, p. 634; Oksenberg and Tong, "Evolution of Central-Provincial Fiscal Relations," p. 24.

154. Lok Sang Ho, "Central-Provincial Fiscal Relations," in Joseph Cheng Yu-shek and Maurice Brosseau (eds.), *China Review 1993* (Hong Kong: Chinese University Press, 1993), pp. 12.8.

155. "Zhejiangsheng renmin zhengfu guanyu jubu tiaozheng caizheng guanli tizhide tongzhi" (Circular of the people's government of Zhejiang province concerning partial adjustments to the financial management system), *ZJJJNJ 1989*, pp. 84-85; Jae Ho Chung, "Beijing Confronting the Provinces: The 1994 *Fenshuizhi* Reform and Its Implications for Central-Provincial Relations in China," *China Information*, Vol. 9, Nos. 2–3 (1994-95), p. 7.

156. *ZJRB*, January 17, 1995 in FBIS-CHI-95-023, pp. 49-50.

157. Tsang Shu-ki and Cheng Yuk-shing, "China's Tax Reforms of 1994: Breakthrough or Compromise?" *Asian Survey*, vol. 35, no. 9 (1994), pp. 781, 784-85.

158. See Li Xiaonan (cadre in the policy and law department of the Ministry of Personnel), "Zhongyang zhengfu yu difang zhengfu jingji guanxide jiben taishi ji zouxiang" (The basic state of affairs and trends in the economic relations between the central government and local governments), *Jingji yanjiu cankao*, No. 673, May 11, 1995, p. 6.

159. At a taxation work meeting held in late 1996 those in attendance were reminded by Deputy-governor Chai Songyue that the collection of the two central taxes had to be fulfilled. Between January and September of that year the province had collected 72 percent of its quota, an increase of 19 percent on the same period for 1995. However, Chai warned bluntly that if the target was not met, the balance would have to be made up from local taxes, while if the target was met the province would be rewarded. He stated that in the future the two taxes would be linked with the export rebate paid to provinces, a clear warning that the center would withhold this revenue in the event of a failure to meet central tax collection targets. *ZJRB*, October 30, 1996.

160. "Guowuyuan guanyu shixing fenshuizhi caizheng guanli tizhide jueding" (Decision of the State Council concerning the implementation of the tax-sharing fiscal management system), *Caizheng*, No. 2, 1994, pp. 18-20; "Shixing 'fenshuizhi' caizheng tizhi hou youguan yusuan guanli wentide zanxing guiding" (Provisional regulations concerning budget management issues as a result of implementing the "tax-sharing" fiscal system), Caizhengbu tiaofasi bian, *Zhonghua renmin gongheguo caizheng fagui huibian (1993 nian 1 yue–1993 nian 12 yue)* (Fiscal Laws and Regulations of the PRC) (Beijing: Zhongguo caizheng jingji chubanshe, 1993), pp. 9-17.

161. *ZJTJNJ 1994*, p. 323; *Zhongguo caizheng nianjian 1994*, p. 430.

162. Tsang Shu-ki and Cheng Yuk-shing, "China's Tax Reforms of 1994: Breakthrough or Compromise?" *Asian Survey*, Vol. 35, No. 9 (1994), p. 787.

163. Another layer was added to the fiscal administrative system in 1984 when the province revived village finance offices which had been experimented with during the Great Leap Forward. By the following year almost half of the province's villages had set up finance offices. See *Zhejiang shengqing*, p. 635; *Dangdai Zhongguode Zhejiang*, Vol. 1, p. 542.

164. *Zhejiang shengqing*, pp. 634-35.

165. See "Zhejiangsheng renmin zhengfu guanyu gaijin caizheng guanli tizhide tongzhi" (Circular of the people's government of Zhejiang province concerning improving the system of fiscal management), *ZJJJNJ 1986*, pp. 76-77, translated in On-kit Tam and Keith Forster (eds.), *Chinese Economic Studies*, Vol. 24, No. 2 (1990-91), pp. 28-37; *Dangdai Zhongguode Zhejiang*, Vol. 1, pp. 541-42.

166. *China: Revenue Mobilization and Tax Policy*, pp. 271-73.

167. *ZJNJ 1993*, pp. 133-34; *1994*, pp. 134-35.

168. *Zhejiang 1979-1988 nian jingji fazhan baogao*, pp. 27-28.

169. *ZJJJNJ 1991*, p. 262.

170. *ZJNJ 1994*, pp. 226-29.

171. In the third round of China's 100 economically strongest counties selected in 1994 Zhejiang was represented by 23 (the second greatest number behind Jiangsu province). Shaoxing was listed 10th in the country, and Yiwu city, which was not represented in either the first or second rounds of 1991 and 1992, came in at 8th overall, and 1st in terms of per capita GDP, labor productivity and the number of secondary students per million people. Of the 23 counties 4 were located in Hangzhou, 2 in Huzhou, 5 in Jiaxing, 3 in Shaoxing and 5 in Ningbo (all in north Zhejiang), while there were 2 located in Wenzhou, 1 in Jinhua and 1 in Taizhou (central and south Zhejiang). *ZJRB*, October 12, 1995, March 13, 1996.

172. See Christine P. W. Wong, "Central-Local Relations in an Era of Fiscal Decline: The Paradox of Fiscal Decentralization in Post-Mao China," *China Quarterly*, No. 128 (1991), pp. 699-715.

173. Lok Sang Ho, "Central-Provincial Fiscal Relations," p. 12.7. In 1990 the provincial-level budgetary revenue in Sichuan province comprised only 7 percent of total revenue. See *Caizheng yanjiu (Studies in Public Finance)*, June 1992, p. 24.

174. *ZJRB*, March 20, 1991; Zhejiang government decision, December 31, 1994, concerning revising the methods for managing extra-budgetary funds, dated January 28, 1991, *ZJZB*, No. 6, 1995, pp. 7-12.

175. *ZJRB*, March 24, 1995.

176. *Zhongguo caizheng tongji (1950–1991)*, pp. 200, 224.

177. *Zhongguo caizheng nianjian 1994*, pp. 430-31. A note at the bottom of both pages states that due to an adjustment in the scope of extra-budgetary funds in 1993 the figures are not comparable with earlier years. It is unclear whether this refers to a change in definition or of substance.

178. A recent article has confirmed that this did occur. See Lin Lin (fiscal and monetary department, State Planning Commission), "Yusuanwai zijinde bianhua fazhan qingkuang ji zhengce jianyi" (Changes and developments in extra-budgetary funds and policy suggestions), *Jingji yanjiu cankao*, No. 760 (October 16, 1995), pp. 31-32.

179. Yang, "Patterns of China's Regional Development Strategy," pp. 230-57.

180. Zhu Jialiang, "Zhejiang diqu jingji buju zhanlüe tantao" (A discussion of the strategic disposition of Zhejiang's regional economy), *Zhejiang jingji yanjiu*, No. 3, 1986, pp. 9-14.

181. *Dangdai Zhongguode Zhejiang*, Vol. 1, pp. 102-106.

182. For Wenzhou see Chow and Chen, "Wenzhou: Development in Regional and Historical Contexts," pp. 188-90; also see Christine P. W. Wong, "Material Allocation and Decentralization: Impact of the Local Sector on Industrial Reform," in Elizabeth Perry and Christine P.W. Wong (eds.), *The Political Economy of Reform in Post-Mao China* (Cambridge: Harvard University Press, 1985), p. 205; Naughton, "Industrial Policy during the Cultural Revolution: Military Preparation, Decentralization, and Leaps Forward," in William A. Joseph, Christine P.W. Wong and David Zweig (eds.), *New Perspectives on the Cultural Revolution* (Cambridge, Mass: The Council on East Asian Studies, Harvard University, 1991), p. 319, fn 16 for reference to a mini third front strategy in Shanghai.

183. This did not prevent the provincial leaders in the Cultural Revolution from ear-marking 21.6 million yuan for the construction of a residence for Lin Biao in Hangzhou. See *Dangdai Zhongguode Zhejiang*, Vol. 1, pp. 538-39.

184. *ZJJJNJ 1987*, pp. 16-31.

185. Some of the more important of these new projects included: new airports in Wenzhou and Ningbo, expansion of Hangzhou Airport, double-tracking of the Shanghai-Hangzhou railroad (110.4 kilometers in Zhejiang), extension of two hydropower stations, the new Beilun Power Plant in Ningbo, Hangzhou City's computerised switchboard project, expansion of the 2.5 million-ton refinery of the Zhenhai Petrochemical Plant on the north-east coast of Zhejiang, the Zhejiang Acrylic Fibre Plant, the Ningbo Paper Mill, and new projects at Ningbo University. In addition, construction of a second bridge across the Qiantang River in Hangzhou, the Qinshan Nuclear Power Plant in the north-east of the province, the Zhejiang Provincial Broadcasting and Television Center, the Hangzhou Gas Supply Center, and other key projects were commenced.

186. *ZJRB* April 4, 1991.

187. *ZJNJ 1992*, pp. 8-20.

188. Zhou Zhili (Zhejiang province People's Bank), "1994 nian Zhejiangsheng jingji jinrong xingshi fenxi yu 1995 nian xingshi zhanwang" (Analysis of the economic and

financial situation in Zhejiang province in 1994 and prospects for 1995), *Jingji yanjiu cankao*, No. 621, February 6, 1995, pp. 46-52; *Jingji yanjiu cankao*, No. 645, March 20, 1995, pp. 18-28.

189. Barry Naughton, "The Decline of Central Control over Investment in Post-Mao China," in David M. Lampton (ed.), *Policy Implementation in Post-Mao China* (University of California Press, Berkeley and Los Angeles, 1987), pp. 51-80, argues that one of the clearest indicators of the center's decline in control over investment during the reform period has been the failure of local governments to direct more of the share of investment into the energy and transport sectors which have been given priority by Beijing. Naughton describes this trend as an "implementation bias."

190. *ZJTJNJ 1994*, p. 238.

191. *Zhejiang 1979-1988 nian jingji fazhan baogao*, pp. 16-23.

192. Ibid., p. 90.

193. Ibid., pp. 29-30.

194. David Denny, "Regional Economic Differences During the Decade of Reform" (unpublished paper), pp. 26-32.

195. Nevertheless, economic co-operation between the two has, of necessity, strengthened in recent years. In late 1994 it was claimed that there were 180,000 construction workers from Zhejiang working in Shanghai. *ZJRB*, October 19, 1994. See also *ZJRB*, January 24, 1996. In March 1996 the leaders of the two administrations met in the "neutral" city of Ningbo to discuss economic co-operation. *ZJRB*, March 23, 1996.

196. Keith Forster, "Reform in Zhejiang: The Paradoxes behind Restoration, Reinvigoration and Renewal" in David S.G. Goodman (ed.), *China's Provinces under Reform* (London: Routledge, 1997), pp. 233-71.

197. For a discussion of these issues, see Wong , "Fiscal Reform and Local Industrialization," pp. 200, 210; Yang, "Reforms, Resources and Regional Cleavages," p. 49.

198. *Zhejiang 1979-1988 nian jingji fazhan baogao*, p. 25.

199. After eight years, work on double-tracking the line was finally completed in November 1995, at a cost of 2.1 billion yuan. See *ZJRB*, December 4, 1995.

200. See reports on the meetings convened by the provincial government and attended by Governor Wan Xueyuan in *ZJRB*, April 4, 21, 29, 1995.

201. *Jingji yanjiu cankao*, No. 58, June 1992, pp. 39-40.

202. Zhang Xuwei, "Zhejiangsheng shichang jingji fazhande xianzhuang, wenti he duice" (The current situation, problems and counter-measures in the development of Zhejiang's market economy), *Jingji yanjiu cankao*, No. 246, July 24, 1993, pp. 24-25.

203. See Li Zemin's report on leading bodies in *ZJRB*, May 25, 1993.

204. Zhejiang People's Radio, January 7, 1995, in FBIS-CHI-95-009, p. 89.

4

One Step Behind

Shaanxi in Reform, 1978–1995

Kevin P. Lane

Shaanxi's experience with reform has not been a walk in the park. The province has struggled since 1978 to define a reform strategy and execute it. Provincial officials have been slow to implement reform policies, and the province has dropped dramatically in national economic rankings. Part of the reason for Shaanxi's difficulties are structural: as an interior province, it has been deliberately excluded from the focus of the national reform campaign. This is true in part by design, since coastal provinces have been selected to "get rich first," and in part by circumstance, since Shaanxi's location and economy leave it poorly equipped to compete effectively with the coast. During the period of reform, the province has suffered from a dramatic drop in central largess, in terms of both capital and favorable policies.

But part of the explanation for Shaanxi's relatively poor economic results during the past eighteen years involves the performance of its leadership. Shaanxi's leaders have responded cautiously and indecisively to the challenges presented by the reform environment. They have moved slowly to articulate provincial policies and to mobilize resources on their behalf. Shaanxi has been dealt a weak hand, but the province's leaders have played that hand poorly.

This chapter demonstrates the importance of the spatial dimension to understanding reform in China; interior provinces like Shaanxi have faced a different set of options and challenges than their coastal counterparts. It also demonstrates the ways in which leaders—both as individuals and members of a leadership "corps"—interact with structural variables to shape outcomes. Shaanxi's relationship with the Center and the decisions of provincial leaders concerning allocation of scarce resources have shaped in significant ways the direction of provincial development during the reform era.

Shaanxi's Historical Role in China's Economic Development

Shaanxi has for centuries played host to critical developments in Chinese politics and society. The nation itself was born within Shaanxi's borders, when Qin Shihuang in 221 B.C. completed his military conquests and established a unified nation with its capital there. Between the eleventh century B.C. and the twelfth century A.D., eleven dynasties established capitals in Shaanxi, making it a center of Chinese civilization and the heart of China's development. The Silk Road, which connected China to Central Asia and Europe, originated in Shaanxi, which was better situated for land travel with the West than the coastal provinces that later dominated China's foreign contacts. The Tang dynasty (618–907 A.D.) capital, Chang'an, thrived as a cosmopolitan center with no rival in the world— economically advanced, socially sophisticated, culturally rich.

After China's political and cultural centers shifted east beginning in the twelfth century, Shaanxi cast a much smaller shadow on the national scene. The province was barely brushed by the nineteenth-century confrontations with the West that shook China to its roots and helped create the conditions for both modernization and revolution. As eastern China became a cauldron of intellectualism and political activism in the first half of the twentieth century, Shaanxi maintained its reputation for being backward and closed. As trade, colonialism and extraterritoriality transformed the economies and cultures of the coast, Shaanxi remained very much a part of traditional China, remote and relatively inaccessible. The province was connected by rail to eastern China only in 1935, and by 1949 it could boast only 275 miles of rails and less than 3000 miles of poor quality roads.[1] The arid northern and mountainous southern regions of the province remained particularly remote from developments elsewhere in China.

Shaanxi's inaccessibility was partly responsible for its return to the center stage of Chinese politics during the civil war. Yan'an in North Shaanxi provided safe haven for the Communist Party to recover from the Long March in the late 1930s, and it was there that the party under Mao's leadership built the political and military institutions that eventually defeated Chiang Kai-shek's Nationalists. Yan'an became the cradle of the Chinese revolution and earned a lasting place in the hearts of party members who lived there. Even Xi'an reemerged into the spotlight: it was there that the dramatic kidnapping of Chiang took place in December 1936, leading to a second "united front" of Communist-Nationalist cooperation against the Japanese.

After the revolution, Shaanxi took on still new significance as the focus of a campaign to develop China's hinterland for economic and national security reasons. The First Five-Year Plan (1953–1957) targeted the province as a key site for industrial development, and 24 of the plan's 156 major projects undertaken with Soviet assistance were located there. Labor, expertise and capital were shifted from the coast to the interior, and Shaanxi—particularly the Guanzhong region in the province's center—quickly took on some of the features of a heavy industrial center.

Shaanxi's significance waned somewhat when national priorities shifted back toward the coast beginning in 1956. But with the inauguration in 1965 of China's "Third Front" (*san xian*) campaign to develop an industrial belt in the hinterland, Shaanxi reemerged as a strategic center for industrial development. The province undertook major projects in a wide variety of areas, but primarily in rail construction, energy resources, defense technology and civil aviation.[2] The radical phase of the Cultural Revolution delayed aggressive pursuit of the Third Front between 1966 and 1969, but then it took off. Shaanxi's investment in basic construction in 1970 was more than double that of 1969, and the pace of construction remained high through the Fourth and Fifth Five-Year Plans (1971– 1975 and 1976–1979). Personnel and material were moved from coastal cities to Xi'an to aid in the development projects, and Shaanxi mobilized large numbers of PLA troops and private citizens to join in the campaign.[3]

Policies of state-directed economic development that began in the 1950s changed the face of Shaanxi. The province remained comparatively backward by the late 1970s, but it was nevertheless far advanced from the abject poverty that had characterized the province in the past. At the same time, Shaanxi's economy in the late 1970s was a monument to the economics of socialist planning and redistribution. By pursuing unrealistically rapid growth and injecting ever-increasing amounts of cash into large-scale construction projects, the Third Front had been terribly wasteful. Of the campaign's more than four hundred major projects, nearly 90 percent were scattered about in remote regions, far from major cities and from each other. Capital accumulation during this period far exceeded the national average while real wages declined by 5.64 percent between 1966 and 1976 and consumer goods became harder to find. According to provincial bank statistics, Shaanxi wasted more than one billion yuan in basic construction investment funds between 1966 and 1980.[4] Studies in the province show that the rate of increase in industrial output value fell far short of the rate of increase in investment in fixed assets between 1956 and 1986.[5]

Shaanxi had developed an industrial base by the late 1970s, but it was inefficient, wasteful, and dependent on Beijing. Levels of worker productivity and product quality stood well below national averages. The number of factories operating at a loss increased during the 1970s to about one-third of the total number of plants.[6] Sixty-five of the province's 101 counties operated in the red in 1975; the number rose to 83 in 1978.[7] Shaanxi's economy was a creation of Beijing and of a particular complex of policies of socialist economic development—precisely those policies that Deng's reforms intended to undo.

Shaanxi's Spatial Economy

Although Shaanxi is a single administrative unit, its political economy operates in distinct regional contexts. With territory that stretches five hundred miles from north to south, Shaanxi is really three provinces in one. Guanzhong is the province's geographic and economic core. Located in the province's center, the Wei River Valley, Guanzhong has the most fertile soil, the most developed agriculture, and the most advanced industry. It hosts six of Shaanxi's eight municipalities, including the capital, Xi'an, which is the province's cultural and intellectual heart. With about 60 percent of the province's population, Guanzhong is responsible for about two-thirds of provincial GNP and more than four-fifths of industrial output value. It is thus also the major source of provincial revenue.[8]

North Shaanxi is both Shaanxi's poorest region and the bearer of its most important political legacy. Its arid territory, mostly loess plateau, accounts for almost 40 percent of the province's terrain but only 14 percent of its population. North Shaanxi holds substantial coal reserves, but the low price of coal and an inadequate transportation system have kept mines operating in the red. Agriculture in the north accounts for only about 6 percent of the provincial total, and industry, at about 5 percent, is extremely underdeveloped. North Shaanxi's greatest pride is Yan'an, the site of the Communist Party's "Camelot," and that legacy helps keep the region in the minds of provincial and national leaders. Significantly, the north, for all its remoteness, has also provided a steady stream of provincial leaders steeped in the lessons of poor peasant life and committed, they say, to perpetuating the "Yan'an Spirit."

South Shaanxi is also poor and remote, but for different reasons. It has traditionally been described as "eight parts mountain, one part water, and one part fields," which is only a bit off the mark: 95 percent of the region is mountainous, leaving little land to till. The region, which resembles neighboring Sichuan more than it does any other part of Shaanxi, is rich in natural resources, but poor access has constrained their exploitation. South Shaanxi accounts for about 34 percent of the province's territory and 27 percent of its population, but its GNP represents only about one-fifth of the provincial total. Many people in Shaanxi look to the south as a valuable resource, but one that will only bear fruit in the distant future.

Implementing Economic Reform in Shaanxi

The View of Reform from Shaanxi

For several reasons the prospect of economic reform in 1978 looked decidedly less promising from Shaanxi than from some other parts of China. First, Deng's reform program emphasized coastal development. The coast was to get rich first, leaving Shaanxi and other hinterland provinces lagging behind. Second, the reform program for logical reasons emphasized those industries and sectors in which coastal provinces held an advantage. Prices for natural resources, for example, were to be kept low while prices of consumer goods were allowed to rise. Light industry was to take preference over heavy industry and large state-owned firms were to make way for smaller enterprises. These priorities worked against Shaanxi's strengths. Third, some aspects of the reform program, such as tax policy or production contracts, would require extensive training to insure that cadres could carry them out. Shaanxi's provincial bureaucracy had relatively low levels of education and relatively little experience with the kinds of market-oriented reforms that were emerging. Whereas Shanghai and Guangzhou could hope to rejuvenate strong trade and market traditions, Shaanxi could not draw on such a rich past. Fourth, the prospect of having to rely more on local funds and less on national coffers was troubling for Shaanxi, which had grown attached to its annual fiscal supplements and had a weak economic base on which to draw for self-support. Thus, while the reform program might have promised higher production and greater wealth in absolute terms, it also threatened to drive Shaanxi down China's provincial economic rankings in relative terms.

That is exactly what happened. Shaanxi's economic growth rate during the reform period has been the second slowest of all China's provinces.[9] The province ranked twelfth in the nation in peasant income in 1978 but dropped to twenty-eighth by 1985 and hovered around twenty-sixth or twenty-seventh through 1993. Between 1979 and 1989, it ranked twenty-seventh out of 29 listed provinces in growth rate of peasant income.[10] Worker wages began the reform period higher than average but have grown at only half the national rate. They fell to 4.6 percent below the national average in 1990, then to 20.4 percent below in 1994.[11] Between 1978 and 1986 Shaanxi's share of combined national output in agriculture and industry declined steadily, dropping the province from seventeenth to twentieth place, then to twenty-first by 1995, and its position in per capita national income slipped from nineteenth to twenty-fifth, then to twenty-seventh in 1995. Between 1981 and 1986, Shaanxi's share of total national investment in basic construction dropped from a post-1949 average of 3.7 percent to 1.9 percent, well below its share of national population, which is about 2.7 percent. On a per capita basis, Shaanxi's share of investment in basic construction moved from 35 percent above the national average to 35 percent below.[12] Xi'an, the provincial capital and the most developed city in Northwest China, ranked last in economic development among fourteen "central economic cities" (*jihua danlie shi*) nationwide that had separate budgetary arrangements at the end of the 1980s. And while Xi'an enjoyed rapid growth in agricultural and industrial output between 1978 and 1988, its share of national output value dropped from 0.73 percent to 0.65 percent.[13] Meanwhile, between 1979 and 1991, 89.7 percent of foreign investment and 81.5 percent of foreign-funded projects went to coastal provinces.[14] Shaanxi's fortunes improved in some areas in the first half of the 1990s, but only marginally, and its performance relative to the rest of China remained weak. Reform did not come as an unalloyed blessing for Shaanxi.

Even before Deng's program began to take concrete form at the subprovincial level across China, there were signs that economic reform would require a particularly dramatic about-face in Shaanxi. The province had aggressively pursued "leftist" economic policies during the post–Cultural Revolution period. In November 1977, for example, when a conference in Beijing called for roughly 10 percent of brigades to test implementation of brigade accounting, Shaanxi, under the leadership of First Party Secretary Li Ruishan, quickly established test points in two counties and declared that 70–80 percent of all brigades in Shaanxi would implement brigade accounting within one or two years. This move was seen as the first step in a province-wide transition from team to brigade accounting. Between the winter of 1977 and the spring of 1978, 70–80 percent of the brigades in Chang'an County, 90 percent of the brigades in Lintong County, and 30 percent of the brigades in Weinan County implemented brigade accounting. By January 1978, 8.9 percent of all brigades in the province had implemented the policy, a rate well ahead of most of the rest of the country. As part of the process, personal property (such as bicycles used for transporting goods) was confiscated, private plots were recalled to the collective, and household sideline production and free markets were attacked as "capitalist."[15] During this period, provincial agricultural policy emphasized the importance of rapid growth. A critical decision on agricultural policy in May 1978 appeared to make concessions to liberalization, for example by calling for the autonomy of production teams and increased household sideline production, but in fact the document promoted movement toward brigade accounting and forbade all labor outside the collective.[16] As late as January 1979, after the reform program had been approved nationally, Shaanxi's provincial newspaper praised one county for making the transition from team to brigade accounting;[17] that process was not reversed until later in the year.

Shaanxi also energetically followed the Center's lead in pursuing a "new leap forward" by raising industrial targets to unattainable levels after 1976. To help meet those new targets, Shaanxi's state budget in 1978 included a remarkable increase of 46.7 percent in basic construction investment compared to 1977. A provincial survey in 1978 found more than three thousand projects under way, requiring 35 percent more funds than budgeted. Supplies ran short: available quantities of steel and aluminum wire, for example, met only 40 percent and 13 percent, respectively, of demand.[18] Thus, when Deng Xiaoping's reform campaign began to take shape in 1978, Shaanxi was running at breakneck speed in the opposite direction.

An Overview of Developments in Agriculture and Industry

Shaanxi turned toward reform slowly and suspiciously. At each stage of the reform process, from the late 1970s to the mid-1990s, Shaanxi failed to move aggressively to implement center policies. And as Shaanxi lagged behind in implementation, so it did in results. The province's economic performance during most of the reform period, including such measures as industrial growth, agricultural growth, attraction of investment and export growth, failed to meet national averages and fell far short of the pace set by coastal provinces. Part of the explanation for those results has to do with objective conditions within the province that left it ill-suited to cope with new economic priorities. But part of the explanation undoubtedly has to do with the way in which Shaanxi's officials implemented—or failed to implement—the reform program.

Agricultural reforms were central to Deng's program, but they took root only slowly in Shaanxi. The policy of "taking agriculture as the base," which established a broad context for rejuvenating the rural economy beginning in 1978, did not receive a warm welcome in Shaanxi. Some cadres at the provincial and subprovincial levels worked to thwart its implementation and to maintain policies, from budgeting to prices, that worked against agriculture.[19] The household responsibility system, which was so critical to sparking China's agricultural boom, was promoted on a large scale only beginning in the summer of 1982, two to three years after much of the rest of the nation.[20] On several occasions between 1980 and 1982, provincial party leaders explicitly restricted implementation of some household responsibility systems, warning of their negative consequences. Thus, while the policy was implemented widely across China in 1980 and 1981, by early 1982 in Shaanxi it was used in only 40 percent of production teams, almost all of those in North and South Shaanxi.[21] Shaanxi's agricultural reforms and agricultural results continued to play catch-up. A party rectification campaign in 1983–1984 revealed that agricultural development in Shaanxi lagged behind that of other provinces. That lag was reflected consistently in statistics that showed growth in rural incomes well below national averages.[22]

Shaanxi reformed its industrial sector at the same sluggish pace. The center-mandated shift in resources from heavy industry to light industry moved slowly in the province and was met with reluctance at all levels. Between 1980 and 1985, heavy industry grew at twice the pace of light industry.[23] Not until 1988 did the province undertake a rigorous campaign to develop light industry by offering preferential policies, and in the mid-1990s, growth of heavy industry continued to outpace growth of light industry.[24] As a result, Shaanxi began the race to produce consumer goods one step behind the coastal provinces. In some cases, the province began producing large quantities of consumer goods, such as refrigerators, washing machines and television sets, just as demand began to slacken. Growth of consumer goods industries was further limited by the quality of Shaanxi products, which failed to match their coastal competitors. Thus, throughout the late 1980s Shaanxi's share of sales both inside and outside the province dropped, and in the early 1990s the sales rate for Shaanxi's consumer products languished at the bottom of the national charts. In the textile industry, one of Shaanxi's most important, more than 70 percent of goods produced consisted of printed and dyed cotton, and only a very small portion were high value-added clothing or synthetics. By the early 1990s, Shaanxi imported from other provinces more than 70 percent of the market's most popular consumer products, including such items as fashionable clothing, cosmetics and toys. The province's own industries appeared to be sliding downhill, with losses mounting rapidly.[25]

Township enterprises, which experienced explosive growth in coastal provinces during the 1980s, also expanded rapidly in Shaanxi. However, the reluctance of local cadres to promote rural "capitalism," their inexperience in managing the new enterprises, and restrictions on the availability of capital all complicated the process. As credit availability fluctuated in the first half of the 1980s, for example, the number of collective-run township enterprises also fluctuated, dropping from 42,000 in 1980 to 37,000 in 1983, then climbing precipitously to 48,000 after credit was relaxed in 1984, and declining again to 45,000 after tightening in 1985. Enterprise failures were common.[26] And while the absolute number of enterprises and amount of revenue increased substantially in the early 1990s, reaching nearly 77,000 enterprises and 36.8 billion yuan, Shaanxi suffered a marked decline in relative terms. Between 1990 and 1993, Shaanxi's share of the total national income from township enterprises declined by 27.4 percent, so that by the end of 1993 the province accounted for a mere 1.3 percent of the national total.[27]

The performance of local cadres was also critical to the development of township enterprises. As Ma Shanshui argues, conservative cadres in power in the countryside easily blocked enterprise growth, while in some regions frequent shifting of cadres created an atmosphere of uncertainty that was counterproductive to establishing new enterprises and expanding old ones. As elsewhere in China, cadres also complicated the process by establishing bureaucratic hurdles and restricting enterprise autonomy.[28]

Reluctance to move aggressively on enterprise reform appeared at both provincial and subprovincial levels. For example, Shaanxi was slower than most provinces to establish the enterprise responsibility system (*chengbao zhi*), waiting until May 1987 to promote this most critical aspect of enterprise reform.[29] Even as late at 1992, party and government organs continued to interfere in enterprise management more than in other provinces.[30] Similarly, reports from Xi'an in 1986 confirmed that ten months after the municipal party committee promulgated policies designed to encourage lateral economic ties among research institutions and enterprises, cadres in government offices had still not taken steps to implement the changes.[31]

It should come as no surprise, then, that private enterprises (*geti qiye* and *siying qiye*) also emerged at a sluggish pace in Shaanxi. In 1988, Shaanxi's private enterprises produced 0.35 percent of the provincial gross value of industrial output, compared to a national average of 2.0 percent.[32] By 1993, despite some growth, Shaanxi's private economy appeared to be going nowhere slowly—the number of enterprises had stood near 30,000 for a few years, a per capita rate below the national average. Shaanxi's private enterprises were also smaller, with an average capitalization at the time of opening that was 25 percent below the national average.[33] In 1994, the proportion of output value produced by private enterprises was less than half the national average.[34]

Shaanxi's performance was perhaps least impressive in foreign trade. Unlike coastal provinces, which made rapid leaps in attracting foreign investment and penetrating foreign markets, Shaanxi's external relations developed slowly. This was clearly the area for which Shaanxi was least prepared, for several reasons. The province had little modern historical experience with foreign trade. Its major products were not those most likely to find a profitable international market. And Shaanxi's low productivity and low quality of consumer goods meant that the province would find it difficult to compete with coastal areas for market share.

Shaanxi's leaders took initial formal steps toward developing foreign trade as early as 1979, when the province held its first-ever conference on foreign trade. In 1980, Shaanxi received permission for the first time to participate fully in the Guangdong Trade Fair. But the province had much ground to gain. A 1983 provincial report claimed that Shaanxi lagged well behind national averages in its foreign trade.[35] Shaanxi's leaders pursued foreign trade more aggressively after 1983, and the province held its first international trade convention in December 1984, with representatives from twenty-five countries and territories traveling to Xi'an to sign contracts for trade and technological cooperation.[36] But development remained sluggish. By 1992, Shaanxi could claim only 1 percent of China's total exports and 1.4 percent of foreign investment.[37] Substantial increases in 1993 and 1994 demonstrated that Shaanxi, led by its capital, Xi'an, was devoting more attention to developing foreign trade and encouraging foreign investment, but it still lagged well behind. One sign of the province's relative backwardness in this area of economic reform is that Shaanxi's "opening to the outside" has been promoted in two contexts: opening to foreign countries and opening to other provinces in China.

The defining characteristics of reform in Shaanxi have thus been "slow" and "conservative." The two terms are, of course, connected: ideological conservatism led to conservatism in implementation. Thus, whereas officials in many areas of China, and most obviously on the coast, quickly seized the opportunity to implement responsibility systems, open free markets, build private enterprises, and establish foreign trade and investment, many of Shaanxi's officials responded cautiously and reluctantly. For example, the *lianchan daolao* responsibility system, which ties labor within the collective directly to income, met with opposition from all levels of cadres and was implemented in a relatively small number of production teams when the policy was first issued.[38] Rural reforms were stymied at the grassroots because cadres continued to pursue "petty egalitarianism" (*xiao pingjun zhuyi*) even after the old policies of brigade accounting and egalitarian distribution had been formally abandoned. Shaanxi's top leaders explicitly confirmed this tendency to move slowly in late 1987, after inspection tours in the province and in the wake of the party center's Thirteenth

Congress. The Shaanxi officials pointed out that rural reforms were implemented 2–3 years later than in other provinces, that village and township enterprises were also started later, and that in general Shaanxi officials, still steeped in old attitudes, failed to pay sufficient attention to economic results.[39] Provincial Party Secretary Zhang Boxing formally confirmed Shaanxi's late start at a meeting of the provincial party Standing Committee in August 1988.[40]

Evidence of Shaanxi's leftism has emerged repeatedly throughout the reform period as a source of obstruction to reform. Both the New China News Agency and the *Renmin ribao* (People's Daily) publicly criticized Shaanxi for leftism in 1979.[41] Provincial Party Secretary Ma Wenrui in January 1979 called Shaanxi a "disaster area" in terms of the damage caused by Lin Biao and the Gang of Four. Unlike the rest of the nation, which Ma claimed had already moved on from a campaign to undo the leftism of the Cultural Revolution to reform-based construction, Shaanxi still needed to "make up that lesson" before it could take further steps.[42] A month later Li Erchong, a deputy party secretary, explicitly drew a link between Shaanxi's resistance to agricultural reform and leftism among leaders, some of whom continued to refuse to implement policies:

> Responsibility for the slow pace of agricultural development and the various errors that exist in rural work in Shaanxi is not at the lower levels, among the numerous rural cadres, but is foremost at the provincial party committee. Most of the many problems that have occurred at the lower levels have come about because the party committee established incorrect rules or raised unrealistic demands or issued inappropriate praise and criticism . . .[43]

The problem of leftism at all levels did not disappear once reform got under way, and official provincial forums continued to produce complaints about the problem through the mid-1980s and even into the 1990s. Governor Li Qingwei, for example, claimed in 1984 that the influence of "leftism" was Shaanxi's worst shortcoming in economic work.[44] Ma Wenrui argued that based on evidence from a provincial rectification campaign, leftism was the main cause behind Shaanxi's slow implementation of reforms.[45] In 1985 Hu Yaobang, then CCP general secretary, argued that conservatism, rather than the limits of Shaanxi's natural environment, was the main cause of Shaanxi's inability to keep up with the rest of the nation.[46] And Shaanxi's governor, Bai Qingcai, appealed to Shaanxi's leaders to overcome the leftism that he said continued to obstruct the course of implementing reform and opening up to the world beyond Shaanxi's borders.[47] The evidence suggests that the governor's statements were not merely sloganeering.

The record of reform in Shaanxi leaves the province with little to cheer about, not because conditions in the province have declined—indeed, they have improved measurably—but because Shaanxi seems to have struggled more than other provinces to get reform right. In its broad strokes, reform in Shaanxi has resembled reform elsewhere in China, but in its detail, the reluctance to move quickly has made the reform campaign look substantially different, and the consequences of that difference have made a considerable impact on the lives of the province's citizens.

Fiscal Policy and Results in Shaanxi

A Deficit Province

The story of reform in China's coastal provinces appears to be about coping with vastly increased amounts of wealth. In places like Guangdong and Shanghai, provincial leaders have been faced with the difficult task of retaining revenues generated by rapidly growing economies. In interior provinces like Shaanxi, by contrast, the story of reform has been about a constant struggle to generate revenue. While absolute measures of wealth and social welfare have risen in Shaanxi under reform, the province at the same time has experienced a deepening fiscal crisis.

Part of that crisis is reflected in revenue and expenditure figures for the reform period (see Table 4.1). These numbers do not reveal the full financial picture; for example, they exclude extra-budgetary revenue, and they are subject to obfuscation and errors in reporting. Nevertheless, they reveal a clear trend: after nearly three decades of modest budget surpluses, Shaanxi in 1979 began to run increasingly high deficits. With central investment sharply curtailed, the province was left to develop its own sources of revenue. At the same time, however, fiscal reforms limited the capacity of the provincial government to raise tax revenue, and the economic reform drive itself created incentives for increased spending. Thus, while revenue grew at an average of 8.84 percent per year between 1979 and 1993 (after which a radically different tax regime took effect), expenditures grew by 10.35 percent per year.

Shaanxi has become a deficit province under reform. That deficit has been made up for by disbursements from the central government or ministries within the central government. Commonly, units in Shaanxi address requests to their respective administrative branches in Beijing. But particularly in recent years, the annual shortfalls have not been made up in full, leaving Shaanxi with an accumulating deficit and little means to close the gap.

Shaanxi's Fiscal Relationship with Beijing

Shaanxi's economy in the pre-reform era has been described as a "transfusion economy" (shuxue jingji), since its economic growth and development relied on constant transfusions of capital from Beijing.[48] Shaanxi enjoyed a rate of central investment considerably higher than the national average, and the central government established new industries that came to dominate the local economy.

Table 4.1

Shaanxi Revenues and Expenditures, 1950–1995 (million yuan)

Year	Total revenues	Total expenditures	Surplus or deficit	Change in revenues (%)	Change in expenditures (%)
1950	85.81	31.36	54.45	—	—
1951	135.48	78.97	56.51	57.9	151.8
1952	180.91	111.40	69.51	33.5	41.1
1953	241.97	155.52	86.45	33.8	39.6
1954	294.14	183.38	110.76	21.6	18.0
1955	294.77	193.06	101.71	0.2	5.3
1956	327.86	282.91	44.95	11.2	46.5
1957	340.01	261.58	78.43	3.7	−7.5
1958	741.13	589.46	151.67	118.0	125.3
1959	990.09	922.51	67.58	33.6	56.5
1960	1,045.96	1,116.48	−70.52	5.6	21.0
1961	672.41	473.58	198.83	−35.7	−57.6
1962	572.43	314.44	257.99	−14.9	−33.6
1963	542.02	382.70	159.32	−5.3	21.7
1964	586.11	432.73	153.38	8.1	13.1
1965	654.91	579.46	75.45	11.7	33.9
1966	839.13	711.69	127.44	28.1	22.8
1967	619.16	564.25	54.91	−26.2	−20.7
1968	336.72	429.54	−92.82	−45.6	−23.9
1969	753.55	714.77	38.78	23.7	66.4
1970	977.53	929.04	48.49	29.7	30.0
1971	1,162.37	1,034.17	128.20	18.9	11.3
1972	1,357.30	1,186.31	170.99	16.8	14.7
1973	1,410.05	1,215.82	194.23	3.9	2.5
1974	1,396.79	1,269.09	127.70	−0.9	4.4
1975	1,522.58	1,283.98	238.60	9.0	1.2
1976	1,359.71	1,314.51	45.20	−10.7	2.4
1977	1,502.64	1,382.62	120.02	10.5	5.2
1978	1,975.87	1,830.26	145.61	31.5	32.4
1979	1,680.10	1,956.17	−276.07	−15.0	6.9
1980	1,581.05	1,828.37	−247.32	−5.9	−6.5
1981	1,345.38	1,638.87	−293.49	−14.9	−10.4
1982	1,356.22	1,729.93	−373.71	0.8	5.6
1983	1,454.07	1,880.76	−426.69	7.2	8.7
1984	1,531.24	2,274.71	−743.47	5.3	20.9
1985	2,029.67	2,750.07	−720.40	32.6	20.9
1986	2,409.07	3,559.31	−1,150.24	18.7	29.4
1987	2,818.05	3,780.51	−962.46	17.0	6.2
1988	3,387.88	4,458.35	−1,070.47	20.2	17.9
1989	3,896.03	5,078.70	−1,182.67	15.0	13.9

(continued)

Table 4.1 (continued)

1990	4,119.01	5,390.62	−1,271.61	5.7	6.1
1991	4,513.91	5,827.81	−1,313.90	9.6	8.1
1992	5,095.39	6,526.54	−1,431.15	12.9	12.0
1993	6,289.82	7,539.85	−1,250.03	23.4	15.5
1994*	4,258.86	8,551.58	−4,292.72	−32.3	13.4
1995*	5,130.11	10,269.17	−5,139.06	20.5	15.5

Source: Shaanxi tongji nianjian 1994 (Shaanxi Statistical Yearbook 1994) (Beijing: Zhongguo tongji chubanshe, 1994), p. 141; Shaanxi tongji nianjian 1992 (Shaanxi Statistical Yearbook 1992) Beijing: Zhongguo tongji chubanshe, 1992), p. 153.
*Figures for 1994 and 1995 reflect new tax regulations.

Between 1950 and 1983, 83.2 percent of public investment in basic construction came from the Center, and the proportion reached as high as 99.3 percent at its peak. The average central contribution to total investment was 79.1 percent.[49] The shift in priorities to the coast that came with Deng Xiaoping's reform program put a crimp in the transfusion tube; suddenly, Shaanxi found itself enjoying central largess at a rate far below the national average. For a province whose economic growth had depended heavily on investment from the center, this created a severe obstacle to further development. Shaanxi in the early 1980s watched as its life's blood drained away: investment in fixed assets, for example, grew 97 percent in Shaanxi between 1982 and 1985 compared to a national average of 200.9 percent and an average among China's eleven western provinces of 197.6 percent. Shaanxi's share of national investment in fixed capital assets dropped from 3.7 percent to about 1.9 percent between 1979 and 1987. Just as troubling, Shaanxi's share of investment among western provinces fell substantially as well.[50] The central government's share of investment in basic construction in Shaanxi fell from 82.9 percent in the six years before reform to 51.8 percent in the six years after.[51] Moreover, in the reform environment Shaanxi's large number of state enterprises became a burden, because the province had to provide infrastructural and social service support for enterprises and their workers without gaining the benefit of their profits.

New tax regimes also made life more difficult for Shaanxi. The focus of tax reform in the 1980s and 1990s has been the desire to distinguish central and provincial revenues, to "eat from separate kitchens" rather than from a single iron rice bowl. But the iron rice bowl had served Shaanxi well, since Beijing had always ensured that it was full. Beginning in 1980, Shaanxi, along with other provinces, began to implement the "separate revenues and expenditures, contract by level" (huafen shouzhi, fenji baogan) fiscal system. As a deficit province, Shaanxi was permitted to retain 88.01 percent of industrial and commercial tax revenues.[52] There is no evidence in Shaanxi of intense bargaining over retention rates, of the type that has been detailed in other provinces, particularly Guangdong. Rather, observers in the province report that Shaanxi went along easily with Beijing's mandated retention rates, in part because the province had little economic clout with which to bargain, and in part because of a proclivity among provincial leaders not to argue with the center over such matters.

The introduction of "tax for profit" (*li gai shui*) in 1983 did not help Shaanxi's fiscal fortunes. With a high proportion of firms operating at a loss or with small profit margins, and with a large proportion of state-owned enterprises whose revenues were submitted directly to Beijing, efforts to establish a genuine tax-based fiscal system served to limit the province's access to revenue. The same is true of the "tax sharing" system (*fen shui zhi*) instituted nationally in January 1994. By clarifying central and provincial tax sources, it took one step further the process of cutting Shaanxi's "transfusion" tube from Beijing. In addition to limiting sources of provincial tax revenues, the new system increased tax burdens on township enterprises in interior provinces, where township enterprises currently need development most. By cutting tax concessions, it also raised the burden on older, less productive enterprises, including those in the defense industry, thus complicating the process of updating old plants and equipment. Early reports indicated that the new system would reduce expected tax revenues substantially in Shaanxi and other underdeveloped provinces.[53] Two years of data show those reports to be accurate: provincial tax receipts in 1994 fell by 39 percent from 1993, then rose by 20 percent in 1995, but still stood close to 1991 levels.[54] These efforts to make Shaanxi responsible for its own fiscal circumstances, while possibly advantageous in the long term, have only exacerbated the province's fiscal crisis in the short term.

Subprovincial Fiscal Relations

Shaanxi's subprovincial tax regimes have followed the broad outlines laid down by the Center, though implementation has been slower than elsewhere. The dominant factor shaping the province's revenue situation has been the high proportion of deficit counties—between 60 and 75 percent of the total during the reform era. Not all of these are in fact as poor as they seem, because borderline counties sometimes use creative accounting methods to maintain the policy advantages of official "deficit" status, and because budget figures do not reveal all revenue sources. But the burden placed on provincial coffers is nonetheless apparent. Table 4.2 provides a representative snapshot from 1993 of subprovincial budgetary finances. It shows virtually all of North and South Shaanxi running budget deficits, leaving the province to rely heavily on the Guanzhong region for its revenue. Xi'an is the major source of income, providing almost one-third of the provincial total. During the reform period, Xi'an has contributed 50–70 percent of its earnings to the provincial government. Fixing that proportion has constantly generated friction between the provincial government and its capital city, contributing to a tense relationship similar to that found between other provincial governments and major cities.

Table 4.2

Revenues and Expenditures for Shaanxi Cities and Prefectures, 1993
(million yuan)

City/prefecture	Revenues	Expenditures	Surplus/deficit
Provincial total	6,289.82	7,539.85	−1,250.03
Province level	868.89	1,871.13	−1,008.24
Xi'an City	1,856.26	1,311.67	544.59
City level	1,113.77	691.07	422.70
Xincheng district	101.00	55.75	45.25
Beilin district	100.33	60.18	40.15
Lianhu district	100.45	58.26	42.19
Baqiao district	49.30	41.41	7.89
Weiyang district	60.80	42.44	18.36
Yanta district	58.35	39.93	18.42
Yanliang district	34.10	24.87	9.23
Chang'an County	51.73	62.62	−10.89
Lantian County	21.55	38.47	−16.92
Lintong County	65.07	58.67	6.40
Zhouzhi County	29.02	49.00	−19.98
Hu County	56.97	62.51	−5.54
Gaoling County	13.82	26.49	−12.67
Tongchuan City	131.72	163.68	−32.14
City level	78.93	72.88	6.05
Urban district	13.75	16.67	−2.92
Suburban district	9.21	19.88	10.67
Yao County	25.48	38.01	−12.53
Yijun County	4.35	16.42	−12.07
Baoji City	715.53	604.89	110.64
City level	360.14	230.58	129.56
Weibin district	79.43	43.97	35.46
Jintai district	38.68	29.11	9.57
Baoji County	57.00	54.54	2.46
Fengxiang County	39.33	41.29	−1.96
Qishan County	33.22	35.81	−2.59
Fufeng County	21.46	37.99	−16.53
Mei County	26.18	32.09	−5.91
Long County	23.11	30.49	−7.38
Qianyang County	8.90	18.82	−9.92
Linyou County	5.15	14.67	−9.52
Feng County	14.93	21.17	−6.24
Taibai County	8.00	14.36	−6.36
Xianyang City	579.58	633.48	−53.90
City level	198.73	144.98	53.75
Qindu district	47.47	45.86	1.61
Weicheng district	51.47	45.23	6.24
Yangling district	5.40	13.96	−8.56
Xingping City	40.04	43.74	−3.70

Sanyuan County	30.96	43.64	−12.68
Jingyang County	26.98	33.85	−6.87
Qian County	24.88	36.65	−11.77
Liquan County	22.16	42.23	−20.07
Yongshou County	27.58	29.22	−1.64
Bin County	30.39	35.43	−5.04
Changwu County	12.53	21.85	−9.32
Xunyi County	24.26	37.38	−13.12
Chunhua County	18.84	30.03	−11.19
Wugong County	17.62	29.43	−11.81
Weinan Prefecture	507.01	652.85	−145.84
Prefecture level	−0.29	95.12	−95.41
Weinan City	90.55	86.02	4.53
Hancheng City	55.20	66.44	−11.24
Huayin City	24.50	28.62	−4.12
Hua County	23.35	31.07	−7.72
Tongguan County	37.59	36.29	1.30
Dali County	41.72	51.92	−10.20
Pucheng County	48.49	59.70	−11.21
Chengcheng			
County	86.33	67.84	18.49
Baishui County	30.31	35.65	−5.34
Heyang County	28.10	46.11	−18.01
Fuping County	41.16	48.07	−6.91
Hanzhong Prefecture	731.37	696.17	35.20
Prefecture level	−12.41	121.13	−133.54
Hanzhong City	111.00	76.20	−34.80
Nanzheng County	366.21	173.12	−193.09
Chenggu County	96.34	72.81	−23.53
Yang County	35.85	48.62	−12.77
Xixiang County	20.30	37.60	−17.30
Mian County	43.32	43.94	−0.62
Ningqiang County	14.31	30.35	−16.04
Lueyang County	39.66	42.60	−2.94
Zhengba County	9.36	27.66	−18.30
Liuba County	4.41	10.88	−6.47
Foping County	3.02	11.26	−8.24
Ankang Prefecture	177.64	344.07	−166.43
Prefecture level	22.59	53.60	−31.01
Ankang City	49.94	80.88	−30.94
Hanyang County	12.48	25.13	−12.65
Shiquan County	12.26	22.48	−10.22
Ningshan County	8.52	13.46	−4.94
Ziyang County	10.21	29.51	−19.30
Langao County	8.29	22.49	−14.20
Pingli County	7.96	23.05	−15.09
Zhenping County	2.26	10.65	−8.39
Xunyang County	36.06	42.74	−6.68
Baihe County	7.07	20.08	−13.01

(continued)

Table 4.2 *(continued)*

Shangluo Prefecture	104.92	296.87	−191.95
Prefecture level	14.54	45.48	−30.94
Shangzhou City	16.79	48.47	−31.68
Luonan County	27.00	61.79	−34.79
Danfeng County	8.51	27.13	−18.62
Shangnan County	8.19	26.64	−18.45
Shanyang County	11.84	33.11	−21.27
Zhenan County	10.85	32.12	−21.27
Zuoshui County	7.20	22.13	−14.93
Yan'an Prefecture	402.36	507.05	−104.69
Prefecture level	191.40	131.16	−60.24
Yan'an City	35.64	66.60	−30.96
Yanchang County	17.05	27.24	−10.19
Yanchuan County	10.54	27.09	−16.55
Zichang County	12.11	28.5	−16.39
Ansai County	17.42	28.87	−11.45
Zhidan County	7.09	21.79	−14.70
Wuqi County	6.36	21.43	−15.07
Ganquan County	11.42	18.16	−6.74
Fu County	16.18	25.40	−9.22
Luochuan County	25.08	33.68	−8.6
Yichuan County	11.03	20.27	−9.24
Huanglong County	5.19	16.29	−11.10
Huangling County	35.85	49.51	−13.66
Yulin Prefecture	214.54	451.81	−237.27
Prefecture level	41.68	75.72	−34.04
Yulin City	25.05	44.42	−19.37
Shenmu County	48.51	54.39	−5.88
Fugu County	33.39	38.15	−4.76
Hengshan County	7.25	26.54	−19.29
Jingbian County	10.13	31.33	−21.20
Dingbian County	14.65	33.30	−18.65
Suide County	15.29	31.80	−16.51
Mizhi County	3.44	24.42	−20.98
Jia County	4.75	26.16	−21.41
Wubao County	3.58	13.81	−10.23
Qingjian County	3.87	25.22	−21.35
Zizhou County	2.95	26.55	−23.60

Source: Shaanxi tongji nianjian 1994 (Shaanxi Statistical Yearbook 1994) (Beijing: Zhongguo tongji chubanshe, 1994), pp. 141–43.

Peter T.Y. Cheung argues in this volume that fiscal policy in Guangdong has been critical to the successful implementation of other reform measures. In Shaanxi, a similar connection between fiscal policy and overall economic performance is apparent, but the results have been quite different. For example, beginning in 1979 Shaanxi adopted measures to transfer fiscal responsibility to lower administrative levels. Beginning in the early 1980s, the provincial government encouraged counties and townships (after the disbandment of communes, which began in 1983) to establish their own fiscal administrative offices and train cadres to manage the new tax regimes that were being established. Greater administrative responsibility was accompanied by greater control over resources; between 1979 and 1986, the proportion of profits retained by state enterprises increased from less than 5 percent to 34 percent.[55]

These changes did nothing to help Shaanxi's fiscal difficulties, and they may have aggravated the problems. There are three reasons why. First, the province had, and continues to have, a high percentage of firms operating at a loss. In 1994, 54 percent of enterprises operated in the red, 63 percent in Xi'an.[56] Profit retention means nothing without profit. Second, Shaanxi's enterprises operated at relatively low levels of efficiency, so no matter how favorable the tax terms, they found it difficult to generate rapid revenue growth. In 1986, for example, Shaanxi realized only 12.5 yuan in profits and tax for every 100 yuan of capital in publicly owned industries, compared to a national average of 20.70 yuan.[57] By 1989, Shaanxi was still almost 5 yuan below the national average.[58] Third, decentralization made it difficult for the province to control spending at precisely the time that costs in all areas of the economy—from labor to public administration—grew rapidly. Thus, while provincial leaders struggled to generate more revenue using new tax systems, they watched spending spiral out of control.

The Search for Capital

With reduced investment from the Center and an ever-increasing demand for capital, Shaanxi has been faced with on ongoing struggle to find new money. The task has not been easy. Because of the relative inefficiency of Shaanxi enterprises, the province has had a very difficult time attracting investment from outside, whether foreign or domestic. Indeed, Shaanxi has experienced a substantial outflow of capital to coastal regions, where investments are much more profitable. The capital follows several routes: individuals invest their savings in the Shenzhen and Shanghai stock markets; Shaanxi banks lend money to coastal customers, who are better credit risks than local customers; Shaanxi individuals and collectives invest directly in coastal enterprises, particularly in booming areas like Shanghai's Pudong district; and Shaanxi individuals and collectives buy property in coastal areas where appreciation is likely to bring them a healthy profit. The outflow of capital exceeded 2 billion yuan in the first half of 1993. Provincial authorities took measures to slow it down, but not before Shaanxi had borrowed more than one billion yuan at high interest rates from Guangdong to meet the crisis.[59] The costs for Shaanxi have been high, since capital sent to the coast would otherwise fund the province's own development. Local observers have found particularly troubling the widespread participation of Shaanxi's own banks in coastal investment. And with the province's capital heading for the coast, it is easy to see why Shaanxi should find it difficult to attract funds from elsewhere.

The obvious solution for cash-starved enterprises in these circumstances has been to borrow, but borrowing has created problems of its own. Liu Ronghui, provincial deputy party secretary, reported in 1994 that 78 percent of the capital in Shaanxi's state-owned large and medium-sized enterprises was debt and only 22 percent equity.[60] At subprovincial levels, there were reports that cadres used their authority to force banks to make unsound loans. Even without that administrative pressure, the drive to invigorate local economies created great demand for cash, so that by the end of the 1980s provincial leaders were pointing to a "grave financial crisis." In the first seven months of 1988, for example, the province had placed 29 percent more money in circulation than had been designated in the entire annual plan.[61] Enterprises took advantage of lax regulation in the banking system to grab more capital. One commentary described the problem:

> At present banks are in a tight monetary position and find it difficult to continue their business not because of less money supply but because of large cash outflows. Some comrades say there is now gold everywhere. Some enterprises have several tens of thousands and even more than a million yuan in hand but they do not want to deposit them in the bank for fear that as long as the money is deposited in the bank, it will be inconvenient for them to withdraw. Some enterprises have large amounts of savings deposits in the bank but they refuse to pay off overdue loans because they fear that if they repay their loans it will be difficult for them to request them again. Some specialized banks dare not recall loans from enterprises for fear that their relations with them will be affected. Furthermore, due to mismanagement of the banking system, dead loans have doubled and redoubled and the turnover of funds is very slow, thus tightening the money market.[62]

The Fight to Control Spending

If the search for capital is 90 percent of the story of Shaanxi's finances under reform, the other half, as Yogi Berra might say, is the struggle to control spending. This problem has been a major preoccupation of provincial leaders, and for good reason: Shaanxi's revenues have increased at a respectable rate since 1978, but expenditures have grown even faster (see Table 4.1).

Shaanxi has engaged in the same kinds of wasteful spending that have become common throughout China: banquets, bonuses, gifts, cars, travel, and other perks. Official figures show growth in fixed capital investment of approximately 81 percent per year between 1978 and 1994, while basic construction investment in state economic units grew at an annual rate of 41 percent.[63] Of course, these budgetary figures do not reflect the full extent of spending, particularly at the local level. And in Shaanxi more than in most provinces, nonproductive investment has been especially high. Between 1981 and 1989, for example, nonproductive investment as a share of total investment was higher in only four other provinces.[64] As enterprises and administrative units have sought to jump on the money-making bandwagon, they have spent increasing amounts of money on capital expenditures. Decentralization of fiscal authority, as in other provinces, has facilitated that process. The result has been a fifteen-year struggle on the part of provincial leaders to control spending at all levels—including the provincial level itself. Perhaps the most notorious case of overspending in Shaanxi was the construction in 1983 of a new provincial office building and luxury residences for provincial leaders. The Central Committee learned of the project and objected to the opulence of the living quarters, but construction of the office building went ahead.[65] At a cost of 100 million yuan, it was reported to be the most expensive office building in China at the time.

At times following Beijing's lead and at times acting on their own initiative, Shaanxi's leaders attempted to curtail capital expenditures by putting a stop to projects under construction and limiting approval for new proposals. In August 1983, for example, the Shaanxi government suspended or postponed 131 projects valued at 34 million yuan.[66] Another major round of cuts took place in late 1988, when the province suspended or cut 194 projects valued at 500 million yuan. The provincial government pointed to three "trends" that limited the effectiveness of the cuts during implementation at subprovincial levels: refusing to cut projects already under way, ignoring projects financed by collectives, and ignoring projects outside the state plan. As a result, many projects, including large numbers of nonproductive projects for offices, residence buildings, and guest houses, went ahead unhindered.[67] It is not surprising, then, that Vice Governor Bai Qingcai in 1993 claimed that the excessive scale of basic construction was the major reason for Shaanxi's shortage of funds.[68]

It is important to note that Shaanxi's excessive spending, like its capital shortage, has been driven by the reform campaign. The devolution of fiscal authority to lower levels has made rampant spending possible; the demands of competing in the reform environment—whether for profit, social welfare or cadre perks—have made it necessary, at least from the perspective of local officials making spending decisions. The structural incentives to spend have been almost irresistible, producing what Shaanxi leaders have publicly recognized as fiscal chaos.

It also bears noting that capital shortages and uncontrolled spending have not been unique to Shaanxi. The same incentives have operated elsewhere in China, producing similar fiscal pressures. But there are two factors that make Shaanxi and other interior provinces different. First, they have operated with a much weaker economic base than coastal regions. Thus, for example, Shaanxi's weak infrastructure has made it critical for the province to spend funds on basic construction. Second, Shaanxi and other interior provinces have not enjoyed the preferential policies granted to those provinces at the center of the reform program, so they have not benefited from the same opportunities to increase revenues. This has made the fiscal crunch even more acute.

Development Strategy and Budgetary Priorities

In general terms, economic reform policies in Shaanxi have echoed the themes established by the Center. Given the nature of the Chinese state, that should be no surprise. Shaanxi's leaders have established responsibility systems in agriculture and industry that, though late in appearing, have been consistent with Beijing's demands. They have tried to shift the focus in labor from quantity to quality. They have tried to increase efficiency in enterprises, in administrative units, and in the countryside. They have called for streamlining the bureaucracies and promoting new leaders on grounds of professional merit. They have followed Beijing's lead in implementing new fiscal systems. Despite the province's recent history as an isolated heavy industrial center, Shaanxi's leaders have even made efforts to emulate coastal regions in promoting production of consumer goods and external trade.

As every chapter in this volume indicates, however, a focus on national outcomes and cross provincial consistency obscures meaningful cross provincial variations in reform implementation and results. Shaanxi faced its own set of circumstances—some unique to the province, some resembling other interior provinces—and produced its own response, what Governor Bai Qingcai once referred to as "the road to opening with hinterland characteristics."[69] Shaanxi's experience with reform, particularly as it relates to the important area of resource allocation, should be understood in the context of sectoral and regional policies.

Shaanxi began the reform era dominated by heavy industry, and it remains so today. Indeed, much of the debate over reform strategy in Shaanxi concerns the conflict of priorities among agriculture, light industry, and heavy industry. Agriculture would on the surface appear to be critical for Shaanxi, an underdeveloped province with four-fifths of its work force in agriculture. But the reality is different. Agriculture accounts for less than one-third of the province's total output value, and provincial leaders have frequently downplayed its significance. Shaanxi was slower than most other provinces to adopt the "taking agriculture as the base" policy during the early stages of reform, and Shaanxi's investment in agriculture has stood well below the national average. Peasant income has risen slower than in other provinces, dropping Shaanxi in the national rankings. And even while provincial leaders have paid lip service to the importance of agriculture in the provincial economy, they have appeared reluctant to devote a substantial portion of scarce resources to this sector. Only in the Seventh Five-Year Plan, beginning in 1986, did the provincial leadership make a substantial fiscal commitment to agriculture by dedicating 20 percent of surplus revenues to that sector. By 1990, expenditures on agriculture accounted for 12.5 percent of budgetary expenditures.[70] This shift in resources alone was apparently not sufficient to solve the problem. In December 1988, provincial officials adopted an emergency policy to divert capital construction funds and provincial foreign exchange funds to agriculture, after recognizing that the low procurement price for grain and decreased investment in agriculture had severely aggravated grain shortages. Among other problems, decreased investment had contributed to reduced irrigation, a reduction in the total area of irrigated fields, and decreased soil fertility.[71] In the important agriculture prefecture of Weinan, as one symptom of the problem, fiscal assistance to agriculture had decreased from 7.6 percent of agricultural output value to 1.7 percent between 1980 and 1987. Ironically, Shaanxi's bumper harvest of 1984 may have contributed to reduced interest and investment in agriculture, since some officials used the occasion to claim that agriculture had already achieved a critical level of success.[72]

Light industry would seem a logical sector for Shaanxi to develop aggressively. The province enjoys traditional strengths in textiles and electronics, and light industrial development would be consistent with national development priorities under the reform program. Indeed, Shaanxi's leaders have officially favored a policy of light industrial growth since the late 1970s. In practice, however, the promised transition from heavy to light industry has not happened. Growth of light industry has consistently lagged behind the national pace and has trailed Shaanxi's heavy industry at an increasing distance. Between 1978 and 1993, the value of light industrial output grew 5.5 times while the value of heavy industrial output grew 8.6 times, a difference of 56 percent.[73] Heavy industry has continued to enjoy the lion's share of investment funds, including more than half of all basic construction investment into the early 1990s.

Shaanxi's light industry received a boost after 1988, when provincial authorities issued a new policy to promote the sector. The announcement was significant because it represented a clear sign of an emerging development strategy, but also because it arrived so late in the reform process. On its face, the policy promised to allocate substantial new resources to light industrial development. It gave priority in assigning raw materials, electric power, credit, and transportation to selected light industrial products. It lifted price restrictions on certain light industrial products and broadened limits on employee compensation. It provided tax benefits, including deductions for capital raised through shares and dividends paid on them, plus exemptions for moving from profit-losing to profit-making status. New urban collectives that raised 50 percent of their own capital and 60 percent of whose employees came from the ranks of the previously unemployed would be exempt from taxes for three years. The scheme also granted three-year tax exemptions for production attributed to the sale of new shares and capital raised by the enterprise itself.[74]

This package of policies appears to have represented a dramatic shift, but its long-term effects were mixed. Output figures showed that light industry's performance relative to heavy industry continued to decline. Between 1989 and 1993, output value of light industry increased 66.6 percent, while heavy industrial output rose 115.4 percent, representing a wider gap than in the first years of reform.[75] While Shaanxi officials may want to raise the performance of light industry, they also must deal with the reality of an economic structure that is weighted heavily in favor of heavy industry. Transforming that structure—a process that must include raising the output of agricultural products that are used in light industrial production and resolving bottlenecks caused by serious infrastructural weaknesses—has been an explicit goal of Shaanxi officials, but it is necessarily a long-term goal, and the process of transformation has been slower in Shaanxi than in many other provinces.

By the early 1990s, 54 percent of Shaanxi's total capital was tied up in six pillar industries: coal, textiles, chemicals, machines, transportation and communications, and electronics. The problem is that enterprises in these industries were losing money. Every one of Shaanxi's coal mines operated at a loss. In 1992, the textile industry lost 159 million yuan, the machines industry lost 177 million yuan, the transportation and communications equipment industry lost 77 million yuan, and the chemicals industry lost 87 million yuan. In addition, the province has supported a large and unproductive defense sector with a profit rate almost one-half the provincial average.[76] In the short term, Shaanxi's leaders have tried to forge a reform and development strategy based on those industries with the strongest growth potential. The list has changed somewhat during the past fifteen years—itself a reflection of the leadership's inability to settle on a single strategy—but it has generally included machines, textiles, electronics, defense technology, tourism, natural resources, and processed foods and medicines. These are industries in which Shaanxi already has large firms operating and which are supported by local resources, such as strong education and research facilities or, in the case of tourism, a wealth of important historical sites. In recent years, Shaanxi's leaders have also pinpointed large and medium-sized industries, which produce more than two-thirds of the value of industrial output, to lead industrial reform and growth.

In addition to coping with Shaanxi's underproductive industry and irrational industrial structure, provincial leaders have faced the challenge of pursuing a single development strategy in the context of significant subprovincial variations. Their solution has been to adopt the same logic that national policy makers applied to China's regional disparities: let Guanzhong get rich first and promise that the other two regions will follow. Some provincial leaders have even referred to Guanzhong as the "South China of the north." The argument in favor of this approach is obvious. The Guanzhong region is far more advanced than North or South Shaanxi, and it occupies a superior position to take advantage of the reform environment. Eighty-five percent of large and moderate-sized enterprises, which provincial leaders have targeted as the focus of their growth strategy, are located in Guanzhong.[77] And while leaders promise to devote resources to the poor North and South, they recognize that the province's real promise lies in Guanzhong. The cost of devoting substantial resources to developing North and South Shaanxi at this time would be extremely high, the likelihood of returns very low. Of course, pursuit of a Guanzhong-based strategy also carries costs: regional inequality in Shaanxi, as elsewhere in China, will continue to grow.

In policy addresses since 1978, Shaanxi's leaders have repeatedly drawn the broad strokes of their reform and development strategy. They have targeted specific industries and firms of a certain size, have promised to pursue development by relying on the province's strength in science and technology, and have declared that Guanzhong would lead the way with North and South Shaanxi to follow. They have paid somewhat less attention to the details of provincial strategies, however, and for much of the reform period it has been difficult to identify a precise strategy. More important, Shaanxi officials appear to have found it difficult to implement the strategies that they have produced. The continued dominance of heavy industry after the policy shift of 1988 offers one example of this problem, as does a continuing failure to support strongly and maintain the province's corps of scientists and technicians. Allocation of provincial resources and economic results both point to Shaanxi's difficulty in choosing a strategy and then executing it.

Reform and Leadership in Shaanxi

Shaanxi's disappointing economic performance since the beginning of the reform program has been strongly conditioned by the province's geography, economic history, and status in the national policy program. Given those circumstances, it would be unreasonable to expect Shaanxi to produce the same rates of growth and development as Zhejiang or Fujian. Nevertheless, Shaanxi's performance has also been shaped by the decisions of its leaders. The story of implementing reform in Shaanxi, as in other provinces, is about how leaders responded to the objective conditions they faced.

In this regard, it is important to keep in mind the distinction between outputs and outcomes. "Outputs" refers to those aspects of policies that are actually carried out, while "outcomes" refers to the results of the policies. Shaanxi officials cannot always determine outcomes, which are significantly shaped by objective factors beyond the control of individual leaders and by the nature of the policies themselves. They are in a better position to shape outputs, although doing so means mobilizing a large administrative machinery and persuading the targets of policies to go along. Ultimately, as the Shaanxi case shows, the outputs that provincial leaders produced affected outcomes; in other words, there is a link between the ways in which leaders implemented policies and provincial economic performance.

Provincial Leaders

Any generalizations about provincial leadership will necessarily obscure important details about specific officials. It is nevertheless possible in Shaanxi, as elsewhere, to identify general characteristics of the leadership "corps" that help explain why policies took the course they did in the province. In Shaanxi, one obvious characteristic is leftism. Since the 1950s, Shaanxi's leaders at all levels have earned a reputation for favoring leftist policies typically associated with Maoism. Thus, during the Anti-rightist Campaign, the Socialist Education Campaign and the Cultural Revolution, Shaanxi moved more aggressively than many other provinces to take action against perceived "rightists," "capitalists," "revisionists," and other enemies. Particularly during the Socialist Education Campaign, Shaanxi was noted for far harsher treatment of peasants and lower-level cadres than was the case in other provinces. During the Cultural Revolution, Shaanxi was unusual in that physical violence and destruction of property actually worsened after revolutionary committees were established as the new organs of government in 1968.[78] Similarly, when national policy shifted toward economic liberalization, such as in 1956–1957 and 1961–1965, Shaanxi responded slowly and reluctantly.[79] Even in the case of leftist policies, however, Shaanxi's leaders have never strived to ride the cutting edge of political change. Rather, they have typically acted cautiously, using opportunities to shape policy implementation but refraining from standing out in the manner of, for example, Guangdong or Henan.

Shaanxi's tendency to lean to the left may stem from the dominance in provincial politics of the North Shaanxi Gang. This is a loosely-knit group (not a "faction") of officials known for their ideological conservatism. Many have family roots in the conservative North Shaanxi region, though such roots are not a prerequisite for membership in the group. (Another group, the Guanzhong Gang, is said to hold influence in municipal and county politics in central Shaanxi, primarily in the city of Xi'an.) The North Shaanxi Gang has held influence in province-level politics, but observers in the province say that its main strength lies in the bureaucracy's middle levels, where cadres can easily delay, alter, or otherwise thwart the policy instructions of provincial officials. Indeed, some sources within Shaanxi attribute the difficulties Hu Yaobang experienced as Shaanxi's first party secretary between 1964 and late 1965 to the obstruction of pervasive conservative forces within the provincial party bureaucracy. Hu clearly did not fit the characteristic conservative mold of Shaanxi leaders, and he did succeed in reversing some of the severe sanctions taken against cadres during the Socialist Education Campaign. However, some observers point out that the provincial bureaucracy and Liu Lantao, first party secretary of the Northwest Bureau, refused to cooperate with Hu and that they ultimately helped drive him from the province.[80]

The vision of Shaanxi as a backward, closed province is solidified by the fact that the province has a tradition of native leadership. Shaanxi's most important leaders from the 1950s through the present day have been Shaanxi natives. These include Zhang Desheng, first party secretary from 1954 to 1964, a North Shaanxi native who spent his entire career in Northwest China.[81] Xie Huaide, who held top party and government posts from the 1950s to the 1980s, was born in Shaanxi and served as mayor of Yan'an during the Anti-Japanese War. Zhao

Shoushan, Shaanxi's governor from 1952 to 1959, was the son of poor peasants in central Shaanxi. He spent his career working in northwest China. Zhao Shoushan's replacement, Zhao Boping, was a central Shaanxi native who worked in the Shaanganning border region government, then in the Xi'an municipal government, before gaining a provincial post. His successor, Li Qiming, was born in neighboring Shanxi and spent his entire career in public security in the Northwest. The most important figure in Shaanxi during the Cultural Revolution was Li Ruishan. Born in 1920 in North Shaanxi's Yan'an Prefecture, Li Ruishan worked in the Shaanganning border region during the Yan'an period, then in Heilongjiang Province. After 1949, he held senior party posts in Hunan Province before returning to Shaanxi in 1966, first as second secretary, then as first secretary and chairman of the revolutionary committee. Li Ruishan is still much revered by peasants in Shaanxi for his leadership in irrigation projects, but many others view him as a leftist who led Shaanxi too far down the wrong path. Indeed, the party center's criticism after 1978 of extreme leftism in Shaanxi's leadership was directed first and foremost at Li Ruishan.

Leaders During Reform

Shaanxi remained under the leadership of Li Ruishan immediately after the Cultural Revolution, and the province continued to display leftist traits. Central officials took preliminary efforts to turn the province around beginning in July 1978, when Shaanxi's top party and government officials attended a three-and-a-half-week conference in Beijing devoted to reporting on conditions in Shaanxi. At that meeting, top officials in the party center, including Li Xiannian and Hu Yaobang, criticized Shaanxi's leaders for failing to pursue the campaign to criticize the Gang of Four, suggesting that "leftism" and leftist leaders had survived in Shaanxi longer than in other provinces. The party center also shuffled the provincial leadership, most importantly by appointing Wang Renzhong as second party secretary and first deputy secretary of the provincial revolutionary committee. He was promoted to first secretary in December before being replaced at the end of the month.[82] Wang was a native of Hebei who had held senior positions in Hubei from 1949 until he was purged in 1966. Wang was already in Xi'an before his appointment, since he had been assigned work selling meal coupons at the Northwest Agricultural Institute during the Cultural Revolution.[83]

Wang's role in Shaanxi was to serve as a caretaker who could bring the province into line with central policies. Immediately after the Beijing conference, he led a month-long province-level conference to criticize the provincial leadership for its leftism in economic policy. The key reason that Shaanxi lagged beyond the rest of the nation in agricultural policy, the meeting claimed, was that leaders had failed to implement party policies. Indeed, as a provincial directive on agricultural policy confirmed in November, the party's provincial committee

Table 4.3

Shaanxi First Party Secretaries and Governors Under Reform

First party secretaries	Governors
Wang Renzhong(Aug. 1978–Dec. 1978)	Yu Mingtao (Dec. 1979–Feb. 1983)
Ma Wenrui(Dec. 1978–Aug. 1984)	Li Qingwei (May 1883–Dec. 1986)
Bai Jinian (Aug. 1984–Aug. 1987)	Hou Zongbin (Sept. 1987–April 1990)
Zhang Boxing(Sept. 1987–Dec. 1994)	Bai Qingcai(April 1990–Dec. 1994)
An Qiyuan (Dec. 1994–)	Cheng Andong (Dec. 1994–)

had defied central policies in 1977 and 1978 by opposing private plots, free markets and other liberalization measures.[84]

Ma Wenrui took over the provincial party leadership in December 1978 and held the position until August 1984. Ma is a native of North Shaanxi who was born in 1912 and spent much of his career working in Shaanxi. A true veteran of the revolution, he joined the Communist Youth League at the age of 14 and the CCP at 16. He served in several capacities in North Shaanxi party organizations before 1949, including as secretary-general of the Shaanxi party committee, and he studied at the party school in Yan'an. After 1949 he worked in the Northwest Bureau before being transferred to Beijing in 1955. Between 1955 and his return to Shaanxi in 1979 (except 1967–1974, when his career was interrupted by the Cultural Revolution), Ma held senior positions in Beijing, including minister of labor, vice chairman of the State Planning Commission, and vice president of the Central Party School.

Ma Wenrui pursued a public campaign to correct past leftist errors so that Shaanxi might catch up with the nationwide movement toward reform. It was not an easy task, since the policies of rapid growth and reliance on the state budget had been deeply embedded in the province's political culture and economic practice. At a January meeting of provincial, prefectural, and county cadres, provincial leaders hammered away at the themes of "taking agriculture as the base" and reversing the exclusive focus on grain. The meeting also began the process of reversing verdicts from the Cultural Revolution era, admitting that criticism of Hu Yaobang's work as party secretary just before the Cultural Revolution had been wrong and that many other officials had also been wrongfully purged.[85] But Ma Wenrui demonstrated no aggressive commitment to the policies of reform. In fact, under his leadership Shaanxi fell behind in critical areas of agricultural policy. Ma did develop a reputation for his aggressive commitment to retaining his job, however. Cadres in Shaanxi and at the CCP's Organization Department joked that Shaanxi cadres would not retire until Ma led the way. Their expression was: "Tui butui, kan Wenrui" (As for whether to retire, look to Wenrui).[86]

Ma Wenrui was removed from office by "promotion" to the Chinese People's Political Consultative Conference in 1984. He was replaced by Bai Jinian. Born in 1926, Bai is fourteen years younger than Ma, and he comes from a neighboring county in North Shaanxi. Bai spent his teenage years studying in Yan'an, then his entire career working in Shaanxi. His most important appointments have been in rural work. Bai's term as party secretary was not noted for particular achievements, and he did not leave a significant mark on the course of reform in the province. Long recognized as conservative, he has been considered the head of the North Shaanxi Gang.

Zhang Boxing, who replaced Bai Jinian in 1987, served longer than any other party secretary in Shaanxi during the reform era and clearly had the greatest impact on provincial development. Unlike every other first party secretary, Zhang was not a Shaanxi native—he was born in Hebei in 1930—and he is too young to have played a significant role in Yan'an. But he spent his entire career, beginning in the 1950s, in Shaanxi, working in the areas of defense technology, industry, and petrochemicals. Zhang's reputation in the province is generally poor; he is seen as a leader who lacked both conviction and skill, and his background did not prepare him well for transforming Shaanxi's economy away from its old structure. People frequently refer to him by the nickname, "Zhang Buxing," a pun on his name that means "No-good Zhang."

Zhang was replaced in December 1994 by An Qiyuan, a Guanzhong native who was born in 1933. An Qiyuan's training and work experience have been limited almost exclusively to the oil industry, including an assignment at the Daqing oil fields in 1954–1965. Nevertheless, he has had a somewhat more varied background than many of his predecessors and, significantly, spent most of the 1980s in Beijing. He held senior positions in the Ministry of Petroleum Industry and the Bureau of Seismology in the 1970s and 1980s before being transferred back to Shaanxi in 1988 as party secretary of Xi'an, then promoted to deputy secretary of the provincial party committee. His appointment was welcomed by many people in Shaanxi who were disappointed with his predecessors, but it is still early at the time of this writing to assess his impact on the course of reform.

For obvious reasons, provincial governors have had far less impact on policy making and implementation than party secretaries. And in Shaanxi, the backgrounds of governors have looked quite different from those of their party counterparts. Yu Mingtao, the first governor of the reform era, was born in Hebei in 1918 and joined the party in 1936. He spent his pre-1949 career working in several different posts at the county and prefectural level in Hebei. After 1949, he held a series of party positions in Hunan, where he worked alongside Li Ruishan. After being purged in 1968, Yu was named a Hunan party secretary in 1971. He was transferred to Shaanxi as a vice chairman of the revolutionary committee in 1977 and named to the Central Committee the same year. Two years later, with the reconstitution of the provincial government and the departure of Li Ruishan, Yu became governor. Yu brought with him a reputation as a leftist, and his views were shared by some of his top deputies in the provincial government.

Yu's successor, Li Qingwei, was born in 1920 less than a hundred miles from Yu's home. He served in his home county in Hebei until 1950, when he began a long career in Henan Province, working primarily in economics. Li rose to become a vice governor and party secretary in that province before his transfer to Shaanxi in 1983. Li Qingwei was replaced by Hou Zongbin, who was born in 1929 only several miles from Li's home. Hou worked as deputy party secretary in an electric motor plant in Hunan before the Cultural Revolution. From 1975 until his appointment to the Shaanxi governorship in 1987, Hou worked in senior positions, primarily related to industry, in Gansu Province.

The most influential of Shaanxi's reform-era governors has been Bai Qingcai. Born in 1932 in Shanxi, Bai joined the Communist Youth League in 1949 and the CCP in 1955. He worked in finance in Shanxi Province beginning in 1952, eventually rising to the vice governorship in 1983. Like his two immediate predecessors, Bai had no experience in Shaanxi before he was appointed to the top position. He was generally thought to be more capable than other top officials, but he did not earn a good reputation as governor. His term of office is best remembered for constant battles over policy and power with Zhang Boxing. And although Bai is generally considered to have been more competent than Zhang, he was not effective in advancing reform policies in the early 1990s. Bai also has been blamed for some serious policy mistakes, including initiation of a large infrastructural development program for which Shaanxi did not have adequate funds.

Cheng Andong, who was appointed governor after Bai Qingcai's dismissal in December 1994, thus stepped into a difficult position. Born in Anhui in 1936, Cheng did not join the party until 1980. He earned a university degree in mining in 1962, then worked in the mining industry in Jiangxi Province, where he rose to become mayor of Nanchang from 1984 to 1990. Cheng was appointed secretary of the Xi'an party committee in 1990 and held that position until his promotion to governor. Like An Qiyuan, Cheng Andong's appointment has been greeted with both hope and skepticism. One factor working in his favor may be his prior experience in Shaanxi. Although, like his predecessors, Cheng Andong spent almost all of his career outside Shaanxi, he served for four years in Xi'an before his recent promotion. That may make it easier for him to manage the province. Indeed, while it is still too early ath the time of this writing to draw conclusions, the new leadership "team" of An Qiyuan and Cheng Andong seems to work more effectively its predecessors.

Shaanxi Natives and Provincial Leadership

One striking characteristic of Shaanxi's politics during the reform period is that Shaanxi natives have continued to dominate party leadership. Excluding Wang Renzhong, who was a transitional figure, three of the four party leaders have been Shaanxi natives, two of those from North Shaanxi. The fourth, Zhang Boxing, spent his entire career working in the province and is considered by residents there to be "half" a Shaanxi native.

Repeated appointments of natives to the top provincial post is unusual in China, and the reasons in this case are unclear. They may be linked to both culture and institutions. Shaanxi is known to be insular and parochial, making it difficult for outsiders to operate effectively. Thus, leaders in Beijing may have believed that only Shaanxi natives could manage the province. Shaanxi is also reputed for its strong internal party networks, which may complicate the efforts of outsiders to pursue their own agendas. Hu Yaobang's brief and difficult tenure as first party secretary provides supporting evidence for these arguments, as does the experience of Zhang Boxing. The party center's decision to appoint Zhang was based in part on his extensive career in Shaanxi combined with non-native status; it was thought that he would bring local knowledge to the job but would also be able to break the stranglehold of natives on provincial politics.[87] Ultimately, the results disappointed officials in Beijing, who turned to another Shaanxi native—significantly, this time from Guanzhong—to take Zhang's place.

In contrast to the party leadership, Shaanxi's reform-era government has consistently been led by outsiders. Three of the governors were Hebei natives, one was from Shanxi, and the current governor is from Anhui. They have brought some experience in economics and industry, though their backgrounds are limited to a narrow geographical range: Hunan, Henan, and Gansu. The placement of non-natives in Shaanxi's government may have been designed to dilute the influence of the natives in party leadership without eliminating native control.

Whatever the intended relationship between Shaanxi's party and government leaders, the actual experience has been characterized by constant conflict. Such conflict occurs in every province, but it was particularly severe in Shaanxi, and most notably under the leadership of Zhang Boxing and Bai Qingcai. The conflict between the two grew so serious that central leaders, apparently believing that the friction had created an obstacle to effective government, ousted them both simultaneously in December 1994. In an unusual move that reflected the seriousness of the situation, the party center did not consult other provincial leaders before making its decision.[88]

The appointments of An Qiyuan and Cheng Andong that followed appear, at least in part, to have been made with the party-government conflict in mind. An Qiyuan, like his predecessors, is a Shaanxi native, but he has spent considerable time working outside Shaanxi. His three immediate predecessors had spent their entire careers in the province and the fourth, Ma Wenrui, was a Yan'an veteran who was personally and professionally steeped in provincial traditions. Cheng Andong, for his part, resembles previous governors in his extensive experience outside Shaanxi, but he also spent four years in Xi'an before his appointment as governor. Of his four predecessors, only Yu Mingtao worked in Shaanxi prior to taking the governorship. In addition, An Qiyuan and Cheng Andong both served in Xi'an. That shared experience may provide the double bonus of facilitating their cooperation while smoothing relations between the province and its capital.

Shaanxi's Conservatism

As in the pre-reform era, Shaanxi leaders during the reform period have been noted for their conservatism. None of the party secretaries or governors has earned a reputation, either in Shaanxi or elsewhere, for aggressiveness in pursuing reform. Zhang Boxing and Bai Qingcai both went through the public motions of supporting the reform agenda—for example, by making a publicized trip to Shanghai's Pudong zone—but in practice moved very cautiously. The tendency toward caution and conservatism has been equally apparent at the lower levels of leadership in Shaanxi. From the beginning of the reform program, many sub-provincial cadres demonstrated their suspicion of the new policies by moving slowly or, in some cases, refusing to implement certain measures altogether. This practice is not new to Shaanxi, which has long had a reputation for conservatism. Nor should it be surprising: Shaanxi's cadres legitimately feared that the reform program would dismantle the ideology and institutions that they had come to associate with their way of life. For all the waste and inefficiency of China's pre-1978 economy, it did bring measurable benefits to an interior province that had known centuries of relative backwardness.

At one level, Shaanxi's slowness in implementing reforms may be linked to the relatively poor educational backgrounds of its cadre corps. Shaanxi officials, products of a remote and backward province, are less worldly and less well educated than their coastal counterparts, characteristics that have contributed to suspicion of certain aspects of the reform program and a lack of sophistication in implementation. Provincial leaders have missed opportunities to exploit the reform environment and lower-level officials have had difficulty applying new methods of accounting and management. Shaanxi cadres are said to be "early to rise but late to get out of bed" (*xinglaide zao, qilaide wan*); they may realize quickly that a new campaign is under way, but they only slowly grasp the steps needed to implement it.

The low general level of education among Shaanxi officials is an old problem. Although systematic data for the early years is unavailable, the evidence suggests that compared to coastal provinces since 1949, Shaanxi has had a relatively low percentage of officials educated beyond middle school and a relatively high percentage of officials with little or no formal education.[89] Illiteracy was not uncommon among grassroots officials in the 1950s and 1960s. As late as 1980, Shaanxi still had inadequately low levels of education in key governmental departments. In the province's financial system, for example, 76 percent of the personnel had either an elementary school or middle school education; only 3 percent held a university diploma. Only 67 percent were listed as being fully competent in their fields, including 53 percent of personnel with ranks at the county level or the section (*ke*) level in the provincial government.[90] This is true despite the province's position as one of China's largest educational centers, featuring more than 1100 research institutes and 58 universities and colleges.[91] Shaanxi in 1983 had 20.6 university students per 10,000 residents, compared to a national average of only 11.8 students.[92] Yet intellectuals in Shaanxi have typically not played a meaningful role in provincial politics. In fact, one pressing problem that the province has yet to address effectively is its rapid brain drain. Only a small proportion of Shaanxi's top graduates stay in the province, and senior intellectuals, with experience in fields ranging from the sciences to administration, have deserted the province in droves since 1978. Like many Chinese intellectuals who leave the country and fail to return, Shaanxi intellectuals prefer to remain in a place where they earn more money and more respect.

Better educated and more experienced cadres would certainly have helped technical aspects of implementing reforms in Shaanxi, and greater familiarity with the experience of coastal provinces would have broadened the horizons of officials in need of creative approaches to new problems. Education can transfer skills and change perspectives. But the conservatism of Shaanxi officials during the reform era goes deeper than either of these factors. Shaanxi's status in national affairs has changed dramatically since 1978. Once at the center of national development and a major beneficiary of Beijing's largess, Shaanxi now operates on the fringes of the reform program, one of the provinces that must wait to get rich, and must do so largely on its own. The province's influence in Beijing has waned, too: In the mid-1990s, not a single Shaanxi native sat on the Politburo or headed a government ministry. Hu Yaobang made several publicized trips to Shaanxi during the 1980s, and Beijing still views the province as a leader in the hinterland, but its relative position on the national agenda has undoubtedly fallen. It is easy to understand why provincial officials might be reluctant to embrace these changes.

At the same time, because Shaanxi since the 1950s has relied heavily on Beijing for its development, Shaanxi officials have come to see themselves as dependent on the Center. Their attitudes toward the Center have not changed as quickly as their actual status. Officials in Shaanxi and Beijing both report that, unlike their counterparts in some coastal provinces, Shaanxi's leaders have not employed aggressive bargaining tactics to seek advantages from Beijing. Despite the province's dire need for assistance, the behavior of Shaanxi's leaders toward Beijing has reflected a traditional Shaanxi mindset known as the "three don'ts" (*san bu zhuyi*): don't come unless called, don't take something unless it is offered, and don't make a fuss (*bujiao budao, bugei buyao, buchao bunao*). That attitude has persisted even though Shaanxi's status in national affairs—and Beijing's proclivity to offer benefits—have declined markedly.

Conservatism in Shaanxi is also linked to ideology. Many Shaanxi officials seem to feel organically linked to the glorious days of Yan'an and its legacy of socialist virtue. Appeals to the "Yan'an Spirit" have often appeared in provincial propaganda. From the 1950s through the 1970s, Maoist thinking and policy found a warm welcome in Shaanxi, and the evidence suggests that some officials were genuinely reluctant to see it weakened after 1978. Thus, whereas Shaanxi was slow to implement economic reforms, it moved quickly to implement the "leftist" campaigns of the 1980s.

Perpetuation of conservative attitudes has been aided by the structure of the Shaanxi party organization.[93] The control of the North Shaanxi Gang and the Guanzhong Gang (especially in the Xi'an government) encourages conservatism by selecting cadres who accept the dominant values and agenda. It is not clear whether, in fact, Shaanxi's cadre corps has a tighter structure and stronger local elite than those of other provinces. However, some reform-minded officials in Shaanxi believe that one advantage of the recent leadership shift is that it weakened the stranglehold of the North Shaanxi Gang, which suggests that they see the provincial party structure as a barrier to reform.

Understanding Shaanxi's Experience

Guangming ribao (Guangming Daily) published a column in December 1994 that caused a great stir in Shaanxi. Titled "Shaanxi Leads in Science and Technology, Why Does it Lag Behind Economically?" the column posed a troubling question: Why should Shaanxi, a leading center for scientific research with a record of technological accomplishment, have performed so poorly since 1978?[94] The author, Ling Xiang, argues that the causes have less to do with Shaanxi's geography than with the perspectives of people who make critical decisions. Leading cadres, for example, have failed to allocate the kinds of resources necessary to exploit existing scientific resources. Whereas officials in Beijing, Shanghai, and Jiangsu have granted land and capital to leading research institutions, Xi'an's officials have instead blocked requests for more resources and watched silently as top institutions have lost property to encroachment from other units. Leaders in coastal provinces have provided financial and administrative support to specific industries, while Shaanxi's leaders have allowed theirs to fail in the competitive national market by refusing to provide the resources needed to succeed.

Of course, one must be careful not to overstate the degree of Shaanxi's distress. Shaanxi remains in better shape than several other provinces, and in many respects it remains a leading interior province. Because of decades of central government support, Shaanxi enjoys a stronger economic base than, for example, Gansu, Ningxia or Yunnan. But Shaanxi's performance is troubling for two reasons. First, Shaanxi has dropped in national rankings of economic performance, indicating that its relative achievements have been poor. Whereas in 1978 Shaanxi's economy would have compared with Zhejiang's, in 1995 Zhejiang makes Shaanxi look like a poor cousin. Second, Shaanxi's glorious past and its rich endowment of expertise seem to represent unrealized potential. These factors drive Ling Xiang's argument and animate much of the discourse, frequently filled with bitterness and frustration, in Shaanxi today.

One critical question to be answered, whether in regard to Shaanxi's reform program generally or to its resource allocation policy specifically, is whether a different group of leaders would have made a difference. The evidence from fifteen years of experience suggests that the answer is a guarded yes. It is guarded because any leaders in Shaanxi would have found their actions circumscribed by the realities of the province's economy and Beijing's policies. And all implementation efforts rely on compliance of lower level officials. The problem of provincial leadership is a problem of the leadership "corps" rather than a few top officials. But the answer is still yes, because it is clear that Shaanxi's leaders consciously established their own agenda in the reform period, that they chose to move slowly, that they chose to allocate resources—however scarce—in ways that limited the scope of reform policies.

A 1990 World Bank report on the Chinese economy pointed out that decision making has differed substantially across regions during the reform era. The authors argued, "Some provinces are capable of implementing intelligent development programs, whereas others seem largely at the mercy of events."[95] Shaanxi falls into the latter category. To be sure, central policies have placed Shaanxi in a difficult position. But by failing to develop a comprehensive reform strategy early and pursue it aggressively, provincial leaders have aggravated the problem rather than mitigated it. Many subprovincial officials have contributed to the problem.

Shaanxi's Future

By 1996, some signs of improvement had appeared in Shaanxi. New provincial leadership may have weakened old patterns of conservatism and party-government conflict. The province adopted a new slogan for reform and identified key industries that would drive development into the next century. But daunting challenges remain. Shaanxi still needs capital, but it continues to suffer a capital outflow to the coast. It needs to expand industry and trade but suffers from a seriously inadequate infrastructure. It desperately needs to make better use of its human resources, but the brain drain continues. It could use more help from Beijing, but the province's influence in the capital has never been weaker. To emerge from this hole, Shaanxi will require unusually creative management and marketing skills. Its challenge in the foreseeable future will not be to catch up with the coast, but to keep from falling further behind.

Notes

Research for this article was made possible by a Faculty Research Grant and a Faculty Summer Travel Grant, both from Franklin and Marshall College. I benefited greatly from the use of resources at the Universities Service Centre in Hong Kong, from the generous assistance of Nancy Hearst, and from the insightful comments of Peter T.Y. Cheung and Alan Wachman on an earlier draft.

1. *Zhongguo shengqing* [Conditions in China's Provinces] (Beijing: Hongqi chubanshe, 1986), pp. 807–15; The Consulting Group, Bank of America Asia, Ltd., "China: Provincial Economic Briefing Series," Vol. 6 (1982), pp. 23–46; Eduard B. Vermeer, *Economic Development in Provincial China: The Central Shaanxi Since 1930* (Cambridge: Cambridge University Press, 1988), pp. 1–5.

2. In the Fourth Five-Year Plan, for example, four key industries accounted for the following shares of total investment in basic construction: rail, 27.2 percent; coal-fired electric power, 13.8 percent; defense technology, 15.1 percent; civil aviation, 7.6 percent. See Zhang Ze, Bai Wenhua, and Guo Qi (eds.), *Dangdai Zhongguode Shaanxi* [Shaanxi in Contemporary China] (Beijing: Dangdai Zhongguo chubanshe, 1991), p. 141.

3. Zhang Ze et al., *Dangdai Zhongguode Shaanxi*, p. 141.

4. Ibid., pp. 152–54.

5. According to a provincial report, Shaanxi's investment in fixed assets between 1956 and 1986 rose by a factor of forty and labor by a factor of seven, but industrial output value rose only eighteen times. See Shaanxi Provincial Service, June 9, 1988, in Foreign Broadcast Information Service, *Daily Report: China* (hereafter, FBIS), June 10, 1988, p. 50.

6. Zhang Ze et al., *Dangdai Zhongguode Shaanxi*, p. 153.

7. *Shaanxi sheng zhi* [Annals of Shaanxi Province], Vol. 37 [Financial Annals] (Xi'an: Shaanxi renmin chubanshe, 1991), p. 600.

8. Figures for all three regions come from Zhao Bingzhang and Zhang Baotong, *Shaanxi jingji fazhan zhanlue zonglun* [A Survey of Shaanxi's Economic Development Strategy] (Xi'an: Sanqin chubanshe, 1988), p. 12; *Zhongguo xibu diqu kaifa nianjian, 1979–1982* [Yearbook of Development in China's Western Region, 1979–1982] (Beijing: Gaige chubanshe, 1982), pp. 378–79.

9. Ling Xiang, "Shaanxi keji lingxian yuanhe jingji zhihou" [Shaanxi Leads in Science and Technology, Why Does it Lag Behind Economically?], *Guangming ribao* [Guangming Daily], Dec. 6, 1994, p. 1.

10. Office of Shaanxi Province Finance Department, *Shangbannian wosheng caizheng yusuan zhixing lianghao, dan zhengti jingji xiaoyi chade wenti jidai jiejue* [Implementation of Shaanxi's Budget in the First Half of the Year Has Been Very Good, But the Problem of Overall Weak Economic Results Urgently Awaits Resolution], *Shaanxi zheng bao* [Shaanxi Government Report], No. 16, 1991, p. 48; *Zhongguo nongcun tongji nianjian 1991* [Statistical Yearbook of Rural China 1991] (Beijing: Zhongguo tongji chubanshe, 1994), p. 281. This list excludes Qinghai.

11. "Shaanxi zhigong gongzi yu quanguo pingjun shuiping bijiao fenxi" [An Analysis of Shaanxi's Worker Wages Compared to the National Average], *Tongji yu shehui* [Statistics and Society], No. 2 (April 1995), p. 33.

12. Shaanxi Commission for Structural Reform of the Economy, *Shaanxi gaige*

gouxiang [Concepts of Reform in Shaanxi] (Xi'an: Shaanxi renmin chubanshe), pp. 75–76; *Zhongguo tongji zhaiyao: 1994* [China Statistical Summary: 1994] (Beijing: Zhongguo tongji chubanshe, 1994), pp. 11, 16.

13. Research Group of the Xi'an Finance Institute, "Xibei diqu guangche jinsuo zhengcede jige wenti" [Some Problems in Implementing Retrenchment Policies in the Northwest Region], *Jingji gaige* [Economic Reform], No. 2, 1990, pp. 30–32.

14. Total contract volume was US$52.3 billion. Xinhua News Agency, Haikou, Oct. 2, 1994.

15. Li Ping'an et al. (eds.), *Shaanxi shehuizhuyi jingji jianshi* [A Brief History of Shaanxi's Socialist Economy] (Xi'an: Shaanxi renmin chubanshe, 1988), pp. 355–56.

16. Li Ping'an et al. (eds.), *Shaanxi jingji dashiji* [A Chronology of Shaanxi's Economy] (Xi'an: Sanqin chubanshe, 1987), pp. 437–38.

17. *Shaanxi ribao* [Shaanxi Daily], Jan. 10, 1979, p. 1.

18. Li Ping'an et al., *Shaanxi shehuizhuyi jingji jianshi*, pp. 357, 493.

19. *Shaanxi ribao*, February 11, 1979, p. 1.

20. Xiang Dongfang and Cheng Huaigang, "Shaanxi jingji fazhan mianlinde kunjing yu xuanze" [Difficulties and Choices that Shaanxi Faces in Economic Development], *Jingji gaige*, No. 1, 1988, p. 39; Zhang Ze, et al., *Dangdai Zhongguode Shaanxi*, pp. 157–58.

21. Li Ping'an et al., *Shaanxi shehuizhuyi jingji jianshi*, pp. 381–83.

22. Ibid., pp. 370–71.

23. Heavy industry grew 79.4 percent while light industry grew only 40.4 percent. See Li Ping'an et al., *Shaanxi shehuizhuyi jingji jianshi*, p. 481.

24. *Shaanxi ribao*, Feb. 25, 1994, p. 2.

25. Liu Taosheng, "Shaanxi gongye jingji xiaoyi xiajiang yuanyin hezai" [Why the Economic Results in Shaanxi's Industry Have Declined], *Jingji gaige*, No. 6, 1992, p. 57.

26. Ma Shanshui, "Shaanxi sheng xiangcun jiti qiye fazhan xianzhuang jiqi duice" [Current Conditions and Policy Responses in the Development of Rural Cooperative Enterprises in Shaanxi], *Jingji gaige*, No. 1, 1988, pp. 42–43.

27. *Shaanxi tongji nianjian 1994* [Shaanxi Statistical Yearbook 1994] (Beijing: Zhongguo tongji chubanshe, 1994), p. 241; *Zhongguo nianjian 1993* [China Yearbook 1993] (Beijing: Zhongguo nianjian she, 1993), p. 440; *Zhongguo nianjian 1994* [China Yearbook 1994] (Beijing: Zhongguo nianjian she, 1994), p. 412.

28. Ma Shanshui, "Shaanxi sheng xiangcun jiti qiye," p. 44.

29. Xiang Dongfang and Cheng Huaigang, "Shaanxi jingji fazhan," p. 39.

30. Liu Taosheng, "Shaanxi gongye jingji," p. 57.

31. Shaanxi Provincial Service, May 8, 1986, in FBIS, May 9, 1986, p. T2.

32. Xiang Dongfang and Cheng Huaigang, "Shaanxi jingji fazhan," p. 41.

33. Yang Yongshan, "Dui dali fazhan Shaanxi geti, siying jingjide jianyi" [Suggestions for Vigorously Developing Shaanxi's Private and Privately-Operated Economy], *Jingji gaige*, No. 3, 1993, p. 58.

34. "Shaanxi shengwei Liu Ronghui fushuji zai jingji shehui zonghe pingjia hui shangde jianghua (zhaiyao)" [The Remarks of Shaanxi Deputy Party Secretary Liu Ronghui at the Comprehensive Assessment Conference of the Economy and Society (Excerpts)], *Tongji yu shehui* [Statistics and Society], No. 6 (Dec. 1994), p. 2.

35. Li Ping'an et al., *Shaanxi jingji dashiji*, p. 515.

36. Li Ping'an et al., *Shaanxi shehuizhuyi jingji jianshi*, p. 437.

37. *Gongchandangren* [Communist Party Man], No. 8, 1992, p. 4.

38. Eduard Vermeer, "Collectivization and Decollectivization in Guanzhong, Central

Shaanxi, 1934–1984," in Ashwani Saith (ed.), *The Re-emergence of the Chinese Peasantry* (London: Croom Helm, 1987), p. 20.

39. Shaanxi Provincial Service, Dec. 10, 1987, in FBIS, Dec. 16, 1987, p. 34.

40. Shaanxi Provincial Service, Aug. 3, 1988, in FBIS, Aug. 4, 1988, pp. 50–51.

41. Eduard Vermeer, "Collectivization and Decollectivization," p. 20.

42. *Shaanxi ribao*, Jan. 23, 1979, p. 1.

43. *Shaanxi ribao*, Feb. 11, 1979, p. 1.

44. Li Ping'an et al., *Shaanxi jingji dashiji*, p. 537.

45. Ibid., pp. 539–40.

46. Ibid., p. 544.

47. Bai Qingcai, "Zou you neilu tesede kaifang zhi lu" [Take the Road to Opening with Hinterland Characteristics], *Shaanxi zheng bao* [Shaanxi Government Report], No. 22, 1992, p. 6.

48. Zhao Bingzhang and Zhang Baotong, *Shaanxi jingji fazhan zhanlue zonglun*, p. 14.

49. Li Ping'an et al., *Shaanxi shehuizhuyi jingji jianshi*, p. 493; Zhao Bingzhang and Zhang Baotong, *Shaanxi jingji fazhan zhanlue zonglun*, p. 327.

50. Xiang Dongfang and Cheng Huaigang, "Shaanxi jingji fazhan," p. 37; Yang Zongyue, "Shixian Shaanxi chanye jiegou helihuade jiben silu" [Basic Ideas on Achieving the Rationalization of Shaanxi's Industrial Structure], *Jingji gaige*, No. 4, 1988, p. 47.

51. Li Ping'an et al., *Shaanxi shehuizhuyi jingji jianshi*, p. 493.

52. Ibid., p. 456.

53. Finance Research Group of the Gansu Branch, People's Bank of China, "Caishui, jinrong tizhi gaige dui bu fada diqu jingji fazhande yingxiang ji duice" [The Impact of Tax and Finance Reform on Economic Development in Underdeveloped Regions, and Policy Responses], *Jingji yanjiu cankao* [Economic Research Reference], No. 29 (Feb. 20, 1995), p. 17; *Shaanxi tongji nianjian 1996* [Shaanxi Statistical Yearbook 1996] (Beijing: Zhongguo tongji chubanshe, 1995), p. 180.

54. *Shaanxi tongji nianjian 1996*, p. 181.

55. Zhang Ze et al., *Dangdai Zhongguode Shaanxi*, p. 173.

56. "Shaanxi shengwei Liu Ronghui fushuji zai jingji shehui zonghe pingjia hui shangde jianghua (zhaiyao)," p. 2.

57. By contrast, Shanghai produced 50 yuan. See Xiang Dongfang and Cheng Huaigang, "Shaanxi jingji fazhan," p. 37.

58. Shaanxi Provincial Service, April 10, 1989, in FBIS, April 11, 1989, p. 54.

59. Bai Qingcai, "Zai sheng zhengfu quanti huiyide jianghua" [Address to the Full Meeting of the Provincial Government] (July 10, 1993), *Shaanxi zhengbao*, No. 17, 1993, p. 4; Fan Wangbang, "Shaanxi jingji tengfei: jiegou tiaozheng yu guannian zhuanbian" [Shaanxi's Economy Soars: Adjusting the Structure and Transforming Attitudes], *Jingji gaige*, No. 6, 1993, p. 410.

60. "Shaanxi shengwei Liu Ronghui fushuji zai jingji shehui zonghe pingjia hui shangde jianghua (zhaiyao)," p. 2.

61. Shaanxi Provincial Service, Sept. 6, 1988, in FBIS, September 8, 1988, p. 71.

62. Shaanxi Provincial Service, Oct. 7, 1988, in FBIS, Oct. 14, 1988, p. 62.

63. *Shaanxi tongji nianjian 1994*, p. 67; *Shaanxi sheng 1994 nian guomin jingji he shehui fazhande tongji gongbao* [1994 Shaanxi Statistical Report on the People's Economy and Social Development] (Xi'an: Shaanxi tongji ju, 1995), pp. 6–7.

64. Jiang Yue and Liu Yin, *Zhongguo diqu jingji zengzhang bijiao yanjiu* [A Comparative Study of Regional Economic Growth in China] (Shenyang: Liaoning renmin chubanshe, 1991), pp. 216–19. This list of provinces excludes Tibet and Guangdong. Things may be improving: the proportion of nonproductive investment in Shaanxi appeared to have fallen by the end of 1994.

65. Xinhua, Aug. 21, 1983, in FBIS, Aug. 31, 1983, p. T2.

66. *Shaanxi ribao*, Sept. 2, 1983, in FBIS, Sept. 22, 1983, p. T7.

67. Shaanxi Provincial Service, Dec. 25, 1988, in FBIS, Dec. 30, 1988, p. 74; Beijing Domestic Service, Dec. 26, 1988, in FBIS, Jan. 3, 1989, p. 70.

68. Shaanxi People's Radio, April 25, 1993, in FBIS, May 10, 1993, pp. 51–52.

69. Bai Qingcai, "Zou you neilu tesede kaifang zhi lu," p. 6.

70. Office of Shaanxi Province Finance Department, "Youlide cujin le quansheng jingji he shehuide fazhan, wo sheng 'qi wu' caizheng shouzhi zhixing qingkuang lianghao" [Aggressively Promoting the Entire Province's Economic and Social Development, Shaanxi Has Had Very Good Implementation of the "Seventh Plan's" Financial Arrangements for Revenues and Expenditures], *Shaanxi zhengbao*, No. 2 (Nov. 5, 1991), p. 37.

71. Shaanxi Provincial Service, Dec. 16, 1988, in FBIS, Dec. 16, 1988, p. 65.

72. Weinan diqu jingji fazhan yanjiu zhongxin ketizu, "Yingxiang nongmin dui nongye tourude yuanyin ji duice" [Causes Influencing Peasant Investment in Agriculture and Policy Responses], *Jingji gaige*, No. 1, 1990, p. 34.

73. *Shaanxi tongji nianjian 1994*, p. 251.

74. Shaanxi Provincial Service, June 6, 1988, in FBIS, June 6, 1988, p. 65; Shaanxi Provincial Service, March 22, 1988, in FBIS, March 24, 1988, p. 81.

75. *Shaanxi tongji nianjian 1994*, p. 251.

76. Liu Taosheng, "Shaanxi gongye," p. 57.

77. Shaanxi Provincial Service, March 30, 1989, in FBIS, April 3, 1989, p. 84.

78. *Shaanxi ribao*, March 3, 1979, p. 1.

79. See Kevin P. Lane, "The Life of the Party: Implementing Agricultural Policy in China, 1956–1957 and 1961–1965" (Ph.D. Dissertation, Harvard University, 1992).

80. It is worth noting that Hu was not entirely alone. He reportedly enjoyed the support of Li Qiming, Chen Yuanfang, and Zhao Shouyi among the top provincial elite. The official evaluation of Hu's performance in Shaanxi, not surprisingly, was revised in his favor in 1979. See Guo Qi et al. (eds.), *Shaanxi wuqian nian* [Five Thousand Years of Shaanxi] (Xi'an: Shaanxi shifan daxue chubanshe, 1989), pp. 914–15.

81. Biographical details for Shaanxi officials come from interview sources and from Donald W. Klein and Anne B. Clark, *Biographic Dictionary of Chinese Communism, 1921–1965*, 2 vols. (Cambridge: Harvard University Press, 1971); *Who's Who in Communist China* (Hong Kong: Union Research Institute, 1966); *Who's Who in Communist China*, 2 vols. (Hong Kong: Union Research Institute, 1969); Wolfgang Bartke, *Who's Who in the People's Republic of China* (Armonk, N.Y.: M. E. Sharpe, 1981); Wolfgang Bartke, *Who's Who in the People's Republic of China*, 2 vols. (N.Y.: K. G. Saur, 1991); *Who's Who in China: Current Leaders* (Beijing: Foreign Languages Press, 1989 and 1994); Liao Gailong, Zhang Pinguang, and Liu Yousheng, (eds.), *Xiandai Zhongguo zhengjie yaoren zhuanlue daquan* [A Collection of Brief Biographies of Major Chinese Political Figures in Modern China] (Beijing: Zhongguo guangbo dianshi chubanshe, 1993).

82. Zhang Ze et al., *Dangdai Zhongguode Shaanxi*, p. 163.

83. Interviews, China, June 1995.

84. Li Ping'an et al., *Shaanxi jingji dashiji* , pp. 443–47.

85. Ibid., p. 452.

86. Interview, China, June 1995.

87. Interview, China, June 1995.

88. Interview, China, June 1995.

89. See, for example, "Guanyu Shaanxi sheng diyi ci ganbu wenhua jiaoyu huiyide baogao" [Report Concerning Shaanxi Province's First Conference on Cadre Cultural Edu-

cation], *Shaanxi zhengbao*, No. 18 (Dec. 1956), p. 904.

90. *Shaanxi sheng zhi*, p. 756.

91. Xinhua News Agency, Shaanxi, Dec. 3, 1994.

92. Zhao Bingzhang and Zhang Baotong, *Shaanxi jingji fazhan zhanlue zonglun*, p. 418.

93. I am indebted to Lynn White for suggesting this point, though I do not hold him responsible for my interpretation of its relevance to Shaanxi.

94. Ling Xiang, "Shaanxi keji lingxian yuanhe jingji zhihou."

95. World Bank, *China: Macroeconomic Stability and Economic Growth Under Decentralized Socialism* (Washington, D.C.: World Bank, 1990), p. 201.

Part II

Provincial Reform Strategy and Policy
Toward Foreign Capital Investment

5

Shandong's Strategies of Reform in Foreign Economic Relations

Preferential Policies, Entrepreneurial Leadership, and External Linkages

Jae Ho Chung

Coastal provinces have been the main players as well as the principal beneficiaries of the economic reform of the post-Mao era. It seems that there have been manifest differences and variations among the coastal provinces in terms of their pace, patterns and strategies of development. In the context of China where standardization and uniformity (*yidaoqie*) had so long dominated the process of decision making and policy implementation, regional variation was a rather unfamiliar territory. Given the limited coverage of post-Mao reform from a sub-national angle—most studies have employed either macro-national perspectives or micro-village/enterprise viewpoints—a comparative exploration of provincial reform strategies seems both timely and worthwhile.[1]

This study, focusing on the strategy of provincial economic development, takes Shandong as its core case. Two reasons justify the selection. First, while most studies of China's coastal development deal with the southern provinces of Guangdong, Fujian, Jiangsu, Shanghai, and the special economic zones, very few have examined northern provinces in general and Shandong in particular. Such neglect is unwarranted given that Shandong is the most populous coastal province and the third most populous in China after Sichuan and Henan. Second, Shandong's path of development merits special attention since it has successfully attained a very rapid pace of growth from the late 1980s and shed its long-held image of an "atypical coastal laggard."[2] As a matter of fact, the province has already become one of the key models of development to be emulated by other provinces.[3]

Shandong's developmental path has evolved from a slow start in the beginning (especially compared with its southern counterparts), through a rapid catch-up from the late 1980s and eventually to a virtual take-off during the 1990s. Two questions emerge from this observation. First, what factors deterred Shandong from actively pursuing reform initiatives during much of the 1980s? Second, what factors have been responsible for its successful "telescoping" of development since the late 1980s? Both questions demand an investigation of more or less the same set of variables. These variables are: (1) policy orientations of key provincial leaders; (2) selective policy support and resource allocation by the central government; (3) innovative and entrepreneurial policy measures adopted by the provincial authorities as the province's key reform strategies; and (4) changes in external strategic and economic environments as a critical source of opportunity for promoting provincial-international nexuses.

These variables may be sequentially linked.[4] In the case of Guangdong, for instance, central policy support (e.g., the special economic zone designation) was contingent upon the province's proximity to Hong Kong. Beijing's preferential policies then facilitated the rise of the reform-minded provincial leadership which in turn came up with innovative initiatives in order to attract foreign capital and technologies. In the case of Shandong, too, it took much of the 1980s for its provincial leadership to break out of conservatism. Only when Beijing decided to include the Shandong Peninsula region in its "open coastal development" scheme in 1988 did its leadership begin to manifest reformism. The subsequent provision of various preferential policies and the rise of Jiang Chunyun, as well as the timely Sino–South Korean rapprochement contributed principally to the making of Shandong as a highly successful late comer. Shandong's advantages in geographical location and resource endowments were no doubt important, yet the fundamental propellant seems to have been of a political nature. And this is not surprising, since reform is inherently a highly political process.

This chapter consists of six sections. The first provides background information on Shandong, including an overview of its historical legacies, geographical and resource configurations, and its economic development. The second deals with an intricate issue of "provincial culture"—that Shandong may have cultivated through its interactions with Beijing over the years—as part of the explanation for its post-Mao developmental path. The third investigates the role of Shandong's provincial leaders in the post-Mao era to see how critical each of these leaders was in determining the pace and path of the province's development. The fourth elaborates on the subtle relationship between the province's heavy fiscal contribution and Beijing's provision of selective preferential policies. The fifth explores Shandong's "recipe for development" with respect to regional, industrial and infrastructural policies. The sixth examines the role of external linkages in Shandong's development, focusing on foreign trade, foreign investment, foreign borrowings, policy and organizational innovations, and local-international linkages.

Shandong in Retrospect: Legacies, Endowments, and Development

Located on the eastern coast of China, along the lower reaches of the Yellow River, Shandong is a region full of histories, myths and folklore, including those of the *Water Margin* during the Song dynasty and the "immortal boxers" at the turn of this century. Throughout its history, Shandong was replete with natural disasters, making the lives of its people unbearably miserable and forcing them to adopt a highly "protective" attitude toward anyone and anything that came from outside their territory. The province's predominantly Han-based ethnic composition (over 99 percent) also reinforced such "anti-outsider" (*paiwai*) sentiments.[5]

Encompassing 157,000 square kilometers, Shandong's land area constitutes 1.6 percent of China's total. In contrast, its population, 87 million as of 1995, marks 7.2 percent of China's total, making the province the third most populous. And its population density (553 people per square kilometer) was second only to Jiangsu.[6] With 65 percent of its total area in the plain region with thick and fertile soil, the province is well suited to agricultural production, particularly that of wheat, cotton, soybeans, and millet. With its coast line totaling more than 3,000 kilometers (one-sixth of China's total), Shandong's deep-water ports of Qingdao, Yantai, Weihai and Longkou position the province well for foreign trade. Shandong is also very well endowed with a variety of natural resources that number more than ninety kinds, including gold that ranks number one in terms of its deposits, and diamonds, petroleum and copper deposits that all rank second.[7]

In the last forty-odd years, Shandong's economy underwent significant changes. Between 1949 and 1979, its gross value of industrial and agricultural output (GVIAO) increased at an average rate of 8.9 percent per annum. In 1979, the total GVIAO was 45 billion yuan, almost fifteen times that of 1949. During 1949–1979, the share of gross value of industrial output (GVIO) in GVAIO rose from 29 percent to 70 percent. Shandong's contribution to the national economy also changed over time. For instance, Shandong's contribution to China's total national income (*guomin shouru*) was 6.9 percent in 1952, 6.5 percent in 1978, and 9.2 percent in 1993. Shandong's share in total fixed asset investment in the state sector (*guoyou guding zichan touzi zonge*) was 2.6 percent in 1957, 4.4 percent in 1978, and 6.6 percent in 1995.[8]

The pace of Shandong's economic growth was relatively slow in the early years of reform. It was in the 1990s that its pace of development took off to make Shandong one of the fastest developing provinces. In 1993, for instance, only eight provinces managed to mark a per-annum growth of gross domestic product (GDP) higher than 20 percent over that of 1989. Among these, Shandong only fell behind Zhejiang, Fujian and Hainan while equaling Guangdong.[9] Table 5.1 provides average annual growth rates for the 1949–1995 period on Shandong's gross value of agricultural output (GVAO), GVIO, GDP,

Table 5.1

Shandong's Key Growth Indicators, 1949–95 (%)

	GVAO	GVIO	GDP	Foreign Trade
1949–78	3.9	13.5	9.0	N/A
1981–85	9.8	12.0	11.1	10.3
1986–90	3.7	20.8	8.3	6.5
1991–95	11.9	24.8	16.7	25.7

Sources: Figures for 1949–78 are from Shandong Provincial Statistical Bureau, *Shandong tongji nianjian 1994* (Beijing: Zhongguo tongji chubanshe, 1994), pp. 11–13; and other figures are from *Shandong tongji nianjian 1996*, pp. 13–15.

Table 5.2

Comparison of Key Growth Indicators 1991–95

(%)	Shandong	National
GDP	16.7	12.0
GVAO	11.9	6.7
GVIO	24.8	22.2
Foreign Trade	25.7	19.7

Sources: *Zhongguo tongji nianjian 1996* (Statistical Yearbook of China 1996) (Beijing: Zhongguo tongji chubanshe, 1996), pp. 23, 25, 27; and *Shandong tongji nianjian 1996* (Statistical Yearbook of Shandong 1996) (Beijing: Zhongguo tongji chubanshe, 1996), pp. 13–15.

and foreign trade. The positive effects of decollectivization and price adjustments for agricultural products were clearly manifested in the rapid growth of GVAO in 1981–85. The pace of growth in GVAO, however, significantly slowed down in the following years due to the well-publicized nationwide problems of the lack of state support and technological bottlenecks. The pace picked up again in the 1990s, making Shandong the most successful case of agricultural development. In the case of GVIO and GDP which had grown relatively slowly during the early 1980s, their growth rates quickly outpaced that of GVAO in the second half of 1980s and the process was accelerated in the 1990s. Shandong's foreign trade also showed a similar path of development in that it grew at 10 percent per annum in the early years of the reform and stagnated for several years eventually to pick up significantly during the 1990s.[10]

Table 5.2 compares Shandong's annual growth rates in GDP, GVAO, GVIO, and foreign trade with the national average for the period of the Eighth Five-Year Plan. Shandong's figures exceeded the national average in all four categories, and its edge seems to reside more in agriculture and foreign trade. In terms

Table 5.3

Rank of Shandong's Foreign Economic Relations, 1986–95

	1986	1990	1991	1992	1993	1994	1995
Exports	4	4	4	4	4	5	4
Foreign Funds Utilized	6	7	4	4	4	4	5
Foreign direct investment	8	6	6	4	4	4	5

Sources: *Zhongguo duiwai jingji maoyi nianjian 1987* (China Foreign Economic Relations and Trade Yearbook 1987) (Beijing: Zhongguo shehui chubanshe, 1987), pp. 329, 549; *Quanguo zhuyao shehui jingji zhibiao paixu nianjian 1992*, pp. 116–117; and Ibid., 1993 issue, pp. 116–117. Export ranking is from *Zhongguo duiwai jingji maoyi nianjian 1994/95* (China Foreign Economic Relations and Trade Yearbook 1994/95) (Beijing: Zhongguo shehui chubanshe, 1994); for 1993 figures for foreign funds, see *Zhongguo tongji nianjian 1994*, p. 530; for 1994 ranking, see *Zhongguo tongji nianjian 1995*, pp. 551, 557; and for 1995 ranking, see *Zhongguo tongji nianjian 1996*, pp. 595, 600.

of its national ranking on GVIO, GVAO, GVIAO, and per capita GVIAO, Shandong consistently ranked second on GVAO, GVIO, and GVIAO during 1990–1993 and number one for GVAO in 1993–95, while it ranked only eighth on per capita GVIAO for the same period.[11] Shandong's foreign economic relations also made a big stride in the 1990s, particularly in terms of utilizing foreign capital. As Table 5.3 illustrates, while Shandong's ranking in exports remained consistent during 1990–1995, its ranking on foreign fund utilization and foreign direct investment rose from sixth and eighth in 1986, respectively, to fifth in 1995.

Shandong's Policy Behavior in Historical Perspective

In this section, we examine Shandong's policy behavior by investigating its pattern of compliance with central policy. A key underlying assumption here is that there may be distinct local norms of interacting with Beijing and such norms may not change frequently. The relative resilience of such norms thus allows the province to respond to central policies in a relatively consistent manner. During Mao's rule (especially after the traumatic experiences of the anti-rightist campaign in 1957), "bandwagoning" constituted a widely adopted pattern of local compliance in China.[12] Bandwagoning consists of two key elements. First, such provinces initially maintain an extremely cautious stance toward central policy and try to remain inconspicuous by not implementing it too fast or too slowly. Second, once the Center's preference for the given policy appears fixed, these provinces quickly popularize it, very often without due regard for its province-wide applicability. Since getting too far ahead of others in implementing controversial policies (i.e., "pioneering") or lagging too far behind others (i.e., "resisting") always entailed enormous political risks during the highly politicized Maoist period (and it still holds true for the current period to a considerable extent), most provincial leaders remained largely unwilling to opt too early for an uncontested innovation, and they chose rather to wait and see how the Center would respond to a handful of "pioneer" provinces.[13]

Available data on Shandong's implementation of several key policies during the pre-reform era suggest that the province was *rarely* a "resister." Shandong ranked thirteenth in its pace of implementing the cooperativization policy of 1954–56, but its cooperativization is considered to have been carried out hastily without an adequate preparation, clearly displaying the symptom of "bandwagoning." The province ranked eighth, sixth, and seventh, respectively, in its pace of implementing land irrigation, grain purchase, and communization policies during 1957–59. In establishing its provincial revolutionary committee, however, Shandong ranked second only after Heilongjiang by completing the task within two months after the January 1967 directive. Limited and fractured as they may be, these data seem to characterize Shandong as having moved between bandwagoning and pioneering, staying clear of resisting the Center.[14]

It may be that Shandong's learning over time to give up the "bandwagon" option with reference to non-economic policies from the Center had a lot to do with its geographical proximity to Beijing. Although the factor of physical distance alone may not suffice to explain varying patterns of implementation by all provinces (e.g., Guangdong versus Sichuan or Heilongjiang versus Yunnan), the case of Shandong rather seems to be a confirming one. One Chinese interviewee stated that "Shandong is a very typical case in which its geographical proximity to Beijing has considerably limited the range of policy alternatives available to the provincial leadership." Some scholars, too, suggest that Beijing is geographically—and possibly politically—close enough to some provinces to cast a significant shadow over the latter's implementation behavior.[15]

While Shandong had largely been a complier of central policy, the province was not necessarily always willing to reveal its policy preferences. Perhaps due mainly to Beijing's heavy political shadow over it, Shandong had been highly opportunistic by remaining extremely cautious in revealing its preferences, particularly when the central political stage was full of uncertainties. During the critical period of January 1976 through January 1977, for instance, many provinces stressed the Maoist principle of "taking the class struggle as the key link" in their efforts to rectify party organizations. Shandong, however, along with a few other provinces, refused to take a side by remaining silent. More importantly, in late 1976 when most provinces concerned themselves in some manner with criticizing the decade-long abuses of the Gang of Four, it was only Shandong that refrained from making any comments on the issue at all.[16]

Shandong's opportunism and bandwagoning seem to have continued well into the post-Mao period. The province displayed its typical bandwagoning pattern

Table 5.4

Shandong's Pace of Decollectivization Compared with Anhui and Heilongjiang

	Dec. 1980	June 1981	Dec. 1981	June 1982	Dec. 1982
Nationwide	14.4	28.2	50.0	71.9	78.2
Shandong	27.6	38.2	55.9	69.3	96.8
Anhui	66.9	69.3	84.6	97.0	98.8
Heilongjiang	—	0.7	—	—	12.0

Source: Chung, *The Politics of Policy Implementation in Post-Mao China*, Table 3–1.
Note: Figures represent the percentage of production teams implementing two household-based responsibility systems of *baochan daohu* and *baogan daohu*.

during agricultural decollectivization in 1979–83. Table 5.4 compares Shandong's pace of decollectivization with that of Anhui and Heilongjiang as well as with the national average. While Anhui (as a pioneer) and Heilongjiang (as a resister) consistently either went far ahead of others or lagged far behind most other provinces, Shandong's pace remained inconspicuous, closely matching the national average almost throughout the period of decollectivization. Toward the end of 1982, however, it suddenly pushed for swift province-wide popularization in order to accommodate Beijing's changed preference for its nation-wide implementation.

If Shandong had indeed developed a certain "culture" as to how to respond to a variety of policies emanating from the central government—a set of operational norms that guide the province to opt for the most risk-averse response to a potentially controversial policy—these particular norms might constitute a partial explanation for the slow pace of economic reform in Shandong during much of the 1980s, when the imperative of systemic reforms was still under intense debates at the Center.[17] On the other hand, Shandong's catch-up with its southern counterparts in the late 1980s and its take-off in the 1990s should be explored from a perspective that focuses upon the role of its provincial leadership which, in line with Beijing's priorities for the reform, made efforts to minimize the impact of cultural and structural constraints imposed on it.

Policy Orientations of the Provincial Leaders in Shandong, 1949–95

In China where personnel decisions for the top provincial leadership are tightly controlled by the *nomenklatura* system, the problem of "bureaucratic careerism"—a tendency of career bureaucrats not to associate themselves too closely with potentially controversial policies when there is even a slight chance of reversal—is particularly pervasive.[18] This problem of bureaucratic careerism can be pushed to an extreme in "totalitarian" or "authoritarian" systems where advocating local interests against the priorities of the central government may be interpreted as representing an "incorrect" ideological or political line and very often meets with severe punishment. The following excerpt from the *People's Daily* from the heyday of the reform elucidates how fears of political persecution fueled bureaucratic careerism which seriously undermined the rational operation of the policy process:

> Under the circumstances where people are constantly told that they must not revise any document from the center and must follow documents in everything they do, how can they ever solve new problems whose solutions are not provided by the central documents? . . .
> [The most important problem is that] they dare not speak of irrational orders, inflated production statistics, and policies unsuitable for local conditions. . . .
> [The core reason lies in] nothing but fears.
> The fear of being labeled as a "capitulationist"; the fear of being dismissed from one's post; the fear of being expelled from the party; the fear of being divorced by one's wife; the fear of serving a prison term; and the fear of being beheaded.[19]

Under these fears, however crucial certain local interests might be, they could never become as important as the careers of local officials. Thus, when bureaucratic careerism becomes the shared norm of local implementors, the most widely adopted mode of response among local officials is to play safe by staying away from controversial policies and waiting for the optimal point to bandwagon. Several key leaders of Shandong, particularly of the earlier years of the reform, were no exception to this rule. Let us first examine some key characteristics of the province's top leaders.

Provincial Leaders of Shandong, 1949–1995

Counting only the two most important positions—provincial (first) party secretary and governor—there are twenty-four tenures held by fourteen people for the period of 1949–95 (see Table 5.5). In the pre-reform era, it was quite common for the party secretary (then called first secretary) to serve concurrently as governor as in the cases of Kang Sheng, Tan Qilong, Wang Xiaoyu, Yang Dezhi and Bai Rubing. During the reform period, however, no party secretary concurrently served as governor (in accordance with the principle of "separation of party and government"), but serving as governor seems to have become a pre-requisite for assuming the party secretary position.[20]

Table 5.6 provides profiles of these top leaders. Five out of eleven provincial party secretaries—Kang Sheng, Wang Xiaoyu, Liang Buting, Jiang Chunyun, and Zhao Zhihao—are natives of Shandong, and one of the remaining six comes from

Table 5.5

Names and Tenures of Shandong's Provincial Leaders, 1949–1995

Party Secretary	Governor
Kang Sheng (3/49–8/54)	Kang Sheng (10/49–3/54)
Shu Tong (1/55–10/60)	Zhao Jianmin (3/55–11/58)
Zeng Xisheng (11/60–4/61)	Tan Qilong (11/58–12/63)
Tan Qilong (4/61–?/66)	Bai Rubing (12/63–?/66)
Wang Xiaoyu (2/67–3/71)	Wang Xiaoyu (2/67–3/71)
Yang Dezhi (4/71–1/74)	Yang Dezhi (3/71–11/74)
Bai Rubing (11/74–12/82)	Bai Rubing (11/74–12/79)
Su Yiran (12/82–6/85)	Su Yiran (12/79–12/82)
Liang Buting (6/85–12/88)	Liang Buting (12/82–6/85)
Jiang Chunyun (12/88–10/94)	Li Chang'an (6/85–6/87)
Zhao Zhihao (10/94–)	Jiang Chunyun (6/87–12/88)
	Zhao Zhihao (3/89–2/95)
	Li Chunting (2/95–)

Table 5.6

Profiles of Shandong's Provincial Leaders, 1949–1995

	Shandong natives	Previous work experience in Shandong	Central positions*
Party Secretaries(N=11)	45% (5/11)[a]	82% (9/11)[b]	100% (11/11)
Governors (N=13)	54% (7/13)[c]	77% (10/13)	85% (11/13)[d]
Party Secretaries and Governors (N=24)	50% (12/24)	88% (21/24)	92% (22/24)

Sources: Wolfgang Bartke, *Who's Who in the People's Republic of China*, 3rd ed. (München: K. G. Saur, 1991); Donald Klein and Anne B. Clark, *Biographic Dictionary of Chinese Communism, 1921–1965*, two vols. (Cambridge: Harvard University Press, 1971); *Shandong nianjian 1993* (Shandong Yearbook 1993) (Ji'nan: Shandong nianjianshe, 1993), pp. 659–661; and *Zhongguo renming dacidian* (Who's Who in China: Current Leaders) (Beijing: Waiwen chubanshe, 1994). Information on Wang Xiaoyu is from interviews in Ji'nan on March 14, 1995.

Notes: *Central positions refer to memberships of the Politburo and the Central Committee (both full and alternate).

[a] Kang, Wang, Liang, Jiang, and Zhao Zhihao are natives of Shandong.

[b] Bai and Liang had no previous work experience in Shandong.

[c] Zhao Jianmin and Li Chunting are natives of Shandong.

[d] Zhao Jianmin and Bai Rubing (at the time of his appointment as governor in 1963) did not have any central party positions.

the neighboring province of Anhui (Su Yiran). In the case of governors, three governors of the Maoist era (Kang Sheng, Zhao Jianmin and Wang Xiaoyu) and the last four (Liang Buting, Jiang Chunyun, Zhao Zhihao and Li Chunting) are natives of Shandong. The "native ratio" of Shandong's party secretaries and governors rose sharply from 36 percent (5/14) during 1949–79 to 70 percent (7/10) during 1980–95. Compared to the national average—21 percent for 1949–78 and 44 percent for 1988—Shandong's native ratios are rather high.[21] The ratios for party secretaries with previous work experience in the province, 82 percent for 1949–95 and 100 percent for 1949–78, are also well above the national average of 57 percent for the 1949–78 period.[22] Additionally, all party secretaries and 85 percent of governors of Shandong concurrently held central party positions including one Politburo member. While all provincial party secretaries became full members of the Central Committee at the Eleventh Central Committee in 1977, that was not the norm before 1977. Therefore, Shandong's case where all of its party secretaries were members of the Central Committee even before the Eleventh Central Committee is rather exceptional.[23]

On the basis of the foregoing discussion, it may be suggested that during 1949–95 only one-half of twenty-four tenures of provincial party secretaries and governors of Shandong were held by "non-natives" who nevertheless mostly had previous work experience in the province and concurrently held prestigious central party positions. On the party side, except for the rather extraordinary periods of nation building (Kang Sheng for 1949–54) and the Cultural Revolution (Wang Xiaoyu for 1967–71), "outsiders" had dominated Shandong politics up until Liang Buting became the party boss in 1985. It seems that the management of Shandong's top party leadership was tightly controlled by Beijing, reinforcing its heavy political shadow over the province. In the reform era, however, natives have dominated both the party and government sides in Shandong.

Shandong's slow pace of reform in the early years of the post-Mao era may be attributed to the prevalence of bureaucratic careerism facilitated by Beijing's tight control over Shandong's personnel arrangement, in addition to the absence of selective preferential policies (such as that of special economic zones granted to Guangdong and Fujian). In Shandong, fundamental changes in these two areas occurred almost simultaneously. The first batch of measures of "opening up" Shandong were pronounced by the State Council in 1984, while the province's first native party boss in the post-Mao era—Liang Buting— was appointed in mid-1985. We now turn to Shandong's leaders in the post-Mao era.

Bai Rubing and Su Yiran as "Bandwagoners"

As his tenure spanned eight years from 1974 through 1982, Bai Rubing was the last to serve concurrently as governor and first party secretary. Bai was born in 1912 in Shaanxi Province and joined the Communist Party in 1927. Both before and after the Liberation, Bai worked mostly in the northwest region, and his functional affiliation was with finance. After serving briefly in Beijing, he was transferred in 1958 to Shandong as a deputy governor. Bai became governor in 1963 and fell from power in 1966. Bai reappeared in 1974 to replace Yang Dezhi as Shandong's party secretary and governor. Born in Anhui, Su Yiran had served as a deputy governor of Anhui before his transfer to Shandong in 1963. After a four-year disappearance during the Cultural Revolution, Su resurfaced in early 1971 as a vice-chairman of the Shandong Revolutionary Committee, and later became the first political commissar of the Shandong Military District in 1978 and governor of Shandong in 1979. In 1982, Su became the first party secretary of Shandong, a position which he held until June 1985.[24]

The bandwagon behavior of these two leaders is best exemplified by Shandong's implementation of agricultural decollectivization in 1979–83. According to interviewees, provincial leaders at the time displayed extremely opaque attitudes toward the highly controversial policy of household farming. According to them, Su Yiran, then governor, "did not oppose but did not support the policy, either"; and Bai Rubing, first party secretary, kept silent until Beijing clearly made its preference known by pushing hard for its nationwide popularization in late 1982. Once the center demanded swift popularization of the policy, however, Shandong became one of its fastest implementors (see Table 5.4) even at the expense of replacing recalcitrant local leaders like Lu Shengyuan of Yantai Prefecture.[25]

The prevalence of bureaucratic careerism, repeatedly reinforced by abrupt policy changes and subsequent persecution of local deviation, induced many provincial leaders to opt for the opportunistic but safe option of bandwagoning. Furthermore, Shandong was under the particularly strong influence of "leftist" ideology as late as 1985. Therefore, key provincial leaders (referring to Bai and Su) were very often unwilling to implement reformist policies, so long as such lukewarm attitudes did not constitute an explicit violation of Beijing's overall policy framework. Many interviewees in Shandong characterized both Bai Rubing and Su Yiran as "highly compliant but very conservative at the same time" (hen tinghua danshi ye hen baoshou)—i.e., they listened to whatever the Center told them, but they generally complied only within the boundary of their own ideological convictions.[26] This being the case, it may be suggested that conservative orientations of these leaders might have significantly contributed to the slow pace of reform in Shandong during these early years.

Liang Buting and Li Chang'an as "Failed Pioneers"

A potential watershed came in June 1985 when Beijing appointed two new leaders, Liang Buting as first party secretary and Li Chang'an as governor. Although born in Shandong, Liang hardly worked in the province as his functional affiliation was mainly with the center—as a member of the standing committee of the Communist Youth League (1957) and deputy director of the State

Office for Agriculture and Forestry (1964). After the Cultural Revolution, Liang reappeared in 1978 as secretary of the Qinghai provincial party committee. After serving as Qinghai's first party secretary, Liang was transferred to Shandong as its governor in 1982 and party secretary in 1985.[27]

As a native of Liaoning, Li Chang'an also worked mainly in Beijing first as a factory engineer in 1968–73, then as vice-chairman of the Planning Commission in the Beijing People's Government, and later as a vice-minister of the Seventh Ministry of Machine Building. In 1983, Li was transferred to Shandong as a deputy secretary and became its governor in 1985. As a son of Li Fuchun, Li was then one of the "rising princes" well connected to the central party and government authorities. At the age of 49, Li was identified as the key person in charge of the Party Rectification Work Office under the Shandong Provincial Government. He served as governor until July 1987 when he was transferred to the State Council as its deputy secretary-general.[28]

As a protégé of Hu Yaobang (through the Communist Youth League network), Liang is considered to have been much more reform-oriented than his two predecessors, occasionally pushing for reformist policies, particularly in the area of foreign economic relations. Yet, several interviewees noted that Liang's contribution to Shandong would have been much larger if the overall policy environment had been more favorable and if Liang's personal relationship with Li Chang'an had been smoother. First, as far as Shandong was concerned, the period of 1985–87 was still marked by high uncertainties. Despite the designation of Qingdao and Yantai as "coastal open cities" in April 1984, no concrete policy support was followed from the Center. In fact, the State Council's plan of extending "open policy" to the whole Jiaodong Peninsula in Shandong was shelved in 1985 in the midst of the infamous Hainan scandal. Despite some continued support from the Center (e.g., from Gu Mu in September 1985) and indigenous efforts by Shandong (i.e., issuing provincial regulations on preferential treatment of foreign investment in 1986), the initiative was once again killed by the anti-bourgeois liberalization campaign during 1986–87.[29] Second, according to some interviewees in Ji'nan, Liang did not get along with Li very well, which not only adversely affected the reform process in the province, but also eventually pushed Li to return to Beijing.[30]

Jiang Chunyun as a Successful Pioneer

As the first party boss of Shandong to serve *concurrently* as a Politburo member, Jiang Chunyun's career is rather exceptional. Jiang never left Shandong in his entire administrative career until his recent transfer to Beijing, yet he managed to join the top echelon of the provincial and national leadership.[31] Born in 1930 in Laixi County in the eastern part of Shandong, Jiang joined the party in 1947.[32] After the Liberation, Jiang served as a secretary of Laixi County party committee. In 1957–60, he was a deputy section chief of the Qingdao branch of the China

Souvenir Import and Export Corporation and deputy section chief of the Foreign Trade Bureau of Qingdao. In 1960–66, Jiang worked in the Department of Propaganda of the Shandong provincial party committee. In 1966 Jiang was sent down to a village in Huimin County and later to the "May Seventh Cadre School" in Qihe County, where he remained until 1970. After Wang Xiaoyu—Shandong's Maoist boss—stepped down in March 1971, Yang Dezhi took over the province's party and government work. In the same year, Su Yiran, then a member of the Provincial Revolutionary Committee, "liberated" Jiang and appointed him as the head of the secretarial group for the administrative office of the Provincial Revolutionary Committee. Su's rescue of Jiang is allegedly rooted in their friendship cultivated during their residence in Qihe's "May Seventh Cadre School."[33]

In 1975, Jiang became the deputy director of the administrative office of the Provincial Revolutionary Committee under Bai Rubing who succeeded Yang Dezhi. In 1977, Jiang became deputy secretary-general of the provincial party committee. When Su Yiran succeeded Bai Rubing in 1982, Jiang was immediately appointed secretary-general of the provincial party committee. In 1983, Su promoted Jiang to the concurrent positions of deputy secretary and secretary-general of the provincial party committee. In 1984, Jiang became a deputy provincial party secretary and the party secretary of Ji'nan. When Su retired in June 1985, Jiang attended the China Self-Learning Institute of Languages and Literature (*Zhongguo yuyan wenxue zixiu daxue*), from which he acquired a college diploma in 1987. Then, he succeeded Li Chang'an as governor. In December 1988, Jiang was appointed as Shandong's leading party secretary, while the governorship was succeeded by his protégé and Shandong native, Zhao Zhihao.[34] At the 1992 Fourteenth Party Congress, Jiang was appointed a member of the Politburo, along with four other provincial bosses from Beijing, Tianjin, Shanghai and Guangdong. In October 1994, Jiang, along with Shanghai's Wu Bangguo, was inducted into the Central Committee Secretariat and appointed deputy premier in charge of agriculture at the second plenary session of the National People's Congress held in March 1995.[35]

Very little is known about Jiang's personal relationships, except for the aforementioned patron-client relationship with Su Yiran. Given his ordinary family and educational backgrounds, Jiang must not have had any substantial ties with key central-level figures, particularly in the earlier stage of his career. There are some speculations as to certain personal ties Jiang might have utilized in advancing his career and promoting provincial interests. Hong Kong media noted Jiang's alleged ties with Chen Yun, but none has explained how such friendship was generated in the first place and how it affected Jiang's career.[36] Others speculate that Jiang's relationship with Deng Xiaoping's children might have helped the development of his career as well as that of Shandong.[37] Still others stress Jiang's utilization of the so-called Shandong faction (*Shandong bang*). According to these reports, Jiang made the best out of the "Shandong network" within the central party and government organizations, including Song Ping, Wan Li, Tian Jiyun and Luo Gan, who at one point or another represented Shandong's interests at the Politburo, the National People's Congress, and the State Council, as well as many others who currently occupy key positions at the center.[38]

Interviews in Ji'nan revealed that Shandong's provincial officials themselves did not assign too much weight to Jiang's personal relationships with central officials. Despite the widely held notion that many Shandong-born officials in Beijing pay special attention to the development of their home province, there seem to be certain structural limitations as to how much they could actually do to help. One interviewee, who had frequently visited Beijing for negotiations with the relevant units of the State Council over large-scale investment projects, commented that, given Shandong's fiscal contribution to Beijing's coffer over the years, the Center's provision of preferential policies exclusively for Shandong has been relatively fewer than that for its southern counterparts. Another interviewee suggested that, while provincial officials might no doubt seek to elicit support from Shandong-native officials at the Center, their help could be effective only with the policies that were selectively applied to Shandong and a few other places, and the same could not be said of many other policies with a nationwide scope.[39]

Despite the different explanations given to Jiang's success, there is no doubt that Jiang was the successful "pioneer" of the reform in Shandong.[40] As will be further elaborated in the sections that follow, Jiang was responsible for designing Shandong's regional development strategies and devising a series of innovative policies in the areas of industrial development, agriculture, infrastructural development and, most importantly, in foreign economic relations. Clearly, Jiang had what his predecessors had not: the highly favorable policy environment due to Beijing's provision of many selective preferential policies. But he was at the same time highly entrepreneurial by making the best use of Beijing's selective policies. And we now turn to the question of how Shandong came to obtain these exclusive preferential policies.

Shandong's Fiscal Contribution to the Center and Beijing's Provision of Preferential Policies

Shandong's most important contribution to the central government can be found in their fiscal relations. Table 5.7 provides detailed information on Shandong's budgetary arrangements with the central government during 1980–94. Shandong was one of the fifteen provinces designated in 1980 to implement the system of "sharing specific revenues" (*fenlei fencheng*), under which Shandong had to remit 90 percent of its revenues from the consolidated industrial and commercial tax (*gongshangshui*) which had accounted for about one-quarter of its total fixed incomes.[41] According to a knowledgeable interviewee, as of 1980, Shandong

Table 5.7

Shandong's Budgetary Arrangements with Beijing, 1980–94

Year	Fiscal Arrangement	Retention Rate	Ownership Change
1980	system of "sharing specific revenues"	about 40%	—
1981	system of "sharing overall revenues"	48.9%	—
1982	same as above	52.93%	Shandong Electricity Bureau and Ji'nan Automobile Corp. recentralized
1983	same as above	51.5%; later 55.7%	Qilu Petrochemical and Ji'nan Petroleum recentralized
1984	same as above	55.6%	Weifang Diesel Co. and Shandong Aluminium recentralized*
1985	same as above	59%	—
1986	same as above	76.75; later 77.47%	Shandong Tobacco Co. and resource tax on petroleum recentralized
1987–93	fixed-sum remittance	287 million yuan	—
1994	tax-sharing system	—	—

Source: Interviews in Ji'nan in 1994 and 1995; and *Shandong jingji yanjiu* (Studies of Shandong's Economy), eds. Pang Xiuzheng, Lin Shuxiang and Wang Yongchang (Ji'nan: Shandong renmin chubanshe, 1996), Vol. 2, pp. 1019–34.

*In 1984, the retention rate remained the same despite the ownership change of two large enterprises. The reason was that the Center paid an unknown amount of compensation to the province for that year. But, in 1985, the change was reflected in the increase of the retention rate by 3.4 percent.

remitted about 60 percent of all the "income produced within the province" (*jingnei shouru*) to Beijing.[42] In 1981, Beijing took a "forced loan" of 421 million yuan and Shandong's revenue suffered considerably. Subsequently, Beijing permitted Shandong to opt out of the system of "sharing specific revenues" and to adopt that of "sharing overall revenues" (*zonge fencheng*) which it maintained until 1987.[43]

From 1981 to 1986, Shandong's retention rate continued to rise from 48.9 percent to 77.47 percent. However, such a rise in Shandong's retention rate can be highly misleading, as it did not guarantee any considerable increase in the revenue incomes for the province. Each increase in the retention rate was accompanied by Beijing's recentralization of some highly profitable enterprises formerly owned by the province. The magnitude of the ownership recentralization was such that only the largest and most profitable enterprises in each sector were claimed by the Center, including the Shandong Electricity Bureau which monopolized the supply of electricity, the Ji'nan Automobile Corporation with over twenty thousand workers, and the Shandong Tobacco Company which produced profits well over 2 billion yuan every year.

In 1985 when Shandong enjoyed an increased retention rate of 59 percent, it was not a high rate compared to those of other provinces. Excluding the three centrally administered municipalities, nine provinces operated under the same system of "sharing overall revenues" in 1985 and Shandong's retention rate was the fourth lowest after Jiangsu, Liaoning, and Zhejiang.[44] Furthermore, the recentralization of tobacco-related revenues in 1986 was not a national policy but applied only to Shandong.[45] The switch to a more favorable system of "fixed-sum remittance" (*dinge shangjiao*) in 1987 did not come cheap, either, since Shandong had to give up huge revenue remittances from Qingdao which became a "central economic city" (*jihua danlie chengshi*) in the same year. In other words, Beijing allowed Shandong to adopt the fiscal contract system as a package of compensation for its fiscal loss of Qingdao.[46]

Shandong's fiscal contribution to Beijing went well beyond budgetary sharing. All the special levies collected and funds appropriated from the better-off provinces—including the State Energy, Transportation and Key Construction Fund (*guojia nengyuan jiaotong jianshe jijin*), State Budget Adjustment Fund (*guojia yusan tiaojie jijin*), "local government loans" (*difang zhengfu jiekuan*), "specific-items remittances" (*zhuanxiang shangjiao*), "extra contribution" (*duozuo gongxian*) remittances, and a share of various incomes generated within the provinces such as incomes from banking and insurance businesses and foreign exchange earnings—were also imposed on Shandong.[47] In the case of the State Energy, Transportation and Key Construction Fund which began in 1982, 10 percent levies were imposed on the after-tax profits of the provincial enterprises and these were divided by the central and provincial governments in the ratio of 7 to 3.[48] In the case of the "extra contribution" remittances, after 1987 Shandong was held responsible for paying 20 percent of the "tax refund for export products" (*chukou tuishui*) which had previously been paid entirely by the Center. Beginning in 1989, Shandong also paid 0.5 percent of its provincial extra-budgetary funds to the Center in the name of "Budget Adjustment Funds." In 1982–85, Beijing imposed "forced loans" on Shandong (as well as several other well-off provinces) which "loaned out" 140 million yuan to the Center every year. In 1986, this amount became a part of the budgetary remittance baseline figure. Additionally, from 1990 onwards, Shandong also provided a so-called fiscal contribution (*caizheng gongxian*) fund by remitting an extra 200 million yuan.[49]

Most importantly, there are many large and medium-sized enterprises in Shandong that fall under the central government's jurisdiction. As of 1994, for instance, only 190 (3.7 percent) out of 5,034 state enterprises in Shandong were owned by the central government. But these enterprises accounted for 34.3 percent of the total GVIO produced by the province's state enterprises. One interviewee went so far as to suggest that Shandong's annual budgetary remittance to Beijing during 1987–93—287 million yuan—was insignificant compared to the total amount of income generated within Shandong but accrued to the central coffers—estimated to be about 15 billion yuan in 1993, and precisely 16.9 billion yuan in 1994 which accounted for about 40 percent of all revenue income created within the province. For the period of 1986–93, 54.5 percent of all income generated within Shandong was remitted to Beijing.[50]

A crucial question remains. What has Shandong received in return for its extraordinary fiscal contribution to the central government over the years? Most interviewees in Ji'nan responded to this question in almost a unanimous way: "not much."[51] They nevertheless pointed out two characteristics of Beijing's management of Shandong's top leadership as plausible indicators of the Center's special consideration for the province. First, there was an extraordinary degree of leadership continuity in the sense that, with only one notable exception of Li Chang'an, each of the other four governors succeeded their predecessors to become provincial party secretaries in the post-Mao period (see Table 5.5). This is remarkable, particularly compared with other provinces, since it may reflect the fact that at least in the post-Mao era Shandong did not suffer much from Beijing's arbitrary interposition of outsiders. Instead, the provincial leaders came to have a bigger say in making their own personnel arrangement which was then approved by the Center.[52]

Second, as Table 5.8 illustrates, Shandong ranked first, along with Guangdong, in the total number of its provincial officials holding central party positions—seven people with their weighted scores of 13. With seven provincial leaders holding central party positions including one Politburo member (when Jiang Chunyun was still with Shandong), there was no doubt that Shandong had a better chance than many other provinces in getting its views across to the central party and government apparatus. In the column to the far right—the differences in the weighted scores between 1990 and 1994—Shandong marked the highest increase of five, which at least partially reflects the consistently expanding power of Shandong in national politics.[53]

Many of the interviewees pointed out the crucial role played by Song Ping in promoting Shandong officials to the Center and planting others in various provin-

Table 5.8

Distribution of Central Party Positions by Province (1990/1994)

Province	PB	CC	CC(a)	Total*	Scores**	94–90
Gansu	0/0	2/0	1/2	3/2	5/2	-3
Zhejiang	0/0	3/1	1/1	4/2	7/3	-4
Henan	0/0	3/1	3/2	6/3	9/4	-5
Fujian	0/0	2/1	1/2	3/3	5/4	-1
Shanxi	0/0	3/1	1/3	4/4	7/5	-2
Jiangxi	0/0	2/2	1/1	3/3	5/5	0
Guangxi	0/0	2/2	1/1	3/3	5/5	0
Hainan	0/0	1/1	2/3	3/4	4/5	+1
Ningxia	0/0	1/2	2/1	3/3	4/5	+1
Xizang	0/0	3/2	1/2	4/4	7/6	-1
Guizhou	0/0	2/1	2/4	4/5	6/6	0
Hebei	0/0	2/2	2/2	4/4	6/6	0
Jilin	0/0	2/2	1/2	3/4	5/6	+1
Hunan	0/0	1/3	3/0	4/4	5/6	+1
Jiangsu	0/0	2/2	1/2	3/4	5/6	+1
Liaoning	0/0	1/2	2/2	3/4	4/6	+2
Tianjin	0/0	1/2	2/2	3/4	4/6	+2
Anhui	0/0	1/2	2/2	3/4	4/6	+2
Hubei	0/0	2/2	0/2	2/4	4/6	+2
Yunnan	0/0	1/2	2/2	3/4	4/6	+2
Shaanxi	0/0	2/2	0/2	2/4	4/6	+2
Qinghai	0/0	1/2	0/2	1/4	2/6	+4
Sichuan	1/0	1/1	2/5	4/6	9/7	-2
Xinjiang	0/0	3/2	3/3	6/5	9/7	-2
Neimenggu	0/0	2/2	1/3	3/5	5/7	+2
Shanghai	0/1	1/1	6/2	7/4	8/9	+1
Beijing	1/1	1/2	2/1	4/4	9/10	+1
Guangdong	0/1	4/2	1/4	5/7	9/13	+4
Shandong	**0/1**	**3/2**	**2/4**	**5/7**	**8/13**	**+5**

Sources: *China Directory 1991* and *1995* (Tokyo: Radiopress, 1990 and 1994).

Notes: PB, CC, and CC(a) refer to Politburo, Central Committee and alternate Central Committee members, respectively.

*For the 13th and 14th Central Committees—represented by 1990 and 1994, respectively—there were 107 (2 PB, 57CC and 48 CCa) and 117 (4PB, 49CC and 64 CCa) members. The scores for Shanghai and Shandong did not take into consideration the resignation of Wu Bangguo and Jiang Chunyun in late 1994.

**Scores were calculated by assigning 5, 2, and 1 to PB, CC, CC(a) members.

cial governments. At the central level, they include Jiang Chunyun (a member of the Politburo as well as the Secretariat), Zhang Quanjing (formerly the chief of the Shandong organization department who became the director of the Central Organization Department), Zhang Jingyuan (deputy secretary of the State Organizational Work Commission—*guojia jiguan gongzuo weiyuanhui*—under the State Council), and so on. At the provincial level, examples include the party secretaries of the Inner Mongolia Autonomous Region (Liu Mingzu who was formerly the party secretary of Linyi Prefecture) and the Xinjiang Autonomous Region (Wang Lequan who was formerly a vice-governor of Shandong), and governor of Henan (Ma Zhongchen).[54]

More important is perhaps the expanded authority of the province in selecting its own leadership. In selecting a successor to Zhao Zhihao who resigned the governorship to perform solely as the party secretary, three people were allegedly considered: Yu Zhengsheng (Qingdao party secretary and Zhejiang native allegedly recommended by Beijing), Wang Jiangong (former vice-governor in charge of agriculture and Hebei native allegedly recommended by Zhao Zhihao) and Li Chunting (former executive vice-governor and Shandong native allegedly recommended by Jiang Chunyun). Eventually, Jiang's influence prevailed and Li—the only Shandong native among the three candidates—was appointed the governor. While the political dynamics between Jiang and Zhao are difficult to assess, Shandong seems to have been able to resist Beijing's implicit pressure by selecting a native of Shandong to rule the province.[55]

Shandong has also benefited considerably from a variety of preferential policies (*youhui zhengce*) which the central government granted only to a highly selective group of provinces. In fact, with the most notable exception of "special economic zones" (hereafter SEZs) granted only to Guangdong, Fujian, and Hainan, Shandong has always obtained its share in all other preferential policies. In April 1984, the State Council designated fourteen cities as "coastal open cities" (*yanhai kaifang chengshi*: hereafter COCs) which were empowered to implement preferential policies to attract foreign investment and promote export-oriented industries. Among these fourteen cities located in ten province-level units, only four provinces managed to have two cities designated as COCs: Jiangsu, Zhejiang, Guangdong, and Shandong (with Qingdao and Yantai). In 1984–85, the State Council also designated eleven "economic and technological development zones" (*jingji jishu kaifaqu*: ETDZs) among the fourteen COCs, and this time only three provinces managed to have two of their cities designated as ETDZs: Jiangsu, Guangdong and Shandong (again with Qingdao and Yantai).[56]

Beginning in 1983, the central government designated a dozen cities as "central economic cities" (*jihua danlie chengshi*: hereafter CECs). As one of the most innovative developmental strategies of the post-Mao Chinese leadership, the CEC designation enabled the so-designated cities to enjoy a provincial-level status in making decisions pertaining to economic polices. Chongqing became the first CEC in early 1983, followed by Wuhan, Guangzhou, Xi'an, Shenyang, Harbin and Dalian. In 1987 Qingdao and Ningbo also obtained the privileged status, and they were soon joined by Xiamen and Shenzhen in 1988, and by Nanjing, Chengdu and Changchun in 1989. While Shandong did not join Guangdong, Liaoning and Sichuan in having two of their cities designated as such, this later proved to be a blessing since all sorts of disagreements and conflicts were generated between the provinces and those CECs which were provincial capitals. Subsequently, in the summer of 1993, the controversial CEC policy was finally pronounced terminated with regard to provincial capitals, thus allowing only six CECs out of the original fourteen to remain.[57] While Shandong kept Qingdao, at this point it is difficult to gauge whether it is a blessing for the province or not.

In 1987, Shandong obtained another highly preferential policy that was initially granted only to Shandong. According to a knowledgeable interviewee in Ji'nan, the State Council held a meeting at the end of 1987 where a crucial decision was made to designate Shandong as the key province (*zhongdiansheng*) in dealing with South Korea on a non-governmental and economic basis. The interviewee suggested that such a decision was never put into writing (perhaps out of Beijing's political concern with Pyongyang at the time), but various preferential arrangements followed this decision, such as the opening of ferry routes between Weihai of Shandong and Inchon of South Korea, and the authorization for the Shandong provincial authorities to issue entry visas to South Korean businessmen upon their arrival in China.[58]

Beginning in 1990, the State Council designated a dozen cities to establish "bonded zones" (*baoshuiqu*). The first zone was established in Shanghai in 1990, and in 1991 three other zones were established in Tianjin, Shenzhen and Shatoujiao. In 1992, nine more bonded zones were set up in Dalian, Guangzhou, Zhangjiagang, Haikou, Xiamen, Fuzhou, Ningbo, Shantou and Qingdao. Bonded zones are granted the most favorable terms of trade and investment among all existing preferential arrangements approved by the Center. Guangdong was able to have four of its cities designated and Fujian had two. Shandong, too, managed to obtain a share in this highly privileged policy when Qingdao joined the list in November 1992.[59] In addition, the State Council authorized selected areas to establish the so-called "new and high technology industrial development zones" (*gaoxin jishu chanye kaifaqu*) in March 1991. Shandong once again obtained its share in this new preferential policy when Qingdao was authorized to set up a zone in 1992. As of 1994, the total number rose to five with the addition of Weihai, Zibo, Weifang and Ji'nan. In terms of the number of open ports authorized for the international flow of people, commodities, and so on, Shandong (along with Jilin and Xinjiang) ranks fourth with its nine open ports, while Guangdong, with forty, ranks first.[60] Finally, Shandong joined another list of exclusive membership by having Shilaoren District of Qingdao designated as one of the eleven "state tourism and leisure zones" (*guojia luyou dujiaqu*) in China.[61]

To sum up, due mainly to Shandong's generally compliant relationship with Beijing and its significant fiscal contributions to the central coffers over the years, both the provincial leadership and its supporters at the Center may have found it relatively easier to lobby for Shandong's expanded discretion in the selection of provincial leadership and for the provision of more preferential policies essential to effective implementation of economic reform. The cultivation of good relationships with central officials and the attainment of favorable policies alone, however, may not suffice to bring about such an accelerated pace of economic transformation since, in most cases, developmental reforms require concrete strategies of change. Shandong's particular choice of developmental strategies is the subject to which we now turn.

Strategies of Economic Reform: The Shandong Recipe

This section examines the strategies which Shandong's provincial leadership devised and utilized in promoting economic development in the post-Mao era. More specifically, its regional development policy (*diqu buju zhengce*), industrial policy (*chanye zhengce*), and infrastructural development (*jichu shebei*) are discussed.

Regional Development Strategies

During 1978–83, there was no regional development strategy to speak of, not only because the provincial leadership (under Bai Rubing and Su Yiran) was then not geared toward the sort of reform under way in the southern provinces, but because this particular period was fully devoted to the historical reversal of collectivized agriculture.[62] According to interviewees in Ji'nan, up until 1990 Shandong's regional development strategy was largely to support a few key-point cities—most notably Qingdao, Yantai and Weihai—authorized by Beijing to implement preferential policies in promoting foreign economic relations. A so-called "two-three-six" strategy was researched during 1990–91 and proposed in 1991 by the Provincial Economic Research Center, and formally endorsed in 1992 by the provincial government.[63] The first "two" stands for "two large chunks" of the province: (1) the Shandong Peninsula development zone—covering eight open cities of Qingdao, Yantai, Weihai, Rizhao, Weifang, Zibo, Ji'nan and Dongying—geared toward "outward-oriented" development[64] and (2) the inland western Shandong—encompassing nine cities and prefectures of Jining, Taian, Heze, Liaocheng, Dezhou, Zaozhuang, Linyi, Laiwu and Binzhou—specializing in agriculture, animal husbandry, mining and energy development.

The "three" component refers to "three industrial concentration belts" (*sange chanye jujidai*) along the key railways in the province. The most important belt spans the Jiaoji Railway linking Dezhou in the northwest, the two central cities of Ji'nan and Jiaozhou, and Qingdao in the east. This belt gives priority to export-oriented agriculture, and processing and hi-tech industries including precision-machinery, pharmaceuticals, and electronics. The second belt spans the Dongming Railway linking Heze in the southwest with Rizhao in the southeast, focusing on energy and construction materials industries such as electricity, coal, cement, marble, steel and petrochemicals. The third belt is located along the Delong Railway linking Dezhou and Longkou covering the northern part of the province—i.e., the so-called "Yellow River Delta region"—concentrating on grain and cotton production, animal husbandry, and oil refining.[65]

The final "six" denotes six areas grouped together according to their levels of economic development and geographical location. These areas include: (1) the Jiaodong region encompassing Yantai and Weihai; (2) the Jiaowei region of Qingdao and Weifang; (3) the northwestern region covering Ji'nan, Taian, Dezhou and Liaocheng; (4) the northern region composed of Zibo, Dongying and Binzhou; (5) the southern region of Linyi and Rizhao; and (6) the southwestern region covering Zaozhuang and Heze.[66]

Whichever configuration of Shandong's regional development strategies is chosen, one area always stands out—the Jiaodong Peninsula region.[67] Most of the provincial officials interviewed in Shandong regarded Qingdao as the "dragon head" (*longtou*) of Shandong's economic development, and Yantai and Weihai as "two wings" of the developmental scheme. While they acknowledge that the province's infatuation with Qingdao significantly cooled down after Beijing's designation of the city as a "central economic city" in 1987, they nevertheless agreed that the positive effects Qingdao brings to other areas in the province have been very crucial, particularly in spreading the developmental ideology and diffusing reform strategies and business networks.[68]

Key Industrial Policies

Despite Shandong's reputation as a "large agricultural province" (*nongye dasheng*), the share of its GVAO in GVIAO has continued to decline over the years. Although there were some fluctuations due to ideologically driven campaigns (as in the case of 1960) or to agricultural decollectivization (as in the case of 1985), the share consistently dropped from almost three-quarters in 1949 to about one-sixth in 1995 (see Table 5.9). Within agriculture, too, diversification was actively pursued so that the share of forestry, animal husbandry, and fishery in GVAO rose from 38.6 percent in 1990 to 50.7 percent in 1995. The ratios for light and heavy industries as percentages of GVIO, which had considerably fluctuated before the reform, became stabilized and remained largely equal in the post-Mao period. An interviewee in Ji'nan commented that such a stabilized balance between light and heavy industries was not coincidental, but it was an outcome of the provincial government's conscious efforts in policy coordination.[69]

The far-right column in Table 5.9 presents data on the evolving balance among the primary, secondary and tertiary industries. The provincial government uses different "formalized language" (*tifa*) to promote each of these industries: (1) "further strengthen" (*jiaqiang*) for the primary industry; (2) "improve" (*youhua*) for the structure of the manufacturing industry; and (3) "extensively develop" (*dali fazhan*) for the tertiary service industry. The provincial government paid special attention to the development of the tertiary industry by setting the goal of raising its share in GDP to 30 percent by the year 2000.[70] Such concern on the part of the provincial government is understandable since Shandong ranked twenty-seventh and thirtieth (out of thirty provincial-level units)

Table 5.9

Key Indicators of Industrial Development in Shandong, 1949–95

Year	Agriculture versus industry (% of GVIAO)	Light versus heavy industry (% of GVIO)	Comparison of primary, secondary, and tertiary industries (% of GDP)
1949	71:29	87:13	—
1955	58:42	79:21	61:20:19
1960	23:77	45:55	29:44:28
1965	42:58	60:40	49:34:17
1970	31:69	50:50	41:43:16
1975	37:63	47:53	39:45:15
1980	29:71	51:49	36:50:14
1985	40:60	55:45	35:43:22
1990	23:77	51:49	28:42:30
1991	23:77	51:49	28:41:30
1992	19:81	49:51	24:45:30
1993	14:86	45:55	21:39:30
1994	14:86	48:52	20:49:31
1995	17:83	49:51	20:48:32

Sources: *Shandong tongji nianjian 1986* (Shandong Statistical Yearbook 1986) (Beijing: Zhongguo tongji chubanshe, 1987) pp. 32–33; *Shandong tongji nianjian 1994*, pp. 10, 14, 17; *Shandong tongji nianjian 1995*, pp. 14–15; and *Shandong tongji nianjian 1996*, pp. 13, 16, 20.

in 1990 and 1991, respectively, in the share of its tertiary industry in provincial GDP.[71]

One most important reason for Shandong's remarkable success in recent years resides in its consistent growth in agriculture.[72] Shandong's success in agriculture was materialized by four key measures, only to name the principal ones, all of which were allegedly devised and promoted under Jiang Chunyun's direction. First, the effective decentralization of policy-making authority to the county level in 1987 contributed significantly to the activation of local initiatives, thus avoiding standardized policy (*yidaoqie*) regardless of varied local conditions. As of 1991, there were a dozen county-level models—including those of Laixi and Pingdu—for different sectors of the economy. As grass-roots information is becoming increasingly valuable, township and village governments have also been given more latitude in pursuing varied models of agricultural development keyed to their local conditions.[73] Second, Shandong's success is also attributed to its steady budgetary investment in agriculture, which rose from 384 million yuan in 1980 to 883 million yuan in 1994, in addition to various other sources of funding that include foreign investment and bank loans.[74]

Third, the development of township and village enterprises (TVEs) has been actively promoted and, as a key result, their share of industrial output in total rural production value rose from 24 percent in 1978 to 67 percent in 1993. This development was also linked up with a novel strategy of combining different sectors of the rural economy—say, peasants produce, process and market their farm products (*nong jia xiao*), or they farm, manufacture and export (*nong gong mao*) without relying on intermediaries.[75] Finally, the prioritized development of wholesale markets was another important factor. County governments played a crucial role in funding the establishment of specialized wholesale markets for farm products and in creating national and regional marketing networks. In 1992 alone, the provincial government spent 1.5 billion yuan to build more than three hundred wholesale markets and over seven thousand farmers' markets.[76]

With regard to structural adjustments within industry, Shandong has adopted a "three-tier" strategy by which the development of labor-intensive, capital-intensive, and high-technology industries is pursued simultaneously. By the year 2000, the respective output share of these three industries is to become 30 percent (no change from 1995), 40 percent (from 50 percent), and 30 percent (from 10 percent). According to the plan, such transformation will take place mainly through restructuring and renovating large and medium-sized enterprises with the help from internationally renowned firms.[77] In order to attract foreign capital and technology, however, a sound infrastructural foundation is a prerequisite. Infrastructural development is the issue that we now focus on.

Infrastructural Development

One of Shandong's most important accomplishments in the post-Mao era is considered to be infrastructural development. During the Sixth Five-Year Plan period, Shandong concentrated on increasing its production capacity for electricity, and by 1986 Shandong replaced Liaoning as number one in China.[78] The most crucial accomplishment of the Seventh Five-Year Plan period (1986–90) concerns the progress in its transportation linkages. Shandong's achievements in railway and road construction are highly noted in China, and the newly opened superhighway linking Ji'nan and Qingdao (*Jiqing gaosu gonglu*) particularly stands out in its effects on promoting intra-provincial cooperation by linking the coastal and inland regions of the province. The total length of Shandong's first- and second-rate roads—25,596 kilometers as of 1992—ranked first in China and its 3,040 kilometers of railway is also far above the national average.[79]

Shandong's provincial leadership—Jiang Chunyun in particular—played a pivotal role in improving transportation linkages by providing active policy support. One of the first policy measures Jiang adopted upon his assumption of the governorship in June 1987 was to ask the Provincial Transportation Bureau to establish funds for managing transportation links more effectively, and building more roads and railways. In late 1987, the bureau disseminated document No. 60 stipulating that, beginning in 1988, the so-called "road maintenance fee" (*yanglufei*) was to be levied on the owners of motor vehicles and tractors, and its baseline figure would increase annually by 7.3 percent for automobiles and by 16.2 percent for tractors during the 1989–92 period. Fees so collected were equally divided between the provincial and local transportation bureaus, and used for the maintenance of old roads and construction of new roads. In 1991 alone, the income from road maintenance fees amounted to 1.2 billion yuan.[80]

Second, the provincial government also established five specialized funds (in the form of low-interest or interest-free loans) in 1991 for the purpose of supporting the construction of various transportation linkages including river transport, road transport, harbor construction, airport construction, and railways. Third, Shandong made efforts to diversify the sources of funds for the construction of transportation linkages. In October 1992, the Shandong Provincial Government Document No. 158 stipulated that the Provincial Transportation Bureau set up the Shandong Provincial Transportation Development and Investment Corporation to take charge of soliciting external investment. The provincial leadership allowed a variety of sources of funds, including bank loans, ministerial investments and foreign investment, to be used in the development of its transportation linkages. In constructing the Qingyang Railway (linking Qingzhou and Yangkou), for instance, 35.5 percent of the investment came from Shandong's funds while the remaining investment came from the Ministry of Railways, Ministry of Light Industry and the Shandong Petrochemical Corporation. The construction of the Jiqing superhighway also relied on five sources of funds from the World Bank, Beijing, domestic banks, the provinces, and prefectures and cities of Shandong. The construction of Longkou harbor was also funded in significant part by investments from South Korea.[81]

Shandong's Foreign Economic Relations: Reform, Management, and Linkage-Weaving

Effective management of foreign economic relations entails three key dimensions. First, it is highly imperative for the provinces (and other local governments) to obtain as many preferential policies as possible from the Center. Since the Beijing government very often lacks sufficient funds to support all local projects, it has instead chosen to provide a variety of favorable policy environments to appease discontented local governments (*zhigei zhengce bugei qian*).[82] Second, as preferential policies alone do not suffice to guarantee success in foreign economic relations, strategic efforts must be made by local governments themselves in reforming and improving rules and institutions of foreign trade and investment. Finally, the fortuitous presence of a "friendly neighbor" which is both willing and able to engage in meaningful economic exchanges is also an indispensable prerequisite.

In the case of Shandong, as discussed earlier in detail, various preferential policies were granted by Beijing. In this section, therefore, we are concerned primarily with two questions: (1) what sort of ideas, strategies, and organizational innovations were employed to promote foreign trade and attract foreign capital; and (2) what measures were adopted to expand Shandong's external linkages.

Shandong's Foreign Economic Relations in the Post-Mao Era

Like other provinces in China, except Guangdong and Fujian, Shandong's efforts toward "opening" were minimal during 1978–83. This was natural, since during this period even the central government was still in the middle of heated debates, controversies, and conflicts regarding whether "opening" was necessary at all for China's economic reform, and whether the establishment of four special economic zones in South China could be readily justified.[83] Under such uncertain circumstances, Shandong's provincial leaders—Bai Rubing and Su Yiran in particular—chose to play safe by not moving too fast toward the controversial option of "opening" and, as a consequence, Shandong's foreign economic relations were highly limited in their scope and intensity.[84]

The first watershed year in Shandong's foreign economic relations was 1984 not only because Beijing designated Qingdao and Yantai as "coastal open cities" but because this was also the year when the Import, Export and Trade Commission (*jinchukou maoyi weiyuanhui*: usually referred to as *jinchukouwei* and abbreviated here as ImExCom) was established within the provincial government. This was a significant measure in that its intention was to decentralize much of the central government's foreign trade authority to the provincial government. In principle, ImExCom was put in charge of supervising the province's foreign trade activities by overseeing "general foreign trade corporations" (*waimao zonggongsi*) stationed in Shandong (mainly in Qingdao) and formerly controlled exclusively by the Ministry of Foreign Trade. According to interviewees in Ji'nan and Qingdao, despite such stipulations as to the delegation of foreign trade authority to the provincial level, the period of 1984–86 was still characterized by the Center's planned control through the State Planning Commission (SPC) and the Ministry of Foreign Trade (which was later renamed Ministry of Foreign Economic Relations and Trade and abbreviated as MOFERT). Comparatively speaking, while Guangdong had set up and managed its first batch of provincial foreign trade corporations as early as 1980, as of 1986 Shandong's foreign trade corporations were still controlled by both "functional" (referring to MOFERT) and "territorial" (referring to ImExCom) authorities, with the former exerting more influence.

The second watershed came in 1987–88. First, provincial foreign trade corporations were finally separated from the general foreign trade corporations under MOFERT's control. What this meant was that from 1987 onwards these provincial foreign trade corporations were controlled solely by ImExCom under the provincial government.[85] Second, ImExCom was reorganized as the Foreign

Economic Commission (*duiwai jingji weiyuanhui*: usually referred to as *waijingwei* and abbreviated here as FEC) in 1987 with a mission to supervise the province's foreign trade activities. The establishment of the FEC, however, generated serious inter-agency conflicts over vested interests and lines of authority. The most serious conflict stemmed from the presence of an old organization called the Foreign Trade Commission (*duiwai maoyi weiyuanhui*: hereafter FTC) located in Qingdao and formerly placed under the functional (*tiaotiao*) control of MOFERT. The bifurcation of provincial foreign trade authority and the resulting redundancy and confusion were by no means desirable, but the issue could not be easily resolved due to the FTC's staunch opposition to the merger with the FEC.[86]

More importantly, 1988 witnessed the long-waited opening of the Shandong Peninsula region encompassing six cities (Qingdao, Yantai, Weihai, Weifang, Rizhao, and Zibo) and forty-four counties. With this opening, the ceiling of Shandong's authority in approving foreign-invested projects was raised from US$ 5 million to US$ 30 million.[87] In its immediate aftermath, Jiang Chunyun, in his keynote speech at the Provincial Work Conference on Opening to the Outside, called for an "all-directional opening" toward socialist and capitalist countries alike. Jiang further argued that, "without fundamental changes in ideas and attitudes toward opening, an outward-oriented economy would be impossible to achieve."[88] In May, the project-approving authority for "processing with imported materials" (*lailiao jiagong*) was delegated to the county level, and that for the "three foreign-invested firms" (*sanzi qiye*) was also decentralized to the prefectural level.[89] Furthermore, Shandong enacted thirteen local economic laws to accelerate the opening process. During the seven-month period of January–July 1988, over 600 projects worth US$ 4.4 billion were signed, an amount twenty times larger than that for the same period in 1987.[90]

The third key year for Shandong's foreign economic relations was 1990, because in this year the two competing provincial trade authorities—FEC and FTC—were finally merged to form the Foreign Economic and Trade Commission (abbreviated as FETC). As foreign trade and investment were becoming increasingly crucial for the province's economy, Jiang Chunyun allegedly intervened to unify the bifurcated structure. Fearing continued factional struggles after the merger, the provincial leadership transferred the heads of both the FEC and the FTC to other units, and instead invited an outsider to head the newly formed FETC.[91] In 1990, Shandong's open area was further expanded with the addition of Ji'nan and its nine counties, covering about 40 percent of the province's total population and making the region the largest open area in China.

The final key year was 1992—probably a critical year for many other provinces as well owing to Deng Xiaoping's southern tour. In its immediate aftermath, Jiang Chunyun personally directed a series of surveys and investigations on "outward-oriented economies" by dispatching two vice-governors to four provincial-level units—Beijing, Dalian (as a central economic city), Fujian, and Guangdong—to assess their experiences in promoting foreign economic relations. On the basis of these surveys and investigations, the provincial party committee held a series of "work conferences on opening" in March 1992 attended by three-level (provincial, prefectural and county) party secretaries. At these conferences, "further liberation of ideas" was called for. Additionally, the provincial government approved the establishment of thirty-six "export-oriented industrial processing zones" (*waixiangxing gongye jiagongqu*) in the Shandong Peninsula Coastal Open Region; of twelve "opening and development comprehensive experimental zones" (*kaifang kaifa zonghe shiyanqu*) in the western region; of seven "new and high-tech industrial development zones" (*gaoxin jishu kaifaqu*); and of two "tourism development zones" (*lüyou jingji kaifaqu*) and three "tourism and leisure zones" (*lüyou dujiaqu*).[92]

There was another important development in 1992: the establishment of diplomatic normalization between China and South Korea. While there were already extensive economic exchanges between Shandong and South Korea during 1988–91, the diplomatic normalization provided a catalyst in expanding the bilateral economic relationship. With over 90 percent of twenty thousand overseas Chinese residents in Korea originally from Shandong, geographical proximity and the special attention Shandong's provincial leaders paid to the bilateral relationship (Jiang Chunyun, Zhao Zhihao and Li Chunting—governor since 1995—all visited South Korea), by 1994 South Korea became number two destination for Shandong's exports and the third largest investor in Shandong only after Hong Kong and Taiwan.[93]

In March 1993, Dongying was designated by the State Council as an open area and Shandong's open area thus covers eight of its seventeen prefectural-level cities and fifty-six counties. In 1993, Weihai was authorized to set up an "economic and technological development zone" (ETDZ) to compete with Qingdao and Yantai. In 1993, thanks to Shandong's effective lobbying, Weifang, Weihai, Zibo and Ji'nan were all approved by the State Council to establish "new and hi-tech industrial development zones," which had until then been reserved only for Qingdao.[94]

Shandong's Foreign Trade

In 1978–1995, Shandong's foreign trade increased about fourteen times from US$ 872 million to US$ 13.1 billion. Its per-annum growth rate was 18.2 percent, while the national average was only 10.6 percent for the period of 1978–94. Although very high growth rates were noted for some earlier years—such as 56 percent in 1978–79 and 37.5 percent in 1979–80—the reason was that it had started from such a low base in 1978. On the other hand, a very slow growth characterized the province's foreign trade during 1981–86, in part because Shandong did not have its own foreign trade authority until 1987 (its foreign trade was mostly planned by MOFERT and carried out by its general foreign trade corporations). In contrast, during the subsequent period, and particularly in

Table 5.10

Key Destinations of Shandong's Exports in Select Years

Rank	1987	1991	1993	1994	1995
1	Japan	Japan	Japan	Japan	Japan
2	Hong Kong	Hong Kong	Hong Kong	Hong Kong	S. Korea
3	Singapore	U.S.A.	U.S.A.	S. Korea	Hong Kong
4	Brazil	S. Korea	S. Korea	U.S.A.	U.S.A.
5	U.S.A.	Singapore	Germany	Germany	Germany

Sources: *Shandong tongji nianjian, 1989* issue, p. 306; 1993 issue, p. 478; and 1996 issue, p. 474.

the 1990s, when Shandong came to plan and control its own foreign economic relations, not even once did Shandong's foreign trade score a negative growth as it marked a steady growth in 1987–90 and a virtual take-off in 1991–95 (with a per-annum growth rate of 25.7 percent as opposed to 6.5 percent for 1985–90).[95] In terms of trade balance, Shandong's exports far exceeded its imports throughout the entire period of 1978–95. Obviously, foreign exchange earnings were one important priority. In fact, as early as 1988 the provincial leadership laid down the policy framework—in the case of Shandong, importing raw materials should be minimized as most of them were available within the province or the country.[96]

While Shandong's foreign trade has expanded significantly during the 1990s, it also has had some structural problems. First, in 1993, 43 percent of Shandong's foreign trade was carried out by provincial foreign trade corporations as opposed to municipal and prefecture-level foreign trade corporations and non-governmental firms. Compared to Guangdong (4 percent) and Fujian (10 percent), Shandong's reliance on provincial-level planning and coordination was relatively heavier. As of 1996, however, the share of provincial foreign trade corporations in the province's total exports declined to 21 percent, while that for foreign-invested enterprises (*sanzi qiye*), municipal and prefecture-level foreign trade corporations and non-governmental firms with their own export authority was 43, 25 and 12 percent, respectively. While Shandong has about 820 enterprises with their own import and export authority as of 1996, this figure is even smaller than that of Guangdong, 900, for 1987.[97] Second, the share of industrial products in Shandong's exports was 74.9 percent in 1995, among which 14.4 percent was electronic goods. Given that the national average was 85.5 percent and the figure for Jiangsu was over 90 percent, Shandong has a lot of room to improve on this front.[98]

Table 5.10 lists the top five destinations of Shandong's exports. Japan and

Hong Kong maintained their top two positions throughout 1987–94, a trend which applies to most other provinces in China as well, while the United States kept its number three position in 1991–93. In the case of Shandong, however, South Korea's increasing importance stands out as it moved from a virtually unknown player in 1987, to a steady number four in 1991–93, to number three in 1994, and to number two overtaking Hong Kong in 1995.[99] By contrast, the significance of Singapore has been gradually reduced from number three in 1987 to number six in 1993.

Foreign Investment in Shandong

Having started with five "compensation trade" projects worth US$ 1 million in 1979, Shandong's utilization of foreign capital has made very impressive progress in the last sixteen years. By 1995, the total accumulated number of foreign-invested projects was 26,087, with their contracted and actually utilized foreign capital totaling US$ 27.3 billion and US$ 11.9 billion, respectively. The number of foreign direct investment projects in Shandong for the period of 1979–95 was 19,446, with their contracted and actually utilized foreign capital totaling US$ 22.4 billion and US$ 8.5 billion, respectively. In 1995 alone, the size of actually utilized foreign funds reached US$ 3.3 billion, while that for foreign direct investment was US$ 2.6 billion.[100] Shandong's utilization of foreign direct investment was very minimal in 1978–83: the contracted amount of foreign investment in 1979–83 was merely US$ 0.1 million. In 1984–91, thanks to Beijing's provision of selective preferential policies and active promotion of foreign investment by the provincial leadership (particularly since 1988 under Jiang Chunyun), the annual contracted amount of foreign direct investment rose from US$ 5.6 million in 1985 and US$ 39 million in 1988 to US$ 180 million in 1991. With the new "opening" incentive initiated by Deng's southern tour and, more importantly, the South Korea–China diplomatic normalization, the figure skyrocketed to US$ 973 million in 1992 and US$ 2.6 billion in 1995.[101]

While "processing and assembling" (*jiagong zhuangpei*) projects constituted a major portion of foreign funds committed in Shandong during the early years, beginning in the mid-1980s joint ventures increased very rapidly. Since 1987 when foreign businesses were permitted to establish wholly-owned ventures, and especially after 1989–90 when the risk of joint ventures was raised by the trauma of the June Fourth Incident, the number of foreign wholly-owned ventures (FWOs) has risen rapidly. From Table 5.11, three patterns are discernible with regard to the type of foreign investment committed in Shandong. First, after FWOs were permitted, the respective share of compensation trade, processing and assembling, and cooperative ventures significantly declined in the 1990s.[102] Second, while it still remains the most dominant form of investment, the share of joint ventures began to go down in 1993. Third, the share of FWOs has increased rapidly, and the average amount of investment for FWOs (US$ 1.7

Table 5.11

Distribution of Foreign Investment Types in Shandong (%)

	JVs	CVs	FWOs	CT	P&A
1988	29.4	19.4	4.3	15.3	32.1
1989	44.0	6.8	0.02	14.6	32.1
1990	10.1	45.8	0.01	3.5	39.1
1991	56.5	12.3	14.2	0.02	14.7
1992	71.1	6.9	19.3	0.01	0.02
1993	61.9	6.9	28.9	0.01	0.02
1994	53.9	3.8	21.3	1.13	19.9
1995	49.9	7.1	29.7	3.0	4.7

Source: Shandong tongji nianjian 1994, p. 410; and *Shandong tongji nianjian 1996*, p. 477.

Notes: The acronyms refer to joint ventures (JVs), cooperative ventures (CVs), foreign wholly-owned enterprises (FWOs), compensation trade (CT), and processing and assembly agreements (P&A). Figures are for contracted investments.

million) was more than twice as large as that for joint ventures (US$ 0.8 million). Despite the provincial government's wishes to have more joint-equity ventures for the purpose of utilizing foreign capital in renovating old state enterprises and upgrading their outdated technologies, FWOs may soon catch up with joint-venture investment in Shandong.[103]

In sectoral terms, foreign investment in Shandong seems fairly well diversified. While textile, chemical and machinery industries constituted the top three sectors in both the number of projects and the amount of investment, many other sectors ranging from commerce, eateries, circulation and electronics to construction, transportation and agriculture have also attracted a significant size of foreign investment.[104] The Shandong government also stressed the need to integrate the rural economy with foreign economic relations. Locating foreign-invested enterprises in suburban and rural areas to transform township and village enterprises has been a priority policy in Shandong. Another priority policy was to allow foreign firms to rent or buy land at discounted prices for "combined production" of farming, food processing, marketing and other export-oriented activities. For instance, an Israeli firm invested US$ 6 million to rent a huge area in Dongying to process various agricultural products for export.[105]

In geographical terms, all of the top five recipient cities in 1992–95 were "open areas," with Qingdao leading all other cities (Table 5.12). This reflects the uneven effect of the open policy in intra-provincial terms. The combined share of the top five recipients in Shandong's total foreign direct investment declined from 76 percent in 1992 to 73 percent in 1995. And the gap between Qingdao and the number two city for 1992–94, Yantai, also decreased from 8.2 percent in 1992 to 4 percent in 1994, but it rose again to 18 percent, with Weifang outpacing Yantai in

Table 5.12

Foreign Direct Investment in Shandong by Cities, 1992–95

Rank	1992	1993	1994	1995
	(% of provincial figures)			
1	Qingdao (29%)	Qingdao (19%)	Qingdao (23%)	Qingdao (32%)
2	Yantai (21%)	Yantai (17%)	Yantai (19%)	Weifang (14%)
3	Weifang (10%)	Ji'nan (12%)	Weifang (18%)	Yantai (13%)
4	Weihai (8%)	Weifang (11%)	Weihai (9%)	Ji'nan (9%)
5	Zibo (8%)	Weihai (9%)	Ji'nan (8%)	Zibo (5%)

Source: Shandong tongji nianjian 1993, p. 484; 1994 issue, p. 414; 1995 issue, p. 475; and 1996 issue, p. 481.

Table 5.13

Foreign Direct Investment in Shandong by Country, 1988–1995

Rank	1988	1989	1991	1993	1994	1995
1	Hong Kong	Hong Kong	Hong Kong	Hong Kong	Hong Kong	Hong Kong
2	Japan	USA	Taiwan	Taiwan	Taiwan	S. Korea
3	FRG	Japan	USA	USA	S. Korea	Taiwan
4	USA	S. Korea	Japan	S. Korea	U.S.A.	U.S.A.
5	Singapore	Taiwan	S. Korea	Japan	Japan	Japan

Sources: Shandong tongji nianjian 1989, p. 314; 1990 issue, p. 458; 1992 issue, p. 474; and 1996 issue, p. 479.

Note: Ranks are based upon the actual amount of foreign funds utilized.

1995. The rise of Weifang and Ji'nan is particularly noteworthy since it seems to reflect a gradual process in which developmental ideologies have gradually spread into the middle-belt areas away from the Jiaodong Peninsula region.[106]

Table 5.13 breaks down Shandong's foreign direct investment by the country of origin. While Hong Kong has been an indisputable number one investor in Shandong (as it has been for many other provinces as well), Japan's significance has continued to decline over the years. Instead, two new players have emerged: Taiwan and South Korea. Owing to its eight hundred thousand residents of Shandong origin and key preferential policies toward their investment, Taiwan ranked second in successive years of 1991–94. Due to Shandong's priority given to investments from South Korea, the significance of South Korea has continued to rise from a virtually unknown player in 1988, to number five in 1991, to number three in 1994, and to number two in 1995.[107]

Foreign Borrowing

Foreign borrowing is not an indicator of provincial economic performance per se, but perhaps it may be an indirect indicator of the central government's concern with a particular province or of the given province's bargaining power vis-à-vis the Center. The main reason lies in the process of approval for local utilization of foreign funds in China. According to a provincial official, all foreign borrowing and loans are controlled solely by the State Planning Commission under the State Council regardless of their size. Two issues are pertinent here: (1) how the foreign borrowing of Shandong compare to other coastal provinces; and (2) which type of foreign lender is preferred by the provincial authorities. First, the overall size of Shandong's foreign loans became increasingly smaller over the years as the provincial leadership was trying hard to reduce its dependence on foreign borrowing.[108] In 1992–93, for instance, the size of Shandong's foreign loans was much smaller than those of Guangdong Shanghai, Liaoning, and Tianjin. Furthermore, the share of Shandong's foreign loans in its total foreign funds utilized also became very small—2.3 percent in 1992 and 0.5 percent in 1993—compared to the other four provinces.[109] One key implication of such a low level of dependence on foreign loans is that the province may fare better with Beijing's intermittent adoption of "austerity measures" to cool down the overheated economy.

Table 5.14 breaks down Shandong's foreign borrowing of 1988–1994 by three types of lenders: foreign governments, international organizations, and commercial lending institutions. If we compare the compositions of these three types of loans during 1988–95, the respective share of all three types was highly

Table 5.14

Foreign Borrowings of Shandong by Lender, 1988–1995 (US$ million)

	Foreign governments	International organizations	Foreign commercial loans	Yearly total	Accumulated total
1988	41 (51)	9 (11)	30 (38)	80	362
1989	195	—	—	195	557
1990	132	—	—	132	689
1991	66 (30)	118 (54)	36 (16)	220	909
1992	106 (16)	460 (68)	114 (16)	680	1,589
1993	132 (40)	56 (17)	138 (42)	326	1,915
1994	226 (57)	40 (10)	128 (33)	394	2,309
1995	167 (57)	34 (12)	92 (31)	293	2,602

Sources: Shandong tongji nianjian 1989, p. 311; 1990 issue, p. 324; 1991 issue, p. 457; 1992 issue, p. 471; 1993 issue, p. 480; and 1996 issue, p. 477.

Note: Figures in parentheses refer to their respective share in yearly totals.

unstable, producing no discernible patterns.[110] While the national as well as provincial priority is on "foreign government loans" (*waiguo zhengfu daikuan*) with longer repayment schedules and low rates of interest (or often interest-free), the year-end figures tend to reflect the loans approved for the projects that the central government liked to see implemented most—i.e., such infrastructural development projects as the Longkou harbor funded by a South Korean loan and the Jiqing superhighway relying on World Bank funds. Despite Beijing's wish to avoid commercial loans with relatively higher rates of interest and to reduce debt dependence on a few individual countries, it seems that Beijing's priorities may not always prevail since certain commercial loans may be worked out within the "banking system" (*yinhang xitong*) that is becoming increasingly independent of the planning system, and for some highly efficient sectors utilizing commercial loans would not necessarily be a bad idea.[111]

Provincial Strategies for Expanding External Linkages

Shandong's provincial leadership, particularly that under Jiang Chunyun and Zhao Zhihao, strongly emphasized the expansion of the province's interactions with the outside world. As embodied in the slogan of "all-directional opening," Shandong's leadership has strived to "open up" more areas to foreign economic relations. As a key result, a total of 56 cities and counties were opened up by early 1993, covering 54,000 square kilometers and more than 40 percent of the province's population. And this makes Shandong's open area the second largest in China only after Guangdong with 42 cities and counties covering 93,000 square kilometers and 52 million people.[112]

There are several indicators of the extensive external linkages Shandong has established over the years. First, by the end of 1995, all of Shandong's seventeen prefectures and prefecture-level cities as well as 62 counties acquired import-export authority. Shandong established economic and trade relations with over 179 countries and maintains "friendship relations" (*youhao guanxi*) with over 60 provinces, states and cities overseas. Of these 60 linkages, 34 were established since 1988.[113] Second, Shandong maintains a total of 64 overseas offices (*guowai banshichu*) in 17 countries. Some of these are managed directly by provincial government units, others by provincial enterprises, and still others by various cities and prefectures of the province. In South Korea, for instance, Shandong has six offices: two managed by the province's Foreign Economic Relations and Trade Commission; another by the provincial tourism corporation; and the remaining three by Qingdao, Yantai, and Weihai.[114]

Third, the increase in Shandong's overseas firms and factories also reflects its deep concern with expanding international linkages (see Table 5.15). Shandong's overseas investment has grown rapidly during the 1990s. As of 1994, Shandong has a total of 87 overseas trading firms that fall under the jurisdiction of various provincial, prefectural and city foreign trade corporations (examples include the

Table 5.15

Shandong's Overseas Networks, 1980–1995

Year	Year-end cumulative total (number of overseas firms, factories, and liaison offices)
1980	2
1990	47
1992	120
1993	226
1994	266
1995	359

Sources: Figures for 1980–1993 are from Zhao Huajian, "Shandongsheng haiwai qiye fazhan de xianzhuang, wenti yu duice"(The Current Situation of the Development of Overseas Investment by Shandong), in *Shandong jingji* (Shandong Economy), No. 4, (1995), p. 18; and the 1994 and 1995 figures are from interviews in Ji'nan in 1995 and 1997.

Luxing Corporation in New York and the Hualu Corporation in Hong Kong).[115] Shandong also has a total of 115 factories located overseas with the total amount of investment reaching US$ 115 million (an average of US$ 1 million for each plant). Fourth, the total number of Shandong firms with their own import and export authority was 820 at the end of 1995 (an increase by 570 from 1993).[116] Finally, Shandong has tried hard to get connected with other countries through transportation networks. In terms of sea routes, as of 1993, Shandong had 24 coastal ports with 195 berths and maintained 17 international shipping lines sailing to more than 300 destinations overseas. And, in terms of air routes, Shandong is linked to Hong Kong, Macau, South Korea, Singapore, and Japan. While still in its development stage, Shandong has also managed to establish its own aviation system—Shandong Air Line—with the blessings from the State Council and the State Administration of Civil Aviation.[117]

Also noteworthy is the provincial leadership's efforts to extend local-international nexuses into the inland areas of the province with structural disadvantages in conducting foreign economic relations. Three key measures were employed to link the coastal and inland regions of the province. First, the provincial leadership maximally utilized its own administrative authority to designate several dozen localities to enjoy similar privileges granted to the seventeen cities and development zones designated by Beijing. As Table 5.16 illustrates, with the exception of the bonded zone, Shandong designated a total of sixty zones to enjoy almost the same privileges granted to the Center-designated zones.[118]

Second, the provincial leadership adopted a variety of policies that were to link more advanced and open coastal regions with backward inland areas—called "pairing" (*jieduizi*). In 1992, the provincial government selected 26 coun-

Table 5.16

State- and Province-Designated Special Zones in Shandong (1996)

Province-designated	Beijing-designated
36 "export-oriented industrial processing zones"	8 "coastal open cities"
12 "opening and reform comprehensive experimental zones"*	3 "economic and technological development zones"
7 "high-tech development zones"	5 "high-tech development zones"
2 "tourism development zones"	
3 "tourism and leisure zones"	1 "tourism and leisure zone"
none	1 "bonded zone"

*All of these twelve zones were located in the inland areas.

ties of the coastal region and linked them with another 26 counties of the inland region. Rongcheng County of Weihai Prefecture, for instance, was linked up with Sishui County of Jining Prefecture, and Rongcheng was supposed to utilize surplus labor of Sishui by encouraging its enterprises to give processing work to the latter. The provincial government also selected 26 government units (such as the Electricity Bureau and the Finance Department) to help these 26 poor counties. Additionally, key provincial leaders were also assigned to supervise a few counties each: Jiang Chunyun, for instance, was put in charge of three counties. Such "pairing" did not stop at the county level: Qingdao Municipality was linked up with Heze Prefecture, Yantai with Binzhou, and Weihai with Liaocheng.[119] Finally, exchange of cadres is another key strategy devised by the province. The main goal is to transfer cadres of coastal regions to inland areas so that they can pass on their experiences with reform and opening. The appointment in 1993 of Zhang Huilai—formerly Qingdao deputy party secretary—as Dezhou party secretary is a good example in point.[120]

Provincial Strategies of Reform: Concluding Observations from the Shandong Case

In this chapter, we examined three key components of Shandong's strategy of development: (1) the transformation of the local environment for reform through the maximum acquisition of preferential policies from Beijing; (2) the maintenance and acceleration of the pace of developmental reform through political intervention and policy innovations by the provincial leadership; and (3) the province-wide promotion and expansion of local-international nexuses to secure necessary funds and technologies. While it is difficult to weigh the relative importance of each component, the experiences of Shandong may enable us to ponder about sequencing these components.

Reform is a risky political undertaking as it presupposes radical changes of the established routines and vested interests. High uncertainties associated with reform, therefore, generally produce conservatism among policy makers as well as implementors. Particularly in systems where career advancement is largely determined on the basis of ideological and political conformity, bureaucratic careerism reinforces such conservatism among local implementors. What enables them to break out of such conservative norms is an explicit stipulation by the Center that certain policies favor changes rather than the status quo. In this respect, a variety of preferential policy packages Beijing bequeathed on Shandong since 1988 were vital to the transformation of the provincial atmosphere for reform.[121] And such transformation of the provincial atmosphere proceeded in two different but related realms: (1) Beijing's provision of preferential policies eased fears and suspicion on the part of the provincial implementors with respect to the intentions of the Center; and (2) these preferential policies significantly improved the provincial position in attracting foreign trade and investment by offering special terms of transaction with Beijing's official guarantee.

Once bureaucratic conservatism is mitigated by the Center's guarantee on the imperative of reform, the role of local leaders becomes very crucial, which is obviously context-variant. As the case of Liang Buting and Li Chang'an indicates, there seem to be clear limits as to what can be accomplished by an innovative leadership without the Center-endorsed policy framework for changes. The magnitude of accomplishments by Jiang Chunyun and Zhao Zhihao, on the other hand, is illustrative of what could grow out of the combination between central support and entrepreneurial leadership. It may be true that we cannot provide a clear-cut assessment as to which of the two was more important in facilitating Shandong's rapid growth in recent years. One thing is clear, however: Shandong would not have developed so fast without its provincial leadership which performed like a skillful statesman in dealing with the Center to obtain more preferential policies and, at the same time, as an innovative entrepreneur in attracting foreign trade and capital. As (post)socialist systems will maintain for quite a long period what Kornai has termed a "dual economy," where the role of private entrepreneurs continues to be limited by the state, the role of local governments as skillful entrepreneurs will remain crucial.[122]

Finally, the expansion of external linkages was indispensable in Shandong's success. The huge literature on "newly industrializing economies" (NIEs) notes the importance of international linkages in economic development.[123] There is no doubt that Shandong's geographical location (i.e., proximity to South Korea and Japan) and rich resource endowment were crucial to its attainment of preferential policies from the Center. Although these preferential policy packages were important in offering highly attractive terms of foreign investment, given the intense inter-provincial competition in China, conscious efforts on the part of Shandong to differentiate itself from other provinces enjoying the same privileges were also vital. Equally important was the presence of a willing and capable partner—South Korea—which has been a real blessing for Shandong, as Hong Kong and Taiwan have been for Guangdong and Fujian.[124]

Shandong may not be unique among China's coastal provinces, although the degree to which the developmental experiences of coastal provinces converge is to be assessed in the conclusion of this volume. The Shandong case suggests that, as long as there is appropriate central policy support, a capable and astute leadership to utilize it to a full extent, and international networks to provide industrial capital, technology and marketing routes, Shandong's success may well be replicated. Given that many inland provinces are still predominantly agricultural and have yet to exhaust the extensive phase of their growth process, its replication is not completely out of the question.[125] If the experiences of the NIEs are any guide, however, the particular choice of economic strategy alone may not necessarily produce a similarly successful emulation in other areas of the developmental process.[126] Political decisions that provide a powerful boost and catalyst for local economic development in China are situation-contingent and historically bound. Yet, such political decisions always come with a premium which, therefore, makes them relatively scarce.[127]

Notes

An earlier version was presented at the Contemporary China Studies Seminar Program, Centre of Asian Studies, University of Hong Kong, on March 24, 1995, and at the 47th Annual Meeting of the Association for Asian Studies in Washington D.C. on April 6–9, 1995. I would like to thank Peter T.Y. Cheung and Keith Forster for their comments and Roy Man for research assistance. Three trips to Ji'nan and two trips to Qingdao in 1994–95 were supported by the faculty research support fund from the Division of Social Sciences, and a Direct Allocation Grant (DAG-HSS03 1994/95) from the Hong Kong University of Science and Technology.

1. Initial contributions along this line were recently made by David S. G. Goodman (ed.), *China's Provinces in Reform* (London: Routledge, 1997), David S.G. Goodman, and Gerald Segal (eds.), *China Deconstructs: Politics, Trade and Regionalism* (London: Routledge, 1994) and Jia Hao and Lin Zhimin (eds.), *Changing Central-Local Relations in China: Reform and State Capacity* (Boulder, Colorado: Westview, 1994), although the latter provides only two case studies on Guangdong and Shanghai. While a strategy of comparing two or more provinces is highly desirable, given the inherent difficulties associated with comparative research, doing collaborative projects on multiple provinces— what this volume aims to accomplish—may constitute the second best alternative. For key conceptual and methodological issues in the study of central-local dynamics, see Jae Ho Chung, "Studies of Central-Provincial Relations in the People's Republic of China: A Mid-Term Appraisal," *China Quarterly*, No. 142 (June 1995), pp. 487–508.

2. For Shandong's earlier image as a "laggard," see Peter Ferdinand, "Shandong: An Atypical Coastal Province?" in David S. G. Goodman (ed.), *China's Regional Development* (London and New York: Routledge, 1989), pp. 153–163.

3. For the calls to emulate Shandong's reform strategies, see Xing Chongzhi, "Xuexi Shandong jingyan jiakuai wosheng jingji fazhan" (Learn from Shandong's Experiences and Accelerate the Economic Development of Our Province), *Gongchandangyuan* (Communist Party Members), July-August 1988, pp. 22–26; "Xinjueqi de jingji dasheng—

Shandong" (A Newly Emerging Economic Giant — Shandong), *Liaowang zhoukan* (Outlook Weekly: overseas edition), July 2, 1990, pp. 8–9; "Shandong jingji fazhan kuai de aomi" (The Mystery of Shandong's Fast Economic Development), *Qiushi zazhi* (Seeking the Truth Magazine), No. 15 (1992), pp. 19–23; "Gaige kaifang shi Shandong yueju quanguo qianlie" (Reform and Opening Put Shandong in the Front Line) in *Guangjiaojing yuekan* (Wide Angle Monthly), March 1992, pp. 20–25; "Shandong jingji gaosu fazhan gei women de qishi" (Revelations from Shandong's Accelerated Growth), *Qinghai ribao* (Qinghai Daily), April 16, 1993; "Guangdong: zhenshi xianshi zaizhao youshi—Yuelu liangsheng jingji fazhan duibi ji qishi" (Guangdong Must Face the Reality and Once Again Create Its Own Advantages—A Comparison of Economic Developments in Guangdong and Shandong), in *Guangdong tongji nianjian 1994* (Guangdong Statistical Yearbook 1994) (Beijing: Zhongguo tongji chubanshe, 1994), pp. 19–27; and "Shandong weilai fazhan zhanlue" (Shandong's Strategies for Future Development), in *Guangjiaojing yuekan*, January 1997, pp. 44–54.

4. For the importance of "sequencing" in reform, see Michel Oksenberg and Bruce J. Dickson, "The Origins, Processes, and Outcomes of Great Political Reform," in Dankwart A. Rustow and Kenneth Paul Erickson (eds.), *Comparative Political Dynamics: Global Research Perspectives* (New York: Harper Collins, 1991), pp. 248–249; and Robert W. Campbell, *The Socialist Economies in Transition: A Primer on Semi-Reformed Systems* (Bloomington: Indiana University Press, 1991), pp. 219–222.

5. For such an "anti-outsider" culture in Shandong, see Zhang Yufa, *Zhongguo xiandaihua de quyu yanjiu: Shandongsheng, 1860–1916* (Regional Studies of Modernization in China: Shandong, 1860–1916) (Taipei: Academia Sinica, 1982), p. 136. Also see Xin Xiangyin (ed.), *Shuodao Shandongren* (Speaking of the Shandong People) (Beijing: Zhongguo shehui chubanshe, 1995), pp. 50–51.

6. *Zhongguo tongji nianjian 1996* (China Statistical Yearbook 1996) [hereafter *ZGTJNJ*] (Beijing: Zhongguo tongji chubanshe, 1996), p. 24; *ZGTJNJ 1995*, p. 60; and *Shandong tongji nianjian 1996* (Statistical Yearbook of Shandong 1996) (Beijing: Zhongguo tongji chubanshe, 1996), p. 13.

7. Shandong's petroleum (heavily deposited near Dongying) accounts for more than one-fifth of China's total deposits and its Shengli oilfields produce 20 million tons annually, ranking second in China. Information from *Dangdai Zhongguo de Shandong* (Contemporary China's Shandong) (Beijing: Zhongguo shehui kexue chubanshe, 1989), Vol. 1, pp. 10–11; and Zhou Shunwu, *China Provincial Geography* (Beijing: Foreign Languages Press, 1992), pp. 231, 235, 238, 241.

8. See Zhou, *China Provincial Geography*, p. 236; *ZGTJNJ 1995*, p. 137; *ZGTJNJ 1996*, p. 23; *Shandong tongji nianjian 1994*, p. 12; *Shandong tongji nianjian 1995*, pp. 11, 86; and *Shandong tongji nianjian 1996*, p. 91.

9. See *ZGTJNJ 1994*, p. 35.

10. More discussion on this is given in the later section on foreign trade.

11. State Statistical Bureau, *Quanguo zhuyao shehui jingji zhibiao paixu nianjian 1992* (Yearbook of the Ranking of Key National Social and Economic Indices) (Beijing: Zhongguo tongji chubanshe, 1993), pp. 19, 31, 51, 153, 156; Ibid., 1993 issue, pp. 19, 31, 51, 156; *ZGTJNJ 1995*, pp. 332, 378; and *ZGTJNJ 1996*, p. 356.

12. Regarding the deleterious effect of the anti-rightist campaign on central-provincial relations, David Bachman notes as follows: "[D]uring and after this campaign, no one dared to contradict the views coming down from above for fear of being sentenced to labor reform." See his *Bureaucracy, Economy, and Leadership in China: The Institutional Origins of the Great Leap Forward* (Cambridge: Cambridge University Press, 1991), p. 5.

13. Such a risk-averse behavior is described as "hanging on" in Kenneth Lieberthal and Michel Oksenberg, *Policy Making in China: Leaders, Structures and Processes*

(Princeton: Princeton University Press, 1988), p. 335. For a fuller discussion of these three patterns (pioneering, bandwagoning, and resisting), see Jae Ho Chung, *The Politics of Policy Implementation in Post-Mao China: Central Control and Provincial Autonomy under Decentralization*, Ph.D. dissertation, Department of Political Science, University of Michigan, 1993, pp. 191–192, 215–217.

14. The data on Shandong's ranking in the five policy areas are from Frederick C. Teiwes, "Provincial Politics in China: Themes and Variations," in John M. H. Lindbeck (ed.), *China: Management of Revolutionary Society* (Seattle: University of Washington Press, 1971), pp. 155, 168–170, 172. For the hasty execution of cooperativization in Shandong, see Nicholas R. Lardy, "Economic Recovery and the First Five-Year Plan," in Roderick MacFarquhar and John K. Fairbank (eds.), *The Cambridge History of China*, Vol. 14, The Emergence of Revolutionary China 1949–1965 (London: Cambridge University Press, 1987), p. 167. And for the swift establishment of the revolutionary committee in Shandong, see Harry Harding, "The Chinese State in Crisis," in MacFarquhar and Fairbank (eds.), *The Cambridge History of China*, Vol. 15, *Revolutions within the Chinese Revolution 1966–1982* (London: Cambridge University Press, 1991), p. 173.

15. The quoted information is from the author's interview with a central government official in Hong Kong in 1994. For the significance of physical distance from Beijing, see Lieberthal and Oksenberg, *Policy Making in China*, p. 338; concerning its effect on Shandong, see Ferdinand, "Shandong," p. 159; and for a view that also emphasizes "political distance" as opposed to physical distance alone, see David S. G. Goodman, "Political Perspectives," in *China's Regional Development*, p. 29. For an interesting study that utilizes infrastructural indicators — such as the frequency and convenience of transportation to and communication with Beijing — for the variable concerned, see James Tong, *The 1989 Democracy Movement in China: A Preliminary Spatial Analysis* (Hong Kong: Hong Kong Institute of Asia-Pacific Studies, 1994), pp. 23–24.

16. See Lewis M. Stern, "Politics without Consensus: Center-Province Relations and Political Communication in China, January 1976–January 1977," *Asian Survey*, Vol. 19, No. 3 (March 1979), p. 275.

17. Added to such bureaucratic careerism was Shandong's "conservatism" (*shoujiu sixiang*) that many Shandong people themselves regard as a key deterring factor of reform in the early years. For Shandong's traditional conservatism, see *Renmin ribao* (People's Daily), May 15, 1988.

18. For the issue of bureaucratic careerism, see Joel S. Migdal, *Strong Societies and Weak States* (Princeton: Princeton University Press, 1988), pp. 239–242. For a study of the Chinese case in this respect, see Barbara Krug, "Regional Politics in Communist China: The Spatial Dimension of Power," *Issues & Studies*, Vol. 21, No. 1 (January 1985), pp. 70–75.

19. *Renmin ribao*, December 7, 1978.

20. Li Chang'an was the only exception as he was transferred to Beijing as a deputy secretary-general of the State Council. According to an interviewee in Ji'nan, Li's personal relationship with Liang Buting was not very good and Li's transfer was supposedly made upon his own request to leave Shandong.

21. Some studies which examined the "native" issue with a large set of aggregate data found that the native proportion was very high in the 1950s, radically declined afterward to hit its nadir during the Cultural Revolution decade, and rose again during the 1980s. See David S. G. Goodman, "The Provincial First Party Secretary in the People's Republic of China, 1949–78: A Profile," *British Journal of Political Science*, Vol. 10, No. 1 (January 1980), pp. 52–53; and Zang Xiaowei, "Provincial Elite in Post-Mao China," *Asian Survey*, Vol. 31, No. 6 (June 1991), p. 516. According to a recent study, Shandong's native ratio ranked ninth for the 1949–94 period and fourth among the coastal

provinces (after Jiangsu, Fujian, and Guangxi). See Zhiyue Bo, "Native Local Leaders and Political Mobility in China: Home Province Advantage?" in *Provincial China*, No. 2 (October 1996), pp. 4–8.

22. The national average is from Goodman, "The Provincial First Party Secretary in the People's Republic of China," p. 59.

23. With the exception of Tan Qilong who was an alternate member, all others were full members. The one Politburo member refers to Jiang Chunyun who joined the prestigeous body in 1992 at the Fourteenth Party Congress. At the Fifteenth Party Congress of September 1997, Shandong's new party boss since April 1997, Wu Guanzheng, also jointed the Politburo as its full member. Wu, a Jiangxi native with no working experience in Shandong, was formerly the provincial party secretary of Jiangxi.

24. Biographical information on Bai is from *Zhongguo gongchandang renming dacidian, 1921–1991* (Who's Who in the Chinese Communist Party, 1921–1991) (Beijing: Zhongguo guoji guangbo chubanshe, 1991), p. 130. Biographical information on Su is from Wolfgang Bartke, *Who's Who in the People's Republic of China*, 3rd ed. (München: K. G. Saur, 1991), Vol. 2, p. 531.

25. Author's interviews in Beijing in 1992 and in Ji'nan in 1992 and 1994. The resister-cum-bandwagoner position of the provincial leadrship under Bai and Su was well manifested in a commentary published in the province's official newspaper, *Dazhong Daily* on December 20, 1981. Such a pattern of implementation was not unique to Shandong, however: in fact, bandwagoning was very popular among the majority of provinces. For an observation of a similar process in Hubei, see Daniel Kelliher, *Peasant Power in China: The Era of Rural Reform 1979–1989* (New Haven: Yale University Press, 1992), p. 65. For a detailed analysis of this process in operation in Shandong, see Chung, *The Politics of Policy Implementation in Post-Mao China*, chapter 4.

26. For the pervasive "leftist" influence in Shandong in the 1980s, see Ferdinand, "Shandong," pp. 155–156. Chinese used to call Shandong "an area severely inflicted by the remnants of leftist ideologies" (*zuoqing yudu zhongzaiqu*). See Research Office of the Shandong Provincial Party Committee, *Shandong sishinian* (Forty Years in Shandong) (Ji'nan: Shandong renmin chubanshe, 1989), p. 140.

27. Biographical information on Liang is from Bartke, *Who's Who in the People's Republic of China*, Vol. 1, p. 333.

28. Biographical information on Li is from Bartke, *Who's Who in the People's Republic of China*, Vol. 1, p. 274.

29. See Jude Howell, *China Opens Its Doors: The Politics of Economic Transition* (London: Lynne Rienner, 1993), pp. 68, 72, 84.

30. There are three different versions of explanation for their bumpy relationship: (1) merely the matter of personal chemistry; (2) a result of factional conflict between natives and non-natives of Shandong; and (3) differences in attitudes toward reforms.

31. Kang Sheng is rumored to have been a Politburo member during his tenure as Shandong's party boss. See Klein and Clark, *Biographic Dictionary of Chinese Communism*, Vol. 1, p. 426.

32. Biographical information on Jiang Chunyun, unless noted otherwise, is from He Pin and Gao Xin, *Zhongguo xinquangui: zuixin lingdaozhe qunxiang* (China's New Power Elite: The New Leadership Group) (Hong Kong: Contemporary Monthly Publishing, 1993), pp. 252–265.

33. According to a source, this was when Jiang's career as a secretary (*mishu*) began, as he was linked to Su Yiran. Interview in Ji'nan in 1995.

34. Relatively little is known about Zhao except for his administrative career. As a Shandong native born in 1931, Zhao worked entirely in Shandong taking various responsibilities that include territorial positions of county (Deng County), prefectural (Zibo), and

provincial government, and party work and functional positions ranging from the customs administration, tax bureau, party schools and so on. He is largely considered to be on good terms with Jiang by actively supporting Jiang's policy positions. For Zhao's administrative career, see *Shandong nianjian 1993*, pp. 659–660 and *Guangjiaojing yuekan*, January 1997, pp. 48–49.

35. See *South China Morning Post*, November 15, 1994 and March 18, 1995.

36. For the alleged ties between Jiang and Chen, see *South China Morning Post*, October 18, 1994.

37. According to this view, supposedly, Shandong is one of the places that the Deng household likes to visit most, and Jiang Chunyun and his associates have been very enthusiastic in making use of their visits to offer generous donations to charity projects run by Deng's children, most notably the China Welfare Fund for the Handicapped. See *South China Morning Post*, January 25, 1995.

38. In China, one colloquial expression is gaining popularity: "Guangdong relies on opening, Fujian depends on Taiwan, Shandong utilizes its hometown networks, and Heilongjiang resorts to Mao Zedong Thought" (*Guangdong kao kaifang, Fujian kao Taiwan, Shandong kao laoxiang guanxi, Heilongjiang kao Mao Zedong sixiang*). For a list of people who are supposedly the members of the "Shandong faction," see *Qianqiao* (The Front-Line), April 1994, p. 91 and Ibid., May 1995, pp. 33–35.

39. Interviews in Ji'nan on June 27 and 28, 1994. For a theoretical exploration of the distinction between so-called selective and encompassing policies, see Chung, "Studies of Central-Provincial Relations in the People's Republic," pp. 504–506.

40. Jiang's success can be deduced from Shandong's pace of growth during the Eighth Five-Year Plan period (1991–95) which closely paralleled his tenure as the province's party boss (refer to Tables 5.1 and 5.2). Shandong officials, too, view the Eighth Five-Year Plan period as the most crucial phase. See "Shandongsheng jingji fazhan de jiben moshi" (A Basic Pattern of Shandong's Economic Development), *Jingji yanjiu cankao* (Reference Materials for Economic Research), No. 892 (June 14, 1996), pp. 24–26.

41. Compared to Shaanxi, Henan and Sichuan which kept 88.1, 75.9 and 72 percent of their industrial commercial taxes, Shandong was indeed contributing significantly more to Beijing. See Audrey Donnithorne, "New Light on Central-Provincial Relations," *Australian Journal of Chinese Affairs*, No. 10 (July 1983), p. 97.

42. Interview in Ji'nan in 1995.

43. For detailed descriptions of these systems, see Song Xinzhong, *Zhongguo caizheng tizhi gaige yanjiu* (Study of China's Fiscal Reform) (Beijing: Zhongguo caizheng jingji chubanshe, 1992), pp. 52–54. For the rationale behind the 1981 change, see Pang Xiuzheng, Lin Shuxiang and Wang Yongchang (eds.), *Shandong jingji yanjiu* (Studies of Shandong's Economy) (Ji'nan: Shandong renmin chubanshe, 1996), Vol. 2, p. 1020.

44. Shanxi, Hunan, Henan and Anhui enjoyed more preferential rates of 97.5, 88, 81 and 80.1 percent, respectively. See *Dangdai Zhongguo caizheng* (Contemporary China's Finance) (Beijing: Zhongguo shehui kexue chubanshe, 1988), Vol. 1, p. 376.

45. Interview in Ji'nan in 1995.

46. Interview in Ji'nan in 1994. Qingdao was still obliged to remit to Shandong 10 percent of its fixed incomes and the rate was later readjusted to 5 percent. See *Shandong jingji yanjiu*, Vol. 2, p. 1024.

47. For a nationwide discussion of these issues, see Jae Ho Chung, "Beijing Confronting the Provinces: The 1994 Tax-Sharing Reform and Its Implications for Central-Provincial Relations," *China Information*, Vol. 9, No. 2/3 (Winter 1994–95), pp. 11–12.

48. In 1983, the levy rose to 15 percent on a nationwide basis. Yet, Shandong seems to have maintained the original rate of 10 percent. For the nationwide change, see *Dangdai Zhongguo caizheng*, Vol. 1, p. 310.

49. Interviews in Ji'nan in 1994 and 1995.

50. Interviews in Ji'nan in 1994 and 1995; and *Shandong jingji yanjiu*, Vol. 2, pp. 1010–11. An interviewee argued that "no province-level units in China, except Shanghai, contributed to Beijing more than Shandong." In 1994, however, for the first time Shandong is alleged to have exceeded Shanghai in the overall amount of its fiscal contribution to the Center.

51. This unanimity may have a lot to do with their expectations with regard to their due share of preferential policies. Or, they might not have wished to reveal to an outsider their views on such sensitive issues.

52. In the post-Mao period, both Guangdong and Shaanxi had no governor who later became the provincial party secretary. In the cases of Fujian and Zhejiang, only one governor each became the provincial party secretary (Jia Qinglin of Fujian and Xue Ju of Zhejiang). In the case of Shanghai, Jiang Zemin, Zhu Rongji and Huang Ju are such cases. With the appointment of Wu Guanzheng from Jiangxi in 1997, this norm was broken.

53. More interesting are the profiles of these seven Shandong provincial officials with central party positions. With the only exception of Yu Zhengsheng (party secretary of Qingdao) who is from Zhejiang, all other six are Shandong natives with extensive work experiences in the province. Even the political commissar of the Ji'nan Military Region and Central Committee member, Song Qingwei, who has served in the province since 1985, is from Shandong. For these profiles, see *Shandong nianjian 1993*, pp. 659–661.

54. Background information is from the "personnel trend" (*renshi dongtai*) section in *Zhonggong yanjiu* (Studies of Chinese Communism), various issues in 1994–95. On Song Ping, see Jae Ho Chung, "Song Ping," in *Dictionary of the Politics of the People's Republic of China*, eds. Colin Mackerras, Donald McMillen and Andrew Watson (London: Routledge, 1998).

55. Information from interviews in Ji'nan. For biographical backgrounds to these three, see *Shandong nianjian 1993*, pp. 660, 667. In fact, Shandong's top leaders in recent years —say, Jiang Chunyun (Laixi), Zhao Zhihao (Longkou) and Li Chunting (Xixia)—all come from the Jiaodong Peninsula region encompassing Qingdao and Yantai. And, among the fifteen members of the fourteenth provincial party committee elected in 1992, eleven were Shandong natives.

56. See *Zhongguo gaige kaifang dacidian* (Dictionary of China's Reform and Opening) (Xiamen: Xiamen daxue chubanshe, 1993), pp. 855, 873. As of 1994, Shandong had eight COCs (with the addition of Weihai, Zibo, Weifang, Rizhao, Ji'nan and Dongying) and three ETDZs (with the addition of Weihai in 1993). A total of 60,000 square kilometers constituted an "open area, covering 40 percent of the province's total area and 38 percent of its population."

57. For the background to the CEC policy, see Paul E. Schroeder, "Territorial Actors as Competitors for Power: The Case of Hubei and Wuhan," in Kenneth G. Lieberthal and David M. Lampton (eds.), *Bureaucracy, Politics and Decision Making in Post-Mao China* (Berkeley: University of California Press, 1992), pp. 286–291; and Dorothy J. Solinger, "The Place of the Central City in China's Economic Reform: From Hierarchy to Network?" in *China's Transition from Socialism: Statist Legacies and Market Reforms 1980–1990* (Armonk: M. E. Sharpe, 1993), p. 212. And for the changes in 1993–94, see Jae Ho Chung, "Central-Provincial Relations," in Lo Chi Kin, Suzanne Pepper, and Tsui Kai-yuen (eds.), *China Review 1995* (Hong Kong: Chinese University Press, 1995), pp. 3.22–24.

58. Interviews in Ji'nan in 1994. For a report on the official designation of Shandong, see *South China Morning Post*, October 25, 1988.

59. For the background and the details of the preferential treatment granted to "bonded zones," see "Zhongguo baoshuiqu de jianli yu fazhan" (The Establishment and Development of Bonded Zones in China), in *Jingji yanjiu cankao*, No. 424 (February 7, 1994), p. 43.

60. For the open ports, see Hui Feng, "Dalu duiwai kaifang kouan diaocha" (Survey of Open Ports on Mainland China), in *Zhonggong yanjiu*, Vol. 27, No. 6 (June 1994), p. 64. Among these nine ports, three (Qingdao, Rizhao, and Longkou) are managed by the Center while the four ports of Yantai, Weihai, Dongying, and Binzhou are subject to provincial management.

61. Interview in Qingdao on December 16, 1994.

62. A Shandong source indicates that the first real regional strategy was conceived in 1988 when the goal of "open the east, develop the west, and combine both" (*dongbu kaifang, xibu kaifa, dongxi jiehe*) was articulated. See Chen Guanglin, "Shandong jingji fazhan de shige wenti—sishinian huigu conghengtan" (Ten Questions of Shandong's Economic Development—A Recollection of the Last Forty Years), in *Dongyue luncong*, No. 5 (1989), p. 6.

63. The following descriptions of the "2–3–6" strategy draw from the author's interviews in Ji'nan in 1994 and 1995. For brief descriptions of this strategy, see Wang Yu'an and Lin Shuxing (eds.), *Shandongsheng jingji kaifa: xianzai yu weilai* (Shandong's Economic Development: Its Present and Future) (Beijing: Jingji guanli chubanshe, 1991), pp. 70–71; and *Shandongsheng jingji he shehui fazhan zhanlue yanjiu* (Study of Shandong's Strategy for Economic and Social Development), eds. Wang Guangxin and Zhu Zhiming (Beijing: Zhongguo chengshi chubanshe, 1996), pp. 110–113.

64. Qingdao and Yantai were opened up in 1984 and another four in 1988 when the State Council designated the Shandong Peninsula as a "coastal economic open area" (*yanhai jingji kaifangqu*). Ji'nan and Dongying joined these six cities in 1990 and 1993, respectively. See the Special Zones Office of the State Council (ed.), *Zhongguo duiwai kaifang diqu touzi huanjing he zhengce* (The Investment Climate and Policies of China's Open Areas) (Kunming: Yunnan renmin chubanshe, 1993), p. 152.

65. Among these three industrial belts, the first has received the highest priority since, as of 1990, localities situated along the Jiaoji Railway produced 63 percent of the province's GVIO. See *Shandongsheng jingji kaifa*, p. 71. And for a description of these three belts," see Ji Yangwen, Gu Yu'an, Dong Wenyan, and Liang Zhencai, "Dui Shandongsheng diqu jingji buju de gousi" (Thoughts on the Regional Economic Arrangement of Shandong) in *Jihua jingji yanjiu* (Studies on the Planned Economy), No. 6 (1993), pp. 57–59. For a policy recommendation that the Yellow River Delta region should develop hi-tech industries centered around Dongying, see Li Youfeng, "Bawo jiyu tuchu zhongdian jiakuai huanghe sanjiaozhou waixiangxing jingji fazhan" (Grab the Opportunities, Highlight the Key Points, and Accelerate the Development of an 'Outward-Oriented Economy' in the Yellow River Delta Region) in *Shandong jingji* (Shandong Economy), No. 3 (1994), pp. 22–23.

66. According to some interviewees, many people in the provincial government argued that six was too many and probably four was enough. Yet, these six regions seem to have been endorsed by the provincial authorities by 1995. See the industrial configurations of these regions in *Shandong jingji yanjiu*, Vol. 1, pp. 272–345.

67. The Jiaodong Peninsula region covers the four municipalities of Qingdao, Yantai, Weihai, and Weifang. This is also the conventional coverage of the "eastern" region of Shandong. The Shandong Peninsula region, on the other hand, includes three additional cities of Zibo, Ji'nan and Rizhao.

68. Since Qingdao's designation as a central economic city, the provincial authorities have tended to give more support to Yantai and Weihai than to Qingdao in regional planning. For instance, the first South Korea–China ferry route was given to Weihai in 1989 despite strong lobbying efforts on the part of Qingdao. In 1993, when Qingdao was finally granted its own ferry route to South Korea, the privilege had to be shared with Yantai. The information on the ferry route was provided by interviews in Ji'nan in 1994.

69. For the perception that equal attention to both light and heavy industries is neces-

sary for a sound management of the provincial economy, see *Shandong jingji yanjiu*, Vol. 1, p. 197.

70. This goal was accomplished in 1992. The figures for 1990–91 in Table 5.9 are rounded and do not reach 30 percent.

71. See *Quanguo zhuyao shehui jingji zhibiao paixu nianjian 1992*, p. 159; and 1993 issue, p. 159.

72. For reports that point out agricultural development as a key to Shandong's success, see "Shandong jingji fazhan kuai de aomi," p. 22, *Qinghai ribao*, April 16, 1993; and "Guangdong: zhenshi xianshi zaizhao youshi", p. 20. Jiang Chunyun's promotion to the center as the vice-premier in charge of agriculture is also related to the positive assessment by Beijing of Shandong's success on the agricultural front.

73. Gao Changli, "Shandong nongcun gaige yu xianyu jingji fazhan" (Shandong's Rural Reform and Its County-Level Economic Development), in *Nongye jingji wenti* (Problems of Agricultural Economy), No. 8 (1991), pp. 14–15; and Zhan Wu, "Shandongsheng nongcun gaige de qishi" (Lessons from Shandong's Rural Reform), in *Nongye jingji wenti*, No. 9 (1991), p. 23. One crucial example concerns the scale and pattern of agricultural production management. For intra-township variations in terms of household, collective, and hybrid management in Shandong, see Li Hua, "Shandongsheng tudi guimo jingying shidian de xianzhuang yu sikao" (The Current Situation and Some Reflections on the Scale of Land Management in Shandong), in *Nongye guimo jingji yanjiu* (Study of Agricultural Management of Scale) (Beijing: Kexue jishu wenxuan chubanshe, 1989), pp. 100–109.

74. See "Jiakuai nongye touzi tizhi gaige tuidong wosheng nongye shang xintaijia" (Accelerate the Reform of the Agricultural Investment System and Push Our Province's Agriculture Further Ahead), in *Shandong jihua jingji* (Shandong's Planned Economy), No. 5 (1988), pp. 19–20. The figures on the budgetary investment are from *Shandong tongji nianjian 1995*, p. 129. In 1993 alone, 209 foreign investment projects were contracted with US$ 147 million in agriculture-related areas. *Shandong tongji nianjian 1994*, p. 413.

75. See Gao Changli, "Shandong nongcun gaige," p. 18; and *Dazhong ribao*, December 25, 1992. The figures are from *Shandong tongji nianjian 1994*, p. 203. Also see Liu Jingyun, "Zhuchengxian de chuanghui nongye shi zenyang fazhan qilaide" (On How Export-Oriented Agriculture Was Developed in Zhucheng County), in *Shandong jihua jingji*, No. 6 (1986), pp. 19–22; and Xu Qingguang, "Shandongsheng xiangzhen qiye shixian dierci daojun tuqi de silu" (The Idea of Creating the Second Eruption in Shandong's Township and Village Enterprises), in *Shandong jingji*, No. 3 (1994), pp. 45–46.

76. Zhan Wu, "Shandongsheng nongcun gaige de qishi," p. 24; and *Dazhong ribao*, December 25, 1992 and February 10, 1993.

77. See Sui Yinghui, "Jiakuai Shandongsheng chanye jiegou tiaozheng" (Accelerate the Structural Adjustment of Shandong's Industry), in *Jingji yanjiu cankao*, No. 697 (June 22, 1995), pp. 42–45.

78. See "Shandong jingji fazhan kuai de aomi," p. 22; and "Guangdong: zhenshi xianshi zaizhao youshi," p. 20. As of 1994, the province's total power production was 675 million kilowatts per hour, almost double that of 1988.

79. Guangdong lags far behind Shandong in this respect. As of 1992, the former's railway freight constituted 71 percent of Shandong's, while the ratio for road freight was a mere 5.5 percent. See "Guangdong: zhenshi xianshi zaizhao youshi," p. 21. For the progress during the 1991–95 period, see *Shandongsheng jingji he shehui fazhan zhanlue yanjiu*, pp. 57, 61.

80. See *Shandong nianjian 1993*, p. 458; and Guang Xinwei and Zhang Haibo,

"Shandongsheng fazhan jiaotong yunshu de jingyan yu qishi" (Shandong's Experiences in Developing Transportation and Their Lessons), in *Jingji yanjiu cankao*, No. 289 (June 11, 1993), pp. 42–43. According to an interviewee, while the "road maintenance fees" were a nationwide policy enacted by Beijing, Shandong's adoption was about one year earlier than Jiangsu and Anhui, and its rates were also higher than most other provinces. In fact, according to him, several provinces sent investigation teams to Shandong to learn from its experiences. Interview in Ji'nan in 1995.

81. Guang and Zhang, "Shandongsheng fazhan jiatong," pp. 42–43; *Shandong nianjian 1993*, p. 457; and interviews in Ji'nan on March 14 and 15, 1995.

82. The relative significance of Beijing-provided preferential policies has become somewhat blurred recently, as local governments have competitively introduced various, often more favorable, policies of their own. Yet, the center-provided preferential treatment still seems to carry more secure and persuasive power for foreign investors. In fact, during 1993, due to Beijing's clampdown, over 90 percent of various development zones approved by provincial and sub-provincial authorities were closed down. See *Zhongguo gaige kaifang shiwunian dashiji 1978–1993* (Chronology of China's Reform and Opening for Fifteen Years) (Beijing: Xinhua chubanshe, 1994), p. 238.

83. See Howell, *China Opens Its Doors*, chapter 1, esp. pp. 56–63.

84. One key example concerns the locational decision in 1984 for the Huangdao Economic and Technological Development Zone (ETDZ) in Qingdao. According to interviewees, the ETDZ could have originally been located in the eastern part of the city with better transportation linkages and infrastructural support, but the provincial and municipal leadership preferred the then controversial ETDZ to be located as far away from the city proper as possible. Consequently, the overall condition of the Huangdao ETDZ proved much poorer than those of Tianjin and Dalian, resulting in only very limited foreign investment. Interview in 1994. Even in 1992, the Huangdao ETDZ's foreign exchange earnings were less than half of those of the Yantai ETDZ. See *Shandong tongji nianjian 1993*, p. 489.

85. The institutional relationship was not completely severed, however, since provincial foreign trade corporations were still required to pay up to 13 percent of export rebates (*zhekou*) to their respective general corporations. For this point, see Chen Lianwen, "Shandongsheng waimao jingying tizhi gaige tansuo" (On the Reform of Shandong's Foreign Trade Management System), in *Dongyue luncong*, No. 6 (1989), p. 19.

86. This section draws from interviews in Ji'nan in 1994.

87. Special Zones Office of the State Council (ed.), *Zhongguo duiwai kaifang zhinan* (Guide to China's Opening to the Outside) (Kunming: Yunnan renmin chubanshe, 1992), p. 164.

88. See *Dazhong ribao*, March 13, 1988. One crucial target of Shandong's "all-directional opening" at this juncture was South Korea, as discussed earlier, in line with the State Council's decision in December 1987 to designate Shandong as the key-point province in dealing with Seoul.

89. *Renmin ribao*, May 14, 1988.

90. *Renmin ribao*, August 12, 1988.

91. Interviews in Ji'nan in 1994. The outsider inducted was Wang Yu'an, who had served as the director of the provincial planning commission before taking charge of the FETC.

92. *Shandong nianjian 1993*, p. 367; and the Shandong Provincial Foreign Economic and Trade Commission, "Shandongsheng gelei kaifaqu fenbu qingkuangbiao" (Regional Distribution of Development Zones), April 20, 1994. These sixty zones were approved and supported by the provincial authorities, but came to enjoy similar privileges to those of the Beijing-designated zones.

93. For the impact of Sino-South Korean normalization, see "Shandong bandao disanci hanshang touziri" (The Third-Time Fever for Korean Investment in Shandong Peninsula) in *Liaowang Weekly* (overseas edition), November 16, 1992, p. 16; and Jae Ho Chung, "The Political Economy of South Korea-China Bilateralism: Origins, Progress, and Prospects," in Ilpyong J. Kim amd Hong Pyo Lee (eds.), *Korea and China in A New World: Beyond Normalization* (Seoul: Sejong Institute, 1993), pp. 276–278.

94. Interviews in Ji'nan in 1995; and *Zhongguo gaige kaifang shiwunian dashiji*, p. 198.

95. The relatively slow growth in 1986–90 is attributed in part to the complex bureaucratic process in which foreign trade authorities were being transferred to the provincial government from MOFERT. Interview in Ji'nan in 1995. Trade figures are from *Shandong tongji nianjian 1996*, p. 471.

96. Du Xiaofen and Gao Jun, "Guanyu wosheng yanhai fazhan zhanlue jingji moshi de yidian tantao" (On the Economic Model of Coastal Development in Shandong), in *Shandong jihua jingji* (Shandong's Planned Economy), No. 3 (1988), pp. 19, 21.

97. Figures are from interviews in Ji'nan in 1997 and Wu Ming, "Guanyu wosheng waimao zhuanye gongsi chukou de xianzhuang yu fenxi" (The Current Situation and Analysis of Shandong's Foreign Trade Corporations), in *Shandong duiwai jingmao* (Shandong's Foreign Economic Relations and Trade), No. 1/2 (1995), pp. 16, 19.

98. See *Zhongguo tongji nianjian 1996*, p. 581; and *Shandong tongji nianjian 1996*, p. 472.

99. Shandong did not have any trade with South Korea in 1987 (until then, provincial foreign trade corporations were not allowed to engage in foreign trade independently of MOFERT). The volume of Shandong's trade with South Korea for the period of 1988–1994 was US$ 50 (no imports), US$ 110 (no imports), US$ 233, US$ 405, US$ 620, US$ 930 and US$ 1,479 million, accounting for 1.3, 2.7, 5.6, 8.7, 10.5, 12.3, and 13.8 percent of Shandong's total. Interviews in Ji'nan in 1994 and 1995. For an explicit emphasis on expanding economic contact with South Korea by Li Chunting (then vice-governor in charge of foreign economic relations) even before diplomatic normalization, see *Tuanjie bao* (Consolidation Daily), February 17, 1992.

100. For 1979, see *Dangdai Zhongguo de Shandong* (Contemporary China's Shandong) (Beijing: Zhongguo shehui kexue chubanshe, 1989), Vol. 2, p. 34. For the 1995 figures and the accumulated total, see *Shandong tongji nianjian 1996*, p. 476.

101. *Shandong tongji nianjian 1996*, p. 476.

102. For some reason, the share of processing and assembling has risen sharply to 19.9 percent in 1994. It may well be that foreign manufacturers wished to minimize their risk when Beijing was contemplating various measures to tighten its control over the flow of foreign capital since late 1993.

103. For various problems related to joint-equity ventures, see Jonathan R. Woetzel, *China's Economic Opening to the Outside World: The Politics of Empowerment* (New York: Praeger, 1989), pp. 114–123. Compared with the nationwide trend in which the respective share of joint ventures, cooperative verntures and foreign wholly-owned ventures was 64.9, 16.0 and 9.0 percent, respectively, for 1979–93, Shandong was moving relatively fast toward accepting FWOs. For the national figures, see "Woguo liyong waishang zhijie touzi de jiben fazhan taishi fenxi" (An Analysis of the Basic Trends in China's Utilization of Foreign Direct Investment), in *Jingji yanjiu cankao*, No. 556/557 (October 12, 1994), p. 4.

104. See *Shandong tongji nianjian 1993*, p. 483; and 1996 issue, p. 480.

105. Information on Shandong's priority policies on cultivating rural-foreign linkages is from the author's interview in Ji'nan in 1994. As of 1993, 193 South Korea–invested

enterprises were located in the suburban and rural districts of Qingdao, constituting 75 percent of all South Korea–invested firms in Qingdao. The percentage was calculated from "Hanguo zaiqing touzi qiye yilanbiao" (A List of South Korea–Invested Firms in Qingdao) compiled by the Qingdao Sub-Council of the China Council for the Promotion of International Trade in April 1994.

106. For a detailed analysis of intra-provincial disparities in Shandong and the province's efforts to mitigate them, see Jae Ho Chung, "The Political Economy of Development and Inequality in Shandong" in David S. G. Goodman (ed.), *China's Provinces in Reform: Class, Community, and Political Culture* (London: Routledge, 1997), pp. 138–147.

107. See Zhao Haicheng, "Lun Shandong jingji kaifangqu yu dongya diqu de jingji hezuo" (On Shandong's Economic Open Areas and Their Economic Cooperation with the East Asian Region), in *Tequ yu Gangao jingji* (Special Zones and Economies in Hong Kong and Macau), No. 2 (1991), p. 52; "Shandong bandao disanci hanshang touziri," p. 16; *Tuanjie bao* (Consolidation News), February 17, 1992; and *Shandong tongji nianjian 1996*, p. 479. According to the January–September 1996 data, South Korea became the largest investor for the first time.

108. See, for instance, Shi Liyuan, "Shandong liyong waizi he waizhai guanli de zhuyao wenti ji yingcaiqu de cuoshi" (Problems in Shandong's Utilization and Management of Foreign Funds and Loans, and Measures to Resolve Them) in *Shandong jingji* (Shandong's Economy), No. 3 (1990), p. 49.

109. The comparable figures for Tianjin were 59 and 1.6 percent; 24 and 8.4 percent for Liaoning; 45 and 0.6 percent for Shanghai; and 22 and 23 percent for Guangdong. See *Zhongguo tongji nianjian 1994*, p. 530.

110. Given that increasingly loans from international organizations will go to the inland regions, Shandong's reliance on foreign government loans may continue to increase.

111. Interview in Ji'nan in 1995.

112. See *Zhongguo duiwai kaifang diqu touzi huanjing he zhengce*, pp. 142, 152–153.

113. For a list, see *Shandong tongji nianjian 1995*, p. 479.

114. Interview in Ji'nan in 1997.

115. For an earlier list of these firms, see Wang and Lin, *Shandongsheng jingji kaifa*, pp. 597–598.

116. In 1988 only 60 firms had such authority. See Chen, "Shandongsheng waimao jingying tizhi gaige tansuo," p. 15. For the 1993 figure, see Wu Ming, "Guanyu wosheng waimao zhuanye gongsi," p. 19. For a detailed analysis of Shandong's overseas investment, see *Shandong jingji yanjiu*, Vol. 2, pp. 732–740.

117. The information on Shandong Air Line is from an interview in Ji'nan in 1995.

118. Author's interview in Ji'nan in 1995.

119. The strategy of "pairing" is becoming increasingly popular. According to interviewees in Ji'nan, Zhu Rongji adopted it for nationwide implementation, and Shandong was paired with Qinghai. See *Qinghai ribao*, April 16, 1993. For the nationwide practice, see Chung, "Central-Provincial Relations," p. 3.30. Information on Shandong is from author's interviews in Ji'nan in 1995.

120. For a detailed analysis on Shandong's efforts to help the inland region, see Chung, "The Political Economy of Development and Inequality in Shandong," pp. 143–147. Also see Joint Investigation Team, "Wosheng yituo jingjiu fazhan Luxi waixiangxing jingji de zhanlue xuanze" (Strategic Choices for Developing the Outward-Oriented Economy in the Western Region of Shandong), in *Shandong duiwai jingmao* (Shandong's Foreign Economic Relations and Trade), No. 8 (1996), pp. 4–10.

121. More often than not, there are crucial backgrounds to the provision of preferential policies for some provinces but not for others. In the case of Shandong, its heavy fiscal contribution and consistent compliance with Beijing seemed to have made the province obtain a variety of preferential policies in foreign economic relations. The granting of exclusive privileges to Guangdong in the earlier period of reform was related to Beijing's concern with the sensitivity of "opening" (i.e., Guangdong was sufficiently far away from Beijing) and Guangdong's mediocre status in the national economy (i.e., the failure of the experiment would not seriously affect the country as a whole), as well as the province's geographical proximity to Hong Kong and Macau. See Samuel P. S. Ho and Ralph W. Huenemann, *China's Open Door Policy* (Vancouver: University of British Columbia Press, 1984), p. 51. For the centrality of Beijing's preferential policies in Guangdong's economic development, see David S. G. Goodman and Feng Chongyi, "Guangdong: Greater Hong Kong and the New Regionalist Future," in *China Deconstructs*, pp. 185–186; and Peter T. Y. Cheung, "Relations between the Central Government and Guangdong," in Y. M. Yeung and David K. Y. Chu (eds.), *Guangdong: Survey of A Province Undergoing Rapid Change* (Hong Kong: Chinese University Press, 1994), pp. 33–34.

122. See János Kornai, *Highway and Byways: Studies on Reform and Post-communist Transition* (Cambridge: MIT Press, 1995), p. 212.

123. See, for instance, Anis Chowdhury and Iyanatul Islam, *The Newly Industrialising Economies of East Asia* (London: Routledge, 1993), chs. 2, 7, 11.

124. Interviews in Heilongjiang and Yunnan revealed that provincial officials of these provinces held the belief that, despite the burgeoning cross-border trade, their economic progress was kept largely stagnant due mainly to the absence of economically dynamic neighbors who are willing to commit large amounts of development capital and provide advanced management know-how and technologies. Author's interviews in Harbin and Kunming in July 10–15 and August 13–17,1994.

125. For this observation, I am indebted to Andrew G. Walder, "China's Transitional Economy: Interpreting Its Significance," *China Quarterly*, No. 144 (December 1995), p. 971.

126. See Stephan Haggard, *Pathways from the Periphery: The Politics of Growth in the Newly Industrializing Countries* (Ithaca: Cornell University Press, 1990), pp. 15–21.

127. For many inland provinces, therefore, the sequence of development may differ from that for coastal provinces, since they first have to devise various innovative preferential policies of their own to attract foreign businesses. Then, Beijing's postfacto endorsement may come to legitimize the already popular practices. Yet, considering the current atmosphere of "recentralization" since late 1993, as well as the recent clampdown on locally initiated development zones, too much "pioneering" without prior approval from Beijing may be a move with high risk. How the "aid the west" program stipulated in the Ninth Five-Year Plan will be implemented, and with what results, remains to be seen.

6

Provincial Leadership and the Implementation of Foreign Economic Reforms in Fujian Province

Shawn Shieh

The reform era has been one of tremendous opportunities for provincial leaders in Fujian. Together with Guangdong, Fujian has been at the forefront of the reforms in the foreign economic sector from the very outset. Integral to this arrangement was a set of "special policies" that enlarged the province's economic decision-making autonomy, and provided it with greater flexibility in foreign trade and investment matters. For provincial leaders, the "special policies" presented an unprecedented opportunity to bring the province out of thirty years of relative obscurity and poverty, and give full play to its traditional strengths in the foreign economic field. The results over the last fifteen years have been impressive. On the eve of the reforms, Fujian was one of China's poorest provinces, cut off economically from both the rest of the country and the outside world. By the early 1990s, it had vaulted into the front ranks among provincial-level units in a number of economic indicators, ranking twelfth in gross value of industrial output (GVIO), sixth in exports, third in foreign investment, and seventh in per capita income of urban residents (see Table 6.1). The provincial leadership has benefited as well, commanding more resources and prestige than it ever did in the past. The provincial government controls numerous investment and trading companies and offices, while provincial Party secretaries and governors regularly lead business groups to far-off destinations in the U.S., Europe and Japan, and are the subject of numerous interviews and reports in the foreign press.

The other side to this increase in autonomy and status for provincial leaders has been the addition of new responsibilities and demands. Fujian, of course, is by no means unique in this respect. As other scholars of provincial and local politics in China have detailed, the reforms have involved a devolution not only

Table 6.1

Fujian's National Ranking and Percentage of National Totals for Key Socioeconomic Indicators

	Ranking (1978)	Percentage (1978)	Ranking (1993)	Percentage (1993)
Population	18	2.75	18	2.66
GDP	22	1.85	13	3.28
GVIO	22	1.50	12	2.94
GVAO	18	2.40	12	3.59
Exports	12	0.98	6	6.35
Foreign investment	n/a	2.40(1983)	3	7.46

Sources: Zhang Ruiyao and Ni Shidao (eds.), *Fujian jingji gailun* (An Introduction to Fujian's Economy) (Fuzhou: Fujian sheng jiwei jingji yanjiusuo, n.d.), pp. 30–32; *Zhongguo tongji nianjian 1994* (China Statistical Yearbook 1994); *Fujian jingji nianjian 1994* (Fujian Economic Yearbook 1994); Hsueh Tien-tung et al. (eds.), *China's Provincial Statistics, 1949–1989* (Boulder, CO: Westview Press, 1993).

of authority but also of responsibilities to provincial and local officials.[1] Provincial officials are now asked to make more decisions on a wider range of affairs than ever before: fiscal expenditures; economic development strategies; foreign investment; social welfare; and reform experiments. Their job is further complicated by the fact that authority, resources, and responsibilities are rarely delegated to them in a consistent manner. Sounding much like governors and mayors in the U.S. railing against unfunded mandates from the federal government, provincial and local authorities frequently complain that the powers and resources they are given are often not enough to carry out the tasks they have been assigned by central authorities. At the same time, provincial leaders must contend with an ever-growing number of emerging institutional interests that were either quiescent or nonexistent before the reforms. These include subprovincial authorities and agencies, enterprise managers, local People's Congress representatives, and a new stratum of foreign and quasi-private entrepreneurs, all of whom have become increasingly vocal in defending their local or institutional turf over the reform period.[2]

This chapter examines the ability of the provincial leadership in Fujian to make the most of the opportunities presented them in the context of rising demands and pressures coming from above, below, and outside of the party-state hierarchy. It presents first an overview of certain features of the province's economy, society and politics that act as one set of constraints on provincial leaders. Secondly, it examines the provincial leaders themselves, their education, careers, alliances with central leaders and leadership style. The third section then look at the strategies that provincial leaders adopted to carry out the reforms, while the fourth focuses in particular on provincial efforts in acquiring foreign capital.

Economy, Society and Politics in Fujian:
The Historical Legacy

One set of parameters that shapes the choices available to provincial leaders lies in historical or internal features that are distinctive to that province. For those leaders who came to Fujian during the reform period, three such features stood out: the province's traditional dependence on the outside world; its relative isolation and backwardness during the Maoist period; and complex social and political cleavages within the province.

Historically, and for obvious geographical reasons, Fujian's economy has been intimately linked with the outside world. With mountain ranges cutting the province off from much of the rest of the country, little arable land, and a long, winding coast line second only to Guangdong's in length, the province has looked outward for much of its livelihood. Fujian's coastal cities have historically been major centers of trade and commerce.[3] The southern city of Quanzhou was one of the first seaports in China to open to foreign trade, and a major conduit for silk, sugar and tea during the Tang and Song dynasties. As the Quanzhou port gradually silted up during the Ming, its position as the province's major port was usurped by Fuzhou and Xiamen. Both of these port cities developed substantial trade links with Taiwan and Southeast Asia from the sixteenth to the eighteenth centuries. During the seventeenth and eighteenth centuries, trade activities suffered a setback in the province as a result of Qing efforts to restrict trade off the Fujian coast. However, by the mid-nineteenth century, Fuzhou and Xiamen had recovered some of their earlier prominence as trading centers when they were designated as two of China's five treaty ports.

The province's link to the outside is also reflected in its substantial overseas Chinese population. Fujian claims some seven million overseas Chinese who are of Fujian ancestry, a figure that represents a third of the Chinese living abroad, and is second nationally only to overseas Chinese of Guangdong ancestry.[4] Many of these overseas Chinese began migrating to Taiwan and Southeast Asia in the eighteenth century as a result of rising population pressures and chronic grain deficits in the province. While the migration stopped after 1949, the overseas population continued to make substantial contributions to the provincial economy. From 1950 to 1965, overseas Chinese from Indonesia, Hong Kong, Singapore, and the Philippines invested nearly 80 million yuan in the provincial economy. Among the beneficiaries of this investment were some of the province's major light industrial and chemical enterprises.[5] In 1978 alone, overseas Chinese remittances to relatives in the province totaled more than US$ 100 million, accounting for almost all of the province's nontrade-related foreign exchange.[6]

If the province's fortunes have hinged on its connections with the outside world, its decline into relative obscurity and backwardness during the Maoist period was the result of a severing of these connections. Several developments were responsible for this trend: rising tensions across the Taiwan Straits during the late 1950s; China's estrangement from the West; and the autaurkic development strategy that Mao promoted after 1958. All of these developments effectively undercut prospects for reviving industry and trade in the province. Being on the front line of the Taiwan Straits conflict, Fujian was accorded low priority for central investment for much of the Maoist period. From 1949 to 1978, Fujian received a paltry 1.5 percent of the country's total capital investment, fourth lowest among the provinces. During the same period, it failed to get a single major investment project from the center.[7]

This combination of central neglect and international isolation during the Maoist period only added to Fujian's plight as one of the country's more impoverished and backward provinces. In 1949, the province was already the poorest of the coastal provinces, with little industrial base to speak of. From 1957 to 1975, Fujian's contribution to the national income actually declined from 1.56 percent to 1.26 percent.[8] Despite modest improvements to the province's industrial and infrastructural base after 1949, progress in these areas generally lagged behind developments in the rest of the country. On the eve of the reforms, Fujian was still the poorest and least industrialized province along the coast, ranking twenty-second out of twenty-nine provincial-level units in GVIO (see Table 6.1).[9] It was also one of the more inaccessible. In 1978, it had no international airport, and its major ports and railroad system were inadequate for moving large volumes of freight and passengers, both within and outside of the province. While the railway system linked the major coastal cities of Fuzhou and Xiamen with the interior, it did not connect the two cities themselves, nor did it link them directly with major economic centers along the coast such as Guangzhou and Shanghai. As one provincial leader lamented, " . . . if people wanted to go to Xiamen [from outside the country], they had to go first to Guangzhou and then endure the fatigue of a long journey by car. Another 'shortcut' was to go from Shenzhen to Guangzhou by train, then go to Fuzhou by plane, and then travel to Xiamen by car."[10]

The third distinctive feature of the province lies in the complex divisions that characterize its society and politics. Fujian's population mirrors the homogeneity found in many of China's other provinces. Nearly 99 percent of the province's 30 million people are Han Chinese. Yet behind that homogeneity are numerous ethnic, linguistic, and regional divisions. Ethnically, Fujian is home to a variety of minorities who number around 467,000 according to the 1990 census.[11] Moreover, the province's Han Chinese population is itself divided by distinct linguistic and regional features. There are, for example, marked regional and cultural differences between the wealthy and outward-looking coastal population, and the poorer, inward-looking population in the mountainous inland areas, and between the northern Fujianese (*minbei*) and southern Fujianese (*minnan*). The latter two groups, in particular, have historically viewed the other as cultural, economic and political rivals.

Fujian's legacy of an internally divided society, together with its relative political and economic isolation from the rest of the country, have translated into politics in very complex ways. Localism is certainly an undeniable part of the province's political tradition, although it would be difficult to argue that it translates in any way into a desire for separatism. Like other provinces with a distinct language and culture, tensions between "natives" and "outsiders" have played a part in provincial politics. Provincial origin, or at least extensive association with the province, was an important consideration in the make-up of the new provincial leadership which emerged after 1949. As Victor Falkenheim shows, the top leadership posts in the Party and government hierarchy were fairly evenly distributed among local cadres who saw guerrilla action in Fujian and cadres who came with the southbound workteams and military forces, although the latter dominated the highest posts. Eight of the nineteen in these leadership posts were Fujianese, including the top three cadres, Zhang Dingcheng, Ye Fei and Fang Yi.[12]

Intraelite factionalism in Fujian, however, was more complicated than the division between "natives" and "outsiders" would indicate. According to Falkenheim, Kuomintang sources described Fujian politics during the 1950s as being dominated by two factions: the "local" faction, meaning the old revolutionary cadres engaged either in the underground movement or in guerrilla action in Fujian; and the "newcomer" faction, represented by those who had arrived with the southbound workteams.[13] This distinction between the "local" and "newcomer" factions, however, appears to have rested more on differences in organizational experience than on differences in provincial origin. Both Ye Fei and Fang Yi, for instance, were Fujianese, yet they came to the province as part of the southbound contingent. Moreover, Ye Fei, who served as first party secretary in the province from 1955 to 1967, went to some effort to distinguish himself from the local cadres. In a speech given to the provincial People's Congress in December of 1957, he explicitly criticized the "anti-southbound cadre sentiment" of local cadres. He also played a leading role in purging members of the "local faction" for "localism" during the rectification campaign carried out that same year.[14]

The Cultural Revolution introduced into the province other organizational, ideological and regional cleavages that cut across the divisions between locals and outsiders. One analysis describes the period from 1967 to 1973 as one of "virtually open warfare between the forces of Ye [Fei], who fell early in the Cultural Revolution, and the forces of the regional military commander Han Xianchu," and the 1974–1977 period as a "multi-sided struggle between military factions, outsiders and localists, leftists and rightists, and northern and southern Fujianese."[15]

With the onset of reform in the late 1970s, Fujian's distinctive legacy presented provincial leaders with a mix of opportunities and challenges. On one hand, with the Party's decision to liberalize ties with the international economy and pursue peaceful reunification with Taiwan, provincial conditions that were previously a hindrance suddenly worked to the province's advantage. The clearest instance of this turn of events came when the center extended a set of "special policies and flexible measures" to Fujian and Guangdong in July of 1979. Both provinces were singled out for special treatment, in large part, because of their traditional involvement in foreign economic activities, their proximity to Hong Kong, Macao and Taiwan, and their large overseas Chinese populations.[16] Even Fujian's relative isolation and backwardness appear to have strengthened its case for getting favorable treatment. As Ezra Vogel points out, central leaders felt more inclined to allow experiments in these provinces because both provinces were far away from Beijing, and did not constitute important centers of industry or sources of revenue.[17] Any political or economic fallout that resulted from opening up to the outside world would thus be limited. On the other hand, many of these same features also complicated the job of provincial leaders over the long term. Caution and inexperience arising from years of isolation, an underdeveloped industrial and infrastructural base, and long-standing divisions among local cadres were all obstacles that even the most reform-minded leaders would struggle to overcome in their efforts to further the reform process in the province.

Provincial Leadership in Fujian, 1979–1993

The evolution of provincial leadership in Fujian can be divided into three distinct phases, each corresponding with the tenure of the three first party secretaries that led the province from 1979 to the end of 1993: Liao Zhigao; Xiang Nan; and Chen Guangyi (see Table 6.2). Each of these men assumed the predominant leadership role during his time in office, while governors, deputy secretaries and vice-governors played important supporting roles. Of these three, Liao was by far the least successful and possessed all the hallmarks of a laggard. During his time in office, the pace of reform in the province was slow and attracted sharp criticism from central authorities. The next first secretary, Xiang Nan, was a strong supporter of reform and the person most responsible for getting the reforms moving in the province. Yet despite his obvious pro-reform sentiments, Xiang's role best fit that of a bandwagoner. Conditions in the province upon his arrival made it difficult for him to be pioneering, even if he had wanted to be so. The early part of his tenure was occupied largely with preparatory work such as resolving divisions within the provincial elite, unifying them around the reform cause, and building a foundation for the province's opening to the outside. Xiang Nan's replacement, Chen Guangyi, served the longest of the three during this period. Like Xiang, his role belongs in the bandwagoning category. Unlike Xiang, however, Chen and the two governors who served with him tended to be identified with a more cautious approach to reform.

Provincial Leaders, 1979–1981

During the early reform years, Fujian's leadership was dominated by men who were from outside the province and had risen to top posts in the province during

Table 6.2

Fujian's Provincial Leaders, 1949–1996

First Party Secretary	Governor
Zhang Dingcheng (1949.6–1955.4)	Zhang Dingcheng (1949.8–1954.10)
Ye Fei (1955.4–1967.??)	Ye Fei (1954.10–1959.1)
Han Xianchu (1971.4–1974.11)	Jiang Yizhen (1959.2–1962.12)
Liao Zhigao (1974.11–1982.2)	Wei Jinshui (1962.12–1967.??)
Xiang Nan (1982.2–1986.3)	Han Xianchu (1968.8–1973.12)
Chen Guangyi (1986.3–1993.12)	Liao Zhigao (1974.11–1979.12)
Jia Qinglin (1993.12–1996.10)	Ma Xingyuan (1979.12–1983.1)
Chen Mingyi (1996.10–)	Hu Ping (1983.1–1987.9)
	Wang Zhaoguo (1987.9–1991.4)
	Jia Qinglin (1991.4–1994.4)
	Chen Mingyi (1994.4-1996.10)

Source: Ma Qibin et al. (eds.), *Zhongguo gongchandang zhizheng sishinian* (Forty Years of the Chinese Communist Party in Power) (Beijing: Zhonggong dangshi chubanshe, 1989), p. 575; *Who's Who in China: Current Leaders*, 1994 ed. (Beijing: Foreign Languages Press, 1994); Su Xi, "Jia Qinglin tiao Jing, Chen Mingyi zhu Min," *Guangjiaojing* (Wide Angle, Hong Kong) November 1996, pp. 34–35.

the Cultural Revolution decade. Foremost among these were Liao Zhigao, who served as chairman of the provincial Revolutionary Committee from 1970 to 1975 and first party secretary from 1975 to 1981, and Ma Xingyuan, who was vice-chairman of the Revolutionary Committee from 1978 to 1979 and governor from 1979 to 1983.

Liao was born in 1908 in Xikang, a region in the western part of Sichuan, and a separate province until 1955 when it was incorporated into Sichuan. As a member of the Long March generation, Liao was already in his late sixties when he became the first party secretary of Fujian.[18] In his early years, he attended Qinghua University in Beijing, worked for a while as a teacher in Tibet before joining the Red Army in the mid-1930s, and later studied at the Central Party School in Yanan. Liao spent much of his pre-Fujian career in high-level positions in the southwest. In his home province of Xikang, he served as the political commissar of the Xikang Military Region, secretary of the provincial Party Committee, and governor from 1950 to 1955. With the incorporation of Xikang into Sichuan, he was made a secretary in the Sichuan Party Committee in 1956, and promoted to first party secretary in 1965. During the Cultural Revolution, he was purged early on and did not make a reappearance until 1973 when he was an alternate member to the 10th Central Committee.[19] In the mid-1970s, Liao was transferred to Fujian where, in November of 1974, he replaced Han Xianchu as first party secretary and chairman of the provincial Revolutionary Committee. Two years later, he was elected to a seat on the Central Committee.

Liao's counterpart in the government hierarchy, Ma Xingyuan, also came from outside the province. Unlike Liao, however, Ma spent most of his career in Fujian. He was a deputy director of the provincial Rural Work Department as far back as 1959. In 1975, he was promoted to secretary of the provincial party committee, and in December of 1979 became provincial governor. As governor, he was also a member of the Eleventh and Twelfth Central Committees. Ma was actively involved in the implementation of the "special policies" given Fujian and Guangdong. Judging from various documents and meetings concerning the "special policies," he was the main liaison between the province and central authorities during the 1979–81 period. Xiang Nan, Fujian's new first party secretary, took over that role after 1981, although Ma continued to accompany him as late as 1984, more than a year after he had stepped down as governor.[20]

Little is known about the prereform careers of Liao and Ma in Fujian. What is clear is that neither Liao nor Ma implemented reform policies to the satisfaction of the central leadership, or were they successful in managing the factional divisions that continued to plague the provincial elite. By early 1981, amid reports criticizing the slow pace of the reforms in the province, Liao was already ceding his leadership role to his replacement, Xiang Nan.[21] Liao formally stepped down from his position in February of 1982. Ma stayed on for another year as governor, and did not resign until early 1983 when he was replaced by Hu Ping.

Liao, in particular, distinguished himself by his lack of enthusiasm for reform. As one former high-ranking provincial official described him, "Liao was a conservative, but not a leftist (*zuopai*). His biggest fault was being overly cautious in implementing Deng's reforms."[22] This assessment is consistent with reports that were critical of the provincial leadership's handling of reform policies during the 1979–80 period.[23] In one instance, Liao was criticized for not implementing the production responsibility system in agriculture.[24] He, along with the rest of the provincial leadership, also came under fire for not moving more quickly in implementing the "special policies and flexible measures," and particularly in constructing the Xiamen Special Economic Zone. Finally, Liao did little to heal the deep divisions among the provincial elite, and mobilize them around the cause of reform. Long-simmering feuds between "local" and "outsider" cadres, and thousands of unresolved cases of cadres who had been criticized and struggled against during the Cultural Revolution, had a paralyzing effect on cadres in the province. Many, afraid of being labeled "capitalists," were content to adopt a wait-and-see attitude toward the reforms and the province's newly acquired "special policies."

Provincial Leadership, 1982–1986

Liao's replacement as first party secretary, Xiang Nan, offered Fujian a very different leader, one who was closely connected with central reformers, and outspoken in his support of the reform effort. Xiang also had other virtues that Liao lacked for the position. He was a Fujian native from Liancheng county in the west of the province, and he had some experience with the outside world, having spent part of his youth overseas in Southeast Asia.[25]

Born in 1916, Xiang was already at the ripe age of sixty-six by the time he was promoted to the post of first secretary in February of 1982. While a native Fujianese, he had spent nearly twenty-five years of his career in Beijing, working first in the Youth League and later in various ministries. Xiang's career included experience both in ideological work, and in economic work, primarily in the area of agricultural mechanization. He was director of the Propaganda Department of the Youth League from 1955 to 1957. From 1957 to 1964, he served in the Youth League's Central Committee and Secretariat. In 1957, he spoke in defense of the Hundred Flowers Movement, an act which reportedly drew criticism during the anti-rightist movement later that year. During the Cultural Revolution, he dropped out of public view although there is no evidence that he was criticized. He is said to have spent much of this period at a May Seventh school in Heilongjiang driving a tractor. After the Cultural Revolution, Xiang made his first public appearance in 1977 as a vice-minister in the First Ministry of Machine-Building. In 1979, he was transferred to a vice-ministerial post in the Ministry of Agricultural Machinery where he stayed until his transfer to Fujian in 1981. Shortly after his appointment as the province's first secretary, Xiang was elected to the Central Committee.

Xiang Nan was a fervent supporter of the reforms. Ruan Ming, a former theoretician in the Central Party School and confidant of Xiang, calls him "the most thorough reformer among all provincial first Party secretaries."[26] Xiang was also widely regarded by a number of officials and scholars whom I interviewed as Fujian's most popular and effective leader during the reform period. From all accounts, he was active both in familiarizing himself with the situation at the grass-roots level, and in meeting with journalists from Hong Kong and Macao to publicize Fujian's opening to the outside world. He is often portrayed as having a down-to-earth style, and his many speeches, articles, and interviews reflected that homespun quality.[27] They are often to-the-point and detailed, even when addressing problems within the province, and largely free of the stilted, formulaic language that characterizes the speeches of many other leaders.

Among central leaders, Xiang enjoyed the close support, and friendship, of two in particular: Deng Xiaoping and Hu Yaobang. During his many years at the Center, he came to know both of these men well. According to Ruan Ming, Deng had known Xiang for many years. Their relationship was close enough, in fact, that when Deng came to visit Fujian in early 1984, Xiang showed little compunction in proposing to the preeminent leader the astonishing idea of allowing Taiwan to develop Fujian with Chiang Chingkuo in charge, and the Dalai Lama to run Tibet. Xiang's rationale, according to Ruan, was that "[s]uch a policy would eliminate any temptation for Taiwanese and Tibetan independence by the indigenous populations and would be beneficial both to the process of reunification and to further development."[28] Xiang's other high-level patron, Hu Yaobang, had worked with Xiang in the Youth League during the 1950s and 1960s. In Ruan Ming's account, Hu had nominated Xiang to replace Hua Guofeng as president of the Central Party School in the summer of 1981. Hu backed off, however, when he was opposed by Chen Yun and Deng Liqun, both of whom supported Wang Zhen, and decided instead to keep Xiang in Fujian.[29]

Hu Ping, who served as governor from 1983 to 1987, provided a nice complement to Xiang's age and experience at the central level. At fifty-three years of age, he was part of a younger generation of cadres that was entering leadership positions in Fujian, and other parts of the country, during this period. He also had the advantage of being a veteran Fujian cadre who had moved up through the provincial hierarchy. Born in Zhejiang, he spent most of his career in Fujian where he concentrated on industry and planning work.[30] During the 1950s and 1960s, he held minor positions in the Party Committee of Xiamen city, and the Fujian provincial government. He then went on to work in various posts in the Fujian Planning Commission before becoming the director of the commission in 1981. He was promoted to vice-governor in the same year, became a secretary of the provincial party committee in September of 1982, and then rose to the governorship in 1983. After stepping down as governor in September 1987, he was transferred to Beijing where he served briefly as a vice-director of the State Economic Commission, and then as minister of commerce. He served as a full member of the Central Committee during his tenure as governor and minister of commerce.

Under the direction of Xiang and Hu, the provincial leadership moved quickly in the early 1980s to address a number of pressing problems left unresolved by Liao Zhigao and Ma Xingyuan. Foremost among these was the factionalism, and lack of reform initiative, among the provincial elite. During Xiang's first two years in Fujian (1981–82), provincial leaders focused their efforts on restoring the prestige of the local underground Party organization, and some of its leading cadres who were purged in the late 1950s; settling thousands of cases left over from the Cultural Revolution; and bringing a corps of younger, more educated cadres into leadership positions. They also worked to speed up the implementation of the production responsibility system and the "special policies" in the province.[31] These efforts bore fruit in the mid-1980s when the reforms reached new heights in the province. In 1984, central authorities approved the expansion of the Xiamen SEZ to the entire city, and designated Fuzhou an open city. In 1985, the province's "special policies" were reaffirmed and extended, and selected cities and counties in the southern Fujian triangle were designated as open areas enjoying preferential policies for attracting foreign investment. In addition, the 1984–1985 period saw the provincial economy grow at rates that outstripped the national averages.

The resolve and speed with which Xiang moved on these tasks clearly indicate an able, reform-minded leader. During periods of central retrenchment, and campaigns against economic crime and smuggling, Xiang continued to be a vigorous supporter of reforms in the province. While careful to acknowledge the criticisms of conservative leaders, he made it clear that these criticisms were not to be used as an excuse to stifle the reform effort or to slow down on opening to the outside. Once, when asked by a Hong Kong reporter about the prevalence of smuggling and corruption in the province, Xiang was quick to point out that these problems had always existed, and that they should not be used as a reason to reverse China's opening to the outside.[32]

Yet if Xiang was a committed reformer, he was also more likely to play the role of a bandwagoner than that of a pioneer, especially when compared with his counterparts in Guangdong. This may have reflected Xiang's own inclinations. But it also is an indication of certain constraints on Xiang that were not present to the same degree for Guangdong leaders. One is that he lacked the stature, and powerful personal and organizational support at the center enjoyed by Guangdong leaders such as Xi Zhongxun, Yang Shangkun, Ren Zhongyi, and Ye Xuanping. While Xiang had the ear of Hu Yaobang and Deng Xiaoping, his career path suggests that his main support was among intellectuals, rather than senior Party and military leaders. This interpretation is supported by the circumstances surrounding Xiang's resignation as first secretary. According to sources who were close to Xiang, Chen Yun and other conservatives took advantage of two highly publicized cases in 1985—the "Quanzhou Fake Medicine Scandal" in Fujian and the "Hainan Car Scandal"—to oust Xiang and Ren Zhongyi from their posts. Significantly, only Xiang emerged from the affair with an "inner-Party administrative warning" (*dangnei jinggao chufen*).

Secondly, Xiang was simply burdened with too many problems to take a pioneering stance. He had to deal not only with personnel problems, but also with limitations related to the province's poor industrial and infrastructural base, and the preliminary nature of economic ties between Taiwan and the mainland. In contrast, Ren Zhongyi, who was first secretary at the same time as Xiang Nan, had the luxury of plentiful Hong Kong capital and expertise, a more developed infrastructure, and subordinates who were more unified and reform-minded. Ren also had the benefit of succeeding Xi Zhongxun and Yang Shangkun who did much of the preparatory work in terms of rehabilitating cadres, furthering rural reforms, establishing the special economic zones and gaining the cooperation of local military forces.[33] In Fujian, Liao Zhigao's recalcitrance in carrying out reform policies only complicated Xiang's job. As Xiang himself admitted in an interview early in 1983, three full years after Fujian had been given the "special policies":

> strictly speaking, Fujian has just made a first step in opening to the outside. Up to now, our main efforts have not been truly concentrated on this. We are still

focusing our efforts on a series of problems left over from the past. . . . All these problems have to be solved. From now on, that is to say, from 1983, we will gradually shift our main efforts onto economic work.[34]

Provincial Leadership, 1986–1992

The third stage of provincial leadership in Fujian began in March of 1986, when Chen Guangyi replaced Xiang as first party secretary. Like Xiang before him, Chen was a Fujian native who had spent his career in other parts of the country. He was born in 1933 in the coastal city of Putian to a family of workers.[35] At the age of seventeen, he left the province for the northeast and northwest parts of the country where he would spend the next thirty-six years of his life. Like many other "third echelon" cadres who began their careers after 1949, his own career path marks him as an almost stereotypical technocrat. He joined the Communist Party in 1959 after graduating from the Electric Motors Department of Northeast Engineering College. In the early 1960s, he was a deputy division chief in the Heavy Industry Department of Gansu Province. During the Cultural Revolution, he escaped serious criticism and worked as a director of an office in a design institute under the Ministry of Metallurgical Industry. From 1977 to 1980, he rose to the position of division chief of the Gansu Metallurgical Department, and then to vice-director of the Gansu Provincial Planning Commission from 1980 to 1983. In 1983, he was promoted to deputy secretary of the Gansu Party Committee, and then to governor in April of the same year. As governor, he paid special attention to preventing soil erosion, poverty work, and mining. He was elected to the Central Committee in September 1985, and in the following year, at the age of fifty-three, was transferred to Fujian. Chen's status as a "third echelon" cadre, his Fujian roots, and his work as governor in Gansu all appear to have worked in favor of his appointment in Fujian.

Three men worked alongside Chen as governor: Hu Ping, who stepped down a year after Chen became first party secretary; Wang Zhaoguo, who served only three years before being transferred back to Beijing; and Jia Qinglin, who assumed the post of first party secretary in 1994. Wang Zhaoguo's arrival in September of 1987 broke a pattern of promoting veteran Fujian cadres such as Ma Xingyuan and Hu Ping to the highest positions in the province, and was greeted with a cautious wait-and-see attitude among cadres in the province.[36] Before coming to Fujian, Wang enjoyed the reputation of being one of the Party's youngest and fastest rising stars. Born in Hebei in 1941, he joined the Party in 1965 and graduated from Harbin Polytechnic University in 1966. During the Cultural Revolution, he served as a secretary of the Youth League branch in the No. 2 Motor Vehicle Plant. In 1982, after Deng Xiaoping's inspection of the No. 2 Plant, he rose to first secretary of the Youth League's Secretariat. In 1984, he was promoted to director of the Central Committee's General Office. One year later, under the tutelage of Deng and Hu Yaobang, he was made a member of the CCP Central

Secretariat. In 1987, he was transferred to Fujian where he was made vice-governor and then acting governor of the province. In September of 1987, he was appointed governor, and deputy secretary of the provincial party committee. As governor, he was also a member of the Central Committee.

Jia Qinglin replaced Wang as governor in January of 1991. Like his predecessor, he was young (fifty-one), a native of Hebei, and a graduate of an engineering college.[37] Unlike Wang, whose career path was centered in Party administration work, Jia rose through the ranks on the basis of his work in foreign trade and industry. In fact, of all the top leaders who came to the province during the late 1980s and early 1990s, Jia was the only one with previous experience in foreign economic matters. He was general manager of the China National Machinery and Equipment Import/Export Corporation from 1978 to 1983, and then party secretary and director of the Taiyuan Heavy Machinery Plant from 1983 to 1985. In 1985, he was transferred to Fujian where he became the number three man in the provincial party committee behind Xiang Nan and Hu Ping. According to one account, Jia came to Fujian as a replacement for Xiang who was nearing retirement age. But as a result of opposition from provincial cadres, who were unhappy with a northerner being given the top post, Jia was not promoted. The position was given instead to Chen Guangyi. Jia remained a deputy party secretary responsible for organizational and foreign economic matters until his promotion to governor in 1991.[38]

If the provincial leadership under Xiang Nan was generally identified with making substantial and consistent progress during the early and mid-1980s, the record of the leadership cohort under Chen Guangyi during the late 1980s and early 1990s was mixed. During this period, Fujian saw its best chance for an "economic takeoff" as a result of an infusion of Taiwanese investment beginning in 1988. That year, economic growth and foreign investment reached record levels. At the same time, provincial leaders once again encountered criticisms concerning "conservative thinking" and "poor implementation" that had plagued the province in the early 1980s. Complaints were heard about Chen's lack of support of the Xiamen SEZ, and his lukewarm response to Deng's 1992 trip to the south. To his credit, Chen's response was quick and effective. Throughout the rest of that year, he met with officials in the southern Fujian cities of Xiamen, Quanzhou and Zhangzhou, to smooth over differences and agree on a common strategy for increasing foreign investment and exports. The following year, Fujian's economy was once again performing strongly, and experiencing record levels of growth that outstripped the national average.

The Strategy of Economic Reform in Fujian

For provincial leaders, the challenge of fashioning an effective reform strategy rested primarily on their success in three areas. One was their ability to introduce reforms when the conditions were ripe. Usually, this meant acting when reform, rather than retrenchment, was the prevailing mood at the national level. But it also required prompt responses to pressures within the province, changes in the international environment, and reform developments in other provinces. Secondly, provincial leaders had to be skillful in managing relations between the province and Center. The support of central patrons and agencies was a resource that provincial leaders often had to call upon both to get reform experiments approved, and to have them carried through. Thirdly, they had to build support for the reforms within the province itself, both among local officials and the population at large. Such support was especially critical in ensuring the smooth implementation of reforms, and in building a constituency that would sustain the reform momentum in the province.

Formulating an Effective Reform Program

Timing is a crucial part of any political strategy. In the case of Fujian, the timing of the reforms has hinged most critically on opportunities provided by central authorities. This was most evident in the case of reforms in the foreign economic sector. As the recipient of the "special policies," the province was able to get a headstart on most other provinces in introducing changes that played to its strengths. As early as March of 1979, several months before the "special policies" were formally approved, the province won approval to establish the Fujian Investment Enterprise Corporation (*Touzi qiye gongsi*). The Huafu Corporation, as it was also called, was headed by Vice-governor Zhang Yi and was the first provincial organization of its kind. Modeled after the China International Trust and Investment Corporation (CITIC), it was given the authority to borrow from overseas financial institutions and issue bonds and stocks to attract overseas Chinese and foreign capital.[39] A year after Huafu's establishment, in December of 1980, provincial leaders received approval from the State Council for a special economic zone (SEZ) in Xiamen's Huli District that would enjoy preferential policies for attracting foreign investment, technology and management methods.[40] In 1984 and 1988, provincial leaders once again took advantage of an acceleration of the reform process at the national level, and a show of support from central leaders visiting the province, to carry out further reforms in the foreign economic sector. Following visits by Deng and other central leaders during the winter months of 1983–1984, Fujian won permission from the State Council to have the SEZ's area expanded from the Huli District to the entire city, and its scope broadened from export-processing to include commerce, tourism, and overall industrial development. During that same year, the city of Fuzhou was approved as one of fourteen open cities (*kaifang shi*), and given greater authority in foreign economic matters and preferential measures to attract foreign investment and technology. In 1985, a similar set of measures was extended to eleven counties/districts in the southern Fujian delta which was declared an economic open zone (*jingji kaifang qu*).[41] One month later, a State Council document

(No. 46) was issued approving the continuation of the "special policies" in Fujian and Guangdong for another five years.[42]

Zhao Ziyang's visit to Fujian in January of 1988, shortly after a strong reform push at the thirteenth Party Congress the previous fall, produced a similar round of reform initiatives in the province. Soon after Zhao's visit, and as part of his proposed coastal development strategy, the number of open counties and districts in the southern Fujian region was expanded from eleven to thirty.[43] Several months later, Fujian was designated an experimental comprehensive reform area (*zonghe gaige shiyanqu*), which would be geared toward the development of an export-oriented economy. This policy essentially reaffirmed, and expanded on, the autonomy that Fujian was already receiving in various economic sectors under the earlier "special policies" provision.[44]

Reform proposals in the province did not always come about in reaction to events at the center. As the reforms grew in scope and complexity, the timing of reforms in the province increasingly became tied to other developments outside of Beijing. These included social reactions to reforms within the province, opportunities offered by the international economic environment, and reform experiments in other provinces. Some of the impetus for enterprise reforms in the mid-eighties, for instance, came from demands by enterprise managers in the province for greater autonomy. In early 1984, in what turned into a nationally publicized affair, fifty-five enterprise managers and directors in Fuzhou complained publicly to provincial leaders that various reforms delegating decision-making powers to enterprises had not been carried through. Provincial leaders responded by carrying out measures expanding the autonomy of collective enterprises, and experimenting with a variety of contracting arrangements with state-owned industrial and commercial enterprises in the province.[45]

Other reform measures can be seen as a response to new opportunities in the foreign economic environment. For Fujian, the most dramatic instance of this came in 1987 with the relaxation of controls over Taiwanese entering the mainland for business and personal reasons. Beginning in 1988, Taiwanese investment began flowing into China in significant numbers, the majority of it concentrated in Fujian and the Xiamen SEZ.[46] This influx of Taiwanese investment no doubt strengthened the provincial leadership's case that year for increasing the number of open counties in the southern Fujian area, and gaining designation as a comprehensive reform area. Indeed, even before Taiwanese investment became significant, the province had been able to play on its role as a bridge between the mainland and Taiwan as a way of gaining support for certain reform measures. In 1984 and 1986, respectively, for example, the province won central approval to set up the nation's first local airline and joint-venture bank in Xiamen.

The growth of Taiwanese investment in the province had an even more direct impact on two later reform measures that expanded the power and scope of the Xiamen SEZ. One was the decision in 1988 to list Xiamen separately from the province on the state plan (*jihua danlie*). This decision granted the city provincial-level authority in economic matters. It meant that city authorities would no longer have to go through the province in the chain of command, but would be directly subordinated to the center. According to city economic and finance officials, Xiamen did not meet the criteria for *jihua danlie* status, but was given it anyway because it was a magnet for Taiwanese investment.[47] Another measure was the designation in June of 1989 of three Taiwanese investment zones near Xiamen and Fuzhou that would enjoy SEZ-type preferential policies for land and industrial development.[48]

Finally, the introduction of reforms in Fujian was influenced by reform experiments in other provinces. With Xiang Nan's encouragement, administrative reforms decentralizing enterprises and decision-making powers to cities, and measures encouraging the growth of township enterprises, were both preceded by provincial studies of similar reform experiments in the provinces of Sichuan and Jiangsu, respectively.[49] In other instances, Fujian's efforts to acquire preferential policies were helped by the fact that the same policies had already been given to other provinces. The establishment of an open zone in southern Fujian in 1985, for example, followed the establishment of open areas in Guangdong's Zhujiang Delta region and the Yangtze Delta region. Similarly, the designation of Fujian as a comprehensive experimental province in 1988 followed the center's decision to grant Guangdong the same policy the previous year. In both cases, Fujian's ability to win central approval was strengthened by arguments that other provinces had received preferential treatment.[50]

Provincial leaders in Fujian were not always as opportune or astute as the preceding paragraphs suggest in formulating an effective program of reform. Problems cropped up both in the timing and sequencing of reforms during the reform period. In the clearest instance, Liao Zhigao's foot-dragging in the early stage of reform cost the province much of its head-start. By the mid-eighties, when reforms in the province finally began to gain momentum, other coastal provinces and cities, with more developed industrial and infrastructural foundations, were beginning to receive similar preferential policies, and luring domestic and foreign investment away from Fujian. More recently, provincial leaders, and Chen Guangyi in particular, have come under criticism for their lukewarm response to Deng's call for accelerating the pace of reform during his 1992 trip to the south. Soon after Deng's trip, the province reportedly introduced few new reforms, and took a back seat to provinces such as Guangdong, Shanghai and Shandong, which were showcased at the fourteenth Party Congress held at the end of that year.[51]

Managing Central-Provincial Relations

Fujian's achievements over the reform period suggest that the provincial leadership generally did well in managing central-provincial relations. First, they were successful in getting their "special policies" reaffirmed and expanded in 1985 and 1988. As part of the "special policies" deal, the province maintained a "fixed-sum" fiscal arrangement which allowed it to retain all of its revenue for a period of several years, while receiving a fixed-sum subsidy. In comparison with many other provinces, Fujian was also able to retain a higher percentage of its foreign exchange, and enjoyed greater autonomy in the areas of taxation, banking, prices, wages, personnel, and foreign economic matters. In the 1988 agreement, the province also acquired the right to manage and distribute a larger portion of the bank deposits in the province than other areas, and greater flexibility in levying local taxes.[52] Second, as we saw above, provincial leaders won central approval for a multi-tiered system of open areas that consisted of the Xiamen SEZ, the Fuzhou Technological Development Zone, the Southern Fujian Economic Open Zone, the Taiwan Investment Zones around Fuzhou and Xiamen, and comprehensive reform sites in the Quanzhou area. In addition, they were able to get the Xiamen SEZ, and the Southern Fujian Economic Open Zone, expanded in 1985 and 1988, respectively.

Two caveats, however, must be added to using this list of achievements as an indicator of the provincial leadership's job in managing central-provincial relations. One is that not all the credit for these achievements should go to provincial leaders. Other factors independent of the leadership often played a significant role. One of the most important of these was Fujian's close association with Guangdong throughout the reform period. While Fujian was the beneficiary of the "special policies," it was not the focal point of the reform experiment. Guangdong was. A reading of the meetings and documents regarding the "special policies" suggests that Guangdong received the lion's share of attention from central leaders.[53] Fujian leaders occasionally injected their own opinions, and were responsible for crafting their own proposals. However, these tended to reflect opinions and proposals that had already been raised by Guangdong authorities. To be sure, Fujian authorities can claim much of the credit for selecting and cultivating specific reform sites in the province, such as the Quanzhou area. They also played a major role in securing central approval for reforms not extended to Guangdong, such as the expansion of the Xiamen SEZ in 1985, the creation of the country's first local bank and first local airline in the mid-eighties, and the establishment of Taiwan Investment Zones in 1989. But the fact that Guangdong played a leading role in many of the reforms carried out in the two provinces suggests that a number of the province's achievements may have had less to do with efforts by provincial leaders and more to do with Fujian's association with Guangdong.

A second caveat is that these accomplishments were not quite as rosy as they appear on paper. A closer examination of the reforms in Fujian reveals that provincial leaders had more than their share of problems in managing central-provincial relations, particularly in the latter part of the 1980s and early 1990s. These problems become especially apparent when the reforms in Fujian are compared with those in Guangdong.

First, Fujian leaders have encountered numerous problems in carrying out SEZ policy. Originally, provincial authorities had pushed for the establishment of two SEZs in Xiamen's Huli District and on Langqi, an island on the mouth of the Min River near Fuzhou. The Langqi location was apparently preferred for political reasons: it was near Fuzhou and thus could be better controlled by the province.[54] Xiamen, on the other hand, has historically had fractious relations with the province and was expected to assert its autonomy. Langqi, however, was eventually rejected by the center because the island had little infrastructure and would have been costly to develop.[55]

Even after Xiamen was formally designated an SEZ in December of 1980, provincial authorities were slow to extend support to developing the zone. They encountered difficulties, for example, in passing a set of basic regulations governing enterprise registration, land and labor management, and technology imports in the SEZ. These regulations were reported ready as early as March 1982, but were never ratified by the provincial People's Congress or publicized until 1984. From 1980 to 1984, Xiamen simply used Guangdong's SEZ regulations which had been in effect since 1980.[56] This delay in passing a set of regulations for the Xiamen SEZ is cited by zone officials as hurting Xiamen's ability to attract more foreign investment.[57] More recently, criticism has been levied at provincial leaders, and Chen Guangyi in particular, for not giving Xiamen the fiscal autonomy it should enjoy as a *jihua danlie* city, and for diverting investment from Xiamen to Fuzhou and the Meizhou Bay area near his hometown of Putian.[58]

Second, the provincial leadership has not been as entrepreneurial or creative as Guangdong's in dealing with the center in areas such as funding and the implementation of reform policies. Unlike Guangdong, which attracted large amounts of central ministerial investment into Shenzhen, Fujian has not been very successful in attracting investment either from the center or from other provinces until only recently. In the early 1980s, the province was unable to secure central funding to expand and renovate the international airports in Fuzhou and Xiamen.[59] In another case related by an official in Xiamen, the province turned down an offer from the Ministry of Communications in 1983 to invest 500 million yuan in expanding the Xiamen port in return for the right to manage it. Provincial authorities reportedly told the ministry it could do so only on the condition that it also invest the same amount in Fuzhou's port. The Communications Ministry refused the offer and put the money instead into expanding the port at Ningbo.[60]

There is also a perception among cadres, and the general public, in the province that Fujian's leadership has been more conservative in implementing reform policies than Guangdong's. The usual story is that Fujian leaders stick to the letter of the policy and do not attempt anything that does not appear in print. Conversely, Guangdong leaders are known for carrying out policies in ways that go beyond the printed character. To use the familiar traffic light analogy, Fujian cadres tend to stop when the light turns red, while Guangdong cadres find a way to go around the light.[61] While this story no doubt exaggerates the differences between the two provinces, officials in Fujian displayed an impressive ability to call forth examples to support their point. One former high-ranking SEZ official recalled that Guangdong authorities were more flexible in interpreting the rules regarding tax exemptions for foreign investors. While Xiamen was offering two years of tax exemption, some localities in Guangdong were offering three years.[62] Another example was related to me by an official in the provincial economic system reform office. He recalled that Fujian and Guangdong had once applied to the center for permission to carry out price and wage reform in 1988. The center approved the price reform measure, but denied wage reform for both provinces. Guangdong, however, went ahead with wage reform, and covered the increase in the total wage bill from its own revenues. This official noted that Fujian had the financial capacity to cover a rise in wages, but did not go through with wage reform because its leaders were not as bold as Guangdong's.[63]

Finally, Fujian's leadership has been less successful than Guangdong's in having local veterans promoted to the highest positions in the province. This became especially evident in the latter half of the 1980s and early 1990s. Prior to that period, the top leaders in both provinces, i.e., Xiang Nan in the case of Fujian, and Xi Zhongxun and Ren Zhongyi in the case of Guangdong, had come from outside the province. But after 1985, Guangdong saw local cadres, such as Ye Xuanping, Lin Ruo, Xie Fei and Zhu Senlin, promoted to the top posts in the province. In contrast, no local veterans in Fujian have made it to the top with the exception of Hu Ping who served as governor until 1987. Fujian's top leaders in the post-1985 period have all come from the north of China. Chen Guangyi was a Fujian native, but spent his entire career in the northeast and northwest. In addition, the two governors who succeeded Hu Ping—Wang Zhaoguo and Jia Qinglin—were both Hebei natives with established careers in the north of China.

Mobilizing Support within the Province

An effective provincial reform strategy requires support from both provincial and subprovincial cadres, and the population as a whole. Provincial leaders cultivated that support using a variety of measures. Some were directed solely at gaining the support of cadres within the province. These included the decentralization of power and resources down the hierarchy, and personnel policies aimed at resolving factional divisions among the provincial elite and recruiting and promoting able and reform-minded cadres to high-ranking positions. Other measures, such as the adoption of popular reforms, were intended to appeal to the broader interests of the local elite and the population they administered.

Decentralization was carried out in the province with both an administrative and political rationale in mind.[64] Administratively, it was seen as a means of reducing the inefficiency and bureaucratic red tape associated with the highly centralized prereform system. Under this system, local authorities had to get approval from higher-level authorities for any major economic decisions. Enterprises had even less autonomy. A number of the larger state-owned enterprises came under the jurisdiction of multiple levels of local governments and their supervising bureaus. By reducing higher-level interference in the affairs of lower levels, decentralization was seen as an important means of stimulating local initiative and efficiency. Politically, as Susan Shirk has argued, decentralization also served as a means of purchasing the support of local cadres for reform measures and reform-minded leaders.[65]

Decentralization in the province took place gradually over the reform period, although, like other reform measures, it tended to coincide with peaks in the reform cycle. Some decentralization occurred in 1981 when the province gave prefectures and prefectural-level cities the authority to manage their own exports for selected commodities.[66] Decentralization, however, did not make substantial progress until 1984 when a major decentralizing push was carried out in conjunction with the nationwide introduction of the urban economic reforms that same year. In April of 1984, the provincial government expanded the foreign investment approval powers of prefectures, cities and counties. That same year, prefectures, cities, counties and enterprises also received greater authority to approve technical renovation projects in existing enterprises.[67] In 1985, provincial departments pledged to further decentralize control over selected export commodities to prefectures and cities, and to simplify the procedures needed to obtain import licenses.[68]

Accompanying this delegation of powers in the foreign economic sector was a major decentralization in the industrial and commercial systems. From 1983 to 1985, the provincial government transferred 594 of its industrial enterprises, or 73.2 percent of all provincially-controlled enterprises, to the control of the prefectures and cities in which the enterprises were located. Similarly, hundreds of provincially-controlled commercial enterprises were transferred to counties and cities in 1983.[69]

Beginning in 1988, administrative decentralization entered a new phase with the establishment of "comprehensive reform" (*zonghe gaige*) sites. Borrowing from the concept of the "central cities" reform that expanded the decision-making powers of selected large cities, provincial leaders in Fujian began designating certain county-level cities comprehensive reform areas. These cities were given prefectural-level powers in various areas of economic management, such as foreign investment approval, exporting, and the leasing of land. Shishi city was the first to be designated a comprehensive reform city in December of 1987 and achieved results that made it a national model. In 1992, encouraged by the success of Shishi, provincial officials decided to expand this experiment to three other county-level cities, and were considering plans to carry it out province-wide.[70]

In addition to delegating powers and resources to lower levels, provincial leaders sought to build support for the reforms by resolving divisions among local cadres, and promoting younger, more reform-minded cadres into the top leadership groups at various levels of government. Xiang Nan, in particular, saw the resolution of personnel issues as a necessary precondition for successful reform in the province. As we saw earlier, he spent much of his early years in the province healing long-standing rifts between native cadres and outsiders, and resolving cases of cadres who had been wrongly persecuted during the Cultural Revolution.[71]

Another top priority for Xiang was the recruitment and promotion of younger, outward-looking, college-educated cadres to leadership positions in the province and its major cities. In the government, these included the governor, Hu Ping, and vice-governors, Huang Changxi, Cai Ningling, You Dexin, Chen Mingyi and Chen Binfan, who were all promoted to that post under Xiang. In the party committee, they included Jia Qinglin, Wang Yishi, and Zhang Kehui.[72] The large majority of these younger leaders had prior administrative or economic management experience in the province. Some came from leadership positions in the province's major cities. You Dexin was a former mayor of Fuzhou from 1980–1983; Huang Changxi served as vice-mayor of Xiamen from 1980–1982; and Wang Yishi was former head of the Xiamen SEZ Management Committee during the early 1980s. Still others were promoted from high-level management positions in the province. Cai Ningling, for example, was a former director of the Mindong Electric Machinery Plant in eastern Fujian, while Chen Binfan had been the former chairman and general manager of the Huamin Corporation, the province's main business presence in Hong Kong.

At the subprovincial level, cadres who would later earn reputations as popular and able leaders, such as Hong Yongshi, Yuan Qitong, and Xi Jinping, were promoted to leadership positions in the province's two major cities. Hong was selected mayor of Fuzhou in 1984; Yuan became a party secretary of Fuzhou the same year; and Xi was made a vice-mayor of Xiamen in 1985. Like many of the newcomers to the provincial leading bodies, Hong, Yuan, and Xi were around fifty and possessed extensive administrative experience in the province. Xi—the son of former Guangdong first party secretary and Politburo member, Xi Zhongxun—was from the north, but had spent much of his career in the province where he had worked his way up the ranks from the county level.

Chen Guangyi built on Xiang's work in personnel matters by continuing to promote a number of the younger cadres Xiang had brought in. Both Cai Ningling and Yuan Qitong won a spot on the provincial party committee in 1986, the year Chen became first party secretary. Yuan was later promoted to the post of deputy secretary in 1990. Xi Jinping was promoted to first party secretary of Fuzhou in 1988, while Hong Yongshi, who earned a reputation as a popular and capable mayor in Fuzhou, was picked to be mayor of Xiamen in 1992, replacing the long-standing Zou Erjun.

Several noticeable lapses in personnel management during Chen's time of office, however, suggest that he lacked either the commitment, skills or support that Xiang brought to personnel matters. One such lapse was the absence of Xiamen cadres being promoted into the provincial leadership, a slight that must have aggravated the already tense relations between the province and the SEZ. Chen also encountered strong opposition among Xiamen cadres in the election of the city's mayor in 1988, when Zou Erjun was up for reelection, and again in 1992, when Hong Yongshi replaced Zou. In both cases, the local delegates involved in the election voiced their dissatisfaction with the province's choice of mayor, narrowly rejecting Zou in 1988 and turning down the province's choice for executive vice-mayor in 1992.[73] In another instance, problems arose in the selection of governor soon after Chen's arrival in the province. Jia reportedly lacked the support of provincial cadres for the position, despite having been brought in as the number three man behind Xiang Nan and Hu Ping. The position was given, instead, to Wang Zhaoguo, a fast-rising star in the party apparatus, but someone who possessed little in the way of background or experience that qualified him to be governor of the province.

Finally, provincial leaders sought to garner support for the reforms by carrying out popular measures that appealed to local interests. One such measure was to channel more investment into areas that had previously been neglected before the reforms, such as public works and the renovation and beautification of urban areas. In a number of cities along the coast, this shift in priorities was visible in the air, which was thick with dust from workers tearing up sidewalks and laying new sewer lines, and in the cranes that dotted the skyline erecting fancy new hotels and convention centers. Provincial leaders also championed employment-generating measures, such as those encouraging the growth of foreign-invested, urban collective, and township and village enterprises, in the labor-intensive, export-processing sectors.[74] Other popular measures were aimed at resolving some of the undesirable consequences of reform. These included redistributive fiscal policies and poverty work programs to deal with the growing gap between the coastal and inland areas, and the establishment of a social security system (*shehui baoxian*) in state-owned and collective enterprises in the late 1980s. Lastly, provincial leaders cultivated support at the local level by protecting local reform experiments, even when they went counter to central policies. A good example of this was the extensive smuggling and entrepôt trade in the Quanzhou area that provided the initial capital for that region's booming private and township enterprise sectors.[75]

Provincial Policy Toward Attracting Foreign Capital and Investment

As one of two provinces at the forefront of opening to the outside world, Fujian's role in the larger reform process was determined primarily by its ability to acquire foreign capital. Central authorities made clear early on to the province that the "special policies" given to Fujian in 1979 were not so much a grant of money, but of authority. Provincial authorities were to make use of this grant, and their own native strengths, to attract capital, technology and skills from the outside world to make up for what the center could not provide. The implementation of these "special policies," however, did not involve the carrying out of detailed policies and regulations. As the vice-premier in charge of the "special policies," Gu Mu admitted, the central authorities themselves had little experience in foreign economic matters. Their strategy was to learn from Guangdong and Fujian by giving them a certain degree of autonomy and encouraging them to experiment. The "special policies," and other subsequent policies in foreign economic matters given to Fujian and Guangdong were, as a result, frequently vague and left the provinces with substantial latitude in fleshing out the details. In this section, we examine both the formal authority Fujian received, and its use of that authority to attract foreign capital to the province.

Provincial Autonomy and the Acquisition of Foreign Capital

The formal authority that Fujian enjoyed in the area of foreign economic affairs has been shaped primarily by a series of central policies that were directed largely at Fujian and Guangdong. These include the "special policies and flexible measures" (*teshu zhengce linghuo cuoshi*) given to the two provinces in July 1979, and elaborated on in subsequent documents throughout the 1980s, as well as policies establishing open areas in selected areas within the two provinces. For much of the 1980s, these policies gave Fujian and Guangdong more autonomy than other provinces in two areas.[76]

First, they instituted a "comprehensive responsibility system" (*da baogan*) that gave Fujian and Guangdong more decision-making authority in virtually all areas of the economy than other provinces. This arrangement institutionalized a certain amount of autonomy for the two provinces by setting a single baseline (*jishu*) or target in areas such as fiscal revenue and expenditure, and foreign trade earning, for a fixed number of years. Fujian and Guangdong were then given a portion of any revenue, or foreign exchange, earned above that baseline as an incentive for exceeding the target. In the area of foreign exchange, the target for both provinces was fixed at the amount of foreign exchange each had earned in 1978. For a five-year period (1980–1984), Guangdong could retain 70 percent of any above-target foreign exchange earned from trade activities, while handing the remaining 30 percent to the center. Fujian, which was poorer and had a weaker economic base, was allowed to keep all of its above-target foreign exchange earned from trade for the 1980–1981 period. After that, it would revert to the arrangement carried out by Guangdong. In 1985, when the "special policies" were renewed for another five years, the foreign exchange contract system was retained. In addition, Fujian was extended a foreign exchange subsidy of US$25 million a year.

As part of this "comprehensive responsibility system," the two provinces were also given greater authority in areas of planning, investment, taxation, materials allocation, wages and prices. In addition, they could approve all foreign-investment projects, including processing and assembly projects, compensation trade, and joint ventures, that did not affect central plan balances. This authority was tightened somewhat during the retrenchment in 1982 when the center set a limit of US$10 million on foreign-invested projects the province could approve without going through central authorities.[77] The 1985 document, which renewed the "special policies" for another five years, continued the $10 million limit for productive foreign-invested projects. It also allowed the provinces to approve all nonproductive projects that did not affect central plan balances. In 1988, the approval limit for productive investments was raised once again to US$30 million, while limits were abolished for certain categories of projects involving exports, infrastructure, and raw materials.

In addition, the two provinces were permitted to establish the country's first special economic zones, and international trust and investment corporations such as Fujian's Huafu Corporation, specifically for attracting foreign capital. In Fujian, the Xiamen SEZ featured the most preferential tax policies for foreign investors, better infrastructural conditions, and more flexible procedures and terms for customs, land use, profit repatriation, labor and wages than other localities in the province. The Huafu Corporation was vested with the authority to engage in a wide range of foreign business activities that included acquiring capital from international lending institutions, importing advanced technology and equipment, and investing in joint ventures. Over the years, the Huafu Corporation would play a major role in attracting foreign capital to finance some of the larger commercial and infrastructure projects in the province.[78]

Secondly, central policies provided the two provinces with preferential policies designed to attract foreign investors. The Xiamen SEZ, for example, offered foreign investors a low income tax rate of 15 percent, which was half of the standard rate. With the expansion of the Xiamen SEZ, and the designation of Fuzhou, the Mawei Economic and Technological Development Zone, and the southern Fujian triangle as open areas in the mid-1980s, the number of localities enjoying preferential policies proliferated. Each of these open areas was given varying degrees of preferential policies. Thus the Mawei Economic and Technological Development Zone enjoyed the same low income tax rates as the Xiamen SEZ, while Fuzhou and the counties and cities in the southern Fujian area were given a rate of 24 percent, which was higher than the SEZ rate but still lower than that in the rest of the country.[79] All of these areas also enjoyed preferential rates in custom duties, the unified industrial-and-commercial tax, local taxes, and fees for the use of land and facilities.

The autonomy and flexibility given Fujian under the "special policies" arrangement have been a major reason for the rapid growth of the foreign economic sector in the province. During the 1979–1993 period, exports in the province rose more than 140 fold to more than US$4 billion in 1993. During the same period, contracted foreign investment in the province skyrocketed from US$1.05 million in 1979 to US$11.4 billion in 1993, for an aggregate of US$22.5 billion. In 1993 and 1994, the province ranked sixth and fourth respectively in exports, and third both years in foreign investment. These achievements in the foreign economic field have, in turn, been largely responsible for the explosive growth of the provincial economy. By 1993, foreign-invested enterprises were exporting 51.6 percent of the province's total exports, and generating roughly 38 percent of the province's GVIO and 17 percent of the province's tax revenue.[80]

At the same time, Fujian has seen its advantage over other provinces erode as other coastal provinces and cities began receiving more autonomy and preferential policies in the foreign economic sector in the latter half of the 1980s. By 1985, other municipalities and cities, such as Tianjin, Shanghai and Dalian, were enjoying similar approval powers in foreign investment.[81] In 1988, central authorities expanded the number of cities and counties in other coastal provinces designated as open areas. These included the province of Hainan, which became an SEZ, and the Pudong Development Zone near Shanghai. By the early 1990s, Fujian officials began complaining that there was nothing all that special about their "special policies." In their eyes, Fujian was losing its edge to other coastal provinces and places such as Jiangsu and Shanghai. As one official in the Fujian Foreign Economic Relations and Trade Commission summed up the situation, "Our strong points are getting weaker. The beneficial policies which only we enjoyed before are beginning to expand [to other areas]. It is a lot of pressure on us."[82]

Provincial Priorities in Acquiring Foreign Capital

With Deng's decision to open China to a wider range of foreign economic activity in the late 1970s, foreign capital and investment began entering the country in a variety of forms. One was foreign exchange earnings from traditional sources such as exports and overseas Chinese remittances, as well as new nontrade-related sources such as tourism, labor exports, and overseas engineering projects. Exports were by far the largest foreign exchange earner in this category. A second involved various forms of borrowing. These consisted of loans from foreign governments and banks, as well as funds raised from issuing bonds overseas. A third was direct foreign investment in various forms of joint ventures (*hezi or hezuo qiye*) and solely foreign-invested (*duzi qiye*) enterprises. A fourth consisted of various forms of processing and assembly projects (*lailiao jiagong or lailiao zhuangpei*), and compensation trade (*buchang maoyi*). This last category came under the umbrella term "*sanlai yibu*," and involved importing raw materials and equipment into the province where they would be made into finished goods in return for a processing fee or payment for the equipment, or exchanging foreign goods and technology for domestically produced products.

While all of these forms were present in Fujian during the reform period, provincial priorities have focused on the following areas. First, in an effort to modernize state-run enterprises, provincial leaders have encouraged forms of foreign capital and investment that brought in new foreign technologies and management skills.[83] These included processing and assembly, compensation trade, and joint-venture projects that provided production equipment, technology, and patents to the Chinese side as part of the agreement. During the 1980s, the majority of foreign-invested projects in the province involved the technological renovation of old enterprises (*lao qiye gaizao*). By 1988, this category accounted for nearly 80 percent of all industrial foreign-invested projects in the province, and nearly half of all technical renovation investment in the province. Provincial authorities have encouraged this trend by decentralizing approval authority for foreign-invested, and technological renovation, projects to lower levels and providing enterprises undergoing renovation with preferential measures such as tax breaks. They have also set aside a certain portion of their foreign exchange to purchase imported equipment for modernizing certain key enterprises.[84]

Provincial efforts to bring in newer technologies and management skills to update the domestic industrial base have shown steady improvement, and contributed to a growing export base in the province. During the early 1980s, the technology brought in tended to be low-grade technology for labor-intensive processing projects. Much of it dated back to the 1960s and 1970s.[85] This mix changed somewhat in the mid-1980s as the number of projects involving more advanced technology increased steadily. In 1985, nearly 90 percent of the technology introduced was at the 1970s and 1980s levels. In overall terms, this strategy has been effective in raising industrial productivity and output, improving product quality, and increasing exports within the province. Fujian's electronics industry is the most outstanding example. With products such as televisions, Fujian's industry now employs very recent technology and produces products that are competitive on the international market. In 1991, the province was the country's largest exporter of televisions, accounting for 37 percent of the national total.[86]

Secondly, provincial authorities have focused predominantly on attracting loans, and direct investment. Foreign borrowings by the province made a major contribution during the 1979–1990 period, totaling nearly US$582 million, or a third of all foreign capital utilized in the province for that period.[87] Since 1990, however, foreign loans have declined rapidly both in terms of the absolute amount and as a share of total foreign capital (Table 6.3). Nearly half of the province's foreign borrowings was raised through bond issuances, primarily in Japan. The remainder has come from loans from foreign governments and banks, as well as from international organizations such as the World Bank. Most of the money raised through borrowing has gone into infrastructural projects and basic industrial plants involved in manufacturing paper and cement. Loans from the Kuwaiti government and the World Bank, for example, helped finance the expansion of the Xiamen International Airport and the province's two largest hydroelec-

Table 6.3

Contracted Foreign Capital in Fujian, 1979–1995 (U.S. dollars, millions)

	Foreign loans	Foreign direct investment	Other	Total
1979–1990	578	3,349	99	4,026
1991	84	1,149	4	1,537
1992	42	6,351	7	6,400
1993	32	11,366	7	11,405
1994	51	7,179	1	7,232
1995	96	8,906	5	23,367
1979–95	882	38,600	122	39,607

Sources: *Fujian jingji nianjian 1996* (Fujian Economic Yearbook 1996), p. 317.
Notes: The "Other" column refers to processing and assembly, and compensation trade projects.

tric power plants, while the construction of several large paper mills has relied on loans from the governments of several European countries.

Direct foreign investment constitutes the largest, and fastest growing, portion of foreign capital in the province. Between 1979 and 1993, the amount of foreign investment actually utilized came to nearly US$5.98 billion, or almost 88 percent of all foreign capital entering the province. The large part of this investment came during a remarkable spurt during the early 1990s. Foreign investment in 1993 alone nearly equaled the total amount for the 1979–1992 period (see Table 6.3). During the 1980s, most of the foreign investment in Fujian was in the form of joint ventures. During the early 1990s, however, solely-owned foreign enterprises have predominated and now make up the bulk of direct foreign investment in the province (see Table 6.4).

Two prominent features characterize direct investment in the province during the reform period. One is that the lion's share has been concentrated along the coast. During the late 1980s, foreign investment began making inroads into the province's interior as efforts were made to orient the entire province towards the international economy. But as of 1993, foreign investment in those area continued to remain a very small percentage of total investment in the province. The other feature is the concentration of direct investment in small, labor-intensive, processing enterprises in light and consumer industries. Up until 1988, foreign-invested projects averaged about US$700,000, while projects above US$1 million accounted for only about 20 percent of all foreign-invested enterprises. By the end of 1988, the province had only 28 projects above US$3 million, and 6 above US$10 million. In addition, many of the smaller foreign-invested enterprises were concentrated in the labor-intensive, export-processing sectors, producing light industrial and consumer products. By 1988, these types of enterprises accounted for around 80 percent of all productive foreign-invested projects.[88]

Table 6.4

Contracted Foreign Direct Investment in Fujian, 1979–1996
(U.S. dollars, millions)

Ventures	Joint ventures	Contracutal joint ventures	Solely-owned foreign enterprises	Total
1984	122	65	14	201
1985	242	130	5	377
1988	245	75	142	463
1990	285	73	804	1,162
1991	361	235	853	1,449
1992	1,580	911	3,860	6,351
1993	2,399	1,462	7,506	11,367
1994	2,119	879	4,181	7,179
1995	1,754	1,011	6,141	8,906
1979–95	9,543 (25%)	4,948 (13%)	24,109 (62%)	38,600

Sources: *Fujian tongji nianjian 1996* (Fujian Statistical Yearbook 1996), p. 317.

Provincial authorities initially welcomed foreign investment in small, labor-intensive, processing enterprises because they did not require large investments by the Chinese side, yet delivered quick results in the form of profits, foreign exchange, and jobs. Being labor-intensive, such enterprises were also the province's strongest drawing card for foreign investors looking for cheap labor costs.[89] Over time, however, authorities have been more selective about the kind of foreign-invested projects being established in the province as the drawbacks of concentrating foreign investment in the light industrial processing sector became more apparent. Faced with growing bottlenecks in funds, materials and transportation, they have increasingly sought to develop medium and long-range plans to coordinate the allocation of foreign investment in the province. In the mid-1980s, the provincial leadership began identifying certain priority sectors in which foreign capital should be concentrated. These included the construction of infrastructure and raw materials industries; the technical transformation of light, chemical, machine-building and electronic industries; projects producing selected export commodities in which the province has a comparative advantage;[90] and technology-intensive projects. At the same time, provincial authorities called for a reduction in investment in general processing projects, and nonproductive projects such as hotels and buildings.[91]

These efforts to readjust the industrial structure and channel more foreign investment into infrastructure and raw materials industries have met with mixed success. Up until 1988, the ratio of foreign investment in small, processing projects continued to be high, aggravating the already existing bias in the province's industrial structure toward the light industrial sector. Since 1988, however, the number of large projects in heavy industry and infrastructure has grown steadily, although they have not been able to keep up with the demands imposed by the continued rise of processing industries.[92] As part of the province's Eighth Five-year Plan, Chen Guangyi and other provincial leaders formulated ambitious plans to concentrate even more resources on twenty key infrastructure and basic industrial projects, with funding to come mainly from foreign investment and international loans.[93] Provincial authorities prefer the former because it is often accompanied by imported technology. Yet given the existing track record (foreign loans have mostly funded these projects), the province will have a difficult time finding foreign investors willing to invest in long-term infrastructure and basic industrial projects. Nevertheless, the continuing trend toward larger projects in the early 1990s is encouraging. In 1993 alone, the province brought in 286 projects of US$10 million or more, six of which involved amounts of over US$100 million.[94]

A third priority area has been in attracting foreign capital from overseas Chinese, Hong Kong and Macao, and Taiwanese investors. Most of the capital from this group has come from Hong Kong, rather than overseas Chinese in Southeast Asia, and in the form of direct investment rather than loans. During the 1979–1991 period, investment from Hong Kong/Macao alone totaled US$2.65 billion, or nearly half of all contracted foreign direct investment in the province. Investment from Southeast Asian countries with large overseas Chinese populations such as Singapore, Indonesia, Malaysia and the Philippines has been disappointing, lagging far behind Hong Kong's contribution. In fact, except for Singapore and perhaps the Philippines, none of these countries has made a significant contribution to the province (see Table 6.5).

Apart from Hong Kong, Taiwan has been the other major investor in the province, although it did not figure prominently until after 1987 when the Taiwanese government relaxed restrictions over visits to the mainland. In 1988, the amount of contracted Taiwanese investment shot up from nearly nonexistent levels the year before to US$95.66 million. Contracted Taiwanese investment continued to escalate during the next two years, but then fluctuated during the early 1990s, increasing rapidly to record levels in 1992 and 1993 before dropping off in 1994 (Table 6.5). By the end of 1993, Taiwan was second only to Hong Kong with 16.3 percent of all contracted foreign investment in the province.

The high priority that provincial authorities have placed on overseas Chinese investment should come as no surprise. Fujian, after all, was given "special policies" in large part because of its substantial connections to overseas Chinese, and its proximity to Hong Kong and Taiwan. Central and provincial authorities alike saw the overseas Chinese as a potential goldmine for rebuilding the provincial economy. In a 1984 talk concerning the SEZs, Deng Xiaoping pointed out that "[of the ten richest men in the world] five were overseas Chinese, and three of these five were from Fujian."[95]

Table 6.5

Contracted Foreign Capital in Fujian by Selected Countries, 1985–1995 (U.S. dollars, millions)

	Hong Kong & Macao	Taiwan	Japan	Singapore	U.S.	Total
1985	273	2	55	22	9	429
1986	42	1	2	55	11	115
1987	90	1	81	5	3	219
1988	263	96	136	18	16	625
1989	600	242	13	7	5	961
1990	693	460	25	15	21	1,236
1991	713	424	10	21	16	1,537
1992	4,841	891	76	138	75	6,400
1993	7,795	1,549	107	593	264	11,366
1994	n/a	n/a	116	424	106	7,179
1995	4,513	n/a	220	564	235	8,906

Sources: *Fujian tongji nianjian 1996*, p. 320; Zhang Shoushan et al. (eds.), *Fujian duiwai jingmao sishinian* (Forty Years of Fujian's Foreign Economy and Trade) (Fuzhou: Fujian sheng ditu chubanshe, 1989). The figures for Taiwanese investment for the years 1989–1993 were taken from: *Fujian sheng jingji kaifa xianzai yu weilai* (The Present and Future of Fujian's Economic Opening) (Beijing: Jingji guanli chubanshe, 1992), p. 52; and the 1992–1994 issues of *Fujian jingji nianjian*.

The province's performance in attracting overseas Chinese investment, however, has not always lived up to these high expectations. In the initial stages, progress was slow, primarily as a result of the province's underdeveloped infrastructural and industrial base, and the preliminary nature of construction in the Xiamen SEZ. These conditions particularly discouraged direct foreign investment, which was the form that overseas Chinese and Hong Kong investment tended to take. From 1979 to 1983, investment and contributions from overseas Chinese, and Hong Kong and Macao investors, accounted for only a third of all foreign capital in the province.[96] Most of the foreign capital during this period came instead in the form of loans from the U.S., Japan and Kuwait for infrastructure projects, and deals involving processing and compensation trade.

Provincial efforts to attract overseas Chinese, Hong Kong and Taiwanese investors only began to pay off during the latter half of the 1980s and early 1990s as a result of initiatives introduced by Xiang Nan and Chen Guangyi. Provincial authorities made substantial improvements to the province's infrastructure and put forth a number of measures to raise the level of overseas Chinese investment in the province. First, they decentralized foreign-investment approval authority to lower levels in 1984, 1988 and 1991, giving preferential treatment to areas in southern Fujian with close links to overseas Chinese capital. Secondly, in 1986, they began setting up small industrial zones in townships with a large concentration of overseas Chinese in a move to encourage the creation of a foreign-invested township enterprise sector. By 1990, there were sixty such zones involving a total investment of US$295 million. The large majority of these projects were township enterprises invested in by overseas Chinese.[97] Third, provincial authorities won central approval in 1989 to set up Taiwanese investment zones in Xiamen and Fuzhou that would offer preferential policies similar to SEZs. Finally, they authorities began a more aggressive campaign in 1990 to channel foreign investment into real estate and land development projects.[98]

The biggest payoff for the province came with the rapid influx of Taiwanese investment and visitors in the late 1980s. This development provided a much-needed infusion of capital into the province and revived earlier expectations within the province of an economic takeoff fueled by overseas Chinese and Taiwanese capital, much like Guangdong's economic boom has been driven by Hong Kong capital. As a result of the inflow of Taiwanese investment, foreign investment in Fujian was reaching new highs after the suppression of the student demonstrations in June of 1989, even as other areas of the country were experiencing a decline in foreign investment.

Over time, however, the province's growing dependence on Taiwanese investment gave rise to various problems that tempered the initial enthusiasm of officials in the province. Taiwan investors, for example, have not always been as reliable as their Hong Kong counterparts. Nor have local authorities, in their eagerness to cash in on the Taiwanese investment boom, always been careful about the kind of projects they sign with Taiwanese investors. In 1988, the percentage of contracted Taiwanese investment that was actually used came to about 11.5 percent, a very low ratio considering the average for foreign investment as a whole in the province was around 46 percent.[99] Local authorities, particularly in the Xiamen SEZ where most of the Taiwanese investment has been concentrated, have also been criticized for overlooking blatant acts of prostitution, corruption, and land speculation for fear that a crackdown would drive Taiwanese investors away.[100] In addition, provincial and local authorities have shown themselves susceptible to inflated expectations, and internal politics in Taiwan. A good example is the case of Wang Yongqing, the owner of Formosa Plastics who expressed an interest in moving a large part of his petrochemical facilities to the Xiamen SEZ during the late 1980s, only to pull out of talks several years later after negotiations with Taiwan authorities. In response to Wang's declared intention to invest in Xiamen, provincial and local authorities bent over backwards to accommodate him, promising to commit more than a billion yuan into readying the Haicang District of Xiamen for his project.[101] Xiamen's mayor, Zou Erjun, is said to have spent so much time trying to arrange the deal that he ended up neglecting other foreign investors, as well as local concerns.[102] Finally, the growth of Taiwanese investment in the province has subsided somewhat in the early 1990s as Taiwanese entrepreneurs have been lured to other provinces and cities with better infrastructure and similar preferential policies to Fujian. Thus, Taiwanese investment in Fujian accounted for 84.5 percent of all Taiwanese investment in the country in 1992, but only 49 percent in 1993.

Despite these problems, Fujian has continued to tie its fortunes to Taiwan, hoping eventually for the "three openings" (*santong*): the opening of direct aviation and shipping services, direct mail, and direct commercial links between Taiwan and the mainland.[103] Under Chen Guangyi's leadership, the province has planned ambitious improvements in its infrastructure for the 1990s in preparation for direct trade and transportation links. These include building a new four-lane highway linking Fuzhou and Xiamen along the coast; upgrading and extending the railway network; and enlarging the ports in Fuzhou, Xiamen, and Meizhou Bay. The province has also remained committed to widening the range of economic activities that it conducts with Taiwan. These efforts by Chen and other provincial leaders appear to be paying off as Taiwanese investment in the province, indirect trade and fishing contracts between the two sides, and labor exports to Taiwan all registered significant gains in 1992 and 1993.[104] Still, given the many limitations the province faces—its weak economic base, its lack of a hinterland and thus access to markets in China's interior, competition from other coastal provinces and cities, and the uncertainty surrounding Taiwan-mainland ties—it remains to be seen whether direct ties will provide the province with the impetus it needs to catch up with some of its more developed neighbors.

Conclusion

Political leaders, as a number of scholars have argued, play a critical role in initiating political change in communist countries.[105] We only have to look at the tremendous changes introduced in China under Deng, or the Soviet Union under Gorbachev, to see the truth in that statement. This examination of provincial leadership in Fujian's economic reforms shows that provincial leaders, while not the catalyst for change that national leaders are, do play an important role in determining the pace of reform and development at the local level. The question is, in what particular areas is their influence felt and how much of a difference can they make? Here, the answer is more complicated and, in the case of Fujian, appears to depend on the stage the province is at in the reform process.

The experiences of Liao Zhigao and Xiang Nan suggest that, in the early stages of reform, the areas in which provincial leaders made a significant difference were those where they have traditionally had a large say. One of these areas was personnel matters. Provincial leaders can play a critical role in resolving divisions among cadres in the province, unifying them around common goals, and recruiting and promoting reform-minded subordinates to top leadership posts. While the center has the final say on the top leadership posts in the province, the provincial first party secretary has an important voice in proposing candidates for those posts. The province's turnaround under Xiang Nan offers a clear illustration of just how much impact a capable and committed leader can make in the reform process. That turnaround, moreover, came about largely because of Xiang's early commitment to redress urgent personnel issues in the province. Only when those issues were resolved was it possible to accelerate the reform process in the province.

Another area where provincial leaders left their mark, for better or worse, was in the management of central-provincial relations. Here, their success (or lack of it) rested on their relations with central leaders, their ability to cultivate support at the central level, and their sense of timing in accelerating reforms in their province. Liao Zhigao clearly missed the mark on all these counts, and accomplished little as a result. Xiang Nan, on the other hand, generally fared well in this area. He won approval for a number of reform experiments and open areas during his tenure, and pulled the province through retrenchments and campaigns against smuggling in the early 1980s with its reform momentum intact. While Xiang lacked the stature and connections enjoyed by Guangdong leaders at the central level, he was nevertheless helped by his strong rapport with central leaders such as Deng and Hu Yaobang.

Chen Guangyi's long tenure from 1986 to 1993 offers less clear-cut evidence on these matters. Compared to Xiang, Chen fared less well in these areas. He did not have a good working relationship with central reformers, and this was reflected in criticisms of the provincial leadership both before 1989, and after Deng's 1992 trip to the south of China. He also lacked a sense of timing. In 1992, for instance, Chen was criticized for being slow to respond to Deng's call for accelerating the reform process in the spring of 1992. According to one report, by late 1992, Fujian was still carrying out post-Tiananmen retrenchment policies such as the socialist education campaign which sent local cadres to the villages.[106] And yet, in appraising Chen's tenure as a whole, these lapses in managing central-provincial relations do not appear to have significantly diminished his performance in the province. Indeed, while Xiang was clearly the more reform-minded and better connected of the two, it was under Chen's tenure that the provincial economy really began to make major strides. Much of this improvement, of course, can be attributed to the groundwork laid by Xiang, and the rapid influx of Taiwanese capital beginning in 1988. Yet Chen should be given credit for carving out a concrete strategy for accelerating the pace of overseas Chinese and Taiwanese investment in the late 1980s, and for responding quickly and effectively to criticisms from central leaders after Deng's 1992 trip. In the big picture, then, Chen and Xiang were not all that far apart: both fit reasonably well into the mold of bandwagoners.

Chen's ability to compensate for his various handicaps in the later stages of reform presents two possible lessons for the study of provincial leadership in post-Mao China. For one, it suggests that the categories of pioneers, bandwagoners and laggards may not necessarily capture important differences between individual leaders. Xiang and Chen are cases in point. It also raises questions about the complex link between motivation (or ideology) and action (or implementation) in a constantly changing environment.[107] In Xiang's case, a pioneering mentality and close connections to central reformers did not translate into pioneering actions for the most part. Was this due to Xiang's inclinations to stick to the script provided by his central patrons, or to unfavorable provincial conditions, or both? On the other hand, Chen was able to compensate for his more technocratic mentality and lack of rapport with central reformers, thanks to the liberalization in Taiwan's mainland policy in the late 1980s.

Secondly, Chen's case suggests that the performance of provincial leaders in the later stages of reform may depend less on traditional concerns, such as personnel issues and central connections, and increasingly on issues outside of the Center's jurisdiction. This is not to say that the Center no longer looms large in the political calculus of provincial leaders. Certainly, one conclusion that emerges from this study is that the Center continues to be the dominant constraint on provincial leadership. The various changes of provincial first party secretaries and governors—and in particular the removal of Xiang Nan, an outspoken reformer with enemies among conservatives—are unambiguous indications that the Center retains the authority to dictate personnel decisions at the top of the provincial hierarchy. Moreover, central policies establish the broad framework within which provincial leaders can maneuver. As this study shows, the timing of the reforms in the province was linked closely to developments at the center. Provincial leaders in Fujian generally accelerated reforms in the province when central authorities were encouraging reform and growth, and bided their time during periods of retrenchment.

Chen's experience, however, is evidence that success for provincial leaders has come to depend more and more on their ability to cultivate the growing interests and opportunities that have emerged both inside and outside of the province as the reforms have grown in scope and complexity. These include institutional interests that have been strengthened with the decentralization of power to subprovincial governments and enterprises, as well as changes in the international economy. Thus, provincial leaders can and do appeal to their subordinates for support and take advantage of new sources of foreign capital in order to advance reform in the province. To an extent, of course, this is what central reformers had in mind when they gave provinces like Fujian a set of "special policies." But in doing so, they have also erected a set of incentives that encourage provincial leaders to turn their attention and loyalties toward their own provinces, and away from Beijing.

Notes

This paper is based on fieldwork that was carried out in Fujian in 1992–1993 and supported by a Committee on Scholarly Communications with China Graduate Fellowship, and a Tiananmen Memorial Foundation dissertation fellowship. I wish to thank Peter T.Y. Cheung, Jae Ho Chung, Zhimin Lin, and Andrew J. Nathan for comments on an earlier draft. Any errors are of course my own.

1. See Christine P.W. Wong, "Central-Local Relations in an Era of Fiscal Decline: The Paradox of Fiscal Decentralization in Post-Mao China," *China Quarterly*, No. 128 (December 1991), pp. 691–715.

2. See Kenneth G. Lieberthal, "Introduction: The 'Fragmented Authoritarianism' Model and Its Limitations," in Kenneth G. Lieberthal and David M. Lampton (eds.), *Bureaucracy, Politics and Decision Making in Post-Mao China* (Berkeley: University of California Press, 1992), pp. 1–30.

3. See Susan Naquin and Evelyn S. Rawski, *Chinese Society in the Eighteenth Century* (New Haven: Yale University Press, 1987), pp. 167–176.

4. He Shaochuan (ed.), *Dangdai Zhongguo Fujian* (Fujian in contemporary China) (Beijing: Dangdai Zhongguo chubanshe, 1991), p. 15.

5. Zhang Ruiyao and Ni Shidao (eds.), *Fujian jingji gailun* (An Introduction to Fujian's Economy) (Fuzhou: Fujian sheng jiwei jingji yanjiusuo, n.d.), p. 41; Lin Changzhong, "Liyong qiaozi waizi cujin jingji fazhan" (Using Overseas Chinese Capital to Promote Economic Development), in Zhang Shoushan et al. (eds.) *Fujian duiwai jingmao sishinian* (Forty Years of Fujian's Foreign Economy and Trade) (Fuzhou: Fujian sheng ditu chubanshe, 1989), pp. 38–39.

6. Lin Guangsong, "Fujian sheng waihui shouzhi qingkuang, wenti yu duice" (The Situation, Problems, and Countermeasures Regarding Fujian Province's Foreign Exchange Revenue And Expenditures), *Yanjiu baogao* (internal study reports) No. 22, 1988, pp. 6–7.

7. He, *Dangdai Zhongguode Fujian*, p. 160. Also see Xiang Nan's interview in "Fujian shengwei diyi shuji Xiang Nan" (Fujian province's first party secretary, Xiang Nan), *Guangjiaojing* (Wide Angle, Hong Kong), September 16, 1982, p. 7.

8. Edith Terry, "Fujian Province: Decentralizing Foreign Trade," *China Business Review* (September-October 1980), p. 21.

9. Zhang and Ni, *Fujian jingji*, p. 32.

10. "Secretary Xiang Nan Talks on Eight Major Issues," *Wen wei po* (HK), 8 November 1983; trans. *FBIS*, 9 November 1983, p. W5.

11. These figures are taken from *Fujian jingji nianjian 1992* (Fujian Economic Yearbook 1992) (Fuzhou: Fujian renmin chubanshe, 1992), p. 25.

12. "Provincial Leadership in Fukien," in Robert A. Scalapino (ed.), *Elites in the People's Republic of China* (Seattle: University of Washington Press, 1972), pp. 234–235.

13. *Ibid.*, p. 335.

14. *Ibid.*, pp. 335–336. During the same session of the first provincial congress, four prominent members of the Fujian underground Party and guerrilla corps were labelled a "localist anti-Party organization" (*difang zhuyi fandang jituan*) and purged from the Party. Similar struggles in other parts of the province during this period implicated a number of other members of the underground Party and guerrilla organizations. This round of criticism and purges was said to have had very serious, and long-standing, consequences for cadre unity within the province. See He, *Dangdai Zhongguode Fujian*, pp. 102–103.

15. Robert Silin and Edward Winckler (eds.), *South/Southeast China*, vol. 5 of *China Provincial Economic Briefing Series* (Hong Kong: BA Asia, 1982), p. 25.

16. Ezra Vogel, *One Step Ahead in China: Guangdong Under Reform* (Cambridge: Harvard University Press, 1989), pp. 83–84; Zhang and Ni, *Fujian jingji*, pp. 40–41.

17. Vogel, *One Step Ahead*, pp. 83–84.

18. The following biography of Liao Zhigao is based on Wolfgang Bartke (ed.), *Who's Who in the People's Republic of China* (Armonk, NY: M.E. Sharpe, 1981), p.

212. Other sources used for the biographies of provincial leaders include: Wolfgang Bartke and Peter Schier (eds.), *China's New Party Leadership: Biographies and Analysis of the Twelfth Central Committee of the Chinese Communist Party* (Armonk, NY: M.E. Sharpe, 1985); *Who's Who in China: Current Leaders*, 1989 ed. (Beijing: Foreign Languages Press, 1989); *Who's Who in China: Current Leaders*, 1994 ed. (Beijing: Foreign Languages Press, 1994).

19. "Fujian Reshuffle in the Cards," *South China Morning Post*, May 9, 1981, p. 5; trans. *FBIS*, May 13, 1981, p. W3.

20. On meetings between central officials and Fujian officials, see the documents involving Fujian in Guangdong shengwei, ed., *Zhongyang dui Guangdong gongzuo zhishi huibian, 1979–1985* (internal) (A Collection of Central Directives on Guangdong's Work, 1979–1985) (Guangzhou: Zhonggong Guangdong shengwei bangongting, n.d.).

21. "Taipei Paper Predicts New Fujian First Secretary," *Lian he bao*, April 18, 1981; trans. *FBIS*, April 22, 1981, p. V2.

22. Interview File 6.4.

23. See, for example, He, *Dangdai Zhongguode Fujian*, pp. 156–158; "Fujian to Improve Economic Policy Implementation," *Xinhua*, March 24, 1981; trans. *FBIS*, March 25, 1981, p. O1.

24. The production responsibility system in agriculture was contained in the Third Plenum's "Decision Concerning Certain Questions in Accelerating Agricultural Production." It was intended to counteract the egalitarian ethic practiced under the commune system by contracting agricultural production to small groups and households within the larger production teams.

25. "Hsiang Nan—First Secretary of the CCP Fukien Provincial Committee," *Issues & Studies*, Vol. 18, No. 7 (1982), pp. 106–109. The following paragraph is also based on Bartke and Schier, *China's New Leadership*; Guan Nuo, "Fujian shengwei diyi shuji Xiang Nan" (Fujian's first party secretary, Xiang Nan), *Guangjiaojing*, September 16, 1982, pp. 6–13.

26. Ruan Ming, *Deng Xiaoping: Chronicle of an Empire*, trans. and ed. Nancy Liu, Peter Rand and Lawrence R. Sullivan (Boulder, CO: Westview Press, 1994), p. 140.

27. Guan Nuo, "Xiang Nan," p. 6.

28. Ruan Ming, *Deng Xiaoping*, pp. 140–141.

29. *Ibid.*, p. 121. For more on Xiang's association with Hu Yaobang, see "Hu Yaopang's Clansmen from the Communist Youth League," *Issues & Studies*, Vol. 18, No. 4 (1982), pp.71–77.

30. Biographical material on Hu comes from *Who's Who in China*, and "Sheng renda changwei hui guanyu Hu Ping fushengzhang daili Fujian sheng shengzhangde jueding" (The Decision of the Standing Committee of the Provincial People's Congress Concerning Vice-governor, Hu Ping, as Fujian's Acting Governor) *Fujian ribao*, January 12, 1983, p. 1.

31. See Xiang's speech to the 4th Provincial Party Congress, "Fujian ying zou zai sihua jianshede qiantou" (Fujian Should March at the Forefront of the Four Modernizations Drive), *Fujian ribao*, July 5, 1985, 1; trans. *JPRS*, August 29, 1985, pp. 14–38.

32. *Wen wei po* (HK), January 16, 1983, pp. 1–2; trans. *JPRS*, February 2, 1983, p. 76. Also see his 1982 speech to the fourth session of the Fifth Provincial People's Congress, *Fujian ribao*, 13 March 1982, pp. 1–2.

33. Vogel, *One Step Ahead*, pp. 87–88.

34. *Wen wei po* (HK), January 16, 1983; trans. *JPRS*, February 2, 1983, p. 78.

35. Biographical material on Chen is based on the following sources: "Ch'en Kuang-i—Secretary of the CCP Fukien Provincial Committee," *Issues & Studies*, Vol. 22, No. 8 (1986), pp. 152–155; *Who's Who in China*.

36. Biographical information on Wang comes from: *Who's Who in China*; Min Zhongren, "Wang Zhaoguo churen Fujian shengzhang" (Wang Zhaoguo Becomes Fujian's Governor), *Guangjiaojing*, September 16, 1987, pp. 12–13; Guan Qingfu, "Wang Zhaoguo shangdiao shuomingle shenma?" (What is the Significance of Wang Zhaoguo's Transfer?), *Guang jiaojing* November 1990, pp. 10–13.

37. Biographical information on Jia is based on *Who's Who in China*.

38. Guan, "Wang Zhaoguo shangdiao," pp. 12–13. In 1994, Jia finally did become first secretary of the province, replacing Chen Guangyi. At the end of 1996, Jia left Fujian to become mayor of Beijing.

39. The content of these "special policies," including the province's request to establish the Huafu Corporation and the Xiamen SEZ, are contained in Central Committee Document No. 50 (July 15, 1979) (hereafter Document 79.50). See CCP Secretariat Research Office, ed., *Duiwai kaifang zhengce wenxuan huibian, 1979–1985* (A Collection of Policy Documents Concerning the Opening to the Outside, 1979–1985) (Beijing: Zhonggong zhongyang dangxiao chubanshe, 1985), pp. 34–51.

40. *Fujian ribao*, Dec. 6, 1980, p. 1.

41. On all these measures, see *Fujian ribao*, March 19, 1984, p. 1; *Fujian ribao*, April 7, 1984, p. 1.

42. State Council Document No.46 (March 28, 1985) (hereafter Document 85.46), in CCP Secretariat Office, *Duiwai kaifang zhengce*, pp. 545–552.

43. *Fujian ribao*, January 29, 1988, p. 1.

44. See State Council Document No. 58 (April 11, 1988) (hereafter Document 88.58), in State Economic System Reform Office, ed., *Shiyijie sanzhong quanhui yilai jingji tizhi gaige zhongyao wenjian huibian* (A Collection of Important Economic System Reform Documents Since the Third Plenum of the Eleventh Central Committee) (Beijing: Gaige chubanshe, 1990), pp. 510–514.

45. He, *Dangdai Zhongguode Fujian*, pp. 179–181.

46. In 1987, Fujian alone took in 80 percent of Taiwan capital invested in the country. And by the end of 1988, Xiamen itself accounted for about a third of Taiwanese investment both in terms of the number of enterprises and amount of investment. See Huang Shanhe, "Factors Limiting Development of Fujian's Externally Oriented Economy, and Possible Remedies," *Zhongguo jingji wenti*, No. 1, 1990, pp. 54–65; trans. *JPRS*, April 30, 1990, p. 63.

47. Interview Files 30.3 and 34.1. See also *Fujian ribao*, June 6, 1988, 1. *Jihua danlie* cities were part of the administrative decentralization reforms that were intended to give cities a more central role in economic coordination. *Jihua danlie* status was first given to Chongqing in 1983, and then extended to other major cities over the course of the reforms. For a case study of one *jihua danlie* city, see Paul Schroeder, "Territorial Competitors for Power: The Case of Hubei and Wuhan" in Lieberthal and Lampton (eds.), *Bureaucracy, Politics, and Decision Making*, pp. 283–307.

48. *Fujian ribao*, June 21, 1989, p. 1.

49. "Xuexi Sichuan Jiangsu jingyan jiakuai jingji gaige bu fa" (Study the Experience of Sichuan and Jiangsu to Speed Up the Pace of Economic Reform), *Fujian ribao*, October 5, 1984, p. 1; "Renzhen xuexi Sichuan jingji tizhi gaige jingyan gaohuo qiye gaohuo liutong gaohuo zhongxin chengshi" (Earnestly Study Sichuan's Economic System Reform Experience in Enlivening Enterprises, Circulation and Central Cities), *Fujian ribao*, October 20, 1984, p. 1.

50. This interpretation is supported by Vice-premier Gu Mu's talk at a December 1984 meeting on Guangdong and Fujian. There, Gu assuages the fears of Fujian officials that they might not get the same preferential policies as the Zhujiang and Changjiang deltas by proposing similar policies for the southern Fujian region. See *Zhongyang dui Guangdong, 1983–1985*, pp. 235–236.

51. Geoffrey Crothall, "Fujian half-hearted over reform," *South China Morning Post*, March 24, 1992, p. 10; Xi Chang and Wang Jian, "Deng Xiaoping jujian Min gaoguan" (Deng Xiaoping Refuses to Meet with High-level Fujian Officials), *Ming Bao*, February 1, 1993, p. 44.

52. See Documents 79.50, 85.46, and 88.58. Fujian did see its subsidy decrease over the 1980s from about 300 million yuan to around 100 million yuan as its fiscal situation improved (Interview File 19.1).

53. This was confirmed by a former vice-mayor of Xiamen who had also been vice-director of the Xiamen SEZ Management Committee in the early 1980s (Interview File 18.1).

54. Interview File 31.1.

55. Interview File 18.1. According to one source, the cost of developing the island was conservatively estimated at US$350 million. See Terry, "Fujian Province," p. 20.

56. Interview File 18.1.

57. Jin Yan, "Xiamen jingji tequ jianshede qingkuang diaocha" (An Investigation into the Situation of Constructing the Xiamen SEZ), *Fujian jingji*, No. 7, 1983, p. 4; *Fujian ribao*, July 10, 1984, p. 1.

58. Both of these criticisms came out repeatedly in interviews with provincial and Xiamen city finance and economic officials. See Interview Files 6.7, 7.1, 15.2, and 34.1.

59. See Susan Shirk, "The Domestic Political Dimensions of China's Foreign Economic Relations," in Samuel S. Kim (ed.), *China and the World: Chinese Foreign Policy in the Post-Mao Era* (Boulder, CO: Westview Press, 1984), p. 70.

60. Interview File 15.2.

61. Interview File 18.1. The disparity between Guangdong's and Fujian's cadres was openly admitted by Fujian officials. For one example, see *Fujian ribao*, January 4, 1988, p. 1.

62. Interview File 18.1.

63. Interview File 31.1.

64. Franz Schurmann distinguishes between two different kinds of decentralization carried out in communist China: administrative and economic. See *Ideology and Organization in Communist China*, 2nd ed. (Berkeley: University of California Press, 1968), pp. 175–178. The former is the focus here, and refers to the devolution of resources to lower-level authorities, as opposed to enterprises.

65. *The Political Logic of Economic Reform in China* (Berkeley: University of California Press, 1993).

66. *Fujian ribao*, March 27, 1981, p. 1.

67. *Fujian jingji nianjian 1985*, pp. 208–209 & 559–560.

68. *Fujian ribao*, September 16, 1986, p. 1.

69. He, *Dangdai Zhongguode Fujian*, p. 181; *Fujian ribao*, June 26, 1983, p. 1.

70. Interview File 31.1.

71. The importance of recruiting cadres who were younger, better-educated, and possessed skills in line with foreign economic work was a major theme in a number of Xiang's speeches and interviews. See his speech, "Lun rencai" (On Human Talent), *Fujian ribao*, January 20, 1983, p. 1; and his interview in *Wen wei po* (HK), trans. *JPRS*, February 2, 1983, pp. 77–78.

72. *Ibid.*, pp. 73–79.

73. In 1988, a number of delegates supported Xi Jinping for mayor. In 1992, local cadres were unhappy that the province had not selected someone from Xiamen to lead the city. The fact that Hong was a native of southern Fujian, however, did make him a more palatable choice. See Interview Files 6.7, 7.5, and 15.2.

74. See, for example, Liao Zhigao's speech encouraging the growth of collectives,

"Fazhan jiti suoyouzhi shengchan dayou kewei" (Develop the Collective Ownership Sector to Produce Bright Prospects), *Fujian ribao*, July 18, 1979, p. 1; and Xiang Nan's talk on expanding the township and village enterprise sector, "Dui xiangzhen qiye yinggai jiji fazhan dui gaohuo jingji yingdang duodong naojin" (We Should Actively Develop Township Enterprises, and Put Our Minds to Enlivening the Economy), *Fujian ribao*, January 11, 1986, p. 1.

75. Interview File 22.1. For a representative view, see "Zai jiyu he tiaozhan mianqian" (In the Face of Opportunities and Challenges), *Fujian ribao*, April 1, 1988, p. 1.

76. The discussion in the following paragraphs draws primarily from the following central documents: 79.50; 85.46; and 88.58.

77. "Guangdong, Fujian shixing teshu zhengce, linghuo cuoshi he shiban jingji tequde qingkuang—zhongyang shujichu huiyi huibao tigang (11/14/82)" (The Situation of Guangdong and Fujian Implementing Special Policies and Flexible Measures and Experimenting with SEZs—a Proposal Reported at the Central Secretariat Meeting) in *Zhongyang dui Guangdong, 1979–1982*, pp. 405–406; This limit was US$5 million higher than that enjoyed by Beijing, Shanghai, Tianjin and Liaoning. See *Duiwai kaifang zhengce*, p. 296.

78. For more on the Huafu Corporation, see "Huafu gongsi xishou yonghao waizi qude chengxiao" (The Achievements of the Huafu Corporation in Acquiring and Using Foreign Capital), *Fujian ribao*, November 2, 1981, p. 1; Victor Falkenheim, "Fujian's Open Door Experiment," *China Business Review* (May-June 1986); "Huafu gongsi: Fujian Duiwai Kaifangde Chuangkou" (Huafu Corporation: Fujian's Window for Opening to the Outside) *Guangjiaojing*, August 16, 1986.

79. He, *Dangdai Zhongguode Fujian*, pp. 529–530.

80. *Fujian jingji nianjian 1994*, p. 180.

81. *Duiwai kaifang zhengce*, p. 480.

82. Andrew Quinn, "Competition Worries Special Zone," *Japan Times*, May 1992. Also see Xu Yiming, "Fujian gaige kaifang jinru xin jieduan" (Fujian's Reform and Opening Enters a New Stage), *Liaowang*, November 11, 1992, p. 9.

83. See Hu Ping's report on Fujian's 1981 economic plan, trans. *JPRS*, July 23, 1981, p. 11; and Hu Ping's 1984 government work report, trans. *JPRS*, May 25, 1984, pp. 10–11.

84. Lin Changzhong, "Liyong qiaozi waizi cujin jingji fazhan" (Utilizing Overseas Chinese and Foreign Investment to Promote Economic Development), in *Fujian duiwai sishinian*, p. 42; Chen Bing, "Jishu yinjin shi chunqiu" (Technology Imports), in *Fujian duiwai*, pp. 44–45; *Fujian jingji nianjian 1985*, pp. 208–209, 220, 559–60.

85. Chen, "Jishu yinjin," pp. 44–45.

86. Chen Shangyou, "Sanzi gongye dui Fujian gongye jiegoude yingxiang" (The Influence of Foreign-invested Industry on Fujian's Industrial Structure), *Fazhan yanjiu*, No. 10 (1990), p. 24; Elizabeth Cheng, "Fujian: Emergency Measures," *China Trade Report* (July 1991), p. 6.

87. The information in this paragraph is drawn from the following sources: *Fujian tongji nianjian 1994* (Beijing: Zhongguo tongji chubanshe, 1994), p. 184; *Fujian duiwai tongji ziliao 1986*, pp. 30–31; *Fujian jingji nianjian 1990*, p. 188; *Fujian jingji nianjian 1988*, p. 188.

88. Lin Changzhong, "Liyong qiaozi waizi," p. 42.

89. See Hu Ping's 1981 government work report, trans. *JPRS*, July 23, 1981, p. 11.

90. These include aquatic products, shoes, canned food, electronics, textiles and apparel, tea, timber products, jewelry, and chemicals.

91. See "The 1985 Provincial Government Report," *Fujian ribao*, May 8, 1985; trans. *JPRS*, July 15, 1985, pp. 9–11; "Fujian Province's Seventh Five-Year Plan," *Fujian ribao*,

June 8, 1986,. trans. *JPRS*, August 4, 1986, pp. 45–46; *Jingji daobao*, July 14, 1986, p. 25; trans. *JPRS*, December 1, 1986, p. 65.

92. Chen Shangyou, "Sanzi gongye," p. 24; "Fujian sheng 'qiwu' jihuade huigu he chubu pingjia" (A Review and Preliminary Commentary on Fujian's 'Seventh Five-Year Plan'), *Yanjiu baogao* (internal), No. 60, 1990, p. 27.

93. *Fujian jingji nianjian 1992*, pp. 230–231; Total investment in these key projects is estimated to run from 100 to 200 billion yuan. See *China Trade Report* (August 1991), pp. 8–10; Xu Yi, "Fujian gaige kaifang jinru xin jieduan" (Fujian's Reform and Opening Enter a New Stage), *Liaowang*, 30 November 1992, p. 11.

94. *Fujian jingji nianjian 1994*, pp. 180–181. Many of these, however, appear to be in real estate projects, rather than in infrastructure or basic industry.

95. "Deng Xiaoping tongzhi tan tequ deng wenti" (Comrade Deng Xiaoping Talks about the Special Economic Zones and Other Problems), in *Zhongyang dui Guangdong, 1983–1985*, p. 125.

96. Zhang and Ni, *Fujian jingji*, p. 402.

97. *Fujian ribao*, August 9, 1986, p. 1; trans. *JPRS*, September 21, 1990, pp. 85–86.

98. "Xiyin waishang touzi banhao chengpian kaifa tuidong kuoda kaifang" (Attract Foreign Investment, Do a Good Job in Land Development, Promote and Expand Opening), *Fujian ribao*, July 6, 1990, p. 1.

99. This figure was calculated from statistics provided in Zhang Shoushan, *Fujian duiwai sishinian*, pp. 101–103.

100. Elizabeth Cheng, "Setback for Xiamen," *China Trade Report* (August 1991), p. 1.

101. Kent Chen, "Attempt to Lure Taiwan Tycoon," *South China Morning Post*, March 24, 1992, p. 10.

102. Interview File 6.7; Xi Chang and Wang Jian, "Wang Yongqing Haicang zhibu Xiamen shangxiaxin busi" (Wang Yongqing Has Halted His Haicang Project, but Xiamen Refuses to Give Up), *Ming bao*, February 1, 1993, p. 43.

103. Wang Yong, "Fujian Will Straighten Links with Taiwanese," *China Daily*, March 26, 1993, p. 1; *China Trade Report* (August 1991), pp. 8–9.

104. Wang Yong, "Fujian Will Straighten Links," p. 1; *Fujian jingji nianjian 1994*, p. 183.

105. See Valerie Bunce, *Do New Leaders Make a Difference? Executive Succession and Public Policy under Capitalism and Socialism* (Princeton: Princeton University Press, 1981); Seweryn Bialer, *Stalin's Successors* (Cambridge: Cambridge University Press, 1980).

106. Xi and Wang, "Deng Xiaoping," p. 44.

107. This point was raised by Kevin Lane in his discussion at the 1995 Association for Asian Studies panel, "Provincial Strategies of Economic Reform in Post-Mao China."

7

Hainan Province in Reform

Political Dependence and
Economic Interdependence

Feng Chongyi and David S.G. Goodman

Since the mid-1980s and with reform in the People's Republic of China (PRC) Hainan Island has become something of a legend for being China's equivalent of "the wild west." Lawlessness is not so much a problem as the reputation for laxity—emphasized by a series of spectacular cases of corruption. Physical as well as political distance from the mainland and Beijing are obvious characteristics of Hainan's place in contemporary China, and in the wake of the events of June 1989 many took refuge in Hainan.

However, these aspects of its reputation are best understood in the context of the dramatic and rapid changes in Hainan's policy environment during the last decade. Long-term local claims for provincial status were finally granted by Beijing in 1988. At the same time, the province—previously part of Guangdong Province—also became a Special Economic Zone (SEZ). The drives to establish Hainan's political independence from Guangdong and its economic interdependence with both the rest of the PRC and the international economy are the keys to understanding the political behavior of provincial leaders in the late 1980s and first half of the 1990s, as well as the development of a new Chinese province.

Hainan Province: Society, Economy, and Politics

On April 13, 1988, the PRC State Council established Hainan as both a province and a Special Economic Zone. Hainan Island has a land area of 34,000 square kilometers—2,000 square kilometers smaller than Taiwan—and a population of 7.1 million.[1] However, Hainan Province is much larger than Hainan Island. Its administrative jurisdiction includes not only the island but also the 2 million square kilometers of the South China Sea, which accounts for about two-thirds of China's sea area, and around 200 islands to the south of Hainan, including the Spratly Islands.

Hainan is a new province, but China's rule over the island dates back to the Han dynasty. Hainan was formally incorporated into China's territory in 110 BC. Immigration has been substantial, particularly at times of imperial stress. Immigration from the mainland has been no less spectacular since the establishment of the PRC. According to the 1982 census, 830,000 migrated between 1950 and 1981—mostly cadres and ex-servicemen, many of whom settled or were settled in the state farms. Those migrants and their families now account for about 18 percent of the total population of the island. In addition, a further 15 percent or so of the population have migrated from the mainland since the start of the reform era. The 1990 census indicated that mainland migrants accounted for one-third of population growth in Hainan during 1950–1989. In the 1990s numbers have continued to grow with migrants attracted by economic dynamism, and the lack of political controls compared to North China.

Hainan remains as it has been for some time, a predominantly Han Chinese culture. However, there are non-Han Chinese on the island. There are about a million Li and small communities of other nationalities. The largest of these other minority nationality communities is the Miao. The Hainan Miao share common characteristics with the Miao of Southwest China, though they have largely been assimilated by the Li. The origins and ethnicity of the Li, on the other hand, remains a subject of considerable dispute.

Hainan is also an important center for overseas Chinese activity. More than 2 million overseas Chinese living in over 50 countries are of Hainan origin, with particularly sizable concentrations in Hong Kong and Southeast Asia. There are over 1 million returned overseas Chinese and their dependents now living in Hainan: the highest proportion of overseas Chinese in the total population of any province. overseas Chinese have been a most important source of foreign capital in the development of southern China generally during the reform era[2] and Hainan has been no exception. This had also been the case before 1949: the production of many important tropical crops—such as rubber, coffee, pepper, cocoa, pineapple, palm oil, sisal hemp and lemon grass—was first introduced by overseas Chinese, who also founded the first modern factories, schools and hospitals in Hainan.[3] Thousands of overseas Chinese returning to China from Southeast Asia for various reasons in and after the 1950s were settled in Hainan and participated in the development of tropical agriculture and other undertakings.

Hainan has been a largely multi-cultural island throughout its written history. The Li have their own culture, in terms of speech, dress, customs, and religious beliefs. The majority Han Chinese on Hainan developed their own culture to some extent different from that of mainland China. They speak Hainanese, similar to southern Fujianese but entirely different from Mandarin. Due to the close relationship with Southeast Asia, some Malay and English vocabulary has been incorporated in the daily speech of Hainanese villagers. While the Li have become assimilated by the Han in many ways, the Han Chinese on Hainan have come to share some of the religious beliefs of the Li.

The Struggle for Provincial Status

Hainanese are very conscious of their physical and political distance from Beijing, and indeed mainland, and mainstream, China. In their minds distance is the main explanation for all the differences between Hainan and mainland China. The Hainanese consider that the Chinese central government always, whatever the complexion of the government, discriminates against their island. Relations between Hainan and the national capital have rarely been considered harmonious.

In ancient times, when those who lived in southern China generally were labeled as "southern barbarians," Hainan was regarded by the imperial government as "the remotest corner of the earth"—only suitable for the exile of criminals from mainland China. In the eighteenth century a high-ranking official of the Qing dynasty reported to the emperor that Hainan Island was so barbarous and far away that "it was a waste of money to build cities, schools, government offices, and granaries there."[4]

Where regionalism in Guangdong Province in modern times has manifested itself in the pursuit of greater autonomy for the province from central government, the dream for Hainanese has been to separate Hainan from Guangdong Province and establish a separate Hainan Province. Several attempts had been made by Hainanese, sometimes even with the support of national leaders but all failed until 1988. The idea was put forward during the late Qing dynasty by Pan Chun; and proposed several times with no success by Sun Yat-sen (married to Song Qingling, herself a Hainanese). Though Chiang Kai-shek planned to establish a Hainan Province, its Preparatory Committee collapsed with the Nationalist regime in 1949.

After 1949 the drive to establish a Hainan Province fell foul of new political tensions. Hainan was the last area formally taken over by the Chinese Communist Party (CCP) except for Tibet. However, native Hainanese communists were and have remained very proud that the Qiongya Revolutionary Base Area was the only long-term CCP base area anywhere with a sustained presence from 1927 through to 1950.[5] When the Fourth Field Army of the People's Liberation Army (PLA) came to "liberate" Hainan in 1950, they enjoyed the substantial assistance of the local Qiongya Column with 25,000 guerrillas.[6] At first the central leadership of the CCP attempted to accommodate the Hainanese guerrillas, under Feng Baiju. However, Feng's proposal that Hainan become a separate province proved counter-productive, causing suspicion within the leaderships in both Guangzhou (the provincial capital) and Beijing. As increasing numbers of Hainan's local cadres were replaced by members of the "great southbound army" and the Southbound Work Team, sent from the mainland with Beijing's blessing and support, resentment rapidly built up among local people. Resentment led to open complaints by local communists during the Hundred Flowers Movement of 1957, and even an armed uprising in Lingao County, which in turn led to repression of Feng Baiju's so-called independent kingdom and the removal of many native Hainan cadres.

Hainan's status within the PRC remained unaltered until the reform era when the central government tried to turn Hainan into a *de facto* SEZ. The process was interrupted by the "Hainan Car Scandal" of 1985 but Hainan finally achieved provincial status in 1988. The motive for this change appears more political than economic. A most important factor was the strategy to unify mainland China and Taiwan peacefully. Comparison between Hainan and Taiwan is inevitable but embarrassing for Beijing: during the 1940s Taiwan's level of economic development was only slightly higher that of Hainan; by the 1980s the per capita GNP of Taiwan was about twenty times than that of Hainan, in spite of Hainan's much richer natural resources and much smaller population.

Hainan also became important as a testing ground for the central government to try bolder economic and political reforms during the late 1980s. The then general secretary of the CCP, Zhao Ziyang, and other Chinese leaders believed that Hainan was expendable. It was such a small economy, accounting for only half a percent of the nation's GNP, and its physical separation from the mainland meant that it would not do much harm to China as a whole if experimental reform on the island led to unpleasant results or even chaos. On the other hand, unlike the other four SEZs which were all small coastal cities, Hainan's experience of reform would be more relevant to China as a whole. A comprehensive social-economic entity, with a per capita GNP at around the national average level and 80 percent of its population engaged in agriculture or agriculture-related activities, it replicated some of the important features of the whole country, if on a much smaller scale.

Economic Development before 1988

The economy of Hainan has developed from colonial tutelage during 1950–1980 to a more export-oriented and internationally-interdependent development strategy that came with provincial status in 1988. During the earlier era, the Hainan economy was characterized by its dependency on the mainland, the result of a deliberate policy of underdevelopment. Hainan has always had abundant natural resources, but there was little attempt from either the central or Guangdong governments to provide the additional processing industries or infrastructural projects for their development. All strategic resources—iron ore, rubber, and salt—were directly controlled by Beijing or Guangdong and Hainan's output was allocated to other parts of China for the development of industry elsewhere. As a result, Hainan was an island with productive iron mines (unlike the rest of

Guangdong Province) but no iron and steel industry; an island of vast rubber plantations without the associated industries and enterprises; an island of vast forests without a timber processing industry; and an island with 1,528 kilometers of coast line but no major harbor facilities.

During 1952–1980 state investment in Hainan was only 4.3 billion yuan, less than one-tenth of total state investment in Shanghai's Baoshan Iron and Steel Plant. Moreover, most state investment in Hainan went into the extraction of rubber, iron ore and other raw materials for the mainland, leaving little to improve local infrastructure. In 1980, the level of economic development in Hainan was very low: gross industrial and agricultural output value for Hainan was only 1.7 billion yuan, less than a well-developed county on the mainland. There was only one small airport for both military and civilian use, suitable only for the small An-24 aircraft, with four flights a day to Guangzhou and Zhanjiang only; more than half of Hainan's factories in the light industrial sector were completely unautomated; and Hainan's urban population was less than 9 percent of the total, the same as in the 1950s.

In 1980, Document 202 of the State Council—"A Summary of the Forum on the Hainan Island Problem"—authorized Hainan to "copy the experience of Shenzhen and Zhuhai in its economic activities with the outside world" and Hainan entered its "open era." In April 1983, the State Council and the Central Committee of the CCP jointly issued a document known as "A Summary of the Forum on Speeding up the Development of Hainan Island" to elaborate on the "Quasi-Special Economic Zone" policy adopted for Hainan, particularly preferential policies for importing foreign goods and attracting foreign investment. Hainan established its first foreign capital enterprise in 1980, and made use of its first foreign loan in 1983. During 1980–1985, Hainan signed 272 contracts for foreign investment with a total committed investment of US$ 252 million, and actually made use of US$ 36.44 million. Construction started on a number of large-scale projects, and industrial and agricultural output value in Hainan grew at a rate of over 14 percent in 1983 and 1984.

Unfortunately, Hainan lost almost all preferential rights when the central government decided to punish the island in 1985 after the "Hainan Car Scandal." Various enterprises had taken advantage of one of the loopholes in the regulations under which foreign-made cars—and indeed a whole range of white goods—could be imported into Hainan without paying any tax, and then immediately re-exported to mainland China at a profit. The central and Guangdong governments severely punished this practice by revoking Hainan's preferential status and removing the leading reformist cadre, Lei Yu, from the leadership. As a consequence, the Hainan economy lost its momentum. In 1986, Hainan's per capita GDP was only 744 yuan, about 83 percent of the national average. The fixed assets of industry were only 1.9 billion yuan. Total island power capacity was only 397,000 kw, 80 percent of which depended on unreliable hydroelectric production. The value of industrial output was only 1.5 billion yuan, accounting

Table 7.1

Major Economic Indicators of Hainan, 1987–1994

Year	Population (million)	GDP (billion yuan)	National income (billion yuan)
1987	6.15	5.59	4.55
1988	6.27	7.50	6.15
1989	6.39	8.50	7.16
1990	6.51	9.50	7.70
1991	6.61	10.79	8.77
1992	6.71	14.08	11.11
1993	7.01	22.52	17.07
1994	7.11	33.09	—

Sources: Hainan Province Statistics Bureau, *Hainan tongji nianjian 1988–1990* (Hainan Statistics Yearbook); Liao Xun, et al (eds.) *Hainan nianjian 1991–1995* (Hainan Yearbook); Hainan Province Statistics Bureau, "Statistical Communiqué on Social and Economic Development in 1993," in Hainan Ribao, February 28, 1994; Hainan Province Statistics Bureau, "Statistical Communiqué on Social and Economic Development in 1994," in *Hainan Ribao*, February 23, 1995.

for less than a quarter of social output value. The yield per unit area of rice was only 57 percent of the national average. Only 0.35 percent of its population had tertiary education; one-third of its population lived beneath the national poverty level; and more than one-third of its population above the age of 12 was illiterate or semi-illiterate.

Economic Performance since 1988

Economically the Hainan SEZ was not established at an opportune moment, for the end of 1988 marked the beginning of three years of economic austerity in China. Nevertheless, the new-born Hainan SEZ managed to nurse its economy through both favorable and adverse environments. As Table 7.1 indicates, during 1988–93 the province's GDP growth rate averaged 14 percent annually, substantially higher than the national average. In the same period, the annual growth rate for national income was 11 percent; and the annual growth rate for local financial income was 47.6 percent.

After 1988 the most difficult year for the Hainan economy was 1989, when the growth rates in GNP and national income over the previous year were only 5.2 percent and 4.3 percent respectively. The growth rate of the Hainan economy climbed to double digits for the first time in 1991, followed by two years of fast growth in 1992 and 1993, when GDP growth rates stood at 22.4 percent and 22.8 percent respectively. Hainan's per capita GDP growth rates outstripped the national average in 1992, when the province also fulfilled its goal to be self-sufficient in grain staples. These economic achievements enabled 1.6 million people in the province to rise above the poverty level: some 80 percent of the population having previously lived under the poverty line before the establishment of the province.

The momentum of and potential for economic development in Hainan has attracted the attention of those on the mainland and abroad in the most obvious of ways. During 1988–1993 a total of 6,484 foreign firms from 52 countries registered in the province, with contracted investment amounting to US$ 7.64 billion. At the same time, provinces from mainland China registered 17,700 domestic-linked enterprises on the island, with contracted investment totaling 49.5 billion yuan.

In the new round of China's economic advance that started with Deng Xiaoping's "Southern Tour" in 1992 Hainan has been one of the best economic performers, due primarily to the involvement of foreign capital. Renewed economic resurgence came to Hainan earlier than elsewhere, particularly in the development of the property market. While the real estate market in other coastal areas began to flourish during the second half of 1992, in Hainan it had advanced dramatically when news of Deng's trip first filtered out to a small circle of influential figures at the beginning of 1992. In the nine months from January to September of that year the number of property development firms in Hainan increased from about 300 to over 900. A total of 1.2 billion yuan was poured into real estate, including the establishment of more than 80 property development districts. The average price for houses on the open market increased from 2,000 yuan per square meter to 4,000 yuan per square meter, reaching a peak of 9,800 yuan per square meter.[7]

At the same time, Hainan has been somewhat more resistant to the central government's economic restraint measures than elsewhere. In the spring of 1993 when the central government began to tighten the money supply, the economic high tide ebbed away later in Hainan than in other provinces. In contrast to elsewhere, the surplus of bank savings in Hainan increased steadily from 3.6 billion yuan in January 1993 to 17.9 billion yuan in June 1993 before beginning to decrease.[8]

Provincial Leaders in the Reform Era

Hainan's leaders have played key roles in the development of the island during the reform era. Almost all have been nationally high profile figures, and often have been surrounded by considerable controversy. The rise and fall of both Lei Yu and Liang Xiang has been spectacular and dramatic, and certainly have had a major impact on Hainan's development. However, Hainan's development has been influenced significantly by every leadership change, if only because different leaders have had different perspectives on that process. Lei Yu emphasized the idea of free trade, highlighting the advantages of a free flow of goods, capital, technology and personnel between Hainan and the outside world. Xu Shijie and Liang Xiang concentrated on a program of marketization and partial privatization. Ruan Chongwu preferred to emphasize the transformation of government functions, and the consequent changes in economic management.

While it is easy to attribute the consequences of controversy to personalities and individual leadership styles, it is also likely that the novelty of Hainan's institutions and its rapidly changing economic environment have consequences that are largely uncontrollable by anyone. Certainly, the development strategies devised by Hainan's leaders since 1983 have featured in the forefront of China's experiments with reform and "openness." Hainan has experimented with free trade, privatization, full-scale social security, a convertible currency, and with various ideas related to the "market economy" and the notion of "small government."

Lei Yu as a Pathbreaker

The first party secretary and governor of Hainan Province were Xu Shijie and Liang Xiang, but in every sense the history of Hainan's leadership in the reform era dates back to Lei Yu, who formulated the first comprehensive program for the island's reform and opening. In 1980, when the central government decided to open Hainan to the outside world, the island, then known as the Hainan Administrative Area (of Guangdong Province), was under Party Secretary Luo Tian and Director of the Administrative Office Wei Nanjin. In order to ensure that Hainan moved in the same direction and at the same pace as other parts of Guangdong, the provincial leadership put the young and ambitious Lei Yu in charge of the Hainan government in August 1982.

Lei Yu was born to a poor family and brought up by his widowed mother in Guangxi's Heng County in 1934. He joined the PLA in 1949 and participated in the Korean War. In 1952, Lei was decorated as a war hero and sent to study industrial economics at People's University. On graduation he was assigned to a coal mine in North-East China and later appointed director of its planning section. It is generally believed that during his twenty years in North-East China he developed a close relationship with Ren Zhongyi, who became secretary of the Guangdong Provincial Party Committee in the 1980s and subsequently appointed Lei to important positions. Lei returned to South China in 1980 and served successively as deputy director of the General Office of the CCP Guangdong Provincial Party Committee and director of its Policy Research Institute. In the summer of 1981 he led a group of officials from the Provincial Party Committee to Hainan to make an on-the-spot investigation of its circumstances and problems. The group's proposal was well received by both the provincial and central leader, who selected Lei Yu to be Hainan's new leader.

In his late forties, Lei was relatively young for the position. Certainly, at the seventeenth grade of the cadre salary scale, Lei was the lowest ranked official ever sent to lead Hainan. Nevertheless, he was clearly able and it was a calculated gamble by the Guangdong provincial authorities. Alongside Lei Yu they appointed the more experienced Yao Wenxu as party secretary, doubtless in the hope that at critical moments the elder Yao would be able to counsel Lei Yu. In the event, it transpired that Yao Wenxu always gave Lei Yu a free hand in his work in Hainan.

In order to concentrate on his new appointment, Lei took his secretary rather than his family from Guangzhou to Hainan. He essentially abandoned family life in favor of his new work and even ate in the public dining hall, a practice increasingly shunned by ranking officials in the 1980s. He made use of every opportunity to raise his public profile, particularly through the mass media of communication. Interviews were arranged with journalists from all over the world, and he started a special column—*Hainan Takes Off*—on the front page of *The Hainan Daily* to publicize new undertakings and achievements.

After four months in Hainan, Lei Yu announced his administrative program in a public speech. Hainan was to change in five years and become an advanced economy by the end of the century. He summarized his measures as "one foundation," "two breakthroughs," "three industries," and "four new prospects." By the "one foundation" Lei Yu meant the development of tropical agriculture in Hainan, including high yield grain crops, high return economic crops, tropical forests, aquatic breeding, and livestock husbandry. The "two breakthroughs" were to strengthen Hainan's two weakest links: infrastructure and education. Many large-scale projects were designed to this end, including the Changpo Coal Mine, the Daguangba Hydropower Station, off-shore oil exploration of the South China Sea, flights between Hainan and Hong Kong, railways along the western coast line of the island, improvement of the three major highways between the north and south of the island, improvement of the major harbors around the island, and preparations for the establishment of Hainan University. The "three industries," which Lei Yu believed to be Hainan's comparative advantage, and therefore to receive priority in development, were mining, processing based on the agricultural and mineral resources of Hainan, and tourism. The "four new prospects," according to Lei, were a range of Hainan manufactured goods popular on the national and international markets; a complete industry system centered around mining and processing; large-scale tropical agriculture; and the utilization of capital from abroad for development.[9] There can be little doubt that Lei Yu's strategy appealed to almost everyone concerned with the development of Hainan, particularly the Guangdong Provincial Government and the central government. Guangdong Provincial Party Secretary Ren Zhongyi and Governor Liu Tianfu visited Hainan on 16 January 1983; followed by the then Premier Zhao Ziyang on 18 January, and the then General Secretary of the CCP Hu Yaobang on 10 February. All of them, and Hu Yaobang in particular, sent very positive and public messages to Lei Yu.

One of Lei Yu's major problems was that there was almost no capital to finance his plan. He attempted to solve this deficiency in three ways. The first was to attract financial support from both the central government and Guangdong Province. At the end of 1982 and the beginning of 1983, he personally visited more than twenty departments and bureaus within the Guangdong Provincial Government; and more than twenty ministries and commissions of the central government to lobby for funding for projects in Hainan. In the event, this strategy reaped only limited rewards for both the Guangdong Provincial Government and the central government granted preferential policies rather than concrete financial support.

Lei Yu's second tactic was to attract investment from abroad and other parts of China. This was in line with central government thinking. As already noted, when "A Summary of the Forum on Speeding up the Development of Hainan Island" was jointly issued by the State Council and the Central Committee of the CCP in April 1983, it granted Hainan similar preferential policies to those enjoyed by the SEZs. Lei Yu publicized these policies through the media, particularly when he visited Hong Kong. In Lei Yu's view, Hainan was even more "special" than the SEZs: in addition to tax holidays and other preferential arrangements available in the SEZs, foreign investors in Hainan could engage in mining and agricultural development, and could contract large areas of land for comprehensive development.[10] This maneuver proved to be effective. A "Hainan Fever" resulted with literally thousands of highly qualified technologists, managers, and entrepreneurs crossing to the island from the mainland; and large numbers of business people coming from outside the PRC to look for opportunities in Hainan during 1983–1984.

However, Hainan's infrastructure remained inadequate for foreign investment, and local governments had too little power to deal with the problems that emerged with development. The mines and industrial enterprises were controlled by either the Guangdong Provincial Government or by the central government; rubber and other important tropical crops were controlled by the Guangdong Provincial Bureau of Agricultural Reclamation; the central and the western parts of the island were under the jurisdiction of the Hainan Li and Miao Autonomous Prefecture; and the Hainan government only had power to approve projects worth less than US$ 5 million. In October 1984 Lei Yu managed to arrange for the Hainan Administrative Office to be replaced by a Hainan People's Government—a level of government between the province and the prefecture—but without any great success. This level of government did not fit easily into the existing hierarchy, and Lei Yu himself, ironically, was left without a proper title, hidden weakly behind the description of "major responsible person in charge of Hainan People's Government."

The third solution advocated by Lei Yu was to make money by taking advantage of Hainan's special policies. Lei Yu and his colleagues were impressed by the experience of Shenzhen and other parts of Guangdong which made use of their special policies to earn money through importing low tax or tax-free goods from abroad and re-selling them to other parts of China. In "A Summary of the Forum on Speeding up the Development of Hainan Island," the document Lei Yu had played an important part in drafting, there was a provision that Hainan could import state-controlled consumer goods, including cars and household durables.

These imported goods could not be resold to the mainland, but there was no regulation that forbade people in Hainan selling their "secondhand" goods to the mainland. In the light of later developments it is at least possible to believe that this was a loophole deliberately created.

In early 1984 Lei Yu, his partner Yao Wenxu, and his deputy Chen Yuyi, who was in charge of foreign trade, began to cautiously loosen the controls on the trade of imported cars between the island and the mainland. In late July of that year, a deputy director of the marketing section of the State Administrative Bureau of Industry and Commerce stated at a forum in Shanxi that units and individuals from elsewhere in China could buy imported cars in Guangdong and Fujian. Stimulated by this speech, the car trade in Hainan grew rapidly, even to the extent that it was reported sensationally in the Hong Kong and Western media. In September Lei Yu was warned by his superiors that the car trade would have to be kept in bounds, and he appears to have made efforts to slow imports in a planned way that would not adversely affect local people too suddenly. He apparently still felt justified in encouraging car imports, not only because he himself did not gain financially from the trade, but also because of the benefit to the Hainan economy.

Nevertheless, it was unlikely to prove a viable policy in the long term, not least because of the uncertainties of national-level politics. In November 1984 Lei Yu was summoned to Guangzhou and asked to explain his actions. In March 1985 an investigation team with members from the CCP Central Discipline Inspection Commission, Supreme People's Procuratorate, the State Audit Office, the State Economic Commission, the Ministry of Foreign Economic Relations and Trade, the Office of Special Economic Zones, the State Bureau of Goods and Materials, Guangdong Provincial Party Committee and Guangdong People's Provincial Government gathered in Hainan to examine the so-called car scandal. According to the team's report, during January 1984 to March 1985, 89,000 cars and mini-buses were imported to Hainan and more than 10,000 were then resold to 27 provinces on the mainland. The punishment was severe: all cars and mini-buses unsold on the island were confiscated by the central government; Yao Wenxu received an "inner-party warning" and Lei Yu and Chen Yuyi were removed from office, though no one was found to have behaved corruptly. Hainan's preferential policy in foreign trade was rescinded. The incident was a clear set-back to the development of Hainan's economy and it did not recover until 1987.

Xu Shijie and Liang Xiang as Pioneers

Notwithstanding the car scandal on 24 February 1985, Deng Xiaoping told Hu Yaobang, Zhao Ziyang and other important Chinese leaders that Hainan should catch up with Taiwan in twenty years.[11] In late 1986 and early 1987, Zhao Ziyang successively sent a number of important figures such as Liang Xiang, Xu Shijie, Liang Lingguang (all from Guangdong) Xu Jiatun (then head of the New China

News Agency in Hong Kong) and Chen Junsheng (secretary-general of the State Council) to inspect Hainan. All of them came to the conclusion that Hainan should become a separate province and be granted SEZ status and functions. The proposal was approved by Zhao Ziyang, Hu Yaobang and Deng Xiaoping, who first revealed the idea publicly when talking to guests from Yugoslavia on 12 June 1987: "We are setting up a larger Special Economic Zone, namely the Hainan Special Economic Zone."[12] The decision to establish a provincial SEZ was unprecedented, as was the decision to appoint two retired officials to head the province. In September 1987 Xu Shijie and Liang Xiang, party secretary and governor of Hainan Province respectively after August 1988, were appointed to prepare for the establishment of Hainan Province. At that time Xu had been retired for more than a year from his previous post as party secretary of Guangzhou; Liang had similarly been retired for more than a year as deputy governor of Guangdong, and mayor of Shenzhen. It seems reasonable to assume that Xu's appointment was because of his past experience in Hainan; whereas Liang's success in Shenzhen and his close relationship with Zhao Ziyang probably accounted for his appointment.

In a move clearly chosen for its symbolism Xu and Liang crossed the Qiongzhou Straits on 22 September to attend celebrations of the sixtieth anniversary of the founding of the Qiongya Base Area. Strangely, at the time they told friends they were too old to care about their personal futures and ready to risk everything, even ill-health or jail, in the attempt to develop Hainan. In the event during their tenure of office in Hainan, Liang was disciplined and almost jailed in September 1989, and Xu was hospitalized and forced to resign in July 1990.

Xu Shijie was born in Guangdong's Chenghai County in 1920. After completing high school in his hometown, Xu joined the CCP in 1938 and became a professional revolutionary. Before 1949 Xu became a county party secretary and a deputy secretary of a prefectural party committee in the CCP base area in Guangdong. After 1949 he became the first party secretary in his native Chenghai County. He then successively served on the Standing Committee of the Shantou Prefectural Party Committee, as deputy director of the General Office of the Guangdong Provincial Party Committee, as deputy director of the Policy Research Institute of the Guangdong Provincial Party Committee, as deputy director of the Rural Department of the Guangdong Provincial Party Committee, and as party secretary of Xinhui County. In 1964 Xu was appointed as deputy secretary of the Party Committee of the Hainan Administrative Area and remained there for seven years before being transferred elsewhere in Guangdong. In 1981 he was promoted to secretary of the Guangzhou Party Committee, first political commissar of Guangzhou Military Sub-district, and a member of the Standing Committee of the Guangdong Party Committee. He is well-known for his cheery disposition and optimism, as well as for his fondness for composing poems.

According to the formal division of labor, party affairs were Xu's major concern in Hainan. At the same time he and Liang Xiang clearly cooperated closely in all important decisions about the development of Hainan. Moreover, although Liang had the more important initiating role, Xu's personal contribution was important in gaining the support of local cadres for new programs. Unlike other provinces, all the senior officials in Hainan were the direct appointment of central authorities. At subordinate levels where Xu had control he set the general principles for recruitment, promoting local officials as far as possible, and only importing personnel from the mainland when local people were not professionally qualified. Although not all local officials were Hainanese, locals did benefit from the upgrading of Hainan from a prefecture to a province. In the process, Xu became one of the few mainlanders to gain local support, and created a strong community of interest for reform and economic development. Given traditions of favoritism and factionalism within China's politics it is more usual to expect political and enterprise leaders from the mainland to recruit their subordinates from their former positions: this has been a source of increasing tension and conflict in Hainan during the 1990s.

From all accounts it would seem Xu did his best to assist Liang Xiang, although, judging by his criticism of the latter after Liang's downfall, their personal relations were by no means close and Xu was not usually consulted by Liang. The original blueprint for Hainan as a provincial SEZ was drafted by a team that included Liang Xiang, Zhao Ziyang, and Liu Guoguang. However, Xu Shijie's contribution to its implementation was essential. Although he had been cautious on reform and not very flexible when party secretary of Guangzhou, in Hainan he cooperated very well with Liang to promote economic liberalism and flexibility in dealing with their regulatory environment. "It is a greatest happiness" he told cadres from all over Hainan at one conference "to make use of the autonomous powers granted to Hainan by the central authorities. . . . The policies only prohibit us from doing a few things, whereas we can do everything else. We in Hainan have the power to do everything not proscribed."[13] Despite his past Xu Shijie appeared as one of the most liberal provincial party secretaries in 1988 when he wrote "Hainan can adopt special methods. State enterprises can be leased out, contracted out, turned to joint-stock companies, and even sold off. Or, they can be converted into shares and become joint-ventures with foreign investors."[14] He repeated this idea in his report to the First Provincial Party Congress, "We should accelerate the reform of enterprises: firstly, making up our mind to auction off those enterprises running at a loss for a long time, turning them from state enterprises to private enterprises, and encouraging investors from home and abroad to buy them; secondly, establishing joint-stock companies, eventually forming a pluralist enterprise system in which the state, collectives, individuals, and national and international investors all have their shares."[15]

Liang Xiang was born in Guangdong's Kaiping County in 1919. He joined the CCP and participated in the party's underground operations in Guangzhou in 1936 when he was a schoolboy. In 1937 he was sent to study at the Central Party

School in Yan'an, where he later became the secretary of the general party branch and deputy director of the dean's office. After the victory of the Anti-Japanese War in 1945 Liang served in the CCP base area in Liaoning Province successively as head of Xian County, deputy director of the Organization Department of the Xian Prefectural Party Committee, and secretary of Shenyang's Daxi District Party Committee. In 1949 Liang was transferred back to his home province of Guangdong. He served successively as the director of the Guangzhou Bureau of Communications, director of the Industrial and Commercial Bureau of Guangzhou, deputy director of the Financial Committee of Guangzhou, director of the Guangzhou Planning Committee, and deputy mayor and party secretary of Guangzhou. During 1981–1985, Liang was extremely high profile when he held appointments as the first mayor and party secretary of China's first SEZ in Shenzhen, and simultaneously deputy governor of Guangdong.

When he became the first governor of Hainan Province in 1988 Liang Xiang was very conscious of his reputation as the first mayor of Shenzhen, and his role as a hero and symbol of China's reform and opening. His self-confidence and sense of mission enabled him to take even bolder steps in Hainan, especially as he felt "there was not much time left for him.[16] In his report on Hainan to central authorities after his visit in November 1986, Liang had suggested that Hainan be developed as China's most open province, with a free flow of goods, capital and personnel. His proposal was approved by the then Premier Zhao Ziyang and that report become the original version of the blueprint to establish Hainan as a provincial SEZ.[17] It was also his idea to invite in October 1987 a group of scholars from the Chinese Academy of Social Sciences to work out a development strategy for Hainan in detail. The group of scholars led by Liu Guoguang, a famous economist, coined the concepts of the "socialist market economy" and "small government, big society" for the first time as guiding principles to develop Hainan's new economic and political system.

At the turn of 1987–1988 Liang Xiang and his colleagues succeeded in persuading the central government to develop Hainan's economy rapidly through the adoption of policies "more special than for other special zones," even though at the time they themselves were not exactly sure as to the precise content of "more special." Liang's tactic was to tap all sources, Hong Kong business circles in particular, for ideas which could then be converted into policies. As a result, two key State Council documents—"A Summary of the Forum on Further Opening and Faster Development of Hainan Island" and "Regulations of the State Council Regarding the Encouragement of Investment to Develop Hainan Island" of December 1987 and May 1988 respectively—sought to detail some of Hainan's "more special" policies. These included such innovations as the lease of large tracts of land, initially for seventy years; the establishment of foreign banks; and the issuing of entry visas to foreigners upon arrival.

Later in his work report to the first Hainan Provincial People's Congress in August 1988, Liang summed up those "more special policies" in three areas. The

Hainan economy would be regulated by the market, where government would only indirectly intervene to settle the problems which the market and enterprises were unable to solve. Hainan would build up its own diversified ownership structure, which would not be dominated by public ownership and where foreign capital enterprises would be allowed to account for a relatively large proportion of the economy. Hainan would establish a "second line of customs" between the island and the mainland so that foreigners, capital and goods could flow freely in and out of Hainan, allowing enterprises in Hainan to be run according to international practice.[18]

Liang Xiang's program had sounder economic foundations than Lei Yu's ideas. All mines, enterprises, farms and other undertakings on Hainan formerly controlled by the central government or Guangdong provincial authorities were transferred to the provincial government. The central government provided an annual 200 million yuan in low interest loans to Hainan Province. The Hainan Provincial Government was empowered to approve projects worth up to US$ 30 million. At the same time, Liang Xiang was clearly personally in a much more favorable position to secure "original accumulation" for Hainan. For example, he persuaded Zhao Ziyang to agree on a share of the gas from the Yingehai gas field off Hainan; and he made use of his previous contacts from Shenzhen to persuade the Hong Kong–Macau International Trust & Investment Corporation to fund a 250,000 kw capacity power plant.

Just as new prospects started to open for Hainan, Liang Xiang was dismissed from office in September 1989. The official reason provided at the time was that he had abused his position to find work for his son in Hong Kong and to assist his wife in property speculation.[19] However, even more than in the dismissal of Lei Yu it is clear that Liang Xiang's downfall was a function of national politics. It was an open secret that Liang Xiang had provided whole-hearted support for Zhao Ziyang during and after the events of April-June 1989 in Beijing. According to Xu Jiatun, one of Liang's close friends and a political ally, during the June 4th period the Hainan Provincial Government sent a message to the central government, supporting Zhao Ziyang in his handling of the student movement and its demonstrations. Following the downfall of Zhao Ziyang, Liang Xiang was summoned by Li Peng to Beijing to "discuss the development of Yangpu" and was held at Beijing Airport.[20]

Liu Jianfeng and Deng Hongxun as Bandwagoners

Liu Jianfeng and Deng Hongxun, who succeeded Liang Xiang and Xu Shijie in September 1989 and July 1990 respectively, had few problems with the changed national political environment. They did not share their predecessor's beliefs, concerns, or commitment. Though they both attempted to work within the constraints set by Jiang Zemin and Li Peng, they had greater difficulty working together. In the event their conflict proved disastrous to both.

Liu Jianfeng was born in Tianjin's Ninghe County in 1936. He joined the CCP in 1956 and was sent to the Soviet Union to study at the Kiev Industrial Institute. After completing his study he returned to Beijing to work as a technician at the thirteenth Institute of the State Commission of National Defense Science in 1961, later becoming its deputy director, and acting party secretary. He was appointed deputy minister of the Ministry of Electronics Industry in 1984, and it was during his tenure of office at the Ministry of the Electronics Industry that Liu first became associated with Li Peng, who later recommended Liu for the governorship of Hainan Province in 1989 when Liang Xiang was dismissed. Liu Jianfeng actually took over the governorship before his formal appointment on 14 September 1989, a week after Liang Xiang's formal discharge. In a speech at a meeting of provincial party leaders on September 4, Liu stressed that because of the underdevelopment of Hainan's economy and its unsound market system, the island would have to experience "a fairly long transitional period in which the planned economy and the commodity economy run parallel"; and that the right strategy for Hainan's cadres was to implement the policy of the central authorities "to the letter." [21] Ten days later, in his inaugural speech, Liu further emphasized his cautious and conservative approach when he defined the general direction of Hainan government as to "use policies, lay down foundations, and pay close attention to implementation."[22]

Deng Hongxun was born in Wuxi city (in Jiangsu) in 1931. He joined the CCP and participated in its underground operation in 1947. Two years later he was sent to study industrial management at Jiangnan University. After graduation from the university in 1952 he became an engineer and cadre in several iron and steel companies. Deng was promoted to mayor and deputy party secretary of Zhengjiang in 1983, party secretary of Wuxi in 1984, and deputy party secretary of Jiangsu Province in 1989. According to the introduction provided by Meng Liankun, deputy director of the CCP Central Committee's Organization Department, Deng was appointed party secretary of Hainan Province because of his "rich experience in party and government leading positions" and "his familiarity with economic work."[23] However, it is commonly assumed that Deng had powerful backers: he is Jiang Zemin's fellow townsman, and reportedly a close friend of Qiao Shi.

It was expected that Deng Hongxun would at least bring benefit to Hainan through his advanced experience in southern Jiangsu, which had been an advanced economy in China since the late 1970s, especially in terms of the rapid development of rural enterprises. However, during his tenure as party secretary in Hainan Deng did little to make use of his past experience in speeding up economic reform and development. Instead, he focused on "cadre building." When asked why he put so much emphasis on "cadre building" in an interview in November 1990, he quoted Mao Zedong's saying that cadres were the decisive factor once the political line had been determined, and emphasized that "cadre building" was the crux of construction of the Hainan SEZ.[24] These statements, as well as other acts, made Deng Hongxun extremely unpopular in Hainan, especially among native officials who rapidly became alienated. In the guise of importing talent he brought a number—seen as too high by locals—of his friends and trusted followers from Jiangsu to Hainan. He also launched a campaign to crack down on cadres' practice of building private houses for themselves, which in particular adversely affected the life-styles of native officials.

Particularly at the provincial level the almost three years from early 1990 through to the end of 1992 were not a stable period for Hainan. Liu Jianfeng and Deng Hongxun never settled and appeared unable to work together. They rapidly clashed and their fierce wrangling was not only dysfunctional to Hainan's development but it seems reasonable to assume it was also an embarrassment to Jiang Zemin and Li Peng. Deng Hongxun in particular rapidly gained an anti-Hainan reputation. Conflict between the governor and party secretary came to a head at the end of 1992 as both Liu and Deng tried to drive the other out of Hainan. It is rumored that at Deng Hongxun's instigation, a high-ranking provincial official—Li Shanyou—lodged a false criticism of Governor Liu Jianfeng, accusing him of visiting a prostitute. When the conspiracy was brought to light and Li Shanyou was sent to prison, Governor Liu launched a follow-up investigation to unmask the hidden instigator behind his accusation. Consequently, both Liu Jianfeng and Deng Hongxun were transferred to Beijing for other appointments in January 1993.

Ruan Chongwu as a Cautious Reformer

Liu Jianfeng and Deng Hongxun were replaced in January 1993 by one man—Ruan Chongwu. At the time, Ruan was minister of labor and already a member of the CCP Central Committee, and clearly the most senior official sent to Hainan since the 1950s. He is widely believed to be a member of Jiang Zemin's circle, having served under Jiang in Shanghai during the 1980s. Two months after Ruan's appointment, Jiang Zemin came to Hainan to celebrate the fifth anniversary of Hainan Province.

Ruan Chongwu was born in May 1933 in Hebei's Huailai County. His father, Ruan Muhan, was an early participant in underground CCP operations, and later served as mayor of Huhehaote in Inner Mongolia. Ruan Chongwu's education does not seem particularly reform-oriented: he attended primary and secondary schools along with the children of other cadres in Yan'an and the Jin-Cha-Ji base areas. He attended the Beijing Engineering Institute in 1951 and joined the CCP in the same year. In 1953, he went to the Soviet Union for advanced training at the Moscow Institute of Automotive Mechanics, and stayed there for four years.

Ruan's first position on his return from Moscow in 1957 was at the Shenyang Institute of Casting, heading the research division. In 1962 he was transferred to the Shanghai Materials Research Institute and later rose to become its deputy director. During 1969–71 Ruan was sent to perform manual labor at a May 7 cadre school. In 1978 he was appointed to the Chinese Embassy in West Germany as counselor for science and technology. A recall to Shanghai in 1983 saw his promotion to deputy secretary of the Shanghai Municipal Party Committee. He became deputy mayor of Shanghai before his appointment as minister of public security in 1985. From 1987 to 1989 he was in charge of the State Commission for Science and Technology, and then in 1989 he was appointed minister of labor and personnel.

Ruan is reputed to be a man of action rather than talk, and he prefers to maintain a low public profile, having asked—in contrast to some of his predecessors—that the Hainan media not focus on him. His first official speech—"Unite and cooperate to strive for steady development and new objectives" (in Hainan)—overwhelmingly stressed the need for "solid work."[25] Ruan's leadership strategy is not at all at odds with the new national political environment facing Hainan, where since 1992 other provinces have been able to enjoy the "special policies" previously reserved for Hainan.

Ruan's achievements in Hainan so far have been relatively small scale, simple but significant reforms that have had substantial benefits and caught nationwide attention. Three of them are particularly well known. The previously complicated procedure for approval of the establishment of a new firm has been replaced with a simple system of registration. It now only takes one or two days to complete procedures whereas previously three months was normal. Tax collection has been computerized with the result that government financial income has increased, and loopholes in tax collection have been closed. All road fees—including the costs of maintenance—have been converted to a single petroleum tax, in an attempt to produce a simple and effective road management scheme.

For Ruan Chongwu these reforms all point to the transformation of government into a market economy–supporting activity. In one article he argued that "the market economy is an economic system which allocates resources through market mechanisms. It is imperative that the government transform its functions. We are required to make our own power the first target of attack, and sacrifice ourselves for the overall cause of reform."[26] In an interview he vividly depicted what he was doing in this regard as "reducing the gate guards and increasing the cleaners."[27]

At the same time, Ruan Chongwu has been very cautious especially where "guiding principles" are involved. For example, when the question of whether privatization in Hainan had gone too far was raised by some leaders in the central government, Ruan immediately instructed the General Office of the provincial government to write a document which showed that since the founding of Hainan Province "the strength of public ownership has grown without interruption, and the public sector retains its dominant position."[28]

Policy Toward Foreign Capital and Investment

Hainan has never had any choice about the extent of foreign capital and investment in its domestic economy. Even before its establishment as a province,

Hainan's development was predicated on its ability to attract foreign capital and investment: this has been both its advantage and a principal source of difficulties. In the early 1980s when its economic transactions with the outside world were negligible it seemed decidedly over-ambitious for Hainan to adopt an externally oriented development strategy. For thirty years from 1950–1979 the total earnings from exports were only US$ 104 million and the total value of imports was only US$ 25,000, US$ 862 per annum.[29] However, Hainan's international trade witnessed a meteoric rise after 1980 with reform. In 1993 the total turnover of international trade was US$ 2.6 billion, an increase of 51 percent over the previous year. Of this, exports were US$ 902 million, an increase of 2 percent, whilst imports reached US$ 1.7 billion, twice the level of 1992.[30]

When the blueprint for the SEZ was drafted in 1987 it was estimated that some 200 billion yuan in investment would be needed were Hainan to reach the mid-1980s level of Taiwan's economic development within twenty years. It was hoped that this investment would come from outside Hainan in the beginning of the 1990s when the necessary infrastructure had to be established. This was then a very bold plan. On the one hand, the amount of investment expected was absolutely beyond the capacity of Hainan—Hainan's total income in 1987 was only 290 million yuan and its annual investment in fixed assets during 1951–1986 had only been 254 million yuan on average. On the other hand, it was far too ambitious to expect huge investment from abroad. In 1986 total investment in fixed assets in Hainan was 1.3 billion yuan, of which the shares of Hainan, mainland China, and foreign capital were 60 percent, 32 percent, and 8 percent respectively.[31]

Nevertheless, Hainan has so far managed to achieve its goals. The total investment in fixed assets between 1988–1992 was 21.7 billion yuan, 3.7 billion yuan more than the original plan of 18 billion. Among the 16.9 billion yuan of the investment in fixed assets for 1993, 2.5 billion yuan came from foreign capital enterprises, accounting for 15 percent of the total, close to the amount of 17 percent set in the original plan six years earlier.[32] According to other statistics, one-third of Hainan's investment in fixed assets during 1988–94 came from foreign sources.[33]

Foreign Investment

Foreign economic involvement in Hainan predominantly takes the forms of loans and direct investment. Investment in the forms of processing and compensatory trade, unlike elsewhere in China (and particularly Guangdong Province) is negligible. By the end of 1993 the province had signed 6,648 investment contracts with governments and enterprises in more than fifty countries and regions. Table 7.2 provides data on the leading countries and regions investing in Hainan. Contracted foreign investment had reached US$ 9.1 billion, and the actual utilization of foreign capital stood at US$ 2.2 billion. Hainan only started to receive

Table 7.2

Major Countries and Regions Investing in Hainan 1992

Country or region	Items	Contractual capital (million US dollars)	Actually utilized capital (million US dollars)
Hong Kong	1,190	1,511.3	291.8
Taiwan	327	298.2	53.5
Japan	37	257.2	53
United States	84	122.4	29
World Bank	3	76.1	15
Italy	5	68.5	19
Singapore	54	67.7	16
Thailand	34	47.5	15

Source: Liao Xun (ed.), *Hainan gaikuang 1993* (A Survey of Hainan) (Haikou: Hainan Nianjian She, 1993), p.93.

foreign loans in 1990, notably from Japan, the World Bank and France. In the four years from 1990 to 1993 a total of US$ 453 million in foreign loans was utilized in Hainan, accounting for 25 percent of the total utilized foreign investment in that period.

A total of 6,484 foreign capital enterprises had registered to engage in direct foreign investment in Hainan by the end of 1993, mainly from the Asia-Pacific region, with Hong Kong, Taiwan, Japan and the United States the largest geopolitical sources in order of US dollar value. Contracted direct investment for 1990–93 was US$ 7.6 billion, but only US$ 1.7 billion had been utilized.[34] Hong Kong has been the predominant source of investment in Hainan since the early 1980s, accounting for more than 60 percent of the total foreign investment. However, investment from Taiwan has started to increase rapidly. Direct foreign investment from Taiwan began with twelve small enterprises in 1988 and had grown rapidly to more than 500 enterprises with a total of more than 500 million yuan in contracted investment by the end of 1992.[35]

From a broad ethnic perspective, foreign investment in Hainan is to a great extent still Chinese capital, for the overseas Chinese are the dominant group of foreign investors in the province. This has of course been a characteristic of all foreign investment in China since the late 1980s. By any variable—the number of enterprises, the amount of contracted investment, or the amount of actually utilized capital—investment by overseas Chinese accounts for more than 80 percent of total investment in Hainan. In addition, overseas Chinese of Hainanese origin donated more than 400 million yuan to build schools, hospitals and other public facilities in Hainan in the period 1978–1993.[36]

While foreign loans to Hainan have been used exclusively for infrastructural projects, such as airports, highways, ports and communications, the major areas for foreign direct investment have been property and industry. In 1992 for example, foreign direct investment in property and industry in Hainan accounted for 63 percent and 25 percent of the totals respectively. The share of contracted foreign investment in the total investment in the primary, secondary, and tertiary industries is 3.4 percent, 34.4 percent, and 62.2 percent respectively.[37]

Policy Settings

In order to attract foreign capital to Hainan the provincial government has placed particular emphasis on developing the island's economic infrastructure—notably, transport, energy, and finance—and has attempted to present an attractive tax environment. In his Government Work Report to the Provincial Congress on 1 March 1994 Ruan Chongwu emphasized the importance of a favorable tax regime:

> We will continue to perfect a "fair, light, and simple taxation system." While implementing the unified national tax laws, in accordance with the tax levying management jurisdiction assigned to our province by the central authorities, . . . we will . . . combine strict tax levying management with the low tax policies of the SEZ. The preferential policies of the Hainan SEZ will have to be maintained and be kept relatively stable, so as to create the economic conditions which continue to attract domestic and foreign funds.[38]

His statement reflects exactly the current features of the Hainan tax regime. Lower tax and longer tax holidays have been one of the most important factors enabling Hainan to attract investment from the mainland and abroad. There is a range of preferential treatments toward investors in Hainan in terms of tax exemptions, tax deductions and tax holidays. Since mid-1992 all provinces in China have been competing for foreign investment with favorable tax regimes, but it is unlikely that many can match Hainan's offer of for the most part no tax for the first ten years and only half rates for the next ten.[39]

Taking advantage of the preferential policies granted by the central government, Hainan Provincial Government has also taken steps to open mining and agricultural areas to foreign investment, alongside the opening of its property and financial markets to the outside world. Hainan is the first province to allow foreign investment in all sorts of mining, mineral extraction and natural resource exploitation, including oil, gas and gold. Foreign investment in agriculture in Hainan is unique among the SEZs, largely of course because there is so little agriculture in the other SEZs. The policy of establishing long-term leases on large areas of land originated in Hainan, although it has become a common practice throughout China. In Hainan this policy has particularly benefited property development, large infrastructure projects, large-scale tourism projects and agricultural development. The idea of establishing branches of foreign banks in

China also originated in Hainan and has now been extended to Shanghai and elsewhere. Several foreign banks have been set up in Hainan, and some enterprises and investment trusts are entitled to issue shares and bonds for foreign investors.[40]

Hainan as a Special Customs Zone

From the perspective of reform, Hainan's biggest failure has been the demise of the idea of establishing a Special Customs Zone. Among other things this failure indicates the extent to which Hainan's economic dependence on the mainland still inhibits provincial autonomy. The consequences of this failure were obvious to a small circle in the leadership as early as 1989. However, the consequences have become increasingly obvious to government officials and the wider public in Hainan since Deng Xiaoping's "Southern Tour" in 1992, for other parts of China have been vying to follow the experience of Hainan and the other SEZs.

The idea of a Special Customs Zone was formally proposed by Zhao Ziyang. At a workshop in January 1988 organized by the Financial and Economic Leading Group of the CCP Central Committee to discuss basic policies for establishing Hainan Province and the Hainan Special Economic Zone, the then general secretary of the CCP told the audience: "The prerequisite to opening up Hainan is to separate Hainan from the national customs system and make it a second customs zone. This has been decided from the beginning. If this cannot be done, it is pointless to discuss any special policy."[41] Zhao and other reformist leaders intended to kill two birds with one stone. By turning Hainan into a free port—fully integrated into the international economy along the lines of another Hong Kong—they anticipated that external investment would flow in rapidly, thereby avoiding the need for massive state investment. At the same time they hoped that by isolating Hainan from the rest of the country they could both bypass China's existing systems (and their problems) and experiment with more dramatic reform measures: privatization, the termination of state monopolies, the introduction of currency convertibility, the establishment of a relatively free capital market, the development of a social security system, and the marketization of government functions.

Surprisingly, Hainan's leadership was apparently not confident enough at the time to take advantage of the offer. In March 1988 Xu Shijie told a meeting of officials above the county level:

> The problem for Hainan today is that we have little capacity to take advantage of the preferential policies granted by the center. For example, the general secretary [of the CCP] told us to remove the customs posts between Hainan and other countries, and set them up instead between Haikou and the Leizhou Peninsula [in Guangdong]. Dare we do that? I discussed this matter with comrade Liang Xiang over and over again, but we dare not. All goods from the

mainland would then be treated as foreign imports. We do not and cannot produce soap, toothpaste, nor high-quality toothpicks. Eighty percent of all goods come from the mainland. All goods would be treated as imported from abroad and charged the appropriate duty by the customs. Could we afford that?[42]

Undoubtedly, there would have been a considerable price to pay were Hainan to become a special zone separated from China's national customs system in 1988. At that time there were few factories in Hainan and 80 percent of producer goods and consumer durables came from the mainland. Customs duties added to their costs would cause a general, inflationary and unacceptable price rise. Chaos might come from another direction too. Officials on the island had no experience in managing a market economy, let alone a free port. On the other hand, it was equally true that in the long run Hainan had much more to gain than to lose. To remove the protection of China's customs area would do little harm to Hainan's industry since it hardly existed. The rise in the prices of major exports from Hainan such as rubber, iron ore, salt, and sugar would largely compensate for the rise in the costs of major imports from the mainland such as steel, cement, fertilizer, petrol and grain. Management would not be an insurmountable difficulty since it was likely that the various international communities, Hong Kong in particular, would offer help in training qualified personnel. Moreover, the management of a free economy would not be much harder to establish and develop functionally than the management of ambiguity created by the "double-track system." The potential gain was enormous. As a huge free trade zone Hainan could attract massive investment from both the mainland and abroad. This, combined with its rich natural resources, could probably have enabled Hainan to easily produce those goods formerly supplied by and from the mainland. By late 1988 Hainan's provincial leadership began to regret its inaction. Hainan was particularly victimized by central government policy designed to curb inflation and overheating in the economy. The nationwide economic rectification and the CCP's reimposition of a high degree of conformity rendered many of Hainan's preferential policies meaningless. For example, the high expectations for the development of foreign trade in Hainan, particularly exports, were dashed by the introduction of state export quota management. Massive construction projects were canceled or delayed as a result of the tight money policy and new credit controls which generally targeted extra-budget and special-permit projects. The proportion of retained foreign currency earned from exports and foreign trade initially promised to Hainan reverted to the central government, and the latter also did not permit Hainan to open wider areas to foreign investment, such as banking and trade. As a solution to the crisis, the Hainan Provincial Government formally applied to establish the Hainan Special Customs Zone in December 1988. By that time Zhao Ziyang and his colleagues at the Center were already under attack on a range of issues, and further reform and opening in Hainan were definitely not their priority. The June 4 incident in 1989 did not destroy all prospects for the establishment of a Special Customs Zone in Hainan. Although Jiang Zemin and Li Peng were not as keen as Zhao Ziyang to grant further freedoms to Hainan, the provincial leadership after Liang Xiang's removal misjudged national politics and failed to press on with preparations for the establishment of a Special Customs Zone. They waited until Deng's Southern Tour in early 1992 to lobby through a series of meetings and consultative conferences attended by influential national leaders and foreign guests,[43] but all to no avail. Essentially they were too late: the central government had shifted its focus to Shanghai. At the same time, Beijing had become preoccupied with the issue of rejoining GATT and later of joining the WTO and moved to formulate a new package of tariffs for the whole country. Hainan lost its opportunity to become the most favored target of foreign investment in China. For the conceivable future it is likely to remain in a weak position in its trade with the mainland, still fundamentally dependent on the mainland for investment as well as consumer goods.

Conclusions

As a new province and Special Economic Zone Hainan's policy settings and political environment are clearly radically different from those of other provinces. Through its economic integration with the outside world it has something in common with Guangdong Province. However, Hainan was an extremely underdeveloped economy before the 1980s, probably best described in terms of its internal colonial relationship with the mainland.[44] Moreover, where Beijing was prepared to express confidence in Guangdong's development and the political behavior of its leadership through the 1980s and into the 1990s, the central government has been considerably more uncertain about allowing Hainan's leaders to have their lead. Hainan's drives for increased autonomy—politically from both Beijing and Guangzhou—and substantial interdependence—economically with the rest of China and the outside world—were always likely to result in uncertainty during the reform era. Despite considerable support within Hainan, as the analysis of provincial (and pre-provincial) leadership during the 1980s and 1990s clearly indicates, it was also a high risk strategy. Hainan's growth rates particularly during the 1990s have been spectacular. However, the Hainan economy remains substantially underdeveloped, and the economic achievements such as they are have not resulted in much if any political stability. Politically, provincial leaders still depend disproportionately on their off-island relationships, and within the province many of the issues that dominated the pre-1980s era remain. The establishment of a Hainan Province has not completely localized provincial politics, or at least not for all. For example, few native Hainanese have been appointed to positions above the level of deputy director at the departmental level within the provincial government. The relationships between on the one hand the different communities in Hainan—particularly the Hainanese speakers, the Li, overseas Chinese, the mainlander immigrants of the 1950s, and the reform-era mainlander immigrants—and on the other the drives for political independence and economic development clearly are not to be ignored. It is far from clear that provincial status in 1988 has meant the same to each of Hainan's communities, or that they have all participated equally or commonly in the drive for economic development. To understand the uncertainties of Hainan politics within the island—and not just between Haikou and the mainland—one avenue for future research is to disaggregate the political behavior and economic locations of each of those communities.

APPENDIX: HAINAN'S LEADERS SINCE 1949

Chinese Communist Party

Party Secretary, Hainan Administrative Area

May 1950–August 1954	Feng Baiju
August 1954–July 1955	Chen Renqi
July 1955–May 1956	Zhang Weilie
May 1956–December 1957	Zhang Yun
December 1957–October 1960	Lin Liming
October 1960–August 1966	Yang Zejiang
August 1968–January 1970	Sun Ganqing
	(Head, Revolutionary Leading Group)
January 1971–April 1973	Feng Jingqiao
December 1974–November 1975	Li Ziyuan
November 1975–December 1976	Li Erzhong
December 1976–August 1983	Luo Tian
August 1983–September 1987	Yao Wenxu

Secretary, Preparatory Group for the Establishment of Hainan Province

September 1987–August 1988	Xu Shijie

Secretary, Working Committee for the Establishment of Hainan Province

February 1988–August 1988	Xu Shijie

Provincial Party Secretary

September 1988–July 1990	Xu Shijie
July 1990–January 1993	Deng Hongxun
January 1993–	Ruan Chongwu

People's Government

Director, Hainan Administrative Office

May 1950–April 1951	Deng Hua [Chairman, Military-Political Committee]
April 1951–November 1953	Feng Baiju
November 1953–October 1955	Xiao Huanhui
October 1955–July 1957	Wang Jue
July 1957–January 1958	Huang Kang
June 1958–September 1965	Xiao Huanhui
September 1965–April 1968	Wei Nanjing
April 1968–January 1970	Sun Ganqing
January 1970–December 1974	Feng Jingqiao
December 1974–November 1975	Li Ziyuan
November 1975–December 1976	Li Erzhong
December 1976–April 1980	Luo Tian
April 1980–August 1982	Wei Nanjing
August 1982–September 1984	Lei Yu

Head, Hainan People's Government

October 1984–August 1985	Lei Yu
August 1985–April 1988	Meng Qianping

Head, Hainan Provincial People's Government

April 1988–August 1988	Liang Xiang

Governor, Hainan Province

August 1988–September 1989	Liang Xiang
September 1989–January 1993	Liu Jianfeng
February 1993–	Ruan Chongwu

Notes

1. All statistics are 1994 unless otherwise indicated.
2. Asia Research Centre, *Southern China in Transition* (Canberra: Australian Government Publishing Service, 1992).
3. Li Liangduan, "Relations between overseas Chinese of Hainan origin and the development of Hainan: the past and the future," paper presented to the workshop on *The Development of Hainan and the Opportunity for Australia*, Haikou, May 9–14, 1994.

4. Quoted in Xu Shijie (ed.), *Hainan sheng* (Hainan Province) (Beijing: Shangwu Yingshuguan, 1988), p. 115.

5. Li Zhimin and Wang Houhong (eds.), *Hainan sheng qing gaiyao* (A Survey of the Current Situation in Hainan) (Haikou: Hainan Chubanshe, 1992), p. 11.

6. Office for the History of Armed Struggle in Hainan (ed.), *Qiongya zongdui shi* (A History of the Qiongya Column) (Guangzhou: Guangdong Renmin Chubanshe, 1986), p. 298.

7. Zhao Guochuan and Lang Yanfen, "The current situation and prospects for real estate in Hainan" in Liao Xun, Fu Dabang and Tang Yong (eds.), *'92 Hainan shehui jingji fazhan yanjiu* (A Study on Social and Economic Development in Hainan in 1992) (Haikou: Nanhai chuban gongsi, 1993), pp. 452–453.

8. Liao Xun, "How to assess the current economic situation of Hainan" in Social and Economic Development Research Centre of Hainan Provincial Government (ed.), *Jiyu yu tiaozhan* (Opportunities and Challenges), 1993, p. 27.

9. Lei Yu, "Tuanjie xilai, nuli kaichuang Hainandao shehui zhuyi xiandaihua jianshe de xin jumian: zai Hainan dangxiao de baogao" (Unite to open up a new prospect in constructing socialist modernization on Hainan Island: a speech at the Hainan Party School), *Hainan ribao*, December 22, 1982.

10. Shixing gengjia kaifang zhengce, gei waizi yi youhui daiyu, Hainan yi kaifang chu kaifa: Lei Yu jiu youguan wenti da *Nanfang ribao* jizhe wen (Policies to be more open and preferential toward foreign capital, Hainan to use opening as a means of development: interview with Lei Yu by a journalist from *Nanfang ribao*), *Hainan ribao*, February 9, 1983.

11. Research Office of Hainan Party History, *Xin Hainan jishi* (A Chronicle of New Hainan) (Beijing: Zhonggong dangshi chubanshe, 1993), p. 565.

12. "Zhongguo tequ sheng de jueqi" (The rise of a provincial Special Economic Zone in China), *Hainan ribao*, August 20, 1988.

13. Xu Shijie, "Zai shi xian wei shuji kuoda huiyi shang de zongjie jianghua" (Summary speech at an enlarged meeting of city and county party secretaries), Research Office for System Reform and Policy Research Office, CCP Hainan Provincial Party Committee (ed.), *Fangzhen, zhengce, fagui, zhanlue: Guanyu Hainan jian sheng ban da tequ wenjian ziliao huibian* (Guiding Principles, Policies, Regulations and Strategies: A Collection of Documents Regarding the Establishment of Hainan Province and Hainan Special Economic Zone), Vol. 1, 1988, pp. 131–132.

14. Xu Shijie, "Zhili yu fazhan shengchanli: Hainan jian sheng shexiang" (Work for the development of productive forces: A proposal for the establishment of Hainan Province), Research Office for System Reform and Policy Research Office, CCP Hainan Provincial Committee (ed.), *Fangzhen, zhengce, fagui, Zhanlue: Guanyu Hainan jian sheng ban da tequ wenjian Ziliao Huibian* (Guiding Principles, Policies, Regulations and Strategies: A Collection of Documents Regarding the Establishment of Hainan Province and Hainan Special Economic Zone), Vol.1, 1988, p. 151.

15. Xu Shijie, "Fangdan fazhan shengchanli, kaichuang Hainan tequ jianshe xinjumian" (Take bold steps to develop productive forces and open up new prospects for the construction of Hainan SEZ), Research Office for System Reform and Policy Research Office, CCP Hainan Provincial Party Committee (ed.), *Fangzhen, zhengce, fagui, zhanlue: Guanyu Hainan jian sheng ban da tequ wenjian ziliao huibian* (Guiding Principles, Policies, Regulations and Strategies: A Collection of Documents Regarding the Establishment of Hainan Province and Hainan Special Economic Zone), Vol. 4, p. 28.

16. Liang Xiang, "Wei Hainan renmin zaofu" (Bring benefit to Hainan people) *Hainansheng touzi zhinan* (Guidebook to Investment in Hainan Province) (Haikou: Hainan renmin chubanshe), p. 12.

17. "Zhongguo tequ sheng de jueqi" (The Rise of a Provincial SEZ in China), 20 August 1988 *Hainan ribao*; "Liang Xiang xiangshu Hainan jiansheng jinguo" (Liang Xiang talks in detail on the process of establishing Hainan Province") Research Office for System Reform and Policy Research Office, CCP Hainan Provincial Party Committee (ed.), *Fangzhen, zhengce, fagui, Zhanlue: Guanyu Hainan jian sheng ban da tequ wenjian Ziliao Huibian* (Guiding Principles, Policies, Regulations and Strategies: A Collection of Documents Regarding the Establishment of Hainan Province and Hainan Special Economic Zone), Vol.1, 1988, pp. 166–180.

18. Liang Xiang, "Hainan jian sheng de xingshi, mubiao yu renwu" (Circumstances, objectives and the tasks of establishing Hainan Province), Research Office for System Reform and Policy Research Office, CCP Hainan Provincial Party Committee (ed.), *Fangzhen, zhengce, fagui, zhanlue: Guanyu Hainan jian sheng ban da tequ wenjian ziliao huibian* (Guiding Principles Policies, Regulations and Strategies: A Collection of Documents Regarding the Establishment of Hainan Province and Hainan Special Economic Zone), Vol.4, 1988, pp. 95–96.

19. CCP Central Committee, "Guanyu chexiao Liang Xiang tongzhi dang neiwai zhiwu bing jixu diaocha de tongzhi" (Notice about dismissing comrade Liang Xiang from his posts within and outside the party and carrying on further investigation), Joint Investigation Team of the CCP Central Committee, "Guanyu Liang Xiang tongzhi wenti de diaocha baogao" (Report on the investigation on the problem of comrade Liang Xiang).

20. Xu Jiatun, *Xu Jiatun xianggang huiyilu* (Xu Jiatun's Hong Kong Memoirs) (Hong Kong: Xianggang Lianhebao, 1995), p. 451.

21. Liu Jianfeng, "Zai Shengwei changwei kuoda huiyi shang de zongjie jianghua" (A speech at an enlarged meeting of the standing committee of the provincial party committee), Zhonggong Hainan Shengwei Zhengce Yanjiushi, Hainansheng Tizhi Gaige Bangongshi, *Hainan shehui zhuyi shichang jingji tizhi de jiben shijian* (Basic Practice of the Socialist Market Economy System in Hainan), Vol. 1, 1993, pp. 42–43.

22. Liu Jianfeng, "Zai sheng renmin daibiao huiyi disanci huiyi shang de jianghua" (Speech at the third session of the Provincial People's Congress), Zhonggong Hainan Shengwei Zhengce Yanjiushi, Hainansheng Tizhi Gaige Bangongshi, *Hainan shehui zhuyi shichang jingji tizhi de jiben shijian* (Basic Practice of the Socialist Market Economy System in Hainan), Vol. 1, 1993, p. 58.

23. *Hainan ribao*, July 7, 1990.

24. "Jianding de tuijian gaige kaifang, jiashu Hainan de jingji fazhan: Deng Hongxun shuji chang tan Hainan gaige kaifang wenti" (Firmly carry forward reform and openness and speed up economic development in Hainan: Secretary Deng Hongxun speaks glowingly of reform and openness in Hainan) *Hainan ribao*, November 7, 1990.

25. Ruan Chongwu, "Tuanjie hezuo, wending fazhan, wei shixian xin de mubiao er nuli fendou" (Unite and cooperate to strive for steady development and new objectives), quoted from Zhong Yuechang, "Ruan Chongwu zhuzhen Hainan jishi" (An account of Governor Ruan Chongwu on Hainan), *Hainan qingnian bao*, November 25, 1994.

26. Ruan Chongwu, "Shehui zhuyi shichang jingji tiaojian xia de zhengfu zeren" (The responsibility of government under the socialist market economy,) in *Kaifang yu kaifa* (Opening & Development), No. 2, 1994, p. 3.

27. Ai Feng and Bao Hongjun, "Jianshao 'kanmende' zengjia 'gao weisheng de': fang Hainan shengzhang Ruan Chongwu" (Reducing "gate guards" and increasing "cleaners": An interview with Hainan governor Ruan Chongwu), in *Kaifang yu kaifa* (Opening & Development), No. 3, 1994, p. 2.

28. Hainan Provincial People's Government, "Guanyu Hainansheng suoyouzhi jiegou xingkuang de baogao" (A report on the ownership structure in Hainan Province), 1994.

29. Xu Shijie (ed.), *Hainan sheng*, p. 282.

30. Hainan Provincial Statistical Bureau, "Statistical communique of social and economic development for 1993," *Hainan ribao*, February 28, 1994.

31. Liu Guoguang, *Hainan jingji fazhan zhanlue* (Strategy for Economic Development of Hainan) (Beijing: Jingji guanli chubanshe, 1988), p. 17.

32. Liao Xun, "Bu ru gaosu fazhan: liu nian lai de Hainan jingji" (At the beginning of high speed development: Hainan's economy in the last six years), paper presented to the conference on *The Development of Hainan and the Opportunities for Australia*, May 9–14, 1994.

33. Wu Guanghua, "Hainan jingji tequ liyong waizi de xianzhuang yu zhanwang" (The current situation and the prospects of utilizing foreign capital in the Hainan SEZ), paper presented to the conference on *The Development of Hainan and the Opportunities for Australia*, May 9–14, 1994.

34. Wu Guanghua, "Hainan jingji tequ liyong waizi de xianzhuang yu zhanwang" (The current situation and prospects for utilizing foreign capital in the Hainan SEZ), paper presented to the conference on *The Development of Hainan and the Opportunities for Australia*, May 9–14, 1994.

35. *Hainan tongji nianjian 1988–1990* (Hainan Statistics Yearbook); "*Touze zai Hainan xingchen xin geju*"(Investment from Taiwan is taking new shape in Hainan), *Renmin ribao*, Overseas Edition, January 26 and February 9, 1993.

36. Li Liangduan, "Haiwai Hainan ren yu Hainan de kaifa jianshe jixi fazhan xushi" (The development of Hainan and overseas Chinese of Hainan origin: Past, present and prospects for the future), paper presented to the conference on *The Development of Hainan and the Opportunities for Australia*, May 9–14, 1994.

37. Wu Guanghua, "Hainan jingji tequ liyong waizi de xianzhuang yu zhanwang" (The current situation and the prospects of utilizing foreign capital in the Hainan SEZ), paper presented to the conference on *The Development of Hainan and the Opportunities for Australia,* May 9–14, 1994.

38. Ruan Chongwu, "Government Work Report," *Hainan ribao*, March 19, 1994.

39. Article 31 of "Preferential Policy and Rules of the Hainan Special Economic Zone on Foreign Investment" approved by the Standing Committee of the People's Congress of Hainan Province at its Fifteenth Session on March 16, 1991 and operational upon promulgation on May 4, 1991.

40. Zhou Liangxian, "Hainan yu qita tequ touzi zhengce bijiao" (A comparison of investment policies in Hainan and other SEZs), Hainan Provincial Government Centre for Research on Social and Economic Development (ed.), *Hainan sheng touzi zhengce* (Policies Regarding Investment in Hainan Province) (Haikou: Sanhuan chubanshe, 1991), pp. 148–168.

41. Zhao Ziyang, "Zhao Ziyang tongzhi zai zhongyang caijing lingdao xiaozu taolun Hainan jian sheng ban da tequ jiben zhengce hui shang de tanhua yaodian" (The gist of the speech made by comrade Zhao Ziyang at the Financial and Economic Leading Group of the CCP Central Committee workshop on basic policies for setting up Hainan Province and Hainan Special Economic Zone), in Research Office for System Reform and Policy Research Office, CCP Hainan Provincial Committee (ed.), *Fangzhen, zhengce, fagui, zhanlue: Guanyu Hainan jian sheng ban da tequ wenjian ziliao huibian* (Guiding Principles Policies, Regulations and Strategies: A Collection of Documents Regarding the Establishment of Hainan Province and Hainan Special Economic Zone), Vol. 3, 1988, p. 3.

42. Xu Shijie, "Zai shi, xian wei shuji kuoda huiyi shang de zongjie jianghua" (Summary speech at the enlarged conference of county and city party secretaries), in Research Office for System Reform and Policy Research Office, CCP Hainan Provincial Party Committee (ed.), *Fangzhen, zhengce, fagui, zhanlue: Guanyu Hainan jian sheng ban da tequ wenjian ziliao Huibian* (Guiding Principles, Policies, Regulations and Strategies: A

Collection of Documents Regarding the Establishment of Hainan Province and Hainan Special Economic Zone), Vol. 1, 1988, p. 133.

43. For details see Research Office for System Reform and Policy Research Office, CCP Hainan Provincial Party Committee (ed.), *Hainan shehui zhuyi shichang jingji tizhi de jiben shijian (9): "Tebie guanshui qu" yanjiu* (The Basic Practice of the System of Socialist Market Economy in Hainan (vol. 9): A Study on "The Special Customs Zone), March 1993.

44. See, Feng Chongyi and David S.G. Goodman, "Hainan: communal politics and the struggle for identity," in David S.G. Goodman (ed.), *China's Provinces in Reform: Class, Community and Identity* (London: Routledge, 1997), pp. 53–88.

8

Provincial Leadership and Its Strategy Toward the Acquisition of Foreign Investment in Sichuan

Lijian Hong

Sichuan and Its Position in China

Situated at the northeast corner of China's southwest region (including Sichuan, Guizhou, Yunnan, and Tibet), Sichuan has a total area of 570,000 square kilometers, which is approximately 6.9 percent of the national total. In terms of area, it is the fifth largest provincial-level administrative unit in the People's Republic of China and the largest among Han Chinese provinces.[1] Surrounded by mountains and hills, the eastern part is a basin, known as the Red Basin by the outside world. With a total area of 160,000 square kilometers, the basin is one of the largest in China. The central part of the basin is the Chengdu Plain, one of the richest places in ancient China. From the surrounding mountains, the rivers of Yalong, Dadu, Ming, Tuo, Fu, and Jialing run from north to south and the Wu River from south to north. These rivers, plus many smaller ones, join the Yangtze River which runs through the southern part of the basin. The upper reach of the Yangtze, the Jinsha River, separates Sichuan from Tibet. The western part of Sichuan is a highland. Mountains in this area are above 3,000 meters above sea level. The northern part of the highland is an extension of the Qinghai-Tibet Plateau, with an average of 3,500 meters to 4,500 meters in elevation. The southern part of the highland is part of China's Hengduan Mountains running from south Sichuan down to Yunnan. The Hengduan Mountains is an area where the land is separated by deep gorges and rapid rivers running from north to south.[2] This topography of Sichuan presents three basic features: first, it is difficult to access from outside, "the road to *Shu* is as difficult as to heaven"; second, thanks to the Yangtze and other rivers, it is relatively easy for Sichuanese to travel to the outside world; third, once in Sichuan, especially in the basin area, internal transportation is easy and convenient. "In a time when inter-regional exchanges only amounted to a low percentage of gross national product, this external isolation," according to Adshead, "was less significant than the excellent internal communications in determining the life and character of Szechwan."[3] Since the beginning of this century, communication with the outside world has been dramatically improved. Compared with China's coastal regions, however, the topography of Sichuan was one of the major obstacles for local modernization.

Sichuan is a province of rich mineral resources which are characterized by relatively concentrated large deposits. Of the 150 kinds of mineral resources found in China, Sichuan has 123. The province has rich natural gas deposits, ranking second in the nation (44 percent of the national total), especially in the southern part of the basin. In the western part of the basin, phosphate rock deposits account for one-fourth of the national total. Symbiotic iron ores in southwest Sichuan are unique in China for the large number of elements and the large deposits (number two in China). In southwest Sichuan, around Panzhihua area, more than twenty elements (including vanadium, titanium, nickel, and cobalt) are interspersed with iron. A large and high grade titanium deposit has been found there, which accounts for about 90 percent of the national total. Panzhihua Steel Complex is one of China's major production bases of ferrous and non-ferrous metals and rare minerals. It produces more than eighty varieties of steel and nearly forty steel products.[4] Around Zigong City in south Sichuan, well salt production has a long history dating back to the Song Dynasty. Sichuan today is the largest well salt producer in China. Coal concentrates are found mainly in the east and south of Sichuan. The soft coal reserve in the northwest highland is the largest deposit in China.[5]

With more than 1,400 rivers in the province, Sichuan has a potential hydropower resource of 91.66 million kilowatts, ranking number one among the provinces.[6] Sichuan also has the nation's second largest forest area of 7.46 million hectares, with 80 percent of Sichuan's timber growing in the western part of the province, in the middle and upper reaches of the Yangtze River.[7]

The first railway of commercial value began construction in 1950 immediately after communist rule was set up in Sichuan, dramatically improving travel to and from Sichuan. The province is now accessible by four major railways (Chengdu-Baoji, Chengdu-Kunming, Sichuan-Guizhou, Chongqing-Xiangtan) and their branches. Airlines connect Sichuan with almost all major capital cities in China, Southeast Asia, Hong Kong, and Japan. In addition, the Yangtze River forms the backbone of provincial waterway transportation, linking Sichuan with central China.

Sichuan has been one of the most important provinces in China ever since the first emperor unified the province more than two thousand years ago. In more modern times, however, the collapse of central authority in 1911 led to continuous chaos in the province. If ancient Sichuan had shown loyalty to a unified

China, modern Sichuan showed a certain strong localism, if not a desire for independence, against the central government. From the 1911 Revolution until the communist takeover in 1949, the central authorities never effectively ruled the province. During the war period, as the Nationalist government built its wartime capital in Chongqing and armies loyal to the central government poured into the province, the relation between the Center and local warlord generals intensified. When the People's Liberation Army (PLA), led by two Sichuan natives, Liu Bocheng and Deng Xiaoping, swept into Sichuan in 1949, local warlords went over to the communists and destroyed the Nationalist government's attempt to use Sichuan as a strategic position from which to resist the communist victory.

Even so, Sichuan was the last mainland province "liberated" by the communist armies. Immediately after 1949, Sichuan was divided into five administrative units. Chongqing, the former wartime capital of the Nationalist government, maintained its special position as a city under the direct leadership of the Military and Administrative Committee of Southwest China and, later, of the central government. The rest of Sichuan was controlled by four subprovincial administrative units of the East, West, South and North Sichuan Administrative Offices. In 1952, during a nationwide restructuring of the local governmental system, Sichuan was reorganized as a province. In 1955, as a result of an agreement between the Chinese central government and the Tibetan local government, Xikang, a province between Sichuan and Tibet, was divided into two parts with the western part being returned to Tibet and the area east of Jinsha River to Sichuan. Since then, the area of Sichuan has remained unchanged until the hiving off of Chongqing into a centrally administered city in 1997.

Over the past forty years, Sichuan, under the communist government, has played an important role in the national economy — as it did for the previous governments. On the other hand, the communist style of modernization has also brought tremendous changes to this remote province of China. For example, Sichuan now has one of China's largest concentrations of defense-related industries and nuclear industries. One of the nation's two space centers was set up in the southwest corner of the province. The province is also one of four national bases of metallurgical, engineering, electronic and chemical industries.[8] Table 8.1 shows that unlike other peripheral provinces, the economic performance of Sichuan in absolute terms is not too far behind more advanced coastal areas. Sichuan's gross domestic product, for example, came after only the three richest coastal provinces of Guangdong, Jiangsu and Shandong in 1995. Sichuan's gross output value of farming, forestry, animal husbandry and fishery was ranked number three after Guangdong and Jiangsu, while grain production ranked number one in China. For its gross value of industrial output, however, Sichuan was behind the industrially advanced provinces of Jiangsu, Guangdong, Shandong, Zhejiang, Shanghai, Liaoning and Henan, but ahead of all northwest, southwest and most central provinces. As for foreign trade, Sichuan ranked behind the coastal provincial-level units: Guangdong, Beijing,

Table 8.1

Economic Performance of Sichuan in China (1995)

	National	Sichuan	% of national total	ranking in China
population (million)	1,211.21	113.25	9.35	1
GDP (billion yuan)	5,727.73	353.40	6.17	4
total investment in fixed assets (billion yuan)	2,001.93	90.14	4.5	6
GVIO (billion yuan)	9,189.38	442.64	4,82	8
GOVA (billion yuan)	2,034.09	152.03	7.47	3
grain production (million tons)	466.62	43.65	9.35	1
total value in wholesale and retail sales (billion yuan)	4,054.53	180.09	4.44	8
number of institutes of higher education	1,054	64	6.07	3
scientific and technical personnel in state-owned research and development institutes (above county level)	10,128.04	97,713	9.65	1
telephones (million sets)	57.62	2.17	3.77	11
freight traffic volume (million tons)	12,348.10	900.77	7.29	2
foreign trade (US$ billion)	280.85	3.48	1.24	9
actual foreign investment (US$ million)	48,132.69	619.36	1.29	15

Source: Zhongguo tongji nianjian 1996 (China Statistical Yearbook), pp. 70, 43, 140, 404, 558, 662, 534, 506, 594 and 600.

GOVA = Gross output value of farming, forestry, animal husbandry and fishery.

GVIO= Gross output value of industry.

Shanghai, Jiangsu, Fujian, Shandong, Liaoning and Zhejiang. In terms of actual foreign investment, Sichuan was placed number fifteen, not very far behind the central China province of Henan and the northeast province of Heilongjiang, but far behind all of coastal provinces.[9]

While Sichuan can be safely defined as one of the largest regional economies in China in absolute terms, its per capita economic figures are among the poorest provinces in China due to its huge population. The communists' achievement of modernization is, however, remarkable especially considering Sichuan's geographic disadvantages, the large number of non-productive defense-related industries, a huge rural population and low investment in agriculture.

Since the 1980s, however, when the Chinese central government changed its strategy of economic development and granted preferential policies to the coastal areas, Sichuan, once a pioneer of the post-Mao reform, seems to have been seriously disadvantaged, especially in terms of central investment. The transition from Mao's China to Deng's China has not only affected political and economic development of the nation in general, but the impact caused by the policy change of the Center has also affected local governments and their leaders. As leaders of China's most populous province, the party secretaries and governors of Sichuan have had to face challenges in a dramatically changed political and economic environment and to survive the increasing pressures from both central demands and local interests. On the other hand, the new social and political order of post-Mao China has also provided local leaders with new opportunities for them to display their initiative and leadership.

This chapter aims to examine some of the most influential leaders in post-Mao Sichuan and their management of Sichuan in a rapidly changing period. It is well known that rapid economic development in coastal regions in post-Mao China has largely been the result of foreign investment. In comparison, the slow economic growth of the inland provinces has been mainly due to the lack of investment, both domestic and foreign. Apart from other factors such as geographic inconvenience, the lack of preferential policies granted by the Center were seen by many local leaders as the main reason for local backwardness. While using every opportunity to create their own policies to attract foreign investments, local leaders also had to bargain with the Center for more preferential policies, not only for economic benefit, but also for political protection. Without strong political support from the Center, local leaders would face political risk in initiating policies. We shall discuss the local leadership in Mao's China, its formation, and its structure in the following section.

Local Leadership Prior to 1978

From 1952, when it was reorganized as a province to the outbreak of the Cultural Revolution, Sichuan was ruled mainly by one person, "Political Commissar" Li Jingquan. Li was the former political commissar of the Eighteenth Corps of the First Field Army. When the main communist force, formed by the Second Field Army and part of the Fourth Field Army, swept into Sichuan from the south and southeast, Li and his commander, He Long, led the Eighteenth Corps against the Nationalist army from the north.[10] Although the Second Field Army had a strong presence across the whole area of the southwestern provinces of Sichuan, Yunnan, Guizhou and Tibet, the First Field Army controlled half of Sichuan (north and west Sichuan) and Xikang Province. Table 8.2 shows the distribution of power in early communist Sichuan.

The political influence of the Second Field Army in Sichuan was further weakened when both Deng Xiaoping and Liu Bocheng were soon transferred to work in the Center.[11] When Sichuan was reorganized as a province in 1952, He Long and his First Field Army had a stronger position than the Second Field Army. Li Jingquan, the then Party and government leader of West Sichuan, was appointed head of the newly established provincial Party committee and govern-

Table 8.2

List of Party and Government Leaders of the Southwest Region and the Five Sub-provincial Administrative Units of Sichuan

Southwest Region: Liu Bocheng (Chairman of the Southwest Military-Administrative Committee, Commander of the Second Field Army)

Deng Xiaoping (Secretary of the Southwest Sub-Bureau of the Party Central Committee, Political Commissar of the Second Field Army)

He Long (Commander of the Southwest Military Region, Commander of the Eighteenth Corps of the First Field Army)

Chongqing: Chen Xilian, Mayor and Party Secretary (Commander of the Third Corps of the Second Field Army)

East Sichuan: Yan Hongyan, Government Leader (Director of the Political Department of the Third Corps of the Second Field Army)

Xie Fuzhi, Party Secretary (Political Commissar of the Third Corps of the Second Field Army)

Wang Jinshan, Military Commander (Deputy Commander of the Third Corps of the Second Field Army)

South Sichuan: Li Dazhang, Government Leader and Party Secretary, (civilian)[a]

Du Yide, Military Commander (Deputy Commander of the Third Corps of the Second Field Army)

North Sichuan: Hu Yaobang, Government Leader and Party Secretary (Director of the Political Department of the Eighteenth Corps of the First Field Army)

Wei Jie, Military Commander (Commander of the Sixty-first Army of the First Field Army)

West Sichuan: Li Jingquan, Government Leader and Party Secretary (Political Commissar of the Eighteenth Corps of the First Field Army)

Zhang Zuliang, Military Commander (Commander of the Sixtieth Army of the First Field Army)

Sources: *Dangdai Sichuan dashi jiyao bianjibu* (ed.), *Dangdai Sichuan dashi jiyao (Major Events in Contemporary Sichuan)*, (Chengdu: Sichuan Renmin Chubanshe, 1991) pp. 3–4. He Husheng, et al., *Zhonghua renmin gongheguo zhiguanzhi (Party, Government and Army Leaders of the People's Republic of China)*, (Beijing: Zhongguo shehui chubanshe, 1993) pp. 682, 684.

a: Zhang Guohua, commander of the Eighteenth Army of the Second Field Army, was formerly appointed the Party and government leader of South Sichuan, but was soon ordered to march to Tibet. He was replaced by Li Dazhang.

ment and political commissar of the Sichuan Military Region.[12] The former West Sichuan Party and government formed the core of the new provincial power structure. During the Great Leap Forward, Li was elected to be a member of the Politburo in 1958, one of four provincial-level Party secretaries among the twenty-three members.[13] During the period between 1952 and the outbreak of the Cultural Revolution, the highly centralized power of "Commissar Li," as local people called him, remained unchanged.[14]

Sichuan under Li was mainly ruled by "outsiders." Cadres from the First and Second Field Armies formed the backbone of the Party and government institutions down to the county level. Records from the 12 county annals of Dayi, Wushan, Kaijiang, Emei, Pujiang, Qianwei, Jingyan, Renshou, Chongqing (County), Jiajiang, Shifang and Nanchuan show that for the period from 1950 up to the outbreak of the Cultural Revolution, of the 88 secretaries of county Party committees, 42 were from Shanxi, 19 from Shandong, 16 from Hebei, 3 from Henan, 1 from Shaanxi and 2 from the southern provinces of Hubei and Jiangsu. There were only 5 from Sichuan, representing 5.68 percent of the total. Of the 96 county magistrates, 39 were from Shanxi, 18 from Shandong, 5 from Hebei, 3 from Henan, 3 from Shaanxi, and 5 were unknown. There were 16 Sichuanese, or 16.66 percent of the total.[15] These statistics also suggest that among the northerners in local Sichuan Party and government institutions, people from the former communist base area of Jin-Sui (northern Shanxi and southern Inner Mongolia), the main base area of the Eighteenth Corps, had the strongest position. This group of people was referred to by the local Sichuanese as the "Shanxi Bang" (Shanxi Gang), or jokingly, the "Potato Clique" (*shanyaodan bang*).[16]

The unbalanced political forces caused certain tensions between the First Field Army group and the non–First Field Army groups, which was one of the explanations for a prolonged conflict between the provincial leadership in Chengdu (based on the First Field Army and the West Sichuan government) and the city leadership of Chongqing (based on the Second Field Army and cadres of the old Southwest Sub-bureau). During the 14 years of Li Jingquan's rule, no Party or government leaders from Chongqing, still the largest industrial city in the whole southwest region and one of the largest in China, were promoted to the top position of the provincial leadership.[17] Apart from the outsider groups, there were also a large number of former underground Party members. Most of those members joined the Chinese Communist Party when the Communist Party and the Nationalist Party formed the second United Front against the Japanese invasion. On the eve of Sichuan's liberation, underground Party organizations played an important role in agitating anti-government sentiment among the masses, especially among intellectuals, and protecting factories, power stations and railways for the new rulers. They paid heavily under a bloody suppression by the Nationalist government in 1949. After liberation, however, many former underground Party members were considered by the "liberators" as unreliable because of their family background and connections with the Nationalist government. In

1956–57, a purge was launched against alleged localism among underground Party members who felt that the outsiders did not pay enough attention to the local situation but slavishly implemented central instructions. They were not rehabilitated until after 1979.[18]

Politically, Li's governance in Sichuan was characterized by his loyalty to Mao and strong determination against those who were unable to keep pace with the increasingly radical line of Mao. In August 1958, for example, in the midst of the national campaign against rightist deviation, more than 50 local Party and government leaders above county level who opposed the ultra-left line of Li Jingquan were criticized. Later that year, a similar campaign was carried out among local Party and government officials. A total of 160,000 cadres were involved. A report to the Party Central Committee admitted that "an unprecedentedly large number of leading people were criticized" during the campaign.[19] By 1960, a total of 3,951 officials at various levels in Sichuan were "criticized" or purged.[20] Moreover, in August 1959, immediately after the Lushan Conference where Li Jingquan stood firmly on Mao's side against Peng Dehuai, a closed book test was conducted among 1,300 senior provincial Party and government officials. Cadres were required to give opinions on a document without knowing it was Peng's letter to Mao. Those who supported Peng Dehuai's view and expressed their dissatisfaction about the Great Leap Forward were purged as rightists.[21] Economically, after the initial success in restoring local economic order through the early 1950s, mismanagement by local leaders during the Great Leap Forward cost Sichuan dearly, both in terms of livelihood and of resources. In the steel industry, for example, it was estimated that of the 1,100 million yuan invested, 430 million yuan worth of projects was unable to operate after completion.[22] According to an investigation conducted in 1963, a total of 60 million yuan worth of materials were wasted during the period.[23]

In agriculture, the Great Leap Forward led to an even greater disaster in Sichuan. Although real growth in grain production in 1958 was only 5.4 percent, commodity grain consumption increased 42.8 percent due to a dramatic increase in the urban population and the wastage of grain in 610,000 public canteens which provided free food to 96 percent of the rural population.[24] Furthermore, despite the serious shortage of food, state purchase of grain was still carried out as planned. One local official said that in the three years from 1958 to 1960, a total of 5.87 million tons of grain were delivered to the Center, leaving Sichuan with only 3.53 million tons.[25] The direct consequence of food wastage and the central government's surplus purchases was a wide-spread famine. The number of people who died during the famine has never been published,[26] but official statistics show an extraordinarily high mortality rate and continuous negative population growth rate from 1959 to 1961.[27] Local historians believe that a total of more than one million people died of hunger during the Great Leap Forward.[28] Table 8.3 below shows the situation of Sichuan during that period.

If mismanagement was the main cause of a wide-spread famine in the coun-

Table 8.3

Birth Rate, Death and Natural Growth Rates of Sichuan Population, 1957–61
(in millions)

Year	Total	Urban	Rural	Birth rate (0/00)	Death rate (0/00)	Natural growth
1957	70.81	6.71	64.10	2.92	1.21	1.72
1958	70.78	7.64	63.14	3.40	2.52	0.89
1959	68.97	8.35	60.62	1.67	4.70	-3.03
1960	66.20	8.44	57.76	1.17	5.40	-4.22
1961	64.59	7.77	56.82	1.18	2.94	-1.76

Source: Guojia tongjiju (ed.), *Quanguo ge sheng, zizhiqu, zhixiashi lishi tongji ziliao huibian* (A Compendium of Historical Statistical Data of Provinces, Autonomous Regions and Centrally Administered Cities in China) (Beijing: Zhongguo tongji chubanshe, 1990), p. 690.

tryside, it was Li Jingquan's policy that caused unnecessary deaths in the major cities. When food shortage was serious, the provincial government called on urban people to tighten their belts and save food. Many people responded to the call positively and saved their food coupons. In September 1960, however, the provincial government suddenly announced the abolition of old provincial food coupons, equivalent to 48 million kilograms of food. Millions of urban people suffered untold heavy losses.[29] The official explanation was that this was a special measure to save grain for people in Beijing, Tianjin and Shanghai where there were only a few days of food supply available, an explanation that was a typical reflection of Li's principle: to sacrifice the interest of the local people for the interest of the Center when there was a conflict between the two. Although Li was generally considered a radical follower of Mao Zedong in the first 17 years of Mao's China, he was dumped by Mao in May 1967, one year after the outbreak of the Cultural Revolution, because of his close connection with He Long, Lin Biao's enemy in the Chinese military.

From 1967 to 1975, Sichuan was ruled by military leaders. The highly centralized rule of Li Jingquan was replaced by General Zhang Guohua, former commander of the Tibet Military Region, who concurrently held the posts of head of the provincial Party committee, head of the provincial revolutionary committee (i.e., government) and political commissar of the Chengdu Military Region. Zhang died in 1972 and he was succeeded by another military man from the Guangdong Military Region, Liu Xingyuan. The period of military rule was a total chaos. Although Zhang had a strong military background as he was a former Second Field Army general, his military talent did little to help his political career. Sichuan during the Cultural Revolution resembled Sichuan in ancient times when China was in disintegration. The decline of Li Jingquan and his Shanxi Clique led to wide-spread chaos which paralyzed local Party and government functions, forcing many factories to close down. Not forced to close down were the military enterprises whose products sustained a prolonged armed confrontation between rebel organizations and cost thousands of local people's lives. Although the provincial revolutionary committee was established in May 1968, the situation did not improve until trouble makers in the revolutionary committee were removed by the Party Central Committee at the end of 1969.[30] Nevertheless, Zhang still had to face challenges from local rebels and another strong military man, Liang Xingchu (Fourth Field Army system). Liang, commander of Chengdu Military Region, was a former Korean War hero. Zhang remained deeply concerned about the deteriorating agricultural and industrial production, the delay of the Third Front Project, the power struggle within the leadership and the split between local PLA troops, with the Thirteenth Army in Chengdu supporting one rebel group and Fifty-fourth Army in Chongqing supporting the other. However, Zhang was unable to control any of them. The heavy pressure took a toll on Zhang's life and he died of a heart attack in 1972. Military rule in Sichuan was sustained for another three years. During a nation-wide process of de-militarization of local Party and government leadership in 1974–75, Zhao Ziyang, a future political star of China, was transferred to Sichuan.

Post-Mao Leadership in Sichuan

One important consequence of the Cultural Revolution in Sichuan was that the dominance of Li Jingquan and his Shanxi clique in local politics was destroyed. The decline of Li Jingquan's rule meant an end to Mao's radical line in Sichuan, providing an opportunity for local leaders to take the initiative. Locally initiated reforms, encouraged by Zhao Ziyang, have eventually changed the social, political and economic order of Mao's China. The decline of Li Jingquan and his outsiders' rule also encouraged the rise of native Sichuanese politicians in the power center of the province. Finally, the decline of Li Jingquan and his First Field Army faction in Sichuan led to an increase in leaders from Chongqing, most of whom belonged to the Second Field Army faction. Table 8.4 below provides a list of Party and government leaders of Sichuan since 1978.

Of the above leaders, Zhao Ziyang, Tan Qilong and Zhang Haoruo were from outside the province. Lu Dadong and Song Baorui were not native Sichuanese, but they had worked in the province for a long time. Lu had been a local leader since 1949. Song Baorui had been working in Sichuan since he graduated from university. Lu Dadong, Jiang Minkuan and Xiao Yang were three leaders from Chongqing. Yang Rudai, Xie Shijie, Yang Xizong and Song Baorui were all Party secretaries of subprovincial cities other than Chengdu and Chongqing before they assumed the provincial leadership. Yang Rudai, Xiao Yang, Xie Shijie and Yang Xizong are native Sichuan leaders. Most of them began their

Table 8.4

List of Party Secretaries and Governors of Sichuan Since 1978

Party Secretaries	1975–80	Zhao Ziyang
	1980–81	Tan Qilong
	1981–93	Yang Rudai
	1993–	Xie Shijie
Governors	1975–79	Zhao Ziyang
	1979–82	Lu Dadong
	1983–85	Yang Xizong
	1985–88	Jiang Minkuan
	1988–93	Zhang Haoruo
	1993–95	Xiao Yang
	1996–	Song Baorui

Source: Yang Chao (ed.), *Dangdai Zhongguo de Sichuan* (Sichuan in Contemporary China) (Beijing: Dangdai Zhongguo chubanshe, 1990), Vol. II, pp. 769–89. Also see various issues of *Sichuan ribao*.

communist careers in Sichuan and worked continuously in Sichuan before being promoted to the top provincial position. Among "outsiders," Zhao Ziyang was famous for his bold economic reforms. Tan Qilong, as we shall discuss in detail later, was more or less a transitional leader who contributed little to local development. Zhang Haoruo was said to belong to China's "princeling clique," whose strong family background and personal connections guaranteed his political future. His appointment was generally considered a temporary arrangement and that he would return to the Center for a more important position after certain years of service. Apart from the Chongqing group, all other locally promoted leaders—Yang Rudai, Xie Shijie, Yang Xizong and Song Baorui—were from subprovincial units. None of them were from the capital city Chengdu. Of these two groups of leaders, Yang Rudai was the first native since 1949 to assume the top provincial position. As a member of the Politburo, he also had the highest political position among his native colleagues. Yang Xizong did not stay in his post for long before being moved to Henan Province. Xie Shijie was considered a representative of the second generation of native leaders. It is believed that Xie played a leading role in driving out Xiao Yang, but this cannot be confirmed. Although not a native Sichuanese, Song Baorui had worked in Sichuan since the late 1960s. He later replaced Xiao Yang and was said to be active in promoting Sichuan's opening up. Jiang Minkuan also endeavored to promote Sichuan's opening up. He was the pioneer in attempting to link Sichuan more closely with the former Soviet Union and other Eastern European countries. (We shall discuss this in detail later.) Of all of the leaders from Chongqing, Xiao Yang was perhaps the most controversial. He was viewed by some as a reformer, but by others as a totally corrupt official. His removal in disgrace from his post was welcomed by certain factions within the provincial Party and government institutions, but was seen by others as a sign of the decline of Deng Xiaoping's authority in Sichuan.[31] (We shall also discuss this later.)

In the sections below, three provincial leaders—Zhao Ziyang, Yang Rudai and Xiao Yang — are used as case studies. These three leaders represent three different local leadership types in Sichuan. They also represent three different periods of post-Mao Sichuan: Zhao Ziyang initiated profound economic reform in Sichuan in the early days of Deng's China; Yang Rudai was leader during the period when the Center changed its strategy of economic development and focused upon the southeast coastal regions. Sichuan was felt to have been abandoned and was forced to find its own way to survive; Xiao Yang was the most controversial leader in a dramatically changing period. Through an investigation of these three Sichuan leaders, this chapter attempts to understand the changing relationship between Center and locality in post-Mao China and local leaders' reactions to this change.

Zhao Ziyang: A Pioneer Cautious in Politics but Bold in Economics

Zhao Ziyang was well known for his bold economic reforms both in Sichuan and in China. He may be safely categorized as a pioneer in economic reform, but not so in political reform. It is said that Zhao himself once said that to be politically correct, one must be bold in economic reform, but be conservative in politics.[32] When Zhao Ziyang replaced Liu Xingyuan as the leader of the provincial Party government, Sichuan was on the verge of economic bankruptcy. At the worst point of the Cultural Revolution (1967–68), the national figure for the total output value of agriculture and industry declined 9.6 percent and 4.2 percent respectively, while Sichuan registered an 11 percent and 23.8 percent reduction respectively. By 1976, however, the national figure had increased 134 percent over 1965, a per annum increase of 8 percent. In Sichuan, by contrast, total output increased only 76.5 percent compared with that of 1965, a per annum increase of 5.3 percent. Productivity per capita in state-owned enterprises in 1966 was 6,282 yuan in Sichuan, falling to 2,126 yuan in 1968. By 1976, it had only reached 4,912 yuan. State purchase of grain in 1957 was 5.49 million tons. By 1976 when the Cultural Revolution ended, this figure had fallen to 3.64 million tons. For the first time since the Great Leap Forward, Sichuan became a grain-importing province.[33]

Not only did Zhao have to feed the most populous province with a poor local economy, but he also had to handle local politics carefully. The 1975–76 period was a period of dramatic changes in Chinese politics. The power struggle at the top caused tension between local military leaders in the revolutionary committees at various levels and bureaucrats who were survivors of the old Party and government institutions; between local military and administrative leaders on the one side and local rebels on the other; and among various factions of local rebel organizations. The downfall of the Gang of Four saw a decline of both local military leaders and rebels. The political vacuum left was filled by a large number of old bureaucrats. As a new outsider and a recently rehabilitated official, Zhao Ziyang maintained a low profile in the province while the political situation remained unclear. After the Gang of Four was arrested, however, Zhao still exercised caution in local politics and tried to maintain balance between various factions. In a campaign to eliminate the influence of the Gang of Four, for example, instead of showing a resolute determination to root out radical followers of the Gang of Four in Sichuan, Zhao repeatedly warned against treating people in the same way as the Gang of Four had or, in his own words, not to *fan shaobing,* literally meaning not to turn over a pancake repeatedly.[34] Zhao's political moderation aroused discontent from old bureaucrats who had suffered greatly during the Cultural Revolution.[35] Rumors spread that some old subordinates of Li Jingquan even asked Li to return and take over the leadership.[36]

Zhao also maintained a careful balance between different political forces in the Center. While he openly disagreed with the "whateverist" faction for not "seeking truth from the facts" under the new circumstances, he also showed his deviation from Deng Xiaoping's idea to stress the importance of scientists. In a speech to the provincial science conference, held following the national science conference, Zhao emphasized: "We must acquire full understanding of Chairman Hua's strategic thought of raising the scientific and cultural level of the entire Chinese nation . . . and arming the broad masses with up-to-date scientific knowledge."[37] At the time when both Deng Xiaoping and Hua Guofeng needed support from the localities, a "wait and see" attitude may have been the safest policy for local leaders. Probably because of Zhao's political ambiguity, he was seen by both sides as being cooperative and not a threat. It is not strange, therefore, that when Hua Guofeng visited Romania and Yugoslavia in 1978, Zhao was chosen to be the second head of the delegation. However, Deng Xiaoping, Hua's challenger, also saw Zhao as a firm supporter of his reform program. What was in Zhao's mind in the first two years after the collapse of the Gang of Four and how he viewed the future of political development in post-Mao China remains a question that needs further study.

From 1978, however, Zhao's attitude toward post-Mao reform became clearer. During his visit to Romania and Yugoslavia with Hua Guofeng, Zhao saw how far economic liberalism, if not political liberalism, could be undertaken under the banner of socialism. He returned with many books on Yugoslavia's non-Stalinist type of socialism.[38] The ideas expressed by Yugoslavian ideologues apparently inspired his ideas about enterprise reform. In the same year, Zhao also led a provincial delegation to visit Jiangsu where collective rural enterprises were fast replacing state-owned enterprises in the local economy. According to Xu Jiatun, the then Party secretary of Jiangsu, Zhao told him after the visit that rural reform could go even further. Although he did not say how far he could go, Zhao obviously had some ideas in mind.[39] Developments in Sichuan showed that

Zhao's visit to Jiangsu had convinced him that rural reform in Sichuan was politically safe, just as his visit to Eastern Europe had inspired his reform of urban enterprise.

The radical reform encouraged by Zhao in the rural areas of Sichuan abolished the egalitarian reward system, illustrated by the agricultural model of Dazhai, and introduced (or re-introduced) the contract system. The contract system was not novel to peasants in Sichuan, especially in the poor areas of the province. In early 1959, in the aftermath of the Great Leap Forward, two Party secretaries, Deng Zili of Zigong Prefecture, and Zhang Fengwu of Jiangjin Prefecture, abolished the mess halls and established a contract system. Li Jingquan abruptly stopped the "reform." The contract system was banned immediately after the Lushan Conference and prefectural Party leaders Deng Zili and others were purged.[40] In early 1978, local Party leaders in Guang'an County re-introduced the contract system. To reduce any possible political risk, contracts were made between government and production teams, i.e. between the state and collectives, not individuals. Zhao authorized the practice and introduced it to other parts of the province.

In the same year as rural reform unfolded, reforms in Sichuan's state-owned enterprises began.[41] Six enterprises in Chongqing and Chengdu were chosen as "experimental sites." A new policy was granted to give these enterprises the right to retain profits for bonus payments to advanced workers; to expand production and to engage in production outside the state plan; and to be able to market their products after the plan targets were met. The new policy gave enterprises the right to deal directly with foreign companies and to reserve part of their foreign exchange earnings for importing new technology, raw materials, advanced equipment and other products necessary to improve production. The new policy also gave factory managers the right to penalize workers who brought heavy losses to the factory.[42] A modified policy was soon extended to another 100 enterprises and then a further 200 enterprises in 1980. In the same year, a more radical policy was adopted in several enterprises such that the factories were allowed to "manage independently, pay tax, rather than profit, to the state and assume full responsibility for profit and losses."[43] The results were encouraging. Of the 403 experimental enterprises, industrial output increased 29.9 percent compared with that in 1978, productivity increased 12.72 percent, profit increased 29.2 percent, and tax paid to state increased 23.34 percent.[44]

In terms of economic reform, therefore, Zhao can be considered a pioneer in post-Mao China. The reforms he introduced in Sichuan obviously increased local productivity. More importantly, these reforms also had strong political implications: they had broken Mao's social, political and economic order and suggested an alternative to the Maoist strategy of economic development.

While Zhao did take risks to exploit the opportunities offered in the reform era, other factors should also be considered. Local reform was possible during the late 1970s and early 1980s because policy differences existed among the top leaders in Beijing. While factional struggle in the Center often required support from local political leaders, it was still politically risky for such leaders to adopt an unsanctioned policy. In September 1978, the official press published an article praising Zhao's role in local agricultural development, but it did not mention the contract system being carried out in the rural areas of Sichuan.[45] Whether this suggested an appreciation or a disapproval of Zhao's experiment was unclear. But one thing is almost certain, should Deng Xiaoping have lost his battle with Hua Guofeng, Zhao Ziyang would probably have had to pay for his boldness. Zhao possibly understood this and maintained a certain balance between Deng Xiaoping and Hua Guofeng, at least in the early days of reform. His visit to Romania and Yugoslavia with Hua was, in fact, seen by many as Hua's effort to build up a stronger tie between the two men.

Within the province, Zhao's reform ideas were not always shared by other provincial leaders. Most of them were remnants of Li Jingquan or followers of Mao's radical line. Before Zhao's reform was formally accepted by the Center, he was actually very isolated in Sichuan.[46] Even Zhao himself implemented the contract system with great caution and hesitation. He repeatedly stressed that various methods could be tried and compared, but not a contract system between a people's commune and individual households. He was also strongly opposed to the division of land or the encouragement of household farming.[47] Only after 1981, when rural reform swept across China and the contract system between government and individual households was practiced in other provinces did Zhao admit that his reluctance had hampered the initiatives of local Party and government leaders in Sichuan.[48] If Zhao's bold economic reform categorized him as a pioneer, his political opportunism ranked him as a bandwagoner.

Yang Rudai: A Party Secretary from the Grass-roots Level

Yang Rudai was a leader who took initiatives in economic reform, but could hardly be considered a pioneer. He only took initiatives when the general situation was favorable, but stayed firmly in line with the Center politically and economically, when told to do so. Therefore, he may well be considered a bandwagoner.

The promotion of Yang Rudai to the position of Party secretary in Sichuan was significant for several reasons. He was the first native Sichuanese promoted to the top position since 1949. Secondly, he was the first provincial Party secretary without a pre-1949 revolutionary background. Thirdly, at the time when Yang was promoted to the top position in 1981, educational background was one of the most important factors for cadres to become Party and government leaders. However, of all the Party secretaries in the province, Yang's educational level was the lowest. He only had primary school education, an educational level lower than that was required of a provincial Party secretary.[49]

Yang's career is relatively simple. He came from a poor peasant family in a very rich southern Sichuan county, Renshou. He was very active in the early 1950s when the land reform was carried out in his hometown and his performance was rewarded. After the land reform, Yang joined the Party, just when Sichuan was reorganized into a province in 1952. Within two years, Yang was promoted from a land reform team leader to a deputy Party secretary of Renshou County. From the early 1960s, as domestic politics became increasingly radical, family background often determined one's political future. Yang apparently benefited from this situation. He was promoted to the first Party secretary of Renshou as a model of Li Jingquan's "class line." Because of his ties with Li, Yang suffered a lot during the Cultural Revolution. Nevertheless, he still worked very hard and led the local people to complete a 300 million cubic meter reservoir which solved a key irrigation problem for local agriculture. His success impressed the new provincial leader, Zhao Ziyang. Soon after Zhao came to Sichuan, Yang was promoted to Party secretary of Leshan Prefecture in 1977. Only a year later, Yang became Zhao's close assistant, vice governor of Sichuan Province. Before Zhao left Sichuan to work in the Center, it was widely believed that Yang would succeed Zhao as the new governor and Party secretary of Sichuan. But to everyone's surprise, a senior official of the revolutionary generation, Tan Qilong, came to succeed Zhao.[50] The explanation was that among all the provincial-level Party and government leaders, Yang was the only one who joined the Party after 1949. He needed senior people to "assist" him for a period of time before he could work independently. There might also have been a compromise between the Center and Tan Qilong, whereby Tan would succeed Zhao as the Party and government leader of Sichuan after Zhao left. Then, in two to three years, Tan would be completely retired from politics and he would be succeeded by Yang. As a result of this arrangement, Yang was promoted as a provincial Party secretary among others, but he was the Party secretary in charge of day-to-day operation.

Two years later, in 1982, Tan retired. In a complete reshuffling of the provincial leadership, most senior Party and government leaders of the revolutionary generation were retired. Yang and three other native Sichuanese (including a person of Yi ethnicity) were selected Party secretaries of Sichuan with Yang as the first among equals. For the first time in post-1949 Sichuan, a Sichuan native became the Party leader of the province. At the Party's Thirteenth National Congress held in 1987, Yang was even elected as a member of the Politburo of the Central Committee.

A cadre from a rural village of Sichuan with limited education, Yang probably knew agriculture and local peasants much better than industry, foreign trade, education, science and technology, Party and government bureaucrats, and intellectuals and factory workers. Local officials and scholars believed that Yang was chosen as the top leader of Sichuan, not because of his ability, but because he was a man of action without much political ambition. Therefore, he did not constitute a threat to anyone and was consequently accepted by almost everyone.

As a communist leader from the countryside, Yang's private life was very simple. His wife worked as a contract worker in a collective-owned factory even after he became the Party secretary of Sichuan. He was cautious and careful not to make any major political mistakes or form any factions. But many people in Sichuan believed that just because of his carefulness, Sichuan did not achieve any breakthrough in reform and lagged behind other provinces after Zhao Ziyang left. This charge might not be fair since Sichuan's slowdown was the result of many factors: a huge population, a large number of non-productive defense industries, geographic inconvenience. Most importantly, Yang Rudai became the Party secretary of Sichuan at a time when the Center changed its policy from a balanced development strategy to a preferential strategy favoring the coastal regions. Apart from the decline of central investment, which will be discussed in detail later, there were many new social, economic and political problems that challenged Yang's leadership.

Unemployment of Industrial Workers

Communist industrialization in Sichuan was mainly sponsored by central investment. Like other industrial centers formed during Mao's period, Sichuan has a large number of state-owned enterprises (SOEs). In 1995, the average annual wage of staff and workers in state-owned units in Sichuan was 4,952 yuan, ranking it twenty-fifth among the provinces. The national average was 5,625 yuan. Sichuan's average annual SOE wage was only 52 percent that of Shanghai (9,578 yuan) and 58 percent that of Guangdong (8,540 yuan). Per capita consumption in the province was 1,261 yuan, ranking it twenty-second in China. The national average was 2,311 yuan. Per capita consumption was only 24 percent that of Shanghai (5,345 yuan) and 47 percent that of Guangdong (2,699 yuan). In 1995, Sichuan had one of the highest unemployment rates in China (3.7 percent), ranking eighth in the nation. The national average was 2.9 percent.[51] The real situation was probably even worse. The situation in the old industrial city of Chongqing, for example, was appalling. Although the official newspapers never reported it, local officials said privately that industrial strikes had occurred in major cities like Chengdu and Chongqing every year since 1992, involving thousands of workers from defense-related industries who were underpaid, or seldom paid, because their factories were unable to survive in an increasingly marketized economy. These demonstrations set alarm bells ringing for both central and provincial leaders. With few funds to dispense, the Center asked local governments to look for their own solutions. Yang Rudai had to instruct the local Party and government to seek donations from society, a campaign called "showing your concern" (*song ai xin huodong*) and also persuaded banks and relevant departments of the central government to provide special funds.[52] In 1994, government subsidies for financial losses of the SOEs was 621.41 million yuan, most of which were actually used to pay workers salaries.[53]

The Third Front Project

The embarrassing situation of the Third Front Project exemplifies the disadvantages of Sichuan in a new environment. From 1965, the central government invested heavily in Sichuan to build a new strategic defense-related industrial center there. This effort turned Sichuan into an industrialized province, but the project also created problems in the post-Mao era.[54]

Changes in the Chinese leaders' conception of the world and a departure from the Maoist economic development strategy since the late 1970s have seriously affected the Third Front Project. When the Center originally attempted to transfer the project to Sichuan, local leaders in Sichuan were, in fact, not happy to accept it. The reasons were apparent. First, enterprises of the Third Front Project were designed for military production without considering economic efficiency. In 1978 the realized output value for every 100 yuan invested in fixed assets of the Third Front Project enterprises was 30 percent lower than that of the national average. The capital-tax rate was 40 percent lower than that of the national average and much lower than those of the coastal areas. The total value of fixed assets in the Third Front Project accounted for 56 percent of the national total, but its total output value accounted for only 39 percent of the national total.[55] The introduction of a market economy in the 1990s meant that this Maoist legacy could be a burden rather than a source of wealth.

Second, although the Third Front Project included a relatively high level of technology, its military-related technology could not be easily converted into civilian production. In a market-oriented economy, many enterprises were not competitive. Moreover, the transfer of modern technology from western countries to the coastal areas meant that the Third Front areas lost their position as a hi-tech center within China after the 1980s.

Third, the sudden termination of the Third Front Project construction in the late 1970s left many of the supporting projects unfinished. As a result, many key projects had difficulties maintaining even normal production.[56]

Fourth, the project's construction was by nature a "blood transfusion" project from an industrially advanced area to a poor area. When the process ceased, the poor area was not able to continue by itself.

Finally, there were both profitable enterprises and loss-making enterprises among the Third Front Projects. When the central government decided to transfer the Third Front Projects to Sichuan, relevant departments of the State Council were willing to hand over only non-profitable enterprises while keeping profitable ones for themselves.

Within the province, Yang Rudai was said to be willing to help the Center to solve the above-mentioned problems, while other provincial leaders were very reluctant to accept the project without any compensation from the Center. After repeated negotiations between the central government and functional departments on the one side and the provincial government, its functional departments and leaders of the enterprises concerned on the other, the central government agreed in 1985 to provide a special fund for Sichuan to convert the military production of the Third Front Project into civilian production. However, of the more than 2,000 enterprises, the Center agreed to sponsor only 7 percent. Of the total fund provided (2 billion yuan), the central government provided only 40 percent (in the form of a construction loan). For the other 60 percent, the enterprises had to raise half by themselves (30 percent of the total), while the other half would be shared by the provincial government and relevant departments of the State Council.[57] While local revenues decreased continuously since 1985, the provincial government had to spend millions of dollars to subsidize the SOEs, many of them belonging to the Third Front Project: 1.26 billion yuan in 1985, 0.9 billion yuan in 1986, $1.31 billion yuan in 1988, 1.58 billion yuan in 1989–90 and 1.3 billion yuan in 1991.[58] For an already tightened local budget, the Third Front Project was a heavy financial burden. The Third Front Project was built with the assistance of the entire nation, but Sichuan alone had to shoulder the responsibility of the mismanagement of the central government. Yang's cooperation with the central government was rewarded: in 1987 he was promoted to be a member of the Politburo.

Relations between the Party and Government

Relations between the Party and government were not a serious problem in Sichuan before the Cultural Revolution as Li Jingquan dominated local politics and assumed leadership of the local Party, government and military apparatus. In post-Mao China, the division of work between Party and government was adapted as a principle of the Party at the Thirteenth Party Congress. As a provincial Party secretary and a member of the Politburo, Yang Rudai generally was not considered to be an ambitious politician. His working relations with Governor Yang Xizhong were considered good, probably because both men grew up in the rural areas. Yang's relations with other governors who had different backgrounds, however, did not seem very smooth.

Governor Jiang Minkuan (1985–88), for example, was a Shanghai native. Originally a chief engineer of a defense-related modern aluminum processing factory in Chongqing, Jiang studied in the Soviet Union in 1953–55. He joined the Party in 1961 when the Sino-Soviet split became open. He moved to Sichuan as an engineer with his factory during the Third Front Project period. In 1985, Jiang was elected the governor of the Sichuan provincial government. As a government leader from a large modern factory, Jiang spent a lot of time attempting to improve the performance of Sichuan's industry and foreign trade, while Yang, as a Party leader from the countryside, was more familiar with agriculture and the rural economy. At a time when China's foreign trade with western countries was controlled by the Center and dominated by the coastal regions, Jiang proposed to develop foreign relations with the former Soviet

Union and the Eastern European countries. The proposal, which will be discussed later, was rejected by the then Premier Zhao Ziyang as unrealistic. Within the province, Yang criticized Jiang's idea, without mentioning the governor's name, as "an interference" in the strategy of the Central Committee.[59] As a result, the relationship between the provincial Party committee and the government was not good during the period of 1985–88, with tensions apparent between the two men. Jiang was later transferred from Sichuan to work in the Center.

Zhang Haoruo succeeded Jiang as the new governor in 1988. Returning from the former Soviet Union in 1954 as a government-sponsored student, Zhang worked as a chemical engineer in the Chinese petroleum industry for many years until 1986. Before his appointment as governor of Sichuan in 1988, he worked as a vice minister of foreign economic relations and trade.[60] Zhang's father was said to be a senior official working in the Ministry of Coal Industry of the State Council in the 1950s and his two brothers were leading officials in Tianjin and Hainan. Thus, Zhang was considered a member of China's "princeling clique." With his family background, Zhang had close relationships with many key persons in the central government, in particular Li Peng. These wide political and personal connections gave Zhang a very strong position in the province.

In early 1992, a resolution to build the world's biggest dam at the Three Gorges of the Yangtze River was passed at the Fifth Meeting of the Seventh National People's Congress. It is estimated that by the time the project is completed in the year 2008, Sichuan will lose, either entirely or in part, 15 counties and cities, representing a total of 503 square kilometers of land. A total of 955,000 people will have to be relocated along with 555 factories (including 4 modern industrial complexes and 11 medium-size factories, with a total value of 712 million yuan), 106 power stations, 595.4 kilometers of roads, 747.3 kilometers of power lines and 1,325.7 kilometers of telephone lines. The project is designed to provide protection against flooding for the middle and lower Yangtze River valley areas and to generate electric power for industrially advanced central and eastern China. Sichuan, however, will not benefit directly from the project.[61]

Within the province, Yang Rudai originally opposed the decision and supported local deputies at the National People's Congress in making strong protests against the project. But Governor Zhang firmly supported the central decision. One local official who has attended every National People's Congress since the early 1980s said that before the Fifth Plenary Meeting, the Center warned the provincial leaders not to oppose the project at the forthcoming National Congress. Governor Zhang was the first to express his resolute support of the central decision. Under central pressure, Yang Rudai changed his position and supported the decision, but at the same time he also asked other provincial leaders to take the opportunity to urge the Central Committee to seriously consider Sichuan's difficulties. Finally, local leaders reached an agreement among themselves: while supporting the Center's decision, they should also negotiate with the Center. As a result, Sichuan agreed to support the project at the Fifth Plenary Meeting. As a concession, the central government agreed to increase the investment to 18.5 billion yuan in the Three Gorges areas as a compensation for Sichuan's losses. When the deal was reached, Governor Zhang Haoruo expressed his support of the project, on behalf of Sichuan, at a press conference. Yang remained conspicuously silent.

Serious conflicts between Yang and Zhang intensified during the student demonstrations in 1989. Yang sent a telegram to the Party Central Committee before martial law was imposed in May. He expressed his desire that the conflict be handled peacefully. After the imposition of martial law, Governor Zhang decided to publish an open statement in support of the central government. The statement was sent to the local Party organ, *Sichuan Daily*, to be published. Yang was informed before the statement went to press. He ordered the paper not to publish the letter and went to the provincial government to discuss with the governor how to "coordinate" between the provincial Party committee and the government. After the meeting, a joint statement by the provincial Party committee and the government was published in support of the Center's decision, with Yang adopting a harsh policy towards local student demonstrators. Thousands of armed policemen were sent to the city center of Chengdu and many student demonstrators were arrested. Severe conflicts between local people and armed police broke out. The largest shopping center of the city was burnt down.[62]

Yang was the first Sichuan native to rise to the top position in local leadership. With limited education, a lack of strong political connections with the Center and no experience in industry and foreign trade, Yang worked very cautiously during his office term. He made several efforts to push local reforms, but with unimpressive results. (These will be discussed in detail later.) He tried to protect local interests on several occasions, but ultimately gave up under central pressure.

Xiao Yang: A Sichuanese Who Speaks Mandarin

Of all of Sichuan's Party and government leaders in the post-Mao era, Xiao Yang may be the most controversial. It is very difficult to fit him into a single category. His bold economic proposals, however impractical they were, place him as a pioneer, but his poor political performance damaged his reputation.

Xiao Yang is a Sichuan native, but he spent most of his revolutionary career in Beijing. He joined the Party in 1947 when he was a student at Qinghua University. Liberation provided him with new opportunities. After 1949, he became a staff member of the Beijing Military Control Committee and was sent to work as a military representative in the Beijing Glass Factory. When the situation normalized, Xiao was appointed head and Party secretary of the factory. In the early 1950s, like many promising young communists with higher education, Xiao was sent to East Germany to study at post-graduate level. After returning to China in 1956, he was appointed head and Party secretary of a modern glass factory, the Beijing General Glass Factory, until the Cultural Revolution. Local people say that Xiao's political life changed after he led a group of specialists to make a crystal coffin for the dead leader, Mao Zedong. This cannot be confirmed, but Xiao was promoted quickly after 1976 and was believed to be on the list of the "Third Echelon"—officials who would assume important Party and government positions when the old revolutionaries retired. Before Xiao was appointed deputy Party secretary and vice mayor of Chongqing in 1984, he had already been promoted to be the vice director of the Foreign Economic and Trade Committee of the Beijing Municipal Government.[63]

When Xiao Yang moved to Chongqing in 1983, many people thought that, as a selected member of the "Third Echelon," Xiao would only stay in the position for a couple of years before returning to Beijing for a higher position. In March 1985, however, Xiao was promoted to the third higher ranking position in the city Party committee, after Yu Hanqing, the then mayor of Chongqing and deputy secretary of the city Party committee. People quickly realized that it would only be a matter of time before Xiao Yang would replace either the first Party secretary, Liao Bokang, or the mayor. In September of that year, at the Third Plenary Meeting of the Tenth People's Congress of Chongqing, Yu resigned and Xiao took over his position. In 1988, Xiao swapped this position for city Party secretary.

In the same year as Xiao's transfer to Chongqing, the city was promoted as one of the four centrally planned cities, along with Wuhan, Shenyang and Dalian, having provincial-level economic power and under the direct leadership of the State Council. The aim was to rebuild Chongqing into a trade and industrial center of southwest China.[64] However, economic independence did not give Chongqing any real corresponding political or administrative independence. The province was still a direct superior of the city. After Chongqing was upgraded, it suddenly found that it became very difficult for the city to have materials supplied and to market for its products within the province and as such, many of its factories experienced losses.[65] Provincial leaders made it clear that, since Chongqing had a new boss, it should ask the Center, not the province, to solve these problems. With Xiao's appointment, local people hoped that Xiao's connection with the Center would help the city to solve its problems. But Xiao's performance at one crucial moment was rather disappointing and embarrassed Chongqing.

In early 1992, prior to the forthcoming annual meeting of the Seventh National People's Congress, Xiao Yang began urging the central government to build an even higher dam than the Center had originally planned.[66] Xiao's support of the central decision was considered by local officials, including those from Chongqing, to be a betrayal of local interests. But Xiao's political performance rewarded him. Despite strong opposition from local leaders, Xiao was appointed by the Center as a deputy secretary of the provincial Party committee.

People said that because of Xiao Yang's close relations with Deng Xiaoping, and because of his support for central decisions on many occasions, he had originally been selected to replace Yang Rudai both as the new provincial Party secretary and as a member of the Politburo.[67] However, local Party workers believed that since Xiao's poor reputation in the province might not win him enough votes,[68] the Center had planned that Li Boyong, the then vice governor, should be promoted as governor of Sichuan and Yang Rudai would remain as the Party head until after a new provincial Party congress was held following the Fourteenth Party Congress. Yang would then retire and Xiao would be appointed by the Party Central Committee as the new provincial Party secretary and member of the Politburo without election. However, with Li Boyong being appointed minister of labor of the State Council, Xiao was appointed deputy governor of Sichuan before the Fourteenth Party Congress and would replace Zhang Haoruo as governor of Sichuan after the congress. The Center decided that Xiao should be elected to the Politburo at the Fourteenth Congress while Yang was out. The decision proved to be a disaster for Sichuan. Xiao's performance during the Party Congress elicited a strong negative response from deputies of other provinces.[69] He was elected as the last alternate member of the Central Committee[70] and, accordingly, was not eligible to be elected to the Politburo. As a result, Sichuan lost its seat in China's power center, and officials in Sichuan believed that Xiao Yang himself was to be blamed for this debacle.

Xiao Yang was made governor of Sichuan in 1993, but scandals surrounded him since he took up the position. Rumors spread that the new governor is a satyr. His men in Chongqing were removed after he left. Thousands of shareholders held a demonstration in front of the provincial government building in 1994 after a futures company supported by Xiao went bankrupt and the owner fled overseas.[71] During a provincial Party congress in late 1995, Xiao resigned at the behest of local officials.[72] His position as governor was taken by Song Baorui, a Beijing native who has been working in Sichuan since 1968.

Some local officials argue that despite his poor political performance, Xiao should not be considered a conservative. Since gaining the leadership position, Xiao took several bold initiatives to open Sichuan. In about 1994, for example, he proposed building Chengdu into the largest international city in China's southwest in order to attract more foreign investment.[73] He also organized several large foreign investment and trade conferences in Chengdu, Hong Kong and Hungary in 1993–95, aimed at attracting foreign capital to Sichuan and promoting exports from the province.[74] He pushed the central government to allow foreign banks to open branches in Sichuan.[75] He pioneered the proposal that in order to attract foreign investment, foreign enterprises should be allowed to sell all their products in Sichuan's domestic market.[76] However, many of his proposals were not translated into feasible working policies for local government, while others were not permitted by the Center. Nor did his investment and trade conferences attract as much foreign investment as people expected. Xiao Yang's bold economic proposals could label him a pioneer, but his lack of political skill in persuading the Center to support these proposals damaged his reputation. It is very difficult to fit local leaders such as Xiao Yang into categories of either pioneer or bandwagoner.

Foreign Economic Policy

The foreign economic policy of a province is the product of a complex political process. Individual initiatives may involve a balancing of different opinions among top provincial leaders; conflicting interests and compromise between different groups; and negotiations between central and local governments. The political and economic situation, the personal characteristics and the attitudes of individual leaders toward reform are all important factors. The previous sections provided an overview of three typical provincial leaders whose roles in post-Mao Sichuan all affected the decision-making process for foreign economic policy. In the following sections, we focus specifically on the foreign economic policy of the provincial leadership in the post-Mao period.

General Situation

As a remote inland province, Sichuan's connection with the outside world has been obstructed by its geographical isolation. Under the highly centralized management of the Mao era, Sichuan conducted little direct foreign trade activity. The province functioned mainly as a supply of resources for export. Most of its products, including grain, vegetable oil, meat and other agriculture-related products, were exported through other border provinces or coastal cities. Meanwhile, through the central government's arrangement, Sichuan also received foreign aid projects or technology transfer from the former Soviet Union, other Eastern European socialist countries and a few western countries. Modern factories built during the period included defense-related industries, such as heavy machinery, chemical industry and textile plants. In the 1960s, when China was further isolated from the rest of the world, Sichuan's connection with the rest of China improved somewhat. Ironically, it was Sichuan's geographical isolation that attracted the Center to invest heavily in Sichuan and build the Third Front Project in preparation for a possible world war. After the 1970s however, when China's relations with the western world improved, Sichuan's export position declined as many of its agricultural products did not suit western markets. Sichuan's provincial position in exports dropped from fifth in the 1950s to nineteenth in 1969–74.[77]

The decline in foreign trade was only one aspect of the generally deteriorating local economy. A detailed study shows that in 1978, Sichuan had the highest GDP among three provinces (24.48 billion yuan in Sichuan, 22.91 billion yuan in Shandong and 15.1 billion yuan in Hubei). By 1990 GDP had increased 367 percent in Sichuan (114.4 billion yuan), 482 percent in Shandong (133.21 billion yuan) and 424 percent in Hubei (79.2 billion yuan). National income per capita in 1978 in Sichuan, Shandong and Hubei were respectively 238 yuan, 321 yuan and 332 yuan but by 1990, it was 1,063 yuan, 1,569 yuan and 1,496 yuan. The difference between Sichuan and Shandong in 1978 was 83 yuan, but it increased to 506 yuan by 1990. Since population growth in Shandong (18.63 percent) was higher than Sichuan (11.48 percent) during the same period, the difference was obviously caused by Shandong's faster economic development.[78]

Another study shows that the annual growth rate of total industrial output in Sichuan was 11.8 percent in the period from 1953 to 1978, higher than that of the national average (11.4 percent) and Guangdong (10.6 percent). From 1981 to 1989, however, growth in Sichuan was 12.2 percent, lower than both the national average (13.2 percent) and Guangdong (20 percent). The annual growth rate of income in Sichuan in the period from 1952 to 1957 was 11.1 percent, again higher than the national average (8.88 percent) and Guangdong (9.20 percent). From 1979 to 1989, however, the growth rate in Sichuan dropped to 8.3 percent, lower than the national average (8.7 percent) and Guangdong (11.6 percent).[79]

The economic success of China's coastal areas is mainly the result of increasing investment, both Chinese and foreign. Since 1978, the preferential policies granted by the Center have attracted large sums of foreign investment into China's coastal areas in the southeast and provided a strong foundation for this economic take-off. In comparison, the lack of capital investment, whether central or foreign, has been one of the major problems in the decline of Sichuan's local economy. Despite its rich natural resources and development potential, geographic isolation and the lack of immediate benefits for foreign investors are seen as the main reasons for low foreign investment.[80] By the end of 1993, the number of foreign enterprises registered in Sichuan was 2.26 percent of the national total, 8.47 percent that of Guangdong. Foreign investment accounted for 1.98 percent of the national total, or 5.75 percent that of Guangdong. Foreign capital actually used accounted for 1.47 percent of the national total, only 5.81 percent that of Guangdong. In terms of per capita figures, in 1993 every Cantonese attracted US$ 133.84, while every Sichuanese attracted only US$ 5.14 (national average was US$ 32.87).[81]

On the other hand, central investment in Sichuan, the primary force for economic modernization in the previous years, has dropped continuously since the 1980s. Average state investment in Sichuan has also decreased continuously from 95.65 percent of the total investment in the third five-year plan (1966–70), 89.83 percent in the fourth five-year plan (1971–75), 75.44 percent in the fifth five-year plan (1976–80), to 42.53 percent in the sixth five-year plan (1981–85). Average state investment in the sixth five-year plan was 53.12 percent lower than that in the third five-year plan.[82]

Since the 1980s, Sichuan has made great efforts to attract foreign investment. In 1988, for example, the provincial People's Congress passed "Regulations Encouraging Foreign Investment in Sichuan." According to this document, Sichuan would offer part of its market, its local resources, its interests and property rights for foreign investment. No compulsory demands would be made on potential joint ventures or sole foreign investment regarding the share of its products to be exported. The regulation also said that whatever preferential treatment or encouragement was made available in other provinces or regions could be extended by Sichuan to foreign investors in a similar manner. Sichuan also adopted a policy known as "six non-restrictions" toward foreign investment, meaning that there would be no restrictions on foreign investment in the areas of their special fields, the size of the enterprises, the nature of the ownership, the methods of cooperation, the channels of cooperation and the prospective partners for foreign investment.[83]

Other major preferential policies for foreign investment issued by the province included: (1) long-term projects of foreign investment in the fields of energy, communication, transportation, agriculture and forestry are entitled to expand their business into other related areas with the approval of the provincial government; (2) corporate income tax for foreign investment is 33 percent. Foreign investment in manufacturing enterprises operating in special areas with preferential policies similar to those adopted in the coastal open areas have a corporate income tax of 24 percent. Enterprises operating in the economic-technological zones and those in the high-tech development zones which are recognized by the State Council as high-tech enterprises[84] have a corporate income tax rate of 15 percent; (3) for all foreign invested enterprises with a business record of over 10 years, corporate income tax is exempted completely for the first two years, starting from the year when profit is realized, and corporate income tax is reduced to 50 percent for the third to fifth years; (4) all lands obtained by the foreign-invested enterprises in the form of leases are entitled to release, rent or mortgage according to the law.[85]

After 1992, the provincial People's Congress and local people's congresses in Chengdu and Chongqing adopted new regulations to encourage foreign investment. The new regulations gave more powers to the subprovincial cities to approve foreign investment. While Chengdu and Chongqing enjoyed preferential policies similar to those of the coastal cities, the provincial government gave other sub-provincial cities the right to approve any foreign investment up to US$ 10 million.[86] In reality, the provincial Party and government relied on the Center to allocate more investments from foreign governments to Sichuan while attempting to attract foreign investment through the foreign investment and trade conferences mentioned earlier.

Since 1978, tremendous achievements have been made in attracting foreign investment. From 1979 to the end of 1994, the province attracted a total of US$ 9.4 billion in contracted investments, of which foreign loans (US$ 3 billion) accounted for 32.3 percent; direct foreign investment (US$ 6.1 billion) was 64.2 percent of the total; and other foreign investment (US$ 0.3 billion) accounted for 3.5 percent of the total. Of the total contracted foreign investment, 45 percent was actually placed (US$ 4.3 billion, including US$ 2.6 billion foreign loans).[87]

During the same period, 34.4 percent of the foreign investment went to industry, 23.1 percent to energy and transportation, 16.2 percent to real estate, 10 percent to city construction, 5.9 percent to farming, 5 percent to tourism and other recreation industry.[88] Of the total foreign loans, government loans, arranged by the central government, accounted for 60 percent (US$ 1.8 billion).[89] World Bank loans accounted for 39.7 percent (US$ 1.19 bilion).[90] Most government loans were used in energy (67.5 percent), chemical fertilizer (11.1 percent) and communications (7.9 percent).

Foreign investment loans have made a significant contribution to the improvement of the infrastructure of the province, which has directly or indirectly provided a better environment for economic development of the province. According to the provincial government, for example, the completion of the Ma Hui Hydraulic Power Station and the Wei Tuo Hydraulic Power Station were assisted by loans provided by the Austrian government, the Jiang You Power Station and the Luo Huang Power Station in Chongqing were built with the loans from the French government. All contributed to the easing of power shortages in Sichuan. The introduction of the programmed telephone system aided by Spanish, Swedish and Canadian government loans improved telecommunications in the province. Loans provided by the Japanese government were used to improve Chengdu's water supply.[91]

Another important foreign investment source came from loans provided by the World Bank. Of the total World Bank loans invested in Sichuan, the province was responsible for US$ 890 million, or 74.8 percent of the total. Of this, US$ 380 million (42.7 percent) was used for the Ertan Hydraulic Power Station (the largest of its kind in China), US$ 186 million (20.9 percent) for provincial projects (89 percent of which were used to build the Chengdu-Chongqing Highway and the Luzhou Natural Gas Chemical Plant). A further US$ 324 million (36.4 percent) was used to support economic development of poor areas in the province.[92]

The third and largest form of foreign investment was private foreign investment. Since 1983, 5,286 enterprises have registered as foreign-invested enterprises.[93] Between 1990 and 1993, Sichuan had an annual increase in contracted foreign investment of US$ 1 billion, with actual foreign investment increasing US$ 0.2 billion annually.[94] Unlike foreign government loans and low interest loans provided by the World Bank, private foreign investments were mainly concentrated in industries like foodstuffs, textiles and electronics. In recent years, this form of investment has spread to the areas of real estate (25.3 percent), light industry, foodstuffs and garments (20.6 percent), building materials (14.8 percent), machinery (9.8 percent), catering service and recreation (5.3 percent), transportation and communication (5.1 percent), electronics (3.6 percent), chemical industry (3.6 percent) and others.[95]

If compared with other areas, Sichuan's effort to attract foreign investment was not very impressive. In 1995, for example, actual foreign investment in

Sichuan was US$ 619.36 million, 1.29 percent of the national total and 5.8 percent that of Guangdong. Registered foreign-invested enterprises numbered 5,897, 2.52 percent of the national total and 9.9 percent that of Guangdong.[96]

Strategies to Attract Domestic and Foreign Investment

While continuing to persuade the central government to invest in the western regions of China and attract foreign investment, Sichuan has also undertaken various efforts to attract domestic investment from other provinces. Five strategies deserve special attention.

The Great Southwest Development Strategy

Provincial leaders, and especially Party Secretary Yang Rudai, have urged Sichuan to strengthen its links with other provinces in China's western areas. Sichuan felt disadvantaged in the 1980s. The feeling was justified when the Center published its new program of development based on a theory of "development by stages" (tidu kaifa lilun), according to which the central government would give first priority to industrially advanced eastern regions, followed by the central regions. Sichuan and other poor provinces in southwest and northwest would wait until the next century. Strongly opposing this strategy of economic development, scholars from the Sichuan Academy of Social Sciences took an initiative in inviting local administrators, veteran Sichuanese who worked in the central government, and scholars from Yunnan and Guizhou (later including Chongqing, Guangxi and Tibet) to form an "Economic Cooperation Conference of the Great Southwest." Since March 1983, this semi-government organization has held annual meetings with participants from provincial Party and government units.

The unity of China's west, which includes the nine provinces of Sichuan, Yunnan, Guizhou, Tibet, Gansu, Ningxia, Shaanxi, Qinghai and Xinjiang, has formed a strong local lobby to persuade the central government to shift its focus of economic development from the coastal regions to China's western areas. Although local Party and government leaders were not the pioneers of this policy, they encouraged and supported the idea of building a united front among western regions. The idea has particular significance for Sichuan since the latter enjoys a leading position in regional development. Statistics show that in 1995, GDP in Sichuan was 353.40 billion yuan, accounting for 43.36 percent of the regional total. The gross value of industrial output was 442.64 billion yuan, accounting for 47.32 percent of the regional total. Local revenue was 16.71 billion yuan, representing 59.59 percent of the total. Fixed asset investment was 90.14 billion yuan, or 37.69 percent of the total. The gross output value of farming, forestry, animal husbandry and fishery was 152.03 billion yuan, or 28.29 percent of the total. Foreign trade was US$ 3.48 billion, 33.66 percent of the total. Actual foreign investment was US$ 619.36 million, or 41.24 percent of the total.[97]

Apart from drawing the Center's attention to the western and southwestern regions, the concept of the Great Southwest Development Strategy has also helped Sichuan to attract domestic investments from other provinces in the region. It is reported that during the first finance and trade conference of the southwest region held in 1987, a total of 46 deals were completed among six parties (Sichuan, Yunnan, Guizhou, Guangxi, Tibet and Chongqing), involving 2.27 billion yuan. In the same year, mutual investment among the southwestern provinces and Chongqing reached 75.72 million yuan.[98] By 1990, a total of 14,800 economic and technological cooperation agreements had been reached between Sichuan and other provinces and between different subprovincial regions within Sichuan. Contracted investments totaled 2.7 billion yuan, of which 1.25 billion yuan was invested in Sichuan.[99]

"Boat-Borrowing" Policy

While attracting domestic investment from other provinces, Sichuan has also spent part of its already tightened budget investing in the coastal areas in order to share in the benefit of fast economic growth. The policy was encouraged by the top leaders of the province. In a new tide of reform stimulated by Deng Xiaoping's southern China inspection tour in 1992, Party Secretary Yang Rudai openly urged Sichuanese to invest in coastal areas and summarized Sichuan's strategy as to "borrow a hen to lay eggs and to borrow a boat to go overseas" *(jie ji xia dan, jie chuan chu hai)*.[100]

Sichuan's investment in the coastal areas actually started in the late 1980s. By the end of 1990, Sichuan had established more than 700 "window enterprises" in Shenzhen, Hainan, Guangdong, Fujian and Shanghai with a total investment worth 1 billion yuan.[101] In Shenzhen alone, 200 enterprises were run by Sichuan-owned companies with a total investment of 460 million yuan. Industrial output value of these enterprises was believed to account for 10 percent of the city's total in 1989.[102] In Hainan, Sichuanese enterprises were the first in number and third in investment (after Guangdong and Beijing). In 1990, "window enterprises" produced a total output value of 0.3 billion yuan and exported US$ 50 million worth of goods. More importantly, 30 million yuan was sent back to Sichuan.[103]

Local officials said that, although in 1992 a total of 10 billion yuan was needed for capital investment in Sichuan, the province invested 7 billion yuan in the coastal areas, including 3 billion yuan in Beihai alone. In fact, Sichuan has invested so much in Beihai that people jokingly refer to the city as Beihai City of Sichuan Province.[104]

Despite these achievements, investment from Sichuan into coastal areas also caused a serious shortage of funds within the province. During the worst period of 1992–93, some local governments did not even have enough money to pay for grain purchased from the peasants. Meanwhile, local government officials used various kinds of excuses to increase peasants' taxes, levies and other charges. When rumors spread that local leaders had lost peasant funds which were to be used to build traffic roads through real estate speculation in Beihai, thousands of angry peasants in Renshou County, Yang Rudai's hometown, surrounded the county Party committee and government offices and burnt down buildings. Fearful of negative reactions from other parts of the province, Yang Rudai was said to have refused to use force, instead promising peasants that he would take responsibility for the case personally and no one would be punished.[105]

Another heavy blow to Sichuan's "boat-borrowing" policy was the central government's decision in late 1992 not to approve any loan to real estate businesses following Vice-premier Zhu Rongji's strict financial policy. Local officials said that Beihai became a new hot spot in real estate speculation when Li Peng inspected the city. After pushing land prices up and skimming enough profits from land speculation, companies run by various departments of the central government and the "princeling clique" quickly withdrew before the Center changed its policy. For late-comers like Sichuan, which was not aware of the sudden change, most of its funds were trapped in the real estate speculation, causing an even more serious shortage of funds for the province. Insiders said that Yang Rudai tried to negotiate with the Center and wanted the Center to relax its financial policy so that Sichuan could withdraw at least part of its investment from Beihai. Zhu Rongji was said to have refused Yang's request, fearing that any new financial deregulation would cause the whole system to collapse. Yang failed. Some people in Sichuan even believed that Yang's opportunistic policy in Beihai cost him his political career.[106]

Multi-dimensional Open-door Policy

As mentioned earlier, little progress had been made in Sichuan to attract foreign investment in the initial reform period after 1978, mainly because of the lack of preferential policies. Failing to attract foreign investment from the West, Governor Jiang Minkuan proposed turning to the former Soviet Union and other Eastern European socialist countries and using Sichuan's agricultural products to bargain for Soviet technology and, perhaps, attract investment.[107] He argued that China's open policy should be a multi-dimensional one (*quan fangwei*), meaning China should not only open its door to the western world, but also to East European communist countries. The idea was significant, especially at a time when Sino-Soviet relations had relaxed, if not totally normalized. There was a rumor that in order to normalize Party and government relations with China, Russians suggested that they would use advanced technology to upgrade more than one hundred large enterprises that the Soviet Union had built for China during the honeymoon period of Sino-Soviet relations in the 1950s. If this were true, Sichuan would have benefited from the proposal, since most of its modern enterprises built in the 1950s were Soviet-aid projects. It is hard to know whether Jiang's idea had any connection with this.

In practice, however, exporting to non-western countries or any trade between a Chinese province and Russia and other Eastern European countries still had to be approved by the central government. Politically, any increase of trade or technological transfer between China and the former Soviet Union might cause diplomatically sensitive problems for the Chinese government when its relations with western countries were improving. Most importantly, Jiang seemed not aware that the former Soviet Union and other Eastern European countries had economic difficulties of their own. It is very hard to believe that these countries were financially capable of investing in China. As mentioned earlier, Governor Jiang's idea was rejected by the Center.

Ironically, after 1989 when the western world imposed economic sanctions against China in the wake of the June Fourth incident, Jiang's idea of multi-dimensional opening was adopted by the Center. Trade between China and the former Soviet states and other Eastern European countries increased dramatically after the communist system collapsed there. Importantly, many of these trades were made not between two governments as they used to be, but between private business companies. Sichuan took a lead in such private transactions. In 1992, a private entrepreneur, Mu Qizhong from Chengdu, used China made products of daily necessities to exchange four Russian made Tu-154M airplanes. The whole deal was believed to be worth more than SF800 million.[108] It is so far the largest private international trade China has had since 1978.

The Sale of State-owned Enterprises to Foreign Investors

Another important policy local leaders made to attract foreign investment to Sichuan was to sell state-owned enterprises to foreign investors. The policy was made after Deng Xiaoping's southern inspection tour in 1992. As a traditionally agricultural province, most of Sichuan's modern industries were built after the 1950s. Many of them were state-owned, defense-related, non-productive enterprises. Despite initial success in industrial reforms, many of these enterprises had difficulties surviving in a market economy. Beginning from 1984, Sichuan organized several international investment and trade conferences in Hong Kong, Thailand, Macao, South Korea, as well as in Beijing, Chengdu and Chongqing. The provincial government also held several Sichuan Festivals in Moscow and Sofia, and participated in similar investment and trade conferences in other cities of China, trying to persuade foreign investors to buy property rights to these enterprises.

At least four types of sales of state-owned enterprises to foreign investors can be analyzed.

The first is a "joint enterprise through property rights transfer." It requires that an asset assessment of a state-owned enterprise is made, and then a part of the assets are transferred to the overseas investor in order to establish a joint venture. Once a joint venture is established, a board of directors and an operation and management structure are set up jointly by the local and foreign parties.

The second type is called "exclusive foreign capital enterprise through property rights transfer." The process of asset assessment is similar to the first type, but the property right is sold entirely to the foreign investor who then organizes a sole foreign capital enterprise. The Chinese staff of the original enterprise can be re-employed by the foreign investor. Those who are not employed are rehabilitated by government institutions.

The third type is a "limited liability company under joint Chinese-foreign management." The foreign investor will form a joint venture with the Chinese party by subscribing specific amounts of shares of a Chinese enterprise. With the approval of the concerned authorities, this kind of company is entitled to issue bonds to foreign investors.

The last type is a "joint enterprise or sole foreign capital enterprise established through international tender call." No asset assessment is required, but the bid margin of the enterprise is fixed according to an index showing the present-day value of the net cash inflow of the enterprise over the years to come. After that, open invitations are sent to foreign investors with an indication to transfer part or total property rights.[109]

It was believed that by selling state-owned enterprises to foreign investors, Sichuan would receive foreign capital, advanced management and technology. Most importantly, it would solve the problems of the state-owned enterprises by privatizing them.

Although Sichuan wants to use advanced foreign management and technology to transform its large number of state-owned enterprises into modern joint ventures or sole foreign enterprises, foreign investors may hesitate to put their money into a remote inland province. On the other hand, while Sichuan wants to use foreign investment to upgrade its enterprises so that they can compete in the international market, foreign investors want their products to enter into a local market with over 100 million people.

During a foreign investment and trade conference held in Hong Kong in 1992, about 100 enterprises or projects were presented. All of them were state-owned. Most of them did not have a good record of profit making and their products did not have a market. The conference was not very successful. Only a few enterprises were sold. Again in 1994, a larger foreign investment and trade conference was held in Chengdu. More than 300 enterprises and projects, including a wide range of industries, like metallurgy, electronics, building materials, light industry, chemical industry, energy, agriculture and food processing were marketed. It is believed that only a few contracts were signed during the Chengdu conference. The director of the provincial Foreign Trade Commission admitted that the enterprises presented did not show good performance in the past. "We just try to use this method to attract advanced technology, management and speed up reform."[110]

Sell the Market for Hi-tech

In recent years, the investment shortage in Sichuan seems to have relaxed for three reasons. Firstly, the increasing cost of production in coastal areas has given Sichuan a chance to attract foreign investment. It is believed that labor cost in Sichuan is only one-third to one-quarter that of the coastal areas. The cost of similar products produced in Sichuan is 20 percent lower than those made in coastal areas.[111]

Second, reforms in the financial and taxation systems by the central government have given local governments more flexibility in their own financial management.[112] Finally, in recent years, central government has apparently changed its policy of granting preferential policies only to coastal areas and tried to reduce the gap between the advanced east and the backward west in China. Statistics show that in 1988, six coastal provinces and cities attracted US$ 3,732.8 million in foreign investment, while 12 inland provinces attracted US $638.3 million, accounting for only 17 percent that of coastal areas. In 1992, foreign investment in coastal areas increased to US$ 10.59 billion, while inland provinces increased to US$ 0.92 billion, accounting for 8.69 percent that of the coastal areas.[113] In 1995, fourteen coastal open cities and four special economic zones attracted actual foreign investment of US$ 19.89 billion, while 12 inland provinces attracted US$ 4.24 billion, 21.31 percent that of the former.[114]

With these new developments, two local academics believed that Sichuan's financial shortage should relax into the foreseeable future if the current macroeconomic policies of the central government continue.[115] Meanwhile, they argue, international economic competition in recent years has increasingly relied on advanced science and technology. Thanks to the Third Front Project, Sichuan has a very good foundation to develop a modern science and technology base. Once the shortage of investment is no longer an immediate problem, Sichuan should quickly change its policy from merely providing preferential policies to attract foreign investment. Instead, Sichuan should open its huge local market to big foreign companies in exchange for their advanced technology. Foreign banks and financial institutions should be allowed to open branches in Sichuan. Joint venture or sole foreign capital enterprises in Sichuan should be allowed to run more tertiary industry businesses, including department stores. The proportion of internal sales of joint venture and foreign enterprises' products should be increased in order to attract more foreign investment with high technology. To attract hi-tech foreign enterprise into Sichuan, the provincial government has provided a series of preferential policies for foreign enterprises with advanced technology. Such enterprises will be exempted from income tax for the first two years and pay only 50 percent from the third to the fifth years. The 50 percent discount could be extended for another three years subject to approval. Foreign enterprises with advanced technology will also be exempted from land tax for the first three years.[116] In 1991, the province established a leading group headed by the governor to guide science and technology work in Sichuan. Party Secretary Yang Rudai also expressed clearly that the development of science and technology would be the major task of Sichuan for the next ten years.[117]

Conclusion

By investing heavily in the province, the central government has helped Sichuan to become modernized in a relatively short period. High political pressure and Party discipline reduced the damage caused by the mismanagement of communist bureaucrats. Economically, Sichuan's continued dependence on central investment and the central government's control over local economic activities also secured communist rule in the province. In post-Mao China, however, the reduction of central investment has caused many problems for Sichuan. Although local leaders have more autonomy than their predecessors, they still do not have any institutionalized guarantee "to do the best according to the local situation." The fact that local leaders have repeatedly asked the Center to grant special policies reflects Sichuan's political dependence upon the Center. Between local interest and Party discipline, no local leaders are willing to risk their careers in a changing political climate. With the death of Deng Xiaoping, control over local development by the new central leadership has increased. This was especially apparent after a new financial and taxation policy was introduced in 1994. Should no power struggle engulf the Center, which may damage the authority of the Center over the localities, we can expect that central-local relations in post-Deng China, which could be traced to the legacies of the past decades, would experience little change.

Notes

1. The first four largest provincial-level administrative units are: Xinjiang (1,600,000 square kilometers), Tibet (1,200,000 square kilometers), Inner Mongolia (1,100,000 square kilometers), Qinghai (720,000 square kilometers). Zhongguo ditu chubanshe (ed.), *Zuixin shiyong Zhongguo dituce* (The Latest Practical Atlas of China) (Beijing: Zhongguo ditu chubanshe, 1995), pp. 99, 88, 25 & 95.
2. *Zhonghua renmin gongheguo fen sheng ditu ji* (Maps of Provinces of the People's Republic of China) (Beijing: Zhongguo ditu chubanshe, 1974), p. 115.
3. S.A.M. Adshead, *Province and Politics in Late Imperial China: Viceregal Government in Szechwan, 1898–1911* (London: Curzon Press, 1984), p. 5.
4. Yang Chao (ed.), *Dangdai Zhongguo de Sichuan* (Sichuan in Contemporary China) (Beijing: Zhongguo shehuikexue chubanshe, 1990), Vol. 1, p. 4. Gu Zongzhen and Tang Zejiang, *Xi'nan jingjiqu gaikuang* (A Survey of the Southwest Economic Region) (Chengdu: Sichuan shehuikexueyuan chubanshe, 1989), p. 239.

5. Yang Chao (ed.), *Dangdai Zhongguo de Sichuan*, Vol. 1, p. 4. Gu Zongzhen and Tang Zejiang, *Xi'nan jingjiqu*, p. 240.

6. Hongqi chubanshe (ed.), *Zhongguo shengqing* (Provincial Conditions in China) (Beijing: Gongshang chubanshe, 1986), p. 672.

7. Yang Chao (ed.), *Dangdai Zhongguo de Sichuan*, Vol. 1, pp. 4–5. Zhou Shunwu (ed.), *China Provincial Geography* (Beijing: Foreign Languages Press, 1992), pp. 361–62.

8. Pu Haiqing, "Changkai tianfu damen, jiakuai Sichuan fazhan" (To open wide the gate of the Heavenly Kingdom and speed up Sichuan's development), *Jingji tizhi gaige* (Reforms of Economic System), No. 4 (1994), p. 31.

9. Guojia tongjiju (ed.), *Zhongguo tongji nianjan 1996* (China Statistical Yearbook 1996) (Beijing: Zhongguo tongji chubanshe, 1996), pp. 70, 43, 140, 404, 558, 662, 534, 506, 594 & 600.

10. Marshal He Long, commander of the eighteenth Corps of the First Field Army, led his troops, occupied north Sichuan and later became commander of the Southwest Military Region and the third Party secretary of the Southwest Bureau.

11. Liu Bocheng was appointed vice chairman of the Revolutionary Committee of the Central Government and president and political commissar of the newly established Military Academy of the PLA in Nanjing. Deng Xiaoping was appointed vice premier of the Political Administrative Council (later the State Council) and General Secretary of the Central Party Committee. See Liu Jintian and Shen Xueming (eds.), *Lijie Zhonggong zhongyang weiyuan renming cidian, 1921–1978* (A Biographical Dictionary of Central Committee Members of the Chinese Communist Party, 1921–1978) (Beijing: Zhonggong dangshi chubanshe, 1992), pp. 50 & 97.

12. Bianji bu (ed.), *Dangdai Sichuan dashi jiyao* (Major Events in Contemporary Sichuan) (Chengdu: Sichuan renmin chubanshe, 1991), pp. 47–48. During a restructuring of local military regions in 1955, Sichuan Provincial Military Region became Chengdu Military Region, one of twelve first level local military regions. Li consequently became political commissar of the Chengdu Military Region.

13. The other three were Peng Zhen, Party secretary of Beijing, Ke Qingshi, Party secretary of Shanghai, and Ulanfu, Party secretary of Inner Mongolia. Both Peng Zhen and Ulanfu concurrently had positions in the Center. Ke and Li were local leaders.

14. Li kept his position as the provincial Party secretary until early 1965. He was succeeded by Liao Zhigao who in the early 1950s was the Party secretary of Xikang Province.

15. See county annals of the above counties, published by Sichuan People's Publishing House and Sichuan University Press, Dayi, pp. 156–57, 202–5, Wushan, pp. 359, 389–90, Kaijiang, pp. 379, 441, Emei, pp. 106, 145–46, Pujiang, pp. 493–95, 541–43, Qianwei, pp. 444–45, 486, Jingyan, pp. 418, 444, Renshou, pp. 324–25, 353, Chongqing (County), pp. 178–79, 205–9, Jiajiang, pp. 435–36, 442–4, Shifang, pp. 4–5, 40–41 (section 5), Nanchuan, pp. 379–82, 420–21. Calculations are mine.

16. Because potatoes are the main staple food of the peasants in Shanxi.

17. Only after 1979, Lu Dadong, Jiang Minkuan and Xiao Yang, all from Chongqing, assumed the position of provincial governor.

18. Gong Zide (ed.), *Zhonggong Sichuan difangshihuanti jishi—shehui zhuyi shiqi* (Chronicles of Major Events of the History of the Sichuan Local Communist Party: The Socialist Period) (Chengdu: Sichuan renmin chubanshe, 1991), p. 336.

19. Yang Chao (ed.), *Dangdai Zhongguo de Sichuan*, Vol. 1, p. 99, cited from the Sichuan provincial Party committee's report to the Party Central Committee, dated December 11, 1959.

20. Gong Zide (ed.), *Zhonggong Sichuan difangshi*, p. 151.

21. Ibid., p. 147.

22. He Haoju (ed.), *Dangdai Sichuan jiben jianshe, 1950–1985* (Basic Construction in Contemporary Sichuan, 1950–1985) (Chengdu: Sichuan shehuikexue yuan chubanshe, 1987), p. 15.

23. Ibid., p. 19.

24. Yang Chao (ed.), *Dangdai Zhongguo de Sichuan*, Vol. 1, p. 91.

25. According to Yang, state purchase of grain in the years from 1959 to 1961 accounted for 48.9 percent, 46.2 percent, and 38.8 percent of total grain production respectively, 9.2 percent, 10.7 percent, and 9.2 percent higher than the national average. Peasants' annual consumption of grain per person in these three years was 139 kg, 130 kg, and 129 kg; 26.3 percent, 26.4 percent, and 29.9 percent lower than the national average, see Yang Chao (ed.), *Dangdai Zhongguo de Sichuan*, p. 104. Unconfirmed information believes that Li Jingquan deliberately concealed the real situation when the Central Committee asked him whether Sichuan was able to deliver surplus grain to the central government in the wake of general famines in the central and eastern Chinese provinces.

26. Cong Jin estimated that a total of 40 million died during the famine. See Cong Jin, *Quzhe fazhan de suiyue* (Years of Tortuous Development) (Zhengzhou: Henan renmin chubanshe, 1989), pp. 272–3. Bramall's book contains a detailed study of the famine in Sichuan. Chris Bramall, *In Praise of Maoist Economic Planning: Living Standards and Economic Development in Sichuan since 1931* (Oxford: Clarendon Press, 1993), pp. 291–304.

27. A decrease of 3.03 per thousand, 4.22 per thousand and 1.76 per thousand, respectively. Guojia tongjiju (ed.), *Quanguo ge sheng, zizhiqu, zhixiashi lishi tongji ziliao huibian* (A Compendium of Historical Statistical Data of Provinces, Autonomous Regions and Centrally Administered Cities in China) (Beijing: Zhongguo tongji chubanshe, 1990), p. 690.

28. *Yibin shizhi* (History of Yibin City), cited from Ding Shu, "Cong Dayuejin dao da jihuang" (From the Great Leap Forward to Great Famine), special issue of *Huaxia Wenzhai* (Chinese Magazine), No. 75 (January 6, 1996).

29. Yang Chao (ed.), *Dangdai Zhongguo de Sichuan*, Vol. 1, p. 105.

30. *Dangdai Sichuan dashi jiyao*, pp. 275–6.

31. The above information was gained from the author's interviews with local Party and government officials during his field research in Sichuan in 1993, 1995 and 1996. See also Zhonggong zhongyang wenxian bangongshi (ed.), *Zhonggong di shisijie zhongyang weiyuan minglu* (List of the Members of the Fourteenth Party Central Committee) (Beijing: Zhongyang dangxiao chubanshe, 1993); Bianji weiyuanhui (ed.), *Zhongguo renmin da cidian: xianren dangzhengjun lingdao renwuzuan* (Who's Who in China: Current Party, Government and Army Leaders) (Beijing: Foreign Languages Press, 1989).

32. This has never been confirmed, but some overseas Chinese journals have mentioned this from time to time.

33. In 1976, 510,000 tons of grain were imported from northeast China provinces. Yang Chao (ed.), *Dangdai Zhongguo de Sichuan*, Vol. 1, pp. 184–5, 191.

34. Chengdu, Sichuan Province Service, November 22, 1976. Cited by David L. Shambaugh, *The Making of a Premier: Zhao Ziyang's Provincial Career* (Boulder: Westview Press, 1984), p. 79.

35. Ironically, their discontent with Zhao's political moderation was mixed with their discontent with Zhao's radical economic reform in Sichuan. We shall discuss this later.

36. Li was reportedly said to be willing to return to Sichuan. But strong resistance from other local officials, especially those from the non-Shanxi clique, stopped him. It is also believed that the Center did not want Li to interfere in Zhao's work in Sichuan.

37. *Sichuan ribao* (Sichuan Daily), July 28, 1978. Cited by Shambaugh, *The Making of a Premier*, p. 85.

38. After returning to China, Zhao sent many books published by the Yugoslavs to the Sichuan Academy of Social Sciences and asked that they be translated.

39. Xu Jiatun, *Xu Jiatun Xiang Gang huiyilu* (Memoirs of Xu Jiatun) (Taibei: Lianjing chubanshe, 1995), Vol. 2, p. 531.

40. Zhang Fengwu was not "disclosed" until December 1960. Deng was later "conditionally" rehabilitated after the Enlarged Working Conference (the 7,000 People's Conference), which was held in January 1992. Gong Zide (ed.), *Zhonggong Sichuan difangshi*, pp. 149–50, 152–3.

41. In his speech to the Eighth National Party Congress, Li Jingquan also suggested a reform of the current incentive system in enterprises which would allow enterprises to share profit with the state according to a certain percentage. To what extent Li's idea was put into practice remains to be studied. See Li Jingquan, "Comrade Li Jingquan's Speech at the Eighth National Congress of the Chinese Communist Party," in *Zhonggong gongchandang di baci quanguo daibiao dahui wenxian* (Documents of the Eighth National Congress of the Chinese Communist Party) (Beijing: Renmin chubanshe, 1957), p. 171.

42. Shambaugh, *The Making of a Premier*, pp. 88–9.

43. Gong Zide (ed.), *Zhonggong Sichuan difangshi*, pp. 365–7. Yang Chao (ed.), *Dangdai Zhongguo de Sichuan*, Vol. 1, p. 202.

44. Ibid., Vol. 1, p. 202.

45. Wu Shaoqiu & Chen Fangyuan (ed.), *Ershi shiji Zhongguo dashi ji* (Chronicle of China: 20th Century) (Guangzhou: Beiyu wenyi chubanshe, 1995), p. 1049.

46. Of the provincial senior officials, Tian Jiyun might be the only one who openly supported Zhao's reform. The future vice premier was then the head of the provincial Department of Finance.

47. Gong Zide (ed.), *Zhonggong Sichuan difangshi*, p. 347.

48. Yang Chao (ed.), *Dangdai Zhongguo de Sichuan*, Vol. 1, p. 199.

49. Although his official biography always says that Yang's educational level is "equivalent to secondary school." Yang used to be a laughing stock because he always misread what his secretary wrote for him at various meetings.

50. Tan joined the revolution in 1928 when he was only 14. He was the Party secretary and governor of Shandong before the Cultural Revolution. After he was rehabilitated, he was appointed the Party and government leader of Fujian, Zhejiang and Qinghai. It is said that while in Qinghai, Tan complained repeatedly about the hard living and working conditions in Qinghai and asked the Center to transfer him to a better province for health reasons.

51. *Zhongguo tongji nianjian 1996*, pp. 114, 117 & 280.

52. Report from *People's Daily*, December 25, 1995, p. 3.

53. Guojia tongjiju (ed.), *Sichuan tongji nianjian 1995* (Sichuan Statistical Yearbook 1995) (Beijing: Zhongguo tongji chubanshe, 1995), p. 165.

54. The section below is a summary of ideas expressed by Lin Lin, Li Shugui, Wang Xiaogang, Tang Zejiang and local officials in the cities of Chengdu and Mianyang gained from the author's interviews in 1993 and 1995.

55. Lin Lin and Li Shugui, *Zhongguo sanxian shengchan buju wenti yanjiu* (A Study of the Problems of the Distribution of the Third Front Production in China) (Chengdu: Sichuan keji daxue chubanshe, 1992), p. 149.

56. A total of 100 million yuan had to be spent as an annual "maintenance fee" at least to 1990. Wang Xiaogang, "Woguo sanxian gongye zhengce de tiaozheng" (The Adjustment of the Third Front industries in our country), *Zhongguo gongye jingji yanjiu* (Studies of Chinese Industrial Economics), No. 5 (1989), p. 60.

57. Ibid., p. 60.

58. Guojia tongjiju (ed.), *Sichuan tongji nianjian 1992* (Sichuan Statistical Yearbook 1992) (Beijing: Zhongguo tongji chubanshe, 1992), p. 307.

59. Yang made this remark on several occasions of the provincial Party committee. The information is from interviews with local government officials.

60. *Zhongguo renmin da cidian: xianren dangzhengjun lingdao renwujuan*, p. 927.

61. Jin Xiaoming, *Fengyu sanxia meng* (Winds and Rains of the Dream of the Three Gorges) (Chengdu: Sichuan renmin chubanshe, 1992), pp. 196–7.

62. From interviews with local people.

63. *Zhonggong di shisi jie zhongyang weiyuan minglu*, p. 69.

64. A document of the Provincial Party and Government of Sichuan, "Guanyu zai Chongqing jinxing jingji tizhi zonghe gaige shidian de yijian" (Opinions on the Experiment of Comprehensive Reform of the Economic Structure of Chongqing), in Quanguo renda fazhi weiyuanhui (ed.), *Yanhai, yanjiang, yanbian kaifang falu, fagui ji guifan xing wenjian huibian* (Collections of Laws, Regulations and Legal Documents Regarding the Opening of Coastal Areas, the Border Areas and the Areas Along the Yangtze River) (Beijing: Falu chubanshe, 1992), p. 500.

65. Yang Weimin, "Woguo lao gongye jidi fazhan chizhi de yuanyin ji gaizao yu zhenxing de silu" (Reasons for the Slow Development of the Old Industrial Bases in China and the Considerations of how to Reform and Vitalize Them), *Jingji xuejia* (The Economists), No. 4 (1993), p. 75.

66. Chongqing became a centrally planned city in 1983 and enjoyed economic power equal to a province. Xiao Yang, a native Sichuanese, was the vice director of the foreign trade commission of Beijing before he was appointed mayor of Chongqing. In 1988, he became the Party secretary of the city. See *Zhonggong di shisi jie Zongyang weiyuan minglu*, p. 69.

67. It is believed that Xiao became a good friend of Deng's second daughter, Deng Nan, when he studied at the Central Party School as a member of the "Third Echelon" in early the 1980s. But this cannot be confirmed.

68. Partly because of the prolonged tension between Chongqing and Sichuan, partly because Xiao was considered by local cadres as Beijing's man. This was especially so after Xiao led Chongqing to show support for the Three Gorges Project.

69. During the congress, Xiao urged deputies of Sichuan to write an open letter to Deng Xiaoping to express their gratitude to the paramount leader. People also said that when the deputy Party secretary, Xie Shijie, held a press conference during the meeting, Xiao, instead of sitting with Xie to show the unity of the provincial leadership, and talked to correspondents outside the meeting room.

70. Reliable sources said that the number of alternate members was expanded in order to include Xiao Yang.

71. It is said that the owner of this futures company had donated US$ 1 million to China's Hope Project, a project helping children from poor families to continue their schooling. Premier Li Peng had a meeting with him and introduced him to Xiao Yang.

72. Unconfirmed information believes that Xiao and some other senior leaders of the province were involved in a financial scandal. Xie Shijie strongly requested the Center to investigate the case. Finally, an agreement was made whereby the Center would not investigate the case, but Xiao and those senior officials who were involved should resign. Xiao was later appointed vice director-general of the Three Gorges Project, but he was apparently hit by his political disgrace and has since fallen ill. The dismissal was a surprise to Xiao himself.

73. The proposal was made during a local people's congress session and was widely publicized in local newspapers.

74. Luo Rulan, "Miaozhun Sichuan" (Aiming at Sichuan), *China Times*, No. 71 (May 9–15, 1993), pp. 10–11.

75. Ibid., p. 11.

76. Luo Rulan, "Rang chu neixiao shichang" (To Trade in the Domestic Market), *China Times*, No. 71 (May 9–15, 1993), p. 14.

77. Lin Lin (ed.), *Sichuan—Zhongguo Neilu dasheng de duiwai kaifang* (Sichuan: The Opening of a Big Chinese Inland Province) (Chengdu: Sichuan keji daxue chubanshe, 1992), p. 3.

78. Ma Lieguang (ed.), *Zhongguo ge shengqu jingji fazhan bijiao* (A Comparison of Economic Development of Various Provinces and Regions) (Chengdu: Chengdu keji daxue chubanshe, 1993), p. 127.

79. Guoweyuan yanjiushi, *Zhongguo lao gongye jidi gaizao yu zhenxing* (The Reform and Development of China's Old Industrial Bases) (Beijing: Kexue chubanshe, 1992), pp. 10, 52.

80. Lin Lin and Li Shugui (eds.), *Zhongguo sanxian shengchan buju wenti yanjiu*, p. 18.

81. Guojia tongjiju (ed.), *Zhongguo tongji nianjian 1994* (Statistical Yearbook of China 1994) (Beijing: Zhongguo tongji chubanshe, 1994), pp. 530–1. Calculations are mine.

82. He Haoju, *Dangdai Sichuan jiben jianshe, 1950–1985*, pp. 415–7. Absolute figures in these periods were: 12.38 billion yuan in the third Five-Year Plan, 12.45 billion yuan in the fourth five-year plan, 9.45 billion yuan in the fifth five-year plan, 6.70 billion yuan in the sixth five-year plan.

83. Sichuansheng zhengfu, *A Report on Sichuan's Utilization of Foreign Capital for Greater Economic Progress*, 1995 (internal document), p. 257.

84. There are two high-tech development zones in Sichuan recognized by the central government, one in Chengdu and one in Chongqing. Government officials said, however, that there were many more locally established such zones in almost all major cities in Sichuan since 1992. Most of them have not been recognized by the state. Preferential policies regarding foreign investment in these zones were mainly locally initiated.

85. *A Report on Sichuan's Utilization of Foreign Capital for Greater Economic Progress*, p. 261.

86. Chen Yaobang (ed.), *Zhongguo zhongxibu diqu kaifa nianjian 1995* (Yearbook of the Development of China's Central and Western Regions 1995) (Beijing: Gaige chubanshe, 1995), p. 466. Another source said that Chongqing had the right to approve foreign investment up to US$30 million, Chengdu, US$10 million and other subprovincial cities US$5 million. See Luo Rulan, "Rang chu neixiao shichang," p. 10.

87. *A Report on Sichuan's Utilization of Foreign Capital for Greater Economic Progress*, p. 228.

88. Ibid., p. 169.

89. Ibid., p. 230.

90. Ibid., p. 251.

91. Ibid., pp. 230–1.

92. Ibid., pp. 352–5.

93. Ibid., p. 235.

94. Ibid., p. 174.

95. Ibid., p. 238.

96. *Zhongguo tongji nianjian 1996*, pp. 600, 601.

97. Ibid., pp. 43, 140, 230, 356, 404, 594, and 600.

98. Editorial Office (ed.), *Zhongguo jingji nianjian 1988* (Economic Yearbook of China 1988) (Beijing: Zhongguo jingji chubanshe, 1988), p. VI-257.

99. Lin Lin (ed.), *Sichuan*, p. 233.

100. Yang Rudai, "Jin yi bu jiefang sixiang, jiakuai gaige kaifang, fanrong Sichuan

jingji" (Further Emancipate People's Minds, Speed Up Reform and Openness and Enliven Sichuan's Economy), *Jingji xuejia* (The Economists), No. 4 (1992), pp. 120–1.

101. Lin Lin (ed.), *Sichuan*, p. 234.

102. Li Guoqiang, "Jiang Zemin dui Sichuan you xin zhishi, Sichuan shixing di erci da gaige" (Jiang Zemin has a new instruction for Sichuan and Sichuan starts the second major reform), *Guangjiaojing* (June 1991), p. 33.

103. Lin Lin (ed.), *Sichuan*, p. 234.

104. The following information is based on the author's interviews with local government officials during his visits to Sichuan in 1993–4 and 1995.

105. The official newspaper did not openly report the incident, but it was widely reported by overseas Chinese and foreign newspapers.

106. The above information was gained during the author's interviews with local officials.

107. The following information is from interviews with local government officials. The author himself also worked in Sichuan during that period. Governor Jiang made this proposal on many occasions in the 1980s.

108. He Bosheng (ed.), *Zhongguo baiwan furong (Chinese Millionaires)* (Xi'an: Shaanxi renmin chubanshe, 1993), pp. 112–3. Another source believes the total deal was worth SF240 million. Lu Jun (ed.), *Zhongguo dangdai yiwan furong* (Contemporary China's Rich Men with One Hundred Million) (Nanjing: Yilin chubanshe, 1993), p. 41.

109. *A Report on Sichuan's Utilization of Foreign Capital for Greater Economic Progress*, pp. 195–6.

110. Luo Rulan,"Rang chu neixiao shichang," p. 11.

111. Pu Haiqing, "Changkai tianfu damen, jiakuai Sichuan fazhan," p. 32.

112. Qi Xianwang and He Xiangui, "Zouchu neilu shengqu duiwai kaifang de xin luzi" (To Find a New Path for Inland Provinces' Opening), *Jingji tizhi gaige* (Reforms of the Economic System), No. 2 (1995), p. 86.

113. The twelve inland provinces include Guizhou, Sichuan, Henan, Anhui, Hunan, Jiangxi, Shanxi, Hubei, Ningxia, Qinghai, Gansu, and Shaanxi. Xin Wen (ed.), *Neibu diqu gaige kaifang yanjiu* (A Study of Reform and Opening of Inland Regions) (Chengdu: Sichuan daxue chubanshe, 1995), p. 108.

114. *China Statistical Yearbook 1996*, pp. 331, 600.

115. Qi Xianwang and He Xiangui, "Zouchu neilu shengqu duiwai kaifang de xin luzi," p. 86.

116. Chen Yaobang, *Zhongguo zhongxibu diqu kaifa nianjian 1995*, pp. 115–6.

117. Li Guoqiang, "Jiang Zemin dui Sichuan you xin zhishi, Sichuan shixing di erci da gaige," *Guanjiaojing* (June 1991), p. 29.

Conclusion

Provincial Leadership and Reform

Lessons and Implications for Chinese Politics

Zhimin Lin

The eight case studies contained in this book are among some of the first detailed looks into the relationship of reform and provincial leadership in China. As a result, they have raised as many questions as they have provided answers. Still, what emerged from these studies is a new level of appreciation of the dynamics behind the momentous reform movement since the late 1970s. In particular, this study helps us understand how and why the provincial leaders shaped the course of local reform and development. The goal of this chapter is to compare the findings of the preceding chapters in the context of the changing politics in China.

One of the basic questions this study focuses on is: did the provincial leaders matter in China's reform? The answer of the preceding chapters is that they not only mattered but mattered a great deal. China's reform opened the door for growing provincial autonomy in deciding the direction and pace of local changes. The reform also provided the provincial leaders with more resources and alternatives than before, hence putting them in a much better position to carry out their own agendas. Moreover, China's reform is highly complicated, uneven in its process across different regions and without an integrated blueprint. To take full advantage of the changed environment, individual provinces need to capture "policy windows" and supplant the latter with innovative tools of implementation. All these made the provincial leaders the key to the reform as what they did could either accelerate or hinder local changes, mitigate or exacerbate the adverse effects of the reform, and help use or misuse local resources.

If the provincial leaders were responsible for the results of reform in their respective localities, the next question this book focuses on is: why did such results differ sharply in different provinces? The case studies in this book argue that it was the differences in provincial leadership that played a critical role in the divergent reform processes and results in China's provinces. In particular, they show that the political and policy orientations of key provincial leaders and the quality of reform strategy and implementation under their stewardship have major impacts on the course of local reform and development.

Political and Policy Orientations and Impact

The preceding chapters argue that the political and policy orientations of the key provincial leaders, namely party secretaries and governors, were of critical importance in China's reform. Reform represents a radical departure from established norms, values and policy guidelines. To guide local reform under such circumstances, the top provincial leaders often had to rely on their own perceptions, attitudes and preferences or even instincts. Their personal background, education, career paths and central patronage were thus prominent factors influencing their political orientations, namely how they defined the goals and boundaries of the reform efforts at the provincial level. One of the key indicators of the political orientations of the provincial leaders was the level of their commitment to reform. While few provincial leaders openly opposed reform, not all of them shared the same enthusiasm for radical changes. The differences in the level of commitment to reform had major impacts on the reform processes of the eight provincial studies in this book.

Among the eight provinces, for example, only the leaders in Guangdong showed strong and unwavering support for radical reform throughout the reform period. The province was not known for its national leadership in socio-economic experiments in the pre-reform era. Since 1978, however, Guangdong became the leader in China's open policy and other reform policies from the beginning to this day. It is true that the preferential policies, such as the fiscal contract between Guangdong and the Center and its proximity to Hong Kong played a major role in promoting the province's remarkable economic growth. In the final analysis, however, it was the domination of consecutive batches of reform-minded leaders that gave Guangdong the courage and leadership to try controversial reform programs and to be successful. From the early reformers such as Ren Zhongyi, Lin Ruo and Ye Xuanping to more recent leaders such as Xie Fei and Zhu Senlin, it was their unquestionable commitment to reform, including the determination to embrace bold reform policies before they were accepted by the majority and defend them in the face of heavy criticism, that set the stage for Guangdong's success. Through their personal endorsement and involvement, these leaders not only made Guangdong a model in market-oriented reform but also introduced a brand new local culture that encouraged and rewarded subprovincial officials who supported the reform programs as aggressively as they did.

By contrast, Fujian's record in the reform period was less impressive even though it received a similar policy package from the Center as Guangdong did. The gap can ultimately be attributed to the differences in provincial leadership in the two provinces. With the exception of Xiang Nan (1982–1986) who supported bold reform and was an effective leader, but whose success was constrained by his lack of personal and organizational support, most of Fujian's top leaders were for reform but inclined to stay on the more conservative way, especially when the reform involved controversial issues. As a norm, they would rather wait for other provinces such as Guangdong to try out these programs first or simply stick with the narrow interpretations of the instructions on these programs as a means of self-protection. As a result, Fujian often either missed opportunities or failed to maximize the potential of the reform programs already introduced.

The importance of political and policy orientations among top provincial leaders can also be seen in the cases of Shanghai and Shandong. Both provinces experienced a rather slow start in China's reform. Yet, both turned around to become very successful late-comers after the mid- and late 1980s. One of the key contributing factors to the turnaround was the arrival of more reform-oriented leadership teams in both cases. In Shanghai, the city had been long marred by economic stagnation. It took the arrival of such reform-minded leaders as Rui Xingwen, Jiang Zemin and Zhu Rongji after 1985 to finally break the stagnation and move the city in a direction of renewed growth. Previous leaders had supported the reform in general. But they were hesitant to launch bold reform programs that could easily outlive their tenures. Nor did they have the full backing of the central government to effectively mobilize the huge amount of resources needed for the city's renewal. The new leadership team changed both. They had the blessing of the central government which began to realize the mistake of overlooking Shanghai in its national campaign of reform. But more importantly, the new leadership team was determined to use central assistance as a stimulus to introduce a broader program which was designed not only for overhauling Shanghai's economy but also for paving the way for the city to reemerge as a leader in China's reform and economic development. Compared with their predecessors, the new leadership team and their successors were not only younger and better educated, but they were also more motivated to embrace radical changes as their performance in Shanghai could have a major impact on their future careers. As a result, Shanghai after the mid-1980s experienced an unexpected double-boom—in economic growth as well as urban renovation—thanks largely to the strong show of leadership by the top city officials.

Shandong's turnaround was equally impressive. Until the late 1980s, Shandong was described as a laggard in reform relative to other coastal provinces. Many provincial leaders, especially Bai Rubing (1974–1982) and Su Yiran (1982–1985), long preferred a cautious approach to reform. In addition to their personal reasons, their orientation reflected the influence of a local culture that encouraged the political elite to take an opportunist stance on major reform programs for fear of adversely affecting their own careers. Indeed, the influence of such a local culture was so strong that until after Qingdao and Yantai were designated as "coastal open cities" in 1984 and the arrival of more reform-minded leaders such as Liang Buting (1982–1985) and Li Chang'an (1985–1988), there was still little radical change in Shandong. The province remained a passive follower of Beijing's general policy but without much enthusiasm and innovation. It took the ascendance of Jiang Chunyun in 1988 to finally break the resistance to bold reforms. Jiang's personal commitment was obvious. But more importantly, he managed to receive a series of highly favorable treatments from the Center and he used the changed environment to convince the other provincial and local elites of the benefits of moving along with him. Within a short period of time, Jiang was able to introduce an effective strategy of regional development and a series of innovative policies to boost the local economy through more international links. The success of these policies in turn helped consolidate a new norm within the political elite that favored aggressive reform rather than the status quo.

The political orientations of the provincial leaders were even more important in deciding the course of reform among the inland provinces. China's reform had a clear bias against these provinces as most preferential policies and investment went to the coastal region. To many provincial leaders in the inland region, the reform was more than an opportunity for rapid growth; it was a very tough adjustment that involved enormous costs and difficulties. It was thus essential for them not only to establish a strong commitment to reform but also to demonstrate the knowledge and skills in how to do it amid adversity. Unfortunately, neither of the two inland provinces studied in this book, Shaanxi and Sichuan, passed the test, although Sichuan's record was somewhat mixed.

Shaanxi has a rich revolutionary past. Most of its top leaders came from North Shaanxi where the revolutionary bases were located during the anti-Japanese and Civil War periods. Shaanxi also benefited from the old system of central planning and had become highly dependent on the Center for investment and other policy support. More importantly, Shaanxi had been strongly influenced by leftism whose impact lasted years after the Cultural Revolution ended. The task facing the provincial leaders during the reform period was formidable. To make things worse, with the exception of the latest leadership team, most of the leaders who ruled Shaanxi from 1978 to 1994 suffered from two deficiencies. First, there was a general lack of strong commitment to bold reform. During Ma Wenrui's tenure (1978–1984), he was credited with organizing a campaign to correct the leftist errors. However, neither his background nor his strong desire to retain his job prepared him to take aggressive action in reform. Similarly, when Bai Jinian, the head of the so-called "North Shaanxi Gang," served as the first party secretary from 1984 to 1987, he also left little mark on the reform process. Secondly, even for those provincial leaders who were generally pro-reform, their incompetence in leading the transition to a market-oriented economy often undercut the very reform efforts they introduced. Zhang Boxing, for example, led Shaanxi from 1987 to 1994, but his expertise was mainly in managing state-owned heavy industries. Even though he had the opportunity to make a difference in Shaanxi's reform process as he occupied the post longer than any other top leader after 1978, he had little to offer that could generate strong momentum or public support for reform. As a result of the consecutive show of poor leadership, Shaanxi fell to the bottom of national ranking in economic growth.

Sichuan's case was more complicated. As the most populous province located in a landlocked region, Sichuan was obviously not in the best position to lead the nation in reform and development. However, this was also the province that produced such reformers as Zhao Ziyang in the late 1970s and Xiao Yang in the early 1990s. Why then did Sichuan have so many difficulties in catching up with the coastal provinces? Sichuan's objective conditions clearly took a toll on its reform process. For example, even though the province was rich in resources, it had little experience in dealing with the international market directly. Like many other inland provinces, Sichuan was hit twice by the recent reform when it tried to increase the financial input in local economy: the investment from the central government fell sharply while the inflow of overseas investment was so slow that it could only make up a fraction of the lost state appropriations. Ultimately, however, it was the weakness in the provincial leadership that made Sichuan's revival more difficult than what it had already been. Zhao introduced bold reform in the rural areas but his tenure was cut short when he was transferred to the Center in 1980. Generally regarded as an earthy leader, Yang Rudai (1981–1993) was one of the longest serving provincial party secretaries in the reform era. However, his narrow background, caution in approaching new things, or even the lack of political ambition made him unable to seek breakthroughs in Sichuan's reform process. On the other hand, when Xiao Yang (1993–1995) emerged as governor and as a proponent for radical reform and an alternative path to development, his image of being a spokesman for the Center and not for the natives and his association with several scandals diminished his ability to be an effective pioneer in reform. As a result, despite the fact that there were periods and areas where bold reform programs were introduced and some of them proved to be rather successful, Sichuan failed to find a path toward sustained reform and growth in the post-Mao era.

The two other case studies in this book, Hainan and Zhejiang, provide a different but interesting angle to examine the relationship between the basic orientations of the provincial leaders and the results of reform. Hainan's leaders were among the most aggressive in reform efforts. The island was poor, underdeveloped and sometimes treated by the Center and others as an outcast. The reform era provided the only hope for the island to become economically prosperous and politically independent from its traditional master in Guangzhou. Even before Hainan became a province in April 1988, prominent leaders such as Lei Yu had already shown striking boldness in reform plans and actions. His successors such as Liang Xiang (1988–1989) and Xu Shijie (1987–1990) were equally determined to carry out bold, though sometimes controversial, reform programs. However, the strong commitment to reform alone did not always bring about the desired results. The 1985 "Hainan Car Scandal" cost the island some critical privileges in foreign trade which were initially part of the incentives for the island to move more quickly toward an open economy. In 1989, the political fallout of the Tiananmen crackdown further dampened Hainan's ambition in economic development as many of its bold reformers were replaced by more cautious leaders such as Liu Jianfeng (1989–1993) and Deng Hengxun (1990–1993).

Zhejiang's approach was almost the opposite. Throughout the reform period, Zhejiang leaders maintained a low-key approach to reform. They rarely took bold initiatives. When they tried to define the priorities of local reform, they would often simply copy what the central directives suggested, even if the latter had little bearing on Zhejiang's actual needs. Furthermore, Zhejiang leaders showed little consistency in reform efforts. For example, they were slow in agricultural reform, indecisive on urban reform and shifted back and forth frequently between advocating more openness and embracing protectionism. However, the absence of pro-reform orientations among Zhejiang's top officials did not seem to have too much negative impact on local economic growth and the march toward a market-oriented economy. In fact, Zhejiang's economic record was among the best in the nation for the most part of the reform period. Why was this the case?

Zhejiang's experience does not refute the general argument that the quality of provincial leadership played a key role in local reform and development. What it suggests is that the show of strong provincial leadership could take different forms. In Zhejiang's case, the loosening of government intervention played well with the unique economic structure of the province. Zhejiang had few state-owned enterprises (SOEs) but possessed some of the most dynamic and seasoned private and semi-private sectors long waiting for an opportunity to assert themselves in the local and provincial economy. Moreover, there was a high degree of dependence of Zhejiang's economy on its powerful neighbor—Shanghai. For Zhejiang to embrace bold but controversial reform programs, especially if that entailed some form of conflict with the Center, might not serve the best interests of the province. On the other hand, Zhejiang did not try to reimpose strict government control over the economy. It was in fact practicing quiet but de facto decentralization. The decentralization in turn had the real effect of encouraging lower levels of government and other economic entities to embrace radical reforms beyond what the provincial government tried.

Several conclusions can be drawn from the above comparisons. The political and policy orientations of the provincial leaders are a complex issue. China's reform downplayed the traditional ideological division among the political elite. On the other hand, the range of choices facing the provincial leaders was such that their responses inevitably revealed their preferences. While our analytical framework constitutes a first step in studying leadership types in reform China, it is nevertheless useful to link the general patterns of behavior to the different results of reform in the provinces.

The leaders in Guangdong, Shandong (since the late 1980s) and Shanghai (since the mid-1980s) were more aggressive in reform and more effective in achieving the desired goals. Moreover, what they did often inspired reactions and changes far beyond the state apparatus. Consequently, the overall results of reform in the three provinces tended to be more successful than the rest of the nation. The leaders in Shaanxi in general and several particular leaders in other provinces were much less reform-minded. They either opted for no action, or slow action when under pressure to reform or they tried to limit the content and thrust of the reform programs to the extent that the latter became virtually ineffective. As a result, Shaanxi fell further behind other provinces. The leaders of the rest of the provinces were basically followers of reform. Their common behavior was to defer decisions or actions until the dust of the reform programs settled. Then they would act according to the generally accepted norms and rules. Under this type of leadership, the process of reform would proceed, but rather slowly. Moreover, this type of leadership tended to miss critical opportunities. There was a fourth group of provincial leaders such as Xiang Nan and Xiao Yang. They were bold reformers and sometimes could leave a major impact on local reform. However, they still failed eventually. The reasons for their failures varied. Some had to do with their personalities. But more often than not, their failures had roots in the deficiency in their leadership, like the failure to build up sufficient organizational support or to break the bureaucratic resistance to change. Some of them were actually the victims of the power struggle at the Center. From the point of view of reform at the provincial level, the inability of these leaders to lead the reform process should still be considered a failure.

Secondly, the political and policy orientations of the top provincial leaders reflected the influence of a number of factors. Under normal circumstances, a single issue such as the native background of leaders did not constitute a decisive factor. For example, most of Shaanxi's leaders were natives, yet their conservatism was rather obvious. The recent leaders in Shanghai and Guangdong were also natives or veteran officials who spent most of their careers in the two provinces. However, they campaigned more aggressively on behalf of the localities they served since they had no other places to draw support and build up their own political capital. On the other hand, if the "mixture" was right, it was easier for reform-mined leaders to excel. This mixture, based on the preceding chapters, tends to include at least the following conditions: a local culture favoring radical changes over status quo, a general identification with the overall reform goal by the key personnel involved, a high personal stake in the success or failure of local reform, good timing, strong backing from the Center, coherence and unity among the top provincial leaders and some basic qualities on the part of the key leaders such as communication skills and the ability to build institutional support.

Finally, the political and policy orientations do not have to be a constant or limited to a particular person. In fact, the preceding chapters show that with proper leadership and organizational skills, a particular type of orientation can pass onto other political elite within a particular province. Moreover, given the fact that the changes under China's reform were momentous and that the turnover rate of top provincial leaders was higher than before, the basic orientation of the provincial leaders could change rather quickly. In both Shanghai and Guangdong, there is evidence that the most recent leaders were not as aggressive in initiating bold and controversial reform programs as their predecessors had been. The reason is simple. The risk of breaking new ground now is sometimes higher than keeping the current economic programs intact. By contrast, the latest leadership team in places such as Shaanxi began to show a more pro-reform stance.

Provincial Reform Strategies, Successes and Failures

The importance of provincial leadership can also be seen in terms of the quality of reform strategies different provinces adopted and implemented. With a few exceptions, China's reform was heavily influenced by government policies and programs. The success of local reform was tied intimately to the effectiveness of the reform strategy of the provincial government. The strength of the provincial leadership was hence severely tested. In particular, as the preceding chapters show, the provincial leadership had to meet a number of challenges in searching for and implementing an effective reform strategy. Moreover, while the details of these challenges might differ from province to province given their huge differences in natural endowment, historical legacies and unique positions in China's economy and reform, the basic thrust of these challenges was surprisingly identical.

Managing Central-Provincial Relationship

The first challenge was to develop a strategy to manage the relationship with the Center that fit the changed environment. The preceding case studies show that this was not a simple task. Despite several rounds of decentralization and the gradual process of marketization, the power to make decisions on major policy issues and to appoint or remove top provincial leaders was still in the hands of the central government. A poorly managed relationship with the Center could be highly detrimental not only to the career prospects of individual leaders but also to the interests of the very provinces they presided over. On the other hand, China's reform had created a more dynamic pattern of interactions between the Center and the provinces. Unlike in the past when the provinces could expect guaranteed central appropriations as long as they complied with the directives from the Center, the recent reform had opened an era in which preferential policies were given only to select provinces and the implementation of such policies involved a high degree of flexibility. Moreover, the influence of the provinces on national policies was also on the rise. During the recent reform, some central leaders "played to the provinces" and used it as a means to circumvent the resistance to reform within the central government. There was also an increasing emphasis on recruiting prominent provincial leaders to central posts. In short, the management of the relationship with the Center has become even more critical and demanding. It requires not only efforts to seek preferential policies but also an ability to maximize the return of these policies and skills to develop certain leverage over the central government.

The responses from the eight provinces studied in this book varied sharply, reflecting the differences in the quality of their reform strategies. Guangdong, Shandong (since the late 1980s) and Shanghai (since the mid-1980s) were among those that managed their relationship with the Center reasonably well. Fujian, Zhejiang, Hainan and Sichuan had ups and downs in dealing with the Center. Shaanxi was unable to fashion a new approach to its relationship with the Center and hence was hit hardest by the fundamental shift in the patterns of central-provincial relationship. The differences in their handling of the relationship with the Center showed up in their record books accordingly.

The approaches adopted by Guangdong, Shandong and Shanghai had several common features. For example, all three targeted special concessions from the Center as a key to help jump start the reform process. Guangdong did so by riding the wave of open policy promoted by Deng Xiaoping himself. Shanghai received such concessions after convincing the Center of the negative consequences if the city were to continue to be excluded from the more favorable revenue-sharing regimes. Shandong took advantage of a new round of open policy but managed to add a few things that proved to be extremely beneficial, like being designated the key province to expand trade with South Korea. Secondly, none of the three provinces was content at just receiving the preferential policies. Instead, they used these policies as a starting point to build a more complete and local-oriented reform program. For example, not only did Guangdong use the fiscal contract it obtained from the Center in 1979 to launch a series of fiscal deals with subprovincial governments in an attempt to encourage revenue collection and economic reform. But it also decentralized investment authority to local units to motivate their efforts in mobilizing resources for development. Shanghai used the authorization to borrow money in international markets to open up more channels in resource mobilization and help generate a more favorable environment for local growth after 1985. Shandong's practice was less grandiose but equally effective. It rode a new wave of open policy in the late 1980s with the establishment of the diplomatic relationship between China and South Korea in 1988 to obtain several preferential policies. It then used the policies to complete the long-waited drive toward opening up the whole Shandong Peninsula region and to serve as a stimulus for similar changes in the rest of the province.

Not all the provinces were able to handle the relationship with the Center with this degree of confidence and sophistication. Fujian, for example, received the same preferential policies that Guangdong did in 1979 but it failed to supplant them with more local-specific and viable measures. Nor was it able to identify the critical shift in central policy, as reflected, for instance, in its cautious response to Deng Xiaoping's 1992 southern tour, which undermined its relationship with the Center.

Zhejiang and Sichuan shared one thing in common when they managed their relationships with the Center. They were important provinces in their own right but not as prominent as such places as Guangdong and Shanghai in nationwide reform. As a result, they often received "normal" treatment from the Center in that they were neither given exclusive preferential policies nor excluded from more general preferential policies, especially when the latter were applied to multiple provinces. The top leaders of the two provinces were thus faced with a decision as to how much political capital they wanted to invest in implementing the watered-down versions of preferential policies. Zhejiang's approach was characterized by the avoidance of tough decisions. For example, the province had difficulties in identifying a well-articulated reform strategy to attract more attention from the Center. Nor was it able to take real advantage of its strong revenue base to elicit more concessions from the Center. If Zhejiang's weakness in handling the relationship with the Center was partially offset by a vibrant local economy that benefited from an environment of generally weak government regulations, Sichuan's inability to fashion an effective strategy in dealing with the Center proved to be far more detrimental. Under Yang Rudai, a leader often described as "a man of action without much political ambition," Sichuan maintained a generally smooth relationship with the Center. Yet, the lack of aggressiveness and the generally coastal-biased reform strategy of the Center had long prevented Sichuan from receiving major help from Beijing. The lack of central support in turn made it more difficult for the province to seek breakthroughs in local reform and development. Xiao Yang succeeded Yang in 1993. During his brief tenure as the party secretary, Xiao showed greater enthusiasm in building up a good relationship with particular central leaders. Given Sichuan's predicament, Xiao's approach was not unreasonable especially if the improved relationship with the central leadership could yield Sichuan much needed assistance from the Center. However, Xiao's overplay of this approach backfired as he lost local support while Sichuan as a political unit lost its crucial seat in the all powerful Politburo.

Shaanxi failed to adjust its relationship with the Center. As a budget-deficit province, Shaanxi did not have the same leverage over the Center as Guangdong or Shanghai did. However, the problem was exacerbated by the province's unwillingness to accept the fact that the Center was no longer willing to make up whatever budgetary shortfall the province encountered in the wake of reform. Unlike other provinces, Shaanxi did little to develop effective countermeasures to minimize the negative effects of the new revenue-sharing regimes introduced under the current reform or to search for alternative sources of revenue that could replace the sharp decline of direct government investment. The conservative approach in handling the fiscal relationship with the Center did not win praise from Beijing. Instead, it kept Shaanxi out of the ranks of those who managed to adjust their relationship with the Center on a more timely and practical basis.

Putting in Place Effective Reform Programs

In the reform era, China's provinces were encouraged to develop specific reform programs with a distinctive local flavor. Some of these programs reflected the overall goals and priorities of local development. Shanghai's strategy of making the city the national center of international commerce, finance and high-tech industries and Shandong's so-called "two-three-six" strategy (two economic regions, three industrial concentration belts and six central cities) are good examples in this regard. Other reform programs were designed to deal with more specific issues in particular areas or sectors. As the case studies of this book show, to design these programs was one thing, to make them operational, viable and mutually supportive of one another in pursuit of the basic goals of the reform and development in a particular province was another.

The performance of the eight provinces studied in this book can be roughly divided into two categories. Shandong, Fujian, Shanghai and Guangdong were able to design and carry out reform programs generally appropriate for the local conditions and needs. For example, Shandong's reform programs under Jiang Chunyun were highly successful because they used multiple models to boost the growth in agriculture, linked the expansion of foreign economic relations with the need to restructure and upgrade local industries, and made infrastructural development a centerpiece in an effort to attract foreign investment and integrate the local economy with the market system. Fujian's management of the timing of its reform programs provided another positive example. Even though Fujian was less aggressive and innovative in pursuing bold reform programs, it nevertheless did well in timing the initiation of particular reform programs in such a way that they tied nicely to what happened at the Center. As a result, these programs had a better chance of getting seriously implemented. Moreover, since the mid-1980s, Fujian further tied the introduction of major changes with the outburst of local demands and the new opportunities appearing in the external economic environment, particularly the changing relationship with Taiwan. While Fujian generally took a backseat to Guangdong and other leaders in reform, effective management of reform programs helped the province to use its geographic location and the policy advantage it received from the Center to attract a large amount of foreign investment. The investment in turn helped Fujian sustain a relatively high growth rate throughout the reform period.

The other four provinces, Hainan, Zhejiang, Sichuan and Shaanxi experienced various problems in setting up effective reform programs. Accordingly, the overall reform efforts in these places were negatively affected. Hainan, for example, placed high priorities on developing the island's infrastructure and a favorable tax regime as a means to attract foreign investment. It was also the leader in introducing innovative practices such as wholesale land leasing and the opening of foreign bank branches on China's soil. However, Hainan's efforts in these areas were undercut by deficiencies in other areas of reform. Hesitancy to seek status as a Special Customs Zone in 1988, for example, cost the province the opportunity to consolidate its position as a leader in China's open policy. The unregulated inflow of funds into the local real estate market, on the other hand, made the province highly vulnerable to fluctuations caused by price speculation and fraud.

Zhejiang also had to pay for its weakness in developing effective reform programs. The province's economy, as discussed above, benefited from the robust private and semi-private sectors and the geographic proximity to and close economic links with Shanghai. However, the inability to introduce forward-looking programs and the lack of follow-up measures to implement the existing programs posed a threat to Zhejiang's long-term development goals. For example, despite its high economic growth rate up to this point, Zhejiang has lagged behind Guangdong in developing high-tech industries and in active engagement with the international economy. All these problems will hinder Zhejiang's future growth if they are not corrected on a timely basis.

Perhaps the best example of how the failure to coordinate various reform programs could negatively affect the reform process happened in Sichuan. In the early 1990s, a new policy known as "boat-borrowing" was introduced. The policy was designed to set up "window enterprises" in the coastal provinces to help learn the key to the success of the open policy in these areas and attract more external investment via established windows. However, the new policy led to a net outflow of funds which not only undercut the very purpose the policy was designed to serve but also led to serious social problems such as the inability to pay cash to farmers for the grain the state had purchased.

Securing Institutional and Popular Support

The third pillar of an effective reform strategy involves efforts to seek and maintain a high level of institutional and popular support for the reform programs. China's reform upset the traditional organizational routine and balance. It took some carefully crafted policies and serious efforts from the provincial leaders to re-command the loyalty and support from their subordinates. The reform also undermined the social foundation of the regime. With growing social fragmentation, income disparities and regional imbalances, the need to reach out and seek as broad popular support as possible became crucial not only to social stability but to the success of the planned reform programs. The reform also raised expectations among the populace, making it increasingly difficult to insulate the decision-making and implementation process from public scrutiny. How to mobilize both internal and societal support for reform was thus an urgent task facing all the provinces. Several common practices were used in response to this challenge, with varying results in different provinces.

Guangdong, for example, used fiscal and investment decentralization to secure institutional support from subprovincial government units. To be sure, many of the provinces used similar measures to force the sub-provincial governments to share the burden of revenue collection. However, Guangdong's efforts went beyond the traditional patterns. Its fiscal decentralization programs included, on a consistent basis, clauses that favored local economic development, special treatment for low income regions and a gradual shift of authority in fiscal management to the cities and prefectures. Similarly, the decentralization of investment greatly empowered these local governments. In short, Guangdong tried to ensure that the benefits of fiscal and investment decentralization for the localities were real and reliable. In return, the provincial leadership could count on these localities not only to support the general thrust of their reform efforts but also to take their own reform initiatives. Fujian, Shandong and Shanghai pursued a similar path. Zhejiang's decentralization efforts were more subtle but had similar effects.

Promoting pro-reform cadres to key party and government posts was another commonly used measure to build institutional support for reform. Although China's reform called for promoting younger and more reform-minded cadres in general, it often took the personal involvement of key provincial leaders to make this happen on a consistent basis and a large scale. On the other hand, once these cadres were recruited, they could provide the crucial support for the reform programs. From Fujian's Xiang Nan and Shandong's Jiang Chunyun to the top officials in Guangdong and Shanghai, the efforts to promote pro-reform cadres were a major contributing factor to their strong performance during the reform period. By contrast, in provinces such as Shaanxi, the domination of more conservative-minded leaders made it difficult to recruit and promote reform-minded leaders. This lapse in building institutional support explains why in Shaanxi it was not just the provincial leaders but the local officials as well who were more resistant than those in most other provinces to reform .

China's reform also put the seeking of popular support on the top of the provincial leaders' agenda. Shanghai and Fujian's experiences were good examples. Shanghai's top leaders had introduced a more explicit populist theme in their plan to revitalize the local economy after the mid-1980s. They did so to help win support for the ambitious transformation. They also used such themes and related programs to preempt possible outbursts of public anger at the high costs associated with the revitalization plan, such as urban reconstruction. As a result, even though the economic recovery of Shanghai created many social problems, the city officials were able to maintain a relatively high level of public approval for their plan. The public support, in turn, helped accelerate the pace of change in Shanghai. In Fujian, popular programs like renovating public works and other infrastructures vital to the lives of common citizens were also introduced. The purpose was to appeal to the broad interests of the local elite and the population they administered so that more controversial, or even painful, reform programs could be launched. Neither Shanghai's nor Fujian's use of popular programs was a panacea to all the problems generated during the reform process. They did, however, help mitigate some of the most damaging consequences and hence contributed to the effectiveness of provincial leadership in leading local reform.

Mobilizing and Allocating Resources in Determined Ways

Finally, any effective reform strategy must include certain measures to help mobilize and distribute resources in determined ways. Almost without exception, China's provinces have embraced a development strategy that used intensive inputs, especially investment, as a key to achieve a high rate of economic growth. This emphasis on growth was understandable since only through rapid economic expansion could the local governments meet the soaring public demand for higher living standards and complete the difficult transition from a transitional economy to a market economy. There was also a political consideration behind this emphasis since the performance of the provincial and local leaders was often measured by the speed of economic growth in their respective areas. However, the high-input, high-growth-rate strategy put a heavy burden on the provincial leaders to mobilize and distribute resources in determined ways.

Several provinces studied in this book, especially Shandong, Shanghai, Fujian, Guangdong and to a less degree, Hainan, were more successful in this endeavor. Their methods included efforts to seek greater control over locally generated revenue, stretch central policies to the extent that they could maximize returns without violating these policies, use creative methods and institutions to multiply the benefits associated with preferential policies, encourage the use of non-conventional and non-governmental sources of investment on projects promoted by the provincial government, diversify the responsibilities in resource mobilization so that the lower-level government units could contribute to the efforts, restructure the patterns of local spending in accordance with the changed need and priorities caused by reform and local development, and, above all, seek the inflow of a large amount of overseas funds as a major driving force for economic take-off.

Not all the provinces did equally well in this regard, of course. Indeed, in some cases such as Hainan, if the efforts to attract foreign investment had been more successful, the overall results of the reform process might have been different. But there is no question that the strong capacity of these coastal provinces to mobilize and allocate resources was critical to their overall performance under the current reform. The inability of Sichuan and Shaanxi to match the coastal provinces in resource mobilization, on the other hand, did more than anything else to slow the pace of reform and development in these two inland provinces.

The Rise of Provincial Leadership and National Politics

What are the implications of the rise of the provincial leadership to China's politics in general? The above discussion touches upon the impact of central policies on the reform process at the provincial level. This section will identify some of the areas where the evolution of the provincial leadership has a clear impact on national politics. A more systematic examination of the topic will be provided by Jae Ho Chung's appendix that follows this chapter.

It is difficult to underestimate the impact of the rise of the provincial leadership. Most people still see the relationship between Beijing and the provinces as an essentially central-local relationship. However, if the portrait of the preceding chapters is accurate, the provinces themselves have already emerged as a "center" in their own right. The provincial leaders now control substantial policy autonomy, command a huge amount of organizational and economic resources, maintain a high degree of control over the local economy, and have established multiple channels of communication with the international market. They in some sense possess the capability to serve as an important political force not only at the provincial level but at the national level as well. The question is in what direction and how much this political force is going to affect the overall political process.

The preceding chapters have shed new light on this question. China's reform and the provincial responses to the changes have altered the dynamics of the relationship between the two. In some provinces where the reform was more advanced and the provincial leadership stronger, the relationship with the Center has clearly become more interactive. There were areas in the relationship where the Center still called the shots, like the selection of top provincial officials and the granting or retracting of preferential policies. There were areas, on the other hand, where mutual dependence prevailed. For example, Guangdong received preferential treatment in China's open policy but thereafter became an indispensable core of China's success in expanding foreign economic relations. Shanghai received central assistance to help develop the Pudong area and rebuild the city's infrastructure. In return, Shanghai became a new source of growth for the leaders in Beijing and a competing model of development vis-à-vis the model represented by Guangdong. There were still other areas where the Center gave nominal guidelines but it was the provincial leadership that exercised real control, and the number of these areas is growing. Based on the preceding chapters, such areas at least include the handling of the relationship with subprovincial government units, the crafting and implementation of local development strategies, the mobilization and allocation of local resources and the search for institutional and procedural solutions in dealing with the various consequences of reform. It is still too early to predict which trend is going to overwhelm the central-provincial relationship. Based on the findings of the preceding chapters, one thing is certain: if current developments hold, it will be very difficult to continue to regard China as a monolithic state dominated by hierarchical control.

As the preceding chapters show, the provincial leaders now pay more and more attention to what happens below them and not just to the orders they receive from above. In addition, there is increasing pressure on them to adopt populist policies to cater to the rising demands of their local constituencies. There are strong reasons for this shift of political locus and loyalty according to the case studies in this book. The Center no longer provides the majority of support needed for local development; local sources do. The management of local reform is highly complicated and requires local-specific solutions. More and more top provincial officials are natives, better educated, and eager to seek popular support as a source of political capital. However, the shift of political locus and loyalty could have serious consequences for Chinese politics. At the very least, it may accelerate the "hollowization" of central authority. More seriously, it may lead to the rise of powerful centrifugal forces further making the maintenance of even nominal political unity difficult. There is another possibility. As the provincial leaders become more sensitive to popular demands and politics at the provincial level reflect different kinds of interests, eventually there will be spill-over effects on national politics.

Another area where the changes at the provincial level could threaten the current political order is the increasing inter-provincial gap in reform and the level of economic development. A large portion of this book is devoted to assessing and explaining such a gap. But the gap's impact on national politics is substantial as well. For example, China's reform is created essentially a three-tiered ranking among the provinces: the most advanced provinces, the provinces seeking to catch up, and the provinces hopelessly left behind. It has become increasingly difficult for the Center to initiate and implement national policies in a uniform manner. The ineffectiveness of national policies, on the other hand, encourages provinces to seek greater autonomy and control at the expense of the central government. It is also possible that some form of regional alliances may emerge as alternative political centers in Chinese politics in the future.

Finally, the rise of the provincial leadership highlights the potential of a wild card in influencing the future of Chinese politics. As the role of the provinces becomes more prominent, the importance of the personal factor also rises. A major contribution of this book is to call attention to the critical role of top provincial leaders through a detailed account of their contributions to local reform and development in their respective provinces. However, the future roles of these leaders still remain unpredictable, hence making this one of the most important wild cards in Chinese politics. Will these leaders become standard bearers of the so-called bureaucratic authoritarianism in that they become the staunchest defenders of the current political and economic system not because of ideological reasons but because of the fact their personal interests are best served by integrating a rigorous market economy with a corrupt, bureaucrat-dominated local government system? Or will they use their enhanced control of policy and resources to seek more independence from the Center and promote their own agendas, even if some of these might not be consistent with central directives? Or will the current provincial leaders prove to be no more than transitional figures as their backgrounds and education limit their ability to complete the transformation from an authoritarian and semi-market system to a more pluralist society with a full-blown market economy? This book alone cannot provide all the answers to these questions. It requires more efforts like this project to develop a better understanding of this extremely important shift in Chinese politics.

Appendix

Study of Provincial Politics and Development in the Post-Mao Reform Era

Issues, Approaches, and Sources

Jae Ho Chung

With a very few notable exceptions, provinces have always constituted the most critical level of local administration in the People's Republic of China. Supra-provincial "administrative regions" (*xingzhengqu*) were always short-lived, while subprovincial "prefectures" (*diqu*) were rarely given sufficient or legitimate power to challenge the provinces. While the extent to which Beijing was able to rein in the provinces at different times may be subject to varying interpretations, and while the growing importance of counties situated on the interface of state and society is duly noted, it seems indisputable that the provinces are still the most important sub-national units of administration in China.[1]

Although certain measures of decentralization, both fiscal and administrative, were intermittently implemented during the period of Mao's rule, they were never fully materialized so as to "institutionalize" local participation in decision making and local discretion in policy implementation. More often than not provinces performed as faithful agents of the central authorities rather than as sincere representatives of local interests. In short, central imposition, local compliance, and standardized implementation characterized much of this period's policy dynamics.[2]

The last eighteen years of reform have changed much of what has just been described. Despite occasional reassertion of the powerful Center, successive phases of decentralization encompassing various policy areas have gradually transformed the command-compliance relationship between Beijing and the provinces into much more complex dynamics involving more actors, interests and negotiations. Now, local compliance is no longer simply taken for granted; political imposition of Beijing's priorities is becoming increasingly difficult and costly; and variation, rather than standardization, more closely depicts the dominant pattern of local policy implementation.

This appendix attempts to lay out some key features of provincial dynamics in the reform era since 1978 and to explore some ways to approach this highly complex topic. The chapter is divided into three sections. The first surveys the expanding "space" of provincial politics in the post-Mao reform era. More specifically, four relational "spaces" in terms of who the provinces interact with— i.e., central-provincial, inter-provincial, intra-provincial and subprovincial dynamics—are discussed. The second section explores a couple of thematic approaches, including institutional and procedural changes, the scope and pattern of local variation, and the intensity and rationale of conflict and cooperation among the Center, the provinces and subprovincial units. The third section provides a select list of indispensable and newly available source materials on the study of provincial politics and development.

The Expanding Space of Provincial Politics in the Reform Era

Reform as Providing Incentives for Provincial Assertiveness

In pre-reform China, the role of the provinces was relatively simple: disseminating Beijing's policy directives and monitoring subprovincial compliance with state plans. Particularly after the traumatic experiences of the anti-rightist campaign, there was a kernel of truth to the "totalitarian" interpretation of the policy dynamics in Maoist China that provinces were no more than the loyal agents of the Center.[3] One fundamental change induced by the post-Mao reform was the emergence of assertive localities. "Assertive" does not necessarily denote that local interests were always accommodated. It rather suggests that, compared to the pre-reform era, localities have become more aggressive in articulating and protecting their vital interests. Post-Mao measures of fiscal and administrative decentralization have gradually generated a new set of problems in central-provincial relations.

As the topic of central-provincial relations has recently received heavy attention both in and outside China, a large number of studies were produced in efforts to understand the evolving dynamics between Beijing and the provinces. Many of these studies point to a similar assessment that, compared to the pre-reform era, the overall balance of power has increasingly tilted toward the provinces. Some even point to a possibility of China being split up, although they differ considerably on the nature of such a division.[4] One key question is whether the central government has actually become so weak as to facilitate a situation where even territorial disintegration is a serious possibility. The power of Beijing has indeed been reduced by a series of extensive decentralizations. But, at the same time, the Center has also been tolerant of local perversities due mainly to its ultimate concern with the hoped-for gains of the reform as a whole.[5] Therefore, we need to be careful about making generalizations as to the evolving balance of power between the central and provincial governments in the reform era.[6]

One fairly common conceptualization is that central-provincial relations are necessarily of a zero-sum nature. That is, if a seemingly high level of provincial discretion is identified, then it is almost automatically equated with the Center having lost its overall control over the provinces. Alternatively, if the capacity or willingness of the Center to regulate local affairs seemingly increases, we tend to presume that the room for provincial autonomy must have decreased accordingly. Although there are times when central-provincial dynamics do resemble a zero-sum game, more often than not a reduction in the Center's imposition does not necessarily result in increased local autonomy. Thus, decentralization reforms should not be construed as necessarily and automatically weakening the overall control capacity of the Center. A case can even be made that decentralization, under certain circumstances, may strengthen the overall control capacity of the Center by creating additional "space" for sub-national units and thereby deflecting the regionalist temptation.[7]

While the overall scope of provincial discretion might have expanded in the post-Mao era, it seems wrong to infer that the Center has been rendered completely helpless in restricting provincial autonomy. Available evidence shows that Beijing has been both willing and able (at least partially) to regulate provincial fiscal behavior for the purpose of promoting its own preferences.[8] The overall effects of the post-Mao reform seem to have been more diluted than what is commonly supposed. While the decline of ideology and economic decentralization have expanded the scope of local discretion, the Center still retains much of its capacity in controlling local personnel appointments through the *nomenklatura* system.[9] Policy instruments are also becoming increasingly important as more localities seek preferential policies (e.g., state designations for special economic zones and other development zones). The central government, as the sole legitimate provider of such policies, can reward or punish the provinces with the provision or withdrawal of these highly selective incentives. Moreover, the post-Mao reform seems to have significantly improved Beijing's ability to monitor and supervise local policy behavior. For instance, the staff size of the State Statistical Bureau (SSB) increased from 46 in 1976, to 280 in 1981, to 580 in 1988, and to over 1,000 in 1994. the Center is also believed to have created new organizations and strengthened old units to help improve its capacity to monitor and enforce local compliance.[10]

Another common conceptual fallacy is to assume that a change in intergovernmental structural arrangements is bound to have across-the-board effects. It is suggested here that the effects of decentralization are not necessarily indiscriminate among different types of policy, since the Center may be more willing to solicit local initiatives on some policies, while insisting on total compliance on others. Three factors—the number of policy targets, the extent to which a policy entails resource allocation, and the degree to which a policy proposes to depart from the status quo—may determine the scope of local discretion. First, in terms of their scope of application, policies can be divided into encompassing and selective policy: encompassing policy is applied to all local units, while selective policy is applied only to some units. It is suggested that the larger the number of policy targets (i.e., if a policy is more encompassing than selective), the more restricted is local discretion. Due to the Center's limited monitoring capacity and its "unwritten" obligation to treat all localities impartially, policy with a large number of targets tends to be highly standardized (i.e., provincial performance becomes easier for the Center to monitor) and, therefore, leaves relatively smaller room for local discretion. Selective policy with a smaller number of policy targets tends to render the task of interest coordination much easier by making the Center willing to accommodate some local preferences through the process of bargaining and negotiation.[11]

Second, policy may be categorized by its functional characteristics into allocative and non-allocative policy. Allocative policy concerns the allocation of tangible resources and includes budgetary arrangements, material allocation, project location, and so on. Non-allocative policy does not involve direct transfer of fiscal or material resources between central and provincial governments and includes institutional reorganization, personnel appointments, political campaigns, and so on. Non-allocative policy may demand much stricter compliance mainly because implementation of such policies without resources at stake is more likely to be dictated by political values. On the other hand, allocative policies are more susceptible to bargaining and, therefore, may provide larger room for local maneuvering as they are dictated by economic rationale.[12]

Third, policy may also be categorized by extent of radicalism—how much the proposed policy departs from the established structure of interests. Such "newness" of policy is contingent upon limited information and experiences possessed by central policy makers. The "uncertainty factor" may thus dictate the degree to which policy makers become willing to allow local experimentation and adaptation of central policy and to solicit the support of local implementors in popularizing the potentially controversial policy. A crucial implication of this division is that the more radical the nature of the proposed change, the larger the scope of local discretion in implementation.[13]

To summarize, a higher level of local discretion may be associated with the policy: (1) that is radical (i.e., less susceptible to standard operating procedures); (2) that is allocative (i.e., more likely to involve intensive bargaining); and (3) that involves a relatively small number of implementors so as to reduce the degree of standardization. When a policy is targeted at all local units, when the nature of the policy is routinized, and when the policy requires relatively few resources to allocate, the Center's priority is more likely to dominate and local discretion likely to be restrained. A majority of policies fall somewhere between these two extremes. Since most reform policies are quite new and radical, two other criteria seem more crucial. Policies related to project location (such as the "Three Gorges Dam") are selective and allocative and, thus, more susceptible to local discretion and intergovernmental bargaining. The new policy of "tax shar-

ing," on the other hand, is allocative but encompassing, thus perhaps less susceptible to local discretion than project location policies. Election campaigns are
encompassing and non-allocative policies and personnel reshuffles are selective
and non-allocative policies. Both seem to allow relatively less local discretion
than the former two types.

In studying provincial politics in the post-Mao reform era, it is necessary for
us to chart the key changes that have occurred in central-provincial dynamics. In
doing so, however, we need to pay an equal amount of attention to the measures
favoring decentralization and local discretion, as well as to those favoring recentralization and central control. Perhaps, we have so far focused rather too exclusively on the former dimension. Our study of central-provincial interactions must
also diversify in its policy coverage. More specifically, we need to go beyond
resource policies and cover as many different types of policies as possible in
order to derive meaningful generalizations about the differential effects of policy
type on the scope of local discretion.[14]

Reform as Activating Inter-Provincial Linkages and Politics

In pre-reform China, by design or default, provinces were largely left to rely on
themselves, although the Center intermittently intervened to correct local perversities
and to "equalize" regional inequalities. This strategy of "cellular" development produced a nationwide replication of various "self-sufficient" but inefficient units, large
or small (*da xiao er quan*). In the absence of well-conceived inter-provincial networks, all but a very few provinces suffered in silence. By introducing market
principles and stressing competition and efficiency, the post-Mao reform has
fundamentally altered much of the way China's economy had operated. A new
rule of the game is that those willing to compete on the basis of their comparative advantages are to survive, while those clinging to the old ways will lag
behind.

Competition did not take place in a vacuum, however. As the post-Mao
reform began with a regionally discriminating design that favored the coastal
region, initial competition was mainly among the coastal provinces. Since the
crucial boost for provincial economic development came from Beijing's granting
of preferential policies, coastal provinces fiercely competed for more special and
exclusive policy designations.[15] Competition was not just for more preferential
policies. Coastal provinces also competed among themselves in order to obtain a
higher share of export quotas and to secure key raw materials like silk, wool, and
cotton crucial to their textile and garment industries.[16] While some provinces
have recently come to value "horizontal economic linkages" (*hengxiang jingji
lianxi*) as a venue for reducing inter-provincial conflicts and for promoting cooperation on the basis of comparative advantages, better-off provinces in the
Yangtze River Delta and Guangdong still seem to prefer to bargain individually
with Beijing rather than collectively.

Inter-provincial competition for preferential policies gradually spilt over to the inland provinces which have increasingly felt that they were being discriminated against. A predominant majority of the special policies were initially applied only to coastal provinces under the name of the "coastal development strategy." It was only in the early 1990s that Beijing adopted an "all-round development strategy" by opening up border and inland areas.[17] Yet, in most cases, the belated granting of special policies to non-coastal provinces was not followed by concrete policy and resource support from the Center. Although Beijing occasionally made pledges to provide more funds and policy support— which, more often than not, turned out to be empty rhetoric—inland provinces did not simply wait for the Center's initiatives. Some devised their own preferential policies to attract foreign investment without getting prior approval from Beijing. Many others joined collective efforts to compete against their coastal counterparts by forming regional organizations. Currently, the number of inter-provincial and other regionally-based organizations in China amounts to more than one hundred, including, to name only the principal ones, the Regional Association of Northwest China, the Regional Economic Coordination Association of Southwest China, the Northeast Economic Zone Coordination Office, the Shanxi, Gansu and Sichuan Economic Cooperative Region, the Nanjing Association for Regional Economic Coordination, and so on. In mid-1994, for instance, party bosses of five northwest provinces of Shaanxi, Gansu, Qinghai, Ningxia and Xinjiang held a "summit meeting" where they agreed to join in efforts to obtain more preferential policies from Beijing. They went further to produce a pledge that they would explore the possibility of an "economic cooperative zone"—a regional entity to cope with their economic backwardness.[18]

Inter-provincial organizations constitute only one, though important, manifestation of "horizontal linkages" created at the sub-national level. Some linkages were the creation of the Center which has sought to alleviate the inland provinces' problems by linking them with the relatively well-off coastal provinces. As early as 1980, in accordance with a State Council regulation, Gansu was "teamed up with" (*jie duizi*) Tianjin, Qinghai with Shandong, and Xinjiang with Jiangsu with the hope that the coastal partners would actively help their inland counterparts to develop their economies. In southern China, too, comparative advantages were utilized as the project of building power plants in Yunnan was linked to the goal of supplying electricity for Guangdong enterprises.[19] In the case of Tibet, Beijing specifically ordered twenty-nine provinces and municipalities to come up with at least one project for which "teaming up" would be made to promote infrastructure development in the autonomous region. Beijing's administrative order was very effective since all provinces responded within two months. Provinces like Guangdong, Shandong, Shanghai, Jiangsu and Zhejiang committed themselves to projects with investments ranging from 39 to 60 million yuan, while poor and backward provinces like Qinghai, Jiangxi, Anhui, Gansu and Inner Mongolia contributed 3 to 6 million yuan.[20]

The more and the faster these horizontal linkages are created, the more difficult may Beijing find it to deal with various groups of provinces which put
forward their demands on a collective and egalitarian basis. While such inter-
provincial linkages may help the provinces to cope with the Center and to utilize
their respective comparative advantages, they may also significantly expand the
issue "space" of provincial politics by introducing new actors and interests. Such
"interdependence" among the provinces will constitute an indispensable part of
the local process of decision making and may often create delicate conflicts
when their expectations and preferences happen to differ. To what extent the
newly emerging interprovincial linkages will work in the direction of cooperation, as opposed to conflict, remains to be seen.

Reform as Instilling Economic Logic into Intra-Provincial Politics

In pre-reform China, provincial politics were largely a replica of national politics, implementing central plans and policies (very often to the letter), launching
"movements" and "campaigns" in accordance with the ideological whims of the
Center (and Mao), whipping up the wind of production wars, and so on. Too
much of provincial politics was ideologized so that there was very little room for
the utilization of economic logic.[21] It seems that the degree to which ideological
and political imposition dictated the developmental imperative was significantly
reduced in the reform era. As visible accomplishments on the production front
are becoming a major criterion of career advancement, many provincial and local
leaders are forced to deliver the "fruits of reform." In doing so, however, they
have to rely on some economic logic suitable for the promotion of comparative
advantages, competition, efficiency, and so on, as opposed to autarky, organizational dependence, equality, and so forth.[22]

The expanded role of economic logic can be found in various dimensions.
The prevalence of economic logic is partly manifested in the changing proportion of "native" officials in the provincial leadership. In the reform era which has
continuously stressed the principle of "comparative advantage" and "local adaptation of central policy" (yindi zhiyi), it seems that high priority is given to
"natives" (as opposed to "outsiders") who are supposedly more familiar with
local conditions. Compared to the pre-reform era, the share of "natives" at the
provincial-level leadership has risen both consistently and significantly. For the
whole of China, the native ratio was 34 percent in 1965, which rose to 41 percent
in 1988 for the provincial party secretaries. As for the provincial governors and
deputy-governors, the 1988 figure was 44 percent.[23] The chapters included in
this volume also generally support the emerging trend that "natives" are rising in
the provincial politics of the reform era: Fujian, Shandong, Shaanxi, and
Guangdong have had an increasing number of "natives" as their key provincial
leaders and party secretaries in particular.[24]

The revival of old ties and the creation of new factions can also be attributed to the impact of economic logic on intra-provincial politics of the reform era. One manifest example of the revival of old ties is found in Anhui. There, the long-persecuted followers of Zeng Xisheng, Anhui's party boss during the early 1960s who had fallen due to his controversial push for the "responsibility plots" (*zerentian*), made a gradual comeback with the triumph of the household responsibility reform in the early 1980s. Although their comeback was aided partly by local forces based in Chuxian Prefecture and Maanshan City, the revival of the Zeng faction has constituted an important variable in Anhui politics.[25] The creation of new factions or groups are also found. Since cadres from the coastal regions are generally considered to have better expertise and more experience in promoting "reform," many key provincial posts are increasingly occupied by such cadres. In the case of Shandong, for instance, many key provincial leaders are believed to have come from the eastern Jiaodong Peninsula region (encompassing Qingdao, Yantai and Weihai). Among the fifteen members of the fourteenth provincial party committee elected in 1992, eleven were Shandong natives and seven of them (64 percent) were from the peninsula region. Considering the peninsula region's very small population (only 18 percent of the province's total population), its share in the provincial party committee is disproportionately high. Moreover, through the intra-provincial "cadre transfer" program, many of the key inland posts are also taken up by cadres from the peninsula region, while the same cannot be said about the opposite direction.[26]

The rise of certain bureaucratic organizations at the expense of others is another salient characteristic of the reform era. At the national level, this trend has already been observed for quite a while.[27] As the economic reform introduced many changes in the way resources were allocated and decisional authority was exercised, provincial government units favored by the reform gradually expanded their influence, while those at loggerheads with the proposed changes were sidelined or left out in the cold. At the provincial level, at least two types of bureaucratic organizations have become the main beneficiaries: (1) "administrative units" closely related to the reform and "opening"—such as the foreign economic relations and trade commission (*waijingmaowei*), the foreign affairs office (*waiban*), and the economic system restructuring commission (*tigaiwei*); and (2) "business units" related to foreign trade, foreign investment, taxation, insurance, and banking. As a matter of fact, it will be a worthwhile exercise to conduct systematic surveys to see (1) whether youths actually prefer to work in these units as opposed to the conventionally prestigious ones like the planning commission (*jiwei*) and the propaganda apparatus; and (2) whether key provincial leaders tend to have backgrounds in these newly emerging functional areas more closely related to the reform.[28]

As China's economic reform relies heavily on its cooperation with foreign countries, overseas and foreign connections may also be a critical issue in understanding provincial politics of the reform era. Since one's career advancement will indisputably depend upon one's ability to deliver such "goods of reform" as increased exports, foreign direct investment and technology transfer, those with close overseas and foreign connections are more likely to have a competitive edge in making authoritative decisions pertaining to local development policy. Whether or not such connections will work only as an advantage—as opposed to burdens and even handicaps if the wind blows in the reverse direction—remains to be seen.[29]

Finally, the rise of a new generation of provincial-level leaders merits our attention. Despite many earlier studies,[30] we still lack more systematic, updated, and comprehensive aggregate studies on the backgrounds of provincial leaders in the reform period.[31] In addition to the "native" issue, it is important to examine the extent to which the new generation of key provincial leaders has been consciously "cultivated" by the Center—as opposed to having "gradually made their way to the top on their own." Another question concerns how many of these new generation provincial leaders have "good" family backgrounds. Limited evidence shows that quite a few children of high-level officials were groomed at the local levels as potential "successors" (jiebanren) to rule certain provinces. Many are well educated with engineering backgrounds and, therefore, are presumably able to deliver the "goods of reform."[32]

Reform as Compounding Subprovincial Politics

In pre-reform China, the hierarchy of local administration was both rigid and clear-cut. Provinces, as the highest sub-national unit of administration, took charge of supervising the prefectures and prefectural cities which in turn governed counties on behalf of provincial authorities. Such a highly institutionalized system of top-down administration came in very handy when the principal function of local government was only to monitor and control. In the post-Mao era, however, local initiatives and incentives were actively promoted for the sake of economic reform and, consequently, a variety of new local units were created and many already existing ones had their bureaucratic status readjusted.

As an increasing number of local units have become involved in policy making in the reform era, whether we put our analytical focus on the top-down imposition by the province or on the exercise of local discretion by subprovincial units may result in significantly different explanations. The rise of subprovincial cities has been particularly noteworthy, since not only their number rose dramatically in the reform era but also their role as "agents of development" has been assessed very positively.[33] Particularly, such highly preferential designations as "special economic zones" (jingji tequ: hereafter SEZs), "coastal open cities" (yanhai kaifang chengshi: hereafter COCs), and "central economic cities" (jihua danlie chengshi: hereafter CECs) allowed some two dozen subprovincial cities to grow strong enough to compete with the provinces. These new developments have largely undercut the power of both the Center and the provinces, thus further complicating central-provincial policy dynamics as well as intra-provincial politics.[34] One crucial implication is that in studying provincial politics and development we now have to go beyond the conventional practice of looking exclusively at the provincial level: subprovincial politics and intra-provincial variation will become as important as central-provincial dynamics.

Since some preferential policies bestowed a considerable amount of authority in policy making and project approval on subprovincial units, the problems of control and coordination constitute an increasingly important issue. Such problems are particularly manifest in the province's relations with SEZs, COCs and CECs as well as with many flourishing "development zones" designated by prefectures and counties without prior approval from the provincial authorities. One novel way by which these subprovincial cities undercut the power of their respective provincial authorities is to conduct inter-city diplomacy. By getting themselves organized and constantly informed about what is taking place in other localities, SEZs, COCs, and CECs use such information in lobbying for more privileges from the Center and their respective provinces. For instance, there are a series of annual meetings that leaders of CECs attend to discuss common problems and issues.[35] Subprovincial cities also maintain liaison offices in other regions. After Qingdao became a CEC in 1987, Qingdao established its Beijing office under the approval of the State Council.[36] Other than Beijing, Qingdao also established liaison offices in Guangzhou, Shanghai, Shenzhen and Xiamen. As of 1994, Harbin, Shenyang, and Ji'nan, too, maintained thirteen, eight, and seven offices, respectively, in other provinces and cities.[37]

The contradictions of control were particularly acute in the provinces' relations with CECs. Since CEC status enabled so designated cities to enjoy a provincial-level status in various economic policy issues, the confrontation between the two levels of administration was rather inevitable. Between 1983–89, a total of fourteen CECs were approved, among which eight were "provincial capitals" (shenghui). Despite the wishes that benefits from the CECs would overshadow the loss of revenue and control, all sorts of disagreements, tensions and conflicts were generated between the provinces and the CECs.[38] While such contradictions were common for all CECs, the particular degrees of "unhappiness" on the part of the provincial governments were more considerable in the case of the eight CECs which housed both provincial and municipal governments. The ensuing conflicts between the provincial and CEC governments became so disruptive that Beijing finally abolished the controversial CEC status for the eight provincial capitals in the summer of 1993.[39] These eight former CECs did not lose all of their privileges: administratively, they were still categorized as "deputy-provincial level" (fushengji) units. In 1994, Ji'nan of Shandong and Hangzhou of Zhejiang were added to the list of "deputy-provincial level" cities.[40]

In any case, the rise of subprovincial cities (which include deputy-provincial, prefectural and county-level ones) has introduced a highly complex equation into intra- and subprovincial politics.[41] And it is not entirely inconceivable that Beijing is perhaps cultivating these key cities to utilize them as counterweights to the growing autonomy and regionalism of provincial authorities.[42] In our study of provincial politics and development of the reform era, therefore, it will become increasingly important to figure out the general pattern of interactions among these subprovincial units, as well as between them and central and provincial authorities, and key factors that produce the dominant pattern of such interactions.

Approaches to the Exploration of Provincial Politics in the Reform Era

Institutional and Procedural Changes

Perhaps one of the most important tasks facing scholars of contemporary China, particularly of its reformist phase, is to identify and document the key changes that have occurred in the institutional and procedural dimensions of provincial politics.[43] A couple of suggestions follow. First, it would be a worthwhile project to draw an organizational chart of the provincial organizations including party, government, people's congress, and other civilian as well as military units, and compare its composition with that of the pre-reform period. Some old units went through a series of merger, separation and reorganization, while certain units, though new, may carry considerable political weight in accordance with the shifting policy preferences for growth and efficiency.[44] Research efforts along this line will probably have to be replicated in a relatively large number of provinces in order to have some basis of generalization. Relatedly, we may also explore a key organizational puzzle of why, despite several serious attempts, the number of provincial government units and the size of their staff have continued to expand.[45] While this phenomenon of "thickening" dates back to the pre-reform era, how the economic reform might have affected the particular pattern of organizational growth at the provincial level seems an interesting topic of research.

Second, we may wish to get some impression about how key decisions are actually made at the provincial level, and about whether and how the process differs from the past as well as from the process at the Center. More specifically, how may we evaluate the role of the provincial party standing committee? Is the provincial secretary still the ultimate arbiter in all cases, or is he but one important member of the collective provincial leadership? How has the relationship between the party secretary and governor been evolving? What is the role of "work conferences" (gongzuo huiyi) and "transmission meetings" (chuanda huiyi)? What is the nature of the relationships among the provincial party and government bodies and the provincial people's congress? What kind of weight do demands from subprovincial units carry in the provincial-level decision-making process?

Third, we may also want to find out about the nature of concrete changes that have been implemented in key areas of interaction among Beijing, the provinces and subprovincial governments. Methodologically, it may be done at the nationwide aggregate level or with a case province or two. A hybrid method of combining both may also be utilized. A couple of key questions in this regard are: (1) are central-local interactions really being transformed into a predominantly bargaining relationship? (2) how generalizable is such an argument? and (3) how can we assess the impact of post-Mao decentralization in fiscal and administrative terms? Studying Beijing's *nomenklatura* control of local personnel appointments is a crucial example in point. Such research may produce very meaningful contributions if it investigates the changes in the scope and nature of Beijing's personnel control over the provinces from a longitudinal perspective.[46] Similar efforts were made in the fiscal dimension to account for the changes and continuities with reference to Beijing's budgetary relationships with various provinces.[47] We probably need to do similar research along this line on a variety of other policy areas which have so far received relatively scant attention.[48]

Identifying and Explaining Local Variation

With extensive measures of decentralization for more than a decade, the policy process in the reform era is likely to become increasingly bottom-heavy in its demands for resources and information. A crucial implication is that variation, rather than uniformity, will characterize what transpires at sub-national level politics. With the decline of ideology and the introduction of markets and profits, provincial politics will also be increasingly shaped by local interests as much as by the Center's priorities. Since local interests may vary quite significantly among different provinces and municipalities, how provincial politics are played out with regard to particular policies may also differ accordingly. In sum, the study of provincial politics and development in the reform era should focus on identifying such variations and explaining why they occur in such a way as they do.

Identifying and explaining variations is not as easy as it seems. First of all, in order to identify local variation, the minimum number of provinces (and sub-provincial units) needed is two, which thus requires some sort of comparative method. In empirical research, comparative studies are much more difficult and time-consuming to carry out than single-case studies. Particularly when one deals with units of analysis that are large-scale organizations (as opposed to individuals or groups), readily available yet persuasive indicators are rather difficult to locate. Therefore, the task of identifying the magnitude of local variation is a very tough challenge.[49]

Having found local variation, how are we going to explain it? The field of contemporary China studies has too few exemplary studies to shed any meaningful light on this crucial question. We do not even have an agreed-upon list of general variables that affect inter-provincial variation. It seems that there are three broad categories of variation that merit our attention: (1) differences in the pattern of structural arrangements between Beijing and the provinces (e.g., revenue-sharing frameworks for Guangdong and Shanghai); (2) the divergent pace and mode of economic development among different provinces (e.g., the developmental paths of Guangdong and Zhejiang); and (3) the variations in the pace and pattern of implementation of public policy (e.g., the pace of decollectivization in Anhui and Heilongjiang).[50] It seems that our attention has previously been focused too much on the first type of variation, largely ignoring the remaining two.

Once certain variations are identified, we may then proceed to explain them on the basis of the following list of variables, which is presented here only for illustrative purposes and is by no means exhaustive.[51]

1. Economic Variables: wealth—various production, sales and income standings, budgetary conditions, grain self-sufficiency, foreign exchange earnings, and many other policy-specific factors
2. Strategic and Geographical Variables: strategic locale (i.e., border areas), the degree of influence by the PLA (state farms and military settlements), coastal-inland differences, and physical distance from Beijing
3. Cultural Variables: regionalism (history, linguistic barriers, entrepreneurial traditions, and so on)
4. Political Variables: provincial internal solidarity, characteristics of provincial leadership, intra-regional standing of the province, and patron-client relationships between central and provincial leaders[52]

Some of these variables have readily available indicators (usually in statistical yearbooks), while others are very difficult to operationalize. And in many cases we may have to come up with a set of additional variables closely related to the particular policy of concern. Yet, our future research must move toward this direction of working with a more or less common set of variables and seek to evaluate and specify their relative explanatory power for different policy issues as well as for different sets of provinces.

Intensity and Rationale of Local Compliance and Resistance

One fundamental component of provincial politics concerns the making of strategic decisions with regard to how the province should respond to the priorities and demands of the central government. When the Center's demands do not diverge too much from provincial interests, provinces will more often than not comply with the Center. When there are significant differences between Beijing's priorities and provincial preferences, however, the province has to make a choice concerning to what extent it should accommodate the Center's demands and at what costs. Compared to the pre-reform era, detecting local resentment, resistance, and non-compliance has recently become relatively easier since local governments have become increasingly more vocal about protecting their interests.[53]

A crucial question concerns how we may become able to understand the rationale of compliance and, more importantly, of resistance. How can we empirically substantiate that provincial interests coincide with the Center's demands, and vice versa? How can we distinguish provincial resistance on the basis of public (provincial) interests from provincial non-compliance due to personal conviction and ambitions of individual leaders? One related issue concerns how provincial behavior is monitored and supervised, and how provincial resistance is overturned by the Center. How the Center keeps itself informed about provincial and local policy processes also needs to be explored.

Reference and Source Materials: A Select List

During the earlier decades, researchers had serious difficulties in securing stable access to both systematic and reliable data and information on provinces and other units of local administration.[54] In the 1990s, however, we can no longer complain about the paucity of materials; instead, we are literally flooded by so many source materials on the provinces, prefectures, and counties.[55] Under these circumstances, we need a sort of "screening and evaluating" mechanism to review, on a regular basis, key categories of reference and source materials on provincial issues.

General Reference Materials

Numerous reference materials are currently available on various aspects of politics, economy, society, and many other issue areas of contemporary China. One key source concerns dictionaries on "who's who in the People's Republic," examples of which include *Zhongguo renwu nianjian 1994* (Yearbook on China's Key Figures 1994) (Beijing: Huayi chubanshe, 1994) and *Guangdong jinxiandai renwu cidian* (Dictionary on Modern and Contemporary Figures of Guangdong) (Guangzhou: Guangdong keji chubanshe, 1992). A very complete biographical reference on key CCP figures is *Zhongguo gongchandang renming dacidian, 1921–1991* (Dictionary of Who's Who in the Chinese Communist Party, 1921–1991) (Beijing: Zhongguo guoji guangbo chubanshe, 1991). For references on more current leaders, *Zhongguo renming dacidian: xianren dangzhengjun lingdao renwujuan* (Who's Who in China: Current Leaders in the Party, Government, and Military) (Beijing: Waiwen chubanshe, 1994), 2nd ed., is useful. An extensive yearly compilation of personnel of central and local government organizations and non-governmental organizations is *China Directory* (Tokyo: Radiopress, every year). And for accumulated lists of leading figures in regional and provincial government bodies, see Malcomb Lamb, *Directory of Chinese Officials and Organizations in China: A Quarter-Century Guide* (Armonk: M. E. Sharpe, 1994) and *Zhonghua renmin gongheguo zhiguanzhi* (List of Office Holders in the People's Republic of China) (Beijing: Zhongguo shehui chubanshe, 1993) which goes back to the era of the base areas. For detailed lists of provincial government organizations, see *Zhongguo zhengfu jigou minglu* (List of Government Organizations in China) (Beijing: Xinhua chubanshe, 1996), vol. 2.

The State Statistical Bureau (SSB) as well as various functional ministries publish a wide range of publications that contain key information and data on the provinces. In addition to the well-known China Statistical Yearbook (*Zhongguo tongji nianjian*), China Agricultural Yearbook (*Zhongguo nongye nianjian*), and Yearbook on China's Foreign Economic Relations and Trade (*Zhongguo duiwai jingji maoyi nianjian*) published by the SSB, the Ministry of Agriculture, and the Ministry of Foreign Trade and Economic Cooperation, respectively, the SSB also publishes statistical yearbooks on such areas as rural economy, urban economy, markets, population, labor, commodity prices, industrial economy, and labor unions.[56]

The SSB also published a wide range of one-shot and non-periodic data compilations for particular sectors and issue areas. Examples include *Guomin shouru tongji ziliao huibian 1949–1985* (Compilation of Statistical Materials on National Income 1949–1985) (Beijing: Zhongguo tongji chubanshe, 1987), which contains provincial data on such items as national income, gross national products, consumption, and so on; *Zhongguo guding zichan touzi tongji ziliao 1950–1985* (Statistical Materials on China's Fixed Asset Investment 1950–1985) (Beijing: Zhongguo tongji chubanshe, 1987); *Quanguo gesheng zizhiqu zhixiashi lishi tongji ziliao huibian 1949–1989* (Statistical Compilation on China's Provinces, Autonomous Regions, and Centrally Administered Cities 1949–1989) (Beijing: Zhongguo tongji chubanshe, 1990); and *Quanguo zhuyao shehui jingji zhibiao paixu nianjian 1993* (Yearbook on National Rankings of Key Socio-Economic Indicators 1993) (Beijing: Zhongguo tongji chubanshe, 1993). While it is not a SSB publication, *Zhongguo jingji tizhi gaige nianjian 1994* (Yearbook on China's Economic System Reform 1994), provides helpful information on documents and other references to reform policies related to enterprises, markets, circulation, macro-economic control, rural reform, foreign exchange regulation, science and technology, and so on. Additionally, *Zhongguo xianqing daquan* (Comprehensive Overview of China's Counties) (Beijing: Zhongguo shehui kexue chubanshe, 1993) provides invaluable information on China's counties contained in six volumes.

Chronologies

There are a variety of chronologies relevant to the study of provincial politics. Some chronicle major events in the concerned provinces, while others have more specific issue-oriented foci. An example of the latter type is *Heilongjiang nongye hezuoshi* (History of Heilongjiang's Agricultural Cooperativization) (Beijing: Zhonggong dangshi ziliao chubanshe, 1990), and an example of the former is Party History Research Office of Heilongjiang Provincial Party Committee (eds.), *Zhonggong Heilongjiang dangshi dashiji* (Chronology of Heilongjiang Communist Party History) (Harbin: Heilongjiang renmin chubanshe, 1991). Such publitions as *Shandong shengqing* (Facts and Figures of Shandong) (Ji'nan: Shandong renmin chubanshe, 1989) also include a significant portion of chronological data pertaining to the respective province. Of course, provincial volumes of the Contemporary China (*Dangdai Zhongguo*) series also have detailed chronologies.

Province-specific chronologies also include those with longer time frames: *Jilinsheng biannian jishi, 1653–1985* (Jilin Province's Annual Chronicles, 1653–1985) (Changchun: Jilin renmin chubanshe, 1989), two volumes; *Shanxi dashiji 1840–1985* (Shanxi's Chronicle 1840–1985) (Taiyuan: Shanxi renmin chubanshe, 1987); *Hubei zhengfa dashiji 1838–1986* (Chronology of Hubei's Political and Legal Affairs 1838–1986) (n.p., 1987); and *Hebei shengzhi dashiji, yuangu–1988* (Hebei Provincial Chronology from Ancient Times to 1988) (Baoding: Hebei daxue chubanshe, 1992). Those with shorter time frames include *Jiangsusheng dashiji 1949–1985* (Jiangsu Province's Chronology 1949–1985) (Nanjing: Jiangsu renmin chubanshe, 1988) and *Henan gaige dashiji 1978–1988* (Chronology of the Reform in Henan 1978–1988) (Zhengzhou: Henan renmin chubanshe, 1988). There are also party and government organizational histories which are now available for most provincial-level units (and for prefectures and counties as well). Examples include *Zhongguo gongchandang Shanghai shi zuzhishi ziliao 1920–1987* (Materials on the Organizational History of the CCP in Shanghai) (Shanghai: Shanghai renmin chubanshe, 1991); *Zhongguo gongchandang Shanxisheng zuzhishi ziliao 1924–1987* (Materials on the Organizational History of the CCP in Shanxi Province) (Taiyuan: Shanxi renmin chubanshe, 1994), two volumes; *Zhongguo gongchandang Fujiansheng Xiamenshi zuzhishi ziliao 1926–1987* (Materials on the Organizational History of the CCP in Xiamen in Fujian Province) (Fuzhou: Fujian renmin chubanshe, 1990); and *Zhongguo gongchandang Shanxisheng Yushuxian zuzhishi ziliao 1932–1987* (Materials on the Organizational History of the CCP in Yushu County of Shanxi Province) (Taiyuan: Shanxi renmin chubanshe, 1994).

Document Compilations

of document compilations are available on a wide range of policy nstance, with regard to the decollectivization reform in the late 1970s 980s, a comprehensive compilation of provincial documents of al- rovince-level units is available in a two-volume internal publication: *un jingji zhengce huibian 1978–1981* (Collection of Rural Policy Docu- 1978–1981) (Beijing: Nongcun duwu chubanshe, 1982); and (2) *Nong- i zhengce huibian 1981–1983* (Collection of Rural Policy Documents in 983) (Beijing: Nongcun duwu chubanshe, 1984). Concerning the reforms ectivization and decollectivization, Shandong also published a two-vol- ternal compilation of key documents and pertinent data in *Shandongsheng e hezuohua shiliaoji* (Collection of Historical Materials on Agricultural Col- ization in Shandong Province) (Ji'nan: Shandong renmin chubanshe, 1989). A similar effort was made by Anhui: Historical Archives Commission of the Anhui Provincial Political Consultative Conference (ed.), *Nongcun gaige de xingqi* (The Rise of Rural Reform) (Beijing: Zhongguo wenshi chubanshe, 1993).[57]

Central-Local Dynamics and Local Governments in General

An increasingly large number of publications are being produced on this topic, although the quality of scholarship and data provided varies considerably. Some "internal" (*neibu*) research outputs are particularly helpful in providing key information and data about the issue areas in which provinces most frequently interact with Beijing. Examples include the Policy Research Office of the State Planning Commission, "Woguo zhongyang yu difang jingji guanli quanxian yanjiu" (Study of Boundaries of Economic Management between China's Central and Local Governments), in *Jingji yanjiu cankao* (Reference Materials for Economic Research), No. 434/435 (1 March 1994); and Guo Yanzhong, "Fenshuizhi yanjiu zhuanji" (Special Edition on the Study of the Tax-Sharing System), *Jingji yanjiu cankao*, No. 401 (1 January 1994).

There is also an increasing number of monographs published in this area: Quan Zhiping and Jiang Zuozhong, *Lun difang jingji liyi* (On Economic Interests of the Locality) (Guangzhou: Guangdong renmin chubanshe, 1992); Wang Shaoguang and Hu Angang, *Zhongguo guojia nengli baogao* (Report on China's State Capacity) (Shenyang: Liaoning renmin chubanshe, 1993); *Difang zhengfu de zhineng he zuzhi jiegou* (Functions and Organization of Local Government), ed. Zhang Jianshi (Beijing: Huaxia chubanshe, 1994), two volumes; Wu Yang and Zhang Jianxi (eds.), *Zhongguo difang jingji fazhan fenxi* (Analysis of Local Economic Development in China) (Beijing: Zhongguo jingji chubanshe, 1994); and Wei Liqun (ed.), *Shichang jingji zhong de zhongyang yu difang jingji guanxi* (Central-Local Economic Relations in the Market Economy) (Beijing: Zhongguo jingji chubanshe, 1994); Dong Fureng et al., *Jiquan yu fenquan* (Centralization and Decentralization) (Beijing: Jingji kexue chubanshe, 1996); and Zhou Weilin, *Zhongguo difang zhengfu jingji xingwei fenxi* (Analysis of Local Government Economic Behavior in China) (Shanghai: Fudan University Press, 1997).

Regional and Provincial Monographs

Broadly speaking, there are three types of monographs concerning specific regions and provinces. First, there are series of monographic publications on the histories of provinces, the most important of which is the *Contemporary China* (*Dangdai Zhongguo*) series published initially by the China Social Science Publisher and later by the Contemporary China Publisher. With the volumes on Hainan and Shanghai published in 1993, one or two volumes were published on all province-level units in China. Second, both national and local publishers put out a large number of monographs covering various aspects of the development in one particular province. The quality of writing and data contained varies greatly among them, but some of these monographs provide helpful insights, collections of documents, sets of data and so on. Examples include Liao Jianxiang and Guan Qixue (eds.), *Guangdong duiwai jingji guanxi* (Foreign Economic Relations of Guangdong) (Guangzhou: Guangdong gaodeng jiaoyu chubanshe, 1988); *Yunnan chanye zhengce yanjiu* (Study of Industrial Policy in Yunnan) (Kunming: Yunnan nianjian chubanshe, 1990); Liu Yuhua (ed.), *Shandong guoyou qiye shichanghua gaizao* (The Marketization Reform of Shandong's State Enterprises) (Beijing: Renmin chubanshe, 1994) and Yue Chifeng (ed.), *Liaoning jingji fazhan silu zhi tansuo* (In Search of the Path of Economic Development in Liaoning) (Beijing: Zhonggong zhongyang dangxiao chubanshe, 1995). Third, there are many monographs with regional foci and many of these include detailed chapters on individual provinces. These volumes often implicitly provide a comparative framework. Examples include Ma Lieguang (ed.), *Zhongguo geshengqu jingji fazhan bijiao* (Comparison on China's Economic Development in Provinces and Regions) (Chengdu: Chengdu keji daxue chubanshe, 1993), which compares Shandong, Hubei and Sichuan; and *Zhongguo daxinan zai jueqi* (The Rise of China's Southwest) (Nanning: Guangxi jiaoyu chubanshe, 1994), which has sixty-page chapters each on Sichuan, Yunnan, Guizhou, Xizang and Guangxi.

Regional and Provincial Yearbooks

Some regional yearbooks[58] which contain key provincial and other local information and data include *Dongbei jingjiqu tongji nianjian 1988* (Statistical Yearbook on the Northeast Economic Region) (Shenyang: Liaoning renmin chubanshe, 1988) which deals with Liaoning, Jilin, Heilongjiang and Neimenggu; *Huadong diqu tongji nianjian* (Statistical Yearbook on the East China Region) (Beijing: Zhongguo tongji chubanshe, 1990–) focuses on Shanghai, Jiangsu, Zhejiang, Anhui, Fujian, Jiangxi and Shandong; *Zhongguo huangjin haian nianjian 1994* (Yearbook on China's Gold Coast 1994) (Ji'nan: Qunyan chubanshe, 1994) provides information on Beijing, Shanghai, Tianjin, Liaoning, Hebei, Shandong, Jiangsu, Zhejiang, Fujian, Guangxi, Guangdong, Hainan and coastal open cities; and *Zhongguo xibu diqu kaifa nianjian 1994* (Yearbook on the Development of China's Western Region) (Beijing: Gaige chubanshe, 1994) deals with Guangxi, Sichuan, Guizhou, Yunnan, Xizang, Shaanxi, Gansu, Qinghai, Ningxia, Xinjiang and Neimenggu.

Currently, all provincial-level units publish their own yearbooks, statistical yearbooks, and many other more specialized yearbooks on various sectors and issue areas. Provincial yearbooks provide a detailed overview of key changes, new policies and current developments in the province for each year. Provincial "statistical yearbooks" provide key socioeconomic and some administrative data of the provinces. Some provinces (such as Shanghai and Shanxi) also publish "economic yearbooks" (*jingji nianjian*), and others (such as Liaoning and

Heilongjiang) publish "economic statistical yearbooks" (*jingji tongji nianjian*), while still others (such as Jilin) produce "social and economic statistical yearbooks" (*shehui jingji tongji nianjian*). Many provinces also published a "forty-year" (*sishinian*) review of the respective provinces.[59]

Provincial yearbooks may also be categorized in accordance with their functional specialization. First, many provinces publish industrial yearbooks and examples include: *Shanghai gongye nianjian 1992–93* (Shanghai Industrial Yearbook 1992–93) (Shanghai: Shanghai cishu chubanshe, 1994) and *Shandong gongye tongji nianjian 1994* (Statistical Yearbook of Shandong's Industry 1994) (Ji'nan: Shandong yatai chubanshe, 1994). Provincial yearbooks are also published on agricultural economy: *Heilongjiangsheng nongye nianjian 1989* (Agricultural Yearbook of Heilongjiang 1989) (Harbin: Harbin chubanshe, 1989); *Fujian nongcun tongji nianjian 1993* (Statistical Yearbook of Fujian's Agriculture 1993) (Beijing: Zhongguo tongji chubanshe, 1993); and *Guangdong nongcun tongji nianjian 1994* (Statistical Yearbook of Guangdong's Agriculture 1994) (Beijing: Zhongguo tongji chubanshe, 1994). For foreign economic relations, see *Heilongjiang duiwai jingji maoyi nianjian 1993* (Yearbook of Heilongjiang's Foreign Economic Relations and Trade 1993) (Harbin: Heilongjiang renmin chubanshe, 1993); *Guangdongsheng duiwai jingji tongji ziliao 1992* (Statistical Materials on Guangdong's Foreign Economic Relations in 1992: internal publication) (n.p.: Guangdong tongjiju, 1993); and *Jiangsu duiwai jingji tongji daquan 1952–1991* (Comprehensive Overview of Jiangsu's Foreign Economic Relations Statistics) (Nanjing: Nanjing daxue chubanshe, 1993).

Provincial yearbooks are also available on more specialized sectors like transportation, civil affairs, commodity prices, internal trade, electricity and fixed asset investment. Examples follow: *Sichuan jiaotong nianjian 1994* (Yearbook on Sichuan's Transportation 1994) (Chengdu: Sichuan renmin chubanshe, 1994); *Zhejiang minzheng tongji nianjian 1990* (Statistical Yearbook on Zhejiang's Civil Affairs) (Hangzhou: Hangzhou daxue chubanshe, 1991); *Shandongsheng wujia yu renmin shenghuo diaocha tongji nianjian 1994* (Statistical Yearbook of the Surveys on Commodity Prices and People's Livelihood 1994) (Ji'nan: Shandongsheng tongjiju, 1994); *Shandong guonei maoyi tongji nianjian 1994* (Statistical Yearbook on Shandong's Internal Trade 1994) (Ji'nan: Shandong renmin chubanshe, 1994); *Yunnan dianli nianjian 1994* (Yearbook on Yunnan's Electricity 1994) (Kunming: Yunnan dianli nianjian chubanshe, 1994); and *Shandongsheng guding zichan touzi he jianzhuye tongji nianjian 1993* (Statistical Yearbook on Shandong's Fixed Asset Investment and Construction Industries 1993) (Ji'nan: Shandongsheng tongjiju, 1995).

Provincial Periodicals

There are thousands of provincial-level journals and periodicals on almost all key issues and sectors. Many are published by administrative units of the provincial government, and others by academic associations. All provinces have their "administrative offices" (*bangongting*) publish monthly or bi-weekly "government reports" (*zhengbao*) which provide information on key policy documents, current developments, personnel and organizational changes and so on.[60] Provincial party committees also have their own mouthpieces, usually published monthly: Heilongjiang's *Fendou* (Struggle), Jilin's *Xin changzheng* (New Long March) and Hunan's *Xuexi daobao* (Studies Bulletin) are such examples. Provincial people's congresses have their official outlets such as Shandong's bimonthly *Renda gongzuo wenzhai* (Digests of the Work of the People's Congress), Gansu's monthly *Renda yanjiu* (Study of the People's Congress), and Guangdong's monthly *Renmin zhi sheng* (Voices of the People). Provincial discipline inspection commissions publish their own journals including *Sichuan jiancha* (Inspection in Sichuan), *Dangfeng* (Party Discipline) in Guangdong, and *Dangji* (Discipline of the Party) in Guangxi. Propaganda apparatuses, too, have their voices heard; an example of such a channel is *Sichuan xuanchuan* (Propaganda in Sichuan) published monthly by the Propaganda Department of the Sichuan provincial party committee.

More economy-oriented periodicals include those published by the provincial economic system restructuring commission (*tigaiwei*)—e.g., Henan's *Gaige yu lilun* (Reform and Theory), Zhejiang's *Gaige yuebao* (Reform Monthly), and Shaanxi's *Jingji gaige* (Economic Reform); by the provincial planning commission (*jiwei*) and "development research center" (*fazhan yanjiu zhongxin*)—e.g., *Fujian jingji*, *Guangdong jingji*, and *Henan jingji*; and by provincial industrial and commercial management bureaus (*gongshang guanliju*)—e.g., *Anhui gongshang* and *Hebei gongshang*. On agriculture, different units are in charge of publishing provincial agricultural journals: the provincial agricultural commission (*nongwei*) in the case of Gansu's *Gansu nongye*; the provincial agriculture, animal husbandry, and fishery bureau (*nongmuyuye ting*) in charge of Heilongjiang's *Heilongjiang nongye*; and the provincial rural work department (*nongcun gongzuobu*) in the case of Jiangsu's *Jiangsu nongcun jingji*. In terms of labor issues, the provincial labor bureau (*laodongting*) gets out *Hunan laodong*; and the provincial personnel bureau (*renshiting*) publishes *Jiangxi laodong*. The provincial foreign economic commissions are responsible for *Fujian duiwai maoyi*, *Guangdong dajingmao*, *Shandong duiwai jingmao*, and so on. In Guangdong, the provincial statistical bureau publishes a monthly report entitled *Guangdong tongji yuebao*.

Many provincial academies of social sciences publish monthly and bimonthly publications entitled "Social sciences" (*shehui kexue*), while others publish under such names as *Dongyue luncong* (Shandong), *Fujian luntan*, *Jianghan luntan* (Hubei), and *Jianghuai luntan* (Anhui). Many journals and periodicals on provincial finances, budgets, taxation, and insurance are published by academic associations. Examples include *Guangdong jinrong* (Guangdong's Finance), *Guangxi nongcun jinrong* (Guangxi's Rural Finance), *Hubei caishui* (Hubei's Taxation), and *Shandong baoxian* (Shandong's Insurance).

Toward a Further "Disaggregation" of China

Over a decade ago, a scholar characterized the study of contemporary China during the decade of the 1970s as an era of "disaggregation," during which individual provinces and cities, as opposed to the national system as a whole, were examined in detail.[61] In retrospect, however, such a tendency toward the geographical disaggregation of China has further intensified in the 1980s to culminate in the 1990s with an almost explosive level of research on provinces, cities and counties.[62] In light of the current state of the field as well as China's systemic reforms involving extensive measures of deregulation and decentralization, study of sub-national levels of government will certainly continue to be a principal subject of scholarly inquiry in contemporary China studies in the coming years.[63]

If "geographical disaggregation" is indeed a continuing trend—in fact, a major one—how can we benefit from it in the longer run? How can we relate a variety of separate research projects on sub-national governments to the advancement of our systematic knowledge of contemporary China? One way to answer this question is to increase our reliance on general disciplinary studies in order to more or less "standardize" our modes of discourse without necessarily sacrificing the obvious advantages of area studies. On the other hand (or at the same time), we may seek to create a highly interactive "scholarly community" on China's sub-national politics, which will work together on a relatively similar set of questions and variables with reference to different groups of provinces and localities. Both of these suggestions have been made before but neither have materialized very successfully.[64] As the overall number of case provinces, cities and counties studied in the field increases, we will somehow have to come up with a way to assess our knowledge and improve our understanding of this ever-important topic in the study of China. In this respect, it is hoped that suggestions and comments made in this chapter can be of some help for the efforts to "further disaggregate" China.

Notes

I would like to thank Peter T.Y. Cheung, David S. G. Goodman and Barry Sautman for their comments on an earlier version.

1. Two periods are associated with the rule by the supra-provincial regions: (1) the era of the six great administrative regions in 1949–54; and (2) the period of 1961–66 when Beijing desired tight recentralization in the aftermath of the Great Leap fiasco. While there were some debates as to the desirability of resurrecting the regions in the late 1970s, the idea never materialized. See Dorothy J. Solinger, "Some Speculations on the Return of the Regions: Parallels with the Past," *China Quarterly*, No. 75 (September 1979), pp. 623–638. For the growing importance of counties, see Marc Blecher and Vivienne Shue,

Tethered Deer: Government and Economy in a Chinese County (Stanford: Stanford University Press, 1996), pp. 3–5.

2. This does not necessarily mean that there was no variation at all among the provinces in implementing central policy. Compared to the reform period, however, the scope of local discretion and variation was undoubtedly much smaller in the pre-reform period. For instance, in the pre-reform era, we hardly, if at all, talked about the possibility of a "split China."

3. Of course, there were occasions of non-compliance, resistance, and fait accompli. But, overall, especially with regard to national priority policies, localities had very little, if any, discretion in pursuing their own preferences and priorities. See, for instance, Alfred Chan, "The Campaign for Agricultural Development in the Great Leap Forward: A Study of Policy-Making and Implementation in Liaoning," *China Quarterly*, No. 129 (March 1992), pp. 52–71; and Penelope B. Prime, "Central-Provincial Investment and Finance: The Cultural Revolution and Its Legacy in Jiangsu Province," in William A. Joseph, Christine P. W. Wong and David Zweig (eds.), *New Perspectives on the Cultural Revolution* (Cambridge: Harvard University Press, 1991), pp. 197–215.

4. Studies that point to the possibility of China's disintegration include Wu Guoguang and Wang Zhaojun, *Deng Xiaoping zhi hou de Zhongguo* (China after Deng) (Taipei: Shijie shuju, 1994), pp. 181–282; Edward Friedman, "China's North-South Split and the Forces of Disintegration," *Current History*, No. 575 (September 1993), pp. 270–274; Maria Hsia Chang, "China's Future: Regionalism, Federation, or Disintegration," *Studies in Comparative Communism*, Vol. 25, No. 3 (September 1992), pp. 211–227; and Gerald Segal, *China Changes Shape: Regionalism and Foreign Policy*, Adephi Paper, No. 287 (London: International Institute for Strategic Studies, 1994). For more cautious approaches, see John Fitzgerald, "Reports of My Death Have Been Greatly Exaggerated: The History of the Death of China," in David S. G. Goodman and Gerald Segal (eds.), *China Deconstructs: Politics, Trade and Regionalism* (London: Routledge, 1994), pp. 21–58; Yasheng Huang, "Why China Will Not Collapse," *Foreign Policy*, No. 99 (Summer 1995), pp. 54–68; and Jae Ho Chung, "Central-Provincial Relations," in Lo Chi Kin, Suzanne Pepper, and Tsui Kai-yuen (eds.), *China Review 1995* (Hong Kong: Chinese University Press, 1995), pp. 3.31–32.

5. As Dali Yang has correctly pointed out, "it is difficult to differentiate between the case of the centre choosing not to exercise its prerogatives and the centre being unable to do so." See "Reform and the Restructuring of Central-Local Relations," in Goodman and Segal (eds.), *China Deconstructs*, p. 74.

6. The remainder of this section is drawn, though modified, from Jae Ho Chung, "Studies of Central-Provincial Relations in the People's Republic of China: A Mid-Term Appraisal," *China Quarterly*, No. 142 (June 1995), pp. 501–506.

7. For the largely undetermined outcome of decentralization, see Douglas Durasoff, "Conflicts between Economic Decentralization and Political Control in the Domestic Reform of Soviet and Post-Soviet Systems," *Social Science Quarterly*, Vol. 69, No. 2 (June 1988), pp. 388–389; and Joel Samoff, "Decentralization: The Politics of Interventionism," *Development and Change*, Vol. 21, No. 3 (1990), pp. 513–530.

8. Beijing's measures employed in this respect included: (1) the downward readjustment of provincial budgetary sharing rates; (2) the establishment of new taxes and reclassification of tax categories to increase central government revenues; (3) the appropriation of profitable local enterprises; (4) the institutionalization of "forced loans" (*difang jiekuan*), by which Beijing "borrowed" money from the provinces under a variety of pretexts but never paid it back; (5) the distribution of provincial quotas for the mandatory purchase of national bonds; and (6) most importantly, a complete overhaul of the revenue-

sharing and taxation arrangements. See *Dangdai Zhongguo caizheng* (Contemporary China's Finance) (Beijing: Zhongguo shehui kexue chubanshe, 1988), Vol. 1, pp. 309–311; Christine P. W. Wong, "Central-Local Relations in an Era of Fiscal Decline: The Paradox of Fiscal Decentralization in Post-Mao China," *China Quarterly*, No. 128 (December 1991), p. 701; and Song Xinzhong, *Zhongguo caizheng tizhi gaige yanjiu* (Study of China's Fiscal Reform) (Beijing: Zhongguo caizheng jingji chubanshe, 1992), p. 64. For the case of Guangdong, see Peter Tsan-yin Cheung, "The Case of Guangdong in Central-Provincial Relations," in Jia Hao and Lin Zhimin (eds.), *Changing Central-Local Relations in China: Reform and State Capacity* (Boulder: Westview, 1994), pp. 226–227. For Beijing's control over local investment behavior, see Yasheng Huang, *Inflation and Investment Controls in China: The Political Economy of Central-Local Relations During the Reform Era* (Cambridge: Cambridge University Press, 1996).

9. For a view that discounts Beijing's authority in personnel appointments for economically better-off provinces (like Guangdong), see John P. Burns, "Strengthening Central CCP Control of Leadership Selection: The 1990 *Nomenklatura*," *China Quarterly*, No. 138 (June 1994), pp. 470–474.

10. For the Center's increased capacity in collecting information about local behavior, see Nina P. Halpern, "Information Flows and Policy Coordination in the Chinese Bureaucracy," in Kenneth Lieberthal and David M. Lampton (eds.), *Bureaucracy, Politics and Decision Making in Post-Mao China* (Berkeley: University of California Press, 1992), pp. 125–148; Nicholas Eftimiades, *Chinese Intelligence Operations* (Annapolis: Naval Institute Press, 1994), chapter 6; and Chung, "Central-Provincial Relations," pp. 3.18–21. For the staff size of the SSB, see Yasheng Huang, "Information, Bureaucracy, and Economic Reforms in China and the Soviet Union," *World Politics*, Vol. 47, No. 1 (October 1994), pp. 127–128 and *South China Morning Post*, October 24, 1994. For a perceptive study of administrative monitoring by Beijing, see Yasheng Huang, "Administrative Monitoring in China," *China Quarterly*, No. 143 (September 1995), pp. 828–843.

11. See Max O. Stephenson, Jr. and Gerald M. Pops, "Conflict Resolution Methods and the Policy Process," *Public Administration Review*, Vol. 49, No. 5 (September-October 1989), p. 467; and Ruth Hoogland DeHoog, "Competition, Negotiation, or Cooperation? Three Alternative Models for Contracting for Services," in Miriam K. Mills (ed.), *Conflict Resolution and Public Policy* (New York: Greenwood Press, 1990), pp. 155–176.

12. See Susan Barrett and Michael Hill, "Policy, Bargaining and Structure in Implementation," in Michael J. Goldsmith (ed.), *New Research in Central-Local Relations* (Aldershot: Gower, 1986), pp. 50–52.

13. Brian W. Hogwood and Lewis A. Gunn, *Policy Analysis for the Real World* (New York: Oxford University Press, 1984), pp. 206, 213–214.

14. In this respect, this volume also has a limited coverage since both fiscal and foreign economic relations policies are resource-related. Nor are these policies encompassing since there are as many variations as there are similarities among the eight case provinces in policy terms. The diversification of policy coverage involves serious difficulties associated with data collection and other research activities (i.e., for many policies, there are no readily available data or indicators). Yet, cooperative research endeavors may provide a useful venue for overcoming some of these problems.

15. For the centrality of Beijing's preferential policies in Guangdong's development, see David S. G. Goodman and Feng Chongyi, "Guangdong: Greater Hong Kong and the New Regionalist Future," in Goodman and Segal (eds.), China Deconstructs, pp. 185–186. For the case of Shandong, see Jae Ho Chung, "The Political Economy of Development and Inequality in Shandong," in David S. G. Goodman (ed.), China's Provinces in Reform: Class, Community, and Political Culture (London: Routledge, 1997), pp. 132–142.

16. For the case of "silk wars" between Jiangsu and Zhejiang, see Yong-Nian Zheng, "Perforated Sovereignty: Provincial Dynamism and China's Foreign Trade," *The Pacific Review*, Vol. 7, No. 3 (1994), pp. 313–314; and Barry Naughton, *Growing Out of the Plan: Chinese Economic Reform 1978–1993* (Cambridge: Cambridge University Press, 1995), pp. 162–163.

17. See Jude Howell, *China Opens Its Doors: The Politics of Economic Transition* (London: Lynne Rienner, 1993), pp. 95–112; and Liu Baorong and Liao Jiasheng (eds.), *Zhongguo yanbian kaifang yu zhoubian guojia shichang* (The Opening of China's Border Areas and the Neighboring Markets) (Beijing: Falu chubanshe, 1993).

18. For the list, see Jia Hao and Wang Mingxia, "Market and State: Changing Central-Local Relations in China," in Jia Hao and Lin Zhimin (eds.), *Changing Central-Local Relations in China*, p. 44; Yong-Nian Zheng, "Perforated Sovereignty," pp. 316–318; and *Zhongguo hengxiang jingji nianjian 1992* (Yearbook on China's Horizontal Economic Linkages 1992) (Beijing: Zhongguo shehui kexue chubanshe, 1993). For the 1994 "summit," see *South China Morning Post*, May 20 and August 23, 1994. For the northwestern organization, see Xu Bingwen et al., *Zhongguo xibei diqu fazhan zhanlue gailun* (Survey of Economic Development Strategies in China's Northwest Region) (Beijing: Jingji guanli chubanshe, 1992), pp. 51–55. For the southwestern organization — encompassing Sichuan, Guizhou, Yunnan, Guangxi and Xizang — see *Zhongguo daxi'nan zai jueqi* (The Rise of China's Southwest) (Nanning: Guangxi jiaoyu chubanshe, 1994), pp. 10–18.

19. For the "teaming up" in northwest China, see Xu Bingwen et al., *Zhongguo xibei diqu fazhan zhanlue gailun*, pp. 246–255. And for the pairing of Yunnan and Guangdong, see Segal, *China Changes Shape*, p. 18.

20. *World Tibet Network News* (on Internet), September 21, 1994 and *Liaowang* (Outlook), No. 558 (September 26, 1994), pp. 14–23.

21. See, for instance, Carl Riskin, "Neither Plan Nor Market: Mao's Political Economy," in Joseph, Wong, and Zweig (eds.), *New Perspectives on the Cultural Revolution*, pp. 133–152.

22. Of course, it is not suggested that economic logic has replaced political logic. Rather, economic logic has been mixed with political logic to produce tension and conflicts in the process of reform. See Vivienne Shue, "Grasping Reform: Economic Logic, Political Logic, and the State-Society Spiral," in *China Quarterly*, No. 144 (December 1995), pp. 1174–1185.

23. Xiaowei Zang, "Provincial Elite in Post-Mao China," *Asian Survey*, Vol. 31, No. 6 (June 1991), p. 516.

24. Hainan was an exception in that none of its post-Mao party secretaries were from Hainan, although two were from neighboring Guangdong and Guangxi. In Fujian, both Xiang Nan (1982–86) and Chen Guangyi (1986–94) were natives; in Shandong, Liang Buting (1985–88), Jiang Chunyun (1988–94), and Li Chunting (1995–) were natives; and, in Shaanxi, Ma Wenrui (1978–84), Bai Jinian (1984–87), and An Qiyuan (1994–) were natives.

25. Interviews in Hefei in July 1994.

26. For a list of the committee members and their background information, see *Shandong shengqing 1993* (Facts and Figures of Shandong 1993) (Ji'nan: Shandong shengqingshe, 1993), pp. 49, 659–667. For details of Shandong's intra-provincial cadre transfer program, see Chung, "The Political Economy of Development and Inequality in Shandong," pp. 146–147.

27. For the sectoral and bureaucratic conflicts at the national level, see Susan Shirk, "The Domestic Political Dimensions of China's Foreign Economic Relations," in Samuel S. Kim (ed.), *China and the World: Chinese Foreign Policy in the Post-Mao Era* (Boul-

der: Westview, 1984), pp. 64–70; and Jonathan R. Woetzel, *China's Economic Opening to the Outside World: The Politics of Empowerment* (New York: Praeger, 1989), pp. 146–147.

28. For the expansion of local foreign trade bureaucracies in the reform period, see David Zweig, "'Developmental Communities' on China's Coast: The Impact of Trade, Investment, and Transnational Alliances," *Comparative Politics*, Vol. 27, No. 3 (April 1995), p. 255.

29. "Overseas connections" — often sarcastically called "southern wind" (*nanfeng*) — are important even among ordinary people. In view of their concern with career advancement, local officials must regard them as an invaluable asset in the reform era. For the metaphor, see *Nanbeiji yuekan* (North and South Poles Monthly), November 1988, p. 45.

30. For an extensive list of studies on this issue, see Chung, "Studies of Central-Provincial Relations in the People's Republic of China," p. 498, footnote 26.

31. A one-shot, but comprehensive, study on mayors is found in Cheng Li and David Bachman, "Localism, Elitism, and Immobilism: Elite Formation and Social Change in Post-Mao China," *World Politics*, Vol. 42, No. 1 (October 1989), pp. 64–94. For an aggregate analysis of provincial leaders for 1949–94 on the native issue, see Zhiyue Bo, "Native Local Leaders and Political Mobility in China: Home Province Advantage?" in *Provincial China*, No. 2 (October 1996), pp. 2–15.

32. The most well-known examples include Xi Jinping (son of Xi Zhongxun) in the Fujian provincial standing committee; Yu Zhengsheng (son of Huang Jing) in the Shandong provincial standing committee; Liu Zhen (Liu Shaoqi's son) as the secretary-general of the Inner Mongolian People's Government; Wang Hui (Wang Bingqian's son) as the director of the Shanxi provincial economic commission; Xi Zhengning (son of Xi Zhongxun) as the director of the Henan provincial justice department; and Bo Xilai (son of Bo Yibo) in the Liaoning provincial standing committee.

33. The total number of subprovincial cities was 191 in 1978, 318 in 1985, 476 in 1991 and 619 in 1994. The first three figures are from Wu Peilun, *Dangdai Zhongguo zhengfu gailun* (Overview of Contemporary China's Government) (Beijing: Gaige chubanshe, 1993), p. 182. For the 1994 figure, see *Zhongguo tongji nianjian 1995* (Statistical Yearbook of China 1995) (Beijing: Zhongguo tongji chubanshe, 1995), p. 3.

34. The emergence of cities and counties merits a close examination particularly with regard to their relations with the provinces and the Center (in the cases of special economic zones and central economic cities) and their roles in intra-provincial politics. For studies on subprovincial units, Paul E. Schroeder, "Territorial Actors as Competitors for Power: The Case of Hubei and Wuhan," in Lieberthal and Lampton (eds.), *Bureaucracy, Politics and Decision Making in Post-Mao China*, pp. 283–307; Dorothy J. Solinger, "City, Province and Region: The Case of Wuhan," in Bruce L. Reynolds (ed.), *Chinese Economic Policy* (New York: Paragon, 1988), pp. 233–284; idem., "The Place of the Central City in China's Economic Reform: From Hierarchy to Network?" in Dorothy Solinger, *China's Transition from Socialism: Statist Legacies and Market Reforms 1980–1990* (Armonk: M. E. Sharpe, 1993), pp. 205–222; and idem., "Despite Decentralization: Disadvantages, Dependence and Ongoing Central Power in the Inland — the Case of Wuhan," in *China Quarterly*, No. 145 (March 1996), pp. 1–34.

35. For the information on the annual meetings of the CECs, I am indebted to Dorothy Solinger, "Decentralization in Wuhan" (Draft) which was prepared for the "Decentralization in China" project of the World Bank, September 1994, p. 15.

36. See Qingdao Municipal Office for Historical Research, *Qingdao nianjian 1992* (Qingdao Yearbook 1992) (Qingdao: Zhongguo baike quanshu chubanshe, 1993), pp. 70–71.

37. These figures are from an interview in Qingdao in December 1994.

38. For a detailed analysis of these problems, see Zhu Limin et al., "Zhongyang yu difang zhengfu shiquan huafen yu zhineng peizhi wenti yanjiu" (Study of How to Distribute the Rights and Functions of Central and Local Governments), in Wu Peilun (ed.), *Difang jigou gaige sikao* (Thoughts on the Reform of Local Organizations) (Beijing: Gaige chubanshe, 1992), pp. 182–187.

39. See *Foreign Broadcast Information Service: Daily Report-China* (hereafter FBIS), August 12, 1993, p. 16. Also see Ibid., November 9, 1993, p. 33.

40. Interview in Ji'nan in June 1994.

41. The new designation of Chongqing as the fourth centrally administered city will create new tensions and problems in its relations vis-à-vis Sichuan and Beijing.

42. This speculation has benefited from Vivienne Shue, *The Reach of the State: Sketches of the Chinese Body Politic* (Stanford: Stanford University Press, 1988), pp. 54–55.

43. See, for instance, Gong Ting and Chen Feng, "Institutional Reorganization and Its Impact on Decentralization," in Uia Hao and Lin Zhimin (eds.), *Changing Central-Local Relations in China*, pp. 67–88; and Wu Guoguang and Zheng Yongnian, *Lun zhongyang difang guanxi* (On Central-Local Relations) (Hong Kong: Oxford University Press, 1995).

44. An example of the former refers to agriculture-related units such as the "agricultural commission" (*nongwei*), the "rural affairs office" (*nongban*), and the "bureau of agriculture" (*nongyeju*). And an example of the latter is the "economic system restructuring commission" (*tigaiwei*). Other new units include the "economic research center" (*jingji yanjiu zhongxin*), the "poverty alleviation office" (*fupinban*), the "economic cooperation office" (*jingxieban*) and, most recently, the "local tax bureaus" (*difang shuiwuju*).

45. The average number of party and government units at the provincial-level administration was 48 per province in 1983. The figure rose to 68 in 1991. See "Xingzheng guanli tizhi he jigou gaige de shexiang ji jingyan" (Ideas and Experiences Regarding the Administrative Management System and Organizational Reform), in *Jingji yanjiu cankao*, No. 275/276 (May 18, 1993), p. 13.

46. John P. Burns, "China's Nomenklatura System," *Problems of Communism*, Vol. 36, No. 5 (September-October 1987), pp. 36–51 and idem., "Strengthening Central CCP Control of Leadership Selection: The 1990 *Nomenklatura*" constitute such examples.

47. Examples include Jae Ho Chung, "Beijing Confronting the Provinces: The 1994 Tax-Sharing Reform and Its Implications for Central-Provincial Relations," *China Information*, Vol. 9, No. 2/3 (Winter 1994/95), pp. 1–23; Wang Shaoguang, "Central-Local Fiscal Politics in China" and Lin Zhimin, "Reform and Shanghai: Changing Central-Local Fiscal Relations," in Jia Hao and Li Zhimin (eds.), *Changing Central-Local Relations in China*, pp. 91–112, 239–260; Dali Yang, "Reform and the Restructuring of Central-Local Relations"; Christine Wong, "Central-Local Relations in An Era of Fiscal Decline," pp. 691–715; and Michel Oksenberg and James Tong, "The Evolution of Central-Provincial Fiscal Relations in China, 1971–1984: The Formal System," *China Quarterly*, No.125 (March 1991), pp. 1–32.

48. See, for instance, Wei Liqun (ed.), *Shichang jingji zhong de Zhongyang yu difang jingji guanxi* (Central-Local Economic Relationship in the Market Economy) (Beijing: Zhongguo jingji chubanshe, 1994), pp. 33–163.

49. For more detailed discussion of this methodological point, see Chung, "Studies of Central-Provincial Relations in the People's Republic of China," pp. 495–496.

50. For studies on the first type, see note 47; this volume is a good example of the second type, and an effort to combine the first and second is Linda C. Li, *Shifting Central-Provincial Relations in China: The Politics of Investment in Shanghai and*

Guangdong 1978–1993 (Oxford: Oxford University Press, 1998); and for a third-type study, see Jae Ho Chung, *The Politics of Policy Implementation in Post-Mao China: Central Control versus Local Autonomy under Decentralization*, Ph.D. dissertation, University of Michigan, 1993.

51. The degree to which ideological indoctrination and political "witch-hunts" dominate the policy process constitutes an environmental variable for central-provincial dynamics and provincial politics in general (e.g., the impact of the Great Leap Forward and the Cultural Revolution). Yet, this variable becomes largely a constant in explaining interprovincial variation since ideological control tends to have indiscriminate effects across the board.

52. This list is indebted in part to David S. G. Goodman, *Centre and Province in the People's Republic of China: Sichuan and Guizhou, 1955–1965* (Cambridge: Cambridge University Press, 1986), p. 193; Kenneth Lieberthal and Michel Oksenberg, *Policy Making in China: Leaders, Structures, and Processes* (Princton: Princeton University Press, 1988), pp. 330–331, 336–339; and Frederick C. Teiwes, "Provincial Politics in China: Themes and Variations," in John M. H. Lindbeck (ed.), *China: Management of A Revolutionary Society* (Seattle: University of Washington Press, 1971), pp. 116–189.

53. For the "veiled" and indirect articulation of provincial positions in the pre-reform era, see Teiwes, "Provincial Politics in China," pp. 135–136. For more outright expressions in the reform period, see Chung, "Beijing Confronting the Provinces: The 1994 Tax-Sharing Reform and Its Implications for Central-Provincial Relations in China," pp. 16–20.

54. An earlier version of this section on sources appeared in Jae Ho Chung, "Reference and Source Materials in the Study of Provincial Politics and Economics in the Post-Mao Era: A Select List," in *Provincial China: A Research Newsletter*, No. 1 (March 1996), pp. 2–8.

55. "Local gazetteers" (*difangzhi*), alone, amount to over 6,000 different kinds. All provincial-level units except Tibet have so far published about 2,000 gazetteers and 4,000 more will be produced by the end of the century. See *Ming Pao*, October 7, 1995. For the importance of local gazetteers, see Stig Thorgersen and Soren Clausen, "New Reflections in the Mirror: Local Chinese Gazetteers in the 1980s," *Australian Journal of Chinese Affairs*, No. 27 (January 1992), pp. 161–184.

56. They are *Zhongguo nongcun tongji nianjian, Zhongguo chengshi tongji nianjian, Zhongguo shichang tongji nianjian, Zhongguo renkou tongji nianjian, Zhongguo laodong tongji nianjian, Zhongguo wujia tongji nianjian, Zhongguo gongye jingji tongji nianjian,* and *Zhongguo gonghui tongji nianjian*.

57. Some provinces published chronologies instead of document compilations on the issue of decollectivization. See, for instance, *Heilongjiang nongye hezuoshi* (Beijing: Zhonggong dangshi ziliao chubanshe, 1990); and *Hubei nongcun jingji, 1949–1989* (Beijing: Zhongguo tongji chubanshe, 1990).

58. These regional yearbooks are particularly helpful to those whose research focus is on regional comparisons and variations, because they provide lots of intra-regional comparative data.

59. This category of "forty-year" reviews also has two sub-categories: (1) an encompassing version such as *Shandong sishinian* (Shandong in the Last Forty Years) (Ji'nan: Shandong renmin chubanshe, 1989); and (2) a more issue-oriented review like *Guangxi guding zichan touzi sishinian* (Guangxi's Fixed Asset Investment in the Last Forty Years) (Nanning: Guangxi renmin chubanshe, 1990) and *Henan dianli sishinian 1949–1989* (Henan's Electricity in the Last Forty Years) (n.p.: Henan renmin chubanshe, 1992).

60. Most "government reports" are monthly, while a few (such as those of Guangdong and Shaanxi) are bi-weekly.

61. See Harry Harding, "The Study of Chinese Politics: Toward a Third Generation of Scholarship," *World Politics*, Vol. 36, No. 2 (January 1984), pp. 292–293.

62. See, for instance, Harry Harding, "The Evolution of American Scholarship on Contemporary China," in David Shambaugh (ed.), *American Studies of Contemporary China* (Armonk: M. E. Sharpe, 1993), pp. 25, 28; and Avery Goldstein, "Trends in the Study of Political Elites and Institutions in the PRC," *China Quarterly*, No. 139 (September 1994), pp. 729–730.

63. See, for instance, Michel C. Oksenberg, "China Studies toward the Twenty-First Century," in Shambaugh (ed.), *American Studies of Contemporary China*, pp. 325–326. Similar trends can be observed in non-western communities of contemporary China studies. See, for instance, Ryosei Kokubun, "The Current State of Contemporary Chinese Studies in Japan," *China Quarterly*, No. 107 (September 1986), pp. 515–517; and Mark Sidel, "The Re-emergence of China Studies in Vietnam," *China Quarterly*, No. 142 (June 1995), p. 522.

64. The initiation of the new journal *Provincial China: Research, News, Analysis* is one crucial step forward in this direction. For descriptions of international cooperative projects on provincial politics and reform strategies currently under way, see the first issue of the above journal, pp. 29–33 and the second issue, pp. 79–81.

Contributors

Peter T.Y. Cheung is Associate Professor in the Department of Politics and Public Administration, University of Hong Kong. He holds a Ph.D. in political science from the University of Washington, Seattle. His current research interests concern the role of local government in economic reform in Guangdong province, the development strategies of coastal cities, the politics of central-provincial relations, and the external relations of provinces in post-Mao China. He is a member of the editorial committee of *Provincial China*, a foundation fellow of the Centre for Research on Provincial China, Sydney, and a fellow of the Centre of Urban Planning and Environment Management at the University of Hong Kong.

Jae Ho Chung is Assistant Professor in the Department of International Relations at Seoul National University, Korea. He holds a master degree in Chinese history from Brown University and a Ph.D. in political science from the University of Michigan. He previously taught at the Hong Kong University of Science and Technology during 1993–1996. He has contributed more than a dozen of articles to such journals as *The China Quarterly, Studies in Comparative Communism, China Information* and *Pacific Affairs*. He is a foundation fellow of the Centre for Research on Provincial China, Sydney, and member of the editorial committee of *Provincial China*. He is currently editing a book entitled *Sub-provincial Recipes of Development: Cities in Post-Mao China* and authoring a book on the provincial implementation of agricultural decollectivization.

Feng Chongyi is Lecturer in China Studies at the Institute for International Studies, University of Technology, Sydney. He is the author of four Chinese books, *Peasant Consciousness and China, Bertrand Russell and China, Chinese Culture in the Period of the War of Resistance Against Japan,* and *Breaking out of the Cycle: Peasant Consciousness and China this Century*. He also published (with David S.G. Goodman) *China's Hainan Province: Economic Development and Investment Environment*. He is also an adjunct Professor of History at Nankai University, Tianjin.

Keith Forster is currently teaching Asian Studies at Southern Cross University, Australia. He has published widely on the politics and economics of contemporary China, including *Rebellion and Factionalism in a Chinese Province: Zhejiang, 1966–76* and (with Dan M. Etherington) *Green Gold: the Political Economy of China's Post-1949 Tea Industry.* He taught at a Chinese university in the late 1970s and has made extensive research trips there since the late 1980s. In 1998, he will carry out research in China and Holland under the auspices of an Australian Research Council Large Grant and as Senior Visiting Fellow at the International Institute of Asian Studies in Leiden.

David S.G. Goodman is Director of the Institute for International Studies, University of Technology, Sydney. His most recent publications are *China's Provinces in Reform: Class, Community and Political Culture* and (with Gerald Segal) *China Rising: Nationalism and Interdependence.*

Lijian Hong is Lecturer of Chinese at the Department of Asian Languages and Studies, Monash University, Australia. A former research fellow at the Institute of Political Science, Sichuan Academy of Social Sciences, he finished his Ph.D. studies at the Australian National University. His research interests are contemporary Chinese politics, economics and military affairs, with special emphasis on central-local relations in post-Mao China. He has published widely on these areas in both English and Chinese.

Kevin P. Lane is a consultant living in China. He has taught at Dartmouth College and Franklin and Marshall College. He is the author of *Sovereignty and the Status Quo: the Historical Roots of China's Hong Kong Policy*, and currently is working, with Jacques deLisle, on a book that evaluates the dispute over Hong Kong through the lens of legal theory.

Zhimin Lin is Associate Professor in the Department of Political Science at Valparaiso University, Indiana. He holds a master degree in public affairs from Princeton University and a Ph.D. in political science from the University of Washington, Seattle. He co-edited *Changing Central-local Relations in China: Reform and State Capacity* and is currently working on a project on the changing patterns of local politics in Shanghai.

Shawn Shieh received his Ph.D. from Columbia University and is Assistant Professor of Political Science at Marist College in Poughkeepsie, New York. He is currently researching local property rights structures in urban China.

Index

1857 2007 The Harvard Club of Chicago

150 Years of The Harvard Club of Chicago
1857–2007

Edited by Walter L. Keats

Contributing Editors:

Paul L. Choi, Michael J. Cronin, Robert A. Hastings,
Suzanne F. McCullagh, Margaret I. McCurry,
Julie Gage Palmer, M. Faye H. Sinnott

With the assistance of Ethel C. Gofen, Andrew B. Pacelli, and Michael S. Saper

The Harvard Club of Chicago
P.O. Box 350
Kenilworth, Illinois U.S.A. 60043-0350

The Harvard Club of Chicago
P.O. Box 350
Kenilworth, Illinois U.S.A. 60043-0350

ISBN 978-0-9792524-0-2

Front cover: Map of Chicago, 1857. Drawn by James T. Palmatary, lithographed by Herline and Hensel, and published by Braunhold and Sonne. Chicago History Museum.

Back cover: Johnston Gate, Harvard College, 1920. Photograph by Leon Abdalian.

The Harvard Club of Chicago
is honored to dedicate
this sesquicentennial history to
its members, past and present, and to
Drew Faust
Lincoln Professor of History and
Twenty-eighth President
Harvard University

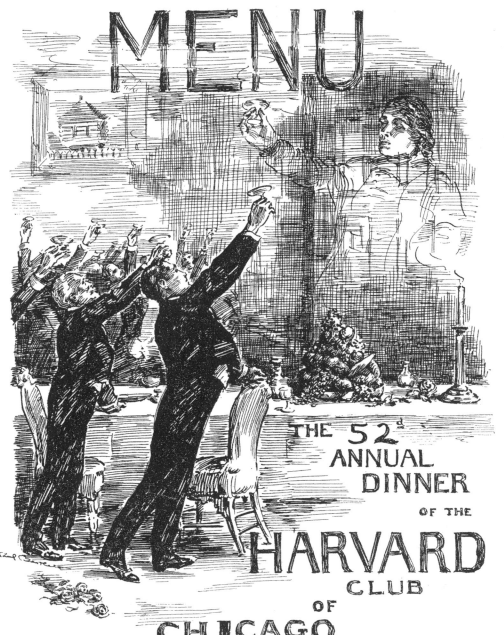

MENU

THE 52ᵈ
ANNUAL
DINNER
OF THE
HARVARD
CLUB
OF
CHICAGO

Contents

Foreward

As one contemplates the history of the Harvard Club of Chicago in this its sesquicentennial year, it is clear that the Club's evolution over the past 150 years has been commensurate with the evolution of the University. The Club grew from a convivial men's club concerned with connectivity across the 1,000-plus miles that separated its original founders not only from their alma mater but from their eastern roots as well. These college men of privilege, while seeking their fortunes in the wild and wooly "West" also sought fellow alumni to share their emigrant experiences. This we are told occurred over strawberries and cream at a Chicago confectionery.

Today, the Club, through all the obvious new communication technologies, maintains close ties to Harvard, and the miles between are breached in nanoseconds, but its current diverse membership (reflecting that of the University) still treasures the camaraderie that inspired its founders to seek out fellow alumni. It continues to send Midwestern contingents in the form of directors and overseers east to strengthen that connectivity and to ensure that voices and views from this city on the inland sea are heard on the eastern seacoast. Club officers return to Cambridge each year to participate in the Club Leadership Conference sponsored by the Harvard Alumni Association (HAA), where best practices are shared.

Proud of being one of the earliest contributors to Midwestern scholarships, the club continues that tradition on a yearly basis. More recently it has raised monies for summer and yearlong undergraduate student internships in not-for-profits, as well as support for graduate students, in each case connected to community service. Many alumni volunteer as tutors and mentors at Walter Payton College Prep, while countless others join the Schools Committee to interview prospective students.

Each year the Club celebrates the accomplishments of its Chicago graduates through numerous conversations and social occasions. Members also enjoy frequent erudite discussions with visiting University professors, and every few years we welcome the current president of the University for a special dinner. This year the Club is proud that Harvard president Drew Faust will celebrate the culmination of our sesquicentennial year with us at a gala dinner in the fall.

Ever with an eye toward invigorating the club while increasing the connectivity of Chicago alumni to the University and to each other, the board is currently engaged in long-range planning analyzing all aspects of its activities as they relate to its mission. In response to present-day University initiatives as presented by the HAA, the Club is about to embark on a long-distance on-line learning experiment entitled "Justice Now" with a most respected Harvard professor, Michael Sandel.

In summary, from our earliest members, the merchant kings, we have added queens and an infinitely broader range of professional leaders. We boast of alumni who head our important universities and cultural institutions and a limitless number of firms, corporations, and not-for-profits, all contributing to the cultural, economic, and civic fabric of Chicago. The threads that weave us together in this interlocking textile are many, in particular, loyalty to the University and fellow alumni, coupled with a desire to participate in the University's pursuit of educational excellence. We Midwesterners value our educational experience in the East and the lifelong learning initiatives instilled in us during those years as we celebrate, in this city of broad shoulders, 150 years of membership in a Club that has maintained its connectivity and commitment to its alma mater for a century and a half.

It has been my pleasure to serve as president of the Harvard Club of Chicago during the preparation of this History.

Margaret I. McCurry

Preface and Acknowledgements

The Harvard Club of Chicago is celebrating its sesquicentennial anniversary in 2007. It is acknowledged as the oldest continuous Harvard Club in existence, leading its near contemporaries, the Harvard Clubs of Boston and Cincinnati. The club in Chicago owes its early success to the determination of a small group of graduates to retain their ties to Harvard and to each other, but its long-term success is due in no small part to the fortunes of the city of Chicago. This historical volume traces the dual trajectories of the Club's relations with the city and the University, a thousand miles to the east, as well as the contributions made by the Club's members to each of them and to the Club itself.

The Harvard Clubs in Boston and Cincinnati had good reasons to consider themselves probable frontrunners as the oldest continuous club. A club for graduates remaining near the University had been founded in Boston in 1855 with lofty goals. However, when the goals proved more ambitious than the members were willing to support, the club folded two years later, and another one was not formed until 1908. For some time the Harvard Club of Cincinnati expected its founding in 1858 might qualify it to be the oldest continuous club. Cincinnati was an early boomtown founded in 1788, forty-five years before Chicago was born in 1833. Cincinnati was also a much larger city in the mid-1800s, according to the 1850 Census, making it the sixth largest city in the United States, with a population of 115,435. At that time Chicago was in twenty-fourth place with just 29,963 inhabitants.

For the first two hundred plus years after its founding in 1636, Harvard remained a fairly small regional university with a traditional educational focus. In the 1850s Harvard still had only twenty-six faculty members teaching forty-eight courses to an enrollment of 529 students (a figure, it should be noted, in line with other well-known schools of the time). The courses were heavily oriented toward Latin, Greek, mathematics, and philosophy, with little to connect students to the realities of a life in commerce or agriculture. Even into the 1880s Harvard had more courses in Latin than in any other subject, reflecting its original mission to provide ministers who could read, write, and speak Latin and Greek, thus able to interpret the Bible for their congregations. Indeed, several of the Chicago Club's founders began their careers after graduation as teachers, for which they were better prepared than for other occupations.

However, major changes were taking place in the mid-1800s that began to draw people to the West, and to Chicago in particular, as a place of opportunity. In 1848, completion of the Illinois and Michigan Canal linked the Great Lakes with the Mississippi River via Chicago. Chicago quickly became the largest inland port.

The city was becoming a main hub for new rail lines that would cross the country and by 1852 it was connected to New York by rail, not through Cincinnati but through Cleveland. By 1854 the railroads that intersected Chicago had crossed the Mississippi River, finally to reach the Pacific Coast in 1869.

The earliest recorded graduate of Harvard to arrive in Chicago was from the class of 1844, with others following from the classes of 1847, 1848, 1849, and then 1855. None had been raised in Chicago. Two were doctors, one a lawyer, one a surveyor (who trained at Rensselaer Polytechnic Institute after graduating from Harvard), and one was in the insurance business. But within the next several decades, sons born and raised in Chicago would attend Harvard to get a "proper" education and then return, often becoming engaged in commerce. While Abraham Lincoln rose to the presidency after educating himself by the light of candles and fireplaces, he would send his son Robert Todd Lincoln to Harvard as a member of the class of 1864.

Fascination with the opportunities available in Chicago led to its rapid growth into a position of great prominence in American industry and culture in the latter part of the nineteenth century. By 1890 the recorded population had surpassed a million persons, making Chicago the second largest city in the United States. The prominence of the Harvard Club of Chicago grew with it.

So too, Harvard as a college, and later as a university, was changing, albeit slowly. Only gradually did it focus on the West, which in the early days meant west of the Hudson. In the 1850s, only 8% of Harvard students came from the West. Theodore Roosevelt, AB 1880, who certainly knew his West, told the Club that Harvard needed more Western men. Harvard eventually set up scholarships to encourage "Western" applicants. The tradition continues today, as aspiring young scholars from across the country and around the world are encouraged to apply to Harvard.

This broadening of outlook and diversification is a dominant theme in the histories of both the University and the Club.

The University has evolved from the early Puritan-dominated college training a few select graduates, many of whom would become ministers, to a University comprised of fourteen "schools." In addition to the College and the Graduate School of Arts and Sciences there are professional schools— Business, Dental, Design, Divinity, Education, Engineering, Government, Law, Medical, and Public Health—as well as the large continuing education school and the Radcliffe Institute, successor to Radcliffe College, a separate institution for the education of women.

The slowly changing demographics of the student body, which reflect both nationwide cultural changes and deliberate admissions policy changes, are an important part of a thread of increasing openness and diversity woven throughout the book. To be admitted to Harvard in the first two and a half centuries of the school's existence, one had to be fluent in Latin and have some knowledge of Greek—a degree of learning that was mainly open only to the privileged and far beyond the offerings of most public schools. As an illustration of the limited access to the school in these early years, the founders of the Harvard Club of Chicago generally came from families that boasted other Harvard alumni and enjoyed relative financial security. It is interesting to note that the Club's first scholarship, given in 1893, was for graduate, not undergraduate, study, presumably reflecting the fact that undergraduates typically had the financial means to attend the College without further assistance from the school.

These changes can be clearly seen as one contrasts some of the earlier biographical sketches with more recent ones. In particular, the Chapter 6 vignette of Katherine Shortall Dunbaugh, AB '12, who received the Medaille d'Argent for her work in France after the 1918 Armistice, reveals vestiges of the earlier pattern of ethnicity, privilege, and interconnectivity interspersed with service and heartbreak. Covered in various later chapters are the dramatic changes in admissions and financial aid policies, including aid-blind admissions, that have allowed minorities and women equal access to Harvard. These changes were undertaken by Harvard out of a sense of the rightness and fairness of these policies, as well as a realization that without them Harvard would begin to lose promising students to more progressive schools around the country.

As changes in the student body occurred, they have in turn been manifested in the Club in a more diverse membership and leadership, particularly in the years since World War II. The Club saw its first woman on the Club's board of directors, Margaret MacGregor Magie, AB '28, in 1954. Others followed on the board and then as officers, a trend culminating in 1984–1986, when Mari DeCosta Terman, AB '57, became the first female president of the Club. Many of the people who benefited from Harvard's more open policies now participate on the Schools Committee, which interviews and recommends prospective students. The Club's first Asian-American president, Desmond C. Wong, MBA '77, presided in 1994–1996. While it has yet to have its first African-American president, African Americans are now common on the board and have been associated with the Club at least since the early 1900s, when Richard T. Greener, AB 1870, the first African-American graduate of the College, retired to Chicago. Today the Club is no longer, as it was for many years, the domain of white men. In 2007, as the Club prepares to welcome Drew Faust, Harvard's first female president, as speaker at its gala centennial dinner on November 9, the Club is led by its second female president, Margaret McCurry, LF '87.

Other themes run through this book, such as the changing commitment of Harvard and its alumni to national service, particularly in the military during wartime. Samuel S. Greeley, AB 1844, relates that during the Civil War, "the quintette of the Harvard Club took ardently to the practice of the infantry drill and the double-quick in a vacant sail loft, though none of the five, so far as I know, enlisted for active service. The roster of the present Club holds the names of many men who served honorably in the war." Steady support continued through subsequent wars, with the Club itself financing a complete ambulance and crew in World War I. During World War II, President Conant could describe Harvard as the second largest military academy in the country. Support for military engagements continued through the Korean War but tapered off significantly with the Vietnam War. Beginning in the

Kennedy years, students were drawn to the Peace Corps and other alternative forms of service in large numbers. In 1969 ROTC programs were eliminated from Harvard altogether, although in recent years interested students have been able to participate via MIT. At present, an unknown but likely small number of graduates have served in the conflicts in Kuwait, Afghanistan, and Iraq.

•   •   •   •   •   •

When I considered how to organize the ample but often disparate materials that document the Club's history, it became readily apparent that a chronological presentation would allow for exploration of not only the facts of that history but also the "whys." Very fortunately, the history falls nicely into three segments of about fifty years. This structure paralleled the digital filing system that was set up to store the several thousand documents and images that had accumulated over many months of intense research prior to the actual writing. The database, which includes much more than the materials used in this book, will be placed online for future historians and those interested in further pursuit of a particular topic.

We owe a great debt to previous Club historians for their contributions. Samuel Sewall Greeley, AB 1844, one of the five founding members of the Club, documented the early years of the Club in an article "The Harvard Club of Chicago," which was published in the *Harvard Graduates' Magazine* in June, 1903. For the second fifty years we turned to a small pamphlet published in 1958 entitled *The Harvard Club of Chicago: A Centennial History*, written by Arthur T. Hamlin, AB '34, university librarian at the University of Cincinnati, as part of his research on the history of the Cincinnati Club.

For the third fifty-year period we had considerable archival materials, both in the Club's Chicago office and available from University records, with which to reconstruct the events, personalities, and social contexts of Harvard-Chicago relations in the modern era. The Harvard University Archives, located in the Pusey Library were particularly helpful. Staff in these and other locations contacted were generous in providing information, referrals, and copies of materials not in the Club's own archives. Very special thanks are due to Marvin Hightower, AB '69, university historian, and Barbara Meloni of the Archives. Among those at the University who graciously filled information requests were Molly Constable, Wallace Dailey, Warren M. Little, AB '55, and Jane Knowles, Kate Moynihan, and Amanda Schmidt of the Schlesinger Library.

A major source for local information on the Club, its activities, and its members was the online digital archives of the *Chicago Tribune*, which go back to 1852. They contained more than 420 articles relating to the Club. Additional materials were found in the Newberry Library, Chicago, and the Chicago History Museum (formerly the Chicago Historical Society). We thank the staff of these institutions for their many hours of assistance in tracking down historical records and images.

The Greeley School in Winnetka, Illinois, and Richard S. Greeley, SB '49, provided information on Samuel S. Greeley, AB 1844. Several Magie family members provided background on the various Harvard relationships of their lineage. Rush Medical College provided information on Edward L. Holmes, AB 1849. Assistance with research on African Americans at Harvard and in the Club graciously came from Caldwell Titcomb, AB '47, AM '49, PhD '52, co-editor of the excellent *Blacks at Harvard*; Alexander L. Jackson IV, AB '70, who helped with background on his family history in Chicago; and Ayana Haaruun of the Chicago Defender.

Many people have helped in hundreds of ways with the research and preparation of this book. At the risk of overlooking some contributions, the Club and the authors wish to express their thanks for the valued assistance of Club members Nancy Berman; Tony D. Brooks, AB '72, MBA '79; Richard C. Burnstine, AB '50, MD '54; John A. Challenger, AB '77; Kellogg Fairbank, Jr., AB '63; John C. Gabbert, AB '68; Ethel Caro Gofen, MAT '59; William P. Hall, AB '45, MBA '48; Alan H. Hammerman, AB '55; C. Anderson Hedberg, AB '57; Christopher G. Janus, SB '36; Sharon E. Jones, AB '77, JD '82;

Joseph V. Messer, AB '53, MD '56; Susan J. Oliver, AB '78; Michael S. Saper, JD '65; Joel H. Schneider, MCRP '82; Adele Smith Simmons, AB '63; Mari DeCosta Terman, AB '57; Clark L. Wagner, LLB '57; and Charles E. Zeitlin, AB '53, LLB '56. Those who contributed chapters and also contributed in many other ways as well are Paul Choi, AB '86, JD '89; Michael J. Cronin, AB '83; Robert A. Hastings, AB '57, MBA '59; Suzanne F. McCullagh, MA '74, PhD '81; Margaret McCurry, LF '87; Julie Gage Palmer, AB '84; and M. Faye H. Sinnott, MBA '74. Andrew Pacelli, AB '04, provided crucial research and writing assistance as press date drew near. Immediate past president Robert Hastings supported the project from the beginning, and current president Margaret McCurry has given unstintingly of her time to guide it toward a successful conclusion.

Particular thanks are due to Karin Kuzniar, our very creative book designer, and Marjorie Pannell, who ably provided editorial services, both of whom endured our late submissions and changes. My wife, Winnie Lu also deserves special thanks for her tireless assistance.

All of us who have been involved with the writing and editing have worked diligently to minimize the possibility of errors in information or attribution, or of other mistakes. Any that have occurred are ours to bear, and corrections of fact would be welcome. The creation of this book and the associated Web site to follow are overwhelmingly the result of innumerable volunteer hours. We hope these efforts will in turn prove useful to those who prepare the bicentennial history of the Club, and to historians interested in relations between Harvard University and its longest continuous and first "Western" club.

Walter L. Keats

Fair Harvard

Fair Harvard! we join in thy jubilant throng,
　　And with blessings surrender thee o'er
By these festival rites, from the age that is past,
　　To the age that is waiting before.
O Relic and type of our ancestors' worth,
　　That hast long kept their memory warm,
First flow'r of their wilderness! Star of their night!
　　Calm rising through change and through storm.

Farewell! be thy destinies onward and bright!
　　To thy children the lesson still give,
With freedom to think, and with patience to bear,
　　And for right ever bravely to live.
Let not moss-covered error moor thee at its side,
　　As the world on truth's current glides by,
Be the herald of light, and the bearer of love,
　　'Til the stock of the Puritans die.

Part I

The Early Years:

1909

1857

From the age that is past . . .

As the Harvard Club of Chicago, the oldest continuous Harvard Club in the country, looks back on the past 150 years, it is fitting to step back and take a fresh look at the history of the Club, the environment in which it developed, how it was formed, how it grew and prospered, and who some of the main actors were in its modest drama. This record recounts the Club's story in the historical context of the city of Chicago, which grew from a small outpost of thirty souls to a major industrial and population center in the time covered by the narrative, and of the much older university a thousand miles to the east. Welcome to "the age that is past."

Chapter 1

The Creation Story

In the beginning there was the pristine prairie, and the large lake. But slowly, almost imperceptibly, the serenity of the prairie felt the tread of inquisitive visitors from the east. In the fall of 1673, thirty-seven years after the founding of Harvard College, Father Jacques Marquette, a French-born Jesuit missionary, and Louis Joliet, a Canadian-born explorer and mapmaker, became the first Europeans to travel through the area. The ensuing years saw only the occasional trader or explorer until late in the century, when two Indian villages were established. In 1696 the French Jesuit missionary Father François Pinet founded the Mission of the Guardian Angel, but abandoned the project in 1700 when his proselytizing efforts proved fruitless.

It wasn't until 1779 (143 years after the founding of Harvard College) that the first permanent settlement was begun, near the mouth of the Chicago River at the site of the present-day Tribune Tower. The pioneer settler was the Haitian Jean Baptiste Point du Sable (c. 1745–1818), the son of a French mariner and a slave mother. Du Sable enjoyed good relations with the indigenous people of the area, marrying the daughter of a Potawatomie chief, and the early name of the settlement, Eschikago, was derived from a Native American word whose exact meaning—possibly "wild onion" or "strong"—has been lost.

Du Sable's homestead saw many firsts for the future city of Chicago, including the first marriage, the first child born, the first election, and the first court of justice. Over the years his settlement became a trading post for travelers crossing the region, attesting to the vigor of the Great Lakes, the Ohio River, on the southern border of the state, and the major north-south rivers—the Illinois, Kankakee, Wabash, and Mississippi—as transportation conduits. For unknown reasons, however, on May 7, 1800, du Sable sold his entire property to John Kinzie, a settler from Canada, and moved further west, to Iowa.

The first trace of the future Chicago appears in the Treaty of Greenville, signed on August 10, 1795, between General Anthony "Mad Anthony" Wayne and various Indian tribes at Greenville, Ohio. The Indians had been defeated the previous year by General Wayne at the Battle of Fallen Timbers, and the peace treaty called not only for opening up the Ohio territory for settlement but also for certain tracts of land in the Indian country to be used by the United States for forts and portages—including the tract described as "one piece of land six miles square, at the mouth of the Chicago River, emptying into the southwest end of Lake Michigan." No one at the time could have anticipated that this small, sparsely inhabited tract would, within a few decades, become the bustling center of a fast-growing America.

Even with peace, there were few settlers during this period. The six weeks of overland travel from New York City to Chicago proved an impediment, and there was sparce development perceivable upon arrival. The first settlers entered the territory mainly from the south, following the Ohio and Mississippi Rivers, working their way north and gradually building their numbers until by 1818 the population had climbed above 40,000, and the state of Illinois was formed. Reflecting this pattern of migration and settlement, the capitals of Illinois have all been in the southern half of Illinois. The first capital was in Kaskaskia, at the junction of the Kaskaskia and Mississippi Rivers, about seventy miles north of the confluence of the Mississippi and Ohio Rivers. In 1819 the capital moved to Vandalia, about eighty miles further north along the Kaskaskia River, and from 1839 on it was located in Springfield, another sixty-five miles north. No one in the early years of the state could have anticipated that Chicago would for a time surpass in size and economic importance all but one city in the country.

The gradual northward drift of the population eventually saw an increasing convergence at the mouth of the Chicago River, where the venerable Old Fort Dearborn was first built in 1803. By 1830 the land around the river's mouth had been platted—surveyed into large squares—and was for sale for $1.25 per acre. Travel time from New York City to Chicago had by then fallen to three weeks. In only three more years, in 1833 (197 years after the founding of Harvard College), there were 350 people living in the area, enough to qualify as a town in early Illinois, and Chicago was legally incorporated. Over the next twenty years migrants arrived at the rate of almost five per day, until by the 1850 Census 29,963 residents were recorded within Chicago's boundaries. This was no town of shacks and scruffy pioneers, however. Many of the newly arrived Chicagoans came from New England and brought their Greek Revival–style, wooden homes to the former prairie. They also brought their business skills to take advantage of the economic opportunities available there.

Two developments were most influential in this rapid growth of Chicago. First, the National Road, authorized by Congress in 1806 under Thomas Jefferson, began construction from Cumberland, Maryland, in 1811. It reached Wheeling, Virginia (now West Virginia) on the Ohio River by 1818, allowing travelers to switch from their stagecoaches or Conestoga wagons to river transport. This was the first and only highway in the nation built entirely with federal funds. It was a major catalyst for settlement and trade in the Ohio River Valley and the Midwest. Towns all along the route of the road saw the development of ancillary businesses such as inns, taverns (some estimates are that there was one tavern per mile, all offering food, drink, and accommodations), blacksmith shops, livery stables, boat building, freight hauling,

View of Chicago looking west from Lake Michigan, c. 1830.

View of Chicago looking east toward Lake Michigan, c. 1845.

and the like (By the 1850s, railroads had begun to replace the National Road as the main means of east-west travel. By the 1920s, with the rise of automobiles, the National Road saw new life as U.S. Route 40, but was then superseded in the 1970s by Interstate 70.)

The second development was the construction of the Illinois and Michigan Canal, which linked Lake Michigan via the Chicago River to the Illinois River and on to the Mississippi River and New Orleans. This project had been envisioned and planned from 1822, but construction did not start until 1836 and ended only in 1848, at a cost of more than

$6 million. With the opening of the I&M Canal, Chicago became the largest inland port in the country. Trade, which had been mostly restricted to moving from north to south and from east to west, could now move from south to north and from west to east as well. The railroads quickly saw the opportunities in Chicago, and the succeeding decades saw Chicago become the rail hub of the nation.

In the decade from 1850 to 1860, over 80,000 more migrants arrived in Chicago—an average rate of more than twenty a day. The 1860 Census lists 112,172 residents in the burgeoning city, making it the ninth largest population center

Demographic Statistics from the 1850 Census

Of the top ten cities in population size from the 1850 Census, only four were in the West (considered in the nineteenth century to be west of the Hudson River). Three of the ten were river towns and six seaports, underscoring the significance of waterways for trade and personal transport. The total U.S. population was 23,191,876, a 336% increase from 5,308,483 in 1800.

New York City	515,547	Cincinnati	115,435
Baltimore	169,054	Brooklyn	96,838
Boston	136,881	St. Louis	77,860
Philadelphia	121,376	Spring Garden, PA	58,894
New Orleans	116,375	Albany, NY	50,763

Chicago ranked 24th, with 29,963; Milwaukee ranked 35th, with 20,061; Cambridge, Mass. ranked 45th, with 15,215; and Indianapolis ranked 87th, with 8.091. No other Illinois or California cities, other than Chicago, were in the top 100. A city needed to have more than 7,250 people to rank in the top 100 cities in the United States in 1850. The population was divided 15% urban and 85% rural (it was 6% and 94% respectively in 1800). By 1850 the geographic population center had shifted from near Baltimore in 1800 to western West Virginia, clearly in the West. The national population density had increased from 6.1 per square mile in 1800 to 7.9 in 1850.

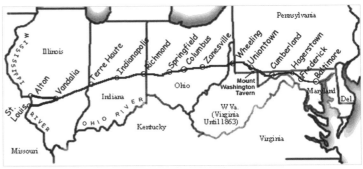

The National Road, now U.S. Route 40.

Chicago River, view east from Rush Street Bridge, c. 1869.

Edward Everett, AB 1811, AM 1814
(PhD 1817 University of Göttingen, Germany)
1794–1865
President of Harvard University 1846–1849
Everett, a clergyman and orator, served in the
U.S. House of Representatives, as governor
of Massachusetts, and as the U.S. minister to
Great Britain before becoming President.

Jared Sparks, AB 1815, AM 1818
(Harvard Divinity School studies 1818)
1789–1866
President of Harvard University 1849–1853
Sparks, a clergyman and historian, served
as the first McLean Professor of Ancient
and Modern History at Harvard.

James Walker, AB 1814, AM 1817
(Harvard Divinity School studies 1817)
1794–1874
President of Harvard University 1853–1860
Walker was the Alford Professor of Natural
Religion, Moral Philosophy, and Civil Polity
at Harvard.

in the United States. With the extension of the railroads to Chicago, travel time from New York City was dramatically reduced to only two days by 1860.

It is in this context that the first Harvard graduates, all from the College, began to filter into Chicago between 1850 and 1857. At least five graduates of Harvard College are known to have been in Chicago by 1857, when two in particular decided to get together with their fellow alumni in the area. In an article published in the *Harvard Graduates' Magazine* in June 1903, Samuel Sewall Greeley, class of 1844, picks up the story of the first meeting of what was to become The Harvard Club of Chicago.

It was probably in the year 1857 that Charles A. Gregory and the present scribe met by chance one day in the early summer, and inquired each of the other, "How many sons of Harvard now dwell in Chicago?" and one answered, "Peradventure we be five." Whereupon it was agreed that as many such as could be found should be summoned to eat, drink, and make merry in good fellowship and in loving memory of Alma Mater."

So said, so done. So far as my memory goes, the men who then met were Samuel S. Greeley (olim Greele), 1844; Dr. Charles G. Smith, 1847; Dr. Edward L. Holmes, 1849; Charles A. Gregory, 1855, and probably Frederick P. Fisher, 1848, five in all. Gregory came to Chicago in 1857, not earlier. The others came some years before that time.

But the individual memory is treacherous, and often shuffles and deals the facts "in ways that are strange and in tricks that are vain." At the historic dinner given by this Club to Mr. Lowell in February, 1887, President Charles G. Smith said that "he could hardly realize that thirty years had passed since eight or ten graduates met at Ambrose & Jackson's restaurant on Clark Street, near where the Grand Opera now is, and organized the Harvard Club." The worthy Doctor clinches his facts with all the minuteness of detail of Dame Quickly's indictment of Falstaff: "Thou didst swear to me upon a parcel-gilt goblet, sitting in my dolphin chamber, at the round table, by a sea-coal fire, upon Wednesday in Wheeson week." Both hostess and Doctor fix time and place beyond cavil and forever.

President Smith was then speaking from a point sixteen years nearer than today to those doings "quaeque ipse omnia vidit, et quorum pars magna fuit." If we may reset an old saw to present use—"Nil nisi verum a mortuis"—the testimony of lips now long sealed in death must be taken as final, and we must record the date as 1857, and the guests as "eight or ten." But what smiling and jovial unboltered Banquos were these that filled the stools, unseen by all save one, and swelled our company from five to eight or ten? We shall never know till dear Doctor Charlie call the roster "d'outre tombe!"

Ambrose & Jackson's restaurant, No. 91 Clark St., first appears in the City Directory of 1861. Our "Noctes Ambrosiannae" must have lasted until that date at least.

Of the original five, named above, the survivors are Greele[y], 1844, and (so far as known) Gregory, 1855, who is no longer living in Chicago.

Our thinking was perhaps high: certainly our fare was plain; strawberries and cream were the limit.
We were, like the conies, but a feeble folk, and I think there was no serious idea that we could ever be of

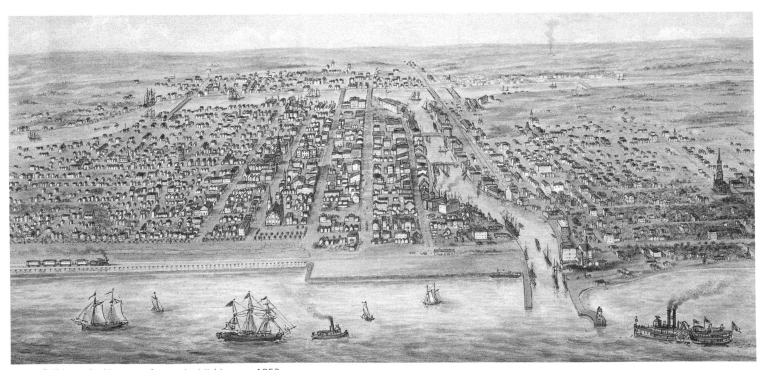

View of Chicago looking west from Lake Michigan, c. 1853.

Soda parlor similar to that of the first meeting of the founders of the future Harvard Club of Chicago, c. 1888.

service to the University. It was good comradeship and the abounding spirits of early manhood that called and held us together. We were pilgrims starting on the voyage of life. We took neither scrip nor purse. We appointed no leader, wrote no record, gathered no treasure. We held perhaps some three or four annual strawberry festivals from 1857 to 1861, at one of which, I think, it was informally agreed that the oldest graduate should be respected as the president, and that Gregory should act as reminding secretary to call the meetings, etc.

Hon. George E. Adams reminds the writer that in the summer of 1860, when he came home, as the first graduate, i.e., the first man who, as undergraduate, hailed from Chicago, The Harvard Club proposed to escort him with a torchlight procession from the station to his home. The plan was abandoned because the members of the Club were not numerous enough to produce the proper impression.

Then in 1861 the war cloud burst upon the land, Fort Sumter fell, there was hurrying to and fro, and the tramp of half-armed men was heard rush to the front at Baltimore and at Cairo. Rifle clubs and companies for military drill were formed in every town and city. The quintette of the Harvard Club took ardently to the practice of the infantry drill and the double-quick in a vacant sail loft, though none of the five, so far as I know, enlisted for active service. The roster of the present Club holds the names of many men who served honorably in the war.

The interest of the Civil War dwarfed all other interests, and the forgotten Harvard Club entered upon the long sleep of the chrysalis, "the world forgetting—by the world forgot."

Although questioning the words of the founding fathers regarding the events of their time is a delicate matter, today's research finds no mention of the Ambrose and Johnson ice cream parlor prior to 1861 in the old city directories. It was Dr. Charles Smith who in 1887 identified this specific ice cream parlor as the site of the historic first meeting, a recollection more than thirty years old at the time. Samuel Greeley did not mention a specific place, although Arthur T. Hamlin in his centennial history of the Club, published in 1958, felt that it was more likely the Anderson's Ice Cream Saloon and Restaurant. There is no conclusive record of the venue, and at a time so far removed from the event itself, probably little need for such specificity.

The early Chicago directories, however, do show that all of the founding members except Gregory are listed prior to and including 1857. Interestingly, the 1857 directory mentions a G. W. Spofford, a teacher at "School No. 9" in Chicago, as having studied at Harvard (he is not listed in the directories from 1837 on, which may only mean that he did not graduate). He is the only teacher listed as having gone to Harvard, whereas at least three are listed as being from Yale. There is no satisfying explanation for this collegial imbalance.

Along these lines, it is noteworthy that Samuel Greeley and Edward Holmes were both teachers after graduation from Harvard. It was only after Greeley attended Rensselaer Polytechnic Institute that he learned the practical skills in math and engineering that led to his future career in surveying. It is highly probable that graduates without family wealth or sinecures were ill-prepared for anything but teaching. Among the original five, two became doctors, one a lawyer (all having had additional training), one a surveyor (again with additional training), and one an insurance agent. None went into the ministry, although all were involved in various church organizations.

Demographic Statistics from the 1860 Census

Of the top ten cities in population from the 1860 Census, only four were in the West (that is, west of the Hudson River). All were located on water. Three of them were river towns and six seaports. The total U.S. population was 31,443,321, a 36% increase from 23,191,876 in 1850.

City	Population	1850 Rank
New York City	813,669	1st
Philadelphia	565,529	4th
Brooklyn	266,661	7th
Baltimore	212,418	2nd
Boston	177,840	3rd
New Orleans	168,675	5th
Cincinnati	161,044	6th
St. Louis	160,773	8th
Chicago	112,172	24th
Buffalo	81,129	16th

San Francisco ranked 15th, with 56,802; Milwaukee ranked 20th (35th), with 45,246 (20,061 in 1850); Cambridge, Mass. ranked 33rd (45th), with 26,060 (15,215); Indianapolis ranked 48th (87th), with 18, 611 (8,091); Peoria ranked 65th, with 14,045; and Quincy ranked 69th with 13,718. A city needed to have more than 9,550 people to rank in the top 100 cities in the United States in 1860, a 32% increase from 1850. The population was divided 20% urban and 80% rural (15% and 85% in 1850). The geographic population center had moved further west, to near Chillicothe, Ohio.

It would also be of interest to know whether any of these Harvard men in Chicago had been exposed to the short-lived Harvard Club of Boston, the first Harvard Club to be established, in May 1855. Charles A. Gregory was certainly at Harvard during this period, as he stayed on after graduation in 1855 to study law for two more years, exactly the period the club was in existence. Arthur T. Hamlin, AB '34, author of *The Harvard Club of Chicago: A Centennial History*, describes the first Boston Club's rise and fall as follows:

It is interesting to compare the Chicago Club with its predecessor, the Harvard Club of Boston, which was established in May, 1855, and went bankrupt in 1857. The Boston group, led by Charles W. Eliot [later to become president of Harvard] and Edward H. Ammidown, had ambitious plans for a social club. They circularized 1,400 alumni, raised several thousand dollars, rented and furnished their club rooms and hired an attendant. In addition they formed an impressive organization of committees and officers. Had these two talented and enthusiastic young men, both 21 years old, made less ambitious plans their club would undoubtedly have prospered. The failure of the original Boston club in 1857 is undoubtedly a principal reason for the relatively late date (1908) of the organization of the current Harvard Club of Boston.

It was Chicago's advantage to have only a few Harvard men on whom to call. The Chicago club lived because it took on increasing responsibilities only as it grew in membership and funds.

In light of the closure of many bricks-and-mortar clubs in the past few decades, it is worth noting the wisdom of the Chicago approach.

Harvard alumni/ae today might not know the meaning of the Latin in Greeley's history, but his contemporaries would have known. Even into the 1880s, thirteen Latin courses, the most for any subject, were taught at Harvard, with Greek a close second. The 1880 Quinquennial directory, although the last to do so, continued to list alumni with Latinized names—for example, "Radulphus-Waldo Emerson, class of 1821" and "Theodorus Roosevelt, class of 1880." This longlasting convention reflected the original mission of Harvard, namely, to train ministers for the colonists, men who had to be conversant in Latin and Greek in order to read and spread the Word. It also marked them as educated men. The dual focus on education and religion—the Puritan legacy—is evident in the language of a tract written by Harvard's first president, Henry Dunster (served 1640–1654), that is thought to be the first historical account of the founding of Harvard College:

After God had carried vs safe to New England and wee had bvilded ovr hovses, provided necessaries for ovr lively hood, reard convenient places for Gods worship and settled the civill government one of the next things we longed for and looked after was to advance learning and perpetvate it to posterity dreading to leave an illiterate ministery to the chvrches when ovr present ministers shall lie in the dvst.

Dunster's work was published in London in 1643 by Thomas Weld and Hugh Peter under the title *New England's First Fruits*. Its function seems to have been to publicize the College to a candidate population across the Atlantic. Dunster himself had been educated in England, holding a BA (1631) and an MA (1634), both from Magdalene College, Cambridge University. The words of the preceeding paragraph are reproduced on a pillar of the famed Johnston Gate, facing Massachusetts Avenue, through which for decades each commencement procession passed.

The end of this period saw the return of the first alumnus of Harvard from Chicago, George Everett Adams, class of 1860. Born in New Hampshire in 1840, he moved to Chicago with his parents in 1853. He attended Phillips Exeter Academy prior to entering Harvard but was a resident of Chicago at the time of his matriculation and for the rest of his life.

George Everett Adams, AB 1860, LLB 1865

June 18, 1840–October 5, 1917

George Everett Adams, class of 1860, was born in Keene, Cheshire County, New Hampshire, on June 18, 1840. He moved with his parents to Chicago in 1853. He attended Phillips Exeter Academy, Exeter, New Hampshire, before entering Harvard, where he graduated eighth in his class of 110.

After returning to Chicago, during the Civil War he enlisted in the First Regiment Illinois Light Artillery. Later he attended and graduated from Harvard Law School. He was admitted to the bar in 1865 and commenced practice in Chicago. He was elected to the Illinois State Senate and served from 1880 until March 3, 1883, when he resigned to enter the U.S. Congress. He was elected as a Republican to the Forty-eighth Congress and the three succeeding Congresses, serving from March 4, 1883, to March 3, 1891. He was an unsuccessful candidate for reelection in 1890 to the Fifty-second Congress, whereupon he resumed his law practice in Chicago.

In 1892, after years of lobbying by Western clubs (now defined as west of the Allegany Mountains) to be allowed to vote for overseers of Harvard, Adams was elected as the first Harvard overseer from the West and served from 1892 to 1904. He died at his summer home in Peterborough, Hillsborough County, New Hampshire, on October 5, 1917. He is buried in Pine Hill Cemetery in Dover, New Hampshire.

Chapter 2

The Founding Fathers

A fair amount of information is available on the five Founding Fathers of the Harvard Club of Chicago. The vignettes provided here reflect what is known of these men. Almost all of the information comes from Arthur T. Hamlin's (AB '34) 1958 *The Harvard Club of Chicago: A Centennial History* and from contemporary articles and obituaries published in Chicago newspapers. The men appear here in order of their graduation from Harvard.

Samuel Sewall Greeley, AB 1844
October 11, 1824–March 8, 1916

Samuel Sewall Greeley, the acknowledged progenitor of our historic Club, was born in Boston on October 11, 1824, the fifth Samuel descended from Andrew Greele (as the name was originally spelled), who arrived in Massachusetts around 1638, only a few years after the founding of Harvard College. One of Samuel Sewall Greeley's relatives, Samuel Sewall, entered Harvard College in 1667. Greeley's father graduated from Harvard College, and several more generations of Greeleys also attended Harvard College.

Samuel Sewall Greeley was only nineteen when he graduated from Harvard in 1844. After teaching in Akron, Ohio, and Plymouth, Massachusetts, he went to live with an uncle who was a minister for a Unitarian Church in Syracuse, New York. This uncle influenced him to be an abolitionist and also to continue his studies for a year at Rensselaer Polytechnic Institute in Troy, New York, where he studied mathematics and surveying. This professional training led to a job in Boston for the next two years helping to survey and build the city's new waterworks. With the money he earned from this work, he and a friend spent several months traveling in Europe, stopping in London, Paris, Rome, Florence, and Liverpool. On his return to the States he secured a job surveying a railroad near Bull Run, Virginia. He was not happy working in the South, however, owing to his colleagues' views on slavery and Northerners. He rejoined his uncle in Syracuse, where he met Frederick Douglas. Back in Boston working for the city again he met two young ladies from Chicago, Ms. Annie M. Larned (whom he later married, in 1855) and Mrs. Joseph Ryerson. Together, they convinced him to come to Chicago, which he did in the fall of 1854.

In Chicago he first tried his hand at bookkeeping but shortly set up his own surveying company, which remained in business until the 1940s. He was elected the city surveyor of Chicago in 1855 on the Know-Nothing ticket and served several terms. During the Great Fire of 1871 his home was destroyed, but he was able to save many of his surveying records, which were of immense help during the reconstruction of the city.

Eventually Greeley and his family moved north of the city to Winnetka, where his descendants have lived to the present day. For his service to the community and his support of education generally, Greeley Elementary School was named for him.

In June 1903, the *Harvard Graduates' Magazine* published his nine-page article, "The Harvard Club of Chicago," which summarized the early history of the Club from its first meeting in 1857. This article serves as the primary source for most of the information known about the early Club.

In 1916, when Greeley died peacefully at the age of ninety-two, he was the oldest living graduate of Harvard.

Samuel Sewall Greeley. AB 1844
A painting by Marriotti hanging in the Greeley School in Winnetka, Illinois

Charles Gilman Smith, AB 1847
January 4, 1828–January 10, 1894

Arthur Hamlin's centennial history offers an intriguing look at the men who gathered to form the Club:

Charles Gilman Smith, AB 1847
A sketch published in an obituary
in the Chicago Daily Tribune

Of the five men known to be at the first meeting, two were physicians in their late twenties. Charles Gilman Smith was born in Exeter, New Hampshire, in 1828. He attended Phillips Academy, entered Harvard in 1844, and graduated with the class of 1847. Smith was a student at the Medical School when that most famous of all Harvard scandals, the Webster-Parkman case, disrupted his studies. He transferred to the University of Pennsylvania and received his medical degree in 1851. Dr. Smith began his practice in Boston and moved to Chicago in December 1852. In Chicago he took part in many civic and professional enterprises. [Alfred T.] Andreas [in his 1886 *History of Chicago*] sums up his life by describing him as "one of Chicago's oldest and most respected practitioners, a leader in social as well as professional circles." Dr. Smith was the first president of the [revived] Chicago Harvard Club. He died in Chicago in 1894.

Dr. Smith in fact served three consecutive terms as president of the Chicago Harvard Club, from 1874 to 1877. Service to others seems to have been a distinct character trait, and one that shaped his life. The obituary that appeared in the *Chicago Daily Tribune*, the city's major newspaper, on January 11, 1894, the day following Dr. Smith's death, paid tribute to a highly skilled physician who sought out opportunities to aid those in need:

During the war he was one of the six physicians placed in charge of the prisoners at Camp Douglas in this city, and in this position he added largely to his reputation as a skillful practitioner. In 1868 Dr. Smith went abroad to study in the hospitals of France, Germany, and England. On his return he lectured in the Women's Medical College for some time. He was next made consulting physician at the Women's and Children's Hospital and at the Presbyterian Hospital. He was also a trustee for several years for the Peck Home for Incurables, in which he took an active interest. Dr. Smith, in addition to his private practice, served a number of the more important insurance companies as their examining physician, a line in which he had an extensive experience. Dr. Smith was recognized as a leader among the most eminent physicians in the Northwest.

The obituary writer also noted Dr. Smith's skills as a toastmaster, and the heartbreaking loss of his 1,500-volume library to the Great Fire. He then "devoted himself to the accumulation of another library . . . including a collection of some seventy volumes of epitaphs." A personal friend of Oliver Wendell Holmes, Dr. Smith was as much at home in literary circles as on the medical wards.

Frederick Pitkin Fisher, AB 1848
Unknown–August 28, 1886

From Hamlin's centennial history:

Frederick P. Fisher, class of 1848, was a native of Oswego, New York. He attended Williston Seminary before entering Harvard College. After graduation he entered the employ of the Oswego Insurance Company in that city. In 1850 Fisher moved to Chicago and went into insurance. Later on he formed a partnership with his [twin] brother, Francis P. Fisher [AB 1848], which was not unexpectedly named "Fisher Bros." A long newspaper obituary mentions his leadership in church work and in social, literary, and charitable movements.

In its words, "Few of our citizens were more active or better known in the business or social circles of Chicago for the last thirty years. . . . He had a high sense of honor, sterling integrity, and was conspicuous for fidelity to every trust." Fisher served as vice-president of the Harvard Club for 1880–81, and died in Chicago, August 28, 1886.

Edward Lorenzo Holmes, AB 1849, MD 1854
January 28, 1828–February 12, 1900

From Hamlin:

Of equal stature in the community with Dr. Smith and of greater national reputation was Edward L. Holmes of the class of 1849. He was born in Dedham, Massachusetts, in 1828. Family reverses forced him to live extremely frugally during his college years. He taught school for two years to finance his further education, then entered the Harvard Medical School and graduated with the class of 1854. He spent nearly two years in study abroad and began practice in Chicago late in 1856. Dr. Holmes took an active and often leading role in the creation of nearly all the local charitable, educational, and cultural organizations of his day. He was nationally famous as a physician, and for some years was president of Rush Medical College. Dr. Holmes was a leading citizen in the best sense

Edward L. Holmes, AB 1849, MD 1854 in a photograph taken in 1888.

of the term. He served several terms as vice-president of the Harvard Club. He died in Chicago in 1900.

Dr. Holmes's life and contributions to Chicago were celebrated in two eulogies in the *Chicago Daily Tribune* around the time of his death on February 12, 1900. One focused on his professional achievements, noting that he was "connected either in an honorary or in an active capacity with almost every medical institution of importance in Illinois." The second showed the esteem held for him by his colleagues and students, as can be heard in these testimonials:

"Dr. Holmes was as good a man as he was great," said Dr. Nicholas Senn. "He was a remarkable scholar, an influential practitioner, and a great teacher. He never wrote much, but rather directed his energies toward material accomplishments. Rush College, as it stands today, practically owes its existence to him. Personally he was loved by everybody. Although he was severe and exacting, he never resorted to drastic measures. He hardly ever took a vacation. He was kind to the poor, and he was never a money-maker."

. . .

"Dr. Holmes was, perhaps, the leader of specialists in eye and ear diseases," said Dr. George W. Webster. "He was a great General, for he was not contented with knowing all that could be known himself, but he insisted that those subordinate to him assist in the advancement of medical science. In this respect he was a powerful inspiration to young physicians. He urged them to gain rudimentary knowledge early, and to become proficient in practice while they were young."

Charles Augustus Gregory, AB 1855
Unknown–June 2, 1915

Hamlin's biography of Gregory describes the meeting with Greeley as though it was the same day as the first meeting of the five alumni, but Greeley's words are less specific, noting only that they "met by chance one day in the early summer, and inquired each of the other, 'How many sons of Harvard now dwell in Chicago?' and one answered, 'Peradventure we be five.' Whereupon it was agreed that as many such as could be found should be summoned to eat, drink, and make merry in good fellowship and in loving memory of Alma Mater."

We return to Hamlin for the biography of the last Founding Father:

Charles A. Gregory, who chanced to meet Greeley on the street that day when the Harvard Club was conceived, was a graduate of 1855, the youngest member of the group of founders. He had remained in Cambridge an additional year to study law, and was admitted to the Suffolk County bar in April, 1857, following which he went at once to Chicago. In June of that year, when the Club held its first dinner meeting, Gregory must have been just a little homesick and eager to cultivate friends who had attended his college. In later years Gregory prospered in law and real estate. He is mentioned in [Alfred T.] Andreas's [1886] *History of Chicago: From the Earliest Period to the Present* as active in Masonic circles, and stopping his buggy to pick up neighbors fleeing the Chicago Fire on foot. The Secretary's reports of the class of 1855 (Boston, 1865, and Boston, 1880) give details of his business and personal life.

The *Chicago Daily Tribune* of November 21, 1857, showed Gregory already involved with the Chicago Association for the Ministry at Large as its secretary. This association's purpose was the "collection and care of vagrant or neglected children." He was also active in the YMCA organization. By November 9, 1860, he was secretary of the newly formed Chicago Law Institute, apparently a precursor to the Chicago Bar Association. His interests in law and land gave him opportunities on the speakers' circuit. In 1889, he gave a lecture at Harvard under the auspices of the Harvard Natural History Society on the great American desert. According to Gregory, "the arid region extends from the 100th meridian to the Pacific Ocean. . . . The question is how to make this region profitable for agriculture." On April 3, 1895, the *Tribune* reported that "Charles A. Gregory, a member of the bar in Chicago, delivered an address to the collected classes of the law college of the Northwestern University at the Masonic yesterday on 'The Genesis and the Evolution of the Power Behind the Writ.'"

Beginning in the early 1880s, Gregory became involved in a mining transaction that would haunt him for the next twenty years. In 1883 he entered into negotiations with George Butterfield and others for the purchase of some mining property in Maine. Gregory and a business colleague together gave Butterfield 160,000 shares of the Great Sierra Mining Company in exchange for some notes and cash intended to be used to purchase the mining property from one Frederick Pike. Gregory and others involved in the transaction then sailed for England, where they hoped to sell the mining property they had contracted to buy. The sale in London fell through, and the transaction went bad. The resulting lawsuits brought by Gregory against Pike and others wound its way through multiple courts on multiple issues before reaching the U.S. Supreme Court in 1892. Related issues lingered on in several courts until 1902. Gregory's activities through this period suggest that he was in fact functioning at a high level, contrary to Hamlin's contention. The cessation of legal actions in 1902 is the last known evidence of Gregory's life until his reported death on June 2, 1915.

Chapter 3

The Chrysalis Period

S amuel Greeley, our source for the early years of the Club, continues the story, describing the Club's "chrysalis" period, which lasted from the 1861 outbreak of the Civil War through the tragic assassination of the state's most famous citizen, Abraham Lincoln, and concluded with the massive destruction wrought on the city by the Great Fire of 1871:

The interest of the Civil War dwarfed all other interests, and the forgotten Harvard Club entered upon the long sleep of the chrysalis, "the world forgetting—by the world forgot."

The thirteen years following the beginning of 1861 were filled with stirring events, that moulded the life of both the nation and the individual citizen. There were the varying fortunes of the civil war, the failure of the Western and Southern wildcat banks, the financial tragi-comedy of the "stumptail money," the currency famine and the issue of United States greenbacks and postal currency, and

the wild speculations of 1865, the murder of President Lincoln, the close of the war, and then the burning of Chicago. Through these historic events the Harvard Club, made small by its great surroundings, peacefully slumbered, giving no sign of life for fourteen years.

The life of the Harvard Club of Chicago we think may be properly divided into three epochs: the grub, 1858 to 1861; the chrysalis, 1861 to 1874; and the butterfly, 1874 to the present date. Its birth as the grub, like the beginnings of many other high enterprises, lies in the domain of myth; it is prehistoric—that is, being interpreted, it happened before the great Chicago fire of Oct. 9, 1871, which consumed in a night and a day the greater part of the city. It is from this "hegira," or flight of her people, that new Chicago dates.

With the destruction of thousands of buildings, of nearly all public records, and of private papers and

Cornelius Conway Felton, AB 1827, AM 1830
1807–1862
President of Harvard University 1860–1862
President Felton, the Eliot Professor of Greek Literature at Harvard, also served on the Massachusetts Board of Education and as a regent of the Smithsonian Institution.

Thomas Hill, AB 1843, AM 1846 (Harvard Divinity School degree, 1845)
1818–1891
President of Harvard University 1862–1868
President Hill was a clergyman, mathematician, and educator. He served as president of Antioch College immediately prior to becoming Harvard's president.

The Grand Pacific Hotel after the Great Fire of 1871. The Harvard Club held its Annual Dinner of 1874 in the restored building.

monuments, in that grim and unforgotten night, all was lost that could serve to recall to living men the memory that such a club had ever lived. Of the handful of men who had personal knowledge of it and its doings in those distant days, "there lives not three good men unhanged, and one of them is fat and grows old."

A reader from another club might ask, "How can the Harvard Club of Chicago claim to be the oldest continuous Harvard Club in the country when there was an extended period of inactivity, a time that can only be described diplomatically as a chrysalis period?" In answer, several arguments can be made on behalf of the Club.

The first argument is that during the 1800s, a dinner, preferably annual, was the normal way to get together and celebrate. This certainly did not happen. But it is clear that the little band of brothers did maintain contact and have other relationships with each other. Holmes and Smith worked at some of the same institutions, possibly even assisting one or the other to become involved. Greeley stated that "the quintette of the Harvard Club took ardently to the practice of the infantry drill and the double-quick in a vacant sail loft," clearly indicating that the club members engaged in activities together outside of the annual dinner meeting.

The second argument is that there truly were extenuating circumstances at work. A civil war that engulfed the entire nation required the complete attention of its citizens, leaving little time for the social and fraternal activities appropriate to a more leisurely era. Although Chicago was spared actual combat, it was engaged in supplying many of the materials of war, and was even the site of a major prisoner-of-war camp, Camp Douglas, built on sixty acres of land on the South Side that had previously been owned by Illinois's famous senator, Stephen A. Douglas.

Originally built as a training camp for some of the six regiments Illinois assembled for the conflict, it became a prison camp from 1862 through the end of the war. At its peak, it held more than 8,000 prisoners. More than 6,000 prisoners died of wounds and illness and were originally buried in the old City Cemetery in present-day Lincoln Park, with the remains later moved to Oak Woods Cemetery near Jackson Park, the largest Confederate cemetery in the North. A forty-six-foot monument was dedicated at the site in 1895, with President Cleveland and his cabinet in attendance.

Third, the assassination of President Lincoln, a favorite son of Illinois, was a major national tragedy that further darkened the horizon for all citizens, much as the assassinations of President Kennedy, his brother Robert, and Martin Luther King affected the nation in the 1960s.

President Abraham Lincoln's Funeral Procession in Chicago, 1865

Hush'd Be the Camps Today

Hush'd be the camps today,
And soldiers let us drape our war-worn weapons,
And each with musing soul retire to celebrate,
Our dear commander's death.
No more for him life's stormy conflicts,
Nor victory, nor defeat—no more time's dark events,
Charging like ceaseless clouds across the sky.
But sing poet in our name,
Sing of the love we bore him—because you, dweller in
camps, know it truly.
As they invault the coffin there,
Sing—as they close the doors of earth upon him—one verse,
For the heavy hearts of soldiers.

Walt Whitman

And finally, the Great Fire of 1871 added to the inactivity of the Club. The fire destroyed 17,500 buildings, one-third of the buildings in the city, leaving more than 100,000 people, or about one-third of the population, homeless, including Samuel Greeley (and, according to Hamlin, the other four founders). Records were destroyed, and tragically, more than three hundred lives were lost. Interestingly, it appears that Samuel Greeley was able to save his surveying records, which were of great help in reestablishing property lines during the reconstruction.

In a peculiar twist of fate, this gap is not inconsistent with Harvard's own early historical record. Although the date of 1636 is well known and documented, it is less well known that in the succeeding decade or two there were several years when, owing to lack of finances or other reasons, there were no students or graduates. Similarly, the Chicago Club was officially revitalized in 1874. All five of the early members—Greeley, Gregory, Holmes, Smith, and Fisher—and first Chicago alumnus, Adams were present and active in the rebirth, providing living continuity with the earlier, more informal years.

Demographic Statistics from the 1870 Census

Of the top ten cities in population in the 1870 Census, five were in the West (that is, west of the Hudson, and then west of the Alleghany Mountains), a pattern that will hold until the 1960 Census. All were on water. Four were river towns and six seaports. The total U.S. population was 38,558,371, a 23% increase from 31,443,321 in 1860.

City	Population	1860 Rank
New York City	942,292	1st
Philadelphia	674,022	4th
Brooklyn	396,099	3rd
St. Louis	310,864	8th
Chicago	298,977	9th
Baltimore	267,354	4th
Boston	250,526	5th
Cincinnati	216,239	7th
New Orleans	191,418	6th
San Francisco	149,473	15th

Milwaukee was ranked 19th (20th), with 71,440 (45,246); Indianapolis was ranked 27th (48th), with 48,244 (18,611); Cambridge, Mass. was ranked 33rd (33rd), with 39,634 (26,060); Quincy was ranked 55th (69th), with 24,052 (13,718); Peoria was ranked 59th (65th), with 22,849 (14,045); and Springfield was ranked 84th, with 17,364. A city needed to have more than 14,930 people to rank in the top 100 cities in the United States in 1870, a 56% increase from 1860. The population was divided 26% urban and 74% rural (it was 20% and 80% in 1860). The geographic population center has moved further west, to near Cincinnati, Ohio.

Not to be overlooked during this period was the historic year when Richard Theodore Greener, AB 1870 became the first African American to graduate from Harvard College since its founding, 234 years earlier. Upon his retirement from the U.S. Foreign Service in 1905 he relocated to Chicago and was an active participant in the community until his death in 1922.

Perhaps it was the dynamism of a period in which people rallied to overcome the setbacks of the previous decade that motivated these men, or perhaps it was the arrival of reinforcements that turned the tide. By 1870, Chicago's population had almost tripled over that of 1860, to 298,977. The record of the first meeting of the revived Club, officially called the Harvard Association of Chicago, which was held on June 27, 1874, at the rebuilt Palmer House Hotel, indicated an attendance of thirty men, a decided increase from the five participants only seventeen years earlier.

From this distance it is difficult to say precisely what caused the renewal, particularly as no records document it, but the history is clear that from 1874 onward, the Club was fully awake. It would remain so through the end of the 19th and the 20th centuries to the sesquicentennial year of 2007.

Palmer House Hotel in 1875.

Women and Harvard Law

Midwestern states took an early lead over the East in recognizing and educating women for the practice of law, but that lead was hard won. The first licensed woman lawyer in the United States was Arabella Mansfield, who was admitted to the Iowa bar in June 1869. From 1869 to 1873, three women in Illinois—Myra Bradwell, the founder and editor of the *Chicago Legal News*, and Alta Hulett and Ad Kepley, the first women law school graduates in the United States (from the University of Chicago Law School)—attempted to join the Illinois bar but were rejected for various gender-based reasons. The language of the bar admission statute in Illinois used the pronoun he, and was interpreted literally. Ms. Bradwell took her case to the U.S. Supreme Court, which ruled against her. The only dissenting vote came from Chief Justice Salmon P. Chase, who had been appointed by Abraham Lincoln.

Alta Hulett and others drafted a bill that was passed by the Illinois legislature on March 22, 1872. The bill "prohibited gender as a bar to any occupation or profession." Ms. Hulett was required to take the bar examination again, which she passed with the highest score in her class. On June 6, 1873, just two days after her nineteenth birthday, she became the first woman admitted to the Illinois bar.

In that same year two young women, Ellen Martin and Mary Fredrika Perry, applied to Harvard Law School but were denied admission because "it was unacceptable for men and women to use the library at the same time." This did not stop them from becoming lawyers, however, and in 1876 they were the second and third women to be admitted to the Illinois bar.

In 1894, Ida Platt, originally from Cleveland, graduated from the Chicago College of Law and became the first African-American woman to be admitted to the Illinois bar. One source says she was also a cousin of Richard Theodore Greener, AB 1870, the first African American to graduate from Harvard College, and that he lived with her after he retired to Chicago around 1906 until his death in 1922.

Harvard Law School did not open its doors to women until 1950, making it one of the last law schools to do so.

Chapter 4

The Rebirth

As the Club awakens from its temporary slumber, Samuel Greeley continues his story:

On June 27, 1874, in the words of Secretary Goward, "a meeting of the graduates of Harvard University, resident in Chicago, was held at the Palmer House, for the purpose of organizing an alumni association, for an annual meeting and banquet." It was resolved that this association be called "The Harvard Association of Chicago." Secretary Goward reports an attendance of thirty.

From that time forward the Secretary's record and the Chicago papers give evidence of annual business meetings and annual banquets; but no recognition of the real origin of the Club is found till the dinner of December 28, 1884, which is noted as the twenty-eighth. The newspaper report states, erroneously, that the Club was founded in 1856.

Charles William Eliot, AB 1853, AM 1856
1834–1926
President of Harvard University 1869–1909
The longest serving president in Harvard history, Eliot previously had been a professor of mathematics and chemistry at Harvard, and then chemistry at MIT.

As the Club becomes stronger in numbers and influence, it has filial yearnings and a desire for some personal and visible connection with the University, and at the meeting of December 13, 1881, it instructs its committee "to invite the President of the University and several of its Professors to attend the coming dinner, the Club to pay the expenses of the journey." The invitation was accepted, and on January 27, 1882, President Eliot, with Professors Goodwin, Thayer and James, first ate the bread and drank of the cup of a Western Harvard Club. It was the baptism and adoption of an infant already well stricken in years.

Not mentioned in Mr. Greeley's report was the fact that the president for the first three years of the newly revived Club was none other than Dr. Charles Gilman Smith, class of 1847, who was present with him in 1857 at the historic "strawberries and cream" meeting. The vice president was Robert Todd Lincoln, class of 1864, son of the late president, who had co-founded the law firm of Isham, Lincoln and Beale a few years earlier. The revitalized club was called the Harvard Association of Chicago but was not incorporated.

From this modest rekindling the Club renewed its custom of holding regular annual dinners, on October 28, 1875, at the Gardner House with twenty-four attending, and on January 24, 1877, at Kinsley's with twenty attending. On December 31, 1877, a dinner was held at Samuel Johnston's home with fifty attending, followed by another dinner on June 10, 1879, at George E. Adams's home.

Samuel Greeley reports on the memorable dinner at Samuel Johnston's, the Club's president that year, as follows:

It was on the last night of that year that President Johnston gave the Club at his own home the memorable supper, which has since passed into "the annals of a quiet neighborhood." It was a bachelor's abode, and there was no gentle hostess to temper the spirit of revelry. The punch was mixed by the rules laid down by Father Tom in his apocryphal supper of "potluck with the Pope"—"a little hot water, lemon, sugar, and plenty of whiskey; after that every drop of water goes to the spoiling of the punch!" The survivors of that Walpurgis Night may haply still hear in fancy the "Highpiping Pehlevi" of Sam Johnston's quavering song, "It was my last cigar"; and may remember how, when Gregory cheerfully offered to enliven the proceedings with the "Skeleton in Armor," fifty stalwart skeletons in fleshly panoply thundered a prohibitory chorus.

"The night drave on wi' songs and clatter;
And aye the punch was growing better;
The mirth and fun grew fast an' furious,"—

and when the merry crew burst out of doors, some two or three offering with tipsy gravity to help the others home, "The Skeleton in Armor," "The Last Cigar," and "The Harvard 'Rah," were so blended and softened by the crisp, sweet midnight air—"so hallowed and so gracious was the time," that a devout and saintly invalid, lying sleepless in her house, hard by, protested she heard the "Christmas Waits," returned to chant anew the heavenly chorus—"Peace on earth, good will to men!" Alas! We wag the "frosty pow" over follies long since condoned, which we should perhaps now blush to commit anew. Let not the Recording Angel blot the page with a tear "Forsitan et haec olim meminisse jubavit."

Greeley also reports on the memorable but more decorous dinner at the Honorable George E. Adams's home the following year:

In June, 1879, the Club amply redeemed its character for decorum and sobriety at a delightful open air fete given by Pres. and Mrs. George E. Adams on their ample piazzas and lawns, overlooking Lincoln Park and Lake Michigan. But why rehearse in detail the banquets of the Club between the great awakening and the present time, rather than those Barmecide feasts, the undined dinners, in the 14 years' gap—"Hiatus valde flendus"—between the old and the new?

Technological innovation was making Chicago more attractive economically. The development of refrigerated rail cars in 1874 cut the cost of shipping beef to the East Coast by 50%. The population of Chicago rose to 503,185 by 1880, almost doubling from its pre-fire count.

For a third of a century from its founding the Club had kept on the even tenor of its way, eating the appointed dinners for which it seems to have been created, and mainly occupied with its own domestic affairs.

Demographic Statistics from the 1880 Census

Of the top ten cities in population size in the 1880 Census, five were in the West. Four of them were river towns and six seaports. The total U.S. population was 50,189,209, a 30% increase from 38,558,371 in 1870.

City	Population	1870 Rank
New York City	1,206,299	1st
Philadelphia	847,170	2nd
Brooklyn	566,663	3rd
Chicago	503,185	5th
Boston	362,839	7th
St. Louis	350,518	4th
Baltimore	332,313	6th
Cincinnati	255,139	8th
San Francisco	233,959	10th
New Orleans	216,090	9th

Milwaukee was ranked 19th (also 19th in 1870), with 115,587 (71,440); Indianapolis was ranked 24th (27th,) with 75,056 (48,244); Peoria was ranked 67th (59th), with 29,259 (22,849); Quincy was ranked 73rd (55th), with 27,268 (24,052); and Springfield was ranked 100th (84th), with 19,743 (17, 364), for its last appearance in the top 100. A city needed to have more than 19,740 people to rank in the top 100 cities in the United States in 1880, a 31% increase from 1870. The population was divided 28% urban and 72% rural (26% and 74% in 1870.) The geographic population center was still near Cincinnati, Ohio.

On March 21, 1881, the Club changed its name from the Harvard Association of Chicago to The Harvard Club of Chicago, its name to this day. Feeling their oats, the Club members invited, at the Club's expense (presumably meaning at certain wealthy members' expense), President Eliot and several faculty members to attend a Club dinner in Chicago only six weeks after issuance of the invitation. This appears to be the first example of a Harvard president visiting a so-called Western club. As mentioned in an earlier Greeley quote, this historic dinner on January 27, 1882, in the dead of winter, attracted ninety attendees to the fashionable Grand Pacific Hotel.

The Newberry Library in Chicago has a copy of the very elegant cloth-covered menu from the historic 1882 evening (displayed on the following page). In addition, the Club printed a fifteen-page "Book of Songs" for the occasion. The songs were led by the Club Chorister, Frederick S. G. Reed,

Grand Pacific Hotel in 1873, corner of Clark Street and Jackson Boulevard.

class of 1881. This book is also at the Newberry Library. It appears the Club made a "good showing" for this first outing by a Harvard president to the West, as President Eliot came back at least four more times during his tenure (presumably paid for by Club members). In the same year, 1882, the Club produced the first known directory of Chicago Club members. A copy of this hardbound, seventeen-page membership directory is in the Harvard University archives, apparently given to President Eliot. It shows a "membership" of 102 alumni, indicating a tremendous turnout for the dinner for President Eliot. The directory lists four alumni from classes earlier than Samuel Greeley's, including a Rev. Charles Fay, 1829, Cyrus Leland, 1832, Sabin Smith, 1840, and Richard W. Swan, 1842. These four men probably arrived in Chicago some time after 1857, as did the more than ninety other alumni. All five of the original founders are listed as members, as is George E. Adams. Not listed is Robert Todd Lincoln, who had been appointed secretary of war in 1881 by President Garfield and was in Washington during that period.

A local paper described the evening thus:

The tables were very prettily decorated with smilax and baskets of flowers, the former extending from end to end, and the latter being placed at intervals in the centre. The menu was an excellent one, and the service was remarkable even for the Grand Pacific. About a quarter of 11, when the cigars were lighted, Mr. Larned made a neat little speech to which he spoke of their love for their alma mater, and of the work of President Eliot, concluding by introducing him.

The article goes on to describe President Eliot's comments in some detail, including his comments on the fact that at that time, there were only thirty-one students at Harvard from Illinois out of 857 total college students. He asked the assembled alumni to assist in finding and encouraging suitable young men to attend Harvard from the area, as Harvard was becoming more of a national university.

Samuel Greeley goes on to describe the impact President Eliot's visits had not only on the Club but also on the city of Chicago.

The five pastoral visits of President Eliot, the unmitred bishop of a diocese of letters as broad as this boundless continent of ours, have been occasions of the greatest interest. While the President has always aroused the greatest enthusiasm within the Club, the whole city has been his audience. His masterly address on "Municipal Finance" before the Commercial Club, and his noble oration, addressed to the public at large, on "The Aims of the Higher Education," and other minor addresses, have made the people of Chicago his friends and the friends of Harvard.

> By 1883 Harvard had increased the number of faculty to sixty-nine. They taught 160 courses to 969 students, 13% of whom came from the West. There were by then 118 scholarship funds established. Two years later, in 1885, Jeannette Swan Brown became one of the first graduates of the Society for the Collegiate Education of Women. She then moved to Chicago (Maywood) and lived there until her death in 1953.

Bill of Fare
Blue Points on Shell.
Consommé.
Lake Superior Trout Lobster Sauce.
Hollandaise Potatoes.
Braised Capon with truffles.
Fillet of Beef with Mushrooms.
Baked mashed Potatoes. Asparagus.
Sweet Breads.   French Peas.
Croquettes of Chicken.   Cream Sauce.
Roman Punch.
Red Head Duck.   Quail on toast.
Dressed Lettuce.   Shrimp Salad.
Roquefort cheese.   Biscuit.
Cake.   Confectionery.
Fruit Ices. Tutti Frutti. Ice Cream.
Fruit.   Coffee.
The Grand Pacific Hotel
Jan: 27th 1882.

Samuel Greeley describes the period of the 1880s as follows:

For many years the Club has held rigidly to its original purpose as set forth at the meeting of reorganization in 1874. But, relations being now established, it is ready for broader and more practical activity. In June, 1882, "the Secretary is instructed to correspond with the President of the University with reference to nominating a member of the Club to be voted for Overseer at Commencement."

In March, 1885, it orders that a "letter be written to John Williams White, Chairman of the Faculty Committee of Harvard University on athletic sports, expressing hearty sympathy with the late advisory committee of graduates in its action and advice in University boating matters."

By October of the same year we have grown cosmopolitan, though we are still modest. We do not yet suggest an all Europe and America International Regatta of Ironclads on the neutral waters of Lake Michigan. We coyly appoint a committee "to correspond with other Harvard Clubs, and with the University Boat Club, respecting the sending [of] an invitation to the Oxford Boat Club to row a race with Harvard in this country." Later records give no further information as to the correspondence, or the proposed race.

At the annual meeting of October 12, 1886, a resolution was passed looking to "the founding of a University Club after the plan of similar clubs in other cities." The need had begun to be felt for the massing of the forces of the higher life of the community, for cooperation among the alumni of all learned institutions, and for a common home for college men, where they could assemble daily for lunch and for friendly intercourse. A committee was appointed to invite men of other colleges to join Harvard in this enterprise. In January, 1887, at a meeting of this committee it was voted "to ask a committee of Yale men to cooperate with Harvard at once, and that, if they did not, to proceed without their cooperation to take out a charter for the University Club of Chicago." It was further agreed that, with the consent of Yale, the committee ask the cooperation of at least three other colleges with associations in Chicago. Princeton, Williams and Ann Arbor were named as the allies to be sought.

Under these instructions the committee consulted with Yale and other colleges, and on February 15, 1887, at a meeting of college men held at the Grand Pacific Hotel, the University Club was duly started. The organization papers had already been taken out by Messrs. LeMoyne and deWindt of Harvard, Browning of Ann Arbor, and Waller of Princeton. After the early struggles and defeats incident to the youth of such undertakings, the University Club of Chicago is now strong and successful; around its tables and in its parlors may daily be found many of the active and guiding men of the city, sons of many colleges, each ready, when need be, with the war-cry of his clan, but meeting here in the love of the humanities, and in the genial kindliness born of healthy appetites properly appeased.

On February 15, 1887, members of the Harvard Club William M. Le Moyne, AB 1884, and Heyliger A. de Windt, AB 1881, at the request of the Club, convened a meeting at the Grand Pacific Hotel with representatives from the Yale, Princeton, and Ann Arbor (University of Michigan) clubs to found the University Club of Chicago, which was to become the site of many Club meetings and programs.

Of note to all alumni of Harvard but probably not known to them was that in 1889, the Club's second president in the new era, Samuel Johnston, Class of 1855, donated the Johnston Gate to Harvard. Designed by the venerable New York architectural firm of McKim Mead & White, the gate still stands and is a main entrance used at commencement.

YOU ARE INVITED TO ATTEND A MEETING TO ORGANIZE THE

UNIVERSITY CLUB,

TO BE HELD AT THE GRAND PACIFIC HOTEL, CLUB ROOM "A," ON TUESDAY EVENING, FEBRUARY 15, AT EIGHT O'CLOCK.

ALLISON V. ARMOUR,
YALE.

WM. M. LE MOYNE,
HARVARD.

JAMES B. WALLER, JR.,
PRINCETON.

GRANVILLE W. BROWNING,
ANN ARBOR.

HEYLIGER A. DE WINDT,
HARVARD.

Meeting notice to form the University Club of Chicago, February 15, 1887.

THIRTY-THIRD ANNUAL DINNER

THE HARVARD CLUB

SATURDAY FEBRUARY FIFTEENTH

EIGHTEEN HUNDRED AND NINETY

HOTEL RICHELIEU CHICAGO

Top: February 15, 1890, Annual Dinner program showing the new Johnston Gate.
Bottom: The Johnston Gate in 2006.

Samuel Greeley describes it thus:

Annual business meetings and annual dinners occur in order, and are duly registered in the Secretary's book. Upon St. Valentine's Day, 1890, the menu cards of the annual dinner bore an etching of the new memorial "Harvard Gateway," given by bequest to the College by Samuel Johnston, '55. Johnston was the second president of the resuscitated Harvard Club, having been elected in January, 1877.

Samuel Johnston died on October 5, 1886, and, among other public and private bequests, gave "the sum of $10,000 to Harvard University to be used in erecting a Gateway at the main entrance to the Yard." May the Johnston Harvard Gate swing wide to an ever increasing throng of youthful seekers in perpetual memory of the genial giver!

At the close of the 1880s, it was clear the revitalized Club was on its way with an influx of new members from the East (that is, east of the Hudson), a new, closer relationship with Harvard itself in the form of regular visits by the president and other faculty members, and a fraternal relationship with other university graduates in the Chicago area. The coming decades would see even more growth of the Club, and active involvement in the Chicago community, with other newly formed clubs, and with Harvard University.

Samuel Johnston, AB 1855

Unknown–October 5, 1886

Samuel Johnston, AB 1855, a Chicago financier and real estate entrepreneur, was active in civic circles and left a historic legacy through the bequests of his will. Born in Cincinnati in 1833, he took up permanent residence in Chicago after graduating from Harvard. He was Club president for the 1878–1879 year and remained active with the Club while out of office. The *Chicago Daily Tribune*, in naming attendees at the Club's Twenty-eighth Annual Dinner, on December 27, 1884, listed Johnston immediately after the Club president, Henry S. Boutell.

Johnston served as director of the Chicago City Railway Company beginning in 1875, as vice president of the Chicago Exposition of 1876, and on the board of directors of the Interstate Industrial Exposition of 1877—all positions consistent with his professional interest in land development. He also served on the Committee for the 1882 May Festival, a city festival organized by Theodore Thomas, founder and first music director of the Chicago Symphony Orchestra.

Johnston never married. At his death, on October 5, 1886, his will disposed of his fortune along a number of philanthropic avenues. The famed Johnston Gate, the first of the several gates and enclosures that replaced the earlier post-and-beam fence around Harvard Yard, was only one. An equal sum went to the city of Chicago to erect a bronze statue of Shakespeare in Lincoln Park. Far larger sums, however, went to two orphanages, one in Cincinnati, one in Chicago, with the greatest share bequeathed to St. Luke's Hospital, Chicago.

Chapter 5

The Golden Age

With the close of the 1880s and the beginning of the 1890s, the Club's golden age begins. Samuel Greeley, looking back from his perspective in 1903, continues his report in the *Harvard Graduates' Magazine* as follows:

On February 9, 1888, President Eliot honored the Club by paying a second visit. The total absence of all report of the proceedings need not prevent the truthful annalist from declaring that dinner one of the notable incidents in our history.

Several documents from that evening are preserved at the Newberry Library. They show that the dinner was held at the Hotel Richelieu, with approximately one hundred in attendance. A songbook was printed for this occasion as well.

February 9, 1888, Annual Dinner program showing Sanders Theater.

At the end of that year, on December 29, 1888, the Harvard Glee Club and the Harvard Banjo Club entertained Club members at the Central Music Hall, with "not a vacant seat," according to the *Chicago Tribune*.

Demographic Statistics from the 1890 Census

In the 1890 Census, the city of Chicago posted a population of 1,099,850 to pass Philadelphia as the second largest city in America. Chicago continued to hold this No. 2 ranking for 100 years, until the 1990 Census, when it was finally overtaken by Los Angeles. The top ten rankings continue to show five cities each in the West and East. All ten cities were on the water, an indication of the continued importance of water transportation. Four of them were river towns and six seaports. The total U.S. population was 62,979,766, a 26% increase from 50,189,209 in 1880.

City	Population	1880 Rank
New York	1,515,301	1st
Chicago	1,099,850	4th
Philadelphia	1,046,964	2nd
Brooklyn	806,343	3rd
St. Louis	451,770	6th
Boston	448,477	5th
Baltimore	434,439	7th
San Francisco	298,997	9th
Cincinnati	296,908	8th
Cleveland	261,353	11th

Milwaukee was ranked 16th (19th), with 204,468 (115,587); Indianapolis was ranked 27th (24th), with 105,436 (75,056); Cambridge, Mass. was ranked 41st (31st), with 70,028 (52,669); Los Angeles was ranked 57th, with 50,395; Peoria was ranked 71st (67th), with 41,024 (29,259); and Quincy was ranked 96th (73rd), with 31,494 (27,268), for its last appearance in the top 100. A city needed to have more than 30,800 people to rank in the top 100 cities in the United States in 1890, a 56% increase from 1880. The population was divided 35% urban and 65% rural (it was 28% and 72% in 1880.) The geographic population center has moved further west, to near Columbus, Indiana.

Henry Sherman Boutell
AB 1876, AM 1877
March 14, 1856–March 11, 1926

Henry Sherman Boutell, AB 1876, AM 1877, served two terms as president of the Harvard Club of Chicago, from 1885 to 1887. He was admitted to the Illinois bar in 1870 and enjoyed an impressive career as a barrister, politician, and diplomat. In Chicago, he practiced law with Boutell, Currier & Freeman. After becoming a member of the Illinois legislature in 1884, he was elected to Congress on the Republican ticket in November 1897 to fill an unexpired term. His Sixth Illinois District constituents reelected him to serve a full term, from 1898 to 1900. He then represented the Ninth Illinois District from 1902 to 1908. In 1911 President Taft appointed him minister plenipotentiary to Switzerland, in which capacity he served for two years. Upon his return to the United States he took up a position teaching law at Georgetown University, Washington, D.C., from 1914 to 1923. He also served as trustee of Northwestern University and as president of the Phi Beta Kappa Society, the Illinois Society of the Sons of the American Revolution, and the University Club.

During the 1880s and 1890s, many milestones were passed by the Club, the University, and the city. In 1892, after years of prodding by the Harvard Club of Chicago, other Western clubs, and the Associated Harvard Clubs, Harvard allowed George Everett Adams, AB 1860, the first resident of Chicago to attend Harvard, to stand for and be elected an overseer of the University, the first Westerner to hold that office.

Greeley continues:

With the increasing number of Western students at Harvard, and the current of Harvard graduates flowing westward in search of homes and fortunes, it was early felt that the government of the University should not be limited to residents of Massachusetts—that the interests, both of the University and of its Western sons, would be served if one or more Western men should be placed upon the Board of Overseers. This feeling found expression at the informal meeting of June, 1882, already referred to, when the Secretary was instructed to correspond with the President of the University with reference to nominating a member of this Club to be voted for Overseer at Commencement. For several years the matter was kept alive by occasional mention, and at the meeting of November 24, 1891, a committee was appointed to confer with other Harvard clubs on the question of a Western Overseer. At the next annual dinner, on January 3, 1892, the committee reported the answers received from various Harvard clubs, and nominated the Hon. George Everett Adams, '60, as the Western candidate. I find no report by the Secretary of this important meeting, but one of the newspaper reports of the dinner states that "the name of Mr. Adams came as an out of town suggestion, as the only man upon whom the West could combine."

It is part of the history of the University, as well as of this Club, that Mr. Adams was elected at Commencement, 1892, re-elected in 1898—that he has been present at all meetings, except when absent, for short periods, from the country, and that he has rendered efficient and intelligent service as a member of the Board. The thousand miles of travel hence to Harvard have been no greater hindrance to Mr. Adam's attendance than the crossing of Charles River is to members of the Board who dwell in Cambridge and its vicinity.

In 1893 the city of Chicago had its "coming-out" party for the world. It hosted the World's Columbian Exposition in honor of Columbus's "discovery" of the New World four hundred years earlier (yes, it was one year late; it should have been in 1892). Given the devastation of the city in the

Great Fire of 1871 only twenty-two years earlier, it was a great accomplishment and one of which the citizens were duly proud. Four times larger than any previous world's fair, the Exposition covered more than 630 acres and had more than two hundred temporary structures. Only one survived, as the Museum of Science and Industry, which was rebuilt along the Midway Plaisance in permanent materials. During its six-month run, the Exposition recorded more than 27 million visitors, equivalent to 43% of the U.S. population at the time.

Harvard had a significant connection to the Exposition in the person of Frederick Ward Putnam, director of the Peabody Museum of American Archaeology and Ethnology at Harvard. Putnam was hired to put together the Anthropology: Man and His Work exhibit. The exhibit would have almost 50,000 anthropological objects from around the world. Recognizing the importance of this collection, Putnam proposed that it form the nucleus of a new museum in Chicago. This proposal was realized after the fair in the form of the Field Museum of Natural History, one of the great research museums of the world.

The *Harvard Graduates' Magazine* from July 1893 has an article by Merritt Starr, class of 1881 and a lawyer in Chicago, titled "The Sources of Harvard's Population." In the article he reported that for the school year 1892–1893, there were forty-seven undergraduates from Illinois, thirty-one of whom were from the Chicago area. Those thirty-one students

1893 World's Columbian Exposition.

were exceeded only by students arriving from New York City and the state of Massachusetts. Starr also pointed out that although the normal trend at Harvard was for a class to decrease in size from freshman to senior year, for students from the West, the trend seemed to be in the opposite direction. He attributed this to two reasons: one, the number of colleges springing up in the West where students could get a good education closer to home, thus draining away the candidate freshman population at Harvard; and two, a trend for some students who received degrees from colleges in the West to attend Harvard for a second senior year to get a Harvard degree as well. He also noted that at least 75% of the college students were from large cities rather than rural areas, reflecting the national trends toward urbanization and centralization.

Greeley's history now turns to a more serious side of the Club, its early identification of support to Harvard-bound students as a critical part of its mission:

But a Club, however strong in numbers and college enthusiasm, wholly fails of its highest and best life, if it have no other business than to elect officers, eat dinners, and encourage intercollegiate athletics and smokers. The Harvard Club felt the impulse toward the higher living and nobler service, when, at the meeting of November 24, 1893, on motion of William Eliot Furness, '60, it resolved unanimously to appropriate $300 to support a graduate scholarship at Harvard, to be open to graduates of Illinois colleges; and as if to mark the beginning of effective work for others, the splendid silver loving cup, the gift to the Club of J. B. Galloway, '70, "patera mero impleta," made the joyous circuit of the company.

In the autumn of 1894 the committee on scholarship appointed, as the first beneficiary, Mr. John Albrecht Walz, a graduate of the Northwestern University, who was reappointed for a second year. From the first the scholarship has been constantly filled by able young men of high standing in their respective colleges, all of whom have amply justified the choice of the appointing committee. By an amendment to the constitution adopted on December 14, 1897, the scholarship became a permanent constitutional feature of the Club.

The Club's $300 graduate scholarship was only the second scholarship to be offered by a Harvard Club or Association. John Walz, who graduated from Northwestern University and received the award in each of its first two years, went on to become professor of German language and literature at Harvard.

February 21, 1896, Annual Dinner program

This award appears to have been a cash award, not from any endowment fund. The Club records show recipients of this award for nineteen straight years, from 1894 through 1913. In twelve of these years the award went to students from Northwestern, in four years to students from Knox College, in two years to a student from Wheaton College, and in one year to a student from Illinois Wesleyan. The *Chicago Daily Tribune* of May 15, 1930, records the award of the Club's graduate scholarship to William K. Maxwell, Jr., the salutatorian of his class at the University of Illinois. Award recipients were selected by a committee of the Club, not by Harvard. It is interesting to speculate from today's perspective that this initial scholarship effort was for graduate studies, since Club members may have presumed, with some justification, that most undergraduates at that time did not require any financial assistance.

Radcliffe College

In 1894 the Society for the Collegiate Education of Women was officially renamed Radcliffe College after Lady Ann Moulson (née Radcliffe; 1576–1661), an early benefactor of Harvard College who in 1643 donated money for the first endowed scholarship. In 1898, Alberta V. Scott became the first African-American woman to graduate from Radcliffe College. After graduating she was recruited by Booker T. Washington to teach at Tuskegee Institute in 1900, but sadly, she became ill and died in 1902.

On February 21, 1896, the Hon. Theodore Roosevelt, class of 1880, addressed the Club's 39th Annual Dinner at the Auditorium Hotel. At the time, Roosevelt was the president of the Board of Police Commissioners of New York City. He had resigned his position as a U.S. civil service commissioner the previous year and would resign this position in 1897 to become the Assistant Secretary of the Navy. Presiding at the dinner was Club president Robert Todd Lincoln, class of 1864.

Scholarship Support

Providing financial support to Chicago-area students at Harvard became, as Greeley notes, a major thrust of the Club's mission. In a losing battle to keep up with the rising costs of tuition and living expenses, the Club established its own Scholarship Endowment Fund (now administered by Harvard), which had a cumulative value of more than $2 million in 2007. In addition, there are a half-dozen other named scholarships, all focused on financial aid for Chicago-area freshman.

Greeley's report continues:

On November 18, 1890, the Club seems to have been awakened to its potential influence in the affairs of the University by a circular from Prof. William M. Davis of the Lawrence Scientific School, presented and supported by H. A. de Windt, '81, "asking the votes of those graduates of the Academic Department, who desired that the other Departments of the University should have a voice in the election of Overseers." No action seems to have been taken upon the proposition at that time.

The Auditorium Hotel's main dining room in the 1890s.

On November 20, 1895, the matter is again brought before the Club; after some discussion in which one man argues at length against the proposed extension, the question is laid over to the next annual meeting, and a committee appointed, who shall investigate the subject and report at the next meeting. George A. Carpenter, '88, Merritt Starr, '81, and Moses J. Wentworth, '68, composed the committee.

On January 6, 1897, in the absence of the Chairman, Mr. Starr submitted the report of the committee. In this report Mr. Starr strongly favors what is known as the "middle ground" plan of extension, recommended to the Board of Overseers in a report made to them on April 12, 1893, by C. J. Bonaparte and A. T. Lyman. Mr. Starr's report is able and exhaustive in its treatment of the subject, and shows a careful, thorough, and dispassionate study of the condition of the Professional Schools, and of their relation to the University. It is one of the most valuable contributions to the literature of this great debate. Resolutions, offered by Mr. Starr, were adopted, approving the principles and conclusion of the "middle ground" report to the Overseers referred to above.

After 17 years of agitation the question is still before the Board of Overseers, undecided, with an increasing minority in favor of the extension of the franchise. It is hoped and expected that the more liberal counsel will prevail and that the desired extension of the franchise may be granted at no distant day.

The Associated Harvard Clubs (AHC) was founded in 1897 with eleven charter members, all "Western" clubs—Chicago, Indianapolis, Kansas City, Louisville, Maryland, Milwaukee, Minnesota, Omaha, Rocky Mountains, St. Louis, and Washington, D.C. As its name implies, this was an association of the various Harvard Clubs west of the Hudson River that had by then sprung up around the country. According to the history of the Harvard Alumni Association, the AHC consisted of fifty-four clubs by 1913, with a combined membership of more than 12,000 alumni.

The new AHC held its first annual meeting on December 18, 1897, in Indianapolis, with George B. Leighton, AB 1888, of St. Louis as chairman and Frederick W. Burlingham, AB 1891, of Chicago as secretary. Subsequent annual meetings were hosted by various clubs around the country, with Chicago known to have hosted meetings in 1899, 1906, 1914, 1926, and 1938.

Arthur T. Hamlin reports the primary impetus for the AHC's formation as "militant action to include western alumni on the Board of Overseers." He goes on to quote George B. Leighton, the first chairman, as follows:

Formerly the belief was general that a Harvard man, when he had crossed the Hudson, passed from all further contact with the college or material interest in her future. He was simply the manufactured article destined to find his sphere of usefulness like a machine distant from the factory and never to return. These days and ideas are past. Harvard looks to the youth of America for her pupils and to the council of her graduates in America for aid and support.

Hamlin continues, noting that at the second annual meeting of the AHC in St. Louis on December 3, 1898,

The Associated Clubs then recommended that constituent member clubs support "a graduate scholarship at Harvard University, open to graduates of the colleges of the state where the club is located."

It is possible that this action was inspired in part by the Harvard Club of Chicago's graduate school scholarship, begun in 1893.

A University sponsored alumni organization, the Harvard Alumni Association (HAA), had been founded in 1840 prior

Avery Coonley, AB1894

Avery Coonley, AB 1894, commissioned Frank Lloyd Wright to design his home, which was constructed in 1907–1908. Now known as the Avery Coonley House, the estate consists of several buildings on the banks of the Des Plaines River, including a Wright-designed playhouse intended for the kindergarten education of Coonley's young daughter. Indeed, the education of children was a primary Coonley interest. The Coonleys founded a school in Downers Grove, Illinois, whose "mission is to provide a learning environment that is appropriate both for academically bright and gifted children, preschool through eighth grade." Coonley was a vice president of the Harvard Club of Chicago in 1913–1914.

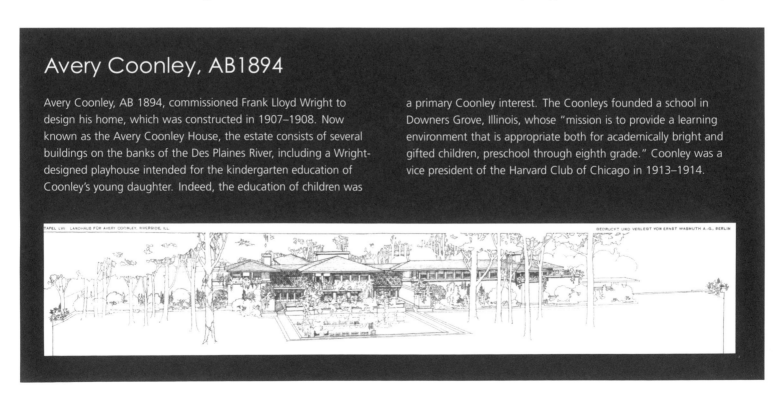

to formation of the Associated Harvard Clubs. Robert Todd Lincoln, AB 1864, was elected the twenty-fourth president of the HAA (and the first from Chicago) in 1898 after he returned from his service in Washington as secretary of war and then as minister plenipotentiary to Great Britain. The AHC and HAA continued as separate organizations until they merged in 1965 under the name Associated Harvard Alumni. In 1982, prior to Harvard's 350th Anniversary celebration, the University-wide alumni organization returned to the original HAA name. Other Chicagoans who later served as presidents of the HAA or the AHA, with their year of service, include William C. Boyden, AB 1886 (1922), Frederic A. Delano, AB 1885 (1932), Laird Bell, AB '04 (1947), Clarence E. Randall, AB '12 (1950), Hermon Dunlop Smith, AB '21 (1958), J. Harris Ward, AB '30 (1966), Henry G. Van der Eb, AB '42 (1981), and most appropriately during the Club's 150th anniversary year, Paul J. Finnegan, AB '75, MBA '82, (2007).

On May 9, 1899, the Club was finally able to officially secure its desired name. A local social club located on the South Side of Chicago at 6325 Harvard Street had incorporated as the Harvard Club in 1889, preventing the Club from incorporating the name. By 1899 the Harvard Club on Harvard Street had become moribund and the "real" Harvard Club was able to have it amicably dissolved and finally incorporate itself as The Harvard Club of Chicago, a "not for pecuniary profit" organization, which it remains to this day.

The other Harvard Club, a social club headquartered on Harvard Street on Chicago's South Side, c. 1870s.

Robert Todd Lincoln, AB 1864
August 1, 1843–July 26, 1926

Born on August 1, 1843, in the Globe Tavern in Springfield, Illinois, where his parents were staying at the time, Robert Todd Lincoln was the oldest and only surviving child of the Lincolns' five. His father, not wanting his son to lack a proper education, saw to it that he attended the University of Illinois, then Phillips Exeter Academy, before entering Harvard with the class of 1864. After graduating and spending four months at Harvard Law School, he entered the army as a captain on the staff of General Grant, in which capacity he witnessed the fall of Petersburg and Lee's surrender at Appomattox.

Tragically, Robert Todd Lincoln was present not only at the assassination of his father but also at the assassination of President Garfield in 1881, and was within sound of the gunshots that killed President McKinley in 1901. After the death of his father, Robert moved with his mother to Chicago to manage the family affairs and to practice law. He was admitted to the Illinois bar in 1867 and was a founding partner of the firm Isham, Lincoln and Beale in 1872. He practiced law in Chicago until 1881, when he was appointed secretary of war by President Garfield and subsequently by President Arthur, serving for four years. In 1889 President Harrison appointed him minister plenipotentiary to Great Britain. He served in this position for four years, returning to Chicago in time for the 1893 World's Columbian Exposition. Upon his return he built a mansion at 1234 Lake Shore Drive, on the northwest corner at Scott, where he lived with his family until 1911. He was elected president of the Harvard Club of Chicago and served two terms, from 1894 to 1896. He became president of the Pullman Company in 1897 and served as president and later chairman until his retirement in 1911. He was also president of the Chicago Historical Society and a member of the Chicago Club and the Union League Club. After retirement he moved to Vermont, where he passed away peacefully at the age of eighty-two on July 26, 1926.

Demographic Statistics from the 1900 Census

The top ten rankings of cities from the 1900 Census show five cities each in the West and in the East (respectively west and east of the Alleganies). All ten cities were on the water, showing the continued importance of water and water transportation. The total U.S. population was 76,212,168, a 21% increase from 62,979,766 in 1890.

City	Population	1890 Rank
New York	3,437,202	1st
Chicago	1,698,575	2nd
Philadelphia	1,293,697	3rd
St. Louis	575,238	5th
Boston	560,892	6th
Baltimore	508,957	7th
Cleveland	381,768	10th
Buffalo	352,387	11th
San Francisco	342,782	8th
Cincinnati	325,902	9th

Milwaukee was ranked 14th (16th in 1890), with 285,315 (204,468); Indianapolis was ranked 21st (27th), with 169,164 (105,436); Los Angeles was ranked 36th (57th), with 102,479 (50,395); Cambridge, Mass. was ranked 41st (41st), with 91,886 (70,028); and Peoria was ranked 67th (71st), with 56,100 (41,024). A city needed to have more than 38,300 people to rank in the top 100 cities in the United States in 1900, a 24% increase from 1890. The population was divided 40% urban and 60% rural. (It was 35% and 65% in 1890, 15% and 85% in 1850, and 6% and 94% in 1800.) It achieved a 50-50 ratio by 1920. The geographic population center was still near Columbus, Indiana. The national population density had increased from 6.1 per square mile in 1800 to 7.9 in 1850 and to 21.5 in 1900.

By the 1890s, both Chicago and the Club were ready to assume more responsibility in the greater community. Samuel Greeley's article in the Harvard Graduates' Magazine notes the philanthropic turn in evidence at the 1903 Annual Dinner:

The annual dinner of the 46th year of the Club's life was held on February 21, 1903, President Benj. Carpenter, '88 presiding. President Eliot was the chief guest of honor, Mr. Orville Franz, 1903, representing the undergraduates, and Prof. G. E. Vincent, of the University of Chicago, speaking for Yale.

F. A. Delano, '85, chairman of the Dunlap Smith Scholarship Committee, after a brief but feeling eulogy of the late Dunlap Smith, reported that nearly $5,000 had been raised, which the Committee hoped soon to increase to $6,000, which this Club "presents to the University for the foundation of a scholarship in memory of one of its ex-presidents—Dunlap Smith, of the Class of 1884, a foremost citizen of Chicago, a loyal alumnus of the College, and a beloved member of the Club, with the request that the foundation shall be forever known as the Dunlap Smith Scholarship."

"The Club requests that the income from this fund shall be paid annually to some meritorious student in the undergraduate department of Harvard College, or in the Lawrence Scientific School, preference being given, upon application, however; first, to the sons of Dunlap Smith; second, to sons of present members of the Harvard Club resident in Chicago or vicinity; third, to other residents of Chicago or its vicinity." Dunlap Smith was a native and lifelong resident of Chicago. Graduating in 1884, he at once went into the real estate business, and soon reached the front rank of the profession. He was the best type of the scholar in trade, conducting the most important transaction with delicacy and skill, handling large trust funds with prudence and fidelity. He died on Christmas morning, 1901, mourned by all who knew him.

President Eliot gave, in his usual clear and persuasive manner, an elucidation and defense of the elective system of Harvard, as offering to each student those courses of study in which he was most likely to succeed in after life.

Mr. Frantz spoke modestly, but with force, of the present interests and pursuits of the undergraduates, and set forth the great benefits already derived from the Harvard Union.

President Carpenter and the Yale champion, the Hoplite of the Eli force, waged a merry war over the merits of their respective colleges; each launched his keenest darts, but neither pierced the other's armor:

"Doubtful it stood;
As two spent swimmers that do cling together.
And choke their art."

That the champion of Yale, after his brilliant philippic, leaning wearily back in his chair, cried faintly to the Ganymede in waiting, "Give me some drink, Titinius," the present deponent is not prepared to affirm.

Just at the close of President Eliot's address, unseen hands displayed from the balcony a banner with this strange device: "In the little village of Winnetka dwell

Theodore Roosevelt giving a speech in Evanston in April 1903.

21 Harvard men, with 57 children, 30 boys and 27 girls. Who says we don't know how to multiply? In the directory of Winnetka, there is no such word as Yale!"

In this, its 46th year, this Club is a united and prosperous body, firm in its loyalty to its Alma Mater, and steadily increasing in numbers and influence. It is hoped that it will always be a valued adjunct to the University, and a potent factor in fostering the higher life of the community wherein its lot is cast.

And thus ends the reading from the Club's first and foremost scribe. Without his prescient efforts to record the Club's early history we would forever be in the dark about these first fifty years. The Club and Harvard owe a great debt to this dedicated, thoughtful alumnus.

To cap this golden age, the Club still had a few arrows in its quiver, Theodore Roosevelt, class of 1880, now President Roosevelt, was the featured attraction of the Club for a reception on May 10, 1905, at the Hamilton Club, a powerful Republican in its day. The *Chicago Daily Tribune* reported that 350 local alumni lined up to greet the president and shake his hand. Included in the line were Samuel S. Greeley, his son Louis Greeley, a classmate of the president at Harvard; William M. Scudder, class of 1899, who had served with the president in Cuba; and Kellogg Fairbank, class of 1890, LLB 1893, president of the Harvard Club. In his remarks to the gathering, President Roosevelt said, "My pet theory has been that the best thing which could happen [to] Harvard would be for the west to win it. I hail every Harvard club west of the Alleganies even more than I do those east, for I feel that Harvard's mission to the country can be incalculably furthered if it has a sufficient amount of western blood, the blood that 'does things' in it. For that reason I am particularly pleased to greet the Harvard Club of Chicago again in as pleasant circumstances as I ever have had the pleasure of greeting it before."

In the following year the 10th Annual Meeting of the Associated Harvard Clubs was held in Chicago. The featured speaker was Col. Henry Lee Higginson, AB 1857, who had donated Soldiers' Field at Harvard (and founded the Boston Symphony Orchestra). He came out to Chicago with a delegation of alumni from Boston and New England. It was estimated that 250 alumni from around the country would join the 500 Club members for the annual meeting. The two-day program began with a "smoker" on Friday evening at the University Club, where, according to the report in the *Chicago Daily Tribune*, alumni smoked "cherished cob pipes and well colored meerschaums" while drinking "steins of cooling beverages" and singing "all the old Harvard songs." The next day the activities included a "special train" to Lake Forest and the Onwentsia Club. Another special train would bring the group back in time for the concluding dinner at the Auditorium Hotel. Over the decades the Harvard Club of Chicago hosted at least six AHC annual meetings and provided many of its presidents, including William C. Boyden, AB 1886, Benjamin Carpenter, AB 1888, and Robert J. Cary, AB 1890.

Radcliffe Club of Chicago Founded

The following news item was reported in the April 1908 edition of the Radcliffe Magazine:

Radcliffe students in and near Chicago have formed a club this winter to unite Radcliffe women of the vicinity in the interests of the college and to make its fame and advantages more widely known. Edith R. Goldthwait, '02, is Secretary-Treasurer of this club.

Richard Theodore Greener, AB 1870
January 30, 1844 – May 2, 1922

Richard Theodore Greener was born in 1844 in Philadelphia to free African-American parents. His father left the family to pursue mining opportunities in California when Greener was about nine, and was later presumed dead. Richard's mother moved to Boston and then to Cambridge in search of educational opportunities for her son. Greener attended the progressive Broadway Grammar School until he was about fourteen, when he left school to support his mother.

Greener was later accepted to Oberlin College, the first American college to admit blacks, through the assistance of one of his employers, teacher and reformer Franklin B. Sanborn. After three years Greener left to pursue his dream, to study at Harvard College. In preparation, he studied at Phillips Andover Academy, excelling in all his courses and graduating in 1865. He entered Harvard that fall at twenty-one, but despite his rigorous preparation had to retake his freshman year. By his sophomore year, and again as a senior, however, Greener won a Boylston Prize for elocution. He received his AB in 1870 with a Bowdoin Prize for his dissertation, becoming Harvard College's first African American graduate.

After graduation Greener became principal of the Male Department at Philadelphia's Institute for Colored Youth (later Cheyney University). In 1873, during Reconstruction, he was appointed professor of mental and moral philosophy at the University of South Carolina, and assisted in the Latin and Greek, Mathematics and Constitutional History departments. Greener also was studying at the Law School, receiving an LLB with honors in 1876. He was admitted to the Supreme Court of South Carolina in 1877 and to the bar of the District of Columbia the next year. Appointment as dean at Howard University's Law Department followed in 1879. Greener also had been elected in 1875 the first African American member of the American Philological Association, the learned society for classical studies.

During the administrations of President McKinley and then President Roosevelt, Greener rose to prominence in national and international affairs. In 1898, he was appointed U.S. Consul to Bombay, India. Transfer to Vladivostok, Russia, as the first American to hold this post, followed. During the Russo-Japanese War in 1904, he represented not only the United States but also the Japanese and British interests in the Russian Far East. After retiring from the Foreign Service in 1906, he traveled and lectured throughout the South. He settled in Chicago in 1910, where he was shown in several reports as a member of the Club.

Part II

1953

1909

The Middle Years

Chapter 6

The Lowell Years

1909–1933

Abbott Lawrence Lowell, AB 1877,
LLB 1880
1856–1943
President of Harvard University
1909–1933
Lowell was a professor of government
and served as the Eaton Professor of
the Science of Government at Harvard.

Abbott Lawrence Lowell (1856–1943) led the University during one of its most vital and challenging eras of definition and growth, from the grace of the Edwardian era in 1909 to the agitated modern world that endured the Depression and saw the rise of dictators in 1933. A strong and visionary president, ironically, Lowell is now remembered more for the shortcomings and errors in judgment that tied him to his past than for his many positive ambitions and accomplishments that were essential to the creation of Harvard as we know it today. Most importantly, Lowell is remembered for his spirited defense of academic freedom.

Born into a prominent Boston family, Lowell was one of five children and the sixth generation of Lowell men to attend Harvard. His younger brother Percival, AB 1886, became a famous astronomer, his younger sister Amy, a renowned poet. In her first poem, written as a child on a family visit to Chicago en route east from California, her family's focus on Boston was made explicitly clear. Unimpressed by the city or its setting, she wrote:

The folks go / on the lake / in sailboat / and barge. / But for all / of its beauty / I'd rather go home / to Boston, / Charles River, / and the / State House's dome.

Lawrence proved to be both a talented athlete and a superior scholar at Harvard, earning his AB in 1877 cum laude with highest honors in mathematics and his LLB in 1880. In his history, *The Harvard Century*, Richard Norton Smith notes that

"[a]s a sophomore, Lowell took both the half-mile and mile races on the same afternoon and annoyed his competitors by looking over his shoulder at them."

Lowell practiced law for seventeen years, marrying his partner's sister, a remote cousin. They never had any children. They must have traveled broadly, as it is said their Marlborough Street home was filled with medieval arms and armor gathered on their journeys. Lowell found the practice of law rather disappointing, and turned to writing about issues of government. Based on his scholarship and involvement in Boston schools, in 1897 he was invited to be a part-time lecturer at Harvard, and was "the first to give his entire attention to Government," as Samuel Eliot Morison observed. His lectures were extremely popular, and the excessive crowding that ensued inspired Lowell in 1903 to anonymously contribute $84,000 to construct the New Lecture Hall (now called Lowell Hall), with a capacity for almost 1,000 students.

In 1900 he was appointed full professor, and quickly became involved in University affairs. As John Bethell in *Harvard Observed* notes, Lowell was Eliot's "most persistent critic." Lowell had criticized Eliot in the *Harvard Graduates' Magazine*:

It is certainly true, whatever the reason may be, that at present we fail to touch the imagination of the students. We awake little spontaneous enthusiasm for knowledge or thought. We arouse little ambition for intellectual power. The elective system, with its liberty for each man to pursue the subject in which he is most interested, was expected to cure that evil; but the elective system, while in some form a necessity, is not a panacea. By encouraging every man to follow his own bent it has, in fact, isolated him; and while promoting individuality, it has broken down the common scholastic bond among the higher students which furnished a strong incentive to excel.

Lowell continued to write. His magnum opus, *The Government of England*, was published in 1908 to great critical acclaim.

Eliot put him at the head of the Committee on Improving Instruction, and in 1909 the faculty approved the Lowell Committee's report calling for less pedagogical emphasis on factual details and more on broad principles and ideas. When President Eliot decided to step down after forty years of leadership in 1909, hoping his colleague Jerome Green would succeed him, there was little question that Lowell was the best candidate for the job. As Samuel Morison wrote,

Lowell's character, talents, background and activity in university reform made him the one logical candidate for the succession; he was elected by the Corporation on January 13, 1909, promptly confirmed by the Overseers, entered upon the duties of the office when President Eliot retired in May, and was formally inaugurated in October. He had high ambition to promote scholarship in Harvard University and to raise the standards of higher education in America. . . . Mr. Lowell's mind has the Greek agility that Eliot's lacked; it acquires knowledge easily and imparts it eagerly. His personality is outgoing and vivacious; he converses rapidly and listens little, yet what he says is always worth hearing.

Whereas Eliot had developed the graduate schools of Harvard, Lowell attended to the undergraduate, and was renowned for mixing with the students more than Eliot ever had. Lowell dismissed Eliot's laissez-faire attitude toward electives and housing in favor of more stringent academic requirements, and he was deeply concerned about the quality of collegiate life. John Bethell further portrays him: "Unlike Eliot, Lowell started his own workday at a relatively late hour, though he was always at Appleton Chapel for daily prayers at 8:45. In morning coat, striped trousers, and starched shirt, set off by a bright red tie, he cut a striking figure. Subordinates found him difficult. He was notoriously unpunctual, and was apt to lose himself in administrative detail."

Admiral Morison observed, "An intellectual aristocrat himself, Mr. Lowell disliked the social divisions that he found in the College. . . . The traditional union of religion, learning and social life no longer existed." While Eliot had sought to shorten the college experience to three years, beginning at age eighteen, Lowell propounded the advantages of men entering college at seventeen for four years, saying, "I believe their character depends not merely on being instructed, but mostly on their living together in an atmosphere of good fellowship." Although Lowell seemed to have won the day, he was haunted throughout his career by the success and continuing presence of his predecessor: Eliot sat on the board of overseers, closely observing his successor.

Morison wrote of the two presidents years later: "The writer, who had the best of both worlds—entering at the zenith of free electives, taking the first distinction examinations, and teaching in the stimulating and challenging atmosphere of the Lowell regime, feels that something was lost when we turned away from Eliot and liberty; but that more was gained."

It would seem that the year 1909 was a time of "no little plans" for either Chicago, with the Burnham Plan for preservation of an open lakefront, or Cambridge, which began construction of the subway in Harvard Square. Just a week after Lowell's election by the Harvard Corporation, he and Eliot spoke at the First Annual Dinner of the Harvard Club of Boston.

Three weeks later, on February 11, 1909, Eliot addressed the 52nd Annual Dinner of the Harvard Club of Chicago at the Congress Hotel–Auditorium Annex, saying, "I have learned tonight what a privileged place the presidency of Harvard is and what a reward awaits the man who serves long with industry, truth, and devotion in that capacity. I do not know how a happier life well could be imagined so far as the work and contact with human life goes." The *Chicago Daily Tribune*, reporting the event the next day, went on to say, "In closing, President Eliot spoke of his successor, Prof. Lawrence Lowell, as in every way fitted for the presidency of the university and declared that the progress of the institution will not suffer from his selection to the office."

Lowell's inauguration on October 6, 1909, characterized by

the usual pomp and circumstance, had in addition substance and vision. In remarks that would inspire educational institutions throughout America, the new president outlined his ideals and his plans for achieving them at Harvard. But before turning to his ideas and eloquent prose, some of the pomp and circumstance with a Chicago connection deserves mention. On the very day of the inauguration, Harvard House at Stratford-on-Avon, England, was formally opened and placed in trust for the University. Built in 1596 by John Harvard's maternal grandfather, it was restored by novelist Marie Corelli with funds from Edward Morris, a wealthy Chicagoan, as a rendezvous place for Americans.

The new president opened his remarks with a dire forecast: "College life has shown a marked tendency to disintegrate, both intellectually and socially." Speaking eloquently and from the heart, Lowell proclaimed: "Surely the essence of a liberal education consists in an attitude of mind, a familiarity with methods of thought, an ability to use information rather than in a memory stocked with facts, however valuable such a storehouse may be. . . . The best type of liberal education in our complex modern world aims at producing men who know a little of everything and something well."

From the first declaring his concern for undergraduate education, Lowell maintained: "If we can increase the intellectual ambition of college students, the whole face of the country would be changed. The object of the undergraduate department is not to produce hermits, each imprisoned in the cell of his own intellectual pursuits, but men fitted to take their places in the community and live in contact with their fellow men."

To achieve this, he suggested requiring undergraduates to make a concentration in one chosen field of at least five of their sixteen elective courses, with a careful distribution of the rest. Taking inspiration from the British Oxbridge system, he advocated instituting a new tutorial system for upper classmen. And to bring a more democratic and enriching life to the campus, he projected the need for freshman housing, saying:

College ought to give its students a wide horizon and it fails therein unless it mixes them together so thoroughly that the friendships they form are based on natural affinities, rather than similarity of origin. Now these ties are formed most rapidly at the threshold of college life, and the set in which a man shall move is mainly determined in his Freshman year. It is obviously desirable, therefore, that the Freshmen should be thrown together more than they are now. . . . One object of a university is to counteract rather than copy the defects in the civilization of the day.

This ambitious vision would not be achieved overnight. One of Lowell's favorite sayings was that you cannot lift a blanket by one corner. As Morison observed, "There must be effort at several points in order to raise the general standard."

On New Year's Day, 1910, President Lowell was fêted at a reception at the University Club of Chicago. Reflecting back on his sister Amy's disdain for Chicago's lakefront, it is amusing to think that in that same year, 1910, Cambridge began tidying up its waterfront with the installation of the Charles River dam, turning mudflats into one of the greatest assets of the University. Lowell began to institute his riverside plan for freshman housing, insisting on the maintenance of red brick Georgian Revival architecture despite great pressure to adopt Gothic Revival. Privately, Lowell and his wife contributed $100,000 for the construction of the third residence hall. As Bethell writes, "The architecture and landscaping of the new halls would transform a dingy commercial riverfront into an arcadian shoreline of handsome buildings and stately trees."

Less than two months later, on February 21, 1910, the Harvard Club of Chicago's 53rd Annual Dinner was held at the University Club, with over 300 attending. The *Chicago Daily Tribune* heralded the occasion, saying "There's always fun to ignite at a function of Chicago's Harvard club, the oldest alumni organization in the west." The guest speaker was Harvey Wiley, "national pure food commissioner" and "chief of the division of chemistry of the United States" (also known as the "Father of the Pure Food and Drugs Act"). The *Chicago Daily Tribune* reported the next day:

Jollity was the keynote of the evening . . . even Prof. Eduard Meyer of the University of Berlin, who is the exchange professor at Harvard, fell a victim to the sway of joviality. "I heard a good illustration of education in the east," he said. "Harvard is the à la carte, Princeton is the table d'hôte, and Columbia the quick lunch.

Discussing the widespread demand that Harvard be made a co-educational institution, Dr. Wiley took up the cudgels for the women and before finishing he nearly committed himself to the proposition of woman suffrage. . . . "What are we going to do with the women anyhow?" he asked. "They are now beating at the gates of Harvard. They are the Trojan horses of the university, and some day they will scale her walls and enter. The women will not be denied. They some day will do the voting, and why should they not? We have not time to stop and argue against them. There is no argument. We had better quit now and let them have their rights. Harvard recognizes the fact that woman is a human being and deserving of an education on an equality with man."

Of more parochial interest, the *Tribune* also heralded one of the local Harvard legends:

The Harvard club of Chicago is particularly fortunate in its quota of real "old grads." It has a choice selection and they never miss a chance to appear before the young and middling collegians and give an object lesson in the beauty of living to an age when you are throned and revered, cherished and cheered. There is a higher eminence even than that, of "old grad"—just one. It is the pinnacle known as "grand old grad." The holder of that gilded title is Samuel S. Greeley of Winnetka, who graduated at Cambridge in 1844—pardon, '44. Mr. Greeley also was a charter member of the Harvard club of Chicago when it was organized in 1857. They didn't have a charter then, for there were only five Harvard men to be raked in the whole city of Chicago. Not until 1874, after a meeting in the new Palmer house, was there any sort of real organization and the cohesion of the first group of five had long since been disrupted. Of the original squad which formed an infant citadel of New England culture in the raw Chicago of 1857, all save Mr. Greeley have gone. The others were Dr. Charles G. Smith, '47; Dr. Edward D. Holmes, '49; Charles A. Gregory, '55; and Frederick P. Fisher, '49. Those were salad days for the Harvard pioneers, but there wasn't any mayonnaise spread on.

Lowell's undergraduate concentration and distribution requirements went into effect in the fall of 1910; students in the class of 1914 also would be the first to be required to pass a language exam in French or German by their junior year. Lowell would comment in his first annual report, "The ordinary student is too apt to treat courses as Cook's tourists do the starred pictures in foreign galleries, as experiences to be checked off and forgotten." Also in that year, Roscoe Pound was called from Chicago to assume the Story Professorship as dean of the Law School.

In 1911, a new city hall was erected in Chicago. In Cambridge, Lowell's building boom was well under way. To promote solidarity, members of the class of 1911 were urged to live in the Yard as seniors. In what Dean Briggs called "a belated tribute to modern civilization," Yard dorms were fitted with bathrooms and showers. Further laurels were bestowed on Chicago with the announcement early in the new year that William C. Boyden of Winnetka had received formal notification of his appointment as chief marshal at the Harvard commencement exercises in June. A member of the class of 1886, LLB 1889, he was a past president of the University Club, of the Harvard Club, and of the Associated Harvard Clubs.

The Associated Harvard Clubs, founded in 1897, pooling alumni from all points west of the Hudson to Minneapolis, celebrated a Harvard Day Banquet at the University Club of Chicago on June 8, 1911. The Chicago Daily Tribune ran the following article on June 4:

"Good Old Hah-vahd" to Have Its Day
Automobile parades and a banquet at the University club will be features of the Chicago stopover celebration. . . . Special cars will arrive in Chicago in the afternoon from Cincinnati and Indianapolis. . . . In the evening, following the banquet, the entire Harvard battalion will march from the University club to the trains, preceded by a band. The "Chicago special" to the Twin Cities will be made up of solid compartment sleeping cars, plus two parlor smoking cars and a diner. Over 100 Chicago men "signed up" for the trip.

A similarly boisterous meeting was reported in the Chicago Daily Tribune of February 22, 1912:

'Frats' Defended Against Wilson; Speaker Before Harvard Club of Chicago Says Good Offsets Evils

Woodrow Wilson, erstwhile president of Princeton University and now Democratic presidential aspirant, last night was assailed before the Harvard Club of Chicago for his assertion that college fraternities are breeders of a false aristocracy and snobbishness. Stevens Heckscher, a Philadelphia lawyer, did the assailing. . . . President Emeritus Charles W. Eliot also was criticized by the Harvard graduate from Philadelphia. "What are the relations between the faculty and students?" he asked. "I remember when I was at Harvard we conferred once at the opening with the adviser and then bid him godspeed for the rest of the year. Students were utterly out of touch with the faculty. We might pass the then president of the university and get a dignified bow, which caused us to look upon him as the head of foreign affairs. I would suggest that relations between students and teachers are not as close as they should or

William Cowper Boyden
AB 1886, LLB 1889
April 6, 1864–May 30, 1929

William Cowper Boyden was a founder of the law firm of Fisher, Boyden, Kales and Bell and became president of the American Bar Association. He served as secretary-treasurer of the Harvard Club of Chicago under Robert Todd Lincoln and as vice president under Samuel Sewall Greely before ascending to the presidency himself in 1899–1900. Both his son and grandson also attended Harvard. William Cowper Boyden, Jr., AB '16, joined his father's law firm, but Boyden III died in a car crash before he could graduate with the class of 1957.

Harvard alumni en route to an annual Associated Harvard Clubs meeting in Minneapolis–St. Paul arriving at the University Club for a banquet, June 8, 1911.

could be. The president of today seems to appreciate the situation and is meeting with the students in their clubs now and then, but in the past there has been a woeful lack of proper relations."

Further measures to tighten up were instituted in 1912, as the Medical and Divinity Schools instituted general exams.

Lowell returned to Chicago for an informal dinner at the University Club on May 8, 1913. He spoke about the progress made on the freshman dormitories, the building of Widener Library (a memorial to Harry Widener, AB '07, who perished in the *Titanic*'s sinking), and outlined "the desirability of men going to college young, preferably not over 17 years of age, so that they might attend a graduate school and still begin their business careers at a reasonably young age and be in a position to marry before they were 30 or during that period," as he said, "when the blood runs strong." The account in the September 13 *Harvard Graduates' Magazine* continued: "Many members of the Club had never before heard Pres. Lowell speak, and the general opinion was that he was perhaps the most absorbing speaker and the one who held his audience best that the club had heard in many years."

Again and again in 1914 Lowell revisited Chicago, attending the Annual Award Dinner on February 21, 1914, at the University Club, and participating in the Associated

Harvard Clubs parade and banquet on June 6, 1914, at the Blackstone. The seeds he sowed on his first visit were expanded during his second. The *Chicago Daily Tribune* for February 22 ran the provocative banner: "SAYS HARVARD IS FOR THE POOR MAN: President Lowell Declares It No Longer Is Merely "Rich Man's College." REVOLUTION IS BREWING." "We hear a great deal about Harvard being 'a rich man's college,'" said President Lowell. "It is, but it is a poor man's college, too. Next fall we will open three new dormitories where men can get rooms for $1 a week. True, they will be chummed with six other men, but that will not hurt them. There is no reason why the poor man at college should not associate with others better off, or they with him."

Consumed with his crusade, Lowell cited "a growing feeling . . . that the tendency of the wealthy students to live in private dormitories outside the yard, involves great danger of a snobbish separation of students on lines of wealth, and is thereby bringing about a condition of things that would destroy the chief value of the College as a place for the training of character. I fear, that with the loss of that democratic feeling which ought to lie at the basis of university life, we are liable to lose our moral hold upon a large part of the students."

As early as 1877 he had advocated construction of dorms large enough to house the great bulk of the students within the College walls. "A college . . . to be successful must be

Freshman residence halls along the Charles River in 1914, later to become part of Winthrop House.

a democracy; and a democracy cannot continue to exist if the richer men live apart by themselves in expensive private dormitories, and the poorer men by themselves in other places, as is becoming more and more the case in Harvard at the present day."

Touting what they predicted would be the largest meeting of Harvard men ever held outside the eastern states, the Chicago Daily Tribune announced, "One Thousand Graduates Will March in Parade June 6." In fact the throng of alumni at the Auditorium Hotel numbered 838, as again they reported: "President Lowell urged a campaign to induce parents to send their boys to college at a younger age. He decried the practice of men leaving school before graduation. He strongly emphasized the importance of the collegiate course as a broad foundation for a professional career." But this was an extraordinary occasion. The Tribune continues:

Previous to the speechmaking, class songs were sung and yells were given. Old men seized younger ones and tangoed between the tables. President Lowell was greeted with a prolonged, deafening Harvard cheer. *What Would John Harvard Say?* "What would he think if he saw these middle-aged men dancing the tango? He'd probably think it all improper, but I'm sure . . . he'd realize it was a genuine Harvard reunion. . . . The business of a college is to make men. It is said man is

More than 800 Harvard alumni march with President Lowell on Michigan Avenue for an Associated Harvard Clubs meeting in Chicago on June 6, 1914.

the noblest work of God, and therefore many must be the hardest thing for human beings to attempt to create . . . the purpose of the college is to prepare men for life, distinct from technical training. It gives a man a broad base line of what men have done and said and thought in the past and of what they are doing and saying and thinking today. . . . Let us not take the joy and pleasure out of college life. Happiness is a great thing if you pursue it and don't let it pursue you.

Chicagoans waxed proud when Samuel Greeley was introduced as the "oldest member of any Harvard club in the world, and grandfather of the Associated Harvard clubs." He replied with a reminiscence of Gen. Grant in Paris, most of which was related in French.

Among notable Club scholarship recipients in those years were Max Blanchard, AB '18, and Charles K. Horwitz, AB '15, LLB '19. Blanchard, an all-around athlete at Calumet High School, had surprisingly won both the 1913 and 1914 New Year's Pullman Road Races. He reportedly then pedaled to Cambridge for freshman year in 1914 on his winning bicycle. Horwitz was one of two Chicagoans in his law school class of just sixty-seven.

It is one of the ironies of history that the same year that Chicago suffered the great *Eastland* disaster in Lake Michigan, Harvard celebrated the dedication of Widener Library by Eleanor Elkins (Mrs. George D.) Widener in memory of her son Harry, AB '07, who went down with the *Titanic*. The year opened with Lowell once again attending the Harvard Club of Chicago's 58th Annual Dinner at the University Club on January 19, 1915.

President Lowell continued to pay considerable attention to Chicago alumni and supporters, perhaps to gain support and funding for his ambitious plans. In Cambridge he had helped launch a building boom by providing $155,000 to build a large red brick president's house at 17 Quincy Street, as well as new quarters for the Varsity Club adjoining the Harvard Union across the street. Lowell, who liked to work by a fireplace, had insisted that every study should have one. And each Varsity Club resident was to have his own bedroom and Harvard armchair.

Having no children of his own, he treated all the undergraduates as his own. Supportive of those who wished to enlist in the war effort, he later wrote to every mother of an undergraduate who was lost in the war and commissioned John Singer Sargent to paint murals in Widener Library in their memory. One of the images is inscribed:

Happy those who with a glowing faith
In one embrace clasped Death and Victory.

Lowell later mused, "The fate of those who died was the more heroic, that of the living more continuous and perplexing . . . the soldier dead, who died in the light, and we, who live on in the dark."

In addition to the monumental events being waged on the world stage in those years, there were many other challenges to President Lowell. Several different incidents of unpopular faculty stances rallied his sense of justice and prompted him to become one of the greatest defenders of academic freedom America has known. Even when his personal views ran counter to those he defended, Lowell is reputed to have said, "If the Overseers ask for Laski's resignation, they will get mine." The defense he gave to law professor Zechariah Chafee, LLB '13, caused Chafee to dedicate his next book,

Free Speech in the United States, to Lowell, "whose wisdom and courage in the face of uneasy fears and stormy criticism made it unmistakably plain that so long as he was president no one could breathe the air of Harvard and not be free." In his report for 1916–17 he gave "a definition of Academic Freedom that has become classic." He reiterated his position in 1918: "The teaching by the Professor in his classroom on the subject within the scope of his chair ought to be absolutely free. He must teach the truth as he has found it and sees it. This is the primary condition of academic freedom, and any violation of it endangers intellectual progress."

With housing projects under way and the curriculum realigned for concentration and distribution, Lowell was gradually achieving his vision for Harvard. By 1917 almost every department had devised general exams for the AB to offset the fragmented, isolated nature of individual courses, and he had also set up a tutorial plan for upper classmen to supplement undergraduate lectures and to encourage individual work.

In the postwar years, Lowell once again was faithful in attending the Harvard Club of Chicago Annual Dinners, including one on February 10, 1919, and another the following year on February 21, 1920. Both occasions were again at the University Club, and at the latter, Lowell elaborated on the validation of his approach. In an article

The Henry Elkins Widener Memorial Library at its dedication on June 24, 1915.

HARVARD CLUB OF CHICAGO

The following telegram has been received by the Harvard Club of Chicago:

Boston, May 18, 1917.
"The Medical Department of the Army has asked Harvard to recruit three ambulance units for immediate service in France for the duration of the war.

The units will have special Harvard insignia and be kept distinct Can you put this opportunity before the younger alumni in Chicago who would be interested?

Age limits eighteen to forty-five."

Further information will be furnished on request by

Joseph Husband, Secretary,
58 E. Washington Street.
Telephone: Majestic 7296.

The Harvard Club received a telegram requesting three ambulance units for service in France near the end of World War i.

in the *Chicago Daily Tribune* wittily titled "Washington's 1 Error: Didn't Go to Harvard," President Lowell was quoted as saying, "We are attempting now to treat each man as a unit. Then we are trying to test what a man is when he gets through, what he knows, and what he is able to do. We are interested in the result instead of in the process. When a man comes to graduate he must submit himself to a general examination on the subject he has taken."

Lowell could make fun of George Washington for not having the intelligence even to try to go to Harvard, but there were a number of areas where his own convictions and upbringing produced blind spots and undermined his many good works and intentions. As tensions grew in the world, these shortcomings became more evident. Unfortunately, today he is more often remembered for his failings in dealing with immigrant populations, African Americans, Jews, homosexuals, and women. It is one of the ironies of history that one of Larry Summers's finer moments was the apology he gave for Lowell's bigotry following a 2002 article by Amit R. Paley in the *Harvard Crimson* revealing his expulsion of eight students and one PhD candidate for being homosexual or associating with them; three of these individuals eventually committed suicide.

Richard Norton Smith identified "his lifelong bias against hyphenated citizenship." In 1912, Lowell became national vice president of the Immigration Restriction League, "feeling keenly that the new immigrants—Italians, Greeks, Slavs, Russian Jews— undermined the Anglo-Protestant culture and threatened the well-being of the country." One of the triumphs of Lowell's vision for an egalitarian living situation at Harvard was the opening in 1914 of three freshman halls to 489 first-year students. Andrew Schlesinger observes that "Lowell saw no inconsistency in hailing 'democracy' and excluding blacks from the halls. He assumed that black students were 'anxious to avoid unnecessary antagonism' and therefore happily established themselves in private houses."

This peculiar assumption and wrong-minded attitude finally blew up when Lowell wrote in 1922 to a black undergraduate

Laird Bell, AB '04
April 6, 1882–October 21, 1965

Laird Bell, AB '04, received a law degree from the University of Chicago in 1907. Two years later he married Nathalie Fairbank, with whom he had four daughters. He became a senior partner of Bell, Boyd, Marshall and Lloyd and a board member of the Liquid Carbonic Corporation, the Chicago Title & Trust Company, and the Weyerhaeuser Company, as president of the *Chicago Daily News*. Bell was a man with significant civic and educational leanings. He served as president of the Harvard Club of Chicago in 1921–22, as president of the Harvard Alumni Association in 1947, and on Harvard's board of Overseers from 1948–54. He also served on the board of trustees of the University of Chicago, for which he was chairman from 1949–53, on the board of Carleton College, and as president of the Winnetka board of education.

Laird Bell's professional appointments underscore his deep interest in the role of the United States in world affairs. From 1937 to 1939 he was president of the Chicago Council on Foreign Relations. Subsequently he served the Allied Control Council's military government in U.S.-occupied Germany as deputy director of its economic division, just after Germany's defeat in World War II. He argued against the U.S. administration's postwar policy, warning that a retributive policy making Germany a wasteland would lead to future war. He took on Senator Joseph McCarthy in 1952, and he defended professors who refused to testify before legislative committees about alleged communist influences on the campus of the University of Chicago. President Eisenhower appointed him alternate delegate to the Tenth Assembly of the United Nations in 1955.

who wanted to live in freshman dormitories, "I am sure you will understand why, from the beginning, we have not thought it possible to compel men of different races to reside together." Many prominent faculty and alumni, including Admiral Morison, signed a petition in outrage. In April 1923, a faculty committee on admissions reported to the board of overseers that the College should "maintain its traditional policy of freedom from discrimination on grounds of race and religion." The board accepted the report and approved a resolution stating "up to capacity of the Freshman Halls all members of the freshmen class shall reside and board in the Freshman Halls, except those who are permitted by the Dean of Harvard College to live elsewhere. In the application of this rule, men of the white and colored races shall not be compelled to live and eat together, nor shall any man be excluded by reason of his color."

This very confusing opinion would seem to have half-heartedly supported Lowell, but, ever watchful for his follower's failings, regarding Lowell's position on integration of residence halls, in 1923 President Eliot wrote, "President Lowell's recent errors are by no means 'of merely academic significance.' They indicate that the Corporation and Board of Overseers should keep incessant watch against his defects, of judgment and good sense."

At about the same time, Lowell noted the rising number of Jewish students and urged a 15% admissions quota similar to those imposed by Columbia and New York University, and to a lesser extent Yale and Princeton. Once again, Lowell was apparently unaware of the error in his judgment, believing he was acting in the best interests of all involved, and was surprised by the severity of the reaction he faced when a letter he wrote to Alfred A. Benesch, a Jewish alumnus from Cleveland, was published in the *New York Times* on June 17, 1922: "The anti-Semitic feeling among the students is increasing, and it grows in proportion to the increase in the number of Jews. If their number should become 40 percent of the student body, the race feeling would become intense. When, on the other hand, the number of Jews was small, the race antagonism was small. And such race feeling among the students tends to prevent the personal intimacies on which we must rely to soften anti-Semitic feeling. If every college in the country would take a limited proportion of Jews, I suspect we should go a long way toward eliminating race feeling among the students."

Once again, the "Jewish problem" was turned over to an admissions committee, including three Jews, and once again

no satisfactory, unambiguous conclusion was reached. Instead of speaking to the issue itself, the committee underscored the desirability of greater geographic distribution and recharted their approach to admissions. It was decided to offer positions to any applicants in the top one-seventh of their class without exams, to draw more students from the South and West. In 1923, they decided to limit the class size to 1,000 and to require on the applications an indication of ethnic identity, religious affiliation, and any change in their name from that of their father. As Schlesinger has pointed out, "admissions effectively reduced [the] proportion of matriculating Jews by considering 'character and fitness' was well as scholastic achievement, in admissions and by making 'regional balance' a factor, as most Jews lived in the Northeast. A passport-size photograph was required as part of the admissions application beginning in 1926."

Richard Norton Smith dealt with the dichotomy of Lawrence Lowell's idealistic vision and unfortunately shortsighted limitations:

The living must grope to find their duty in a twilight and through a labyrinth, said Lowell. His own groping produced his landmark defense of academic freedom. It also stumbled over racial barriers and religious quotas. It was the same aristocratic sense of mission and self-certainty that directed each endeavor, the same thirst to assimilate and mold young men. . . . To his admirers, Lowell was consistent with this conscience in both causes. To critics, however, in the second he was sadly at odds with the spirit of the democratic crusade to which he paid tribute in chapel prose and artist's murals.

One can only imagine what Lowell must have thought of co-education. Ada Louise Comstock, the able president of Radcliffe, discretely alludes to the battles she endured in the following: "There was a hard period of four years. . . . President Lowell saw the defects of the relationship between Harvard and Radcliffe, as they have been seen recently but the cure that was proposed, that of splitting Radcliffe off complete from Harvard, would have been fatal to Radcliffe—fatal at any rate to Radcliffe as we know it and as we believe it should be. Mr. Lowell was a resourceful and determined man; and the struggle, for those four years, was pretty nearly incessant and at times gave us all great anxiety. In the long run I think that struggle did us good. It gave us champions and friends whom we otherwise might have lacked."

In 1924 came the good news that honors candidates could reduce their course load from sixteen to fourteen. A luxurious reading period was instituted for all students. In Chicago, on February 25 of that year, the *Chicago Daily Tribune* reported on the creation of the "Harvard, Yale, and Princeton Club" at 316 Federal Street (later relocated to 321 Plymouth Court). The club was organized to meet the need for a social and athletic organization available to younger graduates immediately after leaving college. The building offered a grill, lounge, squash courts, and bedrooms.

In April 1925, Russell Tyson, AB 1890, of Chicago, former president of the University of Chicago and of the Harvard Club of Chicago, was nominated to the HAA board of directors. It is to this era that Lowell's successful new budget system can be traced. His success as a money manager was combined with a fine fundraising ability that his successor envied. As the Kellers observed in *Making Harvard Modern*, "When Conant told Lowell of the problem of preparing appropriate remarks to the Alumni Association, his predecessor sympathized: 'it is difficult to combine the collection and the benediction.'" To the consternation of Harvard's development officers, Lowell even concluded in the 1920s that Harvard needed no more money and probably never would: "a reduction in large gifts would not be fatal to us now. We have enough for a great university if wisely used." Tuition was $400 in 1928, and a distinguished professor's salary was $12,000 in 1930.

June 3, 1926, marked another regional meeting of the Associated Harvard Clubs in Chicago with President Lowell presiding. It was at about this point that he was able to realize his greatest dream regarding student housing. By 1926,

Marita Odette Bonner Occomy AB '22
June 16, 1898–December 6, 1971

Harlem Renaissance writer Marita Bonner published short stories from 1924 to 1941, sometimes under the pseudonym of Joseph Maree Andrew. She also wrote several plays. Her work deals with issues of race, class, and gender, especially the vulnerability of black women. In 1930 she married William Almy Occomy and moved to Chicago, where she had three children and taught school. Her Frey Street stories are set in Chicago. In 1941 she joined the Christian Science Church and died in 1971 from injuries from a fire in her home.

Exterior of the Harvard-Yale-Princeton Club of Chicago, c. 1924–34.

as Samuel Morison observed, practically all divisions of the faculty had a corps of tutors, and the time seemed ripe to decentralize Harvard College. Lowell proposed to house the upper three classes with their tutors in residential units, each with its own dining hall and common room, and see if some of the old social values of a college education could not be restored. It was Lowell's great good fortune Edward S. Harkness, Yale AB 1897, who had encountered lengthy debate on and no commitment to his offer of residences to Yale, approached Lowell in the fall of 1928. Harkness' contribution of over $13 million made Lowell's dream of more collegial living possible through the creation of seven Houses, three newly erected in 1930 (Dunster, Eliot, and Lowell), and four created from existing residential units (Adams, Kirkland, Leverett and Winthrop). These seven became the major undergirding for the House system that continues in 2007 and now numbers twelve residential Houses. It has been said:

Lowell's crowning achievement was the house system, which became the cornerstone of undergraduate education at Harvard. . . . Along with the Yard itself, this is the part of the University that strikes most beholders as quintessentially Harvardian. The "cloistering" of the Yard (1924–30) and the Business School's new campus (1928) were other landmark projects of the Lowell years. . . . All told, Lowell's 24-year presidency saw the construction of some 60 new buildings—more than Harvard had raised in the 273 years since its founding.

The year 1927 was a big year for Chicago. Midway, the municipal airport, opened, and in January, Barrett Wendell, Jr., AB '02, of Chicago, an overseer, was chosen chief marshal of the alumni for the 1927 Commencement. Life was not so steady back in Boston, where President Lowell occasioned the biggest controversy in his own day for his role in the execution of accused murderers Sacco and Vanzetti. When their murder conviction was reviewed in 1927 with Lowell as chairman of the advisory committee, Harvard became stigmatized as "Hangman's House."

Lowell came to Chicago twice in 1928, attending the Annual Dinner on February 21. The *Chicago Daily Tribune* reported the next day that he claimed "Modern Students Are Better." Extolling the virtues of his new reading period to encourage study, Lowell said, "Under our new system, students are allowed a five weeks' period during which they do their own studying and are not required to report on progress during that period. We have found that the plan is very successful, because present day students take their duties seriously." In June, Lowell returned for the 28th meeting of the Associated Harvard Clubs in Chicago, with more than 2,000 regional alumni expected.

With the backing of generous alumni donations, in 1931 Lowell undertook the construction of Memorial Church in the center of Harvard Yard as a tribute to the 11,000 students and alumni who enlisted and a majestic memorial to the 375 who were killed in the First World War. Finished in 1932 with a bell tower and spire that mounts 170 feet above the weighty Doric columns of the porches below, the ensemble

Lowell House in 1930, one of the first undergraduate residential houses built with a gift from Yale alumnus Edward Harkness.

has been described by Professor Howard Mumford Jones (as Reverend Peter Gomes likes to quote) as "Emily Dickinson above, but pure Mae West below."

On February 20, 1932, President Lowell attended yet another Harvard Club of Chicago Annual Dinner, this time at the Palmer House. The *Chicago Daily Tribune* reported the next day that President Lowell declared that the college students of today take greater interest in the welfare of mankind than did those of past generations. In the fall of that year, he announced his intention to step down as president. Sadly, flu prevented him from attending the Annual Dinner of 1933, but in that year he realized his dream of establishing the Society of Fellows, an elite group of scholars that encouraged young faculty and engaged revered masters. It would be a continuing source of interest for Lowell in his retirement.

The twenty-four years he had as president marked a tenure surpassed only by his predecessor, Charles W. Eliot (forty years), and Edward Holyoke (thirty-two years). This time no obvious candidate emerged, and James B. Conant, AB '14, Sheldon Emery Professor of Organic Chemistry, was not even on the first list of about fifty names that were mentioned. It was therefore all too easy for the *Lampoon* to produce a "fake *Crimson*" announcing the election of a mythical Chicago businessman, which fooled the Associated Press. Finally, Conant's appointment was confirmed by the board of overseers on June 21.

Many sought to capture the varied contributions Lowell had made. The *New York Herald Tribune* claimed "that no man, Eliot included, did more to change the current of educational thought in America." David McCord wrote in the *Alumni Bulletin*:

He inherited much but he gave away even more. . . . He chose to be rich by making his wants few, as Emerson said of Thoreau. His approach to everything was direct, and his decisions were unconditional. If he believed in a man, he would back him to the limit. He could, on occasion, be brusque almost to the point of

Katherine Shortall Dunbaugh, AB '12

After attending the Girton School, a prep school for girls in Winnetka, Illinois, and Miss Houghteling's School, Katherine Shortall entered Radcliffe, graduating with the class of 1912. Following in the footsteps of many young Harvard men who served in the Great War, after the Armistice in 1918 she boarded ship for France to help boost American troop morale with the YMCA. Once in France, her skills in French and music proved very useful. Her mother published her letters home in a book, *A 'Y' Girl in France*, in 1919. She stayed on in France with the Radcliffe Unit of the French Red Cross, later receiving the Medaille d'Argent. In 1923 she married Harry J. Dunbaugh, LLB '03, who worked at the law firm of Isham, Lincoln and Beale (the firm co-founded by Robert Todd Lincoln) from 1903 until his death in 1969. The Dunbaughs had four children. Tragically, three died within a year of their birth. A son graduated from Harvard with the class of 1951, then joined the Marine Corps and served as a lieutenant in the Korean War. He was listed as missing in action, presumed dead, in 1952. At the time of her death in Evanston in 1993 at age 102, Katherine Dunbaugh was the oldest living alumna of Harvard or Radcliffe. She was a director of the Huron Mountain Wildlife Foundation in Michigan and a member of both the Chicago and Winnetka Fortnightly Clubs. She was a trustee of Radcliffe from 1932 to 1936, and on the board of the Eli Bates Settlement in Chicago.

Memorial transept in Memorial Church, honoring Harvard's war dead. The centerpiece sculpture, *The Sacrifice*, was designed by Malvina Hoffman, the same sculptress who was commissioned by Stanley Field in 1930 to sculpt the 104 Races of Mankind series for the Field Museum.

rudeness, but he could also be generous to the point of anonymity. We may not know for a long time the extent of his benefactions to the University to which he dedicated his life. . . . From the modified elective system to the Society of Fellows, his influence on scholarship was enormous. . . . Character and ability were the twin criteria by which he chose the new men for his powerful faculty. Most importantly of all, he sought consistently and openly for academic freedom.

Writing in 1936, Samuel Eliot Morison concluded, "Mr. Lowell, becoming President in the shadow of the greatest holder of that office, proved an educational statesman of the first rank. His defense of academic freedom maintained the great liberal tradition of the University; his wisdom and energy invigorated its many departments; his devotion restored to Harvard College the ancient 'collegiate way of living.'"

Most recently, Andrew Schlesinger summarized his accomplishments:

Lowell was proud to have restored the luster to the "scholarly escutcheon. . . ." No longer was admission to the College virtually guaranteed for any white Anglo-Saxon male able to meet certain intellectual standards and pay the tuition.

President Lowell at age seventy-two, near the end of his tenure at Harvard.

Lowell eliminated the famous Gentleman's C and reference to the greasy grind [for serious scholars]. . . . During his tenure, enrollment more than doubled, faculty nearly trebled, endowments increased from $22 to $130 million. . . . New professional schools of architecture, business administration, education and public health were founded. Beginning in 1930, he reorganized an under-graduate body of about 3200 students into seven separate, self-contained residential houses. . . . He encouraged changes in admission and scholarship practices that opened Harvard to public school graduates from the entire country, making it a truly national educational institution. . . . He co-founded the Harvard Society of Fellows and vigorously defended attacks on faculty during and after WWI. He also provided funds for many buildings and enhancements.

In Chicago, the years 1933–34 marked the Century of Progress, but by August 1934, the Harvard-Yale-Princeton Club was forced to close owing to the difficult economic times. Several hundred of its members, those able to pay the dues, were absorbed into the University Club of Chicago. The Harvard-Yale-Princeton Club was officially dissolved in 1936.

At the time of Harvard's tercentenary, former president Lowell was deeply involved in the festivities. There are amusing tales of how he attempted to tell President Roosevelt how long and how apolitical his remarks should be. But the words that Lowell crafted for himself etch a deep and meaningful portrait of a man with every advantage who waged a crusade for his idea of a better university, an educational institution to inspire the entire country:

As wave after wave rolls landward from the ocean, breaks and fades away sighing down the shingle of the beach, so the generations of men follow one another, sometimes quietly, sometimes after a storm, with noisy turbulence. But, whether we think upon the monotony or the violence in human history, two things are always new—youth and the quest for knowledge, and with these a university is concerned. So long as its interest in them is keen it can never grow old, though it count its age by centuries. The means it uses may vary with the times, but forever the end remains the same; and while some principles based on man's nature must endure, others, essential perhaps for the present, are doomed to pass away.

Chapter 7

The Conant Years

1933–1953

James Bryant Conant, AB '13
(Class of 1914), PhD '16
1893–1978
President of Harvard University
1933–1953
Conant, a chemist, served as the
Sheldon Emery Professor of Organic
Chemistry at Harvard.

*"Behold the turtle. He
makes progress only when
he sticks his neck out."*
James Bryant Conant

In 1933, at the relatively young age of forty, James Bryant Conant, AB '13, PhD '16, became the twenty-third president of Harvard University. At his appointment he was sufficiently untested as an administrator to have been passed over not long before by Roxbury Latin, his own high school, for the position of headmaster. Conant proved to be an able administrator, however, and was instrumental in transforming Harvard, until then widely thought of as a finishing school for the upper classes, especially those in New England, into a world-class research university. He introduced the National Scholarship program for gifted boys who did not come from the Eastern boarding schools, Harvard's main supplier of students, and indeed could now come from any economic class. He also oversaw the introduction of aptitude tests—which later became the SAT (Scholastic Aptitude Test)—into the undergraduate admissions system so that students would be chosen on the basis of intellectual prowess and merit rather than social connections. Conant liked the test because he thought it measured raw intelligence rather than the quality of the student's high school.

Conant also worked to expand the scope of each student's education, implementing the General Education Program. This required every undergraduate to take courses in the humanities, social sciences, and natural sciences. He encouraged moving the general undergraduate curriculum away from the traditional emphasis on the classics and toward a more modern and scientific program. Conant promoted the study of the history of science, which became part of the General Education curriculum, and instituted the Harvard Case Histories in Experimental Science. Conant hoped that this approach would help Americans understand the importance of science in the modern world. During and after World War II, American science seemed to be dominated by military funding, and Conant wanted to encourage a scientifically literate population that could understand and manage the difficult issues that would be a part of their future. He also wanted the United States to have top-flight scientific talent.

During his years at the helm, Conant was noted for espousing the three Jeffersonian fundamentals of freedom of the mind, social mobility through education, and universal schooling. His commitment to those principles guided many of his leadership strategies at Harvard and explained the passion with which he spoke out against the tyranny arising in Germany as he ascended to Harvard's presidency. The year 1933, which saw the appointment of Conant to a long tenure at Harvard, also saw Adolph Hitler became chancellor of Germany. The arc of the modern era both for the Western world and for Harvard University might be said to have its origin in that year.

War and the Depression were also much on the minds of Chicagoans as the city in 1933 hosted its second world's fair, the Century of Progress Exposition. Originally intended to celebrate Chicago's past, the exposition came to stand for hope for the future in the aftermath of the Great War and the long-dragged-out economic slump. The exposition was championed by the Chicago Commercial Club, of which Rufus C. Dawes, an oil tycoon, Julius Rosenwald, of Sears, Roebuck, and Frederic A. Delano, AB '85, railroad executive and uncle of President Franklin D. Roosevelt, AB '04, were among its most active members. Dawes was instrumental in giving the fair its thematic direction, heeding the suggestions of several Chicago physicians and scientists, who saw the opportunity to rebuild public trust in science after the devastation caused by the use of mustard gas and other chemical weapons during World War I. The fair became "an exposition of science and industrial development" and rekindled alliances between the scientific and business communities.

At the exposition, the exhibits and displays effectively delivered the message that cooperation among science, business, and government could create the path to a better future. President Roosevelt was so impressed by the power of the fair to stimulate spending on consumer durables and thereby contribute to igniting the economy that he personally urged Dawes to reopen the fair in 1934. The exposition corporation agreed.

In addition to nearly two dozen corporations hosting their own pavilions at the fair and encouraging viewers to modernize everything from their homes to their cars, there were many entertainments. The hit of the fair was a show featuring Sally Rand's fan dance in the "Streets of Paris" concession. Rand, a self-promoting local performer and aspiring actress, had a talent for parody. Rand "originally intended her show as a spoof on Chicago's high-society matrons who insisted on overdressing at a time when many Americans barely had money to clothe themselves. By taking it off, she was putting them on." "The Streets of Paris" was one of the most financially successful of the exposition's venues. Other than midway shows, however, women were largely ignored by the fair's corporate leadership and had no influence in shaping its practices.

Chicago's African Americans, on the other hand, had some limited success in influencing fair management. On the negative side, not only were African-American contributions to Chicago largely ignored in the 1933 version (aside from Jean Baptiste Point DuSable, the African American who established Chicago's roots and whose cabin was reproduced at the fair), there was also active discrimination in Exposition employment and refusal of service in several restaurants on the fair grounds. However, a handful of African-American state legislators held up legislation authorizing the continuation of the fair into 1934—with the help of the National Association for the Advancement of Colored People (NAACP)—until exposition management agreed to wording that forbade racial discrimination. Richard T. Greener, AB 1870, the first African American to graduate from Harvard College, had been instrumental in establishing a Chicago chapter of the NAACP prior to his death in 1922.

The Harvard Club of Chicago took advantage of the unusual opportunities afforded by exposition facilities for convivial get-togethers. In 1933 the annual Spring Strawberry Night, the most informal of the Harvard parties and one of the older traditions, was held at the Century Club at the exposition. Barrett Wendell, AB '02, was in charge of the arrangements for the dinner, which included strawberries and beer. John Spaulding Brown, AB '14, and Clay Judson, AB '14, both classmates of University president-elect Conant, each said a few words about Dr. Conant.

On December 27, 1933 fifty young men from the Harvard University musical clubs arrived to begin a hectic schedule arranged by the Chicago alumni in charge of their entertainment. They arrived just in time to present a concert in Orchestra Hall, after which they were whisked away to the Casino to enjoy the dinner dance hosted by the John P. Kelloggs and W. H. Mitchells in honor of their debutante niece, Miss Helen Hunter.

The following day the Club hosted its annual Christmas luncheon for undergraduates, prospective students, and alumni, with the members of the musical clubs as guests.

Panorama of the Century of Progress Exposition in 1933.

The excitement ran high at the luncheon, as Harvard had defeated Yale the previous week and a Winnetka boy was said to have been largely responsible for Harvard's victory. Dan Wells, the son of Mr. and Mrs. Harry L. Wells of Hubbard Woods, was a first-string halfback who threw two long touchdown passes. Movies of the game were shown at the luncheon, and Wells was prevailed upon to speak. The Harvard vocal group led the singing of football and undergraduate songs and were lustily joined by the alumni.

For that December 1933 Harvard-Yale game, about 170 men and women listened to the telegraphic report in the main dining room of the Harvard-Yale-Princeton Club, where a play-by-play board was located. Even more turned out for the Princeton-Yale game, so many that the overflow had to sit in another room and follow the game over the radio. This 1933 Harvard-Yale game was the first time ladies had been invited to attend football game daytime events, and the ladies were also invited for the Princeton-Yale contest. After the game, squash racquet devotees saw the Harvard-Yale-Princeton Club's team play intra-city matches.

Two months later, Conant made his first trip to Chicago as president, speaking to the Club at the University Club of Chicago on February 21. Conant announced that he contemplated no radical changes from the program of his predecessor, A. Lawrence Lowell. He further noted he thought Lowell had raised the institution's educational standards far enough. Conant hoped to bring gifted and exceptionally talented young men to Harvard. These young men would take full opportunity of its facilities and thereby create a way to spread the school's ideals and learning. Conant also stressed research for the betterment of mankind, and planned to bring the researchers into close contact with the undergraduates to make them teachers as well as developers of new knowledge.

Included in Conant's presentation was a plan to attract talented and gifted applicants from any social and economic stock, up to at least 10% of the student body. These students would be supported by four-year fellowships. Conant noted, "The importance of our universities rests upon the fact they are the guardians of spiritual values of art, literature and science won so laboriously through the centuries. . . . It is not enough that we have a chicken in every pot and a car in every garage. It is not enough that we reduce poverty if we leave no permanent contribution to civilization for the following centuries. No amount of material success can make up for the failure to do that."

Conant went on to explain his vision for encouraging student engagement across department and school boundaries. He broadened the intellectual scope of the undergraduate student body by requiring each undergraduate, regardless of his major, to take courses in the humanities, the social sciences and the natural sciences. Strongly believing in the value of intellectual exchange, Conant established prestigious University Professorships, which gave leading scholars tenured appointments without specific ties to faculties or departments. He developed strategies to encourage intellectual exchange, saying, "There is a great deal one cannot get from books that he can gain in experience with his fellow man. Such associations are profitable. More souls are saved around a dinner table than in lecture courses. This is an important aspect of our undergraduate house plan, which we hope in the future to extend to graduate schools so that law, medicine, art and business students may meet and exchange ideas rather than be bound in the confines of specialized education."

Conant concluded by stating "It is all too easy to make concessions to the present and jeopardize the future." Conant would consistently seek to enhance Harvard's international reputation for academic excellence at the student level, the faculty level, and the school level. Three years later, thanks to the generosity of a Midwestern alumnus (in Milwaukee), Conant helped establish the Nieman Fellowships. These fellowships continue to fund a year of study at Harvard for professional journalists.

Harvard alumni heard Conant's call to create scholarships for talented youth. At the February 21, 1935, Annual Dinner at the Palmer House, with George Cook Kimball, SB '02, presiding, the business considered centered on plans for the

Club's first benefit in twenty-five years. To raise money for its scholarship fund, the Club decided to bring the champion Harvard polo team from Cambridge to play a selected Army team from the 124 Field Artillery Armory on March 2 in Washington Park. Harlow Niles Higinbotham, AB '28, and John Wadsworth Valentine, AB '28, handled all of the arrangements for the event.

The Harvard polo team, 1934 intercollegiate champions, promised a competitive game, as indeed they gave, winning 6 to 5½. The veteran U.S. Army polo players learned a few pointers from the college boys. The event drew an overflow crowd to the armory. The Harvard boys, who had arrived only a few hours before the game, had considerable difficulty with their borrowed ponies in the first chukker. Major C. A. Wilkinson, "who learned to play polo about the time the Harvard boys were outgrowing their rompers," controlled the first period as the Army team had the best of them. The tide turned in the second chukker, with Harvard quickly scoring 3 to make it 4½ to 3 at half time. Harvard scored the only goal in the third chukker. In the final period, a Harvard pony kicked in a goal to give the Crimson the lead. Immediately thereafter, Army regained the lead. It was short-lived, as Harvard came right back to score with a clever near side stroke from 30 yards out.

The Harvard alumni gave the team members a rousing welcome. With their "fairest ladies," and formally clad, they filled the box circle around the arena and mightily cheered the hard-riding and quick, skillful play that brought Harvard

U.S. President Franklin D. Roosevelt at Harvard's Tercentenary, 1936.

victory. The evening was more than a simple appreciation of polo skills. This was the first time that a Harvard athletic team had played in Chicago. Even more impressive, the proceeds from the evening's entertainment swelled the Harvard Club's scholarship fund.

The year 1936 represented not only the 300th anniversary of Harvard, but also the approaching 50th anniversary of the University Club of Chicago, which had been founded in February 1887. A simple invitation to graduates of Yale, Harvard, Princeton, the University of Michigan, and others had been sent out by a group that included William M. LeMoyne, AB 1881, and Heyliger A. De Windt, AB 1881, of Harvard. Only De Windt was alive of the original founders. The original roster reflected seventy members, thirty-five elected to membership on February 15, 1887, and another thirty elected on February 18. Several of the fifteen surviving charter members, including De Windt, attended an anniversary celebration and enjoyed seeing themselves depicted in the eight historical episodes recreated in the program.

The February 27, 1936, Annual Dinner held at the Blackstone Hotel again featured President Conant as special guest and speaker, along with Robert Maynard Hutchins, president of the University of Chicago. The dinner celebrated the 300th anniversary of the founding of Harvard. In his presentation, Conant reported on the early results of Harvard's initiative to recruit the best and brightest regardless of ability to afford tuition. He declared the winners of the prize fellowships Harvard had been awarding to selected high school seniors in Illinois and other Midwestern states have been establishing brilliant scholastic records. The University had decided to continue the awards and extend the plan as fast as funds became available.

During the fall of 1936, as Chicago's North Shore youth returned from vacations, farewell teas dotted social calendars. Twenty five young women were going to Vassar, twelve to Smith, four to Sarah Lawrence and two each to Wellesley and Bryn Mawr. Nine students were headed to Yale and eight to Harvard, including William H. Daughaday, AB '40, MD '43 of Winnetka, who received a Harvard prize fellowship, and his cousin Hamilton Daughaday, Jr., AB '40, SM '41, who received the Harvard Club of Chicago scholarship.

That same fall, the Harvard, Yale and Princeton alumni groups decided to rescind the "men only" rule that generally had prevailed at their broadcast parties for football games. After the Harvard-Yale-Princeton Club was disbanded, the parties had for the most part become stag affairs. "If women are invited to football games, why not to the broadcasts?" asked one Harvard man, reportedly with an especially charming wife. Football widows no more, there were now three important dates on the calendars for buffet luncheons served in the Red Lacquer Room of the Palmer House before the Harvard-Princeton and Yale-Harvard broadcasts, and in the Grand Ballroom before the Yale-Princeton game. Philip W. Moore, AB '31, handled the arrangements for Harvard.

On October 15, 1936, Clay Judson, AB '14, was elected Club president, succeeding Clarence B. Randall, AB '12. Conway Olmsted, AB '29, was elected secretary to succeed John W. Valentine AB '29, and Alex E. Kirk, AB '20, was reelected treasurer. Vice-presidents were Harold V. Amberg, AB '08,

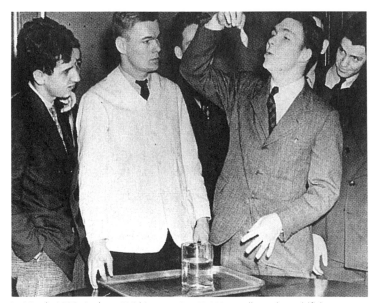

In March 1939, Lothrop Withington, Jr., AB '42, swallowed a goldfish as a publicity stunt for his campaign to be freshman class president. He lost but started a craze in colleges across the country.

Samuel W. White, AB '08, and Dr. Nathan S. Davis III, AB '10. Directors included Mr. Randall, Donald C. Cottrell, AB '15, and Mr. Philip W. Moore, AB '31. Perry Dunlop Smith, AB '11, discussed the University's tercentenary exercises in his role as one of the Club's delegates to the event.

A "nasty blow" was struck the wives and sweethearts of Harvard-Yale-Princeton alumni in the fall of 1938 with the announcement that "by popular demand," the season's football luncheons were reverting to stag affairs. Philip Spaulding Dalton, Jr., AB '31. Harvard luncheon committeeman, was a bachelor, though his compatriots from Yale and Princeton were both married. Dartmouth demurred, however, and prevailed on Yale to include wives and sweethearts at the joint luncheon to hear the direct wire broadcast of the Dartmouth-Yale games.

Times were beginning to change, however, as members of the Tavern Club chose to depart from custom and invite wives and female guests to tea at the club any afternoon except Sunday. Tea service was available between 3 and 5 o'clock. Until then ladies had not been permitted in the Tavern until 6 p.m. on weekdays. The existing weekend policy of allowing invitations to luncheon was not changed.

Although the times were changing, how quickly was not always apparent. In early 1939, students at Harvard demonstrated the swallowing of goldfish to reporters. Later that year, the last remaining Jewish enterprises in Germany were closed, and German troops invaded Poland. In Bombay, Gandhi fasted in protest of the autocratic rule in India. In August 1939, Albert Einstein wrote President Roosevelt about developing the atomic bomb using uranium. Roosevelt implemented the Neutrality Act of 1939, allowing cash-and-carry purchases of weapons to nonbelligerent nations. In November, Al Capone was released from Alcatraz.

Harvard and the University of Chicago had begun playing each other in football in 1938, with a second game scheduled for October 14, 1939 in Chicago. The previous Monday the Club was fortunate to hear from Victor M. Harding, Jr.,

AB 1889, representing Harvard, and Jay Berwanger, former Maroons player, and in 1935 the first Heisman Trophy winner and Silver Football awardee as the most valuable player in the Big Ten. The luncheon was held in the Shoreland Hotel, as was a celebratory cocktail party following Harvard's second lopsided victory by 61-0, achieved without playing the Crimson team captain and star, Toby McDonald, AB '40. An interesting footnote is that later the same year the Maroons would lose to Ohio State by the same score, and in the season final with Illinois only by 46-0.

In late 1939, the *Chicago Daily Tribune* posted a profile on the changing U.S. diplomatic corps. Of the 700 career men in the State Department, fully seventy—10%—were Harvard men. Yale provided fifty-one and Princeton forty-two. Some called the foreign service a glorified Harvard-Yale-Princeton Club. Dartmouth and Cornell supplied fifteen people each. Of the top fourteen posts in the State Department—the board of governors of the Foreign Service—ten had spent time at Harvard. More interestingly, the article went on to note that those career men who did not have the Harvard accent by

Harold Vincent Amberg, AB '08, LLB '10

Harold Vincent Amberg, AB '08, LLB '10, served on the staff of the Federal Trade Commission and as special advisor to the United States Shipping Board. In the latter capacity he acted as special commissioner with the shipping board at the Paris Peace Conference in 1919. He was Club president in 1938–39. He served as president of the Association of Reserve City Bankers in 1940 and as vice president and general counsel of First National Bank of Chicago before being appointed special consultant to the Treasury on tax matters in 1947–48. Friends described Amberg as a "Woodrow Wilson democrat." In 1950, Amberg testified before the U.S. Senate in opposition to President Truman's proposal to put the office of the controller of the currency under the authority of the Treasury Department. Amberg predicted that the president's proposal could be "an incentive to socialize our banking system" and subject banks to "political expediency."

virtue of schooling soon acquired it by association in the State Department or while on duty at the Court of St. James or other posts dominated by British staffers.

In 1939 and 1940 President Conant was receiving a variety of student and alumni inputs regarding the possibility of another war. At his Sunday teas with students he began encountering many with passionate pacifism who held the view the United States had been tricked into entering World War I. On May 21, 1940, the Harvard Crimson published a letter signed by hundreds of students stating the signers were determined "never under any circumstances to follow the footsteps of the students of 1917." The reasoning was not an advocacy of pacifism but because the students believed "that the way in which America drifted toward war in those years was unintelligent and unworthy of our nation." Shortly thereafter there was a meeting of the Associated Harvard Clubs in New York, following which a response appeared in the Crimson from thirty-four members of the class of 1917, possibly written at the meeting. Asserting they had fought for principles, the veterans aggressively rebutted the propaganda that had built up in subsequent decades about how the American people had been deceived.

Conant understood the threat of totalitarianism from Hitler, and, while not an advocate of active involvement, strongly felt the United States should be prepared and should be able to supply Britain, especially after Germany attacked the Low Countries. Yet Conant knew by the signatories it was alumni from the coasts (East and West) that took umbrage at the students' views. He suspected many Midwesterners might agree with the students. In August 1940, Charles Lindbergh spoke to an isolationist rally at Soldier Field in Chicago. However, earlier that same summer Conant had been recruited by Vannevar Bush to join President Roosevelt's National Defense Research Committee (NDRC). A major charge of the committee was to evaluate the possibility of creating an atomic reaction. The arrangement was revolutionary, as rather than creating massive governmental labs and staff, the government would contract with universities and private industry to conduct the work.

In December 1940, Chicagoan Russell Tyson, AB 1890, organized and chaired the Chicago Committee for Aid to China. The committee served a coordinating function for national groups working for China in the fields of education, child welfare, medical aid, and industrial cooperatives. China at this time had suffered under the Japanese occupation. The hope was that assistance appeals could be coordinated through the Chicago committee.

As winter wore on, France fell, British forces were successfully evacuated from Dunkirk, and all eyes were on Britain and its air defenses. In April 1941 Conant visited Salisbury, United Kingdom, where Harvard had set up a joint hospital venture with the American Red Cross and the British Ministry of Health to monitor and treat outbreaks of infectious disease under the adverse civilian conditions then extant in Britain. He met with Prime Minister Churchill. Greece was about to fall, and the mood was somber. Conant flew back to the States from Lisbon, using the new flying boat service. He was now prepared to give the isolationists some frank talk.

The spring meeting of Harvard's board of overseers was a surprise to Conant, as a number of overseers and their wives thought the war could be brought to an end soon with a negotiated peace. Conant was able to assure the overseers that Britain had no thought of compromise, and that to believe otherwise was "utterly fantastic." In mid-May 1941, Conant addressed a meeting of the Associated Harvard Clubs in Baltimore. There he reported on college matters and the professional schools before sharing a few words as a private citizen. Conant spoke about the two great ideas battling in the national conscience, peace and freedom. He ended with these words: "Gentlemen, I have no doubt as to the ultimate decision of the American people, for I have no doubt of the firmness of our sense of moral values. We shall regain peace through defeating evil, and in the fight for freedom throughout the world we shall before long take our proper place." He was greeted with an enthusiastic ovation from the alumni.

In May 1941, the Office of Scientific Research and Development (OSRD) was created by executive order of President Roosevelt to coordinate scientific research for military purposes. It superseded the work of the NDRC and took the research on nuclear fission into deep secrecy. The OSRD was given almost unlimited access to funding and resources, and reported only to Roosevelt. Conant became Bush's deputy in the project, which became the Manhattan Project.

On December 7, 1941, all discussion of interventionism versus isolationism became moot. Pearl Harbor had been bombed, and the United States entered World War II. Between Pearl Harbor and V-J Day in August 1945, Harvard was a university at war. In Conant's words:

Before the academic year 1941–1942 was over, a gradual exodus of professors had begun. Some took commissions in the armed forces, some in civilian war agencies; almost without exception, the physical scientists were enrolling in one or another of the government-supported secret laboratories located in various institutions of higher learning. The number of graduate students rapidly diminished. One could foresee that it was only a matter of time before the War Department would complete its plans for calling to arms many if not all of the young men of college age. (By 1944 the undergraduate enrollment was only 850 as compared with 3,500 before the war.) Special Army, Navy and Air Force schools had come into existence in many universities in the early months of 1942; Harvard had its share; no less than twelve such training courses, accommodating a total of three thousand men, were soon in operation and would continue in full force until the war ended. Young men in uniform swarmed over the Harvard Yard and into the buildings of the Harvard Graduate School of Business Administration across the river. A total of many thousands of officers were thus trained in Cambridge during the years 1942–1945.

On December 2, 1942, Arthur Compton of the University of Chicago led a team that successfully constructed an atomic reaction. However, rather than the crucial experiment being conducted at Argonne Forest outside Chicago, it was conducted under the west stands of the athletic grounds—Stagg Field—at the University of Chicago. Compton and Enrico Fermi and the other physicists involved had been quite certain that under no circumstances would there be a release of energy that could not be controlled. Within hours Compton had called Conant and reported, "Our Italian navigator has just landed in the new world." Conant asked, "Were the natives friendly?" obviously concerned about safety. Compton replied, "Everyone landed safe and happy." It would take three and a half more years to construct a reliable atomic bomb and end the war.

As the nation mobilized for war, Conant was active in exploring whether especially capable students in the sciences or other critical disciplines should be able to enlist in the different services but be deferred from combat, to serve their country in essential industries and research establishments. Indeed, the proposal suggested such students be identified and recruited for full scholarship training. The program did not go forward, in part owing to the complexity of working with the various armed services and government agencies.

This lithograph of the atomic reaction under Stagg Field and the personalities associated with it was printed with ink made from graphite used in the experiment. Portrayed are Leo Sailard, Arthur H. Compton, Enrico Fermi, and Eugene Wigner.

The young Chicagoans who headed off to college in those lovely late summer days now would be caught up in the war. Conant described the leave-taking scene in his autobiography, *My Several Lives*:

On January 10, 1943, we at Harvard acknowledged the closing of the normal functioning of the college by holding a Valedictory Service in the Memorial Church. It was a service we announced of "farewell and Godspeed for some fifteen hundred undergraduates about to enter the armed forces of the United States." Many of those present had completed the requirements for the bachelor's degree but could not wait to participate in the commencement ceremony of awarding degrees in June; others were interrupting their college course. It fell to me as president of the university to make the address. It was no easy assignment. I thought of the occasion as one in which the university saluted all who were leaving Harvard to serve the nation in an hour of need. The realization that some of those to whom we were saying good-bye would never return was never far distant from the center of our thoughts. Quite unashamedly I invoked the past. I concluded as follows:

"Formal education for the present you leave aside, but you will grow in wisdom nonetheless. New knowledge will come to you by virtue of the sacrifices that you will be asked to make. Having been ready to run all risks for freedom, you will comprehend it as those of us at home cannot. On some subsequent commencement day you will return with the understanding born of great events. On that occasion it will be said of you as returning Harvard soldiers in 1865:

Today our Reverend Mother welcomes back
Her wisest scholars, those who understood . . .
Many loved Truth, and lavished life's best oil
Amid the dust of books to find her. . . .

But these, our brothers, fought for her. . . .

"Gentlemen, with anxious pride, Harvard awaits the day of your return."

The departure of young Harvard men to war finally motivated some changes in the relations between Harvard College and Radcliffe. Radcliffe College had been chartered by the Commonwealth of Massachusetts in the early twentieth century as a successor to the Society of the Collegiate Instruction of Women, formed in 1879. In 1880, Harvard had refused to take over the enterprise and firmly declined offering Harvard degrees to women. The Harvard governing boards accepted "visitorial power" and consented to countersigning the women's degree diplomas. In exchange, all instruction would be given by Harvard staff on the women's campus. There were some idiosyncracies, as in the cases where women earned their PhD, fulfilling all of the requirements for the Harvard degree, but received only a Radcliffe degree. Radcliffe's president Ada Louise Comstock would not agree to Harvard graduate degrees without similar arrangements for the undergraduate degrees, as those programs too were taught by Harvard professors.

Specifically, Radcliffe hired the Harvard faculty who staffed the Radcliffe courses. It was an extra stipend for those Harvard professors. This arrangement worked well enough until the war brought to the fore all the background issues in the informal staffing arrangement, as many of the young instructors left to enlist, and many of the older faculty took positions in war agencies. The Harvard-Radcliffe agreement of 1943 resolved the issue. Harvard accepted the responsibility for providing instruction for Radcliffe students in return for Radcliffe's turning over to Harvard all but a small portion of the Radcliffe tuition. This would also result in the Harvard faculty salaries increasing by some 20%, as everyone would have to teach more courses. While the formal agreement stated that Radcliffe students would continue to receive instruction in separate classes, in actuality Harvard and Radcliffe students shared classes. As Conant noted in his account of those years, two jokes began to circulate:

"Harvard was not coeducational in theory, only in practice; and, Harvard was not coeducational, but Radcliffe was." From this beginning, the graduate schools began to change. The School of Education had long accepted women. In 1943, women were accepted into the Medical School.

Back in Chicago, the city hunkered down for the war. At the annual meeting held at a luncheon in the University Club on December 7, 1942, Joseph C. Grew, AB '02, LLD '43 (Hon.) former ambassador to Japan, told the Harvard Club that Harvard University was now the second largest military academy in the country. Grew, president of the Harvard Alumni Association (he found out about his election upon his return from six months' internment), said Harvard had trained more than 9,000 officers and men for the nation's armed forces. A recent football game saw 2,800 men in uniform march on the field. Grew noted that an even greater participation in the war effort was planned for 1943. He observed that almost immediately after the Pearl Harbor attack, "business as usual" ended at Harvard, as University officials decided the school's educational program must be subordinated to the war effort.

The war years saw the passing of several notable Chicagoans who had served as president of the Club. G. Cook Kimball, AB '00, died after a year's illness in 1942. A steel executive, Kimball had been president of the Club in 1935, president of the Associated Harvard Clubs in 1919, and vice president of the Harvard Alumni Association in 1920. On April 20, 1943, the Chicago community lost a giant in the legal profession with the death of John H. Wigmore, AB 1883, dean emeritus of the Northwestern University Law School. Wigmore, who had been president of the Club in 1915, died of injuries suffered in an automobile accident. Educated at Harvard and the University of Wisconsin, Wigmore never lost sight of the human side of either law or man. He found time to represent an obscure taxicab driver in Police Court, attack prohibition as a "huge mistake," and even condemn as "Scroogelike" Evanston's 1931 plan to tax nonresidents using its beaches. Howard F. Gillette, AB 1896, died in October 1943. He too was a former president of the Club (1933), a longtime supporter and executive board member of the Boy Scouts of America, and a national commodore of the Sea Scouts of America, an organization he had helped establish. Mr. Gillette had chaired a birthday ball for President Franklin D. Roosevelt in 1935 in Chicago. In 1944 another former Club president (1908) who spent many years on the federal bench, Judge G. A. Carpenter, AB 1888, died.

When one line of Chicago's first subway project was completed after five years of work on October 17, 1943, it was cause for celebration. Supported by city fathers, among them many Harvard men, Chicago Mayor Kelly and Secretary of the Interior Harold Ickes had turned the first spades of earth. President Roosevelt, impressed with Chicago as a city that could deliver a Democratic victory in tight elections, and with the dramatic social unrest caused by mass unemployment during the Great Depression, had encouraged his agency heads to be generous with New Deal funds. Originally a Public Works Administration federally financed project, subway Route No. 1, under Clybourn Avenue, Division Street, and State Street, and No. 2, under Milwaukee Avenue, Lake Street and Dearborn Street, were unfinished when the United States entered World War II. Mining through the soft, watery clay that lay under the city and connecting tubes to pass under the Chicago River had been a challenging engineering task that was successfully completed without a single cave-in or flood. In addition to the subway, Chicago had used federal funds to complete construction of Lake Shore Drive, build thirty new schools, and landscape numerous parks during the days of the Great Depression.

The Club's 1943 Annual Dinner was held at the Palmer House in February. Guests saw a new color film, *Harvard Goes to War,* and David M. Little, AB '18, AM '22, PhD '35, secretary to the University, provided an informative commentary. Frederick C. Crawford, AB '13, MCE '14, also spoke, and William C. Boyden, AB '16, Club president, presided over the evening. In addition to inviting the area alumni, now numbering some eight or nine hundred, visitors in town for the midwinter meeting of the executive committee of the Associated Harvard Clubs also were encouraged to attend.

The Club's Annual Dinner in 1944 was held in the Crystal Ballroom of the Blackstone Hotel. During the war years, opportunities for local reunions had become rare, as the Club's annual "father and son" luncheon had been called off. At this meeting Dr. Roger I. Lee, AB '02, from Boston delivered an address titled "Harvard Looks to the Future." Gaetano Salvemini, a member of the Harvard faculty who formerly taught at the University of Florence, gave a talk titled "America at the Crossroads in Italy."

In the fall of 1944, Harvard alumni were well represented among the organizers of the Art Institute of Chicago's opening reception, "Art of the United Nations," Wednesday evening, November 15. The Art Institute considered this its most spectacular affair of the new season. More than a year in the planning, the exhibition included one outstanding work of art from each of the thirty-seven allied countries. These ranged from a portrait of Mrs. Richard Yates by Gilbert Stuart lent by the National Gallery of Art in Washington, D.C., to a contemporary Guatemalan costume from the Bartlett collection. Gyorgy Kepes, who had taught at the New Bauhaus in Chicago from the late 1930s to 1943, designed the settings for the show, which featured special lighting and live gardens. Prior to the opening, all consuls or consuls general of collaborating nations stationed in Chicago and their wives were invited to join the institute's trustees for coffee and to participate in the evening's festivities.

Carroll Binder, AB '16, (whose son, a member of the class of 1943, was killed in action over Germany in May, 1944) addressed the Harvard Club of Chicago at lunch at the University Club for the organization's 1944 annual business meeting in November. He was introduced by president Dr. Nathan S. Davis, AB '10, and spoke on current foreign affairs.

For the Annual Dinner in February 1945, Harvard's interest in foreign affairs continued, with Professor Samuel Hazzard Cross, AB '12, AM '15, PhD '16, former chief of the European division of the U.S. Department of Commerce and an authority on Russia, as guest speaker. His address, titled "The Soviet and the West," was of growing interest as thoughtful men looked beyond the end of the war in Europe and began to monitor Russia. Cross's travels in Europe and Russia, his current assignment at Harvard as chair of Slavic Languages and Literature, and his studies at the University of Leningrad and at German universities gave him unique perspectives to share with the club. Snelling S. Robinson, AB '20, Club president, presided at the meeting.

Laird Bell, AB '04, was the 1945 president of the Community and War Fund of Metropolitan Chicago, Inc. He succeeded Elmer T. Stevens, who reported that the 1944 War Fund raised $12,998,870, exceeding the goal of $12,980,000, and had expenses of only 3.7% of the amount raised, the lowest

percentage of any large city in the country. Bell was joined by fellow officers, including Clarence B. Randall, AB '12, who had been the 1944 campaign chairman. The Community and War Fund represented the National War Fund in Cook, Lake, and DuPage counties. Its funds supported U.S.O. Camp Shows, United Seamen's Service, War Prisoners Aid, American Field Service, and seventeen allied relief and refugee agencies. In Chicago, eleven overseas refugee rescue groups, the Jewish Welfare fund, and 187 health and welfare agencies were included.

Germany formally surrendered to the Allies on May 7 and 8, 1945. Hitler had committed suicide in his bunker on April 30, during the Battle for Berlin.

Alexander Louis Jackson, AB '14
Alexander Louis Jackson, III, SB '44
Alexander Louis Jackson, IV, AB '70, MDV '77

The Alexander Louis Jackson family stands out in Chicago not only as one of only a few three-consecutive-generation Harvard families, but also as the only known example among African-American families in Chicago. The first Alexander Louis Jackson was born in 1861 and lived in Great Neck, NY where Alexander Louis Jackson, II was born. Unfortunately the senior ALJ died of ptomaine poisoning when ALJ II was only about 2 years old, so ALJ II never used the II designation. As a good student he was sponsored to attend Williston, Andover and then Harvard. He entered as one of two "Negroes" with the same class, 1914, as future president Conant, Leverett Saltonstall, and a particular friend G. Endicot Peabody. At Harvard he distinguished himself as an orator and athlete. After graduation he moved to Chicago, becoming the Executive Director of a new Negro YMCA branch. In 1915 he was one of the founders of the Association for the Study of Negro Life and History, of which Dr. Carter Godwin Woodson, PhD '12, became the Executive Director until his death in 1950. The Association continues to publish the quarterly "Journal of Negro History." He also became an editor of the Chicago Defender, the major Chicago African-American newspaper. Later he became president of Provident Hospital, a major private hospital serving primarily African-Americans who were normally turned away from other

hospitals in the city. It was also a major teaching hospital in the city for African-American doctors and nurses, who, again, were not allowed to work at other hospitals. ALJ II died in 1973 of brain cancer.

ALJ II had three sons who also went to Williston, with two going on to Harvard, ALJ III, AB '44, and William E. AB '47. There are conflicting reports as to how the Jacksons were treated by the Club, but there is a photograph of a Club luncheon or dinner meeting with ALJ II at one of the tables. There are also entries in the club membership records showing both ALJ II and ALJ III as paid members in 1943-44. After graduation from Harvard ALJ III returned to Chicago to marry Frances Brooks Wills in 1945. Ms. Will's father was a prominent doctor in Chicago. In 1946 they moved to New York city where ALJ IV was born in 1948. ALJ III was a member of the team of overqualified African-Americans who worked for Pepsi beginning in 1947, successfully promoting Pepsi to the "Negro" market. He quit within a short time, unwilling to put up with the Jim Crow laws still prevalent in the country that made traveling difficult, dangerous and humiliating. He died in 2003. ALJ IV graduated from Harvard in 1970, later attending the Harvard Divinity School. He currently works for Smith Barney in Massachusetts.

Meanwhile, after the death of President Roosevelt, President Harry S. Truman created an Interim Committee in May to study the use of atomic bombs against Japan. At the first meeting the committee, composed of Secretary of War Henry L. Stimson, Secretary of State James Byrnes, Harvard's President Conant, MIT physicist and educator Karl Compton, Vannevar Bush, and a few others, heard physicist Robert Oppenheimer, AB '26, predict the atomic bomb would be equal to between 2,000 and 20,000 tons of TNT and with its blast and radiation could kill as many as 20,000 Japanese. After consulting with more scientists and the Joint Chiefs of Staff, the committee recommended that the atomic bomb should be used against a Japanese city with a military facility. For greatest psychological effect, the recommendation advised that the bomb be used without prior warning.

On July 26, 1945, President Truman, joined by Great Britain, told Japan via the Potsdam Declaration to "Surrender or suffer prompt and utter destruction." On July 29, Japan rejected the Potsdam Declaration. On August 6, "Little Boy" was dropped on Hiroshima. On August 9, "Fat Man" was dropped on Nagasaki. V-J Day was announced on August 14, 1945, in U.S. time zones.

Nathan Smith Davis, AB '10

Dr. Nathan S. Davis, a 1910 graduate of Harvard College, graduated from medical school in 1913. He served as a lieutenant in the Illinois National Guard and saw active duty on the Mexican border in 1916 and in the U.S. Army in World War I. Davis was an assistant and associate on the Rush Medical College faculty before joining the staff of Wesley Memorial Hospital, subsequently becoming a professor at Northwestern University Medical School. Davis married Cordelia Carpenter in a ceremony attended by her niece, flower girl Margaret Bell (daughter of Laird Bell, AB '04, and Nathalie), in July 1923. From 1933 to 1941, Davis was a member of the Illinois State Planning Commission. Davis was also a president and secretary of the Chicago Medical Society, which was affiliated with the American Medical Association. In this, Davis followed his grandfather and namesake, Dr. Nathan Smith Davis, who founded the AMA.

In Cambridge at 3 p.m. on December 7, 1945, the fourth anniversary of the United States' entry into World War II, Harvard held a commemorative service in the Memorial Church, honoring the 579 Harvard graduates and staff who died in wartime service. Flags from University Hall flew at half mast.

After the war, President Conant continued to amplify Harvard's footprint on history. While continuing to serve as an advisor to the Atomic Energy Commission, he declined serving as chairman. He also continued to serve as chairman of the National Science Board, and continued to be concerned about the caliber of science and technical students turned out through the U.S. educational system.

Conant also resisted the emotional extension of mandatory military service considered at the end of World War II. While a peacetime draft was reinstated in 1948 and expanded in 1951, Conant thought the nuclear age would change the manpower requirements for the nation's armed forces. More specifically, he believed mandatory conscription should be a question coolly reflected on and not an emotional response to wartime environments.

After six years of war, much of Europe was devastated, its cities and industries destroyed and millions homeless. Millions were also slowly starving. There was a consensus in Washington that the events after World War I—which clearly set the stage for World War II—should not be repeated. The United States also realized that something must be done in the face of the growing Soviet threat emerging in Eastern Europe. At the Harvard graduation on June 5, 1947, standing on the steps of Memorial Church in Harvard Yard, and accepting an honorary degree from President Conant, U.S. Secretary of State General George Marshall announced a major program of American aid to promote European recovery and reconstruction. "It is logical," said Marshall, "that the United States should do whatever it is able to do to assist in the return of normal economic health to the world, without which there can be no political stability and no assured peace. Our policy is not directed against any country, but against hunger, poverty, desperation and chaos. Any government that is willing to assist in recovery will find full cooperation on the part of the U.S.A." The Marshall Plan had been formally announced to the United States at Harvard.

When the Harvard Club held its Annual Dinner in the Crystal Ballroom of the Blackstone Hotel in early March, 1947, wives of Harvard alumni were again temporarily without their husbands. David M. Little, AB '18, AM '22, PhD '35, secretary of the University, and Donald K. David, MBA '20, dean of the University's Graduate School of Business Administration, were the principal speakers. Leaders for the year included Arthur Dixon, AB '16, as president and E. Francis Bowditch, AB '35, current headmaster of Lake Forest Academy, as vice-president.

Life in Chicago for the Harvard Club began to return to normal after the war. The Hasty Pudding Club show was presented at the University Club in December 1947, and Club members and their wives enjoyed an elegant dinner prior to the performance. Harvard-Yale Football broadcasts resumed. The 1948 game, played in Cambridge, was broadcast to members assembled in the University Club, with president Kellogg Fairbank, Jr., AB '30, presiding. The December father-and-son luncheon, at which football coach Arthur Valpey spoke, foreshadowed the changing era of football. As the awarding of substantial scholarships based on athletic ability with minimum regard for academic qualifications grew, Ivy League schools could no longer dominate. In Valpey's words, "Harvard University cannot hold with subsidizing football players. If a player is seeking gifts, my advice to him is to take the highest bidder and sacrifice his education. But the only real way to pick a college is on the basis of what it can do for you in giving an education by which you can earn a living." Valpey noted that Stanford was now on the schedule, because "it is getting more and more difficult to find opponents whose standards are similar to our own in these days of high-pressure football."

In 1949, Chicago had several members playing a national role with the University. The February, 1949 annual meeting featured Wilbur J. Bender, dean of Harvard College; Laird Bell, AB '04, and Clarence B. Randall, AB '12, overseers or trustees of the University; and Herman Dunlap Smith, AB '21, vice-president of the Associated Harvard Clubs. The dinner, held in the Chicago Bar Association's quarters, was traditionally considered by members as the best and largest event of the season's club calendar. Joining Bender at the speaker's table were Club president Kellogg Fairbank, Jr., AB '30, James P. Baxter, IV, AB '41, Lanning Macfarland, AB '19, Howard F. Gillette, AB '36, and Gerald Vanderbilt Hollins, AB '36.

President Conant kept the importance of science and math in the minds of alumni by encouraging Harvard scientists to speak at alumni meetings. The 1951 Annual Dinner, attended

The Harvard Club of Chicago Scholarship Fund

The Harvard Club of Chicago formally established The Harvard Club of Chicago Scholarship Fund in 1947 through the College, with the stipulation: "The income shall be available for scholarships to a student or students, of any department of Harvard University, nominated by the Harvard Club of Chicago and approved by the President and Fellows of Harvard College." Chicago alumni enthusiastically supported the scholarship effort, as suggested by President Conant in his first presentation to the Club in 1934, as a supplement to Harvard's National and regular scholarship programs.

Scholarships to Harvard were very competitive, with candidates from all forty-eight states and several territories and foreign countries. Recipients were selected from one thousand or more applicants based on their prior academic performance and leadership in extracurricular activities, plus the written application and rigorous entrance exam. The scholarships could be renewed for the four years of college, based on the maintenance of honor grades. They were a successful strategy for providing the brightest, most capable young men the financial capability to attend Harvard. Selection of those successful applicants from the Chicago area to receive a Harvard Club of Chicago Scholarship included an interview with its Scholarship Committee.

by some 150 alumni, featured Dr. A. Baird Hastings, a leading scientist, whose address was titled "University Science and the Present Emergency." Dr. Hastings chaired Harvard's chemistry department and was the Hamilton Kuhn Professor of Biological Chemistry at the Harvard Medical School.

The Club's annual father-and-son luncheon had also returned to the schedule. The 1951 December meeting at the Sherman hotel was typical, featuring several undergraduate speakers, including Arnold Horween, Jr., AB '53, Joseph G. Hubbard, AB '53, Miles P. Cuningham, AB '54, and Allen N. Rieselbach, AB '53, LLB '56, all star athletes from the Chicago area. Club president Boyd N. Everett, AB '26, MBA '29, presided, with

a highlight of the lunch motion pictures of the fall's Harvard-Brown football game.

Chicago had regained its strength after the Great Depression. Its civic life was thriving. Chicago alumni were recognized not only in the city but also for their national service. In the words of Meyer Kestnbaum, AB '19, MBA '21, president of Hart, Schaffner & Marx, "I like the city. I like its wonderful community of business men. In Chicago we can still get a group of the city's leaders together to work for the interests of the community. I would describe Chicago as the largest community in the country. In that respect it is different from New York City, which has such a wide

The Fairbank Family

Kellogg Fairbank, Jr., AB '30, (pictured) appears in the middle of a venerable Harvard lineage. His father, Kellogg Fairbank, AB 1890, JD 1893, was elected president of the Harvard Club of Chicago in 1905. The son of Nathaniel K. Fairbank, a prominent Chicago businessman, "Ked" was born in 1869 on the South Side of Chicago. After his Harvard years he returned to Chicago. He had a keen interest in political reform and served as secretary of the Municipal Voters League. The league, one of the earliest political reform groups in Chicago, achieved great success in proposing candidates for election to the Chicago City Council during the early 1900s.

During World War I he served as a director and president of the Chicago Shipbuilding Company. Ked later served as a member of the Committee of Citizens that defeated a proposition to locate an airport on the lakefront. Ked also served for twenty-five years as president of Tiffany Enamel Brick Company in Momence, Illinois. Originally his father's investment, Ked led Tiffany through construction downturns and the Depression, preserving jobs and supporting Momence.

Ked died in 1939, but his son, Kellogg Fairbank, Jr. ("Kel"), followed in his father's foot steps. Born in 1906, Kel received his AB from Harvard

in 1930 just as the Great Depression began. During World War II, Kel headed the Chicago chapter of the American Red Cross, hauling his family out to every five-alarm fire in the city during the war. He also ran Travelers Aid Society during the war and spent time every day greeting servicemen as they passed through the railroad stations of Chicago.

Kel served for many years on the Boards of the Chicago Hearing Society and the Academy of Sciences. Like his father, he believed that the Burnham Plan protected Chicago's lakefront from commercial exploitation, and he led a lawsuit in the 1950s to prevent the state from buying $25 million of bonds to help finance the original McCormick Place. After three years, the Illinois Supreme Court upheld the state, and McCormick place was built at its present site.

Kel was active in the Harvard Club and was elected president in 1949. He never directly told his son, Kellogg Fairbank III (also "Ked"), that he ought to attend Harvard. Kel just took young Ked along to all the Harvard functions, and it never occurred to his son that there were any alternatives. Kel had taken particular pleasure at an Annual Dinner in the 1960s when he overheard Prof. John H. Finley, AB '25, PhD '33, the featured speaker and Eliot House Master, telling a group of alumni about Ked's experiences while directing *Trial by Jury* at the Woman's Prison in Framingham, Massachusetts. Ked graduated from Harvard in 1963, the year his father died. He is currently on the board of directors of the Club.

divergence of interests it is hard to get a truly representative group together."

"Each honest calling, each walk of life, has its own elite, its own aristocracy based on excellence of performance." James Bryant Conant

President Conant resigned the presidency in 1953, having led Harvard to new heights in scholarship and leadership, and became President Eisenhower's high commissioner, later ambassador, to Germany. Upon his return to the United States in 1957, he undertook a series of studies on public education underwritten by the Carnegie Corporation. Later he returned to Germany as an education advisor through the Ford Foundation. He died in 1978 in New Hampshire.

Boyd Nixon Everett, SB '26, MBA '29

Boyd N. Everett, SB '26, MBA '29, served as Club president in 1952. Everett, who served as senior financial vice president of Continental Casualty Company, was named chairman in June, 1957 of a Chicago-area committee to raise funds to strengthen undergraduate education at Harvard University. In 1967 he took an extensive trip to several countries in Africa, from which he returned to write a disgruntled "Voice of the Traveler" piece for the *Chicago Tribune* advising others not to travel to the same destinations. "Frankly, we don't need to go back to Abidjan or Dakar—they aren't that good!" Everett must have been at the height of his career in February 1969, when he announced on behalf of CNA Financial Corporation plans to begin construction of a $36 million, forty-three-story skyscraper on Wabash Avenue, south of Jackson Boulevard. However, any happiness resulting from his business success must have been interrupted just a few months later. On May 1, 1969, the Tribune announced that Everett's son, Boyd N. Everett, Jr., AB '56, MBA '59, had died along with four other Americans and two Sherpa guides on a climbing expedition in Nepal while trying to conquer the Dhaulagiri peak. Everett Jr. had become interested in mountain climbing while at Harvard and had been scaling mountains since 1956. According to his father, he was the only American to have successfully scaled the four tallest mountain peaks in North America. Everett also had three other sons, William C., Torrey, AB '60, and Bruce A., AB '64. In 1975, Everett wrote an opinion piece for the *Chicago Tribune* in support of Henry Kissinger. His words still have relevance today: "It was never in the cards for Kissinger to be successful in the Middle East unless the two sides were willing to make adjustments to reality and particularly the Arab world's acceptance of Israel in being. Failing that even the Almighty could hardly have been expected to accomplish a permanent accommodation."

Part III

1953 2007

The Later Years

. . . To the age that is waiting before

Chapter 8

The Pusey Years

1953–1971

Nathan Marsh Pusey, AB '28,
AM '32, PhD '37
1907–2001
President of Harvard University
1953–1971

In 1953, Harvard selected forty-six-year-old Nathan Marsh Pusey as its twenty-fourth president. Born in the Midwest, in Council Bluffs, Iowa, Pusey was the first Harvard president to come from west of New York state, an indication that the University was moving to a more national perspective. Pusey came east to Harvard for his postsecondary schooling, earning three Harvard degrees in history. Shortly after completing his doctorate, however, he returned to the Midwest and began a teaching career at Lawrence College in Appleton, Wisconsin. Pusey also taught at Scripps College and Wesleyan University before being called to be president of Lawrence, where he served for nine years before returning to Cambridge as Harvard's president in 1953.

A seemingly mild-mannered man who was described by subsequent President Bok as having "kindness, decency and thoughtfulness," Pusey proved forceful when needed. At the time of his death, in 2001, then president Lawrence Summers said of Pusey, "He had a profound sense of the values of the University, which he called 'one of the noblest creations of the mind of man.'" Those values proved invaluable, as Pusey would face many challenges while at Harvard. They included leading the defense of universities and academic freedom against congressional critics and anti-communists during the McCarthy era, the student rebelliousness of the 1960s, and protests over the Vietnam war. For such leadership even in the early years of his presidency he was featured on the cover of *Time* in 1954 and *Newsweek* in 1957.

In December 1953, just two months after his formal installation as president of Harvard, Pusey declared in an address to the New England Association of Colleges and Secondary Schools: "Americanism does not mean enforced and circumscribed belief. . . . Our job is to educate free, independent, and vigorous minds capable of analyzing events, of exercising judgment, of distinguishing facts from propaganda, and truth from half-truths and lies." In June 1957, he would provide his concept of a liberal education in a guest column for "This Week: The National Sunday Magazine": "The true liberal education has larger aims than just cramming its students with facts in order to teach them how to earn a living. First, it must help each student to find himself as an individual; then it must help him to lose himself in interests, causes, and ideas larger and more enduring than he. America has no need for a race of young people fitted to the same pattern, content to sit back and enjoy what has been called 'a prosperous conformity.'" In the midst of the turbulent 1960s he added in a commencement address in 1964: "[I]n my judgment, there is one thing Harvard men must be agreed about. This is the recognition that truth is not something easily identifiable or simply stated, and that this being so, those other qualities for which we all care so much—integrity, concern, and courage—these qualities make serious demands for understanding upon us all."

Nathan Pusey with Martin Luther King, Jr., January 10, 1965.

During Pusey's administration the Program for Harvard College was undertaken. The most successful fundraising effort in the history of higher education to that point, it raised $100 million from 28,000 donors. In addition, the endowment grew from $304 million to over $1 billion, and more than thirty new buildings were constructed. These included the Carpenter Center for the Visual Arts, the Countway Library of Medicine, Gund Hall, Gutman Library, Hilles Library, Holyoke Center, the Loeb Drama Center, and the Science Center. The new construction, along with additions to existing facilities, nearly doubled the floor space of the University.

The January–February 2002 issue of *Harvard Magazine* noted that Pusey was "A deeply religious man and a staunch friend of Memorial Church, he was the last Harvard president to read the lesson at services every Sunday. And he was the prototype of today's college presidents, who must feel equally at ease in the world of academe and that of large-scale fundraising." Visitors to Harvard Yard can find the Pusey name emblazoned in the Nathan Marsh and Anne Woodward Pusey Room in Memorial Church and in the Nathan Marsh Pusey Library—fitting tributes to a man who feared a "world without spirit."

Reflecting the kind of thinking that led to the selection of the first president from the West, in the early 1950s Harvard University also was embarking on a significant transition that would have major benefits for young men from the Chicago area and west. This expansion of Harvard College's admissions efforts to recruit and admit more students from the West and become a more diverse and national institution was informally known as "Boys from the Sparse Country." Incentives to enroll included scholarship assistance, in some cases in the form of National Scholarships, which provided added assistance with the understanding the recipient should not need to work during the school year and thereby feel more able to contribute to extracurricular activities and other broadening aspects of life at the College.

Students from a few well-known Chicago-area schools, such as New Trier in Winnetka and Evanston Township High

Robert A. Hastings, AB '57, MBA '59

Another Midwesterner was admitted in 1953 who would subsequently become president of both Chicago's Harvard Business School and Harvard Clubs, as well as accept many other Harvard-related responsibilities. Granted a National Scholarship was Robert A. Hastings of Austin, Minnesota. While widely heralded as a T-formation football quarterback, when the Harvard coach decided to stick with the single wing and not switch as promised, Bob focused on basketball and baseball, becoming a three-year letter winner in both. In 1957 he was awarded the Dana J. P. Wingate Memorial Trophy as the Best All Around Player on the Harvard Baseball Team, and also won recognition as the Most Valuable Player in the Greater Boston League and as Harvard's first baseball All-American. After completing an MBA at Harvard Business School in 1959, he and his wife settled in Chicago, and he immediately became active in alumni affairs.

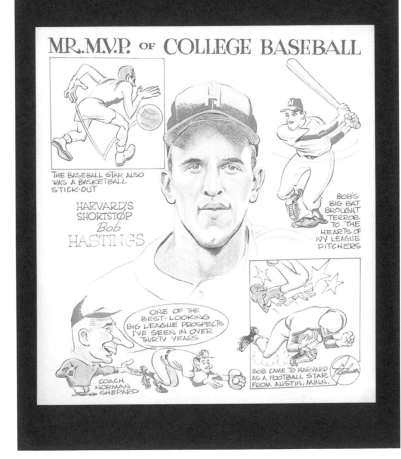

School, already were being admitted in the 1950s. Alan H. "Mickey" Hammerman, who was to return to Chicago and become the longtime head of the Schools and Scholarship Committee of the Club and its president for two years in the 1980s, was admitted in 1951 to the class of 1955, along with five others. Mickey tells a story of one fellow classmate who, because he had an automobile available, was recruited their senior year to drive the dean of admissions from New Trier to Evanston Township High School. Mickey says he was quite surprised when that young man was subsequently admitted. When he later asked the dean how it happened, the dean noted that each member of the admissions committee was entitled to a "wild card" selection, and he had admitted the young man based on their chance acquaintance.

According to reports in the *Chicago Daily Tribune*, a number of students from outlying suburban schools also were beginning to be admitted to Harvard in the early 1950s, often with scholarship assistance granted by the local Club. In 1952, Alex R. Smith of Aurora, Harry S. Jackson of Elmhurst, and David B. Davis of River Forest were admitted to the class of 1956 with Harvard Club scholarships. Admitted to the class of 1957 and granted Harvard Club scholarships, reportedly of $600 to $1,200, were Gil A. Cuatrecasas of Bensenville (who had come to the United States from Spain just five years previously) and Gregory E. Jones of La Grange. Granted regular freshman scholarships that year were Robert L. Bombaugh of Downers Grove and Stephen V. Letcher of McHenry.

Freshman Register pictures of William Cowper Boyden III (left) and William S. North III (right).

The Club was especially active in the years leading up to the 100th anniversary of the Harvard Club of Chicago in 1957, and for several years after that milestone. A favorite event was the Annual Christmas Luncheon, known informally as the "father and son" event. It marked the halfway point in the Club's year and included comments from students home for the holidays, as well as a principal address, usually given by a recognized figure from Cambridge. The 1953 luncheon was held at the Bal Tabarin room of the Sherman Hotel, with football coach Lloyd Jordan as principal speaker. Fullback Ronald Messer of Polo, Illinois, was one of the student speakers, and a film was shown of Harvard's recent 13-0 victory over Yale, always a highlight.

In 1954, Thomas D. Bolles was the featured speaker at the holiday luncheon. He was introduced by Club president Phinney Baxter, AB '41. As appropriate for a school that emphasizes intramural almost as much as intercollegiate competition, Bolles carried the title of Director of Physical Training and Athletics. In his comments, Bolles noted that all eight Ivy schools were now subscribing to the philosophy that athletics were an adjunct to collegiate life rather than a dominant factor. He also reported that while in the last year the Crimson competed in 17 intercollegiate sports, with 349 contests involving 1,600 undergraduates, of perhaps greater importance was an intramural program that included 226 teams in 18 sports, 974 team contests, and 1,954 competitors.

The 1955 holiday luncheon was saddened by the announcement that two undergraduates from prominent Chicago families had been killed December 21 in a tragic accident, when a truck struck their automobile on the way home to Chicago. The Club quickly decided to establish scholarships in each of their names, to be held in an endowment fund by the University's treasurer. Initial and subsequent donations to the William Cowper Boyden III (class of 1957) and William S. North III (class of 1958) memorial funds continue to enable scholarships to be given in their names to enrolling Chicago-area students. The two funds were established early the following year with donations from William C. Boyden, Jr., AB '16, Arthur Dixon, AB '16, and Hermon Dunlap Smith, AB '21, all past presidents of the Club; current president Robert F. Spindell, AB '37; and Adlai E. Stevenson II, whose son was involved in the crash but survived. Visitors to Eliot House who check in the Memorial Dining Room off the regular dining area will find "William Cowper Boyden 1957" inscribed on the fireplace.

In addition to the holiday luncheon, the Club held an Annual Dinner, usually in late February or early March. In most years the dinner featured an address by a speaker affiliated with Harvard. The February 27, 1955, dinner took place at the Sheraton-Blackstone Hotel with speakers Benjamin C. Willis, Chicago Superintendent of Schools; Herold C. Hunt, former Chicago Superintendent and at the time professor of education at Harvard; and Dr. Francis Keppel, dean of the faculty of education at Harvard.

Other meetings held in the mid-1950s did not suffer for lack of Harvard speakers, relationships, or humor. To accommodate broad interest from non-alumni, Orchestra Hall was chosen for a performance by the Harvard Glee Club on April 9, 1954. At a luncheon meeting in late 1955, Dean Horton of the Divinity School recounted the story of a midshipman at Annapolis who was asked on an examination to explain why the Spanish Armada suffered defeat at the hands of the British. "The Armada failed thru a lack of three ships," answered the future admiral. "Leadership, marksmanship, and seamanship."

The award of Harvard Prize Books by the Club continued in the 1950s. A *Chicago Daily Tribune* article of June 9, 1955, noted that Emmons (Pete) Riddle of Highland Park had been awarded the prize "given to the junior male student who 'best combines high character, scholastic ability, leadership, and accomplishment.'"

While Harvard College was not yet accepting women, it was recognizing an obligation to protest racial discrimination. Athletic Director Bolles released the following statement in early October regarding a previously planned southern trip: "Acting in its belief that Harvard alone must decide on the eligibility

of its students to compete, the faculty committee on athletics has withdrawn its approval of the trip which had included two games in locations, where, under present conditions, this control of eligibility would not be possible."

But despite the fact Harvard remained a male-only institution and father-and-son traditions were strong, the Club was beginning to recognize the importance of women, especially graduates of its sister school, Radcliffe. The *Chicago Tribune* reported on December 1, 1954, "It's a WOMAN'S WORLD. Even the Harvard Club of Chicago is acceding that point by electing its first woman director in its 97 year history—Mrs. William A. Magie II (Margaret MacGregor). If being steeped in Harvard tradition qualifies a person for that post, then Mrs. Magie is qualified. A trustee and alumna of Radcliffe College, which practically shares the Harvard campus, she has a Harvard husband and two Harvard sons—William Magie III of the class of '53 and Peter, a sophomore."

The Annual Dinner in 1956 leading up to the Club's 100th anniversary was particularly notable for its further recognition of women. In a significant departure from the ninety-nine-year tradition of a stag dinner since the Club's founding in 1857, wives and special guests were included for the first time. Featured speaker Herman Dunlap "Dutch" Smith entertained the audience with tales of the 41st Annual Dinner in 1898, at which his father Dunlap Smith, AB 1884, had presided as president of the Club and been the speaker. The elder Smith's comments in 1898 included the following:

During the past year the Harvard men of the West have shown their interest in the Alma Mater by holding, for the first time, a convention for the nomination of an overseer who should be representative of the entire West, and on that occasion honored the Chicago Harvard Club by unanimously nominating our distinguished Vice President, George E. Adams. . . .The Harvard club is to be congratulated also that Harvard men in and about Chicago now outnumber those of any Eastern University, a fact we have long suspected, but which this year we have been able to prove officially for the first time. Our efficient Secretary has prepared [a] catalogue that includes the names of 458 Harvard men in and about Chicago thereby leaving Yale far in the rear and placing both Yale and Princeton in the "and others' class. . . .I have no doubt that no man will feel that he has completed his education unless he holds a degree bearing the Harvard seal.

A *Chicago Tribune* article reported the menu of the 1898 dinner as read from a copy of the menu that had been saved: "It ran the gamut from relishes to cheese and coffee, and included oysters, soup, lobster Newburg, larded filet of beef, roast jacksnipe, asparagus, Neapolitan ice cream and cake, red and white wines, Crème de Mandarin punch, cigarettes and cigars!"

The grand year of celebrating the Club's 100th anniversary

in 1957 is well documented in a report from the Anniversary Committee retrieved from Dutch Smith's family collection of Harvard memorabilia. It begins: "In the fall of 1955 the Harvard Club of Chicago received word from the Harvard Archives in Cambridge that The Harvard Club of Chicago was, in fact, the oldest of all Harvard Clubs . . . organized in 1857." The report states the board of directors then asked Dutch to serve as "Chairman of a 100th Anniversary Committee to provide a program that would duly celebrate the occasion and create a favorable impression of Harvard in the Chicago community." A steering committee of eight prominent alumni chairmen was formed to guide the effort.

According to the report nearly 1,000 Harvard and Radcliffe alumni and spouses attended the Club's 100th Anniversary Dinner on February 1, 1957. The event was chaired by Wyndham Hasler and held in the Grand Ballroom of the Palmer House. President Pusey gave the principal address,

First Female Club Director

Margaret MacGregor and William Magie

Margaret MacGregor earned her AB at Radcliffe in 1928, following her sister Helen, AB '24, and preceding her brother Robert, AB '33. She married William A. Magie, AB '28, younger brother of Frank Ogden Magie, Jr., AB '18. William had grown up at 735 Sheridan Road in Winnetka and 1235 Astor Street in Chicago. He was football manager his senior year, served as Class Secretary for his class, and after the couple settled in Chicago was a director and treasurer of the Harvard Club from 1932 to 1935.

Margaret Magie was elected a trustee of Radcliffe in 1953, the year son William, Jr. graduated from Harvard. She served until 1959, and in 1954 also was elected the first female director of the Harvard Club of Chicago. Her son John reports his mother's service for Radcliffe was "an honor she was justly very proud of and took very seriously, traveling often to Cambridge—even after 1959 for other Radcliffe committees."

William, Jr. also moved back to the Chicago area following graduation, first living in Kankakee. During his later childhood he and his family had lived at 695 Prospect Avenue in Winnetka, near the well-known Harvard-connected Greeley family descendents of Samuel Sewell Greeley, AB 1844. In yet another Harvard connection, the landmark house on Prospect was designed by architect Joseph Lyman Silsbee, AB 1869.

titled "The Alumnus of the University." There was particular applause when President Pusey remarked, "It is pleasing to know that The Harvard Club of Chicago not only surpasses the other Clubs in venerability, but also takes its place with the very best of the Harvard Clubs in the number of its members and in their spirit of energy and devotion to Harvard." Arthur T. Hamlin, AB '34, librarian of the University of Cincinnati gave a brief talk on the history of the Harvard Club of Chicago. President Paul P. Swett, Jr., of the Associated Harvard Clubs, which had held their midyear meeting in Chicago earlier in the day to recognize the anniversary, delivered a congratulatory message. Dutch Smith would be elected president of the Associated Harvard Clubs the following year.

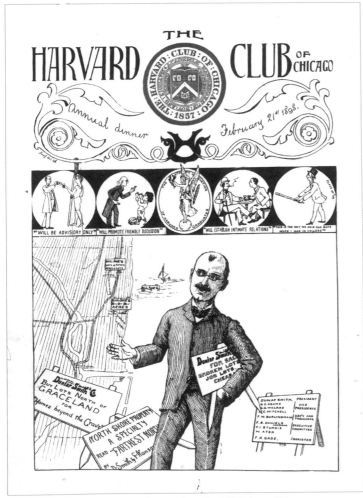

1898 dinner program cover, referenced at the 1956 Award Dinner.

The 100th anniversary stimulated widespread activity in the Chicago alumni community. Meetings were planned that were specifically tailored to graduates of the professional schools, including those for the Harvard Medical School, chaired by Philip Shambaugh, MD '30, and the Harvard Law Society, chaired by William N. Haddad, LLB '26. The most ambitious was a Midwest Business Conference held on April 13 and chaired by Harris Ward, AB '30, MBA '32, executive vice president and subsequently CEO of Commonwealth Edison Company. Harvard Business School dean Stanley F. Teele, Marion B. Folsom, Secretary of Health, Education and Welfare, and a group of senior professors from the Harvard Business School presented an all-day program that was reported to have "caused much excitement in the business community for months to come."

The wide variety of functions also resulted in strong membership gains for the Club, which reached 1,000 for the first time. Special attention was given a newly established Decade Group for college graduates within the preceding ten years. The Decade Group field day, held August 17 at the home of Laird Bell, AB '04, LLD '55 (hon.), in Winnetka, drew about 150 members for fun and games, good food, and reminiscing. Future Club president Philip W. K. Sweet, AB '50, and his wife were among those shown in *Tribune* photographs of those attending. It set a pattern for successful similar events to bring young graduates into the Club's membership and stimulate long-term participation in subsequent years. Many senior members of the Club were willing to act as hosts at their expansive North Shore estates. Before later infill development, the spacious backyard of almost football field size and tennis court at well-known architect Denison B. Hull's (AB '19, MAR '23) home on DeWindt Road in Winnetka provided ample space for summer games and a picnic, as did Laird Bell's woodsy acreage off Tower Road. Former president Bob Spindell was happy to host in the large garden of his home in Kenilworth. Dutch Smith's expansive home bounding Lake Michigan in Lake Forest was great for volleyball, badminton, croquet, and other games on the grass above the bluff, or for swimming off the beach below.

The anniversary year was not without entertainment programs. Samuel S. Greeley AB '36, LLB'39, great-grandson of one of the founders of Club, chaired a heavily attended April 2 Harvard Glee Club concert. It filled the large auditorium of Chicago's skyscraper at the time, the Prudential Building. The calendar year concluded with a very popular performance of the Hasty Pudding Institute of 1770 during the holiday period.

The year 1957 also was notable for the beginning of the successful $82.5 million campaign initiated by President Pusey to raise money for new facilities at Harvard. Boyd N. Everett, AB '26, MBA '29, chaired a kick-off meeting dinner October 29 for the Midwest portion of the campaign.

Alumni activity in Chicago hardly slowed following the 100th anniversary year. The February 21, 1958, Annual Dinner in the Sheraton-Blackstone's Crystal Ballroom continued the Club's tradition of holding the dinner on the eve of George Washington's birthday. Another spectacular event brought the Harvard University Band and two eight-foot novelties for its April 1, 1958, concert at the Eighth Street Theater. One of the novelties was an eight-foot tuba said to produce the loudest "oompah" in the world, made originally for celebrated bandleader John Philip Sousa. The other was an eight-foot

bass drum, which requires a specially designed truck to carry it to performances. Included in the sixty undergraduate players were George J. Klems, AB '58, and Barry L. Berman, AB '57, of Chicago, Jon E. Gudeman, AB '58, of Winnetka, and Philip E. Johnson, AB '61, of Aurora. This concert, to benefit the Harvard Club's scholarship fund, was the first by the band in Chicago since its founding in 1919.

The Harvard Club of Chicago then cooperated with the Adult Education Council to produce a May 14 tribute to the late Supreme Court Justice Oliver Wendell Holmes, including a play written by Francis Coughlin, continuity director for WGN, and William Friedkin. Famed Chicago poet, historian, and biographer Carl Sandburg, who modeled Justice Windom, a central character of his book, *Remembrance Rock*, after Holmes, was a principal speaker, along with Mark DeWolfe Howe, AB '28, LLB '33, Harvard law professor and former secretary to and biographer of Holmes (he had finished the first of a multivolume biography of Holmes). The Chicago and Cook County Bar Associations also cooperated in the program, along with the Decalogue Society.

Radcliffe graduates continued to receive increasing responsibility within the Harvard Club and participated in

The Harvard University Band's "Big Bass" drum.

Radcliffe president Mr. Wilbur Kitchener Jordan, AM '28, PhD '31 and wife (center), at a Radcliffe Club of Chicago dinner with incoming RCC president Zoe Andre Bakeeff Petersen, AB '44, and husband, Edward S. Petersen, MD '45, at the Fortnightly Club, January 24, 1958.

many of its programs during this period, especially working on women's and other committees. However, they continued to maintain a strong separate affiliated club identity and to hold meetings specifically oriented to Radcliffe graduates, such as one chaired by Radcliffe Club of Chicago president Zoe Andre Bakeeff Petersen, AB '44, on January 24, 1958.

In the spring of 1958, Chicago hit a Harvard College scholarship peak, garnering twenty-one of the 300 awardees. Among those who returned to Chicago and were widely known were Harry S. Meislahn, AB '62, MBA '65, who matriculated at New Trier Township High School, and George A. Ranney, Jr., AB '62, who attended Westminster School in England. Both received honorary scholarships.

In early September 1959, Levering Cartwright opened his home in Kenilworth to continue a longstanding tradition of the Club of hosting a welcome party for incoming freshmen at Harvard College. The sixty students enrolling made up one of the largest classes ever admitted from this area. Also joining in the fun were Decade Group members and officers of the Club. In a similar welcoming process, entering Radcliffe freshmen were visited by an alumna and attended a party a few days later hosted by Mrs. William A. Magie II.

The January 1960 Annual Dinner, held in the Guildhall of the Ambassador West, was notable for the inclusion of the presidents of the Yale and Princeton alumni clubs. The heads of alumni clubs of Ivy League schools, the graduate schools at Harvard, and occasionally those of other Harvard Clubs in the Midwest have graced the head table from time to time during the Club's history.

Later in 1960, the Club's December 28 luncheon featured track coach William W. McCurdy as principal speaker, with students home for the holidays particularly invited to attend. Personally greeting the attendees in the Red Lacquer Room of the Palmer House were Edward B. Ayres, AB '50, of Lake Forest, chair of the Schools Committee, Frank L. Bixby, AB '50, chair of the Scholarship Committee, and Robert A. Hastings, AB '57, MBA '59, chair of arrangements for the meeting.

The Club continued in 1961 to host the College's musical organizations and professors. An April 7 Harvard concert band performance at the Germania Club included a wide range of selections, from Berlioz to "Fair Harvard." It was followed in early May by a luncheon featuring Professor George E. Kirk, an associate of the Center for Middle Eastern Studies, the title of whose address was "The Middle East—A Time of Hope?"

One of the fifty-four young men admitted in 1961 was Bruce Douglas Borland. Bruce's father, John J. Borland, AB '33, of Lake Forest, had served as president of the Club in 1957.

Several noteworthy events highlighted Philip Sweet's 1963 year as president of the Club. Legendary and beloved professor John H. Finley, Jr., AB '25, PhD '33, was the guest speaker at the Annual Dinner, held in the Guildhall of the Ambassador West Hotel.

Alumni warmed up for the Hasty Pudding's return to Chicago April 5, 1963, with a luncheon at the Racquet Club at which Walter H. Moses, Jr., of Winnetka played tunes from the present show and the 113th and 114th, for which he wrote the music. John W. Stimpson chaired the show committee for the Club and reminded everyone that both male and female roles are played by the young men in the cast. Undergraduates Walter Benson of Barrington was the producer and Robert Altman the scenery builder for "Tickle Me Pink," which was presented in the New Trier High School auditorium. Stuart Abelson and Telford A. Walker appeared as actors. Walker, a 210-pound football player, brought down the house with his role as a Russian ballerina. It was reported that some notable Chicago business figures who had been members of Hasty Pudding in their undergraduate days were Barrett Wendell, Perry D. Smith, Hermon Dunlap Smith, William C. Boyden, Arnold and Ralph Horween, William H. Mitchell, William F. Borland, Arthur Dixon, and William and Michael Cudahy.

As he concluded his term, Phil Sweet called on Dutch Smith to report at a luncheon session on the May meeting of the University's governing boards. The meeting had been held in

Washington, D.C., and President Kennedy, who like Dutch was a retiring overseer at the time, had hosted a dinner at the White House. An interesting anecdote included in the report was that as the guests proceeded up the stairs to dinner, they were accompanied by the Marine Band dressed in red/crimson uniforms playing Harvard songs.

The year 1963 was another milestone for women in gaining full acceptance at Harvard University. The Graduate School of Arts and Sciences was opened to women and the Radcliffe graduate school closed.

President Denison B. Hull presided over the March 1964 Annual Dinner of the Club in the Guildhall of the Ambassador West Hotel. Dean of the Divinity School Dr. Samuel H. Miller delivered the address, "What Do You Want Out of a Minister These Days?" William S. North chaired the dinner.

Humphrey Doermann, director of admissions for the College, addressed a stag dinner on September 29, 1965, at the Shoreacres Club. Attendees were fascinated by his comments on the admissions process and Harvard's move to need-blind admissions. Doermann worked closely with Chicago Schools Committee members during the 1960s and was particularly interested in the college performance of students admitted from public schools compared with those from traditional prep feeder schools in the East. Bob Hastings recalled a visit with Doermann in his Cambridge office in which the preliminary results of a comparison study were discussed. The indications were that the prep school graduates did better initially, perhaps because the teaching and performance expectations were closer to what would be experienced at the College. However, by sophomore year the public school graduates generally caught up, and over the four years they often would surpass those from prep schools. In an interesting aside concerning admissions competition at the time, it was asked whether a large stack of IBM cards on Doermann's desk were those of the study. The reply: "No, they represent the National Merit Semi-finalists who have applied, and there are more of them than there are places in the entering class."

One of the longstanding traditions in which present and former Club officers have participated over the years is an Annual Ivy League Alumni Golf "Tournament." Usually played as a best ball of pairs event, and hosted in the early years by the former year's winners, the event continues as a once each summer enduring enjoyable excuse for a generally friendly outing with good-natured ribbing about the quality of play. After winning the 1965 event at Glen View Club, Robert F. Spindell hosted the August 19, 1966, event at Knollwood Club along with his partner, W. S. North. Harvard has won a fair share of the titles, which in recent years have been played for at Old Elm Club.

The Hasty Pudding returned to Chicago Saturday, April 9, 1966, with its 118th theatrical production, "Right Up Your Alley." Show members Frederick A. Steadry and Peter Voyseys of Winnetka, and Christopher C. DeMuth of Kenilworth were right at home in the auditorium of New Trier High School. David Foster of Lake Forest also was a member of the cast. Eleanor Page's prominent column in the April 5 *Chicago Tribune* noted the young men would participate with former members and past and present directors of the Club in a stag dinner Friday night. Cast members would be entertained before the show by members of Kappa Alpha Theta sorority at Northwestern. John W. Stimpson chaired the event, with help from committee members President Austin L. Wyman, Stefan S. Anderson, Philip W. K. Sweet, Wolcott H. Johnson, and Robert A. Hastings.

The two year 1967–68 tenure of Christopher G. Janus, SB '36 as president of the Club was notable for imaginative programming and the introduction of a special award given for distinguished service to the community. One of the innovations was a monthly "dialogue luncheon" with a variety of interesting participants. A January 1967 session, for example, had as panelists Chicago Police Superintendent O. W. Wilson; Democratic Representative John Brademus of Indiana; Mortimer J. Adler, director of the Institute for Philosophical Research; and Reverend Paul S. Allen, pastor of the Winnetka Congregational Church.

The first Annual Award Dinner was held March 17, 1967, in the Sheraton-Blackstone Hotel. It was the first of many festive such evenings, with crimson and gold menus. Hermon Dunlap Smith, AB '21, received the first "special award," "ordinarily granted to a person (occasionally persons) who has made a distinguished contribution to the greater Chicago community in some field other than his or her primary occupation. The recipient(s) may be any person, regardless of sex, race, creed, or education, and need not have any Harvard University connection." Mr. Smith was presented a six-inch replica of the John Harvard statue by Marshall Field V, chair of the Award Committee, at a dinner in the Crystal Ballroom of the Sheraton Blackstone Hotel. President Janus stated: "The award was given to him [Smith] especially because he was largely instrumental in keeping the Lewis H. Silver collection of rare books at the Newberry Library. The collection is valued in excess of $2 million."

In his comments as recipient, Smith noted several aspects of public service for young people at the time, and added several quotes along with his own comments as follows:

In the typical urban community in this country, every promising young man, or woman, is approached by an invitation to become involved in some civic activity.

To quote another prominent Harvard man, and a former president of this Club, Clarence Randall: "What counts is the sharing of an ideal and the fighting staunchly side by side with others to bring it to fulfillment. In such projects no one cares what the other man's regular job is, or what his rank is. A network of activity is woven from human friendship, based upon mutual respect. Its bonds are the comradeship that causes like-minded persons to stand together and share responsibility in a common undertaking."

Walter Fisher, when many of his friends spoke to him in high praise of his public spirited sacrifice in giving up a successful and lucrative law practice to serve as Chairman of the Illinois Commerce Commission at a considerable reduction in compensation, said "Just because this is costing me money does not make it a sacrifice. It is really a form of luxurious self-indulgence. Some people indulge themselves in yachts, or race horses, but I don't care for either, and so I felt I was entitled to this form of extravagance."

Aristotle defined happiness as "activity of the soul in accordance with virtue." . . . Almost all Western philosophy from Aristotle to Emerson (there comes Harvard again) has stressed the concept of useful activity as the key to happiness. . . . This should, of course, be its *own* reward, but a charming statue of John Harvard makes very nice frosting on the cake.

At the time "Dutch" Smith was not only a senior executive of the Marsh and McLennon insurance firm but was also serving as president of the Newberry Library and Adlai Stevenson Institute of International Affairs, chairman of the Executive Committee of the Chicago Community Trust, director of the Chicago Council on Foreign Relations, head of the National Merit Scholarship organization, and trustee of the Chicago Planetarium Society and Chicago Horticultural Society. He also was a trustee of Radcliffe College. Congratulatory communications regarding the award were received from senators Everett McKinley Dirksen and Hubert H. Humphrey, Illinois governor Otto Kerner, and Chicago mayor Richard J. Daley.

The speaker at the first Annual Award Dinner was Franklin L. Ford, dean of the Faculty of Arts and Sciences. It was a challenging time in academia, and Dean Ford spoke to the essential nature of education and a concern that the increasing unease among students might threaten the essential quality of the education they hoped to receive: " Our students want to learn something while they are in college, and that seems to me a right which we must respect above all others. . . . What some of them forget is that their right to read and listen and criticize and revise is precisely what their elders in the university community are sworn to defend, whether against the Old Right or against the New Left." Ford called for the preservation of liberalism in education, defining it as the insistence on unrestricted freedom of inquiry and the belief the highest values of civilization are those of individual striving and individual attainment within a community of free men who respect the rights of other men.

Christopher Janus strongly believed in Greece's place in history. It was later reported he would write during the dictatorship of the Greek military in 1970: "The ruling army junta also does not appreciate that Greece does not belong to them. Thru its ancient heritage, which stresses the dignity and personal rights of all individuals, Greece belongs to all nations and people it has helped enrich." Janus was one of the founders of the Greek Heritage Foundation, which he largely controlled. That led to an unusual program opportunity in the fall of 1967. Members were invited to participate in the Fourth Annual Greek Heritage Foundation Symposium in Athens, September 25 to October 9. The lectures provided by Sir Maurice Bowra, vice chancellor of Oxford University, and others and a tour of the Greek Islands proved of interest to more than twenty-five participants. A similar trip was offered in the fall of 1969. It included a week of lectures in Athens, Corinth, and Delphi, with a cruise of the Greek Islands afterward. That year the Greek Heritage Foundation also sponsored an essay contest from which two Chicago-area high school winners would be selected to join the trip. Contestants had to compose a letter of 400 words or less to an imaginary Greek teen on "the advantages of living in a free society."

The second Annual Award Dinner, on January 19, 1968, recognized the contributions of architect William E. Hartmann and Mrs. John V. (Bea) Spachner. Hartman was recognized for helping persuade Pablo Picasso to undertake the commission for the sculpture that stands in the Daley Center Plaza and for his participation in the design of the Civic Center. Mrs. Spachner was instrumental in the preservation and restoration of the Auditorium Theater, for which she spearheaded a nine-year drive that raised almost $2.25 million. Each received a

John Harvard replica statue in recognition of their efforts on behalf of the community. John H. Finley, Jr., AB '25, PhD '33, master of Eliot House for a quarter of a century beginning at age thirty-eight in 1942, during which twenty-six Rhodes Scholars who lived in Eliot were named, returned to Chicago to deliver the keynote address. As reported in a memorial minute from the *Harvard University Gazette* of May 25, 2000, Finley was vice chair of the committee that formulated the educational blueprint "The Objectives of a General Education in a Free Society," and much of the report was formulated by him. Few students of the 1940s to 1960s who took Humanities 2, the course he taught in concert with Harry Levin, or Humanities 103—The Great Age of Athens, or who know Finley as their Eliot House Master missed the opportunity to hear him once again. Mrs. Robert A. (Margaret) Hastings served as chairperson of a Women's Committee for the dinner, which included Mrs. Roger P. (Sally) Eklund, Mrs. Lyman W. (Gretchen) Hull, Mrs. J. Harris (Mary) Ward, and Mrs. William (Ethel) Gofen, president of the Radcliffe Club.

The Sheraton-Blackstone Hotel continued to be a favored location for the Award Dinners into the 1970s. On January 10, 1969, Charles Daggett Harvey was recognized for his community service. Harvey was a strong supporter of the National Parks, especially at the Grand Canyon, and had served as chairman of the Western Conference of National Park Commissioners. He also had initiated an award given to outstanding doctors at Northwestern University's Feinberg School of Medicine and was a supporter of other causes, as well as having served as president of the Chicago Council on Foreign Relations (now Global Affairs) in 1950–53. Edwin O. Reischauer, MA '32, PhD '39 was the featured speaker. Reischauer enchanted the audience with stories from his Japanese experiences. He had been born in Japan in 1910 to American missionary parents and, while living and being educated there until he was seventeen, became fluent in Japanese language, culture and customs. During his career at Harvard he was named director of the Harvard-Yenching Institute in 1956 and also served as chair of the Department of Far Eastern Languages. In 1961 President John F. Kennedy took the unusual step of nominating Reischauer to be ambassador

Harvard Glee Club Snowed Out

William P. Hall, AB '45, MBA '48, president of the Harvard Club of Chicago in 1979–81, provided this reminiscence.

"In early March, 1968 the Harvard Glee Club was scheduled to give a recital at North Shore Country Day School, then stay with club members that night, and bus to Minneapolis the next day. Let's say it was Friday and storm clouds were threatening. I drove in town to my Loop office and picked up the programs from the printer. About noon the snow began to fall and increase in intensity. By mid-afternoon I decided to leave for home, but was waived off by a policeman while half way. I ended up at a bar from which I called home. Ann said that the Glee Club had abandoned its bus and was coming to Winnetka by train. She and others had rounded up two local ladies with four-wheel drive cars who would pick up the lads and take them to the homes to which they were assigned.

"I didn't get out of the bar until after 10:00 p.m. when the radio assured us that plowing had been done. When I reached home, the concert, of course, had been cancelled and we had six (not two, as scheduled) Glee Clubbers in the house. Ann had managed to feed them (plus our family) and assigned them beds. I got the couch in our living room.

"The next morning was bright and gorgeous. The bus arrived at our place about 9:00 a.m. and the ladies brought all members to our house. I'll never forget them kneeling in the snow by the bus and singing a song to Ann as a thank-you. Then off they went to Minneapolis. There never was a more memorable Glee Club non-concert."

other Harvard departments, centers and research institutes, and to respond to scholarly and public interest in Japan from outside Harvard through outreach activities such as lectures, conferences, symposia, exhibitions and films.

In 1970 two awards were given, to Mrs. J. Harris Ward and Daniel Walker. Mrs. Ward, the wife of Commonwealth Edison's CEO, was a major benefactor of many Chicago area charities but was especially noted for her efforts in reviving the Lyric Opera and supporting Know Your Chicago. Daniel Walker was recognized for his leadership of the report covering the conduct of the Chicago police during the 1968 democratic convention. It brought him considerable recognition and was a major contributing factor in his surprising defeat of Lieutenant Governor Paul Simon in the democratic primary and Republican governor Richard B. Ogilvie in the 1972 race to become governor of Illinois. Astronaut Frank Borman, commander of the 1968 Apollo 8 mission that was the first to circle the moon, described the challenges of space travel and its potential risks and contributions in his keynote presentation. He had served in 1967 as a member of the board that investigated the Apollo 204 fire that killed three astronauts, and he later headed the team to reengineer the Apollo spacecraft.

The dialogue luncheon program also continued to be a positive part of the Club's activities. Among provocative offerings during John Stimpson's 1971 year as president were the October and December 1970 events held in the University Club, "Should Public Employees Have the Right to Strike?" and "Pollution—Are We Meeting the Challenge?"

The December 17, 1970, holiday luncheon in the Palmer House honored John Yovicsin, the retiring football coach. Yovicsin had undergone open heart surgery six years previously in the midst of compiling a record of 78-45-5 in his fourteen years, including ten winning seasons in a row and more victories than by any previous Harvard coach. Junior Spencer Dreischarf, a defensive guard on the team, referred to Yovicsin as "the most respected and honored football coach in the East." Yovicsin had been honored four times as

to Japan, which he saw as an opportunity to foster stronger relations between the land of his childhood and his American heritage. Reischauer would later found the Japan Institute in 1973, which in 1985 would be renamed the Edwin O. Reischauer Institute of Japanese Studies in his honor. The Institute is described on its Web site as having "a university-wide mandate to develop and coordinate activities concerning Japan among the various faculties at Harvard through the advancement of instruction and research in the social sciences and humanities. Moreover, the Reischauer Institute seeks to expand and coordinate Japan-related connections with

New England Coach of Year by the New England Football Writers Association, in 1961, 1966, 1968, and 1970. Radcliffe sophomore Kyle Carney of Lake Forest, the first female student to address the Club at what had earlier been known as the "father and son" luncheon, secured a large laugh from the primarily male audience when she noted, "There simply weren't any coed facilities at Radcliffe until about 350 Harvard men moved in."

The Pusey years ended on a high note in early 1971 for the Harvard Club of Chicago when the Club again hosted a "Harvard Comes to Chicago" program and the first meeting in twenty years of the worldwide Associated Harvard Alumni in Chicago, capped by the Club's Annual Award Dinner. Even a Yale graduate, Illinois governor Richard Ogilvie, recognized the importance as he proclaimed January 22, 1971, "Harvard's Day in Illinois."

Participants in the day's activities included John Dunlop, dean of the Faculty of Arts and Sciences, speaking during the morning and afternoon seminars, and Henry Kissinger, assistant to the president for national security affairs, who delivered the keynote address at lunch. Attendees said Kissinger attempted to explain Nixon administration actions in the international arena. He described them as an attempt to establish new directions and methods that would enable the nation to leave the role as security chief for much of the world and spread this responsibility among other nations. In

his view, the Soviet and Chinese blocs were divided, Germany and Japan were capable of providing for themselves, and foreign policy needed to be brought into line with the physical and psychological limitations of the nation.

President Pusey was the featured speaker at the Award Dinner, which capped the day's festivities. It was the last opportunity for Chicago alumni to hear from him in person and wish him well before his retirement that June. In his presentation Pusey noted the many campus incidents of the 1960s and voiced a major concern for academic morale, expressing as the greatest problem a "loss of faith in the simple goal of scholarship—that nothing is more important than learning itself." Co-chairs of the dinner were Eugene P. Heytow and Marshall Field.

Former president of the Club Christopher Janus presented the award for distinguished service to the community to William McCormick Blair at the dinner. Former award winners Hermon Dunlap Smith and Mrs. J. Harris Ward and their spouses of Lake Forest were rumored to be hosting the Puseys and other dignitaries. However, no one seemed to know for publication, perhaps due to the tight security imposed because of a recent threat to Kissinger. The day proceeded without problems and was thoroughly enjoyed by all of the alumni participants and guests.

New football coach Joe Restic spoke at the Annual Meeting in the Kenilworth Club in June 1971, which concluded the year's activities. Restic had coached the Hamilton Tiger Cats of the Canadian Football League for nine years before being lured to Cambridge, and said he would employ the wide-open offense of that experience. Restic was joined in the presentation by senior Kit Starck, a center from Loyola Academy, and junior Steve Hall, a fullback from New Trier East. Gene Heytow, AB '55, was elected president for the 1972–73 year at the meeting.

Left: January 21, 1971 Harvard Comes to Chicago and Associated Harvard Alumni meeting Luncheon. Christopher G. Janus, SB '36; John W. Stimpson, AB '58; President Nathan Marsh Pusey, AB '28, AM '32, PhD '37; Speaker Henry F. Kissinger, BA '50, MA '52, PhD '54, Assistant to the President of the United States for National Security Affairs; Robert F. Spindell, AB '27, LLB '30

Chapter 9

The Bok Years

Derek Bok, AB '51 (Stanford); JD '54, AM '58 (Washington University)
1930–
President of Harvard University 1971–1991
Bok, a lawyer and law professor, served as dean of Harvard Law School.

Derek Curtis Bok, JD '54, became the twenty-fifth president of Harvard in the summer of 1971, at a time when the campus tumult of the late 1960s was still fresh in people's minds. The Vietnam War was still raging at the time of President Bok's ascendancy. The war effort had recently intensified with U.S. troops invading Cambodia, as former Harvard professor and presidential foreign policy advisor, Henry Kissinger, AB '50, AM '52, PhD '54, had discussed at the Harvard Club of Chicago's 1971 Annual Award Dinner. President Bok guided the University with a sure and steady hand until his first retirement as president in 1991.

In keeping with the spirit of a new beginning, Harvard also hired a new football coach, Joe Restic, to lead the Crimson, commencing with the 1971 season. As mentioned at the end of the last chapter, Coach Restic was the Harvard Club of Chicago's speaker at the June 1971 Annual Meeting. The tenure of Restic, the longest serving Harvard football coach to date, almost exactly paralleled the first term of President Bok. Coach Restic retired in 1993, just two years after the termination of Bok's first period of service.

Invited to speak at the Club's January 1972 Annual Dinner, Bok shared his vision for the future of Harvard. As reported in the *Chicago Tribune*, Bok intended Harvard professors to become more intimately engaged in their primary duties as student educators, while maintaining their research and writing endeavors. Bok's emphasis on education was evident early during his watch and undoubtedly contributed to the development of the Core Curriculum, which although under re-evaluation was still in use in 2007. Bok further emphasized

at the 1972 dinner that he hoped to steer Harvard away from excessive reliance on government grants, which he saw as a threat to the University's independence. In subsequent years, Bok led a number of successful fundraising campaigns that helped make the University less reliant on government funding. In his remarks at the Annual Dinner, Bok also decried the increasing cost burden to those seeking to become doctors, lawyers, teachers, or other professionals, thus laying a path for the University's generous financial aid policies in the years to come.

The Annual Awardee in 1972 was Chicago real estate developer and patron of the arts Louis C. Sudler (Yale '25). A gifted baritone, Sudler was a member of the Chicago Civic Opera. He appeared nationally as a soloist, with symphonies, and with concert bands. Sudler performed at functions honoring several U.S. presidents. He established scholarships and awards for promising young musicians through the Louis Sudler Foundation and the Sousa Foundation. He became known for his leadership of the Orchestral Association of the Chicago Symphony Orchestra and for his service on the boards of a number of art institutions throughout the country.

During the early 1970s, China was beginning to emerge from decades of isolation from the West following the communist revolution, and the Harvard Club of Chicago was a participant in this new movement. The Chinese government was initially hesitant to encourage typical tourism and favored culturally oriented visits. Through the efforts of Chris Janus, SB '36, approximately forty members of the Harvard Club of Chicago were granted access to China as part of this new trend. Club members commissioned local artist Edward Weiss to paint a larger-than-life portrait of Mao Tse-Tung to present to the Chinese leader on their trip.

In November 1972, *Chicago Tribune* publisher Harold Grumhaus addressed the Harvard Club at a dialogue luncheon held at the University Club. Freedom of the press and freedom of speech were the topics of discussion. While admitting that the press occasionally made mistakes, Grumhaus contended the American press was the most free and reliable press in the world. Hoping to make some recompense for an honest press mistake, Grumhaus revealed that he intended to present Harry Truman with a plaque bearing a replica of the *Tribune* headline, made prematurely after the 1948 presidential election, which declared "Dewey Defeats Truman." President Truman had reportedly indicated he had a great deal of fun with the erroneous headline over the years. Before the plaque could be presented, however, Truman died, in December 1972. Grumhaus then presented the plaque to the Truman Memorial Library in Independence, Missouri.

The Club honored Harold Grumhaus as its seventh Annual Award Winner in February 1973. Again speaking in favor of a free press, Grumhaus criticized efforts by government agencies to create standards to regulate the press through so-called "fairness doctrines." Also in attendance at the evening festivities was Matina Horner, the new, thirty-two-year-old president of Radcliffe. The guest speaker that evening was Caspar W. Weinberger, AB '38, LLB '41, President Nixon's nominee at the time to run the Department of Health, Education and Welfare. Weinberger lauded the dedication to public service exhibited by both Harvard and Grumhaus. President Nixon sent a telegram that was read at the Annual Award Dinner congratulating his "old friend" Grumhaus and remarked that "the coveted Harvard Club Award for public service is a tribute to the finest qualities of citizenship and community leadership." Just over a year later, on August 8, 1974, under threat of impeachment from the Watergate scandal, Richard Nixon would resign as president of the United States.

David Rockefeller, AB '36, LLD '69, addressed the Club at the February 1974 Annual Award Dinner. Rockefeller was chairman of Chase Manhattan Bank and rumored at the time to replace George Schulz as Secretary of the Treasury. The Arab oil embargo was in full swing, and Rockefeller was reportedly "optimistic" that lower oil prices would return after the embargo was lifted. At the same time, Rockefeller indicated Arab investment of the dollars earned from oil in American corporations and real estate could be "beneficial." Robert E. Brooker, philanthropist and a former president of Montgomery Ward, was the evening's awardee.

The Harvard Club of Chicago acknowledged contributions to culture at the Annual Award Dinner in February 1975. William and Eleanor Wood-Prince were the honorees. Among their contributions was the donation of the Chagall mosaic "Four Seasons," a Chicago treasure for years to come, which was placed in the plaza of the First National Bank of Chicago, later sold and acquired most recently by Chase Bank. Former Harvard Nieman Fellow (1956–57) and Harvard's vice president for financial affairs Hale Champion was the guest speaker. Later that same year, American troops pulled out of Vietnam.

Harvard-Yale Game Broadcasts

James E. Challenger, AB '47, provided the following reminiscence:

"We were having the Harvard-Yale football game at my house in Winnetka. It was a house that lent itself well to parties. We held the Harvard-Yale game party at our home for many years in the 1970s. In the days before satellite TV, the only way to get the game was to ask Illinois Bell to bring in the game feed directly from Cambridge. Early during the week of the game, Illinois Bell would come in to set up their equipment. One year the technician arrived on Saturday morning and discovered that he could not get the game on the line nor was he able to fix the problem. He called into service to get more help and they told him someone could be out by dinner to look at it. This did not make much sense because the game would have long been completed.

"Fortunately, the head of the telephone company lived about a block away from our house. I called him on the phone, told him about our plight, and he offered to try and help. Less than ten minutes later, he arrived at our house. He personally fixed the line and we started to get the feed from Cambridge. He then sent two service people to guard the equipment throughout the entire game to ensure it didn't break down again. We offered them food but they were so worried for fear that a problem might occur that they sat rigidly in their chairs and refused to move. If it wasn't for the head of the phone company, we would have disappointed all those people. Over a hundred individuals showed up each year for this event and I think at that time it was all Harvard people. In those days, people dressed more formally, often showing up in sport coats and Harvard sweaters."

The Club turned its attention to the cosmos at the 1976 Annual Award Dinner with invited speaker Robert C. Seamans, Jr., BS '39. Seamans spent the better part of two decades between 1948 and 1968 working on various projects as a top administrator for NASA and its predecessor organization, the National Advisory Committee for Aeronautics. Seamans served as secretary of the U.S. Air Force between 1969 and 1973. He also spent many years teaching at MIT, eventually becoming dean of its School of Engineering in 1978. Also honored for public service that evening was Helen Regenstein, long-time patron of the arts and education.

Nixon, Watergate, and Vietnam were still fresh in mind when the Club invited former Watergate special prosecutor Archibald Cox, AB '34, LLB '37, LLD '75 (hon.), to speak at the Annual Award Dinner in February 1977. The award winner that night was former vice chairman of the First National Bank of Chicago and trustee chairman of the Newberry Library, Edward F. Blettner, AB '28, MBA '30. Archibald Cox had joined Harvard's law faculty after World War II. He was appointed solicitor general in 1961 by President John F. Kennedy and was widely recognized for pursuing legal remedies to injustice. President Nixon later appointed him to serve as special prosecutor to try to quiet the public storm over the Watergate break-in. However, Cox was fired by Nixon after he subpoenaed tapes of conversations in the White House, just five months after he had been appointed, in what was dubbed "the Saturday night massacre." Cox appeared quite content to work as a Harvard Law School professor, although he voiced no regrets for his time spent in government service. Cox viewed the events of Watergate as leading to a significant victory for American law. In keeping with his great respect for the law, however, Cox viewed President Ford's eventual pardon of Richard Nixon as regrettable.

President Bok returned to speak at the Club's February 1978 Annual Award Dinner, which was presented in conjunction with a "Harvard Comes to Chicago" program. Marshall Field V, AB '63, was the awardee. It was only fitting that Marshall subsequently became a member of the committee assigned

to select the Annual Award winner, and he was still on the committee through the time of the Club's 150th anniversary celebration in May 2007. One of the more notable 1978 speakers was Harvard professor and former U.S. ambassador to Japan Edwin O. Reischauer. Japan had been reshaping itself as an economic world power out of the ruins of World War II. Many Americans felt threatened by the economic revival of the former imperial power and formidable enemy. Reischauer was critical of the protectionist sentiment that had arisen in response to competition from Japanese goods, and noted that similar outcries were not directed against former European rivals. Reischauer derided the attitude as "residual racism" and a grave threat to world stability, advocating instead understanding and the development of constructive trade agreements among the world economic powers.

Perhaps as a precursor to the "Reagan Revolution" looming on the horizon, John LeBoutillier, AB '76, MBA '79, author of *Harvard Hates America*, passed through Chicago in October 1978 on a book promotional tour. While still a sophomore at Harvard, LeBoutillier had gained prominence nationally among conservative Republicans after raising some $250,000

Danny M. Jiggetts, AB '76

One of the few Harvard graduates to play professional football, Danny Jiggetts was an All-American standout his senior year while majoring in government and economics. He spent ten years in the NFL, playing offensive tackle for the Chicago Bears from 1976 to 1982. One of Chicago's most popular media personalities, Jiggetts has served as Comcast SportsNet's host of *Chicago Tribune Live* and studio analyst on *U.S. Cellular Bears Post Game Live*, the 90-minute wrap-up and analysis program following every Bears game during the NFL season. Jiggetts also has worked for CBS, ESPN, and WMAQ-TV, the NBC affiliate in Chicago.

in campaign contributions in an attempt to unseat Senator George McGovern. LeBoutillier's book was critical of what he perceived as a liberal bias at the University. Christopher Janus, a past president of the Harvard Club of Chicago, was quoted by the *Chicago Tribune* as offering the following critique of the book: "It is a long and boring sophomoric bull session, spiced with a lot of kiss-and-tell episodes." Janus took issue with LeBoutillier's thesis, commenting, "Here is a young man obviously bright, but making remarks based on the flimsiest of evidence." Janus concluded, "Maybe Harvard is going down the drain, if he [LeBoutillier] is an example of recent alumni."

Newton N. Minow, IOP '86, was the speaker at the 1979 Annual Award Dinner. His comments about the "TV wasteland" are as appropriate today as they were that evening. The awardee that year was George E. Johnson, founder of Johnson Products Company, the first African-American-owned company to be listed on the American Stock Exchange. Johnson was honored for his dedication to philanthropic, cultural, and civic activities, including his instrumental roles with the George E. Johnson Foundation, Junior Achievement of Chicago, the Chicago Urban League, the Lyric Opera, and the George E. Johnson Educational Fund.

Chicago has been long celebrated for its architectural treasures, and architecture was a central theme at the February 1980 Annual Award Dinner. At that time, the Harvard Club of Chicago honored Marian Despres. A founder of the Chicago Architecture Foundation, Despres helped establish Chicago's ArchiCenter and organized walking tours showcasing the city's famous architectural sites. Her husband, long-time alderman, Leon Despres, was Mayor Jane Byrne's parliamentarian of the Chicago City Council at the time. Also speaking at the 1980 dinner was Harvard astronomy professor Eric Chaisson, MA '69, PhD '72, who intrigued guests with tales of the "big bang" and other cosmic theories.

Marian Despres was instrumental in coordinating the restoration of the Glessner House, in Chicago's Prairie Avenue Historic District. Mrs. Despres told the story of another Harvard connection between Glessner House and Harvard. The landmark Romanesque style Glessner House was designed by Boston architect Henry Hobson Richardson, AB 1859. Harold Glessner, the home's former owner and a founder of International Harvester, had purchased a Steinway piano in 1887 as part of the decor for Glessner House. Glessner later donated the Steinway to the president of Harvard, and it remained in the presidential home. At the time of the Glessner House restoration, Gardner Cowles, AB '25, a Chicagoan and trustee of Harvard, inquired as to the possible return of the Steinway. The University agreed to return the Steinway if a suitable substitute piano could be given in exchange. Cowles was generous enough to donate a new piano to the President's home. In a ceremony that included Sir Georg Solti, director of the Chicago Symphony, the Steinway was returned by Harvard to Glessner House in April 1980.

Robert Brustein, director of the Loeb Drama Center and professor of English at Harvard, delivered remarks to the Club at the February 1981 Annual Award Dinner. A founding director of the American Repertory Theatre, Brustein supervised well over two hundred productions. Club members were enlightened by the insights of this prolific author, director, actor, and critic of the arts. The awardee that evening was noted Chicago jeweler and philanthropist William Swartchild, Jr.

Glessner House piano 1980

Harvard dean Henry Rosovsky, AM '53, PhD '59, delivered remarks concerning the state of the University at the 1982 Annual Dinner, which was actually held in December 1981. Rosovsky joined the Harvard faculty as a professor of economics in 1965. He served as dean of the Faculty of Arts and Sciences from 1973 through 1984, and also served temporarily as acting president of Harvard during 1984 and 1987. Patron of the arts and education Marion M. Lloyd was the awardee honored at the event.

The Club was transported to the Middle Ages when Harvard professor and noted medieval scholar Giles Constable, PhD '50, entertained the guests at the February 1983 Annual Award Dinner. Juxtaposing Giles was an Annual Awardee known for his more contemporary pursuits, Daniel J. Terra. Terra had earlier developed a new ink vehicle that allowed

printing presses to run faster than ever before, which contributed to the creation of the pictorial magazine, Life. Terra founded Lawter Chemical in Chicago, a leading producer of printing inks and chemicals. The Club honored Daniel Terra in part for establishing the Terra Foundation for American Art in 1978. Terra's efforts further led to the opening of two museums focusing on the work of American Artists, the Terra Museum of American Art in Chicago (founded in 1987, which became a part of the Art Institute of Chicago in the early 2000s), and the Musee d'Art American in Giverny, France (founded in 1992). In 1982 President Reagan appointed Daniel Terra Ambassador at Large for Cultural Affairs, a position the president created specifically for Terra.

The Club was fortunate to have renowned economist John Kenneth Galbraith, AM '50 (hon.), as a speaker at the Annual Award Dinner in January 1984. This dinner was the most popular program of the past fifty years, with more than 600 people registering. Jerome Stone, former Chairman of Stone Container Corporation, was the honoree that evening. Stone was a founder and national president of the Alzheimer's and Related Disease Association. The importance of Stone's endeavors to help combat this nefarious disease was underscored by the fact that Alzheimer's disease gradually overtook the sitting president at the time, Ronald Reagan.

Culture was on display in June 1984, when the Harvard Club of Chicago presented a performance by the Hubbard Street Dance Company. In addition to promoting a popular Chicago-based organization, the event also raised funds for charity. Some of the proceeds from the event were donated to the Urban Gateways' arts-in-the-schools programs. The balance of the proceeds went toward scholarships provided in conjunction with the Club's longstanding commitment to Harvard students in need of financial assistance to attend the University.

The Club honored local real estate tycoon Arthur Rubloff at the February 1985 Annual Award Dinner. Although Rubloff had previously stated that he had given up receiving awards, he was more than happy to make an exception for the Club. James Schlesinger, AB '50, AM '52, PhD '56, secretary of

Sharon L. Beckman, AB '80

Sharon Beckman went to Harvard from Park Ridge, Illinois, graduating with honors in 1980. While at Harvard she distinguished herself on the women's swimming team, becoming co-captain her senior year. On August 28, 1982, she completed a successful solo crossing of the English Channel in the time of nine hours and six minutes, making her one of the fastest women swimmers ever.

Beckman attended the University of Michigan Law School, graduating with high honors. She clerked for the Hon. Frank Coffin of the U.S. Court of Appeals for the First Circuit and then for the Hon. Sandra Day O'Connor of the U.S. Supreme Court. Currently she is associate clinical professor of law at Boston College Law School teaching criminal law. She is remembered each year at Harvard through the Sharon Beckman Award, given to the female swimmer who best emulates her outstanding performance, dedication, qualities of leadership, and promotion of Harvard swimming.

1984 (left) Program cover featuring John Kenneth Galbraith and 1986 (right) Annual Award Dinner program cover featuring Peter Sellars.
Artwork by John Holabird, AB '42, MAR '48

defense under Presidents Nixon and Ford, and the first head of the Department of Energy, created under President Carter, was the guest speaker. Schlesinger delivered an informative talk at the dinner titled "Behind the Headlines."

Director and actor Peter Sellars, AB '80, entertained those gathered for the March 1986 Annual Award Dinner. Sellars had gained international renown for his modern stagings of classic operas and plays. Dressed in oriental garb, Sellars overwhelmed those assembled with an entertaining speech.

The honoree that evening was Stanley M. Freehling, long-time patron of the arts and president of the Arts Club of Chicago.

In late 1986, Robert A. Hastings, AB '57, MBA '59, was appointed executive director of the Harvard Alumni Association. The attention in the preceding several years had been focused on the University's 350th birthday celebration, so a part of the call was to address the HAA's internal operations. Hastings noted, for example, "despite recent completion of a multi-million dollar computerized development system, there was only one non-interactive terminal in the HAA offices and major reunion activity was being handled on 3x5 cards." Funding was obtained, and an interactive computer system that would permit downloading of data for various reunion and other alumni communication and activities was soon installed.

Before Hastings resigned at the end of academic year 1989, he was involved in several fascinating negotiations. One involved a sensitive decision regarding upcoming joint twenty-fifth reunions of Harvard and Radcliffe graduates and the position of First Marshal of Commencement, the person who leads the twenty-fifth reunion class into Tercentenary Theatre. There was considerable support for allowing Radcliffe graduates to have a separate first marshal. However, in discussions with Radcliffe president Matina Horner it was agreed "separate is not equal." A voting system was proposed and agreed to by President Horner that would provide an essentially equal opportunity for a Radcliffe graduate to be first marshal. The proposal was initiated in 1989, and in 1990 Ursula K. Oppens, AB '65, became the first woman to lead the combined twenty-fifth reunion classes.

As a benefactor of the alumni interviewing and recruiting process, Hastings felt there was a need to recognize those alumni who worked largely unheralded over many years "in the field." Concern initially was expressed that a new award might detract from the Harvard medals given at commencement to recognize major service at the University level. However, the value of an HAA Alumni Award to be given at an official meeting of the HAA apart from commencement or at another appropriate occasion finally was accepted. Approval was received to award, beginning in 1990, up to six awards in a given year, except in special anniversary years. The awards recognize devoted service reflected in significant commitment to a club, Schools and Scholarships Committee, class, fund, or other activity substantially benefiting Harvard University. Awards have been given to Chicago alumni Alan Hammerman, AB '55, in 1990; Hammond E. Chaffetz, AB '28, LLB '30, and Mari Terman, AB '57, in 1994; and Leo F. Mullin, AB '64, SM '65, MBA '67, in 1995.

When Club members gathered for the February 1987 Annual Award Dinner, they were treated to a talk by David Halberstam, AB '55, who had won a Pulitzer Prize for his reporting on the Vietnam War. A celebrated chronicler of diverse topics, including the Vietnam War generation, the Washington press corps, and baseball, Halberstam was an engaging speaker and drew a large attendance.

Hammond E. Chaffetz, AB '28, LLB '30, was the winner of the 1987 Annual Award. In his early years after law school, Chaffetz became a successful federal prosecutor specializing in antitrust cases. He later helped turn Chicago's Kirkland & Ellis into one of the country's largest law firms. The Club honored Chaffetz for his active support of the arts in Chicago, most notably the Chicago Symphony Orchestra, the Goodman Theatre, and the International Theatre Festival. Chaffetz was instrumental in helping his good friend Sir Georg Solti bring the Chicago Symphony Orchestra to international prominence. Chaffetz also served as chairman of the International Theatre Festival of Chicago, helping to bring the Royal Shakespeare and other acclaimed international companies to Chicago.

Author and entertainer George Plimpton, AB '48 ('51), was the speaker at the February 1988 Annual Award Dinner. Plimpton was a roommate of Robert F. Kennedy, AB '48, at Harvard and was well-known for documenting his full-immersion experiences in professional sports as an amateur. His exploits included stints as a professional football quarterback, an ice hockey goalie, and a sparring partner for professional boxers Sugar Ray Robinson and Archie Moore. Plimpton delivered smiles to a large group that evening. James J. O'Connor, MBA '60, former chairman of Commonwealth Edison Company and its successor, Unicom Corp., was honored for his civic activities.

In 1988 the Harvard Club of Chicago launched its successful Adopt-A-School program. The Club's initial adoptee was ethnically diverse Foreman High School in Chicago. A small army of Club volunteers served as tutors, advisors, coaches, and mentors for students at the Northwest Side school. The effort was led by Club president Thomas S. James, AB '52, AMP '75, Robert T. Gannett, Jr., AB '72, Radcliffe Club of Chicago president Jacquelyn S. Sanders, AB '52, Ellyn Kestnbaum Daniels, AB '83, EdM '85, John Daniels, Laurie Smith, MBA '85, Emile S. Godfrey, Jr. AB '72 and Tony Maier, AB '71. Club members taught English to Mexican and Polish immigrants and math to any student in need of assistance. Harvard volunteers also presented career days, job search seminars, and other programs encouraging students to plan for their life after high school. In October 1990, the Harvard *Crimson* quoted Foreman principal John Garvey as saying about the volunteers' activities, "The Harvard Club's involvement has made a big difference and has come at the perfect time." He continued, "There's something going on every day." The Adopt-A-School program has continued as an important and significant part of the Club's activities, although since 2000 at Walter Payton College Prep High School.

In 1988 Hannah Holborn Gray, PhD '57, then president of the University of Chicago, was elected to Harvard's Board of Overseers and began a long period of service to the University. She formerly had been a teaching fellow from 1955 to 1957 while working on her PhD, an instructor from 1957 to 1959, and an assistant professor in 1959–60.

From left to right: University of Chicago president Hannah Holborn Gray, Phd '57, LLD '95 (Hon.), Radcliffe Club of Chicago president Jacquelyn Sanders, AB '52, and Radcliffe College president Matina Horner in Chicago, c. 1988.

Gray came to the United States at the age of four when her father, Hajo Holborn, and mother, Annemarie Bettman, both of whom held PhDs, left Nazi Germany for Hajo's new position at Yale, where he taught for thirty-five years.

Gray moved to Chicago in 1960 when her husband, Charles Montgomery Gray, AB '49, PhD '56, received an appointment at the University of Chicago. In 1961 she too was offered a position, as an assistant professor in the history department, and when they abolished their nepotism rules in 1964 she was granted tenure and they became the first academic couple.

Gray's ability to combine rational thinking with tough decision making was exhibited as a committee member in a controversial faculty non-reappointment review. It brought her subsequent opportunities as dean of the College of Arts and Sciences at Northwestern University in 1972, provost of Yale in 1974, and acting president of Yale in 1977–78. Shortly after Bartlett Giamotti was named president of Yale, the University of Chicago offered her its presidency in 1978. It continued her rise as the first woman to serve in various academic administrative positions.

After retiring in 1993 to president emerita and Harry Pratt Judson Distinguished Service Professor of History of the University of Chicago, Gray was appointed the first woman member of the Harvard Corporation (and the only Chicago alumnus/a ever to serve in that capacity), effective July 1, 1997. President Rudenstine was quoted in a June 6, 1996, article announcing the appointment as saying: "In 15 years of distinguished leadership at one of America's great universities, she earned the respect of the entire academic community for her willingness to make difficult decisions while standing firm on fundamental principles. I greatly valued Hanna's counsel during her service on the Board of Overseers, and I look forward to working even more closely with her in the years ahead." The article also noted that in 1992–94 she had "chaired a key committee which reviewed the visitation process at Harvard and made a series of recommendations which are now leading to greater coordination between the visitation of various units in the University and the academic planning process." She resigned from the Corporation effective June 2005.

Gray was granted the Medal of Liberty in 1986 and the Presidential Medal of Freedom in 1991. She also has received more than sixty honorary degrees from universities in the United States and abroad, including the LLD from Harvard in 1995.

President Bok returned to Chicago and addressed the Club for a third time at the Annual Award Dinner in February 1989. During Bok's term as president, the programs and faculty at the Kennedy School of Government were greatly expanded. President Bok also led a concerted effort during his tenure to increase public service participation by Harvard students. It was thus perhaps appropriate the awardee that evening was business man and philanthropist Irving Brooks Harris, for whom the Irving B. Harris School of Public Policy at the University of Chicago is named. Harris was particularly well-known for his dedication to charities that benefited disadvantaged children, including those he pioneered, such as the Educare Center and the Ericson Institute.

The Club's special connection with the University Club of Chicago was still evident in 1990. At that time, the University Club was in need of a substantial renovation to its second floor, including the Michigan Room, one of the largest rooms in the Michigan Avenue facility. In retrospect, it was only fitting that the University Club should choose Margaret McCurry, LF '87, who later became president of the Harvard Club in 2006, to spearhead this renovation project. As reported by Thomas Davies Jones in *A Heritage: University Club of Chicago 1887–1987*:

Needless to say, a project as large as this one required not only the direction of a company of Club members, but the talents of the design architect in whom they reposed their confidence. She is Margaret McCurry of Tigerman-McCurry Architects, daughter of the late Paul McCurry, himself an architect and an honored member of the Club. She did her ancestry as well as her assignment proud.

Newton Minow, IOP '86, has the unique distinction of being both a speaker and an awardee at two separate Harvard Club Award dinners.

At the February 1991 Annual Award dinner Newton Minow, IOP '86, added to his previous role as speaker when he was honored as the awardee. Minow, a former chairman of the Federal Communications Commission and the Public Broadcasting Service, was recognized for his many years of public service. Rev. Theodore M. Hessburgh, distinguished president of the University of Notre Dame, entertained the guests as the evening's speaker.

President Bok retired from his first stint of service as president of Harvard in 1991. During his tenure, the Harvard Club of Chicago strengthened its ties to the local community by promoting civic, cultural, and educational opportunities, even as it deepened connections to the University and to the world at large. The programs and partnerships developed during Bok's presidency continue on into the Club's 150th year.

Chapter 10

The Rudenstine Years

1991–2001

Neil L. Rudenstine, BA '56 (Princeton University); BA '59, MA '63 (Oxford University); PhD '64
1935–
President of Harvard University 1991–2001

In March 1991, Neil L. Rudenstine, PhD '64, was appointed twenty-sixth president of Harvard University, succeeding the two-decades-long presidency of Derek C. Bok. President Rudenstine obtained his doctorate in Renaissance literature from Harvard, served as an Adams House tutor, and was assistant professor of English at the University from 1964 to 1968. Apart from these years at Harvard, Rudenstine enjoyed a longstanding affiliation with Princeton University, where he earned his undergraduate degree. Later, after his teaching stint at Harvard concluded, he returned to Princeton to become successively professor of English, dean of students, dean of the college, and finally provost. At the time of his appointment as the new president of Harvard, the former Rhodes Scholar was serving as executive vice president of the Andrew W. Mellon Foundation.

Neil Rudenstine began his presidency with a vision for a more unified University with greater outreach to the broader community. In his Presidential Installation Address on October 18, 1991, he focused his remarks on the state of the major universities in the United States. After describing the unique development and structure of the university system in America, President Rudenstine outlined several proposed measures, applicable both to universities generally and to Harvard specifically, to reverse the erosion in quality of the major universities. Among these proposals were approaches and ideas that ultimately characterized his legacy as president of Harvard: listening carefully to groups and institutions outside the university community; evaluating the universities' performance more carefully and making certain that resources (including financial resources) were used effectively; and, for Harvard, creating a University-wide agenda and a stronger University-wide consciousness.

Rudenstine used his first months in office to put these ideas into practice. He soon developed a reputation for his unassuming style and his willingness to listen to others and engage in frank discussion. Early in his presidency, however, he embarked on a project that ultimately became one of his greatest achievements, the launching of Harvard's first University-wide capital campaign. The campaign targeted $2.1 billion in new funds, the largest amount any university had ever attempted to raise. In October 1999, toward the end of his presidency, he could announce that the University had easily surpassed that goal and had raised a record $2.6 billion. One of Rudenstine's enduring legacies was to place the University on a much stronger financial footing. The University endowment almost tripled, to $15 billion, during his residency, and the operating deficits that once plagued the University's finances soon disappeared. Not surprisingly, this scholar of Renaissance literature is viewed by some alumni as Harvard's most successful fundraiser.

Rudenstine's first few days in office were also devoted to another goal, creating a more centralized University administration. He reinstated the position of university provost, a post that had been discontinued shortly after World War II. Rudenstine viewed the provost position as a means for delegating authority and as a tool for unifying the University. The office continues to this day, with the provost effectively serving in the role of a deputy president.

During the ten years from 1991 to 2001 that Neil Rudenstine served as president of the University, he was a frequent visitor to Chicago and to Club events. He graciously agreed to speak to the Club on five occasions during these years, including three of the Club's Annual Award Dinners.

Shortly after assuming his office, President Rudenstine first spoke at the Club's 1992 Annual Award Dinner, which honored Bernice Weissbourd. Weissbourd, the president of Family Focus, Inc., had dedicated her life to improving the lives of children and families. Her critically important work had had national, state, and local impact. Rudenstine's address that evening was the highlight of a daylong gathering of Harvard alumni, beginning with the "Harvard Comes to Chicago" symposium of presentations by Harvard faculty members at the Drake Hotel. The morning program included lectures by Diana Eck (professor of comparative religion and Indian studies) on religion in America, Alex Krieger (adjunct professor of architecture and urban design) on city planning, and Gregory Nagy (Francis Jones Professor of Classical Greek Literature and professor of comparative literature) on Greek heroic ideals. In the afternoon, the Chicago-area alumni faced a difficult decision of attending either a session on changes in the global environment led by Michael McElroy (Abbott Lawrence Rotch Professor of Atmospheric Science and chairman of Earth and Planetary Sciences) or listening to Robert B. Reich (lecturer in public policy) speak on American competitiveness.

Following the successful "Harvard Comes to Chicago" program, a couple of months later the Club sponsored another installment in its popular Spring Seminar series, an annual opportunity to learn more about an important topic with the leadership of a Harvard faculty member. On April 11, 1992, Jeffrey Masten, assistant professor of English and American literature, led a seminar entitled "Shakespeare(s)." The seminar considered Shakespeare in light of the then recent attention to literature within its historical context. The Spring Seminars concluded with a pair of lectures, one from Christopher Janus, SB '36, and former Club president, discussing a book of memoirs (*Angel on My Shoulder—Remembrances at Eighty*) and one from renowned pediatrician T. Berry Brazelton, clinical professor emeritus of pediatrics, whose address was titled "Kids Need More Than Medicine to Get Well."

Under the stewardship of Club president Richard Burnstine, AB '50, MD '54, the fall 1992 program season saw a stimulating speech by Christoph Wolff, dean of the Graduate School of Arts and Sciences, titled "The Challenge of Blank Paper: Mozart the Composer." Wolff described a story about Mozart that formed the title of his talk: "At work on

an opera, Mozart once reported to his father, 'Everything has been composed, but not yet written down.'" In the spring of 1993, Club members were also treated to a Spring Seminar led by Benjamin M. Friedman, chair of the Economics Department, and Steven Strongin, vice president of the Federal Reserve Bank of Chicago. With the recent election of Bill Clinton as president of the United States and with the uncertain prospects for fiscal and monetary policy under the new administration, Friedman and Strongin offered the Club members their prognostication on taxes and interest rates.

Lester Crown, MBA '49, the 1993 Harvard Club of Chicago Awardee.

The 1993 Award Dinner honored Lester Crown, MBA '49, chairman of Material Service Corporation and executive vice president of General Dynamics Corporation, at a gathering held at the Fairmont Hotel. Crown was recognized for having dedicated himself to the advancement of important civic, humanitarian, and cultural causes. The speaker at the dinner was to have been Madeleine May Kunin, deputy secretary of education in the new Clinton Administration. Kunin had previously been a three-term governor of Vermont, during which time she became known for her achievements on behalf of education, the environment, and children's services. Unfortunately, she was unable to come at the last minute because of a horrific snowstorm, and Peter C. B. Bynoe, MBA '76, graciously filled in with only a few hours' notice.

Later that spring the Club, in conjunction with the Yale Club of Chicago, embarked on an important four-part series of programs under the general title of "Reinventing Government: Business Approaches to Making the Public Sector Work." These off-the-record meetings with government and community leaders were designed to promote a free and open discussion of the pressing issues confronting local, state, and national governments and the taxpayers who fund them. The first speaker in the series was Robert Belcaster, president of the Chicago Transit Authority. Belcaster spoke about new approaches to making the CTA operate with the efficiency, responsiveness, and innovation typical of private sector enterprises. Vincent Lane, chairman of the Chicago Housing Authority, was next. Lane spoke about the challenges of reinventing the largest concentration of public housing in the United States. Ronald J. Gidwitz, chairman of the City College of Chicago, and Martin J. Koldyke, chair of the Chicago School Finance Authority, spoke of their approach to reinventing public education. Finally, the series of programs ended with an address by Jim Edgar, then governor of Illinois. Governor Edgar spoke about his efforts to downsize and streamline the state government in a number of areas while promoting funding for his top priority, education.

Eppie Lederer, better known as Ann Landers, the advice columnist, was the 1994 Harvard Club of Chicago Awardee.

The Club's leadership during the 1994 fiscal year was under a new president, Charles E. Zeitlin, AB '53, LLB '56. During Mr. Zeitlin's tenure as president, the Club honored Eppie Lederer as its 1994 award recipient. Better known to many by her pen name, Ann Landers, Ms. Lederer was a syndicated columnist for the *Chicago Tribune* and the *Los Angeles Times* and the author of numerous books. She once observed, "I have learned that no matter how well educated, well balanced or well bred a person may be, each of us is capable of doing something completely irrational—completely out of character at some time during our lives . . . and this doesn't mean we are crazy. It merely means we are human." The speaker that evening was Lou Dobbs, AB '67, who anchored the award-winning CNN *Moneyline* TV show.

Following the successful "Reinventing Government" series of

programs in 1993, the Club, again in conjunction with the Yale Club of Chicago, launched an ambitious five-part series in the spring of 1994 based on the theme "Life in Chicago." The gatherings were off-the-record breakfast meetings with notable representatives of different facets of life in the city. Rebecca M. Blank, Northwestern University assistant professor of economics, kicked off the series with a speech entitled "Chicago's Vital Signs . . . With a Focus on Poverty in Chicago: Problems and Policies in the 1990s." Her remarks examined how Chicago's poverty issues compared with those facing the rest of the nation and provided an overview of Chicago's economic and demographic "vital signs." Edward J. Noha, chairman of CNA Insurance, spoke a month later; his speech was titled "How Can Chicago Become the Economic Miracle of the 1990's?" Noha addressed the issues Chicago faced in its economic development and vitality. For the third session, the Club welcomed His Eminence, Joseph Cardinal Bernardin. As the archbishop of Chicago, Cardinal Bernardin oversaw and ministered to Chicago's largest religious denomination. In his address, he shared with the audience his perspectives on the importance of religious faith in Chicago's social fabric. A few weeks later, Samuel K. Skinner, president of Commonwealth Edison Corporation, spoke to the Club about the importance of Chicago's transportation infrastructure to the overall economic vitality and quality of life for Chicago-area residents. Finally, U.S. Congressman Luis V. Gutierrez, the first Hispanic congressman from the Midwest, discussed immigration policy and its importance to the Chicago community.

The 1995 Annual Award Dinner saw the return of President Rudenstine to Chicago for his second Club event. His visit to Chicago on March 4, 1995, was particularly noteworthy because it followed his recent return to daily duties from a three-month-long medical leave for exhaustion. Rudenstine's keynote address to the gathering of local alumni at the Chicago Hilton and Towers was preceded by the presentation of the Annual Award to Donald S. Perkins, MBA '51, one of Chicago's most distinguished citizens. Perkins had spent the major portion of his business career with Jewel Companies, Inc., and, following retirement, had served as a director of ten companies around the country. The award recognized his strong commitment to enhancing civic life in Chicago, especially his focus on education.

The Club continued to present multiseries programs under Club president Desmond C. Wong, MBA '77. In the spring of 1995, the Club (along with the Yale Club and the Princeton Club of Chicago) began a three-part program focused on culture wars. This series was intended to elucidate the ways in which America is struggling with fundamental questions of identity, purpose, and meaning. The first meeting examined the ways in which race and language affect our country's present and ongoing search for a common culture. This discussion was led by Henry Louis Gates, Jr., chairman of the Afro-American Studies Department and director of Harvard's W.E.B. Du Bois Institute for Afro-American Research. Professor Gates is America's foremost scholar of African-American literature. Kevin E. Consey, director of Chicago's Museum of Contemporary Art, was the featured speaker at the second meeting. Consey discussed how various works of art express and define contemporary culture and identity in the United States. The final speaker was Richard C. Notebaert, chairman and CEO of Ameritech. Notebaert spoke on the ways in which communications technologies are shaping a new sense of culture in the United States, defining new types of shared communities for Midwestern consumers and developing new avenues through which Midwestern businesses must compete in the global economy.

Meanwhile, important changes were occurring at the College. In May 1995, Dean of the College L. Fred Jewett, AB '57, decided to randomize the selection of students for the twelve undergraduate residential houses. Originally conceived in the 1930s, the residential houses were intended to be a "microcosm" of the College. Until the early 1970s, students were required to apply to live in one of the houses. This application approach was eventually replaced with a system whereby students ranked their top house preferences. The goal of randomization was to promote diversity in each house, but it sparked controversy among students and alumni by finally eliminating the ability of students to choose their undergraduate house, thereby diminishing or eliminating distinct house identities.

One month after announcing his decision on the randomization of the house selection process, Dean Jewett came to Chicago to speak at the Club's 1995 Annual Meeting, held at the 410 Club. Club officers and members were afforded an insider's perspective on the state of the College and the new initiatives that were under way.

There were several highlights to the Club's activities during 1996. In March, Linda S. Wilson, president of Radcliffe College, spoke to a combined audience of Radcliffe Club and Harvard Club members. Her address was titled "The American University in the 21st Century." That same month, the Club held its Annual Award Dinner at the Drake Hotel. The award went to Martin J. Koldyke, chairman of Frontenac Company and chair of the Chicago School Finance Authority. The award honored Koldyke for his civic activities in the area of education, particularly public education in Chicago as founder of the Golden Apple Award to outstanding teachers. After the award ceremony, Adele Smith Simmons, AB '53, president of the John D. and Catherine T. MacArthur Foundation of Chicago, delivered the main address at the dinner.

Irwin K. Carson, AB '66, succeeded Desmond Wong as Club president and served in that role until his untimely death in 1998. Irwin had been an active member and leader of the Club for several decades. The spring of 1997 marked the return of "Harvard Comes to Chicago," with the main address given by President Rudenstine. The Harvard faculty members spoke on a wide range of subjects. In the morning sessions, Felton Earls, professor of human behavior and development and professor of child psychiatry, addressed the causes and consequences of violent behavior in children; James Engell, professor of English and comparative literature, discussed the state of libraries; Margaret Geller, professor of astronomy, spoke on the search for galaxies; and Richard Hunt, senior lecturer on social studies and the University marshal, recounted the announcement of the Marshall Plan at the 1947 commencement. Rudenstine's luncheon speech was his third major address to the Club. In the afternoon, "Art, Art Funding, Public Policy and the First Amendment" was the headline of remarks by Frederick Schauer, Frank Stanton Professor of the First Amendment, and Richard Elmore, professor of education, led a discussion of educational standards.

In a departure from the general practice of recognizing a single awardee, the 1997 Annual Award Dinner honored Robert W. Galvin and Robert A. Pritzker. Galvin was the former chairman of the Executive Committee of Motorola, Inc., and Pritzker was president and CEO of the Marmon

Program cover featuring Adele Smith Simmons, AB '63, the 1996 Harvard Club of Chicago Award Dinner speaker.

Group, Inc. Both of these individuals had been deeply involved in Chicago's charitable community. Most recently, Galvin and Pritzker had presented a $120 million challenge grant to the Illinois Institute of Technology, with the hope that these funds would dramatically enhance the future of the school. The dinner speech was delivered by David Wilhelm, MPP '90, who was the former chairman of the Democratic National Committee and the campaign manager for President Bill Clinton's 1992 campaign. His speech, entitled "Why Americans Hate Their Government—Can We Ever Get Them to Like It Again?" offered insights into the American political process from one its savviest participants.

The following year, at the 1998 Award Dinner, the Club honored Sondra A. Healy for her service to Goodman Theater. She had been instrumental in assisting the Goodman plan to move to the site of the former Harris and Selwyn Theatre complex on North Dearborn Street. The project not only expanded the Goodman, it also preserved two landmark buildings and helped the city in its efforts to restore the Loop area. Rather than having a traditional dinner speaker, the Din & Tonics performed for the assembled guests at the Drake Hotel. The Dins asked the alumni of the Harvard Glee Club, the Krokodiloes, or other Harvard singing groups to join them in their final medley of Harvard College songs and for the singing of the traditional evening ending, "Fair Harvard."

A few months later, Bill Cleary, Harvard's athletic director, was the guest speaker at the Club's 1998 Annual Meeting, which saw the election of Craig I. Coit, '73, as the new president of the Club. Cleary spoke about the current state of the Harvard athletic program, including the football team's record season. Under the direction of football coach Tim Murphy, the Harvard football team had won the 1997 Ivy crown, a campaign that may be regarded as among the finest in 126 years of Harvard football. The squad finished 9-1 overall and 7-0 in League play. The nine wins were the most since the 1919 Rose Bowl team, and the perfect Ivy record was the first in school history.

In the fall of 1998, the new program year began with a gallery talk given by Suzanne McCullagh, MA '74, PhD '81, curator of earlier prints and drawings at the Art Institute of Chicago. The focus of her talk was the work of John Himmelfarb, AB '68, MAT '70, a Chicago resident and nationally recognized artist whose prints and drawings were showing at the prestigious Jean Albano Gallery in Chicago. Himmelfarb graciously agreed to offer a special limited edition of his lithographs for sale, the proceeds of which were donated to the Club's Scholarship Fund.

The arts in Chicago were the theme of the 1999 Award Dinner. The Club paid tribute to John H. Bryan, chairman and CEO of Sara Lee Corporation, and Richard J. Franke, former chairman and CEO of John Nuveen & Co. Both Franke, a Chicago Humanities Festival founder, and Bryan had long and distinguished histories of support for the arts and humanities in Chicago. Bryan later lead the funding effort for Millennium Park. The Club audience then enjoyed the remarks of the speaker, William F. Weld, AB '66, LLB '70, the former governor of Massachusetts.

Meanwhile, back in Cambridge, 1999 witnessed the official merger of Radcliffe College and Harvard University and the creation of the interdisciplinary Radcliffe Institute for Advanced Study. President Rudenstine was instrumental in accomplishing these changes. On January 1, 2001, noted historian Drew Gilpin Faust became the first dean of the Radcliffe Institute. Six years later, she would be named the twenty-eighth president of the University, the first woman to hold that office.

President Rudenstine returned to Chicago in May 1999 for his fourth address to the Club, again as part of the "Harvard Comes to Chicago" program. The day of dialogue with the Harvard faculty members began with a lecture by Gary Orfield, professor of education and social policy and director of the Harvard Project on School Desegregation, on the status of civil rights policy in education, including issues of affirmative action and diversity. Juliet Schor, senior lecturer on women's studies, offered her views in a lecture titled "The Overspent American." Next, Neil Levine, the Emmet Blakeney Gleason Professor of History of Art and Architecture, spoke

about Frank Lloyd Wright's vision for a modern Chicago, and Hermina Ibarra (professor of business administration) spoke on the topic of identity in an address titled "Inauthentic Selves: How Professionals Discover Themselves." After Rudenstine's luncheon remarks, Judah Folkman, Andrus Professor of Pediatric Surgery and professor of cell biology, spoke about the latest developments and controversies in the field of angiogenesis, the process by which chemical signals induce capillary blood vessels to grow, and its relationship to treating cancer.

In the summer and fall of 1999, Club members were invited to two programs that explored the city of Chicago. In August, members walked from the Museum of Contemporary Art to Michigan Avenue and then to the Chicago River to view "Cows on Parade," an exhibition of cows created by prominent artists and architects in the area. The tour was led by Nathan Mason from the City of Chicago's Department of Public Art. In November, Club members were among the first to see the new Peggy Notebaert Nature Museum of the Chicago Academy of Sciences. The gathering, which was hosted by the Chicago Academy of Sciences, allowed the members to tour the state-of-the-art environmental museum, including the collections, which provide a valuable environmental and genetic record of the region's natural history.

The 2000 Annual Award Dinner recognized Shirley Welsh Ryan. Ryan was the president and co-founder of the Pathways Center for Children. Founded in 1985, Pathways is an outpatient individualized neurodevelopmental therapy center. She also served on the board of numerous not-for-profit institutions. Not to be outdone by the Dins, the Harvard Krokodiloes delighted the audience with their harmonies and humor. Dinner guests who were former Kroks, former Dins, former members of the Glee Club, and former members of other University singing groups were once again asked to join the Kroks in their finale of Harvard fight songs and in the singing of "Fair Harvard." A few weeks later, the Club hosted a performance of the Harvard Glee Club at Alice Millar Chapel at Northwestern University, thereby completing the invitations to the three best-known Harvard undergraduate singing groups. Other highlights of the spring 2000 programs included the return to the Club of Jim Edgar, former governor of Illinois, who discussed his thirty years of state government service.

On May 22, 2000, President Rudenstine surprised the Harvard community by announcing that he would resign his office as of June 30, 2001.

In the fall of 2000–2002, the Club was led by Kenneth V. Hachikian, AB '71, MBA '73. One of the first programs of the

Program cover featuring Harvard president Neil Rudenstine, PhD '64, the 2001 Harvard Club of Chicago Award Dinner speaker.

fall 2000 calendar was a gathering with Jonathan Alter, AB '79, on November 16, to discuss the results of the national elections. Alter was a senior editor of *Newsweek* magazine and a contributing correspondent for *NBC News*. The intense focus on the controversies surrounding the 2000 presidential elections made Alter's discussion particularly timely and fascinating. During this time, the Club embarked on a number of initiatives. Following its Adopt-A-School program at Foreman High School, the Club began a new program at the recently established Walter Payton College Prep High School on Chicago's Near North Side. The new program at Walter Payton soon attracted dozens of "Harvols" who volunteered at the school as tutors, coaches, and mentors.

At the 2001 Annual Award Dinner, the Club recognized three generations of the Edward Byron Smith family. The granting of the award to the family reflected the continuing commitment of civic-minded families that has been a Chicago strength and tradition. Moreover, in 1999, the family had donated the Smith Museum of Stained Glass to the city of Chicago, which housed the collection at Navy Pier. This important art medium had helped make Chicago one of the artistic hubs of the United States during the 1880s to the 1930s.

The 2001 dinner was also Neil Rudenstine's fifth and last address to the Club as president of the University. Rudenstine honored the Club by choosing it as one of the few Harvard clubs in the country selected for his farewell tour. In his speech, he returned to the theme of his presidential installation address, speaking on the state of Harvard and higher education. His final speech to the Club is reproduced below.

Not surprisingly, I have been thinking a great deal about Harvard—and higher education more generally—during these last several months. I have also been asked many questions about the contemporary state of education, especially higher education, in the world at large. I want to talk for a few minutes on this subject, before turning back to Harvard itself.

My personal assessment is that the situation is very difficult right now, and that the balance between recent gains in higher education abroad, and recent deterioration, presents us with a major world-wide problem that somehow must be addressed, but will not be solved at all easily.

There are several reasons for this predicament, but I will single out just two of them. The first has to do with recent changes in the way the world now works. The other has to do with the relative lack of change in so many systems of higher education in more than 125 countries and territories.

By any standard, the years since about 1990 have been remarkable. I have talked before about the political, economic, and cultural changes that have taken place—transforming a world that for nearly half a century had seemed bipolar into one that is now multiple in nearly all its dimensions. There is now more openness, more fluidity, and more potential for fruitful development. There are more governments trying to create one or another kind of democratic political process. There is a greater focus on how to help societies become more productive economically.

At the same time, there are many more groups and nations participating actively in our global drama. There is a more intricate web of cross-connections and shifting alliances. There are more complicated human organizational and technological systems to understand, to trace, and to manage.

So life has in many respects become more unpredictable and volatile, subject to sudden swings and new forms of danger, with many examples of national, ethnic, religious, and other forms of tension or strife-all magnified and made ubiquitous by the media in all of its

acoustic, visual, legible, and kinetic forms. As a result, we are conscious—continuously—of events taking place in every briar patch of our planet. It is not surprising, therefore, if the world often seems more complex, less easily managed, and more resistant to melioration than we had hoped. One consequence of the transformations-positive and less positive-that have taken place during the past decade, is that more countries than ever have come to recognize, very explicitly, that there is a powerful link between the quality of their higher education system (including their investment in research) and the well-being of their society-their ability to be productive, healthy, stable, and economically competitive in this globalized habitat of ours. This close link between higher education and different kinds of human or societal development is certainly not a new idea. But the extent of its unusually broad acceptance is new, and it is leading nations as different as South Africa, China, and Mexico to place a much greater priority on higher education than they did even a decade or two ago.

This is obviously a very hopeful sign, and we can see evidence of real progress in many places around the world. Nevertheless, when measured against the actual needs of all societies, the availability of excellent higher education—not to mention primary and secondary education—that now exists, or that is likely to exist at any time in the foreseeable future, is dramatically inadequate. The gap really is enormous.

If we consider just the number and kinds of businesses, school-systems, hospitals and health-care systems, financial systems, legal systems, government agencies, an independent press, and other organizations that must be created, brought to maturity, and managed with real skill in dozens of countries; or if we consider the number and different kinds of leaders that are now needed in nations around the world; or what is required to create an educated citizenry that can sustain democratic institutions: then any metric that we use will show immediately how far short we are from reaching anything like the number of experienced, trained people required to run the complex, demanding, and often dangerous affairs of our world in a way that is not only competent, but also humane.

Demand has already far outstripped supply. Why is this the case? That question brings me to my second point. If the world has changed profoundly in the last decade or so, most systems of higher education have not changed in critical ways. There are several reasons why this is the case, including constant turbulence and even war in a number of societies, but I want to highlight two other reasons. First, excellent modern education is exceptionally expensive. It is not only labor-intensive but increasingly capital-intensive. Very few nations have anything like the resources to create excellent institutions and systems of higher education. In addition, developments of this kind—even if resources were available—take decades and decades to mature. Great universities are created, not over the course of years, but of generations.

Second, the prevailing worldwide organizational and financial model for higher education is now largely obsolete. Yet, changing that model will be unusually difficult, and will at best take a very long time.

The basic difficulty is not hard to explain. Nearly all major higher education systems abroad are supported either entirely, or almost entirely, by government money. There are very few cases where important institutions have much independence or autonomy; much capacity to set their own goals and levels of aspiration; much freedom to inquire openly into all fields of knowledge; or any significant ability to raise their own financial

resources either through student fees, or annual gifts, or endowment growth, or other means consistent with the purposes of universities as we know them.

Without these capacities, the possibility of building truly excellent institutions of higher education at an international level of quality—and then sustaining them—is very remote. Hardly any governments have the financial ability to undertake so huge a task. Beyond that fact, most governments around the world have a great many competing—often more urgent and basic— priorities confronting them.

As a result, if the development of major universities or university systems remains dependent on the financial models and other processes that are now in place, then those systems will continue to be seriously under-funded, as most are now—and that is a major problem for all of us. So just at the moment when we need more and better higher education in the world, we have less of it, relative to our present and future requirements. Highly educated human talent is, and will remain—indefinitely into the future—the scarcest significant resource on our planet.

Now, it is true that if we think only of the best universities in our own country and a few others, we might conclude that we can rest easy, because matters are in quite a good state. But taking so local and restricted a view of the situation is no longer adequate, simply because we now depend so much more on the trained intelligence of people throughout the entire world to make sensible and sane decisions-and to help manage and guide events in ways that are likely to cause the least amount of harm, and to increase the probabilities for peaceful and productive co-existence— or "multiple-existence"—among people everywhere.

One important implication of everything that I have

been saying is that those universities that are already well established and are in a position to lead and to play a significant educational role internationally as well as nationally: those universities, and I include Harvard at the forefront, cannot relax their efforts, because the stakes are simply too high. So when you greet my successor, bear in mind that Harvard's next President will need strong support to carry out Harvard's role in higher education—in all fields, but particularly in relation to the international situation that I have just described.

What are just a few things that Harvard could consider doing to help address the worldwide shortage of educated talent that I have just been describing? First, we should continue and expand our range of excellent mid-career programs for individuals from abroad who are already in positions of responsibility, but who may have had only limited opportunities to do advanced work in medicine and public health, government, law, business, design, urban planning, and many other fields. These mid-career programs are very effective, and Harvard is unusually well positioned to offer them. We have a great deal of experience-and already educate 60,000 "students" a year in this way. This is one important way—if only a limited one—to have an immediate, direct impact on individual—-and on the leadership in entire countries—without waiting for the full creation of major new systems of higher education abroad.

There are also other avenues open to us in the international sphere. Creating significant research projects-of which there are already dozens and dozens of examples involving Harvard-with scholars and practitioners from other nations; continuing to keep the doors of our degree programs open to students from abroad; and, of course, helping our own students and faculty to travel and undertake research in all parts of the world: these and other initiatives matter vitally, and

no other institution is better equipped than Harvard to play a large-scale, powerful leadership role in higher education on a global basis.

Well, far be it from me to set the menu either for you, or for the fortunate person you will entertain so warmly at a dinner next year. Tonight, I am only suggesting what some of the hors d'oeuvres might be. And, in addition to expanding the field of international studies, I suspect that other courses will include large portions of increased research across all of the sciences; expanded systems of-and new uses for-information technology in education and research; and, of course, constant attention to undergraduate education and the College, because a deep and extended grounding in the liberal arts and sciences has never been more important than it is today-when we have to know more, and learn more, than we can possibly know or learn; when we need future leaders who can be intellectually agile without being merely superficial; who are strong enough to contend with intermittent chaos, as well as to seek beneficent forms of order; who can ponder evidence and consequences; and who can act intelligently and decisively.

Lady Asquith once said of a friend that "he has a brilliant mind until he makes it up." We always need-but we now need an even greater number-of people who have, not necessarily brilliance (though that can often help), but an abundant store of rich knowledge, a fund of the right human qualities, and the kinds of experience that can lead to wisdom—especially wisdom converted into action.

There is, alas, no certain or easy way to help students—or any of us—to acquire all these uncommon capacities. But one of the ways that can be most helpful is to be educated at an excellent college-especially a college named Harvard-in the broad and marvelous full range of the sciences, the humanities, the social sciences, and the arts-as well as in the equally challenging arena of everyday residential college life, where one seeks to understand, to learn from, to befriend, and to live on gracious terms with a wide diversity of fellow students who are different from oneself and yet-at other levels-so very much like oneself.

That is what happens now at Harvard College-and at Harvard University as a whole. That is what we must ensure will continue to happen, long into the future. I have said it before, but I want to repeat it this evening: all of you in this room-and thousands of other alumni around the world-understand the purposes and aspirations of a great university more profoundly than any other similar group that I have encountered; and that particular kind of understanding and dedication has-as much as any other single factor-been responsible for making Harvard the very great university that it is.

During this last decade, Angelica and I have had the privilege of being able to work with all of you on behalf of Harvard College and Harvard University. I cannot begin to express how much these years have meant to us, but I can say how deeply we have valued your support, your interest, your constancy, and your friendship.

Together, we have all had one of the world's rare and precious human institutions in our trust. That in itself has been a piece of great good fortune for us, because it is not often in life that we have the opportunity to be so closely associated with something as powerful in its aspirations, as clear in its purposes, and as extraordinary in its range of achievements, as Harvard. For joining us as close companions on this journey, Angelica and I will always be grateful to you, and will always remember you.

Thank you.

Former President Derek Bok congratulates Neil L. Rudenstine on the occasion of the unveiling of his official portrait, which will hang inside University Hall, c. 2006

Chapter 11

The Summers Years

2001–2006

Lawrence H. Summers, BS '75 (MIT),
PhD '82
1954–
President of Harvard University
2001–2006
Summers, an economics professor,
served as secretary of the treasury
under President Bill Clinton.

On a crisp fall day in October of 2001, Larry Summers enthusiastically announced "I accept!" at his inauguration as the twenty-seventh president of Harvard. In his address on this occasion before the Harvard community, which included the directors of the Harvard Alumni Association assembled in Cambridge (and coincidentally among them current Harvard Club of Chicago president Margaret McCurry, LF '87), Summers thanked retiring president Neil Rudenstine for "his vision, his dedication, his care [which] left Harvard far stronger than he found it." It was almost a month to the day after 9/11, and President Summers acknowledged that we were meeting "in the shadow of [those] terrible and tragic events." He stressed that just as sixty-five years before, when Franklin D. Roosevelt stood on the same stage and stated, "It is the part of Harvard and America to stand for the freedom of the human mind and to carry the torch of truth," the process by which we carry that torch today in our present struggle is to "recommit ourselves to the University's enduring service to society—through scholarship of the highest quality and through the profound act of faith in the future that is teaching and learning."

It was an idealistic speech and, at times, often a poetic one that focused on the educational experience and the role of the University in fomenting ideas and the pursuit of "Veritas." He spoke of the specific challenges he saw Harvard facing in the coming years, which were reiterated in his address to the Harvard Club of Chicago's Annual Award Dinner six months later. But here in Cambridge, he stressed the "community of scholars and students . . . united by common convictions and common objectives" by way of mentioning that "every tub may rest on its own bottom, but . . . the strength and reputation of each depend upon the strength of all. We will not sacrifice the flexibility and innovation that autonomy promotes. But we will assure that Harvard as one University exceeds—by ever more—the sum of its parts."

Summers's concluding remarks were to set the tone of his presidency:

In this new century, nothing will matter more than the education of future leaders and the development of new ideas. Harvard has done its part in the past. But that past will be prologue only if all of us now do our part to make it so. We will face difficult choices. We will take risks. Sometimes we will fail. Indeed, if we

President Larry Summers, "It's good to be home."

never fail, we will not have participated as fully as we can in the adventure of our times. Like all great universities, Harvard has always been a work in progress, and it always will be. In the words of the song we are about to sing, let us together renew this great university for the age that is waiting before.

Whether in response to the extraordinary coming together of Americans following 9/11 or as a reaffirmation of Summers's remarks on community, the Harvard Club of Chicago saw record numbers of members turn out that fall at two museum events offered by the Club in conjunction with the other Ivies and the Seven Sisters. The Van Gogh and Gauguin exhibit at the Art Institute drew more than 200 attendees to hear lectures on the Studio of the South, as did the exhibit Cleopatra of Egypt at the Field Museum. Past president Dr. Richard Burnstine's wine-tasting event on a Sunday afternoon in November also brought many Harvardians together. A series of Shakespeare plays for which the Club obtained tickets during the course of its 2001–2002 fiscal year completed the cultural calendar. A sprightly conversation after the holidays with John Lithgow, AB '67, UNV '05, author of the enormously popular "Arts First" event held the first weekend in May on the Harvard campus, drew slightly more attendees than *Richard II*, but undoubtedly his subject matter was less dark than Shakespeare's tragic play, performed as it was less than

John Lithgow AB '67, ArtD '05 (Hon.)

Dr. Serafino Garella, 2002 Award Dinner Honoree

a month after the collapse of the Twin Towers. Of note was the timely talk in January by William A. Graham, professor of religion and Islamic studies at Harvard, whose address was titled "September 11th and the Question of Islam."

Harvard Club of Chicago Annual Awardee Newton Minow, IOP '86, was heard in conversation at a buffet lunch. Evening programs included the Honorable George N. Leighton, LLB '43, and Arne Duncan, AB '86, in his first year as chief executive officer of the Chicago Board of Education. A crowd came to hear his innovative ideas for the future of the Chicago public schools. The Reverend Peter John Gomes, STB '68, head of Harvard's Memorial Church and on the faculty of the School of Divinity, journeyed to Chicago to deliver a talk, "The Good Life: Truths That Last in Times of Need."

The Annual Award Dinner in March 2002 at the Drake Hotel honored Dr. Serafino Garella for service to humanity as the founder of a free Hispanic community health clinic staffed and financed by volunteers. The event drew more than 400 Club members, who also came to hear Larry Summers discuss his vision for Harvard and his goals for his presidency. In his opening remarks, he said, "It was one of the great thrills of my lifetime when I was offered the Presidency of Harvard University." He went on to say to a round of applause, "And if you think about the work of Harvard University, it is the work of new ideas, and it is the work of preparing young people who will bring them to fruition. I believe there is no more important work in this world than developing new ideas and engaging in education which is the ultimate act of faith in the future. I believe there is no institution in this world that does it better than the university we love, Harvard University."

Summers went on to highlight five issues that he felt were the most important ones facing the University. First, he addressed strengthening Harvard College through a review of the core curriculum "for the kinds of programs that are, to a new world, what social studies, and history and literature were to the world of two generations ago." He also pledged more faculty-student contact "whether it is in the common room, or the classroom, the laboratory, or the library."

The second issue was science, "the life sciences . . . because of what science can contribute, but equally, because if war is too important to leave to generals, science is too important to leave to scientists in its social implications. And if we are to come to the right views on questions like cloning, questions like stem cells, questions like privacy in the era of the Internet, we will need thoughtful people, trained in a humanistic tradition, who understand these technologies, and can help us craft solutions that assure that they are used best."

Third, he averred, was "service to a broad world," and to a second round of applause he stated, "If we are to maximize our contribution to an increasingly dangerous world, we must make sure that all the privileges, and all the strengths that have traditionally attended the Harvard professional schools that prepare people for a life in the private sector, also attend those schools that prepare people for a life in public service, whether in education, or health, or law, or any other sector. That is part of how we can maximize our contribution."

The fourth issue was the development of the Allston campus whose acquisition—"the equivalent of three Harvard Yards"—had recently been announced. "I don't know which components of the University will move to Allston. That is the subject of a complex planning process. But I do know this. Those who move will be thanked by their successors because we have an opportunity that no other great university has: to create a brand new, 21st century, modern academic space."

His last "trinity of issues" were "globalization, information technology, and continuing education"—that is, the technology of distance learning. "What we must do at Harvard is make sure that we extend our excellence in every way possible without ever diluting that excellence. And believe me, how successful we are in doing this will have a very profound impact on the world. Because if you think about it, there is no greater global challenge right now than the coming together of rich countries and poor countries; no greater opportunity, but also no greater risk, whether in military conflict, whether in environmental problems, whether in the spread of disease."

In conclusion, President Summers summarized the five issues by saying, "This is a large and ambitious agenda for our university. But its continued greatness demands no less. And it will succeed. It will succeed because of the remarkable students we have. It will succeed because of the faculty who we are able to attract. And it will succeed because it is fortunate in having the loyal support of the remarkable network of 300,000 alumni in every part of the world."

At the Annual Meeting of the Harvard Club of Chicago held at Inas Restaurant on an evening in June 2002, a new slate of officers was introduced to the membership, to be headed for the next two years by President John A. Challenger, '77.

Vice Presidents Stephen W. Baird, AB '75, Adela M. Cepeda, AB '80, and Alan H. Hammerman, AB '55, continued to ably co-chair the Schools and Scholarships Committee. The three oversee the more than 250 volunteers who interview Harvard College's hopeful applicants every year. They also host acceptance parties each summer and plan December get-togethers in alumni homes across the greater Chicagoland area to connect current students with local alumni in a spirit of conviviality. After the 2006 crop had departed for Cambridge, Co-Chair "Mickey" Hammerman led a discussion

Millennium Park, Chicago, 2006

at a wine-and-cheese evening program on early acceptance versus early decision. The Outstanding Contribution Award was presented to board member Alexander "Sandy" Weissent, AB '73, the founding committee chair of the Club's Adopt-A-School program at Walter Payton College Prep. "Harvols," as the more than 200 Harvard alumni volunteers are called, tutor students and assist the school in its mission to provide every student an educational experience that instills integrity and a lifelong love of learning.

Harvard Club members celebrated a late summer evening on the terrace of the Cliff Dwellers Club, overlooking Millennium Park, with the added attraction of Chicago's Wednesday evening fireworks display over the lake. This summer venue was to become a fiscal year kick-off tradition. On this particular August eve, architect Ed Uhlir, Millennium Park design director, explained, in an illustrated format, the evolution of the structures, sculptures, and gardens taking shape obliquely across Michigan Avenue.

Fall programs continued the spirit of the arts in Chicago. Board member Suzanne F. McCullagh, MA '74, PhD '81, curator of earlier prints and drawings at the Art Institute of Chicago, and artist John Himmelfarb, '68, MAT '70, engaged

Harvard-Yale football game telecast, Piece Restaurant, Chicago

in a lively dialogue at the Jean Albano Gallery, where John's paintings were on display. Suzanne also organized a talk by Curator Larry J. Feinberg, AM '70, PhD '86, who discussed his Medici exhibition at the Art Institute, which showed some of the most prized Renaissance treasures of the museums of Florence. Unknown to Club members at the time, the future director of the Art Institute of Chicago, James Cuno, MA '80, PhD '85, then retiring professor at the Harvard University Art Museums, gave a talk in Fullerton Hall titled "A World Changed: Art Museums in the Aftermath of September 11th." The membership announcement of his talk mentioned that Cuno would leave after the first of the year to become director of the Courtauld Institute in London. It also asked, "Did you know that 24 of the world's current art museum directors are Harvard trained?" Two days later Lee Cott, GSD '70, adjunct professor of urban design at the Graduate School of Design, reminded members of another crisis in contemporary American history when he discussed the much admired exhibit Modern Architecture in Pre-Castro Cuba and the aftermath of the revolution, which saw the decline and neglect of once vibrant Havana, the tourist Mecca of the Caribbean. Cott took several GSD Urban Design Studios to Havana, where students developed strategies for revitalizing the city. To complete the fall arts agenda, Chicago's most illustrious nineteenth-century architect, Frank Lloyd Wright, was the subject of a talk by Neil Levine, professor of the history of art and architecture at Harvard and an authority and published author on Wright.

Without doubt, that was a foreshadowing fall! Drew Faust, the first permanent dean of the Radcliffe Institute for Advanced Study, addressed a joint meeting of the Club and the Radcliffe Association on the intellectual agenda being established at the Institute, which will honor its predecessor by sustaining a continuing commitment to the study of women, gender, and society. The telecast party of the Harvard-Yale game annually organized by board member Shu Yan Chan, AB '75, saw Harvard victorious for the second year in a row. In fact, as Larry Summers was to remark in his final Baccalaureate Address in June 2006, "We were here a while, and we never saw Harvard lose a football game to Yale."

2003 Award Dinner Honoree, Carol Lavin (left) and Award Dinner Speaker, Jamie Dimon, HBS '82 (right)

A plethora of stimulating dialogues filled the spring calendar, from discussions with *Wall Street Journal* contributing columnist Joel Henning, AB '61, JD '64, to James Warren, deputy managing editor of the *Chicago Tribune*. From new health care technologies and the future of medicine to masters of the Lyric Opera, the series was capped by a celebration of the publication of the latest book by Christopher X. Janus, '36, the Club's oldest alumnus and former Club president.

Once again held at the Drake Hotel, the 2003 Annual Award Dinner honored most deserving civic-minded Chicagoans. Carol Lavin and the Lavin/Bernick families were the recipients for their generous philanthropic support of numerous institutions. The keynote speaker for the dinner was Jamie Dimon, HBS '82, chairman and chief executive officer of Bank One Corporation, who spoke eloquently on the need for corporations to embrace management strategies for the future.

The board of directors took President Summers's call for support to students who undertake social service careers to heart. Club president John Challenger asked board member Robert A. Hastings, AB '57, MBA '59, to chair the Community Service Committee. Working with the Center for Public Interest Careers (CPIC), housed with the Phillips Brooks House Association at Harvard, Hastings rebuilt the Club's public service internship program, which facilitates summer internships and yearlong fellowships in nonprofit agencies for undergraduates,

in some cases with monetary support for student salaries. A star athlete in his own college years, Hastings also undertook the assignment to coordinate athletic program activities at Walter Payton College Prep High School, the club's Adopt-A-School protégé, subsequently volunteering to coach a freshman basketball team and the junior varsity volleyball team.

At the Kenilworth Club, the site of the annual meeting that closes the club's fiscal year, board member and former president Richard C Burnstine, '50, MD '54, was presented with the Outstanding Contribution Award for his years of dedicated service to the Club. As the official sommelier for countless wine tastings, Richard's spring and fall programs were and are much anticipated convivial occasions.

After an early summer respite, Club members gathered again at the Cliff Dwellers Club in August to hear Dirk Lohan, architect of the addition to the Shedd Aquarium and other civic work, discuss his renovation of Soldier Field, a controversial project in the city. Member families also enjoyed the third annual summer field trip hosted by the Nature Conservancy. On a Saturday in late summer, participants were led on a guided tour through Bluff Spring Fen, a ninety-acre preserve forty miles west of Chicago. City pavements replaced the prairie grasses in September as members toured two Gold Coast condominiums designed by board member Margaret McCurry's firm, Tigerman McCurry Architects. Both apartments also housed spectacular art collections.

This fall's smash hit musical *Mama Mia* regaled members with hit songs, much as the past year's Broadway production of *Suessical* had wowed Harvard families. To add spice to our theatrical offering, Richard Christianson, GSA '53– '54, former theater critic of the *Chicago Tribune*, spoke about the history of theater in Chicago, the subject of his latest book. Communal dinners again took center-stage at the always popular Kendall College School of Culinary Arts.

On a more serious note, the club sponsored discussions on current political events and physical concerns. One such, titled "The Situation in the Middle East and Islamic

Fundamentalism," was delivered by Storer H. Rowley, '49, national editor of the *Chicago Tribune*. For other topical programs, the ever popular Dana Farber/Harvard Cancer Center presented a panel discussion on cancer genetics, and Dean Barry R. Bloom of the School of Public Health and a member of the World Health Organization addressed the issues of immunology and infectious diseases within populations. On an equally serious subject, parents of prospective Harvard College students flocked to a discussion with former senior admissions officer Chuck Hughes, author of *What It Really Takes to Get into the Ivy League*.

In October, Club members were invited to attend a black tie dinner meeting of the Economic Club of Chicago featuring President Lawrence Summers. While Summers was primarily addressing the business community, drawing on his experience as treasury secretary during the Clinton administration, his remarks segued into the importance of universities to establishing a strong foundation for a successful national economy by producing "good thinking and the capacity to think." "It is innovations and ideas that drive our economy," said Summers, harking back to his initial inaugural address, in which he stressed the University's role in fomenting ideas and open inquiry. The conduct of U.S. foreign policy, Summers averred, must rely on allies, and where better a resource than the University "for shaping the perspectives of potential leaders of foreign nations at a time in their lives when their thinking is still malleable." Other themes also emerged in this talk that Summers worked diligently to promote during his presidency, among them the exposure of students to foreign experiences to promote international understanding and the encouragement of diversity in the student body and support for monetary mechanisms to achieve it. In closing, he stressed the importance of inculcating societal values in students as they are educated, noting that this challenge "will be an important issue as we review our curriculum at Harvard."

The calendar year of 2003 closed with a fascinating talk by the Hon. James Zagel, JD '65, of the U.S. district court, a multicareered legal genius who is also an actor, having

Award Dinner Speaker, Frank O. Gehry, GSD '57 ('56–'57), ARD '00 (Hon.) at Millennium Park, 2004

appeared in two feature films as well as writing a best-seller, *Money to Burn*, which tells of a heist at the Federal Reserve Bank committed by a U.S. district judge and his friends.

The New Year 2004 brought a return to the serious subject of international affairs with an address by Dean William A. Graham of the Harvard Divinity School titled "Religion and Politics: The Islamic Case." It was followed by a talk by Marvin Zonis, B '58–59, titled "The Kimchi Matters," which explained how globalization and events like the Iraq War and the 9/11 attacks make understanding the political economies of distant countries most important. On a sister subject, the dean of the Kennedy School of Government, Joseph S. Nye, Jr., addressed the Chicago Council on Foreign Relations, to which Harvard Club of Chicago members were invited, his subject soft power and the war on terrorism. Club president Challenger's involvement on the steering committee of the CCFR provided access to several interesting programs conducted by Harvard professors, just as his position on the board of the Japan America Society of Chicago afforded Club members yearly cultural interactions with consuls general.

Spring also brought the grand opening of Millennium Park, whose construction progress members had watched in consecutive summers from the Cliff Dwellers terrace. The architect of two of the parks most innovative structures, the Pritzker Music Pavilion and the titanium bridge that snakes and undulates across Columbus Drive, Frank Gehry, GSD '57 ('56–'57), ARD '00 (Hon.), was the keynote speaker for our Annual Award Dinner. The creation of buildings such as the Guggenheim Museum in Bilbao and the Walt Disney Concert Hall in Los Angeles, which earned him the Pritzker Prize and the American Institute of Architecture Gold Medal, were subjects Gehry discussed as he shared his unique design methodology with attendees. Gehry had also recently joined the team of New York architects and planners Cooper Robertson as a consultant on the Allston campus. In that capacity he met with President Summers to explore possibilities for a more stylistically diverse building program than that of the adjoining Business School.

The Club's 2004 award recipient was John H. Johnson, LLD '88 (Hon.), a champion of education whose philanthropy and work as a humanitarian was honored. The publisher of *Ebony* and *Jet*, his company is the largest black-owned publishing company in the world.

On a Saturday in April, "Harvard 'Came' to Chicago." At the first session two professors lectured simultaneously on topical subjects, Louise Richardson of the Radcliffe Institute sought to define terrorism, placing it in a historical context and offering lessons from other democracies on how to defeat it without compromising democratic principles. In another room of the Mid-America Club, Marshall Goldman, associate director of the Davis Center for Russian and Eurasian Studies, reminded Club members in his talk, "Putin and the Oligarchs," that the Russian president's actions and the fact that he was a former KGB agent could be returning Russia to the authoritarian ways of the Soviet Union.

The following session paired Robert Stavins, director of the Harvard Environmental Economics Program at the John F. Kennedy School of Government, with Helen Vendler, a professor on the faculty of Arts and Sciences. While Stavins assessed the Kyoto Protocol and proposed alternative solutions to effective global climate control, Vendler discussed two poems of Walt Whitman's, delving into their author's psyche as only a true Harvard Scholar can. As keynote speaker at the

luncheon, John P. Reardon, Jr., AB '60, director of the Harvard Alumni Association, brought attendees up to date on campus activities and Summers's initiatives. Since this Saturday's luncheon was also slated as the Club's annual meeting, President Challenger presided over the conferring of the club's Outstanding Contribution Award to board members Nancy and Bennett I. Berman, LLB '43 (46). As Challenger wrote in the spring newsletter, "Their long years of work on behalf of our club in many areas including the Annual Dinner and Program Committee (Nancy) and Accounting/Finance (Bennett) have been instrumental to our success. The Harvard Club of Chicago would not be nearly as vital as it is today if it had not been for their extraordinary efforts." As the traditional changing of the guard also occurs at this meeting, retiring president Challenger introduced his successor, Robert A. Hastings, whose service to the club spans many decades. Many board members renewed their terms of service, including the current vice presidents, with the addition of John Challenger, who assumed that position and

John H. Johnson, LLD '88 (Hon.)

Bennett I. Berman, LLB '43 and Mayor Richard M. Daley

James Cuno, MA '80, PhD '85

President Summers addressing the College Board Forum in 2004.

the following year became the Harvard Alumni Association's regional director for the Great Lakes region.

At the Club's annual summer gala at the Cliff Dwellers, board member Suzanne McCullagh, MA '74, PhD '81, introduced James Cuno, MA '80, PhD '85, newly appointed president of the Art Institute of Chicago, who discussed his intentions to both maintain this "encyclopedic" museum and expand certain underdeveloped collections. He also affirmed a commitment to building the Renzo Piano addition, and indeed, shortly after his installation, donorship increased exponentially.

Fall's 2004 programs were as interesting and diverse as always. Board member Michael Saper, JD '65, an architectural guru, led another of his well-known famous buildings and neighborhood tours, this time a joint venue with Brown that focused on Bronzeville and the new buildings on the IIT campus, namely, those by Harvard GSD professor in practice Rem Koolhaas and Chicago's own Helmut Jahn. Members heard from the consul general of Mexico, who had just escorted Mexican president Vicente Fox about Chicago. Families journeyed to Green Meadows Farm in Wisconsin for a guided tour of a working farm featuring cow milking and pony rides. Our annual ethnic restaurant exploration settled on the Red Apple Restaurant in the Polish community, where Adam Augustynski, AB '86, spoke on Polish customs and traditions. On the cultural front, the Ivy League Seven

Sisters Round Table announced a joint event with the Chicago Humanities Festival. In and among this plethora of autumnal programs, which ranged from neuroscience to the economy and from CTA art to North Korea, Larry Summers returned to Chicago.

On November 1, the day before the presidential elections, President Summers addressed the College Board Forum in Chicago, which was celebrating its fiftieth anniversary. Summers's speech is condensed as follows:

I want to focus my remarks on a matter of central concern to American families and to the future of the nation—restoring education to its proper role as a pathway to equal opportunity and excellence in our society. . . . The American dream is becoming more remote, as the gap between the life prospects of the children of the fortunate and the less fortunate widens. This is a crucial issue for higher education. Writing a century and a half ago, Horace Mann called education, 'beyond all other devices of human origin . . . the great equalizer of the conditions of men—the balance-wheel of the social machinery.' . . . We need to make sure that we as a nation do everything we can to make sure that adequate financial aid is available to every academically prepared student, and that students know that it will be there. Perception is as important as reality, because perceptions shape the dreams and aspirations of our young people. . . . There is an additional dimension that is particularly important at this point in our history . . . if the United States is to be a major player in the new global world. . . . We can all agree that no child should be left behind, but let us also agree that every child can get ahead. All children, whatever their backgrounds and whatever their schools, must have the opportunity to fulfill their full potential. Equal opportunity must mean equal opportunity for excellence. The imperative of equality must never mean the toleration of mediocrity. . . . This has been an enduring theme in higher education, with great and creative efforts made by many institutions. Earlier this year, we announced a new initiative at Harvard aimed at the students from families of low and moderate income. Under our new program, families with incomes of less than $40,000 will no longer be expected to contribute to the cost of attending Harvard for their children. Families with incomes of less than $60,000 will also see their contributions reduced.

Mayor Daley and Chicago's school leader, Arne Duncan, AB '86, are, with the help of the Gates Foundation, providing the kind of leadership we need to address these issues. . . . Later this morning, I will be visiting the Walter Payton College Preparatory School, a public high school here in Chicago committed to providing students with a strong education in languages and technology so that they are prepared to go to college and to become leaders in an increasingly global world. Payton is an exam school, and there are 40 qualified applicants for every spot. One third of admitted students come from low-income backgrounds. Payton students follow a rigorous and diverse curriculum and perform in the

President Summers playing Ping-Pong with Walter Payton College Prep students, 2004.

top 5 percent academically in the city. . . . In an elitist age, the Duke of Wellington famously observed that the battle of Waterloo was won on the playing fields of Eton. Today, the battle for America's future will be won or lost in America's public schools.

The Club's newsletter covered Summers's tour of its adopted school, remarking that he stopped for a brown bag lunch, where he was warmly received by the Payton students, especially when, during a classroom break, he joined in their favorite activity of Ping-Pong, challenging several students to a game.

New Year 2005 began for Chicago Club members with a mid-January performance of *All Shook Up*, featuring Elvis Presley's musical classics. In Cambridge at the same moment in time, Larry Summers was shaking up the campus, and especially the FAS faculty, with his remarks on women in science at a meeting of the National Bureau of Economic Research. At the NBER conference, "Diversifying the Science and Engineering Workforce," Summers suggested, as reported in The Nation section of the *New York Times* on Sunday, January 23, "that the low representation of women scientists at universities might stem from, among other causes, innate differences between the sexes." A worldwide firestorm followed this statement. Summers sought to extinguish the blaze. He apologized to Harvard's standing Committee on Women. He was he said only trying to "stimulate various kinds of statistical research." The Harvard economist who organized the conference said Summers was asked "to speak in his capacity as a world-class economist, not an institutional leader." Within three weeks of his unfortunate remarks, Summers had announced, (as the *Harvard University Gazette* reported on February 10), "the establishment of two University-wide task forces, charged with developing proposals to reduce barriers to the advancement of women faculty at Harvard and in academic careers more broadly," the task force on Women Faculty and the task force on Women in Science and Engineering. The newspaper went on to quote the president, "I have long been aware of the many challenges women face in pursuing academic careers, but in the past several weeks the nature and extent of these challenges have been made particularly vivid to me. . . . It is time for Harvard to step up and affirm in strong and concrete terms its commitment to the advancement and support of women pursuing academic careers. With that in mind, I have asked Drew Faust, Dean of the Radcliffe Institute for Advanced Study and Lincoln Professor of History in the Faculty of Arts and Sciences, to join with me and Provost Steven E. Hyman in taking the lead on these efforts."

"This is a moment of great opportunity for Harvard," said Radcliffe dean Drew Faust. "These task forces will focus on action. They will propose specific measures that can make a significant difference for women at the University. Harvard seeks to lead in every academic and professional field. Our new initiatives are dedicated to making Harvard a leader in advancing the careers of women faculty by offering strong support for their talents and aspirations and eliminating barriers to women's fullest achievement."

Letters of support for Summers were disseminated to the Harvard community. A senior fellow of the Harvard Corporation wrote one, as did William C. Kirby, dean of the Faculty of Arts and Sciences, who also documented in great detail what FAS was doing "right now" and had done in the past "to address these issues." The *Chicago Tribune*'s editorial on Sunday, February 20, "A Summers Storm at Harvard," also supported the president. With a number of alumni in positions of authority on the newspaper, the editorial critically examined the belatedly released transcript of the NBER Conference and concluded, "Summers' comments were in the best tradition of free intellectual inquiry the attempt to shout him down is not."

But the seeds of discontent planted early in Summers's presidency with respect to his management style (more Washingtonian than collegial) were sprouting and would be in full bloom within the year. As *The New Yorker* had observed in a "letter from Cambridge speechless," written two years before by Jeffrey Toobin, "A big, shambling man, Summers has a provocative conversational style, which seems to involve disagreeing with every proposition that is

put to him. For many at Harvard, that style, like Summers himself, has been unnerving. . . . Since Summers became Harvard's twenty-seventh president, in 2001, he has rejected the reticent, university-focussed manner of his predecessor, Neil Rudenstine, in favor of a broader and more opinionated mode, one notably hostile to campus pieties. Many have welcomed the return of a Harvard president to national debates, but there is little question, too, that Summers has sometimes been ill-served by his own pugnacity."

While the conflagration raged in Cambridge, the Chicago Club's winter program menu once again served up interesting selections. Cultural tidbits included a personal tour by Curator Richard F. Townsend, PhD '75, of his exhibit at the Art Institute, American Indian Art of the Midwest and South. John W. Barr, AB '65, MBA '72, president of the Chicago-based Poetry Foundation and *Poetry Magazine*, discussed his ideas for a strategic plan for the future in light of a major gift that had been developed to "raise poetry to a more visible and influential position in American culture." The Club enjoyed hearing remarks on the transition to being a judge by the Hon. Mark Filip, JD '92, one of the youngest and newest federal judges. Members also listened intently to Dr. Walter Willett, chair of the Department of Nutrition at the Harvard School of Public Health, whose recent book, *Eat Drink and Be Healthy* . . . , had appeared on most best-seller lists.

At the winter meeting of the Harvard Alumni Association in Cambridge, HCC board member Sandy Weissent, AB '73, was recognized as one of two worldwide winners of the Outstanding Club Contribution Award. President Hastings had nominated Sandy, chair of the Club's Adopt-A-School Committee, for his achievements in recruiting more than 200 Harvard volunteers, establishing a structure of coordinators to match Harvols with Walter Payton students in need of tutoring, college counseling, academic decathlon debate, and athletics, as well as overseeing a Web based system for matching students with volunteers. Citywide recognition of the success of the Harvard Club's Adopt-A-School program resulted in Sandy's being asked by the Alumni for Public Schools (APS) board to connect twenty to forty additional

At left, Award Dinner Honoree, David J. Vitale '68, with Award Committee members, Chairman Marshall Field V, AB '63, and Suzanne F. McCullagh, MA '74, PhD '81

Harvard Law School Professor Charles J. Ogletree, JD '78

alumni clubs with that same number of Chicago public schools. To undertake this initiative, Sandy left the Adopt-A-School program and Hastings added overall coordinator to his athletics role until he could recruit very capable Kate Tomford, AB '99, as overall coordinator and Dani Cupps, AB '92, to handle tutoring and college counseling. Together with Richard Sullivan, AB '69, who was doing a marvelous job in helping raise the Payton debate program to national stature, they have led a program recognized by the Friends of Payton at its 2007 auction fundraiser.

Early spring, and the Annual Award Dinner rolled around again. The 2005 recipient, David J. Vitale, '68, was introduced by Arne Duncan, '86. Vitale, a financial executive, director of Bank One, and president of the Chicago Board of Trade, joined the Chicago Public Schools pro bono as chief administrative officer, as well as serving on numerous other charitable boards. The keynote speaker, Ellen Condliffe Lagemann, was at the time dean of the Graduate School of Education. She is a leading historian of education and a nationally known expert on education research. As a former high school social studies teacher, her remarks were apropos to our Chicago Public Schools consortium.

President Hastings arranged for the 147-year-old Harvard Glee Club to sing at a Saturday afternoon venue at the

Winnetka Congregational Church, and Club members offered overnight accommodations for the touring choristers. The performance included the official world premiere of Chicago composer Frank Ferko's commissioned motet, "O coruscans lux stellarum" (with a twelfth-century text by Hildegard von Bingen), with Mr. Ferko attending. The previous weekend, Club members dined at Tiparos Thai Cuisine and Noodle Boutique. This Near North Side restaurant had been featured on WTTW. Hastings also secured highly successful hedge fund manager Kenneth C. Griffin, AB '89, to speak to a joint meeting with the HBS Club of Chicago at a private session at Griffin's Citadel Investment Group offices. Griffin enthralled the audience with his comments on investing, the advantages of being in Chicago rather than New York, and the future outlook for Chicago's financial services companies.

Another public broadcasting event saw Andrew Patner, WFMT critic at large, discuss the state of the arts in Chicago. In a presentation co-hosted by the Black Women Lawyers of Chicago and the ABA Commission on Racial and Ethnic Diversity in the legal profession, Harvard Law School professor Charles J. Ogletree, JD '78, discussed *Brown vs. Board of Education* and the future of the Supreme Court. Some of his well-known former students were in attendance, among them U.S. Senator Barack Obama, JD '91, and his wife, Michelle Robinson Obama, HLS '88. Community Service Day, presented by the Ivy League/Seven Sisters Round Table, and a German Riesling wine-tasting were just some of the events that rounded out the spring calendar.

Larry Summers came to talk to the Club at our annual meeting in June, which drew a very large audience to the Mid-America Club. The president spoke extemporaneously, and no transcript of his remarks exists, but all who heard him remember a brilliant summation of his accomplishments. In spite of the winter's adversity, he spoke confidently and eloquently about the goals set forth early in his tenure (many of which he had outlined when he addressed the Club's Award Dinner three years before) and of how many of them were well on their way to becoming a reality, if not already so de facto. If one reviews the text of his address to the Washington, D.C., club two months earlier, one can extrapolate what was said in Chicago. With respect to admissions and equal opportunity, he announced that 10% of the class of 2009 would be African American and that the Harvard College faculty would also have increased by nearly 10%. Recruitment of faculty will occur not only at the star level from other universities but earlier out of our own graduate schools, where outstanding teachers can be nurtured and put on a tenure track. He cited several examples already in place and assured the audience that the search for extraordinary faculty would include men and women "who are of every race, every ethnicity, and from every part of this world." He also alluded to the earlier controversy by saying that "with the aid of the task forces that we have established as you may have noticed, some of these issues of diversity have rather come into focus in recent months—we believe in taking advantage of opportunities, even if we might wish those opportunities had not presented themselves in quite the same form that they did. With the aid of those task forces we are going to address some of the crucial issues."

By the time Summers spoke in Chicago, those task forces on women had released their findings and recommendations. Dean Drew Faust, who partnered with the provost, said about them, "The task forces have produced recommendations that promise to transform not only opportunities for women and

underrepresented minorities at Harvard, but the culture of the entire University community. It is important to recognize that the issues addressed in these reports are deep seated, and progress will require continuing attention and sustained commitment for many years to come."

Summers also mentioned the ongoing crucial review of the curriculum, which he hoped would allow students more independent choices and the opportunity for substantial student-faculty contact. He promised that the next year "there would be a freshman seminar available for every Harvard undergraduate who wants one" and that "all students . . . would have a meaningful international experience" as part of the Harvard experience. A further part of curriculum review will be access for all students to the sciences so that not only will every student be able to name five plays by Shakespeare, they will also know the difference between a gene and a chromosome. They will have "a basic sense of scientific literacy."

Summers mentioned again that while keeping "Harvard's every-tub on-its-own-bottom system," he had made a major university responsibility the increased financial aid to students of the smaller schools, such as Education or Public Health, where graduates serve the public but their remuneration is not commensurate with their commitment to society.

In recognition of Summers's plea to clubs to support student's public interest endeavors, the Harvard Club of Chicago announced that in the summer of 2005, the Community Service Committee, headed by Bob Hastings and Clare Golla, '95, found positions in the Chicago area for seven summer interns and two full-year fellows in nonprofit organizations. At this same annual meeting the Club's Recognition Award Committee, chaired by Joel H. Schneider, MCRP, '82, once again honored one of its own whose volunteerism and service to the club are above and beyond the call of duty. George "Smokey" Mann, AB '58, was recognized for his more than twenty years of service on the Schools Committee, his chair of the Scholarship Committee, and his securing of McDermott Will and Emery conference space for the Club's monthly board meetings and programs.

Sporting events have always been on the program docket, and the summer and fall of 2005 were no exception. Club members were invited to meet former Harvard rowers and members of the 2004 Athens Olympics Gold Medal boat at a fundraising reception for the U.S. National Team, which raced on the Chicago River one Friday afternoon in August. Later in the fall, Mark Giangreco, chair of the Parents Committee and sports director of WLS-TV, moderated a panel on the business of sports comprised of Peter Bynoe, AB '72, MBA '75, JD '76, former chairman of the Illinois Sports Facilities Authority and managing general partner of the Denver Nuggets; Michael Alter, AB '83, chairman of the new Chicago WNBA franchise; and Jerry Reinsdorf, chairman of the Chicago White Sox and Chicago Bulls. The Harvard women's basketball team also came to Chicago to play in the DePaul Invitational.

The annual summer outing was enlivened by former *Chicago Tribune* critic Richard Christiansen, GSA '53–54, who discussed the Chicago theater scene after the usual hamburger and hot dog spread that followed cocktails on the Cliff Dwellers' terrace. Apropos of theater, the Club again offered members Shakespeare tickets and other cultural opportunities such as the Body Worlds exhibit at the Museum of Science and Industry and a special opportunity to meet Hershey Felder, pianist, playwright, and past scholar in residence at Harvard University's Music Department. George Burditt, AB '44, HLS '48, hosted Felder in his East Lake Shore Drive apartment, where Club members enjoyed a visit with this Gershwin authority.

Gary T. Johnson, JD '77

The newly appointed president of the Chicago Historical Society (now Chicago History Museum), Gary T. Johnson, JD '77, spoke of the museum's ambitious renovation plans, which would be completed in time to celebrate its 150th anniversary the following year. The Harvard Club of Chicago has been collecting memorabilia to celebrate its own sesquicentennial in 2007 and might consider reposing these documents in Chicago's oldest museum.

On a more somber note, the specter of terrorism that reared its head at the start of Summers' presidency was the subject of a joint talk sponsored by the HCC and the Business School club. Brigadier General Nick Halley (U.S. Army, ret.) discussed international terrorism and his ideas on planning and preventative measures. General Halley is a graduate of West Point and the Army War College and is the on-air military and terrorism expert for WGN-TV. The fourth estate was well represented again this year as David D Heller, AB '75, JD '78, CEO of the Chicago Tribune Company, gave a talk titled "Newspapers and the Changing Media World of Blogs, IPods, Tivos and Text Messaging." The Club also had an opportunity to hear an update on the experiences of women at Harvard in science and engineering from computer science professor Margo I. Seltzer, AB '83, in the Division of Engineering and Applied Sciences. Lisa Randall, Harvard professor of theoretical physics, discussed her latest book, *Warped Passages: Unraveling the Mysteries of the Universe's Hidden Dimensions*, which was included in the *New York Times'* 100 Notable Books list for 2005. Programs on health are always sprinkled throughout the Club's yearly calendar, and the winter season brought many, including a discussion on avoiding or coping with Type II diabetes, presented by Dr. Mark Molitch from Northwestern, and another on heart disease and the statins, presented by board member and nationally recognized cardiologist Joseph Messer, '53, MD '56, professor of medicine at Rush University Medical Center. Faculty from the Harvard School of Public Health presented a program titled "The Challenge of Controlling the Next Influenza Epidemic." Several faculty from the Dana-Farber Cancer Institute also spoke.

Other much awaited yearly business topics included the economic forecast presented once again by Paul Kasriel, senior vice president of economic research at the Northern Trust; a talk on the job market by former Club president John Challenger, AB '77, one of the most frequently quoted business executives in Chicago; and a presentation titled "Leadership in a Time of Global Competition," by Carl W. Stern, AB '68, member of the Club's board of overseers and co-chairman of the The Boston Consulting Group.

Less than two weeks before the Club's Award Dinner, members registered through Post.Harvard received startling but perhaps not totally surprising news. On February 21, 2006, the office of Donella Rapier, vice president of Alumni Affairs and Development, issued a short message to the Harvard Community from Larry Summers announcing his resignation:

Dear Members of the Harvard Community,

I write to let you know that, after considerable reflection, I have notified the Harvard Corporation that I will resign as President of the University as of June 30, 2006. I will always be grateful for the opportunity to have served Harvard in this role, and I will treasure the continuing friendship and support of so many exceptional colleagues and students at Harvard.

Below are links [see p. 200] to my letter to the community, as well as a letter from the members of the Corporation and a related news release.

Sincerely,
Larry Summers

Summers' full letter to the community was a lengthy reiteration of some of the goals he had set for the University, as well as the obstacles that still existed to their realization:

I have notified the Harvard Corporation that I will resign as President of the University as of June 30, 2006. Working closely with all parts of the Harvard community, and especially with our remarkable students, has been one of the great joys of my professional life. However, I have reluctantly concluded that the rifts

between me and segments of the Arts and Sciences faculty make it infeasible for me to advance the agenda of renewal that I see as crucial to Harvard's future. I believe, therefore, that it is best for the University to have new leadership.

Summers went on to cite an example of his frustration:

We cannot maintain pre-eminence in intellectual fields if we remain constrained by artificial boundaries of departments and Schools. 'Each Tub On Its Own Bottom' is a vivid, but limiting, metaphor for decision making at Harvard. We will not escape its limits unless our Schools and Faculties increase their willingness to transcend parochial interests in support of broader university goals.

Following closely on the heels of Summers' resignation letter came one from the Office of the Governing Boards, authored by the Fellows of Harvard College and addressed again to members of the Harvard Community:

With regret we have accepted the resignation of Lawrence H. Summers as president of Harvard University, effective at the end of the 2005–06 academic year. Since his appointment five years ago, Larry Summers has served Harvard with extraordinary vision and vitality. He has brought to the leadership of the University a sense of bold aspiration and initiative, a prodigious intelligence, and an insistent devotion to maximizing Harvard's contributions to the realm of ideas and to the larger world. Through his tenure as president, Harvard has both invigorated its academic programs and engaged more keenly with the complex challenges facing society.

We are fortunate that Derek Bok, president of Harvard from 1971 through 1991, has agreed to our request that he serve as interim president of the University beginning this July 1 and continuing until the search for a new president concludes. We are fortunate as well that Steve Hyman, who as provost has brought great insight and vigor to some of the University's central challenges and opportunities, will carry forward in his vital role. Members of the Corporation will stay in close touch with major developments across the University to assure the smoothest possible transition. There will be more to say soon about the search for a new president, which we intend to launch promptly, and about other pending matters that will require attention in the coming weeks and months.

For now, we want to express the gratitude of the University community to Larry Summers, for his vision, his leadership, and his service. We are pleased that, following a sabbatical in 2006–07, he plans to return to the faculty to resume his distinguished academic career, and with that prospect in view we intend to appoint him as one of Harvard's select group of University Professors once he concludes his time as president. Finally, we want to thank each of you for all you do for Harvard. We will greatly appreciate your cooperative effort and thoughtful counsel in the time ahead.

The *Harvard University Gazette* devoted numerous pages to Summers' accomplishments and included complimentary quotes from the fellows and the overseers. It published his complete career history, reminding readers that in 1975, an MIT graduate, Summers began his Harvard career as a doctoral student in economics. He then taught at MIT, becoming an associate professor, and served in Washington in 1982 as an economist for the President's Council of Economic Advisors. When he returned to Harvard, he became one of the youngest tenured professors before he took leave from the University to return to Washington, where he served as chief economist for the World Bank, then as deputy secretary of the treasury, and finally in 1999 as secretary of the treasury upon Senate confirmation, where he oversaw a workforce of

150,000 employees. At the end of his term he was awarded the Alexander Hamilton Medal, the Treasury Department's highest honor. The *Gazette* article concluded with an update on Derek Bok's curriculum vitae. As might be expected, news of these extraordinary events became, in turn, a major media event—the abdication heard round the world!

Sober conversations on the resignation were heard from Chicago alumni at the 2006 Annual Award Dinner, which once again raised funds for scholarship and community service. The dinner honored another Club overseer, John D. Nichols, Jr., AB '53, MBA '55, one of the most accomplished CEOs of a Chicago-based manufacturing company and a business and social problem solver par excellence. In the nonprofit world, as a life trustee, life member, or director, John often charted new directions for important cultural institutions in the city.

2006 Award Dinner Speaker,
David Halberstam, AB '55

The Club welcomed the return of David Halberstam, AB '55, as keynote speaker. A journalist and nonfiction writer as well as a distinguished social and political commentator, Halberstam reminisced on his long career, especially its early phase, when he covered the beginning stages of the Vietnam War. His classic *The Best and the Brightest* is a critical history of America's entanglement in that conflict. Channel 11 interviewer Phil Ponce served as moderator for the "fireside chat" format of the evening, which drew erudite comparisons between Vietnam and the current war in Iraq. Members could have listened late into the night to Halberstam's insightful and sonorous soliloquy. (The following spring, news of his tragic death in a California car crash saddened the entire Harvard community.)

The season's concluding programs were significant ones. They included a talk from Harvard's executive director of planned giving, a presentation titled "The Perilous State of the American School," by Harvard's GSAS, and "The Origins and Maintenance of Poverty," in the format of a panel discussion with Alex Kotlowitz, author of *There Are No Children Here*, and Dr. Orlando Patterson, Harvard professor of sociology and an authority on contemporary America's problems of race, immigration, and multiculturalism.

The Annual Dinner was held on a Sunday in late May to allow members to attend an afternoon performance of Mozart's *Requiem*, conducted by Helmuth Rilling, which was then followed by an after-dinner presentation by pianist and composer Robert Levin, AB '68, professor of humanities in the Department of Music at Harvard, who, commissioned by Rilling, wrote what is considered the most appropriate completion of the *Requiem*, which had been left unfinished at the composer's death.

Levin, who also appeared at the performance, spoke eloquently of his decision to return to Harvard to teach freshman in the core curriculum to guarantee that music is widely studied by a diverse student body to ensure its continued existence as an art form in a world whose focus is shifting away from the humanities.

The slate for the election of the 2006–07 officers, directors, and overseers was presented and approved by the members present. Margaret McCurry, LF '87, was confirmed as president, with Vice President Paul Choi, AB '86, HLS '89, joining Baird and Hammerman, the two Schools Committee

Club President Robert A. Hastings, AB '57, MBA '59, left, with 2006 Award Dinner Honoree John D. Nichols, AB '53, MBA '55

co-chairs already in place. In addition, Walter L. Keats, AB '67, and his wife, Winnie Lu, were awarded the Club's Outstanding Contribution Award. They were honored for extraordinary and selfless contributions to the Club personally, in addition to the thoughtful provision of membership and countless other office services through their association management company, which succeeded Mrs. Olsen's Letter Service in 1980.

Two weeks later, on June 8, 2006, President Lawrence H. Summers gave his last commencement address. After thanking the students, faculty, alumni, and staff and expressing his gratitude for the "opportunity . . . to lead this remarkable institution," he reiterated that "the convictions I expressed as I entered Harvard's presidency I feel with even more urgency these five years later. It is the urgency, and the possibility, of all Harvard can accomplish in the next years that I want to focus on this afternoon." Of the many issues that Summers addressed, those here illuminated shine as the most prophetic:

Globalization is making the world smaller, faster and richer. . . . Still, 9/11, avian flu, Darfur, and Iran remind us that a smaller, faster world is not necessarily a safer world. . . . America today misunderstands the world and is misunderstood in the world in ways without precedent since World War II. A great university like ours has a profoundly important role to play in promoting international understanding.

Our world is bursting with knowledge—but desperately in need of wisdom. Now, when sound bites are getting shorter, when instant messages crowd out essays, and when individual lives grow more frenzied, college graduates capable of deep reflection are what our world needs. . . . Universities are where the wisdom we cannot afford to lose is preserved from generation to generation. . . . And among universities, Harvard stands out.

And yet, great and proud institutions, like great and proud nations at their peak, must surmount a very real risk: that the very strength of their traditions will lead to caution, to an inward focus on prerogative and to a complacency that lets the world pass them by. And so I say to you that our University today is at an inflection point in its history. At such a moment, there is temptation to elevate comfort and consensus over progress and clear direction, but this would be a mistake. The University's matchless resources—human, physical, financial—demand that we seize this moment with vision and boldness. To do otherwise would be a lost opportunity, not only for Harvard but also for humanity. We can spur great deeds that history will mark decades and even centuries from now. If Harvard can find the courage to change itself, it can change the world.

"Yes I have these last years been a man in a hurry. . . . I have loved my work here, and I am sad to leave it. There was much more I wanted, felt inspired, to do. I know, as you do, that there are many within this community who have the wisdom, the love of Harvard, the spirit of service, and the energy that will be necessary to mount the collective efforts that this moment in history demands. I bid you farewell with faith that even after 370 years, with the courage to change, Harvard's greatest contributions lie in its future.

President Lawrence Summers

Chapter 12

The Bok Interregnum and the Inauguration of Drew Faust

Derek Bok, AB '51 (Stanford); JD '54, AM '58 (Washington University)
1930–
President of Harvard University 1971–1991, interim president, 2006–2007
Bok, a lawyer and law professor, served as dean of Harvard Law School.

Even with changes in top leadership, the life of the University goes on, and in mid-June 2006, a week after commencement, the Harvard Graduate School of Design "Came to Chicago." Incoming Harvard Club of Chicago president Margaret McCurry, a Loeb Fellow of the Design School, invited any interested alumni to participate in the conference. The program included Dean Alan Altshuler, AB '87, and Professor Alex Kreiger, MPCUD '77, GSD '85, a member of the Allston Planning Committee. Penny Pritzker, AB '81, a member of the Harvard Board of Overseers, as well as a Harvard Club of Chicago overseer, invited conferees to tour the recently completed Hyatt Center, designed by Henry N. "Harry" Cobb, AB '47 (46), MAR '49.

The Cobb Family

Henry Ives Cobb, AB 1880 was the architect of the original Chicago Historical Society building designed in 1892, and a vice-president of the Harvard Club of Chicago in 1896. His son, Henry Ives Cobb, Jr., received his AB from Harvard in 1929. His grandson, Henry N. Cobb, AB '47 (46), MAR '49, also became an architect and is one of three founding principals of Pei Cobb Freed & Partners. Among many notable works for which Henry Cobb has been lead designer is the Center for Government and International Studies buildings on the Harvard campus, completed in 2005.

Penny Pritzker was involved in the selection of the architectural firm for the first building to be built on the Allston campus, a science complex. The project was awarded to Behnisch and Behnisch, a German firm well known for its environmentally sensitive projects whose work had been exhibited at the GSD, where the partners had also taught a design studio.

On July 1, 2006, Derek Bok, twenty-fifth president of Harvard University, at the request of the Harvard Corporation, became the interim president of the University, a position he agreed to hold until the conclusion of the search for a new president. "I will do my best to carry out the corporation's request," said Bok. "There is no Institution I care about more deeply."

Members of the Harvard Club of Chicago who were students during Bok's earlier twenty-year presidency petitioned the University to invite him to return to Chicago to address the Club. However, the Club was advised that Bok would do no traveling during his tenure or give any official addresses. He clearly intended to maintain a low profile, promising to "make every effort to work with colleagues to further the University's agenda during this transitional period." We were clearly not the only club to request a return visit from this most popular president.

The 2006 midsummer supper on the terrace of the Cliff Dwellers featured Channel 5 investigative reporter Renee Ferguson, who would depart for Cambridge in the fall to begin her Nieman Fellowship. Renee spoke of the state of broadcast journalism and what she felt should be done to improve the quality of news. But it was her patent excitement over her upcoming Nieman year that permeated her remarks and endeared her to the audience.

As the new board reassembled in August to begin its fiscal year, attendees were reminded that the calendar year of 2007 would be the Club's sesquicentennial year. Initial planning for the anniversary had begun earlier under a committee chaired by outgoing president Bob Hastings, which had agreed that the doings of all 150 years should be documented, as had been done at the Club's centennial in 1957. Walter Keats had

Derek Bok
Interim President 2006–2007

Derek Bok served as the twenty-fifth president of Harvard University, from 1971 to 1991. He went on to serve from 1991 to 2003 as Harvard's 300th Anniversary University Professor. He is currently the faculty chair of Harvard's Hauser Center for Nonprofit Organizations. He also chairs the board of the Spencer Foundation and recently announced his intention to step down after eight years as chair of Common Cause. He has written six books on higher education: *Beyond the Ivory Tower* (1982), *Higher Learning* (1986), *Universities and the Future of America* (1990), *The Shape of the River* (1998, with William G. Bowen), *Universities in the Marketplace* (2003), and *Our Underachieving Colleges: A Candid Look at How Much Students Learn and Why They Should Be Learning More* (2005). He has also written two books about the capacity of the United States government to cope with the nation's domestic problems: *The State of the Nation* (1997) and *The Trouble with Government* (2001). A graduate of Stanford University and Harvard Law School, with a master's degree in economics from George Washington University, he was a professor of law and then dean of Harvard Law School before becoming Harvard's president in 1971.

Artist John Himmelfarb, AB '68, MAT '70, with his lithograph for the Harvard Club's 150th Anniversary.

offered to become the Club's scribe. He volunteered the use of the Club's office as repository for collected data, and started to recruit a research committee to delve into archival material.

As it became clear that Harvard's search process would not conclude in time to permit the new president to visit Chicago in the spring, it was agreed that celebrations to honor the oldest Harvard Club in the country should take two separate forms and occur at six-month intervals. Hastings proposed a "Harvard Comes to Chicago" format for the spring, but substituting prominent Windy City alumni for Harvard faculty. For the fall, a black tie gala dinner seemed an appropriate event to conclude the sesquicentennial festivities. On this occasion, the 150th history book would be unveiled and presented to all in attendance. In support of the Club's plans, and cognizant of its desire to host a Harvard president during its sesquicentennial, the HAA offered to send the provost, Stephen Hyman, to deliver the keynote luncheon address in the spring, and promised not to let the 150th year elapse without a new president to usher it out in the fall. The provost oversees the Allston campus planning, among many of his official duties, and his appraisal of the current plans and construction progress as well as other changes in process in Cambridge would be a much anticipated program. So the countdown to the celebration began.

The usual collection of stimulating conversations with alumni had been placed on the fall calendar the previous spring. The kick-off lecture was a sobering report, "The Impending Collapse of Primary Care," by Club board member C. Anderson (Andy) Hedberg, AB '57, an internal medicine doctor and immediate past president of the American College of Physicians. Andy spoke of the imminent shortage of primary care physicians, the reasons for the shortage, the possible results, and proposed remedies. Next came a discussion with artist John Himmelfarb, AB '68, MAT '70, whose *Catalogue Raisonnée 1967–2004* had recently been published by Hudson Hills Press. With works hanging in major museum collections both here and abroad, John was a natural choice to be asked to create a lithograph to grace the cover of the spring sesquicentennial program, which he produced pro bono. Full size copies would be given to patrons of the fall dinner.

James Stockard, MCP '68, LF '78, curator of the Loeb Fellowship at Harvard, came to Chicago to recruit minority applicants for the fellowship and stayed to address Club members over wine and cheese. An expert in affordable housing and community development, his analysis of the strategies necessary to effectuate neighborhood revitalization engendered a lively dialogue with alumni striving to accomplish similar objectives.

Interspersed between a live broadcast of Harvard's first loss to Yale since Summers' presidency began and an "Uncommon Wine Tasting," the Club co-hosted programs involving several Harvard professors. In conjunction with the Kennedy School alums and the Harvard Law Society of Illinois, Club members listened to a discussion of censorship and the Internet. The GSAS sponsored John H. Coatsworth, professor of Latin American affairs, who delivered an address titled "The Resurgent Left in Latin America: Threat Irritant or Ally?" Board member Walter Keats, AB '67, capped the fall agenda with an insightful PowerPoint presentation on North Korea's economic development, highlighting projects such as the Kaesong Industrial Complex, which he had just documented on a September sojourn to the Republic.

Calendar 2007 began with a January visit from Nicholas Delbanco, AB '63, director of the MFA program in creative writing at the University of Michigan, who read excerpts from his just published book, *Spring and Fall*, and in response to questions revisited the creative process and his own muse. Another winter visitor to the club, Ralph J. Hexter, AB '74, president of Hampshire College, discussed this private liberal arts college, founded as an experiment in alternative education by four other colleges in the Pioneer Valley: Amherst, Smith, Mount Holyoke, and the University of Massachusetts. (Chicagoan Adele Smith Simmons, AB '63, a Club Overseer, is a former President of Hampshire College, and also of the John D. and Catherine T. MacArthur Foundation.) Then, on February 11, the Harvard University Gazette's Web site posted the welcome announcement that the twenty-eighth president had been elected by the members of the Harvard Corporation with the consent of the University's Board of Overseers.

Drew G. Faust, an eminent historian and outstanding academic leader who has served since 2001 as the founding dean of the Radcliffe Institute for Advanced Study, will become the twenty-eighth president of Harvard University, effective July 1. . . .

"This is a great day, and a historic day, for Harvard," said James R. Houghton, the senior member of the Harvard Corporation and chair of the presidential search committee. "Drew Faust is an inspiring and accomplished leader, a superb scholar, a dedicated teacher, and a wonderful human being. . . ."

"Drew wears her extraordinary accomplishments lightly," said Houghton. "Her many admirers know her as both collaborative and decisive, both open-minded and tough-minded, both eloquent and understated, both mindful of tradition and effective in leading innovation. Her qualities will serve Harvard well as we plan ambitiously for the future—not only in the college but across the schools, not only in the sciences but across the disciplines and professions, not only in Allston but throughout our campus. We share with Drew an enthusiastic commitment to building on Harvard's strengths, to bridging traditional boundaries, and to embracing a world full of new possibilities."

President-Elect Drew Faust

"I am deeply grateful for the trust the governing boards have placed in me," said Faust. "I will work with all my heart, together with people across Harvard, to reward that trust."

"I'm grateful to the search committee for its extensive efforts to solicit advice from a wide range of alumni during the course of the search," said [Chicagoan] Paul J. Finnegan, president of the Harvard Alumni Association. "Drew Faust is an excellent choice, and I look forward to leading warm rounds of applause for our new president-elect at alumni events to come."

As dean of Radcliffe, Faust has been an influential member of Harvard's Academic Advisory Group, which brings together the president, provost, and deans to consider matters of university policy. A devoted teacher and mentor, she is currently leading an undergraduate seminar on the Civil War and Reconstruction. In the spring of 2005, she oversaw the work of Harvard's Task Forces on Women Faculty and on Women in Science and Engineering. In 2004, she served on the Allston Task Force on Undergraduate Life.

Raised in Virginia's Shenandoah Valley, Faust went on to attend Concord Academy in Massachusetts. She received her bachelor's degree from Bryn Mawr in 1968, magna cum laude with honors in history, and her master's degree (1971) and doctoral degree (1975) in American civilization from the University of Pennsylvania.

Before coming to Harvard, Faust served for 25 years on the faculty of the University of Pennsylvania. She was appointed as assistant professor in the Department of American Civilization in 1976, associate professor in 1980, and full professor in 1984. She was named the Stanley Sheerr Professor of History in 1988, then served as the Annenberg Professor of History from

1989 to 2000. She chaired the Department of American Civilization for five years, and was director of the Women's Studies Program from 1996 to 2000. She was twice honored at Penn for her distinguished teaching, in 1982 and 1996.

Bok had warm words for the president-elect: "Drew Faust is clearly one of the brightest stars in Harvard's firmament, as a dean, a scholar, a teacher, and a leading citizen of the University. Harvard will be the fortunate beneficiary of her wisdom, her experience, her eloquence, and her exceptional talent for academic leadership. I will do all I can to assure her a smooth transition and a running start."

Remarks by President-Elect and Lincoln Professor of History Drew Faust:

I am indebted to everyone whose efforts have made this University great, and especially to my predecessors— Neil Rudenstine, who brought me here as Dean of the Radcliffe Institute, Larry Summers, whose powerful thinking and impatience for results cleared the way for important new initiatives, and Derek Bok, whose steady hand has kept us on course during this past year.

I love universities and I love this one in particular. I can imagine no higher calling, no more exciting adventure than to serve as the President of Harvard.

Dean Barry Bloom and Jack Shonkoff of the School of Public Health braved a Chicago blizzard to address club members two days after the public announcement of the presidential selection. At a dinner following the talk, Dean Bloom was filled with praise for his friend Drew Faust, assuring his tablemates she would be an exceptional president. Harvard's recently appointed vice provost for international affairs, Jorge Dominguez, arrived in Chicago two weeks later to discuss "Cuba, Fidel and the United

States: Today and Tomorrow." As an overseer of University-wide international research and education initiatives and policies, this Summers' appointee also anticipated successful collaborations with the new president-elect. In his note thanking the club for its hospitality, he expressed his hope to be included in future events.

On behalf of the board and membership of the Club, President McCurry sent a congratulatory email to President-Elect Drew Faust. It was one of 1,500 she received, according to the HAA. In it McCurry mentioned the Club's sesquicentennial and expressed the board's hopes that she would make the Chicago Club her first official appearance, in honor of its historic birthday. McCurry also promised that the 150-year history book of the club would be dedicated to President Drew Faust in the spirit of beginning the next chapter in the Club's history concurrent with hers. A week later, word came that the invitation had been accepted, and Friday, November 9, was the agreed-upon date. Wheels were immediately set in motion to secure a venue. To pick up the pace on the production of the Club's history, board members were recruited as producers.

President Margaret I. McCurry, LF '87, with 2007 Award Dinner Speaker Ambassador Peter Galbraith AB '73, KSG '78

Meanwhile, March's Annual Award Dinner, which benefits the club's Scholarship and Community Service programs, attracted hundreds of members, who arrived at the Mid-America Club on a Saturday evening to honor awardees Joanne Alter and Marion Stone. These two philanthropists founded a not-for-profit called WITS, an acronym for Working in the Schools. WITS is an organization of 1,600 trained volunteers who for sixteen years have tutored and mentored K–8 students in twenty-eight Chicago public schools. Adela Cepeda, AB '80, of the Awards Committee introduced awardees Alter and Stone, who gave very moving acceptance speeches elaborating on their extraordinary contribution to education.

Club president Margaret McCurry then introduced former ambassador to Croatia Peter Galbraith, AB '73, KSG '78, a former cabinet member, teacher, and author. His latest book is *The End of Iraq*. In his insightful address to an attentive audience Galbraith outlined the political, religious, and military issues in Iraq that have created the current instability and left America more vulnerable to terrorist activity. He then offered scenarios for U.S. disengagement while maintaining a military presence in the area, ideally in the Kurdish region. At the conclusion of the evening, John Holabird, Jr., AB '42, MAR '48, presented his caricature drawing of the guest speaker to Galbraith. John's drawings have graced the covers of the program for the Annual Awards dinner since its inception.

The Club had launched some new initiatives as it sailed into its 150th year: As part of the activities overseen by the Schools Committee, an expansion of the Early College Awareness (ECA) program was undertaken by board member Andrew Pacelli, AB '04. He selected a Saturday in April for a seminar to encourage Chicago Public School students and their parents to start thinking about college before entering high school. Andy worked with the Chicago International Charter School and host school, the Chicago International Longwood Academy, to publicize the event, which attracted 320 would-be collegians and their families. The keynote address was by Selamawi Asgedom, AB '99, an Ethiopian émigré and noted author of *Of Beetles and Angels: A Boy's*

Remarkable Journey from a Refugee Camp to Harvard. This inspirational autobiography was distributed to all attendees.

At the May board meeting the directors unanimously agreed to adopt an HAA lifelong learning initiative entitled "Justice Now," created by Michael Sandel, professor of government. The Chicago Club was asked to be one of ten to fifteen pilot clubs worldwide that would participate in the program. In brief, Professor Sandel's Justice course, one of the most popular courses taught on campus, would be available to alumni in a recorded version presented as twenty-four online lectures. Monthly discussion groups led by a facilitator could include virtual meetings with Professor Sandel such as Web streaming "office hours," blogs, and other varied media outlets. John Challenger, AB '77, HAA regional director for the Western Great Lakes region, volunteered to coordinate the Club's involvement, assisted by board members Julie Gage Palmer, AB '84, David Mann, AB '97, Elroy A. Rozner, EDM '99, and Club member James A. Star, AB '83. This exciting new long-distance learning opportunity would launch the fall program schedule, with discussion groups assembling monthly from September through December.

At that same meeting the Adopt-A-School Committee announced that Walter Payton College Prep had elevated interim principal Ellen Estrada to the position of principal. A good friend and supporter of the Harvard volunteers (Harvols), Ms. Estrada's appointment would be an opportunity to build more faculty and staff support for the future. Harvol debate coordinator Dick Sullivan, AB '69, was invited to attend the board meeting to explain in person the accomplishments of the Payton team, which in a few short years under his tutelage had progressed from being last in their division to being the top urban debate school in the country, winning the National Urban Debate League Championship in Atlanta in April. Board members agreed that an event featuring an actual student debate would be an extremely entertaining program.

The spring 150th anniversary celebration on May 19 also served as the Club's annual meeting. The invitation was broadcast emailed to all 6,500+ alumni in the Chicagoland area with a post.Harvard address and mailed to others. The Club also reached out to invite the Indianapolis, Milwaukee and Minneapolis clubs. The day long roster, which featured local alumni presenting diverse program offerings also reflected interuniversity dialogue among participants representing differing schools, much as Larry Summers had predicted would be critical to Harvard's continued evolution.

2007 Award Dinner program cover by John Holabird, Jr. AB '42, MAR '48

The morning was divided into two consecutive sessions containing three concurrent programs each. "The Future of Chicago's Museums" featured local museum leaders. Gary T. Johnson, JD '77, president of the Chicago History Museum, showcased the museum's new building and exhibitions, and suggested attendees look for *Is It Real?* opening June 30, which will explore how museums determine authenticity of objects. Next, John McCarter, Jr., MBA '63, president and CEO of the Field Museum, wowed audiences with a trailer from the *Encyclopedia of Life* (www.eol.org), a new initiative to "aggregate all known data about every living species." Representing the Art Institute of Chicago were Meredith Mack, MPP '85, senior vice president of Finance and Operations, and Suzanne F. McCullagh, MA '74, PhD '81, curator, Earlier Prints and Drawings, who presented architect Renzo Piano's dazzling plans for the Modern Wing and discussed updates to the print and drawing collection.

In "Socially Valuable and Sustainable Architecture," Margaret McCurry, LF '87, John Ronan, GSD '91, Kara Boyd representing Jeanne Gang GSD '93, and Dirk Denison, GSD '85, shared details of projects employing energy conscious innovations such as rooftop gardens, rooftop wind-activated turbines, photovoltaic cells, and more. Highlighted projects included the Ford Calumet Environmental Center, for which the architects are utilizing "found" industrial materials and recycling them into usable building products; a house in Sonoma that is clad in zinc, an environmentally friendly material; the Gary Comer Youth Center in Bronzeville, which boasts a "green roof" and serves as an important symbol for community development; and architecture and design initiatives by the Illinois Institute of Technology to respond to environmental concerns.

"Harvard Alumni Support for Chicago's Schools" featured Danielle C. Cupps, AB '92, Paul J. Finnegan, AB '75, MBA '82, John Nichols, AB '53, MBA '55, and David Weinberg, AB '74, discussing their involvement in and support of Chicago Public Schools. Projects range from the Club's Adopt-A-School program at Walter Payton College Prep to strengthening secondary education in partnership with

Teach for America. David Weinberg distributed a handout, *Transparency and Choice in Economically Disadvantaged Communities*, which provided an enlightening view of the challenges facing public schools.

"Creating Imaginative Education Programs and Facilities" began with Larry Stanton, AB '85, the chief officer for planning and development at Chicago Public Schools, offering provocative statistics regarding student achievement and discussing reform initiatives. Next, Ralph Johnson, GSD '73, design director at Perkins & Will, shared designs of schools and cultural institutions and raised interesting questions about the role of design in learning. Highlighted projects included Perspectives Charter School in Chicago and the new national university in Angola.

In "U.S. International Competitiveness and the Rise of Asia" Carl Stern, AB '68, co-chairman of The Boston Consulting Group, drew upon his extensive expertise and travel experience to update last year's presentation and discuss the substantially increased competitive capability of Asian countries. Ross Wimer, GSD '88, international design partner at SOM, shared his understanding of how cooperation among local architecture firms can help maintain a competitive edge.

Legal experts Judy McCue, JD '72, of McDermott Will & Emery, and Howard McCue III, JD '71, of Mayer Brown Rowe & Maw, in the session "Understanding the Prospects of Transfer Tax Reform," described how they advise their clients to plan for potential changes in tax legislation. Their informative handout provided a very useful take-home reminder of the wide range of options for minimizing taxes.

Lunch featured a keynote address by Provost Steven E. Hyman, MD, and his presentation of a plaque from the HAA in honor of the Club's 150th anniversary. President Margaret McCurry accepted on behalf of the club. As part of the annual meeting, the board approved the proposed slate of new officers and directors and presented to Robert Hastings, AB '57, MBA '59, the Recognition Award for his significant

150th Anniversary Keynote Speaker
Provost Steven E. Hyman, MD '80

contributions to the Club. He initiated the 150th Anniversary Committee and chaired the "Harvard and Chicago" program. He also materially strengthened the Club's Community Service Committee working with Harvard's Center for Public Interest Careers to place and support summer interns and full year fellows, helped institute graduate student public service awards, and provided leadership in the Adopt-A-School Harvol program.

After lunch, Leah Zell Wanger, AB '71, AM '71, PhD '79 Harvard Overseer, and Marshall Bouton, AB '64 president of Chicago Council on Foreign Relations, offered perspectives on America's challenges in its relationships with Europe and Asia. Suggested priorities include better recognition of geopolitical power shifts, greater sharing of security responsibilities, more effective participation in global institutions, and dealing with potential instabilities involving fundamentalism and terrorism.

In the second afternoon program, William R. Fitzsimmons, Dean of Admissions and Financial Aid spoke of new opportunities for Harvard College in the Post Early Admission Era. He then chaired a Schools and Scholarships Committee discussion following his session.

The day offered attendees stimulating dialog, lively conversation and a chance to reconnect with colleagues.

At the June board meeting Vice-President Stephen W. Baird, AB '75, was congratulated on becoming a new elected director of the HAA for a three-year term. Class of '57 ex officio board member Dr. Murray Levin eloquently reported on the celebratory activities connected with his fiftieth reunion, held concurrently with the 356th Commencement. He also noted that when Lawrence H. Summers, president emeritus of Harvard University and Charles W. Eliot University Professor, was awarded the honorary degree of Doctor of Laws at the Morning Exercises, the assembled students began a chant of "Larry, Larry, Larry," clearly welcoming back from sabbatical a president popular with a majority of the student body.

A long range planning committee had been formed at the beginning of the club's fiscal year comprised of President McCurry, Vice-President Paul Choi, AB '86, JD '89, and board member Jim Stone, AB '60, MBA '62. The group outlined a number of arenas to be revisited and identified new territories to be explored. Long range planning categories were on the agenda at each board meeting throughout the club's 150th anniversary year, engendering lively discussions and charting some new directions. The Membership Committee under chair Richard Bialek, AB '79, MBA '82, developed a survey designed to assess member preferences. The Decade Group, under David Mann, AB '97, investigated new methods of Internet communication to attract new members and signed up one of the Facebook creators, Christopher Hughes, AB '06, who resided in Chicago, to speak at a summer event. The Schools and Scholarships Committee agreed to try to expand its summer welcome party for newly accepted undergraduates to include one for graduate school admittees as well.

Walter Payton College Prep 2007 National Urban Debate League Champions

Richard W. Shepro, AB '75, JD '79, head of the Parents Committee, volunteered to host the August party at his home.

Two key Harvol volunteers at Payton were profiled in the summer edition of the newsletter, which was expanded to a quarterly to accommodate coverage of the year-end events, the Annual Meeting, and the early fall programs. Besides reporting on the support provided by Richard Sullivan, AB '69 for the Debate Team's success, the Payton article also profiled Paul J. Karafiol, AB '92, the coach of the math team, which won its fourth consecutive Divisional State Championship at the end of April.

Programs to engage young families were researched by board member Clare Golla, AB '95, who sponsored a July visit to the Morton Arboretum. The agenda included tram rides and a tour of the children's garden, followed by a picnic lunch. With former Vice-President Al Gore Jr.'s [AB '69, LLD '94 (Hon.)] Academy Award-winning documentary *An Inconvenient Truth* bringing global warming before the American consciousness, the Club planned its summer dinner program based on the city of Chicago's own video on the subject. Prepared by the Department of the Environment, the video illustrates the city's initiatives on energy conservation and green building programs. First Deputy Commissioner Karen Hobbs showed the video in February at a Harvard Design School Symposium on Climate Change sponsored by the Loeb Fellowship. Chicago Club president McCurry, LF '87, attended the Cambridge conference and subsequently invited Sadhu Johnston, commissioner of the city's Department of the Environment, and Cheryl Hughes, LF '04, director of program development in the Mayor's Office of Special Events, to jointly address the Club on the greening of Chicago and the city's response to global warming.

Sesquicentennial program activities continued into the fall, when Walter Keats, AB '67, primary author of the Club's history, gave a September PowerPoint presentation on the subject. His anecdotally illustrated autumnal talk was guaranteed to whet the appetites of members for the

publication date, scheduled to coincide with President Drew Faust's visit in November. To meet said schedule, all the authors had submitted their chapters and the researchers had completed their documentation by the end of June. The summer belonged to editor Marjorie Pannell and graphic designer Karin Kuzniar, with the History Committee meeting intermittently to review progress. The newsletter had offered tantalizing tidbits of ancient history throughout the year, and a mockup of the cover design had been on display at the 150th Anniversary Celebration in May to further advertise the books fall debut. As the anniversary year moved toward its close, the directors anticipated a busy fall planning special events to highlight Drew Faust's first visit to the windy city as Harvard's twenty-eighth president, a fitting ending to The Harvard Club of Chicago's 150th year and an equally fitting beginning to the next fifty.

Drew Faust, AB '68 (Bryn Mawr); AM '71 and PhD '75 (University of Pennsylvania) *1947–* President of Harvard University 2007–
Faust, a history professor, served as the first dean of the Radcliffe Institute for Advanced Study at Harvard from 2001 to 2007.

The Harvard Club of Chicago | *150 years 1857-2007*

Harvard and Chicago
Schedule

8:30-9:15 am Arrival and Registration

9:25-10:35am **Program Session 1**

The Future of Chicago's Museums
Gary T. Johnson JD77, President, Chicago History Museum
Meredith Mack MPP85, Sr. VP, Finance and Operations, & **Suzanne F. McCullagh** MA74, PhD81, Curator, Earlier Prints and Drawings, The Art Institute of Chicago
John W. McCarter, Jr. MBA63, President & CEO, The Field Museum

Socially Valuable and Sustainable Architecture
Dirk S. Denison GSD85, FAIA, Dirk Denison Architects
Kara Boyd, Project Architect, Studio Gang
Margaret I. McCurry LF87, FAIA, Tigerman McCurry Architects
John J. Ronan GSD91, AIA, John Ronan Architect

Harvard Alumni Support for Chicago's Schools
Danielle C. Cupps AB92 - HCC Adopt-A-School Harvols at Walter Payton
Paul J. Finnegan AB75, MBA82 - Teach for America
John D. Nichols, Jr. AB53, MBA55 - Personal Commitments
David B. Weinberg AB74 – Transparency and Choice for Parents in Disadvantaged Communities

10:35-10:50 am *Break*

10:50 am-Noon **Program Session 2**

US International Competitiveness and the Rise of Asia
Carl W. Stern AB68, Co-Chairman, The Boston Consulting Group
Ross Wimer GSD88, AIA, International Design Partner, SOM

Program Session 2, continued

Creating Imaginative Educational Programs and Facilities
Laurence B. Stanton MPA85, Chief Officer, Strategy and Planning, Chicago Public Schools
Ralph Johnson GSD73, FAIA, Design Director, Perkins and Will

Understanding the Prospects of Transfer Tax Reform, and How We Plan in the Face of Such Prospects
Judith W. McCue JD72, McDermott Will & Emery, Past President, American College of Trust and Estate Counsel
Howard M. (Scott) McCue III JD71cl, Mayer Brown Rowe & Maw LLP

Noon-12:15 pm *Break and Assembly for Lunch*

12:15-2:05 pm *Lunch*
The Annual Meeting
Recognition Award Presentation

Keynote Speaker
Steven E. Hyman, MD80, Provost of Harvard University, Professor of Neurobiology at Harvard Medical School

2:05-2:20 pm *Break*

2:20-3:30 pm **Program Session 3**

U.S. Strategic Relationships in Europe and Asia: Priorities for the Next Administration
Leah Zell Wanger AB71, AM72, PhD79, Harvard Overseer
Marshall M. Bouton AB64, President, The Chicago Council on Global Affairs

New Opportunities for Harvard College in the Post Early Admission Era
William R. Fitzsimmons AB67, EdM69, EdD71, Dean of Admissions and Financial Aid
(Dean Fitzsimmons will chair a Schools and Scholarships Committee discussion following this session, Ballroom A.)

The Harvard Club of Chicago
Founded 1857

OFFICERS
President
Margaret I. McCurry LF87

Vice Presidents
Stephen W. Baird AB75
Paul L. Choi AB86, JD89
Alan H. Hammerman AB55

Secretary
Michael J. Cronin AB83

Assistant Secretary
Elory A. Rozner EdM99

Treasurer
Stephen P. Lucado AB94

DIRECTORS
Class of 2007
Stephen W. Baird AB75
Nancy Berman
Richard W. Bialek, Jr. AB79, MBAR?
Michael I. Cronin AB83
Clare K. Golla AB95
Marcus L. Hall AB90
Alan H. Hammerman AB55
Walter L. Keats AB67
Suzanne F. McCullagh MA74, PhD81
Joseph V. Messer AB53, MD56
Gerald M. Offutt AB73, JD76
Elory A. Rozner EdM99
Benjamin S. Sher AB99
James H. Stone AB60, MBA62
Katherine Tomford AB99
Anne Troy AB82

Class of 2008
Adela M. Cepeda AB80
Shu Yan Chan AB75
Paul L. Choi AB86, JD89
Danielle C. Cupps AB92
John C. Gabbert AB68
C. Anderson Hedberg AB57
Bruce Hochstadt AB81
Carrie A. Jablonski AB98, JD03
Sharon Elaine Jones AB77, JD82
Jana Meader Kubacki AB95
Stephen P. Lucado AB94
David E. Mann AB97
Margaret I. McCurry LF87
Andrew Pacelli AB04
Julie Gage Palmer AB84
Robert S. Rivkin AB82
Michael S. Saper JD65
Joel H. Schneider MCRP82

Ex Officio
John A. Challenger AB77, HAA Regional Director
Chris-Tia E. Donaldson AB00, JD03, HBAS
Paul J. Finnegan AB75, MBA82, HAA President
Robert A. Hastings AB57, MBA59, Past President
Murray L. Levin AB57, HAA 50th Reunion Representative
Alex R. Miller MBA97, HBS
James L. Nagle MAR64, GSD
Sheila O'Shaughnessy MBA80, HBS
Kraig Singleton MPP98, KSG
Christina M. Tchen AB78, HAA Director
Sandra S. Yamate JD84, HLS

OVERSEERS
Doris W. Cheng IAF85
Marshall Field, V AB63
M. Margaret Georgiadis AB86, MBA90
H. George Mann AB58
John D. Nichols, Jr. AB53, MBA55
Adele Smith Simmons AB63
Carl W. Stern AB68
David J. Vitale AB68
David B. Weinberg AB74

Ex Officio (Harvard Overseers)
Arne Duncan AB86(87)
Penny Pritzker AB81
Leah Zell Wanger AB71, AM72, PhD79

PRESIDENTS COUNCIL
Frank L. Bixby AB50
Richard C. Burnstine AB50, MD54
John A. Challenger AB77
Craig I. Coit AB73
Anne Meserve Davis AB58
Susan Seder Freehling HRP62
Anne Black Gauthier HRP58
Ethel Caro Gofen MAT59
Kenneth V. Hachikian AB71, MBA73
William P. Hall AB45, MBA48
Alan H. Hammerman AB55
Robert A. Hastings AB57, MBA59
Quentin George Heisler Jr. AB65, JD68
Lawrence Howe AB42
Christopher G. Janus SB36
Susan J. Oliver AB78
Jacquelyn S. Sanders AB52
Philip W. K. Sweet, Jr. AB50
Mari DeCosta Terman AB57
Anne B. Troy AB82
Desmond C. Wong MBA77
Charles E. Zeitlin AB53, LLB56

The Harvard Club of Chicago

2007 Annual Meeting and 150th Anniversary Celebration,

Harvard and Chicago

Luncheon Program

Welcome
Robert A. Hastings AB57, MBA59

Annual Meeting
Margaret I. McCurry LF87

Recognition Award
Joel H. Schneider MCRP82

Speaker
Steven E. Hyman, MD80
Provost of Harvard University

Saturday, the Nineteenth of May
Two Thousand Seven

The Mid-America Club
200 East Randolph Street, Chicago, Illinois

PATRONS

Stephen & Susan Baird
Richard & Ann Burnstine
LeRoy T. Carlson & Catherine Mouly
Shu Chan & Anne Troy
Paul Choi
Dirk Denison
Pantelis & Margo Georgiadis
Bill & Ethel Gofen
Clare Golla
Mickey Hammerman
Robert & Margaret Hastings
C. Anderson & Junia Hedberg
Bruce Hochstadt
Yoshihiko Kawamura
Walter L. Keats
Ryan & Jana Kubacki
Eric Larson & Barbara Wu

Murray & Joan Levin
Stephen Lucado
Suzanne F. McCullagh
Margaret I. McCurry
Joseph & Nancy Messer
Gerald M. Offutt
Andrew Pacelli
Lambrini Papangelis
James & Laura Rhind
Robert S. Rivkin
Michael S. Saper
Charles & Susan Schwartz
Richard Shepro & Lindsay Roberts
Honey Jacobs Skinner
Ben Kim Suzuki
Tina Tchen
Desmond Wong

150th Anniversary Celebration
and
Book Committee

Robert A. Hastings AB57, MBA59, Chair
Paul L. Choi AB86, JD89, Co-chair
Walter L. Keats AB67, Book Chair
Margaret I. McCurry LF87, HCC President
Nancy Berman, HCC Program Chair
Michael J. Cronin AB83
John C. Gabbert AB68
Ethel Caro Gofen MAAT59
Suzanne F. McCullagh MA74, PhD81
Andrew Pacelli AB04
Julie Gage Palmer AB84
Michael S. Saper JD65
M. Faye Harned Sinnott MBA74

Related Chicago Area
Harvard Alumni Organizations

The Harvard Business School Club of Chicago
The Harvard Law Society of Illinois
The Harvard Medical Society of Chicago
The John F. Kennedy School of Government
Chicago Area Alumni Association
The Graduate School of Design Chicago Alumni

Presidents & Leaders

Presidents 1957–2007

1957–1958

F(rancis) Lee H(igginson) Wendell, AB '38

(Deceased) Lee Wendell was a management consultant with the firm of A. T. Kearney & Co..

1958–1959

Frederick William Burnham, AB '30, MBA '32

(Deceased) After graduating from Harvard Business School, Fred Burnham devoted his professional life to banking, first in Boston, then with the Northern Trust in Chicago. Burnham was known as a stamp collector, a bridge player, and a mentor to young professionals. In retirement he remained active with the Harvard Club, working with former Club president Bill Dunn to meticulously proofread the annual dinner invitations and programs.

1959–1960

Rudy Lamont Ruggles, AB '31, LLB '34

(Deceased) Born in Philadelphia in 1909, Rudy Lamont Ruggles graduated from Harvard College in 1931. After moving to Chicago, he spent much of his life as an attorney with the firm of Chadwell, Kayser, Ruggles, McGee & Hastings. From 1964 to 1970 Ruggles served on the Visiting Committee to Harvard College; he was as well a member of Harvard's Committee on University Resources. In addition to his tenure as president of the Harvard Club of Chicago, Ruggles was a member of the Commercial Club of Chicago and president of the Economic Club of Chicago. He is perhaps best known for his commitment to the Newberry Library, where he was a life trustee and to which he donated a celebrated collection of American historical documents.

1960–1961

John Douglas Hastings, LLM '33

(Deceased) After graduating from Harvard Law School, John Hastings worked for the law firm of Hubachek & Kelly, the Household Finance Corporation and finally State of Illinois as an Assistant Attorney General. He was active in Club affairs including Schools Committee work.

1961–1962

John Colville Donnelly, AB'26, MBA '28

(Deceased) John Donnelly spend most of his career in the utilities industry, capping his career as the president of Consolidated Gas & Service Co.

1962–1963

Philip Whitford Kirkland Sweet, Jr., AB '50

Philip Sweet is the retired chairman of the Northern Trust Company. A onetime Adams House resident, Sweet is a life trustee of Rush University Medical Center and a life member of the Council on the Graduate School of Business at the University of Chicago, where he received his MBA in 1957. Active in many Chicago charities and clubs, Sweet is a member of the Commercial Club and served on the board of directors of the Economic Club.

1963–1964

Denison Bingham Hull, 1919 (1920)

(Deceased) Denison Hull, the son of U.S. Congressman Morton Denison Hull, was a well-known Chicago architect whose work included the First Unitarian Church of Chicago at 5650 S. Woodlawn Avenue. An avid fox hunter and dog breeder, he authored the scholarly monograph, *Hounds and Hunting in Ancient Greece*, published by the University of Chicago Press.

1964–1965

Frank Lyman Bixby, AB '50

Frank Bixby spent his legal career as an estate planning attorney at the Chicago firm of Sidley Austin LLP. He served on the boards of the Chicago Urban League and Evanston Township High School and has been on the board of the Spencer Foundation for more than thirty-five years. Bixby was named Urban League Man of the Year in 1974.

1965–1966

Austin Lowell Wyman, Jr., AB '48

(Deceased) Austin Wyman was a second-generation Harvardian and a Chicago attorney. Born in and raised in Glencoe, Wyman was firmly rooted in Chicago through family and career, and after graduating from Harvard he returned to the city to attend Chicago-Kent College of Law. He worked for several years at his father's firm, Cummings & Wyman, and from 1973 on at the firm of Tenney & Bentley in Chicago. In addition to his tenure as president of the Harvard Club in 1965–1966, Wyman served as president of the Adventurers Club and the Chicago Audubon Society, at one point operating a nature store and art gallery in Andersonville. He was a board member of several educational and relief organizations and founded the Community Bank of Edgewater to encourage investment in his North Side community. He died in 2001.

1966–1968

Christopher George Janus, SB '36

Born in West Virginia, Chris Janus attended Oxford after graduating from Harvard. He traveled extensively around the world, worked for the U.S. State Department after World War II, wrote for the *New York Times*, and became an investment banker in Chicago. He is the author of several books, including *Miss 4th of July, Goodbye*, which was later made into a Disney movie. One of the most creative Club presidents, he was also the originator of the idea of the Harvard Club of Chicago Annual Award for a person who made a distinguished contribution to the Chicago community in a field other than his primary occupation.

1968–1969

William McKee Dunn, AB '30

(Deceased) Bill Dunn worked in the paper industry and then in management consulting. In his later years he worked in fund raising for non-profit organizations. In retirement he remained active with the Harvard Club, working with former Club president Fred Burnham to meticulously proofread the annual dinner invitations and programs.

1969–1970

Joseph May Greeley, AB '25, MBA '27

(Deceased) A descendent of one of the founders of the Harvard Club of Chicago, Samuel S. Greeley, Joseph Greeley was active in the Club while working for the advertising firm of Leo Burnett where he became a director and executive vice president.

1970–1971

John Williams Stimpson, AB '58

After graduation, John Stimpson worked for several years in Boston, then entered the insurance business in Chicago, specializing in risk management for financial institutions. In 1984 he co-founded the Interest Rate Management Corporation, which provides interest rate insurance to real estate developers. While in Chicago he served on the board of the Infant Welfare Society (and as its president), WTTW Chicago Public Television, WFMT, and the Chicago Orchestral Association, and as a regional director of the Harvard Alumni Association, in addition to significant engagement with the Club's schools, scholarship, and commencement programs. In 1987 he returned to the Boston area, where he continues to serve as a private trustee.

1971–1973　　　**Eugene Perry Heytow, AB '55**

Eugene Heytow, a Chicago attorney, became part owner of the old McCormick Inn, built on air rights over the Illinois Central lines west of McCormick Place, and later chairman of Amalgamated Trust and Savings Bank. In 1979, Chicago mayor Jane Byrne appointed him chairman of the Metropolitan Fair and Exposition Authority (the McCormick Place Board).

1973–1975　　　**Edward Hutchins Hickey, AB '33, LLB '36**

(Deceased) Originally from Boston, Edward Hickey became a Chicago lawyer and president of the U.S. 7th Circuit Bar Association in 1974–1975. Hickey's service to the public included participation on the U.S. Judicial Conference Committee on Rules of Practice and Procedure. He died on August 31, 1986.

1975–1976　　　**Lawrence Howe, AB '42**

Lawrence Howe (whose father, brothers, son, and granddaughter also attended Harvard) had a successful business career with Jewel Foods, which he last served as vice chairman until its acquisition by American Stores in 1984. Since then he has dedicated his life to supporting metropolitan Chicago's not-for-profit community with service on numerous boards, such as those of the Metropolitan Planning Council, the United Way of Metropolitan Chicago, Evanston Hospital, Metropolitan Family Services and Loyola University of Chicago. He also has served as a community and church leader in his home town of Winnetka, including two terms as village president. He launched and led the Civic Committee of the Commercial Club beginning in 1985. In recent years he has volunteered as a full-time senior program officer and senior advisor for The Chicago Community Trust, and also served as liaison for it and the United Way of Metropolitan Chicago on a joint study to help them improve the effectiveness of support for community health and human services needs. For his many years of selfless community service he received a 2007 Annual Philanthropy Award given by the Chicago Chapter of the Association of Fundraising Professionals.

1976–1978　　　**Vern Kenneth Miller, SB '42**

(Deceased) A native of Milwaukee, Wisconsin, and famous for his imposing size, Vern Miller was a formidable left tackle on the Harvard Crimson varsity football team in the late 1930s and early 1940s. While the 250-pound Crimson letterman spent most of his time on the field, he carved out enough time to star in the 1942 Winthrop House play. Before coming to Chicago he spent time as a sports correspondent with the *Boston Globe*, which afforded him the opportunity to write a weekly column on his old team. He worked at several companies in his career including one in Mexico, and culminating in a family business H. K. Miller, Inc.

1978–1980　　　**William Putney Hall, AB '45, MBA '48**

William P. Hall, now retired from a career as a Chicago businessman, was associated with the prominent service firms Duff & Phelps and A. T. Kearney. He has served on the board of directors of six corporations and a dozen nonprofits, including St. Leonard's House. In retirement he has been involved with Executive Service Corps as a volunteer consultant, trainer, and board member. The Hall family has a long history of Harvard connections going back to the Civil War and Bill's great-grandfather who was an astronomer at Harvard, down through five generations of alumni including two grandchildren.

1980–1982

Alan Howard Hammerman, AB '55

Chicago attorney Alan "Mickey" Hammerman has an extensive record of engagement both with the Harvard Club of Chicago and with the Harvard Alumni Association. In addition to serving as Club president from 1980 to 1982, he has served in a vice presidential role continuously from 1982 to the present as co-chair of the Schools Committee, has been a director since 1968, and on the HAA National Schools Committee since 1970. His outstanding service has been recognized with the Harvard Alumni Award (1990), the Harvard Club of Chicago's Outstanding Contribution Award (2000), and the Hiram Hunn Award (2004).

1982–1984

Stephen Longfellow Seftenberg, AB '56, LLB '59

Stephen L. Seftenberg practiced law in Chicago for thirty years before moving to Florida. He is co-founder of the Talent Assistance Program, which recruits seasoned volunteer management assistance for minority enterprises in the Chicago area. He also served as chair of the editorial board of the *Chicago Reporter*, a monthly journal reporting on race and poverty in the Chicago area, and on the advisory board of the John R. Marshall, Jr., Environmental Foundation. Currently he is a board member of the Harvard Club of the Palm Beaches.

1984–1986

Mari De Costa Terman, AB '57

Mari De Costa Terman contributed to both the Radcliffe and the Harvard communities in Chicago, a common goal that arose out of the institution's administrative separation of male and female undergraduates. Eventually she served two years as president of the Radcliffe Club, engaging in fundraising and interviewing prospective students. She became a director of the Harvard Club in 1977 and in 1984 she was elected president of the Harvard Club, the first woman to hold that position, and was reelected the following year. She describes this period as one of both fun and tension as she sought to carve out an unambiguous role for women. She was subsequently elected a director and then vice president of the Harvard Alumni Association, and has assisted in organizing the 50th Class Reunion for her Radcliffe class.

1986–1987

Leo F. Mullin, AB '64, MS '65, MBA '67

Leo Mullin grew up in Maynard, Massachusetts, twenty miles from Harvard Yard. After getting three degrees from Harvard he worked as a consultant for McKinsey & Co., eventually settling into a senior role at Consolidated Rail Corp. Mullin's success turning around the fortunes of the struggling railroad led to senior management positions at First National Bank of Chicago from 1981 to 1995. From 1995 to 1997 he served as vice-chairman of Commonwealth Edison and from 1997 to 2004 as CEO of Delta Airlines. Currently a resident of Atlanta, Mullin is on the board of the Carter Center and active in the fight against juvenile diabetes.

1987–1989

Thomas Stuart James, AB '52, AMP '75

Thomas S. James, born in Chicago in 1930, earned his JD degree from Georgetown Law School and was an attorney with the Chicago firm of Meyer Brown and Platt until 1961. From 1961 to 1963 he was regional counsel for the Agency for International Development, Central America/Caribbean region. He then joined the Amoco Corporation as associate general counsel (international), which position he held until his retirement in 1995. During his tenure as the Club's president he was instrumental in starting the Adopt-A-School program. In retirement he has been a visiting lecturer on international business transactions at Fuzhou University and Hangzhou University, China.

1989–1991

Quentin George Heisler, Jr., AB '65, JD '68

George Heisler is a long-time partner with the law firm of McDermott Will & Emery. Heisler's commitment to service has spanned a diversity of civic activities, public and private. He is a trustee of the Shedd Aquarium and an active fundraiser for the Art Institute of Chicago and the Chicago Symphony Orchestra. In his hometown of Winnetka, he has served on both the Village Caucus and on the community's Board of Education.

1991–1993

Richard Carl Burnstine, AB '50, MD '54

Richard C. Burnstine, professor of clinical pediatrics at Northwestern University Medical School and a senior attending physician at Evanston Hospital, notes that serendipity has played a significant role in his life. He went to Harvard because it offered him a scholarship and Penn didn't; he met his wife while at Harvard Medical School, and he entered practice in Chicago because of her connection to the city. He was drawn to serve with the Club out of a sense of obligation to Harvard and made the Schools Committee his primary focus. Elected president for consecutive terms in 1990–1992, he sought to broaden the composition of the board and to draw more graduate school alumni into active roles. He was the recipient of the Club's Outstanding Contribution Award in 2003. He has served as president of the Illinois chapter of the American Academy of Pediatrics and as physician-in-chief for the Cradle, a nonprofit adoption agency in Evanston, where he is also on the board. He has been with North Suburban Pediatrics since its inception in 1968.

1993–1994

Charles Ephraim Zeitlin, AB '53, LLB '56

Coming to Chicago out of Harvard Law School Zeitlin helped the Radcliffe Club of Chicago get legally organized, becoming its first male member. He was active on the Schools Committee of the Club prior to becoming president in 1993. Before his move from Chicago to Washington, D.C., in 1994, Charles Zeitlin balanced his commitment to community service organizations such as Urban Gateways with his legal career at the Chicago firm of Aronberg Goldgehn Davis & Garmisa, where he served as managing partner and chief operating officer. Zeitlin's experience as an attorney specializing in entrepreneurship was later channeled into civic work as an officer of MSO Services, a Virginia-based consultancy to nonprofit organizations.

1994–1996

Desmond C. Wong, MBA '77

Desmond C. Wong is president and CEO of Sino Strategies Group, LLC, a consulting firm specializing in advising Western company boards and CEOs on doing business in China and India. In the early 1980s he was appointed to a U.S. Presidential (Grace) Commission to make efficiency and productivity improvement recommendations at the U.S. Treasury. While corporate director of finance at Sears, Roebuck and Co., he directed Sears's global long-term financing, acquisitions and divestitures, and interest rate risk management, and participated in the successful launch of the Discover credit card. Later, as managing director and CFO of a merchant banking firm, he specialized in bringing Western capital and technology to China. A Chicago resident since graduation, Wong is HBS MBA '77 class secretary and has chaired every MBA '77 class reunion since 1982. He is a former president and director of the HBS Club of Chicago and has served on the boards of both the HBS Alumni Association and the AHA. He currently serves on the board of the Indiana University Foundation, the Indiana Kelley School Dean's Council, Junior Achievement of Chicago, and Nu Skin Enterprises, Inc.

1996–1998

Irwin K. Carson, AB '66

Irwin K. Carson, MD (1944–1997), wrote and directed two Hasty Pudding shows while at Harvard. After receiving his medical degree from the University of Michigan, he became an orthopedic surgeon and started a practice in Chicago's northwest suburbs. In addition to serving as the Club's vice president and president, Irwin was an active participant on the Schools Committee and was program chair for many years. His love of music served the Club well as he orchestrated one or more memorable musical programs each year before his untimely death. He also served on the board of the Arthritis Foundation, the University of Michigan Alumni and Medical boards, the Northbrook Symphony Orchestra, and United Way of Highland Park.

1998–2000

Craig I. Coit, AB '73

Craig I. Coit graduated from Harvard College in 1973 with a degree in economics and earned an MBA from Yale in 1978. After serving for twenty years as a financial manager for Bank One and its predecessor companies, Coit joined Aon (ARSA) in 2001. Elected president of the Harvard Club of Chicago in 1998, Coit built on his past experiences as program chair to ensure a full program agenda that would attract participation from members with diverse interests and backgrounds. During his tenure the Club revived the very successful Dialogue program series and continued to strengthen its relationship with Foreman High School and its principal, Dr. Garvey. Coit currently serves as board president for the Friends of the Chicago River and on the board of the Bank Administration Institute.

2000–2002

Kenneth V. Hachikian, AB '71, MBA '73

Kenneth Hachikian, a Boston native, received a BA in economics and an MBA from Harvard Business School, graduating as a Baker Scholar. From 1973 to 1982 he served with the Boston Consulting Group, focusing on corporate strategy for Fortune 500 clients. For the next twenty years he worked as a CEO or COO for four operating businesses, including a successful start-up in health care services. He and his family moved from Massachusetts to the suburbs of Chicago in 1990, and in 2001 he switched to investment banking and became a partner with the Stonegate Group. Hachikian served on the board of the Harvard Club of Chicago for more than a decade, including two years as president, and on the local school board of Lake Forest for six years, including four as board president. Most recently he has served as chair of the Washington, D.C.-based Armenian National Committee of America, an advocacy group focused on the interests of Armenian Americans.

2002–2004

John A. Challenger, AB '77

John A. Challenger is chief executive officer of Challenger, Gray & Christmas, Inc. A recognized thought leader on workplace, labor, and economic issues, he is frequently sought out by foreign and domestic broadcast and print media. In 2002, at the height of the turmoil over corporate governance, the *Wall Street Journal* invited Challenger to address the issue in a bylined article. In 2003, Challenger gave testimony before the U.S. House Committee on Small Business on the issue of permanent job loss in a global economy. Challenger serves on the President's Circle steering committee of the Chicago Council on Global Affairs. He served on the Labor/Human Resource Committee of the Federal Reserve Bank of Chicago for a three-year term. Currently he is president and board member of the Japan America Society of Chicago. He is a member of the board of directors of the Union League Club and is also active in the Economic Club of Chicago, the Chicago Club, the Commonwealth Club of Chicago, and the Metropolitan Club. In addition to his two-year tenure as president of the Harvard Club of Chicago from 2002 to 2004, he served as regional director for the Western Great Lakes region of the Harvard Alumni Association from 2005 to 2007.

2004–2006

Robert Allen Hastings, AB '57, MBA '59

Robert Hastings has managed several chemical and health care entities and held a wide variety of functional senior management positions with Baxter, American Can and FMC in his business career. He co-founded and serves as Chairman and CFO of Policy and Management Institute, Inc. a consulting firm which advises corporate, educational and not-for-profit organizations. In addition, he has taught at the graduate level and been a secondary school head. After settling in Chicago following business school, he began a lifetime of involvement in Harvard alumni activities as an interviewer for the Harvard Club's Schools Committee and a Decade Group leader. In the 1960s he was elected to the board of directors of both the Chicago Harvard and Harvard Business School Clubs, and for the latter was subsequently elected program chair and then president in 1972. From late 1986 to 1989 he served as executive director of the worldwide Harvard Alumni Association. He was elected to consecutive terms as Harvard Club of Chicago president in 2004-2006, has several times chaired its Scholarship Committee, and initiated and leads the 150th Anniversary Committee. He received the Club's Outstanding Contribution Award in 2007, and continues as athletics coordinator in the Adopt-A-School program at Walter Payton College Prep, and to head the Community Service Committee's efforts to arrange summer and year long public service experiences in Chicago for Harvard students.

2006–2008

Margaret I. McCurry, LF '86/'87

Margaret McCurry is a principal in the architectural and design firm of Tigerman McCurry and a Fellow of the American Institute of Architects. She is the recipient of Honor Awards from the national AIA, Distinguished Building and Interior Architecture Awards from the Chicago chapter, and both National and Local Interior Design Project Awards from the American Society of Interior Designers. Her work has been published in architectural and interior magazines and exhibited at museums and galleries in the United States and abroad. A former member of the board of the Architecture and Design Society at the Art Institute of Chicago, she is currently on the board of the Textile Department at that institution. She received her Loeb Fellowship in advanced Environmental Studies from the Graduate School of Design and while president of the Alumni Council of the GSD implemented several Harvard Design School studios which, in conjunction with IIT architecture students, developed urban design and housing initiatives for Bronzeville, Chicago's historic African-American community abutting the IIT campus. In 2006 she completed a six-year term as an appointed director of the Harvard Alumni Association representing the Graduate School of Design.

Current Harvard Overseers

Arne Duncan, AB '87

Arne Duncan, AB '87, CEO of the Chicago Public Schools, graduated magna cum laude with a degree in sociology. Over the next four years he played basketball professionally in Australia and began working with children who were wards of the state. In 1992 he accepted an offer to direct the Ariel Education Initiative, a program that seeks to improve educational opportunities for youth on Chicago's South Side, and in 1998 he started working with the Chicago Public Schools as deputy chief of staff for former Schools CEO Paul Vallas. He was appointed to his present position by Mayor Richard M. Daley in 2001. His deep involvement in primary school education includes serving on the boards of the Ariel Education Initiative, the Golden Apple Foundation, Junior Achievement, Jobs for America's Graduates, the Renaissance Schools Fund, and the South Side YMCA. He also serves on the Dean's Advisory Board of the Kellogg School of Management, on the Board of Overseers for Harvard, on Harvard's Visiting Committee to the Graduate School of Education, and on the University of Chicago's Visiting Committee to the School of Social Service Administration. In recognition of his extraordinary contributions, the City Club of Chicago named him Citizen of the Year in 2006.

Penny S. Pritzker, AB '81

Penny S. Pritzker, AB '81, earned a degree in economics from Harvard, graduating magna cum laude, followed by an MBA and law degree from Stanford University, where she trained for and ran the Ironman triathlon. A founder of five businesses, she is equally concerned with philanthropy, education, and the welfare of children. Currently she develops senior living facilities under the Classic Hyatt Residence name and heads the Pritzker Realty Group. A former board chair of Chicago's Museum of Contemporary Art, she also serves on the Harvard Board of Overseers and is one of four trustees of the Pritzker Foundation, which runs the family's philanthropic efforts. Among her many civic engagements, she serves on the board of the Chicago Public Education Fund, a venture capital fund that seeks to provide a meaningful way for civic and business leaders to help improve educational achievement. She is noted for her commitment to quality public education and has been active with the Chicago Public Schools and the charter school movement.

Leah Zell Wanger, AB '71, AM '72, PhD '79

Leah Zell Wanger, founding partner of Wanger Asset Management, is former lead portfolio manager for Columbia Acorn International, a $4 billion international small-cap equity mutual fund. Currently she is president of LZW Group LLC, a private investment firm. She is on the Executive Committee of the Chicago Council on Global Affairs and serves as its treasurer. She is also serves on the Executive Committee of the German Marshall Fund Board and is an overseer of the International Rescue Committee and of Harvard University.

2006–2007 HAA President

Paul J. Finnegan, AB '75, MBA '82

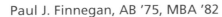

Paul J. Finnegan worked on the business side of international publishing between college and MBA years, serving as director of the Asia-Pacific portfolio for Seavex Ltd., Hong Kong. From 1982 to 1992 he was vice president of First Chicago Venture Capital, where he had oversight of the communications equity portfolio. In January 1993, the principals of First Chicago Venture Capital formed Madison Dearborn Partners, Inc. Finnegan was named co-president and managing director later that year. Currently he serves on the board of directors of iplan LLC and Rural Cellular Corporation. He is 2006–2007 president of the Harvard Alumni Association, a member of the board of the Dean's Advisors at Harvard Business School, and on the Leadership Council of the Harvard School of Public Health. He is the chair of Teach For America in Chicago and chair of the Community Works Advisory Committee of the Evanston Community Foundation. He is also past president and a former board member of Northlight Theatre.

Part IV

Appendices

Chronology

	WORLD • NATION		HARVARD	CHICAGO	HARVARD CLUB OF CHICAGO
1620	Plymouth Colony				
		1632	Founding of Harvard College		
		1640–1654	Henry Dunster 1st President of Harvard		
		1654–1672	Charles Chauncy 2nd President of Harvard		
		1672–1675	Leonard Hoar, '50, AM '53 3rd President of Harvard,		
		1675–1681	Urian Oakes '49, AM '52 4th President of Harvard		
		1682–1684	John Rogers, '49 5th President of Harvard		
		1685–1701	Increase Mather, '56 6th President of Harvard		
		1708–1724	John Leverett, '80, AM '83 7th President of Harvard		
		1725–1737	Benjamin Wadsworth, '90, AM '93 8th President of Harvard		
		1737–1769	Edward Holyoke, '05, AM '08 9th President of Harvard		
		1770–1773	Samuel Locke, '55, AM '58 10th President of Harvard		
		1774–1780	Samuel Langdon, '40, AM '43 11th President of Harvard		
1776	JULY 4 Declaration of Independence				
1797–1801	President of the U.S. John Adams, '55, AM'58				
		1781–1804	Joseph Willard, '65, AM'68 12th President of Harvard		
		1782	SEPTEMBER 19 Founding of Harvard Medical School		
1800	Travel time from New York to Chicago is 6 weeks.				

	WORLD • NATION	HARVARD	CHICAGO	HARVARD CLUB OF CHICAGO
1803	MAY 2 Louisiana Purchase			
	1806–1810	Samuel Webber '84, AM'87 13th President of Harvard		
	1810–1828	John Thornton Kirkland '89, AM 92 14th President of Harvard		
1812	JUNE 12 War of 1812 begins.			
1815	FEBRUARY 18 War of 1812 ends.			
	1816	Founding of Harvard Divinity School		
	1817	Founding of Harvard Law School, the first university law school in the U.S.		
	1818		DECEMBER 3 Illinois achieves statehood as the 21st state	
1825–1829	President of the U.S. John Quincy Adams, '87, AM'90			
	1829–1845	Josiah Quincy '90, AM'93 15th President of Harvard		
1830	Travel time from New York to Chicago is three weeks		Land in newly platted Chicago sells for $1.25 per acre.	
	1833		AUGUST 12 Founding of Chicago: Pop. 350	
	1840	Founding of Harvard Alumni Association (HAA)		
	1846–1849	Edward Everett '11, AM'14 16th President of Harvard		
	1849–1853	Jared Sparks '15, AM'18 17th President of Harvard		
	1850	Only 26 faculty members at Harvard.	Pop. 29,963	Frederick Pitkin Fisher, AB '48, arrives in Chicago.
	1852	Abbot Scholarship created; first scholarship at Harvard College.		

WORLD · NATION		HARVARD	CHICAGO	HARVARD CLUB OF CHICAGO
			1853	**FEBRUARY** Dr. Charles Gilman Smith, AB 1847, arrives in Chicago
	1853–1860	James Walker '14, AM'17 18th President of Harvard		
			1854	**FALL** Samuel Sewall Greeley, AB '44, arrives in Chicago.
	1855	Founding of the first Harvard club, The Harvard Club of Boston. Club was dissolved in 1857		
			1856	Dr. Edward Lorenzo Holmes, AB '49, MD '45, arrives in Chicago.
	1857		Chicago Public Schools have 11 schools with c. 70 teachers and principals and c. 9,000 students	**MAY** Charles A. Gregory, AB '55, arrives in Chicago
				JUNE 1st meeting of the future Harvard Club of Chicago, reputedly at Ambrose & Jackson's restaurant, 91 Clark Street, at a "noctes ambrosianae"
	1858	Founding of Harvard Club of Cincinnati.		
1860	Travel time from New York to Chicago is two days	Number of faculty members at Harvard 26; number of courses 48; number of students 529, 8% from "West"; number of scholarship funds 44. George Everett Adams becomes first male resident of Chicago to attend Harvard College	Pop. 109,260 **MAY 18** Republican National Convention (1st national political convention held in Chicago) nominates Abraham Lincoln, at Wigwam, SE corner of Lake and Market Streets.	**JUNE** George E. Adams '60, 1st "Chicagoan" to attend Harvard, returns to Chicago from Harvard.
	1860–1862	Cornelius Conway Felton 27, AM' 30 19th President of Harvard		
1861	**APRIL 12** Fort Sumter fired on; Civil War begins.			
	1862–1868	Thomas Hill '43, AM '30 20th President of Harvard		

	WORLD • NATION	HARVARD	CHICAGO	HARVARD CLUB OF CHICAGO
1865	APRIL 9 Lee surrenders to Grant at Appomattox; end of Civil War. APRIL 14 Lincoln Assassinated.	Founding of Harvard Club of New York City		
1867	5.8 million telegraph messages sent. Cost for New York to Chicago is $1.30.	Founding of Harvard School of Dental Medicine.		
1869–1909		Charles William Eliot '53, AM '56 21st President of Harvard		
1870		Richard T. Greener becomes first African American to graduate from Harvard College.	Pop. 298,977	
1871		Founding of Harvard Summer School	OCTOBER 9 Great Chicago Fire	
1872		Founding of Harvard Graduate School of Arts & Sciences		
1874	Development of refrigerator cars cuts cost of shipping beef east by 50%			JUNE 27 Meeting of The Harvard Association of Chicago at the Palmer House with 30 attendees.
1877–1881	President of the U.S. Ruthford B. Hayes, LLB'45			
1878		Scholarships awarded by Harvard total $25,000		
1879		Founding of Society for the Collegiate Education of Women (later Radcliffe College)		
1880			Pop. 503,185	
1881		Harvard plays the University of Michigan in football in Ann Arbor and wins		MARCH 21 Name changed to The Harvard Club of Chicago from The Harvard Association of Chicago
1882				JANUARY 27 President Eliot with Profs. Goodwin, Thayer and James attend a "Western" Harvard meeting

WORLD • NATION	HARVARD	CHICAGO	HARVARD CLUB OF CHICAGO
1883	Number of faculty members at Harvard 69; number of courses 160; number of students 969, 13% from "West"; number of scholarship funds 118.		
1885	Jeannette Swan Brown becomes first woman from Chicago (Maywood) to graduate from Radcliffe College.		
1887		FEBRUARY 15 Meeting of representatives from Harvard, Princeton, and the University of Michigan at the Grand Pacific Hotel to found the University Club of Chicago	
1889–1890			Former Club President Samuel Johnston, '55, donates funds for the Johnston Gate
1890	Pop. 1,099,850		
1892			George Everett Adams, '60 is elected 1st Harvard University Overseer from the "West."
1893		World's Columbian Exposition held in Chicago.	NOVEMBER 24 Club unanimously appropriates $300 for a graduate scholarship at Harvard; only 2nd scholarship offered by a Harvard club or association.
1894	Society for the Collegiate Education of Women renamed Radcliffe College		SEPTEMBER John Albrecht Walz of Northwestern University is 1st recipient of graduate scholarship; later becomes Prof. of German Language and Literature at Harvard.
1897	Founding of Associated Harvard Clubs (AHC)		
1898	APRIL 25 Spanish-American War begins. AUGUST 12 Spanish-American War ends.	Robert Todd Lincoln, '64 serves as 24th president of the HAA Alberta V. Scott becomes first African American to graduate from Radcliffe College.		

WORLD • NATION		HARVARD	CHICAGO	HARVARD CLUB OF CHICAGO
	1899			MAY 9 Incorporated as The Harvard Club of Chicago after private social club, The Harvard Club, relinquishes the name.
1900	63.2 million telegraph messages sent; cost for New York to Chicago is 50¢		Pop. 1,698,575	
1901	SEPTEMBER 14 McKinley assassinated; T. Roosevelt becomes President (4th Harvard graduate to become President)			FEBRUARY 21 44th Annual Dinner, with Major Henry Lee Higginson as guest.
1901–1909	President of the U.S. Theodore Roosevelt, '80			
	1903			MAY 3 Harvard Club funds $5,000+ scholarship in memory of Dunlap Smith, '84, managed by the University; $200 award for freshman.
	1905			MAY 10 Harvard Club reception for President Theodore Roosevelt, '80, at the Hamilton Club.
	1907			JUNE 50th Anniversary of Club
1908		Founding of current Harvard Club of Boston OCTOBER 1 Founding of Harvard Business School		
1909		Founding of Harvard Extension School	FEBRUARY 11 A 100-pound black bear cub was found at N. Clark and Diversey Streets (not from the zoo). APRIL 3 Opening of the present University Club of Chicago at 76 East Monroe Street.	FEBRUARY 11 52nd Annual Dinner, with retiring President Charles W. Eliot
1909–1933		Abbott Lawrence Lowell '77, LLB '80 22nd President of Harvard		

WORLD • NATION	HARVARD	CHICAGO	HARVARD CLUB OF CHICAGO
		1910 Pop. 2,185,283	Club charters a special train to attend the Associated Harvard Clubs meeting in Cleveland.
		1912?	Club is responsible for one of 14 state scholarships established by the AHC for freshman from states not or insufficiently represented at Harvard.
		1912	SEPTEMBER First two recipients of new Harvard Club of Chicago freshman scholarships enter college; Harold R. Anderson and John A. Swinson; $300 each.
1914 JULY World War I begins in Europe.			
1917 APRIL 6 U.S. enters World War I.			
1918 NOVEMBER 11 World War I ends with Armistice.			
1920 JANUARY 16 Beginning of Prohibition in the U.S.	Founding of Harvard Graduate School of Education	Pop. 2,701,705	
	1922 Founding of Harvard School of Public Health		
		1924 NOVEMBER 21 Official opening of the Harvard-Yale-Princeton Club of Chicago at 321 Plymouth Court.	
1929 OCTOBER 29 "Black Friday," the stock market crash of 1929.			
	1930 Last Harvard Directory to list all alumni, living and dead	Pop. 3,376,438	
1933–1945 President of the U.S. Franklin D. Roosevelt, '04			
	1933–1953 James Bryant Conant, '13, PhD '16 23rd President of Harvard		
1933 DECEMBER 5 End of Prohibition in the U.S.		A Century of Progress World's Fair held in Chicago	

WORLD • NATION		HARVARD	CHICAGO	HARVARD CLUB OF CHICAGO
	1934	Last Harvard Directory to list "Women Degree Holders"; 498 at the time.	Harvard-Yale-Princeton Club of Chicago closed in the spring; 138 members join the University Club of Chicago.	
	1936	Founding of Harvard Graduate School of Design Founding of Harvard Graduate School of Public Administration		
1937	JULY 7 World War II begins in the Pacific.			
1939	MARCH 15 World War II begins in Europe.			
	1940		Pop. 3,396,808	
1941	DECEMBER 7 Pearl Harbor attacked; World War II begins for America.			
1945	MAY 8 World War II ends in Europe (VE day). AUGUST 6 Atom bomb dropped on Hiroshima. AUGUST 10 World War II ends in the Pacific (VJ day). 236.2 million telegraph messages sent; cost for New York to Chicago is 70¢			
	1948	Harvard Directory shows 88,792 living alumni, 43% from the college, 57% from the graduate schools		
1950	JUNE 25 Korean War begins.			
1953	JULY 27 Korean War ends with Armistice.			
	1953–1971	Nathan Marsh Pusey, '28, AM'32, PhD'37 24th President of Harvard		

WORLD • NATION		HARVARD	CHICAGO	HARVARD CLUB OF CHICAGO
			1957	100th Anniversary of Club
	1960	Harvard Directory shows 140,846 living alumni, 33% from the college, 67% from the graduate schools	Pop. 3,350,404	
1961–1963	President of the U.S. John F. Kennedy '40			
	1965	Merger of Harvard Alumni Association and Associated Harvard Clubs into Associated Harvard Alumni (AHA)		
	1966	Graduate School of Public Administration becomes Kennedy School of Government		
			1967	MARCH 17 111th Annual Dinner; 1st Annual Award Dinner, in honor of Hermon Dunlap Smith, '21.
1970	69.7 million telegraph messages sent; cost for New York to Chicago is $2.25		Pop. 3,369,359	
	1971–1991	Derek Bok, JD '54 25th President of Harvard		
			1974	FEBRUARY 28 1st Annual Award Dinner, program to feature cover art by John A. Holabird, Jr. '42, MAR '48
	1980	Harvard Directory shows 218,255 living alumni, 34% from the College, 66% from the graduate schools	Pop. 3,005,072	Club Scholarship contribution is $15,000.
			1981	Club Scholarship contribution is $25,000.
	1982	Renaming of Associated Harvard Alumni to Harvard Alumni Association (HAA)		
	1990	Harvard Directory shows 249,248 living alumni, 33% from the College, 67% from the graduate schools	Pop. 2,783,726	Club Scholarship contribution is $25,000.

WORLD • NATION		HARVARD	CHICAGO	HARVARD CLUB OF CHICAGO
	1991–2001	Neil L. Rudenstine, PhD '64 26th President of Harvard		
	1999	Founding of Radcliffe Institute for Advanced Study		
	2000	Harvard Directory shows 292,344 living alumni, 31% from the College, 69% from the graduate schools	Pop. 2,896,016	HCC begins Adopt-A-School program with Walter Payton College Prep High School Club Scholarship contribution is $25,000.
2001–2008	President of the U.S. George W. Bush MBA '75			
	2001–2006	Lawrence H. Summers, PhD '82 27th President of Harvard		
	2005	Harvard Directory shows 321,869 living alumni, 29% from the College, 71% from the graduate schools JUNE 30 The university's endowment fund is valued at $25.9 billion SEPTEMBER 19 The university's endowment fund is valued at $29.2 billion		Club Scholarship contribution is $30,000; Club Graduate Scholarship contribution is $10,000
	2006–2007	Derek Bok, JD '54 Interim President of Harvard		Contributions to the Club's Scholarship Fund since 1947 exceed $469,000, with the market value in 2006 of over $2 million.
	2007–	Drew Faust 28th President of Harvard, 1st woman		
			2007	150th Anniversary Celebration

Award Recipients

Annual Award

The Harvard Club of Chicago Annual Award is designed to honor a person (or persons) who has made a distinguished contribution to the greater Chicago community in some field other than his or her primary occupation. The recipient(s) may be any person, regardless of sex, race, creed or education and need not have any Harvard University connection.

1967	Hermon Dunlap Smith, AB '21	1988	James J. Connor, MBA '60
1968	William Edward Hartman	1989	Irving B. Harris
	Mrs. John V. Spachner	1990	James W. Compton
1969	Charles Daggett Harvey	1991	Newton N. Minow, IOP '86
1970	Daniel Walker	1992	Bernice Weissbourd
	Mrs. Mary Ward Wolkonsky	1993	Lester Crown
1971	William McCormick Blair	1994	Eppie Lederer
1972	Louis M. Sudler	1995	Donald Perkins, MBA '51
1973	Harold F. Grumhaus	1996	Martin J. Koldyke
1974	Robert E. Brooker	1997	Robert W. Galvin
1975	William Wood-Prince		Robert A. Pritzker
	Mrs. William Wood-Prince	1998	Sondra A. Healy
1976	Mrs. Joseph Regenstein	1999	John H. Bryan
1977	Edward F. Blettner, AB '28, MBA '30		Richard J. Franke
1978	Marshall Field V, AB '63	2000	Shirley Welsh Ryan
1979	George E. Johnson, AB '63	2001	The Edward Byron Smith Family
1980	Marian DesPres	2002	Serafino Garella
1981	William G. Swartchild, Jr.	2003	Carol Lavin Bernick
1982	Marion M. lloyd	2004	John H. Johnson
1983	Daniel J. Terra	2005	David J. Vitale, AB '68
1984	Jerome H. Stone	2006	John D. Nichols, Jr. AB '57, MBA '59
1985	Arthur Rubloff	2007	Joanne Alter
1986	Stanley M. Freehing		Marion Stone
1987	Hammond E. Chaffetz, AB '28, LLB, '30		

Outstanding Contribution Award

2000	Alan H. "Mickey" Hammerman, AB '55
	Christopher G. Janus, SB '36
2001	Jacquelyn S. Sanders, AB '52
2002	Alexander "Sandy" Weissent, AB '73
2003	Richard C. Burnstine, AB '50, MD '54
2004	Bennett Berman, LLB '43
	Nancy Berman
2005	George Mann, AB '58
2006	Walter L. Keats, AB '67
	Winnie Lu
2007	Robert A. Hastings, AB '57, MBA '59

Historic Officers

1857	Founding Fathers			VP	Frederick Pitkin Fisher, AB1848

Frederick Pitkin Fisher, AB1848

Samuel Sewall Greeley, AB1844

Charles Augustus Gregory, AB1855

Edward Lorenzo Holmes, MD, AB1849, MD1854

Charles Gilman Smith, MD, AB1847

Year	Pos	Name	Year	Pos	Name
				VP	George Alanson Follansbee, LLB1867
				VP	William M. R. French, AB1864
				S-T	Gardner Goodrich Willard, AB1869
				EC	James Buchanan Galloway, AB1870
				EC	Samuel Sewall Greeley, AB1844
				EC	Charles Norman Fay, AB1869
1875	P	Charles Gilman Smith, MD, AB1847	1882	P	Walter Cranston Larned, AB1871
	VP	Robert Todd Lincoln, AB1864		VP	Dr. Edward Lorenzo Holmes, AB1849
	S-T	Gustavus Goward, AB1869		VP	Edward Downer Hosmer, AB1865, AM1871
1876	P	Charles Gilman Smith, MD, AB1847		VP	John L. Thomson, AB1858
	VP	Charles Hastings Allen, AB1831		S	Henry Sherman Boutell, AB1876, AM1877
	VP	Obadiah Jackson, AB1861		T	Francis Almy, AB1879, AM1880
	VP	Robert Todd Lincoln, AB1864		EC	Charles Newton Fessenden, AB1872
	S-T	Gustavus Goward, AB1869		EC	Hiram H. Rose, AB1879
	EC	Francis Porter Fisher, AB1848		EC	Moses Jones Wentworth, AB1868, AM1872
	EC	William Eliot Furness, AB1860, AM1863, LLB1863	1883	P	Gardner Goodrich Willard, AB1869
	EC	James Buchanan Galloway, AB1870		VP	Edwin H. Abbott, AB1855
1877	P	Charles Gilman Smith, MD, AB1847		VP	Dr. Henry Hooper, AB1865
	VP	Charles Hastings Allen, AB1831		VP	Moses Jones Wentworth, AB1868, AM1872
	VP	Obadiah Jackson, AB1861		S	Henry Sherman Boutell, AB1876, AM1877
	VP	Robert Todd Lincoln, AB1864		T	William H. Hubbard, AB1879
	S-T	Gustavus Goward, AB1869		EC	Holdridge Ozro Collins, LLB1867
	EC	Francis Porter Fisher, AB1848		EC	Joseph Shippen, AB1860, AM1867
	EC	William Eliot Furness, AB1860, AM1863, LLB1863		EC	Monroe L. Willard
	EC	James Buchanan Galloway, AB1870	1884	P	Gardner Goodrich Willard, AB1869
1878	P	Samuel Johnston, AB1855		VP	Charles Norman Fay, AB1869
	VP	Walter Cranston Larned, AB1871		VP	William Eliot Furness, AB1860, AM1863, LLB1863
	VP	James I. Tucker, AB1867		VP	Philon C. Whidden
	VP	Frederick H. Winston, AB1853		S-T	Henry Sherman Boutell, AB1876, AM1877
	S-T	Horace Gray Lunt, AB1870		EC	Heyliger Adams de Windt, AB1881
	EC	George Bass, AB1871		EC	James Buchanan Galloway, AB1870
	EC	Col. Henry Weld Farrar, AB1861		EC	Henry Baldwin Stone, AB1873
	EC	Joseph Mosely Moriarty, AB1863, AM1867	1885	P	Henry Sherman Boutell, AB1876, AM1877
1879	P	Hon. George Everett Adams, AB1860, LLB1865		VP	Edwin H. Abbott, AB1855
	VP	Col. Henry Weld Farrar, AB1861		VP	James Buchanan Galloway, AB1870
	S-T	George Bass, AB1871		VP	Moses Jones Wentworth, AB1868, AM1872
	EC	James Buchanan Galloway, AB1870		S-T	Edgar Madden, AB1879
	EC	Dr. Henry Hooper, AB1865, AM1869, MD1871		EC	Heyliger Adams de Windt, AB1881
	EC	Joseph Mosely Moriarty, AB1863, AM1867		EC	Hiram H. Rose, AB1879
1880	P	Col. Henry Weld Farrar, AB1861		EC	Gardner Goodrich Willard, AB1869
	VP	George F. Harding, AB1850	1886	P	Henry Sherman Boutell, AB1876, AM1877
	S-T	Gardner Goodrich Willard, AB1869		VP	Heyliger Adams de Windt, AB1881
	EC	Hon. George Everett Adams, AB1860, LLB1865		VP	Dr. Edward Lorenzo Holmes, AB1849, MD1854
	EC	Cecil Barnes		VP	Joseph Shippen, AB1860, AM1867
	EC	Henry A. Gardner		S-T	Edgar Madden, AB1879
1881	P	Walter Cranston Larned, AB1871		EC	James Buchanan Galloway, AB1870

	EC	Hiram H. Rose, AB1879
	EC	Moses Jones Wentworth, AB1868, AM1872
1887	P	Charles Gilman Smith, MD, AB1847
	VP	Charles Norman Fay, AB1869
	VP	George Alanson Follansbee, LLB1867
	VP	Charles Evans Pope, AB1869, AM1872
	S-T*	Edgar Madden, AB1879
	S-T	Heyliger Adams de Windt, AB1881
	EC	Heyliger Adams de Windt, AB1881
	EC	William Eliot Furness, AB1860, AM1863, LLB1863
	EC	Henry Mascarene Hubbard, AB1882
1888	P	William Eliot Furness, AB1860, AM1863, LLB1863
	VP	James Buchanan Galloway, AB1870
	VP	Rev. Louis Shreve Osborne, AB1873
	VP	Hiram H. Rose, AB1879
	S-T	Heyliger Adams de Windt, AB1881
	EC	Henry Alansin Gardner, LLB1870
	EC	Dunlap Smith, AB1884
	EC	Gardner Goodrich Willard, AB1869
1889	P	William Eliot Furness, AB1860, AM1863, LLB1863
	VP	Dr. Edward Lorenzo Holmes, AB1849
	VP	Rev. Louis Shreve Osborne, AB1873
	VP	Henry Baldwin Stone, AB1873
	S-T	Heyliger Adams de Windt, AB1881
	EC	Henry Mascarene Hubbard, AB1882
	EC	William Murray LeMoyne, C1878
	EC	Charles Gilman Smith, MD, AB1847
1890	P	Moses Jones Wentworth, AB1868, AM1872
	VP	Charles Edwin Rand, C1883
	VP	Joseph Lyman Silsbee, AB1869
	VP	Russell Whitman, AB1882
	S-T	Heyliger Adams de Windt, AB1881
	EC	Henry Cormerais French, AB1882
	EC	Mahlon Hutchinson
	EC	Dunlap Smith, AB1884
1891	P	Moses Jones Wentworth, AB1868, AM1872
	VP	Henry Walker Bishop, AB1853
	VP	M. W. Fuller, AB1854
	VP	Robert Todd Lincoln, AB1864
	S-T	Heyliger Adams de Windt, AB1881
1892	P	James Buchanan Galloway, AB1870
	VP	Henry Walker Bishop, AB1853
	VP	Samuel Adams Lynde, AB1877
	VP	Charles Inches Sturgis, AB1882
	S-T	Heyliger Adams de Windt, AB1881
	C	Lockwood Honore, AB1888
1893	P	Heyliger Adams de Windt, AB1881

	VP	T. B. Bryan, AB1848
	VP	Henry Ives Cobb, AB1880
	VP	Charles Herbert Williams, AB1871, MD181874, AM1875
	S-T	Hon. George A. Carpenter, AB1888
1894	P	J. C. Bartlett, AB1869
1894	P	Henry Baldwin Stone, AB1873
	VP	J. C. Bartlett, AB1869
	VP	Dr. Henry Hooper, AB1865
	VP	Robert Todd Lincoln, AB1864
	S-T	William Cowper Boyden, AB1886, LLB1889
1895	P	Robert Todd Lincoln, AB1864
	VP	William W. Carr, AB1879
	VP	George E. Foss, AB1885
	VP	Charles Inches Sturgis, AB1882
	S-T	William Cowper Boyden, AB1886, LLB1889
1896	P	Robert Todd Lincoln, AB1864
	VP	Henry Ives Cobb, AB1880
	VP	Russell Whitman, AB1882
	VP	John Henry Wigmore, AB1883, LLB1887, AM1887, LLD1909
	S-T	William Cowper Boyden, AB1886, LLB1889
	EC	Charles H. Baldwin, AB1888
	EC	Kellogg Fairbank, AB1890, LLB1893
	EC	Russell Tyson, AB1890
1897	P	Samuel Sewall Greeley, AB1844
	VP	William Cowper Boyden, AB1886, LLB1889
	VP	Rev. William Wallace Fenn, AB1884, STB1887, AM1887, STD1905
	VP	Dr. Henry Hooper, AB1865
	S-T	Frederick W. Burlingham, AB1891
1898	P	Dunlap Smith, AB1884
	VP	Hon. George Everett Adams, AB1860, LLB1865
	VP	Dr. Clifford Mitchell, AB1875
	VP	Gardner Goodrich Willard, AB1869
	S-T	Frederick W. Burlingham, AB1891
1899	P	William Cowper Boyden, AB1886, LLB1889
	VP	Frederic Adrian Delano, AB1885
	VP	William Gardner Hale, AB1870
	VP	William Murray LeMoyne, C1878
	S-T	Frederick W. Burlingham, AB1891
1900	P	Charles Inches Sturgis, AB1882
	VP	Frederick W. Burlingham, AB1891
	VP	Merritt Starr, AB1881, LLB1881
	VP	Russell Whitman, AB1882
	S-T	Robert John Cary, AB1890
1901	P	Frank Hamlin, AB1884
	VP	William Burry, AB1874

	VP	Francis Barrett Daniels, AB1871
	VP	John H. Gray, AB1887
	S-T	Robert John Cary, AB1890
1902	P	Frederic Adrian Delano, AB1885
	VP	Charles Laban Capen, AB1869, AM1872
	VP	Robert John Cary, AB1890
	VP	John F. Holland, AB1885
	VP	John Henry Wigmore, AB1883, LLB1887, AM1887, LLD1909
1903	P	Benjamin Carpenter, AB1888
	1VP	Robert John Cary, AB1890
	2VP	George Higginson, Jr., AB1887
	3VP	Frederic Ives Carpenter, AB1885
	S-T	William Kitchen Otis, AB1898
	C	John Alden Carpenter, AB1897
	C	Edwin Warner Ryerson, AB1895
1904	P	George Higginson, Jr., AB1887
	VP	F. S. Churchill, AB1886
	VP	Louis May Greeley, AB1880
	VP	Hon. Julian William Mack, LLB1887
	S-T	William Kitchen Otis, AB1898
1905	P	Kellogg Fairbank, AB1890, LLB1893
	VP	George E. Foss, AB1885
	VP	John H. Gray, AB1887
	VP	Lockwood Honore, AB1888
	S-T	Ayres Boal, AB1900
	C	Sidney E. Farwell, AB1893
1906	P	Robert John Cary, AB1890
	VP	Hon. Julian William Mack, LLB1887
	VP	Murray Nelson, Jr., AB1891
	VP	Merritt Starr, AB1881, LLB1881
	S-T	Ayres Boal, AB1900
1907	P	Merritt Starr, AB1881, LLB1881
	VP	Blewett Lee, AB1888
	VP	Leverett Thompson, AB1892
	VP	Russell Whitman, AB1882
	S-T	F. W. Blatchford, AB1899
1908	P	Hon. George A. Carpenter, AB1888
	VP	Henry J. Cox, AB1884
	VP	Morton Denison Hull, AB1889
	VP	Russell Tyson, AB1890
	S-T	Charles H. Schweppe, AB1902
1909	P	Hon. Julian William Mack, LLB1887
	VP	Frederick W. Burlingham, AB1891
	VP	Rev. Herman Page, AB1888
	VP	Redmond D. Stephens, AB1896
	S-T	Charles H. Schweppe, AB1902

1910	P	Mitchell D. Follansbee, AB1892
	VP	Morrill Dunn, AB1893
	VP	William Prescott Hunt, Jr., C1881
	VP	Redmond D. Stephens, AB1896
	S-T	Hugh Blythe, AB1901
1911	P	Thomas Taylor, Jr., LLB1885
	VP	Morrill Dunn, AB1893
	VP	William Prescott Hunt, Jr., C1881
	VP	Redmond D. Stephens, AB1896
	S-T	Louis C. Brosseau, AB1907
1912	P	Frederick W. Burlingham, AB1891
	VP	Louis C. Brosseau, AB1907
	VP	E. T. Gundlach, AB1898
	VP	George H. Ingalls, AB1893
	VP	W. George Lee, AB1901
1913	P	Rev. Herman Page, AB1888
	VP	John Alden Carpenter, AB1897
	VP	Avery Coonley, AB1894
	VP	Morton Denison Hull, AB1889
	S-T	George S. Jackson, AB1905
1914	P	Redmond D. Stephens, AB1896
	VP	George A. Dorsey, AB1893
	VP	H. Ernest Peabody, AB1887
	VP	Leverett Thompson, AB1892
	S-T	Louis C. Brosseau, AB1907
	S-T	Theodore Sheldon, AB1905 (Replaced)
	C	Louis C. Seaverns, AB1910
1915	P	John Henry Wigmore, AB1883, LLB1887, AM1887, LLD1909
	VP	Louis C. Brosseau, AB1907
	VP	Walter R. Kirk, AB1901
	VP	Russell Tyson, AB1890
	S-T	Sanger B. Steel, AB1911
1916	P	Morton Denison Hull, AB1889
	VP	Samuel Adams, AB1892
	VP	Arthur Dyrenforth, AB1896
	VP	Theodore Sheldon, AB1905
	S-T	Sanger B. Steel, AB1911
1917	P	George H. Ingalls, AB1893
	VP	Rudolph B. Flersheim, AB1898
	VP	Robert M. Lovett, AB1892
	VP	Charles H. Schweppe, AB1902
	S-T	Joseph Husband, AB1908
	C	Robert B. Whiting, AB1908
1918	P	Arthur Dyrenforth, AB1896
	VP	Laird Bell, AB1904
	VP	L. L. Falk, AB1909

	VP	Joseph Husband, AB1908		S	Arthur Dixon, III, AB1916
	S-T	F. Goddard Cheney, AB1906		T	F. D. Utley, AB1908
1919	P	Kay Wood, AB1892	1927	P	Joseph Loring Valentine, AB1898
	VP	Louis C. Brosseau, AB1907		VP	Nettleton Neff, Jr., AB1892
	VP	Joseph Husband, AB1908		VP	Hathaway Watson, AB1910
	VP	Bertrand Walker, AB1990		VP	Barrett Wendell, AB1902
	S-T	F. Goddard Cheney, AB1906		S	William Zimmerman, AB1910
1920	P	Samuel Adams, AB1892		T	Lanning Macfarland, AB1919
	VP	Lawrence Howe, AB1907	1928	P	Albert Arnold Sprague, II, AB1898
	VP	William Prescott Hunt, Jr., C1881		VP	William Cowper Boyden, Jr., AB1916
	VP	Albert Arnold Sprague, II, AB1898		VP	Lawrence Howe, AB1907
	S	F. Goddard Cheney, AB1906		VP	Lawrence Dunlap Smith, AB1912
	T	F. A. Bonner, AB1907		S	William Zimmerman, AB1910
1921	P	Laird Bell, AB1904		T	Lanning Macfarland, AB1919
	VP	J. O. Carson, AB1902	1929	P	Charles B. Pike, AB1893
	VP	Lawrence Howe, AB1907		VP	Edward E. Brown, AB1905
	VP	Joseph L. Valentine, AB1898		VP	Rev. Charles Whitney Gilkey, AB1903, AM1904
	S	S. P. Griffitts, AB1915		VP	Arnold Horween, AB1921
	T	F. A. Bonner, AB1907		S	William Zimmerman, AB1910
1922	P	Ayres Boal, AB1900		T	Lanning Macfarland, AB1919
	VP	William O. Batchelder, AB1905	1930	P	Lawrence Howe, AB1907
	VP	Arthur Dixon, III, AB1916		VP	Walter T. Fisher, AB1913
	VP	Perry Dunlap Smith, AB1911		VP	C. R. Larrabee, AB1919
	S	S. P. Griffitts, AB1915		VP	Perry Dunlap Smith, AB1911
	T	F. A. Bonner, AB1907		S	K. B. Hawkins, AB1908
1923	P	Russell Tyson, AB1890		T	Leonard C. Larrabee, AB1924
	VP	William O. Batchelder, AB1905	1931	P	Perry Dunlap Smith, AB1911
	VP	L. D. Smith, AB1912		VP	Walter T. Fisher, AB1913
	VP	F. H. Storms, AB1914		VP	Clay Judson, AB1914
	S	Donald F. McClure, AB1920		VP	William H. King, Jr., AB1908
	T	George R. Jones, AB1905		S	William Burry, Jr., AB1918
1924	P	William O. Batchelder, AB1905		T	Leonard C. Larrabee, AB1924
	VP	F. Goddard Cheney, AB1906	1932	P	Barrett Wendell, AB1902
	VP	William C. Hubbard, AB1919		VP	Walter T. Fisher, AB1913
	VP	E. L. Millard, AB1898		VP	Dwight H. Ingram, AB1916
	S	Donald F. McClure, AB1920		VP	William H. King, Jr., AB1908
	T	George R. Jones, AB1905		S	William Burry, Jr., AB1918
1925	P	E. L. Millard, AB1898		T	William J. Louderback, AB1920
	VP	F. W. Copeland, AB1913	1933	P	Howard F. Gillette, AB1896
	VP	George R. Jones, AB1905		VP	William Burry, Jr., AB1918
	VP	W. J. Louderback, AB1920		VP	Clay Judson, AB1914
	S	Arthur Dixon, III, AB1916		VP	William H. King, Jr., AB1908
	T	F. D. Utley, AB1908		S	Dwight H. Ingram, AB1916
1926	P	John Stocker Miller, Jr., AB1911		T	William J. Louderback, AB1920
	VP	F. W. Copeland, AB1913		T	William A. Magie, II, AB1928
	VP	Lanning Macfarland, AB1919	1934	P	Arthur G. Cable, AB1909
	VP	Joseph L. Valentine, AB1898		VP	J. P. Brown, AB1914

	VP	Clay Judson, AB1914
	VP	Clarence Belden Randall, AB1912, LLB1915, LLD1954
	S	Dwight H. Ingram, AB1916
	T	William A. Magie, II, AB1928
1935	P	G. Cook Kimball, AB1900
	VP	Carl E. Ingram, AB1906
	VP	Alexander E. Kirk, AB1920
	VP	Clarence Belden Randall, AB1912, LLB1915, LLD1954
	S	John W. Valentine, AB1929
	T	William A. Magie, II, AB1928
1936	P	Clarence Belden Randall, AB1912, LLB1915, LLD1954
	VP	Harold Vincent Amberg, AB1908, LLB1910
	VP	Carl E. Ingram, AB1906
	VP	Clay Judson, AB1914
	S	John W. Valentine, AB1929
	T	Alexander E. Kirk, AB1920
1937	P	Clay Judson, AB1914
	VP	Harold Vincent Amberg, AB1908, LLB1910
	VP	Nathan S. Davis, III, AB1910
	VP	Samuel W. White, AB1908
	S	Conway H. Olmsted, AB1929
	T	Alexander E. Kirk, AB1920
1938	P	Harold Vincent Amberg, AB1908, LLB1910
	VP	Nathan S. Davis, III, AB1910
	VP	A. M. Kinney, AB1920
	VP	Samuel W. White, AB1908
	S-T	Philip J. Dalton, Jr., AB1931
	AS-T	John Jay Borland, II, AB1933
1939	P	William H. King, Jr., AB1908
	VP	A. M. Kinney, AB1920
	VP	Hermon Dunlap Smith, AB1921
	VP	Evans Spalding, AB1915
	S-T	Philip J. Dalton, Jr., AB1931
	AS-T	John Jay Borland, II, AB1933
1940	P	Hermon Dunlap Smith, AB1921
	VP	William R. Odell, Jr., AB1919
	VP	John I. Shaw, AB1928
	VP	Evans Spalding, AB1915
	S-T	John Jay Borland, II, AB1933
	AS-T	Howard F. Gillette, Jr., AB1935
1941	P	Evans Spalding, AB1915
	VP	John Jay Borland, II, AB1933
	VP	William R. Odell, Jr., AB1919
	VP	John I. Shaw, AB1928
	S-T	Howard F. Gillette, Jr., AB1935
	AS-T	Michael Cudahy, AB1936
1942	P	William R. Odell, Jr., AB1919

	VP	William Cowper Boyden, Jr., AB1916
	VP	Howard F. Gillette, Jr., AB1935
	VP	Snelling S. Robinson, AB1920
	S-T	Michael Cudahy, AB1936
	AS-T	William C. Egan, AB1936
1943	P	William Cowper Boyden, Jr., AB1916
	VP	Thomas H. Beacom, Jr., LLB1923
	VP	Lyell H. Ritchie, AB1920
	VP	Snelling S. Robinson, AB1920
	S-T	William C. Egan, AB1936
	AS-T	R. Gregory Durham, AB1935
1944	P	Nathan S. Davis, III, AB1910
	VP	Meyer Kestnbaum, AB1918, MBA1921
	VP	Lyell H. Ritchie, AB1920
	VP	Snelling S. Robinson, AB1920
	S-T	R. Gregory Durham, AB1935
	AS-T	G. Lyle Fischer, AB1920
1945	P	Snelling S. Robinson, AB1920
	VP	G. Lyle Fischer, AB1920
	VP	Meyer Kestnbaum, AB1918, MBA1921
	VP	Willard O. Thompson, MD, AB1923
	S-T	R. Gregory Durham, AB1935
	AS-T	Kellogg Fairbank, Jr., AB1930
1946	P	Meyer Kestnbaum, AB1918, MBA1921
	VP	E. Francis Bowditch, AB1935
	VP	Arthur Dixon, III, AB1916
	VP	Willard O. Thompson, MD, AB1923
	S-T	Kellogg Fairbank, Jr., AB1930
	AS-T	Snelling S. Robinson, AB1920
1947	P	Arthur Dixon, III, AB1916
	VP	E. Francis Bowditch, AB1935
	VP	Michael Cudahy, AB1936
	VP	Philip W. Moore, Jr., AB1931
	S-T	Kellogg Fairbank, Jr., AB1930
	AS-T	Hobart P. Young, Jr., AB1937
1948	P	Hulburd Johnston, AB1929
	VP	E. Francis Bowditch, AB1935
	VP	Lanning Macfarland, AB1919
	VP	Philip W. Moore, Jr., AB1931
	S-T	Kellogg Fairbank, Jr., AB1930
	AS-T	Ralph Hornblower, Jr., AB1941
1949	P	Kellogg Fairbank, Jr., AB1930
	VP	Howard F. Gillette, Jr., AB1935
	VP	Gerald Vanderbilt Hollins, AB1936
	VP	Lanning Macfarland, AB1919
	S-T	James Phinney Baxter, IV, AB1941
	AS-T	Augustus Thorndike, Jr., AB1941

1950	P	Howard F. Gillette, Jr., AB1936
	VP	William F. Borland, AB1941
	VP	Gerald Vanderbilt Hollins, AB1936
	VP	Herbert Winslow Smith, AB1912
	S-T	James Phinney Baxter, IV, AB1941
	AS-T	Richard Warren Howe, AB1945
1951	P	Herbert Winslow Smith, AB1912
	VP	William F. Borland, AB1941
	VP	Boyd Nixon Everett, SB1926, MBA1929
	VP	Samuel Sewall Greeley, AB1936, LLB1939
	S-T	James Phinney Baxter, IV, AB1941
	AS	Austin Lowell Wyman, Jr., AB1948
	AT	Arthur F. Stake, AB1948
1952	P	Boyd Nixon Everett, SB1926, MBA1929
	VP	William F. Borland, AB1941
	VP	Samuel Sewall Greeley, AB1936, LLB1939
	S-T	James Phinney Baxter, IV, AB1941
	AS-T	Austin Lowell Wyman, Jr., AB1948
1953	P	Samuel Sewall Greeley, AB1936, LLB1939
	VP	James Phinney Baxter, IV, AB1941
	VP	George N. Burns, AB1929
	S	Austin Lowell Wyman, Jr., AB1948
	T	F(rancis) Lee Higginson Wendell, AB1938
	AS-T	Arthur F. Stake, AB1948
1954	P	Samuel Sewall Greeley, AB1936, LLB1939
	VP	James Phinney Baxter, IV, AB1941
	VP	J. Gordon Gilkey, Jr., AB1939
	S	Austin Lowell Wyman, Jr., AB1948
	T	Arthur F. Stake, AB1948
	AS-T	John D. Ingram, AB1950
1955	P	James Phinney Baxter, IV, AB1941
	VP	J. Gordon Gilkey, Jr., AB1939
	VP	Robert Freeman Spindell, AB1927, LLB1930
	S	Austin Lowell Wyman, Jr., AB1948
	T	Thomas William James, AB1947
	AS-T	John D. Ingram, AB1950
1956	P	Robert Freeman Spindell, AB1927, LLB1930
	VP	John Jay Borland, II, AB1933
	VP	J. Gordon Gilkey, Jr., AB1939
	S	Thomas William James, AB1947
	T	John D. Ingram, AB1950
	AS-T	Philip Whitford Kirkland Sweet, Jr., AB1950
1957	P	John J. Borland, AB1933
	VP	Frederick William Burnham, AB1930, MBA1932
	VP	F(rancis) Lee Higginson Wendell, AB1938
	S	Thomas William James, AB1947
	T	John D. Ingram, AB1950

1958	P	F(rancis) Lee Higginson Wendell, AB1938
	VP	Frederick William Burnham, AB1930, MBA1932
	VP	Rudy Lamont Ruggles, C1931
	S	John D. Ingram, AB1950
	T	Philip Whitford Kirkland Sweet, Jr., AB1950
1959	P	Frederick William Burnham, AB1930, MBA1932
	VP	Charles A. Meyer, AB1939
	VP	Rudy Lamont Ruggles, C1931
	S	John D. Ingram, AB1950
	T	Philip Whitford Kirkland Sweet, Jr., AB1950
1960	P	Rudy Lamont Ruggles, C1931
	VP	John Douglas Hastings, LLM1933
	VP	Robert B. Wilcox, AB1944
	S	Philip Whitford Kirkland Sweet, Jr., AB1950
	T	William C. B. Magoun, AB1950
1961	P	John Douglas Hastings, LLM1933
	VP	Wyndham Hasler, AB1934
	VP	J. Dean Vail, Jr., AB1932
	S	Philip Whitford Kirkland Sweet, Jr., AB1950
	T	William C. B. Magoun, AB1950
1962	P	John Colville Donnelly, AB1926, MBA1928
	VP	Denison Bingham Hull, AB1919, MAR1923
	VP	Philip Whitford Kirkland Sweet, Jr., AB1950
	S	William Putney Hall, AB1945, MBA1948
	T	William Morris Weber, AB1954, MBA1958
1963	P	Philip Whitford Kirkland Sweet, Jr., AB1950
	VP	Denison Bingham Hull, AB1919, MAR1923
	VP	Edwin Allen Locke, Jr., AB1932
	S	William Putney Hall, AB1945, MBA1948
	T	William Morris Weber, AB1954, MBA1958
1964	P	Denison Bingham Hull, AB1919, MAR1923
	VP	William Barnes, III, AB1943
	VP	William S. North, AB1934
	S	Thomas E. Ingram, AB1956
	T	James L. Peterson, MBA1958
1965	P	Frank Lyman Bixby, AB1950
	VP	Thomas F. Geraghty, Jr., AB1938
	VP	Austin Lowell Wyman, Jr., AB1948
	S	Thomas E. Ingram, AB1956
	T	David B. Macfarland, AB1953
1966	P	Austin Lowell Wyman, Jr., AB1948
	VP	William McKee Dunn, AB1930
	VP	Thomas F. Geraghty, Jr., AB1938
	S	John A. Griner, III, AB1954, MBA1959
	T	David B. Macfarland, AB1953
1967	P	Christopher George Janus, AB1936
	VP	William McKee Dunn, AB1930

	VP	John A. Griner, III, AB1954, MBA1959
	S	Jon R. Lind, AB1957, LLB1960
	T	David B. Macfarland, AB1953
1968	P	Christopher George Janus, AB1936
	VP	William McKee Dunn, AB1930
	VP	John A. Griner, III, AB, 1954, MBA1959
	S	Jon R. Lind, AB1957, LLB1960
	T	John Williams Stimpson, AB1958
	AS-T	Theodore T. Scudder, III, AB1961
1969	P	William McKee Dunn, AB1930
	VP	John A. Griner, III, AB1954, MBA1959
	VP	Jon R. Lind, AB1957, LLB1960
	S	Charles Ephraim Zeitlin, AB1953, LLB1956
	T	John Williams Stimpson, AB1958
	AS	L. Russell Cartwright, AB1962
	AT	Theodore T. Scudder, III, AB1961
1970	P	Joseph May Greeley, AB1925, MBA1927
	VP	John A. Griner, III, AB1954, MBA1959
	VP	John Williams Stimpson, AB1958
	S	Charles Ephraim Zeitlin, AB1953, LLB1956
	T	Theodore T. Scudder, III, AB1961
	AS	L. Russell Cartwright, AB1962
	AT	Amos J. Coffman, Jr., AB1962
1971	P	John Williams Stimpson, AB1958
	VP	Hammond E. Chaffetz, AB1928, LLB1930
	VP	Eugene Perry Heytow, AB1955
	VP	Edward Hutchins Hickey, AB1933, LLB1936
	S	C. Robert Foltz, AB1960, LLB1963
	T	Theodore T. Scudder, III, AB1961
	AS-T	Amos J. Coffman, Jr., AB1962
1972	P	Eugene Perry Heytow, AB1955
	VP	Alan Howard Hammerman, AB1955
	VP	Edward Hutchins Hickey, AB1933, LLB1936
	VP	Theodore Scudder, III, AB1961
	S	Amos J. Coffman, Jr., AB1962
	T	Stefan S. Anderson, AB1956
1973	P	Eugene Perry Heytow, AB1955
	EVP	Edward Hutchins Hickey, AB1933, LLB1936
	VP	Alan Howard Hammerman, AB1955
	VP	Henry Gerard Van der Eb, SB1942
	S	John A. Bross, Jr., AB1961, LLB1965
	T	John A. Griner, III, AB1954, MBA1959
	AS-T	Norbert S. Jacker, AB1947, LLB1952
1974	P	Edward Hutchins Hickey, AB1933, LLB1936
	VP	Alan Howard Hammerman, AB1955
	VP	John B. Judkins, Jr., AB1947
	VP	Henry Gerard Van der Eb, SB1942

	S	William Putney Hall, AB1945, MBA1948
	T	John A. Griner, III, AB1954, MBA1959
	AS-T	Lincoln V. Janus, AB1970
1975	P	Edward Hutchins Hickey, AB1933, LLB1936
	VP	William Putney Hall, AB1945, MBA1948
	VP	Alan Howard Hammerman, AB1955
	VP	John B. Judkins, Jr., AB1947
	S	Stephen C. Neal, AB1970
	T	Benjamin S. Phinney, AB1970
	AS-T	Lincoln V. Janus, AB1970
1976	P	Lawrence Howe, Jr., AB1942
	S	Bennett I. Berman, LLB1943
	T	Benjamin S. Phinney, AB1970
1977	P	Vern Kenneth Miller, SB1942
	VP	William Putney Hall, AB1945, MBA1948
	VP	Norbert S. Jacker, AB1947, LLB1952
	VP	Margaret Whiting Redding, AB1955
	S	Benjamin S. Phinney, AB1970
	AS	Terence K. Brennan, AB1974
	T	Nicholas Leone, AB1974
1978	P	Vern Kenneth Miller, SB1942
	VP	William Putney Hall, AB1945, MBA1948
	VP	Alan Howard Hammerman, AB1955
	VP	Norbert S. Jacker, AB1947, LLB1952
	VP	Mari DeCosta Terman, AB1957
	S	Benjamin S. Phinney, AB1970
	AS	Edward N. Bothfeld, AB1977
	T	Alexander B. Weissent, AB1973
1979	P	William Putney Hall, AB1945, MBA1948
	VP	Alan Howard Hammerman, AB1955
	VP	Norbert S. Jacker, AB1947, LLB1952
	VP	Mari DeCosta Terman, AB1957
	VP	Robert B. Wilcox, AB1944
	S	Benjamin S. Phinney, AB1970
	AS	Edward N. Bothfeld, AB1977
	T	Alexander B. Weissent, AB1973
	AT	Philip J. Mistretta, AB1977
1980	P	William Putney Hall, AB1945, MBA1948
	VP	Helen McCaig Chandra, AB1951
	VP	Alan Howard Hammerman, AB1955
	VP	Benjamin S. Phinney, AB1970
	VP	Robert B. Wilcox, AB1944
	S	Charles C. Hewitt, III, AB1971
	AS	John Boynton, AB1976
	T	Alexander B. Weissent, AB1973
	AT	Philip J. Mistretta, AB1977
1981	P	Alan Howard Hammerman, AB1955

	AS	Edward Dawson, Jr., AB1981		T	Desmond C. Wong, MBA1977
	T	Craig I. Coit, AB1973	1994	P	Charles Ephraim Zeitlin, AB1953, LLB1956
	AT	David J. Shryock, AB1980		VP	Adela M. Cepeda, AB1980
1990	P	Quentin George Heisler, Jr., AB1965, JD1968		VP	Craig I. Coit, AB1973
	VP	Dr. Richard Carl Burnstine, AB1950, MD1954		VP	Nancy Felton-Elkins, MDV1964
	VP	Irwin K. Carson, AB1966		VP	John C. Gabbert, AB1968
	VP	Adela M. Cepeda, AB1980		VP	Melita M. Garza, AB1981
	VP	Craig I. Coit, AB1973		VP	Alan Howard Hammerman, AB1955
	VP	Robert T. Gannett, Jr., AB1972		VP	Edward S. Nekritz, AB1987
	VP	Alan Howard Hammerman, AB1955		S	Barbara Cherry, JD1980, AM1980
	VP	Jane M. Power, AB1979, MBA1982		AS	Ingrid Sarapuu, AB1975
	S	Lois M. Shelton, AB1979, MBA1983, PhD1985		T	Desmond C. Wong, MBA1977
	T	David J. Shryock, AB1980	1995	P	Desmond C. Wong, MBA1977
	AT	Elisha Gray, III, AB1966		VP	Brian D. Bergstrom, AB1985, JD1989
1991	P	Quentin George Heisler, Jr., AB1965, JD1968		VP	Adela M. Cepeda, AB1980
	VP	Dr. Richard Carl Burnstine, AB1950, MD1954		VP	Ellyn Kestnbaum Daniels, AB1983, EdM1985
	VP	Irwin K. Carson, AB1966		VP	John C. Gabbert, AB1968
	VP	Adela M. Cepeda, AB1980		VP	Melita M. Garza, AB1981
	VP	Robert T. Gannett, Jr., AB1972		VP	Alan Howard Hammerman, AB1955
	VP	Alan Howard Hammerman, AB1955		VP	Cindy McCartney, MPA1990
	VP	Anne Troy, AB1982		S	Ingrid Sarapuu, AB1975
	VP	Charles Ephraim Zeitlin, AB1953, LLB1956		AS	John S. Graettinger, Jr., AB1971
	S	Lois M. Shelton, AB1979, MBA1983, PhD1985		T	Bennett I. Berman, LLB1943
	T	David J. Shryock, AB1980		AT	Amos J. Coffman, Jr., AB1962
	AT	Elisha Gray, III, AB1966	1996	P	Desmond C. Wong, MBA1977
1992	P	Dr. Richard Carl Burnstine, AB1950, MD1954		VP	Irwin K. Carson, AB1966
	VP	Irwin K. Carson, AB1966		VP	Adela M. Cepeda, AB1980
	VP	Adela M. Cepeda, AB1980		VP	Angela Dorn, AB1987, JD1990
	VP	John C. Gabbert, AB1968		VP	Alan Howard Hammerman, AB1955
	VP	Robert T. Gannett, Jr., AB1972		S	John S. Graettinger, Jr., AB1971
	VP	Alan Howard Hammerman, AB1955		AS	Anne Troy, AB1982
	VP	Susan Himmelfarb, MAT1968, MPA1982		T	Bennett I. Berman, LLB1943
	VP	Anne Troy, AB1982		AT	Amos J. Coffman, Jr., AB1962
	S	Barbara Cherry, JD1980, AM1980	1997	P	Irwin K. Carson, AB1966
	AS	Ingrid Sarapuu, AB1975		VP	Adela M. Cepeda, AB1980
	T	Desmond C. Wong, MBA1977		VP	Angela Dorn, AB1987, JD1990
1993	P	Dr. Richard Carl Burnstine, AB1950, MD1954		VP	Alan Howard Hammerman, AB1955
	VP	Adela M. Cepeda, AB1980		VP	Rex Rust, AB1992
	VP	Craig I. Coit, AB1973		S	Eric Eversley, EdD1976
	VP	John C. Gabbert, AB1968		AS	Gerald M. Offutt, AB1973, JD1976
	VP	Robert T. Gannett, Jr., AB1972		T	Bennett I. Berman, LLB1943
	VP	Alan Howard Hammerman, AB1955		AT	Christina M. Ksoll, AB1986
	VP	Anne Troy, AB1982	1998	P	Irwin K. Carson, AB1966
	VP	Charles Ephraim Zeitlin, AB1953, LLB1956		VP	Adela M. Cepeda, AB1980
	S	Barbara Cherry, JD1980, AM1980		VP	Alan Howard Hammerman, AB1955
	AS	Ingrid Sarapuu, AB1975		VP	Susan J. Oliver, AB1978

	S	Eric Eversley, EdD1976
	AS	Gerald M. Offutt, AB1973, JD1976
	T	Bennett I. Berman, LLB1943
	AT	Christina M. Ksoll, AB1986
1999	P	Craig I. Coit, AB1973
	VP	Adela M. Cepeda, AB1980
	VP	Alan Howard Hammerman, AB1955
	VP	Susan J. Oliver, AB1978
	S	Gerald M. Offutt, AB1973, JD1976
	T	Bennett I. Berman, LLB1943
	AT	Christina M. Ksoll, AB1986
2000	P	Craig I. Coit, AB1973
	VP	Adela M. Cepeda, AB1980
	VP	Alan Howard Hammerman, AB1955
	VP	Susan J. Oliver, AB1978
	S	Joel H. Schneider, MCR1982
	AS	Margaret H. Georgiadis, AB1986, MBA1990
	T	Bennett I. Berman, LLB1943
	AT	Christina M. Ksoll, AB1986
2001	P	Kenneth V. Hachikian, AB1971, MBA1973
	VP	Adela M. Cepeda, AB1980
	VP	Alan Howard Hammerman, AB1955
	VP	Gerald M. Offutt, AB1973, JD1976
	S	Christina M. Ksoll, AB1986
	AS	Joel H. Schneider, MCR1982
	T	Bennett I. Berman, LLB1943
2002	P	Kenneth V. Hachikian, AB1971, MBA1973
	VP	Stephen W. Baird, AB1975
	VP	Adela M. Cepeda, AB1980
	VP	Alan Howard Hammerman, AB1955
	S	Joel H. Schneider, MCR1982
	AS	Jana M. Kubacki, AB1995
	T	Bennett I. Berman, LLB1943
2003	P	John A. Challenger, AB1977
	VP	Stephen W. Baird, AB1975
	VP	Adela M. Cepeda, AB1980
	VP	Alan Howard Hammerman, AB1955
	S	Joel H. Schneider, MCR1982

	AS	Amy F. Pritikin, Parent
	T	Bennett I. Berman, LLB1943
2004	P	John A. Challenger, AB1977
	VP	Stephen W. Baird, AB1975
	VP	Adela M. Cepeda, AB1980
	VP	Alan Howard Hammerman, AB1955
	S	Joel H. Schneider, MCR1982
	AS	Amy F. Pritikin, Parent
	T	Bennett I. Berman, LLB1943
2005	P	Robert Allen Hastings, AB1957, MBA1959
	VP	Stephen W. Baird, AB1975
	VP	Adela M. Cepeda, AB1980
	VP	John A. Challenger, AB1977
	VP	Alan Howard Hammerman, AB1955
	S	Joel H. Schneider, MCR1982
	AS	Amy F. Pritikin, Parent
	T	Bennett I. Berman, LLB1943
2006	P	Robert Allen Hastings, AB1957, MBA1959
	VP	Stephen W. Baird, AB1975
	VP	Paul L. Choi, AB1986, JD1989
	VP	Alan Howard Hammerman, AB1955
	S	Michael J. Cronin, AB1983
	AS	Elory A. Rozner, EdM1999
	T	Stephen P. Lucado, AB1994
2007	P	Margaret I. McCurry, LF1987
	VP	Stephen W. Baird, AB1975
	VP	Paul L. Choi, AB1986, JD1989
	VP	Alan Howard Hammerman, AB1955
	S	Michael J. Cronin, AB1983
	AS	Elory A. Rozner, EdM1999
	T	Stephen P. Lucado, AB1994
2008	P	Margaret I. McCurry, LF1987
	VP	Stephen W. Baird, AB1975
	VP	Paul L. Choi, AB1986, JD1989
	VP	Alan Howard Hammerman, AB1955
	S	Michael J. Cronin, AB1983
	AS	Anne Troy, AB1982
	T	Stephen P. Lucado, AB1994

Position codes: AS=Assistant Secretary; AS-T=Assistant Secretary-Treasurer; AT=Assistant Treasurer; C=Chorister; EC=Executive Committee; P=President; S=Secretary; S-T=Secretary-Treasurer; T=Treasurer; 1VP=First Vice President; 2VP=Second Vice President; 3VP=Third Vice President; EVP=Executive Vice President; VP=Vice President.

Harvard Affiliation: Blank=Unknown; B=Business School attendance; C=College attendance; L=Law School attendance.

* Resigned while in office.

Current Members

a

Abboud, A. Robert AB51, JD56, MBA58
Ablin, Donald O. AB55
Abrahamson, Ryan AB00
Abrams, David S. AB98
Ackerman, Allan D. MAR74
Ahern, Mary L. AB74
Akers, James J. AB61
Alfred, Stephen Jay LLB59
Altman, Louis JD58
Ambler, Stuart AB73
Andersen, Wayne R. AB67
Anderson, Douglas Stuart AB95
Anderson, Gary A. PhD85
Anderson, Mark M. MBA05
Anderson, Nicholas AB05
Anderson, Sonya L. EdM01, EdD05
Anderson, Sumner Esten AB92
Anderson, Thomas M. MD70
Andric, Marko AB91
Antes, Deborah L. MAR90
Applebaum, Deborah MPM86
Arekapudi, Smitha SM01, P03 (01–03)
Arewa, Olufunmilayo B. AB85, JD94, P03 (02–03)
Argiris, Van C. AB50
Armour, Nelson MAT68
Arnold, George R. AB80
Artwick, Frederic J. AB66
Aschheim, Joseph AM53, PhD54
Asgedom, Selamawi AB99
Ashenhurst, Robert L. AB50, SM54, PhD56
Attea, Kate L. MBA01
Augustynski, Adam J. AB86
Axel, Lindsey C. MBA02
Axel, Merrick MBA02

b

Bach, Bernard R. Jr MD AB75
Bachmann, Stephen Richard AB72, JD76
Back, Robert W. AB61
Baer, Werner AM55, PhD58
Bagley, Mark R. AB96
Baird, Stephen W. AB75
Baizer, Carrie S. AB05
Bangstad, Kirk AB99
Barash, Anthony H. AB65
Barengolts, Phillip JD01
Barker, Morton D. Jr B43 (41–42)
Barker, R. Lou (Widow)
Barker, Walter L. AB49, MD53
Barnard, Laura AB02
Barnett, Kyle F. MBA02
Barnhart, June E. EdM78
Barreto, Ellen C. AB71
Barrett, William Henry AB75
Barton, Margaret H. AB74
Baskes, Julie Zell AM58
Baskes, Roger S. JD59
Baskin, Sheldon L. JD61
Bauer, Peter Alexander JD52
Bauer, Ronald G. JD71
Baur, Mike (Parent)
Bearrows, Thomas R. MPP84
Beatty, Graham L. AB05
Beatty, Mark AB06
Beavis, Kathleen Gleason, MD AB80
Becker, David A. AB93
Becker, Stephanie MPP97
Beidler, Francis III AB67
Beidler, Prudence AB01
Bellew, Brian F. AB85
Benjamin, Jeffrey A. AMP01
Bennett, Jeffrey I. AB78
Benz, Emily T. EdM03
Berenberg, Anne H. AB67
Bergen, Charles S. AB77, JD81
Bergonia, R. David JD76
Berkson, Stuart M. JD80
Berliner, Robert W. Jr AB67, JD74
Berman, Debbie Moeckler JD90
Berman, Nancy (Widow)
Bern, Megan JD05
Berner, Robert L., Jr LLB56
Berrien, Willard MBA02
Best, William J. AB70
Beverly, James E. AB47
Bialek, Richard W. Jr AB79, MBA82
Bianucci, John Steven AB82
Bienias, Julia L. SD93
Bierig, Jack R. JD72
Bixby, Frank L. AB50
Blackman, Rodney Jay JD60
Blake, James W. AB82
Blettner, Beverly D. (Widow)
Bliss, Charles M. AB43 (42), B44 (42-43)
Block, Bradley S. JD87
Blum, John D. MHS74
Blumberg, Linda H. AB54
Boden, Barbara Davis JD56
Bogart, Susan (Parent)
Boghasen, Rose E. AM66
Boike, Kristen M. AB01
Boiman, Elaine MPP01
Boone, Byron AB01
Boorstein, Ronald L. JD60
Borders, Ann Elizabeth Bryan MD99
Borovsky, James G. MPP83
Bothfeld, Edward N. AB77
Boucher, Bruce Ambler AB70
Bouton, Dr. Marshall M. AB64
Braatz, Margaret Jay EdM93, EdD99
Bradshaw, Gerald M. L76 (73–74)
Brandfonbrener, Eric D. AB83
Brandon, Ann M. W. AB66
Breon, Andrea EdM04
Breuer, Thomas J. MBA66
Bridgman, William L. MBA70
Brock, Mary A. AM56, PhD59
Brody, Jay D. JD01
Bronsteen, John M. AB97
Bross, John A. AB61, JD65
Brown, Anne R. MBA47
Brown, Jeffrey W. AB79
Brown, William G. LLB67
Browne, Rev. C. Bliss Williams MDV74
Browne, Howell E. AB68
Brownie, Pamela F. EdM75
Bruce, Susan Porter EdM74
Bruner, Scott V. JD92
Bruner, Stephen C. LLB67
Buckland, Arthur MBA76
Buckler, Warren AB57
Bump, Thomas E. AB72, MD76
Bunning, David G. AB88
Burditt, George M. AB44, LLB48
Burke, Elizabeth AB04
Burkhardt, Bridget M. MBA00
Burns, Lawrence C. AMP61
Burnstine, Richard C. AB50, MD54
Burrows, Oliver K. Jr AB50
Bynoe, Linda Walker MBA78
Bynoe, Peter C. B. AB72, JD75 (76), MBA75 (76)

c

Caffrey, Liam P. JD99
Calder, William M. III AB54, AM56
Calfee, David L. AB68
Callcott, Rebecca A. MAR95
Campbell, David AB00
Campbell, Richard P. LLB65
Campbell, Robert B. AB79
Canete-Medina, Isabel J. MDS05
Cantwell, Brian AB04
Caplan, Robert (Parent)
Carlson, LeRoy T. MBA41 (42)
Carlson, LeRoy T. Jr AB68, MBA71
Carlson, Walter C. JD78
Carlyle, Christine L. MAU91
Carmel, Marc J. JD00
Carmona, Roberto MPA03
Carr, Kevin W. AB01
Carroll, Martin C. JD51
Castaneda, Lisa Maria AB96
Cavallino, Robert P. AB55
Ceko, Peter AB84
Cepeda, Adela M. AB80
Cerda, Jose III AB88
Cervera, Joe F. Jr AB68
Chaffetz, Sara (Widow)
Challenger, James E. AB47

Challenger, John A.	AB77 (79)	Collins, Judith A.	EdM75

Challenger, John A.   AB77 (79)
Chambers, Anne F. (Parent)
Chan, Shu Yan   AB75
Chandler, James R.   AMP74
Chang, Albert C. (Parent)
Charnetzki, Paul F. III   AB75
Chase-Lansdale,
Dr. Patricia Lindsay   AB74
Chase-Lansdale,
Dr. Wilson Compton   AB74
Chatman, Donald L.   AB56
Cheng, David   AB89
Cheng, Doris Wan   IAF85
Cherry, Daniel R.   JD76
Chertow, Jennifer M.   AB94
Chien, Bruce B.   AB75
Childs, Linton J.   AB85, JD88
Chodacki, Julie Anne   AB89
Choi, Paul L.   AB86, JD89
Choi, Rosellen S.   AB95
Chor, Philip N.   AB68
Choslovsky, William   JD94
Christenson, Paul A. Jr   MBA72
Christiansen, Richard D.   G54
(53–54)
Chung, Sung J.   AB93
Cid, Andrea   AB01
Cisneros, Jose G.   AB84
Claman, Tamara M.   EdM86
Clark, Allison B.   AB92
Clarke, Bennett D.   AB75 (76),
Gp77 (75–77), JD81, L96 (93–95)
Clarke, James J. II   AB71
Clarke, Thomas James   AB04
Clawson, Curtis   MBA90
Clawson, Mitzi   AB90
Cleary, Kevin   AB05
Coffman, Amos J. Jr   AB62
Cohen, Stephen B.   AB61
Cohler, Bertram J.   AM64, PhD67
Coit, Craig I.   AB73
Cole, Linden N.   AB55
Coleman, Delbert W.   AB48
Coleman, W. Bruce   PMD68
Collins, Jacqueline Y.   MPA01,
MTS03

Collins, Judith A.   EdM75
Commanday, David R.   AB76
Conroy, Lorraine M.   SM84, SD88
Cook, Dennis E.   MPA90, AMP94
Cook, John D.   MBA81
Cooper, Laura A.   EdD88
Corrigan, John E. Jr.   AB44, JD49
Cosman, Jeffrey M.   MBA77
Cotting, James Charles   MBA60
Covarrubias, Cristina   AB05
Cox, Brandon L.   AB93
Crane, Charlotte   AB73
Crane, Constance W.   AB56
Crane, Mark   AB56
Craven, George W.   JD76
Creamer, Robert A.   LLB67
Cressey, Bryan C.   MBA74 (76),
JD76
Cronin, Michael J.   AB83
Crossett, Donald S.   AB56
Cruz, Omar R.   DMD06
Cuite, Catherine E.   AB88
Cunningham, Myles P.   AB54
Cuno, James   AM80, PhD85
Cupps, Andrew S.   AB92
Cupps, Danielle Cunningham
AB92
Cyr, Arthur   AM69, PhD71

d

D'Arcy, Dr. Cleora J.   AB73
D'Arcy, Grant   AB06
D'Arcy, Dr. Stephen P.   AB72
Daghestani, Omar   MPP02
Daniels, Ellyn K.   AB83, EdM85
Darlow, Gillian   AB89
Davis, Anne Meserve   AB58
Davis, Chester R., Jr   LLB58
Davis, Muller   JD60
Davis, Tamara Lafay   EdM98
Day, Nancy L.   NF79
de Hoyos, Debora Marie   JD78
DeJong, Judith K.   MAU01
DeLaney, Elaine Jeanette M.   AB37
DeMar, Robert E.   AB53
DePriest, Darryl L.   AB76, JD79

Decker, Sylvia O. (Parent)
Dederick, Robert G.   AB51,
AM53, PhD58
Delaney, Robert O.   AB47
Demich, Mark B.   EdM86
Denison, Dirk S.   MAR85
Diamond, Stephen B.   AB65
Dixon, John M.   LLB65
Doherty, Joseph Steele   MBA67
Dolin, Eliza A.   AB85
Domanskis, Alexander R. (Parent)
Donaldson, M. Scott   AB01
Donovan, Marie Ann   EdD95
Dorris, Thomas B.   MBA67
Douglas, Charles W.   JD74
Douglass, Robert S.   PMD81
Dowling, Brian J.   AB84, MBA89
Drake, Tom and Eileen (Parents)
Drolte, James E.   MPH65
Dubin, Edward   MBA95
Dubravec, Dominik B.   MOB89,
PD89
Duffy, Paula Barker   MBA77
Dugan, Michael J.   MPA81
Duncan, Arne S.   AB86 (87)
Dung, Mary L.   AB83
Dunn, E. Bruce   MBA58
Dunville, Dennis G.   B 85
Duster, Donald L.   K 78
Dwyer, Warren F.   AB44

e

Eakin, Eric L.   AB85
Early, Bert H.   JD49
Ecob, Robert L.   AB73
Edelson, Allan M.   MBA85
Edelstein, Charles B.   MBA87
Edmonds, Howard O. II   AB56
Edwards, Charles E. IV   MBA05
Edwards, Donald J.   AB94
Egan, Ashley A.   AB02
Egan, Kyle P.   AB02
Eggert, John M.   AB90
Egnaczyk, Tiffany   AB05
Eisendrath, Edwin III   AB80
Eisenstein, Marci   AB76

Elden, Gary M.   JD69
Elden, Richard   OPM97
Elkins, Larry Ray   JD63
Ellis, John E. III   AB78
Ellis, Stephen A.   LLB64
Elman, William J.   LLB56
Emerton, Matthew J.   PhD98
Ender, Jon T.   AB64
Engles, Drew Ronald   AB87
Esrick, Jerald P.   JD66
Evers, Christopher G.   AB95
Eversley, Eric L. Jr   EdD76
Ewing, Clarence III   AB93
Eysenbach, Mary   AB05

f

Fabbioli, Anne C.   AB86
Fabbioli, Joseph M.   AB85
Fagan, Shawn F.   JD94
Faier, James M.   MPP86
Fairbank, Kellogg   AB63
Falk, R. Scott   AB85, JD89
Farrell, Elaine E.   MD75
Feely, John George   MBA41
Feingold, Eugene M.   JD53
Feitler, Robert   JD54
Feldman, Jessica T.   MPA89
Feldman, Joe (Parent)
Feldstein, Charles R.   G46 (45–46)
Feldstein, Janice J.   AB47
Felsenthal, Steven A.   JD74
Felton-Elkins, Nancy   MDV64
Ferguson, Mark K.   AB73
Fiddler, Jeffrey Edward   BD67
Field, Marshall V   AB63
Field, Mary Jo   AB60
Fife, John Millar   MBA90
Filippini, Victor P. Jr   AB80
Findley, Blythe M. Olshan   EdD90
Fine, Gary Alan   PhD76
Fink, Jerrold E.   JD71
Finnegan, Paul J.   AB75, MBA82
Fischer, F. Conrad   AB56
Fishbein, Justin M.   AB48
Fisher, David J.   AB73, MBA76
Fisher, Howard S.   AB46

Fisher, Morris A.   MD65 (68)
Fitzgerald, Anne   AB71
Fitzsimmons, Robert G.   AB84
Fitzsimmons, Robert Vincent
      MPP86, JD86
Flood, Timothy P. and
      Suzette L. (Parents)
Flores, Noemi   AB97
Floyd, Richard B.   AB76
Flynn, Hilda M.   AB44,
      Gr47 (46–47)
Folkers, John Paul   PhD93
Foltz, C. Robert   AB60, LLB64
Foote, Edward L.   AB52, LLB55
Ford, Rebecca L.   AB80
Foster, Nabil G.   AB94
Fox, Eric R.   AB73
Fox, Michael Edward   LLB62
Frame, Anne   AB02
Franklin, Cory (Parent)
Franzese, Jennifer N.   AB98
Freehling, Paul E.   AB59, LLB62
Freehling, Susan   HRP62
Freeman, Peter B.   JD69
Fridkin, Michael K.   AB81, JD85
Friedman, Alan M.   AB81
Friedman, David S.   AB79
Friedman, Gregory   A. JD73
Frim, David M.   AB81, AM86,
      MD88, PhD88
Frisch, Henry J.   AB66
Frommer, Barbara (Parent)
Frommer, Michael S. (Parent)
Fung, Christopher H. K.   AB60,
      MD64
Furman, Albert V. III   AB73

g

Gabbert, John C.   AB68
Gabler, Paul W.   AB53
Gadsden, Wilfred W.   AB74
Gallaga, William Clayton   AB95
Galvin, Chris and Cindy (Parents)
Gamino, Ariel   ALM03
Gang, Jeanne K.   MAR93
Gardiner, Judith Kegan   AB62

Garvy, Adeline Harrington   HRP53
Gaspardo, Brian L.   AB91
Gates-Spears, Lorene C.   AB05
Gauthier, Anne B.   HRP58
Gauthier, Janice L.   AB83, JD86
Gavin, John N.   JD75
Gecht, Robert D.   AB73
Geoffrey, Lauren A.   JD04
Geoga, Douglas G.   AB77, JD80
George, John M. Jr   JD82
Georgiadis, Margo Hastings
      AB86, MBA90
Georgiadis, Pantelis Andreas
      MBA90
Gerasimov, Timofei Olegovich
      AB06
Gerdes, Neil W.   BD68
Getzels, Judith N.   AB49
Giancola, James J.   AB70
Gibbons, William J.   AB48, LLB55
Gibson, Mark   C52 (48–52),
      EdM59
Gilbert, Jessie Williams   AB70
Gillett, Henri   PhD78
Ginal, Kathrina   AB01
Ginal, Michael   AB00
Giovannoni, Robert N.   CAS81
Gislason, Eric A.   PhD67
Glass, Stanford L.   JD59
Glerum, James T. Jr   MBA86
Goddard, Alpheus J. III   LLB61
Godfrey, Eleanor P.   AM47, PhD51
Goel, Anubhav S.
      MBA00, MPH04
Gofen, Charles S.   MPP91
Gofen, Ethel C.   MAT59
Gofen, William   MBA54
Goldberg, Geoffrey   MAR82
Goldmeier, Harold   EdD75
Goldstein, Lori J.   AB83
Golitz, Paul T.   C83 (79–82)
Golla, Adam   AB96
Golla, Clare G.   AB95
Gonzalez-Pulido, Francisco J.
      MDS99
Goodman, Gordon L.   AB55, PhD59

Goodman, Linda   AB78
Gordon, Melvin J.   AB41, MBA43
Gottlieb, David E.   AB76
Gould, Andrew C.   AB84
Grabowski, Marianne   JD83
Graettinger, John S. Jr   AB71
Gray, Daniel A.   MBA79
Gray, Elisha, III   AB66
Gray, Laurence   JD55
Green, Harriett Elizabeth   AB03
Green, Orville C. III   AB47
Green, Richard C.   AB79
Green, Ross B.   AB80
Greenberg, Joseph H.   JD88
Greene, Michael C.   AB03
Greenhouse, Lee R.   AB78
Gretz, Hannah Judy   AB78
Griem, Katherine L.   MD82
Griffin, Alais Lachlan Maclean
      AB94
Grinker, Roy R. Jr.   MD52
Gross, Scott E.   AB81
Grossi, Richard H.   AB74
Grossman, David B.   AB99
Grossman, Robert L.   AB80
Guerin, Raymond M.   PMD86
Guzman, Jaime   AB04
Guzowski, Leah-Bellah B.   EdM04

h

Hachikian, Kenneth V.   AB71,
      MBA73
Haddad, William C.   AB61, LLB66
Hagen, Laura J.   LLM78
Hall, A. Lee   MBA72
Hall, Marcus L.   AB90
Hall, Trevor B.   EdM99
Hall, William P.   AB45, MBA48
Hamilton, Daniel W.   PhD03
Hammerman, Alan H.   AB55
Han, Shi   GP92 (90-91, 91-92)
Hanson, David L.   AB59
Harada, John S.   MBA71
Harding, Erin M. Hoffmann   JD02
Harper, Steven J.   JD79
Harrington, Michael James   AB92

Harris, John B.   AB99
Harris, King W. W.   AB65, MBA69
Harris, Martha Tucker   AB47
Harris, Prof. Morton E.
      AM56, PhD60
Harris, Stephanie F.   AB99
Harrison, Nathaniel P.   AB95
Harvey, Bennet B. Jr   JD59
Hastings, Robert A.   AB57, MBA59
Hatch, Marshall E.   AM99
Hatzis, Nicholas M.   AB88
Haug, Bernice   JD92
Hauser, Robert J.   JD70
Hawkins, Richard A.   PhD69
Hayden, Emily M.   AB84, EdM91
Hayes, David J. A. Jr   AB51
Hayes, Holly   AB68
Hayes, Katheryn M.   AB00
Hedberg, C. Anderson   AB57
Heise, Richard Allen Jr   AB85
Heisler, Quentin George Jr
      AB65, JD68
Helm, Thomas E.   BD68
Helmholz, R. H.   LLB65
Henning, Joel Frank   AB61, JD64
Henrys, Paul Jr   AB92
Herbst, Arthur L.   AB53, MD59
Herbst, Lee Ginsburg   AB57
Herbstman, David   AB78
Herbstman, Janet S.   AB78
Hermes, James (Parent)
Hess, Glen Ernest   LLB67
Hickman, Frederic W.
      AB48, LLB51
Hickrod, G. Alan   MAT55, EdD66
Hier, Daniel B.   AB69, MD73
Higgins, Francis J.   LLB61
Higgins, William B.   AB06
Higinbotham, Harlow N.   AB68
Hiller, David D.   AB75, JD78
Himmelfarb, John D.
      AB68, MAT70
Himmelfarb, Susan E.
      MAT68, MPA82
Hinerfeld, Matthew Ben   AB87
Hirsch, John B.   AB54

Hirschtritt, Shelly Matthew   JD98

Hochberg, Jerome E. (Parent)

Hochstadt, Bruce A.   AB81

Hodakowski, George T.   AB80

Hodges, Thomas H.   AB68

Hoffman, Thomas K.   AB74

Holabird, John A. Jr AB42, MAR48

Holleb, Doris B.   AM47

Holleb, Marshall M.

MBA39, JD42 (47), IA41

Holmberg, Gail J.   MPA78

Holtschneider, Rev. Dennis H.

EdD97

Hoplamazian, Mark S.   AB85

Hoppe, John C.   JD75

Hoshino, Yuichi Max   MPA90

Houghton, John William   AB75

House, Garret C.   MBA93

Howard, David Lamont   AB77

Howard, John L.   AMP03

Howe, Lawrence   AB42

Howell, R. Thomas Jr   AMP81

Hsiung, Robert C.   AB80

Hubbard, Ann   PC71

Hubbard, Jonathan V.   AB69

Huber, Col. Steven P.   AM01

Hudnut, Stewart S.   JD65

Huff, Dr. Douglas Morgan

C71 (67 69)

Hughes, Duncan I.   MCP69

Huh, Peter J.   AB99

Hulse, David L.   MPP84

Hunter, Bryan C.   AB83

Hunter, Kimberly Graham   AB'83

Husseini, Rana   EdM02

Hutchison, Andrea Lee   AB01

Hutchison, Andrew   AB01

Huttner, Jan Lisa   EdM75

i

Ingram, John D.   AB50

Israel-Rosen, Judith   MBA82

Istvan, Cheryl L. (Parent)

Istvan, Rudyard L.   AB72,

MBA74 (76), JD77 (76)

j

Jablonski, Carrie   AB98, JD03

Jabon, David C.   AB82

Jackson, Alexander Louis IV AB70

Jackson, Robert S.   STB56

Jackson, William V. AM48, PhD52

Jacobs, Gerard M.   AB76

Jacobs, Thomas Haskins (Parent)

Jacobson, Judy D.   AB66

Jacobson, Richard J. AB65, PhD70

Jacobson-Wenzel, Dorothea

Gp98 (97–98)

Jannotta, Edgar Dalzell Jr MBA86

Jaresko, Natalie A.   MPP89

Jawkowiak, Nora   AB87, MD91

Jentel, Pierre   TUP54

Johnson, Brian A.   JD84

Johnson, Gary Thomas   JD77

Johnson, Jennifer A.   JD99

Johnson, Joni Goldstein   JD84

Johnson, Ralph Everett   MAR73

Johnson, Robert Matthews AB47

Johnson, Scott B.   AB98

Johnson, Timothy B.   MBA75

Johnston, Roger B.   AB49

Jones, Matthew L.   MPP04

Jones, Sharon Elaine AB77, JD82

Judy, Paul R   AB53, MBA57

k

Kahn, David B.   JD67

Kaler, Mark   AB00

Kaplan, James I.   AB77

Kaplan, Jared   LLB63

Kaplan, Steven M.   AM68

Karafiol, Paul J.   AB92

Karanikas, Alexander   AB39

Karasek, Keith R.   PhD80

Karkazis, Demetrios G.   ALM97

Karkazis, Vickie   EdM01

Karp, Jack L.   LLB62

Kassen, Michelle A.   MPH00

Kassen, Patrick J.   JD01

Kataria, Tripti   P 97

Katcha, Joseph R.   MBA86

Katri, Karen   AB02

Katzenellenbogen, Dr. Benita

AM66, PhD70

Katzenellenbogen, Dr. John A.

AB66, AM67, PhD70

Kawamura, Yoshihiko   AMP05

Keats, Walter L.   AB67

Kelly, Charles A.   LLB56

Kempf, Charles P.   AB90

Kempf, Donald G. Jr   LLB65

Kendall, Stephanie N.   AB05

Kersten, Steven A.   AB77

Kessler, Stanton A.   LLB58

Kessler, Timothy R.   AB02

Kessler, Wendy L.   JD92

Kestnbaum, Kate T.

(Parent, Widow)

Khazen, Anthony S.   AB91

Khleif, Baheej B.   ALM92

Khleif, Susan Anderson

AM73, PhD76

Kienitz, Allen C.   AB59

Kies, William S. Jr   PMD85

Kim, Charles.   Gp93 (92–93),

CSS97, OPM99

Kim, Heidi K.   AB01

Kimmel, Wayne A.   K68 (67–68)

Kitchens, Heather L.   AB02

Kleiman, Adina Sue   EdM66

Kleiman, Jay H. MD   MPA98

Klein, William R.   LF91

Klipstein, Sigal   AM02

Kloecker, Robert P. Jr   AB94

Knecht, Joseph R.   AB84

Knoblauch, Loring W.   JD67

Knoebel, John E., Jr   AB79

Koehn, Dennis R.   MDV78

Koh, Jason Lee   AB90

Kohn, Henry L. Jr   AB58

Komaiko, William   AB73, MD78

Korenblit, Allen D. (Parent)

Kouvelas, Gregory G.   AB85

Kraines, Michael B.   JD88

Kravitt, Jason H. P.   AB72, JD72

Kreitzer, Joshua S.   AB93

Kruger, Samuel A.   AB02, AM02

Krumbein, Eliezer   SB47

Kubacki, Jana   AB95

Kubacki, Ryan   AB95, MBA00

Kyriakopoulos, Eleftherea V. AB01

l

LaPlace, Desmond R.

AB54, MBA56

Laff, Charles A.   JD58

Lal, Neeta   AB05

Lal, Raj B. MD   MPA01

Landes, Elisabeth M.   AB67

Lang, Richard A.   AB72

Langan, J. Andrew   JD82

Larson, Eric C.   AB77

Las, Lisa Morel (Parent)

Lasin, Nancy Carson   AB66

Laske, Jeffery T.   MTS92

Latimer, Alfred F. II   AB50

Latimer, Eleanor Larson   AB50

Laurito, Charles E.   AB71

Lavicka, Amber K.   AB02

Lavicka, William (Parent)

Lawlor, William J. III   JD59

Lazar, Flora   AB78

Leahy, Amanda J.   AB00

Leahy, Gaile Beaurline   MBA81

Leahy, James P. (Parent)

Leahy, Tom (Parent)

Lear, William Schureman   MBA68

Learner, Howard A.   JD80

Leary, Anne K.   AB76

Lee, Heeja (Parent)

Lee, Dr. Jadran   AB92

Lee, John Zihun   AB89, JD92

Lee, Nancy H. (Parent)

Lee, Robert M.   AB85

Leighton, George N.   LLB43

Leisten, Arthur G.   LLB66

Lende, Daniel H.   AB91

Leonard, Eva Marie B.

AB44, AM51

Leonard, Henry S. Jr   AM, PhD

Lerner, Alexander (Parent)

Lerner, Lindsey Anne   AB04

Levi, Charles S.   AB72

Levi, John G.	JD72, LLM73
Levin, David S.	JD59
Levin, Murray L.	AB57
Levin, Robert S.	AB'83
Levine, Lara M.	EdM05
Levinson, Michael R.	JD79
Levinson, Stephen E.	AB66
Lewis, Gregory M.	AB79
Lewis, William Theodore Jr	AB57
Leyerle, Richard W.	AB69
Lieberman, Adrienne B.	AB67
Lieberman, Sydney	AB66, MAT67
Lillig, Nicholas A.	AB86
Lind, Andrew (Parent)	
Lind, Jon R.	AB57, LLB60
Lissner, Gary S. (Parent)	
Lodgen, Susanne J.	AB62
Loeb, Beth A.	JD84
Lorenz, Tony	AB06
Lothan, Avram	MAR82
Louie, Eric K.	AB73 (72), MD76 (77), G75 (73–75)
Louie, Karen Giguere	MD79
Love, David S.	AB06
Lowery, George R.	EdD85
Lowry, James H.	PMD73
Lucado, Stephen P.	AB94
Luck, Daniel	MPP87
Luck, Patricia H.	MPP87
Luhrmann, Tanya M.	AB80
Lynch, John D.	OPM82
Lynch, Michael C.	AB74
Lyon, Harvey T.	AB49 (50), AM52, PhD56

m

Mabbs, J. Michele	AB91
MacLeod, John K.	AB79
Mack, Julian C.	AB81
Maher, David W.	AB55, LLB59
Maher, Jill C.	AB55
Maling, Arthur G.	AB44
Mallman, Jennifer Lyn	EdM06
Mann, David E.	AB97
Mann, H. George	AB58
Maraist, Paul W.	AB52

Marasco, Michael A.	MBA91
Mars, Anthony Matthew	AB99
Marsh, Marietta (Widow)	
Marshall, Robert A.	MD68
Martin, Elisabeth M.	AB96
Martin, Jacobina H.	AB92
Martin, Richard W.	MMP57
Martinelli, Andre	AB98, MBA03
Masters, Douglas N.	JD88
Mboma, Eric	MPP06
McCabe, Peter C. III	AB82
McCally, A. Ward III	AB77, MBA79
McCambridge, John R.	AB74, JD77
McCarron, Kevin	EdM94
McCarter, John Wilbur Jr	MBA63
McCarthy, Danielle M.	AB02
McCarthy, Kimberly	AB04
McCarthy, Paul M.	AB68
McCormick, Joseph M.	IA43, MBA46
McCray, Jacque	AB01
McCue, Howard M.	JD71
McCue, Judith Weiss	JD72
McCullagh, Suzanne F.	AM74, PhD81
McCurry, Margaret I.	LF87
McDonald, Kathleen	MPA84
McDonnell, Mary M.	THM83
McFadden, James P.	AB01
McGee, James Louis	SM02
McGirr, William J.	JD64
McGovern, Courtney	PC94
McGrath, Kevin M.	C64 (60–61, 63–65)
McGrath, William Joseph	JD70
McGuire, Matthew T.	PhD99
McIntyre, Judith L.	AB95
McKinney, Peter	AB56
McKinnon, McKay	AB80
McLagan, C. Bruce	MBA59
McLagan, Jane C.	EdM82
McLauchlan, Craig C.	AB96
McNulty, John W.	AB48, L51 (48–49), AM51, PhD62
McNulty, Ted Aymond Jr	AB97

McRae, Harold D.	MBA71
McWhirter, Bruce J.	JD55
Meader, Raymond & Mary (Parents)	
Meadow, Scott F.	AB77, MBA80
Meany, Kathleen T.	MPA84
Medow, Arthur	LLB48
Meites, Thomas R.	AB65, JD69
Mekaelian, Katherine D.	P50 (49–50)
Melas, Andreas Antoniou	CSS92
Meldman, Suzanne Carter	AB48
Mencoff, Samuel M.	MBA81
Merriner, James L.	AB69
Merwin, Davis U.	AB50
Messer, Joseph V.	AB53, MD56
Meyer, Alexander	MBA05
Meyer, Allen H.	AB46
Meyer, Daniel F.	PMD79
Meyer, William E. Jr	AB89
Meyers, Sheldon J.	AB57
Michaels, Linda Louise	AB87
Michalek, Robert J.	EdM63
Mihas, Constantine S.	MBA92
Miller, Alison L.	AB88
Miller, Barry A.	JD78
Miller, Edward J.	MBA48
Miller, Gregory A.	AB75
Miller, Jonathan L.	AB67
Miller, Laura Schenk	MD82
Miller, Paul J.	LLB53
Miller, William Bricen Jr	JD49
Milliken, Diane L.	MBA78
Mills, John W.	LLB58
Mills, Lloyd	AB40, MD43
Miner, Anthony R.	AB85
Minow, Newton N.	IOP86
Mirowski, Ginat W.	DMD86, MOB88, MD90, PD86
Misey, Robert J.	LLB52
Mitchell, Daniel R.	JD66
Mittendorf, Robert Lee	MPH87, DPH91
Model, Rosanne	MPA03
Moevs, Christian R.	AB80
Montano, Albert J.	MBA72

Morales, Isela	AB98
Moran, James B.	LLB57
Moran, Patrick G.	AB72
Morehead, Cynthia	MA61
Morehead, Philip David	AM78
Morehead, Richard H.	LLB61
Moreland, Mary K. Jenks	AB88
Mori, Shigeru	MBA77
Morrison, John H.	JD62
Morrison, Kate Becker	AB52, LLB58
Morrison, Robert W.	AB42
Morrison, William L.	AB52, LLB58
Moss, Harriet	HRP63
Mou, Shanshan	AB04
Mouly, Catherine C.	AB74
Mulliken, William D.	JD64
Munin, Eugene L.	MPA00
Munns, Justin J.	AB04
Munoz, Antonio (Parent)	
Murphy, Mary Elizabeth K.	AB04
Murphy, Robert (Parent)	
Murphy, Thomas (Parent)	
Murphy, William C.	SB42, JD48
Murray, Daniel R.	JD70
Musicant, Ralph C.	JD71
Mycyk, Mark B.	AB92
Myerson, Roger B.	AB73
Myrseth, Kristian Ove Richter	AB04

n

Nadig, Gerald G.	AB67, MBA74
Nadig, Sara	MD05
Nagle, James L.	MAR64
Nammari, Kelly M.	AMP95
Napolitan, James T.	AB69
Narh, Raymond T. MD	MPH98
Neal, John E.	AB72, MBA74
Nechin, Herbert B.	LLB59
Nelms, David S.	
Neskow, Vesna	AB74
Neumeier, Matthew Michael	JD84
Newburn, Jade Earl	JD04
Newburn, Mary Julia	EdM04
Nicholas, John P.	AB85
Nichols, Gerald	K 97

Nichols, John D. Jr   AB53, MBA55
Nicholson, Lewis E. AM51, PhD58
Nicola, Nassira   AB05
Nielsen, Arthur C. III   AB68
Nielsen, Chad   AB98
Niemeyer, Melvin J.   MBA96
Nissen, William J.   JD76
Noback, Roger Allen   AB66
Nobles-Knight, Dolores   04
Noel-Elkins, Amelia V.   AB92
North, Carol L.   HRP57
North, William Denson   JD59
Novack, Tevor D.   MD54
Novatney, Steven Jay   AB93
Novich, Neil S.   AB76
Noyes, Thomas Ellis   MBA60

o

O'Brien, Francis Donal   MPA83
O'Connell, James D.   AB75
O'Connor, James J.   MBA60
O'Donnell, Thomas M.   MBA85
O'Leary, Colleen M.   AB76
O'Malley, Taylor J.   MBA93
O'Rourke, Michael J.   AB73
O'Toole, John E.   MD99
O'Toole, Molly Jane   MPA96
Oberman, Michael Alan (Parent)
Offutt, Gerald M.   AB73, JD76
Olian, Robert M.   AB '74 (73),
JD76 (77), MPP77
Olivas, Luana   AB98
Oliver, Susan J.   AB78
Olson, Bradley J.   AB03, MBA08
Onie, Rebecca   AB97, JD03
Onyeagoro, Linda   AB00
Orput, Alden E.   AB82
Orsic, Eric   JD96
Ossyra, James D.   AB78
Otwell, Ralph M.   NF60
Owens, Elizabeth V. H.
AB80, MBA84

p

Pacelli, Andrew B.   AB '04
Paik, Joon & Sue Chui (Parents)

Paik, Sue K.   AB02
Palay, Robert J.   AB78
Palmer, Julie Gage   AB84
Papangelis, Lambrini   AB84
Pape, Arthur E.   JD65
Parish, Heather D.   MPP90
Park, Jane S.   AB94, JD97
Park, Jason D.   AB06
Parker, John C. Jr   AB80
Parsons, Robert L.   MD55
Pascale, Daniel R.   AB62
Pasch, Rachel   AB80
Paschen, Elise   AB81
Patt, Stephen L.   AB60
Patten, Paul A.   JD90
Patterson, Elissa   ALM97
Pavich, Robert J.   AB69
Pawlowski, Paul L.   AB56, LLB60
Pearce, William H.   AB71
Pekron, Julie Peters   AB95
Pellett, Clark D.   AB76
Pershan, Marc H.   AB82
Persley, Isaac Curtis   AB04
Petersen, Edward S.
C43 (39–42), MD45
Petersen, William O. AB48, LLB52
Petersen, Zoe B.   AB44
Peterson, Richard A.   LLB68
Petravicius, Adam V.   JD95
Pham, Mary Thuy   AB86
Phelps, Craig   AB47
Philipson, Louis H.   AB76
Philipson, Lynn   MHS80
Piatek, Julianne   SM82
Pierce, Daniel M.   AB49, JD52
Pittman, Joseph G.   AB53, MD59
Poholsky, Joel S.   AB70, EdM84
Polelle, Michael J.   JD63
Porter, Jim R.
B64 (62–63), OPM86
Posner, Alan M.   AB74
Potter, Nicholas B.   AB54
Presser, Stephen B.   AB68, JD71
Price, Allan S. and Carla (Parents)
Price, Charles T.   JD69
Priest, Steven J.   MTS88

Primo, Diane   MBA84
Primo, Quintin E. III   MBA79
Pritikin, David T.   JD74
Pritzker, Penny S.   AB81
Prochnow, Herbert V. Jr
AB53, JD56
Przekop, Richard   AB05
Purnell, Kathy   AB91
Py, Pierre O.   MBA05

q

Quanbeck, Maridee A.   JD76
Quantz, Amanda Donna   MTS97

r

Rabinowe, Maxine   AB87
Rafkin, John M.   AB83
Ralph, Brian Edward   AB '98
Ramirez, Adam R.   AB79
Ranney, George   AB62
Ranney, Victoria P.   AB60
Rappa, Colleen & David (Parents)
Rappa, Ryan M.   AB05
Ratain, Mark J.   AB76
Rau, John E.   MBA72
Ray, David C.   AB68
Ray, Leah Ann   MDS96
Read, Thomas   AB49, CAS75
Reagan, Joseph E. III   AB98
Rechtin, James A.   MBA00
Reckinger, Jeffry D.   AB74
Redding, Margaret W.   AB55
Reddinger, James Calvin   AB93
Reenan, Jennifer A.   AB97
Reenan, Neal J.   AB97
Reichert, Susan M.   MBA88
Reilly, Francis X. Jr   JD41
Reliford, Dyisha L.   AB01
Reneau, Andrae P.   AB00
Reneau, Myehla   AB01
Reum, James M.   AB68, JD72
Rhind, James T.   LLB50
Ribaudo, Anthony Joseph   AB93
Ribaudo, Rebecca Chamian   AB93
Richards, Stanley H.   SB44, JD49
Richardson, Peggy A. (Parent)

Ridge, Timothy P.   AB68
Rieger, Mitchell S.   JD49
Rielly, John E.   PhD61
Rinella, Richard A.   AB61
Rios-Meyer, Catalina E.   MBA98
Ristic, Blasko C.   AB91
Rivkin, Robert S.   AB82
Robbins, Ellen S.   JD91
Roberts, Shepherd M. III   EdM96
Robertson, Gary L.   AB57, MD61
Robinson, Daniel V.
AB69, Gp70 (69–70)
Rocca, Bernard T. III   AB68
Rode, Emil C. Jr   EdM84
Rogers, John Edward   JD67
Rogers, Peter W.   AB70, MBA73
Ronan, John J.   MAR91
Rosenberg, Anita Rival   AB85
Rosenberg, Neil F.   AB00
Rosenblatt, Robyn Morgenstern
MAR97
Rosenbluth, Marion E.   AB49
Rosner, Marsha Rich   AB72
Rosner, Robert   PhD76
Ross, Yumi Shilowitz   MAR90
Rothstein, Jeffrey S.   AB78
Rovzar, Leigh Alexander   AB01
Rowley, Guy Anthony   AB68
Rozner, Elory A.   EdM99
Rubin, Rob   AB78 (79)
Rudman, Dr. Irving   C45 (41–43)
Runcie, Diana   AB84, JD87
Runcie, Robert W.   AB84, JD87
Ruschhaupt, Dr. David G.   AB62
Ruschhaupt, Jonathan David AB95
Russell, George L.   AB75
Rutledge, Diane   AM02
Rydholm, Ralph W.   AMP89
Rygiel, Joseph C.   MBA69

s

Sack, Nathaniel   JD65
Saef, David Alan   AB91
Saef, Scott Evan   AB86
Saenz, Jenny   AB06
Safford, Franklin R.   AB57

Safford, Joan B. AB59

Salatich, William G. Jr AB73

Salomon, Richard A. JD79

Samarel, Allen Mark MD76

Sanders, Jacquelyn Seevak AB52

Sandor, Charles S., MD AB80

Santiago, Keith John, MD AB00

Santini, Marina C. AB98

Saper, Michael S. LLB65

Saranow, Mitchell H.
MBA71, JD71

Satin, Howard S. AB51, JD54

Sawyier, David R. AB72, JD77

Schaudt, Peter L. MLA84

Schauer, Louis F. LLB52

Schendel, Mark MAR89

Scher, Paul L. AB57

Scherer, David R. AB93

Scherrer, Philip AB01

Scheub, John E. AB66

Schiff, Patricia Foisie AB77

Schiffman, David M. AB74, JD77

Schilling, Richard M. LLB62

Schlade, Terry M. LLB66

Schlenker, James D. AB66, MD69

Schmetterer, Kenneth L. JD89

Schmitt, Jason AB98

Schneider, Joel H. MCR82

Schorer, Joseph U. JD78

Schultz, John M. MBA76

Schuman, William P. JD79

Schumann, Sarah-Anne H.
AB91, MD99

Schurz, Franklin D. Jr AB52, MBA56

Schutz, Charles E. MPH83

Schwartz, Alan G. MBA54

Schwartz, Charles P. Jr LLB50

Schwartzberg, Hugh J. AB53

Schwartzberg, Joanne
AB55, Gr56 (55–56)

Schwertfeger, Timothy R. AMP86

Scott, Adanna AB06

Scott, Karen AB76

Seed, Randolph W. AB54

Seed, Richard G.
AB49, AM51, PhD53

Seftenberg, Stephen L.
AB56, LLB59

Seith, Alex R. JD60

Selkregg, Leif L. LF89

Seoane-Smithburg, Maria N.
MLA85

Sethi, Savdeep S. AM93, PhD96

Seubold, James H. AB67

Shah, Rachana AB03, JD06

Shapiro, Robert B. AB59

Shapo, Helene Seidner MAT60

Shapo, Marshall AM61, SJD74

Shaw, Nancy M. AB91

Sheffield, Thomas C. Jr
AB58, MBA60

Shepro, Richard W. AB75, JD79

Sher, Benjamin Samuel AB99

Sherlock, Daniel T. (Parent)

Sherman, David A. MBA86

Sherman, Richard S. AB77

Sherrod, Theodore R. Jr JD73

Shields, Mark C. AB70, MD75

Sicher, Steven E. AB71

Sigman, Laura J. JD03

Sikorovsky, Eugene F. LLB51

Silva, Alejandro OPM87

Silverstein, Michael AB66, PhD72

Simmons, Adele Smith AB63

Simmons, John Leroy AB63

Simon, Anthony AB85, MAR89

Simon, Marc S. (Parent)

Simon, Maria AB89

Siner, Jonathan (Parent)

Singer, Paul H. JD61

Singla, Vandana Veenay EdM02

Singleton, Kraig Brandon
AB93, MPP98

Sipples, Timothy F. AB90

Skinner, Honey Jacobs AB78

Sklarsky, Charles B. AB68

Skrodzki, Richard J. (Parent)

Slaughter, William C. AB95

Slichter, Charles P. AB45 (46),
AM47, PhD49, LLD96 (hon)

Sljivic-Simsic, Biljana AM63, PhD66

Smart, Allen Rich II LLB61

Smith, Bryan A. AB05

Smith, Edward B. Jr (Parent)

Smith, Evan T. AB84

Smith, Timothy Dennis AB72

Smyth, Elizabeth E. CSS04

Snow, Richard H. AB50

Snyder, Anna Perry AB97, EdM97

Snyder, John B. LLB57

Soderberg, Leif G. AB76

Sodikoff, Robert N. (Parent)

Sohi, Sunana AB00

Solberg, Timothy G. AB75

Solomon, Scott M. MD AB79

Solow, Michael Barry JD84

Soltes, Anna Lee (Parent)

Soltes, Eugene F. AB04

Soltes, Steven Francis (Parent)

Sorenson, Steven P. AB87

Spring, Bonnie PhD77

Sprowl, Susan W. MAT64

Squires, Vernon T. JD60

Stanhaus, James S. JD70

Stanhaus, Naomi MA68

Star, Alvin D. MBA49

Star, Esta G. AM51

Star, James A. AB83

Stason, E. Blythe Jr LLM57

Stassen, John H. JD68

Steele, Eric H. G64 (63–64), JD67

Steinberg, Bradley D. LLM59

Stekala, Paul C02 (98–01, 02–03)

Stellato, John E. AB88

Stellato, Julene Maree AB90

Stephan, Marjorie H. HRP61

Stephenson, C. Bruce AB74

Stern, Carl W. Jr AB68

Stern, Charles A. JD58

Stern, Janet B. MAT58

Stern, Louis W. AB57

Steuer, Axel D. AM69

Steuer, Loreli Olson MAT60

Stevenson, Adlai E. III AB52, LLB57

Stevenson, George J. III MBA67

Stewart, Donald Mitchell
MPA69, DPA75

Stewart, Jeffrey J. AB01

Stewart, Sarah AB81

Stiles, William R. AB63

Stinziano, Michael P. MPA85

Stokes, Anne Kemble EdM01

Stoll, R. Ryan JD90

Stoll, Ralph W. MD65

Stolper, Matthew W. AB65

Stone, Ellyn JD83

Stone, James H. AB60, MBA62

Stone, Jeffrey Edward JD83

Stracks, Robert J. LLB67

Straus, Francis H. II AB53

Straus, Lorna P. AB55

Strauss, Sarah MBA04 (05), MPA05

Struthers, Harvey J. Jr
AB64, MBA66

Stulberg, S. David AB65

Sudow, Joseph Z. LLB38

Sulkowski, Gregory M.
AB00, MD04

Sullivan, Lawrence E. AM90 (hon)

Sumber, Jeffrey H. MTS95

Sun, Heejoon Y. DMD88, MPH88

Surianarain, Sharmila
AB '01, EdM04

Sutherland, Mary AM73, MBA83

Suzuki, Ben Kim MAR86

Sweet, Philip W. K. Jr AB50

Swett, Daniel R. AB58, LLB61

Swibel, Howard J. AB72, JD75

Swoyer, Vincent H. EdD66

Sylva, David AB02

Szalay, Robert N. MB70

t

Tallas, Gregory G. AB61

Tao, Laurent S. MPH04

Tappin, Anthony Gerald AMP68

Tarbox, Todd AB75

Taswell, Howard F. AB49

Taube, Kenneth P. AB71

Taylor, Bernard AB91

Taylor, Christine R. AB91

Taylor, Prentiss Jr AB73, MD78

Taylor, Ronald L. AB66

Tchen, Christina M. AB78

Tellerman, Judith S.   MAT71
Terman, Mari D.   AB57
Thackray, Andrew   MPA04
Thomas, Pamela Clark   AB67
Thorelli, Norma   MPH00
Thornber, Judy P.   JD66
Thornley, Andrew Maddox   JD05
Tighe, Johanna Aileen   MAT06
Timbers, Stephen B.   MBA68
Tobacman, Joanne Kramer   AB72
Toll, Daniel R.   MBA55
Tomford, Katherine   AB99
Torbert, Preston M.   JD74
Torisky, Donald D.   AMP78
Torshen, Kay P.   EdM64
Totten, Gilbert D.   AM56
Treece, John W.   AB75
Troy, Anne B.   AB82
Trussell, Jacqueline   MTS98
Tsonis, George D.   AB92
Tucker, Todd   HLS85
Turner, Helene J.   EdM83

u

Ung, Feodor   AB92
Ung, Jean Ou   AB95, MD99
Ury, Faryl   AB06
Usiskin, Zalman P.   MAT64

v

Vail, Margaret C.   AB48
Vaingurt, Julia   PhD05
Valdez, Virginia   MPP98
Valerious, Randi L.   JD90
Van Brunt, Constance   MAT72
van der Meulen, Susan Janneke   MAR78
Van Ness, Carroll R. Jr   C65 (61–66)
Van Tine, Matthew E.   AB80
Varones, John N.   AM97
Vender, Kimberly Megan   AB98
Verr, Steven R. AB79, G81 (79–81)
Vickery, Randall G.   JD87
Vieira, Tatiana   AB00
Visin, Robert James   B48 (46–47)

Vitale, David J.   AB68
Vogler, James R.   AB74
Volan, Carolyn   ALM95
Vonau, Matthew F.   AB02

w

Wagner, Stefan, Jr.   MBA54
Walberg, Kim R.   AB96
Waldstein, Sheldon S.   AB45
Walker, Jeffrey A.   AB78
Waller, E. Parker Jr   AB92
Walsh, David J.   GMP00
Walsh, Kathleen Theresa   MPA06
Walsh, Michael Patrick   AB83, MBA87
Walsh, Thomas C.   JD79
Walter, Douglas H.   AB63, JD66
Walter, Kristin L.   AB90, MD97
Walton, Robert S.   JD96
Wanger, Dr Leah Zell   AB71 (72), AM72, PhD79
Ward, Everett S.   JD86
Ward, Sally H. (Parent)
Wardlow, Jesse George Jr   AB77, EdM79
Waterson, Claire M.   MBA74
Watts, Dey Wadsworth   LLB49
Watzke, James N.   PhD72
Wei, Helen H.   EdM96
Weil, Joseph M.   AB39, LLB42
Weinberg, David B.   AB74
Weisbard, Samuel   LLB48
Weissent, Alexander B.   AB73
Weissman, Michael L.   JD58
Welch, Joseph N. II   AB76
Weller, Robert J.   MBA86
Welsh, Kelly R.   AB74, JD78
Wemple, Peter H.   AB80
Werly, James P.   AB78
Wesley, John R.   AB63, MD67
Westin, Craig D.,   M 84
Whitaker, Cheryl Rucker   MPM94
Whitaker, Eric E.   MPH93
Wiebe, Lauren A.   AB00
Wiesen, Sasha J.   ALM04
Wilcox, Robert B.   AB44

Wilcox, Robert B. Jr   AB70
Wilczynski, Aimee V.   MPP05
Wilde, Harold R. Jr   PhD73
Wilder, Keven   AB70
Wilder, Nicholas F.   AB70
Williams, Paul C.   AMP92
Williams, Sandra   AB90
Willis, Nova I.   AB04
Wilson, James Lee II   MBA74
Wilson, Laura S.   MAT72
Wilson, Stephen T.   PhD75
Wintermeyer, Stephen F.   AB85
Wittner, Jennifer L.   AB84
Wolf, Grace W.   JD64
Wolin, Kathleen Y.   SD05
Wong, Desmond C.   MBA77
Wood, Timothy M.   AMP84
Woodman, Lorrin E.   SB37 (38), SM38
Woodruff, Brian D.   MTS84
Woods, David H.   PMD80
Wool, Stephen C.   AB81
Wright, Hannah   AB06
Wright, Jeffrey Michael   EdM03
Wu, Barbara Jil   PhD81
Wuu, Joanne   SM96
Wynne, Ami N.   AB97, JD00

y

Yamate, Sandra S.   JD84
Young, Lauren Jones   EdM79, EdD84

z

Zabelski, Richard E. (Parent)
Zagel, James B.   JD65
Zeitlin, Charles E.   AB53, LLB56
Zessar, Bruce M.   AB87
Zhao, Jia   JD83
Ziegler, Elizabeth A.   MBA98
Zimmerman, Gustavus H. III   AM72, PhD80
Zimmerman, Phil George   MD64
Zinkl, Gregory M.   PhD97
Zonis, Marvin   B60 (58–59)
Zopp, Andrea L.   AB78, JD81

Zourkova, Krassimira J.   JD00
Zucker, David F.   MBA88
Zucker, Karen B.   MBA95

June 30, 2007 member data is based on Harvard University and The Harvard Club of Chicago records, and is presented using the abbreviations and general style of the Harvard Alumni Directory.

Sources

Selected Sources Used in Preparing the Chapters.

Chapter 3 "Women at Harvard Law": Chicago Bar Association Alliance for Women, *Bar None: 125 Years of Women Lawyers in Illinois*, exhibit (1999) and online book (http://www.chicagobar.org/public/barnone/sect1.asp).

Chapter 4 Samuel Johnston and the Johnston Gate: Ken Gewertz, "Enter to Grow in Wisdom," *Harvard University Gazette*, archives, http://www.news.harvard.edu/gazette/2005/12.15/18-gates.html; 28th Annual Dinner, *Chicago Daily Tribune*, Dec. 28, 1884, p. 16; provisions of Johnston's will, ibid., Nov. 5, 1886, p. 8. Biographical information on Avery Coonley: http://en.wikipedia.org/wiki/Coonley_House; www.averycoonley.org/aboutus_mission.htm; http://www.appraisercitywide.com/content.aspx?filename=CustomPage70.x.

Chapter 5 Biographical information on Richard Greener: http://dede.essortment.com/richardgreener_pws.htm; Michael Robert Mounter, unpublished doctoral dissertation, "Richard Theodore Greener: The Idealist, Statesman, Scholar and South Carolinian," 2002.

Chapter 6 Leading references on Harvard University during the Lowell years include Samuel Eliot Morison, *Three Centuries of Harvard*, 1636–1936 (Cambridge, Mass.: The Belknap Press of Harvard University Press, [1936] 2001); William Bentinck-Smith, ed., *The Harvard Book: Selections from Three Centuries*. rev. ed. (Cambridge, Mass.: Harvard University Press, [1953] 1982); Richard Norton Smith, *The Harvard Century, The Making of a University to a Nation* (Cambridge, Mass.: Harvard University Press, 1986); John T. Bethell, *Harvard Observed: An Illustrated History of the University in the Twentieth Century* (Cambridge, Mass.: Harvard University Press, [1953] 1998); Morton and Phyllis Keller, *Making Harvard Modern: The Rise of America's University* (Oxford: Oxford University Press, 2001); John T. Bethell, Richard M. Hunt, and Robert Shenton, Harvard A to Z (Cambridge, Mass.: Harvard University Press, 2004); Andrew Schlesinger, *Veritas: Harvard College and the American Experience* (Chicago: Ivan R. Dee, 2005).

Amy's poem, Smith, p. 65; "as a sophomore," ibid., p. 66; Marlborough Street house description, ibid., p. 66. On Lowell, "the first to give his entire attention," Morison, p. 376; "Eliot's 'most persistent critic,'" Bethell, p. 14; Lowell's criticism of Eliot in the *Harvard Graduates' Magazine*, Schlesinger, p. 150 n. 43. On Lowell's election, Morison, p. 439. "Unlike Eliot," Bethell, p. 46. "An intellectual aristocrat," Morison, p. 441; "I believe their character depends," Smith, p. 63 n. 2; on the two presidents, Morison, p. 387.

Lowell's inaugural remarks, Bethell, p. 45; Lowell's speech, "If we can increase the intellectual ambition," Schlesinger, p. 151; Morison on raising the general standard, p. 445. On the architecture of the new freshman housing halls, Bethell, p. 48. On language examination requirements instituted by Lowell, Bethell, p. 48; Roscoe Pound assumes the Story Professorship, Morison, p. 467. *The Harvard Graduates' Magazine* account of Lowell's May 8, 1913, speech before the Chicago Club, Sept. 1913, p. 135. "The tendency of the wealthy students to live in dormitories," Bethell, p. 24; "A college . . . must be a democracy," Schlesinger, p. 141 n. 29.

On the Pullman road race, *Chicago Daily Tribune*, Sept. 17, 1914; on Charles Horwitz as law school graduate, ibid., Aug. 31, 1919. Every study should have a fireplace, Bethell, p. 52; Lowell writes to mother of war dead, Bethell, p. 87; "The fate of those who died," Smith, p. 80. On free speech: "If the Overseers ask," Bethell, p. 93; "whose wisdom and courage," ibid., p. 94; classic definition of American freedom, Morison, pp. 454–456; "The teaching by the Professor," Bentinck-Smith, p. 23. "Washington's 1 Error," *Chicago Daily Tribune*, Feb. 22, 1920.

On bias: "his lifelong bias," Smith, p. 74; "the new immigrants," Schlesinger, p. 152; exclusion of black students from halls, ibid., p. 154; "shall not be compelled to live and eat together," ibid., p. 168; Eliot on Lowell's errors, ibid., p. 167. Quotas for Jewish students, Bethell, p. 96; letter to Alfred A. Benesch, Schlesinger, p. 164. Ethnic identity required on applications, Bethell, p. 97; photograph required, Schlesinger, p. 168 n. 25. The dichotomy of Lowell's vision and his limitations, Smith, p. 80. Ada Louise Comstock on the difficulties of co-education, Schlesinger, p. 174.

Institution of reading period, Smith, p. 75. Lowell's successful new budget system, Morison, p. 480. "We have enough for a great university," Keller and Keller, p. 147 n. 35. Edward S. Harkness gift, Morison, p. 476. "Lowell's crowning achievement," Bethell et al., p. 22. Construction of Memorial Church, Morison, p. 460; "Emily Dickinson above," Bethell et al., pp. 254–255.

Fake *Crimson* announcing election of Chicago businessman as Lowell's successor, Morison, p. 480. Encomia: *New York Herald Tribune* article, "no man," Smith, p. 71; David McCord's article, Bethell, p. 151; "Mr. Lowell, becoming President," Morison, pp. 480–481; "Lowell was proud," Schlesinger, p. 174. Lowell's speech, "As wave after wave rolls landward," Bentinck-Smith, p. 24.

On Marita Bonner: http://womenshistory.about.com/od/harlemrenaissance/p/marita_bonner.htm.

Chapter 7 Information on James Conant's career from http://en.wikipedia.org/wiki/J._B._Conant, 6/30/2007; http://www.uclearfiles.org/menu/library/biographies/bio_conant-james.htm 6/30/02; http://oasis.harvard.edu:10080/oasis/deliver/deepLink?_collection=oasis&uniqueId=hua08998. On Jeffersonian ideals: "Education for a Classless Society: The Jefferson Tradition," by J. B. Conant, Charter Day Address delivered at the University of California, Mar. 28, 1940. On the world's fair uniting science and business communities, http://www.encyclopedia.chicagohistory.org/pages/225/html; on Sally Rand, ibid. On the annual Spring Strawberry Night, *Chicago Daily Tribune*, June 8, 1933; on the Christmas 1933 luncheon and the December 1933 football games, ibid., Dec. 1, 1933. Conant's February 21, 1934, address to the Club, ibid., Feb. 22, 1934. Account of the Harvard–Army polo game, ibid., Mar. 3, 1935. On the fiftieth anniversary of the University Club, ibid., Feb. 11, 1937, p. 18. Conant's February 27, 1937, address to the Club, ibid., Feb. 27, 1937, p. 18.

Chicago youth to college in fall 1936, ibid., Sept. 22, 1936; women attending previously men-only broadcast parties for football games, ibid., Oct. 16, 1937, decision affirmed in 1938 and introduction of women to the Tavern, ibid., Oct. 27, 1938.

On the United States "tricked" into fighting in World War I by British imperialists and New York bankers, ibid., Nov. 12, 1939, p. 10. Conant's encounters with pacifist students and his response, "The reasoning," in James B. Conant, *My Several Lives* (New York: Harper and Row, 1970), p. 217; utterly fantastic," ibid., p. 267. Conant's speech before the Associated Harvard Clubs in Baltimore, ibid., p. 268. On the atomic reaction beneath Stagg Field, ibid., p. 90.

Valedictory service in Memorial Church, Conant, Lives, p. 350. On coeducational instruction jokes, ibid., pp. 374–380. A university at war, ibid., p. 363. Joseph C. Grews's remarks to the Club on Dec. 7, 1942, *Chicago Daily Tribune*, Dec. 8 1942. On the death of John H. Wigmore, ibid., Apr. 21, 1943; the death of G. Cook Kimble, ibid.; the death of Howard F. Gillette, ibid., Oct. 23, 1943.

On building the Chicago subway and Lake Shore Drive, http://www.chipublib.org/004chicago/timeline/subway1.html, http://www.encyclopedia.chicagohistory.org/pages/1275.html . On the February 1943 Annual Dinner, *Chicago Daily Tribune*, Feb. 19, 1943, pp. 19, 20; on the 1994 Annual Dinner, ibid., Feb. 10, 1944, p. 17. On the Art Institute's exhibit, Art of the United Nations, ibid., Nov. 6, 1944, p. 17. On the 1945 Annual Dinner, ibid., Feb. 21, 1945. On the Community and War Fund, ibid., Feb. 14, 1945.

Recommendation to drop the atomic bomb, http://www.answers.com/topic/manhattan-project?cat=technology. Dropping of "Little Boy" and "Fat Man," http://en.wikipedia.org/wiki/Victory_over_Japan_Day. On the 1947 Annual Dinner, *Chicago Daily Tribune*, Mar. 2, 1947.

On the December 1947 Hasty Pudding show, ibid., Jan. 1, 1948. Arthur Valpey's remarks on the changing era of football, ibid., Dec. 30, 1948. On the February 1949 annual meeting, ibid., Feb. 1, 1949; on the 1951 Annual Dinner, ibid., Feb. 15, 1951, on the December meeting, ibid., Dec. 26, 1951; on the annual Christmas luncheon, ibid., Dec. 30, 1953. Kestnbaum, "I like the city," ibid. May 30, 1953. On Randall serving the Eisenhower administration, Eisenhower Library papers. Conant on mandatory conscription, *Lives*. George Marshall's commencement speech on the Marshall Plan, en.wikipedia.org/wiki/Marshall_Plan.

Bibliographic information on Amberg: Young, "Chicago Banker Blasts Plan to Shift Controler," Chicago Daily Tribune, Apr. 13, 1950; "H. V. Amberg to Aid U.S. as Tax Counsel," ibid., Sept. 2, 1947; "Harold V. Amberg Dies; Expert in Banking Law," ibid., Dec. 25, 1961. On Marita Bonner: http://womenshistory.about.com/od/harlemrenaissance/p/marita_bonner.htm.

Chapter 8 Presidential speeches are available on the Harvard University Web site (Harvard.edu). Information on the Magie family's Harvard involvements courtesy of the Magie family; information on the Smith family from the Smith Simmons family archives courtesy of Adele Smith Simmons.

Chapter 10 Some of Rudenstine's speeches are compiled in a book, *Pointing our Thoughts: Reflections on Harvard and Higher Education 1991–2001* (Cambridge, Mass.: Harvard University Press, 2001). His final speech at the Harvard Club of Chicago is available on the Harvard University

Web site (Harvard.edu). A number of stories in the Harvard Crimson provided background information on developments at Harvard University during Rudenstine's years as president.

Chapter 11 Summers's inaugural address, Office of the President, Address of Lawrence H. Summers, President, Harvard University, Oct. 12, 2001. Summers's speech at Annual Award Dinner in March 2002, Office of the President, Remarks of Harvard University President Lawrence H. Summers, Annual Award Dinner, Harvard Club of Chicago, Mar. 3, 2002. Summers's speech before the Economic Club, Harvard University John F. Kennedy School of Government, Remarks of University President Lawrence H. Summers, Economic Club, Chicago, Ill., Oct. 14, 2003. Summers's remarks before the College Board Forum, Harvard University John F. Kennedy School of Government, "Every Child Getting Ahead: The Role of Education," Remarks of Harvard University President Lawrence H. Summers, College Board Forum, Chicago, Ill., Nov. 1, 2004.

Summers's explanation of remarks on low representation of women in the sciences, James Traub, "Lawrence Summers, Provocateur," *New York Times*, Jan. 23, 2005, The Nation, p. 4. Summers's remarks on establishing a task force on women in academic careers and Faust's response, "Task Forces on Women Established: To Focus on Women on the Faculty and in Science and Engineering," *Harvard University Gazette*, Feb. 10, 2005, vol. C, no. 15, pp. 1, 6. Editorial in support of Summers, "A Summers Storm at Harvard," *Chicago Tribune*, Feb. 20, 2005, sect. 2, p. 8. Jeffrey Toobin's remarks on Summers's style, "Speechless: Free Expression and Civility Clash at Harvard," *The New Yorker*, Jan. 27, 2003, p. 33. Remarks before the Harvard Club of Washington, D.C., Office of the President, Remarks to the Harvard Club of Washington, D.C., President Lawrence H. Summers, Washington, D.C., Apr. 15, 2005. Faust's comment on task force recommendations: Donella M. Rapier, Vice President of Alumni Affairs and Development, Harvard University, "Harvard Task Forces on Women Release Findings and Recommendations," press release, May 16, 2005; Summers's remarks on curricular changes, ibid.

Links to Summer's letter:
http://www.news.harvard.edu/gazette/daily/2006/02/21_summers.html
http://www.president.harvard.edu/speeches/2006/0221_summers.html
http://www.news.harvard.edu/gazette/daily/2006/02/21-board.pdf

Summers's resignation letter, email from Rapier to Alumni and Friends, "Announcement," sent Feb. 21, 2006. Summer's letter to Harvard community regarding his resignation, Office of the President, Letter to the Harvard Community, President Lawrence H. Summers, Feb. 21, 2006. "We cannot maintain," ibid. Letter from the Fellows of Harvard College accepting Summers's resignation, Fellows of Harvard College, Office of the Governing Boards, Feb. 21, 2006.

Chapter 12 "I will do my best," "make every effort," and biographical information on Bok all from "Summers to Step Down as President at End of Academic Year," *Harvard University Gazette* (online), Feb. 21, 2006. "Drew G. Faust" and following quotation from "Harvard Names Drew G. Faust as Its 28th President," *Harvard University Gazette* (online), Feb. 11, 2007. Remarks by Drew G. Faust, "I am indebted," from "Harvard Presidential Announcement: Remarks by President-Elect Drew G. Faust," *Harvard University Gazette* (online), Feb. 11, 2007.

Sources for Illustrations

Except as noted, illustrations in this book are from the Harvard Club of Chicago's archives or from private collections.

Images of Harvard presidents are courtesy of Harvard University.

Images courtesy of others are listed below by organization, with page location(s).

Business Week, New York, NY
Page 122

Chicago History Museum, Chicago, IL
Pages 5, 6, 8, 9, 20, 21, 23, 28, 36, 38, 54, 65, 130, 136

Chicago Public Library, Chicago, IL
Page 40

Chicago Tribune, Chicago, IL
Page 15

City of Chicago, Chicago, IL
Page 120

College Board, Princeton, NJ
Page 125

Glessner House, Chicago, IL
Page 99

Harvard University/Harvard University Archives, Cambridge, MA
Pages 42, 53, 55, 58, 61, 67, 68, 82, 84, 116, 118, 119, 124, 128, 134, 143, 144

The Library of Congress, Washington, DC
Page 40

National Park Service, Washington, DC
Page 6

The Newberry Library, Chicago, IL
Page 29, 31, 34

Rush University Medical Center Archives, Chicago, IL
Page 16

Samuel Greeley School, Winnetka, IL
Page 14

Southern Methodist University, Dallas, TX
Page 132

University Club of Chicago, Chicago, IL
Page 30